CASE
MATERIALS
ON THE
LAW OF TORTS

SEVENTH EDITION

by

ROBERT M. SOLOMON
Professor of Law
University of Western Ontario

MITCHELL McINNES
Professor of Law
University of Alberta

ERIKA CHAMBERLAIN
Assistant Professor of Law
University of Western Ontario

STEPHEN G.A. PITEL
Associate Professor of Law
University of Western Ontario

THOMSON
CARSWELL

The paper used in this publication meets the minimum requirements of American National Standard for Information Sciences - Permanence of Paper for Printed Library Materials, ANSI Z39.48-1984.

Library and Archives Canada Cataloguing in Publication

Cases and materials on the law of torts / Robert M. Solomon ... [et al.]. — 7th ed.

ISBN 978-0-7798-1360-5

1. Torts—Canada—Cases—Textbooks. I. Solomon, Robert M., 1946-

KE1232.A7S64 2007 346.7103 C2007-903702-X
KF1249.S65 2007

Composition: Computer Composition of Canada Inc.

THOMSON CARSWELL™

One Corporate Plaza
2075 Kennedy Road
Scarborough, Ontario
M1T 3V4

Customer Relations
Toronto 1-416-609-3800
Elsewhere in Canada/U.S. 1-800-387-5164
Fax 1-416-298-5094
World Wide Web: http://www.carswell.com
E-mail: orders@carswell.com

This book is dedicated to

the memory of

MYER RALPH SOLOMON

Preface

In writing this book, now in its seventh edition, we have three goals in mind. First, we want to help students to understand the policies, principles and rules of Canadian tort law. Second, through the use of questions, problems and exercises, we want to help students develop analytical and organizational skills. Third, by presenting the raw materials within a larger intellectual context, we want to help students develop an appreciation of the legal, social, moral and philosophical issues that underlie tort law.

Although we wrote this book with introductory courses foremost in mind, we have been careful to include enough detail and nuance to also make it appropriate for advanced courses. Now that a new chapter has been added on defamation, the book addresses every major aspect of Canadian tort law. It was written to accommodate a wide variety of academic interests, teaching styles and pedagogic philosophies. While topics are presented in a logical sequence, we have also, in an effort to maximize flexibility, attempted to ensure that each chapter is capable of standing alone. This allows instructors to teach the chapters in an order which best fits their own approach to the subject. Whenever possible, we have used cases and materials from across Canada and, where appropriate, from abroad.

Readers familiar with previous editions of this book will notice that many features have been retained. They will also notice some important changes. First, we have added a new chapter on defamation (Chapter 27). Second, to improve the clarity of the presentation we have reorganized the structure of some material, such as that on remedies in intentional torts (Chapter 2), causation in negligence (Chapter 16) and the tort liability of public authorities (Chapter 21). Third, we have expanded the definition and explanation of tort law (Chapter 1), the explanation of the defence of lawful authority (Chapter 8), the discussion of recent Supreme Court of Canada decisions on vicarious liability (Chapter 25) and the discussion of corrective justice (Chapter 28). Fourth, new extracts replace older material on negligent infliction of nervous shock (Chapter 12), the use of statutes in establishing the standard of care (Chapter 22), liability for animals (Chapter 25) and intentional interference with economic relations by unlawful means (Chapter 26). Fifth, we have added dozens of recent cases and articles to the notes and several new review problems. Sixth, we have placed greater emphasis on using a consistent style and citation method throughout the book.

Most changes have been necessitated by judicial developments. The implications of the Supreme Court of Canada's decision in *Cooper v. Hobart* continue to be worked out by courts at all levels. Our highest court has remained active in the field of tort law, particularly in the area of vicarious liability in *B.(K.L.) v. British Columbia*, *B.(M.) v. British Columbia*, *G.(E.D.) v. Hammer*, *John Doe v. Bennett*, *B.(E.) v. Order of the Oblates of Mary Immaculate in the Province of British Columbia*, and *Blackwater v. Plint* (all in Chapter 25), and also in cases such as *Fidler v. Sun Life Assurance Co. of Canada* (punitive damages: Chapter 2), *R. v. Paice* (defence of consent: Chapter 6), *Starson v. Swayze* (capacity to consent: Chapter 6), *Canadian Foundation of Children, Youth and the Law v. Canada (Attorney General)* (defence of discipline: Chapter 7),

Childs v. Desormeaux (test for duty of care: Chapter 10; social host liability: Chapter 11), *Hanke v. Resurfice Corp.* (causation: Chapter 16), *Blackwater v. Plint* (thin versus crumbling skull: Chapter 17), *Townsend v. Kroppmanns* (calculation of gross up and appropriate discount rate: Chapter 18), *Young v. Bella* (non-pecuniary damages: Chapter 18), *British Columbia v. Canadian Forest Products Ltd.* (damages for property loss: Chapter 18), *Enterprises Sibeca Inc. v. Frelighsburg (Municipality)* (protection of municipalities from liability: Chapter 21), *Odhavji Estate v. Woodhouse* (misfeasance in a public office: Chapter 21) and *Kirkbi AG v. Ritvik Holdings Inc.* (passing off: Chapter 26).

There have also been substantial developments in other Canadian courts. This edition includes new discussion of, among others, *Thomas Management Ltd. v. Alberta (Minister of Environmental Protection)* (corporate claim for aggravated damages: Chapter 2), *Nagy v. Canada* (false imprisonment: Chapter 3), *Ste-Marie c. Placements J.P.M. Marquis* (invasion of privacy: Chapter 3), *Bartin Pipe & Piling Supply Ltd. v. Epscan Industries Ltd.* (conversion: Chapter 4), *C.(L.) v. Pinhas* (competency to consent to treatment: Chapter 6), *Babiuk v. Trann* (defence of third parties: Chapter 7), *R. v. Wrightman* (obligation to inform the accused of the particulars of a warrant: Chapter 8), *Nespolon v. Alford* (foreseeable plaintiff test: Chapter 10), *Stevenson v. Clearview Riverside Resort* (duty to rescue: Chapter 11), *Cliche c. Baie-James (Commission scolaire)* (duty to supervise: Chapter 11), *B.M. v. British Columbia (Attorney General)* (police role in preventing crime: Chapter 11), *Joudrey v. Swissair Transport Company* (definition of a rescuer: Chapter 12), *Mustapha v. Culligan Canada Ltd.* (nervous shock: Chapter 12), *Conversions By Vantasy Ltd. v. General Motors of Canada Ltd.* (reasonableness of reliance: Chapter 13), *Avco Financial Services Realty Ltd. v. Norman* (negligent misrepresentation and contributory negligence: Chapter 13), *James v. British Columbia* (negligent performance of a service and assumption of responsibility: Chapter 14), *C.S. (Next friend of) v. Miller* (control over children: Chapter 15), *Burbank v. Bolton* (standard of care in police chases: Chapter 15), *McIntyre v. Grigg* (punitive damages for impaired driving: Chapter 18), *Rowe v. Bobell Express Ltd.* (loss of earning capacity: Chapter 18), *Pilon v. Janveaux* (apportionment of liability: Chapter 19), *Snushall v. Fulsang* (failure to wear seat belt: Chapter 19), *Holtslag v. Alberta* (governmental liability: Chapter 21), *Burgess (Litigation Guardian of) v. Canadian National Railway* (use of statute in negligence claim: Chapter 22), *Fullowka v. Royal Oak Ventures Inc.* (occupier's obligation to protect people on the premises: Chapter 23), *Traquair v. National Arts Centre Corp.* (damages under occupiers' liability: Chapter 23), *Lakeview Gardens Ltd. v. Regina (City)* (remedies in nuisance: Chapter 24), *Cowles v. Balac* (liability for animals, contributory negligence and strict liability: Chapter 25), *Reach MD Inc. v. Pharmaceutical Manufacturers Assn. of Canada* (intentional interference with economic relations: Chapter 26), *Culhane v. ATP Aero Training Products Ltd.* (intentional interference with economic relations: Chapter 26), *Carter v. B.C. Federation of Foster Parents Assn.* (internet defamation: Chapter 27) and *Hung v. Gardiner* (defence of absolute privilege: Chapter 27).

This edition analyzes recent leading decisions from other Commonwealth countries, including *Wainwright v. Home Office* (infliction of nervous shock: Chapter 3), *Marcq v. Christie Manson & Woods Ltd. (trading as Christie's)* (conversion: Chapter 4), *Osman v. Ferguson* (police role in preventing crime: Chapter 11), *Harriton v. Stephens* (wrongful life: Chapter 12), *Waller v. James; Waller v. Hoolahan* (wrongful life: Chapter 12), *Cattanach v. Melchior* (wrongful pregnancy: Chapter 12), *Customs and Excise Com-*

missioners v. Barclays Bank plc. (new categories of pure economic loss: Chapter 14), *Kavanagh v. Akhtar* (remoteness of loss: Chapter 17), *Gaca v. Pirelli General plc.* (collateral benefits: Chapter 18), *Vellino v. Chief Constable of Greater Manchester Police* (participation in a criminal act: Chapter 19), *Three Rivers District Council v. Governor and Company of the Bank of England (No. 3)* (misfeasance in a public office: Chapter 21), *Marcic v. Thames Water Utilities Ltd.* (nuisance and public authorities: Chapter 24), *Dennis v. Ministry of Defence* (defence of public interest to private nuisance claim: Chapter 24), *Transco plc v. Stockport Metropolitan Borough Council* (strict liability: Chapter 25), *Mirvahedy v. Henley* (liability for animals: Chapter 25), *Bernard v. Attorney General of Jamaica* (vicarious liability: Chapter 25), *Viasystems (Tyneside) Ltd. v. Thermal Transfer (Northern) Ltd.* (dual vicarious liability: Chapter 25), *Standard Chartered Bank v. Pakistan National Shipping Corp. (Nos. 2 and 4)* (deceit: Chapter 26), *Magill v. Magill* (deceit: Chapter 26) and *OBG Limited v. Allen; Douglas v. Hello! Limited; Mainstream Properties Limited v. Young* (economic torts: Chapter 26).

The seventh edition was prepared by Professors Robert Solomon, Mitchell McInnes, Erika Chamberlain and Stephen Pitel. After working on the past three editions, Professor Rande Kostal has moved on to pursue other projects. We appreciate his efforts over the past decade. Professor Craig Brown has continued to advise us on insurance issues, no-fault liability and the New Zealand accident compensation system. Professor Pitel read over and edited all chapters, and Western Law students Maureen Armstrong, Sean Flaherty, Ryan Neilson, Alessandra Nosko, and Andrew Valentine did a fine job collecting and organizing materials, verifying references and assisting in the editing process. We thank the Law Foundation of Ontario and our respective faculties of law for providing research and administrative support. We have endeavoured to state the law as of May 2007.

Finally, we are grateful to the staff at Thomson Canada Limited, which has made the first seven editions of this casebook possible. In particular, we would like to thank Elizabeth Gillen, Michael Giglio and Ken Mathies, who patiently supervised the preparation of this edition. This book was first published in 1982, so this is its 25th anniversary, a significant milestone for a casebook on Canadian law.

Table of Contents

PREFACE		v
TABLE OF CASES		xxvii
CHAPTER 1	AN INTRODUCTION TO THE LAW OF TORTS	1
	1. Tort Law Defined	1
	Notes and Questions	2
	2. Tort and Contract	3
	Notes and Questions	4
	Review Problem	5
	3. A Brief History of Tort Law	5
	Notes and Questions	8
	4. Trespass and Case: A Brief Review of the Case Law	9
	Scott v. Shepherd	9
	Notes and Questions	12
	Leame v. Bray	12
	Williams v. Holland	13
	Notes and Questions	14
	Holmes v. Mather	14
	Notes and Questions	15
	Cook v. Lewis	15
	Notes and Questions	16
	5. The Bases for Imposing Liability in Tort	17
	(a) Absolute Liability	17
	(b) Strict Liability	18
	(c) Negligence	18
	(d) Intention	19
	(e) No Liability	19
	6. The Functions of Tort Law	19
	(a) Compensation	20
	(b) Appeasement and Vindication	20
	(c) Punishment	21
	(d) Deterrence	21
	(e) Market Deterrence	21
	(f) Justice	22
	Notes and Questions	22
CHAPTER 2	THE BASIC CONCEPTS OF REMEDIES IN INTENTIONAL TORTS	25
	1. Introduction	25
	2. Judicial and Extrajudicial Remedies	25
	Notes	26
	3. Classifications of Damages	26
	Note	27
	4. Nominal Damages	27
	The Mediana	28

Notes and Questions 28
5. Compensatory Damages 29
(a) Assessing Damages for Pecuniary Losses 29
The Mediana 29
Notes and Questions 30
(b) Assessing Damages for Non-Pecuniary Losses 30
Review Problem 31
6. Aggravated Damages 32
Notes and Questions 32
7. Punitive Damages 32
Notes and Questions 33
B.(P.) v. B.(W.) 33
Notes and Questions 35
(a) The Principles in *Whiten v. Pilot* 37
Notes and Questions 38
8. Disgorgement Damages 39
Notes and Questions 39
Penarth Dock Engineering Co. Ltd. v. Pounds 40
Notes and Questions 40
Review Problem 42

CHAPTER 3 INTENTIONAL INTERFERENCE WITH THE PERSON 43
1. Introduction 43
2. Basic Principles of Liability 43
(a) Volition 43
Smith v. Stone 44
Notes and Questions 44
(b) Intent 44
(i) Imputed (Constructive) Intent 45
(ii) Transferred Intent 45
Notes and Questions 45
3. Related Issues: Motive, Mistake and Accident 46
(a) Motive 46
Notes 46
(i) Duress 47
Gilbert v. Stone 47
Notes and Questions 47
(ii) Provocation 48
Miska v. Sivec 48
Notes and Questions 49
(b) Mistake 50
Hodgkinson v. Martin 51
Ranson v. Kitner 51
Notes and Questions 52
(c) Accident 52
Review Problems 53
(d) The Liability of Children and those with a Mental Illness 53
Notes and Questions 53
4. Battery 55
Bettel v. Yim 55
Notes and Questions 58

(a) The Burden of Proof in Sexual Abuse Cases 60
Notes and Questions 61
5. Assault 61
Notes and Questions 61
Holcombe v. Whitaker 62
Police v. Greaves 63
Notes and Questions 64
Review Problems 66
6. False Imprisonment 66
Bird v. Jones 66
Notes and Questions 68
Campbell v. S.S. Kresge Co. 69
Notes and Questions 71
Herd v. Weardale Steel, Coal and Coke Co. Ltd. 73
Notes and Questions 74
7. Malicious Prosecution 75
Nelles v. Ontario 75
Notes and Questions 78
(a) The Tort of Abuse of Process 81
Review Problem 82
8. Intentional Infliction of Nervous Shock 82
Wilkinson v. Downton 82
Notes and Questions 84
Radovskis v. Tomm 85
Samms v. Eccles 86
Notes and Questions 88
(a) The Broadening of Liability 89
Notes and Questions 89
(b) The Innominate Intentional Tort 90
Notes and Questions 90
Review Problems 91
9. Protection of Privacy 92
(a) Introduction 92
Notes and Questions 92
(b) A Common Law Tort Action for the Invasion of Privacy? 93
Motherwell v. Motherwell 93
Notes and Questions 95
(c) Subsequent Common Law Developments 95
Notes and Questions 95
(d) The Statutory Protection of Privacy 99
Hollinsworth v. BCTV 100
Notes and Questions 101
Review Problem 102
(e) Breach of Confidence 103
Notes and Questions 104
Review Problem 104
10. The Common Law Tort of Discrimination 105
Bhadauria v. Board of Governors of Seneca College of Applied Arts and Technology 105
Notes and Questions 108

CHAPTER 4 INTENTIONAL INTERFERENCE WITH CHATTELS 111

1. **Introduction** 111
2. **The Development of the Actions** 111
   (a) Trespass 111
   (b) Detinue 112
   (c) Trover and Conversion 113
   Notes and Questions 114
3. **Trespass to Chattels** 115
   Fouldes v. Willoughby 115
   Notes and Questions 117
4. **Conversion** 118
   (a) General Principles 118
   MacKenzie v. Scotia Lumber Co. 118
   Notes and Questions 120
   Review Problems 125
   (b) Conversion of Cheques and Other Unusual Chattels 127
   373409 Alberta Ltd. (Receiver of) v. Bank of Montreal 127
   Notes and Questions 130
   (c) Remedies for Conversion 131
   Aitken v. Gardiner 131
   Notes and Questions 133
5. **Detinue** 136
   Gen. & Finance Facilities Ltd. v. Cooks Cars (Romford) Ltd. 136
   Aitken v. Gardiner 139
   Notes and Questions 140
6. **Recaption and Replevin** 141
   (a) Recaption 141
   (b) Replevin 141
   Notes and Questions 143
   Review Problems 144

CHAPTER 5 INTENTIONAL INTERFERENCE WITH REAL PROPERTY 145

1. **Trespass to Land** 145
   Entick v. Carrington 145
   Turner v. Thorne 145
   Notes and Questions 147
   Review Problems 149
   Harrison v. Carswell 149
   Notes and Questions 153
2. **Trespass and Nuisance** 156
   Kerr v. Revelstoke Bldg. Materials Ltd. 157
   Notes and Questions 159
3. **Trespass to Airspace and Subsoil** 160
   (a) Trespass to Airspace 160
   Bernstein v. Skyviews & General Ltd. 160
   Notes and Questions 162
   (b) Trespass to Subsoil 163
   Notes and Questions 164
   Review Problems 164

CHAPTER 6 THE DEFENCE OF CONSENT 167
1. Introduction to the Defences 167
2. General Principles of Consent 167
(a) Introduction 167
Notes and Questions 168
(b) Implied Consent 168
Wright v. McLean 168
Notes and Questions 170
(c) Exceeding Consent 170
Agar v. Canning 170
Notes and Questions 171
Review Problems 174
(d) Competency to Consent 174
3. Factors Vitiating Consent: Fraud, Mistake, Duress, and Public Policy 174
(a) Introduction 174
(b) Fraud (Deceit) 175
Notes and Questions 175
(c) Mistake 177
Notes and Questions 177
(d) Duress (Coercion) 178
Latter v. Braddell 178
Notes and Questions 180
(e) Public Policy 181
Notes and Questions 182
Review Problem 183
4. Consent to Criminal or Immoral Acts 183
Notes and Questions 184
Review Problem 186
5. Consent to Treatment and Counselling 186
(a) General Principles of Consent 186
Notes and Questions 187
(b) Exceptions to the General Principles of Consent 188
Marshall v. Curry 189
Malette v. Shulman 190
Notes and Questions 192
(c) The Burden of Proof and Consent Forms 194
Notes and Questions 194
(d) Competency to Consent 195
(i) Minors 195
C. v. Wren 196
Notes and Questions 197
Review Problem 199
(ii) Adults 199
Notes and Questions 199
(e) Substitute Consent 201
Notes and Questions 201
(f) Informed Consent: Battery or Negligence? 203
Review Problem 204

CHAPTER 7 DEFENCES RELATED TO THE PROTECTION OF PERSON AND PROPERTY ... 205
1. **Introduction** ... 205
2. **Self-Defence** ... 205
Wackett v. Calder ... 205
Notes and Questions ... 207
3. **Defence of Third Parties** ... 209
Gambriell v. Caparelli ... 209
Notes and Questions ... 211
4. **Discipline** ... 212
R. v. Dupperon ... 213
Notes and Questions ... 215
5. **Defence of Real Property** ... 217
MacDonald v. Hees ... 217
Notes and Questions ... 219
Bird v. Holbrook ... 221
Notes and Questions ... 221
6. **Defence and Recaption of Chattels** ... 222
Notes and Questions ... 222
Review Problem ... 223
7. **Public and Private Necessity** ... 224
(a) Public Necessity ... 224
Surocco v. Geary ... 224
Notes and Questions ... 225
(b) Private Necessity ... 227
Vincent v. Lake Erie Tpt. Co. ... 227
Notes and Questions ... 230
8. **Apportionment of Fault in Intentional Torts** ... 231
Notes and Questions ... 232
Review Problems ... 234

CHAPTER 8 THE DEFENCE OF LEGAL AUTHORITY ... 235
1. **Introduction** ... 235
Notes and Questions ... 236
2. **The *Canadian Charter of Rights and Freedoms*** ... 237
(a) Liability Under Section 24(1) ... 237
(b) The Impact of Section 52 on the Defence of Legal Authority ... 238
Notes and Questions ... 238
3. **Authority and Privilege to Arrest Without a Warrant** ... 239
(a) Introduction ... 239
Notes and Questions ... 240
(b) A Peace Officer's Power to Arrest Without a Warrant ... 241
Notes and Questions ... 242
(c) Privilege or Justification Under the *Criminal Code* ... 242
Notes and Questions ... 243
(d) A Private Citizen's Authority and Privilege to Arrest Without a Warrant ... 244
Notes and Questions ... 245
4. **Rights and Obligations in the Arrest Process** ... 246
(a) Reasons for the Arrest ... 246
Koechlin v. Waugh and Hamilton ... 246

Notes and Questions 249
(b) The Use of Reasonable Force 251
Notes and Questions 251
5. The Common Law Power to Search Pursuant to a Lawful Arrest 253
R. v. Caslake 253
Notes and Questions 255
6. A Peace Officer's Common Law Power of Entry to Search for a Wanted Person 257
Eccles v. Bourque 257
Notes and Questions 260
Review Problems 262

CHAPTER 9 INTRODUCTION TO THE LAW OF NEGLIGENCE 265
1. Negligence: Defining Terms 265
2. The Historical Development of Negligence 265
Notes and Questions 267
3. The Elements of a Negligence Action 268
(a) Introduction 268
(i) Duty of Care 269
(ii) The Standard of Care and its Breach 269
(iii) Causation 269
(iv) Remoteness of Damages 269
(v) Actual Loss 269
(vi) Defences 270
Notes and Questions 270
(b) Negligence: A Case Illustration 270
Dunsmore v. Deshield 271
Notes and Questions 273

CHAPTER 10 THE DUTY OF CARE 275
1. An Introduction to the Duty of Care 275
(a) The Classical Approach 275
(b) The General Duty of Care Test 276
M'Alister (or Donoghue) v. Stevenson 276
Notes and Questions 280
(c) The Development of the Modern Law of Duty 282
Notes and Questions 284
(d) *Anns* and the Supreme Court of Canada 284
Cooper v. Hobart 285
Notes and Questions 291
(e) Developments Since *Cooper v. Hobart* 293
Notes and Questions 295
2. Application of the Duty of Care Test 295
(a) Foreseeable Risk of Injury 295
Moule v. N.B. Elec. Power Comm. 295
Amos v. N.B. Elec. Power Comm. 297
Notes and Questions 299
(b) Foreseeable Plaintiff 301
Palsgraf v. Long Island Ry. Co. 301
Notes and Questions 304

CHAPTER 11 SPECIAL DUTIES OF CARE: AFFIRMATIVE ACTION 309
1. Introduction to Special Duties of Care 309
2. Introduction to Duties of Affirmative Action 309
Notes 310
3. The Duty to Rescue 311
Osterlind v. Hill 311
Notes and Questions 312
Matthews v. MacLaren; Horsley v. MacLaren 314
Notes and Questions 319
Good Samaritan Act, 2001 (Ontario) 322
Review Problems 322
4. The Duty to Control the Conduct of Others 323
(a) Liability for the Intoxicated 323
Crocker v. Sundance Northwest Resorts Ltd. 323
Notes and Questions 327
(b) Other Duty to Control Situations 332
Notes and Questions 332
(c) The Duty to Prevent Crime and Protect Others 335
Jane Doe v. Metropolitan Toronto (Municipality) Commissioners of Police 336
Notes and Questions 338
Review Problems 343
5. The Duty to Perform Gratuitous Undertakings 344
Notes and Questions 345
Smith v. Rae 346
Zelenko v. Gimbel Bros., Inc. 346
Soulsby v. Toronto 347
Notes and Questions 348
Review Problems 350

CHAPTER 12 SPECIAL DUTIES OF CARE: MISCELLANEOUS CATEGORIES 351
1. Introduction 351
2. The Duty of Care Owed to Rescuers 351
Horsley v. MacLaren 352
Notes and Questions 356
Review Problems 360
3. Duties Owed to the Unborn 361
(a) Pre-Conception Wrongs 361
Notes and Questions 361
(b) Wrongful Birth and Wrongful Life 362
Notes and Questions 363
(c) Wrongful Pregnancy 365
Notes and Questions 366
(d) Pre-Natal Injuries 368
Notes and Questions 371
4. Nervous Shock 374
(a) Introduction 374
Notes and Questions 374
(b) Commonwealth Developments 376
Alcock v. Chief Constable of South Yorkshire Police 377
Notes and Questions 382

(c) The Canadian Position ... 384
Mustapha v. Culligan Canada Ltd. ... 384
Notes and Questions ... 392
Review Problem ... 393
5. **A Health Professional's Duty to Inform** ... 394
Haughian v. Paine ... 395
Notes and Questions ... 396
Review Problem ... 399
6. **A Manufacturer's and Supplier's Duty to Warn** ... 400
Hollis v. Dow Corning Corp. ... 400
Notes and Questions ... 406
Review Problems ... 412
7. **Duty of Care Owed by a Barrister** ... 412
Demarco v. Ungaro ... 413
Notes and Questions ... 416

CHAPTER 13 SPECIAL DUTIES OF CARE: NEGLIGENT MISREPRESENTATION 419
1. **Introduction** ... 419
Notes and Questions ... 421
2. **Negligent Misrepresentation Causing Pure Economic Loss** ... 424
Hercules Managements Ltd. v. Ernst & Young ... 424
Notes and Questions ... 432
3. **Negligent Misrepresentation and Contract** ... 434
(a) Concurrent Liability in Tort and Contract ... 435
BG Checo International Ltd. v. B.C. Hydro & Power Authority ... 435
Notes and Questions ... 441
(b) Pre-Contractual Misrepresentations ... 442
Queen v. Cognos Inc. ... 442
Notes and Questions ... 445
Review Problem ... 446

CHAPTER 14 SPECIAL DUTIES OF CARE: RECOVERY OF PURE ECONOMIC LOSS IN NEGLIGENCE 449
1. **Introduction** ... 449
Note ... 450
2. **New Categories of Pure Economic Loss** ... 450
Martel Building Ltd. v. Canada ... 450
Notes and Questions ... 455
3. **Negligent Performance of a Service** ... 458
B.D.C. Ltd. v. Hofstrand Farms Ltd. ... 458
James v. British Columbia ... 460
Notes and Questions ... 461
4. **Negligent Supply of Shoddy Goods or Structures** ... 462
Winnipeg Condominium Corp. No. 36 v. Bird Construction Co. ... 463
Notes and Questions ... 468
Review Problems ... 472
5. **Relational Economic Loss** ... 472
Bow Valley Husky (Bermuda) Ltd. v. Saint John Shipbuilding Ltd. ... 473

Notes and Questions 479

CHAPTER 15 THE STANDARD OF CARE 483

1. **Introduction** 483
2. **The Common Law Standard of Care: The Reasonable Person Test** 484
   Arland v. Taylor 484
   Notes and Questions 486
3. **Factors Considered in Determining Breach of the Standard of Care** 487
   (a) Probability and Severity of the Harm 488
   Bolton v. Stone 488
   Paris v. Stepney Borough Council 490
   Notes and Questions 493
   (b) Cost of Risk Avoidance 494
   Vaughn v. Halifax-Dartmouth Bridge Comm. 494
   Law Estate v. Simice 495
   Notes and Questions 496
   (c) Social Utility 497
   Watt v. Hertfordshire County Council 497
   Notes and Questions 498
4. **An Economic Analysis of the Standard of Care** 500
   United States v. Carroll Towing Co. 500
   Notes and Questions 502
5. **Special Standards of Care** 503
   (a) The Standard of Care Expected of the Disabled 503
   Fiala v. Cechmanek 503
   Notes and Questions 508
   (b) The Standard of Care Expected of Children 510
   Joyal v. Barsby 510
   Notes and Questions 512
   (c) The Standard of Care Expected of Professionals 513
   White v. Turner 513
   Notes and Questions 515
6. **Degrees of Negligence** 519
   Notes and Questions 520
7. **Custom** 521
   ter Neuzen v. Korn 521
   Notes and Questions 524
   Review Problems 525

CHAPTER 16 CAUSATION 527

1. **Introduction** 527
2. **The But-For Test** 528
   Kauffman v. Toronto Transit Commission 528
   Barnett v. Chelsea & Kensington Hospital Management Committee 529
   Notes and Questions 530
3. **Established Exceptions to the But-For Test** 531
   (a) The Multiple Negligent Defendants Rule 532
   (b) The Learned Intermediary Rule 532
   (c) Informed Consent 532
   Notes and Questions 533

4. **Recent Attempts to Modify the But-For Test** 533
(a) Material Contribution 534
Walker Estate v. York Finch General Hospital 534
Notes and Questions 536
(b) Materially Increased Risk 538
Snell v. Farrell 539
Notes and Questions 543
(c) Proportionate Cause and Loss of Chance 545
Notes and Questions 546
Review Problem 546
5. **Multiple Causes** 546
Notes and Questions 547
(a) Independent Insufficient Causes 548
Athey v. Leonati 548
Nowlan v. Brunswick Construction Ltée 551
Notes and Questions 551
(b) Independent Sufficient Causes 552
Lambton v. Mellish 553
Notes and Questions 554
Review Problems 554
6. **Issues in Assessing the Plaintiff's Loss** 555
(a) Successive Causes of Parallel Injury 555
Penner v. Mitchell 555
Notes and Questions 557
(b) Devaluing the Plaintiff's Loss 557
Dillon v. Twin State Gas and Elec. Co. 557
Notes and Questions 558
Review Problems 559

CHAPTER 17 REMOTENESS OF DAMAGES 561
1. **Introduction** 561
2. **Directness Versus Foreseeability** 562
(a) The Directness Test 562
Notes and Questions 562
(b) The Foreseeability Test 562
The Wagon Mound (No. 1); Overseas Tankship (U.K.) Ltd. v. Morts Dock & Engineering Co. 562
Notes and Questions 565
Review Problems 566
3. **Modifications to the Foreseeability Test** 567
(a) The Kind of Injury 567
Hughes v. Lord Advocate 567
Notes and Questions 568
(b) The Thin-Skulled Plaintiff Rule 570
Smith v. Leech Brain & Co. 570
Marconato v. Franklin 571
Notes and Questions 573
(c) The Possibility of Injury 576
The Wagon Mound (No. 2); Overseas Tankship (U.K.) Ltd. v. Miller Steamship Co. Pty. 576
Notes and Questions 579

Assiniboine South School Division, No. 3 v. Greater Winnipeg Gas Co. 579
Notes and Questions 582
4. **Intervening Causes** 582
Bradford v. Kanellos 583
Notes and Questions 586
Price v. Milawski 587
Notes and Questions 589
Hewson v. Red Deer 590
Notes and Questions 592
Review Problem 593

CHAPTER 18 THE ASSESSMENT OF DAMAGES 595
1. **Introduction** 595
(a) The Purposes of Damage Awards in Negligence 595
Notes and Questions 596
(b) Preliminary Issues 598
Notes and Questions 600
2. **Damages for Personal Injuries** 602
(a) Introduction 602
Andrews v. Grand & Toy Alberta Ltd. 603
Notes and Questions 605
(b) Pecuniary Loss: Future Care 607
Andrews v. Grand & Toy Alberta Ltd. 607
Notes and Questions 611
(c) Pecuniary Loss: Lost Earning Capacity 613
Andrews v. Grand & Toy Alberta Ltd. 613
Notes and Questions 615
(d) Considerations Relevant to Both Heads of Pecuniary Loss 618
Andrews v. Grand & Toy Alberta Ltd. 618
Notes and Questions 620
(e) Non-Pecuniary Loss 621
Andrews v. Grand & Toy Alberta Ltd. 621
Notes and Questions 623
3. **Survival of Actions and Dependants' Claims** 625
(a) Survival of Actions 625
Survival of Actions Act (Alberta) 626
Trustee Act (Ontario) 626
(b) Fatal Accidents Legislation 627
Fatal Injuries Act (Nova Scotia) 627
Family Law Act (Ontario) 628
Notes and Questions 629
(i) The Death of the Family Provider 630
Keizer v. Hanna 630
Notes and Questions 634
(ii) The Death of a Dependant Family Member 635
Notes and Questions 635
4. **Damages for Property Loss** 637
(a) The Assessment of the Damage to the Property Itself 637
(b) The Assessment of Economic Losses Consequent on the Damage to the Property 638

(c) The Plaintiff's Obligation to Mitigate 639
Notes and Questions 639
5. **Collateral Benefits** 642
(a) The Doctrine of Subrogation 643
Notes and Questions 644
Review Problems 645

CHAPTER 19 DEFENCES IN NEGLIGENCE 647
1. **Introduction** 647
2. **Contributory Negligence** 647
(a) The Development of the Defence 647
Notes and Questions 648
(b) Conduct Constituting Contributory Negligence 649
Walls v. Mussens Ltd. 649
Notes and Questions 650
Gagnon v. Beaulieu 652
Notes and Questions 655
(c) Apportionment of Loss 657
Negligence Act (Ontario) 657
Notes and Questions 658
Mortimer v. Cameron 660
Notes and Questions 663
Review Problem 664
3. **Voluntary Assumption of Risk** 665
Dube v. Labar 665
Notes and Questions 668
4. **Participation in a Criminal or Immoral Act** 670
Hall v. Hebert 670
Notes and Questions 673
5. **Inevitable Accident** 675
Rintoul v. X-Ray and Radium Indust. Ltd. 675
Notes and Questions 677
Review Problem 677

CHAPTER 20 PROOF OF NEGLIGENCE 679
1. **The Burden of Proof in a Negligence Action** 679
Wakelin v. London & South Western Ry. Co. 680
Notes and Questions 683
2. **Exceptions to the General Principles Governing the Burden of Proof** 684
(a) Statutes and Shifting Burdens of Proof 684
MacDonald v. Woodard 684
Notes and Questions 685
(b) Directly Caused Injury: Unintended Trespass 686
Dahlberg v. Naydiuk 686
Notes and Questions 687
(c) Multiple Negligent Defendants 688
Cook v. Lewis 688
Notes and Questions 690
3. ***Res Ipsa Loquitur*** 694
Fontaine v. British Columbia (Official Administrator) 695
Notes and Questions 699
Review Problems 700

CHAPTER 21 THE TORT LIABILITY OF PUBLIC AUTHORITIES 703

1. **Introduction** 703
2. **Special Rules for Public Authorities** 704
   (a) Legislative and Judicial Functions 704
   Bradley v. Fisher 705
   Notes and Questions 706
   (b) Crown Immunity 709
   Notes and Questions 710
   (c) Limitation Periods and Special Procedures 711
   Notes and Questions 711
3. **The Negligence Liability of Public Authorities** 713
   (a) Introduction 713
   Just v. British Columbia 713
   Notes and Questions 720
   (b) The Effect of *Cooper v. Hobart* 723
   Notes and Questions 724
4. **Misfeasance in a Public Office** 725
   (a) Introduction 725
   Roncarelli v. Duplessis 725
   Notes and Questions 727
   (b) Modern Developments 728
   Odhavji Estate v. Woodhouse 728
   Notes and Questions 735
5. **Other Torts** 736
   Notes and Questions 736
   Review Problem 737

CHAPTER 22 STATUTORY PROVISIONS AND TORT LIABILITY 739

1. **Introduction** 739
   Note 740
2. **Express Statutory Causes of Action** 740
   Trespass to Property Act (Ontario) 740
   Competition Act (Canada) 741
   Notes and Questions 742
   Trachsler v. Halton 743
   Notes and Questions 744
   Review Problem 745
3. **The Use of Statutes in Common Law Negligence** 746
   R. in Right of Can. v. Sask. Wheat Pool 746
   Notes and Questions 753
   Horsley v. MacLaren 753
   Notes and Questions 754
   Rintoul v. X-Ray and Radium Indust. 754
   Questions 755
   Galaske v. O'Donnell 755
   Ryan v. Victoria (City) 758
   Notes and Questions 761
4. **A Note on the *Canadian Charter of Rights and Freedoms*** .. 762
   Canadian Charter of Rights and Freedoms 762
   Notes and Questions 765
   Review Problems 766

CHAPTER 23 OCCUPIERS' LIABILITY 767
1. **Introduction** 767
2. **The Common Law Principles of Occupiers' Liability** 769
(a) Who is an Occupier? 769
Palmer v. St. John 769
Notes and Questions 771
(b) Categories of Entrants and Corresponding Duties 772
(i) Contractual Entrants 772
Finigan v. Calgary 772
Notes and Questions 774
(ii) Invitees and Licensees 775
McErlean v. Sarel 775
Notes and Questions 777
(iii) Trespassers 780
Veinot v. Kerr-Addison Mines Ltd. 780
Notes and Questions 783
3. **The Provincial Occupiers' Liability Statutes** 784
(a) Introduction 784
(b) *Occupiers' Liability Act* (Ontario) 784
Notes and Questions 788
Waldick v. Malcolm 790
Notes and Questions 794
Review Problem 794

CHAPTER 24 NUISANCE 795
1. **Introduction** 795
2. **Private Nuisance** 796
340909 Ont. Ltd. v. Huron Steel Products (Windsor) Ltd. 796
Notes and Questions 800
Hollywood Silver Fox Farm Ltd. v. Emmett 804
Notes and Questions 806
(a) Defence of Statutory Authority 807
Tock v. St. John's Metropolitan Area Board 807
Notes and Questions 810
3. **Public Nuisance** 814
A.-G. Ont. v. Orange Productions Ltd. 815
Hickey v. Electricity Reduction Co. 817
Notes and Questions 819
4. **Remedies** 820
Mendez v. Palazzi 821
Notes and Questions 822
Miller v. Jackson 823
Notes and Questions 827
Spur Industries Inc. v. Del E. Webb Development Co. 828
Notes and Questions 830
Review Problem 833

CHAPTER 25 STRICT AND VICARIOUS LIABILITY 835
1. **Introduction** 835
(a) Strict Liability 835
(b) Vicarious Liability 836
Notes and Questions 836

2. **Strict Liability for Escape of Dangerous Substances: *Rylands v. Fletcher*** 837
(a) Introduction 837
Rylands v. Fletcher 837
Notes and Questions 839
(b) Escape 840
Read v. J. Lyons & Co. 840
Notes and Questions 843
(c) Non-Natural Use 844
Gertsen v. Municipality of Metropolitan Toronto 844
Notes and Questions 846
(d) Defences to the Rule in *Rylands v. Fletcher* 847
(i) Consent 848
(ii) Common Benefit 848
(iii) Default of the Plaintiff 848
(iv) Act of God 848
(v) Act of a Stranger 849
(vi) Statutory Authority 849
(e) A Comment on *Rylands v. Fletcher* 849
Notes and Questions 851
3. **Strict Liability for Animals** 852
(a) Dangerous Animals 852
Cowles v. Balac 852
Notes and Questions 856
(b) Cattle Trespass 858
Acker v. Kerr 858
Notes and Questions 860
4. **Products Liability: Negligence or Strict Liability?** 861
Notes and Questions 862
5. **Vicarious Liability** 862
(a) Statutory Vicarious Liability 863
Notes and Questions 864
(b) Principal-Agent Relationship 864
T.G. Bright & Co. v. Kerr 864
Notes and Questions 865
(c) Master-Servant Relationship 867
Bazley v. Curry 868
Notes and Questions 873
(d) Independent Contractors 878
671122 Ontario Ltd. v. Sagaz Industries Canada Inc. 878
Notes and Questions 883
(e) Non-Delegable Duties 884
Notes and Questions 886

CHAPTER 26 BUSINESS TORTS 889
1. **Introduction** 889
2. **Deceit (Fraud)** 890
Derry v. Peek 890
Notes and Questions 892
3. **Passing Off** 897
Ciba-Geigy Canada Ltd. v. Apotex Inc. 897
Notes and Questions 901

4. **Intimidation** 903
Central Can. Potash v. Govt. of Sask. 904
Notes and Questions 906
5. **Conspiracy** 907
Posluns v. Toronto Stock Exchange 908
Notes and Questions 909
6. **Interference with Contractual Relations** 912
Posluns v. Toronto Stock Exchange 914
Notes and Questions 917
7. **Intentional Interference with Economic Relations by Unlawful Means** 921
Reach MD Inc. v. Pharmaceutical Manufacturers Assn. of Canada 922
Notes and Questions 924
Review Problem 927

CHAPTER 27 DEFAMATION 929
1. **Introduction** 929
Notes and Questions 930
2. **Elements of a Defamation Action** 931
(a) Defamatory Material 931
Sim v. Stretch 932
Notes and Questions 934
(b) Reference to the Plaintiff 936
Knuppfer v. London Express Newspaper, Ltd. 937
Notes and Questions 937
(c) Publication 939
Notes and Questions 939
3. **Defences** 941
(a) Justification 941
Williams v. Reason 942
Notes and Questions 944
(b) Absolute Privilege 945
(i) Executive Officers 946
Dowson v. The Queen 946
(ii) Parliamentary Privilege 949
(iii) Judicial Proceedings 949
Hung v. Gardiner 949
Notes and Questions 953
(c) Qualified Privilege 954
Hill v. Church of Scientology 956
Notes and Questions 959
(d) Fair Comment 960
Cherneskey v. Armadale Publishers Ltd. 960
Notes and Questions 967
(e) Consent 970
Jones v. Brooks 970
Notes and Questions 972
4. **Remedies** 972
(a) Injunction 972
(b) Damages 973
Hill v. Church of Scientology 973

Notes and Questions 982
Review Question 982

CHAPTER 28 TORT LAW: THEORIES, CRITICISMS AND ALTERNATIVES 985

1. **Introduction** 985
2. **Theoretical Criticism of Tort Law** 985
   (a) Introduction 985
   Notes 986
   (b) Deterrence 986
   Notes and Questions 988
   (c) Compensation 989
   Notes and Questions 991
   (d) Theories of Tort Law Based on Concepts of Justice 992
   Notes and Questions 995
   (e) Feminist Perspectives 996
   Notes and Questions 997
3. **The No-Fault Alternatives** 998
   (a) Introduction 998
   (b) No-Fault Accident Compensation in New Zealand 1000
   Notes and Questions 1000
   (c) Workers' Compensation 1002
   Notes and Questions 1003
   (d) No-Fault Automobile Insurance in Canada 1004
   Notes and Questions 1005
   Review Problem 1007

Table of Cases

A & B Sound Ltd. v. Future Shop Ltd. 920, 924
A.(D.A.) v. B.(D.K.) 32, 60
A.B. v. South West Water Services Ltd. 33
A.G. v. Nissan 226
A.-G. v. Bastow 816
A.-G. v. Cole & Son 815
A.-G. v. Corke 815
A.-G. v. P.Y.A. Quarries, Ltd 815
A.-G. v. Stone 815
A.G. Can. v. Diamond Waterproofing Ltd; Pillar Const. v. Defence Const. (1951) Ltd. 847
A.G. Man. v. Adventure Flights Centre Ltd. 820
A.G. Man. v. Campbell 162, 806
A.G. N.S. v. Beaver 819, 823
A.G. Ont. v. Fatehi 641
A.G. Ont. v. Keller 651, 686
A.G.B.C. v. Couillard 819
A.-G. Ont. v. Orange Productions Ltd. 815
A.K. v. D.K. 182
A.L. v. Ontario (Minister of Community and Social Services) 722
A.U.P.E. v. Edmonton Sun 938
Abbott v. Kasza 593
Abbott (Next Friend of) v. Jarocki 173
Abel v. McDonald 893
Abraham v. The Advocate Co. 938
Acker v. Kerr 858
Ackerman v. Wascana Centre Authority 779
Adair (Litigation administrator of) v. Hamilton Health Sciences Corp. 516
Adam v. Ward 954, 956
Adams v. Beutler 338
Adan v. Davis 194
Agar v. Canning 170, 171
Ahmed v. Stefaniu 55, 531
Air Canada v. M & L Travel Ltd. 913
Air Nova v. Messier-Dowty Ltd. 669
Aitken v. Gardiner 131, 139
Aitkin Agencies Ltd. v. Richardson 125
Akenzua v. Secretary of State for the Home Department 735
Albert v. Lavin 208, 250
Alberta (Minister of Public Works, Supply and Services) v. Nilsson 731
Alberta Wheat Pool v. Northwest Pile Driving Ltd. 660
Alcoa Minerals of Jamaica v. Broderick 575, 638
Alcock v. Chief Constable of South Yorkshire Police 288, **377**, 387
Alcorn v. Mitchell 59
Aldana v. March 516
Aldridge v. Van Patter 839, 844
Aleksic v. Canada (Attorney General) 711
Alexandrou v. Oxford 339
Allan v. Saskatoon 744
Allard v. Manahan 409
Allarie v. Victoria (City) 251
Allen v. C.F.P.L. Broadcasting Ltd. 109
Allen v. Flood 19, 889, 906, 915, 917, 926
Allen v. Head (C.) Ltd. 71
Allen v. Lucas 668
Allen v. Wright 245
Allen (Next friend of) v. University Hospitals Board 484
Alliance & Leicester Building Society v. Edgestop Ltd 652
Allis-Chalmers, Rumely Ltd. v. Forbes Equipment Ltd. 143
Allison v. Rank City Wall Can. Ltd. 341, 771
Alphacell Ltd. v. Woodward 541
Al's Steak House & Tavern Inc. v. Deloitte & Touche 709
Allsop v. Allsop 84
Amar Cloth House Ltd. v. LA Van & Co. 575
Amertek Inc. v. Canadian Commercial Inc. 895
Amin (Litigation Guardian of) v. Klironomos 408
Amos v. N.B. Elec. Power Comm. 297
Andersen v. St. Jude Medical Inc. 862

Anderson v. Excel Collection Services Ltd. 375
Anderson v. Skender 148
Anderson v. Wilson 375
Andrews v. Grand & Toy Alberta Ltd. 31, 601, 602, **603, 607, 613, 618, 621,** 974
Andrews v. R.A. Douglas 801
Angelopoulos v. Machen 685
Annand v. The Merchant's Bank 126
Anns v. Merton London Borough Council 282, 351, 424, 452, 475, 670, 716, 718, 719, 720, 721
Antell v. Simons 570
Antorisa Investments Ltd. v. 172965 Canada Ltd. 894
Apex Mountain Resort Ltd. v. British Columbia 433
Apotex Inc. v. Hoffman-LaRoche Ltd. 911
Arce (Guardian ad litem of) v. Simon Fraser Health Region 611
Archer v. Brown 896
Argyll v. Argyll 104
Aristorenas v. Comcare Health Services 517, 530, 543
Arkwright v. Newbould 891
Arland v. Taylor 484
Armak Chemicals Ltd. v. Canadian National Railway Co. 641
Armory v. Delamirie 124
Armstrong v. Langley (City) 819
Arnault v. Prince Albert (City) Police Commissioners 251
Arndt v. Smith 363, 399, 533
Arneil v. Paterson 552
Arnold v. Teno 602, 615, 974, 991
Arnold v. The King-Emperor 964
Arnott v. College of Physicians and Surgeons (Sask.) 937
Arruda v. Scarborough Hospital 530
Arthur v. Anker 221
Arthur J.S. Hall & Co. v. Simons 413, 416
Asamera Oil Corp. v. Sea Oil & Gen. Corp. 135, 140
Ashby v. White 105, 106, 107, 108, 729, 754, 818
Assiniboine South School Division, No. 3 v. Greater Winnipeg Gas Co. 579
Ashland Dry Goods Co. v. Wages 72
Aspden v. Maniaci 72
Atcheson v. College of Physicians and Surgeons (Alta.) 920
Athans v. Canadian Adventure Camps Ltd. 98, 903
Athey v. Leonati 537, **548,** 574, 589
Atkinson v. Newcastle & Gateshead Waterworks Co. 748
Atlantic Aviation Ltd. v. N.S. Light & Power Co. 160
Atlantic Leasing Ltd. v. Newfoundland 721
Aubry v. Éditions Vice-Versa 98
Augustus v. Gosset 598
Austin v. 3M Canada Ltd. 407, 411
Austin v. Dowling 72
Austin v. Rescon Construction (1984) Ltd. 149, 163
Australian Broadcasting Corp. v. Lenah Game Meats Pty. Ltd. 97, 98
Auto Concrete Curb Ltd. v. South Nation River Conservation Authority 423, 518
Auton (Guardian ad litem of) v. British Columbia (Attorney General) 497
Avco Financial Services Realty Ltd. v. Norman 424, 652
Ayangma v. Prince Edward Island 108

B.(A.) v. J.(I.) 35
B.(D.) v. Children's Aid Society of Durham (Region) 342, 519
B.(D.C.) v. Arkin 54
B.(E.) v. Order of the Oblates of Mary Immaculate in the Province of British Columbia 877
B.(K.L.) v. British Columbia 712, 876, 886
B.(M.) v. British Columbia 339, 876
B.(P.) v. B.(W.) 33, 60
B.(R.) v. Children's Aid Society of Metropolitan Toronto 198
B.C. Elec. Ry. Co. v. Loach 648
B.C. Electric Ry. Co. v. Clarke 600
B.D. v. Halton Region Children's Aid Society 342
B.D.C. Ltd. v. Hofstrand Farms Ltd. 285, **458**
Babcock v. Carr; Babcock v. Archibald 920
Babiuk v. Trann 212
Bachalo v. Robson 600
Bagnell v. Taser International, Inc. 725
Bain v. Calgary Board of Education 333

Bajkov v. Canil 512, 652
Baker v. Bolton 627
Baker v. Market Harborough; Wallace v. Richards 692
Baker v. Willoughby 555
Baldwin v. Daubney 434
Balkos v. Cook 629
Ball v. Manthorpe 220
Balmain New Ferry v. Robertson 68
Banerjee v. K Mart Canada Ltd. 245
Banfai v. Formula Fun Centre Inc. 823
Bank of British Columbia v. Canadian Broadcasting Corporation 944
Bank of Montreal v. Young 421
Bank of N.S. v. Gaudreau 920
Banks v. Bliefernich 80
Banks v. Globe & Mail Ltd. 955
Bannon v. Thunder Bay (City) 484, 712
Banyasz v. K-Mart Canada Ltd. 245
Barclay v. Fournier 54
Barker v. Montfort Hospital 517
Barker v. Saint Gobain Pipelines plc 544
Barkway v. South Wales Transport Co. 695
Barnard v. Carnegie 300
Barnes v. Carter 938
Barnett v. Chelsea & Kensington Hospital Management Committee 348, **529**
Barratt v. District of North Vancouver 714, 720
Barreiro v. Arana 864
Barrett v. Ministry of Defence 329
Barretts & Baird (Wholesale) Ltd. v. Institution of Professional Civil Servants 922
Barron v. Barron 44, 677
Bartin Pipe & Piling Supply Ltd. v. Epscan Industries Ltd. 122
Bartlett v. Children's Hospital Corp. 695
Bartlett et al. v. Weiche Apartments Ltd. 776
Barton v. Weaver 691
Basra v. Gill 677
Bastien v. Ottawa Hospital (General Campus) 375
Bateman v. Doiron 496
Baud Corp., N.V. v. Brook 140
Bauder v. Wilson 238
Baumeister v. Drake 329
Baurose v. Hart 601
Baxter & Co. v. Jones 345, 348
Bazley v. Curry 867, **868**
BBMB Finance (Hong Kong) Ltd. v. Eda Holdings Ltd. 135
Beaudesert Shire Council v. Smith 91, 926
Beaudry v. Tollman 847
Beaulieu v. Sutherland 375
Beaulne v. Ricketts 894
Beausoleil v. Soeurs de la Charité de la Providence 200
Bechard v. Haliburton Estate 304, 383, 574
Beckford v. R. 208
Beebe v. Robb 433
Beecham v. Henderson 548
Beecham v. Hughes 375
Behrens v. Bertram Mills Circus 857
Beim v. Goyer 251
Beljanski (Guardian ad litem of) v. Smithwick 635, 674
Belknap v. Meakes 543
Bell Canada v. Cope (Sarnia) Ltd. 232, 658, 688
Bell-Ginsburg v. Ginsburg 90
Bell Telephone Co. v. The Mar-Tirenno 227
Bellini Custom Cabinetry Ltd. v. Delight Textiles Ltd. 163
Belyea v. Hammond 616
Belzile v. Dumais 570, 582
Benarr v. Kettering Health Authority 367
Bennett v. Kailua Estates Ltd. 794
Bennett v. Stupich 936
Benning v. Wong 849
Benoit v. Farrell Estate 722
Benstead v. Murphy 616
Berardinelli v. Ontario Housing Corp. 712
Berendsen v. Ontario 712
Berezowski v. Edmonton 744
Berkoff v. Burchill 936
Bernard v. Attorney General of Jamaica 874
Bernstein v. Skyviews & General Ltd. 160
Bernstein v. Stoytcheva-Todorova 81
Berntt v. Vancouver (City) 232, 251, 252, 659
Berry v. Pulley 920
Beshada v. Johns-Manville Products Corp. 409
Bessell v. Wilson 255
Betker v. Williams 421

Bettel v. Yim 55
Betts v. Sanderson Estate 331, 668
Beutler v. Beutler 338
Bevilacqua v. Altenkirk 367
Bevis v. Burns 239
Bezusko v. Waterfall 397
BG Checo International Ltd. v. B.C. Hydro & Power Authority 435, 442
Bhadauria v. Board of Governors of Seneca College of Applied Arts and Technology 105, 754, 766
Bianco v. Fromow 637
Bielitski v. Obadiak 46, 85
Bifolchi v. Sherar 616
Big Point Club v. Lozon 163
Bigcharles v. Dawson Creek & District Health Care Society 543
Bigcharles v. Merkel 220
Bijeau v. Pelletier 349
Birch Builders v. Esquimalt (Township) 707
Birchard v. Alberta Securities Commission 417
Bird v. Holbrooke 221
Bird v. Jones 66, 90
Bisoukis v. Brampton (City) 712
Bitton v. Jakovljevic 896
Bjornson v. McDonald 637
Black v. Chrétien 710
Black v. New York, New Haven & Hartford Railroad 312
Blacklaws v. 470433 Alberta Ltd. 456
Blackwater v. Plint 35, 60, 574, 659, 876, 878, 886
Blackwood v. Butler 677
Blades v. Higgs 223
Blair's Plumbing & Heating Ltd. v. McGraw 639
Blake v. Barnard 64
Blake v. Kensche 771
Blakely v. 513953 Ont. Ltd. 185
Blatch v. Archer 541
Blessing v. United States 715
Block v. Martin 589
Bloor Italian Gifts Ltd. v. Dixon 518
Blyh v. Fladgate 865
Blyth v. Birmingham Waterworks Co 485, 489
Bob v. Bellerose 625
Bodley v. Reynolds 132
Body v. Murdoch 918
Boehringer v. Montalto 164
Bohun v. Sennewald 538
Boland v. Globe and Mail Ltd. 969
Bolduc and Bird v. R. 175
Bollinger v. Costa Brava Wine Co. 902
Bolton v. Forest Pest Management Institute 820, 823
Bolton v. Stone 488, 493, 577
Boma Manufacturing Ltd. v. Canadian Imperial Bank of Commerce 127, 130, 232, 659
Bongiardina v. York Regional Municipality 779
Bonham v. Pure Water Association 936
Boomer v. Atlantic Cement Co. 831
Boomer v. Penn 44, 509
Booth v. B.C.T.V. Broadcasting Systems 937
Booth et al. v. St. Catharines et al. 591
Border Enterprises Ltd. v. Beazer East Inc. 82, 422
Boss v. Robert Simpson Eastern Ltd. 589
Botiuk v. Toronto Free Press Publications Ltd. 935, 940
Bottom v. Ont. Leaf Tobacco Co. 831
Boudreau v. Benaiah 393, 417
Boulay v. Charbonneau 516
Boulay v. Rousselle 648
Boulet c. Entreprises M. Canada (Abitibi) Ltée 219
Bourden v. Alloway 10
Bourgoin v. Leamington (Municipality) 590
Bourgoin v. Ministry of Agriculture, Fisheries and Food 735
Bourhill v. Young 378, 390
Boutcher v. Stewart 677
Boutin v. Boutin 148
Bovingdon (Litigation Guardian of) v. Hergott 364, 613
Bow Valley Husky (Bermuda) Ltd. v. Saint John Shipbuilding Ltd. 289, 410, 472, **473,** 648, 659
Bowes v. Edmonton (City) 721
Boyachyk v. Dukes 951
Boyd v. Harris 624
Boyd Knight v. Purdue 433
Boys v. Star Printing and Publishing Co 968
Bradford v. Kanellos 583, 588
Bradford Corp. v. Pickles 804, 806
Bradford-Smart v. West Sussex County Council 334

Bradley v. Fisher 705
Brady v. Schatzel 62
Bradshaw Construction Ltd. v. Bank of Nova Scotia 130
Brandeis Goldschmidt & Co. v. Western Transport Ltd. 120
Brannon v. Airtours plc 332
Bransfield v. Fletcher 548
Brauer v. New York Cent. & H.R.R. Co. 593
Bray v. Palmer 691
Breen v. Saunders 239
Bresatz v. Przibilla 614
Brian v. Mador 601
Bridge v. Jo 358, 359
Bridges Brothers Ltd. v. Forest Protection Ltd. 165
Briffet v. Gander & District Hospital Board 517
Briggs v. Laviolette 245
Brimelow v. Casson 920
Brisson v. Brisson 599
Bristol & West of England Bk. v. Midland R. Co. 139
British Columbia v. Canadian Forest Products Ltd 641
British Columbia v. Imperial Tobacco Canada Ltd 545
British Columbia v. R.B.O. Architecture Inc. 421
British Columbia Public School Employers' Assn. v. British Columbia Teachers' Federation 154
British Railways Board v. Herrington 768, 780
Brito (Guardian ad litem of) v. Wooley 399
Broadfoot v. Ontario (Minister of Transportation and Communication) 329
Brock v. Anderson 397
Brown v. Baugh and Williams 252
Brown v. British Columbia (Minister of Transportation and Highways) 721
Brown v. Cole 659
Brown v. Dunsmuir 674
Brown v. Mack 939
Brown v. Wilson 207
Brown (Next Friend of) v. University of Alberta Hospital 342, 516
Brown and Brown v. B. & F. Theatres Ltd. 773
Brownlie v. Campbell 891
Bruce v. Coliseum Management Ltd. 50, 220
Bruce v. Dyer 62, 208
Brumer v. Gunn 518
Brushett v. Cowan 195, 590
Bryan v. Maloney 471
Buchan v. Ortho Pharmaceutical (Can.) Ltd. 397, 410
Buckland v. Guildford Gas Light & Coke Co. 297, 299
Buckley v. John Allen & Ford (Oxford), Ltd. 631
Buckley v. Smith Transport Ltd. 509
Buckley and T.T.C. v. Smith Transport Ltd. 507
Buehl v. Polar Star Enterprises Inc. 331
Bunyan v. Jordan 85
Burbank v. Bolton 499
Burgess (Litigation Guardian of) v. Canadian National Railway 742
Burmah Oil Co. v. Lord Advocate 226
Burman's Beauty Supplies Ltd. v. Kempster 423
Burnie Port Authority v. General Jones Pty. Ltd. 851, 886
Burrowes v. Lock 891
Burrows v. Burke 896
Buteikis v. Adams 573
Buthmann v. Balzer 471
Butler v. Egg Board 135
Butler v. Southam Inc. 937
Butler v. Standard Telephones & Cables, Ltd 821
Butterfield v. Forrester 648
Byrne v. Boadle 694
Byrne v. Deane 938

C. v. Wren 196, 197
C.B. v. Sawadsky 73
C.(D.) v. Newfoundland (Minister of Social Services) 342
C.(L.) v. Pinhas 198
C.E.S. v. Superclinics (Australia) Pty. Ltd. 367
C.N.R. v. Bakty 358
C.N.R. Co. v. Sask. Wheat Pool 570
C.R.F. Holdings Ltd. v. Fundy Chemical Int. Ltd. 893, 896
C.S. (Next friend of) v. Miller 513
Cachay v. Nemeth 61, 207, 212

Cadbury Schweppes Inc. v. FBI Foods Ltd. 103, 739
Cairns v. John Fairfax & Sons Ltd. 932
Calgary (City) v. Thomas 509
Calliou Estate (Trustee of) v. Calliou 328
Calveley v. Chief Constable of Merseyside 735
Calvert v. Law Society of Upper Canada 417, 708
Cambridge Water Co. v. Eastern Counties Leather plc 801, 850
Cameron v. Morang 117
Campbell v. Calgary Power Ltd. 300
Campbell v. Dominion Breweries Ltd. 135
Campbell v. Hudyma 249, 250
Campbell v. Jones 955
Campbell v. MGN Ltd. 98, 104
Campbell v. Royal Bank of Canada 776
Campbell v. MGN Ltd. 98
Campbell v. S.S. Kresge Co. 69
Campbell v. Spottiswoode 969
Campomar v. Nike 902
Can. Gen. Elec. Co. v. Pickford & Black Ltd. 304
Can. Pac. Ltd. v. Gill 644
Can. Western Natural Gas Co. v. Pathfinder Surveys Ltd. 642, 659
Canada (A.G.) v. Notre Dame Hospital 193
Canada (A.G.) v. Ottawa Carleton (City) 811
Canada (A.G.) v. Vantour 155
Canada (Attorney General) v. Clorey 640
Canada (Attorney General) v. Connolly 507
Canada Cement LaFarge Ltd. v. British Columbia Lightweight Aggregate Ltd. 184, 908
Canada Metal Co. Ltd. v. Canadian Broadcasting Corporation 972
Canada Safeway Ltd. v. Manitoba Food & Commercial Workers Local 832 91, 927
Canada v. Lukasik 80
Canada v. Saskatchewan Wheat Pool 108
Canadian Assn. of Regulated Importers v. Canada (A.G.) 766
Canadian Foundation of Children, Youth and the Law v. Canada (Attorney General) 216
Canadian National Railway Co. v. Norsk Pacific Steamship Co. 288, 472, 474, 479
Canadian National Railway Co. v. Vincent 759
Canadian Newspapers Co. v. Canada (Attorney General) 958
Canadian Pacific Ltd. v. Gill 520, 644
Canadian Pacific Ltd. v. Paul 155
Canadian Training and Development Group v. Air Canada 911
Candler v. Crane, Christmas & Co. 420
Candlewood Navigation Corporation Ltd. v. Mitsui O.S.K. Lines Ltd. (The Mineral Transporter) 284
Canson Enterprises Ltd. v. Boughton & Co. 3, 893
Cant v. Cant 88
Canterbury v. Spence 396
Capan v. Capan 96
Caparo Industries plc v. Dickman 283, 284, 433
Car & General Ins. Corp. Ltd v. Seymour et al. 666
Cardinal v. Loo 686
Carere v. Cressman 517
Caron Estate v. Paneak Estate 630
Carr v. Edmonton (City) Police 72
Carriere v. Bd. of Gravelbourg School Dist. No. 2244 of Sask. 774
Carriss v. Buxton 773
Carroll v. Chicken Palace Ltd 509
Carson v. Thunder Bay 669
Carstairs v. Taylor 848
Carter v. B.C. Federation of Foster Parents Assn. 941
Casey v. Automobiles Renault Canada Ltd. 80
Castle v. Stockton Waterworks 841
Cattanach v. Melchior 365, 366
Cattle v. Stockton Waterworks Co. 449, 479
Caxton Publishing Co. v. Sutherland Publishing Co. 132
Central & Eastern Trust v. Rafuse 436, 437
Central B.C. Planers Ltd. v. Hocker 421, 422
Central Can. Potash v. Govt. of Sask. 904
Central Trust Co. v. Rafuse 518

Chadwick v. British Railways Commission 383
Chae v. Min 664
Chaisson v. Hebert 512
Chamberlains v. Lai 416
Chamberland v. Fleming 664
Champigny v. Ste-Marie 517
Chand v. Sabo Brothers Realty Ltd. 421
Chaoulli v.Quebec (Attorney General) 497
Chapeskie v. Canadian Imperial Bank of Commerce 424
Chapman v. 3M Canada Inc. 109
Chapman v. Hearse 358
Chappel v. Hart 399, 533
Chappell v. Baratti 639
Charing Cross Electric Co. v. Hydraulic Power Co. 841
Charrington v. Simons & Co. Ltd. 163
Chartier v. Quebec (A.G.) 241
Chasse v. Evenson 517
Chatterton v. Secretary of State for India in Council 946
Check v. Andrews Hotel Co. 50
Cheevers v. Van Norden 521
Cherneskey v. Armadale Publishers Ltd. 659, 936, **960**
Cherrey v. Steinke 668
Cherry v. Ivey 81
Cherry (Guardian ad litem of) v. Borsman 366, 517
Chesher v. Monaghan 607
Chessie v. J.D. Irvine Ltd. 820
Chester v. Afshar 533
Cheticamp Fisheries Co-operative Ltd. v. Canada 920
Child and Family Services of Central Manitoba v. Lavallee 193, 203
Childs v. Desormeaux 293, 311, 329
Chilton v. Carrington 138
Chin v. Venning 17
Chmiliar v. Chmiliar 198
Chopra v. T. Eaton Co. 72
Chow (Litigation guardian of) v. Wellesley Hospital 516
Chow v. Hiscock 36
Chretien v. Jensen 331
Chrispen v. Kalinowski 737
Christie v. Davey 805
Christie v. Leachinsky 247
Christie v. Westcom Radio Group Ltd. 969
Christopherson v. Bare 61
Christopherson v. Saanich (District) 251
Chu v. Dawson 801, 847
Ciarlariello v. Schacter 200
CIBA-Geigy Canada Ltd. v. Apotex Inc. 897
Cimolai v. Hall 953
Cinapri v. Guettler 949
City of Brandon v. Farley 776
City of Ft. Smith v. Western Hide & Fur Co. 830
Claiborne Industries Ltd. v. National Bank of Canada 36, 911
Claiter v. Rose 656
Clark v. Canada 89, 109, 333
Clark v. Orr 139
Clark v. Scotiabank 375, 456
Clarke v. Penny 602
Clarke v. Stewart 938
Claxton v. Grandy 675
Clay v. Roberts 934
Cleary v. Hansen 357
Clement v. Leslies Storage Ltd. 635
Cliche c. Baie-James (Commission scolaire) 334
Clissold v. Cratchley 81
Cluett v. R. 251
Clyke v. Clyke 358
Cochran v. Hunter 52
Coco v. A.N. Clark (Engineers) Ltd. 104
Codner v. Gosse 44, 677
Cody v. Leonard 601
Coe Estate v. Tennant 635
Coffyne v. Silver Lake Regional Park Authority 768
Coggs v. Bernard 345
Cohen v. Lion Products Co. 87
Colangelo v. Mississauga (City) 712, 766
Colborne Capital Corp. v. 542775 Alberta Ltd. 920
Colby v. Schmidt 172
Cole v. South Tweed Heads Rugby League Football Club Limited 332
Coleman v. MacLennan 969
College of Dental Surgeons (Saskatchewan) v. Thorvaldson 919
Collin v. Lussier 36
Collins v. Renison 218
Color Your World Corp. v. Canadian Broadcasting Corporation 935
Comeau v. Laliberte 652

Comeau v. Saint John Regional Hospital 525
Comeau's Sea Foods Ltd. v. Canada (Minister of Fisheries & Oceans) 721
Cominco Ltd. v. Westinghouse Can. Ltd. 408
Committee for the Commonwealth of Canada v. Canada 154
Conklin v. Smith 600
Conn v. David Spencer Ltd. 71
Connery v. Gov't. of Man. 567
Conrad v. Crawford 668
Constantine v. Imperial London Hotels, Ltd. 106
Consumers Distributing Co. v. Seiko Time Canada Ltd. 898, 899
Conversions by Vantasy Ltd. v. General Motors of Canada Ltd. 423, 446, 925
Conway v. Jacques 200
Conway v. O'Brien 502
Cook v. Lewis 7, **15**, 532, 537, 547, 686, 687, **688**, 692, 693, 694
Cook v. S. 393
Cooper v. Hobart **285**, 291, 292, 293, 295, 309, 309, 351, 416, 421, 450, 723
Co-operators Insurance Association v. Kearney 882
Cope v. Sharpe 225
Coquitlam School District No. 43 v. D.(T.W.) 54, 335
Cormack v. Mara (Township) 784
Cormier v. Saint John (City) 249
Corothers v. Slobodian 357, 358
Corr v. IBC Vehicles 574
Corrie v. Gilbert 600
Costello v. Blakeson 574
Costello v. Calgary (City) 148, 155
Costello v. Chief Constable of Derbyshire Constabulary 114
Cotic v. Gray 300
Couch v. McCann 771
Couch v. Steel 748
Coueslan v. Canadian Mini-Warehouse Properties Ltd. (c.o.b. Public Storage Canadian) 341
Coughlin v. Kuntz 188, 396, 598
Couillard v. Waschulewski Estate 590
County of Parkland No. 31 v. Stetar; County of Parkland No. 31 v. Woodrow 349
Courchene v. Marlborough Hotel Co. 942
Courdin v. Meyers 625
Cousins v. Wilson 147
Couture-Jacquet v. Montreal Children's Hospital 203
Coward v. Baddeley 61
Cowles v. Balac 232, 659, 670, 683, **852**, 856
Cox v. Fleming 375, 375, 383
Cox v. Coulson 773
Cragg v. Tone 320
Craig v. North Shore Heli Logging Ltd. 149
Crawford v. Halifax 509
Crawford (Litigation guardian of) v. Penney 516
Cresswell v. Sirl 222
Crew v. Nicholson 686
Crocker v. Sundance Northwest Resorts Ltd. 300, **323**, 665, 669, 856
Crofter Hand Woven Harris Tweed Co. v. Vietch 910, 920
Cronk v. F.W. Woolworth Co. 245
Crosby v. Curry 860
Crossman v. R. 37, 737
Crowe v. Noon 242
Crown West Steel Fabricators v. Capri Insurance Services Ltd. 424, 659
Cryderman v. Ringrose 188
Cudmore v. Home Chec Canada Ltd. 669
Culhane v. ATP Aero Training Products Ltd. 925
Cumming (Litigation Guardian of) v. DeSouza 295
Cunningham v. Wheeler 643
Curll v. Robin Hood Multifoods Ltd. 393
Curran v. Northern Ireland Co-ownership Housing Assoc. Ltd. 284
Currie v. Blundell 397
Curry v. Vancouver (City) 417
Customs and Excise Commissioners v. Barclays Bank plc. 457
Culter v. Smith 59

D. v. East Berkshire Community NHS Trust 342
D. & F. Estates Ltd. v. Church Commissioners for England 284, 468, 470
D.(D.R.) v. G.(S.E.) 895
D.(P.A.) v. H.(A.E.) 574
D.C. Thomson & Co. Ltd. v. Deakin 915
D.N. v. Oak Bay (District) 519
Dabous v. Zuliani 518

Dahlberg v. Naydiuk 56, 163, **686**
Dahler v. Bruvold 847
Daigle v. Theo Couturier Ltd 864
Daishowa Inc. v. Friends of the Lubicon 908, 911, 921, 923
Dale v. Munthali 516
Dale's Trad'N Post v. Rhodes 938
Dallison v. Caffery 252, 256
Dalton v. Angus 884
D'Amato v. Badger 472, 480
Dang v. Guiltner 50
Daniels v. Thompson 38, 597
Danku v. Town of Fort Frances 848
Dao v. Sabatino 512
D'Aoust v. Lindsay 304
Darbishire v. Warren 639
Darling v. Attorney-General 886
Davenport v. Miller 88
Davey v. Harrow Corp 821
Davey v. Victoria General Hospital 373
David v. Toronto Transit Comm. 589
Davidson v. Chief Constable of North Wales 71
Davidson v. Connaught Laboratories 409
Davidson v. Toronto Blue Jays Baseball Ltd. 155
Davies v. Gabel Estate 517
Davies v. Mann 648
Davies v. Taylor 600
Davies & Davies Ltd. v. Kott 954
Davis v. Anderson 655
Davis v. McArthur 96, 101
Davis v. Radcliffe 293
Day v. Chaleur Developments Ltd. 771
Day v. Toronto Transit Commission 700
De Gurse v. Henry 686
De Jetley Marks v. Greenwood (Lord) et al. 909
De Vos v. Robertson 496
Deacon v. Canada (A.G.) 181
Deakins v. Aarsen 864
Decock v. Alberta 706, 875
Dee Trading Co. Pty. Ltd. v. Baldwin 125
DeFerrari v. Neville 397
Defosse v. Wilde 50, 212
Delacroix v. Thevenot 940
Delancey v. Dale & Co. Ltd. 79
Delaney v. Cascade River Holidays Ltd. 669
Delaware Mansions Ltd. v. Westminster City Council 803
Dellwo v. Pearson 512
Demarco v. Ungaro 413
Dendekker v. F.W. Woolworth Co. 245
Dennis v. Ministry of Defence 803, 812
Dennis v. Southam Co. 936
Dennison v. Sanderson 28
Depue v. Flateau 219, 229, 231
Deraps v. Coia 433
Dering v. Uris 28
Derry v. Peek 890
Des Brisay v. Canadian Government Merchant Marine Ltd. 484
Des Champs v. Conseil des Écoles séparées catholiques de langue française de Prescott-Russell 712
Desautels v. Katimavik 488
Deshane v. Deere & Co. 411
DeShaney v. Winnebago County Department of Social Services 340
Desjardins v. Arcadian Restaurants Ltd. 789
Devji v. Burnaby (District) 383
Devlin v. Smith 281
Devoe v. Long 223
Devon Lumber Co. v. MacNeill 159, 806
Deyo v. Kingston Speedway Ltd. 843
Dhalla v. Jodrey 516
Dickey v. McCaul 126
Didow v. Alberta Power Ltd. 163
Dietelbach v. British Columbia (Public Trustee) 393
Dilello v. Montgomery 624
Dill v. Excel Packing Company 829
Dillon v. LeRoux 516
Dillon v. O'Brien and Davis 255, 256
Dillon v. Twin State Gas and Elec. Co. 557
Dixon v. British Columbia Snowmobile Federation 669
DNM Mining Pty. Ltd. v. Barwick 557
Dobbs v. Mayer 44, 509, 677
Dobson (Litigation Guardian of) v. Dobson 19, 368, 765
Dodd Properties (Kent) Ltd. v. Canterbury C.C. 29, 638
Doe v. Metropolitan Toronto Board of Commissioners of Police 737
Doe d. Rochester v. Bridges 747
Doem v. Phillips Estate 686
Doiron v. Brideau 669
Doiron v. Caisse Populaire d'Inkerman Ltée. 233
Doiron v. Orr 366

Dokuchia v. Domansch 844
Dom. Securities Ames Ltd. v. Deep 518
Dom. Securities Ltd. v. Glazerman 135
Donnelly v. Jackman 61
Donoghue v. Stevenson. See also M'Alister (or Donoghue) v. Stevenson 7, 267, **276,** 282, 286, 287, 379, 401, 420, 671, 784, 843, 861, 921
Dooley v. C.N. Weber Ltd. 82
Dorschell v. Cambridge 520
Dorset Yacht Co. v. Home Office 721
D'Orta-Ekenaike v. Victoria Legal Aid 416
Doucette v. Parent 159
Doughty v. Turner Mfg. Co. 568
Douglas v. Hello! Ltd. 98, 104, 130, 918, 924, 925
Douglas v. Tucker 957
Douglas College v. Douglas/Kwantlen Faculty Assoc. 765
Dowler v. Bravender 855
Downing v. Moffett 857
Dowson v. The Queen 946
Draper v. Trist 903
Dredger Liesbosch v. Steamship Edison 575, 638
Drouillard v. Cogeco Cable Inc. 925
Dryden v. Campbell Estate 329, 331
D'Souza v. D.P.P. 261
Dubai Aluminium Co. Ltd. v. Salaam 874
Dube v. Labar 665
Dube (Litigation Guardian of) v. Penlon Ltd. 375
Duce v. Rourke; Pearce v. Rourke 562, 593
Ducharme v. Davies 652
Dudeck v. Brown 847
Dudek v. Li 590
Dudley v. Victor Lynn Lines Inc. 348
Dufault v. Excelsior Mortgage Corp 358
Duke v. Puts 954
Dulieu v. White & Sons 376
Dulude v. Canada 239
Dumbell v. Roberts 241
Duncan v. Braaten 779
Duncan v. Cammell Laird & Co. Ltd. 770
Duncan Estate v. Baddeley 629
Dunlap v. Philadelphia Newspapers Inc. 944
Dunlop v. Woollahra District Council 735
Dunn v. Birmingham Canal Co. 848
Dunn v. Dominion Atlantic Railway Co. 219, 326
Dunne v. Clinton 245
Dunsmore v. Deshield 271
Dunster v. Abbott 768
Dupuis v. New Regina Trading Co. Ltd 354
Dushynski v. Rumsey 573
Dutton v. Bognor Regis United Building Co. 423
Duval v. O'Beirne 932
Duval v. Seguin 368
Duwyn v. Kaprelian 375, 389
Dwyer v. Staunton 226, 230
Dyck v. Laidlaw 669
Dyck v. Manitoba Snowmobile Assn. Inc. 438, 669
Dyne Holdings Ltd. v. Royal Insurance Co. of Canada 95

E. Hulton & Co. v. Jones 936
E.(D.) (Guardian ad litem of) v. British Columbia 202
E.D.G. v. Hammer 60
E.(Mrs.) v. Eve 201
E.W. Scripps Co. v. Cholmondelay 938
E.W.B. Venootschap. v. J. Townend & Sons (Hull) Ltd. 902
Eady v. Tenderenda 517
Earl v. Wilhelm 345
Easson v. L.N.E. Rwy. Co. 695
East Suffolk Rivers Catchment Bd. v. Kent 359
Eastern & South African Telegraph Co. v. Cape Town Tramways Cos. 805
Eccles v. Bourque 236, **257**
Ed Miller Sales & Rentals Ltd. v. Caterpillar Tractor Co. 918, 927
Edgar v. Richmond (Township) 486
Edgeworth Construction Ltd. v. N.D. Lea & Associates Ltd. 458
Edmonton (City) v. Lovat Tunnel Equipment Inc. 469
Edmonton Journal v. Alberta (Attorney General) 958, 959
Edwards v. Law Society of Upper Canada 292
Edwards v. Lee's Administrators 41, 164
Egedebo v. Windermere District Hospital Assn. 543
Eid v. Dumas, Hatherly v. Dumas 666, 668

Elder, Dempster & Co. v. Paterson, Zochonis & Co. 439
Elderkin v. Merrill Lynch, Royal Securities Ltd. 421, 422
Eldridge v. British Columbia (Attorney General) 497
Elfassy v. Sylben Invts. Ltd. 848
Eliopoulos (Litigation Trustee of) v. Ontario (Minister of Health and Long-Term Care) 724
Elliot v. Chiarelli 518
Elliott v. Canadian Broadcasting Corporation 938
Elliott and Elliott v. Amphitheatre Ltd. 170
Ellis v. Stenning 137
Ellone v. Mesa 49
Elloway v. Boomars 572
Emeh v. Kensington and Chelsea and Westminster Area Health Authority 366
Emerald Const. Co. v. Lowthian 918
Emerson v. Insurance Corporation of British Columbia 359
Emmonds v. Makarewicz 525
Endean v. Canadian Red Cross Society 694
Engel v. Kam-Ppelle Holdings Ltd. 590, 601, 617
Engemoen Holdings Ltd. v. 100 Mile House 164
Engler v. Rossignol 521
Enterprises Sibeca Inc. v. Frelighsburg (Municipality) 706
Entick v. Carrington 145, 239
Enviro-Tex Products Ltd. v. Fibrex Insulations Inc. 921
Epstein v. Cressey Development Corp. 149, 164
Erie Ry. Co. v. Stewart 349
Erison v. Higgins 695
Erven Warnink B.V. v. J. Townend & Sons (Hull) Ltd. 898
Esanda Finance Corp. v. Peat Marwick Hungerfords (Reg) 433
Esser v. Brown 456
Esso Petroleum Co. v. Mardon 441
Estate of Sinthasamphone v. City of Milwaukee 340
Evans v. MacMicking 895
Everett v. Griffiths 708
Ex parte Drake 125
Execotel Hotel Corp. v. E.B. Eddy Forest Products Ltd. 159
Eyres v. Gillis & Warren Ltd 485

F.(D.) v. S.(A.) 36
F. (J.M.) v. Chappell 101
F.(P.) v. Ontario 98
Fiala v. Cechmanek 44, 55
Fairchild v. Glenhaven Funeral Services Ltd. 543, 692, 693, 694
Falkenham v. Zwicker 566
Fanjoy v. Gaston 774
Fardon v. Harcourt-Rivington 577
Farish v. National Trust Co. 421
Farrell v. Canadian Broadcasting Corporation 982
Federal Sugar Refining Co. v. United States Sugar Equalization Bd. 920
Federic v. Perpetual Investments Ltd. 848
Feener v. McKenzie 686
Feist v. Gordon 397
Feltham v. Terry 117
Fenn v. Peterborough 616, 623
Ferguson v. Hamilton Civic Hospitals 200
Ferguson v. McCann 771
Ferland v. Keith 345
Fiala v. Cechmanek 503
Fidler v. Sun Life Assurance Co. of Canada 32, 38
Fillier v. Whittom 660
Fillion v. New Brunswick International Paper Co 818
Fillipowich v. Nahachewsky 172
Findley v. Driver 652
Fine's Flowers Ltd. v. General Accident Assurance Co. 345, 421
Finigan v. Calgary 772
Finnigan v. Sandiford 261
First National Properties Ltd. v. Highlands (District) 735
Fisher v. Knibbe 596
Fisher v. Prince 135
Fitkin (Litigation Administrator of) v. Latimer 329
Fitzpatrick v. Durham Regional Police Services Board 79
Flame Bar B Q Ltd. v. Hoar 81
Fleming v. Atkinson 857, 860
Fleming v. Fleming 895
Fletcher v. Autocare & Transporters, Ltd. 610
Fletcher v. Bealey 822

Fletcher v. Collins 236, 242
Fletcher v. Manitoba Public Insurance Co. 345, 421
Floyd and Barker 705
Fobel v. Dean 615
Fogden v. Wade 65
Folland v. Ontario 81
Folland v. Reardon 416
Fontaine v. British Columbia (Official Administrator) 695
Fontin v. Katapodis 50
Foran v. Tatangello 707
Forde v. Skinner 59
Foreman v. Chambers 104, 599
Fortey (Guardian ad litem of) v. Canada (Attorney General) 652
Fortier v. Kapeller 148
Foster v. Morton 185
Fouldes v. Willoughby 115
Fowler v. Lanning 686
Fowler v. Schneider National Carriers Ltd 664
Frame v. Smith 88
France v. Gaudet 133
Francis v. Cockrell 773
Francis v. Dingman 893
Francis v. I.P.C.F. Properties Inc. 769
Franklin Supply Co. v. Midco Supply Co. 919
Fraser v. Berkeley 48
Fraser v. Board of School Trustees of School District No. 72 (Campbell River) 518
Fraser v. Westminer Canada Ltd. 295, 456
Fraser Jewellers v. Dominion Electric 669
Fraser River Pile & Dredge Ltd. v. Can-Dive Services Ltd. 868
Fraser-Reid v. Droumtsekas 466
Frawley v. Asselstine 636
Fredette v. Wiebe 367
Free Trade Medical Network Inc. v. RBC Travel Insurance Co. 104
Freeman v. Harrington 142
Freeman v. Home Office (No. 2) 61
Freeman v. Perlman 893
Freeman v. Sutter 462
Freeman-Maloy v. Marsden 735
Freer (Guardian ad litem of) v. Okanagan/Skaha School District No. 67 335
French v. Harbour Grace (Town) 660
Frenchay Healthcare National Health Service Trust v. S. 203
Frey v. Fedoruk 236, 243
Froom v. Butcher 654, 655
Fullerton (Guardian ad litem of) v. Delair 645
Fullowka v. Royal Oak Ventures Inc. 384, 779
Funk Estate v. Clapp 333, 586
Funnel v. Canadian Pacific Railway 232

G.(A.) v. British Columbia (Superintendent of Family & Child Services 342
G.(E.D.) v. Hammer 876, 886
G.(R.) v. Christison 342
G.A. v. McGregor 341
Gaca v. Pirelli General plc. 645
Gagne v. St. Regis Paper Co. 300
Gagnon v. Beaulieu 652
Gala v. Preston 185, 670, 674
Gala Homes Inc. v. Flisar 953
Galantiuk v. Regina 642
Galaske v. O'Donnell 300, 484, 652, 656, **755**
Gallant v. Central Credit Union Ltd. 422
Gambriell v. Caparelli 56, **209**
Gamracy v. R. 249
Garland v. Consumers' Gas Co. 39
Garland v. Rowsell 630
Garrett v. Attorney-General 730, 735
Garratt v. Dailey 46, 54
Garry v. Sherritt Gordon Mines Ltd. 910, 919
Gartside v. Sheffield, Young & Ellis 462
Gaudet v. Sullivan 172
Gaudreault c. Drapeau 321
Gaunt v. Fynney 805
Gazette Printing Co. v. Shallow 957, 959
Geld v. Dehavilland Aircraft of Can. Ltd. 641
Gemco Equipment Ltd. v. Westen 878
Gen. & Finance Facilities Ltd. v. Cooks Cars (Romford) Ltd. 136
General Baking Co. v. Gorman 900
General Motors Acceptance Corp. of Canada v. Fulton Insurance Agencies Ltd. 421
Genik v. Ewanylo 656
George v. Beaubien 706
George v. Skivington 279, 281
Gerigs v. Rose 55

Gerling Global General Insurance Co. v. Siskind, Cromarty, Ivey & Dowler 659
German v. Major 417
Gerrard v. Manitoba 917, 925
Gersham v. Manitoba Vegetable Producers' Marketing Board 736, 927
Gertsen v. Municipality of Metropolitan Toronto 420, 839, **844**, 849
Gervais v. Richard 630
Getejanc v. Brentwood College Assn. 101
Giannone v. Weinberg 612
Gibbons v. Duffell 947, 954
Gibbons v. Port Hope & District Hospital 373
Giffels Associates Ltd v. Eastern Const. Co. 659
Gifford v. Dent 161
Gilbert v. Showerman 829
Gilbert v. Stone 47
Gilles E. Néron Communication Marketing Inc. v. Chambre des notaires du Québec 929
Gillick v. West Norfolk & Wisbech Area Health Authority et al. 196
Gilson v. Kerrier District Council 848
Glamorgan Coal Co. Ltd. v. South Wales Miners' Federation 916, 919
Glanville v. Sutton 857
Glanzer v. Shepard 432
Glasgow Corporation v. Muir et al. 485
Glivar v. Noble 525
Globe & Mail Ltd. v. Boland 955, 964
Gloster v. Toronto Electric Light Co. 494
Gnanasegaram v. Allianz Insurance Co. of Canada 108
Gobin (Guardian ad litem of) v. British Columbia 721
Godin v. Wilson Laboratories Inc. 411
Golden Capital Securities Ltd. v. Holmes 910
Goldhawke v. Harder 590
Goldman v. Hargrave 803, 849
Good-Wear Treaders v. D. & B. Holdings Ltd. 411
Goodwin v. McCully 524
Goodwin v. Pine Point Park 820
Goodwyn v. Cheveley 860
Gootson v. R. 44, 509
Gordelli Management Ltd. v. Turk 423
Gordon v. Denison 255
Gordon v. Greig 603
Gordon v. Moen 433
Gordon v. Wallace 509
Gottardo Properties (Dome) Inc. v. Toronto (City) 300
Gould Estate v. Stoddart Publishing Co. 99
Governors of the Peabody Donation Fund v. Sir Lindsay Parkinson & Co. 284
Graham v. Hodgkinson 677
Graham v. K.D. Morris & Sons Pty. Ltd. 163
Graham v. Persyko 486
Graham v. Picot Gorman and A.E.S. Consultants Ltd. 518
Graham v. Rourke 573, 616
Graham v. Saville 91, 175, 894
Grand Restaurants of Canada Ltd. v. Toronto (City) 423, 652
Grant v. Australian Knitting Mills Ltd. 745
Gray v. Cotic 574, 590
Gray v. Gill 601
Gray v. Macklin 656
Great Atlantic & Pacific Tea Co. v. Roch 87
Greatorex v. Greatorex 375
Green v. Lawrence 251
Green v. Minnes 944
Greenall v. MacDougall 538
Greening v. Wilkinson 132
Greenock Corp. v. Caledonian Railway Co. 848
Greenwood v. Bennett 136, 223
Greeven v. Blackcomb Skiing Enterprises Ltd. 669
Gregg v. Scott 546
Gregory v. Portsmouth City Council 79
Gringmuth v. North Vancouver (District) 712
Grise v. Rankin et al. 676
Groom v. Selby 366
Gros v. Victoria General Hospital 486
Gross v. Great-West Life Assurance Co. 423
Gross v. Wright 174
Grosse v. Purvis 98
Grove Services Ltd. v. Lenhart Agencies Ltd. 349
Groves v. Morton 396
Grzywacz v. Vanderheide 383
Guay v. Sun Publishing Co. 85, 393
Guilford Industries Ltd. v. Hankinson Management Services Ltd. 82

Guimond v. Laberge 177
Gurniak v. Nordquist 642
Guy v. Trizec Equities Ltd. 644
Gwynne v. Dominion Stores Ltd. 768

H.(M.) v. Bederman 341
H.(R.) v. Hunter 363
H.(V.A.) v. Lynch 424
H.G. v. Shamrock School Division No. 38 216
H.L. v. Canada (Attorney General) 484, 642, 876
H. v. R. 61
Hôpital Notre-Dame de l'Espérance v. Laurent 881
Haag v. Marshall 543
Hackshaw v. Shaw 17, 220
Hagblom v. Henderson 518
Haggarty v. Desmarais 329
Hague v. Billings 328, 548
Hague v. Deputy Governor of Parkhurst Prison 69
Haig v. Bamford 421, 426, 518
Haile v. Johns 600
Hale v. Jennings Brothers 849
Haley v. London Electricity Board 306, 509
Haley v. Richardson; McCrae v. Richardson 656
Halifax Building Society v. Thomas 895
Halkyard v. Mathew 398
Hall v. Bennett Estate 462
Hall v. Hebert 184, 331, 663, **670**
Hall v. Smith 865
Hall (Litigation Guardian of) v. Kellar 371
Halprin v. The Sun Publishing Company Ltd. 938
Halushka v. University of Saskatchewan 187
Hambourg v. T. Eaton Co. Ltd. 775
Hambrook v. Stokes Brothers 376, 380
Hamel et al. v. Prather et al. 622
Hamlyn v. Houston & Co 865
Hammond v. Wabana (Town) 498
Hamstra (Guardian ad litem of) v. British Columbia Rugby Union 602
Handcock v. Baker 245, 261
Hanisch v. Canada 72, 241
Hanke v. Resurfice Corp. 534, 537, 694
Hanson v. St. John Horticultural Assn. 669
Hanson v. Wayne's Café Ltd. 68
Hanson et al. v. City of St. John et al. 776
Harbour Equipment v. Canadian National Railway Co. 135
Harbutt's Plasticine v. Wayne Tank & Pump Co. 639
Harder v. Brown 182
Hardisty v. 851791 N.W.T. Ltd. 878
Hare & Grolier Society v. Better Business Bureau 944
Harela v. Powell 518
Harker v. Birkbeck 10
Harland v. Fancsati 896
Harpe v. Lefebvre 547
Harrington (Public Trustee of) v. Pappachristos 709
Harris v. Digital Pulse Pty. Ltd. 3
Harris v. Nashville Trust Co. 939
Harris v. Wong 220
Harrison v. Carswell 28, **149**, 154, 226, 766
Harrison v. University of British Columbia 154
Harriton v. Stephens 363
Harry Winton Investments Ltd. v. CIBC Development Corp. 920
Hartjes v. Carmen 398
Hartlen v. Chaddock 172, 185
Hartman v. Fisette 660
Hasegawa & Co. v. Pepsi Bottling Group (Canada) Co. 471
Hasenclever v. Hoskins 88, 95
Hashem and Hashem v. N.S. Power Corp. 162
Haskett v. Equifax Canada Inc. 434, 456
Haskett v. Univ. of Western Ont. 771
Hatton v. Webb 58
Haughian v. Paine 395
Haward v. Bankes 10
Hawkins v. McGee 31
Hawley v. Bapoo 78, 708
Hay (Bourhill) v. Young 304, 375, 580
Hayduk v. Pidoborozny 864
Haynes v. Nfld. Telephone Co. 147, 164
Hayward v. Thompson 938
Hearndon v. Rondeau 600
Heath v. Weist-Barron School of Television (Canada) Ltd. 98
Heaven v. Pender 266, 277, 278, 280
Hedley Byrne & Co. v. Heller & Partners Ltd. 282, 288, 344, 419, 420, 460, 896, 918

Heeney v. Best 524, 651
Hefferman v. Elizabeth Irving Service Centre 639
Heffron v. Imperial Parking Co. 123
Hegarty v. Shine 176, 183
Heighington v. Ontario 88, 375, 598
Heil v. Rankin 625
Heinicke v. Cooper Rankin Ltd. 457
Heintzman & Co. v. Hashman Const. Ltd. 847
Hellenius v. Lees 695
Heller v. Martens 656, 663
Helmy v. Helmy 911
Hempler v. Todd 331
Hendrick v. De Marsh 420, 519, 586
Hendricks v. R. 349
Henly v. Mayor of Lyme 730
Henry Thorne & Co. v. Sandow 901
Hercules Managments Ltd. v. Ernst & Young 424, 476
Herd v. Weardale Steel, Coal and Coke Co. Ltd. 73
Herman v. Graves 50, 208
Hern v. Nichols 865
Herring v. England (Ministry of Defence) 616
Hersees Ltd. v. Goldstein 910
Hewson v. Red Deer 590
Hickey v. Electricity Reduction Co. 817
Hicks v. Faulkner 75
Higgins v. William Inglis & Sons Pty. Ltd. 857
High Parklane Consulting Inc. v. Royal Group Technologies Ltd. 90
Hilderman v. Rattray 686
Hill v. British Columbia 69
Hill v. Chief Constable of West Yorkshire 284, 339
Hill v. Church of Scientology 33, 36, 624, 766, 929, 930, 955, **956, 973**
Hill v. Church of Scientology of Toronto
Hill v. Hamilton-Wentworth Regional Police Services Board 295, 518
Hill v. Hurst 499, 651
Hill v. Van Erp 462
Hills v. Bridgeview Little League Association 334
Himmelman v. Nova Const. Co. 849
Hinde v. Skibinski 80
Hinz v. Berry 375, 376
Hoare v. McAlpine 848
Hodgkinson v. Martin 51
Hodgson v. Canadian Newspapers Co. 935, 968, 970
Hodgson v. Trapp 642
Hofstrand Farms Ltd. v. B.D.C. Ltd. 518
Holan Estate v. Stanton Regional Health Board 55, 333
Holcombe v. Whitaker 62
Holderness v. Goslin 849
Hole v. Sittingbourne & Sheerness Railway Co. 886
Holinaty v. Hawkins 848, 849
Holland v. Saskatchewan (Minister of Agriculture, Food and Rural Revitalization 724
Hollebone v. Barnard 658
Hollett v. Coca-Cola Ltd. 341, 592
Hollins v. Fowler 120, 121
Hollinsworth v. BCTV 100
Hollis v. Dow Corning Corp. 400, 532
Hollywood Silver Fox Farm Ltd. v. Emmett 804
Holmes v. Mather 14
Holt v. Sun Publishing Co. Ltd. 968
Holt v. Verbruggen 50
Holtby v. Brigham & Cowan (Hull) Ltd. 544, 693
Holtslag v. Alberta 724
Home Office v. Dorset Yacht Co. Ltd. 282, 333
Homer v. Comeau 686
Honan v. Gerhold 864
Hongkong Bank of Canada v. Richardson Greenshields of Canada Ltd. 601
Hooey v. Mancini 331
Hooiveld v. Van Biert 573
Hook v. Cunard SS. Co. 217
Hopp v. Lepp 188, 192, 204, 395, 396, 397, 532
Hooper v. Rogers 822
Horne v. New Glasgow (Town) 376
Hornick v. Kochinsky 600
Horrocks v. Lowe 956
Horseshoe Bay Retirement Society v. S.I.F. Development Corp. 36, 149
Horsley v. MacLaren 108, 319, **352**, 499, **753**
Horton v. Tim Donut Ltd. 903
Hosking v. Runting 98
Host v. Bassett 691
Hotson v. East Berkshire Area Health Authority 546
Hougen v. Kuehn 50

Houle v. S.S. Kresge Co. 779
Houseman v. Coulson 936
Housen v. Nikolaisen 300, 484
Howard v. Furness Houlder Argentine Lines, Ltd. 841
Howarth v. The Queen 708
Howes v. Crosby 601
Hudson v. Brantford Police Services Board 244
Hudson v. Riverdale Colony of Hutterian Brethren 847
Hudson's Bay Co. v. White 155
Hughes v. Lord Advocate 567, 580
Hughes v. Sunbeam Corp. (Canada) 462, 470
Hung v. Gardiner 949, 953
Hunt v. Carey Canada Inc. 544
Hunt v. Sutton Group 331
Hunt v. T&N plc. 409
Hunt (Litigation Guardian of) v. Sutton Group Incentive Realty Inc. 330, 683
Hunter v. Briere 566, 648, 660
Hunter v. Canary Wharf Ltd. 94, 95, 96, 802
Hunter v. Manning 573
Hurley v. Eddingfield 348
Hutchings v. Dow 538
Hutchings v. Nevin 509, 652
Huth v. Huth 939
Hutscal v. I.A.C. Ltd. 134
Hutterly v. Imperial Oil Ltd. 359
Hymas v. Ogden 138
Hynes v. Hynes 823

I.W. Holdsworth Ltd. v. Assoc. Newspapers Ltd. 935
Ilic v. Calgary Sun 82
Innes v. Wylie 59, 62
In re "Agent Orange" Product Liability Litigation 545
In re A.C. 373
Indermaur v. Dames 773, 775
Indian Head Credit Union Ltd. v. A. Hosie & Co. 518
Indust. Teletype Electronics Corp. v. Montreal 641
Ingles v. Tutkaluk Construction Ltd. 721, 723
Ingram v. Lowe 334
Insurance Corp. of British Columbia v. Mandzuk 613
Int. Brotherhood of Teamsters, Local 213 v. Therien 906, 927
Intrawest Corp. v. No. 2002 Taurus Ventures Ltd. 445
Inverugie Investments Ltd. v. Hackett 30
Irvington Holdings Ltd. v. Black 121
Isaack v. Clark 125
Ismail v. Treats Inc. 422, 446
Isreal James Hussey 220
ITO – International Terminal Operators Ltd. v. Miida Electronics Inc. 669
iTrade Finance Holdings Inc. v. Webworx Inc. 896
Iversen v. Purser 331

J.(L.A.) v. J.(H.) 342
J.(M.I.) v. Grieve 68
J.C. Kerkhoff & Sons Contracting Ltd. v. XL Ironworks Co. 907
J.M. v. W.B. 660
J.T. Stratford & Son v. Lindley 906
Jack Cewe Ltd. v. Jorgenson 644
Jacks v. Davis 518
Jackson v. Harrison 185
Jackson v. Kelowna 538
Jackson v. Millar et al. 623, 695
Jacobi v. Griffiths 876
Jacobsen v. Nike Canada Ltd 330
Jacobson v. Kinsmen Club of Nanaimo 331
Jaensch v. Coffey 381
Jaman Estate v. Hussain 875
Jameel v. Wall Street Journal Europe Sprl 960
James v. British Columbia 460
James Street Hardware and Furniture Co. v. Spizziri 640
Jane Doe v. Metropolitan Toronto (Municipality) Commissioners of Police 239, **336**, 736
Janiak v. Ippolito 546, 590, 600, 601
Janigan v. Taylor 895
Jarvis v. Williams 124, 140
Jebson v. Ministry of Defence 332, 570
Jeffrey v. Commodore Cabaret Ltd. 779
Jens v. Mannix Co. Ltd. 640
Jerabek c. Accueil Vert-Pré d'Huberdeau 333
Jill Fishing Ltd. v. Koranda Management Inc. 975
Jinks v. Cardwell 333
Jobling v. Associated Dairies Ltd. 557

John v. Flynn 330, 331
John Bead Corp. v. Soni 185, 674
John Campbell Law Corp. v. Strata Plan 1350 847
John Doe v. Bennett 342, 877
John Lewis & Co. v. Tims 245, 252
John Maryon Int. Ltd. v. N.B. Telephone Co. 642
Johnson v. British Columbia Hydro and Power Authority 147, 155
Johnson v. Leigh 258
Johnson v. Royal Can. Legion Grandview Branch No. 179 182
Johnson v. Webb 669
Johnston v. Re/max Real Estate (Edmonton) Ltd. 421
Jolley v. Sutton London B.C. 569, 587
Jones v. Bennett 968
Jones v. Brooks 970
Jones v. Dowle 137, 139
Jones v. Richard 769
Jones v. Swansea City Council 735
Jones v. Wabigwan 566
Jones (Guardian ad litem of) v. Rostvig 364
Jordan House Ltd. v. Menow 108, 220, 324, 669, 754
Joseph Brant Memorial Hospital v. Koziol 517, 690
Joshi v. Wooley 366
Joslyn v. Berryman; Wentworth Shire Council v. Berryman 668
Joudrey v. Swissair Transport Company 359
Joule Ltd. v. Poole 123
Joy v. Newell (t/a Copper Room) 332
Joyal v. Barsby 510
Jozwiak v. Sadek 938
Juelle v. Trudeau 126
Junior Books Ltd. v. Veitchi 470
Just v. British Columbia 285, 288, 711, **713**

K v. Secretary of State for the Home Department 339
K.J.D. v. Choy 200
K.(K.) v. G.(K.W.) 32, 36, 342
K.(M.J.) v. M.(J.D.) 802
K.(W.) v. Pornbacher 574
Kahler v. Midland Bank Ltd. 124
Kamloops (City) v. Nielsen 284, 471, 475, 670, 716, 718, 720
Kamin v. Kawartha Dairy Ltd. 789
Kamloops (City of) v. Nielsen 471, 475, 670, 721
Kaplan v. Canada Safeway Ltd. 768
Karogiannis v. Poulus 245
Karpenko v. Paroian, Courey, Cohen & Houston 416
Katzman v. Yaeck 589
Kauffman v. Toronto Transit Commission 528
Kavanagh v. Akhtar 574
Kay Aviation b.v. v. Rofe 920
Kealey v. Berezowski 366, 367
Keats v. Pearce 367
Keays v. Honda Canada Inc. 36, 109
Keeble v. Hickeringill 889, 926
Keegan v. Chief Constable of Merseyside Police 79
Keep v. Quallman 52
Keeping v. Canada (Minister of Fisheries and Oceans) 722
Keith Plumbing & Heating Co. v. Newport City Club Ltd. 422
Keizer v. Hanna 619, **630**
Kelly v. Lundgard 421, 525
Kelsen v. Imperial Tobacco Co. (of Great Britain and Ireland) Ltd. 161, 163
Kendall v. Gambles Canada Ltd. 245
Kenlin v. Gardiner 208, 250
Kennaway v. Thompson 828
Kennedy v. Hanes 62
Kennedy v. Hughes Drug (1969) Inc. 566
Kennedy v. Waterloo (County) Board of Education 789
Kent v. Dom. Steel & Coal Corp. Ltd. 801
Kent v. East Suffolk Rivers Catchment Board 718, 720
Kent v. Ellis 124
Kent v. Griffiths 320
Kerlenmar Holdings Ltd. v. Matsqui (District) 804
Kern v. Steele 601
Kerr v. Fleming Financial Corp. 135
Kerr v. Revelstoke Bldg. Materials Ltd. 157
Kettlewell v. Refuge Assurance Co. 895
Kevington Building Corp. v. Lee 639
Keys v. Mistahia Regional Health Authority 372
Khan v. El Al Israel Airlines 74
Khanna v. Royal College of Dental Surgeons (Ontario) 79, 81

Khazzaka v. Commercial Union Assurance Co. of Canada 38
Khorasandjian v. Bush 96, 802
Killip's Television Services Ltd. v. Stony Plain (Town) 498, 517
King v. Fanklin 217
King v. Leith 135
King v. Phillips 304, 580
Kingsbridge Development Inc. v. Hanson Needler Corp. 163
Kirby v. Canadian Tire 411
Kirkbi AG v. Ritvik Holdings Inc. 901, 902
Kirkham v. Chief Constable of Greater Manchester Police 184
Kitchener (City of) v. Robe & Clothing Co. 886
Klein v. American Medical Systems, Inc. 724
Knife (Litigation Guardian of) v. Charles 375
Knockwood v. Cormier 170
Knodell v. New Westminster (City) 722
Knuppfer v. London Express Newspaper, Ltd. 937
Knutson v. Farr 624
Koechlin v. Waugh and Hamilton 246
Kohn v. Globerman 73
Kondis v. State Transport Authority 886
Koperdak v. Wiesblatt 789
Kopka et ux. v. Bell Telephone Co. of Pennsylvania 146
Kovacs v. Ontario Jockey Club 72
Kozak v. Funk 601
Kraft (Next friend of) v. Oshawa General Hospital 596
Kralj v. Murray 484
Krangle (Guardian ad litem of) v. Brisco 363, 612, 642
Kripps v. Touche Ross & Co. 420, 421
Kroeker v. Jansen 616
Krouse v. Chrysler Canada Ltd. 98, 903
Krznaric v. Chevrette 737
Kuddus v. Chief Constable of Leicestershire Constabulary 33, 735
Kuwait Airways Corp. v. Iraqi Airways Co. 134

L.(H.) v. Canada (Attorney General) 35
L.(J.) v. Canada (Attorney General) 333
Létourneau v. Imperial Tobacco Ltd. 411
Labrador School Board v. R.P. 55
Labrecque v. Saskatchewan Wheat Pool 408
LAC Minerals Ltd. v. International Corona Resources Ltd. 40, 103
Lacroix v. R. 163
Lacroix (Litigation Guardian of) v. Dominique 364
Laface v. Williams 328
Laferrière v. Lawson 546
Lafleur v. Maryniuk 331
Lagden v. O'Connor 575, 638
Lai v. Gill 636
Lajeunesse v. Janssens 864
Lajoie v. Kelly 109
Lakefield (Village) v. Black 433
Lakeview Gardens Ltd. v. Regina (City) 827
Lam v. Sorochan Estate 574
Lamb v. London Borough of Camden 593
Lambert v. Lastoplex Chemicals Co. 401, 408
Lambert v. Thomson 939
Lambton v. Mellish 553
Lamine v. Dorrell 135
Lampert v. Simpson Sears Ltd. 779
Lan v. Wu 617
Landry v. Patterson 50
Lane v. Holloway 50, 172, 181, 185
Lang v. Burch 72, 249
Lang v. Giraudo 895
Langridge v. Levy 83, 281
Lankenau v. Dutton 557
Lapensee v. Ottawa Day Nursery Inc. 335
Lapierre v. A.G. Que. 227, 409
LaPlante (Guardian ad litem of) v. LaPlante 335, 513
Lapointe v. Hôpital Le Gardeur 522
Larche v. Ontario 333
Lareau v. La Compagnie d'Imprimerie de la Minerve 935
LaSalle Extension University v. Fogarty 87
Latin v. Hospital for Sick Children 516
Latter v. Braddell 178, 180
Laugher v. Pointer 878
Lauritzan v. Barstead 570
Lavigne v. O.P.S.E.U. 765
Laviolette v. C.N.R. 512, 652, 669
Law Estate v. Simice 495
Lawrence v. Finch 936
Lawson v. Burns 976
Lawson v. Wellesley Hospital 55

Layden v. Cope 516
LeBar v. Canada 69, 72
Le Lievre v. Gould 277, 278, 433
Leake v. Loveday 124
Leaman v. Rea 691, 694
Leame v. Bray 12
LeBlanc v. Canada 735
Lebrun v. High-Low Foods Ltd. 71
Lee v. Dawson 625
Lee v. O'Farrell 652
Lee v. Shalom Branch No. 178 Building Society 159
Lee (Guardian ad litem of) v. Barker 652
Lee v. Dawson 623
Leech v. Leader Publishing Co. 968
Leenen v. Canadian Broadcasting Corporation 968
Lehnert v. Nelson 331
Lehnert v. Stein 666
Leigh v. Cole 255
Leigh and Sullivan Ltd. v. Aliakmon Shipping Co. 284
LeLievre v. Gould 266
Lem v. Borotto Sports Ltd. 409, 410
Leslie v. Ball 413, 415
Letang v. Cooper 17, 687
Letnik v. Metropolitan Toronto (Municipality) 543
Leung v. Campbell 397
Levesque v. Day & Ross Ltd. 677
Levesque v. Wedge 521
Lewis v. Chief Constable 249
Lewis v. Daily Telegraph 935
Lewis v. Oeming 854, 856, 857
Lewis v. Prince Edward Island 721
Lewis v. Todd 620, 634, 651
Lewis (Guardian ad litem of) v. British Columbia 722, 884
Lewvest Ltd. v. Scotia Towers Ltd. 163
Ley v. Hamilton 974
Lian v. Money 636
Lickoch v. Madu 820, 847
Ligate v. Abick 620
Lim v. Titov 164
Lincoln v. Daniels 950, 951
Lincoln v. Hayman 642
Lindal v. Lindal 623
Lindon v. Hooper 117
Lipiec v. Borsa 97
Lippiatt v. South Gloucestershire Council 803
Lister v. Hesley Hall Ltd. 874
Lister v. Romford Ice & Cold Storage Co. 867
Little v. Ottawa (City) 708
Little v. Peers 242
Littleford v. Loanex Financial Services 143
Livingstone v. Canada (Attorney General) 481
Livingstone v. Rawyards Coal Co. 29
Lloyd v. Grace, Smith & Co. 865, 870
Loan v. MacLean 936
Logan Lake (Dist.) v. Rivtow Industries Ltd. 471
London Borough of Southwark v. Williams 226
London Computer Operators Training Ltd. v. British Broadcasting Corporation 944
London Drugs Ltd. v. Kuehne & Nagel International Ltd. 669, 868, 871
London Graving Dock Co. Ltd. v. Horton 776
London Health Sciences Centre v. K.(R.) (Litigation Guardian of) 203
London Passenger Transport Board v. Upson 762
Loney v. Butch 173
Long v. Gardner 50
Lord v. McGregor 97
Long v. R. 121
Long v. Toronto Ry. Co. 648
Longley v. Canada 735
Longmeid v. Holliday 281
Lonrho Ltd. v. Fayed 910, 923
Lonrho Ltd. v. Shell Petroleum Co. (No. 2) 910
Lonrho plc. v. Tebbit 709
Loop v. Litchfield 281
Lord (Litigation Guardian of) v. Downer 630
Lorenz v. Winnipeg (City) 300
Losee v. Clute 281
Lougheed v. Canadian Broadcasting Corporation 936
Louie v. Lastman (No. 2) 88
Lowe v. Guarantee Co. of North America 434, 456
Lowe v. The Guarantee Company of North America 724
Lowns v. Woods 320
Lowry v. Cdn. Mountain Holidays Ltd. 525

Lucas v. Antoniak 656
Ludlow v. Burgess 250
Lumley v. Gye 913, 917
Lumley v. Wagner 914
Lunenburg (County) District School Board v. Piercey 333
Lynch v. Knight 84
Lynch v. Lynch 372
Lyne v. McClarty 517, 574
Lyon v. Village of Shelburne 849
Lyon and Lyon v. Daily Telegraph, Ltd 963
Lysko v. Braley 104, 918, 921
Lyth v. Dagg 182, 341

M. v. Toronto Board of Education 199
M.(A.) v. Matthews 80
MCC Proceeds Ltd. v. Lehman Bros. (Europe) 130
M. Hasegawa & Co. v. Pepsi Bottling Group (Canada) Co. 470
M.(K.) v. M.(H.) 60
M.(M.) v. K.(K.) 181
M.B. v. British Columbia 642
M.S. v. Baker 367
M.Y. v. Boutros 368
MacAlpine v. H.(T.) 708
Macartney v. Warner 629, 630
MacCabe v. Westlock Roman Catholic Separate School District No. 110 333, 335, 518, 617
MacDonald v. Alderson 611
MacDonald v. Hees 217
Macdonald v. Mail Printing Co. 935
MacDonald v. Mitchell 864
MacDonald v. Sebastian 59, 598
MacDonald v. Woodard 684
MacDonald (Guardian ad litem of) v. Neufeld 612
Mack v. Canada (Attorney General) 488
MacKay v. Buelow 90, 96
MacKay v. MacLellan 660
MacKay Estate v. Smith 629
MacKeigan v. Hickman 708
MacKenzie v. Scotial Lumber Co. 118, 135
MacKinnon v. Ellis 860
MacLean v. Liquor Lic. Bd. of Ontario 710
MacLean v. MacDonald 629
Maclenan v. Segar 773
MacMillan v. Hincks 208
MacPherson v. Buick Motor Company 281
Mader v. MacPhee 864
Madge v. Meyer 656
Magnusson v. Bd. of Nipawin School Unit No. 61 of Sask. 335
Mahal v. Young 58, 62, 91
Mainland Sawmills Ltd. v. IWA-Canada, Local 1-3567 Society 88, 96
Mainstream Properties Limited v. Young 104, 130, 918, 924, 925
Mainville v. Ottawa Board of Education 335
Majrowski v. Guy's and St Thomas's NHS Trust 876
Makow v. Winnipeg Sun 945
Malat v. Bjornson (No. 2) 721
Malette v. Shulman 59, **190,** 192
M'Alister (or Donoghue) v. Stevenson. See also Donoghue v. Stevenson 266, **276**
Mallett v. McMonagle 618
Mallet v. New Brunswick 108
Malone v. Metropolitan Commissioner of Police 97
Mandrake Management Consultants Ltd. v. Toronto Transit Commission 811
Manitoba v. Air Canada 163
Manitoba Agricultural Credit Corp. v. Heaman 142
Manitoba Sausage Manufacturing Ltd. v. Winnipeg (City) 420
Mann v. Balaban 207
Mann v. Saulnier 159
Mansfield v. Weetabix 509
Mantella v. Mantella 417
Mantini v. Smyth Lyons LLP (No. 2) 935
Marcic v. Thames Water Utilities Ltd. 813
Marconato v. Franklin 571
Marcoux v. Bouchard 397
Marcq v. Christie Manson & Woods Ltd. (trading as Christie's) 123
Mariani v. Lemstra 445, 470
Market Investigations, Ltd. v. Minister of Social Security 882
Marks v. Campbell 686
Marrinan v. Vibart 953
Marsh v. Keating 135
Marshall v. Curry 189
Marshall v. Saskatchewan 108

Martel Building Ltd. v. Canada 435, **450**
Martin v. Benson 28
Martin v. Capital Health Authority 398
Martin v. Inglis 397
Martin v. Listowel Memorial Hospital 660
Martin v. Murray Estate 691
Martin v. Reynolds Metal Co. 159
Martin v. Watson 80
Marynowsky v. Stuartburn (District) 28
Mason v. Morrow's Moving & Storage Ltd. 345
Mason v. Peters 630, 636
Mason v. Westside Cemeteries Ltd. 375, 639
Masters v. Fox 969
Matharu v. Nam 669
Matheson v. Governors of Dalhousie College and University 170
Matheson v. Smiley 193
Mathison v. Hofer 375
Mathura v. Scarborough General Hospital 543
Matthews v. MacLaren; Horsley v. MacLaren 314, 351
Mattis v. Pollock 875
Maunsell v. Lethbridge Northern Irrigation District 155
Mawe v. Pigott 935
Maxey v. Can. Perm. Trust Co. 345
Mayfair Ltd. v. Pears 148
Mayne v. Kidd 136, 223
Maynes v. Galicz 854, 857
Mayrand v. Cronier 708
McBain v. Laurentian Hospital 195
McC v. Mullan 707
McCarty v. Pheasant Run Inc. 502
McCombe v. Read et al 821
McCutcheon v. Lightfoot 124
McDermott v. Ramadanovic Estate 635
McDonic v. Hetherington 865
McEllistrum v. Etches 511, 512
McErlean v. Sarel 512, **775**
McEvoy v. Capital Motors 652
McFarlane v. Tayside Health Board (Scotland) 366
McGeough v. Don Enterprises Ltd. 779
McGhee v. National Coal Board 538, 692, 694
McGillivray v. Kimber 726
McGinlay v. British Railway Bd. 669
McGinty v. Cook 774
McGivney v. Rustico Summer Haven 774
McHale v. Watson 17
McIntosh v. Bell 675
McIntyre v. Grigg 38, 328, 597, 624
McIntyre v. Sawatsky 521
McKay v. Essex Area Health Authority 363
McKee v. Dumas 878
McKee (Guardian ad litem of) v. McCoy 513
McKew v. Holland & Hannen & Cubitts (Scotland) Ltd. 378, 590
McKinney v. University of Guelph 765
McLachlan v. Canadian Imperial Bank of Commerce 130
McLean v. 366543 B.C. Ltd. 208
McLeod v. Palardy 644
McLorie v. Oxford 256
McLoughlin v. Arbor Memorial Services Inc. 375
McLoughlin v. Kutasy 954, 956
McLoughlin v. O'Brian 377, 378, 379, 381
McMillan v. Rural Municipality of Thompson 1005
McMullin v. F.W. Woolworth Co. 393
McNamara v. Duncan 171
McNeill v. Frankenfield 857
McNichol v. Grandy 939
McPherson v. Daniels 942
McRae v. British Norwegian Whaling Co. Ltd. 817
McTaggart v. Commonwealth Hospitality Ltd. 774
McTaggart v. Ontario 238
McTavish v. MacGillivray 616
McVea (Guardian ad litem of) v. T.B. 636
Mead Johnson Canada v. Ross Pediatrics 927
Mears v. London & South Western Ry. Co. 125
Mee v. Gardiner 148
Meier v. Klotz 942, 945
Mellanby v. Chapple 779
Melnychuk v. Moore 686
Meloche v. Bezaire 857
Meloche v. Hotel Dieu Grace Hospital/Villa Marie 543
Mendelssohn v. Normand Ltd. 441
Mendez v. Palazzi 821
Menear v. Miguna 940

Menna v. Guglietti 345
Mennie v. Blake 141
Meraw v. Curl Estate 331
Mercer v. Gray 589
Mercer v. South Eastern & Chatham Ry. Co.'s Managing Committee 349, 589
Merricks v. Nott-Bower 954
Mersey Docks and Harbour Board v. Coggins & Griffiths (Liverpool) Ltd. 878
Mete v. Mississauga 520
Metrick v. Deeb 82
Meyer v. Parker 357
Meyer Estate v. Rogers 189, 397
Meyers v. Stanley 530
Meyers (Next friend of) v. Moscovitz 517
Michalak v. Governors of Dalhousie College and University 333
Michaud v. Dupuis 334
Middleton v. Humphries 821
Migliore v. Gerard 334
Miles v. Judges 516
Milgaard v. Kujawa 417, 708
Miller v. Decker 185, 666
Miller v. Jackson 160, 493, 801, **823**
Miller v. Wolbaum 499, 651
Miller Dredging Ltd. v. Dorothy Mackenzie (The) 642
Millette v. Kalogeropoulos 744
Milner v. Manufacturers Life Insurance Co. 97
Minister Administering the Environmental Planning and Assessment Act 1979 v. San Sebastien Pty. Ltd. 300, 565
Mintuck v. Valley River Band No. 63A 906, 927
Mirhadizadeh v. Ontario 712, 766
Mirvahedy v. Henley 858
Miska v. Sivec 48
Mitchell v. John Heine and Son Ltd. 76
Mitchell v. McDonald 200
Mitchell v. Times Printing and Publishing Company Limited (No. 2) 968
Mitchell et al. v. C.N.R. Co. 776
Mitran v. Williamson 87
Moar v. Roman Catholic Church of Canada 60
Mochinski v. Trendline Industries Ltd. 886
Moffett v. Downing 857
Mogul S.S. Co. v. McGregor, Gow & Co. 910
Moisan v. Loftus 502
Molnar v. Coates 333
Moloney v. Parry Sound (Town) 789
Molson Canada v. Oland Breweries Ltd. 902
Monahan v. Nelson 600
Monkman v. Singh 582
Montaron v. Wagner 194
Monteith v. N.B. Command, Royal Can. Legion 779
Montgomery v. Thompson 901
Montreal v. Montreal Locomotive Works Ltd. 881
Montreal Tramways Co. v. Léveillé 368
Moore v. Fanning 341, 499, 592, 651, 686
Moore v. R. 250
Moores v. Salter 936
Moorgate Mercantile Co. Ltd. v. Finch 126
Moran v. Wyeth-Ayerst Canada Inc. (c.o.b. Cyanamid Crop Protection) 410
Morash v. Lockhart & Ritchie Ltd. 349
Morel v. Bryden 601
Morgan v. Khyatt 822
Morgan v. Loyacomo 59
Morier v. Rivard 707
Morris v. Baily 857
Morris v. Beardmore 261
Morrish v. Murrey 259
Morrison v. Fishwick 126
Morrison v. Thomas 223
Morrow v. Hôpital Royal Victoria 182, 188
Morse v. Cott Beverages West Ltd. 862
Mortimer v. Cameron 660, 772
Morton v. William Dixon 492
Moss v. Ferguson 525, 592
Mostyn v. Fabrigas 727
Motherwell v. Motherwell 93, 802
Moule v. N.B. Elec. Power Comm. 295, 298, 299
Mount Isa Mines Ltd. v. Pusey 374
Mugford v. Weber 864
Muir v. Alberta 202, 488
Muirhead v. Timber Bros. Sand & Gravel Ltd. 802
Mullen v. Barr & Co. 280
Mullins v. Levy 73
Mummery v. Olsson 368
Municipal Spraying & Contracting Ltd. v. J. Harris & Sons. Ltd. 639
Munir v. Jackson 397

Munn & Co. v. The Motor Vessel Sir John Crosbie 231
Munro v. Canada 417
Munro v. Porthkerry Park Holiday Estates Ltd. 332
Munro v. Toronto Sun Publishing Corp. 969
Munro v. Willmott 139
Munshaw Colour Service Ltd. v. Vancouver 300
Murphy v. Brentwood District Council 283, 469, 470, 474, 479
Murphy v. Culhane 50, 185
Murphy v. LaMarsh 936, 968
Murphy v. Little Memphis Cabaret Ltd. 331, 779
Murphy Oil v. Predator Corp. 104
Murphy v. St. Catharines Gen. Hosp. 407
Murray v. Bitango 772
Murray v. McMurchy 192
Murray v. Ministry 68
Mustafic v. Smith 55, 333, 517
Mustapha v. Culligan Canada Ltd. 375, **384**, 699
Mutual Life & Citizens' Assurance Co. v. Evatt 423
Mutungih v. Bokun 136
My Kinda Town Ltd. v. Soll 903
Mychajluk v. Kolisnyk 936
Myers v. Canadian Broadcasting Corporation 968
Myers v. Haroldson 36
Myers v. Peel County Board of Education 333, 335, 513, 518, 652
Myran v. R. 155

N.B. Telephone Co. v. Wright 639
Nader v. General Motors Corp. 96
Nagy v. Canada 72
Nan v. Black Pine Manufacturing Ltd. 640
Nancy B. v. Hôtel-Dieu de Québec 194
Nantel v. Parisien 149
National Bank of Greece S.A. v. Pinios Shipping Co. (No. 1) 441
National Hockey League v. Pepsi Cola Ltd. 902
National Trust Co. v. Wong Aviation Ltd. 540
Naxakis v. West General Hospital 533
NBD Bank, Canada v. Dofasco Inc. 433
Neate v. Harding 117
Neil v. Equifax Canada Inc 456
Neill v. New South Wales Fresh Food & Ice Pty. Ltd. 497
Nelitz v. Dyck 183
Nelles v. Ont. 75, 417, 708
Nelson v. Welsh 597
Nelson v. Whetmore 119
Nespolon v. Alford 304, 512
Neto v. Klukach 200
Netupsky v. Craig 956
Neufeld v. Foster 328
Neufeld v. Landry 651
Neuman v. Parkland County 721
Nevill v. Fine Art & General Insurance Co 934
New Brunswick Broadcasting Co. v. Nova Scotia (Speaker of the House of Assembly) 765
New South Wales v. Lepore 874, 886
New York Times Co. v. Sullivan 930
Newcastle (Town) v. Mattatall 547
Newfoundland Light and Power Co. v. Furlong Estate 699
Newman v. Halstead 36, 936
Newswest Corp. v. Glendar Holdings Ltd. 911
Newton v. Newton 300
Ng Chun Pui v. Lee Chuen Tat 695
Niblock v. Pacific National Exhibition 331
Nice v. Calgary (City) 700
Nice v. John Doe 660, 686
Nichol v. MacKay 50
Nicholls v. Richmond (Township) 918
Nichols v. Marsland 848
Nichols v. Wal-Mart Canada Corp. 245
Nicholson v. John Deere Ltd. 408
Nickell v. City of Windsor 768
Nielsen v. Kaufmann 630, 636
Nightingale v. Mazerall 637
Nilsson Bros. Inc. v. McNamara Estate 121
Nippa v. C.H. Lewis (Lucan) Ltd. 823
No. 1 Collision Repair & Painting (1982) Ltd. v. Insurance Corp. of British Columbia 920, 924
Nolan v. Toronto (Metropolitan) Police Force 109
Non-Marine Underwriters, Lloyd's of London v. Scalera 60, 167
Norberg v. Wynrib 33, 181, 184

Norman v. Great Western Railway Co. 776
Norman v. Soule 81
Normart Management Ltd. v. West Hill Redevelopment Co. 911
North Vancouver School District No. 44 v. Jubran 334
Northern Territory v. Mengel 91, 730, 735, 926
Northwestern Mut. Ins. Co. v. J.T. O'Bryan & Co. 345
Northwestern Utilities Ltd. v. London Guarantee & Accident Co. 841, 849
Nor-Video Services Ltd. v. Ontario Hydro 802, 806
Nowlan v. Brunswick Construction Ltee 548, **551**
Nowsco Well Service Ltd. v. Canadian Propane Gas & Oil Ltd. 543

OBG Ltd. v. Allan 104, 130, 918, 924, 925
O'Brien v. Clement 965
O'Connor v. Waldron 951
Ocsko v. Cypress Bowl Recreations Ltd. 669
Odhavji Estate v. Woodhouse 293, **728**
O'Fallan v. Inecto Rapid (Can.) Ltd. 410
Ogg-Moss v. The Queen 214
O'Grady v. Brown 373
Ogwo v. Taylor 358, 566
O'Hara v. Belanger 615, 634
Okanagan Exteriors Inc. v. Perth Developments Inc. 341, 593
Oke v. Weide Tpt. Ltd. 313, 586
Oleschak Estate v. Wilganowski 634
Olinski v. Johnson 794
Oliver (Guardian ad litem of) v. Ellison 372
Olsen v. Olsen 36
O'Malley v. O'Callaghan 940
O'Neil v. Van Horne 233
O'Neill v. Esquire Hotels Ltd. 847
Oniel v. Metropolitan Toronto Police Force 78, 80
Ontario (Attorney General) v. Crompton 270
Organ v. Newfoundland and Labrador (Minister of Social Services) 707
O'Rourke v. Schacht 338, 675, 744
Osman v. 629256 Ontario Ltd. 636
Osman v. Ferguson 339
Osman v. United Kingdom 340
Osterlind v. Hill 311
Ottosen v. Kasper 512
Oughton v. Seppings 117
Overseas Tankship (U.K.) v. Morts Dock & Engineering Co. (The Wagon Mound). See also The Wagon Mound (No. 1) 572
Overseas Tankship (U.K.) Ltd. v. Miller S.S. Co. Pty. See also The Wagon Mound (No. 2) 811

P Perl (Exporters) Ltd. v. Camden London Borough Council 593
P.(K.) v. Desrochers 81
P.(N.I.) v. B.(R.) 875
Pac. Blasting Ltd. v. D.J. Byrne Const. Ltd. 639
Pac. Elevators Ltd. v. C.P.R. Co. 639
Pacific Associates Inc. v. Baxter 441
Page v. Smith 384, 387, 390
Pajot v. Commonwealth Holiday Inns of Can. Ltd. 779
Palma v. Stora Kopparbergs Berslags Aktiebolag 847
Palmer v. N.S. Forest Indust 823
Palmer v. St. John 769
Palsgraf v. Long Island Railroad 301, 562, 872, 993
Pannett v. McGuinness & Co. Ltd. 781
Papadimitropoulos v. R. 175
Papp v. Leclerc 589
Paquette v. Desrochers 81
Paragon Properties (Finance) Ltd. v. Del Swan Trucking Inc. 927
Paramount Pictures Corp. v. Howley 902
Paris v. Stepney Borough Council 490
Park v. B & B Electronics Ltd. 408
Parkdale (Village) v. West 155
Parkhurst v. Forster 9
Parkinson v. St. James and Seacroft University Hospital NHS Trust 366
Parkland No. 31 v. Stetar 744
Parmley v. Parmley 177, 192
Parypa v. Wickware 601
Pasley v. Freeman 83, 896
Pasternack v. Poulton 656
Patching v. Howarth 936
Patenaude v. Roy 37, 499
Patry v. General Motors Acceptance Corp. of Canada Ltd. 123
Patten v. Silberschein 593

Pattison v. Prince Edward Region Conservation Authority 848
Pauluik v. Paraiso 589
Pawlak v. Doucette 864
Paxton v. Ramji 362
Payne v. Maple Leaf Gardens Ltd. 170, 669
Payton v. New York; Riddick v. New York 261
Paziuk v. Ewbank 557
Pearson v. Mian 79
Pelletier v. Stewart 486
Pemberton v. Southwark London Borough Council 803
Pembina Resources Ltd. v. ULS International Inc. 639
Penarth Dock Engineering Co. Ltd. v. Pounds 40
Penfolds Wines Proprietary Ltd. v. Elliott 117, 120
Penn v. Singbeil 251
Penner v. Mitchell 555
Penney v. Gosse 148
Penney v. John Doe 342
People Recycling Inc. v. Vancouver (City) 925
Percy v. Glasgow Corp 865
Pereira v. Hamilton Township Farmers' Mutual Fire Insurance Co. 38
Performance Industries Ltd. v. Sylvan Lake Golf & Tennis Club Ltd. 896
Perry v. Fried 249
Perry v. Kendricks Transport Ltd. 839
Perry v. Truefitt 897
Peruvian Guano Co. Ltd. v. Dreyfus Brothers & Co. Ltd. 136, 223
Pesonen v. Melnyk 573
Peters v. Prince of Wales Theatre (Birmingham) Ltd. 848
Peterson v. Windsor (City) 779
Petkovic (Litigation Guardian of) v. Olupona 364
Pettis v. McNeil 172
Phillip v. Whitecourt General Hospital 375, 530
Phillips v. Brittania Hygienic Laundry Co. 676
Phillips v. Calif. Standard Co. 160
Phillips v. Soloway 55
Picka v. Porter 328
Pickard v. Smith 884
Pickering v. Rudd 161
Piercey (Guardian ad litem of) v. Lunenburg (County) District School Board 335
Pierre (Next Friend of) v. Marshall 517
Pilieci v. Lockett 216
Pilliterri v. Nor. Const. Co. 813
Pilon v. Janveaux 658, 668
Pinard v. Coderre 899
Pittman Estate v. Bain 189, 397, 517
Pitts v. Hunt 185, 670, 674
Pizza Pizza Ltd. v. Toronto Star Newspapers Ltd. 944
Pizzolon v. Pedrosa 328, 548
Planned Parenthood Newfoundland/ Labrador v. Fedorik 936
Plas-Tex Canada Ltd. v. Dow Chemical of Canada Ltd. 471
Plester v. Wawanesa Mutual Insurance Co. 38
Ploof v. Putnam 229, 231
Pochwalowski v. Tsai 55
Poirier v. Canada (Minister of Veterans Affairs) 765
Poissant v. Robalo 300
Poitras v. Goulet 660
Police v. Greaves 63
Police Complaints Commissioner v. Dunlop 342
Polly Peck (Holdings) plc v. Trelford 944
Polsinelli v. Marzilli 903
Ponting v. Noakes 848
Poole v. Ragen 96
Pope v. R.G.C. Management Inc. 512
Pope v. Route 66 Clothing Inc. 794
Popovich v. Lobay (No. 2) 940
Posluns v. Toronto Stock Exchange 908, 914
Potechin v. Yashin 919
Potter v. Rowe 918
Potts v. Heutink 722
Potvin v. Stipetic 669
Poulos v. Matovic 82
Pound v. Nakonechny 518
Pound v. Scott 969
Poupart v. Lafortune 243
Powder Mountain Resorts Ltd. v. British Columbia 731, 735, 920
Pozdzik (Next friend of) v. Wilson 372
Pratt & Goldsmith v. Pratt 393
Prefontaine v. Gosman 707
Premakumaran v. Canada 295, 434
Prescott v. Connell 359

Pressler v. Lethbridge 936, 968
Preston v. Canadian Legion of British Empire Service League, Kingsway Branch No. 175 779
Prete v. Ontario 708, 712
Prevost (Committee of) v. Vetter 329, 331
Price v. Chicoutimi Pulp Co. 942, 968
Price v. Garcha 573
Price v. Milawski 587
Price v. Seeley 245
Price Waterhouse v. Kwan 433
Pridgen v. Boston Housing Authority 319
Pridham v. Nash 195
Priestman v. Colangelo 236, 243, 251, 498, 651
Prinse v. Fraser Valley Foods Ltd. 683
Prinzo v. Baycrest Centre for Geriatric Care 90, 108
Procea Products Ltd. v. Evans & Sons Ltd. 903
Pro-Sys Consultants Ltd. v. Microsoft Corp. 911
Proulx v. Quebec (Attorney General) 79, 708
Prud'homme v. Prud'homme 955
Pugsley v. Rahbar 864
Pugh v. London, Brighton and South Coast Ry. Co. 83
Purdy v. Woznesensky 46, 84
Pursell v. Horn 59
Pyke v. TriGro Enterprises Ltd. 159, 812

Q. v. Minto Management Ltd. 341
Qualcast (Wolverhampton) Ltd. v. Haynes 531
Queen v. Cognos Inc. 423, 435, **442**
Queensway Tank Lines Ltd. v. Moise 751
Quinn v. Leathem 917
Quondam v. Francis Belliveau Excavations Ltd. 847

R. v. Asante-Mensah 156, 251
R. v. Aziga 176
R. v. B.(K.) 173
R. v. B.(T.B.) 173
R. v. Baptiste 215
R. v. Beare 252
R. v. Bertuzzi 172
R. v. Biron 241
R. v. Blair 220
R. v. Bogue 208
R. v. Brennan 244
R. v. Brezack 256
R. v. Brisson 216
R. v. Brown 183
R. v. Browne 360
R. v. Carroll 250
R. v. Caslake 253
R. v. Charles 252
R. v. Ciccarelli 172
R. v. Cinous 208
R. v. Clarence 176
R. v. Clark 220
R. v. Colet 208, 261
R. v. Collins 216, 256
R. v. Cote 586
R. v. Cuerrier 176, 177
R. v. Custer 261
R. v. Debot 256
R. v. Delong 260
R. v. Dudley and Stephens 225
R. v. Duffy 210, 212
R. v. Dupperon 213
R. v. East Crest Oil Co. 148
R. v. Elias 250
R. v. Erickson and Hathaway 249
R. v. Feeney 256, 260
R. v. Fennell 210
R. v. Figueira 220
R. v. G.(J.M.) 216
R. v. Gamracy 242
R. v. Garcia-Guiterrez 256
R. v. Godoy 261
R. v. Golden 255
R. v. Golub 241, 256, 260
R. v. Governor of Brockhill Prison (No. 2) 69
R. v. Governor of Brockhill Prison, ex parte Evans (No. 2) 69
R. v. Greffe 255
R. v. Haberstock 215
R. v. Haglof 261
R. v. Halcrow 215
R. v. Harms 175
R. v. Haverstock 220
R. v. Higgins 252
R. v. Huggins 9
R. v. Ireland 65
R. v. J.M. 173
R. v. J.W. 173
R. v. Jackpine 256
R. v. Jennings 744
R. v. Jobidon 172, 181, 185
R. v. Klimchuk 241

R. v. Koszulap 252
R. v. Landry 260
R. v. Larlham 208
R. v. Lauda 257
R. v. Lauzon 216
R. v. Lavallee 208
R. v. Layton 154
R. v. Leitch 250
R. v. Lloyd 817
R. v. Lyons 220
R. v. M.(A.) 216, 257
R. v. M.(M.R.) 216, 236, 257
R. v. Macooh 261
R. v. Macquarie and Budge 68
R. v. Malott 209
R. v. McConnell 209
R. v. McSorley 172
R. v. Meikle 255
R. v. Mellenthin 256
R. v. Nelson 209
R. v. Nord-Deutsche Versicherungs-Gesellschaft 349
R. v. Ogal 206
R. v. Ogg-Moss 216
R. v. Orbanski 250
R. v. Pétel 208
R. v. Paice 173, 181
R. v. Park 216
R. v. Perello 241
R. v. Perka 227
R. v. Peters 150
R. v. Reilly 209
R. v. Roberge 251
R. v. Rousseau 255
R. v. Ruzic 48
R. v. Ryan 208
R. v. Sanderson 261
R. v. Saskatchewan Wheat Pool 724
R. v. Scopelliti 208
R. v. Shoker 181
R. v. Smith 208
R. v. Ssenyonga 176
R. v. St. George 62
R. v. Starson 200
R. v. Stevens 242
R. v. Stillman 256
R. v. Stone 44
R. v. Storrey 241, 252
R. v. Sullivan 373
R. v. Sweet 216, 236
R. v. W.(G.) 173
R. v. Welch 183
R. v. Wetmore 215
R. v. Wheaton 215
R. v. Whitfield 237
R. v. Whynot (Stafford) 209
R. v. Williams 175, 176
R. v. Wood 250
R. v. Wrightman 250
R. in Right of Can. v. Sask. Wheat Pool 740, **746**
R. in Right of Ont. v. Rokeby 737
R. in Right of Ont. v. Schenck 737
R.(J.) v. W.(E.S.) 60
R.(L.) v. Nyp 98, 519
R.F. Fry & Associates (Pacific) Ltd. v. Reimer 135
R.H. Willis and Son v. Br. Car Auctions Ltd. 121
R.W.D.S.U, Local 580 v. Dolphin Delivery Ltd. 764, 765
Rabideau v. Maddocks 663
Racz v. Home Office 735
Radovskis v. Tomm 85
Rahal v. Rahal 39
Rahemtulla v. Vanfed Credit Union 89
Rahman v. Arearose Ltd 589
Rainbow Industrial Caterers Ltd. v. Canadian National Railway Co. 436
Rainham Chemical Works, Ltd. (in Liquidation) et al. v. Belvedere Fish Guano Co., Ltd. 846
Rajkhowa v. Watson 951
Raju v. Kumar 895
Ralston Purina of Can. Ltd. v. Whittaker 134
Ramsay v. Saskatchewan 417
Ranson v. Kitner 51
Rattray v. Daniels 806
Ratych v. Bloomer 643
Rayner v. Knickle 611
Raypath Resources Ltd. v. Toronto Dominion Bank 421
Raywalt Construction Co. v. Bencic 547
Re A (children) (conjoined twins: surgical separation) 202, 225
Re Attorney-General of British Columbia v. Astaforoff 193
Re B (a minor) (wardship: sterilization) 201
Re B (adult: refusal of medical treatment) 193
Re C (adult: refusal of medical treatment) 193, 200

Re Children's Aid Society of Western Manitoba and Daniels 261
Re Indian Residential Schools 342
Re J (a minor) (wardship: medical treatment) 193, 203
Re K. and Public Trustee 202
Re L.D.K.; Children's Aid Society of Metropolitan Toronto v. K. and K. 198
Re Polemis and Furness, Withy & Co. Ltd. 562, 580
Re Royal Can. Legion Branch 177 708
Re Scarth 138
Re Superintendent of Family & Child Service and Dawson 203
Re W (a minor) 198
Re White 217
Re Yoner 708
Reach MD Inc. v. Pharmaceutical Manufacturers Assn. of Canada 922
Read v. Coker 64
Read v. Friendly Society of Operative Stonemasons of England, Ireland & Wales 917
Read v. J. Lyons & Co. 839, **840**, 845
Reckitt & Colman Products Ltd. v. Borden Inc. 898
Reed v. Maley 87
Reekie v. Messervey 616
Rees v. Canada (Royal Canadian Mounted Police) 89, 333
Rees v. Darlington Memorial NHS Trust 366
Reese v. Coleman (No. 1) 304
Reeve v. Palmer 137
Refco Futures (Canada) Ltd. – Refco v. SYB Holdings Corp. 518
Regina v. Walker 881
Reibl v. Hughes 188, 204, 394, 396, 532
Reid v. Webster 71, 79
Reidy v. McLeod 630
Reilly v. British Columbia (A.G.) 79
Rendall v. Ewart 341
Renken v. Harvey Aluminum (Inc.) 801
Revill v. Newbery 220
Rewcastle v. Sieben 656
Reynen v. Antonenko 255
Reynen v. Canada 709
Reynolds v. Clarke 9, 11
Reynolds v. Times Newspapers Ltd. 960
Rhodes v. Canadian National Railway 392
Rhora v. Ontario 333
Rice v. Connolly 250
Richard v. C.N.R. 531, 566
Rickards v. Lothian 845, 846, 849
Rideau Falls Generating Partnership v. Ottawa (City) 811
Rigby v. Chief Constable of Northamptonshire 226, 261
Rinas v. Regina (City) 761
Rintoul v. X-ray and Radium Indust. Ltd. 675, 754
Rioux v. Smith 35
Risk v. Zeller's Ltd. 938
Ristimaki v. Cooper 417
Rivtow Marine Ltd. v. Washington Iron Works 288, 401, 408, 464
Roach v. Long 79
Robb Estate v. Canadian Red Cross Society 699
Robb Estate v. St. Joseph's Health Care Centre 694
Roberge v. R. 651
Robert Addie & Sons (Collieries), Ltd. v. Dumbreck 780
Roberts v. 964639 Ontario Ltd 328
Roberts v. Morana 358, 623
Roberts v. Ramsbottom 508
Roberts v. Wyatt 126
Robertson v. Joyce 251
Robertson v. Stang 341
Robinson v. Kilvert 804
Robinson v. Post Office 589
Robinson v. Williams Estate 668
Robitaille v. Vancouver Hockey Club Ltd. 38, 596
Robson v. Ashworth 333
Robson v. Chrysler Canada Ltd. 420
Rodaro v. Royal Bank of Canada 104
Rodgers v. Maw 117
Rodriguez v. British Columbia (A.G.) 194
Roe v. Dabbs 367
Roe v. Minister of Health 270, 488, 691
Roehl v. Houlahan 907
Rogacki v. Belz 968
Rogers v. Faught 293, 295
Rogers Cable TV Ltd. v. 373041 Ontario Ltd. 919
Rokeby v. R. 160, 813, 847, 849
Rollinson v. R. 135, 238, 638
Rolof v. Morris 397
Roman Corp. v. Hudson's Bay Oil & Gas Co. 706, 921
Roncarelli v. Duplessis 725, 729

Roncato v. Caverly 423
Rondel v. Worsley 413, 414, 415, 416
Rookes v. Barnard 32, 33, 47, 904, 907
Roper v. Harper 177
Rose et al. v. Miles 819
Rosenburg v. Grand River Conservation Authority 819
Rosenthal v. Alderton & Sons, Ltd. 137
Rosewell v. Prior 9
Ross v. Caunters 461, 462
Ross v. New Brunswick Teachers' Association 968
Ross v. United States 340, 348
Roth v. Roth 96, 907
Rothfield v. Manolakos 285
Rothwell v. Raes 409, 525
Rowe v. Bobell Express Ltd. 616
Rowland's Transport Ltd. v. Nasby Sales & Services Ltd. 598
Roy v. Thiessen 470
Roy c. Toxi-Co-Gîtes inc. 333
Royal Aquarium and Summer & Winter Garden Society Ltd. v. Parkinson 949, 953
Royal Bank v. W. Got & Associates Electric Ltd. 135
Royal Bank v. Wilton 918
Royal Bank of Canada v. Intercon Security Ltd. 875
Royal Bank of Canada v. W. Got & Associates Electric Ltd.. 130
Royal Canadian Legion Branch No. 15 v. Burkitt 135
Rozenhart v. Skier's Sport Shop (Edmonton) Ltd. 409, 411, 420
Rozon v. Patenaude 860
Ruckheim v. Robinson 860
Rumley v. British Columbia 342, 593
Rummery v. Matthews 920
Rumsey v. R. 50, 597
Rupert v. Toth 517
Russell v. Esson (M.F.) & Sons Ltd. 590
Russell Transport Ltd. v. Ontario Malleable Iron Co. 813
Russo v. Ontario Jockey Club 153
Ryan v. Auclair 250
Ryan v. Hickson 512
Ryan v. Victoria (City) 285, 487, 663, **758**, 811
Ryder Truck Rental v. Walker 142
Rydzik v. Edwards 744
Rylands v. Fletcher 18, 807, 835, **837**, 842

S.(F.) v. H.(C.) 895
S. v. G. 61
S.(J.) v. Clement 333
Sable Offshore Energy Inc. v. Ameron International Corp. 471
Sabourin v. Ontario 80
Saccardo v. Hamilton 589, 849
Saccone v. Fandrakis 359
Saccone v. Orr 96
Sachs v. Miklos 134, 137
Said (Husain) v. Said 175
Saif Ali v. Sidney Mitchell & Co. (a firm) et al 415
Saint-Jacques v. Canada (Solicitor General) 69
Saltpetre's Case 226
Samms v. Eccles 86
Sammut v. Islington Golf Club Ltd. 827
Sandberg v. Steer Holdings Ltd. 779
Sandhu (Litigation guardian of) v. Wellington Place Apartments 603, 613, 624
Sant v. Jack Andrews Kirkfield Pharmach Ltd 375
Santamaria v. James 90
Saskatchewan (A.G.) v. Pritchard 243
Satara Farms Inc. v. Parrish & Heimbecker, Ltd. 375, 745
Saunders v. Randolph Hotel Co. Ltd., 935
Sauve v. Provost 780
Savage v. Boies 87
Savard v. Urbano 669
Sawatzky v. Riverview Health Centre Inc. 193
Sayers v. Harlow Urban District Council 357, 359
Scandinavia Belting Co. v. Asbestos & Rubber Works of America, Inc. 900
Scardoni v. Hawryluck (2004), 69 O.R. (3d) 700 (S.C.J.) 203
Scarff v. Wilson 612
Scelfo v. Rutgers University 938
Sceptre Resources Ltd. v. Deloitte Haskins & Sells 518
Schacht v. The Queen in right of the Province of Ontario 337
Schact v. R 338
Schell v. Truba 249

Schellenberg v. Tunnel Holdings Pty. Ltd. 699
Schenck v. R. 160, 813, 847, 849
Schentag v. Gauthier 140
Schiavo ex rel. Schindler v. Schiavo 203
Schieber v. City of Philadelphia 340
Schlink v. Blackburn 304
Schmidt v. Sharpe 328
School Div. of Assiniboine South (No. 3) v. Hoffer 761
Schroth v. Innes 864
Schrump v. Koot 600
Schubert v. Sterling Trusts Corp 839, 849
Schultz v. Miki 875
Schulz v. Leaside Devs. 411
Schulz v. Leeside Dev. Ltd. 333
Schwartz v. Canada 300
Schweizer v. Central Hospital 177
Scobie v. Wing 639
Scott v. London and St. Katherine Docks Co. 695
Scott v. R. 256
Scott v. Shepherd 9, 46, 585
Scurfield v. Cariboo Helicopter Skiing Ltd. 669
Sczebel v. Silvertson 557
Seaboard Life Insurance Co. v. Babich 481
Sealand of the Pacific Ltd. v. Robert c. McHaffe Ltd. 421, 893
Searle v. Wallbank 860
Second Cup Ltd. v. Eftoda 982
Secretary, Department of Health and Community Services v. J.W.B. 61, 168
Sedleigh-Denfield v. O'Callaghan 803
Seede v. Camco Inc. 630
Segal v. Derrick Golf and Winter Club 160
Selig v. Mansfield 906
Sellars v. Adelaide Petroleum NL 546
Seraphim v. Sterling Newspapers Ltd. 936
Serhan v. Johnson & Johnson 471
Shackleton v. Knittle 333, 567
Shakoor v. Situ 517
Shanklin Pier Ltd. v. Detel Products Ltd. 441
Shannon v. Westman (Litigation Guardian of) 335
Shaw v. Berman 99
Shaw v. Gorter 50
Shaw v. Roemer 655
Shearman v. Folland 601
Shelfer v. London Electric Lighting Co. 821, 822
Sherrin v. Haggerty 230
Shiffman v. Order of St. John 839
Shilson v. Northern Ont. Light & Power Co. 494
Shkwarchuk v. Hansen 656
Shobridge v. Thomas 598
Shreddfast Inc. v. Oak Point Alignment Ltd. 143
Shultz v. Miki 341
Shute v. Premier Trust Co. 525
Siametis v. Trojan Horse (Burlington) Inc. 896
Sibley v. Milutinovic 61, 168
Sidaway v. Bethlem Royal Hospital Governors 396
Sidhu Estate v. Bains 894
Siemens v. Pfizer C. & G. Inc. 410
Sigouin (Guardian ad litem of) v. Wong 516
Silkin v. Beaverbrook Newspapers Ltd. 960
Sim v. Stretch 932, 965
Simms v. Butt 562
Simpson v. Geswein 59, 208
Simpson v. Mair 968
Sinclair v. Woodward's Store Ltd. 71
Sinclaire v. Boulton 398
Sindell v. Abbott Laboratories 544, 545, 693, 694
Singer Manufacturing Co. v. Loog 897
Singh v. Ali 140
Singleton v. Williamson 860
Sirois v. Gustafson 62
Sirros v. Moore 707
Skelding (Guardian ad litem of) v. Skelding 636
Skelton v. Collins 621
Skelton v. London and North Western R.W. Co. 347
Slaferek v. TCG International Inc. 794
Slater v. Baker 9
Slauenwhite v. Walker 209
Slim v. Daily Telegraph Ltd. 935, 962, 963
Smart v. Sears Canada Inc. 245
Smart v. Simpson Sears Ltd. 71
Smith v. B.C. (A.G.) 333, 486, 518, 586
Smith v. Chadwick 891, 894
Smith v. Eric S. Bush (a firm) 518

Smith v. Jenkins 184
Smith v. Jones 343
Smith v. Leech Brain & Co. 570, 572
Smith v. Littlewoods Organisation Ltd. 341, 570, 593
Smith v. Moscovich 546
Smith v. Ont. & Minnesota Power Co. 849
Smith v. Rae 320, **346**
Smith v. Scott 849
Smith v. Stone 44
Smith v. Tucker 358
Smith v. Widdicombe 847
Smith New Court Ltd. v. Scrimgeour Vickers 895
Smith v. Union of Icelandic Fish Producers Ltd. 446
Smithson v. Saskem Chemicals Ltd. 411
Smythe v. Reardon 175
Snell v. Farrell 539, 691, 692, 694
Snushall v. Fulsang 656, 664
Soccio v. Leduc 36
Sodd Corp. v. Tessis 422
Solloway v. McLaughlin 132
Somwar v. McDonald's Restaurants of Canada Ltd. 95, 99
Sopinka (Litigation guardian of) v. Sopinka 88
Sorensen v. Kaye Holdings Ltd. 893
Sorrell v. Smith 915
Soulsby v. Toronto 347
Southam v. Smout 259
Southern Pacific Co. v. Jensen 151
Southern Portland Cement Ltd. v. Cooper 781, 784
Souto v. Anderson 601
Spagnolo v. Margesson's Sports Ltd. 341, 592
Sparks v. Thompson 663
Spasic Estate v. Imperial Tobacco Ltd. 694
Spectra Architectural Group Ltd. v. Eldred Sollows Consulting Ltd. 919
Spiewak v. 251268 Ont. Ltd. 518
Spur Industries Inc. v. Del E. Webb Development Co. 801, **828**
Squittieri v. De Santis 55
Ste-Marie c. Placements J.P.M. Marquis 97
St. George's Healthcare NHS Trust v. S. 373
St. John (City) v. Donald 886
St. John's (City) v. Lake 811
St. Louis v. R. 694
St. Pierre v. Ontario 802
Stacey v. Anglican Church of Canada (Diocesan Synod of Eastern Newfoundland & Labrador) 778
Stafford v. Motomochi 601
Stamp v. R. in Right of Ontario 691
Standard Chartered Bank v. Pakistan National Shipping Corp. (Nos. 2 and 4) 893, 897
Stanley v. Powell 15, 16
Stansbie v. Troman 593
Stapley v. London, Brighton, and South Coast R.W. Co 347
Stark v. Auerbach 949, 953
Starson v. Swayze 199
State v. Johnson 208
Statler v. Ray Mfg. Co. 281
Steadman v. Erickson Gold Mining Corp. 160
Steagald v. U.S. 261
Steenblok v. Funk 600
Steiman v. Steiman 135
Stein v. Gonzales 819
Stein v. Kathy K (The Ship) 664
Stephens v. Corcoran 174
Stephens v. Myers 62, 65
Stephenson v. Waite Tileman 582
Sterling Trusts Corporation v. Postma 751
Stevens v. Rockport Granite Co. 830
Stevenson v. Basham 85
Stevenson v. Clearview Riverside Resort 320
Stevenson Estate v. Siewert 133
Stevenson Jordan and Harrison, Ltd. v. Macdonald 881
Stewart v. Pettie 300, 328
Stewart v. Stonehouse 59
Stewart v. Traders Trust Co. 177
Stiles v. Hatfield 398
Stoffman v. Veterinary Assn. (Ontario) 79
Stoke-on-Trent City Council v. W. & J. Wass Ltd. 28
Stokes v. Carlson 44
Stott v. Gamble 916
Stovin v. Wise 311, 722
Strachan (Guardian ad litem of) v. Reynolds 600
Strand Electric & Engineering Co. v. Brisford Entertainments Ltd. 40, 41, 140

Stratford (J.T.) & Son Ltd. v. Lindley 918
Strichen v. Stewart 517
Strickland v. St. John's 509
Stringer v. Ashley 789
Strom (Litigation Guardian of) v. White 857
Stuart v. R. in Right of Can. 771
Sturges v. Bridgman 813, 831
Suite v. Cooke 366
Sulz v. British Columbia (Minister of Public Safety and Solicitor General) 109
Sulz v. Canada (Attorney General) 89, 333
Summers v. Tice 689
Sun Life Assurance Co. of Canada v. Dalrymple 957
Sunrise Co. v. Lake Winnipeg (The) 557
Superintendent of Belchertown State School v. Saikewicz 203
Super-Save Enterprises Ltd. v. 249513 B.C. Ltd. (c.o.b. Mike's Auto Towing) 918
Surocco v. Geary 224
Surrey (District) v. Marall Homes Ltd. 911
Sussman v. Eales 950, 953
Sutherland v. Canada (Attorney General) 811, 819
Sutherland Shire Council v. Heyman 283, 722
Swaile v. Zurdayk 148
Swales v. Cox 261
Swami v. Lo 573, 590
Sweeney v. Starrat 223
Swift Current (City) v. Saskatchewan Power Corp. 920
Swinamer v. Nova Scotia (Attorney General) 288, 721
Swinney v. Chief Constable of the Northumbria Police 340
Syms v. Warren 972
Szalatnay-Stacho v. Fink 947
Szarfer v. Chodos 104

T.G. Bright & Co. v. Kerr 864
T.W.N.A. v. Clarke 35, 574, 876
Taller (Guardian ad litem of) v. Goldenshtein 857
Tallow v. Tailfeathers 184
Tame v. New South Wales; Annetts v. Australian Stations Pty. Ltd. 382
Tanner v. Norys 73, 343
Tarasoff v. Regents of the University of California 342
Taylor v. Asody 663
Taylor v. Despard 956
Taylor v. King 300
Taylor v. Morrison 517
Taylor v. Weston Bakeries Ltd. 393
Taylor v. Whitehead 226
Teece v. Honeybourn 185
Teichner v. Bellan 971
Temple v. Hallem 170, 669
Teolis v. Moscatelli 172
Temilini v. Ontario Provincial Police (Commissioner) 80
Tenning v. Manitoba 108
ter Neuzen v. Korn 516, **521**, 599, 624
The Lancashire Wagon Co. Ltd. v. Fitzhugh 126
The Maersk Colombo 646
The Mediana 28, 29, 596
The Quartz Hill Consolidated Gold Mining Co. v. Eyre 81
The Queen v. Jennings 619
The Queen v. Levy Brothers Co. 870
The Schwan 677
The Wagon Mound (No. 1); Overseas Tankship (U.K.) Ltd. v. Morts Dock & Engineering Co. 389, **562**
The Wagon Mound (No. 2); Overseas Tankship (U.K.) Ltd. v. Miller Steamship Co. Pty. 389, **576**
The Winkfield 125
Theaker v. Richardson 936
Theakston v. Bowley 602
Thermo King Corp. v. Proincial. Bank of Can. 920
Thibault v. Fewer 396
Thiele v. Rod Service (Ottawa) Ltd. 593
Thiessen v. Mutual Life Assurance Co. of Canada 884
Thomas v. Hamilton (City) Board of Education 513
Thomas Management Ltd. v. Alberta (Minister of Environmental Protection) 32
Thompson v. Toorenburgh 589
Thomson v. Herman 945
Thomson v. Lambert 940
Thorne v. Deas 344
Thornton v. Byers 241
Thornton (Next friend of) v. Prince George School District No. 57 602, 974

Thorson v. A.G. Can 819
Three Rivers District Council v. Governor and Company of the Bank of England (No. 3) 730, 735
Tillander v. Gosselin 53
Timmermans v. Buelow 85, 88, 91
Timothy v. Simpson 245
To v. Toronto (City) Board of Education 636
Tock v. St. John's Metropolitan Area Board 807, 847
Toews (Guardian ad litem of) v. Weisner 52, 177
Tomizza v. Fraser 590
Tomlinson v. Congleton Borough Council 789
Tompkins Hardware Ltd. v. North West Flying Services Ltd. 659
Toneguzzo-Norvell (Guardian ad litem of) v. Burnaby Hospital 300, 616, 617
Tong v. Bedwell 341, 592
Toogood v. Spryring 954
Torgeson v. Schultz 281
Toronto Dominion Bank v. Forsythe 423
Toronto Ry. Co. v. Grinstead 562
Toronto-Dominion Bank v. Forsythe 424, 433
Toronto-Dominion Bank v. Leigh Investments Ltd. (Trustee of) 421
Torquay Hotel Co. Ltd. v. Cousins 919, 923
Tottrup v. Lund 721, 875
Townsend v. Kroppmanns 612, 620
Townsview Properties Ltd. v. Sun Construction and Equipment Co. Ltd. 147
Toy v. Argenti 359
Trachsler v. Halton 743
Tracy v. Atkins 421
Trafton v. Deschene 939
Tran v. Financial Debt Recovery Ltd. 89, 108, 924
Transco plc v. Stockport Metropolitan Borough Council 839, 844
Trapp v. Mackie 953
Traquair v. National Arts Centre Corp. 790
Treaty Group Inc. (c.o.b. as Leather Treaty) v. Drake International Inc. 422
Tremblay v. McLauchlan 397
Trends Holdings Ltd. (Trustee of) v. Tilson 659
Trevison v. Springman 570
Tridan Developments Ltd. v. Shell Canada Products Ltd. 640
Trizec Equities Ltd. v. Ellis-Don Management Services Ltd. 518
Tronrud v. French 612
Trueman v. The King; Dewan v. The King 743
Tsaoussis (Litigation Guardian of) v. Baetz 605
Tubervell v. Savadge 64
Tucker v. Cadillac Fairview Corporation Limited 156
Tucker (Guardian ad litem of) v. Asleson 548, 617
Tudor Inn Reception Hall (1992) Ltd. v. Merzat Industries Ltd. 862
Turenne v. Chung 600
Turner v. Bederman 397
Turner v. Delta Shelf Co. Ltd. 804
Turner v. Thorne 52, **145**, 177
Tutton v. A.D. Walter Ltd. 304

U.A.W. v. Johnson Controls 361
U.F.C.W., Local 1252 v. Cashin 924
U.S. v. Caltex (Philippines) Inc. 226
U.S. v. Holmes 225
Udale v. Bloomsbury Area Health Authority 366
Ultramares Corp. v. Touche 285, 419, 427, 466
Unident v. DeLong 918
Uni-Jet Industrial Pipe Ltd. v. Canada (Attorney General) 731, 735
United Australia Ltd. v. Barclays Bank Ltd. 39, 135
United Project Consultants Pte Ltd. v. Leong Kwok Onn 457
United States v. Carroll Towing Co. 500
Univ. Hospital Bd. v. Lepine; Monckton v. Lepine 333
Universe Tankship Inc. of Monrovia v. I.T.W.F. 907
Université Laval v. Carriere 350
University of Regina v. Pettick 471, 601
Unruh (Guardian ad litem of) v. Webber 669
Urbanski v. Patel 304, 357, 359

V.K. Mason Construction Ltd. v. Bank of Nova Scotia 422

Valiquette c. Gazette (The) 98
Van de Perre v. Edwards 300
Van Dyke v. Grey Bruce Regional Health Centre 399
Van Mol (Guardian ad litem of) v. Ashmore 198, 396
Vana v. Tosta 637
Vancouver Gen. Hosp. v. McDaniel 525
Vancouver General Hospital v. Fraser Estate 516
Vancouver General Hospital v. Stoffman 765
Vander Zalm v. Times Publishers 968
Vanek v. Great Atlantic & Pacific Co. of Canada 375
Vanvalkenburg v. Northern Navigation Co. 316, 319
Varcoe v. Sterling 518, 761
Vasey v. Wosk's Ltd. 875
Vaughan v. Menlove 505
Vaughn v. Halifax-Dartmouth Bridge Comm. 494
Veinot v. Kerr-Addison Mines Ltd. 780
Veinot v. Veinot 208
Vellino v. Chief Constable of Greater Manchester Police 674
Verchere v. Greenpeace Canada Ltd. 918, 920
Vernon v. Bosley (No.1) 383
Viasystems (Tyneside) Ltd. v. Thermal Transfer (Northern) Ltd. 878
Victorian Railways Commissioners v. Coultas 83, 376
Videan v. British Transport Comm. 352, 354, 356
Videto v. Kennedy 395
Vienneau Assur. Ltée v. Roy 349
Villemure v. L'Hôpital Notre-Dame 333
Vincent v. Lake Erie Tpt. Co. 227
Visanji v. Eaton 518, 700
Vizetelly v. Mudie's Select Library Ltd. 940
Vlchek v. Koshel 38, 408, 597
Vogel v. Canadian Broadcasting Corporation 935, 969
Volkswagen Canada Ltd. v. Spicer 923, 927
Vorvis v. Insurance Corp. of British Columbia 32, 39, 596
Vowles v. Evans 334
Vykysaly v. Jablowski 779
W. v. A. 935
W. v. Essex County Council 383
Wackett v. Calder 205
Wade v. Ball 413, 415
Wade v. C.N.R. 784, 991
Wade v. Hoyt 415
Wade v. Martin 172, 182, 185
Wagner v. Int. Ry. Co. 357
Wagner v. International R. Co. 356
Wainwright v. Home Office 85, 95
Wakelin v. London & South Western Ry. Co. 680
Wakley v. Cooke 942
Walden v. Mitchell 935
Waldick v. Malcolm 769, 784, **790**
Waldman's Fish Co. v. Anderson Ins. Ltd. 518
Walford (Litigation Guardian of) v. Jacuzzi Canada 408
Walker v. CFTO Ltd. 973, 979, 981
Walker v. Ontario 78
Walker v. Ritchie 616, 617, 620, 642
Walker (Litigation Guardian of) v. Region 2 Hospital Corp. 198
Walker Estate v. York-Finch General Hospital 524, **534**
Wallace v. Berrigan 656
Waller v. James; Waller v. Hoolahan 363
Walls v. Mussens Ltd. 649
Walmsley v. Humenick 54, 686
Walt Disney Productions v. Fantasyland Hotel Inc. 902
Walt Disney Productions v. Triple Five Corp. 902
Walters v. W.H. Smith & Son Ltd. 245
Wandsworth Board of Works v. United Telephone Co. Ltd. 162
Ward v. Cannock Chase Dist. Council 593
Ward v. James 622
Ward v. Magna International Inc. 806, 823
Ward v. Vancouver (City) 240
Ware's Taxi Ltd. v. Gilliham 497
Warren v. Green 936
Warren v. Henlys, Ltd. 870
Warren v. King 622
Warriner v. Warriner 620
Waterloo Warehousing & Storage Ltd. v. Swenco Mfg. Ltd. 640
Waters v. Metropolitan Police Commissioner 333, 998

Watkins v. Home Office 735
Watkins v. Olafson 606, 612
Watson v. Jones 954
Watson v. Longsdon 954
Watt v. Meier 97
Watt v. Hertfordshire County Council 497
Webb v. Attewell 153
Webber v. Crawford 656
Webster v. Edmonton (City) Police Services 241
Wechsel v. Stutz 416
WeGo Kayaking Ltd. v. Sewid 969
Wegren v. Prince Albert (City) 722
Weiner v. Zoratti 566
Weingerl v. Seo 875, 876
Weiss c. Solomon 188, 399
Welbridge Hldg. v. Winnipeg 704, 706, 721
Weldon v. Home Office 69
Wellesley Hospital v. Lawson 333
Wells v. Parsons 652
Wells v. Sears 955
Wenden v. Trikha 55, 333, 343, 504, 517
Wennhak v. Morgan 939
Wentzell v. Veinot 223
Werbeniuk v. Maynard 341, 586, 592
Wernikowski v. Kirkland, Murphy & Ain 416
Wessell v. Kinsmen Club of Sault Ste. Marie Ont. Inc. 630
West Coast Finance Ltd. v. Gunderson, Stokes, Walton & Co. 896
Whaley v. Cartusiano 55
Wheeler v. Muri 519
Wheeler v. Somerfield 936
Whelan v. Parsons & Sons Transportation Ltd. 497
White v. Blackmore 669
White v. Chief Constable of South Yorkshire Police 358, 375, 377, 383, 387, 389
White v. Jones 345, 413, 461, 462
White v. Sheaves 677
White v. Turner 513
White Hatter Limousine Service Ltd. v. Calgary (City) 927
Whitehorse (City) v. Domingue 857
Whiteley Ltd. v. Hilt 138
Whiten v. Pilot Insurance Co. 37, 595
Whittingham v. Crease & Co. 345, 413, 461, 462
Whitwham v. Westminster Brymbo Coal and Coke Company 40
Wiche v. Ontario 79, 735
Wickberg v. Patterson 660
Wickline v. California 497
Widdowson v. Newgate Meat Corp. 695
Wiebe v. Canada (Attorney General) 333
Wiebe v. Gunderson 642
Wiebe Door Services Ltd. v. M.N.R. 881
Wieland v. Cyril Lord Carpets Ltd. 589
Wilcox v. Johnston 518
Wilcox v. Police 154, 226
Wildwood Mall Ltd. v. Stevens 153
Wiley v. Tymar Management Inc 772
Wilhelm v. Hickson 462
Wilkinson v. Downton 9, **82**, 108
William Leitch & Co. v. Leydon 117
Williams v. Attorney General of Canada 724, 875
Williams v. Holland 13, 14
Williams v. Mulgrave (Town) 147
Williams v. New Brunswick 333
Williams v. Peel River Land & Mineral Co. Ltd. 40
Williams v. Polgar 433
Williams v. Reason 942
Williams v. St. John (City) 570
Willows v. Williams 938
Wills v. Doe 590
Wills v. Saunders 516
Wilmington Gen. Hosp. v. Manlove 349
Wilsher v. Essex Area Health Authority 538, 692, 694
Wilson v. Bobbie 233
Wilson v. Brett 519
Wilson v. Lind 597
Wilson v. Lombank Ltd. 124
Wilson v. Martinello 607
Wilson v. New Brighton Panelbeaters Ltd. 121
Wilson v. Pringle 59, 61
Wince v. Ball 331
Windrem v. Hamill 860
Winnipeg Child & Family Services (Northwest Area) v. G.(D.F.) 373
Winnipeg Condominium Corp. No. 36 v. Bird Construction Co. 463, 478
Winnipeg Elec. Ry. Co. v. Can. Nor. Ry. 562
Winnipeg Electric Co. v. Geel, 685
Winterbottom v. Wright 281
Wipfli v. Britten 88, 644

Witman v. Johnson 857
Woestenburg v. Kamloops 707
Wood v. Kennedy 80
Woolcock Street Investments Pty. Ltd. v. C.D.G. Pty. Ltd. 471
Woollerton and Wilson Ltd. v. Richard Costain Ltd. 163
Wormald v. Cole 860
Worthman v. Assessmed Inc. 925
Wotta v. Haliburton Oil Well Cementing Co. 691
Wright v. McCrea 592
Wright v. McLean 168
Wright v. Wilson 68
Wright Estate v. Davidson 573, 590
Wyant v. Crouse 148
Wynberg v. Daley 421, 423
Wynberg v. Ontario 721

X (Minors) v. Bedfordshire Country Council 722

Yarmouth v. France 667
Ybarra v. Spangard 691
Yelic v. Gimli (Town) 778
Yellow Submarine Deli Inc. v. A.G.F. Hospitality Associates Inc 918
Yepremian v. Scarborough Gen. Hosp. 606
Yin v. Lewin 599
York v. Alderney Consultants Ltd. 422
York v. Okanagan Broadcasters Ltd. 945
Young v. Bella 295, 342, 458, 518, 624
Young v. Green 854
Yu v. Yu 383
Yuan v. Farstad 653
Yuen Kun Yeu v. A.G. of Hong Kong 284, 287, 293

Z v. United Kingdom 340
Zacharias v. Leys 574
Zanetti v. Bonniehon Enterprises Ltd. 953
Zapf v. Muckalt 669
Zastowny v. MacDougall 674
Zavaglia v. Maq Holdings Ltd. 789
Zbarsky v. Lukashuk 802
Zelenko v. Gimbel Bros., Inc. 346
Zervobeakos v. Zervobeakos 359, 651
Zidaric v. Toshiba of Canada Ltd. 469
Zinck v. Strickland and Blake 182
Zraik v. Levesque Securities Inc. 40

1175777 Ontario Ltd. v. Magna International Ltd. 925
1318777 Ontario Ltd. v. 1004847 Ontario Inc. 893
270233 Ontario Ltd. v. Weall & Cullen Nurseries Ltd. 804
281856 B.C. Ltd. v. Kamloops Revelstoke Okanagan Building Traders Union 154
340909 Ont. Ltd. v. Huron Steel Products (Windsor) Ltd. 796
347671 B.C. Ltd. v. Heenan Blaikie 421
369413 Alberta Ltd. v. Pocklington 920
373409 Alberta Ltd. (Receiver of) v. Bank of Montreal 127
384238 Ontario Ltd. v. The Queen in Right of Canada 117
565486 Ontario Inc. v. Tristone Properties Inc. 920
66295 Manitoba Ltd. v. Imperial Oil Ltd. 471
671122 Ontario Ltd. v. Sagaz Industries Canada Inc. 878
755165 Ontario Inc. v. Parsons 417

1

AN INTRODUCTION TO THE LAW OF TORTS

1. Tort Law Defined
2. Tort and Contract
3. A Brief History of Tort Law
4. Trespass and Case: A Brief Review of the Case Law
5. The Bases for Imposing Liability in Tort
6. The Functions of Tort Law

1. Tort Law Defined

Tort law is difficult to define. The word itself is not commonly used outside of the legal community. It is derived from the Latin word "torquere," which means twisted or crooked. Tort law therefore is concerned with things that have gone wrong, or, to use more technical language, with the *breach of obligations*. It is important to realize, however, that our legal system recognizes various types of wrongdoing, and that only some of those fall within tort law.

At the most general level, a distinction must be drawn between *public wrongs* and *private wrongs*. Public wrongs are addressed through *criminal law*. A crime is committed when a person breaches an obligation that was owed to society as a whole. Because crime is a public matter, action is taken by the Crown (the government) rather than the individual victim (if there is one). That fact is reflected in the *style of cause* (*i.e.* the name of the case). The Crown appears as *Regina* (which is Latin for Queen) in order to prosecute the *accused*: *R. v. Smith*. Likewise, because the primary goals of criminal law are concerned with the protection of society, a successful prosecution, in which the accused is found *guilty*, usually results in some form of punishment, such as imprisonment. Even if the offender is ordered to pay a fine, the money usually is received by the Crown rather than the victim.

Tort law, in contrast, is concerned with private wrongs. The wrongdoer breached an obligation that was owed to an individual, rather than to society as a whole. Consequently, the victim of the wrong (the *plaintiff*) personally takes action against the party in breach (the *defendant*), and the style of cause takes the form of *Smith v. Jones*. Likewise, because a tort is a private matter, successful litigation, in which the defendant is held *liable*, usually results in a remedy that reflects the manner in which the breach affected the parties. For instance, if a benefit is acquired as a result of a wrong, the court may order the defendant to *disgorge* that enrichment to the plaintiff (as when a thief earns a profit by using a stolen car as a taxi). Typically, however, the focus falls upon the plaintiff's loss, rather than the defendant's gain. The appropriate remedy therefore requires the defendant to *compensate* the plaintiff (as when a person wrongfully suffers an injury that entails medical expenses or lost income). Although the plaintiff occasionally is entitled to recover the very thing that was lost (as when a thief steals a family heirloom), compensation usually takes the form of monetary *damages*. Remedies are considered in greater detail in Chapters 2 and 18.

To this point, tort law generally has been discussed in terms of the rights and remedies associated with legal relationships between private parties. That definition, however, is too broad. First, it is necessary to emphasize that since tort law is concerned with wrongdoing, it does not govern situations of true *strict liability*, which do not presume breach of obligation. (As explained later in this chapter, a different conception of "strict liability," which *does* involve the breach of an obligation, *is* part of tort law.) For instance, the law of *unjust enrichment* applies if, in the absence of any juristic reason, the defendant receives a benefit from the plaintiff. That may be true even if the defendant was entirely unaware, and wholly innocent, of the impugned transfer (as when a company mistakenly pays money into the defendant's bank account, rather than its own). The claimant nevertheless is entitled to *restitution* from the recipient.

Moreover, even within the broad category of private wrongdoing, some situations fall outside of tort law. Most obviously, although a breach of contract is a private wrong, it is governed by the law of contract rather than the law of tort. This makes perfectly good sense. The relationship between tort and contract is considered further in the next section. In contrast, it is more difficult to justify the general practice of defining tort law to exclude wrongs that originally developed in the *courts of equity*.

The exclusion of equitable wrongs nevertheless may be defended on purely practical grounds. Tort law is a large subject. The addition of equitable wrongs would contribute substantially to its size. Moreover, if equitable wrongs were included, it would be difficult to justify the exclusion of still more categories of private wrongdoing. That would be true, for instance, of the various causes of action that protect intellectual property rights: breach of patent, breach of copyright, and so on. Some of those wrongs are now governed by statute, but as Chapter 22 demonstrates, tort law already encompasses some statutory wrongs. This book accordingly is confined to the forms of private wrongdoing that traditionally have been characterized as torts. It is important to remember, however, that obligations and liabilities often arise in other ways.

NOTES AND QUESTIONS

1. Although a distinction is now drawn between public wrongs and private wrongs, criminal law and tort law share a common heritage that predates the Norman Conquest of England. See generally Holdsworth, *A History of English Law*, vol. 2 (1932) at 43-54; Malone, "Ruminations on the Role of Fault in the History of the Common Law of Torts" (1970) 31 La. L. Rev. 1; and Hall, "Interrelations of Criminal Law and Torts" (1943) 43 Columbia L. Rev. 753 and 967.

2. A strong argument for subsuming equitable wrongs within the law of tort is made by Birks, "Civil Wrongs: A New World" in *Butterworths Lectures 1990-91* (1992) at 55-112.

3. On the importance of legal taxonomy, see Birks, "This Heap of Good Learning: The Jurist in the Common Law Tradition" in Markesinis, ed., *Law Making, Law Finding and Law Shaping: The Diverse Influences* (1997) at 113-38; and Birks, "Equity in the Modern Law: An Exercise in Taxonomy" (1996) 26 U.W.A.L. Rev. 1.

4. The *Judicature Acts* of the 19th century undoubtedly fused the *administration* of law and equity. There is a debate, however, as to whether Parliament also intended *substantive fusion*. Some commentators, especially in Australia, argue that while law and equity are now administered in a single set of courts, they retain their historical characteristics and therefore remain fundamentally different in outlook and operation: Meagher, Heydon & Leeming, eds., *Meagher, Gummow and Lehane's Equity: Doctrines and Remedies*, 4th ed. (2002); and *Harris v. Digital Pulse Pty. Ltd.* (2003), 56 N.S.W.L.R. 298 (C.A.). Other commentators, however, insist that it is unhelpful, if not irrational, to maintain two perspectives in a single system: Burrows, "We Do This At Common Law But That In Equity" (2002) 22 O.J.L.S. 1; and Birks, "Annual Miegunyah Lecture: Equity, Conscience, and Unjust Enrichment" (1999) 23 Melbourne U.L. Rev. 1.

5. While Canadian courts demonstrate relatively little interest in the fusion debate, the Supreme Court of Canada has suggested that, in some circumstances at least, different principles apply depending upon whether the plaintiff's allegation of wrongdoing lies in equity rather than law: *Canson Enterprises Ltd v. Broughton & Co.*, [1991] 3 S.C.R. 534.

2. Tort and Contract

Although it is important to distinguish tort law from other areas of law, the facts of life do not always fall neatly into place. A single set of facts may support several different analyses. For instance, the same events may support both a claim in tort law and a prosecution in criminal law, as when an offender is privately liable for a victim's injuries and publicly punished for the crime. Likewise, a different set of events may support several claims in tort law, as when a security guard is held liable for both false imprisonment and battery after physically detaining a person erroneously thought guilty of shoplifting. Perhaps the most significant overlap, however, occurs between tort and contract. Very often, for instance, a professional person (such as a lawyer or an accountant) who acts carelessly is held responsible for both breach of contract and the tort of negligence. As a general rule, a plaintiff is entitled to simultaneously sue for several causes of action. If successful on more than one basis, however, the plaintiff normally must *elect* between the options and therefore cannot enjoy *double recovery* for the same loss or gain.

Because of the significance of the overlap between tort and contract, it is necessary to say more about the relationship between those two areas of law.

- *Structure*: Both tort and contract involve *primary* and *secondary* obligations. Primary obligations tell people how they ought to act. For instance, the tort of battery says, "Do not touch another person in an offensive way." The law of contract says, "Keep your promises." Secondary obligations are remedial. They tell people how they must act *after* primary obligations have been broken. In most cases, the defendant is told, "Pay money to the plaintiff as compensation for the losses that you caused." That is true whether the case involves a tort or a contract.

- *Source of Primary Obligations*: Despite sharing the same basic structure, tort and contract differ in several important respects. The first pertains to the source of the primary obligations. Obligations in tort are imposed by law on the basis of circumstance. Consequently, for instance, a motorist will owe a duty of care to a nearby pedestrian, even if the motorist never agreed to take care and even if (remarkably) the motorist is unaware of that duty. In contrast, contractual obligations generally are created by the parties. If contractual parties are required to act in a certain way, it usually is because they voluntarily agreed to do so.

- *Privity*: Because contractual obligations are voluntarily created by the parties, their enforcement is subject to the doctrine of *privity*. As a general rule, only the parties to an agreement can sue or be sued if that agreement is broken. That means, for instance, that an outsider cannot sue for breach of contract, even if the breach caused that person to suffer substantial harm. In contrast, because tort obligations are imposed by law, they apply even if the parties otherwise are complete strangers.

- *Compensation*: Compensation is available in both tort and contract. Once again, however, the underlying obligations result in an important distinction. Suppose that the defendant persuaded the plaintiff to purchase a business opportunity for $100,000 by fraudulently saying that the venture would earn a profit of $50,000. The plaintiff realizes the truth of the matter only after paying the purchase price. An option then arises for suing either in the tort of deceit or in breach of contract. The measure of relief will be different in each instance. Tort obligations are imposed in order to prevent harm and protect an existing state of affairs. Compensation in tort law consequently looks *backward*. It monetarily puts the plaintiff back into the position that would have been enjoyed if the wrong had not been committed. The plaintiff in this case therefore would receive damages of $100,000. Going back in time, that is what was lost. In contrast, contracts are based on promises, and promises pertain to the future. Compensation in contract consequently (usually) looks *forward*. It monetarily puts the plaintiff into the position that would have been enjoyed once the agreement was performed. The plaintiff in this case therefore would be entitled to receive $150,000. Looking ahead in time, that is what the claimant expected to receive.

NOTES AND QUESTIONS

1. Although the orthodox model continues to reflect the general distinction between tort and contract, the line between these two areas of law has become increasingly blurred. For example, contractual obligations are not invariably created by the parties. In many situations, they are imposed upon the parties by operation of law. The *Sale of Goods Act*, R.S.O. 1990, c. S.1, for instance, automatically inserts a large number of terms into contracts for the sale of goods. That is true even if the parties did not consider the matter. Some commentators regard such developments as the "death of contract," in the sense that contractual obligations are not exclusively a function of the parties' volition. See Gilmore, *The Death of Contract* (1974); Atiyah, *The Rise and Fall of Freedom of Conract* (1979); and Blom, "Fictions and Frictions on the Interface Between Tort and Contract" in Burns, ed., *Donoghue v. Stevenson: The Modern Law of Negligence* (1991) at 139.

2. Likewise, while many tort obligations are imposed without regard to volition, others arise only if a person voluntarily enters into a relationship or agrees to undertake certain acts. Various examples will be seen throughout this book.

REVIEW PROBLEM

Angus, a consumer advocate, was conducting a speaking tour criticizing the safety standards of a new Canadian subcompact automobile. The car, which had been hailed as the key to the future of the Canadian automobile industry, was supposed to reverse the trend of falling sales and high unemployment. Several days before his appearance in Windsor, Angus received threatening phone calls. As a precaution he hired Joseph, a local private detective, who agreed to serve as his bodyguard during his speech.

Just before the end of the speech, a man jumped onto the stage shouting, "Canadian jobs first!" and flailed at Angus. Joseph ran off to call the police, but offered no direct assistance. Angus' secretary, Doris, who was an expert in the martial arts, also failed to come to his assistance. The assailant, an unemployed auto worker named Victor, was eventually restrained by two members of the audience, but not before he had severely beaten Angus.

1. As you are probably aware, Victor's attack on Angus is a violation of Canadian criminal law. Who is responsible for bringing charges against Victor, gathering the evidence, and conducting and paying for the prosecution? What role will Angus play at the criminal trial? What private and social benefits result from the criminal prosecution?

2. Victor's attack on Angus also constitutes the intentional tort of battery. Contrast the events involved in bringing a tort suit against Victor with the criminal process. What general distinctions between criminal and tort law emerge?

3. Angus and Joseph are in a contractual relationship. What legal wrong has Joseph done to Angus? What is the public interest in enforcing contractual obligations?

4. Angus also wants to sue Doris, whose legal wrong, if any, was a failure to come to Angus' aid. Distinguish Angus' legal relationship with Doris from his legal relationship with Joseph.

5. A failure to act is referred to as a nonfeasance. In tort law, it has always been more difficult to establish liability for a nonfeasance than for a misfeasance, which is a wrongful positive act. Can you explain why? Provided that a defendant has agreed to act, he or she will generally be held liable in contract for the failure to do so. Why should nonfeasance be more readily actionable in contract than in tort?

6. Should Doris be held liable in tort if she knew of the threats against Angus and promised to protect him? Would your answer be different if: (a) Angus had relied on her assurances and told Doris that he had dismissed Joseph; or (b) Doris was unaware that Angus had dismissed Joseph?

3. A Brief History of Tort Law

The history of tort law is not the evolution of a single idea, but rather the history of how a residual category of civil wrongs came to be formed. The story begins with the separation of public and private wrongs, and continues with the emergence of tort (and other discrete heads of liability) from a general body of civil wrongs.

In Anglo-Saxon England, the primary object of the law was to prevent blood feuds among the clans. There were few divisions in the law, and no distinction was drawn between crimes and torts. The appeasement of the clan's pride and the symbolism of public adjudication were the law's main goals. The wrongdoer paid a *bot* to the other clan for appeasement and a *wite* to the King for having breached the peace. Gradually, as political power became centralized in the King, a distinction between public and private wrongs developed. By the 11th century, the *appeal of felony*, a criminal action that could not be amended by private payment, was recognized. Paralleling this development was a breakdown in the agreed scale of the *bot* among the clans. As a result, there was no legal mechanism for making a private claim for damages.

After the Norman Conquest, there were further attempts to centralize and unify legal authority. In order to consolidate his power and avoid the inconvenience that the diverse local laws caused his tax collectors and judicial officers, William the Conqueror sought to impose a uniform set of laws throughout England. This set of laws came to be known as the *common law*. A central feature of the common law was the writ system – a system that became dominated by an intense concern with procedural formality.

The writs themselves were standardized pleadings issued by the Chancery clerks on behalf of the King, stating that a defendant had committed certain unlawful acts. In order to commence an action in the King's common law courts, a plaintiff had to allege facts that would bring the case within the standard form of the writ. No matter how obviously wrongful the defendant's conduct, no action would lie if it was not governed by an existing writ.

At first, access to the King's courts was limited to suits concerning violent acts – those done with force of arms and against the King's peace (*vi et armis et contra pacem regis*). Causes of action now recognized as torts were grouped into a family of writs called *trespass*. It included actions for assault, battery, trespass to land, and the taking of goods.

The most important factor in the history of tort law after 1200 was jurisdiction, not policy. To meet the demand for access to the King's courts and to expand the King's jurisdiction, it was necessary to broaden the types of wrongs that could be heard. However, this had to be accomplished without increasing the limited number of writs. The solution, as in much of the common law's history, was "a pack of lies": see Langbein, "The Later History of Restitution" in Cornish *et al.*, eds., *Restitution: Past, Present & Future* (1998) at 57. Plaintiffs would plead trespass *vi et armis et contra pacem regis* even if no force or breach of the peace was involved, and the clerks would honour this fiction to assume jurisdiction. For example, if the defendant refused to return goods in storage, the plaintiff would plead that the defendant took them *vi et armis et contra pacem regis* in order to have the case tried in the King's courts.

Although the King's courts eventually assumed jurisdiction over most civil wrongs and the *vi et armis* allegation became unnecessary in the 1300s, the writ system remained. A second writ, called *trespass on the case*, emerged. Its origins are a matter of dispute. The pleadings in an action on the case raised special circumstances which made the act wrongful, whereas in the original trespass action a general plea would suffice.

Before the 19th century, what we would now call actions in tort were not frequently litigated. It appears that most conflicts over intentional and unintentional wrongs were resolved extra-legally. However, the advent in England of more densely populated, impersonal and technologically-advanced communities after 1800 gave rise to increased levels of tort litigation. Just as lawyers for plaintiffs attempted to extend the scope of liability in the writs of trespass and case, so too lawyers for defendants attempted to terminate litigation on procedural grounds. In this context, the longstanding, but conceptually awkward, distinction between trespass and case assumed even more significance. The cases excerpted in the fourth section of this chapter illustrate how the common law judges gradually developed new theories of liability for these torts.

The core normative principle in tort law in the 19th century was the idea of fault or moral blameworthiness. In this era, judges came to agree that, with rare exceptions, liability in tort required proof that the plaintiff's loss had been caused by some wrongdoing of the defendant. For instance, liability in trespass would be established when the plaintiff proved that the defendant had intentionally interfered with his or her rights to security of the person or property. Liability on the case would lie when the plaintiff proved that an actual loss to person or property had been caused by the defendant's carelessness. Although in recent years the "fault-based" conception of liability has been blurred in some types of cases, it continues to underscore most of the contemporary torts of intent and negligence.

After 50 years of debate, the writ system in England was abolished by the *Judicature Acts* in the 1870s. Similar legislation soon followed in other common law jurisdictions, including Canada. It no longer was necessary for a litigant to fit the claim within an existing writ. Instead, the plaintiff pleaded the facts of the case, and if these facts justified relief under any recognized cause of action, the courts would grant that relief. Nevertheless, the break with the old forms of actions was neither sharp nor complete. As F.W. Maitland famously observed, "The forms of action we have buried, but they rule us from their graves": *Equity—A Course of Lectures* (1939) at vi. For example, the intentional torts derived from trespass *vi et armis* have remained strictly defined, typically require proof of direct injury, and have developed little over the years. As *Cook v. Lewis*, [1951] S.C.R. 830, extracted below, illustrates, plaintiffs still benefit if they can prove that they were directly injured.

It was not until the end of the 19th century that academics and lawyers began to speak of torts as a distinct branch of law. Initially, the search for a theoretical basis for tort law centred on the issue of whether there was a general principle of tort liability. J. Salmond argued that tort law was merely a patchwork of distinct causes of action, each protecting different interests and based on separate principles of liability. On that view, the law of torts essentially was a finite set of independent rules, and the courts were not free to recognize new heads of liability. In contrast, writers such as F. Pollock contended that the law of torts was based upon the single unifying principle that all harms were tortious unless they could be justified. On that view, courts were free to recognize new torts.

The debate over the existence of a general theory of tort liability was not limited to academics. The courts, confronted with new claims in the growing area of negligence, also had to decide whether to expand tort liability and, if so, upon what principles. In *Donoghue v. Stevenson*, [1932] A.C. 562 at 580 (H.L.), Lord Atkin suggested that, at least in the tort of negligence, the courts were prepared to expand the scope of recovery and recognize a general theory of liability:

> At present I content myself with pointing out that in English law there must be, and is, some general conception of relations giving rise to a duty of care, of which the particular cases found in the books are but instances. The liability for negligence, whether you style it such or treat it as in other systems as a species of "culpa," is no doubt based upon a general public sentiment of moral wrongdoing for which the offender must pay.

The debate continues today. The increased role of government in all facets of life, the growth of social welfare and social services, the proliferation of liability insurance, and the rapid pace of technological change all continue to influence the development of tort law. Depending upon the legal, social, economic, and philosophical circumstances that prevail in a given time and place, the scope of liability may expand or contract. For instance, as explained in Chapters 9 and 10, the elements of the tort of negligence (the most important of modern torts) occasionally are reformulated or re-phrased, as courts in Canada, England, and Australia attempt to strike an appropriate balance between competing interests. As conditions change, so too does the plaintiff's burden of proof. If the judiciary fears that liability is stifling innovation or creating an insurance crisis, it may narrow the defendant's duty of care. If, in contrast, the courts are concerned that industries are improperly profiting at the expense of injured consumers, they may loosen the reins.

NOTES AND QUESTIONS

1. Anglo-Saxon law was characterized by very strict ideas of causation. The issue of fault was largely ignored and an actor was held liable for even the most remote consequences of his or her actions. It was common, in fact, for offending animals and even inanimate objects which had been the instruments of harm to be destroyed merely because they were part of the causal chain. On the history of Anglo-Saxon law see Winfield, "The Myth of Absolute Liability" (1926) 42 L.Q.R. 37; Baker, *An Introduction to English Legal History*, 3d ed. (1990) at 1-43; and Pollock & Maitland, *History of English Law Before the Time of Edward I*, 2d ed., vol. 1 (1898) at 1-63. See also Arnold, "Accident, Mistake, and Rules of Liability in the Fourteenth Century Law of Torts" (1979) 128 U. Pa. L. Rev. 361.

2. On the origins of the writ of trespass *vi et armis* see Ames, *Lectures On Legal History* (1886-87) at 41-60; Maitland, *Forms of Actions* (1904) at 48-50; Woodbine, "The Origin of the Action of Trespass" (1924) 33 Yale L.J. 799 & (1925) 34 Yale L.J. 343; and Milsom, *Historical Foundations of the Common Law*, 2d ed. (1981) at 283-313. See also Fifoot, *History And Sources of the Common Law* (1952) at 44-65.

3. For a history of the writ of trespass on the case see Landon, "The Action on the Case and the Statute of Westminster II" (1936) 52 L.Q.R. 68; Dix, "The Origins of the Action of Trespass on the Case" (1937) 46 Yale L.J. 1142; Kiralfy, *The Action on the Case* (1951); and Milsom, *supra*.

4. It is debatable whether fault first assumed significance in the 19th century or whether the absence of fault had long provided a valid defence that was simply not apparent from the writ system. See Malone, "Ruminations on the Role of Fault in the History of the Common Law of Torts" (1970) 31 La. L. Rev. 1.

5. Largely as a result of frequent usage, most of the actions in trespass and some of the actions in trespass on the case acquired specific names (*e.g.* battery, assault). As a category, these are known as the nominate actions. There are other torts, innominate actions, that have not been named.

6. With the enactment of the *Judicature Acts*, the plaintiff no longer had to fit the claim into an existing writ. However, these statutes did not address whether the courts could create new tort actions to deal with situations that had not been covered by the writs. In *Wilkinson v. Downton*, [1897] 2 Q.B. 57, discussed in Chapter 3, the court created a new innominate action for intentional, indirectly caused physical injury. This filled some of the gaps left by the established nominate torts. Although it is now generally accepted that courts may recognize new causes of action, plaintiffs have had considerable difficulty establishing new intentional tort claims. In contrast, the scope of liability in negligence has increased dramatically.

4. Trespass and Case: A Brief Review of the Case Law

SCOTT v. SHEPHERD

[1558-1774] All E.R. 296

[The defendant threw a lighted squib, or firecracker, into a crowded marketplace. The squib landed on a stall that was operated by Yates. In order to prevent injury to himself or Yates, or to Yates' goods, Willis picked up the squib and threw it. The squib then landed on a stall operated by Ryal. In order to save himself and his goods, Ryal picked it up and threw it toward another part of the market. The squib struck the plaintiff in the face, exploded, and put out one of his eyes. The plaintiff sued the defendant for trespass and assault.

At the trial before Nares, J., the jury found a verdict for the plaintiff with £100 damages, subject to the opinion of the court on a case. The question for the opinion of the court was whether this action was maintainable.]

NARES, J.:—I am of opinion that trespass would well lie in the present case. The natural and probable consequence of the act done by the defendant was injury to somebody, and, therefore, the act was illegal at common law. The throwing of squibs has by 9 Will. 3, c. 7 [Fireworks Act, 1697: repealed], been since made a nuisance. Being, therefore, unlawful, the defendant was liable to answer for the consequences, be the injury mediate or immediate. YEAR BOOK 21 Hen. 7, 28, is express that malus animus is not necessary to constitute a trespass. ... The principle I go on is what is laid down in *Reynolds v. Clarke* [(1725), 93 E.R. 747], that if the act in the first instance be unlawful, trespass will lie. Wherever, therefore, an act is unlawful at first, trespass will lie for the consequences of it. So, in Y.B. 12 Hen. 4, fo. 3, pl. 4, trespass lay for stopping a sewer with earth so as to overflow the plaintiff's land. In Y.B. 26 Hen. 8, 8, for going on the plaintiff's land to take the boughs off which had fallen thereon in lopping. ... I do not think it necessary, to maintain trespass, that the defendant should personally touch the plaintiff; if he does it by a mean it is sufficient. Qui facit per aliud facit per se. He is the person who, in the present case, gave the mischievous faculty to the squib. That mischievous faculty remained in it until the explosion. No new power of doing mischief was communicated to it by Willis or Ryal. It is like the case of a mad ox turned loose in a crowd. The person who turns him loose is answerable in trespass for whatever mischief he may do. The intermediate acts of Willis and Ryal will not purge the original tort in the defendant. But he who does the first wrong is answerable for all the consequential damages: so held in *R. v. Huggins* [(1730), 92 E.R. 518]; *Parkhurst v. Forster* [(1698), 87 E.R. 746]; *Rosewell v. Prior* [(1701), 90 E.R. 1175]. And it was declared by this court, in *Slater v. Baker* (1767), 2 Wils. K.B. 359, that they would not look with eagle's eyes to see whether the evidence applies exactly or not to the case; but if the plaintiff has obtained a verdict for such damages as he deserves, they will establish it if possible.

BLACKSTONE, J. (dissenting):—I am of opinion that an action of trespass does not lie for the plaintiff against the defendant on this Case. I take the settled distinction to be that, where the injury is immediate, an action of trespass will lie; where it is only consequential, it must be an action on the Case: *Reynolds v. Clarke* [*supra*]; *Haward v. Bankes* [(1760), 97 E.R. 740]; *Harker v. Birkbeck* [(1764), 97 E.R. 978]. The lawfulness or unlawfulness of the original act is not the criterion, although something of that sort is put into Lord Raymond's mouth in *Reynolds v. Clarke* [*supra*], where it can only mean that if the act then in question, of erecting a spout, had been in itself unlawful, trespass might have lain; but as it was a lawful act (on the defendant's own ground) and the injury to the plaintiff only consequential, it must be an action on the case. But this cannot be the general rule, for it is held by the court in the same case that if I throw a log of timber into the highway (which is an unlawful act) and another man tumbles over it and is hurt, an action on the case only lies, it being a consequential damage; but if in throwing it I hit another man, he may bring trespass because it is an immediate wrong. Trespass may sometimes lie for the consequences of a lawful act. If in lopping my own trees a bough accidentally falls on my neighbour's ground and I go thereon to fetch it, trespass lies. This is the case cited from Y.B. 6 Edw. 4, fo. 7, pl. 18. But then the entry is of itself an immediate wrong. And case will sometimes lie for the consequence of an unlawful act. If by false imprisonment I have a special damage, as if I forfeit my recognisance thereby, I shall have an action on the case: per Powell, J., in *Bourden v. Alloway* [(1708), 88 E.R. 975]. Yet here the original act was unlawful, and in the nature of trespass. So that lawful or unlawful is quite out of the case.

The solid distinction is between direct or immediate injuries on the one hand and mediate or consequential on the other, and trespass never lay for the latter. If this be so, the only question will be whether the injury which the plaintiff suffered was immediate, or consequential only; and I hold it to be the latter. The original act was, as against Yates, a trespass; not as against Ryal or the plaintiff. The tortious act was complete when the squib lay at rest on Yates's stall. He, or any bystander, had, I allow, a right to protect themselves by removing the squib, but should have taken care to do it in such a manner as not to endanger others. But the defendant, I think, is not answerable in an action of trespass and assault for the mischief done by the squib in the new motion impressed on it, and the new direction given it, by either Willis or Ryal, who both were free agents and acted on their own judgment. This distinguishes it from the cases put of turning loose a wild beast or a madman. They are only instruments in the hand of the first agent. Nor is it like diverting the course of an enraged ox, or of a stone thrown, or an arrow glancing against a tree; because there the original motion, the vis impressa, is continued, though diverted. Here the instrument of mischief was at rest until a new impetus and a new direction are given it, not once only, but by two successive rational agents. But it is said that the act is not complete, nor the squib at rest, until after it is spent or exploded. It certainly has a power of doing fresh mischief, and so has a stone that has been thrown against my windows and now lies still. Yet if any person gives that stone a new motion and does further mischief with it, trespass will not lie for that against the original thrower. No doubt but Yates may maintain trespass against the defendant. And, according to the doctrine contended for, so may Ryal and the plaintiff. Three actions for one single act! nay, it may be extended in infinitum. If a man tosses a football into the street and, after being kicked about by one hundred people, it at last breaks a tradesman's windows, shall he have trespass against the man who first produced it? Surely only against the man who gave it that mischievous direction. But it is said, if the plaintiff has no action against the defendant, against whom must be seek his remedy? I give no opinion whether case would lie against the defendant for the consequential damage; though, as at present advised, I think that on the circumstances, it would. But I think that, in strictness of law, trespass would lie against Ryal, the immediate actor in this unhappy business. Both he and Willis have exceeded the bounds of self-defence and not used sufficient circumspection in removing the danger from themselves. The throwing it across the market-house instead of brushing it down, or throwing it out of the open sides into the street (if it was not meant to continue the sport, as it is called), was at least an unnecessary and incautious act. Not even menaces from others are sufficient to justify a trespass against a third person, much less a fear of danger to either his goods or his person; nothing but inevitable necessity ... .

It is said by Lord Raymond, and very justly, in *Reynolds v. Clarke* [*supra*]: "We must keep up the boundaries of actions, otherwise we shall introduce the utmost confusion." As I, therefore, think no immediate injury passed from the defendant to the plaintiff (and without such immediate injury no action of trespass can be maintained), I am of opinion that in this action judgment ought to be for the defendant.

GOULD, J.:—I am of the same opinion with Nares, J., that this action is well maintainable. The whole difficulty lies in the form of the action and not in the substance of the remedy. The line is very nice between case and trespass on these occasions. I am persuaded that there are many instances wherein both or either will lie. I agree with Nares, J., that, wherever a man does an unlawful act, he is answerable for all the consequences; and trespass will lie against him, if the consequence be in nature of trespass. But, exclusive of this, I think that the defendant may be considered in the same view as if he himself had personally thrown the squib in the plaintiff's face. The terror impressed on Willis and Ryal excited self-defence and deprived them of the power of recollection. What they did was, therefore, the inevitable consequence of the defendant's unlawful act. Had the squib been thrown into a coach full of company, the person throwing it out again would not have been answerable for the consequences. What Willis and Ryal did was by necessity, and the defendant imposed that necessity on them.

DE GREY, C.J.:—This case is one of those wherein the line drawn by the law between actions on the case and actions of trespass is very nice and delicate. Trespass is an injury accompanied with force, for which an action of trespass vi et armis lies against the person from whom it is received. The question here is whether the injury received by the plaintiff arises from the force of the original act of the defendant, or from a new force by a third person. I agree with Blackstone, J., as to the principles he has laid down but not in his application of those principles to the present case. The real question certainly does not turn on the lawfulness or unlawfulness of the original act; for actions of trespass will lie for legal acts when they become trespasses by accident, as in the cases cited of cutting thorns, lopping of a tree, shooting at a mark, defending oneself by a stick which strikes another behind, etc. They may also not lie for the consequences even of illegal acts, as that of casting a log in the highway, etc. But the true question is whether the injury is the direct and immediate act of the defendant; and I am of opinion that in this case it is.

. . .

I look on all that was done subsequent to the original throwing as a continuation of the first force and first act which will continue until the squib was spent by bursting. I think that any innocent person removing the danger from himself to another is justifiable; the blame lights on the first thrower. The new direction and new force flow out of the first force, and are not a new trespass. The writ in the REGISTER, 95 a, for trespass in maliciously cutting down a head of water which thereupon flowed down to and overwhelmed another's pond shows that the immediate act need not be instantaneous, but that a chain of effects connected together will be sufficient. It has been urged that the intervention of a free agent will make a difference; but I do not consider Willis and Ryal as free agents in the present case, but acting under a compulsive necessity for their own safety and self-preservation. On these reasons I concur with Gould and Nares, JJ., that the present action is maintainable.

Judgment for plaintiff.

NOTES AND QUESTIONS

1. In reference to Blackstone J. and his judgment in *Scott*, Lord Denning stated in *What's Next in the Law* (1982) at 18: "like many learned men, he was not a great judge. He was too technical. He was one of four judges in an important case of those days called *Scott v. Shepherd*... . He had a technical point about the difference in ancient learning between an action of trespass and an action on the case." Do you agree with Lord Denning that Blackstone J. was simply arguing a technical point?

2. In *Scott*, did the court require that intent or negligence be established? If not, on what issue was liability based?

3. Could the court have concluded that the action should have been framed in trespass on the case and nonsuited the plaintiff? As we have already seen, the plaintiff had to predict in advance whether the action properly lay in trespass *vi et armis* or trespass on the case. As *Scott* illustrates, it was not always possible to make such predictions with any assurance.

LEAME v. BRAY

(1803), 102 E.R. 724 (K.B.)

[The plaintiff sued the defendant in trespass. It was alleged that the defendant drove his horse-drawn carriage "with force and arms" into the plaintiff's carriage, that the plaintiff's horses panicked, and that the plaintiff fractured his collar bone when he jumped from his carriage in order to save his own life.]

It appeared in evidence at the trial before Lord Ellenborough C.J. at the last sittings at Westminster, that the accident described in the declaration happened in a dark night, owing to the defendant driving his carriage on the wrong side of the road, and the parties not being able to see each other; and that if the defendant had kept his right side there was ample room for the carriages to have passed without injury. But it did not appear that blame was imputable to the defendant in any other respect as to the manner of his driving. It was therefore objected for the defendant, that the injury having happened from negligence, and not wilfully, the proper remedy was by an action on the case and not of trespass vi et armis; and the plaintiff was thereupon nonsuited.

. . .

LORD ELLENBOROUGH C.J.:—The true criterion seems to be whether the plaintiff received an injury by force from the defendant. If the injurious act be the immediate result of the force originally applied by the defendant, and the plaintiff be injured by it, it is the subject of an action of trespass vi et armis by all the cases both ancient and modern. It is immaterial whether the injury be wilful or not.

... [H]ere the defendant himself was present, and used the ordinary means of impelling the horse forward, and from that the injury happened. And therefore there being an immediate injury from an immediate act of force by the defendant, the proper remedy is trespass; and wilfulness is not necessary to constitute trespass.

[Grose, Lawrence and LeBlanc JJ. concurred.]

WILLIAMS v. HOLLAND

(1833), 131 E.R. 848 (C.P.)

[The plaintiff owned a carriage that was carrying his son, who was also his servant. The defendant owned and operated another carriage. It was alleged that the defendant "so carelessly, unskilfully, and improperly drove, governed, and directed" his carriage that it collided with the plaintiff's. It was further alleged that, as a result of the defendant's "carelessness, negligence, unskilfulness, and improper conduct," the plaintiff's carriage was "crushed, broke to pieces, and damaged," and the plaintiff's son was injured, with the result that the plaintiff was deprived of his services and "put to expense for doctor's bills."]

. . .

TINDAL C.J.:—... The declaration, in this case, states the ground of action to be an injury occasioned by the carelessness and negligence of the Defendant in driving his own gig; and that such carelessness and negligence is, strictly and properly in itself, the subject of an action on the case, would appear, if any authority were wanting, from Com. Dig. tit. Action upon the Case for Negligence; and the jury have found in the very terms of the declaration, that the jury was so occasioned. Under such a form of action, therefore, and with such a finding by the jury, the present objection ought not to prevail, unless some positive and inflexible rule of law, or some authority too strong to be overcome, is brought forward in its support. If such are to be found, they must, undoubtedly, be adhered to; for settled forms of action, adapted to different grievances, contribute much to the certain administration of justice.

But upon examining the cases cited in argument, both in support of, and in answer to, the objection, we cannot find one in which it is distinctly held, that the present form of action is not maintainable under the circumstances of this case.

. . .

Where the injury is occasioned by the carelessness and negligence of the Defendant, the Plaintiff is at liberty to bring an action on the case, notwithstanding the act is immediate, so long as it is not a wilful act; and, upon the authority of that case, we think the present form of action maintainable to recover damages for the injury.

NOTES AND QUESTIONS

1. Why was the plaintiff nonsuited at trial in *Leame*? Why did Lord Ellenborough disagree? What is the *ratio* of the case and what distinction is made between trespass and case?

2. The great significance of *Williams* was that it gave a plaintiff a choice between trespass and case when there was a direct, negligent act. For a detailed consideration of this case see Prichard, "Trespass, Case and the Rule in *Williams v. Holland*" [1964] C.L.J. 234.

3. The immediate result of *Williams* was a marked increase in the number of actions brought in case. Nevertheless, it was still necessary for the plaintiff to frame the action in either trespass or case. It was not until the *Common Law Procedure Act*, 1852 (15 & 16 Vict.), c. 76, that a plaintiff was able to join the two actions. See generally Winfield, "Trespass and Negligence" (1933) 49 L.Q.R. 359.

HOLMES v. MATHER

(1875), L.R. 10 Exch. 261

[The defendant and his servant were driving a horse cart on the highway when the horses became unmanageable. The servant attempted to guide the runaway horses, but with limited success. While turning a corner, the servant led the horses into the plaintiff's path, knocking him down and injuring him. The plaintiff sued in negligence and trespass. The jury found that there was no negligence.]

BRAMWELL B.:—... The driver is absolutely free from all blame in the matter; not only does he not do anything wrong, but he endeavours to do what is the best to be done under the circumstances. The misfortune happens through the horses being so startled by the barking of a dog that they run away with the groom and the defendant, who is sitting beside him. Now, if the plaintiff under such circumstances can bring an action, I really cannot see why she could not bring an action because a splash of mud, in the ordinary course of driving, was thrown upon her dress or got into her eye and so injured it. It seems manifest that, under such circumstances, she could not maintain an action. For the convenience of mankind in carrying on the affairs of life, people as they go along roads must expect, or put up with, such mischief as reasonable care on the part of others cannot avoid. I think the present action not to be maintainable.

That is the general view of the case. Now I will put it a little more specifically, and address myself to the argument of Mr. Herschell. Here, he says, if the driver had done nothing, there is no reason to suppose this mischief would have happened to the woman, but he did give the horses a pull, or inclination, in the direction of the plaintiff — he drove them there. It is true that he endeavoured to drive them further away from the place by getting them to turn to the right, but he did not succeed in doing that. The argument, therefore, is, if he had not given that impulse or direction to them, they would not have come where the plaintiff was. Now, it seems to me that argument is not tenable, and I think one can deal with it in this way. Here, as in almost all cases, you must look at the immediate act that did the mischief, at what the driver was doing before the mischief happened, and not to what he was doing next before what he was then doing. If you looked to the last act but one, you might as well argue that if the driver had not started on that morning, or had not turned down that particular street, this mischief would not have happened.

I think the proper answer is, You cannot complain of me unless I was immediately doing the act which did the mischief to you. Now the driver was not doing that. What I take to be the case is this: he did not guide the horses upon the plaintiff; he guided them away from her, in another direction; but they ran away with him, upon her, in spite of his effort to take them away from where she was. It is not the case where a person has to make a choice of two evils, and singles the plaintiff out, and drives to the spot where she is standing. That is not the case at all. The driver was endeavouring to guide them indeed, but he was taken there in spite of himself. I think the observation made by my Brother Pollock during the argument is irresistible, that if Mr. Herschell's contention is right, it would come to this: if I am being run away with, and I sit quiet and let the horses run wherever they think fit, clearly I am not liable, because it is they, and not I, who guide them; but if I unfortunately do my best to avoid injury to myself and other persons, then it may be said that it is my act of guiding them that brings them to the place where the accident happens. Surely it is impossible.

As to the cases cited, most of them are really decisions on the form of action, whether case or trespass. The result of them is this, and it is intelligible enough: if the act that does an injury is an act of direct force vi et armis, trespass is the proper remedy (if there is any remedy) where the act is wrongful, either as being wilful or as being the result of negligence. Where the act is not wrongful for either of these reasons, no action is maintainable, though trespass would be the proper form of action if it were wrongful. That is the effect of the decisions.

[Cleasby and Pollock BB. concurred.]

NOTES AND QUESTIONS

1. How does Bramwell B. distinguish this case from one in which the defendant has to choose between two evils? Is the distinction meaningful?

2. What is the *ratio*? What is the impact of *Holmes* on the elements of a trespass action?

3. In *Stanley v. Powell*, [1891] 1 Q.B. 86, the principle in *Holmes* was reaffirmed and extended to accidents other than those that occurred on the highway.

COOK v. LEWIS

[1952] 1 D.L.R. 1 (S.C.C.)

CARTWRIGHT J.:—... On the 11th of September, 1948, the plaintiff was hunting with his brother John Lewis and one Dennis Fitzgerald in the vicinity of Quinsam Lake on Vancouver Island. It was the opening day of the hunting season for blue grouse and deer and it was said that the country in which they were hunting was full of hunters. The defendants, accompanied by John Wagstaff, then sixteen years of age, were hunting grouse together. They were using a dog which belonged to Akenhead. They had agreed to divide their bag evenly.

It is said that Cook, Akenhead and Wagstaff were proceeding approximately in line, Cook being on the left, Akenhead in the centre and Wagstaff to the right. The dog, which was some little distance ahead of them, came to a point and at about that moment Fitzgerald, who had come into view on Cook's left, called out a warning and pointed towards a clump of trees which was ahead of Cook and Akenhead and in which at that moment the plaintiff was. Cook heard Fitzgerald's call but did not hear what he said. He thought that Fitzgerald was pointing at the dog and was calling attention to the fact that the dog was on point. Akenhead states that he did not hear Fitzgerald's call. Momentarily after this, a covey of some four or five grouse flew up a short distance in front of the dog. Akenhead says that he fired at the bird which was farthest to the right, leaving the other birds to Cook. Cook says that he fired at a bird straight ahead of him. They appear to have fired almost simultaneously. Immediately afterwards there was a scream from the clump of trees, mentioned above, and the plaintiff appeared. He had received several shot in his face, one of which caused the loss of an eye.

. . .

It was the theory of the plaintiff that either Cook or Akenhead or both of them had shot him and that each was liable even if only one of them had fired the shot which struck him. The theory of the defendant Cook was that he had fired only one shot and had fired in such a direction that it was quite impossible that any shot from his gun could have struck the plaintiff. He also stated that there had been a third shot fired almost simultaneously with those fired by himself and Akenhead and suggested that an unidentified third person had fired the shot which injured the plaintiff. His counsel disclaimed before the jury any suggestion that Akenhead had shot the plaintiff.

Akenhead's position at the trial was that he had fired to the right, that he could not have shot the plaintiff and that if it was either of them it was Cook and not he who had done so.

. . .

With the greatest respect, I think that the learned trial judge did not charge the jury correctly in regard to the onus of proof of negligence. While it is true that the plaintiff expressly pleaded negligence on the part of the defendants he also pleaded that he was shot by them and in my opinion the action under the old form of pleading would properly have been one of trespass and not of case. In my view, the cases collected and discussed by Denman J. in *Stanley v. Powell* [[1891] 1 Q.B. 86] established the rule (which is subject to an exception in the case of highway accidents with which we are not concerned in the case at bar) that where a plaintiff is injured by force applied directly to him by the defendant his case is made by proving this fact and the onus falls upon the defendant to prove "that such trespass was utterly without his fault." In my opinion *Stanley v. Powell* rightly decides that the defendant in such an action is entitled to judgment if he satisfies the onus of establishing the absence of both intention and negligence on his part.

. . .

[The judgment of Estey, Cartwright and Fauteux JJ. was delivered by Cartwright J. Rand J. gave a separate concurring judgment, and Locke J. dissented on a different issue.]

NOTES AND QUESTIONS

1. According to *Cook*, why is this an action in trespass and not case? What are the advantages of suing in trespass? What is the practical significance of this advantage in

cases such as *Cook*? Does the distinction between directly and indirectly-caused harms warrant maintaining these advantages?

2. In *Letang v. Cooper*, [1965] 1 Q.B. 232 (C.A.), the court rejected the approach in *Cook*. Rather, it required a plaintiff to bring the action in negligence even if he or she had been directly injured, unless the defendant had acted intentionally. For a discussion of the Australian position see *McHale v. Watson* (1964), 111 C.L.R. 384 (H.C.A.); *Chin v. Venning* (1975), 49 A.L.J.R. 378 (H.C.); and *Hackshaw v. Shaw* (1985), 59 A.L.J.R. 156 (H.C.).

3. Even in Canada, the rule in *Cook* has been widely criticized. See Wright, "Res Ipsa Loquitur" in Linden, ed., *Studies in Canadian Tort Law* (1968) 41 at 42-45; and Sharp, "Negligent Trespass in Canada: A Persistent Source of Embarrassment" (1978) 1 Adv. Q. 311. But see Sullivan, "Trespass to the Person in Canada: A Defence of the Traditional Approach" (1987) 19 Ottawa L. Rev. 533. See also Fridman, "Trespass or Negligence?" (1971) 9 Alta. L. Rev. 250; and Tindale, "The Burden of Proof in Actions for Negligent Trespass in Canada" (1971) 49 Can. Bar Rev. 612.

5. The Bases for Imposing Liability in Tort

As we have seen, early tort law was dominated by the procedural formalities of the writ system and its focus on directly and indirectly caused injury. It was only in the last half of the 19th century that fault in the form of intent or negligence was established as a prerequisite to liability in most areas of tort law. With the *Judicature Acts* and the abolition of the writ system, fault in various forms emerged as a central organizing principle of tort law. Generally, modern tort law is divided into four categories of actions: (1) intentional torts, (2) negligence, (3) strict liability, and (4) a residual group of actions, such as defamation, which are based on unique principles of liability.

We have used these four categories of actions to structure this book. Nevertheless, in this section we will briefly examine the full range of liability rules, the relationships among them, and the manner in which they may be used to serve specific functions of tort law. We do so in the belief that, before beginning the detailed study of discrete categories of tort law, students should have a broad overview of the course as a whole. The following diagram illustrates various bases for imposing liability in tort.

The Bases of Tort Liability

Absolute Liability	—	Strict Liability	—	Negligence	—	Intentional Torts

(a) ABSOLUTE LIABILITY

Under a rule of absolute liability, the defendant is held liable simply because he or she engaged in proscribed behaviour and thereby caused the plaintiff to suffer a loss. The plaintiff is not required to prove that the defendant's conduct was intentional or negligent. It is enough that the prohibited act caused the loss. Furthermore, no exculpatory defences are available to the defendant. Although none of the modern torts are based on a regime of absolute liability, that concept provides a useful model against which others can be compared.

(b) STRICT LIABILITY

"Strict liability" is an ambiguous phrase. As previously explained, it sometimes refers to a cause of action that does not require proof that the defendant breached an obligation. Liability in unjust enrichment is strict in that sense. As long as there was no juristic reason for the benefit that the defendant received from the plaintiff, liability for restitution will arise even if the defendant was entirely innocent in the transfer.

In contrast, "strict liability" in the tort context means that while an obligation *was* breached, the defendant did not do so intentionally or carelessly. In that sense, strict liability bears a close resemblance to the concept of absolute liability. The two concepts differ, however, in that the defendant enjoys some defences under a regime of strict liability. For instance, as discussed in Chapter 25, the tort of *Rylands v. Fletcher* (1868), [1861-73] All E.R. Rep. 1 (H.L.) imposes strict liability if, as a result of the defendant's non-natural use of land, something escapes from that property and injures the plaintiff. The plaintiff's right to relief does not depend upon proof that the defendant acted intentionally or negligently. Damages nevertheless will be denied if, for instance, the escape was caused by a third party or an act of God against which the defendant could not have guarded, or if the plaintiff's loss was the inevitable result of the defendant's performance of a statutorily authorized activity.

Strict liability is more prevalent in the United States than in Canada. In many American jurisdictions, for instance, manufacturers are held strictly liable for injuries caused by defective products. The plaintiff must prove that the product in question was somehow defective when it left the manufacturer, but does not have to prove that that defect resulted from the manufacturer's intentional or negligent breach. In contrast, the Canadian plaintiff is required to show either intentional or negligent wrongdoing on the part of the manufacturer. In Canada, strict liability tends to be confined to discrete circumstances, such as *Rylands v. Fletcher* and harm inflicted by dangerous animals.

The most common instance of strict liability arises under the doctrine of *vicarious liability*. That doctrine allows a court to impose liability in certain circumstances on one person for the torts committed by another. That is true, for instance, under the rule of *respondeat superior*. An employer may be legally responsible for torts committed by an employee. If so, the plaintiff is entitled to recover damages from either the employee or the employer. The employer's liability is said to be strict because it does not require proof that the employer carelessly or intentionally breached an obligation.

(c) NEGLIGENCE

Negligence consists of a failure to take reasonable care to prevent foreseeable harm to another person. The difference between negligence and strict liability is well illustrated in the context of products liability. In negligence, the plaintiff must prove that the defendant failed to take reasonable care to prevent the defect that caused the harm. However, in strict liability, the plaintiff need merely prove that the defect caused the harm. It should be noted that, in some situations of negligence, the burden of proof may be shifted onto the defendant, thereby providing the plaintiff with some of the benefits of strict liability. This possibility is discussed in Chapter 20.

(d) INTENTION

Liability for intentionally-inflicted harm is, like negligence, based on fault. In most cases, the plaintiff must prove actual subjective intent on the part of the defendant. There are several legal principles that help the plaintiff to do so, however. For example, under the doctrine of imputed intent (discussed in Chapter 3), the law ascribes the requisite intention to the defendant if the plaintiff's loss was certain or substantially certain to follow from the defendant's act. Moreover, in Canada, if the plaintiff proves that an injury was caused directly, the burden of proof shifts to the defendant to disprove intent and negligence. Although this rule arises in some negligence cases, it is more relevant in intentional torts.

(e) NO LIABILITY

Finally, it is important to appreciate that some types of harm simply are not recognized under any rule of tort liability, even if the person who caused the harm did so intentionally or carelessly. Despite the existence of a causal connection between the defendant's conduct and the plaintiff's injury, the type of conduct or the type of harm may lie outside the scope of tort law. *Allen v. Flood*, [1898] A.C. 1 (H.L.) stands for the proposition that, as long as it otherwise acts lawfully, a business will not be liable for financially ruining a competitor, even if it does so intentionally or maliciously. The court in that instance was anxious to encourage competition in the marketplace. More recently, the Supreme Court of Canada held that while a child who is born with injuries sustained *in utero* generally is entitled to hold the perpetrator liable in negligence, no action lies if the injury was caused by the *mother's* careless actions during pregnancy. The court was unwilling to impose any duty of care that might interfere with a pregnant woman's freedom of action: *Dobson (Litigation Guardian of) v. Dobson*, [1999] 2 S.C.R. 753.

6. The Functions of Tort Law

Tort law did not develop from a co-ordinated attempt to achieve specific social goals. The common law process is highly decentralized and modern tort law is a patchwork of judicial decisions and statutory provisions. As the preceding section illustrates, much of tort law has been shaped by procedural concerns rather than policy. Granted, modern legislators and judges do occasionally tailor the law to achieve particular social goals on a case-by-case basis. It nevertheless remains impossible to reduce tort law as a whole to any single principle.

Every judicial decision, legal principle, or set of legal rules favours certain interests over others. The law is not objective or value free. It is a social institution that serves social functions. It therefore is important to raise certain questions with respect to every relevant social concern. Which principles and rules does tort law currently endorse? Which principles and rules *should* it endorse? What mischief does tort law seek to prevent or what benefit does it seek to promote? Can those goals be better served by other legal or non-legal means? To ask such questions is to take a *functional approach* to tort law. It obviously is impossible in this book to resolve all of the debates raised by such an approach. At this point, it is sufficient to focus attention on the social concerns that underlie tort law and to provide the tools required for a functional approach to tort law.

Some of the uncertainty regarding the functions of tort law stems from a failure to delineate various potential perspectives. If one focuses on the litigants' objectives, the goals of tort law will be narrowly defined in terms of the expectations of those parties who have a financial stake in the exercise. And indeed, the parties' motivations certainly are important insofar as they determine the issues that are brought to court. Nevertheless, such a narrow focus overlooks some of the broader social functions of tort law.

Unfortunately, when we adopt a broader focus, the debate regarding tort law's functions becomes largely speculative. There is little empirical evidence on the impact of tort law. That is hardly surprising, given the serious methodological difficulties involved in distinguishing the effects of tort law from the effects of other legal and social forces. Furthermore, tort law is inherently limited in its ability to modify behaviour. Although the prospect of litigation may influence some people, tort law primarily operates through awards of damages. Liability is apt to have little effect on defendants who are impecunious, insured, or otherwise able to avoid the financial burden of being held responsible. Even more clearly, many potential tort claims are never litigated. A potential claimant may be unable to identify and locate the tortfeasor. Alternatively, a potential claimant may be unaware of the relevant laws, may not be able to afford to hire a lawyer, or may refrain from suing for non-legal reasons (*e.g.* a desire to maintain harmonious relations with a valued customer).

The ability of tort law to affect behaviour is also limited by the fact that tort is simply one of many legal and non-legal mechanisms of social control. The role that tort law plays in a particular instance will reflect a broad range of factors, including the crime rate, the effectiveness of the criminal justice system, the existence and enforcement of health and safety standards, the scope of the social welfare system, and the availability of state-funded universal health care. Debates regarding the functions of tort law often mask unstated assumptions about these other issues.

The remainder of this chapter summarizes some of the most commonly cited functions of tort law. You should read this material critically. It is important to assess the empirical basis upon which the various propositions are stated, and to consider the relevance of each purported function to modern Canadian society.

(a) COMPENSATION

From the plaintiff's point of view, compensation, in the sense of reparation for loss, is the most important function of tort law. Society also has a legitimate interest in minimizing the disruptions accompanying an injury by ensuring that the aggrieved party receives compensation. Unfortunately, the current system of tort law has many failings in that respect. First, it provides compensation to a relatively small number of accident victims and then only in very limited circumstances. Second, the accident victim must make a substantial financial investment to initiate the process (*e.g.* by hiring a lawyer). Third, the plaintiff must prove fault, not need, and will recover only if "fortunate" enough to have been injured by a tortfeasor with assets or insurance. Finally, it is generally accepted and clearly documented that tort law is an extremely inefficient mechanism for providing compensation. These failings are further discussed in Chapter 28.

(b) APPEASEMENT AND VINDICATION

A successful tort action may vindicate the plaintiff's position and condemn the defendant's conduct. In the context of incestuous sexual assault, for instance, claimants often are motivated far more by the hope that the tortfeasor will be officially condemned than by the prospect of financial damages (especially against impecunious defendants). It is for such reasons that *nominal damages* are available in response to some torts. Even though the plaintiff suffered little or no loss as a result of the tort, the court may order the defendant to pay a small amount (such as $10) as symbolic recognition of the wrong. However, given the cost and inconvenience of litigation, as well as the possibility of an unfavourable award of *costs* against the claimant, few plaintiffs sue for nominal damages.

(c) PUNISHMENT

As previously explained, criminal and tort law share a common heritage. Although criminal law is most often associated with punishing wrongdoers, tort law has retained traces of its early punitive elements. For example, punitive damages are available to sanction high-handed, vicious, or otherwise outrageous conduct. As tort law has become increasingly dominated by negligence, however, the importance of punishment has declined. As well, most of the morally blameworthy conduct that warrants punishment in tort law also constitutes a federal or provincial offence. It is arguable that the issue of punishment in such circumstances should be left to the criminal justice system.

(d) DETERRENCE

Punishment is different than deterrence. Punishment looks backward at the wrongful act and attempts to mete out a sanction that reflects the wrong. Deterrence, in contrast, is concerned with discouraging the defendant (*specific deterrence*) and others (*general deterrence*) from repeating a wrong. Deterrence and punishment are, of course, closely related insofar as any punishment is capable of deterring. The penalty necessary to achieve optimum deterrence, however, may be quite different from that necessary to achieve just punishment.

In order to be an effective deterrent, tort law must clearly define the undesirable conduct and then provide sufficient inducements for discouraging it. Deterrence works best when the defendant is aware of both the required legal standard and the sanctions for its breach. Tort law therefore has a greater deterrent impact on premeditated conduct than on spontaneous careless behaviour. Even when the conduct is planned, however, the potential damage award must be sufficient to change the defendant's behaviour. The law will have a limited impact if a tortfeasor believes that it is cheaper to pay the various costs associated with liability (*e.g.* damages and adverse publicity) than to alter a course of conduct. If the criminal justice system is any indication, there is little reason for optimism about the deterrent impact of tort law.

(e) MARKET DETERRENCE

Some academics, particularly economists, view tort law as a system of *loss allocation*. *Market deterrence* is an important goal of allocating the costs of accidents. The basic idea is the costs of accidents ought to be incorporated into the price of the activities that generate them. A good example is the rule in most American states that holds manufacturers strictly liable for injuries caused by their defective products. Manufacturers increase their prices to cover their potential liability costs. As prices rise, fewer products are sold and fewer product-related injuries occur. To the extent that a product continues to be purchased at the higher price, economists would say that consumers have demonstrated that they believe that the benefits of the product exceed the cost of the accidents it generates. According to economists, this allocation of accident costs through the market enables society to experience the "optimum" number of accidents. Notice, however, that this theory assumes that damages accurately reflect losses, that all meritorious claims are successfully litigated, and that manufacturers and other well-financed defendants cannot avoid tort liability by securing favourable legislation or threatening to bankrupt potential claimants.

The term "loss allocation" has also been used to describe several other possibly inconsistent schemes. First, R. Posner, an American judge and scholar, argues that an actor should be held liable in negligence whenever the cost of harm exceeds what it would have cost to prevent it. The defendant's fault lies in squandering scarce social resources. Posner's loss allocation system therefore furthers the goal of *efficiency*. Second, the term "loss allocation" sometimes is used to describe a *loss spreading* function, whereby a loss is imposed on the party who is best able to distribute it over time and among a large number of people. Others speak of the *deep pocket* approach to loss distribution, whereby tort law is used to allocate losses to those parties who are best able to bear them. However, even if the courts had sufficient information and expertise to make the correct allocative decision, many argue that it is inappropriate to use tort law as a system to redistribute wealth.

(f) JUSTICE

In recent years, legal philosophers have begun to study tort law. Having found the traditional explanations unsatisfactory, they have focused on the theories of *justice* underlying tort law. Some tort doctrines can be explained in terms of *retributive justice*. Other tort principles apparently are designed to achieve *distributive justice* by ensuring that wealth is properly distributed within society. However, most legal philosophers view tort law in terms of *corrective justice*. Corrective justice accepts the existing distribution of wealth and is concerned with correcting improper deviations from that pattern by annulling "wrongful" gains and compensating "wrongful" losses. The classification of a gain or loss as "wrongful" may be made with reference to several different principles. Depending upon the particular principle, what constitutes a "wrong" may be defined in terms of the actor's conduct, the victim's loss, or a combination of these factors. Corrective justice is discussed further in Chapter 28.

NOTES AND QUESTIONS

1. On the aims of tort law, see generally Wright, "The Province and Function of the Law of Torts" in Linden, ed., *Studies in Canadian Tort Law* (1968) 1; Cane, *Atiyah's Accidents, Compensation and the Law*, 7th ed. (2006), ch. 17; Linden & Feldthusen, *Canadian Tort Law*, 8th ed. (2006), ch. 1; and Englard, "The System Builders: A Critical Appraisal of Modern Tort Theory" (1980) 10 J. Legal Stud. 27. See also Saks, "Do We Really Know Anything About the Behavior of the Tort Litigation System — And Why Not?" (1992) 140 U. Pa. L. Rev. 1147, which casts doubt on our ability to accurately analyze the tort system.

2. Although compensation often is said to be the primary purpose of tort law, the evidence indicates that other systems may achieve the same goal more efficiently. For

instance, a study conducted in connection with Quebec's no-fault automobile insurance scheme found that while the scheme allocates 88¢ of every dollar to compensation, traditional tort schemes spend 64¢ of every dollar on compensation and require the rest for administrative costs. The same report indicated that while the no-fault scheme on average provides compensation within 22 days of the receipt of a claim, tort claimants regularly are required to wait two to ten years: SAAQ, *Quebec's Automobile Insurance Plan* (2001) at 6-11.

3. Even assuming that compensation is an appropriate social goal, the relative effectiveness of tort law in achieving it is questionable. See generally Sugarman, "Doing Away with Tort Law" (1985) 73 Cal. L. Rev. 558; Arlen, "Compensation Systems and Efficient Deterrence" (1993) 52 Md .L. Rev. 1093; Schwarz, "Reality in the Economic Analysis of Tort Law: Does Tort Law Really Deter?" (1994) 42 U.C.L.A.L. Rev. 377; Cane, *The Anatomy of Tort Law* (1997) at 217-225; and Osborne, *Report of Inquiry into Motor Vehicle Accident Compensation in Ontario* (1988).

4. The importance of appeasement in Anglo-Saxon law is illustrated in Malone, "Ruminations on the Role of Fault in the History of the Common Law of Torts" (1970) 31 La. L. Rev. 1 at 2:

> This same demand for appeasement of the sense of honor was manifested in non-fatal injuries. Here the amount of the tariff to be paid was determined to a large extent by the public shame that attended the wound. According to the laws of Ethelbert: "If the bruise be black in a part not covered by the clothes, let bot be made with thirty scaetts. If it be covered by the clothes, let bot be made for each with twenty scaetts." Pound refers to a provision of Howell the Good, King of the Welsh, to the effect that a scar on the face is worth six score pence, whereas the permanent loss of both joints of the thumb (an injury that would virtually disable the hand) brought only seventy-six pence and a half-penny.

5. Linden argues that tort law can act as an *ombudsman*. A private law proceeding may focus public attention on systemic wrongdoing that might otherwise not be detected or prosecuted by the state. The adverse publicity generated by such proceedings may provide a powerful deterrent and motivate the government to take corrective action. Can you suggest a situation in which tort law has served or might serve this function? See Linden, "Reconsidering Tort Law as Ombudsman" in Steel and Rogers-Magnet, eds., *Issues in Tort Law* (1983) 1.

6. Assume that just punishment for a wrong is a fine of $100 and that the perceived conviction rate is 1 in 100. How large must the penalty be in order to actually deter the wrong? Would the imposition of that penalty be unjust? Explain your answer.

7. What do economists mean by the "optimum" number of accidents? Why is the optimum number of accidents not zero? See Englard, "Law and Economics in American Tort Cases: A Critical Assessment of the Theory's Impact on Courts" (1991) 41 U.T.L.J. 359.

8. For a discussion of the deterrent function of tort law, see Calabresi, *The Cost of Accidents* (1970); Dewees & Trebilcock, "The Efficacy of the Tort System And Its Alternatives: A Review of Empirical Evidence" (1992) 30 Osgoode Hall L.J. 57; Posner,

"A Theory of Negligence" (1972) 1 J. Legal Stud. 29; Brown, "Deterrence in Tort and No-Fault: The New Zealand Experience" (1985) 73 Cal. L. Rev. 976; Viscusi, "Toward a Diminished Role for Tort Liability: Social Insurance, Government Regulation, and Contemporary Risks to Health and Safety" (1989) 6 Yale J. on Reg. 65; and Komesar, "Injuries and Institutions: Tort Reform, Tort Theory, and Beyond" (1990) 65 N.Y.U.L. Rev. 23.

9. For a discussion of the loss allocation function of tort law, see Coase, "The Problem of Social Costs" (1960) 3 J.L. & Ecom. 1; Calabresi; "Some Thoughts on Risk Distribution and the Law of Torts" (1961) 70 Yale L.J. 449; and Posner, *supra.*

10. For a philosophical analysis of the functions of tort law, see Fletcher, "Fairness and Utility in Tort Theory" (1972) 85 Harv. L.J. 537; Englard, *The Philosophy of Tort Law* (1993); Epstein, "A Theory of Strict Liability" (1973) 2 J. Legal Stud. 151; Steiner, "Economics, Morality and the Law of Torts" (1976) 26 U.T.L.J. 227; Coleman, *Risks and Wrongs* (1992); and Weinrib, *The Idea of Private Law* (1995).

2

THE BASIC CONCEPTS OF REMEDIES IN INTENTIONAL TORTS

1. Introduction
2. Judicial and Extrajudicial Remedies
3. Classifications of Damages
4. Nominal Damages
5. Compensatory Damages
6. Aggravated Damages
7. Punitive Damages
8. Disgorgement Damages

1. Introduction

In a tort action, the plaintiff must first establish the elements of the specific tort in issue. Even after the plaintiff has proven the requisite elements of the tort, the defendant will not necessarily be held liable. If the defendant can establish a valid defence, he or she will be absolved of liability. Thus, it is only after the plaintiff has proven the commission of the tort and the defendant has failed to establish a valid defence that the issue of an appropriate remedy arises. Therefore, issues relating to remedies are usually addressed last.

There are, however, two reasons for introducing the general concepts of remedies before examining the torts and defences. First, it is important to emphasize that establishing liability is merely a means to an end. The plaintiff is ultimately seeking a remedy for the wrong caused by the defendant. The nature of the available remedy will influence the plaintiff's decision to bring an action. Second, on a more practical level, many of the cases in the following chapters raise issues which cannot be appreciated without some understanding of remedies, particularly damages.

2. Judicial and Extrajudicial Remedies

There are two broad categories of remedies: judicial and extrajudicial. There are four types of judicial remedies, the first and most important of which is an award of damages. An award of damages is available across the range of tort actions. Contrary to what some people may believe, an award of damages does not result in the immediate transfer of money from the defendant to the plaintiff. Rather, it merely grants the plaintiff a legal right to a specific sum. In order to collect the award, the plaintiff may have to pursue creditors' remedies, such as the seizure and sale of assets, that are entirely independent of tort law.

The second type of judicial remedy is an injunction. An injunction is a court order that directs a party to act in a particular manner. There are many types of injunctions. For instance, a court may impose a prohibitive injunction that forbids the defendant from doing something (*e.g.* committing a trespass by walking across the plaintiff's lawn) or a mandatory injunction that compels the defendant to do something (*e.g.* tear down a billboard that he or she wrongfully built on the plaintiff's land). Injunctions have a number of unique features. A person who ignores an injunction may be held in contempt of court and, in an extreme case, imprisoned. Unlike damage awards, injunctions were granted by courts of equity and not courts of law. Equitable remedies were available only if common law remedies were inadequate. Moreover, equitable remedies were discretionary. While a successful plaintiff was generally entitled to compensatory damages as of right, the court had discretion to grant injunctive relief. Today, as a result of the merging of the common law and equitable courts, Canadian courts have authority to grant both legal and equitable remedies. Nevertheless, equitable relief generally remains discretionary and dependent upon whether a damage award would provide adequate relief.

The other two types of judicial remedies are declarations and orders of specific restitution. Declarations are formal statements or decisions of a court which are usually issued to settle a dispute or an issue of legal rights. An order of specific restitution directs a party to restore a pre-existing condition or return an object. Like injunctions, these remedies are granted in limited circumstances and are sought in relatively few tort actions.

Extrajudicial remedies (also called self-help remedies), such as recapture of chattels, re-entry onto land and abatement of nuisance, are also applicable in a small number of cases. These remedies will be discussed when they arise in relation to individual torts.

NOTES

1. For a comprehensive review of the Canadian law of damages see Cooper-Stephenson, *Personal Injury Damages in Canada*, 2d ed. (1996); and Waddams, *The Law of Damages*, 4th ed. (2004).

2. Although frequent reference is made to the general rule that an injunction will only be granted when a damage award would be inadequate, the Canadian courts appear to be adopting a more flexible approach. For a comprehensive analysis of injunctions see Sharpe, *Injunctions and Specific Performance*, 2d ed., looseleaf (1992); and Berryman, *The Law of Equitable Remedies* (2000).

3. For a discussion of the extrajudicial remedies, see Heuston & Buckley, *Salmond and Heuston on the Law of Torts*, 21st ed. (1996) at 572-78; and Dobbs, *The Law of Torts* (2000) at 181-90.

3. Classifications of Damages

Academics, practitioners and judges have classified damage awards according to various criteria, such as the nature of the plaintiff's loss, the way in which the loss is calculated and proven, and the purpose for which the award is made. Since the criteria are unrelated, the corresponding classification systems are not mutually exclusive. The task of mastering the terminology of damages is further complicated by disagreements on the definition of some of the terms.

Perhaps the simplest way to analyze damages is to divide the plaintiff's claims into pecuniary (monetary) and non-pecuniary (non-monetary) losses. Pecuniary losses are those which can be calculated in dollars and cents, such as lost earnings, medical bills and repair costs. In contrast, non-pecuniary losses, such as pain, humiliation and disfigurement, have no monetary equivalent and thus cannot be subject to exact calculation.

In the pleadings of a cause of action, the plaintiff's losses are generally classified as either special or general damages. Special damages are those which can be exactly quantified at the time of trial, whereas general damages are those which are incapable of such quantification. The plaintiff is required to strictly plead and prove special damages, but not general damages because of their speculative nature.

Although both of these classification systems can be applied to damages arising from any torts case, they are most frequently associated with complex damage claims. Since such claims arise most commonly in negligence actions, further discussion of these classification systems will be deferred until Chapter 18.

In intentional torts, damages are most frequently classified according to the purpose for which they are awarded or the function that they are intended to serve. From that perspective, there are four basic categories of damages: nominal (token), compensatory, punitive (retributive, vindictive or exemplary), and disgorgement (restitutionary).

NOTE

1. Although the terms "special" and "general" damages have several distinct meanings, we have used the definitions which are most relevant to the issue of pleadings. See Cooper-Stephenson, *Personal Injury Damages in Canada*, 2d ed. (1996) at 91-94. For a discussion of pecuniary and non-pecuniary losses see Cooper-Stephenson, *ibid.*, at 89-90 and 481-531.

4. Nominal Damages

Nominal damages are awarded in a small sum (*e.g.* $50) to redress a violation of a legal right that the law deems worthy of protection, even in the absence of actual harm. For example, a defendant who steps onto the plaintiff's property causing no harm to the land will be held liable in trespass for nominal damages. The award of nominal damages vindicates the plaintiff's legal right to exclusive possession. Had the defendant crushed several flowers, the plaintiff could have been awarded compensatory damages to redress his or her actual losses. Although the award of nominal damages in the first case would not be much smaller than the award of compensatory damages in the second, it is important to emphasize that the distinction between these awards is based on the purpose for which they are given, not their amounts. Unfortunately, the term nominal damages is not always used consistently, and some judges have used it to refer to a small award of compensatory damages.

According to the traditional view, nominal damages are only awarded for torts that are actionable *per se*; that is, actionable without proof of loss. The intentional torts derived from the writ of trespass *vi et armis*, such as battery and trespass to land, are actionable *per se*. However, the intentional torts derived from trespass on the case, such as malicious prosecution, and torts based on negligence are not actionable *per se*. Rather, the plaintiff must establish actual damages as an essential element of these causes of action. If the plaintiff fails to establish loss in these cases, he or she has no cause of action and the issue of damages does not arise.

THE MEDIANA

[1900] A.C. 113 (H.L.)

EARL OF HALSBURY: ... And, my Lords, here I wish, with reference to what has been suggested at the bar, to remark upon the difference between damages and nominal damages. "Nominal damages" is a technical phrase which means that you have negatived anything like real damage, but that you are affirming by your nominal damages that there is an infraction of a legal right which, though it gives you no right to any real damages at all, yet gives you a right to the verdict or judgment because your legal right has been infringed. But the term "nominal damages" does not mean small damages. The extent to which a person has a right to recover what is called by the compendious phrase damages, but may be also represented as compensation for the use of something that belongs to him, depends upon a variety of circumstances, and it certainly does not in the smallest degree suggest that because they are small they are necessarily nominal damages.

NOTES AND QUESTIONS

1. In contrast to the traditional view, it has been suggested that nominal damages may be awarded with respect to torts that require proof of loss. For example, while the tort of nuisance is premised upon loss, nominal damages may be available if, in the circumstances of a particular case, loss is presumed. See *Stoke-on-Trent City Council v. W. & J. Wass Ltd.*, [1988] 1 W.L.R. 1406 (C.A.). Likewise, nominal damages are sometimes awarded if damage is shown, but the amount is not sufficiently established. See McGregor, *McGregor on Damages*, 17th ed. (2003) at 360-61; Klar *et al.*, *Damages and Remedies in Tort* (1995) at 27-45 to 27-47; and *Marynowsky v. Stuartburn (District)*, [1994] 10 W.W.R. 602 (Man. C.A.). What purpose would such an award serve?

2. A judge may award a trifling sum as contemptuous or derisory damages to express his or her disapproval of the plaintiff's claim, despite its technical validity. In *Dering v. Uris*, [1964] 2 All E.R. 660 (Q.B.), the plaintiff was awarded one halfpenny in damages for the defendant's defamatory comments overstating the extent of the plaintiff's collaboration with the Nazis in a concentration camp. See also *Martin v. Benson*, [1927] 1 K.B. 771; and *Dennison v. Sanderson*, [1946] 4 D.L.R. 314 (Ont. C.A.). Explain the difference between nominal and contemptuous damages.

3. Another mechanism the courts may use to show their disapproval of a plaintiff's claim is an award of costs. Costs are generally awarded to the successful party. However, the court has discretion to deny costs to a successful plaintiff, or perhaps even award costs against him or her, if it feels that the claim was a frivolous attempt at "empty vindication." See Laskin C.J.C.'s dissent in *Harrison v. Carswell*, [1976] 2 S.C.R. 200.

4. Given the current social and private costs of civil litigation, does an action for nominal damages serve a worthwhile purpose for society or the plaintiff? Does your answer depend on whether the case involves personal security, real property or personal property?

5. For a detailed discussion of nominal damages see Cooper-Stephenson, *Personal Injury Damages in Canada*, 2d ed. (1996) at 99-101; and Waddams, *The Law of Damages*, 4th ed. (2004), ch. 10.

5. Compensatory Damages

Most tort actions are brought to obtain financial redress for actual loss. The general principle for assessing compensatory damages was stated by Donaldson L.J. in *Dodd Properties Ltd. v. Canterbury City Council*, [1980] 1 All E.R. 928 at 938 (C.A.): "The general object underlying the rules for the assessment of damages is, so far as is possible by means of a monetary award, to place the plaintiff in the position which he would have occupied if he had not suffered the wrong complained of, be that wrong a tort or a breach of contract."

In *Livingstone v. Rawyards Coal Co.* (1880), 5 App. Cas. 25 at 39 (H.L.), Lord Blackburn stated that the compensatory measure of damages in tort law is: "... that sum of money which will put the party who has been injured, or who has suffered, in the same position as he would have been in if he had not sustained the wrong for which he is now getting his compensation or reparation."

Despite its apparent simplicity, this principle may be extremely difficult to apply in specific situations. The following two subsections examine the types of challenges that may arise in calculating compensatory damages.

(a) ASSESSING DAMAGES FOR PECUNIARY LOSSES

Some claims involve complex damage calculations based on speculative factors stretching far into the future. A young person rendered a paraplegic today may have an almost normal life expectancy, and thus may claim compensatory damages for future medical care, personal assistance services and other support for the next 50 years. In other situations, the challenge may be assigning a value to a particular loss. For example, how should compensatory damages be assessed for the loss of a unique work of art or a prized family heirloom? Similarly, what is the appropriate measure of damages for the defendant's wrongful use of the plaintiff's property which would have otherwise sat idle? *The Mediana*, which was discussed earlier in connection with nominal damages, addresses this issue.

THE MEDIANA

[1900] A.C. 113 (H.L.)

EARL OF HALSBURY: ... Supposing a person took away a chair out of my room and kept it for twelve months, could anybody say you had a right to diminish the damages by shewing that I did not usually sit in that chair, or that there were plenty of other chairs in the room? The proposition so nakedly stated appears to me to be absurd; but a jury have very often a very difficult task to perform in ascertaining what should be the amount of damages of that sort. I know very well that as a matter of common sense what an arbitrator or a jury very often do is to take a perfectly artificial hypothesis and say, "Well, if you wanted to hire a chair, what would you have to give for it for the period"; and in that way they come to a rough sort of conclusion as to what damages ought to be paid for the unjust and unlawful withdrawal of it from the owner. Here, as I say, the broad principle seems to me to be quite independent of the particular use the plaintiffs were going to make of the thing that was taken, except — and this I think has been the fallacy running through the arguments at the bar — when you are endeavouring to establish the specific loss of profit, or of something that you otherwise would have got which the law recognises as special damage. In that case you must shew it, and by precise evidence, so much so that in the old system of pleading you could not recover damages unless you had made a specific allegation in your pleading so as to give the persons responsible for making good the loss an opportunity of inquiring into it before they came into court. But when we are speaking of general damages no such principle applies at all, and the jury might give whatever they thought would be the proper equivalent for the unlawful withdrawal of the subject-matter then in question. It seems to me that that broad principle comprehends within it many other things. There is no doubt in many cases a jury would say there really has been no damage at all: "We will give the plaintiffs a trifling amount" — not nominal damages, be it observed, but a trifling amount; in other cases it would be more serious.

NOTES AND QUESTIONS

1. Do you agree that the plaintiff suffered a loss in the example of the appropriated chair? If so, what precisely was lost? What if the defendant had ridden the plaintiff's horse without the plaintiff's consent and the horse benefitted from the exercise?

2. In the example of the appropriated chair, damages are said to be "at large" because the jury has considerable latitude in quantifying them. The award is not limited to the pecuniary losses that the plaintiff has specifically pleaded and proven. The Earl of Halsbury indicated that, depending on the facts of the case, the jury could award a trifling sum as compensatory damages. Distinguish such an award from an award of nominal damages.

3. The issue raised by the appropriated chair example occasionally arises in connection with trespass to land. In such circumstances, the plaintiff is entitled to "mesne profits" (pronounced "mean" profits) equal to the reasonable rental value of the property. The Privy Council addressed this issue in *Inverugie Investments Ltd. v. Hackett*, [1995] 1 W.L.R. 713. The plaintiff purchased the leasehold to 30 of 164 units in a hotel in the Bahamas. The defendant wrongfully occupied those units for 20 years, during which time it attempted to rent them out to third parties. When the plaintiff claimed compensation for its loss, the defendant presented evidence that the average occupancy rate was only 35%-40%. The Privy Council largely rejected the relevance of that evidence. It held that the quantification of damages was not concerned with the plaintiff's actual loss, nor with the profit made by the defendant. Instead, compensatory damages were assessed in terms of the reasonable rental value of the property. Lord Lloyd explained: "If a man hires a concrete mixer, he must pay for the daily hire, even though he may not in the event have been able to use the mixer because of rain. So also must the trespasser who takes the mixer without the owner's consent. He must pay the going rate, even though in the event he has derived no benefit from the use of the mixer." Consequently, damages in *Inverugie* were calculated on the basis of the wholesale rate paid by tour operators, which accounted for seasonal variations in room rates.

(b) ASSESSING DAMAGES FOR NON-PECUNIARY LOSSES

A different type of challenge arises when a court is asked to award damages for non-pecuniary losses, which by definition have no monetary equivalent. How should compensatory damages be assessed for the humiliation arising from being slapped in the face or for having to endure severe pain? Clearly, there is a loss, but how can seemingly immeasurable values, such as one's public standing or quality of life, be expressed in dollars? Dickson J. addressed this issue in *Andrews v. Grand & Toy Alberta Ltd.*, [1978] 2 S.C.R. 229 at 260-61:

> Andrews used to be a healthy young man, athletically active and socially congenial. Now he is a cripple, deprived of many of life's pleasures and subjected to pain and disability. For this, he is entitled to compensation. But the problem here is qualitatively different from that of pecuniary losses. There is no medium of exchange for happiness. There is no market for expectation of life. The monetary evaluation of non-pecuniary losses is a philosophical and policy exercise more than a legal or logical one. The award must be fair and reasonable, fairness being gauged by earlier decisions; but the award must also of necessity be arbitrary or conventional.

Although such issues arise in intentional torts cases, they are more common in negligence actions. Consequently, a detailed examination of assessing compensatory damages will be left to Chapter 18.

REVIEW PROBLEM

The palm of the plaintiff's hand was severely disfigured by scar tissue. The defendant doctor had a special interest in experimental skin grafting and induced the plaintiff to undergo an operation by stating that he would guarantee to make the hand 100% perfect. The plaintiff agreed and the doctor grafted skin from the plaintiff's chest to his hand. Unfortunately, the operation was unsuccessful. Not only did considerable scar tissue remain, but hair began to grow on the plaintiff's palm.

This fact situation is based on *Hawkins v. McGee*, 146 A. 641 (N.H.S.C. 1929). The court held that the doctor's statement constituted a binding contractual promise to give the plaintiff a perfect hand and that the doctor was strictly liable in contract for breaching this warranty. Assume that a parallel situation arose in tort. For example, if the doctor had made the statement knowing it to be false and there was no contractual relationship between the parties, the plaintiff could have brought an action for the tort of deceit. The following questions illustrate the quantification of compensatory damages in tort, and several differences between tort and contract law.

(a) What damages would you award in tort to compensate the plaintiff for having to live the rest of his life with a scarred and hairy hand? Should this calculation be based on the judge's objective assessment of this disability or on the plaintiff's subjective view?

(b) Applying the principles in *Dodd Properties*, calculate the plaintiff's compensatory damages in deceit. For the purpose of this calculation, assume that the hand had been worth $50 before the operation, $25 after the operation and that it would have been worth $100 had the operation succeeded.

(c) As stated above, the court in *Hawkins* considered the doctor's statement about making the hand perfect to be a contractual warranty. Based on the previously stated values of the hand, what should the plaintiff's compensatory damage award be in contract? If you have calculated correctly, you will have concluded that the plaintiff's compensatory damages are not the same in tort and contract. Can you reconcile this result with the statement in *Dodd Properties*?

(d) Assume that the plaintiff had lost $100 in wages when he missed work to undergo the operation. Based on the values of the hand stated above, calculate the plaintiff's compensatory damages in tort and contract.

6. Aggravated Damages

Although some Canadian courts had used the terms as synonyms, it is now well established that aggravated damages are distinct from punitive damages. Aggravated damages are defined as a form of compensatory damages which are awarded to compensate the plaintiff for additional injuries to dignity and similar feelings arising from the defendant's reprehensible conduct. In principle, aggravated damages are predicated on two requirements. First, given that aggravated damages are compensatory, plaintiffs must establish that they suffered additional injuries to their feelings. Second, the defendant's conduct must be highly offensive or particularly repugnant, and not simply tortious. However, if the defendant's conduct is viewed as being sufficiently outrageous, some courts simply assume that it caused additional injuries to the plaintiff's feelings.

NOTES AND QUESTIONS

1. In *Rookes v. Barnard*, [1964] 1 All E.R. 367 (H.L.), the House of Lords defined aggravated damages in terms of injuries to the plaintiff's "proper feelings of dignity or pride" arising from the defendant's malice or manner of committing the wrong. The Supreme Court of Canada adopted a similar definition in *Vorvis v. Insurance Corp. of British Columbia*, [1989] 1 S.C.R. 1085. See also *Fidler v. Sun Life Assurance Co. of Canada*, [2006] 2 S.C.R. 3.

2. Given that aggravated damages are intended to compensate the plaintiff for injuries to his or her feelings, should they be based on a subjective standard?

3. Can meaningful distinctions be made between the injured feelings that normally arise from being the victim of a tort and the additional emotional injuries stemming from the defendant's reprehensible conduct? See *K.(K.) v. G.(K.W.)* (2006), 40 C.C.L.T. (3d) 139 (Ont. S.C.J.), where the court held that compensation for the defendant's aggravating conduct should be included in the general damage award without attempting to assess a specific amount for aggravated damages. See also *A.(D.A.) v. B.(D.K.)* (1995), 27 C.C.L.T. (2d) 256 (Ont. Gen. Div.).

4. In *Thomas Management Ltd. v. Alberta (Minister of Environmental Protection)* (2006), 64 Alta. L.R. (4th) 206 (C.A.), the court overturned an aggravated damage award that had been made to a closely-held, family-owned corporation. It ruled that corporations could not be compensated for the mental anguish that their shareholders might suffer.

5. For a general discussion of aggravated damages, see Cooper-Stephenson, *Personal Injury Damages in Canada*, 2d ed. (1996) at 94-97.

7. Punitive Damages

The issue of punitive damages has generated considerable judicial and academic attention. Much of the discussion has stemmed from disagreements about the proper role of such awards in tort law. Traditionally, the Canadian courts limited punitive damages to situations in which a defendant's reprehensible conduct warranted punishment. More recently, the courts have recognized that such awards may serve a dual function, providing punishment and/or deterrence. However, a damage award addressing one of these goals may differ significantly from an award focusing on the other.

Punishment looks backwards to condemn the defendant's actions, whereas deterrence looks forward to discourage the defendant and others from committing such wrongs. Since it is generally thought that punishment must be proportionate to the wrongdoing, damages based on punishment will be quantified primarily with reference to the defendant's moral blameworthiness. In contrast, damages based on deterrence will be quantified in terms of the financial disincentive required to discourage future wrongdoing.

In England, punitive damages have been strictly limited and awarded sparingly. In *Rookes v. Barnard*, [1964] 1 All E.R. 367 (H.L.), the House of Lords limited punitive damages to three categories of cases: oppressive, arbitrary or unconstitutional conduct by government officials; conduct calculated to make a profit in excess of the likely compensatory damage award; and situations in which such awards were expressly authorized by statute. Even within these categories, punitive damages had to be awarded with restraint, the plaintiff had to be the victim of the tort and the financial means of the parties had to be considered. Finally, punitive damages were to be awarded if, and only if, an award of compensatory and aggravated damages was insufficient to adequately punish the defendant, denounce the conduct and deter a repetition.

The Canadian courts have rejected limiting punitive damages to these three categories of cases and have made such awards far more frequently than their English counterparts. Nevertheless, punitive damage awards are relatively uncommon in Canada.

NOTES AND QUESTIONS

1. For a discussion of the deterrence function of punitive damages in torts, see *Norberg v. Wynrib*, [1992] 2 S.C.R. 226; and *Hill v. Church of Scientology of Toronto*, [1995] 2 S.C.R. 1130.

2. A common argument for strictly limiting punitive damages is that they constitute a quasi-criminal fine imposed in a civil proceeding in which the defendant is denied the traditional evidentiary and procedural safeguards of a criminal trial. Do you find this argument compelling? See Jeffries, "A Comment on the Constitutionality of Punitive Damages" (1986) 72 Va. L. Rev. 139.

3. In *A.B. v. South West Water Services Ltd.*, [1993] Q.B. 507 (C.A.), the court held that punitive damages were only available in those categories of actions in which they had been awarded prior to *Rookes*. In *Kuddus v. Chief Constable of Leicestershire Constabulary*, [2001] 3 All E.R. 193 (H.L.), the House of Lords rejected this additional "cause of action" limitation.

B.(P.) v. B.(W.)

(1992), 11 O.R. (3d) 161 (Gen. Div.)

[The plaintiff was sexually assaulted from the age of 5 until she was 18 by the defendant, her father. There were other violent incidents and threats, and the defendant raped the plaintiff when she was 20. The defendant pleaded guilty to incest, but two additional charges related to the rape were stayed. He was sentenced to 5½ years imprisonment on the incest conviction.

The plaintiff sued the defendant for assault and battery. He did not defend the action and the case proceeded on the issue of damages. The plaintiff's doctor testified that she was the most traumatized sexual assault victim he had ever seen. He stated that she was left emotionally and socially dysfunctional, and that it was highly unlikely that she would ever be able to function in normal relationships.]

CUNNINGHAM J.: . . .

Non-pecuniary general damages

There can be no doubt that the repugnant and reprehensible conduct of the defendant towards his daughter has severely affected her life. Abuse by fathers has to have a far more negative impact upon children than any other form of abuse. More particularly, a very special relationship exists between fathers and daughters and when that trusting, loving relationship is violated, the results can be catastrophic. They certainly were here. This plaintiff has been, in the words of Dr. Bartashunas, as severely psychologically damaged as anyone he has seen, not only in his practice but in the literature. Not only was there a total breach of trust involved here but also a very significant element of fear. Violence permeated this entire family unit and during her tender years, while being subjected to regular sexual abuse by her father, she often witnessed her mother being beaten by the defendant and indeed had been subjected to his physical violence herself. By the time the plaintiff reached her mid-teens, she began to experience great difficulty coping with her life. She suffered blackouts and before she was brought to the attention of Dr. Bartashunas, she had been through neurological and CAT scan examinations, all of which proved negative.

This case is clearly the most serious I have seen in my review of Canadian authorities. As the plaintiff described in her evidence, it is worse than being murdered. It is something that she has had to live with for a very long time and probably will have to live with every day for the rest of her life. Her great fear, because she recognizes her difficulty in forming meaningful relationships, is that she will grow old alone.

Accordingly, for her non-pecuniary general damages the plaintiff will have the sum of $100,000. [The judge listed a number of cases that he had considered.] . . . In my view, the closest to our case is *Brandner v. Brandner*, where a father sexually abused his daughter, almost continuously from six to 15 leaving her severely traumatized. In that case, the professional witnesses described it as being one of the worst cases of a sexually damaged person ever encountered, a person who would need continual psychotherapy. In fact, most of the difficulties suffered by the plaintiff in that case are very similar to the difficulties being experienced by this plaintiff. Feelings of vulnerability, victimization and profound shame with the attendant lack of self-esteem and self-worth are the results in both cases. In *Brandner*, De Graves J. awarded the sum of $100,000 for psychological trauma and $50,000 for aggravated damages. I intend to deal with aggravated damages separately.

Aggravated damages

Aggravated damages are awarded in cases where, because of the defendant's conduct, the measure of damages is increased. In my view, aggravated damages are not punitive damages which I will deal with later in these reasons. Aggravated damages may be taken into account in the overall assessment of non-pecuniary general damages but in certain circumstances, may be dealt with separately and in addition to general damages where the facts so warrant. This, in my view, is one of those situations. The assaults in this case occurred over a period of many years on a little girl who loved and trusted her father. It was not until she was about 10 years of age that she realized, through interaction with her peers at school, something was wrong with her relationship with her father. This defendant, even during periods of access while the plaintiff was living with her mother, continued his predatory and disgraceful conduct on a young girl approaching adolescence. Even worse, after obtaining custody of the plaintiff in her early teens, he continued his disgusting conduct. Never have I seen a situation where a person in authority has taken such advantage of another and accordingly, I assess aggravated damages at $75,000 for this gross breach of trust. Had it not been for this pattern of abuse, I have no doubt this young woman would today be functioning at a much higher level.

. . .

Punitive damages

In my view, it is clear law that where tortious acts are also crimes and the conduct has already been sanctioned, to award punitive damages in a civil lawsuit would amount of [*sic*] double jeopardy: *B. (A.) v. J. (I.), supra*; *Rioux v. Smith* (1983), 48 B.C.L.R. 126 (C.A.).

In the present case, as I indicated early on, only part of the defendant's conduct was criminally sanctioned. The defendant pleaded guilty to having committed incest upon his daughter between the years 1976 and 1987. From my reading of the proceedings in the criminal court, although there was some brief mention of the 1989 occurrence, the full details of that sexual assault were not documented. The plaintiff has testified that on that occasion she was raped by her father at a time when she was in a particularly vulnerable state. The recitation of the facts in the criminal court indicated that the defendant fondled the plaintiff's breasts and rubbed his penis against her vagina suggesting to her that, despite the fact she was having her menstrual period, it would be a good time to have sex. What the recitation of the facts did not disclose, however, was the fact of the rape. I am satisfied that this conduct in 1989, was not sanctioned. Accordingly, the plaintiff will have punitive damages against the defendant in the amount of $50,000.

NOTES AND QUESTIONS

1. What factors did the judge consider in awarding aggravated damages and punitive damages? Do you agree with the judge's analyses and the amount of these awards?

2. Aggravated and punitive damage awards are common in sexual assault cases. See for example *L.(H.) v. Canada (Attorney General)* (2001), 5 C.C.L.T. (3d) 186 (Sask. Q.B.); *T.W.N.A. v. Clarke* (2003), 20 C.C.L.T. (3d) 165 (B.C.C.A.); and *Blackwater v. Plint*, [2005] 3 S.C.R. 3. Punitive damages have also been awarded against people who

have falsely accused others of such conduct: see *F.(D.) v. S.(A.)*, 2001 CarswellQue 2593 (S.C.) (WLeC); and *Newman v. Halstead*, 2006 CarswellBC 52 (S.C.) (WLeC).

The courts have declined to award punitive damages against: (i) a defendant who sexually abused his younger brother when they were both underage; and (ii) a woman who failed to take steps to prevent her husband from continuing to sexually abuse their daughter over a seven-year period. See respectively *Olsen v. Olsen* (2006), 266 D.L.R. (4th) 209 (B.C.S.C.); and *K.(K.) v. G.(K.W.)* (2006), 40 C.C.L.T. (3d) 139 (Ont. S.C.J.).

3. Does the fact that the criminal justice system is overburdened justify expanding the role of punitive damages in torts, particularly in cases of deliberate and repeated wrongdoing? See Englard, "The System Builders: A Critical Appraisal of Modern American Tort Theory" (1980) 9 J. Legal Stud. 27.

4. Do punitive damages have an important role to play in publicly condemning socially unacceptable behaviour and acknowledging the plaintiff's injuries? Sexual abuse victims occasionally sue in tort, not to recover damages but to obtain official vindication of their grievances. See *Myers v. Haroldson*, [1989] 3 W.W.R. 604 (Sask. Q.B.). However, in *Chow v. Hiscock* (2005), 41 C.C.L.T. (3d) 155 (B.C.S.C.), the court declined to award punitive damages against three young gang members who viciously assaulted the plaintiff. The judge stated that, since the defendants were unlikely to pay even a small fraction of the almost $6 million of compensatory damages, awarding punitive damages was unnecessary because it would be purely symbolic.

5. The Canadian public's perceptions of punitive damages are influenced by media accounts of American cases which often involve very large punitive damage awards. While punitive damage awards are becoming more common in Canada, they remain exceptional and have tended to be relatively modest in size. However, there have been a small number of large awards in Canada. In addition to the cases involving the bad faith denial of insurance benefits that will be discussed shortly, see *Claiborne Industries Ltd. v. National Bank of Canada* (1989), 59 D.L.R. (4th) 533 (Ont. C.A.) (almost $1,500,000 in punitive damages awarded against a bank that breached trust by assisting one customer to defraud another); *Horseshoe Bay Retirement Society v. S.I.F. Development Corp.* (1990), 3 C.C.L.T. (2d) 75 (B.C.S.C.) ($100,000 punitive damage award against a land developer who cut down trees to increase the value of its properties); *Hill v. Church of Scientology of Toronto*, [1995] 2 S.C.R. 1130 ($300,000 in compensatory damages, $500,000 in aggravated damages and $800,000 in punitive damages to Crown counsel who was defamed); *Soccio v. Leduc* (2004), 25 C.C.L.T. (3d) 135 (C.S. Qc.) ($100,000 in punitive damages awarded against a psychiatrist who, under pressure from the plaintiff's employer, falsely reported that the plaintiff was dangerous); and *Keays v. Honda Canada Inc.* (2006), 82 O.R. (3d) 161 (C.A.) ($500,000 punitive damage award in wrongful dismissal case reduced to $77,500). Can you reconcile these punitive damage awards with the award in *B.(P.)*?

6. Section 24(1) of the *Canadian Charter of Rights and Freedoms*, Part I of the *Constitution Act, 1982*, being Schedule B to the *Canada Act 1982* (U.K.), 1982, c. 11 provides that a person whose rights under the *Charter* have been infringed "may apply to a court of competent jurisdiction to obtain such remedy as the court considers appropriate and just in the circumstances." In *Collin v. Lussier*, [1983] 1 F.C. 218 (T.D.), rev'd [1985] 1 F.C. 124 (C.A.), prison officials violated the plaintiff's right to security of the

person under s. 7 of the *Charter* by arbitrarily transferring him to an institution that could not adequately deal with his heart condition. The judge voided the transfer, ordered a new placement and awarded $18,000 in damages, of which $7,500 was for punitive damages. The Federal Court of Appeal quashed the entire award of damages, in part on procedural grounds. Should the courts develop special principles to govern punitive damages in *Charter* cases? See also *Crossman v. R.*, [1984] 1 F.C. 681 (T.D.); and *Patenaude v. Roy* (1994), 26 C.C.L.T. (2d) 237 (Qc. C.A.).

(a) THE PRINCIPLES IN *WHITEN v. PILOT*

The principles governing punitive damages were recently reviewed in *Whiten v. Pilot Insurance Co.*, [2002] 1 S.C.R. 595. The defendant company refused to pay the claim the plaintiffs made under their policy when their house was destroyed by fire. The defendant alleged that the plaintiffs had intentionally burned down their own house, despite the conclusion of the fire chief and the defendant's own adjuster, expert engineer and investigators that the fire was accidental. When its adjuster strongly recommended paying the claim, the defendant replaced the adjuster. Counsel for the defendant pressured his own experts to conclude that the fire was caused by arson and provided them with misleading information. The defendant asserted the arson defence throughout the four-week trial. In the end result, the court restored the jury's $1,000,000 punitive damage award against the defendant. Although the claim arose from breach of contract, Binnie J. undertook a comprehensive review of punitive damage awards in both torts and contracts. Binnie J.'s conclusions are summarized below.

(i) Unlike in the United Kingdom, punitive damages in Canada are not limited to specific categories of cases, but rather can be awarded in any type of case to punish the defendant, deter the defendant and others, denounce the defendant's conduct, or strip the defendant of profits that his or her outrageous conduct generated in excess of the likely compensatory damage award.

(ii) While characterizing the defendant's misconduct as malicious, vicious, high-handed etc. is not helpful, it is clear that only very serious misconduct warrants punishment, deterrence or denunciation and thus punitive damages.

(iii) Punitive damages are most likely to be awarded in intentional torts, but they may also be awarded in nuisance, negligence and other tort actions, as well as in contracts.

(iv) The fact that the defendant has been punished criminally does not preclude a punitive damage award, but rather is only one factor to be considered by the courts.

(v) Punitive damages should be awarded with restraint and then only if an award of compensatory, including aggravated damages, is insufficient to accomplish the specified goal of the contemplated punitive damage award.

(vi) There should be no fixed ratios between compensatory and punitive damages, nor should the latter be subject to a cap. Rather, the size of the punitive damage award should be based on the underlying goal and should be the lowest sum necessary to accomplish that end.

(vii) Juries should be informed of the functions of punitive damages and the factors that govern both the award and the assessment of the amount.

(viii) Appellate courts are entitled to intervene if the punitive damage award exceeds the outer bounds of a rational and measured response to the facts of the case.

(ix) Under s. 24(1) of the *Charter*, the court may award whatever remedy it deems appropriate for a violation of a person's *Charter* rights, including awards of both compensatory and punitive damages. Charter in contracts?

NOTES AND QUESTIONS

1. Can you reconcile the punitive damage award in *Whiten* with that in *B.(P.)*? What public benefit results from the Whitens receiving a $1,000,000 windfall in excess of their compensatory damage award? See Buller, "*Whiten v. Pilot*: Controlling Jury Awards of Punitive Damages" (2003) 36 U.B.C. L. Rev. 357.

2. The issue of insurance companies' bad faith denial of benefits has generated considerable litigation. See for example *Khazzaka v. Commercial Union Assurance Co. of Canada* (2002), 66 O.R. (3d) 390 (C.A.) ($200,000 punitive damage award); *Plester v. Wawanesa Mutual Insurance Co.* (2006), 215 O.A.C. 187 (C.A.) (aggravated damages reduced from $175,000 to $50,000, and $450,000 punitive damage award upheld); and *Pereira v. Hamilton Township Farmers' Mutual Fire Insurance Co.*, 2006 CarswellOnt 3732 (C.A.) (WLeC) ($2.5 million punitive damage award described as "grossly excessive" and "irrational"). In *Fidler v. Sun Life Assurance Co. of Canada*, [2006] 2 S.C.R. 3, the court overturned the $1,000,000 punitive damage award because the insurance company's denial of benefits was "troubling," but was not done in bad faith.

3. As noted in *Whiten*, punitive damages are rarely awarded in negligence cases because they typically involve carelessness and not advertent wrongdoing. However, exceptions exist. In *Robitaille v. Vancouver Hockey Club Ltd.* (1981), 124 D.L.R. (3d) 228 (B.C.C.A.), the plaintiff was told by management that his injury was "all in his head" and he was pressured to continue playing. As a result, the player suffered a permanent and disabling injury. In awarding $35,000 in punitive damages, the court held that the team's conduct had been "arrogant and high-handed." See also *Vlchek v. Koshel* (1988), 52 D.L.R. (4th) 371 (B.C.S.C.), aff'd (1988), 52 D.L.R. (4th) 371n (B.C.C.A.), allowing a claim for punitive damages in a products liability action.

In *McIntyre v. Grigg* (2006), 83 O.R. (3d) 161 (C.A.), the court reduced the $100,000 punitive damage award against an impaired driver to $20,000. The driver, whose blood-alcohol level was two to three times the limit in the *Criminal Code*, R.S.C. 1985, c. C-46, drove through a stop sign, sheared off a lamp post and struck the plaintiff. Should punitive damages be awarded in such cases?

4. In contrast to the current Canadian position, the New Zealand Court of Appeal has held that punitive damages are not available if the facts underlying the plaintiff's tort claim are substantially similar to those that have been, or might be, relied upon in criminal proceedings. The rule applies whether the earlier criminal proceedings resulted in a conviction or an acquittal. See *Daniels v. Thompson*, [1998] 3 N.Z.L.R. 22 (C.A.). Should a wrongdoer be subject to both criminal and civil sanctions for the same act? What considerations militate against the availability of both types of sanctions? What considerations favour the availability of both types of sanctions? Note that a criminal conviction has no bearing on compensatory damages, including aggravated damages.

5. In *Vorvis v. Insurance Corp. of British Columbia*, [1989] 1 S.C.R. 1085, the court said that punitive damages could only be awarded if the defendant's conduct was of a "harsh, vindictive, reprehensible and malicious nature." Other courts described the requisite wrongdoing in terms of "contemptuous," "evil" or "callous" behaviour. Do you agree with Binnie J. that such characterizations are unhelpful?

6. For a discussion of punitive damages, see Waddams, *The Law of Damages*, 4th ed. (2004), ch. 11; and Beaulac, "A Comparative Look at Punitive Damages in Canada" in Beaulac, Pitel & Schulz, eds., *The Joy of Torts* (2002) 351.

8. Disgorgement Damages

The final measure of damages is the least understood and the least often sought. Disgorgement damages are intended to strip defendants of the benefits they obtain as a result of their own wrongdoing. Although such relief is usually called "restitutionary," the term "disgorgement" is preferable. Restitution means to give back and is appropriate when the defendant is required to return to the plaintiff something received from him or her. In contrast, disgorgement means to give up and is appropriate when the defendant is required to give the plaintiff something that he or she wrongfully acquired, regardless of the source.

The plaintiffs will generally prefer disgorgement to compensation whenever the defendant obtains a benefit that exceeds the plaintiff's loss. The law, of course, will not allow the plaintiff to recover both disgorgement and compensatory damages. If both measures are available, the plaintiff must elect one remedy before judgment. See *United Australia Ltd. v. Barclay's Bank Ltd.*, [1941] A.C. 1 (H.L.); and *Rahal v. Rahal*, [1932] 3 D.L.R. 259 (B.C.C.A.).

However, the plaintiff does not always have the option of claiming disgorgement. Some tort actions support disgorgement, but others do not. Unfortunately, the cases are not consistent. The most common view is that disgorgement is available for "proprietary torts," such as trespass to land, conversion and passing-off. With respect to non-proprietary torts, the law is less consistent. Disgorgement is available in some actions, such as inducing breach of contract, but not others, such as assault, battery and false imprisonment.

NOTES AND QUESTIONS

1. For the distinctions between disgorgement and restitution, see McInnes, "Restitution, Unjust Enrichment and the Perfect Quadration Thesis" [1999] R. L. R. 118; and McInnes, "The Measure of Restitution" (2002) 52 U.T.L.J. 163.

2. Properly speaking, restitution is awarded only in response to an action in unjust enrichment. That cause of action, which is entirely independent of tort or contract, consists of three elements: (i) an enrichment to the defendant; (ii) a corresponding deprivation to the plaintiff; and (iii) an absence of any juristic reason for the defendant's enrichment. See *Pettkus v. Becker*, [1980] 2 S.C.R. 834; and *Garland v. Consumers' Gas Co.*, [2004] 1 S.C.R. 629. However, some courts and commentators use the phrase "unjust enrichment" to refer not only to that independent cause of action but also to situations in which disgorgement is awarded in response to tortious or otherwise wrongful

behaviour. See for example *LAC Minerals Ltd. v. International Corona Resources Ltd.*, [1989] 2 S.C.R. 574; and *Zraik v. Levesque Securities Inc.* (2001), 153 O.A.C. 186 (C.A.). In these latter situations, the remedy should be referred to as disgorgement damages for wrongful conduct, rather than as restitution for unjust enrichment. The relevant cause of action lies in a civil wrong, such as a tort, and not in unjust enrichment. The relevant remedy consists of giving up and not necessarily giving back.

3. For a discussion of actions in which disgorgement may be sought, see Jones, *Goff and Jones: The Law of Restitution*, 6th ed. (2002), ch. 36; Jackman, "Restitution for Wrongs" (1989) 48 Cambridge L.J. 302; Weinrib, "Restitutionary Damages as Corrective Justice" (2000) 1 Theor. Inq. L. 1; and McInnes, "Disgorgement for Wrongs: An Experiment in Alignment" [2000] R.L.R. 516.

PENARTH DOCK ENGINEERING CO. LTD. v. POUNDS

[1963] 1 Lloyds' Rep. 359 (Q.B.)

[The plaintiff sold a floating pontoon to the defendant. The defendant agreed to remove the pontoon from the premises that the plaintiff rented from the British Transport Commission by August 9, 1962. However, the defendant did not remove the pontoon until March 25, 1963, and thus committed a trespass to the plaintiff's land. The evidence at trial indicated that the plaintiff suffered no loss as a result of the tort. Accordingly, the plaintiff sought disgorgement of the defendant's gain rather than compensation for its own loss.]

LORD DENNING M.R.: ... The question which remains is, what are the damages? True it is that the Penarth company themselves would not seem to have suffered any damage to speak of. They have not to pay any extra rent to the British Transport Commission. The dock is no use to them; they would not have made any money out of it. But, nevertheless, in a case of this kind, as I read the law, starting with *Whitwham v. Westminster Brymbo Coal and Coke Company*, [1896] 2 Ch. 538, on which I commented myself in the case of *Strand Electric and Engineering Company, Ltd. v. Brisford Entertainments, Ltd.*, [1952] 2 Q.B. 246, at pp. 253 to 254, the test of the measure of damages is not what the plaintiffs have lost, but what benefit the defendant obtained by having the use of the berth; and he has been a trespasser, in my judgment, since Aug. 9, 1962. What benefit has the defendant obtained by having the use of it for this time? If he had moved it elsewhere, he would have had to pay [rent] for a berth for a dock of this kind. ... [The] damages are to be assessed in accordance with the law as I have stated it at the rate of £32 5s. a week for a period commencing from Aug. 9, 1962, which I would let run to Mar. 25, 1963, because the dock has now been removed. I do not know what that sum will come to, but that can be a matter of calculation.

NOTES AND QUESTIONS

1. Should the plaintiff in a tort action be permitted to claim disgorgement, even when this would result in a windfall? In *Penarth*, since the plaintiff would not have rented dock space to anyone else, it realized a profit that it would not have obtained in the normal course of events.

2. Should all torts be capable of supporting both disgorgement and compensation? What arguments can be made for and against that remedial alternative?

3. While both forms of relief are available for certain torts, it is surprisingly difficult to find cases in which the courts have clearly awarded disgorgement. The reason stems partially from the fact that lawyers seldom recognize the possibility of claiming disgorgement. However, it also results from the fact that a single award may often be analyzed as representing either measure of relief. For example *Strand Electric and Engineering Co. Ltd. v. Brisford Entertainments Ltd.*, [1952] 2 Q.B. 246 (C.A.) is frequently cited as a case involving disgorgement. The plaintiff rented electrical equipment to the defendant which retained it after the lease expired and thereby became liable in the tort of detinue. Denning L.J. held the defendant liable for the amount that it gained by not returning the equipment. On that view, the relief was disgorgement. The other two members of the court awarded the same amount, but did so on the basis that the plaintiff had lost a rental fee when the defendant kept its equipment without payment. On that view, the relief was compensation. Similarly, in Sharpe & Waddams, "Damages for Lost Opportunity to Bargain" (1982) 2 O.J.L.S. 290, the authors argue that *Penarth* can be explained in a manner that is entirely consistent with the compensatory theory of damages. They suggest that the plaintiff suffered a real loss, namely the opportunity to rent the dock to the defendant. Do you agree? Given the facts, did the plaintiff in *Penarth* suffer a compensable loss?

4. In *Edwards v. Lee's Administrators*, 96 S.W.2d 1028 (Ky. C.A. 1936), the defendant discovered an entrance to a series of caves that contained spectacular rock formations. He developed a lucrative business conducting tours through the caves. While the entrance to the caves was situated entirely on the defendant's property, approximately a third of the underground cavern was beneath the plaintiff's land. The plaintiff sued in trespass and the defendant was ordered to pay the plaintiff a proportionate share of the net profits. Was that relief compensation or disgorgement?

5. Disgorgement is the subject of misunderstanding on several points. First, it is often misleadingly referred to as "waiver of tort." As indicated, however, the tort is not waived. Rather, the plaintiff relies on the tort action, but claims relief measured by the defendant's gain, and not his or her own loss. See Birks, *An Introduction to the Law of Restitution* (1989) at 314. Second, such relief is occasionally said to be "equitable." However, the historical basis of disgorgement lies primarily in the ancient common law writ of *indebitatus assumpsit*. See Baker, *An Introduction to English Legal History*, 4th ed. (2002) at 343-48.

For a general discussion of disgorgement, see Birks, "The Law of Restitution at the End of an Epoch" (1999) 28 U.W.A.L. Rev. 13 at 49-54; and McGregor, "Restitutionary Damages" in Birks, ed., *Wrongs and Remedies in the Twenty-First Century* (1996) 203 at 206-10.

6. It is important to recognize that a single set of events may support more than one cause of action, and that a single cause of action may support more than one measure of relief. Consider the following situation. John committed the tort of deceit by defrauding Mary. As a result: (i) Mary was tricked into paying John $20,000; (ii) a third party, who

wanted to see Mary suffer, paid John $10,000 to encourage him to defraud Mary; and (iii) Mary suffered a $5,000 loss because of the fraud, in addition to the $20,000 that she had paid to John. Assuming that Mary and John are the only parties before the court, what actions could Mary successfully bring and what damages could she claim?

REVIEW PROBLEM

What damages would be awarded in the following fact situations?

(a) The defendant strikes John and breaks his jaw. The defendant is a known bully with previous criminal convictions for assault. No criminal charge is pending in this case.

(b) The same bully strikes John and breaks his jaw at an office party, attended by the plaintiff's wife, friends and fellow workers. The defendant ridicules the plaintiff while administering the beating.

(c) The bully strikes John and breaks his jaw at the office party, but is unaware that John is in the company of family and friends. The defendant remains silent and bears the plaintiff no personal malice.

(d) The bully is hired for $5,000 to beat the plaintiff. Compensatory damages, other than aggravated damages, are $2,000.

3

INTENTIONAL INTERFERENCE WITH THE PERSON

1. Introduction
2. Basic Principles of Liability
3. Related Issues: Motive, Mistake and Accident
4. Battery
5. Assault
6. False Imprisonment
7. Malicious Prosecution
8. Intentional Infliction of Nervous Shock
9. Protection of Privacy
10. The Common Law Tort of Discrimination

1. Introduction

This chapter begins with the intentional torts that protect an individual's physical integrity. Most of these causes of action – battery, assault and false imprisonment – were derived from the writ of trespass *vi et armis*, and therefore were characterized by direct interference with the person. These actions have remained largely unchanged over the years. The chapter also considers malicious prosecution and the intentional infliction of nervous shock. These torts are also premised on the defendant's intention. However, in contrast to the traditional intentional torts, they derived from the action on the case, rather than the writ of trespass *vi et armis*, and therefore involve indirect interference with the person. Privacy and discrimination, the remaining intentional torts discussed in this chapter, focus on personal interests other than physical integrity. Although these two causes of action have been recognized in some American jurisdictions, their existence is a matter of ongoing debate in Canada.

2. Basic Principles of Liability

Generally, a defendant will be held liable for an intentional tort only if his or her conduct is both voluntary and intentional. Before turning to the specific elements of the individual intentional torts, it is important to carefully define the concepts of volition and intent, and to clearly distinguish them from the related concepts of motive, mistake and accident. This task is complicated by the fact that tort lawyers define many of these terms differently than others do.

(a) VOLITION

The first issue to address in an intentional tort action is whether the defendant's act that gave rise to the tort was voluntary. In general, the requisite element of volition is present if the defendant exercised control over his or her physical actions. A defendant's act is voluntary if it is directed by his or her conscious mind.

SMITH v. STONE

(1647), 82 E.R. 533 (K.B.)

Smith brought an action of trespasse against Stone . . . the defendant pleads this speciall plea in justification, viz. that he was carryed upon the land of the plaintiff by force, and violence of others, and was not there voluntarily, which is the same trespasse, for which the plaintiff brings his action. The plaintiff demurs to this plea: in this case Roll Iustice said, that it is the trespasse of the party that carryed the defendant upon the land, and not the trespasse of the defendant: as he that drives my cattel into another mans land is the trespassor against him, and not I who am owner of the cattell.

NOTES AND QUESTIONS

1. Would the defendant's act have been voluntary if (a) he or she had been chased onto the plaintiff's land by a swarm of bees, or (b) he or she had entered the plaintiff's land to prevent a child from drowning? Would an individual who reaches out instinctively and grasps another's arm to avoid falling have acted voluntarily?

2. In *Stokes v. Carlson*, 240 S.W.2d 132 (Mo. S.C. 1951), the judge defined involuntary actions to include reflex reactions, convulsive movements, and movements during sleep and unconsciousness. Is a person who is acting in a state of automatism acting voluntarily? See *R. v. Stone*, [1999] 2 S.C.R. 290; and Smith, "Automatism – A Defence to Negligence?" (1980) 130 New L.J. 1111.

3. The issue of volition is rarely contentious and consequently there is little reference to it in the case law. In intentional torts, this issue will most likely arise in relation to children and those with a mental illness. The most comprehensive discussion of the question is provided in negligence cases involving drivers who claim to be rendered unconscious by sudden illness. See for example *Gootson v. R.*, [1948] S.C.R. viii (epileptic seizure); *Boomer v. Penn* (1965), 52 D.L.R. (2d) 673 (Ont. H.C.) (insulin reaction); *Dobbs v. Mayer* (1985), 32 C.C.L.T. 191 (Ont. Div. Ct.) (heart attack); *Fiala v. Cechmanek* (1999), 246 A.R. 120 (Q.B.), aff'd (2001), 281 A.R. 248 (C.A.) (manic episode); *Barron v. Barron* (2003), 214 N.S.R. (2d) 76 (S.C.) (choked on coffee); and *Codner v. Gosse* (2003), 227 Nfld. & P.E.I.R. 132 (N.L.S.C. (T.D.)) (blackout). See also Blalock, "Liability of the Unconscious Defendant" (1970) 6:2 Trial 29.

(b) INTENT

In tort law, the term "intent" is used to refer to an actor's desire to bring about the results or consequences of his or her act, rather than his or her desire to do the physical act itself. If the defendant fires at a magpie but the bullet misses and hits a cow, the shooting of the cow is unintentional because the result was not desired. The fact that the defendant desired to pull the trigger is not relevant to the issue of intent to shoot the cow. A single act may bring about several consequences, only some of which may be intentional and only one of which may be relevant to the tort claim in question. For example, assume that Frank, believing that he is alone in a secluded forest, shoots at a tin can and hits it, but the bullet ricochets and strikes the plaintiff. The consequence of hitting the tin can is intentional because Frank desired to shoot that object. However, if the plaintiff sues Frank for the intentional tort of battery, the relevant issue, as we will see, is whether Frank desired to cause an offensive or harmful physical contact with the plaintiff. Since the shooting of the plaintiff was unintentional, the intentional tort claim would fail.

The essential issue is whether the defendant desired to bring about the specific consequence giving rise to the tort in question. The defendant's intent need not be hostile or otherwise blameworthy. For example, a defendant who, at great personal risk, saves a child's life by pushing the child out of the path of a car has the requisite intent to be held liable in battery. The fact that the defendant had intent does not mean that he or she will be held liable – intent is only one element of an intentional tort. One must then analyze the other substantive elements of the action, as well as the associated defences.

However, the fact that the defendant did not desire to bring about the consequence giving rise to the tort may not necessarily resolve the intent issue. As discussed below, the plaintiff may establish intent under the doctrines of imputed and transferred intent.

(i) *Imputed (Constructive) Intent*

The concept of intent includes not only the desired consequences of an act, but also those unintended consequences that are certain or substantially certain to result from it. Thus, a defendant who plants a powerful bomb in the outer office of his or her former boss will be held liable to the staff injured in the ensuing explosion. Although the defendant may not have wished to injure the staff, such an intent will be imputed to him or her if this consequence was certain or substantially certain to follow from the act.

(ii) *Transferred Intent*

The doctrine of transferred intent provides another basis for imposing liability on a defendant for the unintended consequences of his or her act. It is invoked when a defendant intends to commit an intentional tort against one party, but unintentionally commits an intentional tort against the plaintiff. The doctrine also applies if the defendant intends to commit one type of intentional tort against the plaintiff, but unintentionally commits another. In essence, the defendant's wrongful intent regarding the first tort is transferred to the second tort to permit recovery. Traditionally, transferred intent was restricted to directly caused injuries involving hurling, casting and shooting. It was also limited to the intentional torts derived from the writ of trespass *vi et armis*, namely battery, assault, false imprisonment, trespass to chattels, and trespass to land. The Canadian courts have not addressed whether these historical limits on the doctrine should be maintained.

NOTES AND QUESTIONS

1. What is the rationale for the doctrine of imputed intent? American authorities have defined imputed intent in terms of the actor's own belief in the certainty or substantial certainty of the consequences. See *Restatement (Second) of the Law of Torts*

(1965) at §8A; and *Garratt v. Dailey*, 279 P.2d 1091 (Wash. S.C. 1955). What problems, if any, arise in adopting this subjective definition of imputed intent?

2. In *Bielitski v. Obadiak* (1922), 65 D.L.R. 627 (Sask. C.A.) and *Purdy v. Woznesensky*, [1937] 2 W.W.R. 116 (Sask. C.A.) the court applied an extremely broad test of imputed intent, based in part on the criminal law presumption that individuals are deemed to intend the natural and probable consequences of their acts. What is the practical effect of this presumption? For a critique of its use in intentional torts, see Atrens, "Intentional Interference with the Person" in Linden, ed., *Studies in Canadian Tort Law* (1968) 378 at 381-82. But see Epstein, "Intentional Harm" (1975) 4 J. Legal Stud. 391.

3. What is the rationale for the doctrine of transferred intent? Historical factors aside, should it still be limited to torts derived from trespass *vi et armis* and situations involving hurling, casting and shooting? See generally Prosser, "Transferred Intent" (1967) 45 Tex. L. Rev. 650; and Reynolds, "Transferred Intent: Should Its 'Curious Survival' Continue?" (1997) 50 Okla. L. Rev. 529.

4. Give an example in which (a) both transferred and imputed intent would apply, (b) only transferred intent would apply, and (c) only imputed intent would apply. See *Scott v. Shepherd* (1773), 96 E.R. 525 (K.B.), an extract of which appears in Chapter 1.

3. Related Issues: Motive, Mistake and Accident

(a) MOTIVE

The concept of intent refers to the actor's desire to bring about a particular consequence, not his or her motive or reason for wanting that result to occur. A friend who moves your car to prevent it from being impounded, a practical joker who moves it on April Fool's Day, and a thief who steals it all have the intent to commit trespass to chattels, but their motives obviously differ. The plaintiff must prove that the defendant's conduct was intentional, but the plaintiff does not have to establish that the defendant had a blameworthy motive. Unlike intent, motive is generally not an element of the cause of action. Thus, in the example above, all three defendants have committed the tort of trespass to chattels, even though their motives ranged from altruism to greed. The concept of motive is extremely broad, encompassing the full range of factors that induce human behaviour. The following discussions of duress and provocation should be viewed as illustrations of the courts' response to motive.

NOTES

1. Motive is an essential element of some of the intentional torts derived from the writ of trespass on the case. For example, in order to establish the tort of malicious prosecution the plaintiff must prove, among other things, that the defendant acted maliciously or for some other improper purpose.

2. A praiseworthy motive is not a defence *per se*, although it may be an element of a valid defence. For example, to invoke the defence of public necessity, a defendant must establish that he or she was acting to protect the public interest from an impending harm.

3. There are several ways in which the parties' motives may be taken into account in assessing damages. The defendant's highly blameworthy motive may provide grounds for awarding aggravated or punitive damages. It may also influence the size of the general damage award, because the trier of fact has considerable discretion in setting this figure. In some jurisdictions, the fact that the plaintiff provoked the defendant may reduce the size of the compensatory damage award that the plaintiff would have otherwise received. Similarly, the court may express its disapproval of a vexatious plaintiff by awarding only contemptuous damages.

(i) *Duress*

GILBERT v. STONE

(1648), 82 E.R. 539 (K.B.)

Demurrer upon a plea in trespasse.

Gilbert brought an action of trespasse quare clausum fregit [i.e. trespass to land], and taking of a gelding, against Stone. The defendant pleads that he for fear of his life, and wounding of twelve armed men, who threatened to kill him if he did not the fact [sic], went into the house of the plaintiff, and took the gelding. The plaintiff demurred to this plea; Roll Iustice, This is no plea to justifie the defendant; for I may not do a trespasse to one for fear of threatnings of another, for by this means the party injured shall have no satisfaction, for he cannot have it of the party that threatned. Therefore let the plaintiff have his judgement.

NOTES AND QUESTIONS

1. Analyze the issues of volition, intent and motive in *Gilbert*. Distinguish this case from *Smith v. Stone*, an excerpt from which appears at the beginning of this chapter. Is the defendant's conduct in *Gilbert* any more morally blameworthy than that in *Smith*? Can you suggest another rationale for the different results in these two cases?

2. Duress will neither negate volition and intent, nor serve as a defence. Rather, it is simply one factor that the courts may consider in assessing damages. J. Fleming has argued that duress ought to be recognized as a defence, in keeping with the principle of no liability without fault: see Fleming, *The Law of Torts*, 9th ed. (1998) at 107. Outline the competing interests at stake in resolving this issue.

3. Although Stone has no defence in reference to Gilbert, he would have a valid claim in assault against the armed men. As well, their conduct would now give rise to an action for intimidation. In *Rookes v. Barnard*, [1964] A.C. 1129 (H.L.), the House of Lords defined intimidation as coercing a person, by unlawful threats, into doing or refraining from doing that which he or she has a right to do.

4. Is it appropriate that compulsion (duress) is a defence in criminal law, but not tort law? See *Criminal Code*, R.S.C. 1985, c. C-46, s. 17.

5. Under s. 17 of the *Criminal Code*, the defence of compulsion is limited to threats of immediate physical injury and cannot be raised by an accused who is charged with

treason, murder or other serious crimes of violence. In *R. v. Ruzic*, [2001] 1 S.C.R. 687, the court struck down the requirement in s. 17 that the accused be subject to an immediate threat by a person who was present, because that limit violated s. 7 of the *Canadian Charter of Rights and Freedoms*, Part I of *The Constitution Act, 1982*, being Schedule B to the *Canada Act 1982* (U.K.), 1982, c. 11.

6. If duress were recognized as a defence in intentional torts, how would you define it? Should the defendant be able to raise the defence when threatened with (a) immediate and serious physical harm, (b) the destruction of his or her home, (c) being the victim of any federal criminal offence, or (d) being the victim of any illegal act? As in s. 17 of the *Criminal Code*, should a tort defence of duress be unavailable where the defendant has caused serious physical harm?

(ii) *Provocation*

MISKA v. SIVEC
(1959), 18 D.L.R. (2d) 363 (Ont. C.A.)

[Miska sued for injuries that he sustained when Sivec intentionally shot him. Sivec argued self-defence. He claimed that: Miska had cut him off and blocked his car on the road; Miska then emerged from the car and threatened him with a knife and an iron bar; he fled 200 yards to his own house with Miska in hot pursuit; he fired two warning shots after reaching his house; and Miska was injured after he moved into the line of fire. Miska denied that version of events. There was evidence of previous bad blood between the parties.

The jury found in Miska's favour and Sivec appealed. Sivec argued that the trial judge had misdirected the jury on the burden of proof in self-defence and had failed to instruct the jury to take provocation into account when assessing the damages.]

MORDEN J.A.: [delivering the judgment of the court]

. . . In my opinion, Wells J. properly directed the jury on the burden of proof, and the first ground of appeal fails.

The defendant's second ground of appeal was that the learned trial Judge failed and when requested by counsel for the defendant refused to charge the jury on the effect of provocation in mitigation of damages. There is no doubt that where there is evidence of provocation the jury should be instructed to consider it in assessing damages for assault. In this connection, Mr. Goodman submitted that the bad feeling and other incidents between the parties, going back over a period of eight or nine months, should be considered evidence of provocation.

The conduct of the plaintiff to be capable of being considered provocation must have been such as to cause the defendant to lose his power of self-control and must have occurred at the time of or shortly before the assault. In *Fraser v. Berkeley* (1836), 7 Car. & P. 621, . . . three days after the plaintiff published a libel on the defendant and his family, the defendant beat the plaintiff with a heavy whip and his fists and in the action for damages for assault evidence of this libel was given. Lord Abinger C.B. in charging the jury said at p. 624: "The law I think would be an unwise law, if it did not make allowance for human infirmities; and if a person commit violence at a time when he is smarting under immediate provocation, that is a matter of mitigation."

. . .

In deciding in this case whether there was evidence of provocation, incidents occurring between the parties prior to the night of the assault are not to be considered. They were not immediate and by the night in question, if available at all to the defendant, could only be available to show provocation if it were asserted that the effect of the immediate provocative acts upon the defendant's mind was enhanced by those previous incidents being recalled to him and thereby inflaming his passion. There is no such evidence directly or by way of inference to be drawn from the defendant's testimony. A careful perusal of the defendant's evidence of the occurrences on the fateful evening does not disclose any insulting or abusive conduct or language on the part of the plaintiff, nor any sudden passion, lack of self-control or even any annoyance on the defendant's part. His evidence was that the plaintiff had blocked his car and approached him armed with an iron bar and a knife. The defendant then beat a successful retreat back to his house which was about 200 yards away. After he entered the house his wife locked the door and he loaded his shot gun and went upstairs. At this point his wife went to the telephone to notify the police. The defendant took up his position at an open window on the second story from which he fired without any warning at the plaintiff. He did not say that at that time he was annoyed or provoked. His conduct was careful and deliberate and belied the existence of any sudden and uncontrolled passion. In my opinion, there was no evidence of provocation to be left to the jury and the learned trial Judge was correct in refusing to do so.

On both grounds the appeal fails and must be dismissed with costs.

NOTES AND QUESTIONS

1. How did Morden J.A. define provocation? Do you find his application of this definition to the facts convincing? Why did Morden J.A. not consider the previous incidents between the parties as evidence of provocation?

2. In *Miska*, the court appears to use a subjective test which focuses on whether the defendant lost his or her power of self-control. Nevertheless, the test is usually phrased objectively, in terms of whether the plaintiff's conduct caused the defendant, as a reasonable person, to lose his or her power of self-control. Should the defendant's claim of provocation be denied if his or her loss of self-control was reasonable, but the retaliatory behaviour was out of proportion to the plaintiff's provocative behaviour?

3. The courts are careful to confine provocation to situations in which the provocative act occurs shortly before the alleged tort. In *Ellone v. Mesa*, 1997 CarswellOnt 1938 (Gen. Div.) (WLeC), the plaintiff threatened the defendant with a knife. One week later, the defendant went to the plaintiff's house and punched him in the head. The trial judge rejected the plea of provocation on the basis that the two incidents did not occur sufficiently close in time.

4. Research indicates that sudden outbursts of rude, threatening and violent behaviour are not uncommon on Canadian roads. A 2003 study of Ontario drivers found that almost half had been shouted at, cursed at or subjected to rude gestures in the past year,

and that 7.2% were threatened with personal injury or damage to their vehicles: Smart *et al.*, "Road Rage Experience and Behaviour: Vehicle, Exposure, and Driver Factors" (2004) 5 Traffic Injury Prevention 343.

Should the poor or discourteous driving of another motorist ever be viewed as a sufficient basis for establishing provocation? See *Herman v. Graves* (1998), 217 A.R. 275 (Q.B.).

5. One of the most confusing issues is the impact of provocation on the assessment of damages. Initially, the Canadian courts considered provocation a factor in reducing the plaintiff's claim for both compensatory and punitive damages. In *Check v. Andrews Hotel Co.* (1974), 56 D.L.R. (3d) 364 (Man. C.A.), the majority rejected these authorities in favour of *Fontin v. Katapodis* (1962), 108 C.L.R. 177 (H.C.A.) and *Lane v. Holloway*, [1968] 1 Q.B. 379 (C.A.). In both of these cases, the court held that provocation was only relevant in determining whether to award punitive damages. In *Murphy v. Culhane*, [1976] 3 All E.R. 533 (C.A.), Denning M.R. distinguished both *Fontin* and *Lane* as cases in which the plaintiff's conduct was trivial relative to the defendant's savage behaviour. Thus, Denning M.R. concluded that provocation could reduce compensatory damages.

In *Shaw v. Gorter* (1977), 77 D.L.R. (3d) 50 (Ont. C.A.), the Ontario Court of Appeal held that provocation was only relevant in determining whether to award punitive damages. However, in reaching this decision, the court erroneously stated that there were no Canadian cases directly on point. *Gorter* was followed with considerable reservations by MacKinnon A.C.J.O. in *Landry v. Patterson* (1978), 93 D.L.R. (3d) 345 (Ont. C.A.). He indicated that this issue should be resolved by the Supreme Court of Canada. What arguments would you make if you were appealing *Landry* to that court?

Courts in most other provinces have continued to view provocation as a factor that may reduce compensatory damages. See for example *Nichol v. MacKay* (1999), 180 N.S.R. (2d) 76 (C.A.); *Holt v. Verbruggen* (1981), 20 C.C.L.T. 29 (B.C.S.C.); *Hurley v. Moore* (1993), 112 Nfld. & P.E.I.R. 40 (Nfld. C.A.); *Defosse v. Wilde*, [1999] 4 W.W.R. 205 (Sask. Q.B.); *Hougen v. Kuehn*, 1997 CarswellAlta 847 (C.A.) (WLeC); and *Bruce v. Coliseum Management Ltd.* (1998), 165 D.L.R. (4th) 472 (B.C.C.A.).

6. In the jurisdictions in which provocation is not considered in reducing compensatory damages, should it nevertheless be taken into account in terms of aggravated damages? See *Dang v. Guiltner*, 1999 CarswellBC 1775 (S.C.) (WLeC).

7. It has been argued that a plaintiff's provocative act may constitute contributory negligence and thus give rise to an apportionment of damages under the provincial negligence acts. If this argument is accepted, the plaintiff's damages would be reduced by a specified percent to reflect his or her contributory negligence. See *Long v. Gardner* (1983), 144 D.L.R. (3d) 73 (Ont. H.C.); and *Rumsey v. R.*, [1984] 5 W.W.R. 585 (F.C.T.D.).

8. Unlike duress, provocation is not a defence in criminal law. Rather, under s. 232 of the *Criminal Code*, provocation operates to reduce a murder charge to manslaughter.

(b) MISTAKE

In tort law, a mistake occurs when defendants intend the consequences of their acts, but those consequences have a different factual or legal significance than that contemplated. Since mistake, by definition, has no effect on the issue of intent, it is not relevant in establishing the elements of a cause of action. Moreover, neither a mistake of fact nor a mistake of law is recognized *per se* as a defence to intentional tort liability.

HODGKINSON v. MARTIN
[1929] 1 D.L.R. 367 (B.C.C.A.)

MARTIN J.A.: This is an action for trespass to the person and in view of certain unusual incidents I have carefully read the whole appeal book in addition to those portions cited by counsel with the result that it was, in my opinion, open to the Judge below, upon the sharply conflicting evidence to take the view that the defendant, being the deputy minister of industries and industrial commissioner, laid his hands upon the plaintiff and wrongfully put him out of the office premises in question without using any more force than was necessary to effect that object, and that the act was unlawful and therefore a trespass, and that it was done in the sincerely mistaken belief that the defendant was justified in the protection of the interests of the Crown in doing so in order to retain access to the premises which had been in his possession through his servants for 10 days beforehand, and also that his intention in preserving such right of access was not to exclude the custodian in bankruptcy from the premises but to insure their common access thereto.

. . .

It then becomes a question of the amount of damages to be awarded, upon said facts and the appellant submits that the sum of $500 assessed below is excessive and can only be supported on the basis of exemplary damages which are foreign to the case. This, in my opinion, is the proper view to take of the matter which has been made too much of because while the sincere yet mistaken belief of the defendant in the propriety of his illegal action is no excuse therefor yet it is a mitigation of his liability which must be taken into consideration where not the slightest injury has been occasioned to the plaintiff's person, clothing or reputation. It is truly said in that high authority, Salmond on the Law of Torts, 7th ed., p. 145, that: – "Exemplary damages . . . . are given only in cases of conscious wrongdoing in contumelious disregard of another's rights." See Clerk & Lindsell on Torts, 7th ed., p. 140.

It is with reluctance that I feel compelled to interfere in the assessment of damages but having no doubt that nominal damages will amply compensate the plaintiff for the trespass it is my duty to give effect to my opinion by awarding the sum of $10. . . .

RANSON v. KITNER
31 Ill.App. 241 (1889)

CONGER J.: This was an action brought by appellee against appellants to recover the value of a dog killed by appellants, and a judgment rendered for $50.

The defense was that appellants were hunting for wolves, that appellee's dog had a striking resemblance to a wolf, that they in good faith believed it to be one, and killed it as such.

Many points are made, and a lengthy argument filed to show that error in the trial below was committed, but we are inclined to think that no material error occurred to the prejudice of appellants.

The jury held them liable for the value of the dog, and we do not see how they could have done otherwise under the evidence. Appellants are clearly liable for the damages caused by their mistake, notwithstanding they were acting in good faith.

We see no reason for interfering with the conclusion reached by the jury, and the judgment will be affirmed.

NOTES AND QUESTIONS

1. Are *Hodgkinson* and *Ranson* cases of mistake of fact or mistake of law? Can you suggest another example of each type of mistake?

2. What legal impact did the defendant's mistake have in *Hodgkinson* and *Ranson*? What did the judge mean in *Hodgkinson* when he said that the defendant's sincere but mistaken belief "is a mitigation of his liability?" Do you agree with the judge's use of the term "nominal damages" in *Hodgkinson*?

3. Would an individual be liable in intentional torts if he or she shot at a wolf, but the bullet ricocheted and hit a neighbour's dog? Compare this situation to that in *Ranson*.

4. What arguments would you make for recognizing a general defence of mistake? Would your answer depend on (a) the interest invaded by the mistaken defendant, or (b) whether it was a mistake of law or fact?

5. The impact of a mistake of fact on the validity of the defences varies. Thus, a defendant who strikes the plaintiff in a reasonable but mistaken belief that the latter is about to attack him or her may successfully plead self-defence. See *Keep v. Quallman*, 32 N.W. 233 (Wisc. S.C. 1887).

However, an honest but mistaken belief that the plaintiff consented provides no defence if, in fact, he or she has not. See for example *Turner v. Thorne* (1960), 21 D.L.R. (2d) 29 (Ont. H.C.); *Toews (Guardian ad litem of) v. Weisner* (2001), 3 C.C.L.T. (3d) 293 (B.C.S.C.); and *Cochran v. Hunter*, 2004 CarswellBC 2230 (S.C.) (WLeC). For a general explanation of why mistake invalidates some defences but not others, see Keeton *et al.*, *Prosser and Keeton on the Law of Torts*, 5th ed. (1984) at 110-12. See also Forbes, "Mistake of Fact with Regard to Defences in Tort Law" (1970) 4 Ottawa L. Rev. 304; and Hertz, "Volenti Non Fit Injuria: A Guide" in Klar, ed., *Studies in Canadian Tort Law* (1977) 101 at 105-108.

(c) ACCIDENT

In early English common law, the concept of inevitable accident was limited to cases in which the defendant could prove that the tort occurred utterly without fault on his or her part. As the principle of no liability without fault became increasingly entrenched in intentional torts, the definition of accident was broadened. The term "accident" is now used to refer to any situation in which the defendant unintentionally and without negligence injured the plaintiff. By definition, a defendant cannot be held liable in intentional torts or negligence for injuries caused by accident. It is the absence of intent that distinguishes accident from mistake.

REVIEW PROBLEMS

Analyze Mary's conduct in the following situations:

1. John shouted insults at Mary through an open window. In response, Mary threw a rock at John but missed, smashing a neighbour's window. The neighbour sues Mary.

2. Fred insulted Mary for several days. Later that week Mary spotted Fred standing at the window and threw a rock at him. Unknown to Mary, Fred's window was closed. The rock broke the window, but missed Fred. Fred sues Mary for the broken window.

3. Mary attempted to get Bill's attention by gently throwing a few small pebbles at his window. Unfortunately, one of the pebbles cracked the window. Bill sues Mary for the cracked window.

4. As Mary was leaving work she picked up what she thought was her wallet. In fact, it belonged to Ralph. On her way home, Mary was grabbed by a thief armed with a gun, who ordered Mary to hand over her wallet. Mary turned over Ralph's wallet, believing it to be her own. Analyze Mary's conduct (a) when she picked up Ralph's wallet, and (b) when she handed it to the thief.

(d) THE LIABILITY OF CHILDREN AND THOSE WITH A MENTAL ILLNESS

Children and those with a mental illness are governed by the general principles of liability in intentional torts. Thus, it should be determined whether the child's or mentally ill person's act was voluntary and intentional. Nevertheless, rather than applying the accepted tests of volition and intent, the Canadian courts have tended to apply different rules, based on what is now part of the *Criminal Code* defence of mental disorder in s. 16(1). The issue is often framed in terms of whether the specific defendant was capable of "appreciating the nature and quality" of his or her act. The courts have not explained why they have adopted this test, or how it relates to the concepts of volition and intent.

It should be noted that parents, teachers and others who supervise children are not held vicariously liable for the injuries and losses caused by a child. Rather, it must be established that they were a party to the child's wrongful conduct or, as is more often the case, that they were negligent in failing to supervise or control the child. While several provinces have enacted "parental responsibility" legislation, it too requires proof that the parent was personally negligent in supervising or controlling the child.

Similarly, individuals who are treating or supervising the mentally ill are not held vicariously liable for the harms caused by a patient or client. Under both the common law and the mental health statutes, doctors, nurses and other staff can only be held liable if they were a party to the patient's wrong or negligently failed to supervise or control him or her.

NOTES AND QUESTIONS

1. In *Tillander v. Gosselin*, [1967] 1 O.R. 203 (H.C.), aff'd (1967), 61 D.L.R. (2d) 192n (Ont. C.A.), the court held that a child just under the age of three could not be held liable in battery because he did not have "the mental ability to appreciate or know the real nature of the act he was performing." The defendant child had pulled an infant out

of her carriage and dragged her 100 feet. Would the result have been the same if the standard tests of volition and intent had been applied? Is the test used in *Tillander* easier to apply than the standard tests?

The child was also absolved of liability in negligence because he lacked sufficient judgment to exercise reasonable care. How does this test differ from the one that was used to determine liability in intentional torts?

2. See *Walmsley v. Humenick*, [1954] 2 D.L.R. 232 (B.C.S.C.); *Garrett v. Dailey*, 279 P.2d 1091 (Wash. S.C. 1955); and *Barclay v. Fournier* (1991), 112 N.B.R. (2d) 424 (Q.B.). In the first two cases, five-year-olds were held to have insufficient capacity for tort liability, whereas in the third case, the opposite conclusion was reached in regard to a nine-year-old defendant.

3. Section 13 of the *Criminal Code* provides that no child under 12 can be convicted of a criminal offence. Would you favour a statutory provision to govern a child's liability in tort? If so, what should be the age requirement? If not, what is the justification for adopting different principles for criminal and tortious liability?

4. As discussed in Chapter 11, parents, teachers and others are often sued for negligently failing to adequately control and supervise children. In such common law actions, the burden is on the plaintiff to prove that the defendant was negligent. In addition to the references in Chapter 11, see Wilson, "Parental Responsibility for the Acts of Children" (2000) 79 Can. Bar. Rev. 369 at 369-80.

5. The parental responsibility legislation in Ontario, Manitoba and British Columbia is similar. While the statutes impose the burden on parents to prove that they have acted reasonably in supervising their children, they are otherwise far narrower in scope than the common law. First, liability is limited to $10,000 in Ontario and British Columbia, and $7,500 in Manitoba. Second, liability is limited to property damage that the child has intentionally caused. See *Parental Responsibility Act, 2000*, S.O. 2000, c. 4; *Parental Responsibility Act*, C.C.S.M. c. P8; and *Parental Responsibility Act*, S.B.C. 2001, c. 45.

This legislation appears to have considerable political appeal and several other provinces have contemplated introducing such statutes. What are the arguments for and against such legislation? See Adjin-Tetty, "Significance and Consequences of Parental Responsibility Legislation" in Beauluc, Pitel & Schulz, eds., *The Joy of Torts* (2003) 221.

6. Some large retail chain stores have begun sending letters home to the parents of children who have been caught shoplifting. The letters typically inform the parents that they are legally responsible for the child's conduct and offer to settle the matter if the parents pay several hundred dollars to cover the store's alleged costs. Is there any common law or statutory basis for the stores' claims that the parents are civilly liable for these costs? See generally *B.(D.C.) v. Arkin*, [1996] 8 W.W.R. 100 (Man. Q.B.).

7. Although the parental responsibility statutes do not impose vicarious liability on parents, some of the education statutes do. For example, the *School Act*, R.S.B.C. 1996, c. 412, s. 10 requires parents of a student to pay for any damage to school property that results from their child's intentional or negligent acts. In *Coquitlam School District No.*

43 v. D.(T.W.) (1999), 170 D.L.R. (4th) 107 (B.C.C.A.), the defendants were held liable under the statute for $3 million in damages arising from the fire that their son had intentionally started. See also *Labrador School Board v. R.P.* (2003), 229 Nfld. & P.E.I.R. 105 (N.L.S.C. (T.D.)), in which the parents of a student were held liable under the provincial *Schools Act, 1997*, S.N.L. 1997, c. S-12.2, for the $7,000 in property damage that their son had intentionally caused.

8. The defendant in *Squittieri v. De Santis* (1976), 15 O.R. (2d) 416 (H.C.) was found not guilty by reason of insanity at his criminal trial. Even though he appreciated the nature and quality of his act in stabbing Squittieri, he did not know that it was wrong. In holding the defendant liable in battery, the court stated that the issue in a civil action is whether the defendant was capable of understanding the nature and quality of his actions.

Does this test relate to volition, intent or both issues? Why is the issue of whether the defendant knew that his conduct was wrong relevant in criminal, but not tort law?

Similar principles were applied in *Phillips v. Soloway* (1956), 6 D.L.R. (2d) 570 (Man. Q.B.); *Lawson v. Wellesley Hospital* (1975), 61 D.L.R. (3d) 445 (Ont. C.A.), aff'd on other grounds [1978] 1 S.C.R. 893; *Gerigs v. Rose* (1979), 9 C.C.L.T. 222 (Ont. H.C.); and *Whaley v. Cartusiano* (1990), 72 O.R. (2d) 523 (C.A.).

9. For a discussion of the liability of the mentally ill for other torts, see *Pochwalowski v. Tsai* (2003), 41 C.C.L.T. (3d) 124 (Ont. S.C.J.) (defamation); *Wenden v. Trikha* (1993), 135 A.R. 382 (C.A.); and *Fiala v. Cechmanek* (2001), 281 A.R. 248 (C.A.) (negligence). See also Picher, "The Tortious Liability of the Insane in Canada" (1975) 13 Osgoode Hall L.J. 193; and Coleman, "Mental Abnormality, Personal Responsibility, and Tort Liability" in Brody & Engelhardt, eds., *Mental Illness: Law and Public Policy* (1980) 107.

10. As indicated, those supervising or treating the mentally ill are not held vicariously liable for their patients' conduct. Rather, psychiatrists, psychiatric nurses and others providing such services can only be held liable when they are negligent in supervising or treating their patients. See for example *Mustafic v. Smith (G.)* (1988), 55 Man. R. (2d) 188 (C.A.); *Holan Estate v. Stanton Regional Health Board* (2001), 11 C.C.L.T. (3d) 34 (N.W.T.S.C.); and *Ahmed v. Stefaniu* (2006), 216 O.A.C. 323 (C.A.).

4. Battery

BETTEL v. YIM

(1978), 88 D.L.R. (3d) 543 (Ont. Co. Ct.)

BORINS CO. CT. J.: In this action the infant plaintiff, Howard Bettel, seeks damages for assault. His father, Murray Bettel, seeks special damages in the amount of $1,113. . . .

The facts

The events giving rise to this action took place on May 22, 1976, in a variety store owned and operated by the defendant, Ki Yim, situated in a small commercial plaza located in Metropolitan Toronto.

. . .

The defendant testified that the plaintiff, together with six or seven other boys, entered the store and went to the area of the pin-ball machines. Some of the boys were playing with a toy football and toy guns and the defendant told them to leave his store. Half of the boys, including the plaintiff, left and went outside. The defendant saw the plaintiff lighting matches and throwing them into the store. On the first occasion the plaintiff entered the store and retrieved a burning match. The second match that was thrown into the store burned itself out. Then the plaintiff re-entered the store, proceeded toward the pin-ball machines and said "What's the smell?" The defendant smelled nothing, but after 20 or 30 seconds he saw flames coming from the bag of charcoal and proceeded to remove the bag from the store unassisted by the plaintiff who remained inside. The defendant did not see [who had] thrown the match which started the fire.

As the defendant returned to the store he saw the plaintiff walking toward the door. He grabbed the plaintiff by the arm as he did not want the plaintiff to leave. The plaintiff denied that he set the fire. The plaintiff did not try to leave. He stood where he was. Because the plaintiff denied setting the fire the defendant grabbed him firmly by the collar with both hands and began shaking him. His purpose in doing so was to obtain a confession from the plaintiff before he called the police. The plaintiff's constant denials had made the defendant unhappy. He shook the plaintiff two or three times and then his head came down and struck the plaintiff's nose. He relaxed his hold on the plaintiff who fell to the ground. The defendant obtained some kleenex for the plaintiff, who was bleeding from the nose, and helped him to his feet. The defendant then telephoned the police.

In explaining the incident the defendant said: "I shook him maybe three times and my head and his nose accidentally hit; I didn't intend to hit him." In cross-examination he stated that he did not mean to hit the plaintiff with his head and that is why he said it was an accident. . . .

The law

The plaintiff has framed his action in assault. Properly speaking the action should have been framed in battery which is the intentional infliction upon the body of another of a harmful or offensive contact. However, in Canada it would appear that the distinction between assault and battery has been blurred and when one speaks of an assault, it may include a battery: *Gambriell v. Caparelli* (1974), 7 O.R. (2d) 205, 54 D.L.R. (3d) 661. It is on the basis that this is an action framed in battery that I approach the facts in this case.

It would appear to be well established in this country (although not necessarily warmly received), following the dictum of Cartwright, J. (as he then was), in *Cook v. Lewis*, [1951] S.C.R. 830 at p. 839, [1952] 1 D.L.R. 1 at p. 15, that once the plaintiff proves that he was injured by the direct act of the defendant, the defendant is entitled to judgment only "if he satisfies the onus of establishing the absence of both intention and negligence on his part": *Dahlberg v. Naydiuk* (1969), 10 D.L.R. (3d) 319, 72 W.W.R. 210 (Man. C.A.), *per* Dickson, J.A. (as he then was), at pp. 328-9. On the defendant's evidence, his act in grabbing the plaintiff with both his hands and shaking him constituted the intentional tort of battery. It is obvious that he desired to bring about an offensive or harmful contact with the plaintiff for the purpose of extracting a confession from him. Viewed as such, the defendant's own evidence proves, rather than disproves, the element of intent in so far as this aspect of his physical contact with the plaintiff is concerned. Indeed, the defendant's admitted purpose in grabbing and shaking the plaintiff does not fit into any of the accepted defences to the tort of battery – consent, self-defence, defence of property, necessity and legal authority: Fleming, *Law of Torts*, 5th ed. (1977), p. 74 *et seq*. . . .

That there is no liability for accidental harm is central to the submission of defence counsel who argues that the shaking of the plaintiff by the defendant and the striking of the plaintiff by the defendant's head must be regarded as separate and distinct incidents. While he concedes that the defendant intentionally grabbed and shook the plaintiff, he submits that the contact with the head was unintentional. I have, of course, accepted the defendant's evidence in this regard. This, in my view, gives rise to the important question: Can an intentional wrongdoer be held liable for consequences which he did not intend? Another way of stating the problem is to ask whether the doctrine of foreseeability as found in the law of negligence is applicable to the law of intentional torts? Should an intentional wrongdoer be liable only for the reasonably foreseeable consequences of his intentional application of force or should he bear responsibility for all the consequences which flow from his intentional act?

To approach this issue one must first examine what interests the law seeks to protect. A thorough discussion of the history of the old actions of trespass and case is found in Prosser, *Law of Torts*, 4th ed. (1971), p. 28 *et seq.* Terms such as battery, assault and false imprisonment, which were varieties of trespass, have come to be associated with intent. The old action on the case has emerged as the separate tort of negligence. Today it is recognized that there should be no liability for pure accident, and that for there to be liability the defendant must be found at fault, in the sense of being chargeable with a wrongful intent, or with negligence. Thus, "with rare exceptions, actions for injuries to the person, or to tangible property, now require proof of an intent to inflict them, or of failure to exercise proper care": Prosser, *supra*, p. 30.

In discussing battery Fleming writes, *supra*, pp. 23-4:

> Of the various forms of trespass to the person the most common is the tort known as battery, which is committed by intentionally bringing about a harmful or offensive contact with the person of another. The action, therefore, serves the dual purpose of affording protection to the individual not only against bodily harm but also against any interference with his person which is offensive to a reasonable sense of honour and dignity. The insult involved in being touched without consent has been traditionally regarded as sufficient to warrant redress, even though the interference is only trivial and not attended with actual physical harm. "The least touching of another in anger is a battery", and so is such offensive and insulting behaviour as spitting in another man's face, cutting his hair or kissing a woman. The element of personal indignity is given additional recognition in the award of aggravated damages to compensate for any outrage to the plaintiff's feelings . . .
>
> . . . . .
>
> Battery is an intentional wrong: the offensive contact must have been intended or known to be substantially certain to result. On the other hand, it is not necessary that the actor intended to inflict bodily harm, since we have seen that the legal injury is complete without it. Indeed it may be sufficient that he intended only to frighten but in a manner fraught with serious risk of bodily contact or harm. [Footnotes omitted]

. . .

It is my respectful view that the weight of opinion is that the concept of foreseeability as defined by the law of negligence is a concept that ought not to be imported into the field of intentional torts. While strong policy reasons favour determining the other limits of liability where conduct falls below an acceptable standard, the same reasons do not apply to deliberate conduct, even though the ultimate result in terms of harm caused to plaintiff is not what was intended by the defendant. In the law of intentional torts, it is the dignitary interest, the right of the plaintiff to insist that the defendant keep his hands to himself, that the law has for centuries sought to protect. In doing so, the morality of the defendant's conduct, characterized as "unlawful", has predominated the thinking of the Courts and is reflected in academic discussions. The logical test is whether the defendant was guilty of deliberate, intentional and unlawful violence or threats of violence. If he was, and a more serious harm befalls the plaintiff than was intended by the defendant, the defendant, and not the innocent plaintiff, must bear the responsibility for the unintended result. If physical contact was intended, the fact that its magnitude exceeded all reasonable or intended expectations should make no difference. To hold otherwise, in my opinion, would unduly narrow recovery where one deliberately invades the bodily interests of another with the result that the totally innocent plaintiff would be deprived of full recovery for the totality of the injuries suffered as a result of the deliberate invasion of his bodily interests. To import negligence concepts into the field of intentional torts would be to ignore the essential difference between the intentional infliction of harm and the unintentional infliction of harm resulting from a failure to adhere to a reasonable standard of care and would result in bonusing the deliberate wrongdoer who strikes the plaintiff more forcefully than intended. . . .

I have, therefore, reached the conclusion that the defendant must bear the responsibility for the injury suffered by the plaintiff. The defendant intentionally grabbed the plaintiff and shook him. This constituted a battery. While he was shaking the plaintiff, the defendant's head came into contact with the plaintiff's nose and injured it. This was the end result of a brief chain of events set in motion by the defendant. Subjectively, the defendant did not intend to strike the plaintiff's nose. Legally, because it was the result of the defendant's intentional interference with the plaintiff, responsibility for the injury which it caused must fall on the defendant.

NOTES AND QUESTIONS

1. How did Borins J. define battery? Identify the act of the defendant that gave rise to this tort. Why was the burden of disproving intent and negligence imposed on the defendant? Would the result have been the same if the burden of proving these issues had been on the plaintiff? See *Hatton v. Webb* (1977), 81 D.L.R. (3d) 377 (Alta. Dist. Ct.).

2. Are Borins J.'s reasons for holding individuals liable for all the consequences of their intentional acts compelling? Would it have made a difference if he had limited recovery to foreseeable losses? See Klar, "Annotation" (1978), 5 C.C.L.T. 66; and *Mahal v. Young* (1986), 36 C.C.L.T. 143 (B.C.S.C.), a case in which the defendant was held liable for the plaintiff's unforeseeable depressive reaction to the defendant's assault.

3. Could the defendant have successfully argued provocation? If so, what effect would it have had on the damage award? Given the facts of *Bettel*, would you advocate that provocation be taken into account to reduce compensatory damages?

4. The tort of battery is very much concerned with protecting an individual's dignity. Consequently, a plaintiff who is publicly slapped in the face or touched in a sexually inappropriate manner may be awarded far greater damages than a plaintiff who is punched by a friend in horseplay and suffers much greater physical pain and injury.

5. While the defendant must have intent to bring about a physical contact, he or she need not intend that contact to be harmful or socially offensive: see *Wilson v. Pringle*, [1986] 2 All E.R. 440 at 445 (C.A.).

6. The tort of battery prohibits a very broad range of physical interferences with the person. See for example *Stewart v. Stonehouse* (1926), 20 Sask. L.R. 459 (C.A.) (grabbing someone's nose); *Alcorn v. Mitchell*, 63 Ill. 553 (S.C. 1872) (spitting in someone's face); *Pursell v. Horn* (1838), 112 E.R. 966 (K.B.) (pouring water on someone); *Forde v. Skinner* (1830), 172 E.R. 687 (N.P.) (cutting someone's hair); and *Malette v. Shulman* (1990), 72 O.R. (2d) 417 (C.A.) (administering a blood transfusion).

7. A plaintiff may recover in battery even if he or she has suffered no physical harm or injury. See for example *Culter v. Smith* (1977), 25 N.S.R. (2d) 5 (S.C. (T.D.)). Indeed in *Malette*, *supra*, the blood transfusions for which the doctor was held liable in battery likely saved the plaintiff's life. A plaintiff need not be aware of the physical contact at the time in order to recover in battery. Thus, a woman kissed in her sleep would have a battery claim against her assailant.

8. A defendant may also be held liable in battery for intentionally interfering with anything that the plaintiff is carrying, wearing or riding on: see *Morgan v. Loyacomo*, 1 So.2d 510 (Miss. S.C. 1941).

9. In keeping with its historical origins, a battery can only be committed when the defendant undertakes a positive act which causes a physical contact. For example, blocking another's path will not constitute a battery, although it may give rise to liability in false imprisonment. See *Innes v. Wylie* (1844), 174 E.R. 800 (Q.B.). But see *MacDonald v. Sebastian* (1987), 81 N.S.R. (2d) 189 (S.C. (T.D.)), where the defendant landlord was held liable in battery for failing to inform the plaintiff that the water supply was contaminated with arsenic.

10. Battery was traditionally confined to cases of directly caused injury. Consequently, if the plaintiff was indirectly injured by having his or her food poisoned or a trap set in his or her path, the plaintiff could not claim in battery. American authorities have redefined battery to include such indirect physical interferences, and some Canadian authors have followed suit. Most Commonwealth authors, however, have maintained the requirement of direct injury. See *Restatement (Second) of the Law of Torts* (1965) at §13(b); and Sullivan, "Trespass to the Person in Canada: A Defence of the Traditional Approach" (1987) 19 Ottawa L. Rev. 533. What position did the court adopt in *Bettel*?

11. A defendant's conduct will often give rise to both a criminal charge of assault and a civil action in battery. In *Simpson v. Geswein* (1995), 25 C.C.L.T. (2d) 49 (Man. Q.B.), it was held that the certificate of conviction and the judge's reasons in the criminal trial were admissible as evidence in a subsequent civil action arising from the same event. The certificate and reasons were not to be regarded as conclusive proof, but as

strong *prima facie* evidence. Should a defendant be allowed to introduce into evidence the fact that the police did not lay criminal charges or dropped the criminal charges against him or her? Should a defendant's acquittal be admissible as strong *prima facie* proof in a subsequent civil action?

12. As illustrated by *B.(P.) v. B.(W.)* (1992), 11 O.R. (3d) 161 (Gen. Div.), which was included in the previous chapter, there has been an extremely dramatic rise in the number of civil claims brought by the victims of childhood sexual abuse. Many of these cases involve conduct that occurred 10, 15 or even 20 years ago – long after the general limitation period has expired. Limitation periods are set by statute, and they establish the time within which a plaintiff must commence an action. In this particular area, the courts have been increasingly willing to postpone the running of the limitation period until such time as the plaintiff becomes aware of the wrongful conduct and the harms that it has caused, and is psychologically capable of dealing with it and its harmful consequences: *M.(K.) v. M.(H.)*, [1992] 3 S.C.R. 6. Therefore, the commencement of the limitation period therefore may be delayed if (a) the plaintiff was aware of the assaults but did not recognize the physical and psychological problems associated with them, or (b) the plaintiff had no recollection of the assaults, because of the trauma, until sometime after they occurred. See also *E.D.G. v. Hammer*, [2003] 2 S.C.R. 459; and *Blackwater v. Plint*, [2005] 3 S.C.R. 3.

The court in *M.(K.)* also held that since the cause of action for breach of fiduciary duty is equitable, it was not subject to the applicable limitations statute. In several subsequent cases, the limitation period has been avoided by classifying the defendant's wrong as a breach of fiduciary duty. See for example *A.(D.A.) v. B.(D.K.)* (1995), 27 C.C.L.T. (2d) 256 (Ont. Gen. Div.); and *R.(J.) v. W.(E.S.)* (2001), 52 O.R. (3d) 353 (S.C.J.). The wording of some of the limitation statutes may not permit the ultimate limitation period to be avoided. See *Moar v. Roman Catholic Church of Canada* (2001), 205 D.L.R. (4th) 253 (Man. C.A.); and *Limitations Act, 2002*, S.O. 2002, c. 24, s. 15(2). In contrast, other statutes expressly provide that victims of sexual assaults can bring actions regardless of any limitation period that might otherwise apply. See for example *Limitation Act*, R.S.B.C. 1996, c. 266, s. 3(4)(k) and (l).

(a) THE BURDEN OF PROOF IN SEXUAL ABUSE CASES

Until relatively recently, it was generally accepted in Canada that once the plaintiff established that he or she was subject to a direct and intentional physical contact, the burden of proof was on the defendant to establish consent or some other defence. This issue came before the Supreme Court of Canada in *Non-Marine Underwriters, Lloyd's of London v. Scalera*, [2000] 1 S.C.R. 551, a somewhat complex case involving insurance coverage. A majority of the court ruled that the plaintiff had no obligation to establish that she did not consent. Rather, the burden was on the defendant to assert and prove consent. The minority agreed that this principle should generally apply in battery cases, because it is reasonable to assume a lack of consent in most cases. However, the minority contended that a contrary assumption about consent was appropriate for some forms of bodily contact, such as that occurring in sports or sexual situations.

NOTES AND QUESTIONS

1. In *Scalera*, is the majority or minority position more compelling? See generally McInnes, "Sexual Battery and Proof of Consent" (2001) 9 Tort L. Rev. 27.

2. The prevailing view in England and New Zealand is that the plaintiff must prove the absence of consent as an element of his or her battery claim. See *Christopherson v. Bare* (1848), 116 E.R. 554 (Q.B.); *Freeman v. Home Office (No. 2)*, [1984] Q.B. 524 (C.A.); *H. v. R.*, [1996] 1 N.Z.L.R. 299 (H.C.); and *S. v. G.*, [1995] 3 N.Z.L.R. 681 (C.A.). While the issue has yet to be settled in Australia, there is strong *obiter dicta* in the High Court that a *prima facie* case of battery is established once the plaintiff proves a direct interference, such that the issue of consent arises only as a defence. See *Secretary, Department of Health and Community Services v. J.W.B.* (1992), 175 C.L.R. 218 (H.C.A.); and *Sibley v. Milutinovic*, [1990] Aust. Torts Reports 81-013 (A.C.T.).

3. It is generally agreed that accepted social practices, such as gently tapping a person on the shoulder to get his or her attention or jostling a fellow occupant while leaving an elevator, will not give rise to an action in battery. Should such socially accepted practices be excused because they do not constitute batteries or because they are viewed as being justified by implied consent? Is there any practical significance between those two choices? See *Coward v. Baddeley* (1859), 157 E.R. 927 (Ex. Div.); and *Donnelly v. Jackman*, [1970] 1 All E.R. 987 (Q.B.). See also *Wilson v. Pringle*, [1987] Q.B. 237 (C.A.), where the court suggested that ordinary school horseplay might constitute an accepted social practice.

4. Should the plaintiff's, defendant's or society's perspective be adopted in defining acceptable social practices? Should the test be objective or subjective? Would the practice of a hostess, who greeted guests at her party with a kiss, subject her to liability in battery? Would it make any difference if one of the guests considered such conduct to be immoral, unsanitary and extremely offensive? How would you resolve the issue of liability in a case where a female interpreted a male associate's affectionate greeting as a sexual assault and struck him in self-defence? See *Cachay v. Nemeth* (1972), 28 D.L.R. (3d) 603 (Sask. Q.B.).

5. The defence of consent is considered in greater detail in Chapter 6.

5. Assault

The tort of assault may be defined as the intentional creation in the mind of another of a reasonable apprehension of immediate physical contact. It has been stated that conditional threats, future threats, and words alone, without some overt act, cannot constitute assault. However, the courts have reconsidered these limitations and increasingly focus instead on the impression created in the plaintiff's mind.

NOTES AND QUESTIONS

1. The defendant threw a chair at B who ducked, as did C, D and E, the three people standing behind B. The chair hit F and G who were standing nearby. F saw the chair

coming but could not get out of the way, and G had his back turned. Which parties have been assaulted by the defendant?

2. Can a police officer who stands passively in a doorway, blocking the plaintiff's path, be held liable in assault? If the plaintiff continues walking towards the motionless officer, making a collision inevitable, would the officer have a cause of action in assault? See *Innes v. Wylie* (1844), 174 E.R. 800 (Q.B.).

3. Would a 50-kilogram unarmed man be held liable in assault for threatening to hit a 120-kilogram professional boxer who viewed the threat with arrogant indifference? If so, what interests would be served by the tort? See *Brady v. Schatzel*, [1911] Qd. S.R. 206 (S.C.).

4. It has been held that once the defendant has the apparent intent and ability to cause physical contact, whether he or she actually intends, or has the ability, to do so is irrelevant. For example, as a practical joke, the staff of the Club Med in Cancun staged a very realistic bus hijacking. Two guests held at gunpoint for 30 minutes sued, claiming $1,000,000 each in assault and false imprisonment. See "Practical joke victims seek their last laughs in court" *Ontario Lawyers Weekly* (5 April 1985) 14. See also *R. v. St. George* (1840), 173 E.R. 921 (N.P.); and *Kennedy v. Hanes*, [1941] S.C.R. 384.

5. Damage awards for assault unaccompanied by battery are often small. See *Stephens v. Myers* (1830), 172 E.R. 735 (C.P.), where the plaintiff was awarded one shilling. However, in *Mahal v. Young* (1986), 36 C.C.L.T. 143 (B.C.S.C.), the plaintiff was awarded $6,000 damages in assault arising from the defendant's unprovoked threat to kill him. The defendant had previously assaulted the plaintiff and they worked together under circumstances in which the defendant could readily carry out the threat. The plaintiff suffered from severe depression following the threat and missed several months of work. See also *Sirois v. Gustafson*, [2003] 3 W.W.R. 110 (Sask. Q.B.).

6. If the assault is a prelude to battery, the assault may be discussed superficially and not considered in assessing damages. Nevertheless, the occurrence of an assault may colour the court's interpretation of subsequent events. The fact that the defendant was assaulted may provide the basis for a defence of consent or self-defence, or for raising the issue of provocation. See *Bruce v. Dyer* (1966), 58 D.L.R. (2d) 211 (Ont. H.C.), aff'd (1967), 8 D.L.R. (3d) 592 (Ont. C.A.).

HOLCOMBE v. WHITAKER

318 So.2d 289 (Ala. S.C. 1975)

SHORES J.: . . .The next issue argued by defendant [a doctor] concerns the assault count. The plaintiff claimed that the defendant committed an assault when in June of 1971, she went to see him and tried to get him to get an annulment, he said "If you take me to court, I will kill you."; and again in October, 1971, after she had filed the instant suit on September 29, 1971, when he went to her apartment and beat on the door, tried to pry it open, and said again, "If you take me to court, I will kill you." (The complaint was amended to include this act.) The defendant claims this in no way can constitute an assault, because it was merely a conditional threat of violence and because no overt act was involved. . . .

While words standing alone cannot constitute an assault, they may give meaning to an act and both, taken together, may constitute an assault. Prosser, supra (2nd Ed. 1955). In addition, words may negative an act in a manner that apprehension in such a case would be unreasonable. "On the other hand, a show of force accompanied by an unlawful or unjustifiable demand, compliance with which will avert the threatened battery, is an assault." 1 Harper & James, The Law of Torts, page 223 (1956). ". . . the defendant is not free to compel the plaintiff to buy his safety by compliance with a condition which there is no legal right to impose." Prosser, supra, page 40 (4th Ed. 1971). It is obvious that the defendant in the instant case had no right to impose the condition he did on the plaintiff; and we cannot say that this condition explained away his threat to harm her.

The defendant says his conduct cannot constitute an assault because there was no overt action taken by him. The evidence from the plaintiff was that the defendant was pounding on her door making every effort to get into the apartment, and threatening to kill her if she persisted in "taking him to court." We cannot say, as a matter of law, that this was not sufficient to arouse an apprehension of harm or offensive conduct. We think it was a jury question, as was the question of whether the defendant had the apparent ability to effectuate the threatened act.

. . .

According to the testimony offered on behalf of the plaintiff, the doctor succeeded in his efforts to frighten the plaintiff. She was fearful enough to ask friends to stay with her at night; never left the apartment alone after the threats on her life; had her brother-in-law nail the windows closed after the break-in of her apartment; and told one of her friends that she was afraid there might be poison in her coffee. We believe this testimony was relevant under the circumstances of this case. The defendant threatened to kill the plaintiff if she did something she had a legal right to do. We think the evidence of what occurred subsequent to his threats and emanating from them was relevant to the issues being tried.

POLICE v. GREAVES

[1964] N.Z.L.R. 295 (C.A.)

The facts were these – a Mrs. Tolley who occupied with her children a State house situate in Kowhai Street, Naenae, called on the police for help after she had been attacked by the respondent who also resided in the house. It appears that he was somewhat inebriated. When two policemen arrived, the respondent came to the door with a carving knife in his right hand poised at waist height and pointed towards the leading constable, and said, "Don't you bloody move. You come a . . . step closer and you will get this straight through your – guts." The leading constable continued, "The defendant was in a maniacal mood . . . and was not prepared to listen to any reasoning at all. He said, . . .'Get off this – property before you get this in your guts.' "

The constables, faced with this threat, withdrew to obtain further assistance.

The appellant was convicted of assault in the Magistrate's Court but the conviction was quashed in the Supreme Court on the ground that the threat made by the appellant was a conditional one and did not constitute an assault.

The prosecutor appealed by special leave to the Court of Appeal.

. . .

NORTH P.: . . . In our opinion, if the other conditions of the definition were met – as they undoubtedly were – there is no reason why a conditional threat should not constitute an assault. A threat in its very nature usually provides the person threatened with an alternative, unpleasant though it may often be. It is only necessary to recall the oft repeated threat of the highwayman, "Your money or your life" to see that if a pistol be pointed at the victim it would be idle to say that there was not a threat to apply force to the person of another in circumstances in which the person making the threat had, or at least caused the other to believe on reasonable grounds that he had, present ability to effect his purpose, and therefore that an assault had been committed. On the facts of the present case it was enough that the menacing attitude of the respondent caused the police officers to retire. . . . The present case is to be distinguished from such cases as *Tubervell* v. *Savadge* (1669) 1 Mod. 3; 86 E.R. 684, where the person from whom the threat came made it clear that he had no present intention of carrying out his threat. In that case the words used were, "Were it not assize . . . time" he would tell more of his mind.

With all respect for the view of the learned Judge, we do not think that *Read* v. *Coker* (1853) 13 C.B. 850; 138 E.R. 1437 which was relied on by the prosecution is distinguishable from the present case. There the plaintiff, being in the defendant's workshop and refusing to quit when desired, was surrounded by the defendant's servants, who tucked up their sleeves and aprons and threatened to break his neck if he did not go out. It was argued that this did not constitute an assault, but the Court was clearly of opinion that it did, Jervis C.J. saying, "If anything short of actual striking will in law constitute an assault, . . . the facts here clearly show that the defendant was guilty of an assault. . . . There was a threat of violence exhibiting an intention to assault and . . . a present ability to carry the threat into execution" (*ibid.*, 860; 1441). There is not the slightest suggestion in the argument or in the judgment that the fact that the plaintiff was offered an alternative prevented the threat from constituting an assault. Again, in *Blake* v. *Barnard* (1840) 9 Car. & P. 626; 173 E.R. 985, the report of Lord Abinger's summing up to the jury makes no point of the fact that the cocked pistol presented at the defendant's head was accompanied by the statement that "if Blake was not quiet he would blow his brains . . . out." We can see no difference in principle between a demand that the person threatened should retire and a demand that he should not proceed further on his lawful occasions. The policemen were present here on their lawful occasions and their entry was barred; that in our opinion was sufficient. But in any event – though nothing was made of this either in the Court below or before us – it would appear that in fact both kinds of threats were made.

NOTES AND QUESTIONS

1. In *Holcombe*, the judge indicated that words alone, without some overt act, cannot give rise to assault. Although this principle has been accepted in cases of insulting or abusive language, it has been criticized where the words were intended to cause, and in fact caused, a reasonable apprehension of imminent physical contact. As indicated in Keeton *et al.*, *Prosser and Keeton on the Law of Torts*, 5th ed. (1984) at 45: "It is the immediate physical threat which is important, rather than the manner in which it is conveyed." Had the defendant in *Holcombe* merely threatened to kill the plaintiff and not engaged in any other aggressive conduct, would he have been held liable in assault?

See Handford, "Tort Liability For Threatening or Insulting Words" (1976) 54 Can. Bar Rev. 563.

2. In *Fogden v. Wade*, [1945] N.Z.L.R. 724 (S.C.), the accused was convicted of assault when he approached a woman and, while he was close enough to touch her, stated: "Don't go in yet, you've got time for a quick one." The woman screamed and the accused ran off without touching her. Would the accused's conduct have constituted an assault in tort law?

3. How did the court in *Greaves* distinguish the case of *Tubervell*? Given that the essence of assault is the impression created in the plaintiff's mind, is this distinction valid? On what basis, if any, would you distinguish *Tubervell* and *Holcombe*?

In *Greaves*, the court also distinguished between conditional threats that require the plaintiff to take immediate action to avoid the threat and those that do not. Is this distinction justifiable?

4. To what extent was the decision in *Greaves* influenced by the fact that the officers were under a legal duty to apprehend the defendant? Had the defendant made the same threat to a door-to-door salesperson, would he or she have had an action in assault? See *Restatement (Second) of the Law of Torts* (1965) at §30.

5. Generally, future threats will not constitute assault because of the requirement of immediacy. The early cases suggest that the threat must be capable of being carried out at once. See for example *Stephens v. Myers* (1830), 172 E.R. 735 (C.P.). However, given the courts' focus on the impact of the defendant's threat on the plaintiff, the immediacy requirement will likely be relaxed. At what point in the following scenario would the immediacy requirement be met? The defendant, who lives 30 minutes away, calls and threatens to come over and beat up the plaintiff. The defendant calls while en route and repeats the threat. The defendant calls from a pay phone across from the plaintiff's apartment. The defendant knocks on the plaintiff's door.

6. In *R. v. Ireland*, [1997] 1 All E.R. 112 (C.A.), the defendant made a large number of telephone calls to three women and remained silent when they answered. The Court of Appeal held that he was guilty of criminal assault. It stated that the material act was the making of the calls and that it was irrelevant whether words or silence ensued. In either event, the nature of the calls was such that they were likely to cause the victims to apprehend immediate and unlawful violence. The court also stated that it was irrelevant that there was no immediate proximity between the accused and the victims because fear could be instilled over the telephone. Should Canadian courts follow this decision?

7. Even if the defendant's conduct falls short of assault, it may give rise to liability for other torts, such as intentional infliction of nervous shock, defamation or intimidation. The criminal law also prohibits a broad range of offensive, obscene and racist conduct. See for example the *Criminal Code*, s. 264 (criminal harassment), s. 264.1 (uttering threats), ss. 298 and 301 (defamatory libel), ss. 318-320 (hate propaganda), s. 346 (extortion) and s. 372 (indecent or harassing telephone calls and letters).

8. Summarize the legal principles governing the tort of assault.

REVIEW PROBLEMS

1. George drove to a gas station and asked Ralph, the attendant, to fill up his car. Ralph was distracted by some other customers and did not return for 10 minutes. George, furious at the delay, called him an incompetent fool. Ralph, who was 10 metres away, threatened to beat George's brains in if he did not apologize immediately. George approached Ralph, punched him in the head once and walked away. Ralph picked up a wrench and threw it at George, who ducked. The wrench struck Tom, who was walking on the sidewalk 15 metres in front of the station.

Ralph has sought your advice on the legal actions he may bring, and the liability he may have incurred, in assault and battery.

2. The defendant attempted to rob a bank with an unloaded shotgun. When a police officer rushed in, the defendant threatened to shoot Stella, a teller, if the officer came any closer. Stella, who was standing three metres from the defendant, fainted when the threat was made and fell to the floor, fracturing her skull. Stella and the officer wish to know whether they would succeed in an assault action.

6. False Imprisonment

Originally designed to provide a remedy for wrongful incarceration, the tort of false imprisonment now encompasses most situations in which an individual's movement is intentionally restrained. The restraint of movement must be total, even if only momentary. The restraint may be imposed by barriers, other physical means, an implicit or explicit threat of force, or an implicit or explicit assertion of legal authority. Although often discussed as an element of the tort, the issue of whether the imprisonment was lawfully justified *(i.e.* false) is treated by the courts as a defence which the defendant must raise and prove.

BIRD v. JONES

(1845), 115 E.R. 668 (Q.B.)

COLERIDGE J. . . . [T]he plaintiff, being in a public highway [Hammersmith Bridge] and desirous of passing along it, in a particular direction, is prevented from doing so by the orders of the defendant, and that the defendant's agents for the purpose are policemen, from whom, indeed, no unnecessary violence was to be anticipated, or such as they believed unlawful, yet who might be expected to execute such commands as they deemed lawful with all necessary force, however resisted. But, although thus obstructed, the plaintiff was at liberty to move his person and go in any other direction, at his free will and pleasure: and no actual force or restraint on his person was used, unless the obstruction before mentioned amounts to so much. .

. . .

And I am of opinion that there was no imprisonment. To call it so appears to me to confound partial obstruction and disturbance with total obstruction and detention. A prison may have its boundary large or narrow, visible and tangible, or, though real, still in the conception only; it may itself be moveable or fixed: but a boundary it must have;

and that boundary the party imprisoned must be prevented from passing; he must be prevented from leaving that place, within the ambit of which the party imprisoning would confine him, except by prison-breach. Some confusion seems to me to arise from confounding imprisonment of the body with mere loss of freedom: it is one part of the definition of freedom to be able to go whithersoever one pleases; but imprisonment is something more than the mere loss of this power; it includes the notion of restraint within some limits defined by a will or power exterior to our own.

. . .

PATTESON J. . . . I have no doubt that, in general, if one man compels another to stay in any given place against his will, he imprisons that other just as much as if he locked him up in a room: and I agree that it is not necessary, in order to constitute an imprisonment, that a man's person should be touched. I agree, also, that the compelling a man to go in a given direction against his will may amount to imprisonment. But I cannot bring my mind to the conclusion that, if one man merely obstructs the passage of another in a particular direction, whether by threat of personal violence or otherwise, leaving him at liberty to stay where he is or to go in any other direction if he pleases, he can be said thereby to imprison him. He does him wrong, undoubtedly, if there was a right to pass in that direction, and would be liable to an action on the case for obstructing the passage, or of assault, if, on the party persisting in going in that direction, he touched his person, or so threatened him as to amount to an assault. But imprisonment is, as I apprehend, a total restraint of the liberty of the person, for however short a time, and not a partial obstruction of his will, whatever inconvenience it may bring on him. The quality of the act cannot, however, depend on the right of the opposite party. If it be an imprisonment to prevent a man passing along the public highway, it must be equally so to prevent him passing further along a field into which he has broken by a clear act of trespass.

. . .

LORD DENMAN C.J. [dissenting] . . . A company unlawfully obstructed a public way for their own profit, extorting money from passengers, and hiring policemen to effect this purpose. The plaintiff, wishing to exercise his right of way, is stopped by force, and ordered to move in a direction which he wished not to take. He is told at the same time that a force is at hand ready to compel his submission. That proceeding appears to me equivalent to being pulled by the collar out of the one line and into the other.

. . .

I had no idea that any person in these times supposed any particular boundary to be necessary to constitute imprisonment, or that the restraint of a man's person from doing what he desires ceases to be an imprisonment because he may find some means of escape.

It is said that the party here was at liberty to go in another direction. I am not sure that in fact he was, because the same unlawful power which prevented him from taking one course might, in case of acquiescence, have refused him any other. But this liberty to do something else does not appear to me to affect the question of imprisonment. As long as I am prevented from doing what I have a right to do, of what importance is it that I am permitted to do something else? How does the imposition of an unlawful condition shew that I am not restrained? If I am locked in a room, am I not imprisoned because I might effect my escape through a window, or because I might find an exit dangerous or inconvenient to myself, as by wading through water or by taking a route so circuitous that my necessary affairs would suffer by delay?

. . .

It is said that, if any damage arises from such obstruction, a special action on the case may be brought. Must I then sue out a new writ stating that the defendant employed direct force to prevent my going where my business called me, whereby I sustained loss? And, if I do, is it certain that I shall not be told that I have misconceived my remedy, for all flows from the false imprisonment, and that should have been subject of an action of trespass and assault? For the jury properly found that the whole of the defendant's conduct was continuous: it commenced in illegality; and the plaintiff did right to resist it as an outrageous violation of the liberty of the subject from the very first.

NOTES AND QUESTIONS

1. Although the law is settled, do you prefer the majority or minority view of false imprisonment? What problems, if any, would arise from adopting the minority definition?

2. Would it have made any difference to the majority if the plaintiff had been on an urgent business trip that could not have been delayed without serious financial loss? Should it make any difference if the defendant's purpose in obstructing the bridge was praiseworthy?

3. Since false imprisonment will not lie in the absence of total restraint, the court may have to determine if there was a reasonable means of escape known to the plaintiff. Clearly, the plaintiff need not risk physical injury in attempting to escape. Less certain, however, is the exact amount of inconvenience that the plaintiff will be expected to endure in attempting to free himself. See *R. v. Macquarie and Budge* (1875), 13 N.S.W.S.C.R. 264; *Balmain New Ferry v. Robertson* (1906), 4 C.L.R. 379 (H.C.A.), aff'd [1910] A.C. 295 (P.C.); and *Hanson v. Wayne's Café Ltd.* (1990), 84 Sask. R. 220 (Q.B.). But see *Wright v. Wilson* (1699), 91 E.R. 1394 (N.P.), in which the defendant was not held liable in false imprisonment, even though the plaintiff could only escape by trespassing on a third party's property.

4. Alan, Barb and Carol were about to leave the 115th-floor observation deck of the C.N. Tower when they were informed that the elevator service was being discontinued for 30 minutes to permit publicity photos to be taken. All three refused to use the stairs, the only other exit. They now wish to know whether they can maintain a false imprisonment action against C.N. Alan is 30, Barb is 23 and 5 months pregnant, and Carol is 68.

5. Initially, in both England and the United States, the plaintiff had to establish that he or she was conscious of the imprisonment at the time that it occurred. This requirement has been dropped in England and, presumably, in Canada. See *J.(M.I.) v. Grieve*, 1996 CarswellBC 260 (S.C.) (WLeC); and *Murray v. Ministry*, [1998] 1 W.L.R. 692 (H.L.). American authorities have modified their position: the plaintiff may succeed if he or she

was aware of the imprisonment when it occurred or was harmed by it. See Prosser, "False Imprisonment: Consciousness of Confinement" (1955) 55 Columbia L. Rev. 847; and *Restatement (Second) of the Law of Torts* (1965) at §42.

6. A prisoner who is detained after he or she should have been released may sue in false imprisonment. See for example *LeBar v. Canada*, [1989] 1 F.C. 603 (C.A.); and *R. v. Governor of Brockhill Prison, ex parte Evans (No. 2)*, [1998] 4 All E.R. 993 (C.A.). The House of Lords reached this conclusion even though the defendant had used the then accepted sentence calculation approach, which was only later found to be incorrect. See *R. v. Governor of Brockhill Prison (No. 2)*, [2000] 2 A.C. 19 (H.L.); and Cane, "The Temporal Element in Law" (2001) 117 L.Q.R. 5.

More controversial, however, is the issue of whether a false imprisonment action can be brought if a lawfully detained prisoner is improperly held in segregation, improperly transferred to another institution, or held in intolerable conditions. In *Hague v. Deputy Governor of Parkhurst Prison; Weldon v. Home Office*, [1991] 3 All E.R. 733 (H.L.), the court held that such prisoners may have a public remedy and a private action in negligence, but not a false imprisonment action. The court viewed the conduct in issue as affecting the conditions of confinement and not the prisoners' liberty. The result in Canada appears to be different. See *Saint-Jacques v. Canada (Solicitor General)* (1991), 45 F.T.R. 1 (T.D.), where a prisoner was awarded damages in false imprisonment for being wrongfully placed in solitary confinement. See also *Hill v. British Columbia* (1997), 38 C.C.L.T. (2d) 182 (B.C.C.A.) where a prisoner was awarded $500 in general damages for being wrongly placed in segregation, a "prison within a prison," thereby depriving him of the liberty enjoyed by other prisoners.

7. The terms "false imprisonment" and "false arrest" are often used interchangeably. However, false arrest refers to only one category of false imprisonment actions, namely those in which the restraint is imposed by an assertion of legal authority. False arrest actions can be brought against peace officers and private citizens who implicitly or explicitly assert legal authority in detaining others. Thus, peace officers and others may inadvertently commit a false imprisonment when stopping or questioning a person, even if they have no intention of arresting him or her.

There have been sharp increases in the number of false arrest and malicious prosecution actions in Canada. As will be discussed in Chapter 8, the Canadian courts have become far more concerned about civil liberties with the advent of the *Charter*. While some of the pre-*Charter* cases reflected an undue deference to law enforcement officials, some of the more recent cases establish demanding standards for those who detain, arrest and prosecute suspects.

CAMPBELL v. S.S. KRESGE CO.

(1976), 74 D.L.R. (3d) 717 (N.S.S.C. (T.D.))

HART J.: On December 14, 1974, about 6 p.m., the plaintiff went to the K-Mart store of the corporate defendant at Dartmouth to do some pre-Christmas shopping. She took a cart and placed a hockey stick and one or two other articles in the cart and then tried to get the attention of one of the clerks at a counter at the back of the store to make a further purchase. She says that she waited about five minutes while the two clerks discussed their own personal affairs, and decided to wait no longer. She left the cart with the several items in it and proceeded out the main door of the shop.

The defendant, Gary Williamson, was a full-time member of the Dartmouth Police Force with the rank of corporal, who was employed by S.S. Kresge Company Limited as a security officer during his off-duty hours. His chief responsibility for the defendant was the protection of the defendant's property and the catching of shoplifters.

In the early evening of December 14th, while Corporal Williamson was on floor duty in the store, a lady asked him if he was a police officer. He confirmed that he was, and she advised him that she thought she had seen the plaintiff put something in her coat pocket. Corporal Williamson then observed the plaintiff and noticed that she had abandoned her shopping cart and was leaving the store. He followed her outside and confronted her in the parking lot. He showed her his police badge and said that he had reason to believe that she had something that did not belong to her and asked that she come into the store to his office to avoid embarrassment to them both. The plaintiff was upset but went into the store and started towards the back of the store with Corporal Williamson following behind. When she reached the location of the jewellery counter she stopped and demanded to know what it was all about before she went any further. She offered her purse to Corporal Williamson claiming that there was nothing in it that belonged to the store and offered to be searched. At this point Corporal Williamson, not now being able to see the woman who had given him the information, told the plaintiff that he was merely trying to get the facts and that she was free to go. Mrs. Campbell then left the store.

The plaintiff says that she was very upset by this encounter and drove to her mother-in-law's house where she told what had happened. She then returned to the store and spoke to the manager. From this office she proceeded to Mr. Williamson's office to speak with him. They met in the store and she asked if there was a private place where they could talk. He indicated that the security office would be suitable and they went there. The plaintiff then asked why Corporal Williamson had stopped her, and he advised that a woman, who he was not able to identify, had told him that she had put something on her person. He said that he felt this combined with her leaving of the articles in the store cart made him suspicious and that he wanted to get the facts.

In his evidence Corporal Williamson says that he followed the same procedure with Mrs. Campbell that he would have followed if he were certain that a shopper had something on her person taken from the store. He indicates that he probably would have let her go if she had refused to come inside with him, but I am satisfied that the plaintiff being confronted by a member of the police force and being invited inside to avoid embarrassment would have felt that she was obligated to follow the request. It was only when the plaintiff rebelled inside the store and the police officer realized that his source of information was no longer there, and the plaintiff had offered her purse to be searched, that he told her she was free to go.

I am satisfied from the evidence as a whole that the plaintiff was imprisoned by Corporal Williamson, acting in his capacity as agent for the corporate defendant, from the time she was confronted outside the store until the time she was told that she was free to go. In the mind of Corporal Williamson he was not arresting her but merely taking her in in order to get a statement of the facts, but he was using the force of his position as a police officer to take her in a direction that she did not wish to go. She was not consenting to accompany Corporal Williamson, but was going with him out of fear of the consequences should she refuse. If, as Corporal Williamson said, he was not going to arrest her and there was no one present to observe what was going on, then there could have been no "embarrassment" to be avoided and they could easily have had their discussion in the parking lot. The impression he was giving, however, was that she should accompany him or else there might be a scene which would be embarrassing to her. It was the practice of Corporal Williamson to physically detain those suspects whom he believed to have stolen goods on their person, and there is nothing to indicate that he would not have followed the usual procedure had the plaintiff refused to accompany him. He did not know when he was outside the store that his informant would not be present when he returned with the suspect.

[The court proceeded to discuss and then reject the defence of legal authority. Assessing the damages, the court continued.]

The plaintiff alleges that she was greatly upset by this experience and suggests that she was additionally embarrassed that it took place in the presence of many members of the public. I am satisfied from the evidence, however, that the matter was handled discreetly by Corporal Williamson and, although there were shoppers in the vicinity, that no scene was created which would have brought her in disrepute. The damages which she suffered therefore are limited to her personal inconvenience and upset arising from the incident, and I assess these damages in the amount of $500.

NOTES AND QUESTIONS

1. At what point did the officer imprison the plaintiff? In terms of the criminal law, did the officer intend to or, in fact, arrest the plaintiff? Why did the plaintiff submit to the defendant's assertion of authority? Can you distinguish between a situation in which a suspect reluctantly cooperates and one in which a suspect is submitting against his or her will? See *Conn v. David Spencer Ltd.*, [1930] 1 D.L.R. 805 (B.C.S.C.); *Sinclair v. Woodward's Store Ltd.*, [1942] 2 D.L.R. 395 (B.C.S.C.); and *Allen v. Head (C.) Ltd.* (1985), 54 Nfld. & P.E.I.R. 108 (Nfld. S.C.). Even if the plaintiff willingly goes with the security staff, the staff can be held liable in false imprisonment if they subsequently detain him or her. See *Smart v. Simpson Sears Ltd.* (1984), 51 Nfld. & P.E.I.R. 215 (Nfld. Dist. Ct.), aff'd (1987), 64 Nfld. & P.E.I.R. 187 (Nfld. C.A.).

2. An individual may be liable in false imprisonment not only for restraining the plaintiff, but also for ordering another person to do so. For example, if a store manager shouts "Stop that man, he's a thief!" and a police officer does so, then both are responsible for the imprisonment. However, if the manager merely provides information to the officer who, after assessing it, decides to make an arrest, the officer alone is responsible. It may be difficult to distinguish between these situations. If an individual makes the statement "I think that man has my wallet," is he giving an implicit order to arrest or merely providing information? Had the informant in *Campbell* been identified, could she have been held liable in false imprisonment? See *Reid v. Webster* (1966), 59 D.L.R. (2d) 189 (P.E.I.S.C.); *Lebrun v. High-Low Foods Ltd.* (1968), 69 D.L.R. (2d) 433 (B.C.S.C.); and *Davidson v. Chief Constable of North Wales*, [1994] 2 All E.R. 597 (C.A.).

3. A defendant who swears an information before a judicial officer cannot be held liable in false imprisonment when the plaintiff is arrested on the charge. While a police officer may serve as a defendant's agent, a judge is seen as exercising independent,

judicial decision-making authority. The judge is the source of the detention. See *Austin v. Dowling* (1870), L.R. 5 C.P. 534 at 540, where the court explained: "The party making the charge is not liable to an action for false imprisonment, because he does not set a ministerial officer in motion, but a judicial officer. The opinion and judgment of a judicial officer are interposed between the charge and the imprisonment." As we will discuss later in this chapter, in situations in which the defendant has sworn an information, the plaintiff may be able to sue the defendant for the tort of malicious prosecution, which provides redress for the wrongful initiation of criminal charges.

4. Why was the store held vicariously liable for the officer's conduct in *Campbell?* Should the police department have been held vicariously liable?

5. Do you think that the damage award was appropriate in this case? Punitive damages are now often awarded in false imprisonment actions. In *Nagy v. Canada* (2006), 61 Alta. L.R. (4th) 85 (C.A.), the plaintiff was strip-searched, arrested and taken to the hospital for an internal cavity search after arriving at the Edmonton Airport. She sued for battery, unlawful search and false imprisonment. At trial, the police officer and the doctor who conducted the body cavity search were held liable for $150,000 in general damages. The officer was also held liable for an additional $30,000 in general damages for the strip-search and initial imprisonment, and $50,000 in punitive damages. The appeal court upheld the trial judgement and damage awards. See also *Lang v. Burch* (1982), 140 D.L.R. (3d) 325 (Sask. C.A.); and *LeBar v. Canada*, [1989] 1 F.C. 603 (C.A.). But see *Hanisch v. Canada* (2004), 27 C.C.L.T. (3d) 1 (B.C.C.A.), where the appeal court overturned the trial judge's $15,000 punitive damage award against a police officer in a false arrest and imprisonment action.

6. In *Ashland Dry Goods Co. v. Wages*, 195 S.W.2d 312 (Ky. C.A. 1946), the judge held that the seizure of the plaintiff's purse and the statement that she could not leave with the goods until they were wrapped amounted to an imprisonment. Would parents be able to recover in false imprisonment if they remained with their child who had been detained? What factors would be relevant in resolving this issue? See *Carr v. Edmonton (City) Police* (1992), 134 A.R. 61 (C.A.).

7. Even a shoplifter apprehended in the act may easily establish the elements of a false imprisonment action: volition, intent and a total restraint of movement. Once the plaintiff proves that the tort has been committed, the defendant will be held liable unless he or she can establish a defence. The plaintiff's guilt or innocence may be relevant to, but not necessarily determinative of, the validity of the defence. The exact impact of a suspect's guilt on the defence of legal authority will be discussed in Chapter 8.

8. Advise a store detective on how to approach a suspected thief or disruptive customer without committing false imprisonment. See generally *Kovacs v. Ontario Jockey Club* (1995), 126 D.L.R. (4th) 576 (Ont. Gen. Div.); *Chopra v. T. Eaton Co.* (1999), 240 A.R. 201 (Q.B.); and *Aspden v. Maniaci*, 2005 CarswellOnt 974 (S.C.J.) (WLeC).

9. Although most false imprisonment claims involve the police and store detectives, the issue can arise under the civil commitment provisions of the provincial mental health

legislation. See *Tanner v. Norys* (1980), 21 A.R. 372 (C.A.); *Kohn v. Globerman*, [1986] 4 W.W.R. 1 (Man. C.A.); *Mullins v. Levy* (2004), 33 C.C.L.T. (3d) 42 (B.C.S.C.); and *C.B. v. Sawadsky* (2006), 216 O.A.C. 105 (C.A.)

HERD v. WEARDALE STEEL, COAL AND COKE CO. LTD.

[1915] A.C. 67 (H.L.)

The appellant was employed as a hewer at the Thornley Colliery in the county of Durham. The respondents the Weardale Steel, Coal and Coke Company were the proprietors of the colliery, the respondent Curry was the manager, and the respondent Turner was an overman employed at the colliery.

The appellant brought an action against the respondents for damages for false imprisonment. By his statement of claim he alleged that on May 30, 1911, the respondents wrongfully prevented him from using the cage, which was the only means of egress from the mine, whereby he was imprisoned in the mine till 1:30 p.m. The respondents denied the alleged false imprisonment and justified their refusal to raise the appellant on the ground that he had been guilty of a breach of contract in refusing to do some work which he was ordered to do.

. . .

VISCOUNT HALDANE L.C.: My Lords, by the law of this country no man can be restrained of his liberty without authority in law. That is a proposition the maintenance of which is of great importance; but at the same time it is a proposition which must be read in relation to other propositions which are equally important. If a man chooses to go into a dangerous place at the bottom of a quarry or the bottom of a mine, from which by the nature of physical circumstances he cannot escape, it does not follow from the proposition I have enunciated about liberty that he can compel the owner to bring him up out of it. The owner may or may not be under a duty arising from circumstances, on broad grounds the neglect of which may possibly involve him in a criminal charge or a civil liability. It is unnecessary to discuss the conditions and circumstances which might bring about such a result, because they have, in the view I take, nothing to do with false imprisonment.

My Lords, there is another proposition which has to be borne in mind, and that is the application of the maxim volenti non fit injuria. If a man gets into an express train and the doors are locked pending its arrival at its destination, he is not entitled, merely because the train has been stopped by signal, to call for the doors to be opened to let him out. He has entered the train on the terms that he is to be conveyed to a certain station without the opportunity of getting out before that, and he must abide by the terms on which he has entered the train. So when a man goes down a mine, from which access to the surface does not exist in the absence of special facilities given on the part of the owner of the mine, he is only entitled to the use of these facilities (subject possibly to the exceptional circumstances to which I have alluded) on the terms on which he has entered. . . . So, my Lords, it is not false imprisonment to hold a man to the conditions he has accepted when he goes down a mine.

. . .

Now, my Lords, in the present case what happened was this. The usage of the mine – a usage which I think must be taken to have been notified – was that the workman was to be brought up at the end of his shift. In this case the workman refused to work; it may have been for good reasons or it may have been for bad, – I do not think that question concerns us. He said that the work he had been ordered to do was of a kind that was dangerous, and he threw down his tools and claimed to come up to the surface. The manager, or at any rate the person responsible for the control of the cage, said: "No, you have chosen to come at a time which is not your proper time, and although there is the cage standing empty we will not bring you up in it," and the workman was in consequence under the necessity of remaining at the bottom of the shaft for about twenty minutes. There was no refusal to bring him up at the ordinary time which was in his bargain; but there was a refusal, – and I am quite ready to assume that the motive of it was to punish him, I will assume it for the sake of argument, for having refused to go on with his work – by refusing to bring him up at the moment when he claimed to come. Did that amount to false imprisonment? In my opinion it did not. No statutory right under the Coal Mines Regulation Act, 1887, avails him, for the reason which I have already spoken of. Nor had he any right in contract. His right in contract was to come up at the end of his shift. Was he then falsely imprisoned? There were facilities, but they were facilities which, in accordance with the conditions that he had accepted by going down, were not available to him until the end of his shift, at any rate as of right.

. . .

[W]hat we are concerned with at the moment is this and this simply: that no conditions existed which enabled the miner in this case to claim the right which he asserted, and that there was nothing which comes within the definition well known in the law of England which amounts to false imprisonment.

NOTES AND QUESTIONS

1. Did the plaintiff consent unconditionally to go into the mine and remain there until the shift ended? See Amos, "A Note On Contractual Restraint of Liberty" (1928) 44 L.Q.R. 464; and *Khan v. El Al Israel Airlines* (1991), 4 O.R. (3d) 502 (Gen. Div.).

2. To what extent was this decision affected by the then prevailing views of labour and management relations? Would the case be decided differently today?

3. Comprehensive occupational safety standards are now imposed by both federal and provincial legislation. For example, the *Occupational Health and Safety Act*, R.S.O. 1990, c. O.1, s. 43(3) allows employees to refuse to work in unsafe conditions.

4. Outside the entrance of his store, the defendant posted a large sign which read: "The management reserves the right to inspect all unsealed packages and shopping bags." The plaintiff, who is blind, entered the store with her seeing-eye dog. After learning that the store did not carry what she wanted, the plaintiff attempted to leave. The defendant politely explained that she could not leave until her shopping bag was inspected. The plaintiff refused to permit the search and was detained until the police arrived and resolved the issue. Will the plaintiff succeed in false imprisonment? Would the outcome be different if the plaintiff were illiterate, rather than blind? Which party has the burden of proving consent?

5. Summarize the principles of law governing false imprisonment.

7. Malicious Prosecution

Both false imprisonment and malicious prosecution provide redress for unjustified interference with individual freedom and the embarrassment, injury to reputation and other losses that flow from it. Malicious prosecution, however, is derived from trespass on the case. Consequently, it is concerned with indirect interferences, namely those that result from the improper initiation of criminal proceedings against an individual. Moreover, malicious prosecution is not actionable *per se*; rather the plaintiff must establish that he or she has suffered some loss or harm.

NELLES v. ONTARIO
[1989] 2 S.C.R. 170

[The plaintiff was charged with first degree murder in the deaths of four babies at the Hospital for Sick Children in Toronto. After a lengthy and extremely well-publicized preliminary hearing, all charges were dropped against her because of a lack of evidence. She sued several police officers, the Ontario Attorney General and the Crown for false imprisonment, malicious prosecution, negligence and violation of her *Charter* rights.

The following excerpt from the Supreme Court of Canada's decision addresses the issue of malicious prosecution and whether the Attorney General and Crown are immune from such actions.]

LAMER J. (DICKSON C.J.C. and WILSON J. concurring):

. . .

2. *The Tort of Malicious Prosecution*

There are four necessary elements which must be proved for a plaintiff to succeed in an action for malicious prosecution:

a) the proceedings must have been initiated by the defendant;

b) the proceedings must have terminated in favour of the plaintiff;

c) the absence of reasonable and probable cause;

d) malice, or a primary purpose other than that of carrying the law into effect.

(See J.G. Fleming, *The Law of Torts* (5th ed. 1977), at p. 598.)

The first two elements are straightforward and largely speak for themselves. The latter two elements require explicit discussion. Reasonable and probable cause has been defined as "an honest belief in the guilt of the accused based upon a full conviction, founded on reasonable grounds, of the existence of a state of circumstances, which, assuming them to be true, would reasonably lead any ordinarily prudent and cautious man, placed in the position of the accuser, to the conclusion that the person charged was probably guilty of the crime imputed" (*Hicks v. Faulkner* (1878), 8 Q.B.D. 167, at p. 171, Hawkins J.)

This test contains both a subjective and objective element. There must be both actual belief on the part of the prosecutor and that belief must be reasonable in the circumstances. The existence of reasonable and probable cause is a matter for the judge to decide as opposed to the jury.

The required element of malice is for all intents, the equivalent of "improper purpose". It has according to Fleming, a "wider meaning than spite, ill-will or a spirit of vengeance, and includes any other improper purpose, such as to gain a private collateral advantage" (Fleming, op. cit., at p. 609). To succeed in an action for malicious prosecution against the Attorney General or Crown Attorney, the plaintiff would have to prove both the absence of reasonable and probable cause in commencing the prosecution, *and* malice in the form of a deliberate and improper use of the office of the Attorney General or Crown Attorney, a use inconsistent with the status of "minister of justice". In my view this burden on the plaintiff amounts to a requirement that the Attorney General or Crown Attorney perpetrated a fraud on the process of criminal justice and in doing so has perverted or abused his office and the process of criminal justice. In fact, in some cases this would seem to amount to criminal conduct. (See for example breach of trust, s. 122, conspiracy re: false prosecution s. 465(1)(*b*), obstructing justice s. 139(2) and (3) of the *Criminal Code*, R.S.C., 1985, c. C-46.)

Further, it should be noted that in many, if not all cases of malicious prosecution by an Attorney General or Crown Attorney, there will have been an infringement of an accused's rights as guaranteed by ss. 7 and 11 of the *Canadian Charter of Rights and Freedoms*.

By way of summary then, a plaintiff bringing a claim for malicious prosecution has no easy task. Not only does the plaintiff have the notoriously difficult task of establishing a negative, that is the absence of reasonable and probable cause, but he is held to a very high standard of proof to avoid a non-suit or directed verdict (see Fleming, op. cit., at p. 606, and *Mitchell v. John Heine and Son Ltd.* (1938), 38 S.R. (N.S.W.) 466, at pp. 469-71). Professor Fleming has gone so far as to conclude that there are built-in devices particular to the tort of malicious prosecution to dissuade civil suits (at p. 606):

> The disfavour with which the law has traditionally viewed the action for malicious prosecution is most clearly revealed by the hedging devices with which it has been surrounded in order to deter this kind of litigation and protect private citizens who discharge their public duty of prosecuting those reasonably suspected of crime.

3. *Policy Considerations*

In light of what I have said regarding the role of the prosecutor in Canada, and the tort of malicious prosecution, it now is necessary to assess the policy rationales. I would begin by noting that even those decisions that have come out firmly in favour of absolute immunity have described the rule as "troubling", a "startling proposition", "strained and difficult to sustain". . . .

It is said by those in favour of absolute immunity that the rule encourages public trust and confidence in the impartiality of prosecutors. However, it seems to me that public confidence in the office of a public prosecutor suffers greatly when the person who is in a position of knowledge in respect of the constitutional and legal impact of his conduct is shielded from civil liability when he abuses the process through a malicious prosecution. The existence of an absolute immunity strikes at the very principle of equality under the law and is especially alarming when the wrong has been committed by a person who should be held to the highest standards of conduct in exercising a public trust. . . .

Regard must also be had for the victim of the malicious prosecution. The fundamental flaw with an absolute immunity for prosecutors is that the wrongdoer cannot be held accountable by the victim through the legal process. As I have stated earlier, the plaintiff in a malicious prosecution suit bears a formidable burden of proof and in those cases where a case can be made out, the plaintiff's *Charter* rights may have been infringed as well. Granting an absolute immunity to prosecutors is akin to granting a license to subvert individual rights. Not only does absolute immunity negate a private right of action, but in addition, it seems to me, it may be that it would effectively bar the seeking of a remedy pursuant to s. 24(1) of the *Charter*. . . .

It is also said in favour of absolute immunity that anything less would act as a "chilling effect" on the Crown Attorney's exercise of discretion. It should be noted that what is at issue here is not the exercise of a prosecutor's discretion within the proper sphere of prosecutorial activity as defined by his role as a "minister of justice". Rather, in cases of malicious prosecution we are dealing with allegations of misuse and abuse of the criminal process and of the office of the Crown Attorney. We are not dealing with merely second-guessing a Crown Attorney's judgment in the prosecution of a case but rather with the deliberate and malicious use of the office for ends that are improper and inconsistent with the traditional prosecutorial function.

Therefore it seems to me that the "chilling effect" argument is largely speculative and assumes that many suits for malicious prosecution will arise from disgruntled persons who have been prosecuted but not convicted of an offence. I am of the view that this "flood-gates" argument ignores the fact that one element of the tort of malicious prosecution requires a demonstration of improper motive or purpose; errors in the exercise of discretion and judgment are not actionable. Furthermore, there exist built-in deterrents on bringing a claim for malicious prosecution. As I have noted, the burden on the plaintiff is onerous and strict. . . . Finally, the potential that costs will be awarded to the defendant if an unmeritorious claim is brought acts as financial deterrent to meritless claims. Therefore, ample mechanisms exist within the system to ensure that frivolous claims are not brought. In fact, the difficulty in proving a claim for malicious prosecution itself acts as a deterrent. This high threshold of liability is evidenced by the small number of malicious prosecution suits brought against police officers each year. In addition, since 1966, the province of Quebec permits suits against the Attorney General and Crown prosecutors without any evidence of a flood of claims. Therefore, I find unpersuasive the claim that absolute immunity is necessary to prevent a flood of litigation.

As for alternative remedies available to persons who have been maliciously prosecuted, none seem to adequately redress the wrong done to the plaintiff. The use of the criminal process against a prosecutor who in the course of a malicious prosecution has committed an offence under the *Criminal Code*, addresses itself mainly to the vindication of a public wrong not the affirmation of a private right of action. . . . I do however pause to note that many cases of genuine malicious prosecution will also be offences under the *Criminal Code*, and it seems rather odd if not incongruous for reparation to be possible through a probation order but not through a private right of action.

Further, the use of professional disciplinary proceedings, while serving to some extent as punishment and deterrence, do not address the central issue of making the victim whole again. And as has already been noted, it is quite discomforting to realize that the existence of absolute immunity may bar a person whose *Charter* rights have been infringed from applying to a competent court for a just and appropriate remedy in the form of damages.

NOTES AND QUESTIONS

1. Based on *Nelles*, define the elements of a malicious prosecution action. Although not discussed by the court, the plaintiff must also prove that he or she has suffered loss or damage.

2. Explain the objective and subjective elements of reasonable and probable cause. Would a prosecutor meet this test if there were grounds to believe that the accused committed the offence, but the prosecutor did not personally believe that the accused did it? Would the test be met if a prosecutor personally believed on reasonable grounds that the accused committed the offence, but also believed that there was little prospect of obtaining a conviction?

3. How did the court define the element of malice or improper purpose? Would it be improper to charge a suspect with 12 similar break and enters, if there was currently only evidence linking the suspect to 4 of these offences? According to *Nelles*, must there be an element of subjective ill-will or malice? Based on *Nelles*, can the lack of reasonable and probable grounds, in and of itself, satisfy the requirement for malice or other improper purpose?

4. What arguments were made in support of the immunity rule? On what basis did the court reject these arguments? What additional policy issues did the court raise in favour of a no-immunity rule? Would these same arguments justify denying absolute immunity to judges and quasi-judicial decision-makers? Not surprisingly, the Canadian courts have consistently re-affirmed that judges and other decision-makers are subject to immunity at common law.

5. Although the court in *Nelles* denied the existence of a common law immunity protecting the Attorney General and his or her agents as individuals, it did recognize that the Crown itself had statutory immunity from liability with respect to the actions of the Attorney General and the Crown prosecutor. Section 5(6) of the *Proceedings Against the Crown Act*, R.S.O. 1990, c. P.27, states: "No proceeding lies against the Crown under this section in respect of anything done or omitted to be done by a person while discharging or purporting to discharge responsibilities of a judicial nature vested in the person or responsibilities that the person has in connection with the execution of judicial process."

What is the impact of *Nelles* and s. 5(6) on the personal liability of the Attorney General and Crown prosecutors? See *Walker v. Ontario* (1997), 40 C.C.L.T. (2d) 197 (Ont. Gen. Div.); and *Hawley v. Bapoo* (2005), 76 O.R. (3d) 649 (S.C.J.).

6. In *Nelles*, the court suggested that the rigorous requirements of malicious prosecution would limit the proliferation of claims, but this has not been the case.

For example in *Oniel v. Metropolitan Toronto Police Force* (2001), 195 D.L.R. (4th) 59 (Ont. C.A.), the court stated that, in appropriate cases, malice could be inferred from the lack of reasonable and probable cause. Specifically, an officer's failure to make adequate inquiries before continuing a prosecution could amount to malice. In contrast, the English Court of Appeal stated that malice requires more than proof that the officer lacked reasonable grounds, was negligent or incompetent in conducting the investigation, or acted with reckless indifference as to the illegality of his or her conduct: see *Keegan v. Chief Constable of Merseyside Police*, [2003] 1 W.L.R. 2187. The majority of the Canadian cases are consistent with *Keegan*. See *Fitzpatrick v. Durham Regional Police Services Board* (2005), 76 O.R. (3d) 290 (S.C.J.); *Hawley, supra*; and *Reilly v. British Columbia (A.G.)* (2006), 60 B.C.L.R. (4th) 192 (S.C.). Which position is preferable?

Increasingly, police officers are bringing malicious prosecution actions against those who charge them with criminal offences. In addition to *Fitzpatrick, supra*, and *Hawley, supra*, see *Wiche v. Ontario* (2001), 9 C.C.L.T. (3d) 72 (Ont. S.C.J.); and *Pearson v. Mian*, 2006 CarswellOnt 7286 (S.C.J.) (WLeC). What factors do you think have contributed to this trend?

7. The Supreme Court of Canada revisited the malicious prosecution issue in *Proulx v. Québec (A.G.)*, [2001] 3 S.C.R. 9. While both the majority and the dissent purported to apply *Nelles*, they disagreed on whether the plaintiff could establish malice. The fact situation was somewhat complicated. Essentially, the majority was willing to infer malice against the prosecutor from the lack of reasonable and probable grounds for charging the accused with murder, coupled with the prosecutor's hiring of a former police officer who was at that time being sued by the accused for defamation. The dissent held that there was insufficient evidence to establish that the prosecutor had subjectively acted with a malicious or improper intent. See also Harris, "Innocent Albertan got $2.2M payout" *Calgary Sun* (4 October 2006). In this case, a man spent seven years in prison for a rape he did not commit. It was later revealed that the complainant had sex with the investigating officer on several occasions and with a witness who testified against the accused at trial.

8. In *Reid v. Webster* (1966), 59 D.L.R. (2d) 189 (P.E.I.S.C.), the court defined criminal proceedings broadly. It held that a municipal by-law prosecution can give rise to a malicious prosecution action if the by-law provides imprisonment in default of payment, the prosecution affects the plaintiff's trade, and the publicity creates an aura of scandal. See also *Delancey v. Dale & Co. Ltd.* (1959), 20 D.L.R. (2d) 12 (N.S.S.C.) (arrest as a potential absconding debtor).

The Canadian courts have held that the wrongful initiation of disciplinary proceedings against healthcare and other regulated professionals can give rise to a malicious prosecution action. See for example *Stoffman v. Veterinary Assn. (Ontario)* (1990), 73 O.R. (2d) 737 (Div. Ct.); *Khanna v. Royal College of Dental Surgeons (Ontario)* (2000), 47 O.R. (3d) 95 (C.A.); and *Roach v. Long* (2002), 161 O.A.C. 218 (C.A.). However, in *Gregory v. Portsmouth City Council*, [2000] 1 All E.R. 560 (H.L.), the court held that malicious prosecution does not extend beyond the limits of criminal prosecution and special instances of abuse of civil proceedings. Thus, the tort is not applicable to disciplinary proceedings of any kind. In the court's view, defamation and related tort actions provide sufficient protection in cases of wrongful initiation of disciplinary proceedings. For a critique of *Gregory*, see Cane, "The Scope of Malicious Prosecution" (2000) L.Q.R. 346.

9. A defendant cannot be held liable in malicious prosecution for merely providing information to the police or testifying in court. Rather, the defendant must be the driving force in the initiation or prosecution of the action. In most cases, this requirement is met by laying the criminal charge. However, a defendant may also be responsible for initiating the proceedings if he or she lied to the police or wrongfully pressured them to lay the charges. See *Casey v. Automobiles Renault Canada Ltd.*, [1965] S.C.R. 607; *Canada v. Lukasik* (1985), 58 A.R. 313 (Q.B.); *Temilini v. Ontario Provincial Police (Commissioner)* (1990), 73 O.R. (2d) 664 (C.A.); *Hinde v. Skibinski* (1994), 21 C.C.L.T. (2d) 314 (Ont. Gen. Div.); *Wood v. Kennedy* (1998), 165 D.L.R. (4th) 542 (Ont. Gen. Div); and *Sabourin v. Ontario*, 2005 CarswellOnt 133 (S.C.J.) (WLeC).

The House of Lords has adopted a more limited rule on when a person who lies to the police can be held liable for malicious prosecution. In *Martin v. Watson*, [1996] 1 A.C. 74 (H.L.), the court said that individuals who do not lay a criminal charge may nevertheless be held liable in malicious prosecution if: (i) they falsely and maliciously give the police information that the accused committed a crime and offer to testify, making it clear that they want the accused prosecuted; and (ii) the facts are only available to them, such that the police cannot exercise independent judgment in the matter. Is the Canadian or United Kingdom approach preferable?

10. A defendant can be held liable in malicious prosecution not only for the wrongful initiation of the charge, but also for its wrongful continuation. See *Oniel v. Metropolitan Toronto Police Force, supra*. What impact would this principle have on a police officer who laid four charges of theft, but learned prior to trial that the accused could not have been responsible for two of the thefts?

11. In *Casey, supra*, the majority held that the defendant had initiated criminal proceedings by laying a criminal charge before a magistrate who was competent to deal with the matter, even though the defendant withdrew the charge before the magistrate took any action. The court further held that the subsequent withdrawal of the charge amounted to a termination of the proceedings in the plaintiff's favour.

12. In *M.(A.) v. Matthews* (2003), 20 C.C.L.T. (3d) 54 (Alta. Q.B.), it was held that a malicious prosecution claim cannot be commenced until the criminal proceedings on which it is based have been completed.

13. In *Banks v. Bliefernich* (1988), 44 C.C.L.T. 144 (B.C.S.C.), it was held that even though the plaintiff pleaded guilty to one charge, the stay of proceedings on the other charges constituted a termination in the plaintiff's favour. What impact will this case have on plea bargaining?

14. In the past, many criminal cases were prosecuted by private citizens and there were no mechanisms for efficiently co-ordinating the criminal justice system. Therefore, it is not surprising that malicious prosecution was narrowly defined. Has the establishment of an elaborate, publicly-funded system of criminal justice undercut the rationale for restricting this tort?

15. Although malicious prosecution initially provided redress for the wrongful initiation of certain civil actions, it is now limited almost exclusively to penal matters.

The wrongful initiation of bankruptcy and winding-up proceedings are the most notable exceptions. See *The Quartz Hill Consolidated Gold Mining Co. v. Eyre* (1883), 11 Q.B.D. 674 (C.A.); *Clissold v. Cratchley*, [1910] 2 K.B. 244 (C.A.); *Flame Bar-B-Q Ltd. v. Hoar* (1979), 106 D.L.R. (3d) 438 (N.B.C.A.); and *Cherry v. Ivey* (1982), 37 O.R. (2d) 361 (H.C.). See also *Norman v. Soule* (1991), 7 C.C.L.T. (2d) 16 (B.C.S.C.), which suggests that these limited exceptions are not likely to be extended to any other types of civil litigation.

16. It has been suggested that there may be a tort for malicious failure to prosecute. In *Paquette v. Desrochers* (2000), 52 O.R. (3d) 742 at 749 (S.C.J.), McKinnon J. said: "One can contemplate a situation where, as a result of proven malice, an accused is not prosecuted for a vicious attack upon a victim. Subsequently, the same individual viciously attacks the same victim, once again occasioning severe bodily harm. Surely, if malice can be proved, the failure to prosecute may well be alleged as a cause giving rise to the subsequent damage." In a later stage of the same proceedings, the Court of Appeal for Ontario expressly refused to comment on the malicious failure to prosecute: *P.(K.) v. Desrochers* (2001), 9 C.C.L.T. (3d) 317 (Ont. C.A.). Should such a tort be recognized? What are the arguments for and against such a tort?

17. The litigation relating to police and prosecutorial practices has become increasingly complex, particularly in Ontario. As in *Desrochers*, the malicious prosecution issue may be novel, or accompanied by a range of other causes of action. This latter situation is illustrated by *Folland v. Ontario* (2003), 64 O.R. (3d) 89 (C.A.), in which the plaintiff sued the Crown and various police officials for abuse of process, conspiracy to injure and intentional infliction of harm, in addition to malicious prosecution. See also *Khanna v. Royal College of Dental Surgeons of Ontario*, *supra*; and *Bernstein v. Stoytcheva-Todorova* (2007), 44 C.C.L.T. (3d) 181 (B.C.S.C.). This latter case involved claims for malicious prosecution, abuse of process, conspiracy, intentional interference with economic relations, defamation, restitution, unjust enrichment, and breach of various statutes.

18. Summarize the key principles governing malicious prosecution.

(a) THE TORT OF ABUSE OF PROCESS

Until recently, it was widely accepted that no remedy existed for the misuse of civil proceedings. However, courts in some provinces, including Alberta, Ontario and British Columbia, have recognized a common law tort action for abuse of process. Unlike malicious prosecution, abuse of process is not primarily concerned with the wrongful initiation of proceedings. Rather, it focuses on the misuse of civil proceedings for a collateral or illicit purpose other than the resolution of the claim. The plaintiff must prove: (i) that the defendant brought a civil action; (ii) that the defendant did so for some extrinsic purpose; (iii) that the defendant undertook, or threatened to undertake, some overt act, other than the litigation itself, in order to further the improper purpose; and (iv) that the plaintiff consequently suffered a loss. However, in contrast to the tort of malicious prosecution, the plaintiff does not have to prove that the earlier proceedings terminated in his or her favour, or that the defendant lacked reasonable and probable grounds for engaging in the earlier proceedings. Although it appears easier to establish the tort of abuse of process than the tort of malicious prosecution, the need to prove an overt act independent of the litigation itself is usually difficult to demonstrate. See for example *Guilford Industries Ltd. v. Hankinson Management Services Ltd.*, [1974] 1 W.W.R. 141 (B.C.S.C.); *Poulos v. Matovic* (1989), 47 C.C.L.T. 207 (Ont. H.C.); *Dooley v. C.N. Weber Ltd.* (1994), 19 O.R. (3d) 779 (Gen. Div.); *Ilic v. Calgary Sun* (1998), 42 C.C.L.T. (2d) 301 (Alta. Q.B.); *Border Enterprises Ltd. v. Beazer East Inc.* (2002), 216 D.L.R. (4th) 107 (B.C.C.A.); *Metrick v. Deeb* (2003), 16 C.C.L.T. (3d) 298 (Ont. C.A.); and Irvine, "The Resurrection of Tortious Abuse of Process" (1989) 47 C.C.L.T. 217.

REVIEW PROBLEM

Vincent was browsing in the Super Mart. The store detective, Steven, became suspicious because Vincent spent 15 minutes at the cosmetic counter and had a bottle of deodorant sticking out of his shopping bag. When Vincent left without paying for the deodorant, Steven ran after him and tapped him on the shoulder. When Vincent turned around, Steven politely asked him to come to the manager's office. Vincent, who neither spoke nor understood English, smiled and accompanied Steven. John, the store manager, listened to Steven's explanation and called the police. After several minutes, Vincent became nervous and stated in Italian that he was leaving. John told him in Italian that he had to remain, and Steven pushed him towards a chair. Vincent finally realized that he was being arrested, but he had no idea why.

John explained the situation in English to the officers and told them that he was going to press charges. The officers took Vincent into custody and seized his shopping bag as evidence. Once at the station, the desk sergeant explained to Vincent in Italian the reason for his arrest. Vincent replied that there was a receipt in his shopping bag to prove that the deodorant had been purchased at another store. The desk sergeant said that he would look into the matter. The sergeant thought Vincent might be an illegal immigrant and decided to lay the theft charge as a means of holding him until his immigration status could be determined. Vincent was charged with theft, brought before a judge and released on a promise to appear. When the desk sergeant learned later in the day that Vincent was a lawful visitor he looked into the shopping bag for the first time. Upon finding the receipt, he called the prosecutor to withdraw the charge. Vincent has sought your legal advice. He wishes to know what tort actions he can bring against the various parties, the bases for such actions and their likelihood of success.

8. Intentional Infliction of Nervous Shock

WILKINSON v. DOWNTON

[1897] 2 Q.B. 57

WRIGHT J.: In this case the defendant, in the execution of what he seems to have regarded as a practical joke, represented to the plaintiff that he was charged by her husband with a message to her to the effect that her husband was smashed up in an accident, and was lying at The Elms at Leytonstone with both legs broken, and that she was to go at once in a cab with two pillows to fetch him home. All this was false. The effect of the statement on the plaintiff was a violent shock to her nervous system, producing vomiting and other more serious and permanent physical consequences at one time threatening her reason, and entailing weeks of suffering and incapacity to her as well as expense to her husband for medical attendance. These consequences were not in any way the result of previous ill-health or weakness of constitution; nor was there any evidence of predisposition to nervous shock or any other idiosyncrasy.

In addition to these matters of substance there is a small claim for 1*s*. 10½*d*. for the cost of railway fares of persons sent by the plaintiff to Leytonstone in obedience to the pretended message. As to this 1*s*. 101/2*d*. expended in railway fares on the faith of the defendant's statement, I think the case is clearly within the decision in *Pasley* v. *Freeman* [(1789), 100 E.R. 450 (K.B.)]. The statement was a misrepresentation intended to be acted on to the damage of the plaintiff.

The real question is as to the [£]100. . ., the greatest part of which is given as compensation for the female plaintiff's illness and suffering. It was argued for her that she is entitled to recover this as being damage caused by fraud, and therefore within the doctrine established by *Pasley* v. *Freeman* [*supra*] and *Langridge* v. *Levy* [(1837), 150 E.R. 863 (Ex. Ct.)]. I am not sure that this would not be an extension of that doctrine, the real ground of which appears to be that a person who makes a false statement intended to be acted on must make good the damage naturally resulting from its being acted on. Here there is no injuria of that kind. I think, however, that the verdict may be supported upon another ground. The defendant has, as I assume for the moment, wilfully done an act calculated to cause physical harm to the plaintiff – that is to say, to infringe her legal right to personal safety, and has in fact thereby caused physical harm to her. That proposition without more appears to me to state a good cause of action, there being no justification alleged for the act. This wilful injuria is in law malicious, although no malicious purpose to cause the harm which was caused nor any motive of spite is imputed to the defendant.

It remains to consider whether the assumptions involved in the proposition are made out. One question is whether the defendant's act was so plainly calculated to produce some effect of the kind which was produced that an intention to produce it ought to be imputed to the defendant, regard being had to the fact that the effect was produced on a person proved to be in an ordinary state of health and mind. I think that it was. It is difficult to imagine that such a statement, made suddenly and with apparent seriousness, could fail to produce grave effects under the circumstances upon any but an exceptionally indifferent person, and therefore an intention to produce such an effect must be imputed, and it is no answer in law to say that more harm was done than was anticipated, for that is commonly the case with all wrongs. The other question is whether the effect was, to use the ordinary phrase, too remote to be in law regarded as a consequence for which the defendant is answerable. . . . It is, however, necessary to consider two authorities which are supposed to have laid down that illness through mental shock is a too remote or unnatural consequence of an injuria to entitle the plaintiff to recover in a case where damage is a necessary part of the cause of action. One is the case of *Victorian Railways Commissioners* v. *Coultas* [(1888), 13 A.C. 222 (P.C.)], where it was held in the Privy Council that illness which was the effect of shock caused by fright was too remote a consequence of a negligent act which caused the fright, there being no physical harm immediately caused. That decision was treated in the Court of Appeal in *Pugh* v. *London, Brighton and South Coast Ry. Co.* [[1896] 2 Q.B. 248] as open to question. . . . Nor is it altogether in point, for there was not in that case any element of wilful wrong; nor perhaps was the illness so direct and natural a consequence of the defendant's conduct as in this case. On these grounds it seems to me that the case of *Victorian Railways Commissioners* v. *Coultas* [*supra*] is not an authority on which this case ought to be decided.

A more serious difficulty is the decision in *Allsop* v. *Allsop* [(1860), 157 E.R. 1292 (Ex. Ct.)]. . . . In that case it was held by Pollock C.B., Martin, Bramwell, and Wilde BB., that illness caused by a slanderous imputation of unchastity in the case of a married woman did not constitute such special damage as would sustain an action for such a slander. That case, however, appears to have been decided on the ground that in all the innumerable actions for slander there were no precedents for alleging illness to be sufficient special damage, and that it would be of evil consequence to treat it as sufficient, because such a rule might lead to an infinity of trumpery or groundless actions. Neither of these reasons is applicable to the present case. Nor could such a rule be adopted as of general application without results which it would be difficult or impossible to defend. Suppose that a person is in a precarious and dangerous condition, and another person tells him that his physician has said that he has but a day to live. In such a case, if death ensued from the shock caused by the false statement, I cannot doubt that at this day the case might be one of criminal homicide, or that if a serious aggravation of illness ensued damages might be recovered. I think, however, that it must be admitted that the present case is without precedent. . . .

There must be judgment for the plaintiff for [£]100. . . 1*s*. 10½.

NOTES AND QUESTIONS

1. What was the basis on which the plaintiff recovered the small cost of her railway ticket? While she also recovered a larger amount in damages for nervous shock, why was that recovery not on this same basis?

2. How did Wright J. define the principles governing the intentional infliction of nervous shock? Do you agree with the way he applied these principles to the facts? Why was he not bound by *Victorian Railways Commissioners v. Coultas* and *Allsop v. Allsop*, both cited in the extract?

3. Prior to *Wilkinson*, a plaintiff could not recover for nervous shock unless he or she also suffered some physical injury. The courts' attitude to nervous shock was summarized by Lord Wensleydale in *Lynch v. Knight* (1861), 11 E.R. 854 at 863 (H.L.): "Mental pain or anxiety the law cannot value, and does not pretend to redress, when the unlawful act complained of causes that alone; though where a material damage occurs, and is connected with it, it is impossible a jury, in estimating it, should altogether overlook the feelings of the party interested." Why else might the courts have been hesitant to recognize an action for nervous shock? How did Wright J. address these concerns?

4. Did Wright J. consider nervous shock to be an independent action or merely an indirect means of causing physical injury? What is the practical significance of such a distinction?

5. In *Purdy v. Woznesensky*, [1937] 2 W.W.R. 116 (Sask. C.A.), the female plaintiff suffered nervous shock when the defendant punched her husband in the head, knocking

him unconscious. The judge held that the defendant should have foreseen that by causing the plaintiff to witness the attack, he would probably upset her nervous system. Consequently, the judge imputed this intent to the defendant. In *Bielitski v. Obadiak* (1922), 65 D.L.R. 627 (Sask. C.A.), the defendant started a rumour that the plaintiff's son had hanged himself. After being retold several times, the rumour reached the plaintiff, who suffered serious nervous shock and became physically ill. Noting the defendant's failure to explain his conduct, the majority imputed intent to him. Haultain C.J.S. dissented, holding that the plaintiff's injury was not intentionally inflicted, nor the natural, probable or necessary consequence of the defendant's act. Was the doctrine of imputed intent correctly applied in *Wilkinson, Purdy* and *Bielitski*? See also *Timmermans v. Buelow* (1984), 38 C.C.L.T. 136 (Ont. H.C.). Why did the court not apply the doctrine of transferred intent?

Contrast the approach taken in these cases with that in *Bunyan v. Jordan* (1937), 57 C.L.R. 1 (H.C.A.); and *Stevenson v. Basham*, [1922] N.Z.L.R. 225 (S.C.). See also *Restatement (Second) of the Law of Torts* (1965) at §§ 46-47.

6. In *Wainwright v. Home Office*, [2004] 2 A.C. 406 at 425 (H.L.), the court stated that *Wilkinson* was a negligent infliction of nervous shock case which the judge had characterized as an intentional tort action. The judge adopted this approach to avoid having to deny the plaintiff's claim pursuant to the then binding authority of *Victoria Railways Commissioners*. Would you agree with this analysis of *Wilkinson*?

RADOVSKIS v. TOMM

(1957), 9 D.L.R. (2d) 751 (Man. Q.B.)

WILLIAMS C.J.Q.B.: – On August 28, 1956, the infant plaintiff, 51/2 years old Anda Radovskis, was raped by the defendant who was convicted of the offence and is presently serving a lengthy sentence in the Penitentiary.

This action is brought by the child suing by her father Robert Radovskis as next friend to recover damages for the trespass to her person; by the father to recover hospital and medical expenses, loss of wages, and for "worry and inconvenience"; and by the child's mother to recover damages for nervous shock alleged to have been sustained by the mother.

. . .

No medical evidence was offered and the mother did not give evidence. Her husband did say that his wife had not good nerves before and that since they had been bad.

But that is not sufficient to support a claim for damages. In *Guay v. Sun Publishing Co., supra*, Estey J., after discussing the medical evidence before the Court, said (p. 589 D.L.R., p. 238 S.C.R.): "Moreover, it is important to keep in mind what must be proved in order that damages may be recovered, as stated in Pollock on Torts, 15th ed., pp. 37-8, as follows: 'A state of mind such as fear or acute grief is not in itself capable of assessment as measurable temporal damage. But visible and provable illness may be the natural consequence of violent emotion, and may furnish a ground of action against a person whose wrongful act or want of due care produced that emotion. . . . In every case the question is whether the shock and the illness were in fact natural or direct consequences of the wrongful act or default; if they were, the illness, not the shock, furnishes the measurable damage, and there is no more difficulty in assessing it than in assessing damages for bodily injuries of any kind.' "

In this case there was no visible and provable illness within the meaning of this quotation. The mother's action is dismissed without costs.

SAMMS v. ECCLES

358 P.2d 344 (Utah S.C. 1961)

CROCKETT J.: Plaintiff Marcia G. Samms sought to recover damages from David Eccles for injury resulting from severe emotional distress she claims to have suffered because he persistently annoyed her with indecent proposals.

. . .

Plaintiff alleged that she is a respectable married woman; that she has never encouraged the defendant's attentions in any way but has repulsed them; that all during the time from May to December, 1957, the defendant repeatedly and persistently called her by phone at various hours including late at night, soliciting her to have illicit sexual relations with him; and that on one occasion came to her residence in connection with such a solicitation and made an indecent exposure of his person. She charges that she regarded his proposals as insulting, indecent and obscene; that her feelings were deeply wounded; and that as a result thereof she suffered great anxiety and fear for her personal safety and severe emotional distress for which she asks $1,500 as actual, and a like amount as punitive, damages.

. . .

Due to the highly subjective and volatile nature of emotional distress and the variability of its causations, the courts have historically been wary of dangers in opening the door to recovery therefor. This is partly because such claims may easily be fabricated: or as sometimes stated, are easy to assert and hard to defend against. They have, therefore, been reluctant to allow such a right of action unless the emotional distress was suffered as a result of some other overt tort. Nevertheless, recognizing the reality of such injuries and the injustice of permitting them to go unrequited, in many cases courts have strained to find the other tort as a peg upon which to hang the right of recovery.

Some of these have been unrealistic, or even flimsy. For instance, a technical battery was found where an insurance adjuster derisively tossed a coin on the bed of a woman who was in a hospital with a heart condition, and because of this tort she was allowed to recover for distress caused by his other attempts at intimidation in accusing her of gold-bricking and attempting to defraud his company; courts have also dealt with trespass where hotel employees have invaded rooms occupied by married couples and imputed to them immoral conduct; and other similar torts have been used as a basis for such recovery. But a realistic analysis of many of these cases will show that the recognized tort is but incidental and that the real basis of recovery is the outraged feelings and emotional distress resulting from some aggravated conduct of the defendant. The lengths to which courts have gone to find a basis for allowing such recoveries serves to emphasize their realization that justice demands that grossly wrong conduct which causes such an injury to another should be held accountable.

In recent years courts have shown an increasing awareness of the necessity and justice of forthrightly recognizing the true basis for allowing recovery for such wrongs and of getting rid of the shibboleth that another tort peg is necessary to that purpose. Examples are: *Great Atlantic & Pacific Tea Co. v. Roch*, injuries caused by shock where a grocery man included a dead rat in a package as a joke; *Savage v. Boies*, distress caused by false representation that plaintiff's child had been injured in an automobile accident; *Cohen v. Lion Products Co.*, distress to plaintiff's husband resulted from mandatory orders and charges of failure made to him as an employee by defendant's officers.

In *LaSalle Extension University v. Fogarty*, upon defendant's refusal to pay plaintiff's demand, plaintiff sent threatening letters to the defendant, and to his neighbors and employer, for the purpose of harassing him into paying their claim, against which it ultimately proved he had a good defense. Recovery was allowed on his counterclaim for emotional distress thus wrongfully caused him. The court cited the Iowa case of *Barnett v. Collection Service Co.* and quoted the rule which has come to be widely recognized that: "where the act is willful or malicious, as distinguished from being merely negligent, that recovery may be had for mental pain, though no physical injury results."

A case closely analogous to the instant one where such recovery was allowed is the recently decided one of *Mitran v. Williamson*. It holds that a complaint alleging that the defendant had repeatedly solicited plaintiff to have illicit intercourse and had sent obscene photographs of himself to her stated a cause of action.

. . .

Our study of the authorities, and of the arguments advanced, convinces us that, conceding such a cause of action may not be based upon mere negligence, the best considered view recognizes an action for severe emotional distress, though not accompanied by bodily impact or physical injury, where the defendant intentionally engaged in some conduct toward the plaintiff, (a) with the purpose of inflicting emotional distress, or, (b) where any reasonable person would have known that such would result; and his actions are of such a nature as to be considered outrageous and intolerable in that they offend against the generally accepted standards of decency and morality. This test seems to be a more realistic safeguard against false claims than to insist upon finding some other attendant tort, which may be of minor character, or fictional.

It is further to be observed that the argument against allowing such an action because groundless charges may be made is not a good reason for denying recovery. If the right to recover for injury resulting from the wrongful conduct could be defeated whenever such dangers exist, many of the grievances the law deals with would be eliminated. That some claims may be spurious should not compel those who administer justice to shut their eyes to serious wrongs and let them go without being brought to account. It is the function of courts and juries to determine whether claims are valid or false. This responsibility should not be shunned merely because the task may be difficult to perform.

We quite agree with the idea that under usual circumstances the solicitation to sexual intercourse would not be actionable even though it may be offensive to the offeree. It seems to be a custom of long standing and one which in all likelihood will continue. The assumption is usually indulged that most solicitations occur under such conditions as to fall within the well-known phrase of Chief Justice Magruder that, "there is no harm in asking." The Supreme Court of Kentucky in *Reed v. Maley* pertinently observed that an action will not lie in favor of a woman against a man who, without trespass or assault, makes such a request; and that the reverse is also true: that a man would have no right of action against a woman for such a solicitation.

But the situations just described, where tolerance for the conduct referred to is indulged, are clearly distinguishable from the aggravated circumstances the plaintiff claims existed here. Even though her complaint may not flawlessly state such a cause of action, the facts were sufficiently disclosed that the case she proposes to prove could be found to fall within the requirements hereinabove discussed. Therefore, the trial court erred in dismissing the action.

NOTES AND QUESTIONS

1. Why did the mother's claim fail in *Radovskis*? Is the judge suggesting that grief and mental distress are not worthy of compensation or that they are incapable of assessment in the absence of physical injury? Do you agree with either argument?

2. The Canadian and English courts have required the plaintiff to prove either actual physical harm or some serious psychological illness to recover for nervous shock. For example in *Heighington v. Ontario* (1987), 60 O.R. (2d) 641 (H.C.), aff'd (1989), 69 O.R. (2d) 484 (C.A.), the court stated that damages were recoverable in nervous shock for recognizable psychiatric disorders, but not for stress, strain, upset, or anxiety. See also *Wipfli v. Britten* (1982), 22 C.C.L.T. 104 (B.C.S.C.); *Timmermans v. Buelow* (1984), 38 C.C.L.T. 136 (Ont. H.C.); *Hasenclever v. Hoskins* (1988), 47 C.C.L.T. 225 (Ont. Div. Ct.); and *Sopinka (Litigation guardian of) v. Sopinka* (2001), 55 O.R. (3d) 529 (S.C.J.).

3. According to *Samms*, what must the plaintiff establish to succeed in an action for intentional infliction of nervous shock? Based on these principles, would the mother in *Radovskis* have recovered?

4. The courts have identified three difficulties with claims for nervous shock: concern with false, trivial and numerous actions; concern that socially acceptable conduct might cause some unduly sensitive individuals mental distress; and difficulty in assessing damages for mental distress in the absence of physical injury. How did the courts in *Radovskis* and *Samms* address these issues and which approach is preferable? For a thoughtful discussion of the difference between the Canadian and American analysis of the intentional infliction of nervous shock, see *Mainland Sawmills Ltd. v. IWA-Canada, Local 1-3567 Society* (2006), 41 C.C.L.T. (3d) 52 (B.C.S.C.).

5. In *Cant v. Cant* (1984), 49 O.R. (2d) 25 (Co. Ct.), the court entertained a claim for intentional infliction of nervous shock arising out of a custody battle over a child. However, in *Frame v. Smith*, [1987] 2 S.C.R. 99, the court opposed imposing tort liability in family law disputes. Wilson J., who dissented on a different issue, specifically said that intentional infliction of nervous shock claims should not be available in family law because they would provide arbitrary coverage and encourage vindictive litigation. See also *Davenport v. Miller* (1990), 108 N.B.R. (2d) 336 (Q.B.); and *Louie v. Lastman (No. 2)* (2001), 54 O.R. (3d) 301 (S.C.J.), aff'd (2002), 61 O.R. (3d) 459 (C.A.). Do you prefer the approach in *Frame* to that in *Cant*? See Cole, "Intentional Infliction of Emotional Distress Among Family Members" (1984) 61 Denver L. Rev. 553.

6. There has been a trend to advance intentional infliction of nervous shock claims alongside false arrest, wrongful dismissal, sexual harassment, and other employment claims. Does the concern in *Frame* about the multiplicity of actions and vindictive litigation apply equally in false arrest and employment-related litigation?

(a) THE BROADENING OF LIABILITY

The Canadian courts have been expanding recovery for the intentional infliction of nervous shock. This has resulted from either generously interpreting the facts to meet the traditional requirements of the tort or by rephrasing these requirements in broader terms. In *Rahemtulla v. Vanfed Credit Union* (1984), 29 C.C.L.T. 78 (B.C.S.C.), a woman who was accused of theft and summarily fired was awarded $5,000 for the intentional infliction of nervous shock. The court indicated that the defendant need not intend to cause nervous shock. This requirement would be met if the defendant acted in reckless disregard to this possibility, or if it was foreseeable that profound distress would ensue. While the court quoted *Radovskis* for the principle that visible and provable illness was required, it stated that the absence of expert medical evidence was not fatal to the claim. The court acknowledged that the plaintiff's other problems, including the discovery of a tumour in her chest, might well have contributed to her distress, but stated (at 90) that "the most significant cause of her depression and continuing unhappiness" was the defendant's conduct and its effect on her employment prospects.

In *Tran v. Financial Debt Recovery Ltd.* (2000), 2 C.C.L.T. (3d) 270 (Ont. S.C.J.), the plaintiff was barraged with abusive calls at work, threats and lies to pressure him into repaying his student loans, a portion of which he disputed. The plaintiff was awarded $25,000 on a "global basis" in defamation, intentional interference with economic relations and intentional infliction of nervous shock. In regard to the nervous shock claim, the court stated that the plaintiff was entitled to recover for emotional harm falling short of a psychiatric condition or illness.

NOTES AND QUESTIONS

1. In what ways do *Rahemtulla* and *Tran* differ from the traditional principles governing the intentional infliction of nervous shock? Rather than expanding the principles of intentional infliction of nervous shock, should the courts recognize a common law tort of harassment? See Fridman, "The Judicial Response to Non-sexual Harassment Claims" (1998) 77 Can. Bar Rev. 299.

2. In *Clark v. Canada*, [1994] 3 F.C. 323 (T.D.), a female RCMP officer who was driven to resign by the harassing conduct of various male colleagues over a protracted period recovered for the intentional infliction of nervous shock. The court also found her superiors liable in negligence for failing to intervene to protect her. See also *Rees v. Royal Canadian Mounted Police* (2004), 234 Nfld. & P.E.I.R. 347 (N.L.S.C. (T.D.)); and *Sulz v. Canada (A.G.)* (2006), 54 B.C.L.R. (4th) 328 (S.C.), aff'd (2006), 60 B.C.L.R. (4th) 43 (C.A.), in which former RCMP employees successfully sued their former employer for emotional and sexual harassment in the workplace. In both cases, there were large general damage awards, primarily for psychological and emotional distress.

3. In *Prinzo v. Baycrest Centre for Geriatric Care* (2002), 60 O.R. (3d) 474 (C.A.), the plaintiff had worked for 17 years in a beauty shop. She missed work for several months because of a mental illness. During that time, her employer announced that her position was being eliminated for financial reasons and accused her of malingering. There was, in fact, no financial need to eliminate the plaintiff's position and she was not malingering. As a result of the defendant's conduct, the plaintiff's fragile health deteriorated. The plaintiff sued on several grounds, including intentional infliction of mental suffering. The Court of Appeal upheld the $15,000 award of general damages but overturned the $5,000 punitive damage award.

4. For other examples in which the courts have taken an expansive view of intentional infliction of nervous shock, see *Bell-Ginsburg v. Ginsburg* (1993), 14 O.R. (3d) 217 (Gen. Div.); *MacKay v. Buelow* (1995), 24 C.C.L.T. (2d) 184 (Ont. Gen. Div.); and *Santamaria v. James*, 2004 CarswellOnt 790 (S.C.J.) (WLeC). But see *High Parklane Consulting Inc. v. Royal Group Technologies Ltd.* (2007), 44 C.C.L.T. (3d) 169 (Ont. S.C.J.).

5. For a more detailed discussion of the intentional infliction of nervous shock, see Mullany & Handford, *Tort Liability for Psychiatric Damage* (1993) at 283-307.

6. Summarize the legal principles governing the intentional infliction of nervous shock.

(b) THE INNOMINATE INTENTIONAL TORT

Several Commonwealth authors have viewed *Wilkinson* as establishing an innominate intentional tort claim for all unjustified, intentionally-inflicted bodily injuries – nervous shock being but one example. The other illustrations cited include intentionally infecting someone with a disease, setting a trap in someone's path, poisoning someone's food, and removing essential medicine from an incapacitated patient. Although such intentional conduct is morally blameworthy and likely to cause serious injury, it does not come within the traditional definition of the nominate intentional torts. Thus, the innominate action provides a convenient mechanism for redressing such claims without disturbing accepted principles.

NOTES AND QUESTIONS

1. An "innominate tort" is a tort that has not been specifically named. Nominate torts, in contrast, have specific names, such as "battery," "assault" and "false imprisonment."

2. It is difficult to determine the exact scope of the innominate intentional tort action. For example, does it apply solely to bodily injury or does it also include other interferences with physical autonomy? If accepted, would the innominate intentional tort action have provided a remedy in *Bird v. Jones*, extracted above in the section on false imprisonment? Could it be invoked in cases of sexual harassment which did not involve assault, battery or nervous shock? See Fleming, *The Law of Torts*, 9th ed. (1998) at 40-41.

3. In the United States, the courts have tended to deal with indirect injury cases by relaxing the requirements of directness in the nominate actions. This approach eliminates the need for an innominate intentional tort action and permits the intentional infliction of nervous shock to be recognized as an independent tort that is not tied to proof of physical injury.

Nevertheless, there is support in the American case law for a "*prima facie* tort doctrine": a principle that appears to be broader, but otherwise comparable to, the innominate intentional tort action. In the words of one author:

> The *prima facie* tort is generally defined as the "infliction of intentional harm, resulting in damages, without excuse or justification, by an act or series of acts which would otherwise be lawful." The specific applications of this definition vary greatly based on the manner in which courts interpret these elements. These divergencies in interpretation lead courts to apply the *prima facie* tort in inconsistent ways.

See Shapiro, "The Prima Facie Tort Doctrine: Acknowledging the Need for Judicial Scrutiny of Malice" (1983) 63 Boston U.L. Rev. 1101 at 1101.

4. The High Court of Australia recognized a related cause of action in *Beaudesert Shire Council v. Smith* (1966), 120 C.L.R. 145 (H.C.A.). The court stated (at 156) that "independently of trespass, negligence or nuisance but by an action for damages upon the case, a person who suffers harm or loss as the inevitable consequence of the unlawful, intentional and positive acts of another is entitled to damages from that other." However, the High Court subsequently ruled that this principle was unsound and should not be followed: *Northern Territory v. Mengel* (1995), 185 C.L.R. 307 (H.C.A.). See Mullany, "*Beaudesert* Buried" (1995) 111 L.Q.R. 583; and Cane, "The Inexorable Advance of Negligence" (1995) 3 Torts L.J. 205.

5. The Canadian position is difficult to assess because of the dearth of academic and judicial discussion. See Atrens, "Intentional Interference with the Person" in Linden, ed., *Studies in Canadian Tort Law* (1968) 378 at 397-401; *Graham v. Saville*, [1945] O.R. 301 at 310-11 (C.A.); *Canada Safeway Ltd. v. Manitoba Food & Commercial Workers, Local 832* (1983), 25 C.C.L.T. 1 (Man. C.A.); and *Cant v. Cant* (1984), 49 O.R. (2d) 25 (Co. Ct.).

6. Although the innominate intentional tort action, the *prima facie* tort doctrine and *Beaudesert* create distinct causes of action, they all reflect a concern with the inflexibility of the intentional torts. Based on the intentional tort actions discussed in this chapter, is this a legitimate concern? Can you suggest alternative mechanisms for dealing with this concern? As we shall see, at least some Canadian courts have responded to this situation by attempting to create new nominate intentional tort actions.

REVIEW PROBLEMS

1. The torts of assault and the intentional infliction of nervous shock both involve the apprehension created in the mind of the plaintiff. Provide an example of conduct that would give rise to both actions. See *Timmermans v. Buelow* (1984), 38 C.C.L.T. 136 (Ont. H.C.); and *Mahal v. Young* (1986), 36 C.C.L.T. 143 (B.C.S.C.).

2. Jones, a professional boxer, was incensed by a story that had been written about him by Smith, a local sports writer. Jones called Smith and told him to retract the story "or else." While Jones was not a particularly good boxer, he was widely known for his temper and long criminal record for unprovoked assaults. Smith was scared. When he explained to his wife what had happened, she fainted and hit her head on the floor, suffering a concussion. As Smith was preparing to take his wife to the hospital, Jones called again and indicated that he was coming over to "discuss these matters." Smith, who had a weak heart, suffered a minor heart attack brought on by the severe emotional strain of the boxer's threats coupled with his wife's injuries. Mr. and Mrs. Smith survived the incident and now wish to sue Jones. Your initial investigation has revealed that Jones was unaware of Smith's weak heart.

9. Protection of Privacy

(a) INTRODUCTION

In Canada, privacy is protected in a piecemeal fashion by a myriad of civil actions and statutory provisions. The nominate intentional torts were not designed to redress invasions of privacy and only incidentally protect these interests. For example, homeowners will succeed in trespass to land against someone who has planted a listening device on their property, but not against an individual who intercepts their conversations without entering their land. Similar illustrations can be cited involving assault, intentional infliction of nervous shock, defamation, and intimidation. Shortcomings in the existing remedies have prompted consideration of both a common law tort for invasion of privacy and the enactment of various types of privacy legislation.

Perhaps the most challenging problem is defining the concept of privacy. The broader the definition of privacy, the more it will conflict with other interests, such as freedom of speech, movement and association. These problems have led some authors to seriously question the value of privacy as a legal concept. The definitional challenges posed by privacy are unlikely to be resolved in the immediate future, given the heightened public concern about these issues and the accompanying increase in litigation.

NOTES AND QUESTIONS

1. For a discussion of the protection provided by the existing nominate torts, see Burns, "Privacy and the Common Law: A Tangled Skein Unravelling?" in Gibson, ed., *Aspects of Privacy Law* (1980) 21; and Irvine, "The Invasion of Privacy in Ontario: A 1983 Survey" [1983] L.S.U.C. Special Lectures 25.

2. Most American jurisdictions recognize a common law tort for the invasion of privacy. These actions typically reflect the position of the *Restatement (Second) of the Law of Torts* (1977) at §652A which provides that the right of privacy is violated by unreasonable intrusion upon the seclusion of another, appropriation of another person's name or likeness, unreasonable publicity given to another's private life, and publicity that unreasonably places another in a false light before the public. The American Law Institute states that other privacy interests may be recognized as justifying protection. Can you suggest additional privacy interests that warrant recognition?

3. For a review of the American authorities see Post, "The Social Foundations of Privacy: Community and Self in the Common Law Tort" (1989) 77 Cal. L. Rev. 957; and Dobbs, *The Law of Torts* (2000) at 1197-1211.

4. For a searing criticism of the concept of privacy, see Wacks, "The Poverty of 'Privacy' " (1980) 96 L.Q.R. 73. In his conclusion (at 88) he states:

> "Privacy" has grown into a large and unwieldy concept. Synonymous with autonomy, it has colonised traditional liberties, become entangled with confidentiality, secrecy, defamation, property, and the storage of information. It would be unreasonable to expect a notion so complex as "privacy" not to spill into regions with which it is closely related, but this process has resulted in the dilution of "privacy" itself, diminishing the prospect of its own protection as well as the protection of the related interests.
>
> . . .
>
> By locating, as the core of the issue, the regulation of "personal information," the subject is liberated from a tendentiously predetermined general theory, and specific answers may more easily be sought to specific, and frequently disparate, questions. Such progress is possible only if the law eschews the ambiguity, the abstractions and the poverty of "privacy."

Is Wacks opposed to protecting the specific interests that have fallen within the rubric of privacy or to the lumping of all of these matters into privacy? See also Bezanson, "*The Right to Privacy* Revisited: Privacy, News, and Social Change, 1890-1990" (1992) 80 Cal. L. Rev. 1133; Bruyer, "Privacy: A Review and Critique of the Literature" (2006) 43 Alta. L. Rev. 553; and Brown, "Rethinking Privacy: Exclusivity, Private Relation and Tort Law" (2006) 43 Alta. L. Rev. 589.

(b) A COMMON LAW TORT ACTION FOR THE INVASION OF PRIVACY?

MOTHERWELL v. MOTHERWELL

(1976), 73 D.L.R. (3d) 62 (Alta. S.C. (A.D.))

[The defendant, who suffered from a paranoid condition and was mentally unstable, continually harassed the plaintiffs (her brother, sister-in-law and father), making false accusations by way of telephone and mail. After the defendant refused their repeated requests to cease, the plaintiffs brought an action against her for, *inter alia*, invasion of privacy and nuisance, claiming nominal damages and an injunction. The plaintiffs won at trial and the defendant appealed. The defendant argued that "no action lies with the plaintiffs . . . to restrain her lawful communications" with them.]

CLEMENT J.A.: . . .The arguments in appeal advanced by the appellant draw a distinction between nuisance and invasion of privacy. It is said that invasion of privacy does not come within the principle of private nuisance, and that it is a species of activity not recognized as remedial by the common law. It is urged that the common law does not have within itself the resources to recognize invasion of privacy as either included in an existing category or as a new category of nuisance, and that it has lost its original power, by which indeed it created itself, to note new ills arising in a growing and changing society and pragmatically to establish a principle to meet the need for control and remedy;

and then by categories to develop the principle as the interests of justice make themselves sufficiently apparent. . . .

The rule of stare decisis operates, as it seems to me, to regulate the application of precedents to cases which can be said to fall within a category. When the circumstances of a case do not appear to bring it fairly within an established category, they may lie sufficiently within the concept of a principle that consideration of a new category is warranted. The scope of a category may in time be broadened by a trend in precedents which reflect judicial considerations going beyond the disciplines of *stare decisis*. Those same considerations, arising from adequately demonstrated social need of a continuing nature, may lead, when necessary to maintain social justice, to a new category or the review of a principle. . . .

[The court discussed the law of private nuisance at length and made particular reference to the three categories of nuisance recognized in *Clerk & Lindsell on Torts*, 13th ed. (1969) at 781. The third category – the undue interference with a neighbour in the comfortable and convenient enjoyment of his land – was the most germane to the case at bar.]

I think that the interests of our developing jurisprudence would be better served by approaching invasion of privacy by abuse of the telephone system as a new category [of private nuisance], rather than seeking by rationalization to enlarge the third category recognized by *Clerk & Lindsell*. We are dealing with a new factor. Heretofore the matters of complaint have reached the plaintiff's premises by natural means; sound through the air waves, pollution in many forms carried by air currents, vibrations through the earth, and the like. Here, the matters complained of arise within the premises through the use by the appellant of communication agencies in the nature of public utilities available to everyone, which the plaintiffs have caused to serve their premises. They are non-selective in the sense that so long as they are employed by the plaintiffs they have no control over the incoming communications. Nevertheless there are differences between the two agencies of telephone and mail and it does not necessarily follow from their similarities that both should be accepted into a new category.

The telephone system is so much the part of the daily life of society that many look on it as a necessity. Its use is certainly taken as a right at least in a social sense. It virtually makes neighbours not only of the persons close at hand, but those in distant places, other cities, other countries. It is a system provided for rational and reasonable communication between people, and its abuse by invasion of privacy is a matter of general interest. . . . It is essential to the operation of such a system that a call from someone be signalled to the intended receiver by sound such as the ringing of a bell. The receiver cannot know who is calling him until he answers. Calls must be answered if the system is to work. There are not many who would assert that protection against invasion of privacy by telephone would be a judicial idiosyncrasy. Further than that, the people of this Province through the Legislature have expressed a public interest in the proper use of the system in enacting s. 31 of the *Alberta Government Telephones Act*.

In *Clerk & Lindsell*, p. 785, para. 1396, this is said: "A nuisance of this kind, to be actionable, must be such as to be a real interference with the comfort or convenience of living according to the standards of the average man." This statement is amply supported by authority and I take it to be applicable to invasion of privacy. . . .

[Clement J.A. concluded that the respondents had valid claims in private nuisance for the invasion of their privacy through the abuse of the telephone system. He upheld the trial judge's award of nominal damages and the granting of an injunction against further calls. The harassing and offensive mail did not constitute a nuisance because it did not result in a substantial and unreasonable interference with the plaintiffs' use and enjoyment of their property.]

NOTES AND QUESTIONS

1. What was the basis of the decision in *Motherwell*? What factors did Clement J.A. consider in deciding to extend common law protection in nuisance? For a blunt critique of *Motherwell* see *Hunter v. Canary Wharf Ltd.*, [1997] 2 All E.R. 426 (H.L.).

2. What remedies did the plaintiffs seek in *Motherwell*? Why did they not claim compensatory damages? Should that have been fatal to their claim? See *Hasenclever v. Hoskins* (1988), 47 C.C.L.T. 225 (Ont. Div. Ct.), a case in which the inadequacies in pleading damages resulted in the dismissal of a claim that was similar to that in *Motherwell.*

3. As we shall discuss, the Canadian, Australian and New Zealand courts have recognized a common law tort action for invasion of privacy in various categories of cases. In contrast, the English courts have refused to recognize any such claim. According to the House of Lords in *Wainwright v. Home Office*, [2004] 2 A.C. 406 (H.L.), the creation of a tort of privacy requires a comprehensive approach that can only be provided by legislation.

(c) SUBSEQUENT COMMON LAW DEVELOPMENTS

As the following notes and questions illustrate, the common law principles of privacy have evolved piecemeal in Canada, providing redress for some particularly troubling and easily defined categories of privacy cases. While the Canadian courts are moving toward recognizing additional categories of privacy claims, the exact state of the law in these areas cannot be determined with certainty. Several of the relevant cases simply involve unsuccessful pretrial motions to strike out the plaintiff's privacy claim. In other cases, the courts' comments on privacy are made in passing or phrased in equivocal terms. Finally, some courts have awarded global damages for a plaintiff's overlapping claims in intentional infliction of nervous shock, malicious prosecution, harassment, and invasion of privacy without providing much analysis. The tentative nature of the current law is aptly reflected in *Somwar v. McDonald's Restaurants of Canada Ltd.* (2006), 79 O.R. (3d) 172 at 180 (S.C.J.), where the court concluded "it is not settled law in Ontario that there is no tort of invasion of privacy."

NOTES AND QUESTIONS

1. In *Dyne Holdings Ltd. v. Royal Insurance Co. of Canada* (1996), 135 D.L.R. (4th) 142 at 160 (P.E.I.S.C. (A.D.)), the judge stated: "It would seem to me the courts in Canada are not far from recognizing a common law right of privacy if they have not already done so. It is also clear that Canadian courts do not hesitate to protect privacy interests under some recognized tort." What does this statement mean and what are its implications?

2. There has been an increase in the number of "harassment" claims. Like *Motherwell*, some involve offensive phone calls and mail, but others include direct verbal confrontations, threats and stalking. In these latter situations, the courts have held that the conduct constitutes an invasion of privacy, independent of any other tort action that may be brought. See *Capan v. Capan* (1980), 14 C.C.L.T. 191 (Ont. H.C.); *Roth v. Roth* (1991), 4 O.R. (3d) 740 (Gen. Div.); and *MacKay v. Buelow* (1995), 24 C.C.L.T. (2d) 184 (Ont. Gen. Div.). It should be noted that s. 264 of the *Criminal Code* creates an offence of criminal harassment that is commonly referred to as stalking. See MacFarlane, "People Who Stalk People" (1997) 31 U.B.C.L. Rev. 37.

3. As discussed, there has been a trend to add an harassment claim when suing for malicious prosecution or the intentional infliction of nervous shock. The boundary between nervous shock and harassment often appears to be blurred. For example in *Mainland Sawmills Ltd. v. IWA-Canada, Local 1-3567 Society* (2006), 41 C.C.L.T. (3d) 52 (B.C.S.C.), the plaintiffs' harassment claims were dismissed, because their emotional distress fell short of the extreme emotional distress required in the intentional infliction of nervous shock.

The English courts recognized a common law tort action for a range of harassing and threatening conduct in 1993, only to reject it four years later once statutory protection from harassment was enacted. See *Khorasandjian v. Bush*, [1993] Q.B. 727 (C.A.); Bridgeman & Jones, "Harassing Conduct and Outrageous Acts: A Cause of Action for Intentionally Inflicted Mental Distress?" (1994) 14 L.S. 180; and *Hunter v. Canary Wharf Ltd.*, [1997] A.C. 655 (H.L.).

4. The courts have not yet resolved whether watching and following a person in public or questioning a person's friends or neighbours constitutes an actionable wrong. Should there be any limits on such behaviour? Should it make a difference if the person watching is a police officer, private detective, devoted fan, newspaper photographer, or curious member of the public? See *Poole v. Ragen*, [1958] O.W.N. 77 (H.C.); *Nader v. General Motors Corp.*, 25 N.Y.2d 560 (C.A. 1970); and *Davis v. McArthur* (1971), 17 D.L.R. (3d) 760 (B.C.C.A.).

5. In *Saccone v. Orr* (1981), 19 C.C.L.T. 37 (Ont. Co. Ct.), the defendant secretly tape-recorded his telephone call with the plaintiff. When the plaintiff learned about the tape, he warned the defendant not to use it, but the defendant denied its existence. The defendant subsequently played the tape at a municipal council meeting in an effort to clear himself of certain allegations. The local newspaper printed the tape's content, to the embarrassment of the plaintiff. The judge summarized the facts and stated (at 46): "Certainly, for want of a better description as to what happened, this is an invasion of privacy, and despite the very able argument of defendant's counsel that no such action exists, I have come to the conclusion that the plaintiff must be given some right of recovery for what the defendant has in this case done."

Was it the unauthorized recording or the unauthorized playing of the tape, or both, that constituted the invasion of privacy? Would the judge have reached the same conclusion had the defendant revealed detailed written notes of the call that were recorded without the plaintiff's knowledge? Unless the plaintiff demanded and received assurances of confidentiality, why should he assume that the defendant would keep their conversation private? Should different considerations apply when a person who is not a party to the conversation secretly tapes the call?

6. In *Ste-Marie c. Placements J.P.M. Marquis* (2005), 31 C.C.L.T. (3d) 167 (Qc. C.A.), the defendant employer secretly wire-tapped phone lines which the plaintiff employee used at work. The employer gave the police a tape of the employee's conversation with a known safecracker. The employee was arrested but never charged, and was fired. The employee sued for invasion of privacy, claiming breaches of his rights under the *Civil Code of Quebec*, S.Q. 1991, c. 64 and the Quebec *Charter of Human Rights and Freedoms*, R.S.Q. c. C-12. In dismissing the action, the court stated that employees have a diminished expectation of privacy, as their rights must be reconciled with their contractual and other duties to their employer. In contrast to *Saccone*, the Quebec Court of Appeal stated that the fact that the conversation was taped rather than overheard changed nothing, given its content and relationship to the employee's duties.

See also *Malone v. Metropolitan Commissioner of Police*, [1979] 1 All E.R. 256 (C.A.), in which the court held that the plaintiff had no right of privacy protecting him from police wire-tapping of his telephone calls.

7. In *Lipiec v. Borsa* (1996), 31 C.C.L.T. (2d) 294 (Ont. Gen. Div.), the defendants became obsessed with their neighbours' landscaping. Out of spite, the defendants removed a fence that separated the properties and installed a commercial-quality surveillance camera that continuously monitored the plantiffs' backyard. The plantiffs' privacy was lost and their enjoyment of their yard was destroyed. The court held the defendants liable for invasion of privacy. While expressing reluctance to impose liability on the basis of surveillance alone, the judge quoted Fleming, *The Law of Torts,* 8th ed. (1992) at 604 for the proposition that "there is considerable authority which could support redress against overlooking or spying on the premises of others for the sole purpose of causing annoyance." Would liability have been warranted if the defendants had installed the camera partially for security purposes?

8. In *Milner v. Manufacturers Life Insurance Co.* (2005), 36 C.C.L.T. (3d) 232 (B.C.S.C.), the plaintiff applied for long-term disability benefits. However, the defendant believed that her application was based on false claims. Consequently, the defendant arranged for video surveillance of the plaintiff which incidentally captured members of her family. The plaintiff claimed damages for breach of privacy under the *Privacy Act*, R.S.B.C. 1996, c. 373. In dismissing the claim, the court stated that the defendant had a legitimate interest in conducting video surveillance, given the nature of the plaintiff's claim and her questionable credibility. See also *Watt v. Meier*, 2006 CarswellBC 2236 (S.C.) (WLeC).

9. In *Lord v. McGregor* (2000), 50 C.C.L.T. (2d) 206 (B.C.S.C.), the plaintiff's disruptive behaviour during earlier visits resulted in his being barred from the penitentiary. Nevertheless, the plaintiff informed the prison officials that he was going to visit his son and notified the media. The plaintiff's visit, including his altercation with the staff, was videotaped and a copy was released to a television station that broadcasted it. The video was taken in a public reception area in which there were signs advising visitors of the possibility of being videotaped. The plaintiff brought various claims, but the issue

in this case was whether he could recover under the common law for the invasion of privacy. In dismissing the claim, the judge stated that the emerging academic discussion and case law did not support a common law right to privacy on the facts. See also *Australian Broadcasting Corp. v. Lenah Game Meats Pty. Ltd.* (2001), 208 C.L.R. 199 (H.C.A.).

In what circumstances, if any, should video surveillance of an individual in public give rise to a common law tort action for the invasion of privacy? If such an action were recognized, should the defendant's motive for conducting the surveillance be considered in determining if it constitutes an invasion of privacy?

10. Increasingly, the Canadian courts have accepted that unwanted media attention may constitute an actionable invasion of privacy. See for example *F.(P.) v. Ontario* (1989), 47 C.C.L.T. 231 (Ont. Dt. Ct.) (young offender's picture published in local newspaper); *R.(L.) v. Nyp* (1995), 25 C.C.L.T. (2d) 309 (Ont. Gen. Div.) (media disclosing that undercover police officer was sexually assaulted); and *Valiquette c. Gazette (The)* (1991), 8 C.C.L.T. (2d) 302 (Qc. S.C.), rev'd in part, [1997] R.J.Q. 30 (C.A.) (media disclosing that a teacher had AIDS).

These cases are similar to the American privacy concept of unreasonable publicity given to another's private life. The American courts have recognized a cause of action for the public disclosure of private facts. The plaintiff must establish that the facts are true, intimate, offensive to a reasonable person, and of no concern to the public. Many claims fail on the basis that the information is newsworthy or of public concern.

The tort has also recently been recognized in Australia: See *Grosse v. Purvis*, [2003] Q.D.C. 151.

11. In *Aubry v. Éditions Vice-Versa*, [1998] 1 S.C.R. 591, a photographer took a picture of a young woman sitting on the steps of a building in Montreal. When the photograph was subsequently published in an arts magazine, the young woman sued the photographer and the magazine, claiming invasion of privacy. A majority of the court upheld the lower court's $2,000 damage award under Quebec's *Civil Code*. The majority stated that a balance had to be struck in each case between the individual's right to privacy and the right to freedom of expression under the Quebec *Charter of Human Rights and Freedoms*. The plaintiff's right prevailed in this case, partially because the photographer could have asked permission to take her picture and because she was identifiable from the published picture. This need to balance competing interests is also discussed in *Australian Broadcasting Corp., supra*; *Douglas v. Hello! Ltd.*, [2001] 2 All E.R. 289 (C.A.); *Campbell v. MGN Ltd.*, [2004] 2 All E.R. 995 (H.L.); and *Hosking v. Runting*, [2005] 1 N.Z.L.R. 1 (C.A.).

12. The Canadian courts have recognized a common law tort action for the appropriation of personality for the unauthorized use of a person's name or likeness. However, as the following references illustrate, it is not clear if this is viewed as a form of invasion of privacy or as an intentional economic tort. See *Krouse v. Chrysler Canada Ltd.* (1973), 1 O.R. (2d) 225 (C.A.); *Athans v. Canadian Adventure Camps Ltd.* (1977), 4 C.C.L.T. 20 (Ont. H.C.); *Heath v. Weist-Barron School of Television (Canada) Ltd.* (1981), 34 O.R. (2d) 126 (H.C.); Howell, "The Common Law Appropriation of Personality Tort"

(1986) 2 I.P.J. 149; and Abramovitch, "Misappropriation of Personality" (2000) 33 C.B.L.J. 230.

13. In *Gould Estate v. Stoddart Publishing Co.* (1996), 31 C.C.L.T. (2d) 224 (Ont. Gen. Div.), aff'd on other grounds (1998), 39 O.R. (3d) 545 (C.A.), the defendant journalist interviewed and photographed Glenn Gould in 1956, before Gould became famous. Forty years later, after Gould's death, the defendant published a book containing some of those photographs and transcripts of their conversations. Gould's estate sued unsuccessfully for the appropriation of personality. The court stated that it had to balance the individual's privacy interests and the public's interests in freedom of expression and dissemination of newsworthy information. It held that the appropriation of personality is limited to the use of a celebrity's name or image to sell the defendant's product. Consequently, the tort does not extend to situations in which the celebrity is the subject of the work itself, as in a biography. See also *Shaw v. Berman* (1997), 144 D.L.R. (4th) 484 (Ont. Gen. Div.), aff'd (1998), 167 D.L.R. (4th) 576 (Ont. C.A.).

14. In the absence of comprehensive legislation setting out the various situations in which privacy interests will be protected, the patchwork of common law cases will continue to evolve. For example, in *Somwar v. McDonald's Restaurants of Canada Ltd.* (2006), 79 O.R. (3d) 172 (S.C.J.), the court refused to strike out the plaintiff's invasion of privacy claim that undertaking a credit check without the subject's consent gave rise to a common law tort action for the invasion of privacy. For a general discussion of the common law tort of invasion of privacy, see Bell, "Tort of Invasion of Privacy – Has its Time Finally Come?" in Archibald & Cochrane, eds., *Annual Review of Civil Litigation, 2004* (2005) 225.

(d) THE STATUTORY PROTECTION OF PRIVACY

The *Charter* contains various guaranteed rights and freedoms, and provides remedies for their infringement. Although the term "privacy" is not used in the *Charter*, this interest is an integral part of many of the fundamental freedoms in s. 2 and the legal rights in ss. 7 to 15. The Supreme Court of Canada has stated that the *Charter* will be interpreted broadly and purposefully to protect the rights and freedoms it guarantees. If an individual's *Charter* rights have been violated and that violation cannot be justified, the individual may apply to a court of competent jurisdiction under s. 24(1) for a remedy. The court has broad discretion to grant whatever remedy it deems appropriate in the circumstances. However, it should be noted that the *Charter* is limited by s. 32 to federal and provincial laws and governmental actions.

Existing federal and provincial legislation may also serve to protect an individual's right to privacy. For example, Parliament has made the unauthorized electronic interception of private communications an indictable offence punishable by imprisonment for up to five years. The *Criminal Code* also prohibits obscene, racist, threatening, harassing, and other behaviour which may infringe upon an individual's privacy. Similarly, the provincial governments have enacted legislation regulating land use, trespass, noise levels, and the collection and dissemination of academic, medical, legal, and other kinds of personal information. However, the most specific statutory protection of privacy is provided by the British Columbia, Manitoba, Newfoundland, Nova Scotia, and Saskatchewan privacy statutes.

HOLLINSWORTH v. BCTV

[1999] 6 W.W.R. 54 (B.C.C.A.)

LAMBERT J.A. (orally): . . .In 1984 the plaintiff, Mr. Hollinsworth, began to go bald. He started wearing a toupee but he was not content with his appearance. Two years later, in 1986, Mr. Hollinsworth entered into a contract with Look International Enterprises (1983) Incorporated and underwent tunnel graft surgery so that a hairpiece could be attached to his head. Dr. Williams performed the surgery. Mr. Hollinsworth signed a release and consent [that allowed the procedure to be filmed for instructional purposes only.]

Eric Cable, a camera person for BCTV, filmed the operation at the request of Dr. Williams and Look International. Mr. Cable recorded the procedure under a freelance contract entered into with Dr. Williams or Look International or both. He did not do it for his regular employer, BCTV.

The videotape was made for medical instructional purposes only. Dr. Williams knew that. Look International knew that. And Mr. Hollinsworth only consented to that.

Dr. Williams gave the video to Look International after he received it from Mr. Cable following the operation and the filming.

. . .

[S]even years later, BCTV decided to do a five minute feature on baldness after the 6:00. . . news one night. Ms. Aylesworth was assigned to the task by BCTV and Mr. Cable was assigned as her cameraman. . . . Mr. Cable mentioned to Ms. Aylesworth that Dr. Williams did tunnel graft surgery for baldness; that Mr. Cable himself had photographed the procedure; and that there was a videotape.

Mr. Cable and Ms. Aylesworth went to Dr. Williams' office and interviewed him. He was willing or eager to give them the tape. He phoned Mr. van Samang at Look International, found out that the tape was there, and suggested to Ms. Aylesworth and Mr. Cable that they go over to see Mr. van Samang. Dr. Williams said nothing to Mr. Cable or Ms. Aylesworth about confidentiality in relation to his patient, Mr. Hollinsworth.

Mr. van Samang gave Ms. Aylesworth the videotape of the 1986 operation on Mr. Hollinsworth. Ms. Aylesworth was concerned about doctor/patient confidentiality and asked whether the patient in the operation had consented to this use of the videotape. Mr. van Samang assured Ms. Aylesworth that BCTV could use the videotape and that the patient had consented to that. Mr. van Samang also told Ms. Aylesworth that he did not know the current whereabouts of the patient.

. . .

[A]fter the 6:00. . . news one night, BCTV broadcast the feature on baldness. Part of the videotape on Mr. Hollinsworth was shown, including an unmistakable likeness of his full face. He was easily identifiable by his family and by his friends. His full face appeared on the screen for about three seconds.

[The plaintiff sued BCTV, Look International, Mr. van Samang and others for defamation, breach of confidentiality and breach of the provincial *Privacy Act*, R.S.B.C. 1996, c. 373. The trial judge dismissed the actions against BCTV, but awarded the plaintiff $15,000 on his claims against Look International and Mr. van Samang. The plaintiff appealed the dismissal of the claims against BCTV and the damage award.

Lambert J.A. confirmed that BCTV could not be held liable in defamation because it had not made a false statement. Nor was BCTV liable for breach of confidence as there was no evidence that it knew or ought to have known that the videotape was confidential. Lambert J.A. then considered the privacy claim under the statute.]

The claim based on an allegation of a statutory tort under the *Privacy Act* rests on the terms of the Act itself. Section 1, which establishes the tort, reads in this way:

> **Violation of privacy actionable**
>
> 1 (1) It is tort, actionable without proof of damage, for a person, *wilfully* and *without a claim of right*, to violate the privacy of another.
> (2) The nature and degree of privacy to which a person is entitled in a situation or in relation to a matter is that which is reasonable in the circumstances, giving due regard to the lawful interests of others.
> (3) In determining whether the act or conduct of a person is a violation of another's privacy, regard must be given to the nature, incidence and occasion of the act or conduct and to any domestic or other relationship between the parties.
> (4) Without limiting subsections (1) to (3), privacy may be violated by eavesdropping or surveillance, whether or not accomplished by trespass. [emphasis added]

I turn first to the word "wilfully". In my opinion the word "wilfully" does not apply broadly to any intentional act that has the effect of violating privacy but more narrowly to an intention to do an act which the person doing the act knew or should have known would violate the privacy of another person. That was not established in this case.

I move now to the phrase, "without a claim of right". I adopt the meaning given by Mr. Justice Seaton to that very phrase, "without a claim of right" in *Davis v. McArthur* (1969), 10 D.L.R. (3d) 250 (B.C.S.C.):

. . . an honest belief in a state of facts which, if it existed, would be a legal justification or excuse. . . .

It is unnecessary in this case to decide whether the honest belief must be a reasonable one. Here, on the evidence, the belief was both honest and reasonable. I would not accede to this claim under the *Privacy Act*. It is not necessary for me to consider the exceptions under the Act.

In my opinion, the award of $15,000 damages against Mr. van Samang and Look International was neither too high nor too low. I would not vary it. It follows that I would dismiss the appeal.

NOTES AND QUESTIONS

1. Why was the plaintiff in *Hollinsworth* successful against Look International and Mr. van Samang, but not against BCTV? See also *F. (J.M.) v. Chappell* (1998), 41 C.C.L.T. (2d) 26 (B.C.C.A.); and *Getejanc v. Brentwood College Assn.* (2001), 6 C.C.L.T. (3d) 261 (B.C.S.C.).

2. Regardless of whether it is based on common law or statute, how useful will tort law be in controlling invasions of privacy? What role should activity-specific regulation and criminal law play in protecting privacy?

3. It is not possible in this section to discuss all of the *Charter* provisions which may be relevant to the protection of privacy. In order to understand the *Charter*'s impact on privacy interests, it is necessary to analyze each of the relevant rights and freedoms. For the *Charter*'s impact on the tort of invasion of privacy, see Craig, "Invasion of Privacy and *Charter* Values: The Common-Law Tort Awakens" (1997) 42 McGill L.J. 355.

4. The American courts have interpreted their constitution as containing a right to privacy. See for example Tribe, *American Constitutional Law*, 3d ed., vol. II (2000), ch. 15.

5. Individuals convicted of violating the federal wire-tap legislation may be ordered to pay the aggrieved party up to $5,000 in punitive damages. See ss. 183-196 of the *Criminal Code*. See also Cohen, "Invasion of Privacy: Police and Electronic Surveillance in Canada" (1982) 27 McGill L.J. 619.

6. Parliament has enacted legislation regulating the collection and dissemination of information from federal data banks. See the *Privacy Act*, R.S.C. 1985, c. P-21. More recently, the federal government enacted the *Personal Information Protection and Electronics Documents Act*, S.C. 2000, c. 5 which, among other things, governs the private sector collection, use and disclosure of all "personal information" occurring "in the course of commercial activity." The statute applies to both federal and provincial custodians of records, unless the province has enacted comparable commercial data protection legislation.

The provinces have also enacted freedom of information legislation regulating the collection, use and disclosure of provincial and municipal government records. There is also provincial legislation governing credit reporting agencies and other commercial data banks.

For a summary of much of this federal and provincial legislation see McNairn & Scott, *Privacy Law in Canada* (2001); and McIsaac, Shields & Klein, *The Law of Privacy in Canada*, looseleaf (2000).

7. Many provinces have also enacted complex health information protection legislation. This legislation typically applies in addition to similar record-keeping, confidentiality and disclosure provisions contained in the public hospitals, mental health, child welfare and regulated health professions statutes and other related legislation.

REVIEW PROBLEM

John Smith and Mary Jones had been partners in a lucrative business that Mary founded. Their working relationship deteriorated as the business grew. Despite Mary's efforts to resolve their differences amicably, John refused. Finally, Mary left the business and initiated what was likely to be a successful million-dollar action. Mary offered to settle on fair terms but John refused, offering her only a small fraction of what she would likely recover.

John then set about to pressure her into settling on his terms. He hired private detectives to follow Mary in public and collect information on her new business. John directed the detectives to take pictures of anyone with whom Mary met and to question all of her friends, relatives, neighbours, business associates, and acquaintances. John realized that these interviews were unlikely to yield much useful information for the litigation, but he thought that they would increase the emotional pressures on Mary to settle. John told the detectives not to initiate any verbal contact with Mary, enter her property, interfere with her freedom of movement, or physically intimidate her.

Mary became aware of the detectives' activities almost immediately, and her friends and associates complained to her about being approached by the detectives. Although John did not contact Mary, his lawyer called her repeatedly. The lawyer demanded information related to the litigation and the return of all company property, including any documents, business records and even stationery supplies. The lawyer also sent Mary a barrage of complex, time-limited settlement offers, all of which proved to be woefully inadequate. The lawyer's correspondence was so threatening and upsetting that Mary had to stop reading it.

As John expected, these tactics began to take their toll on Mary. Her migraine headaches increased in frequency and duration, she could not sleep and became increasingly reluctant to leave her house. Mary called John and told him that his conduct was making her sick. John showed no remorse, stating that he would "call off the dogs" if she settled on his terms.

This was the last straw. In addition to pursuing her original claim, Mary now wishes to sue John for his conduct and that of his detectives and lawyer in attempting to pressure her into settling on his terms. Your senior partner has asked you to address the following two issues, and to assume for these purposes that John was legally responsible for the conduct of his detectives and lawyer:

(a) Would the detectives' conduct give rise to a common law tort action for the invasion of privacy?

(b) Would John's conduct, coupled with that of his detectives and lawyer, give rise to an action for the intentional infliction of nervous shock?

(e) BREACH OF CONFIDENCE

The tort action for breach of confidence has been used increasingly to protect the privacy of both sensitive business and personal information. In *Lac Minerals Ltd. v. International Corona Resources Ltd.*, [1989] 2 S.C.R. 574, the court held that in order to recover for breach of confidence, the plaintiff had to establish that (i) the information was confidential in nature, (ii) it was disclosed in circumstances creating an obligation of confidentiality, and (iii) its unauthorized use was detrimental to the confider. The same rules apply to the immediate recipients of confidential information and to third parties who receive such information with knowledge of its confidential character. The action for breach of confidence originated in the courts of equity. However, in *Cadbury Schweppes Inc. v. FBI Foods Ltd.*, [1999] 1 S.C.R. 142, the court stated that breach of confidence should be viewed as a hybrid cause of action drawing on principles of both equity and common law. Consequently, the court held that judges have broad discretion in formulating an appropriate remedy in breach of confidence cases.

The action for breach of confidence is most commonly used to protect trade secrets and other secret business information. For example, in *LAC Minerals*, the defendant used confidential information received from the plaintiff to acquire for itself a gold mine that the plaintiff wished to exploit as a joint venture. A majority of the Supreme Court of Canada imposed a constructive trust on the property, thereby requiring the defendant to convey the land to the plaintiff in exchange for indemnification of the expenses that it incurred in developing the mine. In *Cadbury Schweppes*, the defendant wrongfully used the plaintiff's secret formula for Clamato juice to create a similar beverage. The Supreme Court of Canada responded by awarding the plaintiff the profits that it lost as a result of the defendant's breach of confidence.

The action for breach of confidence can also be used to protect sensitive personal information. For example in *Argyll v. Argyll*, [1965] 1 All E.R. 611 (Ch. D.), the court stated that a spouse's disclosure of personal communications made during marriage may be actionable. Although there are numerous Canadian cases on the negligent breach of confidence, there are few cases involving the intentional disclosure of sensitive personal information. Nevertheless, see *Szarfer v. Chodos* (1986), 27 D.L.R. (4th) 388 (Ont. H.C.), aff'd (1988), 54 D.L.R. (4th) 383 (Ont. C.A.), in which the defendant, a lawyer, was held liable for breaching his fiduciary duty by exploiting confidential information about his client's marital problems to have an affair with the client's wife.

NOTES AND QUESTIONS

1. For additional cases on breach of confidence concerning business information see *Coco v. A.N. Clark (Engineers) Ltd.*, [1969] R.P.C. 41 (Ch. D.); *Rodaro v. Royal Bank of Canada* (2002), 59 O.R. (3d) 74 (C.A.); *Foreman v. Chambers* (2006), 41 C.C.L.T. (3d) 175 (B.C.S.C.); *Lysko v. Braley* (2006), 79 O.R. (3d) 721 (C.A.); *Free Trade Medical Network Inc. v. RBC Travel Insurance Co.* (2006), 215 O.A.C. 230 (C.A.); *Murphy Oil v. Predator Corp.* (2006), 44 C.C.L.T. (3d) 58 (Alta. Q.B.); and *OBG Limited v. Allan*; *Douglas v. Hello! Limited*; *Mainstream Properties Limited v. Young*, [2007] UKHL 21.

2. For a discussion of breach of confidence, see Arnold, "Circumstances Importing An Obligation of Confidence" (2003) 119 L.Q.R. 193.

3. Since the English courts do not recognize a common law tort for the invasion of privacy, they have used breach of confidence to protect privacy interests in sensitive personal information. These cases typically involve detailed discussions of the need to balance the plaintiff's privacy interests against freedom of expression. See *Douglas v. Hello! Ltd.*, [2001] 2 All E.R. 289 (C.A.); *Campbell v. MGN Ltd.*, [2004] 2 All E.R. 995 (H.L.); Moreham, "Privacy in the Common Law: A Doctrinal and Theoretical Analysis" (2005) 121 L.Q.R. 628; and Mulheron, "A Potential Framework for Privacy? A Reply to *Hello*!" (2006) 69 Mod. L. Rev. 679.

REVIEW PROBLEM

Phillip and Sarah had been going out for five years and had talked about getting engaged. Phillip suddenly broke off the relationship without warning or any explanation.

Sarah later learned that Phillip had been seeing someone else during the last three months of their relationship. With time, Sarah's initial upset turned to anger.

About three months after their break-up, Phillip and Sarah happened to be at the same party. Phillip was shy, said nothing and tried to avoid Sarah. In contrast, Sarah was seething with anger toward Phillip and began making inappropriate comments. During their relationship, Phillip had shared with Sarah sensitive details of his childhood and troubled youth. These included the fact that Phillip's father had been convicted of manslaughter for killing Phillip's mother, and that Phillip was raised in a provincial orphanage. Phillip had also shared with Sarah that, as a young teenager, he was convicted of a series of break and enters. In an effort to get back at Phillip, Sarah began disclosing these details of Phillip's life in a loud voice that could be readily heard by anyone in the vicinity.

Phillip left the party as quickly as possible. He had worked hard to get an education, succeed at work, establish a network of friends, and leave his past behind. Phillip felt that Sarah had dragged him back to his horrible childhood and youth, and had undermined his years of struggle to make something of himself.

Analyze whether Phillip would have a cause of action against Sarah for (a) the invasion of privacy and (b) breach of confidence.

10. The Common Law Tort of Discrimination

BHADAURIA v. BOARD OF GOVERNORS OF SENECA COLLEGE OF APPLIED ARTS AND TECHNOLOGY

(1979), 105 D.L.R. (3d) 707 (Ont. C.A.), rev'd [1981] 2 S.C.R. 181

WILSON J.A.: [For the Court of Appeal] – The plaintiff in this case complains that she has been discriminated against by the defendant on the ground of her ethnic origin. She makes the following allegations in her statement of claim. She is a highly educated East Indian woman holding a Bachelor of Arts, Master of Arts, and Doctorate of Philosophy in Mathematics. She is also qualified to teach in the Province of Ontario and has seven years' teaching experience. From June of 1974 to May of 1978, she applied for 10 openings on the teaching staff of the defendant college. All of these openings were advertised in the Toronto press. The plaintiff was not granted an interview for any of them although she had the requisite qualifications. She alleges that this was because of her ethnic origin.

The plaintiff, instead of filing a complaint under the *Ontario Human Rights Code*, R.S.O. 1970, c. 318, as amended, issued a writ claiming damages for discrimination and for breach of s. 4 of the Code. In her statement of claim she identifies the nature of her damages. She alleges that she has been deprived of the opportunity to join the defendant's teaching staff and to earn her livelihood as a teacher and that she has suffered mental distress, frustration and loss of dignity and self-esteem.

Section 4(1) of the Code reads as follows:

> 4(1) No person shall,
>
> (*a*) refuse to refer or to recruit any person for employment;
>
> (*b*) dismiss or refuse to employ or to continue to employ any person;

. . .

> because of race, creed, colour, age, sex, marital status, nationality, ancestry, or place of origin of such person or employee.

Counsel for the defendant concedes that the conduct alleged against it in the statement of claim falls within cls. (*a*) and (*b*) above.

. . .

The judgment of Mr. Justice Birkett in *Constantine v. Imperial London Hotels, Ltd.*, [1944] 2 All E.R. 171, is also instructive in this area. In that case the manageress of the defendant hotel, in what was alleged to be a contemptuous and insulting manner, had refused the plaintiff a room because of his colour. He was, however, able to obtain accommodation quite readily at another hotel owned by the defendant. Accordingly, he suffered no special damage. No claim for defamation or slander was made and the learned trial Judge held on the pleadings that the plaintiff's action was an action on the case for the defendant's refusal to accommodate him in the hotel of his choice without any just cause or excuse. The gist of the action on the case, however, is special damage and in this case the plaintiff was unable to prove special damage.

The judgment is a significant one because the learned Judge applied the celebrated principle of *Ashby v. White et al.* (1703), 2 Ld. Raym. 938, 92 E.R. 126, enunciated by Chief Justice Holt at p. 953, as follows:

> If the plaintiff has a right, he must of necessity have a means to vindicate and maintain it, and a remedy if he is injured in the exercise or enjoyment of it; and indeed it is a vain thing to imagine a right without a remedy; for want of right and want of remedy are reciprocal.

Mr. Justice Birkett found that a common law right of the plaintiff was violated in this case. The defendant was an innkeeper under a duty to receive and house the plaintiff. The action was maintainable without proof of special damage because, as Chief Justice Holt had made plain, the injury itself imported damage. He awarded the plaintiff nominal damages in the amount of five guineas.

. . .

Against this background of authorities, we are called on to decide the matter now on appeal before us, namely, assuming that the plaintiff can prove the allegations set forth in her statement of claim, do they give rise to a cause of action at common law and, if they do not, do they give rise to a civil cause of action under the *Ontario Human Rights Code*?

In my view, they give rise to a cause of action at common law. While no authority cited to us has recognized a tort of discrimination, none has repudiated such a tort. The matter is accordingly *res integra* before us.

Prosser in his text, *Handbook of the Law of Torts*, 4th ed. (1971), at pp. 3-4, states:

> The law of torts is anything but static, and the limits of its development are never set. When it becomes clear that the plaintiff's interests are entitled to legal protection against the conduct of the defendant, the mere fact that the claim is novel will not of itself operate as a bar to the remedy.

I think there can be no doubt that the interests of persons of different ethnic origins are entitled to the protection of the law. The preamble to the *Ontario Human Rights Code* reads as follows:

> WHEREAS recognition of the inherent dignity and the equal and inalienable rights of all members of the human family is the foundation of freedom, justice and peace in the world and is in accord with the Universal Declaration of Human Rights as proclaimed by the United Nations;
>
> AND WHEREAS it is public policy in Ontario that every person is free and equal in dignity and rights without regard to race, creed, colour, sex, marital status, nationality, ancestry or place of origin;
>
> AND WHEREAS these principles have been confirmed in Ontario by a number of enactments of the Legislature;
>
> AND WHEREAS it is desirable to enact a measure to codify and extend such enactments and to simplify their administration;
>
> *Therefore, Her Majesty, by and with the advice and consent of the Legislative Assembly of the Province of Ontario, enacts as follows:*

I regard the preamble to the Code as evidencing what is now, and probably has been for some considerable time, the public policy of this Province respecting fundamental human rights. If we accept that "every person is free and equal in dignity and rights without regard to race, creed, colour, sex, marital status, nationality, ancestry or place of origin", as we do, then it is appropriate that these rights receive the full protection of the common law. The plaintiff has a right not to be discriminated against because of her ethnic origin and alleges that she has been injured in the exercise or enjoyment of it. If she can establish that, then the common law must, on the principle of *Ashby v. White et al.*, *supra*, afford her a remedy.

I do not regard the Code as in any way impeding the appropriate development of the common law in this important area. While the fundamental human right we are concerned with is recognized by the Code, it was not created by it. Nor does the Code, in my view, contain any expression of legislative intention to exclude the common law remedy. Rather the reverse since s. 14*a* [enacted 1974, c. 73, s. 5] appears to make the appointment of a board of inquiry to look into a complaint made under the Code a matter of ministerial discretion.

It is unnecessary, in view of the finding that a cause of action exists at common law, to determine whether or not the Code gives rise to a civil cause of action.

I would allow the appeal and set aside the order of Callaghan, J. The defendant shall have 20 days from the date of the order herein to file its statement of defence. The appellant shall have her costs both here and below in the cause.

[The decision was then appealed to the Supreme Court of Canada. Chief Justice Laskin wrote the decision of the court.]

LASKIN C.J.C.: – . . . The view taken by the Ontario Court of Appeal is a bold one and may be commended as an attempt to advance the common law. In my opinion, however, this is foreclosed by the legislative initiative which overtook the existing common law in Ontario and established a different regime which does not exclude the courts but rather makes them part of the enforcement machinery under the Code.

For the foregoing reasons, I would hold that not only does the Code foreclose any civil action based directly upon a breach thereof but it also excludes any common law action based on an invocation of the public policy expressed in the Code. The Code itself has laid out the procedures for vindication of that public policy, procedures which the plaintiff respondent did not see fit to use.

NOTES AND QUESTIONS

1. What factors did Wilson J.A. consider in deciding to recognize a new common law tort of discrimination? How did she use (a) the remarks of Holt C.J., who was dissenting in *Ashby v. White*, and (b) the Ontario *Human Rights Code*?

2. Laskin C.J.C. distinguished *Ashby* as a case in which the plaintiff was granted a remedy for an independent pre-existing right and suggested that Wilson J.A. had relied on *Ashby* to create the right. Do you agree with Laskin C.J.C.?

3. The Commission responsible for enforcing the *Human Rights Code* has broad discretion in deciding whether to initiate an investigation, convene a hearing or take a matter to court. Given the Commission's control over the proceedings and the complainant's subordinate role, is there any reason why the *Code* proceedings and a common law tort action for discrimination should not co-exist?

4. Laskin C.J.C.'s judgment is difficult to reconcile with the Canadian courts' approach to the relationship between common law causes of action and statutes. There is ample support for Wilson J.A.'s use of a statute in deciding to recognize a common law tort action. Laskin C.J.C. himself did the same thing in the landmark cases of *Horsley v. MacLaren*, [1972] S.C.R. 441 and *Jordan House Ltd. v. Menow*, [1947] S.C.R. 239. See also *Canada v. Saskatchewan Wheat Pool*, [1983] 1 S.C.R. 205. Is there something unique about a common law tort action for discrimination that would justify departing from the general trend?

5. Would Bhadauria have a cause of action against the College based on (a) *Wilkinson v. Downton* or (b) the expanded principles of intentional infliction of nervous shock in cases such as *Tran v. Financial Debt Recovery Ltd.* (2000), 2 C.C.L.T. (3d) 270 (Ont. S.C.J.) or *Prinzo v. Baycrest Centre for Geriatric Care* (2002), 60 O.R. (3d) 474 (C.A.), discussed above in the section on intentional infliction of nervous shock?

6. The Supreme Court of Canada's decision in *Bhadauria* has been applied to cases involving the human rights legislation in various provinces. See for example *Marshall v. Saskatchewan*, [1982] 3 W.W.R. 224 (Sask. Q.B.); *Tenning v. Manitoba* (1983), 4 D.L.R. (4th) 418 (Man. C.A.); *Mallet v. New Brunswick* (1982), 43 N.B.R. (2d) 309 (Q.B.), aff'd (1983), 47 N.B.R. (2d) 234 (C.A.); and *Ayangma v. Prince Edward Island* (1998), 168 Nfld. & P.E.I.R. 1 (P.E.I.S.C. (T.D.)).

7. In many cases, the courts have been able to sidestep *Bhadauria* and provide redress for the defendant's discriminatory conduct on the basis of wrongful dismissal or the intentional infliction of nervous shock. See for example *Gnanasegaram v. Allianz*

Insurance Co. of Canada (2005), 251 D.L.R. (4th) 340 (Ont. C.A.) and *Keays v. Honda Canada Inc.* (2006), 82 O.R. (3d) 161 (C.A.) (wrongful dismissal); and *Clark v. Canada* (1994), 20 C.C.L.T. (2d) 241 (F.C.T.D.) and *Nolan v. Toronto (Metropolitan) Police Force*, [1996] O.J. No. 1764 (Gen. Div.) (QL) (intentional infliction of nervous shock). See also Radnoff & Foy, "The Tort of Discrimination" (2002) 26 Adv. Q. 309.

8. Would *Bhadauria* prevent a plaintiff from recovering damages based on a common law tort action for sexual harassment? While some cases have permitted recovery, others have not. For example in *Lajoie v. Kelly*, [1997] 3 W.W.R. 181 (Man. Q.B.) and *Sulz v. British Columbia (Minister of Public Safety and Solicitor General)* (2006), 60 B.C.L.R. (4th) 43 (C.A.), the court stated that the governing human rights legislation did not prevent the plaintiffs from recovering pursuant to a common law tort action for sexual harassment.

However, the reasoning in *Bhadauria* was relied on to strike out harassment claims in *Allen v. C.F.P.L. Broadcasting Ltd.* (1995), 24 C.C.L.T. (2d) 297 (Ont. Gen. Div.) and *Chapman v. 3M Canada Inc.* (1995), 24 C.C.L.T. (2d) 304 (Ont. Gen. Div.), aff'd (1997), 37 C.C.L.T. (2d) 319 (Ont. C.A.).

See Demeyere, "Common Law Actions for Sexual Harassment: The Jurisdiction Question Revisited" (2003) 28 Queen's L.J. 637.

9. Can *Bhadauria* be justified on either doctrinal or policy grounds? See McLaren, "The Intentional Torts to the Person Revived?: Protecting Autonomy, Dignity and Emotional Welfare in a Pluralistic Society" in Beauluc, Pitel & Schulz, eds., *The Joy of Torts* (2003) 67.

10. Section 15 of the *Charter* grants every individual the right to equal protection and benefit of the law without discrimination, and, in particular, discrimination based on race, national or ethnic origin, colour, religion, sex, age, or mental or physical disability. Provided the *Charter* applies, an individual may seek a remedy under s. 24(1) if his or her equality rights under s. 15 have been violated. For a general discussion of s. 15, see Hogg, *Constitutional Law of Canada*, 4th ed., looseleaf, vol. 2 (1997), ch. 52; and Knopff, "On Proving Discrimination: Statistical Methods and Unfolding Policy Logics" (1986) 12 Can. Pub. Pol'y 573.

11. Should the courts or the legislature extend protection against invasions of privacy, discrimination and other similar intentional interference with the person?

12. For a discussion of the civil remedies for discrimination in the United States, see *Restatement (Second) of the Law of Torts* (1979) at §§865-66.

4

INTENTIONAL INTERFERENCE WITH CHATTELS

1. Introduction
2. The Development of the Actions
3. Trespass to Chattels
4. Conversion
5. Detinue
6. Recaption and Replevin

1. Introduction

The modern law governing intentional interference with chattels is the product of a tangled history in which pleadings and procedure preceded the development of substantive principles. Moreover, the origins of this body of law are not contained exclusively within the realm of torts, but rather lie at the intersection of tort, property, and contract.

This chapter begins with a short history of the tort actions governing intentional interference with chattels. We then discuss the three major modern actions – *trespass to chattels*, *conversion* and *detinue* – before concluding with a brief explanation of *replevin* and *recaption*.

As you read through this chapter, ask yourself whether the existing rules satisfactorily serve the needs of modern society. There is growing belief in the need for statutory reform. Although English legislation simplified some of the rules thirty years ago, through the *Torts (Interference with Goods) Act 1977*, considerable confusion and difficulty remain in that country. The problems are, of course, even greater in Canada, where the traditional rules continue to apply.

2. The Development of the Actions

The common law recognized three ways in which a person could be deprived of chattels and it developed an action for each. *Trespass* was designed for cases of wrongful *taking*, *detinue* for cases of wrongful *detention*, and *trover* for cases of wrongful *disposal*. Trespass and detinue remain actionable today. Trover, in contrast, was superseded by *conversion*. As the most modern action, conversion avoids many of the procedural defects that undermine the other two. It therefore is by far the most popular of the proprietary torts.

(a) TRESPASS

The predecessor of the modern action for trespass to chattels – trespass *de bonis asportatis* – emerged in the 13th century. It apparently was an attempt to overcome difficulties affecting the recovery of property under the criminal actions of theft and larceny. Although trespass *de bonis asportatis* initially could be invoked only if goods were taken or destroyed, it later expanded to cover cases of mere damage or interference. In any event, the tort required proof that (1) the defendant's interference was direct and forceful, and (2) the affected goods were in the claimant's possession.

With the abolition of the writ system during the 19th century, intent generally became a prerequisite to liability. The modern tort of trespass to goods therefore now provides a remedy for any direct and intentional interference with chattels in the possession of another. As explained below, however, claimants generally prefer to sue for conversion, rather than trespass, whenever possible.

(b) DETINUE

The origins of the modern action for detinue lie in the *praecipe* writs. Such writs took the form of a command to either do right or provide an explanation to the King's justices. Consequently, in contrast to trespass, the *praecipe* writs were designed to secure compliance with a right, rather than to remedy the breach of a right. The *praecipe* writs took several forms depending upon the circumstances. For instance, a person might be compelled to surrender a piece of land, pay a debt, or (in the case of detinue) return a chattel.

The gist of detinue was that the defendant was wrongfully withholding a chattel to which the plaintiff had a right of immediate possession. The law recognized two possibilities. Detinue *sur bailment* governed those cases in which the defendant had acquired possession of the chattel through bailment. Detinue *sur trover* dealt with cases in which the defendant either found the chattel or acquired possession through some means other than bailment. Bailment occurs when the owner or possessor of a chattel (the bailor) temporarily transfers possession to another person (the bailee) with an expectation that the chattel will be returned at some future time. In common language, bailment refers to the lending of a thing.

Detinue *sur bailment* evolved into a strict action. Once the plaintiff established a bailment and an immediate right to possession, the defendant was required to return the chattel or, if unable to do so, pay its full market value. The fact that the bailee no longer had possession of the item did not provide a defence. Significantly, however, detinue *sur bailment* was not available if the bailee had returned the property in damaged condition. In that situation, the bailor's only claim was in trespass.

Detinue *sur trover* was available in situations not involving bailment. It therefore was used against a finder, a thief, or even an innocent "purchaser" who had acquired possession of the chattel without knowledge of the claimant's underlying rights. However, the action was subject to three major limitations.

- *Chain of Possession*: Possession had to be established in an unbroken chain between the claimant and the defendant. Each link of the chain could be challenged.
- *Continuing Possession*: Liability presumed that the defendant remained in possession of the chattel. Detinue therefore was not available if the defendant had lost, sold, or destroyed the goods. Similarly, it was exhausted once the chattel was returned to the claimant, even if the goods had been damaged.
- *Wager of Law*: Most significantly, a claim in detinue could be defended through the process known as *wager of law*. The defendant could avoid liability by swearing an

oath attesting to his or her innocence and by presenting the requisite number of *compurgators* ("oath helpers") who swore not to the facts, but rather to the purity of the defendant's oath. Whatever its initial merits as a method for finding facts, wager of law deteriorated as society gradually placed greater weight on Earthly matters than on fear of God. Indeed, the situation eventually degenerated to the point where professional compurgators were available for hire! Although wager of law increasingly fell into disrepute, it was not officially abolished until 1833.

(c) TROVER AND CONVERSION

The deficiencies of the various *praecipe* writs led to the emergence of more effective actions. Detinue therefore was supplanted by the action in trespass on the case *sur trover*, or, more simply, the action in trover. The gist of trover was the defendant's wrongful appropriation of the claimant's chattel. The wording of the writ required an allegation that the plaintiff had lost lawful possession of the item, and that the defendant had found it and taken possession. By the end of the 16th century, however, the allegations of losing and finding were obligatory, but non-traversable. The plaintiff continued to assert them, but the court refused to hear argument on point, and the defendant could not escape liability by disproving the allegations of loss and finding. The dispute therefore focussed on the central issue as to whether the defendant, by some positive act, had converted the goods, thereby depriving the plaintiff of possession.

Trover was a clear improvement upon detinue: the defendant could not avoid liability through wager of law, by returning the goods in damaged condition, or by showing that they were no longer in his or her possession. The plaintiff enjoyed other benefits as well. Liability potentially extended to any person who dealt with the claimant's chattels, even if they did so reasonably and innocently. And as a species of *trespass on the case*, trover triggered the remedy of damages. The plaintiff generally was entitled to the monetary value of the chattels at the time of the tort. As discussed below, all of this remains true today.

Although *conversion* (as trover is now called) is the most commonly encountered proprietary tort, claimants continue to use detinue in certain circumstances.

- *Unintentional Loss by Bailee*: Because conversion presumes that the defendant positively and intentionally exercised dominion over the plaintiff's chattel, it is not available if a lawful bailee loses the plaintiff's property or carelessly allows it to be stolen.

- *Specific Recovery*: Detinue is the appropriate form of action if the claimant seeks recovery of the chattel, rather than damages representing its value.

- *Calculation of Damages*: Even if the claimant is content to receive monetary relief, damages are measured differently in conversion and detinue. The former generally proceeds by reference to market value at the *time of the defendant's final act of conversion*; the latter generally calculates compensation on the basis of the market value *at the date of trial*. Accordingly, where both options exist, conversion usually is preferable in a falling market, whereas detinue is advantageous in a rising market.

Likewise, while conversion is far more common than trespass, the older action remains important. Because the remedy for conversion compels the defendant to pay damages representing the chattel's market value, that tort effectively leads to a *forced sale*. The plaintiff receives the value of the item and, in exchange, the defendant acquires the right to retain the item itself (if it is still in possession). The courts recognize, however, that some forms of interference are insufficient to warrant such a result. In such circumstances, the claimant is confined to a claim in trespass and compensation for losses actually suffered.

NOTES AND QUESTIONS

1. The intentional property torts are based on the concept of possession, rather than ownership. Trespass, conversion and, arguably, detinue directly protect the plaintiff's possessory interests. This area of law is not primarily concerned with ownership and title *per se*. The essence of possession appears to be physical custody or control, coupled with the intent to possess. See Palmer, "Possessory Title" in Palmer & McKendrick, eds., *Interests in Goods*, 2d ed. (1998), ch. 3.

2. The fact that the intentional property torts protect the right to possession, rather than ownership, is highlighted by the remarkable case of *Costello v. Chief Constable of Derbyshire Constabulary*, [2001] 1 W.L.R. 1437 (C.A.). From all outward appearances, the plaintiff was in the business of selling stolen cars. He was found in possession of a vehicle that he had purchased from a friend who had numerous convictions for car theft. That vehicle's registration and engine identification numbers had been rubbed off, and a kit for forging car registration numbers was found in the backseat of the plaintiff's vehicle. The police lawfully seized the car, but were never able to determine its true owner. They nevertheless refused the plaintiff's demand to return the car to him. He then sued in conversion. The Court of Appeal held in his favour. Lightman J. held that, according to orthodox property law principles, the plaintiff, as possessor of the vehicle, had a better right to the car than everyone except the true owner. He further explained that, as a matter of tort law, "possession ... is entitled to the same legal protection whether or not it has been obtained lawfully or by theft or by other unlawful means." Do you agree with the result of that decision? How else might tort law deal with such situations? See Fox, "Enforcing a Possessory Title to a Stolen Car" [2002] C.L.J. 27. The defence of *jus tertii*, which may deny liability on the ground that some third party has better rights to the chattel than does the plaintiff, is discussed below. For discussion of the criminal consequences of "stealing" abandoned property, see Hickey, "Stealing Abandoned Goods: Possessory Title in Proceedings for Theft" (2006) 26 L.S. 584.

3. The fact that the proprietory torts are based on the protection of possession limits the types of "things" that can be the subject of claims. Traditionally, for instance, it was impossible to sue in conversion if the defendant interfered with a *chose in action* (such as a debt). As discussed below, however, Canadian courts have begun to adopt a more relaxed approach.

4. For a more detailed account of the history of the intentional property torts see Holmes, *The Common Law* (1881) at 77-129 and 165-205; Ames, "The History of Trover" (1897) 11 Harv. L. Rev. 277-89 and 374-86; Fifoot, *History and Sources of the Common Law: Tort and Contract* (1949) at 24-65 and 102-105; Baker, *An Introduction*

to English Legal History, 4th ed. (2002) at 390-400; and Milsom, *Historical Foundations of the Common Law*, 2d ed. (1981) at 262-75 and 366-79.

3. Trespass to Chattels

FOULDES v. WILLOUGHBY

(1841), 151 E.R. 1153 (Ex. Ct.)

On the 15th October 1840, the plaintiff had embarked on board the defendant's ferry-boat at Birkenhead, having with him two horses, for the carriage of which he had paid the usual fare. It was alleged that the plaintiff misconducted himself and behaved improperly after he came on board the steam-boat, and when the defendant came on board he told the plaintiff that he would not carry the horses over, and that he must take them on shore. The plaintiff refused to do so, and the defendant took the horses from the plaintiff, who was holding one of them by the bridle, and put them on shore on the landing slip. They were driven to the top of the slip, which was separated by gates from the high road, and turned loose on the road. They were shortly afterwards seen in the stables of an hotel at Birkenhead, kept by the defendant's brother. The plaintiff remained on board the steam-boat, and was conveyed over the river to Liverpool. On the following day the plaintiff sent to the hotel for the horses, but the parties in whose possession they were refused to deliver them up. A message, however, was afterwards sent to him by the hotel-keeper, to the effect that he might have the horses on sending for them and paying for their keep; and that if he did not send for them and pay for their keep, they would be sold to pay the expense of it. The plaintiff then brought the present action. The horses were subsequently sold by auction. The defence set up at the trial was, that the plaintiff had misconducted himself and behaved improperly on board, and that the horses were sent on shore in order to get rid of the plaintiff, by inducing him to follow them. The learned Judge told the jury, that the defendant by taking the horses from the plaintiff and turning them out of the vessel, had been guilty of a conversion, unless they thought the plaintiff's conduct had justified his removal from the steam-boat, and he had refused to go without his horses; and that if they thought the conversion was proved, they might give the plaintiff damages for the full value of the horses. The jury found a verdict for the plaintiff with £40 damages, the value of the horses.

In Easter Term last, a rule was obtained calling upon the plaintiff to shew cause why the verdict should not be set aside on the ground of misdirection.

. . .

LORD ABINGER C.B.: – This is a motion to set aside the verdict on the ground of an alleged misdirection; and I cannot help thinking that if the learned Judge who tried the cause had referred to the long and frequent distinctions which have been taken between such a simple asportation [*i.e.* movement] as will support an action of trespass, and those circumstances which are requisite to establish a conversion, he would not have so directed the jury. It is a proposition familiar to all lawyers, that a simple asportation of a chattel, without any intention of making any further use of it, although it may be sufficient foundation for an action of trespass, is not sufficient to establish a conversion. I had thought that the matter had been fully discussed and this distinction established, by the numerous cases which have occurred on this subject; but, according to the argument put forward by the plaintiff's counsel to-day, a bare asportavit is sufficient foundation to support an action of trover. I entirely dissent from this argument; and therefore I think that the learned Judge was wrong, in telling the jury that the simple fact of putting these horses on shore by the defendant, amounted to a conversion of them to his own use. In my opinion, he should have added to his direction, that it was for them to consider what was the intention of the defendant in so doing. If the object, and whether rightly or wrongfully entertained is immaterial, simply was to induce the plaintiff to go on shore himself, and the defendant, in furtherance of that object, did the act in question, it was not exercising over the horses any right inconsistent with, or adverse to, the rights which the plaintiff had in them. Suppose, instead of the horses, the defendant had put the plaintiff himself on shore, and on being put on shore, the plaintiff had refused to take his horses with him, and the defendant had said he would take them to the other side of the water, and had done so, would that be a conversion? That would be a much more colourable case of a conversion than the present, because, by separating the man from his property, it might, with some appearance of fairness, be said the party was carrying away the horses without any justifiable reason for so doing. Then, having conveyed them across the water, and finding neither the owner nor any one else to receive them, what is he to do with them? Suppose, under those circumstances, the defendant lands them, and leaves them on shore, would that amount to a conversion? The argument of the plaintiff's counsel in this case must go the length of saying that it would. Then, suppose the reply to be, that those circumstances would amount to a conversion, I ask, at what period of time did the conversion take place? Suppose the plaintiff had immediately followed his horses when they were put on shore, and resumed possession of them, would there be a conversion of them in that case? I apprehend, clearly not. It has been argued that, the mere touching and taking them by the bridle would constitute a conversion, but surely that cannot be: if the plaintiff had immediately gone on shore and taken possession of them, there could be no conversion. Then the question, whether this were a conversion or not, cannot depend on the subsequent conduct of the plaintiff in following the horses on shore. Would any man say, that if the facts of this case were, that the plaintiff and defendant had had a controversy as to whether the horses should remain in the boat, and the defendant had said, "If you will not put them on shore, I will do it for you," and in pursuance of that threat, he had taken hold of one of the horses to go ashore with it, an action of trover could be sustained against him? There might, perhaps, in such a case, be ground for maintaining an action of trespass, because the defendant may have had no right to meddle with the horses at all: but it is clear that he did not do so for the purpose of taking them away from the plaintiff, or of exercising any right over them, either for himself or for any other person.

. . .

In order to constitute a conversion, it is necessary either that the party taking the goods should intend some use to be made of them, by himself or by those for whom he acts, or that, owing to his act, the goods are destroyed or consumed, to the prejudice of the lawful owner. As an instance of the latter branch of this definition, suppose, in the present case, the defendant had thrown the horses into the water, whereby they were drowned, that would have amounted to an actual conversion; or as in the case cited in the course of the argument, of a person throwing a piece of paper into the water; for, in these cases, the chattel is changed in quality, or destroyed altogether. But it has never yet been held, that the single act of removal of a chattel, independent of any claim over it, either in favour of the party himself or any one else, amounts to a conversion of the chattel. In the present case, therefore, the simple removal of these horses by the defendant, for a purpose wholly unconnected with any the least denial of the right of the plaintiff to the possession and enjoyment of them, is no conversion of the horses, and consequently the rule for a new trial ought to be made absolute.

NOTES AND QUESTIONS

1. Did the defendant's act of removing the horses from the barge constitute a trespass? If so, what would have been the appropriate measure of damages? Why did this act not amount to a conversion? If the defendant had pushed the horses off the barge in the middle of the crossing and they drowned, what damages would the plaintiff have been entitled to in trespass and conversion?

2. Although plaintiffs rarely do so, there is authority for the proposition that, as an alternative to claiming compensation, the plaintiff may choose to use the action in trespass to goods to receive disgorgement of the defendant's gains. See for example *Oughton v. Seppings* (1830), 109 E.R. 776; *Neate v. Harding* (1851), 155 E.R. 577; *Rodgers v. Maw* (1846), 153 E.R. 924; *Feltham v. Terry* (1773), 98 E.R. 613; and *cf. Lindon v. Hooper* (1776), 98 E.R. 1160. Given the ambiguity of the ancient writs, however, many of those cases alternatively may be explained, in modern terminology, as restitution for the cause of action in unjust enrichment.

3. Despite occasional suggestions to the contrary, the better view is that trespass to goods is actionable without proof of loss. See for example *William Leitch & Co. v. Leydon*, [1931] A.C. 90 at 106 (H.L.); Rogers, *Winfield and Jolowicz on Tort*, 17th ed. (2006) at 748-49; and Heuston & Buckley, *Salmond and Heuston on the Law of Torts*, 21st ed. (1996) at 95; *cf. Letang v. Cooper*, [1964] 2 All E.R. 929 (C.A.) (damage required if interference is unintentional). Given that trespass to land and trespass to the person are actionable *per se*, how could a different rule for trespass to chattels be justified?

In the United States, a distinction is drawn between dispossession and mere interference. Dispossession is considered sufficient damage in itself, whereas interference is not actionable without proof of loss. See American Law Institute, *Restatement (Second) of Torts* (1965) at §218. Do you favour the English or American position?

4. The defendant will not escape liability by proving that the trespass occurred as a result of an honest and reasonable mistake. See for example *Cameron v. Morang* (1978), 32 N.B.R. (2d) 22 (Co. Ct.); and *384238 Ontario Ltd. v. The Queen in Right of Can.* (1983), 8 D.L.R. (4th) 676 (F.C.A.). What arguments can be made in favour of this rule? Should a reasonable and honest mistake be recognized as a defence to trespass to chattels?

5. The central importance of possession in trespass is illustrated by *Penfolds Wines Proprietary Ltd. v. Elliott* (1946), 74 C.L.R. 204 (H.C.A.). Penfolds, the plaintiff, made wine and sold it in bottles. The plaintiff at all times retained ownership of the bottles, which were embossed with its name. Customers were expected to drink the wine and return the bottles. An action was commenced in connection with two Penfolds bottles that were delivered to the defendant by his brother. The defendant filled the bottles with a different brand of wine and returned them to his brother. The plaintiff sued in trespass, conversion, and detinue. In addressing the trespass issue, Dixon J. said at 224-25:

> I think that it is quite clear that trespass would not lie for anything which the foregoing facts disclose. Trespass is a wrong to possession. But, on the part of the respondent, there was never any invasion of possession. At the time he filled the two bottles his brother left with him, he himself was in possession of them. If the bottles had been out of his own possession and in the possession of some other person, then to lift the bottles up against the will of that person and to fill them with wine would have amounted to trespasses. The reason is that the movement of the bottles and the use of them as receptacles are invasions of the possession of the second person. But they are things which the man possessed of the bottles may do without committing trespass. The respondent came into possession of the bottles without trespass.

6. Fleming, *The Law of Torts*, 9th ed. (1998) at 60, lists trustees, personal representatives, and franchise owners as exceptions to the general principle that only the person in actual possession is protected in trespass. He also states that a person with a mere right to possession can sue in trespass if his or her servant, bailee at will, or agent had actual possession at the time of the wrong. These exceptions are considered by Rogers, *Winfield and Jolowicz on Tort*, 17th ed. (2006) at 750-51. The author, while acknowledging that these parties can sue in trespass, doubts whether they really are exceptions. What is the significance of this controversy?

4. Conversion

(a) GENERAL PRINCIPLES

MACKENZIE v. SCOTIA LUMBER CO.
(1913), 11 D.L.R. 729 (N.S.S.C.)

RUSSELL J.: – I base my judgment in this case on the learned Judge's findings, as to the facts. The plaintiff was the owner of a raft which had drifted away from its proper, or perhaps improper moorings, and had become, without any interference of the defendants, attached to two rafts belonging to the defendants, which had also gone adrift, all three rafts being stranded on a ledge called "Stopper Rock," in St. Mary's river, Guysborough.

The defendants sent their servants for their own rafts, not for the rafts of anybody else. The servants, finding all three rafts together, and supposing that all three belonged to the defendants, brought them all to the defendants' mill. I take it that the defendants did not know that the raft was at their mill. It is certain that they did not know that the plaintiff's raft was at their mill, but the statement in this form would be equivocal, for although they did not know that the plaintiff's raft was at their mill, they may have known that this particular raft, which was in fact the plaintiff's raft, was at their mill. And it is upon this *équivoque* that the plaintiff bases his claim, contending that if the defendants, under the mistaken idea that the raft was their own, detained it for ever so short a period, treating it as their own, and exercising a dominion over it as their own property, they are liable for a conversion of the raft, even though the moment they discovered the mistake, they returned it to the proper owner.

. . .

The only evidence I can find of a conversion in this case is that of a possible conversion by the servants of the defendants, who, acting without authority from the defendants, did certainly exercise acts of ownership on behalf of the defendants over the raft, under the mistaken idea that the raft belonged to the defendants. Although this proceeding on the part of the servants was not authorized or acquiesced in by any responsible official of the defendant company, I assume that it was so far within the scope of the servants' duty that the company must answer for the act of their servants if that act was a tort.

We are, therefore, I think, obliged to answer the question whether one who takes the property of another person, mistaking it for his own, but returns it to the owner immediately upon discovery of the mistake, can be held liable for conversion of the property. The case must have occurred a thousand times, but the reason why counsel, who argued the appeal, were unable to cite any authority directly bearing upon the question, is probably that, until this case arose, there never was anybody wrongheaded enough to make such an accident the subject of an action at law.

I have examined all the cases collected by Ames and also the selection of cases on torts made by Mr. Wigmore, and I can find none to answer the simple question whether one who, by mistake, takes up the defendant's umbrella in place of his own, but who discovers his mistake before he has reached the street, and immediately returns it to the owner, is, or is not, liable for a conversion of the umbrella. I suspect that he would, strictly speaking, be legally liable, but if upon tender of the umbrella to the owner, the latter were to accept and resume the ownership, I am quite certain it would be a mistake to give damages for the full value of the umbrella and adjudge the property to the defendant. And that is what has been done, in this case. The defendant returned the raft, in the present case, to the plaintiff immediately upon the discovery of the mistake and the plaintiff resumed the ownership, when he asked for the use of a boat to take the raft up the river. From that moment until the action was brought, the plaintiff and defendant were both treating the property as the property of the plaintiff. I suppose that the right of action, having once arisen, the plaintiff must recover nominal damages, but why he should have the full value of the property which was returned to him and which he accepted back from the defendants, I cannot understand, and I think that the judgment of the learned trial Judge is erroneous in this respect.

. . .

The case of *Nelson v. Whetmore*, from South Carolina, 1 Rich. L. 318 (1 Ames' Cases on Torts 349), is also closely in point, but it was decided in favour of the defendant because he did not know that the plaintiff's slave, whom he engaged as a servant, was property at all, and could not therefore have had the intention of converting the defendant's property: "His treatment of Frank as a servant did not indicate an assertion of property." He did not exercise any act of ownership over the defendant's property, because he did not treat the slave as property at all. In this dearth of authority and absence of any clear answer to the question, I think we must hold that the defendants' servants did convert the plaintiff's property, and as they did it in the course of the employment by the defendant company, the latter must be held liable for conversion. But the plaintiff cannot have the property and the full damages for its conversion at the same time. Whether the defendants would have been liable for the full value of the property if the plaintiff had not accepted it, the defendants being ready and willing and offering to return it, may be an open question, but there can be no such question here, because the property was taken back by the plaintiff when the mistake was discovered.

The appeal should therefore be allowed with costs, and there should be judgment for the plaintiff for nominal damages only.

NOTES AND QUESTIONS

1. J. Fleming defines conversion as "an intentional exercise of control over a chattel which so seriously interferes with the right of another to control it that the intermeddler may justly be required to pay its full value": *The Law of Torts*, 9th ed. (1998) at 60-61. See also the American Law Institute, *Restatement (Second) of Torts* (1965) at §222A; and Prosser, "The Nature of Conversion" (1957) 42 Cornell L.Q. 168 at 173-74. Based on Fleming's approach, deliberate wrongdoing will likely result in a finding of conversion even if the chattel can be returned undamaged. In contrast, innocent intermeddling will not amount to conversion unless the plaintiff suffers considerable damage. Is Fleming's view consistent with either *Fouldes* or *MacKenzie*? If not, would you favour the adoption of Fleming's approach?

Even if it finds liability in conversion, the court may permit the defendant to return the chattel and reduce the damages accordingly, if it considers a forced judicial sale to be unwarranted. Given this discretionary power, how significant is the difference between Fleming's approach and that in *Fouldes* and *MacKenzie*?

2. The modern tort of conversion is derived from the *action on the case*. As a general rule, an action on the case requires proof of loss. For that reason, some authorities have held that conversion is not actionable unless the plaintiff establishes the existence of a loss. See for example Law Reform Commission, *Conversion and Detinue* (1971) (18th Report, Cmn. 4774) at 7; Dugdale & Jones, eds., *Clerk & Lindsell on Torts*, 19th ed. (2006) at 1059; and Tyler & Palmer, *Crossley Vaines' Personal Property*, 5th ed. (1973) at 22. Other authorities, however, hold that, history notwithstanding, the tort of conversion is now actionable *per se*: see for example *Brandeis Goldschmidt & Co. v. Western Transport Ltd.*, [1981] 1 Q.B. 864 (C.A.). As explained in an earlier note, trespass to goods is actionable *per se*. Is there any good reason in modern law for treating conversion and trespass differently?

3. In *MacKenzie*, Russell J. cited *Nelson v. Whetmore*, which suggested that the precise nature of a chattel may be significant in determining whether a conversion has been committed. A similar suggestion appears in *Penfolds Wines Proprietary Ltd. v. Elliott* (1946), 74 C.L.R. 204 at 243 (H.C.A.). The facts of *Penfolds* were explained in the previous section. On this point, Williams J. explained:

> The importance of rights attached to ownership vary according to the nature of the particular property. Bottles are meant to be filled so that to fill the bottle of another person is to deprive him of the use of his property. In the present case the brother purported to place the defendant in possession of the bottles as a bailee for him. If they had been 'clean bottles', although in fact the property of the plaintiff, the defendant might not have been guilty of conversion in filling and returning them to the person from whom he got them, unless the plaintiff had made a claim that they were its bottles and had demanded their return. ... But the endorsements on the bottles proclaimed that they were the property of the plaintiff. In *Hollins v. Fowler* (1875), L.R. 7 H.L. 757, at p. 766 (U.K. H.L.), Blackburn J. said that: 'In considering whether the act is excused against the true owner it often becomes important to know whether the person, doing

> what is charged as a conversion, had notice of the plaintiff's title. There are some acts which from their nature are necessarily a conversion, whether there was notice of the plaintiff's title or not. There are others which if done in a *bona-fide* ignorance of the plaintiff's title are excused, though if done in disregard of a title of which there was notice they would be a conversion.' The use which the defendant made of the bottles with knowledge of the plaintiff's title was . . . 'an interference with the property which would not as against the true owner, be justified, or at least excused, in one who came lawfully into possession of the goods.'

4. As *MacKenzie* illustrates, a defendant who makes an innocent and reasonable mistake in handling the plaintiff's chattels may be held liable in conversion. Should such mistakes provide a defence? If so, could you justify recognizing mistake as a defence to conversion, but not to the other intentional torts? In addition to *MacKenzie*, see *R.H. Willis and Son v. Br. Car Auctions Ltd.*, [1978] 2 All E.R. 392 (C.A.); *Irvington Holdings Ltd. v. Black* (1987), 58 O.R. (2d) 449 (C.A.); *Wilson v. New Brighton Panelbeaters Ltd.*, [1989] 1 N.Z.L.R. 74 (H.C.); and *Nilsson Bros. Inc. v. McNamara Estate*, [1992] 3 W.W.R. 761 (Alta. C.A.). For an excellent explanation of why the tort of conversion is strict, in the sense that it can be committed without intentional wrongdoing or carelessness, see Birks, "Personal Property: Proprietary Rights and Remedies" (2000) 11 King's College L.J. 1.

5. There are several exceptions to the rule that an innocent mistake provides no defence to conversion. Two of the more important common law exceptions are the rule governing involuntary bailees and the rule in *Hollins v. Fowler* (1875), L.R. 7 H.L. 757.

An *involuntary bailee* is a person who did not acquire possession by choice. This is true, for instance, when a person receives goods unsolicited through the mail, or when a theatre owner finds a package that a patron left behind. An involuntary bailee will not be held liable in conversion for misdelivering a chattel, provided the act was done with reasonable care and solely for the purpose of returning the item to its rightful owner. The scope of this doctrine remains uncertain and is subject to several complex restrictions. See *Long v. R.* (1922), 63 D.L.R. 134 (Ex. Ct.); Burnett, "Conversion by an Involuntary Bailee" (1976) 76 L.Q.R. 364; Palmer, *Bailment*, 2d ed. (1991) at 689-97; and Tyler & Palmer, *Crossley Vaines' Personal Property*, 5th ed. (1973) at 108-10.

In *Hollins v. Fowler*, Blackburn J. stated at 767:

> [O]ne who deals with goods at the request of the person who has the actual custody of them, in the *bona fide* belief that the custodier is the true owner, should be excused for what he does if the act is of such a nature as would be excused if done by the authority of the person in possession, if he was a finder of the goods, or intrusted with their custody. ... A warehouseman with whom goods have been deposited is guilty of no conversion by keeping them, or restoring them to the person who deposited them with him, though that person turns out to have had no authority from the true owner.

For a discussion of this principle, see Palmer, *supra* at 219-23; Rogers, *Winfield and Jolowicz on Tort*, 17th ed. (2006) at 754-55; and Tyler & Palmer, *supra* at 159.

6. Conversion cases often involve a dispute between two innocent parties. Assume that some third party purports, without authority, to sell the plaintiff's goods to the defendant. This third party then disappears or is judgment-proof. The law therefore must strike a balance between the two innocent parties. The plaintiff seeks protection of a pre-

existing property right under the doctrine of *nemo dat quo non habet* ("one cannot give what one does not have"). If that view prevails, it means that the defendant was unable to acquire title from the third party and therefore converted the plaintiff's property. The defendant, in contrast, seeks protection of a seemingly legitimate commercial transaction under the doctrine of *bona fide* purchase. If that view prevails, it means that, despite the lack of actual authority, the third party was able to pass title to the defendant, and that the defendant's dealings with the item did not constitute conversion of the plaintiff's property.

The tort of conversion generally favours security of title (*nemo dat*) over security of transactions (*bona fide* purchase). In some situations, however, legislation reverses the general rule by favouring the purchaser, rather than the original owner.

One such exception was applied in *Bartin Pipe & Piling Supply Ltd. v. Epscan Industries Ltd.* (2004), 346 A.R. 95 (C.A.). A rogue purchased an oil refinery, and then sold a specific pipe within the refinery to the plaintiff in November. Because the rogue was in the process of dismantling the refinery, it agreed that the plaintiff could collect its new pipe by February. Unfortunately, before the plaintiff could do so, the rogue sold the same pipe to the defendant, who had no reason to suspect anything improper. When the plaintiff eventually discovered that the defendant had removed some of the pipe, it sued in conversion. The defendant sought protection under s. 26(1) of the *Sale of Goods Act*, R.S.A. 2000, c. S-2:

> When a person who has sold goods continues or is in possession of the goods or of the documents of title to the goods, the delivery or transfer by that person or by a mercantile agent acting for that person of the goods or documents of title under any sale, pledge or other disposition thereof, to any person receiving them in good faith and without notice of the previous sale has the same effect as if the person making the delivery or transfer were expressly authorized by the owner of the goods to make it.

The Alberta Court of Appeal agreed and denied liability on the grounds that the defendant (1) had purchased from a "vendor in possession," (2) in good faith, and (3) without being aware of the previous sale to the plaintiff.

Section 26(3) of the same statute likewise provides a defence to a defendant who in good faith purchased goods from a "buyer in possession" (*i.e.* a party who obtained possession, but not title, of goods after agreeing to purchase them from the plaintiff). Similar legislation exists across Canada. See Fridman, *Sale of Goods in Canada*, 5th ed. (2004), ch. 6.

7. As explained in the previous note, the common law generally prefers the doctrine of *nemo dat* to the doctrine of *bona fide* purchase. As a result, a person who honestly and reasonably purports to purchase another's chattel may be held liable for conversion. The general rule is reversed, however, if the chattel in question is money (or, to some extent, a negotiable instrument, such as a cheque). Why is that so? Consider what would happen if a *bona fide* purchase of money (as when a grocer receives $5 in exchange for a bag of carrots) did not ensure clear title. See Fox, "Bona Fide Purchase and the Currency of Money" [1996] C.L.J. 547. For general discussion of exceptions to the *nemo dat* principle, see Ziegel & Duggan, *Commercial and Consumer Sales Transactions*, 4th ed. (2002), ch. 14; and Goode, *Commercial Law*, 2d ed. (1995), ch. 14.

8. Another form of statutory protection for unwitting convertors appears in the Ontario *Factors Act*, R.S.O. 1990, c. F.1 and in similar statutes in other provinces. Such

a statute may apply if an owner provided possession of a chattel to a *factor* or a *mercantile agent* with a view to having the item sold on *consignment*. If a sale occurs on consignment as anticipated, title passes directly from the original owner to the purchaser. The mercantile agent never holds title – it merely enjoys temporary possession of the item for the specified purpose. A difficulty may occur, however, if the mercantile agent exceeds its authority and improperly disposes of the chattel. In that situation, the recipient of the chattel *prima facie* commits a tort by dealing with the plaintiff's property. It nevertheless may enjoy a statutory defence. Section 2(1) of the Ontario *Factors Act*, R.S.O. 1990, c. F.1 (which is typical of the legislation) states:

> Where a mercantile agent is, with the consent of the owner, in possession of goods or of the documents of title to goods, a sale, pledge or other disposition of the goods made by the agent when acting in the ordinary course of business of a mercantile agent is, subject to this Act, as valid as if the agent were expressly authorized by the owner of the goods to make the disposition, if the person taking under it acts in good faith and has not at the time thereof notice that the person making it has not authority to make it.

This provision was applied in *Patry v. General Motors Acceptance Corp. of Canada Ltd.* (2000), 48 O.R. (3d) 370 (C.A.). The plaintiff delivered a boat to X, a dealer in watercraft, on consignment. The boat was treated as part of X's inventory while it was in X's possession. It therefore fell within the terms of a chattel mortgage that X improperly gave to the defendant. When X became bankrupt, the defendant seized the boat and sold it in order to receive payment on X's debt. The plaintiff sued the defendant in conversion. The claim was rejected because (1) X possessed the boat, with the plaintiff's consent, in its capacity as a mercantile agent, and (2) the defendant obtained a chattel mortgage over the boat in good faith. The Court of Appeal for Ontario emphasized that, as long as the defendant acted honestly, it could not be denied protection merely because it failed to investigate true ownership of the boat. The defence would fail only if the defendant refrained from investigating an actual suspicion. The same is true of the "vendor in possession" and "buyer in possession" exceptions that appear in provincial sale of goods statutes.

9. Despite the general rule that an honest and reasonable defendant may be held liable for unwittingly committing a conversion, it sometimes is possible to avoid liability by demonstrating that a purportedly tortious act did not constitute conversion. In *Marcq v. Christie Manson & Woods Ltd. (trading as Christie's)*, [2003] 3 W.L.R. 980 (C.A.), the claimant owned a painting by Jan Steen known as *The Backgammon Players* (1677). The painting was stolen and eventually taken to the defendant's auction house by a third party. The piece failed to sell, however, and the defendant merely returned the piece to the third party. The defendant was not liable in conversion, even though it had intended to sell the painting. The result would have been different, however, if a sale had occurred. The Court of Appeal stressed that liability is based on actions, rather than intentions. It also said that the defendant was under no duty to the claimant to investigate ownership because there was nothing suspicious in the circumstances.

10. Since conversion is an intentional tort, a carrier or custodian can be held liable in conversion for innocently delivering the plaintiff's chattels to a third party, but not for carelessly losing them. Is this result justified? See *Joule Ltd. v. Poole* (1924), 24 S.R. (N.S.W.) 387 (Dist. C.A.); and *Heffron v. Imperial Parking Co.* (1974), 46 D.L.R. (3d)

642 (Ont. C.A.). It should be noted, however, that the careless defendant in these cases may be liable in detinue and negligence.

11. Most authorities state that the right of action belongs to either the party in immediate possession, or the party with a right to immediate possession, at the time of the conversion. Some cases, however, appear to require proof that the plaintiff held a property right in addition to a possessory interest. See for example *Kent v. Ellis* (1900), 31 S.C.R. 110; *McCutcheon v. Lightfoot*, [1929] 1 D.L.R. 971 (Man. C.A.); *Kahler v. Midland Bank Ltd.*, [1950] A.C. 24 (H.L.); *Jarvis v. Williams*, [1955] 1 All E.R. 108 (C.A.); and Warren, "Qualifying as a Plaintiff in an Action for Conversion" (1936) 49 Harv. L. Rev. 1084.

12. A person sued in conversion may establish *jus tertii* ("right of a third party") by proving that someone other than the plaintiff has the best right of possession. The gist of that argument is that tort law should protect only the true owner. As a general rule, however, a claim in conversion will not be defeated by *jus tertii*. This rule is justified on the ground that it avoids the complexity that would arise if a court was required to deal with all possible claims to a chattel, rather than merely those of the parties to the dispute.

An important example occurred in *Armory v. Delamirie* (1722), 93 E.R. 664 (K.B.). A boy found a ring while working as a chimney sweep. He brought it to an apprentice. The apprentice removed the stones from the ring on the pretence of weighing them and then returned the empty ring to the boy. As against the ensuing action in conversion, the apprentice pleaded that the boy was not the ring's true owner. Not only did *jus tertii* fail, but, because the defendant had wrongfully made it impossible to establish the value of the stones, the court assumed that the gems were of "the finest water." See also *Wilson v. Lombank Ltd.*, [1963] 1 All E.R. 740 (C.A.). See generally Jolly, "The *Jus Tertii* and the Third Man" (1955) 8 Mod. L. Rev. 371; Fleming, *The Law of Torts*, 9th ed. (1998) at 73-74; and Tyler & Palmer, *Crossley Vaines' Personal Property* 5th ed. (1973) at 24-25.

13. Notwithstanding the general rule, *jus tertii* may provide a defence in certain circumstances. A distinction must be drawn between two scenarios. If the plaintiff was in possession at the time of the conversion, then the defendant is entitled to raise *jus tertii* only with authority from the true owner. In contrast, if the plaintiff merely had a right to possession, then, according to most authorities, the claimant must establish an absolute title. Assume, for instance, that the plaintiff purchased goods, but temporarily left them in possession of the vendor. The vendor subsequently became bankrupt, and the goods in question were seized and sold. It has been held that the plaintiff does not have an action in conversion against the person who performed the sale: *Leake v. Loveday* (1842), 134 E.R. 399. See Fleming, *The Law of Torts*, 9th ed. (1998) at 73-74; and Tyler & Palmer, *supra* at 24-25.

In England, the defence of *jus tertii* is addressed by the *Torts (Interference with Goods) Act 1977*. Sections 7 and 8 of that statute (1) permit the defence of *jus tertii*, (2) require the claimant to identify other parties interested in the property, (3) allow a court to eliminate any rights that may be held by third parties who fail to appear as commanded, and (4) prohibit double recovery in the event that, for instance, a person liable in conversion is sued successfully by both the finder and the true owner of a chattel. A similar approach has been proposed in Canada: Ontario Law Reform Commission, *Study Paper on Wrongful Interference with Goods* (1989), ch. 12.

14. Alleging *jus tertii* generally will not protect a defendant. More surprisingly, full damages may be awarded to a bailee, even though that plaintiff (1) commenced an action in conversion exclusively on the basis of a possessory interest, and (2) is not liable to account to the bailor. The leading case is *The Winkfield*, [1902] P. 42 (C.A.). The Postmaster-General had possession of mail as a bailee. The defendant negligently caused an accident that resulted in the loss of that mail. The Postmaster-General was entitled to full compensation even though it was not, in turn, liable to the actual owners of the items. What is the rationale for this principle? How does this relate to the issue of who should be permitted to sue in conversion? For more discussion of this case see Welling, *Property in Things in the Common Law System* (1996) at 339-44.

15. The name of "conversion" reflects the historical understanding of the tort. The gist of the claim originally was that property in the chattel had been *converted* or *shifted* to the defendant. That is why, for instance, it initially was impossible to plead both detinue and conversion (or trover) on the same facts. The former presumed that the plaintiff retained property in the item and therefore was entitled to call for its return, whereas the latter presumed that the defendant had acquired property in the thing and therefore was vulnerable to a forced sale. That view reached its peak in *Isaack v. Clark* (1792), 80 E.R. 1143 (K.B.) which held that a refusal to return a chattel provided evidence that property in it had changed and that the item had been converted to the defendant's use. The fiction underlying that development reflected the fact that, for reasons previously discussed, courts and claimants were desirous of extending the scope of conversion at the expense of detinue. Today, of course, it is possible to plead both torts in the alternative. Moreover, while conversion continues to support the remedy of forced sale, property is not thought to pass until the defendant had satisfied judgment by paying the "price." See *Ex part Drake* (1877), 5 Ch. D. 866 (C.A.); and *Sadler v. Scott*, [1947] 1 D.L.R. 712 (B.C.C.A.).

16. Trespass, conversion, and detinue protect the right of possession. Consequently, they cannot be used by a person who, despite being entitled to possess a chattel in the future, does not have a right to immediate possession. That rule may create hardship. For instance, if a car was damaged while on lease, the lessor of the vehicle would not be entitled to demand compensation from the wrongdoer. Fortunately, tort law provides a solution, in the form of an innominate ("unnamed") action, to owners out of possession and people who hold *reversionary interests* in damaged goods. See *Mears v. London & South Western Ry. Co.* (1862), 142 E.R. 1029 (C.P.); and *Dee Trading Co. Pty. Ltd. v. Baldwin*, [1938] V.L.R. 173. Is this action redundant in light of modern negligence law?

REVIEW PROBLEMS

1. Conversion can be committed in various ways. The essential issue nevertheless is always the same: has the defendant intentionally acted in a way that interferes with the plaintiff's right to possess the goods? As the following examples illustrate, this principle is often difficult to apply.

- *Taking Possession*: If Barry takes Allen's car without his consent, Barry will be liable in conversion. Would Barry be liable in conversion if, in an effort to make room for his own vehicle, he pushed Allen's car three metres without damaging it? See *Aitkin Agencies Ltd. v. Richardson*, [1967] N.Z.L.R. 65 (S.C.).

- *Withholding Possession*: If Mary asks Barry to return her chattels in accordance with their storage contract and Barry refuses, he will be held liable in conversion. If she demands that the chattels be delivered at midnight and he refuses, but promises to deliver them the next morning, he will not be liable in conversion. Can you explain these two results? Would Barry be held liable in conversion if he refused to deliver the chattels without receiving proof that Mary was the true owner? See *Scott v. McAlpine* (1887), 6 U.C.C.P. 302; *Annand v. The Merchant's Bank* (1878), 12 N.S.R. 329 (S.C.); and *Morrison v. Fishwick* (1879), 13 N.S.R. 59 (S.C.).

- *Transferring Possession*: Assume that Allen, acting as an agent for Barry, negotiates to purchase goods from Carol which have been stolen from Diane. Assume as well that Allen delivers them to Barry. In this situation, both Allen and Carol will be liable in conversion. If Barry had negotiated the purchase himself and Allen had only picked up the goods from Carol and delivered them to Barry, then Allen would not be liable in conversion. Can you explain these results? If Allen receives goods from Barry which he had not ordered and he mistakenly returned them to Carol instead of Barry, would Allen be liable in conversion? See *The Lancashire Wagon Co. Ltd. v. Fitzhugh* (1861), 158 E.R. 206 (Ex. Ct.); *Dickey v. McCaul* (1887), 14 O.A.R. 166 (C.A.); *Juelle v. Trudeau* (1968), 7 D.L.R. (3d) 82 (Qc. S.C.); and Lawson, "The Passing of Property and Risk in Sale of Goods" (1949) 65 L.Q.R. 35.

- *Destruction, Damage and Use*: If Allen stores ice in a freezer and Barry intentionally opens the freezer door causing some of the ice to melt, Barry will be liable for conversion of the melted ice. Would he also be liable in conversion for the remaining ice? See *Moorgate Mercantile Co. Ltd. v. Finch*, [1962] 2 All E.R. 467 (C.A.).

- *Asserting Ownership*: Assume Allen has stored some chattels on property which Barry subsequently purchased. If Barry refuses to permit Allen to recover the chattels and Barry then removes some of them, he will be liable in conversion. Would Barry have been liable if he had simply refused to permit Allen to recover the chattels? See *Dickey v. McCaul*, *supra*.

2. Mark stole a herd of bison from Meena and sold the animals to you for $50,000. Before you paid, you checked the animals and noticed that they were not branded. You also asked Mark about the herd and were convinced by his answer that he owned the animals. Unfortunately, he has disappeared and Meena has sued you for conversion. Although you had acted honestly, you would probably be held liable for conversion. In buying the animals and treating them as your own, you seriously interfered with Meena's rights. Consequently, you probably would have to pay her $50,000, which was the market value of the animals. Notice that while you will be entitled to keep the herd, you have now paid $100,000 for it. You could try to recover $50,000 from Mark, but he has disappeared, as rogues often do. Are the rules for conversion fair? Why is the law of conversion so strict?

3. Pam owns a computer that she rented to Dave for a period of six months. Although Dave paid the full rent at the beginning of the term, Pam realized that she desperately required the computer after only two months. She therefore re-acquired possession of the computer without Dave's consent. In the circumstances, can Dave successfully sue her for conversion? See *Roberts v. Wyatt* (1810), 127 E.R. 180 (C.P.).

(b) CONVERSION OF CHEQUES AND OTHER UNUSUAL CHATTELS

373409 ALBERTA LTD. (RECEIVER OF) v. BANK OF MONTREAL
(2002), 220 D.L.R. (4th) 193 (S.C.C.)

MAJOR J.: – The outcome of this appeal depends on whether the appellant Bank of Montreal (the "Bank") by itself or with others acted in any way to cause financial loss to the respondents. As the appellant Bank acted with proper authority, the answer is no. The appeal is allowed with costs.

I. Facts

The facts are not in dispute. Douglas Lakusta was the sole shareholder and directing mind of both 373409 Alberta Ltd. ("373409") and Legacy Holdings Ltd. ("Legacy"). The events that give rise to this action occurred after 373409 entered into a General Security Agreement with the respondent Province of Alberta Treasury Branches, but before the respondent Ernst & Young Inc. was appointed as 373409's Receiver and Manager.

Lakusta received a cheque payable to 373409 for the sale of an automobile to a *bona fide* customer, Lea Sanderson. Lakusta altered the cheque by adding "/Legacy" so that the payee read "373409 Alberta Ltd./ Legacy". He deposited the altered cheque into Legacy's account at the appellant Bank. The cheque was not endorsed. The Bank credited Legacy's account with the proceeds of the cheque, and the funds were later withdrawn by Lakusta.

373409 subsequently went into liquidation, and its Receiver and Manager brought the present action in conversion against the Bank for having accepted for deposit 373409's unendorsed cheque into Legacy's account. . . .

IV. Analysis

A. The Tort of Conversion

The tort of conversion "involves a wrongful interference with the goods of another, such as taking, using or destroying these goods in a manner inconsistent with the owner's right of possession": *Boma Manufacturing Ltd. v. Canadian Imperial Bank of Commerce*, [(1996), 140 D.L.R. (4th) 463 (S.C.C.)], per Iacobucci J., at para. 31. It has long been recognized that an action in conversion may be brought by the rightful holder of a cheque against a wrongful dispossessor: *Crawford and Falconbridge: Banking and Bills of Exchange* (8th ed. 1986), vol. 2, at p. 1386 ... The tort is one of strict liability, and although the dispossession must arise as a result of the defendant's intentional act, "it is no defence that the wrongful act was committed in all innocence": *Boma*, *supra*, at para. 31.

An owner's right of possession includes the right to authorize others to deal with his or her chattel in any manner specified. As a result, dealing with another's chattel in a manner authorized by the rightful owner is consistent with the owner's right of possession, and does not qualify as wrongful interference.

...

Boma, *supra*, presented an entirely different factual basis than the case at bar. There, a bookkeeper committed fraud against the companies she worked for by issuing a series of fraudulent cheques made payable to various individuals. The collecting bank deposited the proceeds of the fraudulent cheques into the bookkeeper's account. Iacobucci J. cited (at para. 36) with approval the following passage from *Crawford and Falconbridge*, at p.1386:

> It has been repeatedly held that a bank converts an instrument by dealing with it under the direction of one not authorized, either by collecting it or, semble (although this has not yet actually been decided) by paying it and in either case, making the proceeds available to someone other than the person rightfully entitled to possession. [Footnotes omitted.]

That means a lending institution's liability in conversion is predicated upon finding both that payment upon the cheque was made to someone other than the rightful holder of the cheque, and that such payment was not authorized by the rightful holder. If either of these criteria is not satisfied, there is no tort. On the facts of *Boma, supra*, Iacobucci J. held, at para. 40, that the bookkeeper's actions were beyond the ambit of authority granted to her by the companies she worked for. As a result, the bank's actions were undertaken without the authority of the companies which were rightfully entitled to the cheques' proceeds, and resulted in the dispossession of those companies' entitlements. Consequently, the bank was held to be prima facie liable in conversion for having deposited the cheques' proceeds into the bookkeeper's account.

...

In this appeal, it is acknowledged that the Bank dealt with 373409's cheque in a manner which, if unauthorized, would have created liability in conversion. Before the cheque was brought to the Bank by Lakusta, 373409 was the rightful holder of the cheque and entitled to its proceeds. Lakusta's alteration of the cheque had no effect upon 373409's sole entitlement to it. The deposit of the cheque's proceeds into Legacy's account led to the dispossession of 373409's entitlement. The issue is whether the Bank was authorized by 373409 to deal with the cheque as it did, the result being to deprive 373409 of the cheque's proceeds. If 373409 authorized the Bank to deposit the proceeds of the cheque into Legacy's account, then the Bank's actions cannot be wrongful interference and cannot give rise to liability in conversion because it acted with the authority of the true owner of the cheque.

The respondents' argument turns on their submission that only a proper endorsement of the cheque would have provided the Bank with the authority needed to deal with it. In their submission, Lakusta had to endorse the cheque in accordance with the provisions of the Act. Absent that endorsement, the respondents argue, Lakusta's explicit instructions to the Bank did not constitute authorization to deal with the cheque. The trial judge and the majority of the Alberta Court of Appeal agreed with this analysis. The Court of Appeal stated, at para. 6, that "the Bank cannot argue that Lakusta had authority on behalf of the numbered company without actually obtaining an endorsement to that effect". With respect, that conclusion is wrong as it would remove the possessory rights attached to the ownership of the cheque.

Iacobucci J. stated in *Boma, supra*, at para. 30, that "[a]n individual obtains title to a bill through negotiation". Negotiation, then, refers to the transfer of a bill's title between two parties. As per s. 59(3) of the Act, "[a] bill payable to order is negotiated by the endorsement of the holder". An endorsement, therefore, is the formal mechanism by which the holder of a bill payable to order transfers title in that bill to another party.

The issue in this case, however, is not whether 373409 transferred its title in the cheque to Legacy, but whether the Bank dealt with the cheque on the authority of 373409. As long as the Bank's actions were authorized by 373409, then the criterion of wrongful interference does not arise. An owner's capacity to authorize others to deal with his or her chattel is fundamental to that owner's right of possession. The provisions of the Act do not in any way limit the capacity of a cheque owner to delegate such authority. The rightful owner of any chattel, including a bill of exchange, is capable of authorizing another party to deal with that chattel, notwithstanding the absence of a formal transfer of title.

Consequently, whether 373409 negotiated the cheque and effected a transfer of title to Legacy is not dispositive of whether 373409 authorized the Bank to deal with its cheque as it did. The owner of a cheque is capable of authorizing another party to collect the proceeds of the cheque and transfer those proceeds to a third party. The granting of such authority is not dependent upon a transfer of legal title pursuant to the requirements of the Act.

[A] bank assumes significant risk in accepting an unendorsed third party cheque into a customer's account. An endorsement is the formal mechanism by which a bank is able to verify that it has the authority to deposit a cheque's proceeds into a customer's account. However, where the rightful owner has in fact authorized the bank to deal with the cheque, the lack of endorsement will not negate that authority. [A] bank's ... assumption of that risk ... does not by itself constitute conversion...

In this case, Lakusta instructed the Bank to deposit the proceeds of the cheque payable to 373409 into Legacy's account. As Lakusta was the sole owner of 373409, he could, as he did, authorize the Bank to deal with 373409's cheque, and the Bank played no role in conversion. To state the obvious, if Lakusta was not acting on behalf of 373409, then the Bank would not have had authorization to deal with the cheque and would be liable in conversion for having dispossessed 373409 of the cheque's proceeds.

There can be no doubt that Lakusta's act of directing the Bank to deposit the proceeds of the cheque into Legacy's account can be attributed to and considered authorized by 373409.

...

Here, Lakusta was the sole shareholder, director, and officer of 373409. He was the only person capable of acting as the corporation's directing mind, and he formed the entire "ego" and "personality" of the corporation. In his capacity as sole shareholder and director of the corporation, he had the full capacity to delegate authority to the corporation's agents. He was the sole officer of the corporation, and its only agent. Consequently, any act which he undertook as 373409's agent must be deemed authorized by the corporation. The only conclusion available on the evidence was that Lakusta, *qua* shareholder and director, authorized Lakusta, *qua* officer, to deposit 373409's funds into Legacy's account.

...

The impropriety of the corporation's diversion of funds from its creditors does not undermine Lakusta's authority to deal with those funds on behalf of the corporation. The wrongfulness of an officer's act in relation to a third party does not negate that act's attribution to the corporate body. For instance, a corporation may be responsible for the criminal acts of its agents... The key question in determining attribution is whether that agent's action was within the scope of authority delegated to him or her by the corporation. Since Lakusta was acting within the scope of authority granted to him by 373409, his act of instructing the Bank to deposit the cheque's proceeds into Legacy's account must be attributed to the corporation.

373409, through Lakusta, authorized the Bank, as it was entitled to do, to deposit the cheque's proceeds into Legacy's account. As a result, the Bank did not wrongfully interfere with 373409's cheque, as it did not deal with that cheque in a manner inconsistent with 373409's instructions. Consequently, the Bank is not liable in conversion to 373409's Receiver and Manager for the proceeds of the cheque.

NOTES AND QUESTIONS

1. Explain the concepts of "negotiation" and "endorsement." Were these concepts important for the purposes of Major J.'s decision?

2. When will a bank be held liable for conversion of a cheque?

3. Does Major J.'s decision seem fair to you? What would have been the practical implications of holding the defendant liable? Do banks often receive unendorsed cheques? Consider a situation in which an unendorsed cheque is deposited by way of an automated teller. See Rafferty, "Developments in Contract and Tort Law: The 2002-2003 Term" (2003) 22 S.CL.R. (2d) 175.

4. How did Major J. distinguish the facts before him from the facts of *Boma Manufacturing Ltd. v. Canadian Imperial Bank of Commerce*, [1996] 3 S.C.R. 727? For discussion of *Boma*, see Geva, "Conversion of Unissued Cheques and the Fictitious or Non-Existent Payee – *Boma v. CIBC*" (1997) 28 C.B.L.J. 177; and Ogilvie, "If *Boma* is Wrong, Is the Bank Always Right?: *373409 Alberta Ltd. (Receiver of) v. Bank of Montreal*" (2003) 39 C.B.L.J. 138.

5. The claim in *373409 Alberta Ltd.* pertained to a cheque, which is a *tangible* form of property. Different considerations arise if the plaintiff complains that the defendant wrongfully interfered with an *intangible* piece of property. Conversion traditionally was viewed as protecting the right to possession and it is, of course, impossible to physically possess something that is intangible. For that reason, English courts continue to reject actions in conversion with respect to intangible assets: *OBG Ltd. v. Allan*, [2005] 2 W.L.R. 1174 (C.A.). Canadian courts, in contrast, have imposed liability in such circumstances: *McLachlan v. Canadian Imperial Bank of Commerce* (1987), 13 B.C.L.R. (2d) 300 (S.C.); aff'd (1989), 35 B.C.L.R. (2d) 100 (C.A.); *Bradshaw Construction Ltd. v. Bank of Nova Scotia*, [1993] 1 W.W.R. 596 (B.C.C.A.), additional reasons at (1992), 73 B.C.L.R. (2d) 212 (C.A.); and *Royal Bank of Canada v. W. Got & Associates Electric Ltd.*. (1994), 150 A.R. 93 (Q.B.), additional reasons at (1994), 18 Alta. L.R. (3d) 140 (Q.B.), aff'd (1997), 47 C.B.R. (3d) 1 (Alta. C.A.), aff'd on other grounds [1999] 3 S.C.R. 408. Is this a desirable development? See Tettenborn, "Liability for Interfering with Intangibles: Invalidly Appointed Receivers, Conversion, and the Economic Torts"

(2006) 122 L.Q.R. 31; and Ricks, "Conversion of Intangible Property: Bursting the Ancient Trover Bottle with New Wine" [1991] B.Y.U.L. Rev. 1681.

The House of Lords recently reiterated the orthodox belief that conversion is confined to interference with tangible property: *OBG Ltd. v. Allan; Douglas v. Hello!; Mainstream Properties Ltd. v. Young*, [2007] UKHL 21. The defendants in the first named case improperly acted as receivers of the claimant company. In that ostensible capacity, they liquidated the company's contractual assets. The company subsequently sought relief under the tort of conversion on the basis that the defendants had interfered with its contractual relations. Lord Hoffmann, writing for the majority, emphatically stated (at para. 100) that the "subject matter of conversion or trover must be specific personal property, whether goods or chattels" and said that it would be extraordinary to extend strict liability to people who in good faith, though improperly, had acted as receivers. He also said that since Parliament had examined the area and not taken action, it would be inappropriate, on policy grounds, for the courts to adopt the revisions advocated by the claimant. In a forceful dissent, however, Lord Nicholls believed that the defendants, who had taken over the claimant's entire operation, should be strictly liable for interference with the company's contracts, just as if they had interfered with the company's chattels. He said (at para. 223) "This distinction makes no sense. It has no rhyme or reason." He therefore favoured, as a "modest but principled extension," expanding the scope of conversion to include interference with contractual rights.

In the modern world, much of what people value exists in digitized form. This is true, for instance, of computer software programs. Aside from the physical disks upon which such assets may be impressed, should those digitized assets themselves be protected by the tort of conversion? What are the arguments for and against such protection? See Green, "Can a Digitized Product be the Subject of Conversion?" [2006] L.M.C.L.Q. 568.

6. Because conversion is a *legal* cause of action, it cannot be used to remedy interference with an equitable interest in property. See *MCC Proceeds Ltd. v. Lehman Bros. (Europe)*, [1998] 4 All E.R. 657 (C.A.).

(c) REMEDIES FOR CONVERSION

AITKEN v. GARDINER

(1956), 4 D.L.R. (2d) 119 (Ont. H.C.)

[The defendants purchased share certificates without knowing that they had been stolen from the plaintiff. By the time the action came to trial, the defendants already had sold some of the certificates. Spence J. held that the defendants were liable in either conversion or the old action of detinue *sur trover*. He ordered the defendants to return the remaining certificates they possessed, and then considered the proper measure of damages for the shares they had sold.

The defendants argued that they were liable only in conversion for the sold certificates and that the proper measure of damages was the value of the certificates when they were converted, rather than their much higher value at the time of the trial. Only the portion of Spence J.'s judgment dealing with the measure of damages in conversion is reproduced below.]

SPENCE J.: ... Even if I am in error in concluding that the plaintiff is entitled to assert her claim in an action like the old action of *detinue sur trover*, and is limited to an action for conversion, it is not at all certain that the result of such limitation would be to confine her damages to the small sum of money realized by the defendants upon the sale of these shares. It is true, and it has been stated time after time, that the measure of damages in actions in conversion is *generally* the value of the chattel converted at the time of the conversion.

In 4 C.E.D. (Ont.), 2nd ed., p. 168, it is said: "In an action for conversion the general principle of law, although not an inflexible one, is that the jury can give no more damages than the value of the goods at the time of the conversion."

In *Caxton Publishing Co. v. Sutherland Publishing Co.*, [1939] A.C. 178 at p. 203, Lord Porter said:

> There is no dispute as to the principle on which in general the measure of damages of conversion is calculated. It is the value of the thing converted at the date of the conversion, and this principle was accepted by both sides in the present case.

In *Solloway v. McLaughlin*, [1937] 4 D.L.R. 593 at p. 596, [1938] A.C. 247, Lord Atkin said:

> Their disposal of the deposited shares amounted to nothing short of conversion: and the client on each occasion on which the shares were sold had vested in him a right to damages for conversion which would be measured by the value of the shares at the date of the conversion.

Mayne on Damages, 11th ed., p. 417, explains the latter case further. The defendant stockbroker had converted the plaintiff's shares, but on the closing of the plaintiff's account with him he bought the same number of shares in the same company at a substantially lower price than at the conversion, and tendered these to the plaintiff, who took them without knowledge of the conversion. On discovering this the plaintiff sued for damages and the Court held that the defendants were liable for damages for the conversion and that the measure of damages was the value at the date of the conversion, less the value of the shares bought in replacement at the time when the plaintiff accepted such shares.

In *Salmond on Torts*, *op. cit.*, p. 348, it is said:

> If, on the other hand, the property increases in value after the date of the conversion, a distinction has to be drawn. If the increase is due to the act of the defendant, the plaintiff has no title to it, and his claim is limited to the original value of the chattel...
> If, however, the subsequent increase in value is not due to the act of the defendant, but would have occurred in any case, even had no conversion been committed, the plaintiff is entitled to recover it as special damage resulting from the conversion, in addition to the original value of the property converted: as when goods taken or detained have risen in value by reason of the fluctuation of the market.

The author cites *Greening v. Wilkinson* (1825), 1 Car. & P. 625, 171 E.R. 1344, but adds in a footnote that it is different "if the plaintiff knew or ought to have known of the conversion" for in such case "he cannot claim the benefit of the subsequent rise in value: *Sachs v. Miklos*, [1948] 2 K.B. 23."

Salmond continues at p. 349: "In all actions for a conversion the plaintiff may recover, in addition to the value of the property ... any additional damage which he may have sustained by reason of the conversion which is not too remote." He cites *Bodley v.*

Reynolds (1846), 8 Q.B. 779, 115 E.R. 1066, and *France v. Gaudet* (1871), L.R. 6 Q.B. 199.

It would seem that the damage which a plaintiff suffers due to the defendants' inability to deliver certificates which have increased in value from a few cents to $17.50 per share are not damages which are too remote to enter into the calculation of her loss. Mayne is not so definite as is Salmond, and at p. 416 the author remarks: "Where the article has fluctuated in price, it is by no means settled in England whether it is to be estimated at its value at the time of conversion, or at any later time." And at p. 417 he expresses the opinion that an increase in value of goods from a rise in price is a gratuitous and accidental bonus, obtained by the holder of the goods, and that, consequently, if, in trover for goods, damages were fixed at the time of their conversion, it might deprive the rightful owner of a profit, but that profit might be one which he never would have acquired, and for which he gave no consideration. Nevertheless, I am of the opinion that a person who owns shares and holds them for subsequent sale is a person who intends to acquire a profit if and when those shares increase in value, and that the conversion of those shares has deprived the plaintiff of an opportunity to obtain the profit which the plaintiff planned to obtain should the shares increase in value, and that the deprivation of the opportunity to obtain that profit is a proper element in considering the loss which the plaintiff suffered by the conversion.

. . .

[Spence J. concluded by giving the defendants the opportunity to return share certificates of the same kind to the plaintiff or pay $35,000 damages, the value of the share certificates at the date of trial. He also indicated, in *obiter dicta*, that the proper date for assessing damages was the trial date and not the judgment date if the values on these dates differed.]

NOTES AND QUESTIONS

1. It generally is said that a successful claimant in conversion is entitled to the market value of the chattel at the *time of the conversion*, whereas a successful claimant in detinue is entitled to the market value of the chattel at the *time of trial*. By way of explanation, it should be noted that an act of conversion is perceived a specific event, whereas the refusal to return a chattel that underlies detinue is viewed as an ongoing event. Given that difference, it often is said that, if an option exists, the plaintiff should sue in detinue in a rising market and in conversion in a falling market. That apparently simple proposition unfortunately is not helpful in fluctuating markets, as is often the case with stocks and other investments. Similar problems arise if judgment is awarded in a foreign currency, the value of which fluctuates between the time of conversion and the time of trial: see *Stevenson Estate v. Siewert* (2001), 286 A.R. 181 (C.A.). Problems also may arise if the plaintiff was subject to an obligation to *mitigate* the losses flowing from the defendant's tort.

2. As *Aitken* illustrates, a plaintiff in a conversion action may be entitled to recover not only the market value of the chattel at the time of the conversion, but also *consequential losses* caused by the conversion. Spence J. appears to adopt J. Salmond's analysis of the circumstances in which the plaintiff can recover for consequential economic losses.

What limitations does Salmond impose on such awards? Are they compatible with a plaintiff's obligation to mitigate?

3. In *Kuwait Airways Corp. v. Iraqi Airways Co.*, [2002] 2 W.L.R. 1353 (H.L.), the House of Lords addressed various aspects of the tort of conversion, including the issue of consequential damages. Iraqi forces invaded Kuwait, seized ten aircraft belonging to the plaintiff, moved them to Iraq, and delivered them to the defendant. The Iraqi government, acting through the Revolutionary Command Council, then passed Resolution 369, which transferred property in the aircraft to the defendant. Four of the planes subsequently were destroyed by coalition forces. The other six planes were sent by the defendant to Iran. The plaintiff eventually recovered those planes, but only after paying $20,000,000 in storage fees to the government of Iran. The plaintiff sued the defendant for that amount, plus the revenue that it lost as a result of not being able to use the aircraft during their detention.

As a matter of public law, the defendant enjoyed state immunity with respect to any acts performed prior to the passage of Resolution 369. The defendant's first line of argument therefore was that it could not be held liable for conversion because it received the aircraft during the period covered by state immunity. The House of Lords rejected that argument. It held that, while the defendant had previously come into possession of the aircraft, its actions after Resolution 369 constituted conversion. It had dealt with the aircraft in a manner that was inconsistent with the plaintiff's right of possession (*e.g.* by repainting and insuring the planes) and it had prevented the plaintiff from regaining possession of the aircraft.

On the question of damages, the House of Lords held that the plaintiff was entitled to recover (1) the $20,000,000 that it had paid to the Iranian government to secure the release of the aircraft, and (2) the revenue that it lost during the period of detention. See O'Keefe & Tettenborn, "English Public Policy Internationalised – And Conversion Clarified Too" [2002] C.L.J. 499; Cane, "Causing Conversion" (2002) 118 L.Q.R. 544.

4. In *Ralston Purina of Can. Ltd. v. Whittaker* (1973), 6 N.B.R. (2d) 443 (C.A.), the defendant seized the plaintiff's pigs and sold them. Had the pigs not been converted, the plaintiff would have kept them until they were heavier and then sold them at a higher price. The court awarded the plaintiff the value of the pigs at the date of conversion, plus an additional amount to compensate him for what the pigs would have been worth had they been fattened.

In *Hutscal v. I.A.C. Ltd.* (1974), 48 D.L.R. (3d) 638 (Y.C.A.), the defendant unlawfully repossessed the plaintiff's house trailer. The plaintiff was awarded the value of the trailer at the date of the conversion, but denied damages for the loss of use of the trailer while it was in the defendant's possession. The court held that the plaintiff otherwise would have received compensation twice for the same loss. Do you agree?

Can you reconcile *Hutscal* and *Ralston*? Are these cases consistent with Salmond's analysis of damage awards in conversion?

5. In *Sachs v. Miklos*, [1948] 1 All E.R. 67 (C.A.), the court suggested that there was no practical difference between the measure of damages in detinue and conversion, because the plaintiff can recover any post-conversion increase in the chattel's value by means of a claim for consequential economic loss.

As we shall discuss, the court in *Gen. & Finance Facilities Ltd. v. Cooks Cars (Romford) Ltd.*, [1963] 2 All E.R. 314 (C.A.), specifically rejected this view, while reaffirming that consequential economic loss was available in certain situations involving conversion. That view similarly was rejected in *Steiman v. Steiman* (1982), 143 D.L.R. (3d) 396 (Man. C.A.). The Manitoba Court of Appeal held that damages in conversion must be calculated on the assumption that the plaintiff mitigated by replacing the chattel as early as reasonably possible. A plaintiff who has replaced a converted chattel will not lose any appreciation in a rising market. If awarded damages for consequential economic loss, the plaintiff would recover appreciation twice: once on the converted chattel and again on the replacement chattel. Do you agree with this analysis? Is *Steiman*, in effect, merely trying to ensure that the victim of a conversion mitigate as soon as possible? Can you reconcile *Steiman, Gen. & Finance* and *Aitken*? See *Dom. Securities Ltd. v. Glazerman* (1984), 29 C.C.L.T. 194 (Man. C.A.); and Irvine, "Annotation" (1984), 29 C.C.L.T. 195. See also *Asamera Oil Corp. v. Sea Oil & Gen. Corp.*, [1979] 1 S.C.R. 633; *R.F. Fry & Associates (Pacific) Ltd. v. Reimer*, [1993] 8 W.W.R. 663 (B.C.C.A.); and Waddams, "Damages for Failure to Return Shares" (1979) 3 C.B.L.J. 398.

6. As a general principle, damages in tort are intended to monetarily position the plaintiff as if the wrong had not occurred. Damages are not intended to positively benefit the plaintiff. Does the result in *Solloway v. McLaughlin*, which is discussed in *Aitken*, violate this principle? Can you suggest a countervailing principle that justifies the result in *Solloway*? See *Butler v. Egg Board* (1966), 114 C.L.R. 185 at 189 (H.C.A.); *BBMB Finance (Hong Kong) Ltd. v. Eda Holdings Ltd.*, [1991] 2 All E.R. 129 (P.C.); *Campbell v. Dominion Breweries Ltd.*, [1994] 3 N.Z.L.R. 559 (C.A.); *Kerr v. Fleming Financial Corp.*, [1998] 9 W.W.R. 176 (Man. Q.B.), aff'd (1998), 131 Man. R. (2d) 116 (C.A); and Tettenborn, "Damages in Conversion – The Exception or the Anomaly" [1995] C.L.J. 128.

7. Although many of the cases are ambiguous, the response to conversion may consist of disgorgement of the defendant's wrongful gain, rather than compensation of the plaintiff's loss. This remedial option generally lies with the claimant. See for example *United Australia Ltd. v. Barclays Bank Ltd.*, [1941] A.C. 1 (H.L.) and the older cases *Lamine v. Dorrell* (1705), 92 E.R. 303; *King v. Leith* (1787), 100 E.R. 77; and *Marsh v. Keating* (1834), 131 E.R. 1094.

8. In *Royal Bank v. W. Got & Associates Electric Ltd.*, [1999] 3 S.C.R. 408, the bank was held liable for $100,000 in punitive damages for its high-handed conversion of the plaintiff's business assets. In *Royal Canadian Legion Branch No. 15 v. Burkitt*, 2005 CarswellBC 3013 (S.C.) (WLeC), the defendant secretary stole nearly $200,000 from the plaintiff. The court indicated that it would have awarded punitive damages if it had been asked to do so. And in *Rollinson v. R.* (1994), 73 F.T.R. 16, customs and RCMP officers were held liable in conversion for compensatory, aggravated, and punitive damages for repeatedly seizing the plaintiff's boat and for "escalating their eight-year mistreatment of the Rollinsons, from a very bad, stupid beginning." The court awarded the plaintiffs an additional $8,000 under s. 24(1) of the *Canadian Charter of Rights and Freedoms*, Part I of the *Constitution Act, 1982*, being Schedule B to the *Canada Act 1982* (U.K.) 1982, c. 11 for the defendants' violation of their ss. 7, 8, 12 and 15 rights.

9. In an action for conversion or detinue, the plaintiff exceptionally may obtain recovery *in specie* (that is, of the specific thing). So too, as discussed at the end of this chapter, the owner may retrieve a chattel by means of recaption. While in possession of the property, however, the defendant may have effected considerable repairs or improvements to the item. When, if ever, should the owner be liable in unjust enrichment to provide restitution to the defendant for the value of such benefits? It has been suggested that while an owner who recovers property with judicial assistance must make restitution, one who resorts to the self-help remedy need not pay for the benefit: *Greenwood v. Bennett*, [1972] 3 All E.R. 586 (C.A.); *Peruvian Guano Co. Ltd. v. Dreyfus Brothers & Co. Ltd.*, [1892] A.C. 166 (H.L.); *cf. Mayne v. Kidd* (1951), 1 W.W.R. 833 (Sask. C.A.). Is that rule fair? Should a defendant who honestly repairs a chattel enjoy always an independent claim in unjust enrichment?

In *Mutungih v. Bokun* (2006), 40 C.C.L.T. (3d) 313 (Ont. S.C.J.), the defendant spent considerable money repairing a car that had been stolen from the plaintiff. In awarding relief for conversion, the court noted that the defendant had purchased the stolen vehicle from a third party under suspicious circumstances, and therefore refused to make any allowance for the improvements.

10. Conversion involves a complex, and occasionally difficult, amalgam of tort and property. The proprietary nature of the claim is evidenced by the fact that a judgment in conversion takes priority over the tortfeasor's other personal debts. That proposition becomes tremendously important if the defendant is insolvent. In that situation, tort claimants generally must stand in line with the defendant's other creditors. As a result, they are apt to receive very little, if any, of the money to which they are entitled. In contrast, a successful claimant in conversion enjoys priority and therefore is entitled to receive full payment ahead of most other creditors.

11. The courts at one time allowed the tortfeasor to return the chattel, rather than accept a "forced sale," at least if the goods were undamaged: *Fisher v. Prince* (1762), 97 E.R. 876 (K.B.). Although some modern cases contemplate a judicial power to compel the plaintiff to accept restoration *in specie*, it is not entirely clear when, or if, that power actually exists: *Harbour Equipment v. Canadian National Railway Co.* (1976), 25 N.S.R. (2d) 166 (T.D.); and Fleming, *The Law of Torts*, 9th ed. (1998) at 80. How did the court resolve this issue in the extract from *MacKenzie v. Scotia Lumber Co.* earlier in this chapter?

On the availability of specific relief generally, see Curwen, "The Remedy in Conversion: Confusing Property and Obligation" (2006) 26 L.S. 570.

5. Detinue

GEN. & FINANCE FACILITIES LTD. v. COOKS CARS (ROMFORD) LTD.

[1963] 1 W.L.R. 644 (C.A.)

DIPLOCK L.J.: – This appeal raises a neat point as to the remedies available to a plaintiff who sues for the wrongful detention of goods. The plaintiffs by a specially endorsed writ claimed "the return of a mobile crane index No. OMF 347 or its value and damages for detaining the same." They pleaded their title to the crane and relied on a demand for its delivery updated May 8, 1961. The prayer included an alternative claim for damages for conversion.

There are important distinctions between a cause of action in conversion and a cause of action in detinue. The former is a single wrongful act and the cause of action accrues at the date of the conversion; the latter is a continuing cause of action which accrues at the date of the wrongful refusal to deliver up the goods and continues until delivery up of the goods or judgment in the action for detinue. It is important to keep this distinction clear, for confusion sometimes arises from the historical derivation of the action of conversion from detinue sur bailment and detinue sur trover; of which one result is that the same facts may constitute both detinue and conversion. Demand for delivery up of the chattel was an essential requirement of an action in detinue and detinue lay only when at the time of the demand for delivery up of the chattel made by the person entitled to possession the defendant was either in actual possession of it or was estopped from denying that he was still in possession. Thus, if there had been an actual bailment of the chattel by the plaintiff to the defendant the latter was estopped from asserting that he had wrongfully delivered the chattel to a third person or had negligently lost it before demand for delivery up and the plaintiff could sue in detinue notwithstanding that the defendant was not in actual possession of the chattel at the time of the demand (see *Jones v. Dowle* [(1841), 152 E.R. 9]; *Reeve v. Palmer* [(1858), 141 E.R. 9]). Alternatively the plaintiff could sue in conversion for the actual wrongful delivery of the chattel to the third person, though not for its loss. On the other hand an unqualified refusal to comply with a demand for delivery up of a chattel made by the person entitled to possession may also amount to conversion, but only if the defendant at the time of the refusal was in actual possession of the chattel. If he has wrongfully delivered it to a third person before the date of the demand the prior wrongful delivery constitutes the conversion, not the subsequent refusal to comply with the demand (see *Sachs v. Miklos* [[1948] 1 All E.R. 67]). But even where, as in the present case, the chattel is in the actual possession of the defendant at the time of the demand to deliver up possession, so that the plaintiff has alternative causes of action in detinue or conversion based on the refusal to comply with that demand, he has a right to elect which cause of action he will pursue (see *Rosenthal v. Alderton & Sons, Ltd.* [[1946] 1 All E.R. 583]) and the remedies available to him will differ according to his election.

The action in conversion is a purely personal action and results in a judgment for pecuniary damages only. The judgment is for a single sum of which the measure is generally the value of the chattel at the date of the conversion together with any consequential damage flowing from the conversion and not too remote to be recoverable in law. With great respect to the dictum of Lord Goddard, C.J., in *Sachs v. Miklos* [*supra*], this is not necessarily the same as the measure of damages for detinue, where the same act constitutes detinue as well as conversion, although in many cases this will be so. This dictum was based on the headnote to *Rosenthal v. Alderton* [*supra*], which, in my view, misrepresents the effect of the last paragraph of the actual judgment. The law is in my view correctly stated in the current edition of *Salmond on Torts* at pp. 287 and 288. A judgment for damages for conversion does not, it is true, divest the plaintiff of his property in the chattel (see the analysis of the cases in *Ellis v. Stenning* [[1932] All E.R. Rep. 597]). The judgment, however, does not entitle the plaintiff to the assistance of the court or the executive, videlicet the sheriff, in recovering possession of the chattel.

On the other hand the action in detinue partakes of the nature of an action in rem in which the plaintiff seeks specific restitution of his chattel. At common law it resulted in a judgment for delivery up of the chattel or payment of its value as assessed, and for payment of damages for its detention. This, in effect, gave the defendant an option whether to return the chattel or to pay its value, and if the plaintiff wished to insist on specific restitution of the chattel he had to have recourse to Chancery (see *Re Scarth* [(1874), 10 Ch. App. 234], per Mellish, L.J.). The Common Law Procedure Act, 1854, s. 78, gave the court power to order delivery up of the chattel by the defendant without giving him the option to pay its value as assessed. Such an order was enforceable by execution and if the chattel could not be found distraint could be had on the defendant's lands and goods until he delivered up the specific chattel, or at the option of the plaintiff, distraint could be had of the defendant's goods for the assessed value of the chattel. This, in effect, where the court thought fit to make such an order, gave the plaintiff an option to insist on specific restitution of his chattel if the defendant did not deliver it up voluntarily; but this remedy was not available unless and until the value of the chattel had been assessed (see *Chilton v. Carrington* [(1855), 139 E.R. 735]). This remedy continues to exist under the modern law, but if the plaintiff does not wish to exercise his option to recover the assessed value of the chattel the assessment of its value is no longer a condition precedent to an order for specific restitution (see *Hymas v. Ogden* [[1950] 1 K.B. 246]; R.S.C., Ord. 48, r. 1). In addition to an order for specific restitution of the chattel or for payment of its value as assessed the plaintiff was always entitled to damages for wrongful detention of the chattel.

In the result an action in detinue today may result in a judgment in one of three different forms: (i) for the value of the chattel as assessed and damages for its detention; or (ii) for return of the chattel or recovery of its value as assessed and damages for its detention; or (iii) for return of the chattel and damages for its detention. A judgment in the first form is appropriate where the chattel is an ordinary article in commerce, for the court will not normally order specific restitution in such a case, where damages are an adequate remedy (see *Whiteley Ltd. v. Hilt* [[1918] 2 K.B. 808]). A judgment in this form deprives the defendant of the option which he had under the old common law form of judgment of returning the chattel; but if he has failed to do so by the time of the judgment the plaintiff, if he so elects, is entitled to a judgment in this form as of right (cf. R.S.C., Ord. 13, r. 6). In substance this is the same as the remedy in conversion although the sum recoverable, as I have indicated, may not be the same as damages for conversion, for the cause of action in detinue is a continuing one up to the date of judgment and the value of the chattel is assessed as at that date (see *Rosenthal v. Alderton & Sons, Ltd.* [*supra*]). A final judgment in such a form is for a single sum of money. A judgment in the second form gives to the defendant the option of returning the chattel, but it also gives to the plaintiff the right to apply to the court to enforce specific restitution of the chattel by writ of delivery, or attachment or sequestration as well as recovering damages for its detention by writ of fieri facias (R.S.C., Ord. 42, r. 6). This is an important right and it is essential to its exercise that the judgment should specify separate amounts for the assessed value of the chattel and for the damages for its detention, for if the plaintiff wishes to proceed by writ of delivery for which he can apply ex parte (Ord. 48, r. 1) he has the option of distraining for the assessed value of the chattel if the chattel itself is not recovered by the sheriff. He would be deprived of this option if the value of the chattel were not separately assessed. A judgment in the third form is unusual but can be given (see *Hymas v. Ogden* [*supra*]). Under it the only pecuniary sum recoverable is damages for detention of the chattel. Its value need not be assessed and the plaintiff can obtain specific restitution of the chattel only by writ of delivery, attachment, or sequestration. He has no option under the writ of delivery to distrain for the value of the chattel.

AITKEN v. GARDINER

(1956), 4 D.L.R. (2d) 119 (Ont. H.C.)

SPENCE J.: ... Also, the plaintiff alleges that in order to succeed in an action for detinue he need only prove (1) that the chattel was in the possession of the defendant who refuses to deliver the same, and (2) that, if the defendant on the issuance of the writ no longer had possession of the chattel, he parted with it wrongfully. Counsel for the defendants on the other hand submitted that the action of detinue is restricted to actions based on a bailment by the plaintiff to the defendants.

Clerk & Lindsell on Torts, 11th ed., pp. 441 *et seq.*, points out that the two types of action in detinue are (1) an action in *detinue sur trover*, and the other, an action in *detinue sur bailment*; and the same matter is dealt with in much the same fashion in Potter. Historical Introduction to English Law, 2nd ed., pp. 353 *et seq.* At p. 355 the latter author says: "During the fifteenth century this plea gave rise to a special form of action of Detinue known as *detinue sur trover*, which must be distinguished from the action of Trespass on the Case *sur trover* (shortly called *Trover*), which ultimately took its place ... This distinction [between *detinue sur trover* and *detinue sur bailment*] represented the recognition of the two forms of wrongful detention: one based upon a purely tortious wrong and the other connected with agreement between the parties."

Salmond on Torts, 11th ed. pp. 317-8, quotes Parke B. in *Jones v. Dowle* (1841), 9 M. & W. 19, 152 E.R. 9, as follows: " 'Detinue does not lie against him who never had possession of the chattel, but does lie against him who once had but has improperly parted with the possession of it.' " The author continues: "This being so, it is clear that detinue was available as a remedy for wrongful conversion as well as for wrongful detainer."

The action of detinue declined in popularity because of certain defects – defects which have been largely cured now that, since 1852, the Court has had the option of ordering the actual return of the chattel rather than merely granting damages for it. The fact that the defendants had not possession of the certificate at the time the writ was issued is no answer to an action in detinue so long as they got rid of the possession of the chattel improperly: *Jones v. Dowle*, *supra*, and *Bristol & West of England Bk. v. Midland R. Co.*, [1891] 2 Q.B. 653.

In *Clark v. Orr* (1854), 11 U.C.Q.B. 436 at p. 437, Robinson C.J. says: "It seems clear, we think, on numerous authorities, that it is not indispensable to shew that the defendant in the action of *detinue* had possession of the goods when the action was brought; if he had possession of them before, that may suffice."

In *Jones v. Dowle*, *supra*, the Court said: "Detinue does not lie against him who never had possession of the chattel, but it does against him who once had, but has improperly parted with the possession of it."

See also *Munro v. Willmott*, [1948] 2 All E.R. 983.

Was, then, the defendants' parting with the certificates in question in this action an improper parting? I have found that the certificates were stolen and I have come to the opinion that no principle of negotiability gave to the defendants any right which they could assert as against the true owner of the certificates. In these circumstances I am of the opinion that the sale by the defendants of the shares represented by those certificates was, in law, a conversion, and was therefore an improper parting with possession and was a sufficient basis for the present action in detinue.

[Spence J. held that the plaintiff had an option of suing in either detinue or conversion, and went on to assess damages.]

NOTES AND QUESTIONS

1. Do Diplock L.J. in *Gen. & Finance* and Spence J. in *Aitken* agree on when a detinue action will lie against a defendant who no longer is in possession? If not, which view is preferable?

2. Under what circumstances will the plaintiff have the option of suing in either conversion or detinue? When will the plaintiff be limited to only one?

3. Aside from remedial differences, what are the relative advantages and disadvantages of conversion and detinue? See Law Reform Commission, *Conversion and Detinue* (1971) (18th Report, Cmn. 4774); and Palmer, *Bailment*, 2d ed. (1991) at 241-48.

4. Detinue has been abolished in the United Kingdom by s. 8 of the *Torts (Interference with Goods) Act 1977*. For a discussion of the impact of the legislation see Palmer, "The Abolition of Detinue" (1981) 45 Conv. & Prop. Law 62.

5. In *Baud Corp., N.V. v. Brook* (1973), 12 A.R. 311 (C.A.), varied without reference to this point, [1979] 1 S.C.R. 633 (*sub nom. Asamera Oil Corp. v. Sea Oil & Gen. Corp.*), the court held that a formal demand and refusal is not required for detinue if the plaintiff clearly shows that the demand would have been refused. But see Palmer, "Comment" (1975) 53 Can. Bar Rev. 121.

6. Although there is disagreement, it appears that where detinue is based on an immediate right to possession, a right of property must be established. Unfortunately, it is not clear what the courts mean by "a right of property" in these cases. See for example *Jarvis v. Williams*, [1955] 1 All E.R. 108 (C.A.); and *Singh v. Ali*, [1960] A.C. 167 (P.C.). *Cf. Schentag v. Gauthier* (1972), 27 D.L.R. (3d) 710 (Sask. Dist. Ct.).

7. According to *Gen. & Finance*, in what circumstances is a plaintiff entitled to recover a chattel in detinue? *Cf. Schentag v. Gauthier, supra.* Notice that a claimant in detinue never enjoys a *right* to the detained chattel. That option lies with the court. Judges generally give the defendant a choice between returning the item to the plaintiff or paying compensation. If the chattel is unique or sufficiently special, however, the court may demand restoration.

8. Although many of the cases are ambiguous, a plaintiff in detinue may seek disgorgement of the defendant's gain, rather than either specific recovery or compensatory relief. See for example Lord Denning's analysis in *Strand Electric & Engineering Co. v. Brisford Entertainments Ltd.*, [1952] 2 Q.B. 246 (C.A.).

9. Despite some debate, detinue appears to be actionable *per se*. See *Williams v. Peel River Land & Mineral Co. Ltd.* (1886), 55 L.T. 689 (C.A.); Waddams, *The Law of*

Damages, 4th ed. (2004) at 10.10; Street, *Principles of the Law of Damages* (1962) at 16; and *cf.* Tyler & Palmer, *Crossley Vaines' Personal Property*, 5th ed. (1973) at 22.

6. Recaption and Replevin

While property sometimes is recovered *in specie* under an action in detinue, the plaintiff has no *right* to such relief. A dispossessed owner therefore may attempt to retrieve a chattel by other means. This section considers two possibilities: *recaption* and *replevin*.

(a) RECAPTION

Recaption occurs when a dispossessed owner simply takes back the goods. Although the right of recaption may provide an effective solution to an immediate problem, it ought to be exercised with great care. This is true of self-help remedies generally. There often is considerable risk that tempers will flare and that a minor incident will deteriorate into violence. The right of recaption therefore is limited to results that can be achieved without the use of unreasonable force and without a breach of peace. It may be possible to use *some* force, just as it may be permissible to trespass upon land in order to retrieve a chattel. As always, however, reasonableness depends upon the facts of each case.

(b) REPLEVIN

Even if a dispossessed owner cannot retrieve a chattel through recaption, recovery may be possible by means of *replevin*. Unlike trespass, conversion, and detinue, replevin is *not* a tort. It is, rather, a form of interlocutory relief. Replevin involves two steps.

- *Replevy*: The first stage involves a court order directing an official to seize the disputed property from the defendant and return it to the plaintiff. Although the application normally occurs on notice, the plaintiff may proceed *ex parte* (that is, without notice to the defendant) if there is a risk that the defendant will destroy or dispose of the goods if forewarned. In either event, the plaintiff must provide *security*. That security ensures that, if the matter ultimately is resolved in the defendant's favour, the plaintiff will be able to pay compensation and costs. The initial order also is premised upon the plaintiff's promise to return the goods to the defendant if the court eventually decides in the latter's favour.
- *Action in Replevin*: Having recovered the property, the plaintiff must expeditiously proceed to a full trial for a determination of which party enjoys the better right of possession.

In essence, then, replevin is a means of restoring the *status quo ante*, pending resolution of the matter. That function was explained in *Mennie v. Blake* (1856), 119 E.R. 1078 at 1080 (Q.B.):

> [A]s a general rule it is just that a party in the peaceable possession of land or goods should remain undisturbed ... until the right be determined and the possession shewn to be unlawful. But, where, either by distress or merely by a strong hand, the peaceable possession has been disturbed, an exceptional case arises; and it may be just that, even before any determination of the right, the law should interpose to replace the parties in

the condition in which they were before the act done, security being taken that the right shall be tried, and the goods be forthcoming to abide the decision.

Although the basic process is well-settled, replevin's precise scope is somewhat contentious. Indeed, it has been said that "no action, either in its foundation or in its practice, has given rise to so many contradictory expositions as that of replevin": *Freeman v. Harrington* (1863), 5 N.S.R. 352 at 354 (S.C.). For the purposes of exposition, it is important to draw a distinction between England and Canada.

The doctrine of replevin originated in England. It initially arose, during the medieval period, to remedy cases in which goods were wrongfully subject to *distress* (that is, cases in which a creditor improperly seized a debtor's chattels in an effort to extract payment). Over the ensuing centuries, the procedure expanded to cover *any* wrongful taking, but it fell out of favour during the nineteenth century and today it is seldom, if ever, used in England. The primary explanation for that demise was procedural. While replevin continues to be governed by several complex and technical rules, the tort of detinue was substantially improved and streamlined during the 1800s. Most significantly, the *Common Law Procedure Act 1854* empowered judges in detinue to order specific restoration, without allowing defendants the option of paying damages. Dispossessed owners therefore came to prefer detinue over replevin. Detinue was abolished by the *Torts (Interference with Goods) Act 1977*, but that statute also created a judicial discretion to compel "delivery up of any goods" that are the subject of litigation.

Replevin has followed a much different course in Canada. Although it tends to be neglected in textbooks, it is thriving in practice. Its popularity is largely attributable to its expanded scope. While English courts never extended the doctrine beyond wrongful *takings*, Canadian law also allows replevin to be used in cases of wrongful *detention* (even if the defendant obtained possession lawfully). Moreover, the claimant need not necessarily establish a right of absolute ownership. The interlocutory order is available as long as the plaintiff can demonstrate *any* immediate right to possession (an equitable right, a statutory right, or a mere personal right will suffice): Stewart, "Remedies – Replevin – Recovery *In Specie*" (1984) 62 Can. Bar Rev. 418 at 427. Finally, in contrast to most forms of interlocutory relief (*e.g.* mandatory injunctions and orders for interim preservation of property), replevin does not require proof of irreparable harm or demonstrated danger. Instead, the plaintiff simply must show *prima facie* or "substantial grounds" to support the alleged right to possession: *Ryder Truck Rental v. Walker*, [1960] O.W.N. 70 at 71 (Master).

Even in Canada, however, replevin is, by its very nature, limited in some respects. It cannot, for instance, provide compensatory relief and it obviously is defeated if the defendant no longer has possession of the disputed chattel. Furthermore, because the essence of replevin is a restoration of the *status quo ante*, it presumes that the claimant previously enjoyed possession. That may not be true if, for instance, a creditor seeks possession of a chattel that the debtor provided as collateral for a loan: *Manitoba Agricultural Credit Corp. v. Heaman* (1990), 70 D.L.R. (4th) 518 (Man. C.A.). Finally, even if the formal elements are in place, the requirement of security may be prohibitively expensive for individual claimants.

Replevin is well-established and widely used in Canada. In an effort to simplify and clarify the historically complex rules, however, the procedure has been codified. The traditional process of replevin generally has been replaced by legislated procedures with inelegant names, such as Ontario's "order for recovery of possession of personal property": *Courts of Justice Act*, R.S.O. 1990, c. C.43, s. 104; and Rules of Civil Procedure, R.R.O. 1990, Reg. 194, R. 44. Finally, although several Canadian jurisdictions previously created *Replevin Acts*, the modern approach (as in Ontario) is to deal with the issue through the rules of court.

NOTES AND QUESTIONS

1. Although replevin has fallen into disuse in England, there continues to be debate regarding its formal abolition. In his report to the Chancellor, J. Beatson recommended retention: *Independent Review of Bailiff Law: A Report to the Lord Chancellor* (2000) at para. 16.16. The Lord Chancellor's Department, however, disagreed and saw "little need" for the "ancient remedy": *Towards Effective Enforcement – A Single Piece of Bailiff Law and a Regulatory Structure for Enforcement* (2001) (Cm. 5096) at para. 4.70.

2. In *Allis-Chalmers, Rumely Ltd. v. Forbes Equipment Ltd.* (1969), 8 D.L.R. (3d) 105 (B.C.S.C.), the plaintiff agreed to supply machinery to the defendant on consignment. After the defendant's alleged default, the plaintiff terminated the agreement and sought recovery of the property under the provincial *Replevin Act*. In granting relief, the court stressed that the interlocutory order does not require a determination of the merits of the competing claims. See also *Shreddfast Inc. v. Oak Point Alignment Ltd.* (2005), 192 Man. R. (2d) 169 (C.A.); and *Littleford v. Loanex Financial Services* (1986), 28 D.L.R. (4th) 613 (Man. C.A.).

3. Are recaption and replevin consistent with tort law's general attitude regarding the recovery of chattels *in specie*? Is it possible to reconcile replevin with the fact that both law and equity strongly presume in favour of monetary relief?

4. In exchange for an order of replevin, a plaintiff must undertake to expeditiously bring the matter to court for final resolution. Once the plaintiff gains possession, however, the defendant may decide that the issue no longer is worth fighting.

5. Replevin may be used in small, private disputes, as when a neighbour refuses to return a borrowed lawnmower. Significantly, however, the procedure also is attractive to commercial parties. Consider a situation in which a company sells an expensive machine on credit. The customer is entitled to take the equipment away immediately, but will not receive ownership until the price is paid in full. Consider further that the customer soon becomes bankrupt and is unable to pay its debts. Although the vendor is entitled to the outstanding purchase price, that debt will be unenforceable in effect. Replevin, in contrast, may provide the vendor with a quick and effective remedy

6. See generally Stewart, "Remedies – Replevin – Recovery *In Specie*" (1984) 62 Can. Bar Rev. 418; Simmonds & Stewart, *Study Paper on Wrongful Interference with Goods* (1989) at 40-46; Law Reform Commission of British Columbia, *Report on Replevin* (1978); and Kruse, "Replevin – Repeal or Retain?" (2001) 23 Liverpool L. Rev. 95.

REVIEW PROBLEMS

1. The defendant wrongfully refused to respond to the plaintiff's demand for the return of his shares at a time when they were worth five dollars each. The shares then rose in value to ten dollars, but fell to seven dollars at the date of trial. Can the plaintiff recover ten dollars per share in detinue and in conversion?

2. The defendant took the plaintiff's taxi. Ten days later, the plaintiff demanded its return, while it was still in the defendant's possession. The taxi's value did not change from the date it was taken until the date of trial. Would you suggest suing in conversion or detinue, given that the plaintiff prefers damages to specific restitution?

3. Smith lent his car to Jones to make a return trip to New York City. While in New York, Brown intentionally scratched the car. What action can Smith maintain against Brown? Must Smith wait until Jones returns the scratched car before bringing an action?

Now assume that Smith had agreed with Jones to assume all responsibility for damages while Jones had the car and that Brown stole and destroyed the car in New York. What actions could Jones maintain against Brown? Can Brown raise the agreement between Smith and Jones as a defence? If Brown is held liable to Jones, would Jones be required to compensate Smith?

5. Allan was the owner of an expensive portable TV, but his need to meet pressing debts forced him to sell it. His friend Judy told him that she was interested in buying it, but would like to have it for a week on a trial basis to help her decide. Allan agreed and on Monday evening Judy took the TV, promising either to return it or purchase it by the following Monday.

On Wednesday, Judy took the TV to the beach to watch her favourite programs while tanning. During the late afternoon Judy met a group of friends and went for a walk, carelessly leaving the TV and some clothing behind. While Judy was away, Justin appeared on the scene. Finding the beach deserted and the TV and clothing in danger of being swept away by the advancing tide, Justin took them home for safekeeping. He immediately placed an advertisement in the "lost and found" column of the local newspaper.

Meanwhile, Judy informed Allan of the loss of the TV. On Thursday, Allan spotted Justin's advertisement. Justin refused to return the TV to Allan, explaining that the TV's owner must also be the owner of the clothing which obviously did not belong to Allan. Judy also noticed Justin's advertisement and visited him on Saturday of the same week. Confronted with proof that Judy was the owner of the clothing, Justin was convinced that the TV also belonged to her and agreed to return it. Justin had lent the TV to Sarah on Friday night so he phoned Sarah and told her that Judy would be coming to pick it up. Judy collected the TV from Sarah, but instead of returning it to Allan, she absconded.

One month later, after failing to find Judy, Allan sued Justin. Allan's TV is now worth 40 per cent more than it was two weeks earlier, due to a shortage of portable television parts. Advise Allan.

5

INTENTIONAL INTERFERENCE WITH REAL PROPERTY

1. Trespass to Land
2. Trespass and Nuisance
3. Trespass to Airspace and Subsoil

1. Trespass to Land

The tort of trespass to land may be defined as the direct and intentional physical intrusion onto the land in the possession of another. The tort is actionable *per se*. Given the central role of land in society, the elements of this action were broadly defined under the writ system. Despite the fundamental changes brought about by urbanization and industrialization in the last 200 years, the elements of this tort remain essentially unchanged.

ENTICK v. CARRINGTON
(1765), 19 State Tr. 1029 (C.P.)

[The defendants, claiming authority under a warrant from the Secretary of State, broke into the plaintiff's house and carried away some papers. The plaintiff sued the defendants in trespass.]

PRATT C.J.C.P.: The great end, for which men entered into society, was to secure their property. That right is preserved sacred and incommunicable in all instances, where it has not been taken away or abridged by some public law for the good of the whole. The cases where this right of property is set aside by positive law, are various. Distresses, executions, forfeitures, taxes, &c. are all of this description; wherein every man by common consent gives up that right, for the sake of justice and the general good. By the laws of England, every invasion of private property, be it ever so minute, is a trespass. No man can set his foot upon my ground without my licence, but he is liable to an action, though the damage be nothing; which is proved by every declaration in trespass, where the defendant is called upon to answer for bruising the grass and even treading upon the soil. If he admits the fact, he is bound to shew by way of justification, that some positive law has empowered or excused him. . . . If no such excuse can be found or produced, the silence of the books is an authority against the defendant, and the plaintiff must have judgment.

TURNER v. THORNE
(1960), 21 D.L.R. (2d) 29 (Ont. H.C.)

MCRUER C.J.H.C.: This is an action brought to recover damages sustained by the plaintiff on September 5, 1958. The facts are simple. The defendant Robert N. Thorne operates a business known as the Speedit Delivery Service, and the defendant George Thorne was a driver employed by his co-defendant.

The business of the Speedit Delivery Service is to pick up parcels on request for delivery to designated persons. On the day in question a call was received from a customer of the defendant to pick up 14 cartons of material for delivery to the Gas Machinery Co. (Canada) Ltd., Lime Ridge Rd., on the outskirts of the City of Hamilton. . . .

The Gas Machinery Co. (Canada) Ltd. had done business before in a garage in the rear of some private property and the defendant George Thorne had made deliveries to that garage. On the day in question, on arriving at Lime Ridge Rd., Mr. Thorne without further information assumed that the Gas Machinery Co. was located on the plaintiff's property. He went to the plaintiff's house and rapped on the door but got no answer. In fact, both the plaintiff and his wife were at work. Without making further inquiries Mr. Thorne went to the plaintiff's double garage ... and found it unlocked. . . .

Finding no one at home on the plaintiff's property, Mr. Thorne backed his truck into the driveway and opened the west door and unloaded the cartons which were about 24 ins. long and 9 ins. square, and piled them in the centre of the garage where they would be between the truck and the automobile if the automobile was in the west section of the garage. There is some dispute as to whether the cartons were piled so as to project southerly past the end of the truck. I am satisfied that they were. When the plaintiff came home that evening he and his wife went shopping and returned after dark. The garage was not equipped with any artificial light. For the purpose of opening the west door the plaintiff entered the east door of the garage and walked past the rear of the truck and fell over the cartons which had been deposited in the garage, sustaining serious injuries which were assessed by the jury at $9,626, including out-of-pocket expenses.

. . .

I think the defendant George Thorne is undoubtedly liable in damages. He was a trespasser on the plaintiff's property and it was a trespass to leave the packages in the garage.

. . .

Liability for incidental damage resulting from trespass is most concisely dealt with in the Restatement of the Law of Torts, vol. I, commencing at p. 359. At pp. 375-6 it is stated: "A trespass, actionable under the rule stated in s. 158, may be committed by the continued presence on the land of a structure, chattel or other thing which the actor has tortiously placed thereon, whether or not the actor has the ability to remove it."

A most useful discussion of the relevant law is contained in *Kopka et ux. v. Bell Telephone Co. of Pennsylvania* (1952), 91 Atl. (2d) 232. Although this is a case in the United States Courts I think it accurately states the common law applicable in Ontario. The case arose out of injuries sustained by the owner of land when he fell into a hole dug on his land by servants of the defendant. At p. 235 Mr. Justice Stern, giving the judgment of the Court of Appeal of the State of Pennsylvania, stated:

> Before considering the question of the liability of a trespasser for personal injuries suffered by the possessor of land as an indirect result of the trespass, there are two relevant legal principles to be borne in mind. The first is that the fact that a trespass results from an innocent mistake and, in that sense, is not deliberate or wilful, does not relieve the trespasser of liability therefor or for any of the results thereof.

And on the same page:

> The liability of defendant Company for the trespass involved in the digging of the hole on plaintiff's land without his knowledge or consent being thus established, does such liability extend to the personal injuries sustained by him as the result of his falling into the hole? The authorities are clear to the effect that where the complaint is for trespass to land the trespasser becomes liable not only for personal injuries resulting directly and proximately from the trespass but also for those which are indirect and consequential.

At p. 236 the learned Judge quoted from s. 163 of the Restatement of the Law of Torts as follows: " 'So too, he [a trespasser] is liable for any harm to the possessor ... if such harm is caused by the actor's presence on the land, irrespective of whether it was caused by conduct which, were the actor not a trespasser, would have subjected him to liability.' "

The plaintiff is therefore entitled to judgment in the sum of $9,626, the damages as assessed by the jury.

NOTES AND QUESTIONS

1. For the purpose of a trespass action, the term "land" includes not only the surface area, but also houses, other structures, trees, and anything else that is affixed to it. Thus, throwing a ball against a fence that the plaintiff built on his or her side of the boundary line would constitute a trespass to land.

2. A trespass may be committed by entering the plaintiff's land in person, propelling an object or third person onto the property, or by failing to leave after permission to enter has been terminated. A trespass may also be committed by bringing an object onto the plaintiff's land and wrongfully failing to remove it. The doctrine of continuing trespass applies in such situations, allowing the plaintiff to maintain successive actions until the object is removed. Damages are assessed at the date of each action. For a discussion of continuing trespass see *Johnson v. B.C. Hydro and Power Authority* (1981), 16 C.C.L.T. 10 (B.C.S.C.); *Haynes v. Nfld. Telephone Co.* (1985), 168 A.P.R. 162 (Nfld. Dist. Ct.); and *Cousins v. Wilson*, [1994] 1 N.Z.L.R. 463 (H.C.).

The concept of continuing trespass has an important impact on limitation period issues. In *Williams v. Mulgrave (Town)* (2000), 48 C.C.L.T. (2d) 220, (N.S.C.A.), the defendant ran a drain across the plaintiff's property. The drain caused flooding problems, but the plaintiff took no legal action for several years even after discovering that the defendant had no right to act as it did. The trial judge dismissed the plaintiff's trespass claim as statute-barred, because she had commenced her claim more than six years after when she had discovered the wrongfulness of the defendant's conduct. The Nova Scotia Court of Appeal overturned that decision. It held that, for the purpose of limitation periods, a new cause of action accrued every day that the defendant continued its trespass by leaving its drain on the plaintiff's land. Consequently, while the plaintiff was entitled to damages for only the six years immediately preceding the commencement of her action, her claim was not entirely statute-barred.

3. In order to maintain a trespass action, the plaintiff is generally required to be in possession of the land at the time of the intrusion. For example, in *Townsview Properties*

Ltd. v. Sun Construction and Equipment Co. Ltd. (1974), 7 O.R. (2d) 666 (C.A.), the plaintiff's trespass action failed because the wrongful excavation occurred before it acquired possession.

4. A person with legal title to land is presumed to have exclusive possession and the right to maintain a trespass action. However, even a squatter without title who has possession of land can maintain a trespass action against a subsequent trespasser. As indicated in *Penney v. Gosse* (1974), 6 Nfld. & P.E.I.R. 344 at 346 (Nfld. S.C.), "Any form of possession, so long as it is clear and exclusive and exercised with the intention to possess, is sufficient to support an action for trespass against a wrongdoer. Actual possession is good against all except those who can show a better right of possession in themselves." See also *Swaile v. Zurdayk*, [1924] 2 W.W.R. 555 (Sask. C.A.). In contrast, a person who is merely using land without any possessory interest cannot maintain a trespass action. Why does trespass protect possession, rather than ownership?

It should be noted that possession of Crown land does not provide a sufficient interest to maintain a trespass action. See *Boutin v. Boutin* (1985), 23 D.L.R. (4th) 286 (Sask. Q.B.); and *Fortier v. Kapeller* (1999), 183 Sask. R. 135 (Prov. Ct.).

5. The doctrine of trespass by relation provides an exception to the possession requirement. The doctrine permits a plaintiff, who had only an immediate right to possession when the trespass occurred, to sue in trespass for that intrusion once he or she subsequently acquires possession. This result is achieved through a legal fiction which deems the plaintiff to have been in possession from the moment his or her right to possession accrued. Trespass by relation is most frequently invoked in cases involving vacant land.

6. Trespass to land is limited to direct intrusions onto the land in the possession of another. Consequently, snow thrown onto the plaintiff's land from the defendant's snowblower will give rise to a trespass action, whereas snow blown by the wind from a snow bank on the defendant's land will not. Similarly, roots and limbs of trees growing onto neighbouring property will not support a trespass action. As will be discussed shortly, some of these indirect intrusions may give rise to an action in private nuisance. See *Anderson v. Skender* (1993), 84 B.C.L.R. (2d) 135 (C.A.).

7. As illustrated by *Entick* and *Turner*, the action for trespass to land is strictly defined and applied. Moreover, as Rand J. stated in *R. v. East Crest Oil Co.*, [1945] S.C.R. 191 at 195, "If I walk upon my neighbour's land, I am a trespasser even though I believe it to be my own." See also *Costello v. Calgary (City)* (1997), 38 C.C.L.T. (2d) 101 at 112 (Alta. C.A.), where Picard J.A. stated that "a trespass occurs, regardless of consciousness of wrongdoing, if the defendant intends to conduct itself in a certain manner and exercises its volition to do so." What is the rationale for holding the defendant's motive to be irrelevant and for refusing to recognize mistake as a defence?

8. Once it is established that the defendant is a trespasser, he or she is liable for all the consequences of the trespass, whether or not they are foreseeable. In addition to *Turner*, see *Wyant v. Crouse*, 86 N.W. 527 (Mich. S.C. 1901) (spread of fire); and *Mee v. Gardiner*, [1949] 3 D.L.R. 852 (B.C.C.A.) (tramp spreading skin disease). But see *Mayfair Ltd. v. Pears*, [1987] 1 N.Z.L.R. 459 (C.A.), where the defendant was absolved

of liability for the unforeseeable consequences of his trespass. Which position is preferable?

9. A defendant in a trespass action cannot raise the defence of *jus tertii* claiming that a third party has a better right to possession than the plaintiff, unless that third party authorized the defendant's entry.

10. Trespass to land must be distinguished from ejectment which is not a tort action, but a proprietary action for the recovery of land. Unlike trespass, ejectment does not depend on the plaintiff's possession of, or entry onto, the land. The plaintiff may succeed in ejectment by establishing that he or she has a better right to possession than the defendant. However, the defendant may raise the *jus tertii* defence in an ejectment action.

11. The Canadian courts have awarded substantial punitive damages in trespass cases in which the defendant has acted in a high-handed or arrogant fashion. In *Nantel v. Parisien* (1981), 18 C.C.L.T. 79 (Ont. H.C.), a corporate defendant was required to pay $35,000 in punitive damages when its employees, without warning, broke into the plaintiff's business to demolish the building. The plaintiff had a valid lease and lawful possession. In *Horseshoe Bay Retirement Society v. S.I.F. Development Corp.* (1990), 66 D.L.R. (4th) 42 (B.C.S.C.), the court awarded $100,000 in punitive damages against the defendant for cutting down the plaintiff's trees to enhance the value of its development lots. See also *Craig v. North Shore Heli Logging Ltd.* (1997), 34 B.C.L.R. (3d) 330 (S.C.); *Austin v. Rescon Construction (1984) Ltd.* (1989), 57 D.L.R. (4th) 591 (B.C.C.A.); and *Epstein v. Cressey Development Corp.*, [1992] 3 W.W.R. 566 (B.C.C.A.).

12. For a more detailed discussion of trespass to land see Fridman, *The Law of Torts in Canada*, 2d ed. (2002) at 37-55; Rogers, *Winfield and Jolowicz on Torts*, 17th ed. (2006) at 619-27; and Dobbs, *The Law of Torts* (2000) at 95-112.

REVIEW PROBLEMS

1. Arthur lives in a mansion in one corner of his 500-acre estate. Unknown to him, Bill erected a small home on the opposite corner of the estate and lived there for two years. While Bill was away for several days, Carl moved into his house. What actions can Bill bring against Carl? What actions can Arthur bring against Carl and Bill?

2. Ned rented his house to Tom for a year. After six months, Ned went to see how Tom was faring, only to find that Tom was on holidays and that a squatter had moved in with some old furniture. The squatter left, but refused to take his furniture with him until he could get resettled. Advise Ned on the actions that he may bring against the squatter.

HARRISON v. CARSWELL

[1976] 2 S.C.R. 200

DICKSON J.: The respondent, Sophie Carswell, was charged under the *Petty Trespasses Act*, R.S.M. 1970, c. P50, with four offences (one on each of four days) of unlawfully trespassing upon the premises of the Fairview Corporation Limited, trading under the firm name and style of Polo Park Shopping Centre, located in the City of Winnipeg, after having been requested by the owner not to enter on or come upon the premises. The appellant, Peter Harrison, manager of Polo Park Shopping Centre swore the informations. The charges were dismissed by the Provincial Judge, but on a trial *de novo* in the County Court, Mrs. Carswell was convicted and fined $10 on each of the charges. The convictions were set aside by the Manitoba Court of Appeal . . . and the present appeal followed, by leave of this Court.

With great respect, I am unable to agree with the majority reasons, delivered in the Court of Appeal by Chief Justice Freedman, for I find it difficult, indeed impossible, to make any well-founded distinction between this case and *R. v. Peters* (1971), 17 D.L.R. (3d) 128*n*, decided by this Court four years ago in a unanimous decision of the full Bench. The constitutional issue raised in *Peters* no longer concerns us; the only other issue was whether the owner of a shopping plaza had sufficient control or possession of the common areas, having regard to the unrestricted invitation to the public to enter upon the premises, as to enable it to invoke the remedy of trespass. The Court decided it did. That case and the present case came to us on much the same facts, picketing within a shopping centre in connection with a labour dispute.

. . .

The evidence discloses that distribution of pamphlets or leaflets in the mall of Polo Park Shopping Centre or on the parking lot, has never been permitted by the management of the centre and that this prohibition has extended to tenants of the centre. The centre as a matter of policy has not permitted any person to walk in the mall carrying placards. There is nothing in the evidence supporting the view that in the present case the owner of the centre was acting out of caprice or whimsy or *mala fides*. In a comment entitled *Labour Law – Picketing in Shopping Centres*, 43 *Can. Bar Rev.* 357 at p. 362 (1965), H.W. Arthurs referred to the following as one of the legitimate concerns of the landlord of a shopping centre:

> ... while public authorities may, on behalf of the community, strike a reasonable balance between traffic and picketing on public sidewalks and streets, the shopping centre owner can hardly be expected to make such a choice: he has no authority to speak for the community; to grant picketing or parading privileges to all would invite chaos, while to do so selectively would invite commercial reprisals. He is thus driven to adopt a highly restrictive approach to granting permission to groups who wish to parade or picket in the shopping centre.

It is urged on behalf of Mrs. Carswell that the right of a person to picket peacefully in support of a lawful strike is of greater social significance than the proprietary rights of an owner of a shopping centre, and that the rights of the owner must yield to those of the picketer. . . .

The submission that this Court should weigh and determine the respective values to society of the right to property and the right to picket raises important and difficult political and socio-economic issues, the resolution of which must, by their very nature, be arbitrary and embody personal economic and social beliefs. It raises also fundamental questions as to the role of this Court under the Canadian Constitution. The duty of the Court, as I envisage it, is to proceed in the discharge of its adjudicative function in a reasoned way from principled decision and established concepts. I do not for a moment doubt the power of the Court to act creatively – it has done so on countless occasions;

but manifestly one must ask – what are the limits of the judicial function? There are many and varied answers to this question. Holmes, J., said in *Southern Pacific Co. v. Jensen* (1917), 244 U.S. 205 at p. 221: "I recognize without hesitation that judges do and must legislate, but they can do it only interstitially; they are confined from molar to molecular actions". Cardozo, *The Nature of the Judicial Process* (1921), p. 141, recognized that the freedom of the Judge is not absolute in this expression of his view:

> This judge, even when he is free, is still not wholly free. He is not to innovate at pleasure. He is not a knight-errant, roaming at will in pursuit of his own ideal of beauty or of goodness. He is to draw his inspiration from consecrated principles.

. . .

Society has long since acknowledged that a public interest is served by permitting union members to bring economic pressure to bear upon their respective employers through peaceful picketing, but the right has been exercisable in some locations and not in others and to the extent that picketing has been permitted on private property the right hitherto has been accorded by statute. For example, s. 87 [since rep. & sub. 1975, c. 33, s. 21] of the *Labour Code of British Columbia Act*, 1973 (B.C.) (2nd Sess.), c. 122, provides that no action lies in respect of picketing permitted under the Act for trespass to real property to which a member of the public ordinarily has access.

Anglo-Canadian jurisprudence has transitionally recognized, as a fundamental freedom, the right of the individual to the enjoyment of property and the right not to be deprived thereof, or any interest therein, save by due process of law. The Legislature of Manitoba has declared in the *Petty Trespasses Act* that any person who trespasses upon land, the property of another, upon or through which he has been requested by the owner not to enter, is guilty of an offence. If there is to be any change in this statute law, if A is to be given the right to enter and remain on the land of B against the will of B, it would seem to me that such a change must be made by the enacting institution, the Legislature, which is representative of the people and designed to manifest the political will, and not by this Court.

I would allow the appeal, set aside the judgment of the Court of Appeal for Manitoba and restore the judgment of the County Court Judge.

LASKIN C.J.C. (dissenting): . . . An ancient legal concept, trespass, is urged here in all its pristine force by a shopping centre owner in respect of areas of the shopping centre which have been opened by him to public use, and necessarily so because of the commercial character of the enterprise based on tenancies by operators of a variety of businesses. To say in such circumstances that the shopping centre owner may, at his whim, order any member of the public out of the shopping centre on penalty or liability for trespass if he refuses to leave, does not make sense if there is no proper reason in that member's conduct or activity to justify the order to leave.

Trespass in its civil law sense, and in its penal sense too, connotes unjustified invasion of another's possession. Where a dwelling-house is concerned, the privacy associated with that kind of land-holding makes any unjustified or unprivileged entry a trespass, technically so even if no damage occurs. A Court, however, would be likely to award only nominal damages for mere unprivileged entry upon another's private premises where no injury occurs, and it is probable that the plaintiff would be ordered to pay costs for seeking empty vindication. If the trespasser refuses to leave when ordered, he could be forcibly removed, but, more likely, the police would be called and the issue would be resolved at that point, or a basis for an action, or for a penal charge would arise. In short, apart from privileged entry, a matter to which I will return in these reasons, there is a significant element of protection of privacy in resort to trespass to exclude or remove persons from private dwellings.

The considerations which underlie the protection of private residences cannot apply to the same degree to a shopping centre in respect of its parking areas, roads and sidewalks. Those amenities are closer in character to public roads and sidewalks than to a private dwelling. All that can be urged from a theoretical point of view to assimilate them to private dwellings is to urge that if property is privately owned, no matter the use to which it is put, trespass is as appropriate in the one case as in the other and it does not matter that possession, the invasion of which is basic to trespass, is recognizable in the one case but not in the other. There is here, on this assimilation, a legal injury albeit no actual injury. This is a use of theory which does not square with economic or social fact under the circumstances of the present case.

What does a shopping centre owner protect, for what invaded interest of his does he seek vindication in ousting members of the public from sidewalks and roadways and parking areas in the shopping centre? There is no challenge to his title and none to his possession nor to his privacy when members of the public use those amenities. Should he be allowed to choose what members of the public come into those areas when they have been opened to all without discrimination? Human rights legislation would prevent him from discriminating on account of race, colour or creed or national origin, but counsel for the appellant would have it that members of the public can otherwise be excluded or ordered to leave by mere whim. It is contended that it is unnecessary that there be a reason that can stand rational assessment. Disapproval of the owner, in assertion of a remote control over the "public" areas of the shopping centre, whether it be disapproval of picketing or disapproval of the wearing of hats or anything equally innocent, may be converted (so it is argued) into a basis of ouster of members of the public. Can the common law be so devoid of reason as to tolerate this kind of whimsy where public areas of a shopping centre are concerned?

. . .

It seems to me that the present case involves a search for an appropriate legal framework for new social facts which show up the inaptness of an old doctrine developed upon a completely different social foundation. The history of trespass indicates that its introduction as a private means of redress was directed to breaches of the peace or to acts likely to provoke such breaches. Its subsequent enlargement beyond these concerns does not mean it must be taken as incapable of further adaptation, but must be applied on what I can only characterize as a level of abstraction which ignores the facts. Neither logic nor experience (to borrow from Holmes' opening sentence in his classic *The Common Law*) supports such a conclusion.

Recognition of the need for balancing the interests of the shopping centre owner with competing interests of members of the public when in or on the public areas of the shopping centre, engaged Courts in the United States a little earlier than it did the Courts in this country. Making every allowance for any constitutional basis upon which Courts there grappled with this problem, their analyses are helpful because they arise out of the same economic and social setting in which the problem arises here. Thus, there is emphasis on unrestricted access to shopping centres from public streets, and on the fact that access by the public is the very reason for the existence of shopping centres; there is the comparison drawn between the public markets of long ago and the shopping centre as a modern market place; there is the appreciation that in the light of the interests involved there can be no solution to their reconciliation by positing a flat all or nothing approach. The cases in the United States ... appear to me to reject the appellant's proposition that (as his counsel put it) "the issue is trespass, not picketing" because that, in my opinion, involves a predetermination without regard to the issues of fact.

. . .

A more appropriate approach ... is to recognize a continuing privilege in using the areas of the shopping centre provided for public passage subject to limitations arising out of the nature of the activity thereon and to the object pursued thereby, and subject as well to a limitation against material damage. There is analogy in existing conceptions of privilege as an answer to intentional torts, such as trespass.

. . .

I would agree that it does not follow that because unrestricted access is given to members of the public to certain areas of the shopping centre during business hours, those areas are available at all times during those hours and in all circumstances to any kind of peaceful activity by members of the public, regardless of the interest being prompted by that activity and regardless of the numbers of members of the public who are involved. The Court will draw lines here as it does in other branches of the law as may be appropriate in the light of the legal principle and particular facts. In the present case it is the respondent who has been injured rather than the shopping centre owner.

I would dismiss the appeal.

[Martland, Judson, Ritchie, Pigeon, and De Grandpré JJ. concurred with Dickson J., and Spence and Beetz JJ. concurred with Laskin C.J.C. Note that the order of the reasons for judgment has been reversed.]

NOTES AND QUESTIONS

1. Do you agree with Dickson J. that *Peters* and the statute resolve the issue? Can Laskin C.J.C.'s judgment be reconciled with *Peters* and the statute?

In *Russo v. Ontario Jockey Club* (1987), 62 O.R. (2d) 731 (H.C.), the plaintiff was a skilled bettor who had won a considerable amount of money at the defendant's race tracks. While at Woodbine Race Track, the plaintiff was served with a notice under the provincial trespass act, ordering her to leave and informing her that she would be arrested for trespassing if she returned to any of the defendant's properties. There was no allegation that the plaintiff had engaged in any wrongdoing and no reason was given for banning her. In dismissing the plaintiff's challenge to the notice, the court stated that the defendant, as a property owner, had an absolute right to deny entry to anyone under both the common law and the applicable trespass legislation. See also *Webb v. Attewell* (1993), 88 B.C.L.R. (2d) 1 (C.A.).

2. Would Dickson J.'s analysis and conclusion have been the same if the case had been a common law action for trespass, rather than a prosecution under the *Petty Trespasses Act*, R.S.M. 1970, c. P50? In *Wildwood Mall Ltd. v. Stevens* (1979), [1980] 2 W.W.R. 638 (Sask. Q.B.), the court distinguished *Harrison* on the basis that Saskatchewan had no legislation creating a provincial offence of trespassing. The mall owner's

claim against the picketing workers was then dismissed, because the owner did not have a sufficient possessory interest to exclude all others. Do you agree with the reasoning or the result in *Wildwood*?

3. Would you agree with Colangelo's statement in "Labour Law: *Harrison v. Carswell*" (1976) 34 U.T. Fac. L. Rev. 236, that Dickson J.'s judgment lacks creativity? What values underlie the judgments of Laskin C.J.C. and Dickson J.?

4. Is Laskin C.J.C.'s rationale for modifying the traditional definition of trespass compelling?

What impact would Laskin C.J.C.'s approach have on the provincial offence of trespass and on the common law tort? How does Laskin C.J.C. suggest that the conflicting interests of plaza owners and picketers be resolved? Can meaningful distinctions be drawn between different types of landowners and picketers?

In *Wilcox v. Police*, [1994] 1 N.Z.L.R. 243 (H.C.), ten anti-abortionists were convicted of trespass for continuing to block entry to a hospital after they had been told to leave. The defendants sought to justify the trespass on the need to protect the unborn from unlawful abortions. Although the court accepted the honesty of the defendants' beliefs, it convicted them. How would Laskin C.J.C. have resolved this case?

5. Manitoba amended its trespass legislation shortly after the *Harrison* decision. In general terms, the amendment provided that individuals who peacefully protest outside of premises which are normally open to the public are not guilty of an offence under the Act. See *Petty Trespasses Act*, R.S.M. 1987, c. P50, s. 4. Should the amendment be viewed as a vindication of Dickson J.'s or Laskin C.J.C.'s approach? Is it appropriate for the courts or the legislature to resolve the types of value conflicts raised by *Harrison* and *Wilcox*?

6. Section 2 of the *Canadian Charter of Rights and Freedoms*, Part I of the *Constitution Act, 1982*, being Schedule B to the *Canada Act 1982* (U.K.), 1982, c. 11 guarantees a broad range of fundamental freedoms, including freedom of expression, peaceful assembly and association. However, by virtue of s. 32, the *Charter* does not apply to private persons and associations in a common law tort action. See *281856 B.C. Ltd. v. Kamloops Revelstoke Okanagan Building Traders Union* (1986), 37 C.C.L.T. 262 (B.C.C.A.); *Harrison v. University of British Columbia*, [1990] 3 S.C.R. 451; and Domes, "The Courts, the Common Law, and the Constitutional Imperative: Beyond *Dolphin Delivery*" (1989) 27 Alta. L. Rev. 430.

Nevertheless, since the *Charter* applies to both federal and provincial law, trespass legislation which limits or infringes the rights guaranteed by the *Charter* may be struck down. If the legislation is struck down, there can be no prosecution or statutory cause of action based on such provisions. In *R. v. Layton* (1986), 38 C.C.C. (3d) 550 (Ont. Prov. Ct.), trespass charges against a union organizer who had been distributing material in the public part of a mall were dismissed. The court ruled that the provisions of the trespass act constituted an unjustifiable infringement of the accused's freedom of expression and association under s. 2(b) and (d) of the *Charter*. See also *Committee for the Commonwealth of Canada v. Canada*, [1991] 1 S.C.R. 139; and *British Columbia Public School Employers' Assn. v. British Columbia Teachers' Federation* (2005), 257 D.L.R. (4th) 385 (B.C.C.A.).

7. *Harrison* raises the issue of the revocability of a licence to enter private property. In *Hudson's Bay Co. v. White* (1997), 32 C.C.L.T. (2d) 163 (Ont. Gen. Div.), the court stated that while the public has an implied licence to enter stores to browse and shop, a person entering to shoplift would not be present for any authorized purpose and thus would be a trespasser.

In *Davidson v. Toronto Blue Jays Baseball Ltd.* (1999), 170 D.L.R. (4th) 559, (Ont. Gen. Div.), the plaintiff was arrested under the *Trespass to Property Act*, R.S.O. 1990, c. T.21 when a dispute arose over whether he had to show his ticket when returning to his seat. The plaintiff sued in false imprisonment. The court held that the plaintiff had a licence to be in the stadium pursuant to the contract for the ticket. An implied term of that licence was that the plaintiff had an obligation to show his ticket when entering the stadium, when initially taking his seat, or when resolving a dispute with another patron over the same seat. Since the court ruled that the plaintiff did not have to show his ticket at any other time, his licence to be present remained valid and he should not have been arrested. Given that the defendant had a financial interest in preventing patrons from occupying more expensive seats than those for which they had paid, should the court have concluded that ticketholders had an implied obligation to show their ticket whenever occupying or claiming a seat?

8. Increasingly, trespass actions are being brought in native land claim disputes. See for example *Canadian Pacific Ltd. v. Paul*, [1988] 2 S.C.R. 654, where the court granted a permanent injunction to restrain members of an Indian band from blocking a railway line located on land the band claimed. See also *Myran v. R.*, [1976] 2 S.C.R. 137; *Canada (A.G.) v. Vantour* (1979), 28 N.B.R. (2d) 434 (C.A.); and *Johnson v. British Columbia Hydro and Power Authority* (1981), 16 C.C.L.T. 10 (B.C.S.C.). While a trespass action may resolve a specific legal dispute, it cannot address the native communities' longstanding grievances concerning land claims and treaty rights.

9. The action in trespass is often used following invalid expropriations. For example in *Costello v. Calgary (City)* (1997), 152 D.L.R. (4th) 453 (Alta. C.A.), the defendant city expropriated the plaintiffs' land and took possession of it. The plaintiffs claimed that they were given insufficient notice and, after 11 years of litigation, persuaded the Supreme Court of Canada to declare the expropriation invalid. The plaintiffs then successfully sued the defendant in trespass for the period during which it improperly possessed their land. Picard J.A. saw no relevance in the fact that, but for a mere technical error regarding the statutory notice period, the defendant would have validly expropriated the plaintiffs' land and would not have been a trespasser. See also *Parkdale (Village) v. West* (1887), 12 App. Cas. 602 (P.C.); *Maunsell v. Lethbridge Northern Irrigation District*, [1926] S.C.R. 603; and Todd, *The Law of Expropriation and Compensation in Canada*, 2d ed. (1992) at 29.

10. The plaintiff may have the option of bringing an action under trespass legislation, rather than a common law action. For example the Ontario *Trespass to Property Act*, *supra*, provides:

> 12.(1) Where a person is convicted of an offence under section 2, and a person has suffered damage caused by the person convicted during the commission of the offence, the court shall, on the request of the prosecutor and with the consent of the person who suffered the damage, determine the damages and shall make a judgment for damages

against the person convicted in favour of the person who suffered the damage, but no judgment shall be for an amount in excess of $1,000.

(2) Where a prosecution under section 2 is conducted by a private prosecutor, and the defendant is convicted, unless the court is of the opinion that the prosecution was not necessary for the protection of the occupier or the occupier's interests, the court shall determine the actual costs reasonably incurred in conducting the prosecution and, despite section 60 of the *Provincial Offences Act*, shall order those costs to be paid by the defendant to the prosecutor.

(3) A judgment for damages under subsection (1), or an award of costs under subsection (2), shall be in addition to any fine that is imposed under this Act.

(4) A judgment for damages under subsection (1) extinguishes the right of the person in whose favour the judgment is made to bring a civil action for damages against the person convicted arising out of the same facts.

(5) The failure to request or refusal to grant a judgment for damages under subsection (1) does not affect a right to bring a civil action for damages arising out of the same facts.

Somewhat similar provisions apply in other provinces. See for example *Trespass Act*, R.S.B.C. 1996, c. 462, s. 11; and *Trespass to Property Act*, R.S.P.E.I. 1988, c. T-6, s. 10.

11. Most trespass legislation gives the police, occupiers or both the right to arrest without a warrant anyone whom they reasonably believe is trespassing. See for example the Ontario *Trespass to Property Act*, *supra*, s. 9(1); the British Columbia *Trespass Act*, *supra*, s. 10(2) and (3); and *Petty Trespass Act*, R.S.A. 2000, c. P-11, s. 4. For a discussion of a private citizen's right to use force to arrest without a warrant under s. 9(1) of the Ontario *Trespass to Property Act*, see *R. v. Asante-Mensah*, [2003] 2 S.C.R. 3; and *Tucker v. Cadillac Fairview Corporation Limited* (2005), 200 O.A.C. 140 (C.A.). The latter case involved Reverend Brothers Tucker and Baldasaro soliciting on behalf of the Marijuana Party in the defendant's mall, despite having been previously forbidden to do so. For a discussion of the impact of the trespass legislation, see Parkdale Community Legal Services, "Submissions to the Task Force on the Law Concerning Trespass to Publicly Used Property as it Affects Youth and Minorities" (1997) 35 Osgoode Hall L.J. 819.

12. Section 177 of the *Criminal Code*, R.S.C. 1985, c. C-46 makes it a summary conviction offence to trespass on another person's land at night near a dwelling. Sections 40 and 41(1) give those in possession of a home or other real property broad authority to use force to prevent a trespasser from entering or remaining on their property.

2. Trespass and Nuisance

The law of private nuisance is discussed in detail in Chapter 24. It is introduced at this stage merely to distinguish it from trespass. A private nuisance may be defined as a substantial and unreasonable interference with the use and enjoyment of land in the possession of another. There are several differences between trespass to land and nuisance. First, trespass to land is actionable *per se*, whereas nuisance requires proof of loss.

Second, trespass protects possession, whereas nuisance protects the quality of that possession. Third, the law of nuisance is concerned with the effect of the defendant's conduct on the plaintiff's use and enjoyment of the land, and not with the nature of that conduct. Liability may be imposed in nuisance even if the defendant's conduct was neither intentional nor negligent.

KERR v. REVELSTOKE BLDG. MATERIALS LTD.

(1976), 71 D.L.R. (3d) 134 (Alta. S.C.)

SHANNON J.: In this action the plaintiffs allege trespass, nuisance and negligence. They seek an injunction and damages.

. . .

During his youth Mr. Kerr worked in a general store and later, in 1935, operated a service station and garage at Coleman, Alberta. He and his wife decided that they wanted to build and operate a motel business. ...

The site selected was chosen for its tranquility and scenic beauty. Looking to the south from the site they had a magnificent view of a river valley in a natural state, except for a railway line, and beyond that foothills and a range of rocky mountains dominated by the Crowsnest Mountain peak.

They used approximately two acres of that parcel for the motel site. The remainder was used for agricultural purposes. On the motel site they built a residence and six motel units which were opened for business in 1951. The business was known as "Chinook Motel". In the summer of 1953 two more units were constructed and opened for business. Two additional units were constructed and opened in the summer of 1955. Mr. Kerr was in charge of construction operations and was assisted by his wife and sons. Some outside assistance was obtained but it was primarily a family project as was the motel operation thereafter.

. . .

The defendant is an Alberta lumber company that has carried on an active business in this Province for many years.

It commenced business across the highway from the Chinook Motel in 1958. A planing mill and small teepee burner went into operation that year. The defendant's loading ramp was approximately 800 ft. from the office door of the motel. A sawmill was moved to the same site and commenced operating in 1968. Chipper and debarker operations were added to the sawmill complex in 1971. Also, other industries, such as Phillips Cables Ltd., Sartoga Processing Co. Ltd. and Petro-Chemicals Ltd. were established in the valley. The operation of the defendant's planing mill and teepee burner in 1958 caused the plaintiffs some concern and disturbance but the situation worsened when the sawmill, chipper and debarker operations were introduced later.

It should be noted that the defendant's decision to bring the chipper and debarker operations to the site in 1971 was influenced to some extent by the fact that it received financial inducements from the federal Government to do so. The Crowsnest Pass area was then designated as a depressed economic area and the Government provided incentives to encourage industry to locate there.

From time to time the plaintiffs complained about smoke, sawdust, dust, fly ash and objectionable noises emanating from the defendant's operations. The defendant tried to ameliorate the situation by enclosing a conveyor belt in 1971, lubricating the conveyer belt with rock-drill oil in 1972, enclosing the planer in 1972-73, enclosing the chipper in 1973, enlarging the garage for warm-up of machinery in 1972 and adding an underfire to the teepee burners to improve their efficiency.

Notwithstanding the foregoing efforts on the part of the defendant the plaintiffs continued to complain and in the fall of 1971 they closed their motel operation and it has never been reopened.

I am satisfied on the evidence that they have established a cause of action founded in trespass. The evidence establishes that their premises were invaded from time to time by smoke, sawdust, fly ash and objectionable sounds. The physical invasion of their premises by sawdust and fly ash was so severe on occasion that it interfered with their use and enjoyment of their property. Actual samples of fly ash were collected and placed in vials by the plaintiff James Runciman Kerr, and were entered in evidence as exhibits.

...

I am also convinced by the preponderance of evidence that the plaintiffs are entitled to succeed in nuisance. The fly ash, smoke and dust which assaulted the plaintiff's premises from time to time was serious enough in itself, but the objectionable sounds which emanated from the sawmill operations were such that they constituted a nuisance which was so serious it substantially interfered with the operation of the plaintiff's motel business and with their use and enjoyment of their premises. Also the concern, anxiety and discomfort generated by the situation had a harmful effect on the health of Mrs. Kerr. She became nervous, preoccupied, humourless and irritable and that in turn had a negative effect on her husband and his enjoyment of life. The offensive noises were not constant. They came and went depending upon the state of the lumber market and the resultant activities across the highway at the sawmill.

The intensity and frequency of the objectionable noises increased substantially after the sawmill commenced operating in 1968 and again later in 1971 when the chipper and debarker were added. It is difficult to provide a comprehensive description of the objectionable noises because they were many and varied. Various witnesses, who were guests at the motel, used such adjectives as "squealing, clanking, whining, ear piercing, etc.", to describe them. Another witness referred to the noise as "a high pitched squeal that seemed to go on all night", while another likened the sound to that which is given off by a jet engine. In any event it was so intense at times that it interfered with ordinary conversation in the plaintiff's yard. It also seriously interfered with their rest and sleep and with that of their motel guests because the sawmill carried on its operations at night and during the early morning hours.

...

On the facts of this case I am unable to find that the defendant was negligent in its operations. The simple fact is that the two business operations were not compatible.

In these circumstances an injunction would not be an appropriate remedy and that form of relief will not be granted. However, the plaintiffs are entitled to succeed in trespass and nuisance and the appropriate remedy is damages.

...

The plaintiffs are awarded judgment against the defendant in the amount of $30,000.

NOTES AND QUESTIONS

1. Which interferences did the judge hold to be trespasses and which did he find to be nuisances? Do you agree with his analysis? Would a different characterization of the interferences have affected the damage award? In *Execotel Hotel Corp. v. E.B. Eddy Forest Products Ltd.*, 1988 WL 875157 (Ont. H.C.), the court held that airborne woodchips and particles settling on the plaintiff's property could not give rise to trespass because there was no direct and intentional intrusion. Is the analysis of this issue in *Execotel* more compelling than the analysis in *Kerr*? See also *Devon Lumber Co. v. MacNeill* (1987), 82 N.B.R. (2d) 319 (C.A.).

2. In *Mann v. Saulnier* (1959), 19 D.L.R. (2d) 130 (N.B.C.A.), snow and frost caused the top of the defendant's fence to encroach on the plaintiff's land by several inches. The court held that this was neither a trespass because the injury was indirectly caused, nor a nuisance because no special damages were proven. Can you suggest additional reasons why (i) the trespass and (ii) the nuisance claim should fail?

3. A substantial and unreasonable interference is one that is offensive and inconvenient to a reasonable person. The unreasonableness of the interference is assessed in terms of the plaintiff's use of his or her property, and the relative interests of the defendant and plaintiff. See *Pyke v. TriGro Enterprises Ltd.* (2001), 55 O.R. (3d) 257 (C.A.).

In *Doucette v. Parent* (1996), 31 C.C.L.T. (2d) 190 (Ont. Gen. Div.), the defendant was absolved of liability in nuisance when a tree on her property which showed minimal signs of disease fell on the plaintiff's property. Natural uses of the defendant's land that do not pose a foreseeable risk are unlikely to give rise to a nuisance action. See also *Lee v. Shalom Branch No. 178 Building Society* (2001), 96 B.C.L.R. (3d) 384 (S.C.).

4. Traditionally, trespass to land has been limited to the direct, intentional intrusion of objects that are visible to the naked eye. However, in *Martin v. Reynolds Metal Co.*, 342 P. (2d) 790 (Oregon S.C. 1959), the defendant manufacturer was held liable in trespass because its operations caused invisible fluoride particles to settle on the plaintiff's land, making it unfit for cattle. The judge rejected the argument that the size of the invading object should be a criterion for distinguishing between trespass and nuisance, preferring instead to emphasize the issue of energy and force. As in *Harrison*, the court in *Martin* was faced with the task of applying established legal principles to new situations. Did the court in *Martin* make a compelling argument in favour of altering the traditional principles of trespass to land? What impact would the principles in *Martin* have on the distinction between trespass and nuisance?

While the Canadian courts apparently have not addressed the issue, several American courts have imposed liability in trespass for the physical intrusion of invisible particles that have caused harm. See Dobbs, *The Law of Torts* (2000) at 1322-323.

5. The courts almost always exercise their discretion to grant injunctions in trespass cases, whereas in nuisance they are reluctant to do so. Why do the principles for granting injunctions vary in trespass and nuisance? See Sharpe, *Injunctions and Specific Performance*, 2d ed., looseleaf (1992) at 4-1 to 4-38.

6. What claims are available to the plaintiff in the following situations?

(a) The defendant's seismographic explosions cause vibrations which damage the plaintiff's well. See *Phillips v. Calif. Standard Co.* (1960), 31 W.W.R. 331 (Alta. S.C.).

(b) Golf balls from the defendant's golf course are hit so frequently onto the plaintiff's land that he is unable to use his backyard. See *Segal v. Derrick Golf and Winter Club* (1977), 76 D.L.R. (3d) 746 (Alta. T.D.). See also *Miller v. Jackson*, [1977] Q.B. 966 (C.A.).

(c) The Ministry of Transport's use of salt on the highway results in a salt spray being deposited on the plaintiff's fruit orchards, causing substantial damage. See *Schenck v. R.*; *Rokeby v. R.* (1981), 34 O.R. (2d) 595 (H.C.), aff'd (1985), 49 O.R. (2d) 556 (C.A.), aff'd [1987] 2 S.C.R. 289.

(d) The defendant's construction project causes silt to be carried into the plaintiff's reservoir that contains his domestic water supply. See *Steadman v. Erickson Gold Mining Corp.* (1987), 43 D.L.R. (4th) 712 (B.C.S.C.), aff'd (1989), 56 D.L.R. (4th) 577 (B.C.C.A.).

3. Trespass to Airspace and Subsoil

(a) TRESPASS TO AIRSPACE

The elements of this action are essentially the same as those of trespass to land. Traditionally, defendants were held liable for trespass to airspace for any direct and intentional physical intrusion into the airspace above the plaintiff's land. However, the need for unfettered air traffic has resulted in a distinction being drawn between overflights and other types of intrusions. Although the theories concerning overflights vary, they all tend to limit the landowner's rights in order to facilitate air traffic.

In *Atlantic Aviation Ltd. v. N.S. Light & Power Co.* (1965), 55 D.L.R. (2d) 554 (N.S.S.C.), the court indicated that an overflight at any altitude constitutes a trespass, but the overflight will be privileged if it is done for a legitimate purpose, in a reasonable manner, and at a height that does not unreasonably interfere with the possessor's use of his or her land. On the central issue of the case, the court ruled that aviators have no common law right to prevent landowners from putting up buildings or transmission wires that might impede flights in and out of nearby airports.

BERNSTEIN v. SKYVIEWS & GENERAL LTD.
[1978] Q.B. 479

GRIFFITHS J.: ... By the statement of claim it is alleged that the defendants wrongfully entered the air space above Lord Bernstein's premises in order to take an aerial photograph of his house and were thus guilty of trespass and an actionable invasion of his right to privacy. The defendants admit that they took the aerial photograph but deny that they entered the air space above the premises to do so; they say that the photograph was taken when the aircraft was flying over adjoining land not owned by Lord Bernstein. Alternatively they say that if they did fly over Lord Bernstein's land to take the photograph they had his implied permission to do so....

I turn now to the law. The plaintiff claims that as owner of the land he is also owner of the air space above the land, or at least has the right to exclude any entry into the air space above his land. He relies upon the old Latin maxim, cujus est solum ejus est usque ad coelum et ad inferos ["whomsoever the soil belongs, he owns also to the sky and to the depths"], a colourful phrase often upon the lips of lawyers since it was first coined by Accursius in Bologna in the 13th century. There are a number of cases in which the maxim has been used by English judges, but an examination of those cases shows that they have all been concerned with structures attached to the adjoining land, such as overhanging buildings, signs or telegraph wires, and for their solution it has not been necessary for the judge to cast his eyes towards the heavens; he has been concerned with the rights of the owner in the air space immediately adjacent to the surface of the land....

In *Gifford v. Dent* [1926] W.N. 336, Romer J. held that it was a trespass to erect a sign that projected 4 ft. 8 ins. over the plaintiff's forecourt and ordered it to be removed. He invoked the old maxim in his judgment. . .

That decision was followed by McNair J. in *Kelsen v. Imperial Tobacco Co. (of Great Britain and Ireland) Ltd.* [1957] 2 Q.B. 334, in which he granted a mandatory injunction ordering the defendants to remove a sign which projected only 8 ins. over the plaintiff's property. The plaintiff relies strongly upon this case, and in particular upon the following passage when, after citing the judgment of Romer J. to which I have already referred, McNair J. continued, at p. 345:

> That decision, I think, has been recognised by the textbook writers, and in particular by the late Professor Winfield, as stating the true law. It is not without significance that the legislature in the Air Navigation Act 1920, section 9 (replaced by section 40(1) of the Civil Aviation Act 1949), found it necessary expressly to negative the action of trespass or nuisance arising from the mere fact of an aeroplane passing through the air above the land. It seems to me clearly to indicate that the legislature at least were not taking the same view of the matter as Lord Ellenborough in *Pickering v. Rudd*, but rather taking the view accepted in the later cases, such as the *Wandsworth District* case, subsequently followed by Romer J. in *Gifford v. Dent*. Accordingly, I reach the conclusion that a trespass and not a mere nuisance was created by the invasion of the plaintiff's air-space by this sign.

I very much doubt if in that passage McNair J. was intending to hold that the plaintiff's rights in the air space continued to an unlimited height or "ad coelum" as Mr. Gray submits. The point that the judge was considering was whether the sign was a trespass or a nuisance at the very low level at which it projected. This to my mind is clearly indicated by his reference to *Winfield on Tort*, 6th ed. (1954) in which the text reads, at p. 380: "it is submitted that trespass will be committed by [aircraft] to the air space if they fly so low as to come within the area of ordinary user." The author in that passage is careful to limit the trespass to the height at which it is contemplated an owner might be expected to make use of the air space as a natural incident of the user of his land. If, however, the judge was by his reference to the Civil Aviation Act 1949 and his disapproval of the views of Lord Ellenborough in *Pickering v. Rudd* (1815) 4 Camp. 219, indicating the opinion that the flight of an aircraft at whatever height constituted a trespass at common law, I must respectfully disagree.

I do not wish to cast any doubts upon the correctness of the decision upon its own particular facts. It may be a sound and practical rule to regard any incursion into the air space at a height which may interfere with the ordinary user of the land as a trespass rather than a nuisance. Adjoining owners then know where they stand; they have no right to erect structures overhanging or passing over their neighbours' land and there is no room for argument whether they are thereby causing damage or annoyance to their neighbours about which there may be much room for argument and uncertainty. But wholly different considerations arise when considering the passage of aircraft at a height which in no way affects the user of the land.

There is no direct authority on this question, but as long ago as 1815 Lord Ellenborough in *Pickering v. Rudd* expressed the view that it would not be a trespass to pass over a man's land in a balloon; and in *Saunders v. Smith* (1838) 2 Jur. 491, Shadwell V.-C. said, at p. 492:

> Thus, upon the maxim of law, 'Cujus est solum ejus est usque ad coelum' an injunction might be granted for cutting timber and severing crops; but, suppose a person should apply to restrain an aerial wrong, as by sailing over a person's freehold in a balloon; this surely would be too contemptible to be taken notice of....

I can find no support in authority for the view that a landowner's rights in the air space above his property extend to an unlimited height. In *Wandsworth Board of Works v. United Telephone Co. Ltd.*, 13 Q.B.D. 904 Bowen L.J. described the maxim, usque ad coelum, as a fanciful phrase, to which I would add that if applied literally it is a fanciful notion leading to the absurdity of a trespass at common law being committed by a satellite every time it passes over a suburban garden. The academic writers speak with one voice in rejecting the uncritical and literal application of the maxim... I accept their collective approach as correct. The problem is to balance the rights of an owner to enjoy the use of his land against the rights of the general public to take advantage of all that science now offers in the use of air space. This balance is in my judgment best struck in our present society by restricting the rights of an owner in the air space above his land to such height as is necessary for the ordinary use and enjoyment of his land and the structures upon it, and declaring that above that height he has no greater rights in the air space than any other member of the public.

Applying this test to the facts of this case, I find that the defendants' aircraft did not infringe any rights in the plaintiff's air space, and thus no trespass was committed. It was on any view of the evidence flying many hundreds of feet above the ground and it is not suggested that by its mere presence in the air space it caused any interference with any use to which the plaintiff put or might wish to put his land. The plaintiff's complaint is not that the aircraft interfered with the use of his land but that a photograph was taken from it. There is, however, no law against taking a photograph, and the mere taking of a photograph cannot turn an act which is not a trespass into the plaintiff's air space into one that is a trespass....

NOTES AND QUESTIONS

1. How does the court's approach to overflights in *Atlantic Aviation* differ from liability based on private nuisance?

2. In *A.G. Man. v. Campbell* (1985), 32 C.C.L.T. 57 (Man. C.A.), the defendant built a 70-foot tower on his land to obstruct the adjacent airport and to prevent its further development. The plaintiff's claim in nuisance was successful, and an injunction was granted ordering the defendant to dismantle the tower. How would you reconcile this case with *Atlantic Aviation*? See also *Hashem and Hashem v. N.S. Power Corp.* (1980), 43 N.S.R. (2d) 150 (S.C.), where the defendant's tower and lines, although an unwelcome

annoyance to pilots, did not interfere with the safe use of the plaintiff's aerodrome, and thus did not constitute an actionable nuisance.

3. Summarize the principles governing tort liability for overflights based on *Bernstein*. What is the basic difference between *Bernstein* and *Atlantic Aviation*, and why is that difference significant? Which position do you favour?

4. Although the Canadian courts have clearly rejected the *usque ad coelum* maxim, they have not addressed whether *Atlantic* or *Bernstein* should govern overflights. Nevertheless, the Canadian authorities appear to be more consistent with *Bernstein*. See *Lacroix v. R.*, [1954] 4 D.L.R. 470 (Ex. Ct.); and *Manitoba v. Air Canada*, [1980] 2 S.C.R. 303. See generally Richardson, "Private Property Rights in the Air Space at Common Law" (1953) 31 Can. Bar Rev. 117; Silverman and Evans, "Aeronautical Noise in Canada" (1972) 10 Osgoode Hall L.J. 607; and Abeyratne, "Legal And Regulatory Aspects Of Aircraft Noise" (2000) 25 Ann. Air & Sp. L. 1.

5. As indicated by *Bernstein*, it is generally accepted that any direct and intentional intrusion into the airspace within the plaintiff's zone of use constitutes a trespass. This proposition underlies holding the defendant liable in trespass for shooting across another person's land. See *Big Point Club v. Lozon*, [1943] 4 D.L.R. 136 (Ont. H.C.); and *Dahlberg v. Naydiuk* (1969), 10 D.L.R. (3d) 319 (Man. C.A.). Similarly, a trespass action will arise from erecting a sign, fence or hydro tower that encroaches on the plaintiff's land. See for example *Kelsen v. Imperial Tobacco Co. (of Great Britain and Ireland) Ltd.*, [1957] 2 All E.R. 343 (Q.B.); *Didow v. Alberta Power Ltd.* (1988), 88 A.R. 250 (C.A.); and *Bellini Custom Cabinetry Ltd. v. Delight Textiles Ltd.* (2005), 34 R.P.R. (4th) 93 (Ont. S.C.J.). See also Irvine, "Some Thoughts On Trespass To Airspace" (1986) 37 C.C.L.T. 99.

6. It has been held that the arm of a crane periodically swinging above the plaintiff's land constitutes a trespass. See *Woollerton and Wilson Ltd. v. Richard Costain Ltd.*, [1970] 1 All E.R. 483 (Ch. D.); and *Lewvest Ltd. v. Scotia Towers Ltd.* (1981), 126 D.L.R. (3d) 239 (Nfld. T.D.).

In *Woollerton*, the judge felt compelled by authority to issue an injunction to restrain the defendant's trespass, but suspended its operation until the project was completed. The judge noted that the plaintiff had stubbornly refused to settle and suggested that such matters should be negotiated by the parties outside of the courts. The decision to suspend the injunction has been seriously questioned. In addition to *Lewvest*, see *Charrington v. Simons & Co. Ltd.*, [1971] 2 All E.R. 588 at 592 (C.A.); and *Graham v. K.D. Morris & Sons Pty. Ltd.*, [1974] Qd. R. 1. But see *Kingsbridge Development Inc. v. Hanson Needler Corp.* (1990), 71 O.R. (2d) 636 (H.C.).

(b) TRESPASS TO SUBSOIL

Subterranean intrusions raise the same issue as intrusions into airspace; namely, which interferences should be governed by trespass and which by nuisance. In *Austin v. Rescon Construction (1984) Ltd.* (1989), 48 C.C.L.T. 64 (B.C.C.A.), the defendant was held liable in trespass for inserting steel anchor rods beneath the plaintiff's land at three different unidentified depths. Aside from causing temporary vibrations, the insertion of the rods caused no damage to the plaintiff's land, did not interfere with the foundations of the house or limit the plaintiff's use of his property. In increasing the punitive damage award to $30,000, the court emphasized that landowners may deny entry for any reason they choose and have no obligation to accommodate a contractor or anyone else wishing to enter. In *Epstein v. Cressey Development Corp.*, [1992] 3 W.W.R. 566 (B.C.C.A.), the defendant was held liable for $45,000 in punitive damages for temporarily inserting anchor rods into the plaintiff's subsoil.

The court in *Austin* did not address the issue of whether the depth of the intrusion would affect the cause of action. However, in *Boehringer v. Montalto*, 254 N.Y.S. 276 (S.C. 1931), the court held that the existence of a sewer 150 feet underground was not a trespass. The court concluded that a landowner's title to the subsoil extends only to the depth which he or she can reasonably use.

NOTES AND QUESTIONS

1. Can you reconcile *Austin* and *Epstein* with the cases indicating that landowners have no possessory interest in the airspace above their zone of use?

2. Can you reconcile *Austin* and *Epstein* with *Boehringer*? See also *Haynes v. Nfld. Telephone Co.* (1985), 168 A.P.R. 162 (Nfld. Dist. Ct.); *Engemoen Holdings Ltd. v. 100 Mile House*, [1985] 3 W.W.R. 47 (B.C.S.C.); and *Lim v. Titov* (1998), 56 Alta. L.R. (3d) 174 (Q.B.).

3. In *Edwards v. Lee's Adm'r.*, 96 S.W.2d 1028 (Ky. C.A. 1936), the defendant operated a very profitable cave touring business from an entrance located on his own property. The plaintiff discovered that one-third of the cave was under his property, but there was no entrance from his land to the cave which was 360 feet below. The court concluded that the defendant was a trespasser and granted an injunction and an accounting. Pursuant to the accounting, which is an equitable remedy, the plaintiff was awarded a share of the defendant's net proceeds from the cave tours. Do you agree that the defendant was a trespasser? If so, how would you reconcile *Edwards* and *Boehringer*? Could the plaintiff have recovered in nuisance? Had the plaintiff not sought an accounting, what damages would you have awarded for the trespass?

It has been suggested that *Edwards* involved neither trespass nor nuisance, and should be viewed as bad law based on a "dog-in-the-manger" approach: Keeton, *Prosser and Keeton on The Law of Torts*, 5th ed. (1984) at 82. Do you agree?

REVIEW PROBLEMS

1. Amy and Bruce own adjoining rural properties. Amy has an orchard, and Bruce produces organically grown vegetables for health food stores. On a day when a strong wind was blowing directly onto Bruce's property, Amy sprayed chemicals on her fruit trees. A large quantity of the chemicals drifted onto Bruce's mature vegetables. No apparent damage was done, but Bruce's usual customers refused to purchase the crop because it came in contact with the spray. As a result, Bruce was forced to sell the vegetables as pig food. The spray also killed the bees on Bruce's property, interfering with the pollination and the production of the new crop. Amy knew that Bruce grew

vegetables, but she was unaware that they were sold as organic crops. Bruce now seeks your advice on suing Amy for his losses. See generally *Bridges Brothers Ltd. v. Forest Protection Ltd.* (1976), 14 N.B.R. (2d) 91 (Q.B.).

2. Albert is an experienced private pilot. Early one Sunday morning in February, he and his son rented a plane from his flying club to do some stunts. Although the officer at the club had directed Albert to a particular plane, Albert misunderstood and took a plane of the same model that belonged to Bob, an instructor at the club. The key fit Bob's plane and Albert did not realize his mistake. The plane intended for Albert's use had been cleared for stunt flying, but Bob's had not. The clearance involved a careful check of the plane to ensure that nothing would come loose.

Once Albert got over open country, he decided that it was safe to begin. As the plane somersaulted a tool box came loose and burst through the door of the plane. The box crashed onto a greenhouse some 1,000 meters below, severely damaging it. The cold winter air ruined the valuable orchids that were growing inside. While Albert's son struggled to close the door, Albert rapidly reduced his altitude to bring down the air pressure. He swooped so low over a barn that he frightened a horse, causing it to kick its stall, breaking a back leg. As soon as he could, Albert returned to the airport.

You have been asked to advise Albert on his potential liability.

6

THE DEFENCE OF CONSENT

1. Introduction to the Defences
2. General Principles of Consent
3. Factors Vitiating Consent: Fraud, Mistake, Duress, and Public Policy
4. Consent to Criminal or Immoral Acts
5. Consent to Treatment and Counselling

1. Introduction to the Defences

Even if the plaintiff establishes that the defendant committed an intentional tort, liability may not be imposed. The defendant may be entitled to raise a common law or statutory defence. For analytical purposes, we have divided these defences into three categories: consent, defences related to the protection of person and property, and defences arising from the assertion of legal authority. Consent will be discussed in this chapter, and the remaining categories of defences will be discussed in the following two chapters. It is important to appreciate, however, that the defences are not mutually exclusive. For example, assume that the defendant is sued in battery for pushing the plaintiff during a physical confrontation over a disputed fence. Depending on the specific facts, the defendant may be able to assert defences based on consent, defence of real property, and self-defence. If any of these defences succeed, the defendant will be absolved of liability despite having committed the battery.

2. General Principles of Consent

(a) INTRODUCTION

There is considerable older authority for the view that consent is not a defence, but rather a substantive element of the intentional torts, the absence of which the plaintiff must assert and prove on the balance of probabilities. If the plaintiff cannot establish the absence of consent, no tort will have been committed and his or her action will fail. This remains the prevailing approach in England and New Zealand.

Although the Canadian courts have not squarely addressed this issue in relation to each intentional tort, they have tended to treat consent as a defence that the defendant must plead and prove. For example in *Non-Marine Underwriters, Lloyd's of London v. Scalera*, [2000] 1 S.C.R. 551, the court unanimously agreed that consent is an affirmative defence in "traditional" battery cases. While the majority ruled that this principle applied equally in sexual battery cases, the minority held that the plaintiff should have the burden of proving the absence of consent in such cases.

The issue of consent is inextricably linked to the specific tort in issue. Consequently, the consent issue must be framed narrowly in terms of whether the plaintiff consented to the specific act that gave rise to his or her tort action. The plaintiff may consent explicitly: in writing, verbally or by a gesture such as nodding. Consent may also be given implicitly through participation, demeanor or other behaviour. When a person consents to an act, he or she is generally viewed as consenting to the risks normally inherent in that act. While this principle is easy to apply in some cases, it is extremely difficult to apply in others. For example, while a hockey player in a full-contact league will be viewed as implicitly consenting to being body-checked, is he or she implicitly consenting to the conduct involved in the typical or foreseeable penalties that occur in such games?

NOTES AND QUESTIONS

1. For a discussion of whether consent is an element of the intentional torts or an affirmative defence, see Blay, "Onus of Proof of Consent in an Action for Trespass to the Person" (1987) 61 Aust. L.J. 25; Dobbs, *The Law of Torts* (2000) at 156; and Rogers, *Winfield and Jolowicz on Torts*, 17th ed. (2006) at 1058-59.

2. Although the issue has not been conclusively resolved in Australia, there is strong *obiter dicta* in the High Court that the absence of consent is not an element of the tort of battery, but rather a defence. See *Secretary, Department of Health and Community Services v. J.W.B.* (1992), 175 C.L.R. 218 (H.C.A.); and *Sibley v. Milutinovic*, [1990] Aust. Torts Reports 81-013 (A.C.T.).

3. In order to establish the defence of consent, the defendant must prove that the plaintiff agreed to the act giving rise to the tort. A plaintiff's failure to physically resist the defendant's conduct falls far short of the affirmative conduct, behaviour or demeanor necessary to establish consent. However, it is far more difficult to determine the circumstances in which a failure to object verbally, a failure to withdraw or passivity will be viewed as constituting implied consent. Assume that following a verbal confrontation in a bar, the defendant approaches the plaintiff. Would the plaintiff's conduct in (a) failing to leave the bar, (b) standing his or her ground or (c) standing his or her ground and staring at the approaching defendant constitute implied consent to a fight? Would your answer be different if the parties were men in their 20s, men in their 60s, or women? Should a woman's failure to turn away from, or voice opposition to, her date who is approaching to kiss her goodnight be viewed as implicitly consenting to being kissed?

(b) IMPLIED CONSENT

WRIGHT v. McLEAN

(1956), 7 D.L.R. (2d) 253 (B.C.S.C.)

MACFARLANE J.: . . . Four boys were playing near a mound of earth thrown up in an excavation incident to the construction of a house on a city lot. They were tossing mud balls or lumps of clay found on the pile of earth there at each other. The infant defendant was passing on his bicycle delivering the afternoon paper around 4:30 p.m. One of these mud balls or lumps came up around the infant defendant and another he says went through the spokes of the wheel of the bicycle he was riding. He was not in a hurry, so he dismounted, pushing his bicycle up against a tree and went over toward a mound of this material which he calls the embankment and said "want a fight?" They continued throwing at each other. There is no exact evidence as to how many of these missiles were thrown or how long. One boy said it continued for probably 5 minutes but he says he quit because he was being pelted too much. It would appear that one boy Ross who admits he threw the lumps at McLean while he was on his bicycle, when asked if he was inviting him to play the game, said "In a way I guess so". He appears to have been the leader of the 3 or 4 boys, originally engaged in this play and he and the infant plaintiff and McLean were throwing at each other when the lump or whatever it was which hit the infant plaintiff was thrown by McLean.

. . .

[The plaintiff] put his hand to his temple, cried out and fell or sat down. The play stopped immediately. It is agreed by all the boys that the fighting was not carried on in anger and that there was no malice. The infant plaintiff was then 12 years of age; Ross, a little older, and the other two boys on their side a little younger. McLean was 14. It was not the thought of any of them that the injury was serious as it then appeared as no more than a slight scratch and the infant plaintiff went to a party with the two younger boys and both Ross and McLean went about their ways, after having talked and after McLean had expressed his regrets.

It was not contended that there was any evidence that it was a stone that hit the boy who was injured unless that is to be inferred from the nature of the injuries. McLean quite frankly says that he did not look when he reached down to pick up something to throw, his attention obviously and of necessity being directed to dodging the missiles coming at him, and did not notice just what it was he picked up but threw it in the direction in which they (his opponents) were. He said he would not deliberately pick up a rock or stone and did not intend to do so.

. . .

[The judge then considered the issue of consent and quoted *Pollock on Torts*, 15th ed. (1951) at 112]

"Harm suffered by consent is, within limits to be mentioned, not a cause of civil action." Very briefly, the purport of that paragraph is that in sport where there is no malice, no anger and no mutual ill will, that combatants consent to take the ordinary risks of the sport in which they are engaged. In a note given at the foot of p. 114 in Pollock, there is a reference to an article in the Law Quarterly Review, vol. 6, pp. 111-12. In that article, the author uses this language: "The reasonable view is that the combatants consent to take the ordinary risks of the sport in which they engage, the risks of being struck, kicked, or cuffed, as the case may be, and the pain resulting therefrom; but only while the play is fair, and according to rules, and the blows are given in sport and not maliciously. . . . If these tacit conditions of fair play and good temper are not kept the consent is at an end, and the parties are remitted to their rights."

In all the circumstances where it is agreed that there was no ill will and where the evidence shows that the infant defendant was invited to join the game by the others, then I think that no liability arises apart from culpable carelessness. I think it is quite clear that there is no evidence of that in this case.

. . .

I therefore dismiss the action.

NOTES AND QUESTIONS

1. The action in *Wright* was framed in negligence rather than battery. Nevertheless, the principles articulated by the court are applicable to intentional torts.

2. To what acts did the plaintiff consent? What risks were inherent in those acts? Would it have made any difference if it were established that: (a) the plaintiff's injuries were caused by a stone; (b) the defendant had been completely indifferent as to whether he was throwing a mud ball or a stone; or (c) the defendant realized he had a stone in his hand but threw it anyway?

3. The judge considered the absence of ill will on the defendant's part to be an important consideration in the outcome of the case. Was this element relevant to the issue of the plaintiff's consent? Provide an example in which the plaintiff's consent would be (a) negated and (b) unaffected by the defendant's motive.

4. For other cases involving implied consent and sports injuries see *Matheson v. Governors of Dalhousie College and University* (1983), 25 C.C.L.T. 91 (N.S.S.C. (T.D.)); *Temple v. Hallem*, [1989] 5 W.W.R. 669 (Man. C.A.); and *Knockwood v. Cormier* (1995), 167 N.B.R. (2d) 147 (Q.B.). See also Thiele, "Sports and Torts" (2002) 23 Adv. Q. 348.

5. Do spectators implicitly consent to injuries incidental to attendance at sporting events? In *Elliott and Elliott v. Amphitheatre Ltd.*, [1934] 3 W.W.R. 225 (Man. K.B.), the defendant was absolved of liability for the injuries the plaintiff suffered when hit by a puck that went into the seats. The court held that as an amateur hockey player, the plaintiff was aware of the risks and the protections customarily provided. Would it have made any difference if: (a) this had been the plaintiff's first visit to the arena and the protective screens were substantially lower than those provided at other rinks; or (b) the plaintiff had been visiting from another country and was completely unaware of the possibility of being hit by a puck? See also *Payne v. Maple Leaf Gardens Ltd.*, [1949] 1 D.L.R. 369 (Ont. C.A.); and Kligman, "Tort Liability for Sports Injuries" (1989), 1 C.I.L.R. 153.

(c) EXCEEDING CONSENT

AGAR v. CANNING

(1965), 54 W.W.R. 302 (Man. Q.B.)

BASTIN J.: This is an action by a member of a hockey team against a member of an opposing team, for damages arising out of injuries sustained during the course of a hockey match.

. . . The plaintiff and defendant followed the puck into the south-west corner at the Hartney end of the rink. Defendant body-checked plaintiff, took possession of the puck and started to skate with it, or after it, in the direction of the Killarney goal. Plaintiff attempted to delay defendant by hooking him with his stick and in so doing hit defendant a painful blow on the back of the neck. Defendant thereupon stopped, turned, and holding his stick with both hands, brought it down on plaintiff's face, hitting him with the blade between the nose and right eye. I find that he did this in retaliation for the blow he had received. Plaintiff fell to the ice unconscious and the game terminated at that point.

. . .

Neither counsel has been able to find a reported case in which a claim was made by one player against another for injuries suffered during a hockey game. Since it is common knowledge that such injuries are not infrequent, this supports the conclusion that in the past those engaged in this sport have accepted the risk of injury as a condition of participating. Hockey necessarily involves violent bodily contact and blows from the puck and hockey sticks. A person who engages in this sport must be assumed to accept the risk of accidental harm and to waive any claim he would have apart from the game for trespass to his person in return for enjoying a corresponding immunity with respect to other players. It would be inconsistent with this implied consent to impose a duty on a player to take care for the safety of other players corresponding to the duty which, in the normal situation, gives rise to a claim for negligence. Similarly, the leave and licence will include an unintentional injury resulting from one of the frequent infractions of the rules of the game.

The conduct of a player in the heat of the game is instinctive and unpremeditated and should not be judged by standards suited to polite social intercourse.

But a little reflection will establish that some limit must be placed on a player's immunity from liability. Each case must be decided on its own facts so it is difficult, if not impossible, to decide how the line is to be drawn in every circumstance. But injuries inflicted in circumstances which show a definite resolve to cause serious injury to another, even when there is provocation and in the heat of the game, should not fall within the scope of the implied consent. I have come to the conclusion that the act of the defendant in striking plaintiff in the face with a hockey stick, in retaliation for the blow he received, goes beyond the limit marking exemption from liability.

. . .

Even though provocation was not pleaded, and defendant denied acting on provocation, I have made a finding that defendant acted on provocation so I should take this into account in my assessment of damages.

Special damages amount to $115, consisting of doctor's accounts of $30 and hospital accounts of $85. The medical evidence is that the plaintiff has lost all useful vision of his right eye and has injuries to his nose which will affect his breathing and may require to be corrected by an operation. I allow damages of $250 for pain and suffering and for the injuries to the nose, and $5,500 for the loss of the sight of the right eye. I am reducing these damages by one-third, on the ground that there was great provocation.

[The judge's decision was affirmed on appeal: *Agar v. Canning* (1966), 55 W.W.R. 384 (Man. C.A.).]

NOTES AND QUESTIONS

1. Would any conduct in violation of the rules have exceeded the plaintiff's consent? By breaching the rules himself, did the plaintiff implicitly consent to the risks inherent in other players violating the rules? Had the defendant only retaliated by tripping the plaintiff, could he have availed himself of the defence of consent? See *McNamara*

v. Duncan (1971), 26 A.L.R. 584 (A.C.T.S.C.); *Pettis v. McNeil* (1979), 32 N.S.R. (2d) 146 (T.D.); *Colby v. Schmidt* (1986), 37 C.C.L.T. 1 (B.C.S.C.); and *Gaudet v. Sullivan* (1992), 128 N.B.R. (2d) 409 (Q.B.). See also Yeo, "Determining Consent in Body Contact Sports" (1998) 6 Tort L. Rev. 199.

2. Traditionally, the Canadian courts were reluctant to convict hockey players of assault when they intentionally injured each other in fights. See for example *R. v. Green* (1970), 16 D.L.R. (3d) 137 (Ont. Prov. Ct.); and *R. v. Maki* (1970), 14 D.L.R. (3d) 164 (Ont. Prov. Ct.). However, the Canadian courts have become somewhat less tolerant of hockey violence. In *R. v. Cey*, [1989] 5 W.W.R. 169 (Sask. C.A.), the court stated that it cannot be assumed that players implicitly consent to a specific type of assault simply because it occurs with some frequency in the sport. Moreover, given the nature of the defendant's actions, the plaintiff may not have been able to provide a valid consent for criminal law purposes. See also *R. v. Ciccarelli* (1989), 54 C.C.C. (3d) 121 (Ont. Dist. Ct.); and Elvin, "Liability for Negligent Refereeing of a Rugby Match" (2003) 119 L.Q.R. 560.

After losing a fight to Donald Brashear in the first period of an NHL game, Marty McSorley tried several times without success to persuade Brashear to fight again. With three seconds left in the game, McSorley hit Brashear in the head with his stick. Brashear was knocked unconscious and suffered, among other things, a grand mal seizure and a serious concussion. McSorley was criminally charged. The trial judge held that hockey players implicitly consent to physical contact that is permitted by the rules of the game, as well as to some commonly occurring physical contact that results in penalties. However, he also held that some forms of conduct are "too dangerous for the players to consent to" and that McSorley's conduct fell into this category. Consequently, McSorley was convicted of assault with a weapon and given an 18-month conditional sentence: see *R. v. McSorley*, 2000 CarswellBC 3087 (Prov. Ct.) (WLeC). See also *R. v. Bertuzzi* (2004), 26 C.R. (6th) 71 (B.C. Prov. Ct.).

3. In a fist fight to which both parties consent, one party's use of a knife or other weapon would exceed the other party's consent. See *Teolis v. Moscatelli*, 119 A. 161 (R.I. 1923); and *Fillipowich v. Nahachewsky* (1969), 3 D.L.R. (3d) 544 (Sask. Q.B.).

4. Even if both parties use only their fists, is there a point at which the loser's consent would no longer protect the victor? For example, would the plaintiff's initial consent be exceeded if he or she was punched while lying on the ground or struggling to get up?

5. How would you analyze consent in a fight if it was obvious from the outset that the plaintiff was no match for the defendant? Although the courts have provided redress in these types of situations, they have predicated recovery on the defendant's use of excessive or unnecessary force. Is this rationale compatible with the principles of consent? See *Wade v. Martin*, [1955] 3 D.L.R. 635 (Nfld. S.C.); *Hartlen v. Chaddock* (1957), 11 D.L.R. (2d) 705 (N.S.S.C.); and *Lane v. Holloway*, [1968] Q.B. 379 (C.A.).

6. In *R. v. Jobidon*, [1991] 2 S.C.R. 714, the accused was charged with manslaughter when his fellow combatant died following their consensual fight. The trial judge acquitted

the accused because it was a fair fight and the victim's consent had not been exceeded. The Court of Appeal held that the common law concept of consent applies to the assault provisions of the *Criminal Code*, R.S.C. 1985, c. C-46, and limits consent to cases where bodily harm is neither intended nor caused. The court reasoned that this interpretation was consistent with the goals of protecting the public and keeping the peace. The Court of Appeal overturned the acquittal and entered a manslaughter conviction.

The Supreme Court of Canada affirmed the Court of Appeal's decision. The majority of the court ruled that in a consensual fight between adults the combatants' consent is vitiated if they "intentionally apply force causing serious hurt or non-trivial bodily harm to each other." The majority stated that this principle would not affect the validity of consent to rough sporting activities carried out according to the rules of the game, surgical procedures, or dangerous activities engaged in by qualified stuntmen. The minority expressly rejected this reasoning, but held that the accused knowingly exceeded the victim's consent to fight by continuing to hit him once he was unconscious. It was on this basis that the minority would have upheld the accused's manslaughter conviction.

Was there a compelling public policy basis for invalidating consent in *Jobidon*? Would the court have reached the same decision had the combatant not died? Can you reconcile *Jobidon* with the thousands of bar fights and scores of televised hockey brawls that routinely occur without any criminal charges being brought?

7. *Jobidon* has been roundly criticized on various grounds. For example, the common law concept of consent was not limited to situations in which harm was neither intended nor caused. In any event, why did the court incorporate a "common law" concept into the clear statutory language of s. 265(1)(a) of the *Criminal Code*? That section provides that the offence of assault is limited to situations in which force is applied to another without consent. The lack of consent is a substantive element of the offence which the prosecutor must prove. In effect, the Supreme Court of Canada created a new criminal offence of assault. See Usprich, "Annotation" (1991) 7 C.R. (4th) 235.

8. In *R. v. Paice*, [2005] 1 S.C.R. 339, the court clarified its decision in *Jobidon*, ruling that consent will only be negated if the accused both intends and causes serious bodily harm. In *Paice*, the court refrained from using the term "non-trivial harm," suggesting that *Jobidon* will be limited to incidents involving serious physical injuries. Nevertheless, the courts have continued to struggle in applying *Jobidon*, particularly to schoolyard and other fights involving teenagers. See generally *R. v. W.(G.)* (1994), 90 C.C.C. (3d) 139 (Ont. C.A.); *R. v. B.(T.B.)* (1994), 93 C.C.C. (3d) 191 (P.E.I.C.A.); *R. v. J.M.* (2001), 149 O.A.C. 310 (C.A.); *R. v. J.W.*, [2003] B.C.J. No. 302 (Youth Ct.) (QL); and *R. v. B.(K.)*, 2002 CarswellAlta 1843 (Prov. Ct.) (WLeC).

9. Are *Jobidon* and *Paice* consistent with the common law's preference for autonomy? Our law does not prevent individuals from engaging in various high-risk behaviours such as sky-diving, bungee jumping and automobile racing.

10. What impact, if any, should *Jobidon* and *Paice* have on the defence of consent in tort law? For the application of *Jobidon* in civil cases see *Loney v. Butch*, [1989] O.J. No. 1072 (C.A.) (QL) and *Abbott (Next Friend of) v. Jarocki* (1997), 208 A.R. 133 (Prov. Ct.).

11. For a discussion of exceeding consent in trespass to land, see *Gross v. Wright*, [1923] S.C.R. 214; and *Stephens v. Corcoran* (1965), 65 D.L.R. (2d) 407 (Ont. H.C.).

REVIEW PROBLEMS

1. George, a 110-kilogram college football player, rudely pushed his way to the bar. When Bill, a slight, middle-aged man complained, George challenged him to a "fist fight outside." After ten minutes of verbal abuse, Bill reluctantly agreed. As Bill approached, George held the door open and bowed, stating: "After you, coward." Seizing this opportunity, Bill kicked George in the head once, knocking him unconscious and ending the fight. What tort liability, if any, has Bill incurred as a result of this altercation? Would your answer differ if George had been less specific about the nature of the fight and had merely said "let's settle this outside?"

2. Steve suffered a broken arm when brought down by a well-executed tackle on the first play of a football game at the local playground. He was caught off guard because he thought they were playing touch football. Although he missed the preliminary discussions, he simply assumed the game was touch football: no one was wearing football equipment, his friends rarely played tackle and he had not been told that it was tackle. Advise Steve on whether his battery claim will be defeated by the defence of consent.

(d) COMPETENCY TO CONSENT

In order for consent to be valid, the person giving it must be capable of appreciating the nature and consequences of the act to which it applies. If the person cannot make such a determination due to age, physical or mental illness, intoxication, or other incapacitating factors, the consent will be invalid. The issue of competency to consent addresses a person's ability to understand the information relevant to the act in issue. The fact that the courts or others may view the decision as unreasonable is not necessarily relevant to the issue of competency. This broad test of competency is consistent with the common law's concern with safeguarding autonomy. If a person is competent, the law must uphold his or her right to make both wise and unwise decisions.

It should be noted that some statutes deem certain individuals to be incapable of giving a valid consent for specific purposes. For example, s. 150.1(1) and (2) of the *Criminal Code* provides that the consent of a person under the age of 14 does not generally provide a defence to a charge of sexual assault. Legislation has been proposed to raise this age of consent to 16. A significant number of provincial healthcare and counselling statutes also contain statutory age requirements. The issue of competency to consent will be examined in greater detail in the subsection on consent to treatment and counselling later in this chapter.

3. Factors Vitiating Consent: Fraud, Mistake, Duress, and Public Policy

(a) INTRODUCTION

Once the defendant establishes that the plaintiff consented to the act giving rise to the tort, the plaintiff may raise factors that vitiate his or her consent. If the consent is vitiated, the defendant will be held liable as if there had been no consent. The Canadian courts have tended to rely on criminal law principles and have narrowly defined these vitiating factors. While a narrow definition of these factors may be appropriate in criminal law, it is questionable whether this is the case in tort law, which focuses primarily on compensation.

(b) FRAUD (DECEIT)

The fact that the plaintiff's consent was based on a fraudulently induced belief will not necessarily vitiate the consent. First, it must be established that the defendant was aware of, or responsible for, the plaintiff's misapprehension. Second, the fraud will only negate consent if it relates to the nature and quality of the act, as opposed to a "collateral" matter. In keeping with the approach employed in criminal law, the courts in tort cases have adopted a broad view of what they consider to be collateral matters and have rarely negated the plaintiff's consent. Consequently, a man who lies about his marital status in order to induce a woman to have sex with him will be absolved of liability in battery.

Most cases involving fraud deal with written or verbal statements. However, the defendant's conduct or failure to reveal information may also constitute fraud in some situations. Fraud includes situations in which the defendant either knowingly deceives the plaintiff or acts in total disregard to the truth.

NOTES AND QUESTIONS

1. The distinction between fraud as to the nature of the act and fraud as to collateral matters is well established in criminal law. In *R. v. Williams*, [1923] 1 K.B. 340 (C.A.), a singing teacher was convicted of rape for inducing a 16-year-old student to have intercourse under the pretence that it was a therapeutic procedure to improve her voice. The court emphasized that the girl did not know that she was engaging in a sexual act. In *Papadimitropoulos v. R.* (1958), 98 C.L.R. 249 (H.C.A.), the accused was acquitted of rape for having intercourse with an illiterate woman after he had fraudulently convinced her that they had been married. In this case, the woman was aware that she was participating in a sexual act and consented to it. The court held that the fraud went to a collateral matter and thus did not vitiate her consent. See also *R. v. Harms*, [1944] 2 D.L.R. 61 (Sask. C.A.); *Bolduc and Bird v. R.*, [1967] S.C.R. 667; and Hooper, "Fraud in Assault and Rape" (1967-68) 3 U.B.C.L. Rev. 117.

2. Similar reasoning has been adopted in civil cases. In *Graham v. Saville*, [1945] 2 D.L.R. 489 (Ont. C.A.); and *Smythe v. Reardon* (1949), 23 A.L.J. 409 (Circ. Ct.), the defendant fraudulently claimed to be a bachelor and induced the plaintiff to marry him. In both cases the plaintiff recovered damages based on the tort of deceit, but presumably could not have recovered in battery. What arguments would you make for treating fraud as to collateral matters differently in tort than in criminal law? See Fischer, "Fraudulently Induced Consent to Intentional Torts" (1977) 46 Cinn. L. Rev. 71.

3. Whose perspective should be adopted in determining which matters are collateral? Since the defendant has the burden of proving that the plaintiff consented, should the plaintiff's views prevail? See *Said (Husain) v. Said* (1986), 38 C.C.L.T. 260 (B.C.C.A.).

4. Should the plaintiff's consent be valid if he or she is aware of the nature and quality of the act, but is deceived as to its physically harmful consequences? In *Hegarty v. Shine* (1878), 4 L.R. Ir. 288 (C.A.), the plaintiff contracted a venereal disease from her lover, who knew he was infected but did not inform her. The court concluded that the defendant's failure to disclose his condition did not vitiate her consent. However, the judges appeared to be pre-occupied with denying the plaintiff redress for the consequences of her illicit sexual relationship.

5. Traditionally, as in *Hegarty*, fraud as to the harmful consequences of the accused's act would not vitiate the plaintiff's consent. See for example *R. v. Clarence* (1888), 22 Q.B.D. 23 (C.C.R.); and *R. v. Ssenyonga* (1992), 73 C.C.C. (3d) 216 (Ont. Prov. Div.). The Supreme Court of Canada finally rejected this principle in *R. v. Cuerrier*, [1998] 2 S.C.R. 371.

Cuerrier knew he was HIV-positive. Nevertheless, he had intercourse, mostly unprotected, with the first complainant at least 100 times and with the second complainant 10 times. The accused told the first complainant that he had tested negative for HIV and did not respond to the second complainant's expressions of concern about sexually-transmitted diseases. The accused was charged with two counts of aggravated assault. The trial judge gave a directed verdict, acquitting the accused on the basis that only fraud as to the nature of the act or the identity of the offender could vitiate consent to intercourse. The Court of Appeal upheld the trial judgment.

The Supreme Court of Canada overturned these decisions and ordered a new trial. The court held that fraud as to the potentially harmful consequences of a sexual act could negate consent. First, the Crown had to prove that the accused was dishonest, which could include not only lying, but also non-disclosure. Second, the dishonesty had to result in a deprivation, which could consist of actual harm or exposing a person to a significant risk of serious bodily harm. Given the serious consequences of HIV infection, the court held that the accused's failure to disclose his HIV status prior to having unprotected intercourse with the complainants constituted a deprivation. The majority of the court stated that the careful use of condoms might be found to reduce the risk to the point that there was no longer a deprivation. Finally, the Crown had to prove that the dishonesty induced the complainants to consent to unprotected intercourse when they would not otherwise have done so.

In *R. v. Williams*, [2003] 2 S.C.R. 134, the court suggested that a complainant's consent may be vitiated by fraud even if the complainant was not exposed to a significant risk of serious bodily harm. See also *R. v. Aziga*, [2005] O.J. No. 5983 (S.C.J.) (QL).

6. Should the approach in *Cuerrier* or an even broader principle apply in torts cases involving fraudulently obtained consent? Should a plaintiff's consent be negated, regardless of (a) the severity of the potential physical harm or (b) whether the potential harm was physical, psychological or financial? See generally *Restatement (Second) of the Law of Torts* (1979) at §892(B)(2); Fleming, *The Law of Torts*, 9th ed. (1998) at 89; and Rogers, *Winfield & Jolowicz on Tort*, 17th ed. (2006) at 1061-62.

7. It should be noted that polygamy and feigning a marriage ceremony are offences under ss. 292 and 293 of the *Criminal Code*. In 1985, the *Criminal Code* offence of communicating a venereal disease, unless one was unaware of the infection, was repealed.

(c) MISTAKE

The fact that the plaintiff's consent was induced by a mistaken belief will vitiate the consent only if the defendant was responsible for creating the plaintiff's misapprehension. The American authorities support a broader rule. Presumably, the plaintiff's consent will only be negated if his or her mistaken belief goes to the nature or quality of the act, or to a significant risk of a serious physical harm, as outlined in *R. v. Cuerrier*, [1998] 2 S.C.R. 371. The *Restatement (Second) of the Law of Torts* (1979) at §892(B)(2) provides that the defendant's mere knowledge that the plaintiff consented under a mistaken belief vitiates the consent.

Situations in which the plaintiff consents based on a mistaken belief must be distinguished from those in which the defendant erroneously believes that the plaintiff has consented. In the latter situations, since the plaintiff has not consented to the act giving rise to the tort, the defence of consent is not in issue.

NOTES AND QUESTIONS

1. Explain in your own words the difference between a fraudulently and a mistakenly induced belief. Provide an example of each.

2. There are surprisingly few cases on the impact of the plaintiff's mistaken belief on the validity of his or her consent. See *Roper v. Harper* (1837), 132 E.R. 696 (C.P.); *Stewart v. Traders Trust Co.*, [1936] 4 D.L.R. 139 (Man. C.A.); and *Guimond v. Laberge* (1956), 4 D.L.R. (2d) 559 (Ont. C.A.).

3. Keeton *et al.*, *Prosser and Keeton on the Law of Torts*, 5th ed. (1984) at 119 states that the plaintiff's consent will be vitiated if the defendant knew or ought to have known that the plaintiff's consent was based on a mistaken belief. This position is even broader than that of the American Law Institute in the *Restatement (Second)*. See also Hertz, "Volenti Non Fit Injuria: A Guide" in Klar, ed., *Studies in Canadian Tort Law* (1977) 101 at 113-14, who adopts the Institute's position without comment. See generally Forbes, "Mistake of Fact With Regard to Defences in Tort Law" (1970) 4 Ottawa L. Rev. 304. Which rule should the courts adopt in these situations?

4. Several cases clearly establish that the defendant's mistaken belief that the plaintiff consented provides no defence. See *Parmley v. Parmley*, [1945] S.C.R. 634; *Turner v. Thorne* (1960), 21 D.L.R. (2d) 29 (Ont. H.C.); and *Schweizer v. Central Hospital* (1974), 6 O.R. (2d) 606 (H.C.).

In *Toews (Guardian ad litem of) v. Weisner* (2001), 3 C.C.L.T. (3d) 293 (B.C.S.C.), the defendant was a public health nurse who was providing Hepatitis B vaccinations in schools. The parents of 11-year-old Georgia Toews had not signed the consent form, and Georgia specifically told Weisner that her parents did not want her to be vaccinated. However, Weisner mistakenly believed that Georgia's mother had given verbal consent and vaccinated Georgia. Although no harm resulted and Weisner had a good faith belief that Georgia's mother had consented, she was held liable in battery for $1,000.

(d) DURESS (COERCION)

LATTER v. BRADDELL

(1880), 50 L.J.Q.B. 166 (C.P.)

LOPES J.: This was an action of assault which . . . resulted in a verdict for the defendant [doctor]. The learned Judge . . . withdrew the case against Captain and Mrs. Braddell from the jury, holding that there was no evidence against them upon which a jury could reasonably act.

. . .

I think the case against Captain and Mrs. Braddell ought to have been left to the jury. I do not think it was correct to tell the jury that to maintain this action the plaintiff's will must have been overpowered by force or the fear of violence. This I understand was the direction given by the learned Judge to the jury in summing up the case against the defendant [doctor], and I presume this view of the law induced him to withdraw from the jury the case against Captain and Mrs. Braddell.

I will now call attention to the facts. The plaintiff was a housemaid in the service of Captain and Mrs. Braddell. Captain and Mrs. Braddell had been absent from home, and returned on the 23rd of December. From some information given by a charwoman, Mrs. Braddell came to the conclusion that the plaintiff was in the family way. On the 27th of December Mrs. Braddell told the plaintiff to pack up and leave before twelve o'clock, as she was in the family way. This the plaintiff denied. Mrs. Braddell replied, "The doctor will be here directly". (The doctor had been previously sent for unknown to the plaintiff.) Mrs. Braddell told the plaintiff to go to her room. The plaintiff cried. Mrs. Braddell forbade her to speak. The plaintiff went to her bedroom. The doctor came and went to the plaintiff's bedroom. The plaintiff cried and said she never had such treatment before. She asked the doctor what he was going to do, and said she did not wish to be examined. The doctor said he was a professional man, and told the plaintiff to take off her dress. The plaintiff said she did not like to do so. The doctor said, "Never mind, it would satisfy Mrs. Braddell and him". The doctor told the plaintiff to take off her petticoat. The plaintiff cried and said she did not like to take off her other things. The doctor said, "You must". The plaintiff took off her stays. The doctor said she must take off her chemise. The plaintiff said she did not like to do so. The doctor said she must, and told her to slip her arms through. The doctor then told her to lie on her back on the bed and to loosen the strings of her drawers. He then pinched her breasts and stomach and sounded it. The plaintiff cried all the time. The doctor, after examining her, said she was all right, and he must speak seriously to Mrs. Braddell about it. The plaintiff then dressed.

. . .

If the plaintiff voluntarily consented, or if, in other words, the assault was committed with her leave and licence, the action is not maintainable; and to justify the ruling of the learned Judge, what was done must have been so unmistakably with the plaintiff's consent that there was no evidence of non-consent upon which a jury could reasonably act. It seems to me there was abundant evidence of non-consent to be left to the jury.

The sending for a doctor by a master or mistress and directing him to examine a female servant, without first apprising her, is, in any circumstances, an arbitrary and high-handed proceeding, and cannot, in my opinion, be justified unless the servant's consent is voluntarily given. A submission to what is done, obtained through a belief that she is bound to obey her master and mistress; or a consent obtained through a fear of evil consequences to arise to herself, induced by her master's or mistress's words or conduct, is not sufficient. In neither case would the consent be voluntarily given: it would be consent in one sense, but a consent to which the will was not a party. The plaintiff's case is stronger. She swears she did not consent. I know not what more a person in the plaintiff's position could do unless she used physical force. She is discharged without a hearing, forbidden to speak, sent to her room, examined by her mistress's doctor alone, no other female being in the room, made to take off all her clothes and lie naked on the bed. She complains of the treatment, cries continuously, objects to the removal of each garment and swears the examination was without her consent. Could it be said, in these circumstances, that her consent was so unmistakably given that her state of mind was not a question for a jury to consider? I cannot adopt the view that the plaintiff consented because she yielded without her will having been overpowered by force or fear of violence. That, as I have said, is not, in my opinion, an accurate definition of consent in a case like this.

I do not understand why, if there was a case against the doctor there was none against Captain and Mrs. Braddell. The doctor was employed to see if the plaintiff was in the family way. The plaintiff does not suggest in her evidence that he did more than was necessary for ascertaining that fact. If this is so, the Braddells are responsible for what was done by the doctor.

It is said there ought to be no new trial as against the doctor. I cannot agree with the definition of consent given by the learned Judge, and I think the withdrawing the case against the Braddells influenced the jury in finding for the doctor. They would naturally think the doctor only did what he was told. The Braddells put him in motion, and it would be hard, when the principals are acquitted, to find the agent guilty.

There should be a rule absolute for a new trial.

LINDLEY J.: I am of opinion that, assuming everything said by the plaintiff in this case to be true, a verdict in her favour against the master and mistress could not be supported in point of law, and that as to them she was properly nonsuited.

. . .

The plaintiff's case cannot be put higher than this, namely, that without consulting her wishes, her mistress ordered her to submit to be examined by a doctor, in order that he might ascertain whether she (the plaintiff) was in the family way, and that she (the plaintiff) complied with that order reluctantly — that is, sobbing and protesting — and because she was told she must, and she did not know what else to do. There was, however, no evidence of any force or violence, nor of any threat of force or violence, nor of any illegal act done or threatened by the mistress beyond what I have stated; nor did the plaintiff in her evidence say that she was in fear of the mistress or of the doctor, or that she was in any way overcome by fear. She said she did not consent to what was done; but the sense in which she used this expression was not explained, and to appreciate it regard must be had to the other facts of the case. The plaintiff had it entirely in her own power physically to comply or not to comply with her mistress's orders, and there was no evidence whatever to shew that anything improper or illegal was threatened to be done if she had not complied. It was suggested that her mistress ordered the examination with a view to see whether she could dismiss her without paying a month's wages. But there was no evidence of any threat to withhold wages, nor of any conversation on the subject of wages, until the plaintiff was paid them on leaving. The question, therefore, is reduced to this: Can the plaintiff, having complied with the orders of her mistress, although reluctantly, maintain this action upon the ground that what was done to her by the doctor was against her will, or might properly be so regarded by a jury? I think not. It is said that the jury ought to have been asked whether the plaintiff in effect gave her mistress leave to have her examined, or whether the plaintiff's will or mind went with what she did. But, in my opinion, such questions inadequately express the grounds on which alone the defendants can be held liable. The plaintiff was not a child; she knew perfectly well what she did and what was being done to her by the doctor. She knew the object with which he examined her, and upon the evidence there is no reason whatever for supposing that any examination would have been made or attempted if she had told the doctor she would not allow herself to be examined. Under these circumstances I am of opinion that there was no evidence of want of consent as distinguished from reluctant obedience or submission to her mistress's orders, and that in the absence of all evidence of coercion, as distinguished from an order which the plaintiff could comply with or not as she chose, the action cannot be maintained.

. . .

I do not, however, wish to be understood as being of opinion that the plaintiff had no cause of complaint against her mistress; but, in my opinion, the real substantial grievance was that the plaintiff accused of being in the family way was ordered to be examined, and when the accusation proved to be unfounded was summarily dismissed without any apology. Whether the mistress could or could not have justified such harsh conduct I cannot say, not having heard her evidence. But, harsh as such conduct apparently was, it does not affect the question on which this action turns. I cannot, however, help thinking that if the conduct of the mistress as regards the manner of dismissal had been more considerate, the impossibility of maintaining this action would be more plainly apparent.

As regards the doctor, who is made a defendant, I am of opinion, for the reasons already given, that there was no misdirection in point of law, and that the verdict in his favour was perfectly correct. His conduct throughout was kind and considerate; and whatever grievance the plaintiff may have against her mistress, she has none whatever against the doctor.

. . .

Rule Discharged.

[The Court of Appeal affirmed Lindley J.'s judgment discharging the rule: *Latter v. Braddell* (1881), 50 L.J.Q.B. 448 (C.A.).]

NOTES AND QUESTIONS

1. Did Lindley J. adequately address the issue of consent before focusing on duress? Did the plaintiff in *Latter* consent to the medical examination?

2. How did Lindley J. define duress? What economic threats, if any, would be included in his definition? Do you agree with his application of this definition to the facts? Answer these questions in reference to Lopes J. Which judgment do you prefer?

3. Under s. 17 of the *Criminal Code*, the concept of compulsion (duress) is defined narrowly in terms of a credible threat of immediate death or bodily injury. Although the American Law Institute rejects this type of restrictive definition of duress for civil law purposes, it does not provide an alternative: see *Restatement (Second) of the Law of Torts* (1979) at §892B, comment on subsection (3). See also Keeton *et al., Prosser and Keeton on the Law of Torts*, 5th ed. (1984) at 121. Should the definition of duress differ in tort and criminal law? How would you define duress for the purposes of tort law?

4. Should an employee who submits to her employer's sexual demands to keep her job succeed in battery on the basis that her consent was vitiated by duress? Would your answer differ if the employer's threat of dismissal contravened the provincial labour and human rights legislation?

5. Can policies making treatment a condition of parole be successfully challenged on the basis that the parolee's consent is negated by duress? For a discussion of the *Canadian Charter of Rights and Freedoms*, Part I of *The Constitution Act, 1982*, being Schedule B to the *Canada Act 1982* (U.K.), 1982, c. 11 and other legal implications of such policies, see *Deacon v. Canada (A.G.)* (2006), 352 N.R. 380 (F.C.A.); and *R. v. Shoker* (2006), 271 D.L.R. (4th) 385 (S.C.C.).

(e) PUBLIC POLICY

The courts have increasingly recognized public policy considerations in negating the defence of consent. For example in *Lane v. Holloway*, [1968] 1 Q.B. 379 (C.A.), the court refused to accept the defence of consent, because it was obvious from the outset of the fight that the elderly plaintiff was no match for the young defendant. In *R. v. Jobidon*, [1991] 2 S.C.R. 714 and *R. v. Paice*, [2005] 1 S.C.R. 359, the Supreme Court of Canada held that an accused cannot raise the defence of consent, even in a fair fight, if serious physical harm was intended and caused.

Some courts have negated the defence of consent if the defendant exploited his or her position of trust. In *M.(M.) v. K.(K.)* (1989), 38 B.C.L.R. (2d) 273 (C.A.), the defendant was convicted of the federal offence of sexual exploitation for having sex with his 15-year-old foster daughter. The daughter's civil action was dismissed at trial on the basis that she had initiated and consented to the sexual contact. However, the Court of Appeal reversed the trial judgment. The court rejected the defence of consent because it was dependent on the defendant's wrongdoing, which included criminal misconduct, breach of trust and breach of his duty to act in the plaintiff's best interests.

In *Norberg v. Wynrib*, [1992] 2 S.C.R. 226, the defendant doctor offered to supply an addicted patient with prescription narcotics if she submitted to his sexual advances. She reluctantly agreed only after she failed to secure the drugs from another source. After recovering from her addiction, the patient sued the defendant for battery, negligence and breach of fiduciary duty. The trial and appeal courts dismissed the patient's action and found, among other things, that she had given a valid consent to the sexual contact. The Supreme Court of Canada unanimously upheld that patient's appeal, awarding her $20,000 in general damages and $10,000 in punitive damages. LaForest, Gonthier and Cory JJ. held the doctor liable in battery, stating that the parties' unequal bargaining power and the exploitive nature of their relationship made it impossible for the plaintiff to "meaningfully consent." Sopinka J. held that the plaintiff's consent to the defendant's sexual advances was not vitiated in the circumstances. However, he found the defendant liable in negligence for breaching the requisite standard of care by failing to treat the patient for her addiction. McLachlin and L'Heureux-Dubé JJ. held the doctor liable for breaching his fiduciary duty to the patient by exploiting his position of power and her vulnerability. In their view, this independent cause of action better captured the doctor's wrongful conduct than either battery or negligence.

NOTES AND QUESTIONS

1. Can you identify an underlying principle that explains the result in *Lane, Jobidon, M.(M.)*, and *Norberg*? Do you agree with these decisions?

2. Would the result have been the same in *M.(M.)* if the defendant's conduct had not been illegal, but had merely violated his position of trust? For example, assume that the plaintiff was 18 years old and the defendant was a private music teacher or volunteer basketball coach. See *Lyth v. Dagg* (1988), 46 C.C.L.T. 25 (B.C.S.C.); *Harder v. Brown* (1989), 50 C.C.L.T. 85 (B.C.S.C.); and *A.K. v. D.K.*, [2002] O.J. No. 351 (S.C.J.) (QL).

3. What do you think the majority meant by the phrase "meaningfully consent" in *Norberg*? Would a person who consents to counselling only because it is a term of his or her probation be able to "meaningfully consent?" Which approach in *Norberg* is preferable?

4. *Norberg* raises the issue of the sexual abuse and exploitation of patients. Following a particularly egregious case in the late 1980s, the Ontario College of Physicians and Surgeons established a task force to examine the issue. Among other things, it found that sexual abuse of female patients was not infrequent and that the patients' efforts to obtain redress were largely unsuccessful. See *The Final Report of the Task Force on Sexual Abuse of Patients* (1991).

After the report was released, Ontario enacted legislation requiring regulated health practitioners to report to the appropriate college any situation in which they reasonably believed that a patient had been sexually abused by any regulated health professional. See *Regulated Health Professions Act, 1991*, S.O. 1991, c. 18, ss. 85.1-85.7. Shortly thereafter, Ontario enacted similar mandatory reporting obligations for social workers and teachers.

5. Can you suggest other cases in which public policy considerations should limit the defendant's ability to rely on the plaintiff's consent as a defence?

6. The courts have not reconciled their public policy analysis with the concept of individual autonomy. Nor have they considered the implications of negating a person's consent on policy grounds in other areas, such as healthcare.

There is considerable case law that accepts the plaintiff's consent at face value. In reference to consensual fights, see *Wade v. Martin*, [1955] 3 D.L.R. 635 (Nfld. S.C.); *Zinck v. Strickland and Blake* (1981), 86 A.P.R. 451 (N.S.S.C.); and *Johnson v. Royal Can. Legion Grandview Branch No. 179*, [1988] 5 W.W.R. 267 (B.C.C.A.). In contrast to *Norberg*, see *Morrow v. Hôpital Royal Victoria* (1989), 3 C.C.L.T. (2d) 87 (Qc. C.A.), in which the schizophrenic patient's consent to electroshock therapy was upheld, even though she had not been informed that the defendant doctor was being paid by the CIA to conduct brain-washing experiments. The court held that because the patient was herself a doctor who was aware of the risks, her consent was valid.

7. Should adults be permitted to consent to sadomasochistic sexual practices? In *R. v. Welch* (1995), 25 O.R. (3d) 665 (C.A.), the court held that a victim cannot consent to harm unless the accused is acting in the course of a socially approved purpose. Consequently, inherently dehumanizing or degrading conduct, or conduct that involves sexual gratification from inflicting physical pain, cannot be the subject of consent. See also *R. v. Brown*, [1993] 2 W.L.R. 556 (H.L.), where the court refused to extend the defence of consent to homosexual sadomasochism.

What are the implications of these principles for the professional "sports" of kick-boxing, ultimate fighting and wrestling? Should the courts be the arbiters of what constitutes a socially approved purpose, particularly in regards to criminal liability? Should a similar approach be adopted in tort law? What behaviour should society simply not countenance, regardless of the participants' consent and beliefs?

REVIEW PROBLEM

Following a car accident, the plaintiff sought accident benefits from the defendant insurance company and provided supporting documentation from her physician. The defendant refused to process the claim without additional medical evidence. The insurance contract permitted the defendant to ask the plaintiff to submit to a second assessment. Without consulting the plaintiff, the defendant made an appointment for her with a specialist. The defendant then wrote the plaintiff, instructing her to attend at the pre-arranged date and time. The letter stated that the plaintiff had to submit to the examination or her file would be closed. However, the letter did not inform the plaintiff of her contractual right to challenge the need for a second assessment, propose an alternate specialist, or reschedule the appointment.

In addition to missing work, rearranging her schedule and organizing transportation, the plaintiff was upset about being physically examined by a male physician. The plaintiff had not gone to a male physician since childhood. Nevertheless, she believed that she had no choice. She was ushered into an examining room and told to change into a dressing gown. She was never asked for consent, did not receive a consent form to sign and did not verbally consent to the examination. She followed the instructions that she was given, answered the specialist's questions and complied with his requests concerning the examination.

The plaintiff only deferred to the defendant's demands because she believed that the contract required her to do so. When the plaintiff learned that this was not the case, she approached your law firm. Your senior partner has directed you to assume that the defendant company is responsible for the battery that the specialist committed in physically examining the plaintiff. You have been asked to determine if the defendant can establish a valid defence of consent. See generally *Nelitz v. Dyck* (2001), 52 O.R. (3d) 458 (C.A.).

4. Consent to Criminal or Immoral Acts

As indicated above, in *Hegarty v. Shine* (1878), 4 L.R. Ir. 288 (C.A.), the female plaintiff sued her lover in battery for infecting her with a venereal disease. One of the bases on which the court denied her claim was the principle that a person cannot recover in tort law for the consequences of her own illegal or immoral conduct. This concept, which is often referred to by the Latin maxim *ex turpi causa non oritur actio*, was first applied in contract law. The principle was gradually extended to torts, serving as a complete defence to both intentional torts and negligence. For example, successful combatants sued in battery following a consensual fight often asserted both the defences of consent and *ex turpi causa*.

The principle has generated considerable controversy, in large part because the courts failed to clarify its underlying purpose. Consequently, the principle was applied on a case-by-case basis, making the decisions difficult to reconcile or explain. Nevertheless, the general trend in Canada has been to narrow the principle. For example, some courts held that it only applies to illegal but not immoral acts; others limited it to federal criminal offences and excluded provincial and municipal offences. Finally, some courts concluded that *ex turpi causa* only applies to some federal criminal offences.

Finally, in *Hall v. Hebert*, [1993] 2 S.C.R. 159, the court identified the purpose of the principle and clarified the circumstances in which it applies. The court said that the purpose of the principle was to protect the integrity of the legal system. Thus, for example, *ex turpi causa* would apply to prevent a plaintiff from profiting financially from his or her illegal or immoral behaviour. Conversely, the principle would rarely apply to a plaintiff seeking compensation for actual physical injuries.

NOTES AND QUESTIONS

1. In *Tallow v. Tailfeathers* (1973), 44 D.L.R. (3d) 55 (Alta. C.A.), the *ex turpi causa* defence was limited to truly criminal behaviour, namely violations of federal criminal law, and not provincial or municipal enactments. In the court's words, "anti-social behaviour" and an "aura of criminality" will not suffice. However, in *Canada Cement LaFarge Ltd. v. British Columbia Lightweight Aggregate Ltd.*, [1983] 1 S.C.R. 452, the court held that the principle applies to both criminal and immoral conduct, including involvement in illegal agreements.

2. One concern has been that the concept of immorality is too open-ended and will vary both over time and across jurisdictions. For example, would *Hegarty* be decided the same way now? In *Kirkham v. Chief Constable of Greater Manchester Police*, [1990] 3 All E.R. 246 (C.A.), the plaintiff's husband committed suicide while in police custody. The court rejected the police department's defence of *ex turpi causa* because suicide was no longer viewed as a "moral affront."

3. *Ex turpi causa* is often said to be limited to cases in which the plaintiff's injuries are a direct result of his or her participation in immoral or illegal conduct. However, some courts apply the concept of directness more narrowly than others. For example, the majority in *Norberg v. Wynrib*, [1992] 2 S.C.R. 226 rejected the *ex turpi causa* defence, stating that the plaintiff's criminal conduct in seeking drugs played no causal role in the doctor's sexual exploitation of her. The defence was also rejected in both of the minority judgments, but explicitly on policy grounds.

Should the defence apply to a plaintiff who is injured in a crash caused by the defendant's negligent driving if they are joy-riding together in a stolen car? Contrast *Smith v. Jenkins* (1970), 119 C.L.R. 397 (H.C.A.); and *Tallow v. Tailfeathers*, *supra*, with *Jackson v. Harrison* (1978), 138 C.L.R. 438 (H.C.A.); *Gala v. Preston* (1991), 172 C.L.R. 243 (H.C.A.); and *Pitts v. Hunt*, [1991] 1 Q.B. 24 (C.A.).

4. In *Teece v. Honeybourn* (1974), 54 D.L.R. (3d) 549 (B.C.S.C.), the court held that the defendant police officer could not raise the defence against the deceased, an escaping car thief whom he had negligently shot, because the officer was not one of the deceased's criminal accomplices. This controversial limitation on *ex turpi causa* was specifically rejected by the Supreme Court of Canada in *Hall v. Hebert*.

5. Several courts have simply refused to apply the defence if the loser of a consensual fight was badly injured. The fact that the plaintiff was no match for the defendant and that excessive force was used appears to have influenced these decisions. See *Hartlen v. Chaddock* (1957), 11 D.L.R. (2d) 705 (N.S.S.C.); and *Lane v. Holloway*, [1967] 3 All E.R. 129 (C.A.). But see *Wade v. Martin*, [1955] 3 D.L.R. 635 (Nfld. S.C.); and *Murphy v. Culhane*, [1976] 3 All E.R. 533 (C.A.). Has *R. v. Jobidon*, [1991] 2 S.C.R. 714, discussed earlier in this chapter, rendered these cases moot?

6. Some courts have refused to apply the doctrine to certain *Criminal Code* offences, such as impaired driving. In *Foster v. Morton* (1956), 4 D.L.R. (2d) 269 at 281 (N.S.S.C.), MacDonald J. stated without any explanation that there were weighty reasons why the doctrine should not apply in impaired driving cases. This statement was accepted by both the majority and dissent in *Miller v. Decker*, [1957] S.C.R. 624. See also *Blakely v. 513953 Ont. Ltd.* (1985), 49 O.R. (2d) 651 (S.C.). What impact will *Hall v. Hebert* have on this line of cases?

7. Do you agree with *Hall v. Hebert* that the doctrine should be limited to preserving the "integrity of the legal system?" What other purposes could the doctrine serve? Assuming that the doctrine should be limited to preserving the integrity of the legal system, does it follow that the doctrine would rarely apply to wrongdoing plaintiffs who are seeking compensation for physical injuries?

8. In *John Bead Corp. v. Soni* (2002), 10 C.C.L.T. 318 (Ont. C.A.), the plaintiffs sued the defendants on several grounds including fraud, claiming that they had stolen $1.6 million from the plaintiff's company. The defendants pleaded *ex turpi causa* on the basis that the plaintiffs had also taken money from the company illegally. The court struck out this defence, because the plaintiffs' alleged illegal behaviour was unrelated to their claim against the defendant. The court then gave two examples of situations in which *ex turpi causa* would apply. First, one wrongdoer cannot recover in torts against another for his or her share of their theft or other illegal behaviour. Second, a plaintiff who has been physically injured cannot recover loss of earnings arising from an illegal activity. Thus, a defendant who assaults a forger cannot be held liable for the illegal earnings that the forger lost while his or her hand healed.

9. The defence has generated considerable academic attention. See for example MacDougall, "*Ex Turpi Causa*: Should a Defence Arise from a Base Cause?" (1991) 55 Sask. L. Rev. 1; Klar, "Negligence — Defences — Ex-Turpi Causa Non Oritur Actio — Volenti Non Fit Injuria — The Purpose of Negligent Accident Law: *Hall* v. *Hebert*" (1993) 72 Can. Bar Rev. 553; McInnes, "Ex Turpi Causa and Tort – A Canadian

Perspective" [1993] C.L.J. 379; and Kostal, "Currents in the Counter-Reformation: Illegality and Duty of Care in Canada and Australia" (1995) 3 Tort L. Rev. 100.

REVIEW PROBLEM

Frank and Mary had dated for several months, becoming more emotionally and romantically involved. Mary was reluctant to become physically involved and was cautious about sexually transmitted diseases. Before she agreed to becoming physically intimate, she asked Frank: "Is it safe to have intercourse with you?" Frank responded that she had "nothing to worry about." Unknown to Mary, Frank had been diagnosed with herpes simplex II, a disease that can be transmitted through direct physical contact with an open sore. Once infected, the virus remains in the person's system, resulting in flare-ups of sores from time to time. The sores are unsightly, can be painful and can infect others. If a pregnant woman has an outbreak of genital sores when she goes into labour, she will be advised to have a Caesarean section rather than delivering the baby vaginally. However, the virus is otherwise more of an inconvenience than a significant health risk to the carrier.

Two years ago, when Frank first noticed a sore in his genital area, he sought medical treatment. Frank was so nervous and so relieved that it was due to herpes simplex II and not HIV that he misunderstood what his doctor told him. Frank honestly, albeit erroneously, believed that once that sore went away, he would no longer be capable of infecting others. Frank's doctor had given him a brochure that explained in plain language terms the nature of the disease. Had Frank read the brochure, as his doctor recommended, he would have realized that he remained capable of infecting others if he had intimate contact during a flare-up.

Frank did not tell Mary of his infection, because he did not believe that he could infect her and because of his embarrassment. While Frank realized that he had not been forthcoming, he believed that he had answered Mary's questions honestly. Unfortunately, Mary contracted herpes simplex II from Frank as a result of their sexual relationship. When Mary learned of her infection and realized that Frank was the source, she ended the relationship. Mary now seeks your legal advice about suing Frank in battery for the sexual contact that resulted in her infection.

5. Consent to Treatment and Counselling

(a) GENERAL PRINCIPLES OF CONSENT

As a general rule, healthcare professionals and counsellors must obtain consent to initiate any physical examination, test, procedure, surgery, or counselling. The consent should be obtained in advance and cover the proposed intervention. In order to avoid other potential legal problems, the consent should also address any related issues regarding record-keeping, confidentiality, reporting, and other disclosures of information. The consent must relate to the specific procedure or treatment that is undertaken. If the patient is competent to give a valid consent, it is his or her consent alone that is required. The consent of a patient's next-of-kin is only relevant if he or she is incapable of consenting. Even in these circumstances, there are limits on the validity of substitute consent.

To be valid, the consent must be given "voluntarily," in the sense that the patient's decision must be the product of his or her conscious mind. Consistent with the law's focus on individual autonomy, the legal definition of volition is extremely broad. For example, patients who reluctantly consent to treatment because they have been threatened with termination from a job or expulsion from school will still be held to have "voluntarily" consented.

At common law, the patient's consent had to be based on a full and frank disclosure of the nature of the intervention and its risks. The patient need not understand the technical details of the intervention or the research underlying it. Nevertheless, practitioners and counsellors are increasingly expected to put the proposed treatment into the context of the risks and benefits of its alternatives, including foregoing treatment. A patient may consent implicitly by participation, other behaviour or demeanour, or explicitly, either orally or in writing. The fact that a patient makes an appointment and comes for treatment provides a broad measure of implied consent.

Patients may seek treatment and yet expressly limit the scope of their consent. Healthcare professionals and counsellors may refuse to treat a patient if these limitations render the treatment futile or harmful. However, a patient's express prohibitions cannot be ignored or overridden.

NOTES AND QUESTIONS

1. For a review of the general principles of consent to treatment or counselling, see Nelson, "Chapter 4: The Fundamentals of Consent" in Downie, Caulfield & Flood, eds., *Canadian Health Law and Policy*, 2d ed. (2002) 112; and Osborne, "Chapter 2: Consent to Treatment" in Sneiderman, Irvine & Osborne, eds., *Canadian Medical Law*, 3d ed. (2003) 19.

2. The common law principles of consent are increasingly being supplanted by complex, piecemeal legislation. For example the Ontario government proclaimed in force four statutes relating to consent, counselling and care in April 2005. The next year, the new provincial government repealed, repealed and replaced, or significantly amended the four statutes. Although the government media campaigns suggested that the legislation codified and consolidated the common law principles, this was simply not the case. For example, the *Health Care Consent Act, 1996*, S.O. 1996, c. 2, increased the information that health professionals must provide to patients, and altered the principles governing emergency treatment and substitute consent. Moreover, the treatment provisions of the statute only apply to regulated health practitioners such as doctors and dentists, leaving social workers, addiction counsellors, caregivers, and a broad range of others governed by the common law. While the statute defines the term "treatment" broadly, it then excludes a long list of procedures, examinations and circumstances from the definition. Thus, the statute replicates some common law principles but not others, and only applies to some healthcare and counselling professionals in certain circumstances.

If nothing else, this legislative flurry succeeded admirably in baffling many healthcare and counselling professionals. It should be noted that the courts have largely ignored the legislation in their analysis of tort claims. Can you suggest factors that would encourage governments to introduce and publicize this type of legislation?

3. In *Halushka v. University of Saskatchewan* (1965), 53 D.L.R. (2d) 436 at 443-44 (Sask. C.A.), the court stated that a doctor's obligation to potential research subjects

is at least equal to that owed to patients. Research subjects are entitled to a full and frank disclosure of all the facts, probabilities and opinions that a reasonable person would want before giving consent. See also *Cryderman v. Ringrose* (1978), 89 D.L.R. (3d) 32 (Alta. C.A.); *Weiss c. Solomon* (1989), 48 C.C.L.T. 280 (C.S. Qc.); and *Morrow v. Hôpital Royal Victoria* (1989), 3 C.C.L.T. (2d) 87 (Qc. C.A.).

4. Should a health professional have an affirmative duty to inform patients that a proposed treatment is experimental, novel or not the standard therapy? In *Coughlin v. Kuntz* (1989), 2 C.C.L.T. (2d) 42 (B.C.C.A.), the defendant surgeon had strong and unique views about an experimental surgery of his own design. Unfortunately, the surgery failed, prolonging the plaintiff's suffering and necessitating additional surgery. The doctor was held negligent for misdiagnosing the plaintiff's problem, proceeding with drastic, unsupported, experimental surgery, and failing to adequately inform the patient. In addition to compensatory damages, the plaintiff was awarded $25,000 in exemplary damages to punish the doctor for his arrogant disregard for his patient.

5. See generally Picard & Robertson, *Legal Liability of Doctors and Hospitals in Canada*, 3d ed. (1996) at 86-95; Glass & Lemmens, "Chapter 12: Research Involving Humans" in Downie, Caulfield & Flood, eds., *Canadian Health Law and Policy*, 2d ed. (2002) 459; and Côté, "Adequate Protection for the Autonomous Research Subject? The Disclosure of Sources of Funding and Commercialization in Genetic Research Trials" (2002) 28 Man. L.J. 347.

(b) EXCEPTIONS TO THE GENERAL PRINCIPLES OF CONSENT

Traditionally, the courts have relaxed the strict requirements of consent in three situations. First, in an unforeseen medical emergency, where it is impossible to obtain the patient's consent, a healthcare professional is allowed to intervene without consent to preserve the patient's health or life. This is the basis upon which emergency room staff and, for that matter, members of the public are permitted to provide treatment or first aid to unconscious accident victims. Although the next-of-kin may be consulted, their consent is irrelevant. This right to proceed without consent is narrowly defined.

The second exception to the principles of consent involves patients who have given a general consent to a course of counselling, a treatment program or an operation. In such situations, a patient will be viewed as implicitly consenting to any subsequent counselling sessions or subordinate tests and procedures that are necessarily incidental to the agreed treatment. However, this implied consent can be negated if the patient expressly objects.

Third, at one time, the Canadian courts held that healthcare professionals had a right to withhold information from a patient if its disclosure would undermine the patient's morale and discourage him or her from having needed treatment or surgery. The "therapeutic privilege to withhold information," as it was called, reflected the paternalistic notions of treatment relationships that existed at the time. In two somewhat conflicting cases, the Supreme Court of Canada cast doubt on the continued existence of the privilege: see *Hopp v. Lepp*, [1980] 2 S.C.R. 192 at 208; and *Reibl v. Hughes*, [1980] 2 S.C.R. 880 at 899-90. In keeping with the rise in patients' rights, the subsequent cases have either rejected the privilege altogether or narrowed its scope. See respectively

Meyer Estate v. Rogers (1991), 2 O.R. (3d) 356 (Gen. Div.); and *Pittman Estate v. Bain* (1994), 112 D.L.R. (4th) 257 (Ont. Gen. Div.).

MARSHALL v. CURRY

[1933] 3 D.L.R. 260 (N.S.S.C.)

CHISHOLM, C.J.:—The plaintiff, a master mariner residing at Clifton in the County of Colchester, brings this action in which he claims $10,000 damages against the defendant who is a surgeon of high standing, practising his profession in the City of Halifax.

The plaintiff in his statement of claim alleges: —

(1) That after being employed to perform and while performing an operation on the plaintiff for the cure of a hernia and while plaintiff was under the influence of an anaesthetic, the defendant without the knowledge or consent of the plaintiff removed the plaintiff's left testicle;

(2) In the alternative, that the defendant was negligent in diagnosing the case and in not informing the plaintiff that it might be necessary in treating the hernia to remove the testicle; and

(3) In the further alternative, that in removing the testicle in the above mentioned circumstances, the defendant committed an assault upon the plaintiff.

The defence, in addition to general denials, is, that the removal of the testicle was a necessary part of the operation for the cure of the hernia; that the necessity for removing the testicle could not have been reasonably ascertained by diagnosis before any operation was begun; that consent to the further operation was implied by plaintiff's request to cure the hernia, and that the plaintiff's claim is barred by the Statute of Limitations.

. . .

The defendant states that plaintiff had asked him in July, 1929, what he thought of this hernia. The defendant replied that there was a reasonable chance of curing it; that he thought it was a case suitable for the ordinary hernia operation: the abdominal muscles were in a reasonably good condition. In the operation the defendant found the muscles very much weaker than he had anticipated. In opening the inguinal canal the testicle appeared and was found grossly diseased; it was enlarged, nodular and softened. In order to cure the hernia it was necessary in defendant's opinion to obliterate the canal completely so as not to leave any space. The defendant deemed it necessary to remove the testicle in order to cure the hernia, and also because it would be a menace to the health and life of the plaintiff to leave it. That, he says, was his best judgment in the circumstances. After the operation the defendant cut the testicle in two and found multiple abscesses in it. The defendant gave, as his opinion that if the testicle had not been removed, it might have become gangrenous, and the pus might be absorbed into the circulation, and a condition of blood-poisoning have set up.

[The Court then considered various authorities which supported the following legal principles.]

1. That in the ordinary case where there is opportunity to obtain the consent of the patient it must be had. A person's body must be held inviolate and immune from invasion by the surgeon's knife, if an operation is not consented to. The rule applies not only to an operation but also to the case of mere examination, and it is pointed out in Taylor's Medical Jurisprudence, p. 59, that although the fact that a visit paid by a private patient to a practitioner implies consent to a certain amount of examination it must not be

concluded that such a visit entitles the practitioner to compel an examination more intimate than the patient desires. Such an examination can only be made with the patient's consent; if made without such consent, it is technically an assault.

2. That such consent by the patient may be express or implied. If an operation is forbidden by the patient, consent is not to be implied; and Taylor again says:—"It must be constantly remembered that in this connection silence does not give consent, nor is compliance to be taken as consent."

3. That consent may be implied from the conversation preceding an operation or from the antecedent circumstances. . . .

I am unable to see the force of the opinion, that in cases of emergency, where the patient agrees to a particular operation, and in the prosecution of the operation, a condition is found calling in the patient's interest for a different operation, the patient is said to have made the surgeon his representative to give consent. There is unreality about that view. The idea of appointing such a representation, the necessity for it, the existence of a condition calling for a different operation, are entirely absent from the minds of both patient and surgeon. The will of the patient is not exercised on the point. There is, in reality, no such appointment. I think it is better, instead of resorting to a fiction, to put consent altogether out of the case, where a great emergency which could not be anticipated arises, and to rule that it is the surgeon's duty to act in order to save the life or preserve the health of the patient; and that in the honest execution of that duty he should not be exposed to legal liability. It is, I think, more in conformity with the facts and with reason, to put a surgeon's justification in such cases on the higher ground of duty. . . .

. . .

In the case at bar, I find that the defendant after making the incisions on plaintiff's body, discovered conditions which neither party had anticipated, and which the defendant could not reasonably have foreseen, and that in removing the testicle he acted in the interest of his patient and for the protection of his health and possibly his life. The removal I find was in that sense necessary, and it would be unreasonable to postpone the removal to a later date. I come to this conclusion despite the absence of express and possibly of implied assent on the part of the plaintiff.

Action dismissed.

MALETTE v. SHULMAN

(1987), 47 D.L.R. (4th) 18 (Ont. H.C.)

[The plaintiff was seriously injured in a car accident and taken to the hospital where she was treated by Dr. Shulman. A nurse found a card in Mrs. Malette's wallet indicating that she was a Jehovah's Witness and was not to be given blood under any circumstances. Dr. Shulman was told about the card. However, when Mrs. Malette's condition deteriorated, Dr. Shulman, believing that she would otherwise die, started the first of several blood transfusions. When the plaintiff's daughter, Mrs. Bisson, arrived four hours later, she confirmed that her mother was a practicing Jehovah's Witness and ordered the blood transfusions to be stopped. Dr. Shulman only stopped the transfusions after the plaintiff's condition was stabilized. She was transferred to the Toronto General Hospital and made a good recovery. She then sued Dr. Shulman in negligence and battery.]

DONNELLY J.: Dr. Shulman, on being confronted by an unconscious patient in a life threatening situation in whose possession was found a card refusing blood as a Jehovah's Witness, faced a dilemma of dreadful finality. An immediate decision was required, either to follow the instruction given by the card or to administer the blood transfusion which he regarded as medically essential. He squarely faced the fundamental issue of the conflict between the patient's right over her own body and society's interest in preserving life.

Dr. Shulman acknowledged an awareness of the patient's right to make a decision against a certain treatment in favour of alternative treatment and of his ethical obligation to abide by that decision. However, upon considering the validity of the card, he was not reasonably satisfied that it constituted an adequate instruction because there was no evidence that: (1) it represented the plaintiff's current intent; (2) the instruction applied to the present life-threatening circumstances; (3) at the time the plaintiff made the decision and signed the card she was fully informed of risks of refusal of treatment and accordingly that this was a rational and informed decision.

. . .

The "card" was subject to attack by the defence on the basis of its inherent frailties — that it may have been signed because of religious peer pressure, under medical misinformation, not in contemplation of life threatening circumstances, or that it may not represent current instructions.

It was further argued on behalf of Dr. Shulman that the relatives' participation compounds the problem by adding further uncertainties, such as: is the relative the closest relative in blood; speaking for a unanimous consensus amongst the relatives; competent to give lawful consent; capable of understanding the risks, and devoid of self-interest?

Mrs. Bisson's participation has the effect of rendering unlikely these speculative frailties. It confirms the card and signature as her mother's, her mother's current status as a Jehovah's Witness and her mother's wish not to have blood. It raises nothing inconsistent with the card representing the mother's current intent applying to life threatening situations. The card itself presents a clear, concise statement, essentially stating, "As a Jehovah's Witness, I refuse blood". That message is unqualified. It does not exempt life threatening perils. On the face of the card, its message is seen to be rooted in religious conviction. Its obvious purpose as a card is as protection to speak in circumstances where the card carrier cannot (presumably because of illness or injury). There is no basis in evidence to indicate that the card may not represent the current intention and instruction of the card holder.

I therefore find that the card is a written declaration of a valid position which the card carrier may legitimately take in imposing a written restriction on her contract with the doctor. Dr. Shulman's doubt about the validity of the card, although honest, was not rationally founded on the evidence before him. Accordingly, but for the issue of informed refusal, there was no rationally founded basis for the doctor to ignore that restriction.

. . .

The defence contended that the doctrine of informed consent should be extended to informed refusal on the following analysis. Since there is an obligation on the doctor recommending treatment to advise as to the risks, it must logically follow there is a higher duty where the patient proposes a course of action that the doctor believes to be prejudicial. Thus Dr. Shulman was obliged in law to advise the refusing patient of the attendant risks. Only then could he be satisfied that the refusal was based on a proper understanding of risks. There was no opportunity to fulfill his obligation to ensure there was an opportunity for an informed choice and so he was not bound by the refusal of treatment.

No case has been cited supporting this concept of informed refusal of treatment. Accordingly, I proceed without the benefit of authority and rely upon the following analysis. The principle underlying the doctrine of informed consent finds its roots in the patient's well recognized right to self determination of his body. The patient has the right to decide what, if anything, will be done to his body: *Hopp v. Lepp* (1980), 112 D.L.R. (3d) 67, [1980] 2 S.C.R. 192, [1980] 4 W.W.R. 645. The treating doctor avoids liability for battery only with a valid consent. To be valid that consent must be informed. Hence the need for the doctor to explain risks. The doctor is legally and ethically obliged to treat within the confines of that consent. The same liability considerations do not apply to a patient's refusal to accept treatment. In that instance the doctor is not exposed to a claim in battery. The right to refuse treatment is an inherent component of the supremacy of the patient's right over his own body. That right to refuse treatment is not premised on an understanding of the risks of refusal.

However sacred life may be, fair social comment admits that certain aspects of life are properly held to be more important than life itself. Such proud and honourable motivations are long entrenched in society, whether it be for patriotism in war, duty by law enforcement officers, protection of the life of a spouse, son or daughter, death before dishonour, death before loss of liberty, or religious martyrdom. Refusal of medical treatment on religious grounds is such a value. . . .

. . .

The doctrine of informed consent does not extend to informed refusal. The written direction contained in the card was not properly disregarded on the basis that circumstances prohibited verification of that decision as an informed choice. The card constituted a valid restriction of Dr. Shulman's right to treat the patient and the administration of blood by Dr. Shulman did constitute battery.

[The judge awarded the plaintiff $20,000 in general damages for her mental distress. The Court of Appeal affirmed the trial judgment, but decided that it was unnecessary to address the issue of informed refusal. The court concluded that Dr. Shulman had no reason to doubt the validity of the instructions on the card: *Malette v. Shulman* (1990), 67 D.L.R. (4th) 321 (Ont. C.A.).]

NOTES AND QUESTIONS

1. Based on *Marshall*, what must a doctor establish in order to operate without the plaintiff's consent? Do you agree with the application of these principles to the facts?

In *Murray v. McMurchy*, [1949] 2 D.L.R. 442 (B.C.S.C.), the defendant surgeon tied the plaintiff's fallopian tubes during a Caesarian section when he discovered tumours in the wall of her uterus. The court held that the health hazards posed by the tumours in the event of a subsequent pregnancy did not warrant this drastic action and awarded the plaintiff $3,000 in damages. How would you reconcile *Marshall* and *Murray*? See also *Parmley v. Parmley*, [1945] S.C.R. 635.

2. Could *Malette* have been argued as a case involving an unforeseen medical emergency? Do you agree with the trial judge that a patient's refusal is valid even if it is not premised on an understanding of the risks? Would the decision have been the same if the plaintiff's daughter had not been a Jehovah's Witness and had urged Shulman to start the blood transfusions? See Siebrasse, "*Malette v. Shulman*: The Requirement of Consent in Medical Emergencies" (1989) 34 McGill L.J. 1080.

3. How sure must a health professional be that the patient prefers death to treatment? What should health professionals do if they suspect that a patient who is refusing lifesaving treatment is drunk or drugged, has a concussion, or is in shock?

4. What are the implications of *Malette* for cases of attempted suicide? Would you advise a doctor to pump the stomach of an unconscious patient who had taken a potentially lethal overdose of drugs and left a note explaining why death was preferable to living? Would the patient's reasons for wanting to die be relevant? What if the doctor was convinced that the patient was in a situational crisis and would want to live if he or she could be kept alive for several days?

In *Matheson v. Smiley*, [1932] 2 D.L.R. 787 (Man. C.A.), the deceased attempted to commit suicide and resisted a surgeon's efforts to save his life. Nevertheless, the surgeon recovered from the deceased's estate in unjust enrichment for the services that he had provided. Would the court reach the same result today?

5. In light of *Malette*, can a competent patient give a binding advance directive not to be resuscitated? See Silberfield, Madigan & Dickens, "Liability Concerns about the Implementation of Advance Directives" (1995) 14 Estates & Trusts J. 240; and Sneiderman, "Chapter 24: Patients' Advanced (Health Care) Directives" in Sneiderman, Irvine & Osborne, eds., *Canadian Medical Law*, 3d ed. (2002) 599. For a general discussion of do not resuscitate (DNR) orders see Hashimoto, "A Structural Analysis of the Physician-Patient Relationship in No-Code Decisionmaking" (1983) 93 Yale L.J. 362; and Griener, "Stopping Futile Treatment and the Slide Toward Non-Voluntary Euthanasia" (1994) 2 Health L.J. 67.

6. Can health professionals put a DNR order on a patient's chart when they believe that resuscitation is medically inappropriate, even if the patient or the patient's family objects? See *Re J (a minor) (wardship: medical treatment)*, [1990] 3 All E.R. 930 (C.A.); and *Child and Family Services of Central Manitoba v. Lavallee* (1997), 154 D.L.R. (4th) 409 (Man. C.A.). But see *Sawatzky v. Riverview Health Centre Inc.* (1998), 167 D.L.R. (4th) 359 (Man. Q.B.); and *Scardoni v. Hawryluck* (2004), 69 O.R. (3d) 700 (S.C.J.).

7. For a discussion of an individual's right to refuse lifesaving treatment, see *Re Attorney-General of British Columbia v. Astaforoff* (1983), 6 C.C.C. (3d) 498 (B.C.C.A.); *Canada (A.G.) v. Notre Dame Hospital* (1984), 8 C.R.R. 382 (Qc. S.C.); *Re C (adult: refusal of medical treatment)*, [1994] 1 All E.R. 819 (Fam. Div.); and *Re B (adult: refusal of medical treatment)*, [2002] 2 All E.R. 449 (Fam. Div.). See generally Gochnauer, "Refusal of Medical Treatment: Taking Respect for the Person Seriously" (1987) 2 C.J.L.S. 121; and Sneiderman, "Chapter 13: Decision-Making at the End of Life" in Downie, Caulfield & Flood, eds., *Canadian Health Law and Policy*, 2d ed. (2002) 501.

8. Can a health professional assist or be required to assist in withdrawing a patient from life-sustaining treatment? In *Nancy B. v. Hôtel-Dieu de Québec* (1992), 86 D.L.R. (4th) 385 (Qc. S.C.), the patient was granted an injunction requiring the hospital to turn off her respirator when she directed it to do so, even though this act would cause her death within minutes. Among other problems with the judgment, the court failed to seriously address s. 14 of the *Criminal Code*, which precludes anyone from giving a valid consent to having death inflicted upon him or her, and s. 241, which makes it a federal criminal offence to aid, assist or counsel a person to commit suicide. Nor did the court consider the earlier Québec case of *Notre Dame Hospital, supra*, which held that the right to self-determination was not absolute and could not be used to aid a person in committing suicide.

A distinction can be drawn between stopping ongoing life-sustaining treatment and actively assisting another person in killing him or herself. In *Rodriguez v. British Columbia (A.G.)*, [1993] 3 S.C.R. 519, the plaintiff wanted someone to administer a lethal injection to her when she was no longer physically capable of doing so herself. Consequently, the plaintiff challenged the *Criminal Code* provisions prohibiting assisted suicide as violating her *Charter* rights. In a five-to-four decision, the court upheld the constitutional validity of the assisted suicide provisions.

For a discussion of these and related issues see Gilmour, "Withholding and Withdrawing Life Support from Adults at Common Law" (1993) 31 Osgoode Hall L.J. 473; Canada, *Of Life and Death: Report of the Special Senate Committee on Euthanasia and Assisted Suicide* (1995); and Sneiderman, "Chapter 19: The Mentally Competent Adult Patient and the Refusal of Treatment" and "Chapter 18: Euthanasia, Assisting Suicide, and Termination of Life-Prolonging Treatment: Definitions and Overview" in Sneiderman, Irvine & Osborne, eds., *Canadian Medical Law*, 3d ed. (2002) 423 and 411.

(c) THE BURDEN OF PROOF AND CONSENT FORMS

Although the issue has generated academic debate, the courts have held that health professionals have the burden of proving consent on the balance of probabilities. In the absence of a statute to the contrary, the consent may be given orally or in writing. However, there has been a tendency for health professionals to be lulled into a false sense of security by having a signed consent form. A signed consent form provides only some evidence, not conclusive proof, of consent. The key issue is whether the patient understood the nature of the proposed procedures and their associated risks, and consented to them, not whether he or she signed a piece of paper.

A signed consent form is only as good as the information it contains and the circumstances in which it is signed. A consent form will be of little value if it is written in general terms that do not identify the proposed procedure and explain its risks, is too technical for the patient to understand, or is presented to the patient as a mere formality or in circumstances in which there is no opportunity to read it. Similar problems will arise if the patient signs a consent form while intoxicated, drugged or in severe pain.

NOTES AND QUESTIONS

1. A significant percentage of the Canadian population cannot read English. In *Montaron v. Wagner* (1988), 43 C.C.L.T. 233 (Alta. Q.B.), aff'd (1989), 70 Alta. L.R.

(2d) 86 (C.A.), the plaintiff, who had obvious difficulties in understanding English, signed a form that purported to provide his consent to a procedure that was far more radical than that to which he had orally agreed. Since no attempt had been made to ensure that he understood the procedure, the court held that the consent form was invalid. Would the result have been the same if the plaintiff's inability to read English had not been obvious? In other words, should health professionals assume that patients are functionally literate? See also *Adan v. Davis* (1998), 43 C.C.L.T. (2d) 262 (Ont. Gen. Div.).

2. In *Brushett v. Cowan* (1990), 83 Nfld. & P.E.I.R. 66 (Nfld. S.C. (A.D.)), the plaintiff consented to a muscle biopsy and signed a form that stated, "I also consent to such further or alternative measures as may be found to be necessary during the course of the operation." In performing the muscle biopsy, the defendant observed an abnormal area of bone and did a bone biopsy. The court held that the consent form should be interpreted broadly, consistent with the goal of determining the cause of the plaintiff's medical problem. Consequently, it held that the form provided consent for the bone biopsy. In contrast, the trial court had held that the open-ended wording of the consent form was too general to provide consent for the bone biopsy. Which judgment is preferable? See also *Pridham v. Nash* (1986), 57 O.R. (2d) 347 (H.C.).

3. For a discussion of the burden of proof and its relation to consent, see *McBain v. Laurentian Hospital* (1982), 35 C.P.C. 292 (Ont. H.C.); Blay, "Onus of Proof of Consent in an Action for Trespass to the Person" (1987) 61 Aust. L.J. 25; and Rhoden, "Litigating Life and Death" (1988) 102 Harv. L. Rev. 375.

(d) COMPETENCY TO CONSENT

To be valid, consent must be given by a patient who is legally competent. The common law test of competency focuses on the patient's ability to understand the nature of the proposed treatment and its risks, not his or her ability to make a reasoned or prudent decision. By defining competency broadly, the common law safeguards the autonomy of the individual. A patient may be competent even if he or she is intoxicated, on drugs, young, rash, immature, frail, or developmentally delayed. This test must be applied on a case-by-case basis in terms of the specific risks of the proposed treatment. A patient may be competent to make some treatment decisions, but not others. Similarly, a patient may be competent to make treatment decisions at one point in time, but not at others. If the patient is competent, it is his or her consent alone that is relevant. Indeed, it would be inappropriate to even discuss a patient's treatment with his or her next-of-kin without the patient's consent because that would constitute a breach of confidence.

(i) *Minors*

There is no recognized age of consent at common law for medical treatment or counselling. The test for competency is the same, whether the patient or client is a minor or an adult. If a minor is capable of understanding the nature of the proposed procedure and its risks, his or her consent is valid, and parental consent is not required or relevant. In some cases, the courts have relied on indicia of independence as a guide to the minor's competency.

In contrast to the common law's flexible test of competency, several provincial statutes, such as public hospital, mental health, human tissue gift, and child welfare legislation, may impose a minimum age requirement for consent to specified procedures.

C. v. WREN

(1986), 35 D.L.R. (4th) 419 (Alta. C.A.)

KERANS J.A.: [The judge began by emphasizing that the case was not about abortion, foetal rights or the operation of the hospital abortion committee. Rather, the only issue was the competency of the expectant mother to consent to the proposed procedure.]

. . .

A 16-year-old girl became pregnant by her boyfriend while she was living at home. Several weeks later, she abruptly left home and went elsewhere and has since avoided contact with her parents. She also attended on a physician and surgeon with a view to an abortion and has received approval for it by the statutory committee provided under the *Criminal Code*. The urgency of the matter is that a statutory deadline looms.

The suit here is by the parents against the doctor, and not the child. The doctor is not represented but the child has retained counsel and she intervenes.

. . .

The ground of appeal is that the learned chambers judge erred in finding that the expectant mother had given informed consent to the proposed surgical procedure.

The law in Alberta is that a surgeon may proceed with a surgical procedure immune from suits for assault if she or he has informed consent from the patient. That test was applied by the learned trial judge, and he found on the evidence before him that this child was capable of giving informed consent and had done so. Without more, that is an end to the matter.

It is argued before us today that informed consent means consent after consideration of issues like the ethics of abortion and the ethics of obligation by children to parents. It may be, as Lord Fraser has said in *Gillick v. West Norfolk & Wisbech Area Health Authority et al.*, [1985] 3 All E.R. 402, that doctors have an ethical obligation in circumstances like this to discuss issues of that sort with young patients. If so, the doctor would account to the College of Physicians and Surgeons for the performance of that obligation. That is not the issue before us today. Rather, the issue is whether these issues relate to the defence of consent to assault. In our view, they do not.

We agree with the learned chambers judge that no serious suggestion exists on the evidence here of a lack of informed consent. Accordingly, there are no grounds to enjoin the doctor from proceeding because there is no suggestion that there will be an illegal assault.

The real issue here relates to an obvious and painful dispute between parent and child about the appropriateness in non-medical terms of the proposed abortion. We express in that respect our sympathy both to the parents and the child for this unfortunate confrontation.

The real thrust of argument before us was that children should obey their parents and the courts should intervene to prevent others from interfering with parental control of those children who are committed to their custody and control. That is not quite the suit that has been brought here today, but we will deal with the issue. Parental rights (and obligations) clearly do exist and they do not wholly disappear until the age of majority. The modern law, however, is that the courts will exercise increasing restraint in that regard as a child grows to and through adolescence. The law and the development of the law in this respect was analyzed in detail by Lord Scarman in the *Gillick* case. He analyzes the law back to Blackstone and extracts this principle [at 421]:

> The principle is that parental right or power of control of the person and property of his child exists primarily to enable the parent to discharge his duty of maintenance, protection and education until he reaches such an age as to be able to look after himself and make his own decisions.

He then reviews the application of that principle in cases over the past century, especially in the "age of discretion" cases. He says [at 422]:

> The "age of discretion" cases are cases in which a parent or guardian (usually the father) has applied for habeas corpus to secure the return of his child who has left home without his consent. The courts would refuse an order if the child had attained the age of discretion, which came to be regarded as 14 for boys and 16 for girls, and did not wish to return. The principle underlying them was plainly that an order would be refused if the child had sufficient intelligence and understanding to make up his own mind.

He then concludes that the governing rule is [at 423]:

> In the light of the foregoing I would hold that as a matter of law the parental right to determine whether or not their minor child below the age of 16 will have medical treatment terminates if and when the child achieves a sufficient understanding and intelligence to enable him or her to understand fully what is proposed.

We accept that in that context he says that "understand fully" means understand things like obligation to parents as well as medical matters.

What is the application of the principle in this case? We infer from the circumstances detailed in argument here that this expectant mother and her parents had fully discussed the ethical issues involved and, most regrettably, disagreed. We cannot infer from that disagreement that this expectant mother did not have sufficient intelligence and understanding to make up her own mind. Meanwhile, it is conceded that she is a "normal intelligent 16 year old". We infer that she did have sufficient intelligence and understanding to make up her own mind and did so. At her age and level of understanding, the law is that she is to be permitted to do so.

Accordingly, we dismiss the appeal.

NOTES AND QUESTIONS

1. What was the basis for the decision in *C. v. Wren*? Would the court have reached the same decision if C. had been 14 years old and living at home? What impact, if any, would these factors have had on C.'s competency? See generally Gilmour, "Chapter 7: Children, Adolescents, and Health Care" in Downie, Caulfield & Flood, eds., *Canadian Health Law and Policy*, 2d ed. (2002) 205.

2. Section 215 of the *Criminal Code* requires parents and guardians to provide the "necessaries of life" for a child under the age of 16. The failure to do so without a lawful

excuse constitutes a federal criminal offence. The provincial child welfare legislation typically imposes a similar legal duty on parents and guardians. What impact does this penal legislation have on the common law principles that permit competent children to make their own treatment decisions regardless of their parents' wishes?

3. In *Re Dueck* (1999), 171 D.L.R. (4th) 761 (Sask. Q.B.), a 13-year-old boy refused chemotherapy and surgery, which the paediatric oncologist indicated had a 65% chance of resulting in recovery. The boy believed his father, who told him that God would heal him and that there was a treatment in California and Mexico that had an 85% to 90% cure rate without surgery. This "treatment" was not medically recognized, and there was no evidence that it had any beneficial effect. The psychologist and psychiatrist indicated that the boy had no developmental impairment that would prevent him from being competent. However, the boy was less mature than the average 13-year-old, and his father was a dominating authority figure who made the rules in the house.

The court stated that if the boy was a mature minor (*i.e.* competent), then his wishes would be respected. In making this determination, the court considered the child's age and maturity, the extent of the child's dependence on his or her guardians, and the complexity of the treatment. Given the profound influence of the domineering father and his misguided faith in a non-existent cure, the boy was not able to understand the relevant medical information or appreciate the consequences of the proposed treatment. Consequently, the boy was not a mature minor and an order was made extending the Minister's authority to make medical decisions on the boy's behalf.

For cases involving Jehovah's Witnesses, youth and blood transfusions, see *Re L.D.K.; Children's Aid Society of Metropolitan Toronto v. K. and K.* (1985), 48 R.F.L. (2d) 164 (Ont. Prov. Ct.) (12-year-old); *Walker (Litigation Guardian of) v. Region 2 Hospital Corp.* (1994), 116 D.L.R. (4th) 477 (N.B.C.A.) (15-year-old); and *B.(R.) v. Children's Aid Society of Metropolitan Toronto*, [1995] 1 S.C.R. 315 (infant). For other cases involving the competency of minors see *Van Mol (Guardian ad litem of) v. Ashmore* (1999), 44 C.C.L.T. (2d) 228 (B.C.C.A.); and *Chmiliar v. Chmiliar* (2001), 295 A.R. 140 (Q.B.).

4. In *C.(L.) v. Pinhas*, 2002 CarswellOnt 4793 (S.C.J.) (WLeC), the 15-year-old plaintiff had to be hospitalized for her anorexia. The psychiatrists found that she was not competent (under s. 4(1) of the Ontario *Health Care Consent Act, 1996*, S.O. 1996, c. 2, Sched. A) to make decisions about the proposed tube-feeding to which she had objected. The plaintiff challenged the psychiatrists' finding to the Ontario Consent and Capacity Board. According to the psychiatrists, the illness itself prevented the plaintiff from making informed decisions, even though she intellectually understood the life-threatening risks of continuing to not eat. The Board concluded that she was not competent, and the plaintiff appealed. The court agreed with the Board that the patient's non-compliance was relevant to capacity in psychiatric disorders such as anorexia, where the patient is intellectually capable of understanding the medical risks of refusing treatment. See also *Re W (a minor)*, [1992] 4 All E.R. 627 (C.A.); and Health Canada, *A Report on Mental Health* (2002) at 79-89.

5. As discussed, some courts have negated the plaintiff's otherwise valid consent on "public policy" grounds. Given these cases, can you rationalize upholding a competent minor's refusal of life-sustaining treatment? What is the justification for negating a

competent minor's medical decisions but not the equally life-threatening decisions of competent adults?

REVIEW PROBLEM

The Children's Aid Society received information that Sara, a 13-year-old girl, had been sexually abused by her father. When confronted, Sara denied the allegations and appeared very upset. She expressed concern about the impact that such a charge would have on her father and family. Sara's school friends said that Sara was afraid of her father. The Society has requested that Sara undergo a medical examination at the local Children's Hospital. Both Sara and her parents have vehemently refused consent to the examination. Advise the Society as to its potential tort liability if it proceeds with the examination. See *M. v. Toronto Board of Education* (1987), 38 D.L.R. (4th) 627 (Ont. H.C.).

(ii) *Adults*

The issue of an adult's competency arises most often in cases involving mentally ill or senile patients. However, the fact that a patient is mentally ill or senile does not necessarily mean that he or she is incapable of giving a valid consent. Health professionals must assess the capacity of each patient in relation to the specific procedure or treatment. These principles apply equally to those in custody or under other legal restraints, unless there is express statutory authority to the contrary. For example, the fact that a patient's refusal to consent to treatment may constitute a violation of his or her probation does not alter the healthcare professional's obligation to abide by the decision.

NOTES AND QUESTIONS

1. In *Starson v. Swayze*, [2003] 1 S.C.R. 722, the patient had been frequently institutionalized. His latest psychiatric admission resulted from being found not criminally responsible by reason of mental disability for making death threats. The patient insisted on being called Professor Starson, even though he held no academic position and his family name was not Starson. His psychiatrist concluded that he suffered from a bipolar disorder and prescribed anti-psychotic medication. Starson refused the medication because he believed that similar medication had previously interfered with his research. Although not formally trained, Starson was brilliant, had published extensively and was accepted as a peer by some leading physicists. Starson's psychiatrist believed that he was not competent to refuse consent to the proposed medication. After Starson threatened to kill his first psychiatrist, a second psychiatrist was called in and he also concluded that Starson was not competent. The Consent and Capacity Board upheld the psychiatrists' findings.

Starson appealed the Board's decision. The court was extremely critical of the Board's reliance on the psychiatrists' recounting of Starson's medical and criminal records without introducing the documents into evidence. The court stated that Starson acknowledged that he had mental health problems and showed understanding of his condition. He made a clear choice to reject the medication, because it interfered with the high energy level that he believed was conducive to creative thought. The court concluded that Starson was competent because he understood the relevant information and appreciated the consequences of his decision. The Court of Appeal for Ontario and the majority of the Supreme Court of Canada upheld the trial judgment.

In the Supreme Court of Canada, the three dissenting justices held that there was no basis for overturning the Board's finding of incapacity. There was ample evidence that Starson was in "almost total" denial of his mental illness. This denial was compounded by his inability, because of his delusional state, to understand the information relevant to making a treatment decision. He lacked the ability to appreciate the possible benefits of the proposed medications, that he would be unlikely to return to his previous level of functioning without the medication, that his condition could deteriorate further, and that the lack of treatment would likely prevent his future release.

Starson's subsequent application for release from the facility was denied by the Ontario Review Board and this decision was upheld by the Court of Appeal: *R. v. Starson* (2004), 184 O.A.C. 338 (C.A.). Would the court have reached the same conclusion on Starson's competency had he not been as scientifically accomplished? Is it in society's or mentally-ill patients' interests to be detained in psychiatric hospitals without treatment? See Kelly *et al.*, "Treatment Delays for Involuntary Psychiatric Patients Associated with Reviews of Treatment Capacity" (2002) 47 Can. J. Psychiatry 181.

2. For additional cases on competency and mental health patients see *Re C (adult: refusal of medical treatment)*, [1994] 1 All E.R. 819 (Fam. Div.); *Neto v. Klukach* (2004), 12 Admin. L.R. (4th) 101 (Ont. S.C.J.); *Conway v. Jacques* (2005), 250 D.L.R. (4th) 178 (Ont. S.C. J.); and *K.J.D. v. Choy* (2006), 25 E.T.R. (3d) 41 (Ont. S.C.J.).

3. The Canadian courts have held that consent given while a patient is sedated or in pain may be invalid. See *Beausoleil v. Soeurs de la Charité de la Providence* (1964), 53 D.L.R. (2d) 65 (Qc. Q.B.); and *Ferguson v. Hamilton Civic Hospitals* (1983), 23 C.C.L.T. 254 (Ont. H.C.), aff'd (1985), 33 C.C.L.T. 56 (Ont. C.A.). In *Mitchell v. McDonald* (1987), 80 A.R. 16 (Q.B.), the court held that the plaintiff's agonized plea, "For God's sake, stop," in the middle of an injection did not constitute an express withdrawal of consent, but rather a plea to stop the pain. See also *Ciarlariello v. Schacter*, [1993] 2 S.C.R. 119.

4. Healthcare professionals must refuse police requests to take blood samples or conduct other tests on unwilling or unconscious suspects. This situation must be distinguished from unforeseen medical emergencies in which medical staff intervene in an effort to save the suspect's life. Nevertheless, the samples or test results obtained in the course of emergency treatment should not be given to the police. Rather, the police must obtain a search warrant authorizing the seizure of this evidence. In 1985, Parliament introduced a special warrant authorizing health professionals to take blood samples from unconscious drinking and driving suspects in limited circumstances. See *Criminal Code*, s. 256. In 1995, Parliament introduced special warrant provisions permitting the collection of hair, saliva and blood samples for DNA testing from those suspected of committing "designated" offences. See *Criminal Code*, ss. 487.04-487.09; and *Youth Criminal Justice Act*, S.C. 2002, c. 1, s. 119(6).

5. For a discussion of the consent of prisoners and the mentally ill, see Somerville, "Refusal of Medical Treatment in 'Captive' Circumstances" (1985) 63 Can. Bar Rev. 59; Miller, "The US Supreme Court Looks at Voluntariness and Consent" (1994) 17

Int'l J. L. & Psych. 239; and Schell, Malcolmson & Klassen, "The Hospitalized Psychiatric Patient: Clinical And Legal Aspects of Care" in Bloom & Bay, eds., *A Practical Guide to Mental Health, Capacity, and Consent Law of Ontario* (1996) 255-91.

6. For a discussion of consent and the elderly, see Wahl & Leclair, "The Geriatric Patient" in Bloom & Bay, eds., *A Practical Guide to Mental Health, Capacity and Consent Law in Ontario* (1996) 343-77.

(e) SUBSTITUTE CONSENT

Certain patients, such as young children and the severely mentally ill, are clearly incapable of giving a valid consent to treatment. The practice in such cases has been for health professionals to obtain substitute consent from the patient's next-of-kin. The courts have upheld these consents provided the patient was incompetent, the next-of-kin acted in good faith and the procedure was in the patient's best interest. While relatively easy to state, these principles may be extremely difficult to apply.

The legal issues concerning substitute consent are even more complex when the procedure is performed solely for research purposes. Since these procedures cannot be justified as being in the patient's best interest, the substitute consent may be invalid and the researcher may be exposed, at least in theory, to civil and criminal liability. In response, it is argued that research based on substitute consent is essential to the development of effective treatment for childhood diseases, degenerative mental illnesses and other medical conditions. To date these issues have been discussed in the medical and legal communities but have not been addressed by the legislatures or the courts.

NOTES AND QUESTIONS

1. In *E.(Mrs.) v. Eve*, [1986] 2 S.C.R. 388, the court unanimously held that the non-therapeutic sterilization of a mentally incompetent adult could never be justified as being in the patient's best interests pursuant to a substitute consent. LaForest J., writing for the court, stated that the interests of the parents, the institution or others could not be considered in defining the patient's best interests. But see *Re B (a minor) (wardship: sterilization)*, [1987] 2 All E.R. 206 at 213 (H.L.), where Lord Hailsham stated in regard to LaForest J.'s analysis:

> . . . I find, with great respect, his conclusion . . . that the procedure of sterilisation 'should *never* be authorised for non-therapeutic purposes' (my emphasis) totally unconvincing and in startling contradictions to the welfare principle which should be the first and paramount consideration in wardship cases. Moreover, . . . the distinction he purports to draw between 'therapeutic' and 'non-therapeutic' purposes of this operation . . . [is] totally meaningless. . . . To talk of the 'basic right' to reproduce of an individual who is not capable of knowing the causal connection between intercourse and childbirth, the nature of pregnancy, what is involved in delivery, unable to form maternal instincts or to care for a child appears to me wholly to part company with reality.

Which judgment is preferable? See Keyserlingk, "The Eve Decision — A Common Law Perspective" (1987) 18 R.G.D. 657; Grubb & Pearl, "Sterilisation and the Courts" [1987] C.L.J. 439; and Olesen, "*Eve* and the Forbidden Fruit: Reflections on a Feminist Methodology" (1994) 3 Dal. J. Leg. Stud. 231.

2. In *Re K. and Public Trustee* (1985), 19 D.L.R. (4th) 255 (B.C.C.A.), the court authorized a hysterectomy on a girl with a severe mental disability who had a phobic aversion to blood and would otherwise begin menstruation soon. In *E.(Mrs.)*, *supra*, the Supreme Court of Canada questioned the decision in *Re K.*, but ultimately distinguished it on the grounds that it raised a different issue than sterilization for contraceptive purposes. Do you agree?

3. In *E.(Mrs.)*, the court emphasized that the interests of others cannot be considered in exercising substitute consent on behalf of incompetent patients. Is the court disadvantaging incompetent individuals by ignoring the interests of their caregivers? What are the implications of the court's approach for the validity of substitute consent to tissue and organ donations, circumcision for religious purposes and research? See Baylis, Downie & Kenny, "Children and Decisionmaking in Health Research" (1999) 8:2 Health L. Rev. 3.

4. In *Muir v. Alberta* (1996), 179 A.R. 321 (Q.B.) the Alberta government was held liable for almost $750,000 for wrongfully institutionalizing and sterilizing the plaintiff under the provincial "mental defectives" legislation. Among other things, the province was held liable for: failing to follow its own legislation in institutionalizing the plaintiff as a "moron"; failing to undertake a timely social or psychological assessment; ignoring an expert who indicated that the plaintiff's problems stemmed from her chaotic home life and not from mental disability; administering her anti-psychotic medication from time to time even though she had never been diagnosed as being psychotic; and sterilizing her in 1958 contrary to the statute.

Over 2,900 people had been sterilizing under the provincial statute, which had been enacted in 1928 and was not repealed until 1972, well after the eugenics movement had been discredited. British Columbia and at least 15 American states had similar legislation. After a failed attempt to legislatively limit similar claims, Alberta provided an $80 million compensation package for approximately 290 individuals: see *Edmonton Journal* (2 November 1999). See also Newman, "An Examination of Saskatchewan Law on the Sterilization of Persons with Mental Disabilities" (1999) 62 Sask. L. Rev. 329; and *E.(D.) (Guardian ad litem of) v. British Columbia* (2005), 28 C.C.L.T. (3d) 283 (B.C.C.A.).

5. In *Re A (children) (conjoined twins: surgical separation)*, [2000] 4 All E.R. 961 (C.A.), Jodie and Mary were born joined at the pelvis. The medical evidence indicated that if they were not separated, both would certainly die within three to six months. The evidence also indicated that if they were separated, Mary would certainly die, but Jodie would most likely live. The twins' parents, devout Roman Catholics, refused to consent to the operation on religious grounds. They believed that Jodie and Mary were equal in God's eyes and that one could not be sacrificed for the other. Nevertheless, the court upheld a declaration authorizing the surgery. Although the paramount consideration was the children's welfare, the court stated that it was entitled to prefer Jodie's interests over Mary's given the exceptional circumstances. It had to choose "the lesser of two evils." The court also reiterated that, in the case of young children, the parents' wishes are not always determinative. Finally, the court held that while the surgeon's proposed actions would otherwise constitute a crime, namely killing Mary, the defence of necessity would apply.

Do you agree with the court's decision? Assume that both conjoined twins would certainly die if they were not separated; only one twin would live if separated; and each twin has an equal chance of surviving on her own. On what basis would you decide in favour of one twin over the other? See Bainham, "Resolving the Unresolvable: The Case of the Conjoined Twins" [2000] C.L.J. 49.

6. In what circumstances, if any, is it appropriate for parents to deny or withhold life-sustaining treatment from a disabled child? See *Re Superintendent of Family & Child Service and Dawson* (1983), 145 D.L.R. (3d) 610 (B.C.S.C.); *Couture-Jacquet v. Montreal Children's Hospital* (1986), 28 D.L.R. (4th) 22 (Qc. C.A.); *Re J (a minor) (wardship: medical treatment)*, [1992] 4 All E.R. 614 (C.A.); and *Child and Family Services of Central Manitoba v. Lavallee* (1997), 154 D.L.R. (4th) 409 (Man. C.A.). See also Keyserlingk, "Non-Treatment in the Best Interests of the Child" (1987) 32 McGill L.J. 413; Magnet & Kluge, *Withholding Treatment from Defective Newborn Children* (1985); Griffith, "The Best Interests Standard: A Comparison of the State's Parens Patriae Authority and Judicial Oversight in Best Interests Determinations for Children and Incompetent Patients" (1991) 7 Issues L. & Med. 283; and Sniederman, "Chapter 23: Foregoing of Treatment for Neonates and Pre-Adolescents" in Sneiderman, Irvine & Osborne, eds., *Canadian Medical Law*, 3d ed. (2002) 579.

7. In *Superintendent of Belchertown State School v. Saikewicz*, 370 N.E.2d 417 (Mass. S.C. 1977), the court considered whether a 67-year-old man with a severe disability who was dying of leukaemia should undergo painful chemotherapy to prolong his life. The chemotherapy would not provide a cure, but rather a 30% to 40% chance of a temporary remission. On average, the remission prolonged the patient's life by one year. Saikewicz had an IQ of ten and because of this extremely limited mental capacity he could not co-operate with chemotherapy. He was not in any pain and was expected to die relatively painlessly within weeks or months if he was not given chemotherapy. The trial court held that the chemotherapy was not in Saikewicz's best interests and ordered that no treatment be administered. The appeal court affirmed the decision.

Was it in Saikewicz's best interests to be allowed to die without treatment? Do you think the decision would have, or should have, been the same if the therapy had a 30% to 40% chance of prolonging his life by five years? What are the implications of *Saikewicz* for patients who are in a coma? See for example *Frenchay Healthcare National Health Service Trust v. S.*, [1994] 2 All E.R. 403 (C.A.); *London Health Sciences Centre v. K.(R.) (Litigation Guardian of)* (1997), 152 D.L.R. (4th) 724 (Ont. Gen. Div.); *Scardoni v. Hawryluck* (2004), 69 O.R. (3d) 700 (S.C.J.); and *Schiavo ex rel. Schindler v. Schiavo*, 544 U.S. 957 (2005). See generally "Symposium — Mental Incompetents and the Right to Die" (1977) 11:4 Suffolk U.L. Rev.; and Sneiderman, "Chapter 22: The Mentally Incompetent Adult Patient and Foregoing of Life-Prolonging Treatment" in Sneiderman, Irvine & Osborne, eds., *Canadian Medical Law*, 3d ed. (2002) 551.

(f) INFORMED CONSENT: BATTERY OR NEGLIGENCE?

Traditionally, a doctor's failure to obtain a valid consent was viewed as a basis for a battery claim, whether the lack of consent was due to a failure to disclose the risks or misrepresentation. In the late 1950s, the American courts began to analyze some medical consent cases in terms of negligence, asking whether the doctor failed to exercise a reasonable standard of care in advising the patient of the nature of the procedure and its risks. The Canadian courts adopted a similar approach. As in the United States, this development created uncertainty as to the boundary between medical battery and medical negligence.

The Supreme Court of Canada addressed this issue in *Reibl v. Hughes*, [1980] 2 S.C.R. 880 and *Hopp v. Lepp*, [1980] 2 S.C.R. 192. It held that once patients are aware of the general nature of the treatment, they cannot bring a battery claim alleging that they were not informed of the risks. Rather, battery claims are limited to cases in which the patient did not consent at all, the consent was exceeded, or the consent was obtained fraudulently. In all other cases, the plaintiff must bring a negligence claim for failure to disclose the risks. By requiring a plaintiff to frame these actions in negligence, the Supreme Court of Canada has significantly limited the scope of health professionals' potential liability.

REVIEW PROBLEM

A physician has contacted you about a 62-year-old alcoholic patient in the emergency room. The patient, who lives alone, fell down his stairs and lay at the bottom for several hours before his daughter found him. The patient has a bad gash that requires stitches, but the physician is more concerned about the patient's alcoholism, which has repeatedly brought him into hospital since his wife died two years ago. The physician wants to admit the patient to hospital for about a week in order to "sober him up," conduct medical tests and procedures related to his alcoholism, stabilize his deteriorating physical condition, and encourage him to enter an alcohol treatment program.

The patient is still somewhat intoxicated, but fully aware of his surroundings. At his daughter's urging, he has reluctantly agreed to have the gash sutured, sleep over in the hospital, and undergo "any stupid tests you want." However, the patient vehemently denies that he is an alcoholic or that his drinking has caused any problems in his life. If his past behaviour is any indication, the patient will leave the next day as soon as he feels well enough to get a cab and go home.

The patient's daughter has pleaded with the physician to keep her father in the hospital long enough to get him back on his feet and break his cycle of self-destructive behaviour. In the daughter's view, her father's denial of his alcoholism and rapidly deteriorating physical and mental health provide overwhelming proof of his incompetency. She is willing to sign whatever documents are necessary to give substitute consent for her father's hospitalization and treatment.

The physician has sought your advice on two issues. First, is the patient competent to consent to his admission to hospital and treatment that night? Second, would the patient be competent to refuse treatment and leave the hospital the next day?

7

DEFENCES RELATED TO THE PROTECTION OF PERSON AND PROPERTY

1. Introduction
2. Self-Defence
3. Defence of Third Parties
4. Discipline
5. Defence of Real Property
6. Defence and Recaption of Chattels
7. Public and Private Necessity
8. Apportionment of Fault in Intentional Torts

1. Introduction

In the previous chapter, we began an examination of the defences to intentional torts by considering the defence of consent. In this chapter, we consider several defences pertaining to the protection of person and property.

2. Self-Defence

In order to invoke the defence of self-defence, the defendant must establish on the balance of probabilities that: (i) he or she honestly and reasonably believed that an assault was imminent; and (ii) the amount of force that he or she used to avert the risk was reasonable in all of the circumstances. The defendant's right to invoke the defence ends once the danger has passed. Self-defence is a complete defence. If the plaintiff successfully invokes the defence, he or she will be absolved of liability.

WACKETT v. CALDER
(1965), 51 D.L.R. (2d) 598 (B.C.C.A.)

MACLEAN J.A. (dissenting): The defendant appeals a judgment for damages for an assault following an encounter between the plaintiff and defendant in a beer parlour at Dawson Creek, B.C.

The facts have been found by the learned trial Judge as follows:

> The most accurate account of what occurred outside the hotel is to be found in the evidence of the defendant and of his brother, Raymond Calder, both of whom were truthful witnesses. The plaintiff testified untruthfully on so many occasions as to the events that occurred earlier that afternoon and during the evening in question that it is impossible to give any credence to his evidence except where it is corroborated by other credible evidence. Having arrived outside, the plaintiff reiterated his insulting remarks and invited the defendant to engage in a fight. He endeavoured, without much success,

> to strike both the defendant and his brother. He lurched at them and with his fists pounded them in a rather futile way upon their chests, doing no harm whatever. On one occasion when the plaintiff struck at the defendant, the defendant hit the plaintiff in the face with his fist, knocking the plaintiff to the ground. The plaintiff got up and went for the defendant again. The defendant hit him again and that time the plaintiff "didn't get up so fast." The defendant then returned to the beer parlour, leaving the plaintiff still wanting to fight.

The learned Judge then went on to find that the force used by the defendant was excessive under the circumstances, and finally he concluded:

> The anger of the defendant is easily understood, but it is the policy of the law to discourage violence. Challenges to fight are accepted at some considerable peril, at law. It must have been apparent to the defendant soon after he went outside that the plaintiff's challenge to fight was alcoholic-induced bravado and that, by reason of his intoxication, he was incapable of anything but talk and wild swinging. The defendant could and should have terminated the whole unpleasant episode by returning into the hotel, leaving the authorities to deal with the plaintiff. Instead he delivered two blows to the face of the plaintiff with considerable force — sufficient to knock him down and break a well-protected bone in the cheek. While it is not clear how the plaintiff's wrist got broken, I think it is probable that he must have fallen upon it during the fight.

In my view there is implicit in this judgment a finding that the defendant was not entitled to rely on self-defence — he could have walked away and avoided "the unpleasant episode by returning to the hotel", and secondly, that even if he was entitled to use force to defend himself, he used "excessive force under the circumstances".

I take it that in coming to the latter conclusion the learned Judge was aware of the long line of cases which enunciate the principle that a defendant or accused person when attacked is not required to "measure with complete nicety" the force necessary to repel the attack or apprehended attack: *R. v. Ogal*, [1928] 3 D.L.R. 676, 50 C.C.C. 71, 23 A.L.R. 511, [1928] 2 W.W.R. 465.

In my view the learned Judge's conclusions are supported by the evidence and I would not venture to disturb his judgment.

I would dismiss the appeal.

BULL J.A. [Davey J.A. concurring]: . . . It is clear that what constitutes excessive force beyond what was reasonably necessary under all circumstances depends in each case upon its own facts, and is a matter for the trial Judge, the findings of whom an appellate Court should not lightly question. However, with the greatest deference, it seems apparent that the finding of excessive force was based on conclusions and inferences from evidence which did not wholly support them. Although there was evidence that the respondent was clearly intoxicated, there was no evidence that he was physically incapacitated or unduly unco-ordinated, or in any way incapable of doing serious physical damage to others. He was a man of middle age weighing some 192 pounds and the evidence was clear that he was not staggering, but was in a belligerent and obviously dangerous mood. Again, the learned trial Judge, in giving his views as to what the appellant might have done to end the dispute, seems to have overlooked the evidence of both the appellant and his brother, both of whom he found truthful witnesses, that they were turning away to re-enter the hotel when the respondent attacked and struck the appellant the second time and, received, in turn, the appellant's second blow. It seemed clear that it was this second blow which was the most serious and caused the injury to the defendant's face.

As the learned trial Judge weighed the force used on conclusions which were, in part at least, unsupported by the evidence, an appellate Court is justified in reassessing the evidence directed to this issue and is, I submit with deference, in as good a position as the trial Judge to do so.

The only question here was whether the two blows by the appellant were more than reasonably necessary under all the attendant circumstances, and no question of the use of disproportionate force is involved. The appellant was entitled to reject force with force and, under the authorities, not being bound to take a passive defence, is entitled to return blow for blow. He could act in the light of the apparent urgency of the situation, but he could not trespass beyond the reasonable limits thereof. However, it has been long held that an attacked person defending himself and confronted with a provoking situation is not held down to measure with exactitude or nicety the weight or power of his blows.

In this case there is no evidence whatsoever that the two blows given by appellant were vicious. That one at least was forceful is obvious, but the combined effect of both were not sufficient to render the intoxicated respondent "hors de combat". The first blow was insufficient to stop the respondent's attack on the appellant, and, in my respectful opinion, the second more forceful blow was well justified to put an end to the episode.

Accordingly, on the facts as found by the learned trial Judge, excluding only his conclusions as to the quantum or measure of force used, I would allow the appeal and order the action dismissed.

NOTES AND QUESTIONS

1. Was the defendant in danger of physical injury? Must the defendant prove that the plaintiff posed a threat of physical injury, or merely a threat of any socially offensive or physically harmful contact? See *Cachay v. Nemeth* (1972), 28 D.L.R. (3d) 603 (Sask. Q.B.).

2. Is Maclean J.A. suggesting that self-defence cannot be used by a defendant who ignored an opportunity to walk away from a fight? Would you favour the adoption of this principle? What impact, if any, should the fact that the defendant did not walk away from the threat have on the issue of excessive force?

3. Did the defendant use excessive force in the circumstances? Can you reconcile the principle that the force used must be reasonable and the concept that a person who is attacked is not required to measure with "nicety the weight of his blows?" The burden of proof is on the defendant to establish that he or she was in danger and used only reasonable force: see *Mann v. Balaban*, [1970] S.C.R. 74.

4. In determining whether the force used was excessive, the court should consider the nature of the force used and the circumstances, but not necessarily the resultant injuries. For example in *Brown v. Wilson* (1975), 66 D.L.R. (3d) 295 (B.C.S.C.), the defendant picked up Brown, who was about to hit him, in a "bear hug." In attempting to carry Brown out of the bar, the defendant slipped and Brown fell, hitting his head on the concrete. Although Brown died, the court held that the use of a bear hug was reasonable

in the circumstances even though it led to a tragic result. See also *McLean v. 366543 B.C. Ltd.*, 1995 CarswellBC 2745 (S.C.) (WLeC), aff'd 1997 CarswellBC 2147 (C.A.) (WLeC); and *MacMillan v. Hincks* (2002), 313 A.R. 150 (Q.B.).

5. Evidence that the defendant was convicted of criminal assault provides strong proof against a plea of self-defence in a related civil action. See *Simpson v. Geswein*, [1995] 6 W.W.R. 233 (Man. Q.B.); and *Herman v. Graves* (1998), 217 A.R. 275 (Q.B.).

6. The criminal courts now use a subjective/objective test in determining whether the defendant used excessive force in the circumstances. In *Beckford v. R.*, [1987] 3 All E.R. 425 (P.C.), the court stated that the accused is expected to react to the threat that he or she subjectively perceives as would a reasonable person in the circumstances. See also *R. v. Pétel*, [1994] 1 S.C.R. 3; and *R. v. Cinous*, [2002] 2 S.C.R. 3.

7. The right to use force that is likely to cause death or serious physical injury is limited to situations in which the defendant honestly and reasonably believes that such force is necessary to protect himself or herself from death or serious physical injury. See the *Criminal Code*, R.S.C. 1985, c. C-46, ss. 34-35; *R. v. Smith* (1837), 173 E.R. 441 (N.P.); and *R. v. Bogue* (1976), 30 C.C.C. (2d) 403 (Ont. C.A.). Contrary to some American authorities, the Canadian courts will not permit a person to use deadly force in self-defence merely because the altercation took place in his or her home. Contrast *State v. Johnson*, 136 S.E.2d 84 (N.C.S.C. 1964) and *Veinot v. Veinot* (1977), 22 N.S.R. (2d) 630 (C.A.).

8. For a discussion of self-defence in the context of resisting arrest and search, see *Kenlin v. Gardiner*, [1966] 3 All E.R. 931 (Div. Ct.); *R. v. Larlham*, [1971] 4 W.W.R. 304 (B.C.C.A.); *Albert v. Lavin*, [1981] 3 All E.R. 878 (H.L.); and *R. v. Colet*, [1981] 1 S.C.R. 2.

9. A defendant does not have to wait for the other party to strike the first blow. A defendant who attempts to pre-empt an assault by becoming the aggressor may still invoke self-defence. The plaintiff's reputation for violence or prior violent behaviour can be raised to justify the defendant's decision to strike first. See *R. v. Scopelliti* (1981), 63 C.C.C. (2d) 481 (Ont. C.A.); *R. v. Ryan* (1989), 76 Nfld. & P.E.I.R. 26 (Nfld. C.A.); and *Bruce v. Dyer*, [1966] 2 O.R. 705 (H.C.), aff'd [1970] 1 O.R. 482n (C.A.).

10. A more complex situation arises where the defendant kills a person to end an ongoing relationship of violence. In *R. v. Lavallee*, [1990] 1 S.C.R. 852, a battered woman shot her partner in the back of the head as he was leaving the room. He had beaten her frequently. On that night, he physically abused and taunted her, stating that he would kill her if she did not kill him. A psychiatrist testified at trial about the difficulty battered women have in escaping abusive relationships and the ongoing terror in their lives. He also stated that in his opinion the accused's shooting of the deceased was a desperate act of a woman who sincerely believed that she would otherwise be killed that night. The accused did not testify. She was acquitted at trial, but the majority of the Manitoba Court of Appeal overturned the acquittal and ordered a new trial. The majority's concerns centred on the psychiatrist's evidence.

The Supreme Court of Canada restored the accused's acquittal on the basis of self-defence. It stated that the psychiatrist's testimony was necessary to ensure that the jury understood why the accused was psychologically unable to leave and could assess the reasonableness of her belief that killing him was the only way to save her own life. See *Pétel, supra*; and *R. v. Malott*, [1998] 1 S.C.R. 123.

11. In *R. v. Whynot (Stafford)* (1983), 61 N.S.R. (2d) 33 (C.A.), a woman shot and killed her common law spouse, who had become drunk and passed out. Although the deceased had a history of violence and had often beaten the accused, the Court of Appeal held that self-defence was not available because "no person has the right in anticipation of an assault that may or may not happen to apply force to prevent the imaginary assault." Can you reconcile *Whynot* and *Lavallee*? What non-legal factors might explain the different results in these cases? To what extent should principles developed in criminal law be used in civil actions?

What are the implications of *Lavallee* for a high school student who physically attacks the leader of a gang who has assaulted, threatened and harassed him or her repeatedly over several months? Assume that the student was not in danger at the time he or she acted, but hoped that the attack on the gang leader would prevent further bullying. The student wanted to send the message that he or she would now retaliate physically in response to future threats.

Similarly, can a prison inmate rely on the principles of *Lavallee* to pre-empt a future attack by a fellow inmate? Assume that the inmate had been warned that the victim had planned to knife him or her later that week. Assume as well that there were about 20 to 30 serious assaults among inmates each year in the institution, resulting in at least 1 to 2 deaths. See generally *R. v. McConnell*, [1996] 1 S.C.R. 1075.

12. A person who makes a reasonable and *bona fide* mistake of fact in acting in self-defence can still rely on the defence. See *R. v. Reilly*, [1984] 2 S.C.R. 396; *R. v. Nelson* (1992), 8 O.R. (3d) 364 (C.A.); *Slauenwhite v. Walker* (2000), 186 N.S.R. (2d) 324 (S.C.); and Giles, "Self-Defence and Mistake: A Way Forward" (1990) 53 Mod. L. Rev. 187.

3. Defence of Third Parties

GAMBRIELL v. CAPARELLI

(1974), 54 D.L.R. (3d) 661 (Ont. Co. Ct.)

CARTER CO. CT. J.: . . . At about 5:30 in the afternoon of July 17, 1970, Fred Caparelli, then 21 years of age, and the son of the defendant, decided to wash his automobile which he had parked in the said laneway at the rear of the backyard of his residence. While he was getting the garden hose, the plaintiff (then aged 50), whose car was parked at the rear of his lot, decided to go shopping. In backing out of his lot onto the laneway, the rear of his vehicle came into contact with the rear of young Caparelli's vehicle.

Attracted by the noise of the impact, the Caparelli lad came running out and saw a little dent in the bumper of his car. He and the plaintiff began screaming at each other. Caparelli said he was going to call the police, there was further argument, the plaintiff started to get back in his car, Caparelli grabbed the plaintiff, who then hit Caparelli on the face with his fist. The blow was returned, other blows exchanged. The Caparelli boy, in the course of the fight, was backing up towards the rear of the plaintiff's car and fell back against the car. The plaintiff says that the Caparelli boy kicked him in the chest, leaving a heel mark on the skin, but this is not concurred in by the plaintiff's wife, nor did the plaintiff show this alleged mark to the police.

The Caparelli boy states that the plaintiff then put both hands around his neck and held him down and was choking him and that he was having trouble breathing. The plaintiff said that he never touched the boy's throat.

At this juncture, the defendant, a woman of 57 years at the time, the mother of young Caparelli, appeared on the scene, attracted by the screaming. She said she saw the plaintiff holding her son by the neck, that her son was under the plaintiff and that she thought her son was being choked. She said that she yelled — "stop! stop! stop!". She then ran into her garden and got a metal three-pronged garden cultivator tool with a five-foot-long wooden handle. She said she struck the plaintiff with this three times on the shoulder and then on the head. As soon as the plaintiff saw the blood flowing from his head he released the defendant's son.

. . .

In *R. v. Duffy*, [1967] 1 Q.B. 63, one Kathleen Duffy hit a man named Mohammed Akbar in a tavern. Elizabeth Duffy, sister of Kathleen, appeared from the wash-room and saw Kathleen on her knees on the floor fighting with Akbar, who was holding her by the hair. Elizabeth pulled Akbar's hair to pull him off her sister but did not succeed, and when he kicked her on the leg she hit him on the head with a bottle, as a result of which Akbar received severe lacerations to his face, forehead and head. Elizabeth was convicted of unlawful wounding. On appeal to the Court of Criminal Appeal, the Court quashed her conviction, and at p. 67, Edmund Davies, J. (as he then was), reading the judgment of the Court, said:

> Quite apart from any special relations between the person attacked and his rescuer, there is a general liberty even as between strangers to prevent a felony.

. . .

Again in *R. v. Fennell*, [1971] 1 Q.B. 428 at p. 431, Lord Justice Widgery, delivering the judgment of the Court said:

> Where a person honestly and reasonably believes that he or his child is in imminent danger of injury it would be unjust if he were deprived of the right to use reasonable force by way of defence merely because he had made some genuine mistake of fact.

While the cases I have cited all deal with criminal matters, the principles outlined therein are of equal weight in a civil case of this nature.

It would appear therefore that, where a person in intervening to rescue another holds an honest (though mistaken) belief that the other person is in imminent danger of injury, he is justified in using force, provided that such force is reasonable; and the necessity for intervention and the reasonableness of the force employed are questions to be decided by the trier of fact.

Having regard, therefore, to the facts as I have found them and to the law as I understand it, in my opinion, when the defendant appeared on the scene and saw her son at the mercy of the plaintiff, and being of the belief that her son was in imminent danger of injury, she was justified in using force to prevent that injury from occurring.

. . .

The next question is — Was the force she used reasonable in the circumstances? In the witness-box, the defendant impressed me as a woman who, under normal circumstances, would be quite cool and collected. She is a woman of average build, and as I have indicated, of mature years. As her knowledge of English was slight, her evidence was given in Italian and translated by an interpreter. When she saw her son with the plaintiff's hand about his neck, she shouted for the plaintiff to stop, to no avail. Then she ran and seized the nearest implement she could find, which happened to be a cultivator fork. She struck the plaintiff three times on the shoulder, again to no avail, and finally struck him on the head. I think the fact that the plaintiff sustained only lacerations to his head rather than a fractured skull is indicative of the fact that the force she used in striking the plaintiff was not, in the circumstances, excessive.

In my opinion she had little other choice. If the plaintiff could overpower her son, the empty-handed aid of a woman some seven years older than the plaintiff would have availed little. On the evidence, she was alone in the laneway with the exception of the combatants and Mrs. Gambriell, who did nothing to assist. Had she run for aid, her son might well have been beyond recovery before she returned, especially as, speaking Italian, she may have encountered difficulty in summoning aid. While I am loath to excuse violence, there are times, and I think this is one of them, when the violence inflicted by the defendant on the plaintiff and the degree of such violence was justified and not unreasonable in the circumstances. I would therefore dismiss the plaintiff's case.

I should, in the event that I am in error in my disposition of the plaintiff's claim, assess the plaintiff's damages. No special damages were claimed. The doctor's report indicated that there were no resulting effects from the head injury and that the plaintiff had fully recovered. I am not satisfied that the plaintiff received an injury to his chest. Further, in cross-examination, he indicated that, although he had headaches for two months, it did not interfere with his work at all.

I am of the opinion that the plaintiff was the author of his own misfortune. On the evidence, the plaintiff struck the first blow, and in the course of the fight, the Caparelli boy was backing away from the plaintiff, and the plaintiff could well have desisted. Under all these circumstances, even had I found for the plaintiff, I would not have awarded damages in excess of $1.

I do not, however, think that this is a proper case for costs, and I therefore, as I have said above, dismiss the plaintiff's case, but without costs.

NOTES AND QUESTIONS

1. If the only weapon available to the defendant had been a knife, would the defence have allowed her to stab the plaintiff in defence of her son?

2. The judge indicated that he would have awarded the plaintiff only one dollar had his action succeeded. Could such an award have been justified based on the principles of damages in intentional torts?

3. In *Cachay v. Nemeth* (1972), 28 D.L.R. (3d) 603 (Sask. Q.B.), the plaintiff, while at a party, attempted to kiss the defendant's wife on the cheek. The defendant, who was trained in karate, reacted by striking the plaintiff, fracturing his lower jaw and breaking two teeth. The court rejected the defendant's argument that he acted in defence of his wife because the force used was excessive in the circumstances. Nevertheless, the plaintiff's provocative act was taken into account to reduce damages. Would the result have been the same if: (a) the defendant had not been trained in karate, but had merely struck a lucky blow; or (b) the defendant's wife, untrained in karate, had punched the plaintiff, causing the same injury? See also *Defosse v. Wilde*, [1999] 4 W.W.R. 205 (Sask. Q.B.).

4. As stated in *R. v. Duffy* (1973), 11 C.C.C. (2d) 519 (Ont. C.A.), the defence of third parties is not limited to relatives or others in some special relationship with the person in need of protection. Rather, the defence may be raised by anyone who appears on the scene.

In *Babiuk v. Trann* (2005), 248 D.L.R. (4th) 530 (Sask. C.A.), the defendant, a rugby player, deliberately punched the plaintiff, another rugby player. The plaintiff had just stepped backwards onto the face of one of the defendant's teammates. The court accepted the defendant's evidence that he acted instinctively to protect his teammate, even though the punch was thrown after the whistle ended the play. The claim of the plaintiff, whose jaw was broken in two places, was denied.

5. There is some conflict concerning when an individual will be privileged to intervene to help a third party. The majority of American cases suggest that an intervenor should only be privileged if the person he or she sought to protect had a right of self-defence. Thus, if the third party was a drug trafficker who was unlawfully resisting arrest by an undercover officer, the unwitting intervenor could not raise the defence of a third party. However, the majority of authors have rejected this proposition. See for example Keeton *et al.*, *Prosser and Keeton on the Law of Torts*, 5th ed. (1984) at 129-30; and Fleming, *The Law of Torts*, 9th ed. (1998) at 94.

6. In Canada, it appears that an intervenor's right to raise the defence is independent of the legal rights or position of the person being defended. See the *Criminal Code*, s. 27 (the right to use force to prevent the commission of specified offences) and s. 37 (the right to use force to prevent assault).

4. Discipline

Although attitudes and values have changed dramatically, the common law still recognizes a defence of discipline that parents and guardians can invoke to privilege the use of force in dealing with children. A similar defence to criminal liability exists for parents, guardians and educators in s. 43 of the *Criminal Code*:

> Every schoolteacher, parent or person standing in the place of a parent is justified in using force by way of correction toward a pupil or child, as the case may be, who is under his care, if the force does not exceed what is reasonable under the circumstances.

The Canadian courts have largely assumed that s. 43 governs both the criminal and the civil defences of discipline.

R. v. DUPPERON

(1984), 16 C.C.C. (3d) 453 (Sask. C.A.)

BY THE COURT: The appellant was charged that on or about November 19, 1983, at the City of Saskatoon, in the Province of Saskatchewan, he did in committing an assault on Michael James Dupperon cause harm to him contrary to s. 245.1(1)(*b*) of the *Criminal Code* of Canada.

After a trial before a judge of the provincial court he was convicted, fined $400 and placed on probation for 18 months. He appeals against his conviction.

The evidence is that he strapped his 13-year-old son on the bare buttocks with a leather belt approximately 10 times leaving four or five bruises on the boy's left buttock which were blue and in a linear pattern. Each bruise was approximately four inches long and of a width of one-quarter to one-half an inch.

. . .

In the morning on the day of the assault, Michael had been caught smoking out behind the house and for this he was "grounded". Later that morning the father, Linda Dupperon (his present wife and step-mother to Michael) and Michael were working at the Bingo Palace where the appellant had a janitorial contract. There, Michael admitted, he was "slacking off and doing things I shouldn't have"; and he also used foul language against his father. For this he was grounded for a whole week. When the appellant, Linda Dupperon and Michael returned home from work both the appellant and his wife later left the house and Michael was alone. It was then that he decided to leave home. He left a note to his father which was not produced but concerning which Michael testified: "I think I told him off. I said I wasn't going to come back to home and shit like that." He packed his clothes, radio and some food and left the house. A short time later, Linda Dupperon arrived home, saw the note and telephoned her husband. The appellant came home and about 15 minutes later the telephone rang. It was a call from Michael, who had been at a friend's home down the street, saying he was coming home.

. . .

From the uncontradicted evidence given by Michael there were ample grounds upon which the appellant could conclude that Michael was deserving of a more severe punishment than he had already meted out to him and I am satisfied that he honestly believed that a strapping was required by way of correction. Given the weight of the evidence adduced in this respect, it was unreasonable for the learned trial judge not to have held that the strapping was for correction.

. . .

It is quite clear from both the evidence of Michael and Linda Dupperon that the first strapping consisted of only three or four strokes and that would have been the end of the strapping but for the foul language Michael then employed against his father. This resulted in a further five or six strokes. There is no dispute that the total strapping did not exceed 10 strokes.

. . .

Here the learned trial judge in the course of his judgment said:

> Secondly, I do not view it at all appropriate in the circumstances to pull down a 13-year-old boy's pants and flail him with a strap on his bare buttocks to the extent of this case. It is an unnatural manner of dealing out punishment and is not justified in these circumstances and in the manner in which it was administered.

. . .

While it appears from the above exchange and from other passages in the transcript that the learned trial judge may be opposed, in principle, to corporal punishment, that is his privilege and unless he allowed such views to interfere with his determination of whether the force applied was reasonable under the circumstances, it was not an error to express his personal view.

Put in another way, I think most people would be shocked if corporal punishment were employed in an institution such as Kilburn Hall or in any agency of government designed for the protection of abused children.

. . .

There is some anomaly in the fact that corporal punishment of criminals is now prohibited while corporal punishment of children is still permitted. The *rationale* of s. 43 of the *Criminal Code* has been explained by Dickson J. (as he then was) in the recent judgment of the Supreme Court rendered September 17, 1984, in *Ogg-Moss v. The Queen* [(1984), 11 D.L.R. (4th) 549] . . .

> Section 43 authorizes the use of force "by way of correction". As Blackstone noted, such "correction" of a child is countenanced by the law because it is "for the benefit of his education". Section 43 is, in other words, a *justification.* It exculpates a parent, schoolteacher or person standing in the place of a parent who uses force in the correction of a child, because it considers such an action not a wrongful, but a *rightful* one. It follows that unless the force is "by way of correction", that is, for the benefit of the education of the child, the use of force will not be justified.

In this case I have said that, in my opinion, all of the evidence supports the view that the force used was by way of correction and that the learned trial judge ought to have so found. However, when we come to the second question, namely, whether the force used exceeded what was reasonable under the circumstances, I think the evidence fully supports the finding of the trial judge.

. . .

The only matter with which I am concerned here, therefore, is whether the force used exceeded what was reasonable under the circumstances so as to deprive the appellant of the protection afforded by s. 43 of the *Criminal Code.* In determining that question the court will consider, both from an objective and subjective standpoint, such matters as the nature of the offence calling for correction, the age and character of the child and the likely effect of the punishment on this particular child, the degree of gravity of the punishment, the circumstances under which it was inflicted, and the injuries, if any, suffered. If the child suffers injuries which may endanger life, limbs or health or is disfigured that alone would be sufficient to find that the punishment administered was unreasonable under the circumstances.

. . .

In my opinion, the evidence in this case amply supports the finding of the trial judge. Ten strokes of a leather belt on the bare buttocks is a severe beating, particularly under the circumstances in which it was inflicted here on an emotionally disturbed boy. There is, therefore, no basis upon which this court would be justified in reversing that finding.

[The court accepted the appellant's argument that he should only be convicted of assault and not assault causing bodily harm. However, it held that the sentence imposed at trial was still appropriate.]

NOTES AND QUESTIONS

1. What must the defendant establish to invoke the defence of discipline under s. 43?

2. Do you agree that the force used in *Dupperon* was used for the purpose of correction? What was the intended benefit? Can a parent who hits a child solely to punish him or her for misbehaviour raise the defence of discipline?

Do you agree with the court that the amount of force used was excessive? Would the court have reached that conclusion if the accused had stopped after the first three or four strokes, or the strapping had not left bruises? Would the majority of Canadians in the early 1980s have supported the criminal conviction in these circumstances?

3. It has been held that s. 43 should be interpreted in light of prevailing social standards and customs, rather than those particular to the accused. See *R. v. Baptiste* (1980), 61 C.C.C. (2d) 438 (Ont. Prov. Ct.); and *R. v. Halcrow* (1993), 80 C.C.C. (3d) 320 (B.C.C.A.), aff'd [1995] 1 S.C.R. 440. In *Halcrow*, the court also indicated that the accused's religious beliefs were irrelevant. Although the courts' position is clear, do you think it is necessary to rely on Canadian customs in order to interpret s. 43?

4. Section 43 also permits teachers to use force by way of correction. Initially, educators were given broad latitude to use force not just to correct student behaviour, but also to punish students who were thought to have misbehaved. For example in *R. v. Haberstock* (1970), 1 C.C.C. (2d) 433 (Sask. C.A.), a vice-principal was absolved of criminal liability under s. 43 for summarily slapping three boys in the face in the schoolyard because he believed that they had called him names while leaving on the school bus the preceding Friday. See also *R. v. Wheaton* (1982), 35 Nfld. & P.E.I.R. 520 (Nfld. Prov. Ct.). It is highly unlikely that these cases would be decided the same way today.

Nevertheless, educators appear to be given at least some leeway under s. 43. In *R. v. Wetmore* (1996), 172 N.B.R. (2d) 224 (Q.B.), the accused taught a tenth-grade science class, in which several students including a 20-year-old were frequently obnoxious and disruptive. The teacher, who held a brown belt in karate, called the troublemakers to the front of the class and indicated that he was going to provide a karate demonstration. He took off his shoes and socks and then threw kicks and punches at the students. Although there was some incidental touching of the students, the physical contact was minimal and no harm was caused. The teacher ended the demonstration, called for a discussion and made the troublemakers aware that their offensive conduct, whether directed to him or their classmates, was not acceptable in his classroom. The teacher was subsequently charged with assault. In acquitting the teacher on the basis of s. 43, the court held that his actions were reasonable given the conduct of the troublemakers and the need to teach them respect for authority. See also *R. v. Park* (1999), 178 Nfld. & P.E.I.R. 194 (Nfld. S.C.(T.D.)).

5. Although some courts and lawyers confuse the principles, it is important to distinguish between the narrow defence under s. 43 and educators' broad common law and statutory powers to maintain order and discipline within a school. The Canadian courts have held that the power to maintain order and discipline can be invoked to physically restrain a student who is acting out of control, detain and question a student suspected of violating the school rules or the law, and control a student's movement in school or prevent a student from leaving.

See for example *R. v. Lauzon*, [1991] O.J. No. 968 (Prov. Ct.) (QL); and *R. v. Collins* (1996), 192 A.R. 71 (Prov. Ct.) (subduing an out-of-control student); *R. v. Sweet*, [1986] O.J. No. 2083 (Dist. Ct.) (QL); and *R. v. Brisson* (2000), 262 A.R. 376 (Prov. Ct.) (investigating potentially criminal conduct); *H.G. v. Shamrock School Division No. 38*, [1987] 3 W.W.R. 270 (Sask. Q.B.) (restricting movement); and *Pilieci v. Lockett*, 1989 CarswellOnt 2870 (Dist. Ct.) (WLeC) (preventing a student from leaving in violation of the parents' custody order).

6. In *R. v. G.(J.M.)* (1986), 56 O.R. (2d) 705 (C.A.), the court held that principals, pursuant to their statutory duty to maintain order and discipline, had a legal obligation to investigate any credible allegation of illicit drug use or other serious violation of the school rules. Moreover, if an educator reasonably believed that a student was in possession of drugs, contraband or evidence of a violation of the school rules or the law, the educator could search the student and the student's belongings and locker without a warrant.

In *R. v. M.(M.R.)*, [1998] 3 S.C.R. 393, the court affirmed these principles, explaining that students are subject to a diminished expectation of privacy. In both cases, the principals' detention and search of the students was challenged under the *Canadian Charter of Rights and Freedoms*, Part I of the *Constitution Act, 1982*, being Schedule B to the *Canada Act 1982* (U.K.), 1982, c. 11. The *Charter* challenges were dismissed in both cases. The Supreme Court of Canada has granted leave to appeal from *R. v. M.(A.)* (2006), 79 O.R. (3d) 481 (C.A.) which held that a police canine search for drugs in a school violated s. 8 of the *Charter*.

7. In *R. v. Ogg-Moss*, [1984] 2 S.C.R. 173, the court held that a counsellor of a residential facility for developmentally-delayed adults could not invoke s. 43 because the defence was limited to parents, teachers, and others standing in the position of a parent in relationship to a child or pupil. The court went on to emphasize that s. 43 was to be narrowly interpreted and applied. The decision reflected growing concerns about child abuse, the recognition of the independent legal rights of children and the hardening of attitudes toward the use of corporal punishment.

8. In *Canadian Foundation of Children, Youth and the Law v. Canada (Attorney General)*, [2004] 1 S.C.R. 76, the appellant argued that s. 43 violated the *Charter* rights

of children. Specifically, the Foundation alleged breaches of s. 7 (the right to life, liberty and security of the person), s. 12 (the prohibition against cruel and unusual treatment or punishment), and s. 15 (the guarantee of equal treatment and benefit of the law). While the court upheld the constitutional validity of s. 43, it went to considerable lengths to narrow the defence.

The court stated (at 105) that the defence was generally limited to "minor corrective force of a transitory and trifling nature." First, force can only be used for a corrective purpose that is designed to restrain and control a child or express symbolic disapproval. The defence does not apply to force that is used out of anger or simply to punish a child. Second, the child must be capable of understanding why the force is being used and be capable of benefiting from it. Consequently, the defence does not apply to children under two and other children who, because of a disability, are incapable of learning from the incident. Third, s. 43 does not apply to the use of force that harms or could reasonably be expected to harm a child. Nor will the defence apply where children are hit with rulers, belts or other such objects, or if children are hit or slapped in the head. Fourth, s. 43 does not apply to any use of force that is cruel or degrading. Fifth, the defence cannot be invoked to justify corporal punishment of teenagers, because research indicates that this only generates harmful or antisocial behaviour. Sixth, while teachers may use reasonable force to remove a child from a classroom or secure compliance with instructions, they cannot use force merely as corporal punishment.

Is the court's analysis consistent with the statutory language of s. 43? Has the court conflated s. 43 with educators' common law and statutory powers to maintain order and discipline in schools?

9. Ship captains, pilots and others in similar positions of authority also have a common law right to use physical force to maintain order and discipline. Although at one time this power could be used to punish rebellious crew and passengers, it is probably now limited to maintaining safety and order. See *King v. Fanklin* (1858), 175 E.R. 764 (N.P.); *Hook v. Cunard SS. Co.*, [1953] 1 All E.R. 1021 (Q.B.); and *Re White* (1954), 12 W.W.R. 315 (B.C.C.A.), rev'd on a jurisdictional issue [1956] S.C.R. 154.

It should also be noted that s. 44 of the *Criminal Code* gives ship captains broad powers to maintain order on their vessels. The repeal of this section has been pending proclamation since 2001. Moreover, s. 27.1 of the *Criminal Code*, which was enacted in 2004, gives everyone on an aircraft in flight the right to use as much force as is necessary to prevent the commission of an offence.

5. Defence of Real Property

MACDONALD v. HEES

(1974), 46 D.L.R. (3d) 720 (N.S.S.C.)

COWAN C.J.T.D.: In this action, the plaintiff claims against the defendant for injury, loss and damage said to have been suffered by the plaintiff as a result of an assault alleged to have been committed on the plaintiff by the defendant.

The injuries suffered by the plaintiff were sustained during the early morning of September 23, 1972, when the defendant forcibly ejected the plaintiff from a motel room at the Peter Pan Motel, New Glasgow, Nova Scotia. The defendant, in his defence, in addition to denying any assault, set up the additional defence that, if he used any force upon the person of the plaintiff, he was justified in law and the application of force was due to the unlawful entry of the plaintiff and invasion of the defendant's privacy.

. . .

It is clear that the defendant was in lawful occupation of the motel unit No. 54. That unit had been reserved for his use on the night in question. . . . I find that the defendant had not expressly invited the plaintiff or Boyd to visit him, nor was there any implied invitation to anyone to visit him at the motel unit. However, in my opinion, this is not quite the case of a stranger walking in a motel room without any apparent right. The plaintiff was an officer of the local political party in whose interests the defendant was active that day. The plaintiff wished to introduce Glen Boyd to the defendant, and the circumstances to which I have referred above give some excuse to the plaintiff for his entry to the motel unit occupied by the defendant. The plaintiff was told that there were two units set aside for the defendant's use and, when he went to the area so set aside, it was apparent that the light was on in one of the units, while the other was in darkness. The plaintiff cannot be criticized for his action in knocking on the door of the unit which had the light showing. He then heard someone call from the adjoining unit and assumed, erroneously, that he was being invited to enter that unit.

[The defendant raised both self-defence and defence of property as justifications for his conduct. The judge concluded that there was no basis for claiming self-defence and proceeded to discuss the defence of property.]

With regard to the . . . defence . . . that the defendant was justified in law and that the application of force was due to the unlawful entry of the plaintiff and invasion of the defendant's privacy, it is clear that, as stated in *Salmond, op. cit.*, p. 131:

> It is lawful for any occupier of land, or for any other person with the authority of the occupier, to use a reasonable degree of force in order to prevent a trespasser from entering or to control his movements or to eject him after entry.

It is clear, however, that a trespasser cannot be forcibly repelled or ejected until he has been requested to leave the premises and a reasonable opportunity of doing so peaceably has been afforded him. It is otherwise in the case of a person who enters or seeks to enter by force. In *Green v. Goddard* (1702), 2 Salkeld 641, 91 E.R. 540, it was said that, in such a case:

> . . . I need not request him to be gone, but may lay hands on him immediately, for it is but returning violence with violence; so if one comes forcibly and takes away my goods, I may oppose him without any more ado, for there is no time to make a request.

Even in such a case, however, the amount of force that may be used must not exceed that which is indicated in the old forms of pleading by the phrase *molliter manus imposuit.* It must amount to nothing more than forcible removal and must not include beating, wounding, or other physical injury: Salmond, *op. cit.*, p. 131, and the case of *Collins v. Renison* (1754), Sayer 138, 96 E.R. 830, there cited. In that case, the plaintiff sued for the assault of throwing him off a ladder. It was held a bad plea that the plaintiff was trespassing and refused, after request, to leave the premises, and that the defendant thereupon [at 139] "gently shook the ladder, which was a low ladder, and gently overturned it, and gently threw the plaintiff from it upon the ground, thereby doing as little damage as possible to the plaintiff." It was held that such force was not justifiable in defence of the possession of land.

In the present case, I find that there was no forcible entry by the plaintiff of the motel unit occupied by the defendant. I accept the evidence of the plaintiff and of Glen Boyd, to the effect that the plaintiff, thinking that he had been invited to enter the motel unit occupied by the defendant, opened the unlocked, outside combination screen and storm door and merely touched the door-knob of the inside door when it opened. It was obviously unlocked. The plaintiff then entered the motel unit, at the same time telling the defendant who he was. The plaintiff said that he was about to apologize for the intrusion when he realized that the defendant was in bed. Even if there had been forcible entry, the defendant did not request the plaintiff and his companion to leave and give them any reasonable opportunity of doing so, peaceably. . . . Where the evidence of the defendant conflicts with that of the plaintiff and Glen Boyd, I do not accept his evidence but that of the plaintiff and Glen Boyd.

The evidence of Glen Boyd was to the effect that the plaintiff had merely stepped into the room and made the statement referred to above, and that the time which elapsed from the time when he opened the door to the time when he was thrown back out through the inner door and into the storm door, was very short. Glen Boyd said that it was only long enough for the plaintiff to walk in and be thrown back out. He said that the defendant had not asked the plaintiff to leave before he threw him out.

I find that the use of force by the defendant to eject the plaintiff was not justified, in the circumstances, and that, in any event, the force used was excessive. I find that the defendant threw the plaintiff bodily through the inside motel door which was open, and against the closed combination screen and storm door, in such a way that the plaintiff's head hit the lower portion of the glass in the door, causing it to break and causing severe lacerations to the plaintiff's head.

I therefore find that the defence that the application of force was justified in law, in that it was due to the unlawful entry of the plaintiff and invasion of the defendant's privacy, has not been established. It follows, therefore, that the plaintiff is entitled to recovery against the defendant of damages for the injury, loss and damage which he suffered by the reason of the action of the defendant in assaulting him, and throwing him against the closed combination door.

NOTES AND QUESTIONS

1. As indicated in *Hees*, the defence of real property is based on the legal status of the entrant. According to *Hees*, what principles govern the defence as it relates to trespassers and violent intruders?

2. Why did the court reject Hees' argument that he was acting in defence of property? Assume that Hees had been startled out of a heavy sleep by the plaintiff and awoke knowing only that there was an intruder in his room. Would Hees have been privileged to use the element of surprise to overpower the plaintiff without first asking him to leave? If so, what would be the basis of his defence? See *Boulet c. Entreprises M. Canada (Abitibi) Ltée* (1986), 38 C.C.L.T. 271 (Qc. S.C.), aff'd [1989] R.R.A. 795 (Qc. C.A.).

3. The courts have held that an occupier may be required to tolerate the presence of a trespasser if ejecting him or her would pose a foreseeable risk of physical injury. See for example *Depue v. Flatau*, 111 N.W. 1 (Minn. S.C. 1907); *Dunn v. Dominion*

Atlantic Railway Co. (1920), 60 S.C.R. 310; and *Jordan House Ltd. v. Menow*, [1974] S.C.R. 239.

4. The Canadian courts will not permit an occupier to use force that is likely to cause death or serious bodily injury solely for the purpose of ejecting a trespasser who cannot be induced to leave by less violent means. See *Harris v. Wong* (1971), 19 D.L.R. (3d) 589 (Sask. Q.B.); *Veinot v. Veinot* (1977), 22 N.S.R. (2d) 630 (C.A.); "Bar Patron Tossed Out by Bouncers Awarded $652,400" *The Vancouver Sun* (29 May 1991); and *Bruce v. Coliseum Management Ltd.*, [1999] 4 W.W.R. 178 (B.C.C.A.). While an occupier cannot shoot trespassers, it may be permissible to threaten them with a loaded gun. See *R. v. Haverstock* (1979), 32 N.S.R. (2d) 595 (Co. Ct.); *R. v. Blair*, 1987 CarswellBC 1477 (Co. Ct.) (WLeC); and *Revill v. Newbery*, [1996] 1 All E.R. 291 (C.A.).

5. The older cases indicate that deadly force could be used to repel a violent intruder, prevent being dispossessed or prevent a crime from being committed. See *R. v. Lyons* (1892), 2 C.C.C. 218 (Ont. Co. Ct.); and *Isreal James Hussey* (1924), 18 Cr. App. R. 160 (Ct. Crim. App.). However, the more recent cases prohibit the use of deadly force simply to protect property. See *Bigcharles v. Merkel*, [1973] 1 W.W.R. 324 (B.C.S.C.); and *Hackshaw v. Shaw* (1984), 56 A.L.R. 417 (H.C.A.).

6. The American courts have held that a reasonable and *bona fide* mistake of fact will not negate the defence of real property, unless the intruder is entering as of legal right. See Keeton *et al.*, *Prosser and Keeton on the Law of Torts*, 5th ed. (1984) at 131-32; and *Restatement (Second) of the Law of Torts* (1965) at §77. This issue has not yet been resolved in Canada. See Fridman, *The Law of Torts in Canada*, 2d ed. (2002) at 88. Would you support the American position?

7. The right to eject a trespasser does not necessarily include the right to imprison. See *Ball v. Manthorpe* (1970), 15 D.L.R. (3d) 99 (B.C. Co. Ct.). However, some of the provincial trespass statutes authorize an occupant to arrest trespassers without a warrant. See for example the *Trespass to Property Act*, R.S.O. 1990, c. T.21, s. 9.

8. The use of reasonable force in defending real property and ejecting trespassers is also privileged in criminal law. See the *Criminal Code*, ss. 40 and 41; *R. v. Figueira* (1981), 63 C.C.C. (2d) 409 (Ont. C.A.); and *R. v. Clark* (1983), 44 A.R. 141 (C.A.). See also s. 177, which prohibits trespassing at night, without lawful excuse, on the property of another near a dwelling house and s. 494(2), which permits occupants to arrest without warrant anyone they find committing a criminal offence on, or in relation to, their property.

9. At common law, occupiers were entitled to damage or even destroy the property of another if it was necessary to protect their own property and the damage done was reasonable in relation to the interest protected. Thus, farmers would be privileged to kill a trespassing dog that was attacking their sheep, but not to kill a cow that had merely entered their field. In addition, under the principle of "distress damage feasant," occupiers could seize any chattel that was unlawfully on their land and had caused damage and detain it until they had been compensated. For a discussion of the common law see

Arthur v. Anker, [1996] 3 All E.R. 783 (C.A.); Fleming, *The Law of Torts*, 9th ed. (1998) at 94-98; and Keeton *et al.*, *supra* at 136-37.

BIRD v. HOLBROOK

(1828), 130 E.R. 911 (C.P.)

[The defendant possessed a walled garden in which he grew valuable tulips. Because of previous acts of vandalism, the defendant set up a spring gun with trip wires across the garden. No notice of the spring gun was posted. Indeed, the defendant sought to keep its existence a secret "lest the villain should not be detected."

A peahen escaped from a neighbouring house and landed in the garden. The plaintiff, seeing that a servant girl was upset at not being able to recover the bird, offered to help. He climbed the garden wall and called several times for the occupant. After receiving no answer he jumped into the garden to retrieve the hen. The gun discharged, seriously wounding him.]

BEST C.J.: . . . I am reported to have said, expressly, "Humanity requires that the fullest notice possible should be given, and the law of England will not sanction what is inconsistent with humanity."

It has been argued that the law does not compel every line of conduct which humanity or religion may require; but there is no act which Christianity forbids, that the law will not reach: if it were otherwise, Christianity would not be, as it has always been held to be, part of the law of England. I am, therefore, clearly of opinion that he who sets spring guns, without giving notice, is guilty of an inhuman act, and that, if injurious consequences ensue, he is liable to yield to redress to the sufferer. But this case stands on grounds distinct from any that have preceded it. In general, spring guns have been set for the purpose of deterring; the Defendant placed his for the express purpose of doing injury; for, when called on to give notice, he said, "If I give notice, I shall not catch him." He intended, therefore, that the gun should be discharged and that the contents should be lodged in the body of his victim, for he could not be caught in any other way. On these principles the action is clearly maintainable, and particularly on the latter ground.

. . .

BURROUGH J.: . . . [T]he present case is of a worse complexion than those which have preceded it; for if the Defendant had proposed merely to protect his property from thieves, he would have set the spring guns only by night. The Plaintiff was only a trespasser: if the Defendant had been present, he would not have been authorised even in taking him into custody, and no man can do indirectly that which he is forbidden to do directly.

NOTES AND QUESTIONS

1. Best C.J. premised his decision, in part, on Christian beliefs. Of what relevance are such beliefs in modern Canadian law?

2. In *Bird*, what impact did the defendant's intent have on the defence of real property? The court also discussed the absence of a warning sign. What impact should the presence or absence of a warning sign have on the defence of real property? What other impact would a warning sign have on the defendant's case?

3. Would the defendant have been held liable if his trained dog had attacked the plaintiff causing equally serious injuries? Would the defendant have been held liable if the plaintiff had been an armed and dangerous felon who was planning to break into the house? The liability of dog owners is now often governed by provincial legislation.

4. See generally Bohlen & Burns, "The Privilege to Protect Property by Dangerous Barriers and Mechanical Devices" (1926) 35 Yale L.J. 525; Hart, "Injuries to Trespassers" (1931) 47 L.Q.R. 92; and Palmer, "The Iowa Spring Gun Case: A Study in American Gothic" (1970-71) 56 Iowa L. Rev. 1219. See also s. 247 of the *Criminal Code*, which prohibits the use of traps, devices or other mechanisms for the purpose of causing death or bodily harm to others.

6. Defence and Recaption of Chattels

The legal principles governing the defence of real property generally apply to the defence of chattels. In order to invoke this defence, the defendant must be in possession of the chattel, attempting to immediately regain possession, or in hot pursuit of the person who had just taken the chattel. If a person innocently picks up the defendant's chattel, the defendant must request its return before using any force. However, if a person grabs the chattel out of the defendant's hand, the defendant can use force to retrieve it without first making a request for its return. The specific facts of the case will dictate whether the possessor is privileged to use force and whether the force used was reasonable. For example in *Cresswell v. Sirl*, [1948] 1 K.B. 241 (C.A.), the court held that the defendant would be privileged in shooting a dog if he had no other practical means of protecting his livestock from attack.

Except as outlined above, an individual cannot invoke the defence of chattels once dispossessed. He or she may seek to regain possession by court action or may be entitled to resort to the self-help remedy of recaption, which was discussed in Chapter 4. The remedy of recaption, which is also sometimes called recapture, places the owner of a chattel in the role of a potential aggressor attempting to regain possession of the goods from another person. As a result, the remedy has been narrowly defined. It may only be invoked by an individual who has an immediate right to possession, and then only after a request has been made for the chattel's return. Although the authorities are divided, it appears that only peaceful means can be used to recapture a chattel from a person who came into possession lawfully. Thus, an individual could not use force to recapture a chattel from a bailee who refused to return it. The right to use force is limited to circumstances in which an individual who wrongfully gained possession refuses to hand over the chattel after being requested to do so.

There is a common law privilege to enter another's land to recapture chattels in limited circumstances. If the chattel came onto the land accidentally or was left there by a wrongdoer, the owner could enter the property to retake his or her chattel, provided he or she did not use force or cause a breach of the peace. If the occupier of the land came into possession of the chattel unlawfully, its owner could make a forced entry if his or her request for its return had been denied.

NOTES AND QUESTIONS

1. Although the issue is not completely resolved, it appears that a reasonable and *bona fide* mistake of fact will not negate the defence of chattels, but will negate the

remedy of recaption of chattels. Do you favour this position? On what basis can such a distinction be drawn? See Keeton *et al.*, *Prosser and Keeton on the Law of Torts*, 5th ed. (1984) at 137-38.

2. For a discussion of the defence of chattels, see Keeton *et al.*, *supra*; and *Restatement (Second) of the Law of Torts* (1965) at §§77-87. See also the *Criminal Code*, ss. 38, 39 and 494(2) which create broad authority to use force and make arrests without a warrant to protect chattels.

3. For a review of the law of recaption see *Blades v. Higgs* (1861), 142 E.R. 634 (H.L.); *Morrison v. Thomas* (1922), 65 D.L.R. 364 (Sask. C.A.); *Sweeney v. Starrat*, [1931] 2 D.L.R. 473 (N.S.C.A.); *Wentzell v. Veinot*, [1940] 1 D.L.R. 536 (N.S.S.C.); and *Devoe v. Long*, [1951] 1 D.L.R. 203 (N.B.C.A.).

4. Given the potential for violence, should the remedy of recaption be abolished?

5. It has been suggested that if an owner recaptures a chattel, he or she need not pay for any improvements to it made in good faith by the other party. Conversely, if the owner recovers the chattel through court action, he or she may be required to pay for any such improvements. However, the better view appears to be that the owner may be held liable in an action for unjust enrichment for the value of the improvements in either situation. See *Greenwood v. Bennett*, [1973] 1 Q.B. 195 (C.A.); *Peruvian Guano Co. v. Dreyfus Brothers & Co.*, [1892] A.C. 166 (H.L.); and *Mayne v. Kidd* (1951), 1 W.W.R. 833 (Sask. C.A.).

REVIEW PROBLEM

Al and Bob obtained permission to camp and hunt on the waterfront property of one of their friends. They misunderstood his directions, and beached their canoe and pitched their tent on the wrong property. Al built a fire to keep warm and Bob went for a walk. The owner of the property, Stevens, was hunting nearby when he came across Al and the campsite. Stevens told him to pack up and leave immediately. Al paid little heed. Stevens yelled, "I'm not joking, get off my land or else!" Al poured himself a cup of coffee and replied, "What's your hurry, old man?" Infuriated, Stevens blasted the tent to bits and pointed the shotgun at Al.

Bob heard the shot and came running back as Stevens screamed, "Is there any reason why I shouldn't blow your head off?" Stevens had no intention of shooting Al, he just wanted to scare him. Fearing the worst, Bob picked up a rock and tried to knock the shotgun out of Stevens' hands. Unfortunately, the rock hit Stevens in the head and he fell to the ground unconscious. The shotgun fell beside him, discharging several pellets into Al's shoulder. Both Al and Bob became alarmed when Stevens showed no signs of regaining consciousness. They placed Stevens in their canoe and rushed him to the hospital.

Al and Bob have contacted you from the hospital, wanting to know if they can return to Stevens' land and retrieve their camping equipment. They also want your advice about the civil claims that they could bring against Stevens, and the claims that he might bring against them.

7. Public and Private Necessity

(a) PUBLIC NECESSITY

The defence of public necessity allows an individual to intentionally interfere with the property rights of another in order to save lives or to protect the public interest from external threats of nature, such as fires, floods and storms. Public necessity provides a complete defence, privileging both the interference with the plaintiff's legal rights to the property and any damages resulting from it.

SUROCCO v. GEARY

3 Cal. 69 (Cal. S.C. 1853)

MURRAY, C.J.: This was an action, commenced in the court below, to recover damages for blowing up and destroying the plaintiff's house and property, during the fire of the 24th of December, 1849. . . .

The only question for our consideration is, whether the person who tears down or destroys the house of another, in good faith, and under apparent necessity, during the time of a conflagration, for the purpose of saving the buildings adjacent, and stopping its progress, can be held personally liable in an action by the owner of the property destroyed.

The right to destroy property, to prevent the spread of conflagration, has been traced to the highest law of necessity, and the natural rights of man, independent of society or civil government. "It is referred by moralists and jurists to the same great principle which justifies the exclusive appropriation of a plank in a shipwreck, though the life of another be sacrificed; with the throwing overboard goods in a tempest, for the safety of a vessel; with the trespassing upon the lands of another, to escape death by an enemy. It rests upon the maxim, *Necessitas inducit privilegium quod jura privata* [Necessity provides a privilege for private rights]."

The common law adopts the principles of the natural law, and places the justification of an act otherwise tortious precisely on the same ground of necessity. . ..

This principle has been familiarly recognized by the books from the time of *Saltpetre's Case* (1606), 77 E.R. 1294, and the instances of tearing down houses to prevent conflagration, or to raise bulwarks for the defence of a city, are made use of as illustrations, rather than as abstract cases, in which its exercise is permitted. At such times, the individual rights of property give way to the higher laws of impending necessity.

A house on fire, or those in its immediate vicinity, which serve to communicate the flames, becomes a nuisance, which it is lawful to abate, and the private rights of the individual yield to the considerations of general convenience, and the interests of society. Were it otherwise, one stubborn person might involve a whole city in ruin, by refusing to allow the destruction of a building which would cut off the flames and check the progress of the fire, and that, too, when it was perfectly evident that his building must be consumed. . . .

The counsel for the respondent has asked, who is to judge of the necessity of the destruction of property?

This must, in some instances, be a difficult matter to determine. The necessity of blowing up a house may not exist, or be as apparent to the owner, whose judgment is clouded by interest, and the hope of saving his property, as to others. In all such cases the conduct of the individual must be regulated by his own judgment as to the exigencies of the case. If a building should be torn down without apparent or actual necessity, the parties concerned would undoubtedly be liable in an action of trespass. But in every case the necessity must be clearly shown. It is true, many cases of hardship may grow out of this rule, and property may often in such cases be destroyed, without necessity, by irresponsible persons, but this difficulty would not be obviated by making the parties responsible in every case, whether the necessity existed or not.

The evidence in this case clearly establishes the fact, that the blowing up of the house was necessary, as it would have been consumed had it been left standing. The plaintiffs cannot recover for the value of the goods which they might have saved; they were as much subject to the necessities of the occasion as the house in which they were situate; and if in such cases a party was held liable, it would too frequently happen, that the delay caused by the removal of the goods would render the destruction of the house useless.

The court below clearly erred as to the law applicable to the facts of this case. The testimony will not warrant a verdict against the defendant.

NOTES AND QUESTIONS

1. As *Surocco* suggests, a reasonable and *bona fide* mistake of fact as to the apparent necessity will not negate the defence. See also *Cope v. Sharpe*, [1912] 1 K.B. 496 (C.A.).

To what damages would the plaintiff have been entitled if the defence of public necessity had failed? See generally Finan & Ritson, "Tortious Necessity: The Privileged Defense" (1992) 26 Akron L. Rev. 1.

2. In order to invoke the defence, the defendant must have acted reasonably in terms of the damages caused relative to the likely public benefit. What limits, if any, should be imposed on the exercise of public necessity in cases where only property is threatened?

3. The defence of public necessity has been limited to cases in which the defendant has interfered with the plaintiff's property interests. Should a defendant be privileged to intentionally inflict minor physical injury on the plaintiff to protect another party from serious personal injury or death? Should the law privilege the intentional sacrifice of one innocent person in order to save many other innocent people? In *R. v. Dudley and Stephens* (1884), 14 Q.B.D. 273, the defendants, while adrift in a lifeboat, killed and ate a fellow passenger to save their own lives. The defendants were found guilty of murder, but were subsequently pardoned. Contrast *Dudley* with *U.S. v. Holmes*, 26 F.Cas. 360 (Penn. Cir. Ct. 1842). See also Fuller, "The Case of the Speluncean Explorers" (1949) 62 Harv. L. Rev. 616.

4. *Surocco* suggests that an individual would not be held liable for using force to acquire exclusive possession of a plank that can keep only one person afloat. How does this differ from *Dudley* and *Holmes*? What defence would apply in the example with the plank?

Is this case based on the same principle as *Re A (children)(conjoined twins: surgical separation)*, [2000] 4 All. E.R. 961 (C.A.), discussed in the previous chapter? In that case, the court authorized the separation of the twins even though it would hasten the death of one of them in order to give the more viable twin a good chance for long-term survival.

5. The House of Lords and the United States Supreme Court have both indicated that the government need not compensate people for losses inflicted during wartime operations, presumably because the military is acting under a type of public necessity. See *Burmah Oil Co. v. Lord Advocate*, [1965] A.C. 75 (H.L.); *U.S. v. Caltex (Philippines) Inc.*, 344 U.S. 149 (1952); and "The Burmah Oil Affair" (1966) 79 Harv. L. Rev. 614. However, the courts differed on whether the intentional destruction of private property to prevent it from falling into enemy hands comes within this principle. Contrary to the American decision, the House of Lords held that the plaintiffs were entitled to damages in such circumstances. Nevertheless, the plaintiffs' victory was short-lived as Parliament immediately enacted legislation which negated the decision. For a discussion of the Crown's right to seize property for purposes of war, see *Saltpetre's Case* (1606), 77 E.R. 1294 (K.B.); and *A.G. v. Nissan*, [1970] A.C. 179 (H.L.).

6. In *Rigby v. Chief Constable of Northamptonshire*, [1985] 2 All E.R. 985 (Q.B.), the police burned down the plaintiff's shop by firing tear gas canisters into the building in an effort to force out a dangerous psychopath. The police were absolved of liability in trespass on the basis of public necessity, although they were held liable in negligence for not having any firefighting equipment available. Should the defence of public necessity extend to law enforcement? This issue has not been addressed by the Canadian courts.

7. The defence of public necessity appears to apply to travellers who are forced to cross adjoining land when the public highway is blocked. See *Taylor v. Whitehead* (1781), 99 E.R. 475 (K.B.); and *Dwyer v. Staunton*, [1947] 4 D.L.R. 393 (Alta. Dist. Ct.).

8. Traditionally the defence of necessity has been limited to situations in which the imminent threat is posed by some external force of nature. Thus in *London Borough of Southwark v. Williams*, [1971] 2 All E.R. 175 (C.A.), it was held that homeless squatters could not invoke the defence of public necessity to privilege their entry into vacant houses owned by the Council. Denning M.R. explained at 179:

> If homelessness were once admitted as a defence to trespass, no one's house could be safe. Necessity would open a door which no man could shut. It would not only be those in extreme need who would enter. There would be others who would imagine that they were in need, or would invent a need, so as to gain entry. Each man would say his need was greater than the next man's. The plea would be an excuse for all sorts of wrongdoing. So the courts must, for the sake of law and order, take a firm stand. They must refuse to admit the plea of necessity to the hungry and homeless; and trust their distress will be relieved by the charitable and the good.

Contrast Denning M.R.'s comments with those of Laskin C.J.C. in *Harrison v. Carswell*, [1976] 2 S.C.R. 200 at 210-12. See also *Wilcox v. Police*, [1994] 1 N.Z.L.R. 243 (H.C.), where the court rejected the defence of public necessity asserted by anti-abortion protestors who had blocked the entrance to a hospital.

9. The rationale for absolving an individual of liability when acting under public necessity is clear. However, since the public as a whole benefits, why is the state not required to compensate the party whose property has been sacrificed? What is the justification for imposing the entire burden of public necessity on a single innocent property owner? In maritime law, if part of a cargo is jettisoned to prevent a ship from sinking, the loss is apportioned among all the ship and cargo owners. Should a similar concept be adopted in public necessity cases?

10. In *Lapierre v. A.G. Que.*, [1985] 1 S.C.R. 241, a five-year-old girl was left totally incapacitated after suffering an idiosyncratic reaction to an injection that she received as part of a provincial immunization program. Although such reactions are known to occur, the program as a whole saves lives and reduces illnesses caused by infectious diseases. Neither the manufacturer of the serum nor those who administered the program were negligent. The Supreme Court of Canada dismissed the girl's action, stating that there is no legal principle of necessity that requires damages suffered by individuals for the public benefit to be borne by the community. See Capriolo & Turcot, "Strict Liability for Acts of the State: Liability for Non-Negligent Vaccination" (1985), 13 C.C.L.T. 37.

11. An individual who negligently caused or contributed to the emergency situation will not be allowed to benefit from the defence of public necessity. See *Bell Telephone Co. v. The Mar-Tirenno* (1974), 52 D.L.R. (3d) 702 (F.C.T.D.), aff'd (1976), 71 D.L.R. (3d) 608 (F.C.A.); and *Rigby*, *supra*.

12. Various statutes grant public officials broad powers to invade private property in emergency situations. For example, the fire department may be empowered to invade private dwellings to extinguish a fire or to prevent it from spreading.

13. In *R. v. Perka*, [1984] 2 S.C.R. 232, the accused was smuggling over 33 tons of marijuana from Colombia to the international waters off Alaska when mechanical problems and bad weather forced him to take refuge in a deserted cove on the British Columbia coast. The accused argued that he had never intended to enter Canadian waters and that he was entitled to raise the common law defence of necessity. The court held that the defence was preserved by s. 8(3) of the *Criminal Code* and ordered a new trial. See Wells, "Necessity and the Common Law" (1985) 5 Oxford J. Legal Stud. 471.

(b) PRIVATE NECESSITY

VINCENT v. LAKE ERIE TPT. CO.

124 N.W. 221 (Minn. S.C. 1910)

O'BRIEN J.: The steamship Reynolds, owned by the defendant, was for the purpose of discharging her cargo on November 27, 1905, moored to plaintiff's dock in Duluth. While the unloading of the boat was taking place a storm from the northeast developed, which at about 10 o'clock p.m., when the unloading was completed, had so grown in violence that the wind was then moving at 50 miles per hour and continued to increase during the night. There is some evidence that one, and perhaps two, boats were able to enter the harbor that night, but it is plain that navigation was practically suspended from the hour mentioned until the morning of the 29th, when the storm abated, and during that time no master would have been justified in attempting to navigate his vessel, if he could avoid doing so. After the discharge of the cargo the Reynolds signaled for a tug to tow her from the dock, but none could be obtained because of the severity of the storm. If the lines holding the ship to the dock had been cast off, she would doubtless have drifted away; but, instead, the lines were kept fast, and as soon as one parted or chafed it was replaced, sometimes with a larger one. The vessel lay upon the outside of the dock, her bow to the east, the wind and waves striking her starboard quarter with such force that she was constantly being lifted and thrown against the dock, resulting in its damage, as found by the jury, to the amount of $500.

We are satisfied that the character of the storm was such that it would have been highly imprudent for the master of the Reynolds to have attempted to leave the dock or to have permitted the vessel to drift away from it. One witness testified upon the trial that the vessel could have been warped into a slip, and that, if the attempt to bring the ship into the slip had failed, the worst that could have happened would be that the vessel would have been blown ashore upon a soft and muddy bank. The witness was not present in Duluth at the time of the storm, and while he may have been right in his conclusions, those in charge of the dock and the vessel at the time of the storm were not required to use the highest human intelligence, nor were they required to resort to every possible experiment which could be suggested for the preservation of their property. Nothing more was demanded of them than ordinary prudence and care, and the record in this case fully sustains the contention of the appellant that, in holding the vessel fast to the dock, those in charge of her exercised good judgment and prudent seamanship.

It is claimed by the respondent that it was negligence to moor the boat to an exposed part of the wharf, and to continue in that position after it became apparent that the storm was to be more than usually severe. We do not agree with this position. The part of the wharf where the vessel was moored appears to have been commonly used for that purpose. It was situated within the harbor at Duluth, and must, we think, be considered a proper and safe place, and would undoubtedly have been such during what would be considered a very severe storm. The storm which made it unsafe was one which surpassed in violence any which might have reasonably been anticipated.

The appellant contends . . . that, because its conduct during the storm was rendered necessary by prudence and good seamanship under conditions over which it had no control, it cannot be held liable for any injury resulting to the property of others. . .

The situation was one in which the ordinary rules regulating property rights were suspended by forces beyond human control, and if, without the direct intervention of some act by the one sought to be held liable, the property of another was injured, such injury must be attributed to the act of God, and not to the wrongful act of the person sought to be charged. If during the storm the Reynolds had entered the harbor, and while there had become disabled and been thrown against the plaintiff's dock, the plaintiff would not have recovered. Again, if while attempting to hold fast to the dock the lines had parted, without any negligence, and the vessel carried against some other boat or dock in the harbor, there would be no liability upon her owner. But here those in charge of the vessel deliberately and by their direct efforts held her in such a position that the damage to the dock resulted, and, having thus preserved the ship at the expense of the dock, it seems to us that her owners are responsible to the dock owners to the extent of the injury inflicted.

In *Depue v. Flateau*, 100 Minn. 299, 111 N.W. 1, 8 L.R.A. (N.S.) 485, this court held that where the plaintiff, while lawfully in the defendant's house, became so ill that he was incapable of traveling with safety, the defendants were responsible to him in damages for compelling him to leave the premises. If, however, the owner of the premises had furnished the traveller with proper accommodations and medical attendance, would he have been able to defeat an action brought against him for their reasonable worth?

In *Ploof v. Putnam*, 71 Atl. 188, 20 L.R.A. (N.S.) 152, the Supreme Court of Vermont held that where, under stress of weather, a vessel was without permission moored to a private dock at an island in Lake Champlain owned by the defendant, the plaintiff was not guilty of trespass, and that the defendant was responsible in damages because his representative upon the island unmoored the vessel, permitting it to drift upon the shore, with resultant injuries to it. If, in that case, the vessel had been permitted to remain, and the dock had suffered injury, we believe the shipowner would have been held liable for the injury done.

Theologians hold that a starving man may, without moral guilt, take what is necessary to sustain life; but it could hardly be said that the obligation would not be upon such person to pay the value of the property so taken when he became able to do so. And so public necessity, in times of war or peace, may require the taking of private property for public purposes; but under our system of jurisprudence compensation must be made.

Let us imagine in this case that for the better mooring of the vessel those in charge of her had appropriated a valuable cable lying upon the dock. No matter how justifiable such appropriation might have been, it would not be claimed that, because of the overwhelming necessity of the situation, the owner of the cable could not recover its value.

This is not a case where life or property was menaced by any object or thing belonging to the plaintiff, the destruction of which became necessary to prevent the threatened disaster. Nor is it a case where, because of the act of God, or unavoidable accident, the infliction of the injury was beyond the control of the defendant, but is one where the defendant prudently and advisedly availed itself of the plaintiff's property for the purpose of preserving its own more valuable property, and the plaintiffs are entitled to compensation for the injury done.

LEWIS J.:—I dissent. It was assumed on the trial before the lower court that appellant's liability depended on whether the master of the ship might, in the exercise of reasonable care, have sought a place of safety before the storm made it impossible to leave the dock. The majority opinion assumed that the evidence is conclusive that appellant moored its boat at respondent's dock pursuant to contract, and that the vessel was lawfully in position at the time the additional cables were fastened to the dock, and the reasoning of the opinion is that, because appellant made use of the stronger cables to hold the boat in position, it became liable under the rule that it had voluntarily made use of the property of another for the purpose of saving its own.

In my judgment, if the boat was lawfully in position at the time the storm broke, and the master could not, in the exercise of due care, have left that position without subjecting his vessel to the hazards of the storm, then the damage to the dock, caused by the pounding of the boat, was the result of an inevitable accident. If the master was in the exercise of due care, he was not at fault. The reasoning of the opinion admits that if the ropes, or cables, first attached to the dock had not parted, or if, in the first instance, the master had used the stronger cables, there would be no liability. If the master could not, in the exercise of reasonable care have anticipated the severity of the storm and sought a place of safety before it became impossible, why should he be required to anticipate the severity of the storm, and, in the first instance, use the stronger cables?

I am of the opinion that one who constructs a dock to the navigable line of waters, and enters into contractual relations with the owner of a vessel to moor at the same, takes the risk of damage to his dock by a boat caught there by a storm, which event could not have been avoided in the exercise of due care, and further, that the legal status of the parties in such a case is not changed by renewal of cables to keep the boat from being cast adrift at the mercy of the tempest.

JAGGARD J.: I concur with Lewis, J.

NOTES AND QUESTIONS

1. Upon what bases did O'Brien J. conclude that (a) inevitable accident and (b) public necessity did not apply? What was the basis of Lewis J.'s dissent?

2. The first issue that arises in private necessity, as in public necessity, is whether the defendant is privileged to invade the plaintiff's property interests. As J. Fleming states in *The Law of Torts*, 9th ed. (1998) at 104, "If the emergency is sufficiently great and the good it is intended to do is not disproportionate to the harm likely to result, one may trespass upon the land of another to save himself or his property." This balancing of interests is often expressed in terms of requiring the defendant to act reasonably both in terms of the decision to enter and his or her subsequent conduct. See Keeton *et al.*, *Prosser and Keeton on the Law of Torts*, 5th ed. (1984) at 145-48; and Rogers, *Winfield and Jolowicz on Tort*, 17th ed. (2006) at 1092-96.

3. Should public or private necessity apply if the defendant is attempting (a) to save his or her own life, (b) to protect his or her own interests but in doing so advances the public interest, as in *Dwyer v. Staunton*, [1947] 4 D.L.R. 393 (Alta. Dist. Ct.), or (c) to protect the plaintiff's property, as in *Sherrin v. Haggerty*, [1953] O.W.N. 962 (Co. Ct.)?

4. As with other self-help remedies, such as recaption of chattels, there is a potential for violence inherent in the assertion of private necessity. How is this factor to be taken into account in assessing the appropriateness of the defence? Can you justify granting broader powers of entry in private necessity than in recaption of chattels?

5. What is the significance of the imminent peril requirement? How would you distinguish *Vincent* from a case in which a landowner found it impossible to complete a construction project without trespassing on the adjoining property?

6. Once a court decides that the defendant was privileged to enter, it must then determine who should pay for whatever actual losses ensued. As indicated in *Vincent*, private necessity is generally considered to be a partial or incomplete defence in the United States. In other words, the defendant is permitted to trespass on the plaintiff's land, but must provide compensation for losses inflicted. See Bohlen, "Incomplete Privilege to Inflict Intentional Invasions of Interests of Property and Personalty" (1926) 39 Harv. L. Rev. 307; *Restatement (Second) of the Law of Torts* (1965) at §§196, 197,

262, and 263; and Keeton, "Conditional Fault in the Law of Torts" (1959) 72 Harv. L. Rev. 401.

7. Is it inconsistent to grant defendants a right to trespass but hold them liable for the damages that result? Why would defendants plead private necessity if they still have to pay for the damage they cause? How would the court in *Vincent* have reacted if the dock owner had unmoored the ship, allowing it to be wrecked in the storm? See *Ploof v. Putnam*, 71 A. 188 (Vt. S.C. 1908); Epstein, "Defenses and Subsequent Pleas in a System of Strict Liability" (1974) 3 J. Legal Stud. 165 at 165-70; and Klimchuk, "Necessity and Restitution" (2001) 7 Legal Theory 59.

8. It is not clear whether private necessity is a complete or partial defence in England and Canada. A complete defence would allow a person to trespass without paying compensation for losses inflicted. What arguments would you make in favour of each position? See Williams, "The Defence of Necessity" (1953) 6 Curr. Legal Probs. 216 at 219-23; Sussman, "The Defence of Private Necessity and the Problem of Compensation" (1967) 2 Ottawa L. Rev. 184; and Finan & Ritson, "Tortious Necessity: The Privileged Defense" (1992) 26 Akron L. Rev. 1.

9. The facts in *Munn & Co. v. The Motor Vessel Sir John Crosbie*, [1967] 1 Ex. C.R. 94 were similar to those in *Vincent*, but the case was pleaded and decided in negligence. Although the statement was made in *obiter dicta*, the court expressed a preference for the dissent in *Vincent*. See Sussman, *supra*.

10. Although there is no right to intentionally injure another person in the assertion of either public or private necessity, physical force can be used to overcome resistance to the exercise of necessity. Given the potential for violence inherent in this principle, should it be limited to public necessity? See the *Restatement (Second) of the Law of Torts* (1965) at §196, comment (b) and §197, comment (g). An individual who causes harm or injury in resisting the exercise of public or private necessity can be held civilly liable: see *Depue v. Flatau*, 111 N.W. 1 (Minn. S.C. 1907); and *Ploof v. Putnam*, *supra*.

11. Can you justify the fact that the common law recognizes a defence of public and private necessity but not duress?

8. Apportionment of Fault in Intentional Torts

At common law, the fact that the plaintiff negligently contributed to his or her own injuries provided the defendant with a complete defence to negligence liability. This all-or-nothing approach came to be viewed as inappropriate, for it imposed the entire loss on only one of the two negligent parties. Consequently, legislation was introduced in most common law jurisdictions to apportion losses in negligence actions between the defendant and the plaintiff, according to their respective degrees of fault. This is discussed in greater detail in Chapter 19. Generally, the legislation in Canada's common law provinces applies in any case where the damages have been caused by "fault or neglect." Depending on the courts' interpretation of the word "fault," the legislation may apply beyond the bounds of negligence. The question has arisen whether a defendant in an intentional tort action can invoke the apportionment legislation and use the plaintiff's contributory negligence or other wrongful conduct as a partial defence.

Some recent cases indicate that the apportionment legislation may apply to intentional torts. For example in *Bell Canada v. Cope (Sarnia) Ltd.* (1980), 11 C.C.L.T. 170 (Ont. H.C.), aff'd (1981) 119 D.L.R. (3d) 254 (C.A.), the defendant's damages in trespass to land were reduced by 33% to reflect the plaintiff's contributory negligence. Similarly in *Berntt v. Vancouver (City)*, [1997] 4 W.W.R. 505 (B.C.S.C.), the plaintiff's damages in battery were reduced 75% under the provincial apportionment legislation to reflect his provocative and irresponsible behaviour as a ringleader of a riot following a hockey game. Although the Court of Appeal ordered a new trial on the issue of liability, it did not question the application of the apportionment legislation: *Berntt v. Vancouver (City)* (1999), 46 C.C.L.T. (2d) 139 (B.C.C.A.).

However, in *Boma Manufacturing Ltd. v. Canadian Imperial Bank of Commerce*, [1996] 3 S.C.R. 727, the court stated that as a matter of principle "contributory negligence would not be available in the context of a strict liability tort. . . . While this argument would be available in an action for negligence, the notion of strict liability involved in an action for conversion is *prima facie* antithetical to the concept of contributory negligence." The issue in *Boma* arose in the context of an action for conversion of cheques. It is not clear whether the court intended to preclude other intentional torts as well from the application of apportionment legislation.

The issue of apportionment can arise not only between the plaintiff and the defendant, but also among various defendants. That issue is similarly addressed by statute. For example, the *Negligence Act*, R.S.O. 1990, c. N.1, s. 1 states:

> Where damages have been caused or contributed to by the fault or neglect of two or more persons, the court shall determine the degree in which each of such persons is at fault or negligent, and, where two or more persons are found at fault or negligent, they are jointly and severally liable to the person suffering loss or damage for such fault or negligence, but as between themselves, in the absence of any contract express or implied, each is liable to make contribution and indemnify each other in the degree in which they are respectively found to be at fault or negligent.

NOTES AND QUESTIONS

1. Traditionally, the courts interpreted the words "fault" and "negligent" to be synonyms so as to exclude intentional torts from the scope of the apportionment legislation. See for example *Hollebone v. Barnard*, [1954] 2 D.L.R. 278 (Ont. H.C.); and *Funnel v. Canadian Pacific Railway*, [1964] 2 O.R. 325 (H.C.).

2. In *Boma Manufacturing*, the court stated that contributory negligence is logically incompatible with strict liability torts. In order to establish contributory negligence, the defendant must prove that the plaintiff acted negligently or in an intentionally wrongful manner and that this conduct caused or contributed to the plaintiff's injuries or loss. Given the definition of contributory negligence, do you agree with the court's analysis of the relationship between this defence and strict liability torts? Is the court's characterization of conversion as a strict liability tort accurate?

In *Cowles v. Balac* (2006), 83 O.R. (3d) 660 (C.A.), the plaintiffs were attacked by Bengal tigers at the defendant's drive-through safari zoo. At para. 216 Justice Borins said of *Boma*: "In my respectful view, in stating contributory negligence is not available in the context of a strict liability tort, Iacobucci J. was not intending to state a general principle. Rather, he was referring to the law of bills of exchange." After a detailed review of the cases and academic views, Borins J.A. concluded that contributory negligence should be a defence to strict liability torts. In *Cowles*, Justice Borins was in dissent. The majority held that on the facts the plaintiffs were not contributorily negligent and so did not address this issue.

3. The apportionment legislation only applies when two or more parties have caused or contributed to the same loss or injury. This issue is often framed in terms of whether the loss or injury is "indivisible." The task of determining whether a series of harms should be treated as resulting in a single collective or indivisible injury is often challenging.

For example in *O'Neil v. Van Horne* (2002), 59 O.R. (3d) 384 (C.A.), the defendant was being sued for sexually assaulting the plaintiff when she was three years old. The defendant sought to add the plaintiff's parents and former boyfriend as third parties, because they had allegedly sexually assaulted the plaintiff later in life. The court refused the defendant's motion, stating that while it was inherently difficult to determine which of the plaintiff's damages were attributable to which assaults, the torts were separate and the damages had to be treated as being divisible. Consequently, in this case there could be no joint and several liability and no apportionment. Each defendant would be solely liable for the damages that were attributable to his or her own conduct.

4. Some courts have attempted to avoid the impact of applying the traditional intentional tort defences in cases in which both parties were to blame. For example, the limitations that the courts have imposed on the *ex turpi causa* defence, discussed in Chapter 6, appear to reflect concern about denying a wrongdoing plaintiff any redress. The complex case law governing consensual fights and factors vitiating consent appears to be based on similar concerns. However, by narrowly defining the traditional defences, the courts impose the entire loss on the defendant, despite the plaintiff's at-fault conduct that has contributed to his or her own loss. Is this all-or-nothing approach in intentional torts any more justifiable than the now-discredited all-or-nothing approach to negligence liability? In what other areas of intentional torts would apportionment provisions be appropriate? See generally Crocker, "Apportionment of Liability and the Intentional Torts: The Time is Right for Change" (1982-83) 7 Dal. L.J. 172; and Manchester, "Trespass and Contributory Negligence in Ontario" (1982) 31 I.C.L.Q. 203.

As discussed in Chapter 3, the plaintiff's provocative conduct is taken into account in several provinces to reduce the compensatory damage award that he or she might have received. For a discussion of the relationship between provocation and contributory negligence in intentional torts, see *Wilson v. Bobbie* (2006), 394 A.R. 118 (Q.B.).

5. The debate over the scope of the term fault involves branches of law other than torts. See generally Weinrib, "Contribution in a Contractual Setting" (1976) 54 Can. Bar Rev. 338; Institute of Law Research and Reform, *Contributory Negligence and Concurrent Wrongdoers* (1979) at 11-25; and Klar, "Developments in Tort Law: The 1979-80 Term" [1981] 2 S.C.L.R. 325 at 340-54. See also *Doiron v. Caisse Populaire d'Inkerman Ltée.* (1985), 32 C.C.L.T. 73 (N.B.C.A.).

REVIEW PROBLEMS

1. Although Steven loved to bet on football games, he seldom picked winners. As a result, he became indebted to a local bookmaker named Estelle for $35,000. She made it clear that unless he paid at least $18,000 by the end of the week, he would have to "face the music." Steven was frightened. He knew that Estelle was dangerous and strongly suspected that she was responsible for two unknown thugs severely beating his friend, who was also indebted to Estelle.

Gambling debts were not Steven's only problem. Although entirely oblivious to the fact, Steven had become a prime suspect in the armed robbery of his former employer, Mel. When asked who might have a motive for such a crime, Mel readily suggested Steven, saying "He always hated me, especially after I fired him for insolence."

As Steven was drowning his sorrows in a glass of beer at a local bar, he noticed that two men were watching him. They were very big and looked very tough. Steven quickly paid his tab, finished his drink and left. However, as he was walking toward his car, he noticed that the two men had followed him. When he crossed the street, they did likewise. When he quickened his pace, they did so as well. He could hear their approaching footsteps close behind. Finally, fearing for his safety, he turned and sprayed the two men with a canister of mace. They dropped to the ground, screaming in pain and wiping their eyes. As Steven ran toward his car, one of the men shouted, "Stop or we will shoot. We are the police and you are under arrest." Steven kept running, convinced that the two men were actually Estelle's thugs. Steven then heard a gun shot and felt a searing pain in his leg. As he later learned in the hospital, the two men were indeed undercover police officers. They were following him in connection with their investigation into Mel's robbery.

Steven has come to you for advice. In particular, he wants to know if the police officers can sue him for spraying them with mace, and if so, whether he has any defence. He also wants to know if he can sue the police officer for shooting him and, if so, whether the officer has any defence.

2. There had been bad feelings between the Smith and Jones families for years. In a recent incident, nine-year-old Frank Smith was bitten by Mr. Jones' dog, Max. Frank had been playing with a Frisbee in his own backyard when the wind carried it over the fence and into Mr. Jones' backyard. Frank had just received the Frisbee as a birthday present. He knew from past experience that Mr. Jones would probably take at least a week to return it. Frank was also aware of Max, but he did not see the dog when he peered over the fence and thus concluded that there was no danger. Consequently, although Mr. Jones had previously forbidden him from doing so, Frank climbed over the fence to retrieve his Frisbee. When Mr. Jones saw Frank in his yard, he became furious. Wanting to scare the boy, he opened his back door and let Max run out. To Mr. Jones' surprise, Max not only barked at Frank, he also bit him. Once that happened, Mr. Jones intervened and pulled Max away. Discuss the intentional torts that may have been committed by Mr. Jones and Frank. Also discuss the defences that each party might raise.

8

THE DEFENCE OF LEGAL AUTHORITY

1. Introduction
2. The *Canadian Charter of Rights and Freedoms*
3. Authority and Privilege to Arrest Without a Warrant
4. Rights and Obligations in the Arrest Process
5. The Common Law Power to Search Pursuant to a Lawful Arrest
6. A Peace Officer's Common Law Power of Entry to Search for a Wanted Person

1. Introduction

This chapter deals with legal authority as a defence to intentional torts that may be committed during an arrest, search, seizure, or entry. Although most commonly associated with false imprisonment, the defence of legal authority may be raised in response to actions for battery, trespass to chattels, conversion, trespass to land, and other intentional torts. Initially, the defence was based on both common law civil and criminal cases. Consistent with the common law's concern with autonomy, peace officers and private citizens were given only limited powers to act without a warrant or other prior judicial authorization. In many circumstances, those who acted on reasonable grounds in asserting legal authority were held liable if they arrested the wrong person, seized the wrong goods or entered the wrong property. The early common law viewed law enforcement as a community responsibility, and relatively few distinctions were drawn between the authority of the citizenry and various enforcement officials.

In Canada, these common law principles were largely supplanted by legislation. The statutory provisions greatly expanded the powers of police and others to act without prior judicial approval. Moreover, the courts interpreted these statutory powers very broadly. While this chapter focuses on legal authority under federal criminal law, it is important to appreciate that the police and others are granted broad arrest, entry, search, and seizure powers under various provincial and territorial legislation, including mental health, child welfare, education, liquor, highway traffic, parks, and trespass statutes.

The framework for analyzing the defence of legal authority is essentially the same, whether it is based on the common law or on provincial, territorial or federal legislation. Three issues must be addressed. First, did the defendant have legal authority to undertake the act that gave rise to the tort in issue? Second, was the defendant legally privileged, that is, protected from both civil and criminal liability, in doing the act giving rise to the tort? Third, did the defendant meet all the other obligations imposed upon him or her in the process? For example, even if the police are authorized and privileged in making an arrest, they may be held civilly liable for failing to inform the suspect of the reasons for the arrest or for using excessive force.

It is not possible in this chapter to comprehensively review the defence of legal authority, even if the discussion is limited to federal criminal law or indeed the *Criminal Code of Canada*, R.S.C. 1985, c. C-46. Consequently, we have addressed four common issues that illustrate how the defence of legal authority operates within the federal criminal law: (i) authority and privilege to arrest without a warrant; (ii) rights and obligations in the arrest process; (iii) the common law power to search pursuant to a lawful arrest; and (iv) a peace officer's common law power of entry to search for a wanted person.

As many of the older cases discussed in this chapter illustrate, until the 1980s the Canadian courts broadly interpreted police powers and only reluctantly held police civilly liable. With the advent of the *Canadian Charter of Rights and Freedoms*, Part I of the *Constitution Act, 1982*, being Schedule B to the *Canada Act 1982* (U.K.) 1982, c. 11, judicial attitudes to the police changed dramatically. Nevertheless, it may be some time before the courts' recent concern with civil liberties reshapes the defence of legal authority.

NOTES AND QUESTIONS

1. For a discussion of the English common law enforcement powers, see Harris, *Principles of the Criminal Law* (1877) at 303-12; Stephen, *A History of the Criminal Law of England*, vol. 1 (1883) at 184-206; and Hall, "Legal and Social Aspects of Arrest Without a Warrant" (1936) 49 Harv. L. Rev. 566.

2. In many instances, such as those involving a teacher in a classroom or a doctor in a psychiatric facility, the provincial and territorial legislation creates far broader powers than those given the police to investigate serious *Criminal Code* offences. In regard to educators, see for example *R. v. Sweet*, [1986] O.J. No. 2083 (Dist. Ct.) (QL); and *R. v. M.(M.R.)*, [1998] 3 S.C.R. 393. Under the provincial and territorial mental health statutes, doctors are typically authorized to detain anyone who is mentally ill, poses a significant risk of serious harm to him or herself or others, and is not suitable for admission as a voluntary patient. See for example *Mental Health Act*, R.S.B.C. 1996, c. 288, s. 22; and *Mental Health Act*, R.S.O. 1990, c. M.7, s. 20(1.1).

3. The Canadian courts' reliance on the *Criminal Code* and other federal criminal statutes to define civil liability raises complex issues regarding the constitutional division of legislative authority between the federal and provincial governments. While criminal law falls within the exclusive authority of the federal government, "property and civil rights," which includes tort law, is a provincial matter: *The Constitution Act, 1867* (U.K.), 30 & 31 Vict., c. 3, ss. 91(27) and 92(13), reprinted in R.S.C. 1985, App. II, No. 5. For the most part, the Supreme Court of Canada simply assumed that the *Criminal Code* provisions governed civil liability. See *Frey v. Fedoruk*, [1950] S.C.R. 517; *Priestman v. Colangelo*, [1959] S.C.R. 615; and *Poupart v. Lafortune*, [1974] S.C.R. 175. Even when it has been stated that the criminal and civil defences of legal authority should be treated as distinct issues, the constitutional question has not been squarely addressed. See for example *Fletcher v. Collins* (1968), 70 D.L.R. (2d) 183 at 188 (Ont. H.C.); and *Eccles v. Bourque*, [1975] 2 S.C.R. 739 at 742.

What constitutional argument would you make in support of the courts' reliance on the *Criminal Code* in civil cases? Would your argument vary depending on whether the defendant was a peace officer or a private citizen?

4. Reliance on criminal statutes and cases in tort law is also complicated by the fact that the criminal law concept of arrest does not correspond to the tort concept of

imprisonment. In *R. v. Whitfield*, [1970] S.C.R. 46 at 48, Judson J., quoting 10 Hals. (3d) 342, stated: "Arrest consists of the actual seizure or touching of a person's body with a view to his detention. The mere pronouncing of words of arrest is not an arrest, unless the person sought to be arrested submits to the process and goes with the arresting officer." As discussed in Chapter 3, the tort of false imprisonment may be defined as the intentional bringing about of the total restraint of movement of another person. How do the concepts of arrest and imprisonment differ? What are the legal implications of these differences on the defence of legal authority?

5. Most of the early case law is English and it is difficult to apply in Canada because crimes are categorized differently in the two jurisdictions. The English common law distinction between felonies and misdemeanors was abandoned in Canada with the enactment of our first *Criminal Code*, S.C. 1892, 55-56 Vict., c. 29. Instead, the *Criminal Code* divides offences into those tried by indictment and those tried by summary conviction. There is also a third category, hybrid offences, in which the prosecutor is given discretion to proceed by either indictment or summary conviction.

2. The *Canadian Charter of Rights and Freedoms*

The *Charter* adds another dimension to the analysis of the defence of legal authority. However, the *Charter*'s application is subject to several limitations. Most significantly for our purposes, s. 32 of the *Charter* limits its application to federal and provincial law, and the conduct of government departments, agencies and officials. Consistent with its goal of protecting the public from improper state action, the *Charter* generally does not apply to the actions of entirely private parties.

Some sections of the *Charter* are specifically designed to protect people who are subject to criminal charges or other state-imposed detention, while other sections have a more general application. Sections 7 to 15 of the *Charter* guarantee a broad range of legal rights, including: the right to be secure against unreasonable search or seizure (s. 8); the right not to be arbitrarily detained or imprisoned (s. 9); and the right to legal counsel upon arrest or detention (s. 10(a) and (b)). Section 2 contains broad freedoms, including freedom of expression, assembly and association (s. 2(b), (c) and (d)).

Once an individual establishes that his or her *Charter* rights have been violated, the burden shifts to the government to justify that violation under s. 1. If the government cannot satisfy the requirements of s. 1, the individual may pursue one or more remedies under the *Charter*. Section 24(1) gives a judge discretion to grant the aggrieved individual whatever remedy the judge considers "appropriate and just in the circumstances." Section 24(2), which is primarily relevant in criminal cases, requires the judge to exclude evidence obtained in violation of the accused's *Charter* rights, if its admission would "bring the administration of justice into disrepute." Moreover, s. 52 provides that the *Charter* is the supreme law of Canada, and that any law inconsistent with it is of no force or effect to the extent of the inconsistency. These provisions can affect civil liability in two distinct ways.

(a) LIABILITY UNDER SECTION 24(1)

First, if a person's *Charter* rights are violated, he or she may seek a remedy under s. 24(1). Unlike in a common law tort action, an aggrieved party has no right to a damage award under s. 24(1). Rather, it is simply one of the remedies that a judge may consider granting. In *RJR-MacDonald Inc. v. Canada (A.G.)*, [1994] 1 S.C.R. 311 at 343, the court noted that while it had awarded damages for *Charter* breaches, no body of principles had yet developed governing such awards. The situation has been clarified somewhat in the interim. Several courts have stated that damages should not be awarded under s. 24(1) for *Charter* violations committed in good faith in the absence of reckless or aggressive conduct. See for example *Persaud v. Donaldson* (1997), 32 O.R. (3d) 349 (Gen. Div.); *Chrispen v. Kalinowski* (1997), 148 D.L.R. (4th) 720 (Sask. Q.B.); and *Lucas v. Toronto Police Service Board* (2000), 51 O.R. (3d) 783 (S.C.J.), rev'd on other grounds (2001), 54 O.R. (3d) 715 (C.A.).

However, serious *Charter* violations resulting in significant harm will give rise to substantial damage awards. In *McTaggart v. Ontario*, 2000 CarswellOnt 4808 (S.C.J.) (WLeC), the investigating officer's intentional withholding of exculpatory evidence from the Crown and defence counsel violated the plaintiff's s. 7 *Charter* rights to life, liberty and security of the person. This violation led to the plaintiff's wrongful conviction as a bank robber, 20 months of incarceration in solitary confinement as a dangerous offender, and profound psychological harm. The plaintiff was awarded a total of $230,000 under s. 24(1), made up of $60,000 in lost income, $150,000 in general damages and $20,000 in punitive damages. Similarly, in *Rollison v. R.* (1994), 20 C.C.L.T. (2d) 92 (F.C.T.D.), the plaintiff was awarded $224,000 stemming from a series of unjustified police and customs seizures of his boat. The general damage award included $8,000 specifically for the denial of the plaintiff's *Charter* rights.

(b) THE IMPACT OF SECTION 52 ON THE DEFENCE OF LEGAL AUTHORITY

As indicated, s. 52 provides that any law that is inconsistent with the *Charter* will be of no force or effect to the extent of the inconsistency. Consequently, the *Charter* may eliminate the legal basis upon which a person would have otherwise been able to establish the defence of legal authority. Assume that a peace officer relies upon a *Criminal Code* provision in arresting a suspect and that provision is struck down under s. 52 in the ensuing criminal trial. If the suspect then sues in false imprisonment, the officer will not be able to establish that the detention was authorized by law and the officer may not be able to establish that he or she was privileged from civil liability.

NOTES AND QUESTIONS

1. Although it is often suggested that s. 24(1) of the *Charter* creates a "constitutional tort," is such a characterization appropriate or accurate? Does it assist in resolving the issues raised by damage awards under s. 24(1)? For example, should such awards focus on compensating the aggrieved party, or punishing and deterring the defendant? Should the aggrieved party be able to recover for all of the consequences of the *Charter* violation or only for reasonably foreseeable losses?

2. Initially, the Canadian courts were reluctant to award damages for the *Charter* violation itself, and required the plaintiff to prove actual loss. See for example *Bauder v. Wilson* (1988), 43 C.R.R. 149 (B.C.S.C.); and *Breen v. Saunders* (1986), 71 N.B.R. (2d) 404 (Q.B.). More recently, however, it has been held that proof of actual loss is not

required. See *Bevis v. Burns* (2006), 244 N.S.R. (2d) 211 (C.A.), where the court ordered a new hearing on damages because the trial judge failed to explain the seriousness of *Charter* violations and the need to meaningfully vindicate the plaintiff's rights. Should *Charter* violations be actionable *per se*, like most intentional torts, or should they be actionable only upon proof of loss, like the tort of negligence? See Otis, "Constitutional Liability for the Infringement of Rights Per Se: A Misguided Theory" (1992) 26 U.B.C.L. Rev. 21.

3. As stated in the text above, several courts have indicated that damages should not be awarded under s. 24(1) for *Charter* violations committed in good faith in the absence of recklessness or oppressive conduct. Do you agree? Should negligent breaches of the *Charter* give rise to damage awards under s. 24(1)? Who should bear the burden of proof in these situations?

4. As illustrated by the following discussion of *Dulude v. Canada* (2000), 1 F.C. 545 (C.A.), judicial opinions vary on whether the *Charter* has been violated and whether an infringement constitutes a serious breach. The plaintiff, a member of the armed forces, had obtained sick leave from a military physician, but not his commanding officer. Since the plaintiff was technically absent without leave, the commanding officer was acting within his power in ordering the plaintiff's arrest. The military police who arrested and detained Dulude did not use excessive force and he suffered no physical or psychological injury. The plaintiff sued the Department of National Defence for unlawful arrest. The trial judge ruled that the arrest was lawful and dismissed the claim. The plaintiff appealed. The Federal Court of Appeal held that the commanding officer should not have exercised his power to have the plaintiff arrested and thereby breached the plaintiff's s. 9 *Charter* rights. The court characterized the defendant's conduct as a serious breach of the *Charter* and awarded the plaintiff $10,000 under s. 24(1). See also *Ward v. Vancouver (City)* (2007), 45 C.C.L.T. (3d) 121 (B.C.S.C.).

5. Even if there has been a *Charter* breach, it is unclear when damages will be considered an appropriate remedy. In *Jane Doe v. Metropolitan Toronto (Municipality) Commissioners of Police* (1998), 39 O.R. (3d) 487 (Gen. Div.), the court stated that since the plaintiff was compensated for her injuries as a result of her successful claim in negligence, she was not entitled to an additional damage award under s. 24(1) for the violation of her *Charter* rights. A declaration that the police violated her *Charter* rights was viewed as a sufficient remedy. Do you agree?

3. Authority and Privilege to Arrest Without a Warrant

(a) INTRODUCTION

Peace officers and private citizens often raise the defence of legal authority when a suspect whom they have arrested or detained sues them for false imprisonment or battery. In such cases, the defendant has to prove that the specific act that gave rise to the tort action was authorized by the common law or statute.

Traditionally, the common law did not lightly grant such authority. As illustrated by *Entick v. Carrington* (1765), 19 State Tr. 1029 (C.P.), individuals enjoy a right to freedom of movement unless there is clear legal authority that specifically allows for their restraint. As a result, individuals are generally not required to stop, identify themselves, answer questions, submit to a search, or otherwise co-operate with the police or anyone else purporting to exercise a power of arrest or detention. Although it may be imprudent to do so, individuals are even allowed to use force to physically resist unauthorized police conduct.

However, such a course of action carries not only physical but also legal risks. It is well established that if the police are authorized to arrest or detain an individual, that person is required to defer to their legal authority. An individual who defies or physically resists the lawful exercise of police authority may incur criminal liability for obstructing or assaulting an officer in the execution of his or her duty: see *Criminal Code*, ss. 129(a) and 270(1)(a).

While various sections of the *Criminal Code* authorize arrest in specific situations, the most important sources of authority to arrest are found in the general arrest provisions of ss. 494 and 495.

> 494. (1) Any one may arrest without warrant
> (a) ia person whom he finds committing an indictable offence, or
> (b) a person who, on reasonable grounds, he believes
> (i) has committed a criminal offence, and
> (ii) is escaping from and freshly pursued by persons who have lawful authority to arrest that person.
>
> (2) Any one who is
> (a) the owner or a person in lawful possession of property; or
> (b) a person authorized by the owner or by a person in lawful possession of property,
> may arrest without warrant a person whom he finds committing a criminal offence on or in relation to that property.
>
> (3) Any one other than a peace officer who arrests a person without warrant shall forthwith deliver the person to a peace officer.
>
> 495. (1) A peace officer may arrest without warrant
> (a) a person who has committed an indictable offence or who, on reasonable grounds, he believes has committed or is about to commit an indictable offence;
> (b) a person whom he finds committing a criminal offence; or
> (c) a person in respect of whom he has reasonable grounds to believe that a warrant of arrest or committal, in any form set out in Part XXVIII in relation thereto, is in force within the territorial jurisdiction in which the person is found.

NOTES AND QUESTIONS

1. These seemingly straightforward statutory provisions require careful analysis of several variables, including: the status of the person making the arrest; whether the offence is about to be, is being or has been committed; the category of offence in issue (indictable or criminal); and whether the person making the arrest needs only reasonable grounds or must prove that the person arrested was actually committing or had actually committed the offence.

2. By virtue of the *Interpretation Act*, R.S.C. 1985, c. I-21, s. 34(1)(a), the term "indictable offence" includes hybrid offences. The term "criminal offence" includes summary conviction, hybrid and indictable offences.

3. The legality of arrests under ss. 494(1)(b) and 495(1)(a) and (c) often turns on whether there were reasonable grounds to believe the person arrested committed the offence. The term "reasonable grounds" is typically defined as facts that would create in the mind of a reasonable person a strong and honest belief that the suspect had committed the offence in question. The individual must subjectively believe that the person committed the offence, and that belief must be objectively reasonable. An individual must take into account all of the relevant information in determining whether there are reasonable grounds for the arrest. See *Webster v. Edmonton (City) Police Services* (2007), 69 Alta. L.R. (4th) 205 (C.A.).

Mere suspicion is not sufficient. The fact that a suspect has a prior criminal record, refuses to answer questions or is unhelpful does not, in and of itself, constitute reasonable grounds. See *Dumbell v. Roberts*, [1944] 1 All E.R. 326 (C.A.); *Chartier v. Quebec (A.G.)*, [1979] 2 S.C.R. 474; *R. v. Storrey*, [1990] 1 S.C.R. 241; *R. v. Klimchuk* (1991), 8 C.R. (4th) 327 (B.C.C.A.); *R. v. Golub* (1997), 34 O.R. (3d) 743 (C.A.); *Thornton v. Byers* (1999), 173 D.L.R. (4th) 568 (Ont. Gen. Div.); *Hanisch v. Canada* (2003), 18 C.C.L.T. (3d) 143 (B.C.S.C.), varied (2004), 27 C.C.L.T. (3d) 1 (B.C.C.A.); and *R. v. Perello* (2005), 193 C.C.C. (3d) 151 (Sask. C.A.).

(b) A PEACE OFFICER'S POWER TO ARREST WITHOUT A WARRANT

Several aspects of peace officers' powers to arrest require elaboration. First, although the public and most commentators talk about "police" powers, s. 495 is framed in terms of "peace officers." Under s. 2 of the *Criminal Code*, the term "peace officer" is defined to include police officers, sheriffs, mayors, commercial pilots, fishery officers, and others. However, the term does not include private security guards or private detectives. Second, a peace officer is entitled to invoke the powers in both ss. 494 and 495. Third, peace officers are given broader authority to arrest than private citizens. Perhaps most importantly, s. 495(1)(a) authorizes peace officers to arrest anyone whom they have reasonable grounds to believe has committed or is about to commit an indictable offence. This provision requires individuals who are innocent of any criminal wrongdoing to submit to the peace officer's authority.

Fourth, the Supreme Court of Canada has interpreted s. 495(1)(b) broadly. In *R. v. Biron*, [1976] 2 S.C.R. 56, Constable Maisonneuve arrested Biron for the summary conviction offence of creating a disturbance. Biron struggled while being led to the police wagon by Constable Dorion, causing both of them to fall. As a result, Biron was also charged with resisting a peace officer in the execution of his duty. Following Biron's acquittal on the charge of creating a disturbance, the Quebec Court of Appeal acquitted him on the charge of resisting. The court reasoned that since Maisonneuve had not found Biron committing the offence of creating a disturbance, he had no authority to arrest Biron. Thus, Biron was legally entitled to go on his way, Dorion had no legal authority to detain him, and Biron could not be convicted of resisting a peace officer in the execution of his duty.

The Crown appealed Biron's acquittal on the charge of resisting arrest. It argued that the term "finds committing" means both actually finds committing and apparently finds committing. On that view, since Maisonneuve found Biron apparently committing the offence of causing a disturbance, Biron's initial arrest had been lawful. Consequently,

Dorion had lawfully detained Biron and, by struggling, Biron committed the offence of resisting.

The majority in the Supreme Court of Canada agreed with that argument and restored Biron's conviction. They stated that if the term "finds committing" was interpreted literally, an officer could never know with certainty that an arrest was lawful. The majority reasoned that the validity of an arrest had to be determined in relation to the circumstances that were apparent to the officer at the time of the arrest. In dissent, Laskin C.J.C. stated that the majority's position needlessly expanded police powers, convicted an innocent person of an offence, violated the principles of the statutory interpretation, and was contrary to public policy.

NOTES AND QUESTIONS

1. Why did the Crown in *Biron* not rely on s. 495(1)(a)?

2. As a matter of statutory interpretation, was it appropriate for the majority to hold that the term "finds committing" extends to apparently finds committing? Should the legal consequences of an officer's misapprehension of the facts result in an otherwise innocent individual being convicted of a federal criminal offence?

3. The majority in *Biron* did not define the term "apparently finds committing." Should the test be objective, subjective or a combination of both factors? Must a peace officer witness some aspect of the apparent offence? See *R. v. Stevens* (1976), 18 N.S.R. (2d) 96 (App. Div.).

4. For a discussion of a peace officer's power to arrest under the authority of a warrant see *Fletcher v. Collins* (1968), 70 D.L.R. (2d) 183 (Ont. H.C.); *Crowe v. Noon* (1970), 16 D.L.R. (3d) 22 (Ont. H.C.); *R. v. Gamracy*, [1974] S.C.R. 640; and *Little v. Peers* (1988), 47 D.L.R. (4th) 621 (B.C.C.A.). See also ss. 28 and 29 of the *Criminal Code.*

(c) PRIVILEGE OR JUSTIFICATION UNDER THE *CRIMINAL CODE*

As illustrated by *Biron*, authorizing provisions empower individuals to take specified actions and require others to submit to that exercise of power. In contrast, privileging provisions address the related, but distinct, issue of the criminal and civil liability of those exercising legal authority. As indicated, individuals asserting the defence of legal authority generally must prove that their conduct was both authorized and privileged.

Privileging provisions can be found in a number of provincial, territorial and federal statutes. While the *Criminal Code* contains several privileging provisions, the most important are the general privileging provisions of s. 25.

> 25. (1) Every one who is required or authorized by law to do anything in the administration or enforcement of the law
>
> (a) as a private person,
> (b) as a peace officer or public officer,
> (c) in aid of a peace officer or public officer, or
> (d) by virtue of his office,

is, if he acts on reasonable grounds, justified in doing what he is required or authorized to do and in using as much force as is necessary for that purpose.

[s. 25(2) omitted]

(3) Subject to subsections (4) and (5), a person is not justified for the purposes of subsection (1) in using force that is intended or is likely to cause death or grievous bodily harm unless the person believes on reasonable grounds that it is necessary for the self-preservation of the person or the preservation of any one under that person's protection from death or grievous bodily harm.

(4) A peace officer, and every person lawfully assisting the peace officer, is justified in using force that is intended or is likely to cause death or grievous bodily harm to a person to be arrested, if

(a) the peace officer is proceeding lawfully to arrest, with or without warrant, the person to be arrested;

(b) the offence for which the person is to be arrested is one for which that person may be arrested without warrant;

(c) the person to be arrested takes flight to avoid arrest;

(d) the peace officer or other person using the force believes on reasonable grounds that the force is necessary for the purpose of protecting the peace officer, the person lawfully assisting the peace officer or any other person from imminent or future death or grievous bodily harm; and

(e) the flight cannot be prevented by reasonable means in a less violent manner.

As in the case of the authorizing sections, the Canadian courts have broadly interpreted s. 25, at least until relatively recently. First, the Supreme Court of Canada has established that the term "justified" in s. 25 means protected from both criminal and civil liability. Unfortunately, the Supreme Court of Canada has not addressed the constitutional basis upon which it concluded that the federal *Criminal Code* could govern tort liability, a matter that falls within the province's constitutional authority under property and civil rights. In addition to *Biron*, see *Frey v. Fedoruk*, [1950] S.C.R. 517; *Priestman v. Colangelo*, [1959] S.C.R. 615; and *Poupart v. Lafortune*, [1974] S.C.R. 175.

Second, despite the plain wording of s. 25(1), the Canadian courts have held that peace officers may be privileged under this provision even if they are not, in fact, authorized or required by law to do the act giving rise to the tort. For example in *Biron*, Laskin C.J.C. stated that a peace officer whose actions were not authorized may nevertheless be privileged under s. 25(1), if he or she made a mistake of fact and acted on reasonable grounds. Indeed, that is one reason why the Chief Justice refused to interpret the term "finds committing" to include apparently finds committing. In his view, since s. 25(1) protected the arresting officer from criminal and civil liability, there was no need to distort the plain meaning of the authorizing provision and criminalize the suspect's refusal to submit to an unlawful arrest. In *Frey*, *supra*, the court held that a person who was not authorized would not be privileged under s. 25(1) if he or she had made a mistake of law. See also *Saskatchewan (A.G.) v. Pritchard* (1961), 130 C.C.C. 61 (Sask. C.A.).

NOTES AND QUESTIONS

1. As a matter of policy, should peace officers enjoy a privilege if their actions, however reasonable, were not authorized? By answering that question in the affirmative, the Canadian courts have placed the hardship of any reasonable mistake of fact on an innocent suspect, rather than on an arresting officer.

2. What must an individual establish under s. 25(3) in order to be justified in using force that is intended or likely to cause death or grievous bodily harm?

3. What must an individual establish under s. 25(4) in order to be justified in using force that is intended or likely to cause death or grievous bodily harm?

4. Contrary to the approach in *Biron*, the Court of Appeal in *R. v. Brennan* (1989), 75 C.R. (3d) 38 (Ont. C.A.) interpreted the *Criminal Code*'s authorizing and privileging sections narrowly. The accused police officer attempted to stop the driver of a suspected stolen vehicle. A high-speed chase ensued during which the police officer drove through a stop sign. The court upheld the police officer's conviction for failing to stop at the stop sign. While the officer was authorized to arrest the suspect, he was not authorized to run a stop sign. Since his conduct was not specifically statutorily authorized, he was not privileged under s. 25.

5. In *Hudson v. Brantford Police Services Board* (2001), 204 D.L.R. (4th) 645 (Ont. C.A.), two police officers went to the plaintiff's house in the reasonable belief that he had failed to remain at the scene of an accident. They did not have an arrest warrant, they were not in hot pursuit and they did not have the plaintiff's permission to enter his house. Nevertheless, they entered his house, arrested him and took him to the police station. When charges for leaving the scene of an accident were later dropped, the plaintiff sued for unlawful arrest. The police officers argued that their actions were protected under s. 25 of the *Criminal Code*. The court held that, since the officers had no authority to enter, they were trespassing, and this rendered the subsequent arrest unlawful. It further held that while s. 25 provides protection against civil liability if a defendant acts on a reasonable mistake of fact, it does not apply with respect to a reasonable mistake of law. The officers' mistake in this case pertained to their legal authority to enter the plaintiff's house to arrest him, which was a mistake of law. Since the officers were not privileged under s. 25, the plaintiff's claim was successful.

Should the scope of s. 25 depend on the distinction between mistakes of fact and mistakes of law?

(d) A PRIVATE CITIZEN'S AUTHORITY AND PRIVILEGE TO ARREST WITHOUT A WARRANT

Since the apprehension of criminals was considered a community responsibility, the early common law did not distinguish between private citizens and peace officers in terms of their legal authority and privilege. It was only in the mid-1800s that the common law began to draw such distinctions. In terms of civil liability, peace officers were privileged to arrest without a warrant, provided they had reasonable and probable grounds to believe that the suspect had committed a felony. However, private citizens would only be privileged if they had reasonable and probable grounds to believe both that a felony had been committed and that the suspect was the perpetrator.

In Canada, the arrest powers of private citizens and police are now defined by federal and provincial statutes. For private citizens, the most important provision is s. 494 of the *Criminal Code*. The scope of a private citizen's statutory authority to arrest will depend in part on whether the Supreme Court of Canada's broad interpretation of the term "finds committing" in s. 495(1)(b) is applied to that term in s. 494(1)(a) and

(2). As indicated in the notes and questions that follow, the courts are divided on this issue.

Similarly, the scope of a private citizen's privilege from civil liability will turn on whether the issue is governed by s. 25 of the *Criminal Code* or the old common law principles. Again, the courts are divided on this issue.

NOTES AND QUESTIONS

1. For a discussion of a private citizen's common law powers, privileges and obligations in the arrest process see *Handcock v. Baker* (1800), 126 E.R. 1270 (H.L.); *Timothy v. Simpson* (1835), 149 E.R. 1285 (Exch.); *Allen v. Wright* (1838), 173 E.R. 602 (C.P.); *Price v. Seeley* (1843), 8 E.R. 651 (H.L.); *Walters v. W.H. Smith & Son Ltd.*, [1914] 1 K.B. 595; *Dunne v. Clinton*, [1930] Ir. R. 366 (H.C.); and *John Lewis & Co. v. Tims*, [1952] A.C. 676 (H.L.). See also Hall, "Legal and Social Aspects of Arrest Without a Warrant" (1936) 49 Harv. L. Rev. 566; and Spencer, "Citizens Arrest — At Their Peril" [1992] C.L.J. 405.

2. What must an individual establish to be authorized to arrest under s. 494(1)(a) and (b)? What are the requirements for authority under s. 494(2)?

3. In *Dendekker v. F.W. Woolworth Co.*, [1975] 3 W.W.R. 429 (Alta. S.C.) and *Cronk v. F.W. Woolworth Co.*, [1986] 3 W.W.R. 139 (Sask. Q.B.), the courts indicated that the term "finds committing" in s. 494 should not be defined to include apparently finds committing. The opposite approach was taken in *Karogiannis v. Poulus*, [1976] 6 W.W.R. 197 (B.C.S.C.) and *Banerjee v. K Mart Canada Ltd.* (1983), 43 Nfld. & P.E.I.R. 252 (Nfld. Dist. Ct.). As a matter of statutory interpretation, which line of cases is more compelling? Can you suggest any public policy justification for treating the term "finds committing" differently in ss. 494 and 495?

4. In *Dendekker*, *Karogiannis* and *Banerjee*, *supra*, the court indicated that a private citizen's privilege is defined by s. 25 of the *Criminal Code*. However, in *Kendall v. Gambles Canada Ltd.*, [1981] 4 W.W.R. 718 (Sask. Q.B.); *Banyasz v. K-Mart Canada Ltd.* (1986), 57 O.R. (2d) 445 (Div. Ct.); *Smart v. Sears Canada Inc.* (1987), 64 Nfld. & P.E.I.R. 187 (Nfld. C.A.); *Cronk*, *supra*; and *Briggs v. Laviolette* (1994), 21 C.C.L.T. (2d) 105 (B.C.S.C.), a private citizen's privilege was defined in terms of the common law principles.

The Supreme Court of Canada has repeatedly held that s. 25 of the *Criminal Code* protects peace officers from both criminal and civil liability. Moreover, the section applies to "every one" who is authorized or required by law to undertake an act. What legal or public policy argument would you make in support of the position that the common law governs a private citizen's privilege in civil cases?

5. Most of the Canadian cases that have adopted the common law principles of privilege indicate that private citizens must prove that the crime was in fact committed by the suspect or a third person and that they had reasonable grounds to believe that the suspect was the perpetrator. See *Kendall*, *Smart* and *Briggs*, *supra*, and *Nichols v. Wal-Mart Canada Corp.* (2003), 15 C.C.L.T. (3d) 150 (Ont. S.C.J.).

Even those cases which have held that a private citizen's privilege turns on proof that the suspect committed an offence do not require proof that the suspect was in fact criminally convicted. In a civil case, the defendant need only establish the commission of the crime on a balance of probabilities. See *Cronk, supra.*

6. How should the law balance a shopkeeper's interests in protecting his or her inventory from theft and a customer's autonomy? How would you react if you owned a store and suspected that a shopper was stealing a valuable necklace? What risks are involved in making an arrest? What risks are involved in doing nothing? If you called the police and left the matter to them, is it likely that they could apprehend the suspect in a timely manner?

4. Rights and Obligations in the Arrest Process

(a) REASONS FOR THE ARREST

KOECHLIN v. WAUGH and HAMILTON

(1957), 11 D.L.R. (2d) 447 (Ont. C.A.)

LAIDLAW J.A. (orally): This is an appeal by the plaintiffs from a judgment pronounced by His Honour Judge Shea, in the County Court of the County of York, on May 21, 1956, dismissing with costs an action brought by the plaintiffs for damages for alleged unlawful arrest and imprisonment. . . .

On the evening of October 11, 1955, the infant plaintiff, aged about 20 years, and his friend Victor Wassilgew, attended a picture show in the Township of Scarborough. The show ended about midnight. They went to a restaurant for coffee and, afterwards, started to walk on the sidewalk on Kingston Road in the direction of the home of Wassilgew. They were stopped by the defendants, who are police officers of the Township of Scarborough. The police officers were in plain clothes and were in a police cruiser car. The police called the infant plaintiff and his companion to their car and asked for their identification. Wassilgew gave his identification at once and told the police officers that they were on their way home after the show. The infant plaintiff objected to giving his identification unless the police officer, Hamilton, who spoke to him, first identified himself. The defendant Hamilton produced a badge and said he was a police officer, but the infant plaintiff was not satisfied with that identification and requested the name and number of the officer. The officer did not give his name, but his number was on the badge. The infant plaintiff continued to refuse to identify himself, and a scuffle ensued during which the infant plaintiff fell into a deep ditch. Subsequently, force was used by the police officer and other officers who were called to the scene to put the infant plaintiff into a police car. He was not told any reason for his arrest. He was taken to the police station and told that he would be charged with assault of a police officer.

The adult plaintiff stated in evidence that he was informed about 2 o'clock in the morning that his son was in custody; he went to the police station; he asked the Sergeant of Police the reason his son was there in custody; the sergeant told him it was for assaulting a police officer. The adult plaintiff asked the sergeant how it happened and, according to the evidence of the adult plaintiff, the sergeant said "he would not tell me, that I would hear about it the next day in Court about 10 o'clock in the morning." He says he asked the sergeant if he could see his son and was refused permission. It was 9 or 10 o'clock the following evening before the infant plaintiff was released on bail. On November 18th, the charge against the infant plaintiff was heard and was dismissed.

The learned Judge stated in reasons given by him that the police officers stopped the infant plaintiff and his companion because they were sauntering along the street, and because of "their dress". There was in fact nothing distinctive about the dress of the infant plaintiff, but his companion was wearing rubber-soled shoes and a jacket. The learned Judge referred also to the fact that there had been a number of "break-ins" in the neighbourhood a few nights before and that the police had reported that a person wearing rubber-soled shoes was involved in one or more of those break-ins. After referring to the reasons for stopping the infant plaintiff and his companion and asking for identification, the learned Judge said: "Then, from then on, the actions of Koechlin, and his words, would in my opinion justify the officers in believing that this man either had or was about to commit a crime." Later, he said, referring to Koechlin — "his refusal to co-operate — made the officers still more suspicious and firm in the belief, as I said, that something was wrong."

. . .

A police officer has not in law an unlimited power to arrest a law-abiding citizen. The power given expressly to him by the Criminal Code to arrest without warrant is contained in s. 435 [a predecessor to the current s. 495], but we direct careful attention of the public to the fact that the law empowers a police officer in many cases and under certain circumstances to require a person to account for his presence and to identify himself and to furnish other information, and any person who wrongfully fails to comply with such lawful requirements does so at the risk of arrest and imprisonment. None of these circumstances exist in this case. No unnecessary restriction on his power which results in increased difficulty to a police officer to perform his duties of office should be imposed by the Court. At the same time, the rights and freedom under law from unlawful arrest and imprisonment of an innocent citizen must be fully guarded by the Courts. In this case, the fact that the companion of the infant plaintiff was wearing rubber-soled shoes and a windbreaker and that his dress attracted the attention of the police officers, falls far short of reasonable and probable grounds for believing that the infant plaintiff had committed an indictable offence or was about to commit such an offence. We do not criticize the police officers in any way for asking the infant plaintiff and his companion to identify themselves, but we are satisfied that when the infant plaintiff, who was entirely innocent of any wrongdoing, refused to do so, the police officer has no right to use force to compel him to identify himself. It would have been wise and, indeed, a duty as a good citizen, for the infant plaintiff to have identified himself when asked to do so by the police officers. It is altogether likely that if the infant plaintiff had been courteous and co-operative, the incident giving rise to this action would not have occurred, but that does not in law excuse the defendants for acting as they did in the particular circumstances.

We direct attention to an important fact. The infant plaintiff was not told by either of the police officers any reason for his arrest. The infant plaintiff was entitled to know on what charge or on suspicion of what crime he was seized. He was not required in law to submit to restraint on his freedom unless he knew the reason why that restraint should be imposed. In *Christie v. Leachinsky*, [1947] 1 All E.R. 567, a decision of the House of Lords, Lord Simon, after referring to many authorities, said at pp. 572-3:

> "These citations . . . seem to me to establish the following propositions:
>
> "1. If a policeman arrests without warrant on reasonable suspicion of felony, or of other crime of a sort which does not require a warrant, he must in ordinary circumstances inform the person arrested of the true ground of arrest. He is not entitled to keep the

reason to himself or to give a reason which is not the true reason. In other words, a citizen is entitled to know on what charge or on suspicion of what crime he is seized.
"2. If the citizen is not so informed, but is nevertheless seized, the policeman, apart from certain exceptions, is liable for false imprisonment.
"3. The requirement that the person arrested should be informed of the reason why he is seized naturally does not exist if the circumstances are such that he must know the general nature of the alleged offence for which he is detained.
"4. The requirement that he should be so informed does not mean that technical or precise language need be used. The matter is a matter of substance, and turns on the elementary proposition that in this country a person is, *prima facie*, entitled to his freedom and is only required to submit to restraint on his freedom if he knows in substance the reason why it is claimed that this restraint should be imposed.
"5. The person arrested cannot complain that he has not been supplied with the above information as and when he should be, if he himself produces the situation which makes it practically impossible to inform him, *e.g.*, by immediate counter-attack or by running away.
"There may well be other exceptions to the general rule in addition to those I have indicated, and the above propositions are not intended to constitute a formal or complete code, but to indicate the general principles of our law on a very important matter. These principles equally apply to a private person who arrests on suspicion. If a policeman who entertained a reasonable suspicion that X had committed a felony were at liberty to arrest him and march him off to a police station without giving any explanation of why he was doing this, the *prima facie* right of personal liberty would be gravely infringed. No one, I think, would approve a situation in which, when the person arrested asked for the reason, the policeman replied: 'That has nothing to do with you. Come along with me.' Such a situation may be tolerated under other systems of law, as for instance, in the time of *lettres de cachet* in the eighteenth century in France, or in more recent days when the Gestapo swept people off to confinement under an overriding authority which the executive in this country happily does not in ordinary times possess. This would be quite contrary to our conceptions of individual liberty."

In this case it was held that although the police officers *bona fide* and on reasonable grounds believed the plaintiff had committed an offence, they had not informed him as to why he was being arrested and were, therefore, liable in damages for false imprisonment. In *R. v. Hastings* . . . it was held by the New Brunswick Court of Appeal that a person being unlawfully arrested without a warrant is entitled to resist such unlawful arrest.

There is one further matter that deserves comment. A person who has been arrested should not be held *incommunicado.* We do not find it necessary to find as a fact that the infant plaintiff was denied his right to communicate with his father at the first reasonable opportunity. If, however, the father of the infant plaintiff was refused permission by the Sergeant of Police to see his son at any time before the charge came on for hearing in Court, such practice cannot be justified in this or in any other case. A person in custody should never be denied his right to communicate with his relatives at the earliest reasonable opportunity so that he may avail himself of their advice and assistance. That right ought to be recognized and given effect in all cases, and care should be exercised by police authorities to see that it is not wholly disregarded.

Finally, we are not in accord with the view expressed by the learned trial Judge that the actions of the infant plaintiff in resisting the efforts of the police officers can be regarded as justification for their belief that he "either had or was about to commit a crime." In the particular circumstances he was entitled in law to resist the efforts of the police officers, and they have failed in this case to justify their actions.

It was stated in the course of giving oral reasons for judgment that the Courts would strive diligently to avoid putting any unnecessary obstacle in the way of the detection of crime or the lawful arrest of persons in the proper performance of the duties of a police officer. We repeat an expression of that policy of the Courts. Nothing in these reasons for judgment should be taken as encouragement to any person to resist a police officer in the performance of his duties; on the contrary, it is not only highly desirable, but vitally important, that every person should co-operate to the utmost with police officers for the good of the public and to ensure the preservation of law and order in his community.

In this case the police officers exceeded their powers and infringed the rights of the infant plaintiff without justification. Therefore, the appeal will be allowed with costs. The judgment of the Court below will be set aside and in place thereof there will be judgment for the plaintiffs in the amounts assessed, respectively, for damages suffered by the infant plaintiff and by the adult plaintiff.

NOTES AND QUESTIONS

1. At what point was the plaintiff arrested and on what charge? What authority did the police have to stop and question the plaintiff prior to the arrest? Did the police have any legal authority to use force prior to the arrest?

2. Were the defendants authorized and privileged to arrest the plaintiff in the circumstances? Would they have been held liable, even if they had properly informed him of the reasons? What arguments would you have made on Koechlin's behalf for punitive damages?

3. What impact does the failure to inform a suspect of the reasons for the arrest have on the validity of the arrest? Can the suspect simply leave or use physical force to prevent his or her detention? See *Campbell v. Hudyma* (1985), 66 A.R. 222 (C.A.); *Schell v. Truba* (1989), 79 Sask. R. 27 (Q.B.), aff'd (1990), 89 Sask. R. 137 (C.A.); *Cormier v. Saint John (City)* (1994), 153 N.B.R. (2d) 293 (C.A.); and *Lewis v. Chief Constable*, [1991] 1 All E.R. 206 (C.A.).

4. Laidlaw J.A. was very critical of the defendants for holding the plaintiff incommunicado. Should such conduct result in liability, even if the arrest was lawful and the suspect was informed of the reasons for his or her arrest? See *Perry v. Fried* (1972), 9 N.S.R. (2d) 545 (T.D.); and *Lang v. Burch* (1982), 140 D.L.R. (3d) 325 (Sask. C.A.).

5. Section 29 of the *Criminal Code* also imposes disclosure requirements on an individual making an arrest. However, these provisions have been interpreted as being less stringent than those imposed by civil law. For example, in *Gamracy v. R.*, [1974] S.C.R. 640, the court held that an officer making an arrest pursuant to an outstanding arrest warrant had no obligation to obtain the warrant or ascertain its contents in order to inform the suspect. Upon being informed of the warrant's existence, the suspect was required to defer to the officer's authority. See also *R. v. Erickson and Hathaway* (1977), 5 A.R. 602 (S.C.).

6. In addition to bringing a common law tort action, an individual who is not informed of the reasons for his or her arrest may seek redress under the *Charter*. Section

10 of the *Charter* provides that "everyone has the right on arrest or detention (a) to be informed promptly of the reasons therefor; [and] (b) to retain and instruct counsel without delay and to be informed of that right."

In *R. v. Wrightman* (2004), 72 O.R. (3d) 187 (Ct. J.), the accused was acquitted of charges for resisting an officer's attempt to arrest him under a warrant. The judge held that under s. 10(b) of the *Charter*, the officer had an obligation to inform the accused of the particulars of the warrant; it was not sufficient to simply advise the accused of the warrant's existence. Consequently, the accused was under no obligation to submit to the arrest. Can you reconcile this case with *Gamracy, supra*?

Section 10 of the *Charter* has generated a great deal of litigation and academic debate. For an overview of the various issues, see Hogg, *Constitutional Law of Canada*, 4th ed., looseleaf, vol. 2 (1997), ch. 47.

7. As suggested in *Koechlin*, individuals are generally under no obligation to identify themselves, account for their presence, answer questions, remain on the scene, accompany an officer, or submit to a search. See *R. v. Carroll* (1959), 23 D.L.R. (2d) 271 (Ont. C.A.); *Rice v. Connolly*, [1966] 2 Q.B. 414; *Kenlin v. Gardiner*, [1967] 2 Q.B. 510; *Ludlow v. Burgess*, [1971] Cr. L.R. 238 (Q.B.); *Albert v. Lavin*, [1981] 3 All E.R. 878 (H.L.); *R. v. Wood* (1984), 52 A.R. 356 (Q.B.); and *Campbell v. Hudyma* (1985), 66 A.R. 222 (C.A.). There are, however, many statutory exceptions to this rule. See for example the provincial highway traffic statutes, which typically require drivers to identify themselves.

8. In *Moore v. R.*, [1979] 1 S.C.R. 195, the majority of the court held that a person who violates a provincial statute may have a positive duty to co-operate with the police. Moore had refused to identify himself to an officer who was attempting to ticket him for riding his bicycle through a red light. The officer then arrested Moore under s. 129 of the *Criminal Code* for obstructing a peace officer in the execution of his duty. The majority reasoned that the officer had a legal duty to enforce the provincial highway traffic statute and that Moore's refusal to identify himself prevented the officer from performing this duty. It was on this basis that the majority upheld Moore's obstruction conviction. The decision in *Moore* has been criticized. See for example Cohen, "The Investigation of Offences and Police Powers" (1981) 13 Ottawa L. Rev. 549 at 551-56. See also *R. v. Leitch* (1992), 18 C.R. (4th) 224 (Alta. Prov. Ct.), rev'd (1993), 13 Alta. L.R. (3d) 97 (Q.B.).

In *Ryan v. Auclair* (1989), 60 D.L.R. (4th) 212 (Qc. C.A.), the police arrested two nuns, who were violating a municipal by-law by distributing religious pamphlets, after they refused to identify themselves beyond giving their religious names. When the nuns resisted, the officers used force to overpower them. The Court of Appeal upheld the trial judge's dismissal of the nuns' claim for false imprisonment.

9. Can you reconcile *Moore* and *Ryan, supra* with the cases cited in note 7? In the absence of express statutory authority, should the police have authority to arrest those who refuse to identify themselves in cases involving municipal or provincial offences? Given the courts' increased reluctance to defer to police authority, would *Moore* and *Ryan* be decided the same way now? See generally *R. v. Orbanski; R. v. Elias*, [2005] 2 S.C.R. 3.

(b) THE USE OF REASONABLE FORCE

Both the common law and the *Criminal Code* give those acting pursuant to legal authority broad powers to use force. Nevertheless, as a general rule, suspects must be given an opportunity to submit peacefully before any force is used. If a suspect resists, then as much force as is reasonably necessary may be used to subdue the suspect. In assessing whether the force used was reasonable, the courts examine the nature of the force used in the specific circumstances and not the resulting injuries. A reasonable and *bona fide* mistake of fact as to the need to use force will not defeat the assertion of the right to use force. Provided an individual is acting lawfully, he or she will not be held liable for using force simply because the suspect is innocent.

As discussed earlier, s. 25(1) privileges those who use reasonable force in doing what they are authorized or required by law to do. Section 25(3) limits the use of force that is intended or likely to cause death or grievous bodily harm to individuals who reasonably believe that such force is necessary to protect themselves or others under their protection from death or grievous bodily harm. Section 25(4) permits peace officers to use force that is intended or likely to cause death or grievous bodily harm to apprehend a fleeing suspect who cannot be stopped in a less violent manner. The offence for which the suspect is sought must be one for which he or she can be arrested without a warrant. Moreover, the officer must have reasonable grounds to believe that such force is necessary to protect him or herself or a third person from imminent or future death or grievous bodily harm.

NOTES AND QUESTIONS

1. In what circumstances would self-defence and the right to use force under s. 25(1), (3) and (4) overlap?

2. In *Green v. Lawrence* (1998), 163 D.L.R. (4th) 115 (Man. C.A.), the plaintiff slipped backwards on the stairs into one of the two arresting officers. One of the officers put the plaintiff in a full-nelson hold with sufficient force to break his neck. The plaintiff, who was rendered a paraplegic, sued the officer in battery. The defendant asserted that the plaintiff had thrust himself backwards and that force was necessary to prevent his escape or subdue him. The court held that there was no reasonable basis for believing that the plaintiff was attempting to escape. In any event, the amount of force used was excessive. The defendant was held liable in battery for the plaintiff's injuries.

For other cases on the use of force, see *Cluett v. R.*, [1985] 2 S.C.R. 216; *Penn v. Singbeil* (1986), 44 Sask. R. 312 (Q.B.), aff'd (1987), 56 Sask. R. 314 (C.A.); *Christopherson v. Saanich (District)*, [1995] 4 W.W.R. 381 (B.C.S.C.); *Arnault v. Prince Albert (City) Police Commissioners*, [1996] 4 W.W.R. 38 (Sask. Q.B.); and *R. v. Asante-Mensah*, [2003] 2 S.C.R. 3.

3. The right to use deadly force to prevent the escape of a fleeing suspect is a controversial issue. See *Robertson v. Joyce*, [1948] 4 D.L.R. 436 (Ont. C.A.); *Priestman v. Colangelo*, [1959] S.C.R. 615; *Beim v. Goyer*, [1965] S.C.R. 638; *R. v. Roberge*, [1983] 1 S.C.R. 312; *Allarie v. Victoria (City)*, [1995] 1 W.W.R. 655 (B.C.S.C.); and Abraham *et al.*, "Police Use of Lethal Force: A Toronto Perspective" (1981) 19 Osgoode

Hall L.J. 199. What arguments, if any, would you make for abolishing the right to use deadly force to apprehend fleeing suspects?

4. In addition to s. 25, the *Criminal Code* authorizes the use of force to prevent the commission of certain offences (s. 27), to subdue those committing an offence on an airplane (s. 27.1), to prevent breaches of the peace (s. 30), to suppress riots (s. 32), in self-defence (s. 34), to prevent assaults (s. 37), to defend personal property (ss. 38-39), and to defend real property (ss. 40-41). The Canadian courts appear to assume that these sections govern both criminal and civil liability.

5. *Berntt v. Vancouver (City)* (1999), 174 D.L.R. (4th) 403 (B.C.C.A.) illustrates the factual analysis undertaken to determine if the amount of force used was reasonable in the circumstances. The plaintiff was one of the ringleaders of 50,000 to 70,000 people who rioted in downtown Vancouver after the Canucks lost game seven of the Stanley Cup. After throwing objects at the police and approaching the police line waving a long screwdriver, the plaintiff was shot in the back with a plastic "baton." After receiving treatment, he rejoined the riot. He turned his back to the police to show them the welt caused by the first shot. While he was walking away, he was shot with a second plastic baton. The evidence indicated that although the officer had aimed at the plaintiff's back, the baton hit him in the head.

The plaintiff suffered serious injuries from the second shot and sued for battery and negligence. The trial judge held that only the first shot was justified under s. 32 of the *Criminal Code*, which privileges using force to suppress a riot. The judge reasoned that when the second shot was fired, the police had gained control of the situation, the riot had lessened and the plaintiff posed no immediate threat. Consequently, the firing of the second shot was unnecessary and the officer was liable for damages in battery. The officer appealed. The Court of Appeal ordered a new trial on the issue of the second shot. It stated that the reasonableness of the force had to be assessed in terms of what a reasonable officer at the scene would have believed. The officer need not have been personally endangered to use force under s. 32. If the officer honestly and reasonably believed that firing the second baton was necessary to suppress the riot, then he was justified in doing so.

During the retrial, the judge addressed four questions as directed by the Court of Appeal: (i) did the officer believe that the force he was about to use was necessary to suppress the riot; (ii) did the officer believe that the force he was about to use was not excessive given the apprehended danger from the continuance of the riot; (iii) if the answer to the first question was yes, did the officer have reasonable grounds for that belief; and (iv) if the answer to the second question was yes, did the officer have reasonable grounds for that belief? The trial judge answered all the questions in the defendant's favour. From the officer's perspective, the key to defusing the riot was the removal of the ringleaders, including the plaintiff, and making an arrest was not feasible in the circumstances. Moreover, the plaintiff's brandishing of the screwdriver, an edged weapon, made him very dangerous in a crowd. See *Berntt v. Vancouver (City)* (2001), 209 D.L.R. (4th) 494 (B.C.S.C.).

6. There are additional rights and obligations in the arrest process. For example, once a private citizen made an arrest at common law, he or she had to hand over the suspect to the police or a justice as soon as possible. This obligation is now codified in

s. 494(3) of the *Criminal Code*. Although granted somewhat more leeway to investigate incidents, peace officers were under a similar obligation to bring suspects before a justice without unreasonable delay. See *John Lewis & Co. v. Tims*, [1952] A.C. 676 (H.L.); and *Dallison v. Caffery*, [1965] 1 Q.B. 348 (C.A.). See also the *Criminal Code*, s. 503; and *R. v. Koszulap* (1974), 20 C.C.C. (2d) 193 (Ont. C.A.).

This issue has also arisen under s. 9 of the *Charter*, which guarantees everyone protection from arbitrary detention or imprisonment. In *R. v. Charles* (1987), 36 C.C.C. (3d) 286 (Sask. C.A.), the court held that a 36-hour detention before being brought before a justice violated s. 9. However, in *R. v. Storrey*, [1990] 1 S.C.R. 241, the court held that an 18-hour delay to arrange a line-up did not violate s. 9.

7. For a discussion of the complex pretrial provisions of the *Criminal Code*, see ss. 493-515; and Salhany, *Canadian Criminal Procedure*, 6th ed. (2006), ch. 3. The police powers to fingerprint and photograph arrested suspects are contained in the *Identification of Criminals Act*, R.S.C. 1985, c. I-1. See *Brown v. Baugh and Williams*, [1984] 1 S.C.R. 192; and *R. v. Beare; R. v. Higgins*, [1988] 2 S.C.R. 387.

5. The Common Law Power to Search Pursuant to a Lawful Arrest

R. v. CASLAKE

[1998] 1 S.C.R. 51

[Six hours after the accused was arrested for marijuana possession, his impounded vehicle was subject to an inventory search to safeguard its contents and note its general condition. The vehicle search was conducted without a warrant or the accused's consent. Cash and cocaine were found in the car, and the accused was charged with cocaine possession. The issue before the Supreme Court of Canada was whether the vehicle search constituted an unreasonable search or seizure contrary to s. 8 of the *Charter* and whether the cocaine had to be excluded from evidence under s. 24(2).

The court noted that for a search or seizure to be reasonable under s. 8 of the *Charter*, it had to be authorized by law.]

LAMER C.J.C. (Cory, McLachlin and Major JJ. concurring). . . In this case, the Crown is relying on the common law power of search incident to arrest to provide the legal authority for the search. In *Cloutier* [*v. Langlois*, [1990] 1 S.C.R. 158], my colleague L'Heureux-Dubé J. (for a unanimous Court) discussed this power in detail. She held that it is an exception to the ordinary requirements for a reasonable search . . . in that it requires neither a warrant nor independent reasonable and probable grounds. Rather, the right to search arises from the fact of the arrest. This is justifiable because the arrest itself requires reasonable and probable grounds (under s. 494 of the *Code*) or an arrest warrant (under s. 495). However, since the legality of the search is derived from the legality of arrest, if the arrest is later found to be invalid, the search will be also . . .

She then set out three important limits on the power to search incident to arrest (at p. 186):

> 1. This power does not impose a duty. The police have some discretion in conducting the search. Where they are satisfied that the law can be effectively and safely applied without a search, the police may see fit not to conduct a search . . .

2. The search must be for a valid objective in pursuit of the ends of criminal justice, such as the discovery of an object that may be a threat to the safety of the police, the accused or the public, or that may facilitate escape or act as evidence against the accused. The purpose of the search must not be unrelated to the objectives of the proper administration of justice, which would be the case for example if the purpose of the search was to intimidate, ridicule or pressure the accused in order to obtain admissions.
3. The search must not be conducted in an abusive fashion and in particular, the use of physical or psychological constraint should be proportionate to the objectives sought and the other circumstances of the situation.

If all three of these conditions are met, and the arrest itself is lawful, the search will be "authorized by law" for the purposes of s. 8 of the *Charter*. In the case at bar there is no allegation that the arrest was unlawful or that the search was abusive. Rather, the problem in this case is that the objective and scope of the search exceeded its permissible limits.

C. The Scope of Search Incident to the Arrest

Since search incident to arrest is a common-law power, there are no readily ascertainable limits on its scope. It is therefore the courts' responsibility to set boundaries which allow the state to pursue its legitimate interests, while vigorously protecting individuals' right to privacy. The scope of search incident to arrest can refer to many different aspects of the search. It can refer to the items seized during the search. In *Stillman*, Cory J. for a majority of this Court held, at para. 42, that bodily samples could not be taken as incident to arrest, as a search so invasive is an "affront to human dignity". It can also refer to the place to be searched. The appellant argues that the power of search incident to arrest does not extend to automobiles. I would reject this position. Automobiles are legitimately the objects of search incident to arrest, as they attract no heightened expectation of privacy that would justify an exemption from the usual common law principles referred to above.

Scope can also refer to temporal limits on the power of search, which are at the core of the case at bar. The appellant suggests that the delay between the search and the arrest (six hours in this case) was too long to make the search "incident" to the arrest. In my opinion, the Court should be reluctant to set a strict limit on the amount of time that can elapse between the time of search and the time of arrest.

In my view, all of the limits on search incident to arrest are derived from the justification for the common law power itself: searches which derive their legal authority from the fact of arrest must be truly incidental to the arrest in question. . . . This means, simply put, that the search is only justifiable if the purpose of the search is related to the purpose of the arrest. . . .

To be clear, this is not a standard of reasonable and probable grounds, the normal threshold that must be surpassed before a search can be conducted. Here, the only requirement is that there be some reasonable basis for doing what the police officer did. . . .

As explained above, these limits will be no different for automobiles than for any other place. The right to search a car incident to arrest and the scope of that search will depend on a number of factors, including the basis for the arrest, the location of the motor vehicle in relation to the place of the arrest, and other relevant circumstances.

The temporal limits on search incident to arrest will also be derived from the same principles. There is no need to set a firm deadline on the amount of time that may elapse before the search can no longer said to be incidental to arrest. As a general rule, searches that are truly incidental to arrest will usually occur within a reasonable period of time after the arrest. A substantial delay does not mean that the search is automatically unlawful, but it may cause the court to draw an inference that the search is not sufficiently connected to the arrest. Naturally, the strength of the inference will depend on the length of the delay, and can be defeated by a reasonable explanation for the delay. . . .

[Lamer C.J.C. held that the vehicle search fell outside of the scope of the common law power to search pursuant to a lawful arrest. He did not view the six-hour delay as determinative, especially given the limited staff in the detachment. Rather, he held that the vehicle search was not truly incidental to the accused's arrest. It was conducted for inventory purposes and not to gather evidence or serve some other legitimate ends of criminal justice. Since the vehicle search was not authorized, it violated s. 8 of the *Charter*. Nevertheless, Lamer C.J.C. ruled that the evidence was admissible under s. 24(2) and upheld the accused's conviction.

Bastarache J. (L'Heureux-Dubé and Gonthier JJ. concurring) agreed that the six-hour delay did not preclude the vehicle search from being incidental to the arrest. However, he held that, regardless of the officer's subjective belief about the purpose of the search, the officer had a common law power to search the vehicle incidental to the arrest in the circumstances of the case. Since the vehicle search was authorized by common law, there was no violation of the accused's *Charter* rights under s. 8. It was on this basis that the minority upheld the accused's conviction for cocaine possession.]

NOTES AND QUESTIONS

1. Traditionally, the common law right to search pursuant to a lawful arrest was very narrowly defined. For example, it appears that in order to search the person arrested, the police needed to have reasonable grounds to believe that he or she was in possession of evidence of the offence or a weapon. See *Bessell v. Wilson* (1853), 118 E.R. 518 (Q.B.); *Leigh v. Cole* (1853), 6 Cox C.C. 329 (Oxford Circuit Stftd. Assizes); *Dillon v. O'Brien and Davis* (1887), 16 Cox C.C. 245 (Exch.); and *Gordon v. Denison* (1895), 22 O.A.R. 315. See also Wade, "Police Search" (1934) 50 L.Q.R. 354; and Leigh, "Recent Developments in the Law of Search and Seizure" (1970) 33 Mod. L. Rev. 268.

2. Lamer C.J.C. stated that the police need some reasonable basis for the search, but do not need to meet the standard of reasonable and probable grounds. Can you explain in your own words the difference between these two tests?

3. Do you agree with the majority or minority on whether the inventory search of the vehicle was incidental to the accused's arrest?

4. Based on *Caslake*, summarize the principles governing the common law power to search pursuant to an arrest.

5. The common law power to search pursuant to arrest did not extend to intimate physical searches, seizing bodily samples, or undertaking medical or surgical procedures. Nevertheless, the Canadian courts had permitted a broad range of intrusive and intimate practices to be used in drug cases. See for example *Reynen v. Antonenko* (1975), 54

D.L.R. (3d) 124 (Alta. S.C.) (surgical removal of drugs from the suspect's rectum); *R. v. Meikle* (1983), 9 C.C.C. (3d) 91 (Ont. H.C.); and *R. v. Rousseau*, [1985] R.L. 108 (Qc. C.S.P.) (laxatives and drugs to hasten retrieval of drugs). This accepting attitude in drug cases appears to be changing.

In *R. v. Greffe*, [1990] 1 S.C.R. 755, airport customs officials received a tip that the accused was carrying heroin. However, no heroin was found when he was strip-searched. The R.C.M.P. then arrested the accused for unpaid traffic tickets, and arranged for him to be given a rectal search using a sigmoidoscope. Two bags of heroin were recovered. The Crown admitted that the search violated s. 8, but argued that the evidence should not be excluded under s. 24(2). The majority of the court held that subjecting the accused to a rectal search pursuant to an arrest for traffic tickets, without reasonable grounds that he was carrying drugs, constituted a serious violation of s. 8 that required exclusion of the evidence. As in *Greffe*, the courts now often fail to discuss the scope of the common law authority to search, focusing instead on whether the search was reasonable under s. 8. Nevertheless, it is difficult to imagine that a rectal search could ever be found to be incidental to an arrest for unpaid traffic tickets.

6. In *R. v. Golden*, [2001] 3 S.C.R. 679, the police observed the accused making drug sales and lawfully arrested him. When a pat-down search did not result in finding drugs or a weapon, the police decided to strip-search Golden at the top of the restaurant's back stairwell. When Golden resisted, he was taken to a booth in the back of the restaurant and aggressively strip-searched. The court held that, when necessary, strip-searches could be conducted pursuant to the lawful arrest. However, the court noted that such searches were inherently degrading, regardless of the manner in which they were carried out. Both the majority and the dissent condemned the way in which the strip-search was conducted. While the majority excluded the evidence and ordered an acquittal, the dissent ruled that the evidence was admissible and would have upheld the conviction.

7. In *R. v. Stillman*, [1997] 1 S.C.R. 607, the court held that the common law right to search pursuant to arrest did not extend beyond protecting the arresting officer or seizing evidence that might otherwise be lost. Consequently, the court ruled that the police had no authority to seize hair samples, demand bodily fluids or take dental impressions from a 17-year-old murder suspect who had refused to consent to such procedures. Can you reconcile *Stillman* with the drug cases discussed in note 5 above?

In 1995, Parliament enacted legislation creating a judicial warrant authorizing the taking of hair, saliva and blood samples for DNA testing from those suspected of designated criminal offences. See *Criminal Code*, ss. 487.04-487.092; and *R. v. Jackpine*, [2006] 1 S.C.R. 554.

8. In the absence of specific statutory authority, there is generally no right to search a suspect until after he or she has been lawfully arrested. However, the Canadian courts have created exceptions in drug enforcement. See *R. v. Brezack* (1949), 96 C.C.C. 97 (Ont. C.A.); and *Scott v. R.* (1975), 61 D.L.R. (3d) 130 (Fed. C.A.) in which the courts upheld the use of "throat-holds." Typically, suspects are grabbed by the throat without warning to prevent them from swallowing any drugs that they may be carrying in their mouth.

Despite the *Charter*, the Canadian courts continue to largely ignore the violence and dangers inherent in throat-holds and uphold their use. In *R. v. Collins*, [1987] 1

S.C.R. 265, the court held that the use of a throat-hold would not constitute an unreasonable search if the officer reasonably believed that the suspect was a "drug handler." Does this test adequately balance the physical integrity of drug suspects and the interests of the state? See also *R. v. Debot*, [1989] 2 S.C.R. 1140; and *R. v. Garcia-Guiterrez* (1991), 65 C.C.C. (3d) 15 (B.C.C.A.).

9. Following a lawful arrest, an officer had a common law right to search not only the suspect and his or her personal effects but also the immediate scene, provided the arrest took place in public or in the suspect's premises. It is doubtful whether this search power provided authority for a wholesale search of the suspect's or a third party's home simply because the suspect was apprehended there. See *R. v. Feeney*, [1997] 2 S.C.R. 13; and *R. v. Golub* (1997), 34 O.R. (3d) 743 (C.A.). Similar doubts have been raised about an officer's right to take a suspect home to search his or her residence. See *Dillon v. O'Brien and Davis* (1887), 16 Cox C.C. 245 (Exch.); *McLorie v. Oxford*, [1982] 3 All E.R. 480 (Q.B.); and Wade, "Police Search" (1934) 50 L.Q.R. 354. But see *Dallison v. Caffery*, [1964] 2 All E.R. 610 (C.A.).

10. For a detailed review of the common law power to search pursuant to arrest, see Fontana, *The Law of Search and Seizure in Canada*, 6th ed. (2005) at 460-63 and 518-36.

11. Various federal and provincial statutes contain broad powers to search suspects which may be invoked independently of the common law power. See for example the *Criminal Code*, ss. 117.02-117.06 (search and seizure of weapons); *Controlled Drugs and Substances Act*, S.C. 1996, c. 19, ss. 11-12 (search and seizure of illicit drugs); and the provincial liquor, parks, highway traffic, hunting, and fishing statutes. However, the post-*Charter* cases have limited these provincial powers. See *R. v. Mellenthin*, [1992] 3 S.C.R. 615.

12. The societal interest in conducting a search must be balanced against the individual's reasonable expectation of privacy. However, the weight of that expectation may vary with the circumstances. For instance, the Supreme Court of Canada has held that students have a diminished expectation of privacy while in school. Consequently, a search that might be impermissible if undertaken by a police officer may be permissible if undertaken by a principal. See *R. v. M.(M.R.)*, [1998] 3 S.C.R. 393. But see *R. v. M.(A.)* (2006), 79 O.R. (3d) 481 (C.A.). Similarly, the courts have held that the expectation of privacy with respect to "open fields of land" may be relatively low. See *R. v. Lauda* (1999), 45 O.R. (3d) 51 (C.A.).

6. A Peace Officer's Common Law Power of Entry to Search for a Wanted Person

ECCLES v. BOURQUE

[1975] 2 S.C.R. 739

DICKSON J.: The claim of the appellant, Mr. Eccles, is against the respondents, three constables on the Vancouver Police Force, for damages for trespass alleged to have been committed when the police officers entered the apartment occupied by Mr. Eccles in the City of Vancouver at about 4:00 p.m. on August 12, 1971. The constables were in plain clothes but were armed. The purpose of the entry was to apprehend one Edmund Cheese, also known as Billy Deans, for whom there were three outstanding Montreal warrants. Cheese was not found in the apartment. . . . Mr. Eccles was successful at trial. Mr. Justice Wootton awarded him $300 damages and costs. The Court of Appeal for British Columbia by a majority (Robertson and Taggart JJ.A., with Nemetz, J.A. dissenting) reversed. . . .

There are two issues: (1) Were the respondents authorized by s. 25 of the *Criminal Code* forcibly to enter and search the appellant's apartment pursuant to their right of arrest without warrant under s. 450 [the predecessor to s. 494(1) of the *Criminal Code*] . . . ? (2) If not, were their actions justified on common law principles? On the first issue, s. 450(1)(*a*) of the *Code* provides that any one may arrest without warrant a person who, on reasonable and probable grounds, he believes has committed a criminal offence. There were reasonable and probable grounds for believing that Cheese had committed a criminal offence and had the respondents found him in the apartment or elsewhere there is no doubt they would have been authorized by s. 450(1)(*a*) to arrest him. . . .

It is the submission of counsel for the respondents that a person who is by s. 450 authorized to make an arrest is, by s. 25, authorized by law to commit a trespass with or without force in the accomplishment of that arrest, provided he acts on reasonable and probable grounds. I cannot agree with this submission. Section 25 does not have such amplitude. The section merely affords justification to a person for doing what he is required or authorized by law to do in the administration or enforcement of the law, if he acts on reasonable and probable grounds, and for using necessary force for that purpose. The question which must be answered in this case, then, is whether the respondents were required or authorized by law to commit a trespass; and not, as their counsel contends, whether they were required or authorized to make an arrest. If they were authorized by law to commit a trespass, the authority for it must be found in the common law for there is nothing in the *Criminal Code*. The first issue, therefore, depends upon the second issue, *videlicet*, can the trespass be justified on common law principles? For these principles, we go back to vintage common law, to 1604, and *Semayne's Case*, 5 Co. Rep. 91a, 77 E.R. 194, in which the principle, so firmly entrenched in our jurisprudence, that every man's house is his castle, was expressed in these words [at p. 91b]: "That the house of every one is to him as his castle and fortress, as well for his defence against injury and violence, as for his repose ...". That, then, is the basic principle, as important today as in Biblical times (Deuteronomy 24:10) or in the 17th century. But there are occasions when the interest of a private individual in the security of his house must yield to the public interest, when the public at large has an interest in the process to be executed. The criminal is not immune from arrest in his own home nor in the home of one of his friends. So it is that in *Semayne's Case* a limitation was put on the "castle" concept and the Court resolved that: [at p. 916]

> In all cases when the King is party, the Sheriff (if the doors be not open) may break the party's house, either to arrest him, or to do other execution of the K.'s process, if otherwise he cannot enter. But before he breaks it, he ought to signify the cause of his coming, and to make request to open doors ...

See also, a century later, to the same effect, Hale, *Pleas of the Crown* (1736), 582; Foster, *Crown Law* (1762), 320. Thus it will be seen that the broad basic principle of sanctity of the home is subject to the exception that upon proper demand the officials of the King may break down doors to arrest. The incidental point was made in *Semayne's Case* that [at p. 93a] "the house of any one is not a castle or privilege but for himself, and shall not extend to protect any person who flies to his house ..."

The *Criminal Code* empowers a justice, on proper grounds being shown, to issue a warrant authorizing a search for things but there is no power to issue a warrant to search for persons. Counsel for Mr. Eccles advanced the argument that if a fugitive was in the home of a friend a police officer could not enter to arrest him unless the homeowner gave consent. I cannot agree that this properly expresses the position in law. If that be right, a fugitive could obtain permanent sanctuary merely by residing with a friend. I know of no place that gives a criminal fugitive sanctuary from arrest.

In some of the American jurisdictions a distinction is drawn between entering to arrest a fugitive in his own home and entering the home of another person to arrest the fugitive. I am unable to find any Anglo-Canadian authority supporting a distinction of this nature and in principle it seems to me to be wrong. The fact that the premises to be entered are those of a third person may have a bearing in the determination of reasonable and probable cause. There may be less likelihood of a fugitive being in the home of another than in his own home, but otherwise I can see no good reason for distinguishing between the two types of case.

I would wish to make it clear, however, that there is no question of an unrestricted right to enter in search of a fugitive. Entry can be made against the will of the householder only if *(a)* there are reasonable and probable grounds for the belief that the person sought is within the premises and *(b)* proper announcement is made prior to entry.

(a) Reasonable and probable grounds.

In the case of civil process the rule is that if a sheriff's officer enters the house of A to execute process against the goods of B or to arrest B he enters at his peril and if the goods or B, as the case may be, are not present, he is guilty of trespass. It is said the entry can be justified only by the event: *Johnson v. Leigh* (1815), 6 Taunt. 246, 128 E.R. 1029; *Morrish v. Murrey* (1844), 13 M. & W. 52, 153 E.R. 22; *Southam v. Smout*, [1964] 1 Q.B. 308. But in the execution of criminal process the test is whether there are reasonable and probable grounds for acting. If so, the entry does not become unlawful if the fugitive is not found on the premises. The entry of the police is legal or illegal from the moment of entry and does not change character from the result. . . . If the police officer has reasonable and probable cause to believe that the person named in the warrant for arrest is in the home of a stranger he has the right, after proper demand, to enter the home forcibly, to search and to arrest. In the present case there can be no doubt the police officers believed and in my view had reasonable and probable grounds for believing that Cheese, or Deans as he was known to Mr. Eccles, was in the Eccles apartment. Constable Simmonds had been told by one of his superiors that Eccles was the closest known associate of Cheese. That this information was hearsay does not exclude it from establishing probable cause. Additionally, both Eccles and Cheese had informed Constable Simmonds prior to the entry that Cheese had been staying in the Eccles apartment. On August 12, 1971, the day of the alleged trespass, Cheese had been in the apartment, he had been seen entering and leaving the building and just prior to the impugned entry had been seen to enter the building. Constable Bourque had seen police department bulletins pertaining to both Eccles and to Cheese.

(b) Announcement.

Except in exigent circumstances, the police officers must make an announcement prior to entry. There are compelling considerations for this. An unexpected intrusion of a man's property can give rise to violent incidents. It is in the interests of the personal safety of the householder and the police as well as respect for the privacy of the individual that the law requires, prior to entrance for search or arrest, that a police officer identify himself and request admittance. No precise form of words is necessary. . . . The traditional demand was "Open in the name of the King". In the ordinary case police officers, before forcing entry, should give (i) notice of presence by knocking or ringing the doorbell, (ii) notice of authority, by identifying themselves as law enforcement officers and (iii) notice of purpose, by stating a lawful reason for entry. Minimally they should request admission and have admission denied although it is recognized there will be occasions on which, for example, to save someone within the premises from death or injury or to prevent destruction of evidence or if in hot pursuit notice may not be required. Was proper notice given in this case? The police officers gave notice of presence by knocking on the door of the apartment. After a pause it was opened and an officer gave notice of identity by production of his badge and the words "Vancouver City Police". On August 10th, two days before the alleged trespass, Mr. Eccles had been stopped and searched by two of the respondents. One of the respondents had stopped him on two earlier occasions, so the identity of two of the three persons who appeared at the door of the apartment on August 12th could hardly have been a matter of which Mr. Eccles was ignorant. Whether notice of purpose was given is more difficult. Mr. Eccles testified that when the door was opened one man stood there while the other two ran into different rooms without identifying themselves or their purpose. In his evidence-in-chief, Constable Simmonds, after referring to the opening of the door, said:

> I don't recall if Mr. Eccles answered, I don't recall if he said: "What do you want", or something like that, he probably did and Constable Bourque said: "We're looking for a wanted man and we want to search the premises", so forth —

Constable Wise testified, "Constable Bourque told Mr. Eccles that we were looking for a man wanted on a warrant." Constable Bourque said that when the door opened he observed Mr. Eccles standing in the doorway and he, Bourque, entered the apartment. In reply to the question by Mr. Eccles, "What do you want?" Constable Bourque replied, according to his evidence, "I told him that I had reason to believe a man wanted by our department had just entered this apartment." In my view, the police officers, on the facts of this case, discharged the duty which rested upon them to give notice before forcing entry.

I would, accordingly, dismiss the appeal with costs.

MARTLAND J.: I do not wish to express any view with respect to the application of s. 25(1) of the *Criminal Code* to the circumstances of this case. Subject to this, I agree with the reasons of my brother Dickson and I would dispose of this appeal in the manner which he proposes.

[Laskin C.J.C. and Judson and Spence JJ. concurred with Dickson J., Ritchie, Pigeon, Beetz and de Grandpré JJ. concurred with Martland J.]

NOTES AND QUESTIONS

1. According to Dickson J., what is the source of an officer's authority and privilege to make an entry without a search warrant to arrest a wanted person? What is the effect of *Eccles* on the issue of whether s. 25 can be used as an authorizing provision?

2. Did Dickson J. limit this power of entry to cases involving suspects named in an outstanding warrant? Is the power limited to suspects wanted for indictable offences, rather than summary conviction offences? What is the practical significance of these restrictions?

3. What is required in making a proper announcement? Do you agree with Dickson J.'s application of these requirements to the facts in *Eccles*?

4. The general principles in *Eccles* were affirmed by the Supreme Court of Canada in *R. v. Landry*, [1986] 1 S.C.R. 145. While the court limited the entry power to persons wanted for indictable offences, it held that the police could also enter if they reasonably believed that an indictable offence was about to be committed. But see LaForest J.'s dissent in *Landry*. It has now been established that the principles in *Landry* apply even if the door of the dwelling is open. See *R. v. Delong* (1989), 31 O.A.C. 339 (C.A.).

5. In *R. v. Feeney*, [1997] 2 S.C.R. 13, the majority stated that s. 8 of the *Charter* limits the common law right to enter in search of a wanted person to situations of hot pursuit. The four dissenting judges rejected this limitation. In *R. v. Golub* (1997), 34 O.R. (3d) 743 (C.A.), the court interpreted *Feeney* as permitting such warrantless entries in any exceptional circumstances in which the state interest overrides the general prohibition against warrantless searches of the home.

6. In 1997, Parliament amended the *Criminal Code* to create statutory rights to enter dwellings to arrest a wanted person. The amendments provide for: warrants to enter dwellings to arrest a wanted person; authority to enter without a warrant in exigent circumstances; authority to enter without prior announcement in exigent circumstances; and the issuance of telewarrants if it is impracticable to obtain a regular warrant. These statutory provisions apply in addition to any common law authority the officer may have to make such entries. See *Criminal Code*, ss. 529-529.5.

7. Although not well defined, there was a common law right of forced entry to prevent the commission of murder and other felonies, but it was distinct from the right of entry to search for wanted suspects. Aside from the nature of the impending harm, this right appears similar to that granted in cases of public necessity. See *Handcock v. Baker* (1800), 126 E.R. 1270 (C.P.); and *R. v. Custer* (1984), 32 Sask. R. 287 (C.A.). See also *Re Children's Aid Society of Western Manitoba and Daniels* (1981), 128 D.L.R. (3d) 751 (Man. C.A.); and *Rigby v. Chief Constable of Northamptonshire*, [1985] 2 All E.R. 985 (Q.B.).

In *R. v. Godoy*, [1999] 1 S.C.R. 311, the police received a 911 call from a woman, but the call was disconnected before she could explain the situation. When the police arrived at the apartment, the accused told them that there was no problem and refused them entry. The police made a forced entry, interviewed the wife and then charged the husband with assault. The husband resisted arrest and was charged with assaulting an officer in the execution of his duty. This charge turned on whether the police entry was lawful. The court ruled that the forced entry was justifiable considering all of the circumstances. The court stated that, if it could be inferred that a caller is or may be in some distress, the police had a common law right to demand entry under their common law "duty to protect life." See also *R. v. Sanderson* (2003), 64 O.R. (3d) 257 (C.A.).

8. The House of Lords and the United States Supreme Court have defined the common right of entry to search for a wanted person far more narrowly than the Supreme Court of Canada. See *Payton v. New York; Riddick v. New York*, 100 S. Ct. 1371 (U.S. 1980); *Steagald v. U.S.*, 101 S. Ct. 1642 (U.S. 1981); *Morris v. Beardmore*, [1980] 2 All E.R. 753 (H.L.); and *Finnigan v. Sandiford*, [1981] 2 All E.R. 267 (H.L.).

9. The common law authorizes the police to enter a private dwelling in hot pursuit of a person who had committed an arrestable offence. The crime, pursuit and arrest had to be continuous, forming a single transaction. See *Swales v. Cox*, [1981] 1 All E.R. 1115 (Q.B.); *D'Souza v. D.P.P.*, [1992] 4 All E.R. 545 (H.L.); and *R. v. Haglof* (2000), 149 C.C.C. (3d) 248 (B.C.C.A.). In *R. v. Macooh*, [1993] 2 S.C.R. 802, the court extended this doctrine to provincial offences. What are the justifications for allowing forced entry in hot pursuit? Do you agree with the Supreme Court of Canada that there is no logical reason to distinguish between indictable and provincial offences in analyzing hot pursuit?

10. The common law did not authorize entry without a warrant to seize evidence of an offence or to carry out general investigations. See *Morris v. Beardmore*, *supra*; *Finnigan v. Sandiford*, *supra*; and *R. v. Colet*, [1981] 1 S.C.R. 2.

REVIEW PROBLEMS

1. Fifteen members of a local motorcycle gang pulled into John's Service Station and Restaurant. The owner, aware of the gang's reputation for violent crime, called the police. The gang went to the service centre, where one of the cyclists politely asked to borrow a wrench, which the attendant retrieved from the back of the station. Upon her return, the attendant noticed that two small cans of lubricating oil were missing from the display, but she did not see who took them. Nevertheless, she assumed that one of the gang members had stolen the oil in her brief absence.

When six police officers and their trained dog arrived, the attendant explained that one of the cyclists had stolen some oil, but she had no idea which one it was. Officer Jones approached the gang leader, Steve, and asked him to open his pack. Steve ignored Jones until the dog, on command from Jones, bared its teeth and backed Steve into a corner. In the interim, Jones was informed that no oil had been found in the possession of the other cyclists. He ordered Steve to open his pack. Steve, who was unaware of the attendant's allegation, refused and walked to his motorcycle.

Jones signalled the dog to subdue Steve. It jumped on Steve's back, knocking him to the ground. Just before the dog struck, Jones shouted, "You are under arrest for theft!" Steve was handcuffed and led away to a police car. Although the search of his pack revealed that it was empty, Steve was told that he was under arrest for obstructing a peace officer in the execution of his duty.

The charge against Steve was dropped. He wishes to sue Jones and the attendant in tort and has asked for your advice.

2. Ralph, a former professional football player, owned a small cigar store. Late one night, he heard someone yell "Help! Thief! Help!" As he stepped outside, he saw Gaston running towards him carrying an expensive camera. In hot pursuit, about 30 metres behind, was George. Both were strangers to Ralph, and were unexceptional in size or manner of dress. Gaston turned into a dead-end alley and Ralph, still well ahead of

George, joined in the chase. Just as Gaston slowed down at the end of the alley, Ralph brought him to the ground with a tackle. Gaston attempted to struggle free, but Ralph hauled him to his feet with ease and threw him into a fence with such force that it knocked down an overhanging neon sign. Breathless and badly shaken, Gaston was finally able to scream at Ralph, "I'm not the thief, he is getting away!" When Ralph turned around he saw that George had disappeared, and realized his mistake. Ralph has sought your legal advice regarding his potential tort liability.

3. John was woken by loud banging on his door on Wednesday at 2:00 a.m. When he opened the door, John was confronted by three uniformed police officers, who stated that they were looking for Bobby Seal. John told them to put their guns away and that only his family was in the house. The officers ran past John, stating that he would be arrested if he tried to stop them. The officers entered the bedrooms with their guns at their sides. After thoroughly searching the house, the officers left without providing any further explanation and without apologizing. John's wife was initially fearful, but this soon turned to anger. The children remained upset and had nightmares for several weeks.

The officers knew that Bobby and John were lifelong friends and that they had been convicted of several robberies nine years ago when they were teenagers. While Bobby had had a number of arrests and convictions after that, John had no other arrests. The police were investigating an armed robbery at a jewellery store that had been committed at 8:00 p.m. on Tuesday evening. The security camera had captured pictures of the thief, who resembled Bobby Seal. The thief was carrying a gun. Since the thief wore a ski mask, it was impossible to make a positive identification.

The staff of the bar in the jewellery store plaza told the police that Bobby and John had lunch together in the bar on the day of the robbery. A car somewhat similar to Bobby Seal's was spotted near the plaza at 7:00 p.m. that night. A usually reliable informant had told the police that he wouldn't be surprised if Bobby had robbed the jewellery store, but he doubted that John would get involved. The informant had also told the police that Seal spent time at John's house, particularly when he got in trouble.

The police had checked Bobby Seal's house and his girlfriend's apartment before coming to John's house. However, Bobby's car was not parked nearby and no one reported seeing the car or Bobby in the vicinity of John's house. Nevertheless, the police were anxious to find Bobby as soon as possible. If he was the robber, they did not want to give him an opportunity to dispose of the jewellery.

John has approached your law firm. Your senior partner wants you to analyze the tort claims that John and his family could bring against the officers for entering and searching their home and the defence that the police will likely raise.

9

INTRODUCTION TO THE LAW OF NEGLIGENCE

1. Negligence: Defining Terms
2. The Historical Development of Negligence
3. The Elements of a Negligence Action

1. Negligence: Defining Terms

The term "negligence" is used by tort lawyers in two distinct ways. First, in the broader sense, it refers to a cause of action that constitutes a branch of tort law that is concerned with liability for careless conduct. As discussed below, that cause of action contains a number of elements. Second, in its narrower sense, the term "negligence" refers to one particular element within that cause of action, namely, whether the defendant's conduct met the standard of care. Because of that ambiguity, it sometimes is difficult to know what a court or commentator means when using the term "negligence." Consequently, it may be better to speak of "negligence" only when referring to the cause of action as a whole, and to use the term "carelessness" when referring to conduct that fails to satisfy the standard of care.

Unlike the intentional torts, the cause of action in negligence has few predetermined boundaries. To a large extent, its scope is as wide or as narrow as the judicial interpretation of its core concept, the duty of care. The threshold issue in every negligence case is whether the defendant was subject to a legal obligation, or "duty," to exercise care with respect to the plaintiff's interests. The approach to that issue has varied from time to time and place to place. Toward the end of the 20th century, Canadian judges, in contrast to their English and Australian counterparts, tended to work from a relatively expansive, plaintiff-friendly perspective. As discussed in the next chapter, however, the new millennium has seen a shift in this country towards a more conservative attitude. In any event, the breadth and flexibility of the cause of action in negligence has made it the most frequently litigated tort.

2. The Historical Development of Negligence

The modern law of negligence, like that of intentional torts, has its origins in the writ system. Trespass *vi et armis*, the first writ relating to torts, provided strict liability for direct, forceful interferences with person or property. If the plaintiff established a direct injury, the defendant would be held liable unless he or she could prove that the injury occurred utterly without his or her fault. The stringent nature of liability in trespass *vi et armis* grew out of a strong judicial motivation to vindicate the security of the person and property and to deter public disorder.

The writ of trespass on the case developed after trespass *vi et armis*, and provided a remedy for losses that were not directly and forcefully inflicted. Since such incidents were less likely to cause violent confrontations, trespass on the case was never as stringent as trespass *vi et armis*. The plaintiff was required to prove that he or she had suffered actual loss and that the defendant's conduct was either intentional or negligent. A variety of actions on the case were eventually established, including defamation, nuisance, deceit, and negligence.

The first actions on the case involved defendants in public callings, such as apothecaries, surgeons, common carriers, and innkeepers, who were alleged to have breached the standards of customary practice. Outside of these types of relationships, individuals generally were not held accountable simply because, through carelessness, they indirectly injured others.

As illustrated by the cases in Chapter 1, by the early 19th century, the action on the case was also being used by plaintiffs who had been carelessly run down on public roads. So too by plaintiffs who had been injured through the mismanagement of fire or animals. In all of those situations, judges came to recognize legal duties of care in the absence of contract or, indeed, any prior relationship between the parties. As the number of lawsuits involving inadvertent conduct increased, the judges also began to articulate more clearly a "fault" theory of liability. They eventually held that a plaintiff was entitled to relief only if a defendant was at fault, that is, that the defendant failed to conform to the standard of care required in the circumstances. Both the duty of care concept and the fault principle were used by the courts as means of controlling the expansive tendencies of the tort of negligence.

In a series of cases in the mid and late 19th century, plaintiffs' lawyers attempted to extend the concept of the legal duty of care beyond the established categories, but those efforts were largely unsuccessful. Although lawsuits in negligence became commonplace, they were mainly confined to repetitive situations, such as railroad accidents, which were covered by settled precedent. In *Heaven v. Pender* (1883), 11 Q.B.D. 503 (C.A.), Brett M.R. boldly attempted to promulgate a general theory of the legal duty to take care, one that would apply in any circumstances where the actions of one party had created a foreseeable risk of harm to another. However, that proposition was flatly rejected both by the other justices in *Heaven* and by judges in subsequent decisions, and was even qualified by Brett M.R. himself in *LeLievre v. Gould*, [1893] 1 Q.B. 491 (C.A.) (by which time he had become Lord Esher).

The idea of establishing a synthesized and expansive duty of care in negligence found little support in the English courts until the House of Lords revisited the issue in *M'Alister (or Donoghue) v. Stevenson*, [1932] A.C. 562. The plaintiff alleged that she got sick after consuming the remnants of a decomposed snail in the defendant manufacturer's ginger beer. In what is now regarded as a classic speech, Lord Atkin stated at 580:

> At present I content myself with pointing out that in English law there must be, and is, some general conception of relations giving rise to a duty of care, of which the particular cases found in the books are but instances. The liability for negligence, whether you style it such or treat it as in other systems as a species of "culpa," is no doubt based upon a general public sentiment of moral wrongdoing for which the offender must pay. But acts or omissions which any moral code would censure cannot in a practical world be treated so as to give a right to every person injured by them to demand relief. In this way rules of law arise which limit the range of complainants and the extent of their remedy. The rule that you are to love your neighbour becomes in law, you must not injure your neighbour; and the lawyer's question, Who is my neighbour? receives a restricted reply. You must take reasonable care to avoid acts or omissions which you

can reasonably foresee would be likely to injure your neighbour. Who, then, in law is my neighbour? The answer seems to be persons who are so closely and directly affected by my act that I ought reasonably to have them in contemplation as being so affected when I am directing my mind to the acts or omissions which are called in question.

Donoghue v. Stevenson is the seminal case in modern negligence law because it established a basic framework that could be used for determining when to recognize a duty of care. Despite initial reluctance to adopt a general conception of duty, Lord Atkin's test eventually became widely accepted as governing liability for negligent acts causing physical injury or property damage. There was far greater reluctance, however, to apply the test to those categories of negligence that had previously been subject to restrictive liability rules. These special categories included cases involving a defendant's failure to take affirmative action for the plaintiff's benefit, negligent statements, nervous shock, pure economic loss, and occupiers' liability. During the past 75 years, the courts have gradually, on a piecemeal basis, rejected much of this pre-1932 case law in favour of broader principles more akin to those in *Donoghue*.

NOTES AND QUESTIONS

1. P.H. Winfield identified four areas of the early common law from which the modern negligence action evolved: liability in nuisance; liability based on the control of dangerous things; duties voluntarily undertaken in assumpsit; and the duty cast upon bailees and persons pursuing a common calling. See "The History of Negligence in the Law of Torts" (1926) 42 L.Q.R. 184. See also Wigmore, "Responsibility for Tortious Acts: Its History" (1894) 7 Harv. L. Rev. 315 & 383; Ames, "Law and Morals" (1908) 22 Harv. L. Rev. 97; and Arterburn, "The Origin and First Test of Public Callings" (1926-27) 75 U. Pa. L. Rev. 411.

2. There has been considerable debate over the impact of the Industrial Revolution and the concept of fault on the emergence of negligence as an independent tort action. The orthodox view is perhaps best reflected by C.H.S. Fifoot in *History and Sources of the Common Law* (1949) at 164:

> The prime factor in the ultimate transformation of negligence from a principle of liability in Case to an independent tort was the luxuriant crop of "running down" actions reaped from the commercial prosperity of the late eighteenth and early nineteenth century. Their significance lay rather in their number than in their nature. So long as they could be indulged as the occasional accidents of litigation, they called for no special attention; but when they became a daily occurrence, the judges were forced to recognize a formidable phenomenon which could not be confined, without too gross an artificiality, within the conventional categories.

G.E. White contends that the evolution of negligence in the United States was more complex than the orthodox view suggests. He maintains that the development of negligence was fostered by three 19th century trends: the impulse towards conceptualization among American intellectuals; the collapse of common law writ pleading; and a gradual change in tort cases from those involving parties in "closely defined relations to those involving strangers." Only the last factor is directly related to industrialization and urbanization. See White, *Tort Law In America: An Intellectual History*, expanded ed.

(2003). See also Melamed & Westin, "Anti-Intellectual History" (1981) 90 Yale L.J. 1497.

3. Legal historians continue to debate the question of the social and economic impact of the rise of the negligence tort. In his influential book, *The Transformation of American Law, 1780-1860* (1970), M. Horwitz argued that the judicial development and application of fault-based negligence principles delivered crucial subsidies to American industry, especially in the area of work-related accidents. This view has been substantially revised by more recent scholarship emphasizing the diversity – doctrinal, regional, and temporal – of negligence law and its consequences for American history. See generally, Schwartz, "Tort Law and the Economy in Nineteenth Century America: A Reinterpretation" (1981) 90 Yale L.J. 1717; Kaczorowski, "The Common Law Background of Nineteenth Century Tort Law" (1990) 51 Ohio St. L.J. 1127; Bergstrom, *Courting Danger* (1994); Welke, *Recasting American Liberty* (2001); and Witt, *The Accidental Republic* (2004).

For a study of the relationship between negligence law and the rise of industry in England, see Kostal, *Law and English Railway Capitalism 1825-1875* (1995) at 254-321.

4. As late as 1924, J.W. Salmond argued that negligence was not an independent branch of tort law: *Law of Torts*, 6th ed. (1924). Contrast his position with that of Pollock, *The Law of Torts* (1887) at 22; and Winfield, "The History of Negligence in the Law of Torts" (1926) 46 L.Q.R. 184.

5. Relatively little has been published on the historical development of tort law in Canada. But see Risk, "The Last Golden Age: Property and the Allocation of Losses in Ontario in the Nineteenth Century" (1977) 27 U.T.L.J. 199; and Kostal, "Legal Justice, Social Justice: The Social History of Work-Related Accident Law in Ontario, 1880-86" (1988) 6 Law and Hist. Rev. 1.

6. It should be noted that several academics had formulated theories of negligence which were very similar to that eventually articulated by Lord Atkin. See for example, Pollock, *The Law of Torts* (1887) at 353; and Smith, *A Treatise on the Law of Negligence*, 2d ed. (1887) at 1.

3. The Elements of a Negligence Action

(a) INTRODUCTION

Unlike the nominate intentional torts, the various manifestations of the cause of action in negligence all fall within a single conceptual framework, regardless of the precise nature of the defendant's conduct or the plaintiff's loss. That is not to say that exactly the same rules apply in each instance. For example, the liability rules governing nervous shock are far more restrictive than those governing personal injury. It is correct to say, however, that the basic elements of analysis remain constant.

Unfortunately, while there is broad consensus on that proposition, there is less agreement regarding the manner in which the constituent elements of the claim ought to be named and organized. To a large extent, the incidence of liability should not be affected by the choice of one model over another. Nevertheless, for the sake of consistency and clarity, it is critically important to adopt and adhere to some particular scheme. With that in mind, we have divided the negligence claim into six parts. The plaintiff usually has the burden of proving the first five, while the defendant has the burden of proving the sixth.

(i) *Duty of Care*

The court must decide, as a matter of law, whether the defendant was under any legal obligation to exercise care with respect to the plaintiff's interests in the type of case under consideration. If necessary, the court must also determine the nature and scope of that obligation. Because the duty of care often defines the boundaries of negligence liability, it has historically been the element of negligence most concerned with legal policy.

(ii) *The Standard of Care and its Breach*

Having identified and defined the duty of care, the court must next establish the standard of care required of the defendant. Ordinarily, the defendant is expected to meet the standard of care that would be exercised by a reasonable person in all the circumstances of the case. However, some professionals who have special training or qualifications are expected to meet the standard of their professional colleagues.

The trier of fact will then apply that standard of care to the defendant's conduct to determine whether the defendant breached his or her obligation by acting carelessly (or "negligently").

(iii) *Causation*

Even if the defendant was under a duty of care and breached the standard of care, he or she will not be held liable unless the careless conduct was a cause of the plaintiff's loss. This element of the negligence action is commonly known as cause-in-fact.

(iv) *Remoteness of Damages*

Once it has been established that the defendant carelessly caused the plaintiff's injury, the court must determine whether the relationship between the breach and the injury is too tenuous, or remote, to warrant recovery. In intentional torts, defendants are normally liable for all of the consequences of their wrongful conduct. However, in negligence, liability is generally limited to those losses that were foreseeable consequences of the defendant's negligent act.

(v) *Actual Loss*

Unlike most intentional torts, negligence is not actionable *per se*. The plaintiff must establish that he or she suffered legally-recognized injuries and losses, as well as their nature and extent. Certain losses, such as death and grief, were not recoverable at common law; however, they are generally recoverable under legislation.

(vi) *Defences*

Finally, once the plaintiff has established a *prima facie* claim, the court must address the issue of defences. The plaintiff's damages may be reduced or eliminated on account of his or her own conduct (contributory negligence, voluntary assumption of risk or illegality) or on account of other considerations (inevitable accident). The defendant may also raise general defences, such as lapse of limitation period, that are not peculiar to the action in negligence.

NOTES AND QUESTIONS

1. English authors often divide negligence into three main issues: duty, breach and damages. See for example Heuston & Buckley, *Salmond and Heuston on the Law of Torts*, 21st ed. (1996) at 195-98; and Rogers, *Winfield and Jolowicz on Torts*, 17th ed. (2006) at 132-33. This framework may prove difficult for students because it tends to fuse, rather than isolate, the various issues that must be resolved in a negligence case.

Even more worrying, it has sometimes been suggested that the entire negligence action can be reduced to a single inquiry. In *Roe v. Minister of Health*, [1954] 2 Q.B. 66 at 85 (C.A.), Denning L.J. said that "the three questions, duty, causation, and remoteness, run continually into one another. It seems to me that they are simply three different ways of looking at one and the same problem. . . . Instead of asking three questions, I should have thought that in many cases it would be simpler and better to ask one question: is the consequence within the risk? And to answer it by applying ordinary plain common sense." See also *Ontario (Attorney General) v. Crompton* (1976), 74 D.L.R. (3d) 345 (Ont. H.C.). What does Denning L.J.'s statement say about his view of judging? Would his approach to negligence lead to more or less certainty in the litigation process? Would it make judgments more or less "transparent," in terms of allowing litigants to know why they won or lost?

2. For alternative formulations of the elements of negligence, see The American Law Institute, *Restatement of the Law, Third, Torts: Liability for Physical Harm* (Proposed Final Draft No. 1) (2005), § 6; Fleming, *The Law of Torts*, 9th ed. (1998) at 114-15; and Linden, *Canadian Tort Law*, 8th ed. (2006) at 108-11. See also Gibson, "A New Alphabet of Negligence" in Linden, ed., *Studies in Canadian Tort Law* (1968) 189; and Smith, *Liability in Negligence* (1984). The major differences arise primarily in the authors' approaches to the elements of duty and remoteness.

(b) NEGLIGENCE: A CASE ILLUSTRATION

The following case is typical of many negligence decisions, particularly at the trial level. The facts dominate the court's attention, while legal principles are only briefly discussed. Some issues may be analyzed at length, while others are not mentioned or are discussed only briefly. For example, the judge does not analyze the duty of care because the case falls within an established category and the existence of duty is not contentious. In many cases, judges appear to decide whether the plaintiff has a meritorious claim and then set about the task of legally justifying their initial conclusion. This pragmatic, result-oriented approach makes it difficult to identify the legal basis of the decision.

DUNSMORE v. DESHIELD

(1977), 80 D.L.R. (3d) 386 (Sask. Q.B.)

MACPHERSON J.:—The plaintiff was playing touch football when he collided with another player and one lens of his glasses broke and injured his right eye. The defendant Deshield is the optometrist who supplied the glasses, the defendant Imperial Optical (Imperial) manufactured the lenses.

The plaintiff ordered from Deshield a type of lens known as Hardex which is specially treated by Imperial in a hot and cold process to make it more impact-resistant than ordinary glass lenses. The glasses were supplied as Hardex by Imperial to Deshield and in turn to the plaintiff about February 26, 1973, who wore them off and on until the accident on September 7, 1974.

I am satisfied on the balance of probabilities that the lenses were not Hardex.

The plaintiff sues both defendants for damages alleging that if they were Hardex they would not have broken and he would not have been injured. The action against Deshield is in breach of contract or, alternatively, negligence. Against Imperial he claims in negligence.

The plaintiff is now 34 (then 31). He is a highly educated man who occupies a responsible position in the civil service.

Both defendants plead contributory negligence. The burden of establishing this plea is upon them. They must satisfy me that the plaintiff caused or contributed to his loss and injury by playing touch football with his glasses on. If they were to succeed on this point, the defendants had to show that it was, like football, a game of violence and this they failed to do. The plaintiff said it was a non-contact game but on this occasion he collided with another player. It is a running game in which, he admitted, there has been the odd broken wrist or sprained ankle. There was no evidence that the game involved bodily contact except on this occasion.

I cannot take judicial notice of the rules of the game or how it was played on this occasion. I was not told how many were playing.

I cannot find contributory negligence even on the balance of probabilities.

Imperial was negligent in failing to supply Hardex lenses. Its system of supply and manufacture is not flawless as Mr. Most, its manufacturing optician for 35 years, admitted. Sometimes ordinary lenses are delivered as Hardex. The percentage is small, but is impossible to estimate because it is not known how many are tested by the ophthalmologists or optometrists through whose hands they pass to the consumer. Imperial and many of the optical practitioners possess a small machine called a colmiscope (I think) through which a lens is examined and if it is Hardex a characteristic Maltese cross pattern appears in it. The test is easily done. In addition to its failure to temper the lenses, Imperial failed to test them before delivery to Deshield.

Deshield, likewise, did not test them. He now has a colmiscope but probably did not have one at the time of delivery. In my view he had a duty to the plaintiff to test them but instead relied on Imperial, thus accepting or adopting Imperial's negligence.

But negligence is only part of the plaintiff's cause of action. His more difficult hurdle is causation, the causal relationship between the negligence and the injury. The plea of *res ipsa loquitur* does not help the plaintiff. That involves an inference of negligence not causation. The defendant's wrong cannot be the cause of the injury if it would have happened without the wrong. Therefore, the defendants argue quite rightly that the plaintiff must prove that the impact he received, although sufficient to break the ordinary and untempered lens he wore, would probably not have been sufficient to break a Hardex lens.

Imperial is possessed of another machine, one designed to test the hardness of Hardex lenses. It drops a steel ball having a diameter of 5/8 of an inch onto a lens from a height of 50 ins. Any properly tempered Hardex lens is expected to withstand this blow. Only about one such lens is so tested each month in Imperial's laboratory in Regina, probably enough.

I cannot with certainty conclude that the blow of the steel ball on the lens was lighter or harder than the impact which caused the plaintiff's lens to shatter. I had no expert evidence. But the plaintiff's burden is not to show certainty. He has only to show that more probably than not the one which caused the injury was less violent or of less force than the steel ball test.

I feel the plaintiff has met this burden. The steel ball test shows the strength of Hardex lenses and their ability to withstand a direct blow of considerable force. The momentum of the collision between the plaintiff and the other player would be greater but much diffused, I would think, not as concentrated as the steel ball. All of the force of the bodies in collision at the time of the injury would not be on the lens which broke.

There was evidence suggesting that the Hardex lens breaks in a manner different from an ordinary lens. If acceptable, this evidence would be useful to the plaintiff because the injury might have been less severe or trifling, if, in fact, a Hardex lens had broken in the circumstances. But the evidence on the point is not good enough for me to draw that conclusion. Mr. Most broke an ordinary lens and a Hardex lens of identical prescription in the identical manner and brought the pieces to the trial. My unskilled eye could see nothing but similarity in the glass fragments of the two, but Drs. Griffith and Deshield who have considerable experience seemed to expect smaller fragments. Whether this would cause less injury is too speculative for me to judge.

The plaintiff is not the type of young man who might take unnecessary risks. There seems nothing frivolous about him. If he had known that the lenses were not Hardex, he would not have worn them on this occasion. The defendants by their error failed in their duty to protect the plaintiff against the risk of breakage of ordinary lenses. The risk was foreseeable whether or not they knew that he had athletic pastimes.

The defendants are therefore liable.

In the accident, part of the fractured lens entered the plaintiff's right eye. He was taken to hospital where he saw his family doctor who in turn called Dr. Griffith, an ophthalmologist. He found an irregular laceration of the cornea which healed after removal of a number of small fragments of clear glass from the eye.

Over the next year to 18 months the vision in the right eye improved until it stabilized at 20/25. Before the accident it was 20/20 as was (and is) the left eye. The references are to corrected vision because the plaintiff has been nearsighted all his life.

He was just a few days in hospital and six days off work.

Previously he was able to wear soft contact lenses but now because of the irregularity of the corneal surface he finds them uncomfortable, and wears them only when playing hockey or football. His vision in the right eye is now not as good with contacts as with glasses.

Even with glasses the right eye tires earlier which is a material consideration to a man who plans a career in government requiring much reading and other close work. This factor makes the assessment of damages difficult.

I award the plaintiff $7,500 in general damages and special damages in the agreed amount of $646.50.

Each of the defendants has made a claim over against the other for indemnity.

As I view the facts each of the defendants had a duty to the plaintiff to ensure that he got Hardex lenses and avoided the risk consequent upon the breakage of ordinary lenses. I cannot say that the manufacturer had a greater duty than the optometrist or *vice versa*, but the duty is to the plaintiff. What is their duty to one another? Imperial had no promise or undertaking or contract with Deshield that Deshield would test lenses for hardness before delivery to the plaintiff or any other consumer. Mr. Most does not know today which optometrists have colmiscopes and which do not. How, then, can Imperial say that Deshield had a duty to Imperial to apply the Hardex test? Optical practitioners have colmiscopes to protect their patients not Imperial, I would think. Deshield was entitled to rely on Imperial's duty to supply Hardex lenses notwithstanding Deshield's own duty to his patient, the plaintiff.

Therefore I award judgment against the defendants jointly and severally for the sum of $8,146.50 and costs to be taxed.

The defendant Deshield shall have indemnification from Imperial for the entire judgment plus his own costs.

NOTES AND QUESTIONS

1. As is often the case, the judge did not discuss the basis upon which he concluded that the defendants owed the plaintiff a duty of care. Why do you think the judge imposed a duty on the defendants in this situation?

2. Did the judge specifically address the question of the standard of care that the defendants were expected to meet? How did Deshield and Imperial Optical breach the standard of care? If, as the judge suggests, Deshield did not have a colmiscope, why was he held negligent for not testing the lenses? Considering that Imperial Optical is a large company, should it be found negligent every time it delivers the wrong lenses to one of its clients?

3. What did the plaintiff have to prove in order to establish that Deshield and Imperial Optical caused his injury? If the collision between the plaintiff and the other player was violent enough to shatter a normal glass lens, is it not likely that it would have shattered a Hardex lens? How did the judge decide this issue without expert testimony?

4. How did the judge resolve the issue of remoteness of damages?

5. Summarize the plaintiff's material losses. What was the basis upon which the judge determined that $7,500 was an appropriate award of general damages?

6. Why did the judge conclude that the plaintiff was not contributorily negligent? Do you think that this conclusion would have been different if the game had been tackle football?

7. What is the legal effect of finding the defendants jointly and severally liable? Why did Imperial Optical have to indemnify Deshield for the entire judgment? Would the result have been the same if the judge had relieved Deshield of liability and simply found Imperial Optical liable?

10

THE DUTY OF CARE

1. An Introduction to the Duty of Care
2. Application of the Duty of Care Test

1. An Introduction to the Duty of Care

As discussed in the previous chapter, the core concept within the tort of negligence is the duty of care. Relief is not available unless the court is satisfied that the defendant was under a legal obligation to exercise care with respect to the plaintiff's interests. The materials in this chapter outline the evolution of the duty concept and the current state of duty jurisprudence in Canada.

(a) THE CLASSICAL APPROACH

In the 19th and early 20th centuries, the duty of care was confined to a narrow set of actors and conduct. While the ambit of duty was expanded in isolated cases, the expansion was cautious and piecemeal. Most common law lawyers and judges operated within a fairly rigid set of legal, social and political assumptions about the nature and purpose of negligence law. This set of assumptions may be viewed as the "classical" approach to the duty of care.

The first premise of the classical approach was that legal responsibility for negligence did not flow inexorably from moral responsibility. The classical lawyers respected both precedent and the absence of precedent. If the common law had not established a particular legal duty of care, that was reason enough to doubt its desirability. The conservatism of Victorian judges was driven in part by trust in the wisdom of the common law and in part by a particular vision of social responsibility. In a society committed to individual liberty and self-reliance, legal rights and obligations generally were seen to be a function of voluntary agreements between consenting parties. Legal duties of care imposed by courts, irrespective of individual agreements, did not easily square with these convictions.

The second premise of the classical view was political in nature. As unelected bodies within representative democracies, courts were seen as having a limited role in imposing liability outside the confines of common law precedent. Even if a broader duty of care were required, it was for legislators to enact.

The third premise concerned the theory of legal obligations. Acts were seen to be more culpable than omissions. Consequently, judges drew a distinction between misfeasance and nonfeasance. The courts were much more likely to impose liability if the defendant did something that hurt the plaintiff than if the defendant merely failed to do something that would have helped the plaintiff. For instance, a person would be held responsible for carelessly shooting a stranger, but not for failing to rescue a stranger who had been shot by someone else. Whatever morality might dictate, there was no legal obligation to act as one's "brother's keeper."

Fourth, the classical view rested on assumptions about the value of various interests. Physical injuries to individuals and property were broadly compensable, but emotional harms and loss of commercial profits were not. Physical injuries were seen as more tangible and measurable. The common law also more readily compensated harms caused by deeds than those caused by words. While bankers had a legal duty to prevent their customers' entrusted valuables from being stolen, they had no legal obligation to ensure that their gratuitous financial advice was accurate or sound. Again, the common law focused on what was perceived to be a more concrete and cautious basis for imposing negligence liability.

As we shall see, some of the classical currents are reflected in *Donoghue v. Stevenson*, [1932] A.C. 562 (H.L.), particularly in the dissent of Lord Buckmaster. Even though *Donoghue* marked the beginning of the modern law of negligence, the classical approach to duty – albeit in an altered form – has continued to shape the evolution of the duty of care.

(b) THE GENERAL DUTY OF CARE TEST

M'ALISTER (or DONOGHUE) v. STEVENSON

[1932] A.C. 562 (H.L.)

[The plaintiff's friend purchased a dark, opaque bottle of ginger-beer and gave it to the plaintiff. She drank some before her friend discovered a decomposed snail in the bottle. The plaintiff sued the manufacturer, alleging shock and severe gastroenteritis.]

LORD ATKIN:–My Lords, the sole question for determination in this case is legal: Do the averments made by the pursuer in her pleading, if true, disclose a cause of action? I need not restate the particular facts. The question is whether the manufacturer of an article of drink sold by him to a distributor, in circumstances which prevent the distributor or the ultimate purchaser or consumer from discovering by inspection any defect, is under any legal duty to the ultimate purchaser or consumer to take reasonable care that the article is free from defect likely to cause injury to health. I do not think a more important problem has occupied your Lordships in your judicial capacity: important both because of its bearing on public health and because of the practical test which it applies to the system under which it arises. The case has to be determined in accordance with Scots law; but it has been a matter of agreement between the experienced counsel who argue this case, and it appears to be the basis of the judgments of the learned judges of the Court of Session, that for the purposes of determining this problem the laws of Scotland and England are the same. I speak with little authority on this point, but my research, such as it is, satisfies me that the principles of the law of Scotland on such a question as the present are identical with those of English law; and I discuss the issue on that footing. The law of both countries appears to be that in order to support an action for damages for negligence the complainant has to show that he has been injured by the breach of a duty owed to him in the circumstances by the defendant to take reasonable care to avoid such injury. In the present case we are not concerned with the breach of the duty; if a duty exists, that would be a question of fact which is sufficiently averred and for present purposes must be assumed. We are solely concerned with the question whether, as a matter of law in the circumstances alleged, the defender owed any duty to the pursuer to take care.

It is remarkable how difficult it is to find in the English authorities statements of general application defining the relations between parties that give rise to the duty. The

Courts are concerned with the particular relations which come before them in actual litigation, and it is sufficient to say whether the duty exists in those circumstances. The result is that the Courts have been engaged upon an elaborate classification of duties, as they exist in respect of property, whether real or personal, with further divisions as to ownership, occupation or control, and distinctions based on the particular relations of one side or the other, whether manufacturer, salesman or landlord, customer, tenant, stranger, and so on. In this way it can be ascertained at any time whether the law recognizes a duty, but only where the case can be referred to some particular species which has been examined and classified. And yet the duty which is common to all the cases where liability is established must logically be based upon some element common to the cases where it is found to exist. To seek a complete logical definition of the general principle is probably to go beyond the function of the judge, for the more general the definition the more likely it is to omit essentials or to introduce non-essentials. The attempt was made by Brett M.R. in *Heaven v. Pender*, in a definition to which I will later refer. As framed, it was demonstrably too wide, though it appears to me, if properly limited, to be capable of affording a valuable practical guide.

At present I content myself with pointing out that in English law there must be, and is, some general conception of relations giving rise to a duty of care, of which the particular cases found in the books are but instances. The liability for negligence, whether you style it such or treat it as in other systems as a species of "culpa," is no doubt based upon a general public sentiment of moral wrongdoing for which the offender must pay. But acts or omissions which any moral code would censure cannot in a practical world be treated so as to give a right to every person injured by them to demand relief. In this way rules of law arise which limit the range of complainants and the extent of their remedy. The rule that you are to love your neighbour becomes in law, you must not injure your neighbour; and the lawyer's question, Who is my neighbour? receives a restricted reply. You must take reasonable care to avoid acts or omissions which you can reasonably foresee would be likely to injure your neighbour. Who, then, in law is my neighbour? The answer seems to be – persons who are so closely and directly affected by my act that I ought reasonably to have them in contemplation as being so affected when I am directing my mind to the acts or omissions which are called in question. This appears to me to be the doctrine of *Heaven v. Pender* as laid down by Lord Esher (then Brett M.R.) when it is limited by the notion of proximity introduced by Lord Esher himself and A.L. Smith L.J. in *Le Lievre v. Gould*. Lord Esher says:

> That case established that, under certain circumstances, one may owe a duty to another, even though there is no contract between them. If one man is near to another, or is near to the property of another, a duty lies upon him not to do that which may cause a personal injury to that other, or may injure his property.

And A.L. Smith L.J.:

> The decision of *Heaven v. Pender* was founded upon the principle, that a duty to take due care did arise when the person or property of one was in such proximity to the person or property of another that, if due care was not taken, damage might be done by the one to the other.

I think that this sufficiently states the truth if proximity be not confined to mere physical proximity, but be used, as I think it was intended, to extend to such close and direct relations that the act complained of directly affects a person whom the person alleged to be bound to take care would know would be directly affected by his careless act. That this is the sense in which nearness or "proximity" was intended by Lord Esher is obvious from his own illustration in *Heaven v. Pender* of the application of his doctrine to the sale of goods.

> This (i.e., the rule he just formulated) includes the case of goods, etc., supplied to be used immediately by a particular person or persons, or one of a class of persons, where it would be obvious to the person supplying, if he thought, that the goods would in all probability be used at once by such persons before a reasonable opportunity for discovering any defect which might exist, and where the thing supplied would be of such a nature that a neglect of ordinary care or skill as to its condition or the manner of supplying it would probably cause danger to the person or property of the person for whose use it was supplied, and who was about to use it. It would exclude a case in which the goods are supplied under circumstances in which it would be a chance by whom they would be used or whether they would be used or not, or whether they would be used before there would probably be means of observing any defect, or where the goods would be of such nature that a want of care or skill as to their condition or the manner of supplying them would not probably produce danger of injury to person or property.

I draw particular attention to the fact that Lord Esher emphasizes the necessity of goods having to be "used immediately" and "used at once before a reasonable opportunity of inspection." This is obviously to exclude the possibility of goods having their condition altered by lapse of time, and to call attention to the proximate relationship, which may be too remote where inspection even of the person using, certainly of an intermediate person, may reasonably be interposed. With this necessary qualification of proximate relationship as explained in *Le Lievre v. Gould*, I think the judgment of Lord Esher expresses the law of England; without the qualification, I think the majority of the Court in *Heaven v. Pender* were justified in thinking the principle was expressed in too general terms. There will no doubt arise cases where it will be difficult to determine whether the contemplated relationship is so close that the duty arises. But in the class of cases now before the Court I cannot conceive any difficulty to arise. A manufacturer puts up an article of food in a container which he knows will be opened by the actual consumer. There can be no inspection by any purchaser and no reasonable preliminary inspection by the consumer. Negligently, in the course of preparation, he allows the contents to be mixed with poison. It is said that the law of England and Scotland is that the poisoned consumer has no remedy against the negligent manufacturer. If this were the result of the authorities, I should consider the result a grave defect in the law, and so contrary to principle that I should hesitate long before following any decision to that effect which had not the authority of this House. I would point out that, in the assumed state of the authorities, not only would the consumer have no remedy against the manufacturer, he would have none against any one else, for in the circumstances alleged there would be no evidence of negligence against any one other than the manufacturer; and, except in the case of a consumer who was also a purchaser, no contract and no warranty of fitness, and in the case of the purchase of a specific article under its patent or trade name, which might well be the case in the purchase of some articles of food or drink, no warranty protecting even the purchaser-consumer. There are other instances than of articles of food and drink where goods are sold intended to be used immediately by the consumer, such as many forms of goods sold for cleaning purposes, where the same liability must exist. The doctrine supported by the decision below would not only deny a remedy to the consumer who was injured by consuming bottled beer or chocolates poisoned by the negligence of the manufacturer, but also to the user of what should be a harmless proprietary medicine, an ointment, a soap, a cleaning fluid or cleaning powder. I confine myself to articles of common household use, where every one, including the manufacturer, knows that the articles will be used by other persons than the actual ultimate purchaser – namely, by members of his family and his servants, and in some cases his guests. I do not think so ill of our jurisprudence as to suppose that its principles are so remote from the ordinary needs of civilized society and the ordinary claims it makes upon its members as to deny a legal remedy where there is so obviously a social wrong.

It will be found, I think, on examination that there is no case in which the circumstances have been such as I have just suggested where the liability has been negatived. There are numerous cases, where the relations were much more remote, where the duty has been held not to exist.

. . .

My Lords, if your Lordships accept the view that this pleading discloses a relevant cause of action you will be affirming the proposition that by Scots and English law alike a manufacturer of products, which he sells in such a form as to show that he intends them to reach the ultimate consumer in the form in which they left him with no reasonable possibility of intermediate examination, and with the knowledge that the absence of reasonable care in the preparation or putting up of the products will result in an injury to the consumer's life or property, owes a duty to the consumer to take that reasonable care.

It is a proposition which I venture to say no one in Scotland or England who was not a lawyer would for one moment doubt. It will be an advantage to make it clear that the law in this matter, as in most others, is in accordance with sound common sense. I think that this appeal should be allowed.

LORD BUCKMASTER (dissenting):–. . . The authorities are against the appellant's contention, and, apart from authority, it is difficult to see how any common law proposition can be formulated to support her claim.

The principle contended for must be this: that the manufacturer, or indeed the repairer, of any article, apart entirely from contract, owes a duty to any person by whom the article is lawfully used to see that it has been carefully constructed. All rights in contract must be excluded from consideration of this principle; such contractual rights as may exist in successive steps from the original manufacturer down to the ultimate purchaser are ex hypothesi immaterial. Nor can the doctrine be confined to cases where inspection is difficult or impossible to introduce. This conception is simply to misapply tort doctrine applicable to sale and purchase.

The principle of tort lies completely outside the region where such considerations apply, and the duty, if it exists, must extend to every person who, in lawful circumstances, uses the article made. There can be no special duty attaching to the manufacture of food apart from that implied by contract or imposed by statute. If such a duty exists, it seems to me it must cover the construction of every article, and I cannot see any reason why it should not apply to the construction of a house. If one step, why not fifty? Yet if a house be, as it sometimes is, negligently built, and in consequence of that negligence the ceiling falls and injures the occupier or any one else, no action against the builder exists according to English law, although I believe such a right did exist according to the laws of Babylon. Were such a principle known and recognized, it seems to me impossible, having regard to the numerous cases that must have arisen to persons injured by its disregard, that, with the exception of *George v. Skivington*, no case directly involving the principle has ever succeeded in the Courts, and, were it well known and accepted, much of the discussion of the earlier cases would have been waste of time, and the distinction as to articles dangerous in themselves or known to be dangerous to the vendor would be meaningless.

In *Mullen v. Barr & Co.*, a case indistinguishable from the present excepting upon the ground that a mouse is not a snail, and necessarily adopted by the Second Division in their judgment, Lord Anderson says this:

> In a case like the present, where the goods of the defenders are widely distributed throughout Scotland, it would seem little short of outrageous to make them responsible to members of the public for the condition of the contents of every bottle which issues from their works. It is obvious that, if such responsibility attached to the defenders, they might be called on to meet claims of damages which they could not possibly investigate or answer.

In agreeing, as I do, with the judgment of Lord Anderson, I desire to add that I find it hard to dissent from the emphatic nature of the language with which this judgment is clothed. I am of opinion that this appeal should be dismissed, and I beg to move your Lordships accordingly.

[Lords Macmillan and Thankerton gave concurring speeches and Lord Tomlin gave a dissenting speech. Note that the order of Lord Atkin's and Lord Buckmaster's speeches has been reversed.]

NOTES AND QUESTIONS

1. What role did *Heaven v. Pender* (1883), 11 Q.B.D. 503 (C.A.), play in Lord Atkin's analysis? In his view, what factors justified applying negligence law to products liability?

2. What was the legal basis of Lord Buckmaster's dissent? What considerations did he raise against extending negligence to products liability? Were his concerns about extending negligence to other areas of tort liability justified? Did Lord Atkin adequately address these issues?

3. How did Lord Atkin define the test for determining when a duty of care would be imposed in a products liability case? Based on his analysis, would negligence law extend to a case in which: (a) the retailer or consumer had an opportunity to inspect the bottle's contents before consumption; (b) the product was simply unpalatable, rather than harmful; or (c) the product was a dangerously defective machine intended solely for industrial use?

4. How did Lord Atkin determine that a duty of care was owed to the plaintiff? Explain what this test means in your own words. If a thirsty waiter drank the ginger beer that Mrs. Donoghue had left in the bottle, would he have been owed a duty of care?

5. What standard of care did Lord Atkin suggest ought to apply? How would the plaintiff prove that the defendant breached the standard in a products liability case? For historical background and analysis of the decision, see Burns, ed., *Donoghue v. Stevenson*

and the Modern Law of Negligence: The Paisley Papers (1991); and Rodger, "Mrs. Donoghue and Alfenus Varus" (1988) 41 Curr. Legal Probs. 1.

6. One major problem in interpreting *Donoghue* is that it deals with many of the most important issues in negligence law. This is compounded by the fact that Lord Atkin discusses several of these issues together in the space of about ten lines. First, as a matter of legal policy, does the law of negligence apply to this type of claim or situation? Second, if negligence law does apply, has the defendant's conduct in this case given rise to a duty of care? Third, does the defendant owe this duty of care to the plaintiff in particular? Although Lord Atkin's duty principles have been used for over 70 years, little progress has been made in reaching a consensus on analyzing their component elements.

7. Prior to *Donoghue*, a lack of contractual privity made it extremely difficult for consumers to sue manufacturers in negligence. See for example *Langridge v. Levy* (1837), 150 E.R. 1458 (Exch.); *Winterbottom v. Wright* (1842), 152 E.R. 402 (Exch.); and *Longmeid v. Holliday* (1851), 155 E.R. 752 (Exch.). But see *George v. Skivington* (1869), L.R. 5 Ex. 1. See also Labatt, "Negligence in Relation to Privity of Contract" (1900) 16 L.Q.R. 168; and Palmer, "Why Privity Entered Tort – An Historical Reexamination of *Winterbottom v. Wright*" (1983) 27 J. Am. Leg. History 85.

8. An exception to the privity requirement was found in cases involving articles that were dangerous *per se*. See Barton, "Liability for Things in the Nineteenth Century" in Guy & Beale, eds., *Law and Social Change in British History* (1984). Why would a different set of rules apply to such products? It was not always simple to classify articles as innocuous or dangerous. For example, the New York Court of Appeals had found the category of imminently dangerous articles to include a scaffold (*Devlin v. Smith*, 89 N.Y. 470 (1882)), bottles of aerated water (*Torgeson v. Schultz*, 192 N.Y. 156 (1908)), and a coffee urn (*Statler v. Ray Mfg. Co.*, 195 N.Y. 478 (1909)), whereas articles not imminently dangerous included a defective balance wheel on a circular saw (*Loop v. Litchfield*, 42 N.Y. 351 (1870)) and a boiler that exploded (*Losee v. Clute*, 51 N.Y. 494 (1873)). Moreover, in the watershed duty case of *MacPherson v. Buick Motor Company*, 217 N.Y. 382 (1916), the majority found that an automobile with a broken wheel was imminently dangerous, but the dissent disagreed.

9. For a historical review of duty, see Winfield, "Duty in Tortious Negligence" (1934) 34 Col. L.R. 41. See also Pollock, "The Snail in the Bottle, and Thereafter" (1933) 49 L.Q.R. 22; Buckland, "The Duty to Take Care" (1935) 51 L.Q.R. 637; Morison, "A Re-examination of the Duty of Care" (1948) 11 Mod. L. Rev. 9; Fleming, "Remoteness and Duty: The Control Devices in Liability for Negligence" (1953) 31 Can. Bar Rev. 471; Dias, "The Duty Problem in Negligence" [1955] C.L.J. 198; Heuston, "*Donoghue v. Stevenson* in Retrospect" (1957) 20 Mod. L. Rev. 1; Gibson, "A New Alphabet of Negligence" in Linden, ed., *Studies in Canadian Tort Law* (1968) 189; Symmons, "The Duty of Care in Negligence: Recently Expressed Policy Elements – Part I and Part II" (1971) 34 Mod. L. Rev. 394 & 528; Smith, "The Mystery of Duty," in Klar, ed., *Studies in Canadian Tort Law* (1977) 1; Smith & Burns, "*Donoghue v. Stevenson* – The Not So

Golden Anniversary" (1982) 46 Mod. L. Rev. 147; and Smith, *Liability In Negligence* (1984).

(c) THE DEVELOPMENT OF THE MODERN LAW OF DUTY

Lord Atkin's formulation of the duty of care concept has not been confined to the area of products liability. It has been used to support the proposition that negligence law potentially extends, with limited exceptions, to any act that causes physical injury (as opposed to other forms of loss). This principle is so deeply entrenched in the law that the courts will often simply assume that negligence law applies. For example, a judge will rarely make more than passing reference to the fact that a driver owes a duty of care to other users of the road, or that surgeons owe a duty of care to their patients.

Initially, however, the courts were reluctant to extend Lord Atkin's test to those special categories of cases in which they previously had refused to recognize a duty or had imposed a limited duty. And while the courts did eventually reject much of the pre-1932 case law in favour of broader principles that were more akin to *Donoghue*, they did so on a category-by-category basis. In that sense, *Donoghue* did not effect a wholesale break with the classical approach.

It was not until the 1960s that appellate courts began to use *Donoghue* to overturn traditional, fundamental assumptions regarding the duty of care. In *Hedley Byrne & Co. v. Heller & Partners Ltd.*, [1964] A.C. 465, the House of Lords held that, in certain situations, a duty of care could be imposed for negligent advice. In *Home Office v. Dorset Yacht Co.*, [1970] A.C. 1004, the House of Lords held that public authorities could be held liable in negligence with respect to their statutory functions and operations. These decisions are important not only as leading cases in specific categories of negligence, but also as examples of the evolving and expanding scope of the duty concept. That trend culminated in Lord Wilberforce's now famous speech in *Anns v. Merton London Borough Council*, [1977] 2 All E.R. 492 at 498 (H.L.):

> Through the trilogy of cases in this House, *Donoghue v. Stevenson, Hedley Byrne & Co. Ltd. v. Heller & Partners Ltd.* and *Home Office v. Dorset Yacht Co. Ltd.*, the position has now been reached that in order to establish that a duty of care arises in a particular situation, it is not necessary to bring the facts of that situation within those previous situations in which a duty of care has been held to exist. Rather the question has to be approached in two stages. First one has to ask whether, as between the alleged wrongdoer and the person who has suffered damage there is a sufficient relationship of proximity or neighbourhood such that, in the reasonable contemplation of the former, carelessness on his part may be likely to cause damage to the latter, in which case a prima facie duty of care arises. Secondly, if the first question is answered affirmatively, it is necessary to consider whether there are any considerations which ought to negative, or to reduce or limit the scope of the duty or the class of person to whom it is owed or the damages to which a breach of it may give rise.

Unlike Lord Atkin's speech, this passage does not provide a specific test for determining whether to recognize a duty of care. Rather, it sets out an approach for analyzing existing categories of negligence and for recognizing new categories in novel situations. At the same time, it should be noted that Lord Wilberforce's judgment did not require the general duty principles articulated in *Donoghue v. Stevenson* to be mechanically applied in every case. Indeed, as the House of Lords held in *Anns, Hedley Byrne* and

Dorset Yacht, special circumstances may raise special considerations that justify the formulation of restricted duty principles.

Although the English courts initially embraced the *Anns* approach in a broad range of cases, they began to distance themselves from it by the mid-1980s. After narrowly interpreting *Anns* or ignoring it, the House of Lords decisively overruled it in *Murphy v. Brentwood District Council*, [1991] 1 A.C. 338. *Anns* was criticized as leading to capricious results, providing unworkable tests of liability, unduly expanding the scope of liability, and lacking any foundation in established principle. The leading case in England is now *Caparo Industries plc v. Dickman*, [1990] 2 A.C. 605 (H.L.), in which Lord Bridge offered the following observations.

> [S]ince *Anns's* case a series of decisions of the Privy Council and of your Lordships' House . . . have emphasised the inability of a single general principle to provide a practical test which can be applied to every situation to determine whether a duty of care is owed and, if so, what is its scope. . . . What emerges is that, in addition to the foreseeability of damage, necessary ingredients in any situation giving rise to a duty of care are that there should exist between the party owing the duty and the party to whom it is owed a relationship characterised by the law as one of "proximity" or "neighbourhood" and that the situation should be one in which the court considers it fair, just and reasonable that the law should impose a duty of a given scope upon the one party for the benefit of the other. . . . [T]he concepts of proximity and fairness embodied in these additional ingredients are not susceptible of any such precise definition as would be necessary to give them utility as practical tests, but amount in effect to little more than convenient labels to attach to the features of different specific situations which, on a detailed examination of all the circumstances, the law recognises pragmatically as giving rise to a duty of care of a given scope. Whilst recognising, of course, the importance of the underlying general principles common to the whole field of negligence, I think the law has now moved in the direction of attaching greater significance to the more traditional categorisation of distinct and recognisable situations as guides to the existence, the scope and the limits of the varied duties care which the law imposes.

As a result of *Caparo*, the recognition of a duty of care in England now turns on a three-part test that requires proof that: (i) the plaintiff's loss was a reasonably foreseeable consequence of the defendant's conduct, (ii) there was a sufficiently proximate relationship between the parties, and (iii) it is "fair, just and reasonable" for the court to impose a duty of care in light of the applicable policy considerations. Even more significant than the actual phrasing of that test, however, is the fact that the House of Lords self-consciously distanced itself from the plaintiff-oriented approach of *Anns*.

The experience has been similar elsewhere in the Commonwealth. After an initial honeymoon, *Anns* quickly fell into disfavour in Australia. A leading statement appears in Brennan J.'s judgment in *Sutherland Shire Council v. Heyman* (1985), 157 C.L.R. 424 (H.C.A.):

> It is preferable in my view, that the law should develop novel categories of negligence incrementally and by analogy with established categories, rather than by a massive extension of a prima facie duty of care restrained only by indefinable "considerations which ought to negative, or to reduce or limit the scope of the duty or the class of person to whom it is owed".

The demise of *Anns* outside of Canada reflects a dramatic retreat from the rapid expansion of the duty of care and the spiralling growth in the scope of liability. It also harkens back to the more cautious classical approach.

NOTES AND QUESTIONS

1. In *Anns*, Lord Wilberforce said that a *prima facie* duty of care arises if "there is a sufficient relationship of proximity or neighbourhood such that, in the reasonable contemplation of the [defendant], carelessness on his part may be likely to cause damage to the [plaintiff]." How would you interpret that statement? Specifically, is "proximity" defined entirely in terms of reasonable foreseeability? Or does the first part of the *Anns* test actually consist of two elements: proximity and reasonable foreseeability?

2. There were dramatic increases in the scope of negligence liability as the "neighbour principle" in *Donoghue* was applied to new relationships and to many of the special duty of care situations that had previously been governed by more restrictive principles. This led to concern about the adequacy of these principles for resolving modern tort problems. See Linden, "The Good Neighbour on Trial: A Fountain of Sparkling Wisdom" (1983) 17 U.B.C.L. Rev. 67; and Smith & Burns, "The Good Neighbour on Trial: Good Neighbours Make Bad Law" (1983) 17 U.B.C.L. Rev. 93. See also Little, "Erosion of Non-Duty Rules in England, the United States, and Common Law Commonwealth Nations" (1983) 20 Hous. L. Rev. 959.

3. The Commonwealth courts' growing disenchantment with *Anns* can be traced through a series of cases. See for example *Governors of the Peabody Donation Fund v. Sir Lindsay Parkinson & Co.*, [1985] A.C. 210 (H.L.); *Leigh and Sullivan Ltd. v. Aliakmon Shipping Co.*, [1986] A.C. 785 (H.L.); *Candlewood Navigation Corporation Ltd. v. Mitsui O.S.K. Lines Ltd. (The Mineral Transporter)*, [1986] A.C. 1 (P.C.); *Curran v. Northern Ireland Co-ownership Housing Assoc. Ltd.*, [1987] A.C. 17 (H.L.); *Yuen Kun Yeu v. A.G. of Hong Kong*, [1988] A.C. 175 (P.C.); *D. & F. Estates Ltd. v. Church Commissioners for England*, [1989] A.C. 177 (H.L.); *Hill v. Chief Constable of West Yorkshire*, [1989] A.C. 53 (H.L.); and *Caparo Industries v. Dickman*, [1990] 2 A.C. 605 (H.L.).

4. For commentaries on the rise and fall of *Anns*, see McHugh, "Neighbourhood, Proximity and Reliance" in Finn, ed., *Essays on Torts* (1989) 5; Smillie, "The Foundation of the Duty of Care in Negligence" (1989) 15 Monash Univ. L. Rev. 302; Cooke, "An Impossible Distinction" (1991) 107 L.Q.R. 46; Howarth, "Negligence After *Murphy*: Time to Rethink" [1991] C.L.J. 58; Wallace, "Anns Beyond Repair" (1991) 107 L.Q.R. 228; Markesinis & Deakin, "The Random Element of Their Lordships' Infallible Judgment" (1992) 50 Mod. L. Rev. 619; Stapleton, "In Restraint of Tort" in Birks, ed., *The Frontiers of Liability*, vol. 2 (1994) 83; and Stanton, "Incremental Approaches to the Duty of Care" in Mullany, ed., *Torts in the Nineties* (1997) 34.

More recently, see Witting, "Duty of Care: An Analytical Approach" (2005) 25 O.J.L.S. 33; and Howarth, "Many Duties of Care – Or A Duty of Care? Notes from the Underground" (2006) 26 O.J.L.S. 449.

(d) *ANNS* AND THE SUPREME COURT OF CANADA

The story of *Anns* has been quite different in this country than elsewhere in the Commonwealth. Canadian judges have been, and to some extent continue to be, unusually receptive to Lord Wilberforce's judgment. For many years the leading case was *Kam-*

loops (City) v. Nielsen (1984), 10 D.L.R. (4th) 641 (S.C.C.). Justice Wilson referred to the English authorities and said (at 662-63) that, in determining whether a duty of care should be recognized, two questions should be asked:

> (1) [I]s there a sufficiently close relationship between the parties . . . so that, in the reasonable contemplation of the [defendant], carelessness on its part might cause damage to [the plaintiff]? If so, (2) are there any considerations which ought to negative or limit (a) the scope of the duty and (b) the class of persons to whom it is owed or (c) the damages to which a breach of it may give rise?

See also the Supreme Court of Canada decisions in *B.D.C. Ltd. v. Hofstrand Farms Ltd.* (1986), 26 D.L.R. (4th) 1 (S.C.C.); *Just v. British Columbia* (1989), 64 D.L.R. (4th) 689 (S.C.C.); and *Rothfield v. Manolakos* (1989), 63 D.L.R. (4th) 449 (S.C.C.).

Although it has now been modified by the Supreme Court of Canada, the *Anns/Kamloops* approach is notable for its flexibility and expansiveness. Its first branch merely requires the plaintiff to prove reasonable foreseeability of harm, which, as Major J. said in *Ryan v. Victoria (City)* (1999), 168 D.L.R. (4th) 513 at 525 (S.C.C.), "presents a relatively low threshold." Once that hurdle is cleared, a *prima facie* duty of care exists. The burden then falls on the defendant, under the second branch of the test, to establish why a duty of care nevertheless should be refused or limited. At that point, the plaintiff-oriented nature of the *Anns/Kamloops* test is reinforced. Canadian courts have had a tendency not to seriously engage in the task of examining policy reasons for rejecting or confining a duty of care. Judges appear reluctant to provide explicit analyses of the social and legal choices underlying their duty decisions. For instance, they often neglect opportunities to consider empirical evidence regarding issues of risk, foreseeability and social costs, preferring instead to decide matters on the basis of *ad hoc* policy preferences.

The Canadian approach to *Anns* was also marked by a tendency to broadly apply *Kamloops* as a general test for the duty of care. While Lord Wilberforce's judgment constituted a marked departure from the traditional, category-by-category evolution of the duty of care, it did not provide judges with a blank slate. The special categories clearly remained important insofar as the factors that informed them were directly relevant to the second stage of the *Anns* test. In contrast, the breadth of the *Kamloops* test sometimes encouraged Canadian courts to overlook the distinctions historically drawn between misfeasance and nonfeasance, deeds and words, physical injury and emotional harm, property damage and economic loss.

While recognizing that the "classical approach" was too inflexible for modern purposes, previous editions of this casebook suggested that Canadian courts had strayed too far from the incremental approach that emphasized the special considerations arising in certain circumstances. It also suggested that, as a result, the law had become disorderly and unprincipled. In *Cooper v. Hobart* (2001), 206 D.L.R. (4th) 193 (S.C.C.), the Supreme Court of Canada re-stated the duty of care in a way that may address at least some of the concerns raised by *Anns/Kamloops*. At the same time, however, the decision in *Cooper* has created new uncertainties of its own.

COOPER v. HOBART

(2001), 206 D.L.R. (4th) 193 (S.C.C.)

[The plaintiff, along with thousands of other people, invested money with Eron Mortgage Corp. Eron was governed by the *Mortgage Brokers Act*, R.S.B.C. 1996, c.

313. That statute allowed the defendant, as Registrar of Mortgage Brokers, to investigate complaints, freeze funds and suspend licences of brokers who had breached their statutory obligations. The defendant did in fact suspend Eron's licence. At that point, the company owed more than $180 million to its investors. Faced with the loss of her investment, the plaintiff sued the defendant for negligence. She claimed that if the defendant had acted more quickly in suspending Eron's licence, she would not have suffered the same magnitude of loss. The defendant brought a motion to strike out the plaintiff's statement of claim on the ground that it did not disclose a cause of action. The issue before the court was whether, in the circumstances, the defendant owed a duty of care to the plaintiff.

At first instance, Tysoe J. applied the standard two-part test and held that a duty of care arose between the parties. At the first stage of analysis, he found that it was reasonably foreseeable that the defendant's carelessness would result in the plaintiff's loss. Consequently, a *prima facie* duty of care existed. At the second stage of analysis, he did not find any factors that would negate or limit that duty. The British Columbia Court of Appeal thought otherwise. Newbury J.A. held that even if the plaintiff's loss was reasonably foreseeable, there was not a sufficient relationship of proximity between the parties to support a *prima facie* duty of care. She also held that, even if a *prima facie* duty of care arose, various policy considerations under the second branch of the *Anns/Kamloops* test militated against the possibility of liability. The plaintiff appealed to the Supreme Court of Canada.]

MCLACHLIN C.J.C. and MAJOR J.:–The present appeal revisits the *Anns* test . . . and, in particular, highlights and hones the role of policy concerns in determining the scope of liability for negligence.

. . .

Canadian courts have not thus far recognized the duty of care that the appellants allege in this case. The question is therefore whether the law of negligence should be extended to reach this situation. While the particular extension sought is novel, the more general issue of how far the principles of liability for negligence should be extended is a familiar one, and one with which this Court and others have repeatedly grappled since Lord Atkin enunciated the negligence principle in *Donoghue v. Stevenson* . . . almost 70 years ago. That case introduced the principle that a person could be held liable only for reasonably foreseeable harm. But it also anticipated that not all reasonably foreseeable harm might be caught. This posed the issue with which courts still struggle today: to what situations does the law of negligence extend? This case, like so many of its predecessors, may thus be seen as but a gloss on the case of *Donoghue v. Stevenson*.

In *Donoghue v. Stevenson* the House of Lords revolutionized the common law by replacing the old categories of tort recovery with a single comprehensive principle – the negligence principle. Henceforward, liability would lie for negligence in circumstances where a reasonable person would have viewed the harm as foreseeable. However, foreseeability alone was not enough; there must also be a close and direct relationship of proximity or neighbourhood.

But what is proximity? For the most part, lawyers apply the law of negligence on the basis of categories as to which proximity has been recognized in the past. However, as Lord Atkin [*sic*] declared in *Donoghue v. Stevenson*, the categories of negligence are not closed. Where new cases arise, we must search elsewhere for assistance in determining whether, in addition to disclosing foreseeability, the circumstances disclose sufficient proximity to justify the imposition of liability for negligence.

In *Anns* . . . the House of Lords, per Lord Wilberforce, said that a duty of care required a finding of proximity sufficient to create a prima facie duty of care, followed by consideration of whether there were any factors negativing that duty of care. This Court has repeatedly affirmed that approach as appropriate in the Canadian context.

. . .

The House of Lords in *Anns* for the first time expressly recognized the policy component in determining the extension of the negligence principle. However, it left doubt on the precise content of the first and second branches of the new formulation of the negligence principle. This gave rise to debate – debate which the submissions in this case revive. Was the first branch concerned with foreseeability only or foreseeability and proximity? If the latter, was there duplication between policy considerations relevant to proximity at the first stage and the second stage of the test?

To some extent, these concerns are academic. Provided the proper balancing of the factors relevant to a duty of care are considered, it may not matter, so far as a particular case is concerned, at which "stage" it occurs. The underlying question is whether a duty of care should be imposed, taking into account all relevant factors disclosed by the circumstances. *Anns* did not purport to depart from the negligence test of *Donoghue v. Stevenson* but merely sought to elucidate it by explicitly recognizing its policy component.

We continue in the view, repeatedly expressed by this Court, that the *Anns* two-stage test, properly understood, does not involve duplication because different types of policy considerations are involved at the two stages. In our view, *Anns* continues to provide a useful framework in which to approach the question of whether a duty of care should be imposed in a new situation.

Nevertheless, it is important from the point of view of methodology and clarity in the law to be clear on what falls to be considered at each stage of the *Anns* test. In this connection, it is useful to consider the leading English case on that question. The Judicial Committee of the Privy Council held in *Yuen Kun Yeu v. Attorney-General of Hong Kong*, [1988] 1 A.C. 175, that to find a prima facie duty of care at the first stage of the test there must be reasonable foreseeability of the harm plus something more. As will be seen, we agree with this conclusion. The Privy Council went on to opine that *Anns'* second branch, negation for policy reasons, would seldom come into play. If this is read as a suggestion that policy is not important in determining whether the negligence principle should be extended to new situations, we would respectfully differ. [T]he *Donoghue v. Stevenson* foreseeability-negligence test, no matter how it is phrased, conceals a balancing of interests. The quest for the right balance is in reality a quest for prudent policy. The difference in the two positions, if there is one, may turn on how one defines policy; the Privy Council in *Yuen Kun Yeu* appears to regard policy as confined to practical considerations dictating immunity despite a close relationship and foreseeability.

In brief compass, we suggest that at this stage in the evolution of the law, both in Canada and abroad, the *Anns* analysis is best understood as follows. At the first stage of the *Anns* test, two questions arise: (1) was the harm that occurred the reasonably foreseeable consequence of the defendant's act? and (2) are there reasons, notwithstanding the proximity between the parties established in the first part of this test, that tort liability should not be recognized here? The proximity analysis involved at the first stage of the *Anns* test focuses on factors arising from the relationship between the plaintiff and the defendant. These factors include questions of policy, in the broad sense of that word. If foreseeability and proximity are established at the first stage, a prima facie duty of care arises. At the second stage of the *Anns* test, the question still remains whether there are residual policy considerations outside the relationship of the parties that may negative the imposition of a duty of care. It may be, as the Privy Council suggests in *Yuen Kun Yeu*, that such considerations will not often prevail. However, we think it useful expressly to ask, before imposing a new duty of care, whether despite foreseeability and proximity of relationship, there are other policy reasons why the duty should not be imposed.

On the first branch of the *Anns* test, reasonable foreseeability of the harm must be supplemented by proximity. The question is what is meant by proximity. Two things may be said. The first is that "proximity" is generally used in the authorities to characterize the type of relationship in which a duty of care may arise. The second is that sufficiently proximate relationships are identified through the use of categories. The categories are not closed and new categories of negligence may be introduced. But generally, proximity is established by reference to these categories. This provides certainty to the law of negligence, while still permitting it to evolve to meet the needs of new circumstances.

On the first point, it seems clear that the word "proximity" in connection with negligence has from the outset and throughout its history been used to describe the type of relationship in which a duty of care to guard against foreseeable negligence may be imposed. "Proximity" is the term used to describe the "close and direct" relationship that Lord Atkin described as necessary to grounding a duty of care in *Donoghue v. Stevenson*. . . .

Defining the relationship may involve looking at expectations, representations, reliance, and the property or other interests involved. Essentially, these are factors that allow us to evaluate the closeness of the relationship between the plaintiff and the defendant and to determine whether it is just and fair having regard to that relationship to impose a duty of care in law upon the defendant.

The factors which may satisfy the requirement of proximity are diverse and depend on the circumstances of the case. One searches in vain for a single unifying characteristic. As stated by McLachlin J. (as she then was) in *Canadian National Railway Co. v. Norsk Pacific Steamship Co.*, [1992] 1 S.C.R. 1021 at p. 1151, 91 D.L.R. (4th) 289: "Proximity may be usefully viewed, not so much as a test in itself, but as a broad concept which is capable of subsuming different categories of cases involving different factors". . .

What then are the categories in which proximity has been recognized? First, of course, is the situation where the defendant's act foreseeably causes physical harm to the plaintiff or the plaintiff's property. This has been extended to nervous shock (see, for example, *Alcock v. Chief Constable of the South Yorkshire Police*, [1991] 4 All E.R. 907 (H.L.)). Yet other categories are liability for negligent misstatement: *Hedley Byrne & Co. v. Heller & Partners Ltd.*, [1963] 2 All E.R. 575 (H.L.), and misfeasance in public office. A duty to warn of the risk of danger has been recognized: *Rivtow Marine Ltd. v. Washington Iron Works*, [1974] S.C.R. 1189, 40 D.L.R. (3d) 530. Again, a municipality has been held to owe a duty to prospective purchasers of real estate to inspect housing developments without negligence: *Anns*, *supra*; *Kamloops, supra*. Similarly, governmental authorities who have undertaken a policy of road maintenance have been held to owe a duty of care to execute the maintenance in a non-negligent manner: *Just v. British Columbia*, [1989] 2 S.C.R. 1228, 64 D.L.R. (4th) 689; *Swinamer v. Nova Scotia (Attorney General)*, [1994] 1 S.C.R. 445, 112 D.L.R. (4th) 18. Relational economic loss (related to a contract's performance) may give rise to a tort duty of care in certain situations, as where the claimant has a possessory or proprietary interest in the property, the general average cases, and cases where the relationship between the claimant and the property owner constitutes a joint venture: *Norsk, supra*; *Bow Valley Husky (Bermuda) Ltd. v. Saint John Shipbuilding Ltd.*, [1997] 3 S.C.R. 1210, 153 D.L.R. (4th) 385. When a case falls within one of these situations or an analogous one and reasonable foreseeability is established, a prima facie duty of care may be posited.

This brings us to the second stage of the *Anns* test. As the majority of this Court held in *Norsk*. . ., residual policy considerations fall to be considered here. These are not concerned with the relationship between the parties, but with the effect of recognizing a duty of care on other legal obligations, the legal system and society more generally. Does the law already provide a remedy? Would recognition of the duty of care create the spectre of unlimited liability to an unlimited class? Are there other reasons of broad policy that suggest that the duty of care should not be recognized?

. . .

It is at this second stage of the analysis that the distinction between government policy and execution of policy falls to be considered. It is established that government actors are not liable in negligence for policy decisions, but only operational decisions. The basis of this immunity is that policy is the prerogative of the elected Legislature. It is inappropriate for courts to impose liability for the consequences of a particular policy decision. On the other hand, a government actor may be liable in negligence for the manner in which it executes or carries out the policy. In our view, the exclusion of liability for policy decisions is properly regarded as an application of the second stage of the *Anns* test. The exclusion does not relate to the relationship between the parties. Apart from the legal characterization of the government duty as a matter of policy, plaintiffs can and do recover. The exclusion of liability is better viewed as an immunity imposed because of considerations outside the relationship for policy reasons – more precisely, because it is inappropriate for courts to second-guess elected legislators on policy matters.

. . .

The second step of *Anns* generally arises only in cases where the duty of care asserted does not fall within a recognized category of recovery. Where it does, we may be satisfied that there are no overriding policy considerations that would negative the duty of care. In this sense, I agree with the Privy Council in *Yuen Kun Yeu* that the second stage of *Anns* will seldom arise and that questions of liability will be determined primarily by reference to established and analogous categories of recovery. However, where a duty of care in a novel situation is alleged, as here, we believe it necessary to consider both steps of the *Anns* test as discussed above. This ensures that before a duty of care is imposed in a new situation, not only are foreseeability and relational proximity present, but there are no broader considerations that would make imposition of a duty of care unwise.

. . .

VI. Application of the Test

The appellants submit that the Registrar of Mortgage Brokers owed them, as investors with a firm falling under the Registrar's administrative mandate, a duty of care giving rise to liability for negligence and damages for losses that they sustained. The investors allege that the Registrar should have acted earlier to suspend Eron or warn them of Eron's breaches of the Act's requirements, and that their losses are traceable to the Registrar's failure to act more promptly.

The first question is whether the circumstances disclose reasonably foreseeable harm and proximity sufficient to establish a prima facie duty of care. The first inquiry at this stage is whether the case falls within or is analogous to a category of cases in which a duty of care has previously been recognized. The answer to this question is no.

The next question is whether this is a situation in which a new duty of care should be recognized. It may be that the investors can show that it was reasonably foreseeable that the alleged negligence in failing to suspend Eron or issue warnings might result in financial loss to the plaintiffs. However, as discussed, mere foreseeability is not enough to establish a prima facie duty of care. The plaintiffs must also show proximity – that the Registrar was in a close and direct relationship to them making it just to impose a duty of care upon him toward the plaintiffs. In addition to showing foreseeability, the plaintiffs must point to factors arising from the circumstances of the relationship that impose a duty.

In this case, the factors giving rise to proximity, if they exist, must arise from the statute under which the Registrar is appointed. That statute is the only source of his duties, private or public. Apart from that statute, he is in no different position than the ordinary man or woman on the street. If a duty to investors with regulated mortgage brokers is to be found, it must be in the statute.

In this case, the statute does not impose a duty of care on the Registrar to investors with mortgage brokers regulated by the Act. The Registrar's duty is rather to the public as a whole. Indeed, a duty to individual investors would potentially conflict with the Registrar's overarching duty to the public.

The regulatory scheme governing mortgage brokers provides a general framework to ensure the efficient operation of the mortgage marketplace. The Registrar must balance a myriad of competing interests, ensuring that the public has access to capital through mortgage financing while at the same time instilling public confidence in the system by determining who is "suitable" and whose proposed registration as a broker is "not objectionable". All of the powers or tools conferred by the Act on the Registrar are necessary to undertake this delicate balancing. Even though to some degree the provisions of the Act serve to protect the interests of investors, the overall scheme of the Act mandates that the Registrar's duty of care is not owed to investors exclusively but to the public as a whole.

Accordingly, we agree with the Court of Appeal per Newbury J.A.: even though the Registrar might reasonably have foreseen that losses to investors in Eron would result if he was careless in carrying out his duties under the Act, there was insufficient proximity between the Registrar and the investors to ground a prima facie duty of care. The statute cannot be construed to impose a duty of care on the Registrar specific to investments with mortgage brokers. Such a duty would no doubt come at the expense of other important interests, of efficiency and finally at the expense of public confidence in the system as a whole.

Having found no proximity sufficient to found a duty of care owed by the Registrar to the investors, we need not proceed to the second branch of the *Anns* test and the question of whether there exist policy considerations apart from those considered in determining a relationship of proximity, which would negative a prima facie duty of care, had one been found. However, the matter having been fully argued, it may be useful to comment on those submissions.

In our view, even if a prima facie duty of care had been established under the first branch of the *Anns* test, it would have been negated at the second stage for overriding policy reasons. The decision of whether to suspend a broker involves both policy and quasi-judicial elements. The decision requires the Registrar to balance the public and private interests. The Registrar is not simply carrying out a predetermined government policy, but deciding, as an agent of the executive branch of government, what that policy should be. Moreover, the decision is quasi-judicial. The Registrar must act fairly or judicially in removing a broker's licence. These requirements are inconsistent with a duty of care to investors. Such a duty would undermine these obligations, imposed by the Legislature on the Registrar. Thus even if a prima facie duty of care could be posited, it would be negated by other overriding policy considerations.

The prima facie duty of care is also negated on the basis of the distinction between government policy and the execution of policy. As stated, the Registrar must make difficult discretionary decisions in the area of public policy, decisions which command deference. . . . [T]he decisions made by the Registrar were made within the limits of the powers conferred upon him in the public interest.

Further, the spectre of indeterminate liability would loom large if a duty of care was recognized as between the Registrar and investors in this case. The Act itself imposes no limit and the Registrar has no means of controlling the number of investors or the amount of money invested in the mortgage brokerage system.

Finally, we must consider the impact of a duty of care on the taxpayers, who did not agree to assume the risk of private loss to persons in the situation of the investors. To impose a duty of care in these circumstances would be to effectively create an insurance scheme for investors at great cost to the taxpaying public. There is no indication that the Legislature intended that result.

NOTES AND QUESTIONS

1. Explain the nature of the test that the court articulated in *Cooper v. Hobart*. Did McLachlin C.J.C. and Major J. intend for their test to be applied anew every time that a court is presented with a claim in negligence? Of what relevance are the traditional "categories" of negligence?

2. Prior to *Cooper*, it was commonly said that the first stage of the *Anns/Kamloops* test is generally satisfied by proof of reasonable foreseeability. In *Cooper*, however, the court said that a *prima facie* duty will arise only if there was reasonable foreseeability of harm *plus* "a close and direct relationship of proximity or neighbourhood." Why did the court stress the need for proximity?

3. According to *Cooper*, policy considerations are relevant under both stages of the duty of care analysis. Explain the difference between: (i) the policy considerations that arise in connection with the recognition of a *prima facie* duty of care, and (ii) the policy considerations that arise in connection with the negation or limitation of a *prima facie* duty. Will it always be possible to draw a clear distinction between those two categories? Does the answer to that question really matter?

4. What types of policy considerations are sufficient to override a *prima facie* duty of care, keeping in mind that an otherwise deserving plaintiff would thereby be denied recovery? See Sugarman, "A New Approach to Tort Doctrine: Taking the Best From the Civil Law and Common Law of Canada" in Beaulac, Pitel & Schulz, eds., *The Joy of Torts* (2003) 375 at 388.

5. The court in *Cooper* said that *Anns* continues to provide the proper framework for analysis. Is it accurate to say that *Cooper* merely "highlights and hones the role of policy concerns" as initially expressed by *Anns*?

6. What, if anything, is the difference between the test that the Supreme Court of Canada formulated in *Cooper* and the test that the House of Lords formulated in *Caparo v. Dickman*?

7. What effect will *Cooper* have on the scope of negligence in Canada? As compared with *Anns* or *Kamloops*, is *Cooper* more or less favourable to plaintiffs?

8. Commenting on the *Anns/Kamloops* test, L. Klar argued in "Judicial Activism in Private Law" (2001) 80 Can. Bar Rev. 215 at 221 that, despite standard judicial references to a "two-part test," the Canadian test for a duty of care was "in reality a one stage test":

> Whether a duty of care should exist in any particular case inevitably comes down to whether or not there are any policy considerations which ought to negate or limit a presumed duty. This is because the foreseeability of the plaintiff as a potential victim of harm from negligent conduct is easily established. There have been no Supreme Court of Canada cases, or in fact any reported recent cases from any court, where the plaintiff has failed on the foreseeability test. Injured plaintiffs, even those whose damages are not physical injuries but financial losses are invariably regarded as having been foreseeable. . . . Thus if plaintiffs are always foreseeable, there is always a presumptive duty of care, and the only real issue in negligence actions in so far as the existence of a duty of care is concerned is policy.

How, if at all, has *Cooper* changed that situation?

9. On the same day that it released *Cooper v. Hobart*, the Supreme Court of Canada also delivered judgment in the companion case of *Edwards v. Law Society of Upper Canada* (2001), 206 D.L.R. 211 (S.C.C.). The plaintiff suffered a loss when his lawyer misappropriated funds from his trust account. The plaintiff brought an action in negligence against the defendant, which is the body that regulates lawyers in Ontario. The plaintiff claimed that his loss was caused by the defendant's careless failure to ensure that the lawyer's trust accounts were properly managed. As in *Cooper*, the defendant in *Edwards* brought a motion to strike out the plaintiff's statement of claim on the ground that the circumstances did not support the recognition of a duty of care.

The Supreme Court of Canada affirmed the judgments below and held that the defendant did not owe a duty of care to the plaintiff. Since the facts did not fall within any pre-existing duty category, it was necessary to apply the *Anns/Kamloops* test. The court held that a *prima facie* duty of care did not arise under the first branch of that test because there was insufficient proximity between the parties. In that regard, the court was particularly influenced by: (i) the fact that the plaintiff was not himself a "client" of the lawyer, and (ii) the fact that the legislative scheme under which the defendant operated did not contemplate a private law right of action in the circumstances of the case. The court also held that, even if a *prima facie* duty of care had been established, it would have been negated under the second branch of the test, essentially for the same reasons that would have had effect in *Cooper*. See also *Rogers v. Faught* (2002), 159 O.A.C. 79 (C.A.).

10. On facts similar to *Cooper v. Hobart*, the Privy Council in *Yuen Kun Yeu v. A.G. of Hong Kong*, [1987] 2 All E.R. 705 and the House of Lords in *Davis v. Radcliffe*, [1990] 1 W.L.R. 821 reached the same conclusion as the Supreme Court of Canada.

11. See Pitel, "Negligence: Canada Remakes the *Anns* Test" [2002] C.L.J. 252; Pitel, "A Reformulated *Anns* Test for Canada" (2002) 10 Tort L. Rev. 10; Neyers, "Distilling Duty: The Supreme Court of Canada Amends *Anns*" (2002) 118 L.Q.R. 221; Rafferty, "Developments in Contract and Torts Law: The 2001-2002 Term" (2002) 18 S.C.L.R. 153; and Klar, "Foreseeability, Proximity and Policy" (2002) 25 Adv. Q. 360.

(e) DEVELOPMENTS SINCE *COOPER v. HOBART*

Cooper was intended to clarify the *Anns/Kamloops* test and, in particular, the role of policy considerations in determining the existence and scope of the duty of care. *Cooper* was significant for its affirmation that the first stage of the test involves both foreseeability *and* proximity. Nevertheless, it left several other questions unanswered, some of which are raised in the notes and questions above. Perhaps most critically, it was not clear whether the approach used in *Cooper* was meant as a general test of duty, or was only to be applied in novel situations. Similarly, the decision in *Cooper* did not explain how the recognized categories of proximate relationships were to be treated under the revised test. Were they exempt from stage one of the test, but still subject to stage two, or did they fall outside the scope of the new test altogether? It was also unclear which party bears the burden of proof in the second stage of the test: the court merely stated that "residual policy considerations fall to be considered here." These unanswered questions have been raised again, though not necessarily resolved, in subsequent case law.

In *Odhavji Estate v. Woodhouse*, [2003] 3 S.C.R. 263, Iacobucci J., writing for the court, reviewed the tests from *Anns* and *Cooper* and provided a summary of them. Iacobucci J. explained at para. 52 that, in order to be successful, the plaintiffs needed to establish "(i) that the harm complained of is a reasonably foreseeable consequence of the alleged breach; (ii) that there is sufficient proximity between the parties that it would not be unjust or unfair to impose a duty of care on the defendants; and (iii) that there exist no policy reasons to negative or otherwise restrict that duty." This restatement appears to suggest that the plaintiffs have the burden of proof throughout the test, which would be contrary to previous jurisprudence on the *Anns/Kamloops* test.

However, in the more recent decision in *Childs v. Desormeaux*, [2006] 1 S.C.R. 643, McLachlin C.J.C. clarified the appropriate burden of proof at para. 13: "once the plaintiff establishes a *prima facie* duty of care, the evidentiary burden of showing countervailing policy considerations shifts to the defendant, following the general rule that the party asserting a point should be required to establish it." The decision in *Childs* also provided some assistance on the treatment of established categories under the test from *Cooper*. McLachlin C.J.C. wrote at para. 15:

> The Court in *Cooper* introduced the idea that as the case law develops, categories of relationships giving rise to a duty of care may be recognized, making it unnecessary to go through the *Anns* analysis. The reference to categories simply captures the basic notion of precedent: where a case is like another case where a duty has been recognized, one may usually infer that sufficient proximity is present and that if the risk of injury was foreseeable, a *prima facie* duty of care will arise. On the other hand, if a case does not clearly fall within a relationship previously recognized as giving rise to a duty of care, it is necessary to carefully consider whether proximity is established.

The decision in *Childs* suggests that, at the very least, the proximity analysis from stage one of the *Anns/Cooper* test does not apply to established categories. Moreover, the court in *Cooper* commented that the established categories will seldom be subject to policy considerations under stage two of the test. Thus, the combined effect of *Cooper* and *Childs* indicates that the established categories of duty will not be subject to either stage of the *Anns/Cooper* test, which is generally reserved for novel duty situations.

It may yet take some time for the full effects of *Cooper* to be felt. For the time being, a general guide to determining whether a duty of care exists can be provided as follows:

> (a) As a preliminary matter, is the alleged duty of care within an established category or analogous to an established category? If so, then it will not generally be necessary to proceed through the *Anns/Cooper* analysis. Proximity is established, and overriding policy considerations will rarely arise. Thus, a duty of care exists. As mentioned in the previous chapter, in cases involving established categories, the duty of care frequently goes unmentioned.
>
> (b) If the case alleges a novel duty of care, was the harm reasonably foreseeable? This is typically not a difficult burden for the plaintiff to meet. However, as discussed in the remainder of this chapter, a duty of care may sometimes be rejected because the harm or the plaintiff was not reasonably foreseeable.
>
> (c) Even if the harm was foreseeable, was there a sufficient relationship of proximity between the parties to make it just and fair to impose a duty of care on the defendant? At this stage, the court will consider policy considerations arising from the relationship between the parties. Factors to consider may include expectations, representations and reliance; the types of interests involved (physical, economic, emotional, etc.); and any statutory or contractual framework. Hopefully, as the courts grapple with the concept of proximity, they will provide more guidance on this issue.
>
> (d) If there was foreseeable harm and a sufficient relationship of proximity, a *prima facie* duty of care exists. Then, according to *Childs*, the evidentiary burden shifts to the defendant to raise any residual policy considerations that might negative or limit the scope of the duty of care. These residual policy considerations pertain to the decision's effects on the legal system or society more generally. For example, is there an alternative remedy available, will a duty of care give rise to indeterminate liability, or does the case involve government policy decisions that should be immune from negligence liability? Presumably, the list of residual policy considerations is only limited by lawyers' imaginations. Nevertheless, given that these policy considerations may deny compensation to an otherwise deserving plaintiff, they should not determine the matter if they are merely speculative.

NOTES AND QUESTIONS

1. For recent applications of the *Anns/Cooper* test, see *Rogers v. Faught* (2002), 159 O.A.C. 79 (C.A.); *Fraser v. Westminer Canada Ltd.* (2003), 215 N.S.R. (2d) 377 (C.A.); *Hill v. Hamilton-Wentworth Regional Police Services Board* (2005), 76 O.R. (3d) 481 (C.A.); *Cumming (Litigation Guardian of) v. DeSouza* (2005), 74 O.R. (3d) 197 (Div. Ct.); and *Young v. Bella*, [2006] 1 S.C.R. 108.

2. The next four chapters discuss special categories of duty. As mentioned above, the decision in *Childs* suggests that these special categories are not subject to the *Anns/Cooper* test. Instead, they are subject to the more specific rules that have developed to govern those types of actions in particular. Thus, for example, while a court faced with a claim for nervous shock need not proceed through the *Anns/Cooper* analysis, it must still apply the special principles that define the scope of the duty of care with respect to nervous shock claims. See generally *Premakumaran v. Canada* (2006), 270 D.L.R. (4th) 440 (F.C.A.).

2. Application of the Duty of Care Test

According to *Cooper v. Hobart*, the recognition of a duty of care involves a number of steps. If a case falls within an existing category, either directly or by analogy, then a duty of care will apply on the facts. If a case does not fit within an existing or analogous category, then the court must apply the *Anns/Cooper* test. That test involves three main factors: (i) reasonable foreseeability, (ii) proximity, and (iii) residual policy considerations. The first two factors fall under the first branch of the test and are used to identify the existence of a *prima facie* duty of care. The third factor arises under the second branch of the test and is used to negate or limit the *prima facie* duty of care.

The next four chapters, which deal with special categories of duty, focus on what *Cooper v. Hobart* would classify as considerations of proximity and policy. In the remainder of this chapter, we examine the notion of reasonable foreseeability as it pertains to the duty of care.

In the present context, the essential question is whether, at the time of the alleged tort, it was reasonably foreseeable to a person in the defendant's position that carelessness on his or her part could create: (i) a risk of injury, (ii) to the plaintiff. Although easily stated, the following cases demonstrate that that test is sometimes difficult to apply.

(a) FORESEEABLE RISK OF INJURY

MOULE v. N.B. ELEC. POWER COMM.

(1960), 24 D.L.R. (2d) 305 (S.C.C.)

RITCHIE J.:–. . . At the place where this accident occurred, there was a maple tree which at ground level was some 5 ft. from the pole. This tree really consisted of two intertwined trees and at the height of 33 ft. 6 ins. its trunk was only 3 ft. 2 ins. from the wires; it was cleared of all branches on the side nearest to the wires to a height of about 40 ft. but on the side furthest from the wires there were some branches from about 25 ft. up and there was a crotch in the tree at very nearly the same level as the wires themselves.

A few feet further away from the pole and the wires was a spruce tree which had been cleared of limbs to a height of approximately 13 ft. from the ground but to which some person other than the infant appellant had attached boards which formed a species of ladder so that it was possible for a child to climb up to the lowest remaining branches above which a platform had been constructed going across to the maple tree and just above the platform on the maple tree a board and some straps had been nailed which made it possible to climb up to the lowest remaining branch on the side of that tree which was furthest away from the wires.

About noon on Sunday, September 15, 1957 the infant appellant, who at that time was 10½ years old, had climbed up the spruce tree, crossed on the platform to the maple tree and thence to the crotch of that tree, when he called out to his little friend, Joan Rogers, who came over and who herself climbed up on the platform at which time she says that the appellant "must have been standing in the curve of the tree" and "a little above the wires". The little girl says that she hollered to the boy but got no answer and then saw some smoke coming from where the boy was and she ran for his mother. She and Richard Stewart were the only children who gave evidence except for the appellant himself. They had both been living in the area for 2 or 3 months and neither of them had ever seen any boys climbing the maple tree. The appellant himself says that he had never seen anybody climb as high as he was on the day in question.

The appellant himself does not remember how he got up the tree and in fact says that all he can remember is stepping on a rotten branch. He does, however, admit on cross-examination that he recognized the wires to be dangerous and would not have touched them if he could have avoided them.

. . .

In finding that the respondent "should be held liable for the accident and its consequences" the learned trial Judge said:

> But a tree is much more of an allurement for small boys than a power line pole, and I think it fair to say that it might well be anticipated that they would nail cleats to the tree for climbing purposes. I also think it reasonably foreseeable that a child might slip or fall in his climb and come in contact with a conductor only about 3 feet from the top part of the tree. All of which is not highly probable, but likely enough that where the conductor was such a dangerous source of harm a commensurate degree of care called for removing the tree altogether.

The nature of the boy's injuries make it clear that in falling he not only came "in contact with a conductor about 3 feet from the top part of the tree" but that he did so in such a manner as to bring his body in contact with the tree and the wires at the same time. With the greatest respect for the views of the learned trial Judge, I am nonetheless of the opinion that when this circumstance is considered in conjunction with the presence of the cleats on both trees, the platform between them, the unusual height to which the boy climbed and the fact that he had the misfortune to put his weight on a rotten branch, it discloses a sequence of events which was so fortuitous as to be beyond the range of the foreseeable results which a reasonable man would anticipate as a probable consequence of the presence of the high tension wires, isolated as they were from normal human contact, in the area in question.

Having regard to the proximity of this wooded area to houses occupied by the families of military personnel, it was to be expected that children would play there, and although the respondent was not the owner or the occupier of the land and the pole had been installed by the New Brunswick Telephone Co., the wires were nonetheless a dangerous agency which had been brought into the area by the respondent and it was, therefore, under a duty to take precautions but only against any foreseeable consequence of the presence of that danger which could be said to involve a reasonable probability of causing harm.

That high voltage wires are dangerous goes without saying, and the fact that children are likely to climb trees is certainly a foreseeable circumstance and that it is one to which power companies should give heed in placing their wires so that young climbers will not come unexpectedly on a live wire concealed by the branches of a tree is shown by the case of *Buckland v. Guildford Gas Light & Coke Co.*, [1949] 1 K.B. 410. This does not mean, however, that such a company is necessarily responsible for every accidental contact with its wires by climbing children or that it is deemed to be endowed with prevision of every harmful contingency to which the curiosity, agility and daring of active children may expose them.

In placing the wires 33 ft. 6 ins. from the ground and causing the adjacent trees to be limbed as they were at the place of this accident, I am of opinion that the respondent had taken adequate precautions against such dangers inherent in the presence of the wires as could be reasonably foreseen, and I agree with the learned Judge who, in rendering the decision from which this appeal is taken, has said: "The defendant should not be held guilty of negligence for not having foreseen the possibility of the occurrence of such an unlikely event as happened in this case and provided against it by the removal of the maple tree."

AMOS v. N.B. ELEC. POWER COMM.

(1976), 70 D.L.R. (3d) 741 (S.C.C.)

SPENCE J.:–This is an appeal by leave from the judgment of the Appeal Division of the Supreme Court of New Brunswick pronounced on March 21, 1975. By that judgment, the Appeal Division allowed an appeal from the judgment of Leger, J., given after trial whereby he had allowed the appellants' claim and awarded damages of $36,275.45 and costs.

The infant plaintiff, on July 1, 1970, then nine years old, was visiting his uncle at Kedgwick, New Brunswick, and that afternoon was engaged in play with two other boys Gilbert Le Bourque, age 13, and Leopold Simon, age 10. The uncle's home is located on the edge of a highway and about 25 to 30 ft. therefrom. Along the edge of this highway and within the limits of the highway, the respondent had erected a row of wooden poles carrying various wires, which shall be more particularly described hereafter.

Directly in front of the uncle's house and also on the highway right-of-way, grew a poplar tree. Of course, in July, the tree was in full leaf and made a perfect screen for the series of wires which ran through it. The lowest of those wires was a telephone cable and that cable was 21 ft. above the ground. Some 40 inches farther up was one low voltage line carrying only 110 volts and then some 9 inches to a foot above that two more similar low voltage lines. Above that again, a neutral ground wire and uppermost and 48 inches higher than the neutral ground wire were wires carrying very heavy charges said to be of 7,200 volts. These last three wires were attached to the cross-bar at the top of the pole.

In their play, the three boys devised a contest to determine which one of the three could climb the tree the farthest and the fastest. The plaintiff, although only nine, appears to have been the most agile of the three and he climbed the highest on the tree. He climbed high enough in the tree so that his weight would cause the tree to sway or bend and either the trunk of the tree itself or one of the branches of the tree brushed against these high tension wires. The boy was immediately struck by severe electric shock, knocked unconscious and was actually burning in the tree. A neighbour, at what both Courts below noted was great personal risk, took a chain saw and cut the tree down, so that it fell on the road and the badly injured plaintiff was then taken first to a hospital in nearby St. Quentin and thereafter transferred to a hospital in Montreal.

No issue as to the quantum of damage arose in either the Appeal Division or in this Court, and we are simply concerned with the issue of liability.

In the first place, it may be noted that the power lines and tree were on a public highway and the question of trespass does not arise.

This Court and other Courts have, from time to time, stressed the duty of those who erect electric lines carrying heavy charges to take proper precautions against injury resulting therefrom. . . .

In the present case, the learned trial Judge said [(1974), 9 N.B.R. (2d) 358 at 361]:

> After having considered all of the evidence I have concluded that the tree in combination with the wires constituted an invitation and an allurement for small boys imbued with the natural instinct to climb as high as their strength and energy would permit; that in permitting the power lines to remain without insulation and in failing to maintain the particular tree properly trimmed in proximity to the power lines where the branches or the infant plaintiff could come in contact with them constituted a concealed danger in the nature of a trap for such small infants. The defendant ought reasonably to have foreseen the danger and they must be deemed to have had knowledge of it and ought to have taken the necessary steps to obviate it. Their failure to accomplish this constituted negligence on their part.

With respect, apart from the learned trial Judge's reference to lack of insulation, I agree with him.

Bugold, J.A., giving judgment for the Appeal Division was, in my opinion, ready to accept the law as outlined by the learned trial Judge but was of the opinion that the particular facts in the present case could not result in liability for the respondent because the respondent could not have reasonably foreseen the accident which did occur, and, again, in my opinion, felt that the matter was foreclosed by the decision of this court in *Moule v. N.B. Electric Power Com'n, supra*. . . .

Let us contrast those circumstances and the conduct of the power company in that case with the circumstances of the present case and the conduct of the power company in the present appeal.

The poplar, as noted by the learned trial Judge, is a fast growing tree. The fast growing tree stood directly beneath lines running along the top of the poles and carrying up to 7,200 volts. Yet, the only evidence as to an attempt to keep the tree away from those heavily charged wires was almost casual the inspector of the power company saying it was the practice to trim such trees every four to seven years and so far as he knew the practice had been kept up in reference to this poplar tree. That such practice was indeed insufficient is illustrated by the fact that the accident occurred because it did occur when the tree swayed sufficiently to have the trunk or a branch touch the high tension wires. Those wires were at least 30 ft. above the ground and any contact with those high tension wires could have been avoided by the simple expedient of cutting off the top of the poplar tree. It was left uncut and this heavily leafed tree in mid-summer adequately concealed the presence of the wires from a boy carrying out the perfectly normal play of an active little fellow in climbing the tree.

In *Moule*, in order to get himself injured, the boy had to climb one tree and then cross from it to the maple which had been protected in the fashion I have outlined and then only came in contact with the wire when he stepped on a dead branch and fell. In this appeal, the boy, by climbing what seemed to be a normal poplar tree, caused the tree to bend so that it contacted high tension wires which it should not even have been near. As Ritchie, J., pointed out in *Moule*, that children are likely to climb trees is certainly a foreseeable circumstance. Morris J., said in *Buckland v. Guildford Gas Light & Coke Co.*, [1949] 1 K.B. 410 at p. 419:

> It required no vivid imagination on the part of anyone traversing the route of the wires to appreciate the great peril of having the wires above a tree that could be easily climbed, and whose foliage, being dense in the month of June, would obscure the wires. If anyone did climb the tree he would with every step approach a hidden peril of the direst kind. The facts of the present case show all too dramatically the nature of the peril. It was, in my judgment, easily foreseeable that someone might climb the tree and so might become in close proximity to an unseen deadly peril.

I am of the opinion that those words are particularly applicable to the present appeal.

Although the long series of circumstances which, added together, resulted in the accident in the *Moule* case, could not have been foreseen, I am of the opinion that the accident in the present case was one which could be foreseen and which was almost inevitable when given active boys and a poplar tree running up through and hiding high tension wires, especially when that tree was directly in front of their home.

For these reasons, I am of the opinion that *Moule v. N.B. Electric Power Com'n* does not apply in the present circumstances and that the respondent was liable for the damage caused to the infant plaintiff.

NOTES AND QUESTIONS

1. Do you agree that *Moule* can be distinguished from *Amos*? Specifically, what facts prompted the court to recognize a duty of care in *Moule*, but not in *Amos*? Would the result in *Amos* have been different if the tree had swayed into the wires as a result of the combined effects of the child's weight and an unusually strong gust of wind?

2. The issue of foreseeability of harm is relevant to three elements of a negligence action: duty, standard of care and remoteness of damage. First, a court will impose a duty of care only if the defendant's conduct created a foreseeable risk of injury to the plaintiff. Second, the probability of injury is one of several factors considered in determining whether the defendant breached the standard of care. Finally, the plaintiff's losses will be held to be too remote if they were not a foreseeable result of the defendant's breach of the standard of care. The courts do not always draw a clear distinction between those three concepts.

3. Identify the foreseeability tests used in *Moule* and *Amos*. What was the legal significance of the courts' findings on these issues? Did the courts address the issue of foreseeability in terms of duty, standard of care or remoteness?

4. The different manifestations of reasonable foreseeability were addressed in the Australian case of *Minister Administering the Environmental Planning and Assessment Act 1979 v. San Sebastien Pty. Ltd.*, [1983] 2 N.S.W.L.R. 268 at 295-96 (C.A.) [emphasis in original]:

> [A] recognition has emerged that the foreseeability inquiry at the duty, breach and remoteness stages raises different issues which progressively decline from the general to the particular. The proximity upon which a *Donoghue* type duty rests depends upon proof that the defendant and plaintiff are so placed in relation to each other that it is reasonably foreseeable as a possibility that careless conduct of *any kind* on the part of the former may result in damage of *some kind* to the person or property of the latter. . . The breach question requires proof that it was reasonably foreseeable as a possibility that *the kind* of carelessness charged against the defendant might cause damage of *some kind* to the plaintiff's person or property. . . The remoteness test is only passed if the plaintiff proves that *the kind* of damage suffered by him was foreseeable as a possible outcome of the kind of carelessness charged against the defendant.

Since plaintiffs cannot ultimately succeed without satisfying the narrowest manifestation of reasonable foreseeability at the remoteness stage of inquiry, why should they also be required to separately satisfy the broader manifestations of reasonable foreseeability at the stages of standard of care and duty of care? Does it matter that the duty of care is primarily a question of law, while standard of care and, to a lesser extent, remoteness are primarily questions of fact? Who decides questions of fact and who decides questions of law? When can an appellate court overturn a decision on a question of law and when can it overturn a decision on a question of fact? See *Barnard v. Carnegie* (1924), 26 O.W.N. 264 (C.A.); *Cotic v. Gray* (1981), 124 D.L.R. (3d) 641 (Ont. C.A.); *Galaske v. O'Donnell*, [1994] 1 S.C.R. 670; *Toneguzzo-Norvell (Guardian ad litem of) v. Burnaby Hospital*, [1994] 1 S.C.R. 114; *Gottardo Properties (Dome) Inc. v. Toronto (City)* (1998), 162 D.L.R. (4th) 574 (Ont. C.A.); *Schwartz v. Canada*, [1996] 1 S.C.R. 254; *Van de Perre v. Edwards*, [2001] 2 S.C.R. 1014; and *Housen v. Nikolaisen*, [2002] 2 S.C.R. 235.

5. Since the issue of reasonable foreseeability is framed as a hypothetical question – did the defendant's act create a foreseeable risk of injury? – the fact that injury actually occurred should not colour the resolution of the issue.

6. For additional cases discussing and applying the foreseeability of risk test in duty, see *Munshaw Colour Service Ltd. v. Vancouver* (1962), 33 D.L.R. (2d) 719 (S.C.C.); *Gagne v. St. Regis Paper Co.* (1973), 36 D.L.R. (3d) 301 (S.C.C.); *Crocker v. Sundance Northwest Resorts Ltd.* (1988), 44 C.C.L.T. 225 (S.C.C.); *Campbell v. Calgary Power Ltd.* (1988), 62 Alta. L.R. (2d) 253 (C.A.); *Taylor v. King* (1993), 82 B.C.L.R. (2d) 108 (C.A.); *Lorenz v. Winnipeg (City)*, [1994] 1 W.W.R. 558 (Man. C.A.); *Stewart v. Pettie* (1995), 23 C.C.L.T. (2d) 89 (S.C.C.); *Newton v. Newton* (2003), 17 B.C.L.R. (4th) 1 (C.A.); and *Poissant v. Robalo* (2004), 360 A.R. 101 (Q.B.).

(b) FORESEEABLE PLAINTIFF

PALSGRAF v. LONG ISLAND RY. CO.

248 N.Y. 339 (C.A. 1928)

CARDOZO C.J.:–Plaintiff was standing on a platform of defendant's railroad after buying a ticket to go to Rockaway Beach. A train stopped at the station, bound for another place. Two men ran forward to catch it. One of the men reached the platform of the car without mishap, though the train was already moving. The other man, carrying a package, jumped aboard the car, but seemed unsteady as if about to fall. A guard on the car, who had held the door open, reached forward to help him in, and another guard on the platform pushed him from behind. In this act, the package was dislodged, and fell upon the rails. It was a package of small size, about fifteen inches long, and was covered by a newspaper. In fact it contained fireworks, but there was nothing in its appearance to give notice of its contents. The fireworks when they fell exploded. The shock of the explosion threw down some scales at the other end of the platform many feet away. The scales struck the plaintiff, causing injuries for which she sues.

The conduct of the defendant's guard, if a wrong in its relation to the holder of the package, was not a wrong in its relation to the plaintiff, standing far away. Relatively to her it was not negligence at all. Nothing in the situation gave notice that the falling package had in it the potency of peril to persons thus removed. Negligence is not actionable unless it involves the invasion of a legally protected interest, the violation of a right. "Proof of negligence in the air, so to speak, will not do."

. . .

The plaintiff, as she stood upon the platform of the station, might claim to be protected against intentional invasion of her bodily security. Such invasion is not charged. She might claim to be protected against unintentional invasion by conduct involving in the thought of reasonable men an unreasonable hazard that such invasion would ensue. These, from the point of view of the law, were the bounds of her immunity, with perhaps some rare exceptions, survivals for the most part of ancient forms of liability, where conduct is held to be at the peril of the actor.

. . .

If no hazard was apparent to the eye of ordinary vigilance, an act innocent and harmless, at least to outward seeming, with reference to her, did not take to itself the quality of a tort because it happened to be a wrong, though apparently not one involving the risk of bodily insecurity, with reference to someone else. "In every instance, before negligence can be predicated of a given act, back of the act must be sought and found a duty to the individual complaining, the observance of which would have averted or avoided the injury."

. . .

The argument for the plaintiff is built upon the shifting meanings of such words as "wrong" and "wrongful," and shares their instability. What the plaintiff must show is "a wrong" to herself; i.e., a violation of her own right, and not merely a wrong to someone else, nor conduct "wrongful" because unsocial, but not "a wrong" to any one. We are told that one who drives at reckless speed through a crowded city street is guilty of a negligent act and therefore of a wrongful one, irrespective of the consequences. Negligent the act is, and wrongful in the sense that it is unsocial, but wrongful and unsocial in relation to other travelers, only because the eye of vigilance perceives the risk of damage. If the same act were to be committed on a speedway or race course, it would lose its wrongful quality. The risk reasonably to be perceived defines the duty to be obeyed, and risk imports relation; it is risk to another or to others within the range of apprehension.

. . .

The range of reasonable apprehension is at times a question for the court, and at times, if varying inferences are possible, a question for the jury. Here, by concession, there was nothing in the situation to suggest to the most cautious mind that the parcel wrapped in newspaper would spread wreckage through the station. If the guard had thrown it down knowingly and willfully, he would not have threatened the plaintiff's safety, so far as appearances could warn him. His conduct would not have involved, even then, an unreasonable probability of invasion of her bodily security. Liability can be no greater where the act is inadvertent.

Negligence, like risk, is thus a term of relation. Negligence in the abstract, apart from things related, is surely not a tort, if indeed it is understandable at all.

. . .

Negligence is not a tort unless it results in the commission of a wrong, and the commission of a wrong imports the violation of a right, in this case, we are told, the right to be protected against interference with one's bodily security. But bodily security is protected, not against all forms of interference or aggression, but only against some. One who seeks redress at law does not make out a cause of action by showing without more that there has been damage to his person. If the harm was not willful, he must show that the act as to him had possibilities of danger so many and apparent as to entitle him to be protected against the doing of it though the harm was unintended. Affront to personalty is still the keynote of the wrong.

. . .

The victim does not sue derivatively, or by right of subrogation, to vindicate an interest invaded in the person of another. Thus to view his cause of action is to ignore the fundamental difference between tort and crime. Holland, *Jurisprudence* (12th Ed.) p. 328. He sues for breach of a duty owing to himself.

The law of causation, remote or proximate, is thus foreign to the case before us. The question of liability is always anterior to the question of the measure of the consequences that go with liability. If there is no tort to be redressed, there is no occasion to consider what damage might be recovered if there were a finding of a tort. We may assume, without deciding, that negligence, not at large or in the abstract, but in relation to the plaintiff, would entail liability for any and all consequences, however novel or extraordinary.

. . .

ANDREWS J. (dissenting).:–The result we shall reach depends upon our theory as to the nature of negligence. Is it a relative concept – the breach of some duty owing to a particular person or to particular persons? Or, where there is an act which unreasonably threatens the safety of others, is the doer liable for all its proximate consequences, even where they result in injury to one who would generally be thought to be outside the radius of danger? This is not a mere dispute as to words. We might not believe that to the average mind the dropping of the bundle would seem to involve the probability of harm to the plaintiff standing many feet away whatever might be the case as to the owner or to one so near as to be likely to be struck by its fall. If, however, we adopt the second hypothesis, we have to inquire only as to the relation between cause and effect. We deal in terms of proximate cause, not of negligence.

. . .

But we are told that "there is no negligence unless there is in the particular case a legal duty to take care, and this duty must be one which is owed to the plaintiff himself and not merely to others." Salmond, *Torts* (6th Ed.) 24. This I think too narrow a conception. Where there is the unreasonable act, and some right that may be affected there is negligence whether damage does or does not result. That is immaterial. Should we drive down Broadway at a reckless speed, we are negligent whether we strike an approaching car or miss it by an inch. The act itself is wrongful. It is wrong not only to those who happen to be within the radius of danger, but to all who might have been there – a wrong to the public at large. Such is the language of the street. Such the language of the courts when speaking of contributory negligence. Such again and again their language in speaking of the duty of some defendant and discussing proximate cause in cases where such a discussion is wholly irrelevant on any other theory.

. . .

The proposition is this: Every one owes to the world at large the duty of refraining from those acts that may unreasonably threaten the safety of others. Such an act occurs. Not only is he wronged to whom harm might reasonably be expected to result, but he also who is in fact injured, even if he be outside what would generally be thought the danger zone. There needs be duty due the one complaining, but this is not a duty to a particular individual because as to him harm might be expected. Harm to some one being the natural result of the act, not only that one alone, but all those in fact injured may complain. We have never, I think, held otherwise. Indeed in the *Di Caprio Case* we said that a breach of a general ordinance defining the degree of care to be exercised in one's calling is evidence of negligence as to every one. We did not limit this statement to those who might be expected to be exposed to danger. Unreasonable risk being taken, its consequences are not confined to those who might probably be hurt.

If this be so, we do not have a plaintiff suing by "derivation or succession." Her action is original and primary. Her claim is for a breach of duty to herself – not that she is subrogated to any right of action of the owner of the parcel or of a passenger standing at the scene of the explosion.

. . .

The act upon which defendant's liability rests is knocking an apparently harmless package onto the platform. The act was negligent. For its proximate consequences the defendant is liable. If its contents were broken, to the owner; if it fell upon and crushed a passenger's foot, then to him; if it exploded and injured one in the immediate vicinity, to him also as to A in the illustration. Mrs. Palsgraf was standing some distance away. How far cannot be told from the record – apparently 25 or 30 feet, perhaps less. Except for the explosion, she would not have been injured. We are told by the appellant in his brief, "It cannot be denied that the explosion was the direct cause of the plaintiff's injuries." So it was a substantial factor in producing the result – there was here a natural and continuous sequence – direct connection. The only intervening cause was that, instead of blowing her to the ground, the concussion smashed the weighing machine which in turn fell upon her. There was no remoteness in time, little in space. And surely, given such an explosion as here, it needed no great foresight to predict that the natural result would be to injure one on the platform at no greater distance from its scene than was the plaintiff. Just how no one might be able to predict. Whether by flying fragments, by broken glass, by wreckage of machines or structures no one could say. But injury in some form was most probable.

Under these circumstances I cannot say as a matter of law that the plaintiff's injuries were not the proximate result of the negligence. That is all we have before us. The court refused to so charge. No request was made to submit the matter to the jury as a question of fact, even would that have been proper upon the record before us.

The judgment appealed from should be affirmed, with costs.

POUND, LEHMAN, and KELLOGG, JJ., concur with CARDOZO, C.J.

ANDREWS, J., dissents in opinion in which CRANE and O'BRIEN, JJ., concur.

NOTES AND QUESTIONS

1. How did the majority's analysis of duty differ from that of the dissent? What is the practical significance of this difference?

2. Despite frequent criticism, Cardozo C.J.'s approach has been accepted by the English and Canadian courts. The plaintiff must prove both that the defendant's conduct gave rise to a duty of care and that the duty was owed to him or her. This does not mean that the individual plaintiff must be foreseeable, but rather, that the plaintiff must belong to a class of persons foreseeably at risk. For additional discussions of the foreseeable plaintiff test see *Hay (or Bourhill) v. Young*, [1942] 2 All E.R. 396 (H.L.); *Can. Gen. Elec. Co. v. Pickford & Black Ltd.*, [1971] S.C.R. 41; *Reese v. Coleman (No. 1)*, [1979] 4 W.W.R. 58 (Sask. C.A.); *Tutton v. A.D. Walter Ltd.*, [1985] 3 All E.R. 757 (Q.B.D.); and *D'Aoust v. Lindsay* (2000), 253 A.R. 243 (Q.B.). Few claims are dismissed based on the unforeseeability of the plaintiff.

3. The breadth of the foreseeable plaintiff test varies considerably with the type of interest at stake. For example, a very broad test is applied in cases of rescuers, whereas a narrower test is applied in nervous shock cases. Contrast *King v. Phillips*, [1953] 1 Q.B. 429 (C.A.) with *Urbanski v. Patel* (1978), 84 D.L.R. (3d) 650 (Man. Q.B.).

By manipulating the foreseeable plaintiff test, the courts have been able to control the ambit of recovery in negligence. See also *Bechard v. Haliburton Estate* (1991), 10 C.C.L.T. (2d) 156 (Ont. C.A.); and *Schlink v. Blackburn* (1993), 18 C.C.L.T. (2d) 173 (B.C.C.A.).

4. In *Nespolon v. Alford* (1998), 40 O.R. (3d) 355 (C.A.), the plaintiff suffered nervous shock after he struck and killed an intoxicated teenager who had fallen on a highway. He sued, *inter alia*, the teenager's estate and two of the teenager's acquaintances, who had accepted him into their car knowing that he was "falling down drunk."

Earlier that evening, the acquaintances had assured police that they would safely transport the teenager back to his hometown. At his request, they dropped him off at the roadside, near a house that he recognized as a friend's. The plaintiff claimed that it was foreseeable that, if the intoxicated teenager were abandoned near a highway, he would stumble onto the road, posing a risk to both himself and others.

The Ontario Court of Appeal dismissed the plaintiff's claim. The majority concluded that it was unforeseeable that dropping the intoxicated teenager off would eventually cause nervous shock to someone in the plaintiff's position. Thus, the acquaintances did not owe the plaintiff a duty of care.

5. Since the majority in *Palsgraf* dismissed the plaintiff's action at the duty stage, only the dissent dealt with the other elements of a negligence action. It should be noted that, at the time *Palsgraf* was decided, the courts in both the United States and England used a directness test of remoteness. Thus, Andrews J. framed the remoteness question in terms of whether the plaintiff's losses were a direct result of the defendant's negligence. Given that directness was the test of remoteness, would Andrews J.'s approach have significantly broadened the scope of recovery? Now that foreseeability is the accepted test of remoteness, is there any practical difference between the majority and dissenting judgments?

6. Smith scathingly criticized the foreseeable plaintiff test in "The Mystery of Duty" in Klar, ed., *Studies in Canadian Tort Law* (1977) 1 at 24:

> [T]he courts have created a doctrine of privity in the law of negligence. It is a privity of fault rather than of contract. The doctrine of privity has raised problems and difficulties in the law of contract. It is a freak, an abortion, in the law of torts. The doctrine of privity confuses questions of risk of harm with problems of remoteness, and the language of duty of care is the vehicle of this confusion.
>
> Judges have said that there is no such thing as negligence in the abstract or in the air, and this is, of course, true. A risk of harm must be a risk to someone in order for it to be a risk of harm or negligence. It is often the case, however, that as a result of negligence persons who are not the prime subjects of the risk are harmed as well. It could be someone whose presence could not be anticipated. It might be a person who suffers a nervous shock as the result of witnessing the main or initial harm, or it might be a rescuer who is injured in trying to prevent the harm. These examples all raise questions of remoteness of damage because the legal issue is whether or not the defendant's liability extends to these persons as well as the persons who were the prime subjects of the risk, or, to rephrase the issue another way, whether the damage suffered by these persons is too remote from the original risk which is the foundation of the finding of negligence. We know that injuries to one person will often result in, or bear a causal connection to, other people. No event stands in a causal isolation. We have to place some limits, however, on just how much of this we are going to require the defendant to compensate.

Smith seems to agree with Andrews J. in viewing the foreseeable plaintiff issue as a practical problem of controlling the extent of the defendant's liability, an issue generally considered under remoteness of damages. However, Cardozo C.J. appears to have had an additional concern, namely, that there be a pre-existing relationship between the parties in order to justify a duty of care. For him, this was a theoretical concern as much as a practical one. Is Cardozo C.J.'s concern justified?

7. A question sometimes arises regarding the foreseeability of the plaintiff not because of a bizarre concatenation of events, as in *Palsgraf*, but rather because the plaintiff somehow is unusually vulnerable to harm. *Haley v. London Electricity Board* (1964), [1965] A.C. 778 (H.L.) is illustrative. The defendant's workmen dug a trench outside the plaintiff's house one morning. They intended to refill it by nightfall. As a safety measure, they surrounded it with a barrier about nine inches in height. The defendant, who was blind and used a white cane to find his way about, tripped over the barrier, hit his head and was thereby rendered deaf. He sued in negligence. The defendant denied that it owed a duty of care to him. It argued that it was only obliged to take precautions suitable for able-bodied people and that the barrier that it had used was therefore adequate. Lord Reid rejected that argument, saying that it would mean that "a blind or infirm person who goes out alone goes out at his peril." He then held that the plaintiff's injury did fall within the scope of the reasonable foreseeability test and that the defendant was liable:

> No doubt there are many places open to the public where for one reason or another one would be surprised to see a blind person walking alone, but a city pavement is not one of them; and a residential street cannot be different from any other. The blind people whom we meet must live somewhere, and most of them probably left their homes unaccompanied. It may seem surprising that blind people can avoid ordinary obstacles so well as they do, but we must take account of the facts. There is evidence in this case about the number of blind people in London and it appears from government publications that the proportion in the whole country is near one in five hundred. By no means all are sufficiently skilled or confident to venture out alone, but the number who habitually do so must be very large. I find it quite impossible to say that it is not reasonably foreseeable that a blind person may pass along a particular pavement on a particular day.
>
> No question can arise in this case of any great difficulty in affording adequate protection for the blind. In considering what is adequate protection again one must have regard to common knowledge. One is entitled to expect of a blind person a high degree of skill and care because none but the most foolhardy would venture to go out alone without having that skill and exercising that care. We know that in fact blind people do safely avoid all ordinary obstacles on pavements; there can be no question of padding lamp posts as was suggested in one case. A moment's reflection, however, shows that a low obstacle in an unusual place is a grave danger; on the other hand it is clear from the evidence in this case and also I think from common knowledge that quite a light fence some two feet high is an adequate warning. There would have been no difficulty in providing a fence here. . . .
>
> I can see no justification for laying down any hard and fast rule limiting the classes of persons for whom those interfering with a pavement must make provision. It is said that it is impossible to tell what precautions will be adequate to protect all kinds of infirm pedestrians or that taking such precautions would be unreasonably difficult or expensive. I think that such fears are exaggerated.

Would the court have concluded that the plaintiff was a foreseeable victim of the defendant's carelessness if: (a) only one in 10,000 people in the general population were blind; (b) the barrier was located on a lightly travelled sidewalk that was extremely steep and winding; or (c) the barrier was going to be used for only 20 minutes until a more suitable barrier was delivered?

Given that the *Canadian Charter of Rights and Freedoms*, Part I of the *Constitution Act, 1982*, being Schedule B to the *Canada Act 1982* (U.K.), 1982, c. 11 and both federal and provincial human rights legislation prohibit discrimination on the basis of disability, what assumptions should be made about the foreseeability of disabled people being present in public? What are the implications of holding that a disabled person is not a foreseeable plaintiff?

11

SPECIAL DUTIES OF CARE: AFFIRMATIVE ACTION

1. Introduction to Special Duties of Care
2. Introduction to Duties of Affirmative Action
3. The Duty to Rescue
4. The Duty to Control the Conduct of Others
5. The Duty to Perform Gratuitous Undertakings

1. Introduction to Special Duties of Care

The previous chapter examined the grounds upon which Canadian courts identify duties of care. In *Cooper v. Hobart*, [2001] 3 S.C.R. 537, the Supreme Court of Canada emphasized the role of policy, both in connection with the notion of proximity under the first branch of the *Anns/Cooper* test and in connection with factors that may, under the second branch of the test, negate or limit a *prima facie* duty of care. The court also stressed the need to address policy considerations on a category-by-category basis. Some types of situations raise special concerns regarding either the relationship between the parties or larger societal interests.

This and the next three chapters address policy considerations that arise in various circumstances. This chapter considers the special duties of care applicable in cases of omission. Chapter 12 considers the special duties that may be owed to rescuers, unborn children, and victims of nervous shock, as well as those owed by health care professionals, manufacturers and suppliers of potentially dangerous goods, and barristers. Chapters 13 and 14 consider the special duties of care that may arise in connection with negligent statements and pure economic losses. As you read through these chapters, bear *Cooper v. Hobart* in mind. Ask, in each instance, whether the operative policy factors pertain to the parties' relationship or to larger societal interests.

2. Introduction to Duties of Affirmative Action

The common law has traditionally distinguished between misfeasance (positive acts) and nonfeasance (failures to act). As a general rule, the courts have been willing to impose liability for losses caused by the former, but not by the latter. Granted, duties of affirmative action sometimes were recognized, at least in limited form, if the parties shared a "special relationship" or if the defendant had a contractual or statutory obligation to intervene. In most cases, however, the law merely required the defendant to refrain from interfering with the plaintiff's legal interests. Consequently, while a trespasser who innocently entered a neighbour's land, believing it to be his or her own, was held liable, a person who sat idly by and watched a young child drown was immune from liability.

Although various explanations have been provided for the common law's traditional antipathy to duties of affirmative action, many are now of questionable relevance. The early writs did not easily accommodate complaints arising from omissions. And even if they did, the English courts may have been too overburdened with cases of misfeasance to take much interest in nonfeasance:

> [T]he rough and ready law of the . . . garrison society could not spare the manpower in a world of hot blood and quick death, to punish the subtler harms arising by omissions. (Frankel, "Criminal Omissions: A Legal Microcosm" (1965) 11 Wayne L. Rev. 367 at 371)

Moreover, a duty to rescue was thought to sit uneasily with the English character:

> Self direction or personal autonomy is a mark of the English race. The Englishman, as opposed to one of Latin lineage, does not so easily coalesce with the mass. He distinctly wishes to live his own life, make his own contacts, or as he frequently says, "muddle through" in his own way. (Hope, "Officiousness" (1929) 15 Corn. L.Q. 25 at 29)

Likewise, the rise of capitalism and *laissez-faire* ideologies further fostered the belief that "the struggle of selfish individuals automatically produces the common good of all": Rudzinski, "The Duty to rescue: A Comparative Analysis" in Ratcliffe, ed., *The Good Samaritan and the Law* (1981) at 120. During the 20th century, positive duties seemed to some to constitute "an exalted form of socialism": Minor, "Moral Obligations as a Basis of Liability" (1923) 9 Va. L. Rev. 421 at 422. Along similar lines, it was stressed that positive obligations are necessarily more intrusive than negative duties. A person performing a required act cannot simultaneously do anything else. In contrast, a person who is refraining from committing a prohibited act remains free to do everything else. Finally, especially in more recent times, it has been suggested that it is very difficult, as a practical matter, to define the scope of positive obligations. If a general duty to rescue were recognized, it would be necessary, for instance, to determine how much danger and inconvenience a bystander is required to withstand.

As this chapter and the next illustrate, whatever the explanation, the courts still cling to the general principle that there is no liability in negligence for nonfeasance. Beginning in the late 20th century, however, the scope of liability increased noticeably as courts began to recognize various exceptions to that general rule. The end result is a complex patchwork of specialized principles governing individual categories of cases. The general principle has been preserved, but it applies in fewer and fewer circumstances. Further, the full effect of *Cooper v. Hobart* has yet to be determined in this area of the law.

In this chapter, we examine the expansion of positive duties of care in three situations: (i) the duty to rescue, (ii) the duty to control the conduct of third parties, and (iii) the duty to fulfil gratuitous undertakings.

NOTES

1. The distinction between misfeasance and nonfeasance is often difficult to draw. F. Bohlen suggested that the essential difference is that misfeasance involves worsening the plaintiff's position, whereas nonfeasance involves failing to improve it: "The Moral Duty to Aid Others as a Basis of Tort Liability" (1908) 56 U. Pa. L. Rev. 217 at 220. Although Bohlen's distinction is widely cited and accepted, both courts and academics have continued to find the issue troublesome. See for example E. Weinrib, who describes Bohlen's distinction as "skeletal" and states that its incompleteness undermines its

possible usefulness: "The Case for a Duty to Rescue" (1980) 90 Yale L.J. 247 at 251-58. See also Wright, "Negligent 'Acts or Omissions'" (1941) 19 Can. Bar Rev. 465; McNiece & Thornton, "Affirmative Duties in Tort" (1948) 58 Yale L.J. 1272; and Smith, *Liability in Negligence* (1984) at 29-47.

2. The Supreme Court of Canada used the concept of nonfeasance to justify its decision not to impose liability on social hosts for injuries caused by their intoxicated guests in *Childs v. Desormeaux*, [2006] 1 S.C.R. 643. McLachlin C.J.C., writing for the court, characterized the social hosts' actions as a failure to prevent harm from occurring, and found (at para. 39) that there is no duty to prevent harm unless there is a special relationship between the parties: "[The law] permits third parties witnessing risk to decide not to become rescuers or otherwise intervene. It is only when these third parties have a special relationship to the person in danger or a material role in the creation or management of the risk that the law may impinge on autonomy."

3. The House of Lords discussed nonfeasance at some length in *Stovin v. Wise*, [1996] 3 All E.R. 801 (H.L.). Lord Nicholls affirmed the traditional distinction between misfeasance and nonfeasance:

> The distinction is based on a recognition that it is one matter to require a person to take care if he embarks on a course of conduct which may harm others. He must take care not to create a risk of danger. It is another matter to require a person, who is doing nothing, to take positive action to protect others from harm for which he was not responsible, and to hold him liable in damages if he fails to do so. . ..
>
> There must be some special justification for imposing an obligation of this character. Compulsory altruism needs more justification than an obligation not to create dangers to others when acting for one's own purposes.

4. For a review of liability for nonfeasance, see Little, "Erosion of No-Duty Negligence Rules in England, the United States, and Common Law Commonwealth Nations" (1983) 20 Hous. L. Rev. 959; Markesinis, "Negligence, Nuisance and Affirmative Duties of Action" (1989) 105 L.Q.R. 104; and Rowe & Silver, "The Jurisprudence of Action and Inaction in the Law of Tort: Solving the Puzzle of Nonfeasance and Misfeasance from the Fifteenth Through the Twentieth Centuries (1995) 33 Duq. L. Rev. 807.

3. The Duty to Rescue

OSTERLIND v. HILL
160 N.E. 301 (Mass. S.C. 1928)

. . .

BRALEY J.: – This is an action of tort, brought by the plaintiff as administrator of the estate of Albert T. Osterlind to recover damages for the conscious suffering and death of his intestate. [The plaintiff] alleges that, on or about July 4, 1925, the defendant was engaged in the business of letting for hire pleasure boats and canoes to be used on Lake Quannapowitt in the town of Wakefield; that it was the duty of the defendant to have a reasonable regard for the safety of the persons to whom he let boats and canoes; that the defendant, in the early morning of July 4, 1925, in willful, wanton, or reckless disregard of the natural and probable consequences, let for hire, to the intestate and one Ryan, a frail and dangerous canoe, well knowing that the intestate and Ryan were then intoxicated, and were then manifestly unfit to go upon the lake in the canoe; that, in consequence of the defendant's willful, wanton, or reckless disregard of his duties, the intestate and Ryan went out in the canoe, which shortly afterwards was overturned and the intestate, after hanging to it for approximately one-half hour, and making loud calls for assistance, which calls the defendant heard and utterly ignored, was obliged to release his hold, and was drowned; that in consequence of the defendant's willful, wanton, or reckless conduct the intestate endured great conscious mental anguish and great conscious physical suffering from suffocation and drowning.

. . .

The declaration must set forth facts which, if proved, establish the breach of a legal duty owed by the defendant to the intestate. . . . The plaintiff relies on *Black v. New York, New Haven & Hartford Railroad*, 193 Mass. 448. . ., as establishing such a duty on the part of the defendant. In that case the jury would have been justified in finding that the plaintiff was "so intoxicated as to be incapable of standing or walking or caring for himself in any way." There was testimony to the effect that, "when he fell, he did not seize hold of anything, his arms were at his side." The defendant's employees placed a helpless man, a man impotent to protect himself, in a dangerous position.

In the case at bar, however, it is alleged in every count of the original and amended declaration that after the canoe was overturned the intestate hung to the canoe for approximately one-half hour and made loud calls for assistance. On the facts stated in the declaration the intestate was not in a helpless condition. He was able to take steps to protect himself. The defendant violated no legal duty in renting the canoe to a man in the condition of the intestate. The allegation appearing in each count of the amended declaration that the intestate was incapacitated to enter into any valid contract states merely a legal conclusion. . . . The allegations, therefore, in the counts of the amended declaration to the effect that the intestate was incapable of exercising any care for his own safety is controlled by the allegations in the same counts that he hung to the side of the canoe for approximately one-half hour, calling for assistance.

In view of the absence of any duty to refrain from renting a canoe to a person in the condition of the intestate, the allegations of involuntary intoxication relating as they do to the issues of contributory negligence become immaterial. The allegations of willful, wanton or reckless conduct also add nothing to the plaintiff's case. The failure of the defendant to respond to the intestate's outcries is immaterial. No legal right of the intestate was infringed. . . . The allegation common to both declarations that the canoe was "frail and dangerous" appears to be a general characterization of canoes. It is not alleged that the canoe was out of repair and unsafe.

It follows that the order sustaining each demurrer is affirmed.

NOTES AND QUESTIONS

1. The plaintiff's action was based on two allegations of negligence, each of which arose from a distinct duty of affirmative action. How would you characterize these duties?

2. The judge suggested that Hill would have been under a duty of care if the deceased had been helpless when he rented the canoe. Why did the fact that the deceased was helpless once the canoe overturned not give rise to a duty to rescue?

3. Would the case have been decided differently if: (a) the deceased had been a young child, (b) the deceased had drowned within arm's length of the dock because Hill refused to throw him a nearby rope, or (c) Hill had canoed out to rescue the deceased but changed his mind when he arrived at the scene?

4. Assuming that a duty to rescue had been imposed on Hill, how would you define the standard of care? Should the defendant be required to take action which might involve: (a) a risk of personal injury, (b) a risk of property damage, or (c) considerable inconvenience?

5. There are several situations in which the common law now imposes a duty to rescue. Defendants have an obligation to intervene if they innocently or negligently create the plaintiff's perilous situation. See *Oke v. Weide Transport* (1963), 41 D.L.R. (2d) 53 (Man. C.A.). So too, as discussed below, if they deny the plaintiff other opportunities for aid, or induce the plaintiff to rely upon them to the plaintiff's detriment. How do these situations differ from that in *Osterlind*?

6. The debate regarding the duty to rescue typically arises after high-profile, morally repugnant cases. For example, in 1964 the tenants of an apartment complex idly watched and listened for forty minutes as Kitty Genovese, who was being attacked in the street below, called for help. She was eventually murdered by her assailant. See Rosenthal, *Thirty-Eight Witnesses: The Kitty Genovese Case* (1999). Another notorious case occurred in 1997, when a young girl named Sherrice Iverson was raped and killed in the bathroom of a Las Vegas casino. The murderer was criminally convicted, but the greater controversy surrounded the murderer's friend, David Cash, who watched the attack but did nothing to stop his friend or save the dying girl. The Cash case rejuvenated the duty to rescue debate and prompted some states to take legislative action.

However, empirical data suggest that cases of non-rescue are rare – probably only one or two every year in the United States. In fact, the data indicate that confirmed rescues outnumber non-rescues by a ratio of 740:1, and that for every victim who dies due to non-rescue, there are 70 people who die making rescue attempts: Hyman, "Rescue Without Law: An Empirical Perspective on the Duty to Rescue" (2006) 84 Tex. L. Rev. 653. These data suggest that people are generally altruistic (even foolishly so), and will attempt rescue in the absence of any legal obligation to do so. Given this evidence, is a legal duty to rescue necessary? Do one or two heinous cases justify legislative action?

7. Would a legal duty to rescue change the behaviour of those who are currently non-rescuers? There are many reasons why people fail to rescue: although some people may be morally indifferent to suffering, others fail to respond because of common human emotions – shock, fear, panic, loyalty and guilt. Are such people likely to change their behaviour in response to a legal duty to rescue? Would it be fair to hold them liable for the victim's losses? See Volokh, "Duties to Rescue and the Anticooperative Effects of Law" (1999) 88 Geo. L.J. 105.

8. In spite of its arguably limited practical impact, the debate over the duty to rescue has generated much scholarship, cutting to the heart of fundamental tort concepts like the relationship between law and morality, the distinction between acts and omissions, and the appropriate boundaries of the tort of negligence. See generally Ratcliffe, ed., *The Good Samaritan and the Law* (1966); Heyman, "Foundations of the Duty to Rescue"

(1994) 47 Vand. L. Rev. 673; Fleming, *The Law of Torts*, 9th ed. (1998) at 164-66; Ziegler, "Nonfeasance and the Duty to Assist: The American *Seinfeld* Syndrome" (2000) 104 Dick. L. Rev. 525; "Good Samaritan Symposium" (2000) 40 Santa Clara L. Rev. 957-1103; and The American Law Institute, *Restatement of the Law, Third, Torts: Liability for Physical Harm* (Proposed Final Draft No. 1) (2005) at §§37-44.

•

MATTHEWS v. MACLAREN; HORSLEY v. MACLAREN

(1969), 4 D.L.R. (3d) 557 (Ont. H.C.)

LACOURCIÈRE J.: – These two actions under the *Fatal Accidents Act*, R.S.O. 1960, c. 138, were tried together, and involve the claim of the widows and children respectively of the late Roland Edgar Matthews and the late John Albert Horsley, both of whom lost their lives in a tragedy on Lake Ontario on May 7, 1966. The defendant Kenneth MacLaren was at the material time the owner and operator of an Owens, Empress 30-foot six inch cabin cruiser known as the "Ogopogo" powered by two inboard 100 h.p. engines driving two propellors or twin screws. . . .

On the day of the fatal accident, the late Roland Edgar Matthews and the late John Albert Horsley were gratuitous passengers, or invited guests, of the defendant on this boat, which left Port Credit Yacht Club at approximately 6:30 p.m. for the return voyage to Oakville. The weather at that time was starting to cool and a wind, blowing from the north-west created a light chop on Lake Ontario. The "Ogopogo" with the defendant at the helm was proceeding at a speed of 10 to 12 knots; at that time Matthews, who had looked after the bowline on leaving Port Credit, was still sitting on the port side of the foredeck: another passenger, . . . Richard J. Jones, was in the pilot's cockpit and the other four passengers, *i.e.*, Horsley, one Donald Marck, and the two ladies – Mrs. MacLaren and Mrs. Jones – were in the cabin below. Jones observed Matthews get up and proceed towards the stern along the narrow catwalk on the port side of the boat, holding on to the rail, with his back to the water, and topple over backwards at the level of the windscreen. Jones immediately hollered "Roly's overboard" and the rescue operation began.

The defendant threw the boat controls in the neutral position and on leaning back could see Matthews, floating, with head and shoulders out of the water, some 40 or 50 ft. astern to starboard: he reversed the motors and backed towards Matthews, having pinned the control wheel with his stomach and looking over his shoulder using the throttle to manoeuvre and, according to Jones, swerving a bit, until the man in the water disappeared from his view behind the transom. The defendant then shut the engines down completely to drift towards Matthews: meanwhile, Jones had gone to the stern and thrown a life ring which landed some 10 ft. in front of Matthews, and as the boat got closer Donald Marck, also at the stern, was attempting to hook Matthews with a six-foot pikepole. Matthews was still floating – arms outward with his eyes open and staring, apparently unconscious. The motors had been shut down when the stern of the boat got to within four or five feet of Matthews, who could not be hooked when the boat was blown or drifted away a distance of 10 to 20 ft. The defendant MacLaren started the engines and reversed again towards Matthews. Meanwhile, Jones had thrown a second life-jacket which had fallen on top of Matthews or under his nose.

By then some three or four minutes had elapsed since Matthews had fallen overboard and the situation was getting desperate. Horsley from the stern took off his shoes and trousers and yelling "my friend, my friend!" dived in while the boat was moving, and surfaced some 10 ft. away from Matthews. Mrs. Jones then noticed Matthews' body fall forward – face and head in the water: she then courageously jumped in, one foot away, to hold his head up but Matthews had gone under the starboard quarter and could not be helped. Jones, seeing his wife in the water ran up to the defendant and took over the controls without argument, swung the boat around and approached his wife "bow on", getting her on the starboard side. MacLaren and Marck grabbed her arms and pulled her out of the water. MacLaren reassumed the controls and shortly thereafter Horsley was picked up, but could not be resuscitated and was pronounced dead later at Port Credit.

Although the outside temperature had been warm and pleasant in the afternoon, with a temperature of approximately 65°, the water was extremely cold: the only person who survived the immersion, Jean Jones, described how she felt paralysed, as if in a vat of ice cubes. The witness Burtershaw, chief operator of the Waterworks Department of the Oakville Public Utilities, gave evidence that the recorded water temperature at the intake pipe some 2,400 ft. from shore was a constant 39° on that day, with surface temperature probably five degrees higher.

The pathologist, Dr. D. F. Brunsdon, who examined Horsley's body, ascribed the cause of death to cardiac failure resulting from either sudden shock on immersion or from prolonged immersion in cold water. In the latter case, unconsciousness would precede death. It was his opinion after conducting the autopsy that death was probably due to sudden shock as a result of immersion, in which case death would be immediate or extremely quick; the deceased had been perfectly healthy before and there was no evidence of heart or any other disease. The body of Matthews was never recovered and the cause of his death remains undetermined.

Because of the allegation made in both actions (among other items of negligence) that the defendant was operating his motor boat while his ability to do so was impaired by alcohol, I will summarize the events leading up to the tragic occurrence.

The defendant, then a 51-year-old steel salesman, had earlier in the morning one pint of beer with a sandwich at the Oakville Club, later a hamburger and one beer at the Oakville Powerboat Club with Mr. and Mrs. Jones; the outing was improvised, and a case of 24 pints of beer put on board: the defendant and each passenger had one pint of beer on the trip to Port Credit. The arrival of the "Ogopogo" at the Port Credit Club, and the docking process there was described in great detail by various witnesses because of the incident of damage to the stanchion, a vertical member of the stainless steel pulpit, on the stern of the "Stormalong" which was slightly damaged when hit by the bow of the "Ogopogo". I am satisfied that this was a mere mishap caused by the temporary failure of one engine of the "Ogopogo", which can in no way reflect on the ability of the defendant who was at the helm.

The defendant, as captain of the first boat – so he claimed – to dock at the Port Credit Yacht Club that season, arrived in jovial and exuberant mood and ordered champagne for all present. The steward of the yacht club relates that approximately forty people in the club shared four large (32 oz.) bottles of champagne. The MacLaren party was in the club between 3:30 and 6:30. The defendant admits having consumed two glasses of champagne during that period, intermingling freely with the Port Credit members, many of whom were friends. There is no evidence that the defendant had any of the other drinks being ordered and served that afternoon. After the accident, a glass of amber coloured liquid, presumably containing whisky, was found in a glass-holder near the controls of the cockpit. The defendant disclaims any knowledge of its contents and says that it must have been pressed upon him by friends upon leaving the dock of the Port Credit Yacht Club and forgotten and untouched by him.

Liability:

1. *Re Matthews' Claim*

Notwithstanding the allegations pleaded that the defendant failed to ensure the safety of his passengers and particularly of the deceased Matthews by having them wear life-preservers on board, I am satisfied that in the circumstances this does not constitute actionable negligence. The only negligence argued here relates to the defendant's condition and to his conduct following Matthews' fall into the water. The first question therefore is whether there existed a legal duty on the part of the defendant to come to the rescue of a passenger who fell overboard by reason of his own misfortune or carelessness, and without any negligence on the part of the defendant or any person for whom the defendant would be vicariously responsible. This question, strictly a determination of law for the Court and not a question of fact for the jury, was repeatedly answered in the negative in the 19th century decisions (based on the distinction between "misfeasance" and "nonfeasance") illustrated in Ontario by the 1913 decision of the Ontario Court of Appeal in *Vanvalkenburg v. Northern Navigation Co.* (1913), . . . 19 D.L.R. 649. In that case, a seaman employed on a steamboat had fallen overboard by his own carelessness, and drowned: Mulock C.J.Ex., speaking for the Appellate Division said at . . . p. 652 D.L.R.:

> The question then arises whether the defendants were guilty of any actionable negligence in not using all reasonable means in order to rescue the drowning man. Undoubtedly such is one's moral duty, but what legal duty did the defendants owe to the deceased to rescue him, if possible, from his position of danger, brought about, not by their, but his own, negligence?

And at . . . p. 653 D.L.R.:

> His voluntary act in thus putting himself in a position of danger, from the fatal consequences of which, unfortunately, there was no escape except through the defendants' intervention, could not create a legal obligation on the defendants' part to stop the ship or adopt other means to save the deceased.

This decision was followed by an amendment to the *Canada Shipping Act*, R.S.C. 1927, c. 186, enacting [1934, c. 44, s. 519] what is now s. 526 [R.S.C. 1952, c. 29]:

> 526(1) The master or person in charge of a vessel shall, so far as he can do so without serious danger to his own vessel, her crew and passengers, if any, render assistance to every person, even if that person be a subject of a foreign state at war with her Majesty, who is found at sea and in danger of being lost, and if he fails to do so he is liable to a fine not exceeding one thousand dollars.

The section may not be applicable to or refer to the assistance to a passenger who falls overboard, but the shocking reluctance of the common law to recognize as a legal duty the moral obligation to assist a fellow human being in this predicament has been overcome in cases where a special relation exists, such as that of a carrier to a passenger in peril overboard, by thinly disguising the moral obligation as an "implied contract":

See *Prosser on Torts*, 3rd ed., c. 10, p. 336 under the heading "Duty to Aid One in Peril"; *Fleming on Torts*, 2nd ed., p. 166; *Salmond on Torts*, 14th ed., p. 57.

. . .

It is still in the modern law of negligence that, there is no general duty to come to the rescue of a person who finds himself in peril from a source completely unrelated to the defendant, even where little risk or effort would be involved in assisting: thus a person on a dock can with legal impunity ignore the call for help of a drowning person, even refusing to throw a life ring. The law leaves the remedy to a person's conscience.

There is, however, in the words of Fleming, *ibid.*, at p. 148, ". . . strong support for a duty of affirmative care, including aid and rescue, incidental to certain special relations, like that of employer and employee, carrier and passenger, and occupier and his lawful visitors."

Extending the *quasi*-contractual duty of a carrier to his passenger in peril, it seems to me that the relation between the master of a pleasure boat and his invited guest should also require a legal duty to aid and rescue: Parliament reflecting the conscience of the community has seen fit to impose on the master a duty to render assistance to any stranger, including an enemy alien "found at sea and in danger of being lost" (s. 526, *Canada Shipping Act*); the common law can be no less solicitous for the safety of an invited guest and must impose upon the master the duty to attempt a rescue, when this can be done without imperilling the safety of the vessel, her crew and passengers. The common law must keep pace with the demands and expectations of a civilized community, the sense of social obligation, and brand as tortious negligence the failure to help a man overboard in accordance with the universal custom of the sea.

In any event, if the defendant, as he did here, affirmatively undertakes the rescue operation, he is by law regarded as assuming a duty to act, and will thereafter be liable for his negligence: *Prosser on Torts* (1941), pp. 194-5, puts it this way:

> But further, if the defendant attempts to aid him, and takes control of the situation, he is regarded as entering voluntarily into a relation of responsibility, and hence assuming a duty. Thereafter he will be liable for any failure to use reasonable care in dealing with him, until the emergency has ended, and particularly if he abandons him in a position of danger.

Having found a legal duty to rescue, or a voluntary assumption of duty, the next question is, what is the standard of conduct applicable in the performance of such duty? Bearing in mind that the man in the street would not have any knowledge of a sea rescue operation, the test here is: what would the reasonable boat operator do in the circumstances, attributing to such person the reasonable skill and experience required of the master of a cabin cruiser who is responsible for the safety and rescue of his passengers?

Expert witnesses were called on behalf of the plaintiffs to assist the Court in setting out what such ordinary, prudent, reasonable boat operator would have done in the circumstances. . . . These [experts] agree that there are no statutory regulations or guidelines covering the rescue procedure in a "man overboard" situation, and that none is mentioned in the well-known Canadian booklet "Safety Afloat". This situation, according to them, is a common emergency calling for the common sense of every prudent seaman who should be prepared to react quickly and instinctively, so to speak automatically.

The following should be the procedure followed: having ascertained on which side the man fell, the master first turns his boat towards the same side to clear the propellers and leaves the engine in neutral unless the man overboard is astern and in no danger from them. A life ring is cast, and the master then turns around to approach the man against the wind, allowing him to come on the leeward side where passengers or crewmen can grasp him and haul him in at the lowest point of the boat. The maximum time involved would be one to two minutes or slightly more. Both experts emphasized many reasons why the procedure of reversing the engines and backing should never be adopted, unless in a confined area where the boat cannot be turned around: in addition to loss of control and manoeuvrability, there is the impossibility of keeping sight of the man astern when approaching, the danger of the propellers, and complete loss of control, at the mercy of wind and wave, on shutting down the engines. In the opinion of [one of the experts], the bearing down stern first here adopted by the defendant was the sign of an incompetent operator: the average prudent owner of a 30-foot boat according to both experts should be competent in the rescue procedure described, and if not should not undertake to operate his boat. It is the procedure taught to students, and one in fact known by the defendant and practised by him on many previous occasions.

I can only conclude that the defendant's adoption of the wrong procedure in the circumstances was negligent, being a failure to exercise the reasonable care that the ordinary, prudent, reasonable operator would have shown in effecting the "man overboard" rescue. The defendant in his evidence admitted that he made what he described as an error of judgment and did not attempt to justify the rescue procedure adopted.

Detective Sergeant John Brooks. . ., who had ample opportunity to observe the defendant at the yacht club, and at the Police Station after the accident, formed the opinion that MacLaren's ability to drive an automobile or operate a vessel was impaired by alcohol, and he would have recommended the laying of criminal charges to the Crown Attorney. The admitted consumption by the defendant and the necessary inferences from surrounding circumstances, plus the extraordinary conduct of the defendant during the rescue attempt, force me to the conclusion that the defendant was unable to exercise proper judgment in the emergency created because of his excessive consumption of alcohol.

It is trite law that liability does not follow a finding of negligence, even where there exists a legally recognized duty, unless the defendant's conduct is the effective cause of the loss.

. . .

In the present case the burden is on the plaintiff to prove by a preponderance of evidence that the defendant's negligence was the effective cause of Matthews' death. Obviously the defendant is not responsible for Matthews' fall overboard. There is no evidence in the present case that Matthews was ever alive after falling in the water: all witnesses agree that he was motionless and staring. Bearing in mind that Horsley, a younger man than Matthews, in the opinion of the pathologist probably died of shock immediately or shortly after his immersion, it is reasonable to think that Matthews, 16 years older, did not survive longer, and after he hit the water there never was a sign of life or consciousness. It was impossible in the present case to discharge this burden by a pathologist's report; in the case of a missing body, witnesses' evidence of some struggle or sign of life on the part of the deceased during rescue operations would be required. I am reluctantly forced to the conclusion that, on the balance of probabilities, it has not been shown that Matthews' life could have been saved. The defendant's negligence therefore was not the cause of Matthews' death and there can be no liability.

[Lacourcière J.'s discussion of the action arising from Horsley's death is omitted. It was ultimately resolved by the Supreme Court of Canada on different grounds than Matthews' claim. An extract from that decision is in the next chapter.]

NOTES AND QUESTIONS

1. What was the basis on which Lacourcière J. found that MacLaren was under a duty to rescue Matthews? How would you reconcile this result with the decision in *Vanvalkenburg v. Northern Navigation Co.* (1913), 19 D.L.R. 649 (Ont. C.A.)?

2. Why did Lacourcière J. refer to the *Canada Shipping Act*, R.S.C. 1952, c. 29, s. 526(1)?

3. What standard of care was MacLaren required to meet in rescuing Matthews? What factual evidence did Lacourcière J. rely on in concluding that MacLaren breached this standard?

4. Would the result have been different if the burden had been on MacLaren to prove that his negligence did not cause Matthews' death? For a critical analysis of causation in rescue cases, see Benditt, "Liability for Failing to Rescue" (1982) 1 Law & Phil. 391 at 396-400.

5. What is the *ratio decidendi* of Lacourcière J.'s judgment?

6. In the *Horsley* appeal, both the majority and dissent in the Supreme Court of Canada held that *Vanvalkenburg* was no longer good law and that a special relationship giving rise to a common law duty to rescue exists between boat captains and their gratuitous passengers. The majority held that the trial judge erred in finding that MacLaren had breached the standard of care, whereas the dissent agreed with Lacourcière J. on this issue. See *Horsley v. MacLaren* (1971), 22 D.L.R. (3d) 545 (S.C.C.). For a review of this case, see Binchy, "The Good Samaritan at the Crossroads: A Canadian Signpost" (1974) 25 N.I.L.Q. 147.

7. As illustrated by the Supreme Court of Canada's decision, the courts have greatly expanded the common law duty to rescue in recent years by recognizing new special relationships in which they will impose an affirmative duty to act. What characteristics should the courts consider in determining whether to recognize a special relationship – control, reliance, expertise, or some other factor? Should the relationship that existed between the deceased and the defendant in *Osterlind v. Hill* have been considered a special relationship? See *Pridgen v. Boston Housing Authority*, 308 N.E. 2d 467 (S.C. Mass. 1974). On the expansion of situations involving a duty to rescue in the United States, see Groninger, "No Duty to Rescue: Can Americans Really Leave a Victim Lying in the Street? What Is Left of the American Rule, and Will It Survive Unabated?" (1998-99) 26 Pepp. L. Rev. 353.

8. Should a physician, other health professional, or off-duty police officer or fire-fighter have any special duty to rescue and render aid in an emergency or at the scene of an accident? See McCabe, "Police Officers' Duty to Rescue or Aid: Are They Only

Good Samaritans?" (1984) 72 Cal. L. Rev. 661; and Picard & Robertson, *Legal Liability of Doctors And Hospitals In Canada*, 3d ed. (1996) at 8-10.

In *Stevenson v. Clearview Riverside Resort*, 2000 CarswellOnt 4888 (S.C.J.) (WLeC), Wilson J. dismissed a claim against an off-duty ambulance attendant for failing to advise civilian rescuers on the proper method of stabilizing the victim of a suspected spinal injury. The plaintiff had dived into shallow water and was floating face down. One of his friends entered the water to turn him over so that he would not drown. She and another friend then pulled the plaintiff from the water, possibly causing further damage to his spine. The defendant off-duty ambulance attendant observed the scene, but did not advise the friends that the plaintiff should have been left in the water once it was clear that he could breathe. Wilson J. concluded that there was no special relationship between an off-duty ambulance attendant and a party requiring assistance. At the time, she was simply a private party who had no duty to assist in the rescue.

9. Should physicians have a special duty to respond to a request for urgent medical assistance from one of their regular patients? The early cases suggest not, but the courts have now recognized that health professionals cannot "abandon a patient." Accordingly, a doctor cannot discontinue care without making adequate arrangements for the patient's ongoing medical treatment. Does this principle address the issue of responding to an urgent request for assistance? See generally *Smith v. Rae* (1919), 51 D.L.R. 323 (Ont. C.A.); Picard & Robertson, *supra* at 236-39; and Williams, "Medical Samaritans: Is There a Duty to Treat" (2001) 21 O.J.L.S. 393.

In *Lowns v. Woods* (1996) Aust. Torts Rep. 81 (N.S.W.C.A.), a doctor was held to owe a duty of care to leave his office and render assistance to the plaintiff, who was suffering a severe and prolonged epileptic seizure several hundred metres away. The court emphasized that legislation in New South Wales imposed a clear ethical obligation on doctors to respond to requests for assistance in emergencies. See Haberfield, "*Lowns v. Woods* and the Duty to Rescue" (1998) 6 Tort L. Rev. 56.

10. In *Kent v. Griffiths*, [2000] 2 W.L.R. 1158 (C.A.), the plaintiff suffered an asthma attack in her home. A call was placed to the English equivalent of 911. The defendant, which operated the ambulance service, indicated that it would provide help immediately. Nevertheless, 40 minutes passed before the ambulance arrived at the plaintiff's home. Because of that unreasonable delay, the plaintiff suffered respiratory arrest. She sued the defendant in negligence. The Court of Appeal cautiously held that a duty of care arose in the circumstances. In reaching that conclusion, it stressed that: (i) the ambulance service was part of the health service, and therefore was more akin to a hospital than to a police or firefighting service, (ii) there was, on the facts, no conflict between the plaintiff's interests and the interests of the larger public, and (iii) there was, on the facts, no question of resource allocation. See also *Cragg v. Tone* (2006), 41 C.C.L.T. (3d) 13 (B.C.S.C.).

11. Several countries have enacted broad criminal legislation which imposes a general duty on members of the public to stop and render aid in emergency situations. See Rudzinski, "The Duty to Rescue: A Comparative Analysis" in Radcliffe, ed., *The Good Samaritan and the Law* (1966) 91; Codoppi, "Failure to Rescue and the Continental

Criminal Law" in Menlowe & McCall Smith, eds., *The Duty to Rescue* (1993) 93; McInnes, "The Question of a Duty to Rescue in Canadian Tort Law: An Answer from France" (1990) 13 Dal. L.J. 85; Vranken, "Duty to Rescue in Civil Law and Common Law" (1998) I.C.L.Q. 934; and Tomlinson, "The French Experience with Duty to Rescue: A Dubious Case for Criminal Enforcement" (2000) 20 N.Y.L. Sch. J. Int'l & Comp. L. 451.

In contrast, the *Criminal Code*, R.S.C. 1985, c. C-46, contains only narrow provisions that require an individual to stop and render aid. First, s. 129(b) requires an individual, unless he or she has a reasonable excuse, to comply with an officer's request for assistance in making an arrest or preserving the peace. Second, except in unusual circumstances, s. 252 requires a driver who is involved in an accident to stop and offer assistance if a person is injured. Some of the provincial highway traffic acts contain comparable provisions. See the Law Reform Commission of Canada, *Omissions, Negligence and Endangering (Working Paper 46)* (1985).

12. Quebec's *Charter of Human Rights and Freedoms*, R.S.Q. 1977 c. C-12, s. 2 provides that anyone who is aware of another's peril and is able to assist without risk to himself or herself has a duty to do so. For a successful action to vindicate a breach of this statutory duty, see *Gaudreault c. Drapeau* (1987), 45 C.C.L.T. 202 (C.S. Qc.), where the plaintiff was awarded both compensatory and punitive damages.

13. There are several alternative means of encouraging rescue. Legislation has been enacted in some jurisdictions to provide rescuers with partial immunity from civil proceedings or a statutory right to compensation. See for example the *Volunteer Services Act*, R.S.N.S. 1989, c. 497; the *Compensation for Victims of Crime Act*, R.S.O. 1990, c. C.24, s. 5; and the *Good Samaritan Act, 2001*, S.O. 2001, c. 2 (excerpted below). See also McInnes, "Good Samaritan Statutes: A Summary and Analysis" (1992) 26 U.B.C.L. Rev. 239.

14. In "Waiting for Rescue: An Essay on the Evolution and Incentive Structure of the Law of Affirmative Obligations" (1986) 72 Va. L. Rev. 879, S. Levmore criticizes the existing common law principles because they do not reward those who rescue or punish those who fail to rescue. One author suggests that rewards could be provided by means of restitutionary or salvage awards: McInnes, "Restitution and the Rescue of Life" (1994) 32 Alta. L. Rev. 37; and McInnes, "Life Rescue in Maritime Law" (1994) 25 J. of Maritime L. and Commerce 451.

15. For leading articles supporting a legal duty to rescue, see Weinrib, "The Case for a Duty to Rescue" (1980) 90 Yale L.J. 247; Lipkin, "Beyond Good Samaritans and Moral Monsters: An Individualistic Justification of the General Legal Duty to Rescue" (1983) 31 U.C.L.A.L. Rev. 352; and Prentice, "Expanding the Duty to Rescue" (1985) 19 Suffolk U.L. Rev. 15.

For a sample of arguments against a duty to rescue, see Epstein, "A Theory of Strict Liability" (1973) 2 J. Legal Stud. 151 at 193-204; Denton, "The Case Against a Duty to Rescue" (1991) 4 C.J.L.J. 101; Franklin & Ploeger, "Of Rescue and Report: Should Tort Law Impose a Duty to Help Endangered Persons or Abused Children?" (2000) 40 Santa Clara L. Rev. 991; and Klar, *Tort Law*, 3d ed. (2003) at 174-77.

16. Would you favour or oppose the expansion of criminal or civil liability for failure to rescue? What arguments would you make in support of granting rescuers: (a) some form of civil immunity and (b) a statutory right of compensation? Do you think that the law plays a significant role in encouraging individuals to stop and render aid? Can you suggest additional means of encouraging rescue? See Rosenberg, "The Alternative of Reward and Praise: The Case Against a Duty to Rescue" (1985) 19 Col. J.L. & Soc. Probs. 1. On the behavioural effect of rescue laws, see Brady, "The Duty to Rescue in Tort Law: Implications of Research on Altruism" (1980) 55 Ind. L.J. 551; McInnes, "The Behavioural Implications of Using the Law to Increase the Incidence of Emergency Intervention" (1992) 20 Man. L.J. 656; McInnes, "The Economic Analysis of Rescue Laws" (1992) 21 Man. L.J. 237; Grush, "The Inefficiency of the No-Duty-to-Rescue Rule and a Proposed 'Similar Risk' Alternative" (1998) 146 U. Pa. L. Rev. 881; and Kelley, "A Psychological Approach to Understanding the Legal Basis of the No Duty to Rescue Rule" (2000) 14 B.Y.U. J. Pub. L. 271.

GOOD SAMARITAN ACT, 2001

S.O. 2001, c. 2

Protection from liability

2. (1) Despite the rules of common law, a person described in subsection (2) who voluntarily and without reasonable expectation of compensation or reward provides the services described in that subsection is not liable for damages that result from the person's negligence in acting or failing to act while providing the services, unless it is established that the damages were caused by the gross negligence of the person.

Persons covered

(2) Subsection (1) applies to,

(a) a health care professional who provides emergency health care services or first aid assistance to a person who is ill, injured or unconscious as a result of an accident or other emergency, if the health care professional does not provide the services or assistance at a hospital or other place having appropriate health care facilities and equipment for that purpose; and

(b) an individual, other than a health care professional described in clause (a), who provides emergency first aid assistance to a person who is ill, injured or unconscious as a result of an accident or other emergency, if the individual provides the assistance at the immediate scene of the accident or emergency.

REVIEW PROBLEMS

1. Analyze whether a duty to rescue will be imposed in the following fact situations:

(a) Mike hired a local guide to take him fishing in a canoe. Mike hooked a large carp and stood up in an attempt to land it. The canoe began to rock and Mike, who could not swim, fell into the water.

(b) The guide was paddling while Mike fished from the bow. While daydreaming, the guide paddled into a rock, throwing Mike into the water.

(c) Mike was clinging to a floating log in the water when the guide paddled to his side and urged him to grab his hand and climb back into the canoe. Releasing his hold on the log, Mike lunged for the guide's hand, but missed and fell back into the water.

(d) Luke and John were hunting ducks from a row boat in the vicinity when they heard Mike's screams for help. They rowed close to the log and told Mike to stop yelling, because he was scaring away their game.

(e) When the guide realized that he could not rescue Mike with the canoe, he approached some other hunters for help. They agreed and rowed up to Mike as he was slowly slipping from the log. When they came within five feet of Mike, they changed their minds and rowed off in the opposite direction.

4. The Duty to Control the Conduct of Others

This has been one of the most rapidly expanding areas of negligence law during the last 30 years. While it remains true that there is no general duty to control the conduct of another, the courts have recognized a growing number of special relationships in which a duty will be imposed. The duty to control the conduct of intoxicated people, discussed in the next extract, is simply one example.

(a) LIABILITY FOR THE INTOXICATED

CROCKER v. SUNDANCE NORTHWEST RESORTS LTD.
(1988), 51 D.L.R. (4th) 321 (S.C.C.)

WILSON J.: – The principal issue in this appeal is whether the ski resort had a positive duty at law to take certain steps to prevent a visibly intoxicated person from competing in the resort's dangerous "tubing" competition. The resort contends that it had no such duty but, if it did, it adequately discharged it. The appellant Crocker contends that it had such a duty and failed to discharge it.

I. The Facts

The respondent, Sundance Northwest Resorts Ltd. ("Sundance") operates a ski resort. Sundance held a tubing competition in order to promote its resort. This competition involved teams of two people sliding down a mogulled portion of a steep hill in oversized inner tubes. One evening Crocker went skiing at Sundance with a friend. After their skiing they went to a bar at the resort to drink. At the bar a video of the previous year's race was shown. The video showed people being thrown from their inner tubes. Crocker and his friend did not, however, watch much of this video.

Crocker and his friend decided to enter the competition and attempt to win the $200 in prize money. They signed an entry and waiver form and paid the $15 entry fee. The trial Judge found as a fact, however, that Crocker did not read the form and did not appreciate that it was a waiver.

The race was held 2 days later. On the morning of the race Crocker and his friend drank large quantities of their own alcoholic beverages. They also bought alcoholic drinks from the bar at the resort. They were wearing bibs that identified them as "tubing" competitors when they did so.

Crocker and his friend were the winners of their first heat. During the race the two were thrown from their tube and Crocker suffered a cut above his eye. Between the first and second heats Crocker drank two large swallows of brandy offered to him by the driver of a Molson beer van and was sold two more drinks at the bar.

The owner of Sundance, Beals, saw Crocker between the first and second heats. Noting Crocker's condition Beals asked him whether he was in any condition to compete in another heat. Crocker responded that he was. Beals did nothing more to dissuade him.

At the top of the hill Crocker fell down and his inner tube slid down the hill. The competition organizers obtained a new inner tube for him and his friend. Crocker was visibly drunk and Durno, the manager of Sundance, suggested that it would be a good idea if he did not continue in the competition. But Crocker insisted on competing and Durno took no further steps to restrain him.

Crocker and his friend hit a mogul on the way down the hill. The two were flipped out of their inner tube. Crocker injured his neck in the fall and was rendered a quadriplegic. Earlier that afternoon another competitor had been hospitalized for neck injuries sustained during another heat of the race.

Crocker sued Sundance in tort. At trial Sundance was held to be liable for 75 per cent of the damages suffered by Crocker. Crocker was found contributorily negligent.

. . .

III. The Issue

People engage in dangerous sports every day.

In general, when someone is injured in a sporting accident the law does not hold anyone else responsible. The injured person must rely on private insurance and on the public health care system. The broad issue in the present appeal is whether there is something to distinguish the situation here from the run of the mill sports accident. In order to answer this question the Court must address six sub-issues. . . .

1. *Duty of Care*

The common law has generally distinguished between negligent conduct (misfeasance) and failure to take positive steps to protect others from harm (nonfeasance). The early common law was reluctant to recognize affirmative duties to act. Limited exceptions were carved out where the parties were in a special relationship (e.g., parent and child) or where the defendant had a statutory or contractual obligation to intervene. . . .

Canadian Courts have become increasingly willing to expand the number and kind of special relationships to which a positive duty to act attaches.

. . .

[*Jordan House Ltd. v. Menow* (1973), 38 D.L.R. (3d) 105 (S.C.C.)] is the leading Supreme Court authority on the imposition of a duty to take positive action to protect another. In that case the court held that a licensed tavern owed a duty of care to its intoxicated patron, and was liable when that patron was ejected and was struck by a motor vehicle as he stumbled home on a highway. . .

[Laskin J. writing for the majority in *Jordan House*] . . . considered the relationship between the hotel and Menow and concluded that there was a close enough nexus to require the imposition of a duty of care on the hotel. He stated . . . :

> "The hotel, however, was not in the position of persons in general who see an intoxicated person who appears to be unable to control his steps. It was in an invitor-invitee relationship with Menow as one of its patrons, and it was aware, through its employees, of his intoxicated condition, a condition which, on the findings of the trial judge, it fed in violation of applicable liquor licence and liquor control legislation. There was a probable risk of personal injury to Menow if he was turned out of the hotel to proceed on foot on a much-travelled highway passing in front of the hotel.
>
> . . .
>
> Given the relationship between Menow and the hotel, the hotel operator's knowledge of Menow's propensity to drink and his instruction to his employees not to serve him unless he was accompanied by a responsible person, the fact that Menow was served not only in breach of this instruction but as well in breach of statutory injunctions against serving a patron who was apparently in an intoxicated condition, and the fact that the hotel operator was aware that Menow was intoxicated, the proper conclusion is that the hotel came under a duty to Menow to see that he got home safely by taking him under its charge or putting him under the charge of a responsible person, or to see that he was not turned out alone until he was in a reasonably fit condition to look after himself. There was, in this case, a breach of this duty for which the hotel must respond according to the degree of fault found against it. The harm that ensued was that which was reasonably foreseeable by reason of what the hotel did (in turning Menow out) and failed to do (in not taking preventive measures)."

Thus the relationship between the hotel operator and the patron in this case was close enough to justify the imposition of a duty of care. This duty of care required the defendant to take certain positive steps to avert potential calamity.

The general approach taken in *Jordan House* has been applied in a number of cases. Car owners who have permitted or instructed impaired persons to drive their cars have been found liable . . . The common thread running through these cases is that one is under a duty not to place another person in a position where it is foreseeable that that person could suffer injury. The plaintiff's inability to handle the situation in which he or she has been placed – either through youth, intoxication or other incapacity – is an element in determining how foreseeable the injury is. The issue in the present appeal is whether the relationship between Sundance and Crocker gave rise to this kind of duty.

. . .

Sundance set up an inherently dangerous competition in order to promote its resort and improve its financial future. Sundance employees were in charge of the way in which the event was to be conducted. Sundance provided liquor to Crocker during the event and knew of Crocker's inebriated and injured condition before the start of the second heat. Sundance officials were well aware that Crocker's condition heightened the chance of injury. Both Beals and Durno questioned Crocker's ability to continue. It is clearly not open to Sundance to characterize itself as a stranger to Crocker's misfortune. The nexus between Sundance and Crocker is much too close for that. Sundance must accept the responsibility as the promoter of a dangerous sport for taking all reasonable steps to prevent a visibly incapacitated person from participating.

The jurisprudence in this area seems to me to make this conclusion inevitable. When a railway company removes a drunken passenger from one of its trains it owes a duty of care to this passenger to take reasonable steps to see that the passenger does not come to harm: *Dunn v. Dominion Atlantic Railway Co.* [(1920), 52 D.L.R. 149 (S.C.C.)]. Likewise, when a hotel ejects a drunken patron, it owes a duty of care to the patron to take certain steps to ensure that the patron arrives home safely (*Jordan House*). It would seem a fortiori that when a ski resort establishes a competition in a highly dangerous sport and runs the competition for profit, it owes a duty of care towards visibly intoxicated participants. The risk of calamity in the latter case is even more obvious than in the two preceding cases. I would conclude, therefore, that Sundance was subject to a duty to Crocker to take all reasonable steps to prevent him from entering such a competition. The question that must now be decided is whether Sundance took sufficient steps to discharge that duty.

2. *Standard of Care*

. . .

Numerous steps were open to Sundance to dissuade Crocker from competing. It could, for instance, have disqualified him when it realized he was drunk. This would have been the easiest course to follow. Or it could have tried to prevent him from competing. It certainly did not have to supply him with a fresh tube when he fell down on the slope before the second heat and his tube rolled down to the bottom of the hill! Sundance could have attempted to bring home to Crocker the risk of serious injury in competing while drunk. None of these preventive measures imposed a serious burden on the resort. And yet Sundance did none of them. Sundance officials made mild suggestions that Crocker might not be in any condition to race but this was as far as it went. I agree with the learned trial Judge and with Dubin J.A. dissenting on the Court of Appeal that Sundance failed to meet its standard of care. . . . While it may be acceptable for a ski resort to allow or encourage sober able-bodied individuals to participate in dangerous recreational activities, it is not acceptable for the resort to open its dangerous competitions to persons who are obviously incapacitated. This is, however, what Sundance did when it allowed Crocker to compete. I conclude, therefore, that it failed to meet its standard of care in the circumstances.

3. *Causation*

Sundance strongly urged that, even if it was negligent, its negligence did not cause the injury suffered by Crocker. The argument here is that tubing is inherently dangerous and demands no skill whatsoever. It is thus no more risky to participate in this sport when inebriated than it is to participate in it when sober. Sundance submits, therefore, that Crocker's injury cannot be attributed to his drunkenness. The failure of Sundance to take reasonable steps to prevent Crocker from competing because he was drunk did not cause his injury.

This submission is completely at odds with a finding of fact made at trial.

. . .

4. *Voluntary Assumption of Risk*

The defence of voluntary assumption of risk is based on the moral supposition that no wrong is done to one who consents. By agreeing to assume the risk the plaintiff absolves the defendant of all responsibility for it. . . . Since the volenti defence is a complete bar to recovery and therefore anomalous in an age of apportionment, the Courts have tightly circumscribed its scope. It only applies in situations where the plaintiff has assumed both the physical and the legal risk involved in the activity.

. . .

In the present appeal an attempt could be made to found a volenti defence either on (a) Crocker's voluntary participation in a sport that was obviously dangerous or (b) the fact that Crocker signed a waiver form 2 days before the competition. I will examine each of these bases in turn.

The first basis can be disposed of in short order. Crocker's participation in the tubing competition could be viewed as an assumption of the physical risks involved. Even this, however, is dubious because of the fact that his mind was clouded by alcohol at the time. It is well-nigh impossible to conclude, however, that he assumed the legal risk involved. Sliding down a hill in an oversized inner tube cannot be viewed as constituting per se a waiver of Crocker's legal rights against Sundance.

The argument that Crocker voluntarily assumed the legal risk of his conduct by signing a combined entry and waiver form is not particularly convincing either. The trial Judge, having heard all the evidence, drew the following conclusion on the issue of the waiver. . .:

> "I find that no attempt was made to draw the release provision to Mr. Crocker's attention, that he did not read it, nor in fact, did he know of its existence. Therefore, Sundance had no reasonable grounds for believing that the release truly expressed Mr. Crocker's intention. In fact, in so far as he was signing anything other than an application form, his signing was not his act."

Given this finding of fact, it is difficult to conclude that Crocker voluntarily absolved the resort of legal liability for negligent conduct in permitting him, while intoxicated, to participate in its tubing competition. I would conclude, therefore, that Crocker did not, either by word or conduct, voluntarily assume the legal risk involved in competing. The volenti defence is inapplicable in the present case.

[Wilson J. applied the same analysis to reject the waiver as a contractual defence. She accepted the trial judge's finding that Crocker should be held only 25% contributorily negligent. In the end result, the trial judgment was restored and a new trial was ordered to assess damages.]

NOTES AND QUESTIONS

1. Based on Wilson J.'s judgment, would the Resort have owed Crocker a duty to control his conduct if: (a) he was equally intoxicated, but the Resort had not provided him with any alcohol, or (b) he was sober when allowed to participate in the race? What impact would these factors have on whether the standard of care had been breached?

2. Do you agree with Wilson J.'s analysis of voluntary assumption of risk and contributory negligence? What other steps could the Resort have taken to alert Crocker to the dangers? Would this have changed Wilson J.'s analysis of these issues?

3. *Jordan House*, which is referred to in *Crocker*, generated considerable criticism. In Binchy, "Comment" (1975) 53 Can. Bar Rev. 344, the author was critical of the

apportionment of fault, the dismissal of the *volenti* defence and the failure to consider the *ex turpi* defence. See also Scott, "Negligence: Duty of Care" (1974) 6 Ottawa L. Rev. 622. For more recent reviews, see Klar, "Negligence – Reactions Against Alleged Excessive Imposition of Liability – A Turning Point?" (1987) 66 Can. Bar Rev. 159; Solomon, Usprich & Waldock, "Drink, Drive and Sue: Liability for the Intoxicated" (1993) 4 J.M.V.L. 239; McIvor, "Liability in Respect of the Intoxicated" [2001] C.L.J. 109; and Dalphond, "Duty of Care and the Supply of Alcohol" in Beaulac, Pitel & Schulz, eds., *The Joy of Torts* (2002) 97.

4. The common law duty to control the conduct of the intoxicated person was broadened in a series of cases. In both *Picka v. Porter*, [1980] O.J. No. 252 (C.A.) (QL) and *Schmidt v. Sharpe* (1983), 27 C.C.L.T. 1 (Ont. H.C.), the courts held the alcohol provider liable even though it did not have actual knowledge of the patron's intoxication. In *Hague v. Billings* (1989), 48 C.C.L.T. 192 (H.C.), aff'd (1993), 15 C.C.L.T. (2d) 264 (Ont. C.A.) the Ontario High Court stated that, once the staff realized that Billings was intoxicated and intended to drive, they had a legal duty to take all reasonable steps to stop him. If they failed, they then had a legal duty to call the police. The court also stated that Billings' drinking buddies were equally liable with him for the accident because all three had agreed in advance to go drinking and driving. See *Pizzolon v. Pedrosa* (1988), 46 C.C.L.T. 243 (B.C.S.C.); *Roberts v. 964639 Ontario Ltd.*, [1996] O.J. No. 56 (Gen. Div.) (QL); *Neufeld v. Foster*, 1999 CarswellBC 785 (S.C.) (WLeC); *Laface v. Williams* (2006), 39 C.C.L.T. (3d) 209 (B.C.C.A); and *McIntyre v. Grigg* (2006), 83 O.R. (3d) 161 (C.A.).

5. The trend toward broadening the scope of alcohol-related liability was somewhat checked by *Stewart v. Pettie*, [1995] 1 S.C.R. 131. While an alcohol provider's duty to prevent foreseeable risks of injury posed by intoxicated patrons was reaffirmed, the Supreme Court of Canada held that serving patrons past the point of intoxication did not, in itself, pose a foreseeable risk. Rather, the court held that there had to be some additional risk factor. Since the intoxicated defendant in this case was accompanied by three sober adults, the court held that it was not foreseeable that he would drive. Consequently, the defendant dinner theatre, which had served the intoxicated driver between five and seven double rum and colas, was held not to have breached the standard of care. Given the somewhat convoluted analysis, the unique circumstances, and the fact that the case could have been resolved on the basis of causation, the decision's long-term impact is unclear. See Kostal, "Liability for the Sale of Alcohol: *Stewart v. Pettie*" (1996) 75 Can. Bar Rev. 169.

6. Judicial restraint is also evident in *Calliou Estate (Trustee of) v. Calliou* (2002), 306 A.R. 322 (Q.B.). The defendant hockey team organized and hosted a tournament. In exchange for an entry fee of $350, competing teams were provided with, among other things, beer. A number of people died as a result of an automobile accident that was caused by an intoxicated player. Actions were brought in negligence against the defendant on the basis that it had supplied some of the alcohol that the drunken driver had consumed. The court denied the existence of a duty of care. The judge held that the facts arose somewhere between the model of a social host and the model of a commercial establishment. He held that, in any event, "the thread running through both the commercial host and the social host cases on the question of duty of care, is a knowledge of a state of

intoxication on the part of the guest who drives and injures himself or a third party." On the evidence, however, there is nothing to indicate that the defendant knew, or ought to have known, that the intoxicated driver was drunk.

7. In *Baumeister v. Drake* (1986), 5 B.C.L.R. (2d) 382 (S.C.), the court applied the liability principles from *Jordan House* to a private social host. The claim against the defendant homeowners was dismissed, but only because they had not provided any alcohol to the intoxicated driver. See also *Broadfoot v. Ontario (Minister of Transportation and Communication)* (1997), 32 O.R. (3d) 361 (Gen. Div.); *Fitkin (Litigation Administrator of) v. Latimer* (1997), 35 O.R. (3d) 464 (C.A.); *Haggarty v. Desmarais* (2000), 5 C.C.L.T. (3d) 38 (B.C.S.C.); *Prevost (Committee of) v. Vetter* (2001), 197 D.L.R. (4th) 292 (B.C.S.C.); and *Dryden v. Campbell Estate* (2001), 11 M.V.R. (4th) 247 (Ont. S.C.J.).

The continued authority of these cases may be questionable in light of the Supreme Court of Canada's decision in *Childs v. Desormeaux*, [2006] 1 S.C.R. 643. The defendants hosted a New Year's Eve party at which guests supplied and served their own alcohol. One of the guests was Desmond Desormeaux, who, to the defendants' knowledge, was an alcoholic with several convictions for drunk driving. Although Desormeaux had become obviously and severely intoxicated during the party, the defendants took no steps to dissuade him from driving home. After leaving the defendants' party, Desormeaux caused a crash that left the plaintiff, 18-year-old Zoe Childs, a paraplegic. The plaintiff sued the defendants in negligence.

The trial judge had found that the alleged duty of care owed by social hosts was novel, and applied the *Anns/Cooper* test. He found that a *prima facie* duty of care existed, but was negated for policy reasons. The Court of Appeal for Ontario upheld the result, but on the different basis that there was insufficient proximity on the facts to even establish a *prima facie* duty. The Supreme Court of Canada unanimously agreed. Somewhat curiously, the court decided that allowing guests to become intoxicated in a private residence, and then leave in their vehicles, did not pose a foreseeable risk of harm to other users of the highway. The court also stressed the lack of proximity, distinguishing social hosts from commercial hosts on several bases. First, commercial hosts have a greater ability to monitor alcohol consumption among patrons; second, social hosts are not heavily regulated like those who hold liquor licences; and third, social hosts do not profit from the sale of alcohol. Are these arguments convincing? Would the decision have been different if the hosts actually provided the alcohol to their guests?

See generally Adjin-Tettey, "Social Host Liability: A Logical Extension of Commercial Host Liability?" (2002) 65 Sask. L.R. 515; David, Maroudas & Litchen, "Social Host Liability – A Fresh Approach" (2005) 30 Adv. Q. 457; Kelly, "Before You Host a Party, Read This: Social Host Liability and the Decision in *Childs v. Desmormeaux*" (2006) 39 U.B.C.L. Rev. 371; and Malkin & Voon, "Social Hosts' Responsibility for their Intoxicated Guests: Where Courts Fear to Tread" (2007) 15 Torts L.J. 62. For an American perspective, see French, Kaput & Wildman, "Special Project: Social Host Liability for the Negligent Acts of Intoxicated Guests" (1985) 70 Cornell L. Rev. 1958; and Sparlin, "Social Host Liability for Guests who Drink and Drive: A Closer Look at the Benefits and the Burdens" (1985-96) 27 Wm. & Mary L. Rev. 583.

8. The courts have begun, in some circumstances, to impose a rigorous duty on employers to control the conduct of employees who may be intoxicated. See *Barrett v.*

Ministry of Defence, [1995] 3 All E.R. 87 (C.A.); and *Jacobsen v. Nike Canada Ltd.* (1996), 133 D.L.R. (4th) 377 (B.C.S.C.).

In *Hunt (Litigation Guardian of) v. Sutton Group Incentive Realty Inc.* (2001), 196 D.L.R. (4th) 738 (Ont. S.C.J.), the plaintiff became intoxicated during a Christmas party hosted by the defendant, who was her employer. She attempted to drive herself home from the party. After stopping for two more drinks at a pub, she was severely injured when she lost control of her vehicle on a wintry road. At trial, liability was imposed on both the defendant and the pub (although damages were reduced by 75% on account of the plaintiff's contributory negligence). On the question of a duty of care, the judge said:

> I find that the defendant. . ., as the plaintiff's employer, did . . . owe a duty to the plaintiff, as its employee, to safeguard her from harm. This duty to safeguard her from harm extended beyond the simple duty while she was on his premises. It extended to a duty to make sure that she would not enter into such a state of intoxication while on his premises and on duty so as to interfere with her ability to safely drive home afterwards. This duty was certainly much more evident in the circumstances where the employee was required to travel a substantial distance, at night-time, in the middle of a serious winter storm. [The defendant] ought to have foreseen the dangerous conditions made worse by the intoxicated condition of his employee. He ought to have anticipated the possible harm that could have happened to her and, in fact, taken positive steps to prevent her from driving home.

The Court of Appeal for Ontario ordered a retrial because the trial judge had made several errors, most notably in discharging the jury on the basis that the case was purportedly too complex and had attracted a great deal of publicity: (2002), 215 D.L.R. (4th) 193 (Ont. C.A.). Unfortunately, the appellate court did not squarely address the duty of care issue.

In *John v. Flynn* (2001), 201 D.L.R. (4th) 500 (Ont. C.A.), Shawn Flynn was employed by a company named Eaton Yale. Because he had a severe drinking problem, Flynn had been enrolled in the defendant's "employee assistance program" (EAP) and returned to work under a "last chance agreement" that required him to refrain from drinking on the job. Nevertheless, to the company's knowledge, Flynn continued to abuse alcohol. On the day in question, he drank before reporting to work and during his breaks. At the end of his shift, he drove home without incident, drank more alcohol and then got back into his car. He caused a crash that resulted in injuries to the plaintiffs. The plaintiffs sued Flynn and the defendant company in negligence. The trial judge split responsibility between Flynn and the defendant on a 70%-30% basis. On appeal, the defendant denied that it owed a duty of care to the plaintiff. The Court of Appeal for Ontario agreed. Finlayson J.A. said:

> In my view, the respondents have not established that Eaton Yale owed the Johns a duty of care, which, if breached, could form the foundation of a claim for liability in the circumstances of this case. The fact that Flynn was involved in the EAP . . . and the fact that Eaton Yale was aware that some drinking was occurring on its premises, without more, are not sufficient to establish an expansive duty of care on Eaton Yale to all members of the public who may come into contact with Eaton Yale employees outside the Eaton Yale plant. . . . The trial judge erred in assuming that Eaton Yale, as employer, owed a duty to Flynn, as employee, to protect Flynn from harm, in general, and that this duty of care could be properly extended to hold Eaton Yale liable for all of Flynn's actions following his departure from work. A more thorough examination of the prerequisite issue of duty would have revealed that in the case at bar, there is simply no

basis to hold Eaton Yale liable for the loss suffered by the [plaintiffs], given that Eaton Yale was not aware that Flynn was intoxicated on the night in question, did not provide him with alcohol on that night and did not condone his driving while intoxicated, combined with the fact that the accident was not associated with Eaton Yale in any way other than that one of its employees, who had finished his shift for the night, was involved in the crash. The Johns were not within the class of persons to whom a duty of care was owed by Eaton Yale.

What distinction, if any, would you draw between *John v. Flynn* and *Hunt v. Sutton Group*? Should a duty more readily be recognized if alcohol is provided by the employer, rather than by the employee? If a duty of care is recognized as between the employer and the employee, should the employer also necessarily owe a duty of care to anyone injured by the employee?

9. The liquor licence legislation in many jurisdictions, including Manitoba, Nova Scotia, Ontario, and the Northwest Territories, creates a statutory cause of action against those who sell alcohol to a patron past the point of intoxication. Although these provisions differ in scope, they all create a narrower cause of action than that created by the common law. See for example the *Liquor Licence Act*, R.S.O. 1990, c. L.19, s. 39.

10. Courts may be more likely to impose social host liability where the hosts provide alcohol to or facilitate alcohol consumption by minors. See *Wince v. Ball* (1996), 186 A.R. 156 (Q.B.); *Prevost (Committee of) v. Vetter*, *supra*; and *Dryden v. Campbell Estate*, *supra*.

11. Members of the hospitality industry and private social hosts have long been held liable under principles of occupiers' liability for alcohol-related injuries that occur on their property. See *Lehnert v. Nelson*, [1947] 4 D.L.R. 473 (B.C.S.C.); *Niblock v. Pacific National Exhibition* (1981), 30 B.C.L.R. 20 (S.C.); *Jacobson v. Kinsmen Club of Nanaimo* (1976), 71 D.L.R. (3d) 227 (B.C.S.C.); *Buehl v. Polar Star Enterprises Inc.* (1989), 72 O.R. (2d) 573 (H.C.); *Murphy v. Little Memphis Cabaret Ltd.*, 1996 CarswellOnt 5170 (Gen. Div.) (WLeC), aff'd (1998), 115 O.A.C. 375 (C.A.); *Iversen v. Purser* (1990), 73 D.L.R. (4th) 33 (B.C.S.C.); and *Chretien v. Jensen* (1999), 58 B.C.L.R. (3d) 186 (C.A.).

12. The courts have also held that the owner of a vehicle has a common law duty not to permit an intoxicated person to drive. See *Hempler v. Todd* (1970), 14 D.L.R. (3d) 637 (Man. Q.B.); *Betts v. Sanderson Estate* (1988), 31 B.C.L.R. (2d) 1 (C.A.); and *Hall v. Hebert*, [1993] 2 S.C.R. 159. Should a common law duty of care also be imposed on an owner who lends his or her car to a friend for a week, knowing that the friend has a tendency to drink and drive?

13. Should the police be held civilly liable for failing to detain or otherwise prevent an intoxicated individual from driving? See *Hooey v. Mancini*, [1988] 4 W.W.R. 149 (Man. Q.B.); *Lafleur v. Maryniuk* (1990), 48 B.C.L.R. (2d) 180 (S.C.); and *Meraw v. Curl Estate* (1998), 43 C.C.L.T. (2d) 47 (Ont. Gen. Div.).

14. Given that approximately 40% of all fatal car accidents involve at least one intoxicated driver, and that alcohol is a significant factor in many murders, suicides,

drownings, falls, fires, and other serious crimes and accidents, would you favour creating broader common law and statutory duties for those who provide alcohol to others? See E. Single *et al.*, "Morbidity and Mortality Attributable to Alcohol, Tobacco, and Illicit Drug Use in Canada" (1999) 89 A.J.P.H. 385; Pernanen *et al.*, *Proportions of Crimes Associated with Alcohol and Other Drugs in Canada* (2002); Canadian Council of Motor Transport Administrators, *Road Safety Vision 2010 – The 2000 Update* (2002); and Mercer, *Estimating the Presence of Alcohol and Drug Impairment in Traffic Crashes and their Costs to Canadians: 1999 to 2003* (2005).

15. Alcohol-related liability in Canada is generally broader than in other Commonwealth countries, where it is sometimes even difficult to claim against a commercial host. See for example *Munro v. Porthkerry Park Holiday Estates Ltd.* (1984) 81 L.S.G. 1368 (Eng. Q.B.), where an intoxicated patron was ejected from a club at the defendant's cliff-top resort, fell off the cliff and died. His estate's claim against the resort was denied. See also *Joy v. Newell (t/a Copper Room)*, [2000] N.I. 91 (C.A.). But see the English Court of Appeal's decisions in *Brannon v. Airtours plc*, [1999] T.L.R. 73; and *Jebson v. Ministry of Defence*, [2000] 1 W.L.R. 2055, both of which imposed liability on commercial or institutional party organizers after their guests became intoxicated and sustained foreseeable injury. For an overview, see Chamberlain, "Alcohol Provider Liability in Canada and the United Kingdom: Legal and Cultural Influences" (2004) 33 C.L.W.R. 103. The Australian courts are similarly more cautious in imposing alcohol liability. See generally *Cole v. South Tweed Heads Rugby League Football Club Limited*, [2004] H.C.A. 29; and Solomon & Payne, "Alcohol Liability in Canada and Australia: Sell, Serve and be Sued" (1996) 4 Tort L. Rev. 188.

(b) OTHER DUTY TO CONTROL SITUATIONS

There are a variety of situations in which one person has the ability to control the actions of another. Generally speaking, that relationship of control is not sufficient to trigger the doctrine of vicarious liability. Consequently, for instance, parents normally are not vicariously liable for torts committed by their children. As discussed in Chapter 3, that is true even in jurisdictions that have enacted "parental responsibility legislation." Parents typically are liable only if, by failing to properly supervise their children, they also failed to fulfill a duty of care that they separately owed to the victims of their children's misconduct.

It is therefore important to understand the situations in which one person will owe a duty of care to another person with respect to the behaviour of a third. The duty of care that arises in connection with the parent and child relationship is the most obvious. A duty similarly may arise in connection with relationships between masters and servants, employers and employees, occupiers and entrants, police/guards and prisoners, and coaches/instructors/supervisors and students.

NOTES AND QUESTIONS

1. For general discussions of the duty to control, see Harper & Kime, "The Duty to Control the Conduct of Another" (1934) 43 Yale L.J. 886; and Hall, "Duty to Protect, Duty to Control and the Duty to Warn" (2003) 82 Can. Bar Rev. 645.

2. A duty of care is imposed on those supervising prisoners to ensure that they do not injure themselves, each other or members of the public. See *Williams v. New Brunswick* (1985), 34 C.C.L.T. 299 (N.B.C.A.) (where a prisoner set a fire that killed 21 inmates in jail); *Funk Estate v. Clapp* (1988), 54 D.L.R. (4th) 512 (B.C.C.A.) (where a prisoner committed suicide); *Smith v. B.C. (A.G.)* (1988), 30 B.C.L.R. (2d) 356 (C.A.) (where one prisoner was beaten by other prisoners in a drunk tank); and *Home Office v. Dorset Yacht Co.*, [1970] A.C. 1004 (H.L.) (where prisoners escaped and damaged the plaintiff's property). See also *S.(J.) v. Clement* (1995), 22 O.R. (3d) 495 (Gen. Div.); *Jerabek c. Accueil Vert-Pré d'Huberdeau* (1995), 26 C.C.L.T. (2d) 208 (C.S. Qc.); *Rhora v. Ontario* (2006), 43 C.C.L.T. (3d) 78 (Ont. C.A.); and *Wiebe v. Canada (Attorney General)* (2006), 44 C.C.L.T. (3d) 15 (Man. C.A.).

3. Similar principles apply to those responsible for supervising institutionalized mental health patients. See *Univ. Hospital Bd. v. Lepine; Monckton v. Lepine*, [1966] S.C.R. 561; *Villemure v. L'Hôpital Notre-Dame* (1972), [1973] S.C.R. 716; *Wellesley Hospital v. Lawson* (1977), [1978] 1 S.C.R. 893; *Jinks v. Cardwell* (1987), 39 C.C.L.T. 168 (Ont. H.C.), rev'd [1989] O.J. No. 1492 (C.A.) (QL); *Molnar v. Coates* (1991), 5 C.C.L.T. (2d) 236 (B.C.C.A.); and *Roy c. Toxi-Co-Gîtes inc.* (2004), 33 C.C.L.T. (3d) 87 (C.S. Qc.). See also *Shackleton v. Knittle* (1999), 46 C.C.L.T. (2d) 300 (Alta. Q.B.) for a discussion of the duty and standard of care expected of ambulance attendants in transporting patients with mental illnesses.

See *Robson v. Ashworth* (1987), 40 C.C.L.T. 164 (Ont. C.A.); *Mustafic v. Smith* (1988), 55 Man. R. (2d) 188 (C.A.); *Larche v. Ontario* (1990), 75 D.L.R. (4th) 377 (Ont. C.A.); *Wenden v. Trikha* (1991), 8 C.C.L.T. (2d) 138 (Alta. Q.B.), aff'd (1993), 14 C.C.L.T. (2d) 225 (C.A.); and *Holan Estate v. Stanton Regional Health Board* (2001), 11 C.C.L.T. (3d) 34 (N.W.T.S.C.), where health professionals were absolved of liability when non-custodial mentally ill patients were injured, or committed suicide or acts of violence against third parties. See also Simon, "Tort Law: The Duty to Control the Conduct of a Dangerous Person" (1987) 39 U. Fla. L. Rev. 205.

4. An employer may be held personally or vicariously liable if it fails to prevent abuse or harassment in the workplace. See *Clark v. Canada* (1994), 20 C.C.L.T. (2d) 241 (F.C.); *Waters v. Commissioner of Police for the Metropolis,* [2000] 1 W.L.R. 1607 (H.L.); *L.(J.) v. Canada (Attorney General)* (1999), 175 D.L.R. (4th) 559 (B.C.S.C.); *Rees v. Canada (Royal Canadian Mounted Police)* (2004), 239 Nfld. & P.E.I.R. 1 (Nfld. S.C.T.D.), rev'd on jurisdictional grounds (2005), 246 Nfld. & P.E.I.R. 79 (Nfld. C.A.); and *Sulz v. Canada (Attorney General)* (2006), 54 B.C.L.R. (4th) 328 (S.C.), aff'd (2006), 60 B.C.L.R. (4th) 43 (C.A.).

5. Coaches, instructors and supervisors may be sued on several grounds, including failure to control the participants and failure to provide adequate warnings, instruction and equipment. See *Schulz v. Leeside Dev. Ltd.*, [1978] 5 W.W.R. 620 (B.C.C.A.); *Myers v. Peel County Board of Education*, [1981] 2 S.C.R. 21; *Michalak v. Governors of Dalhousie College and University* (1983), 133 A.P.R. 374 (N.S.C.A.); *Bain v. Calgary Board of Education* (1993), 18 C.C.L.T. (2d) 249 (Alta. Q.B.); *Lunenburg (County) District School Board v. Piercey* (1998), 41 C.C.L.T. (2d) 60 (N.S.C.A.); and *MacCabe v. Westlock Roman Catholic Separate School District No. 110* (2001), 293 A.R. 41 (C.A.). See also Kelly, "Prospective Liabilities of Sports Supervisors" (1989) 63 Aust.

L.J. 669; Davis, "Sports Liability of Coaches and School Districts" [1989] F.I.C.Q. 307; and Noce & von Kaenel, "Individual and Institutional Liability for Injuries Arising from Sports and Athletics" (1996) 63 Def. Counsel J. 517.

In *Bradford-Smart v. West Sussex County Council*, [2002] 1 F.C.R. 425, the English Court of Appeal held that a school may owe a duty of care to protect a student from bullying, not only on school property, but also, in exceptional circumstances, outside the school as well. See Elvin, "The Liability of Schools for Bullying" [2002] C.L.J. 255. See also *North Vancouver School District No. 44 v. Jubran* (2005), 39 B.C.L.R. (4th) 143 (C.A.); and Kendall & Sidebotham, "Homophobic Bullying in Schools: Is there a Duty of Care?" (2004) 9 Austl. & N.Z.J.L. & Educ. 71.

In *Cliche c. Baie-James (Commission scolaire)* (2005), 35 C.C.L.T. (3d) 103 (C.S. Qc.), a municipality was held liable for failing to provide enough lifeguards to supervise a class trip to a municipal pool for 36 kindergarten students. The plaintiff's child was found unconscious in the deep end by a teacher. The child died the following day. Although the teachers were not exempt from the obligation to supervise the children while at the pool, the court found that the municipality took on a duty to ensure the safety of the premises by welcoming the children and teachers into the facility. By failing to provide the required number of lifeguards, the city was at fault.

6. In *Hills v. Bridgeview Little League Association*, 745 N.E.2d 1166 (Ill. 2000), the plaintiff, a little league coach, was severely beaten by coaches from an opposing team. One of those coaches had been yelling and making offensive comments to players and umpires throughout the game. The plaintiff sued the opposing coaches as well as the league for failing to prevent the attack, which was allegedly foreseeable given the coach's continued violent outbursts. The plaintiff also claimed that the umpires and game announcer should have attempted to intervene and end the attack, which lasted for several minutes and included blows with a baseball bat. Although the plaintiff was successful at trial and appeal, his claim was later rejected by the Illinois Supreme Court. The court reasoned that there was no special relationship between the league and the plaintiff. Given what you know of Canadian law, do you think the same result would have been reached in Canada? See D'Amico, "Torts – Negligence in the Protection of Third Parties in Youth Sports Programs" (2002) 12 Seton Hall J. Sport L. 107.

In *Vowles v. Evans*, [2003] W.L.R. 1607 (C.A.), an amateur referee of a rugby match was found to owe a duty of care to players to enforce the rules for their safety. Would a referee also owe a duty of care if his or her failure to enforce the rules caused economic loss to the players, teams, or the league (*e.g.* if a poor decision resulted in a team's elimination from the playoffs)? See Elvin, "Liability for Negligent Refereeing of a Rugby Match" (2003) 119 L.Q.R. 560.

7. The courts readily acknowledge that children cannot be supervised at all times or prevented from getting into mischief. Nevertheless, if parents, teachers or other supervisors are aware of a child's hazardous activities or permit a child to have unsupervised access to snowmobiles, guns and similar objects, the court will impose a rigorous standard of care.

For a discussion of the parental duty to control, see *Ingram v. Lowe* (1974), 55 D.L.R. (3d) 292 (Alta. C.A.) (where a nine-year-old was allowed to have a pellet gun); *Michaud v. Dupuis* (1977), 20 N.B.R. (2d) 305 (Q.B.) (where an 11-year-old had a propensity to throw rocks); *Migliore v. Gerard* (1987), 61 O.R. (2d) 438 (H.C.) (where children were injured, in part because they were not required to wear seat-belts); and *LaPlante (Guardian ad litem of) v. LaPlante* (1992), 93 D.L.R. (4th) 249 (B.C.S.C.), aff'd (1995), 125 D.L.R. (4th) 596 (B.C.C.A.) (where a 16-year-old with physical and mental impairments was permitted to drive).

For examples of actions against parents under parental responsibility legislation, see *Coquitlam School District No. 43 v. D.(T.W.)* (1999), 64 B.C.L.R. (3d) 199 (C.A.); and *Shannon v. Westman (Litigation Guardian of)* (2002), 12 C.C.L.T. (3d) 46 (Ont. S.C.J.).

8. For a discussion of the liability of school authorities see: *Magnusson v. Bd. of Nipawin School Unit No. 61 of Sask.* (1975), 60 D.L.R. (3d) 572 (Sask. C.A.) and *Mainville v. Ottawa Board of Education* (1990), 75 O.R. (2d) 315 (Prov. Div.) (supervision on school grounds); *Myers v. Peel County Board of Education, supra*; *Freer (Guardian ad litem of) v. Okanagan/Skaha School District No. 67*, 2002 CarswellBC 2891 (S.C.) (WLeC); and *MacCabe v. Westlock Roman Catholic Separate School District No. 110, supra* (supervision during gymnastics); *Lapensee v. Ottawa Day Nursery Inc.* (1986), 35 C.C.L.T. 129 (Ont. H.C.), varied (1986), 38 C.C.L.T. 113 (Ont. H.C.) (supervision in home care); and *Piercey (Guardian ad litem of) v. Lunenburg (County) District School Board, supra* (supervision at adventure camp).

See also Hoyano, "The Prudent Parent: The Elusive Standard of Care" (1984) 18 U.B.C.L. Rev. 1; MacKay & Dickinson, *Beyond the "Careful Parent": Tort Liability in Education* (1998); and Batzel, "Negligence and the Liability of School Boards and Teachers Towards Students" in Foster & Smith, eds., *Reaching For Reasonableness: The Educator as Lawful Decision-Maker* (1999) 111.

9. Should parents, teachers and others supervising children be held vicariously liable for the torts committed by children under their authority? Are there any reasons for distinguishing this relationship from that of an employer/employee? See Weinstein, "Visiting the Sins of the Child on the Parent: the Legality of Criminal Parental Liability Statutes" (1991) 64 S. Cal. L. Rev. 859; Chapin, "Out of Control? The Uses and Abuses of Parental Liability Laws to Control Juvenile Delinquency in the United States" (1997) 37 Santa Clara L. Rev. 621; Barton, "Reconciling the Burden: Parental Liability for the Tortious Acts of Minors" (2002) 51 Emory L.J. 877; Andrews, "The Justice of Parental Accountability: Hypothetical Disinterested Citizens and Real Victims' Voices in the Debate over Expanded Parental Liability" (2002) 75 Temp. L. Rev. 375; and Adjin-Tettey, "Significance and Consequences of Parental Liability Legislation" in Beaulac, Pitel & Schulz, *The Joy of Torts* (2002) 221.

(c) THE DUTY TO PREVENT CRIME AND PROTECT OTHERS

The duty to control typically involves situations in which the defendant has direct control over, or supervision of, another. Related issues arise when the defendant has only indirect control or authority, such as the situation with those on probation or out on parole who are living in the community. In other cases, the defendant will simply have an opportunity to prevent or reduce the likelihood of a crime or accident occurring. Several different lines of cases have emerged in this rapidly expanding area of Canadian tort law. The following case illustrates the complex legal and policy issues that must be addressed in these types of cases.

JANE DOE v. METROPOLITAN TORONTO (MUNICIPALITY) COMMISSIONERS OF POLICE

(1998), 160 D.L.R. (4th) 697 (Ont. Gen. Div.).

[The plaintiff sued the police after she was attacked by a serial rapist, Paul Callow, who had raped four other women living in second or third floor apartments in the vicinity. All of the prior attacks had occurred within a one-year period and involved single white women. In each case, the attacker had entered the apartment through the balcony door. The plaintiff's first claim was based on failure to warn. The second claim, based on infringement of rights under the *Canadian Charter of Rights and Freedoms*, Part I of the *Constitution Act, 1982*, being Schedule B to the *Canada Act 1982* (U.K.), 1982, c. 11, has been omitted from this excerpt.]

MacFarland J.: –

. . .

Decision Not to Warn

As I have said Sgts. Cameron and Derry determined that this investigation would be "low key" compared to the investigation conducted into [another serial rapist, Dawson Davidson, who was known as] the "Annex Rapist" and no warning would be given to the women they knew to be at risk for fear of displacing the rapist leaving him free to re-offend elsewhere undetected.

I am not persuaded that their professed reason for not warning women is the real reason no warning was issued.

. . .

There was, I find, no "policy" not to issue warnings to potential victims in these cases – clearly warnings had been given in the Dawson Davidson Annex Rapist investigation – warnings which incidentally all defence expert witnesses agreed were appropriate in the circumstances.

I find that the real reason a warning was not given in the circumstances of this case was because Sgts. Cameron and Derry believed that women living in the area would become hysterical and panic and their investigation would thereby be jeopardized. In addition, they were not motivated by any sense of urgency because Callow's attacks were not seen as "violent" as Dawson Davidson's by comparison had been.

I am satisfied on the evidence that a meaningful warning could and should have been given to the women who were at particular risk. That warning could have been by way of a canvass of their apartments, by a media blitz, by holding widely publicized public meetings or any one or combination of these methods. Such warning should have alerted the particular women at risk, and advised them of suggested precautions they might take to protect themselves. The defence experts, with the exception of Mr. Piers, agreed that a warning could have been given without compromising the investigation on the facts of the case.

. . .

I am satisfied on Ms. Doe's evidence that if she had been aware a serial rapist was in her neighbourhood raping women whose apartments he accessed via their balconies she would have taken steps to protect herself and that most probably those steps would have prevented her from being raped.

Section 57 of the *Police Act*, R.S.O. 1980, c. 381 (the governing statute at the time these events occurred) provides:

> 57. . . . members of police forces. . . are charged with the duty of preserving the peace, preventing robberies and other crimes. . .

The police are statutorily obligated to prevent crime and at common law they owe a duty to protect life and property. As Schroeder J.A. stated in *Schacht v. The Queen in right of the Province of Ontario*, [1973] 1 O.R. 221 at 231-2, 30 D.L.R. (3d) 641 (H.C.J.):

> The duties which I would lay upon them stem not only from the relevant statutes to which reference has been made, but from the common law, which recognizes the existence of a broad conventional or customary duty in the established constabulary as an arm of the State to protect the life, limb and property of the subject.

In my view, the police failed utterly in their duty to protect these women and the plaintiff in particular from the serial rapist the police knew to be in their midst by failing to warn so that they may have had the opportunity to take steps to protect themselves.

. . .

Negligence

My task has been rendered less onerous by the very thorough analysis of Henry J. of the issues raised by the pleading in this case . . . when the matter came before him on a motion to strike out the statement of claim and the succinct reasons of Moldaver J. (as he then was) on behalf of the Divisional Court (1990), 74 O.R. (2d) 225, 72 D.L.R. (4th) 580, when the decision of Henry J. went to that Court on appeal.

After citing section 57 of the Police Act, R.S.O. 1980, c. 381, and observing that by virtue thereof the police are charged with the duty of protecting the public from those who would commit or have committed crimes, Moldaver J. (as he then was) goes on . . . as follows:

> *Do the pleadings support a private law duty of care by the defendants in this case?*
>
> The plaintiff alleges that the defendants knew of the existence of a serial rapist. It was eminently foreseeable that he would strike again and cause harm to yet another victim. The allegations therefore support foreseeability of risk.
> The plaintiff further alleges that by the time she was raped, the defendants knew or ought to have known that she had become part of a narrow and distinct group of potential victims, sufficient to support a special relationship of proximity. According to the allegations, the defendants knew:
>
> (1) that the rapist confined his attacks to the Church-Wellesley area of Toronto;
>
> (2) that the victims all resided in second or third floor apartments;
>
> (3) that entry in each case was gained through a balcony door; and
>
> (4) that the victims were all white, single and female.
>
> Accepting as I must the facts as pleaded, I agree with Henry J. that they do support the requisite knowledge on the part of the police sufficient to establish a private law duty of care. The harm was foreseeable and a special relationship of proximity existed.

. . .

On the evidence I find the plaintiff has established a private law duty of care.

. . .

Do the pleadings support a breach of the private law duty of care?

The law is clear that in certain circumstances, the police have a duty to warn citizens of foreseeable harm. See *Schact v. R.*, [1973] 1 O.R. 221, 30 D.L.R. (3d) 641 (C.A.) affd *sub nom. O'Rourke v. Schact*, [1976] 1 S.C.R. 53, 55 D.L.R. (3d) 96, 3 N.R. 453, and *Beutler v. Beutler, Adams v. Beutler* (1983), 26 C.C.L.T. 229 (Ont. H.C.J.). The obvious purpose of the warning is to protect the citizens.

I would add to this by saying that in some circumstances where foreseeable harm and a special relationship of proximity exist, the police might reasonably conclude that a warning ought not to be given. For example, it might be decided that a warning would cause general and unnecessary panic on the part of the public which could lead to greater harm.

It would, however, be improper to suggest that a legitimate decision not to warn would excuse a failure to protect. The duty to protect would still remain. It would simply have to be accomplished by other means.

In this case the plaintiff claims, *inter alia*, that the duty owed to her by the defendants required (1) that she be warned of the impending danger; or (2) in the absence of such a warning, that she be adequately protected. It is alleged that the police did neither.

Instead she claims they made a conscious decision to sacrifice her in order to apprehend the suspect. They decided to use her as "bait". They chose not to warn her due to a stereotypical belief that because she was a woman, she and others like her would become hysterical. This would have "scared off" the attacker, making his capture more difficult.

The evidence establishes that Det. Sgt. Cameron clearly had linked the four rapes which preceded Ms. Doe's by the early days of August in 1986, and he and Det. Sgt. Derry knew that the rapist would continue to attack women until he was stopped. They knew the rapist was attacking single white women living alone in second and third floor apartments with balconies in the Church/Wellesley area of the City of Toronto.

On the evidence I find the plaintiff has established a private law duty of care.

Det. Sgts. Derry and Cameron determined, in the context of their investigation, that no warning would be given to any women – let alone the specific target group they had identified – and among the reasons given for deciding not to warn was their view that women would panic and compromise the investigation. Det. Sgt. Cameron gave this as a reason to Ms. Doe when he interviewed her following her rape and she asked why women had not been warned.

[The plaintiff was awarded $220,000 in damages for her claim in negligence. Although MacFarland J. found that the plaintiff's rights under ss. 7 and 15 of the *Charter* had also been violated, there were no additional damages awarded on that basis.]

NOTES AND QUESTIONS

1. What were the grounds upon which MacFarland J. found that the police owed the plaintiff a duty of care? What factors did the judge consider in determining that the standard of care had been breached?

2. Was the court's analysis of the causation issue in *Doe* convincing? In *B.M. v. British Columbia (Attorney General)* (2004), 31 B.C.L.R. (4th) 61 (C.A.), the plaintiff's claim against police for failure to prevent crime was dismissed for lack of causation. The plaintiff had an abusive marriage. Her husband had been convicted for assaulting her. When she had another violent confrontation with him, she complained to police. Although the police knew of her husband's violent past (he also had convictions for assault causing bodily harm, unlawful confinement, and manslaughter) they did nothing to intervene and told the plaintiff to see a lawyer to get a restraining order and to stay in public places. Seven weeks later, the plaintiff's husband broke into her home with a gun, killed her friend and seriously wounded one of her daughters. The plaintiff suffered post-traumatic stress disorder as a result of the attack. Her claim against the police was dismissed on the basis that she could not prove causation: human behaviour is unpredictable, and there was no evidence that police intervention would have prevented the violent attack. *Doe* and *B.M.* illustrate some of the difficulties posed by the traditional "but for" test of causation in torts, particularly when predicting what an actor might have done if the defendant had issued a proper warning. For more on causation see Chapter 16.

3. What are the implications of *Doe* for prison and police officials who learn that a convicted rapist, arsonist, pedophile, or bank robber will be released from prison into a community? What policy considerations do these cases pose that were not relevant to *Doe*? See Davenport, "Convicted paedophiles – disclosure of information after release – police duty to protect public – *R. v. Chief Constable of the North Wales Police and ors ex parte AB and CD*" (1998) 3 J.C.L. 141.

4. In *Hill v. Chief Constable of West Yorkshire*, [1989] A.C. 53 (H.L.), the deceased's family sued the police, claiming that, had they acted reasonably, they would have been able to arrest a serial killer before he killed their daughter. The House of Lords struck out the statement of claim, stating that the police owe no duty to victims of crime unless the offender commits the offence while in police custody or after escaping police custody. In particular, the House of Lords was concerned that imposing a duty of care would be detrimental to the conduct of police investigations and decisions about how to distribute police resources. Moreover, there was insufficient proximity between the police and the deceased: she was one of many potential victims of a yet unidentified killer. Is the narrow scope of the police duty in *Hill* preferable to the broad duty in *Doe*? *Hill* has since been followed to deny police or government liability for the failure to prevent crime. See for example *Alexandrou v. Oxford*, [1993] 4 All E.R. 328 (C.A.) (negligent response to a burglar alarm at the plaintiff's shop); and *K v. Secretary of State for the Home Department*, [2002] E.W.C.A. Civ. 983 (failure to deport a violent criminal who committed further crimes).

5. In *Osman v. Ferguson*, [1993] 4 All E.R. 344 (C.A.), a teacher became obsessed with one of his students and began stalking him. The student's family complained to the police and the parties were interviewed several times. The police did not intervene to protect the student. The teacher subsequently rammed a car in which the student was a passenger, killing the student's father. The student brought a negligence action against the police for failing to protect him in light of the teacher's threatening behaviour. While the Court of Appeal found that there was greater proximity in *Osman* than in *Hill*, in that

both the perpetrator and the intended victim were identified, the claim was struck out based on the authority of the policy reasons provided in *Hill.*

However, in *Osman v. United Kingdom* (1998) 29 E.H.R.R. 245, the European Court of Human Rights found that the effectively "blanket immunity" extended to police violated Article 6 of the European Convention on Human Rights, which guarantees access to the courts for the determination of civil rights and obligations. According to the European Court, the plaintiff's claim should not have been struck out at such a preliminary stage. While *Osman v. United Kingdom* had the potential to open wide claims for police and government negligence, its effects were dampened by the subsequent decision in *Z v. United Kingdom* (2002), 34 E.H.R.R. 2. See Gearty, "Unravelling Osman" (2001) 64 Mod. L. Rev. 159.

6. The English courts are not completely hostile toward claims against police for failure to prevent crime. For example in *Swinney v. Chief Constable of the Northumbria Police*, [1997] Q.B. 464 (C.A.), the Court of Appeal refused to strike out a claim against police for failing to protect an informant. The plaintiff had provided information to the police regarding a suspected police killer, and had requested that the information be kept confidential. The suspect was known to be violent. Nevertheless, the police left the information in an unattended police vehicle, which was broken into by criminals and later came to the attention of the suspect. The suspect subsequently threatened the plaintiff and her family. The Court of Appeal acknowledged that a special relationship of proximity might exist between police and informants, and that the policy considerations employed in *Hill* had to be weighed against other factors such as the need to protect informants and to encourage them to come forward.

7. For discussions of this issue, see "Police Liability for Negligent Failure to Prevent Crime" (1981) 94 Harv. L. Rev. 820; Krause, "Municipal Liability: The Failure to Provide Adequate Police Protection" [1984] Wis. L. Rev. 499; Moroz, "*Jane Doe* and Police Liability for Failure to Apprehend: The Role of the *Anns* Public Policy Principle in Canada and England" (1995) 17 Adv. Q. 261; Childs & Ceyssens, "*Doe v. Metropolitan Toronto Board of Commissioners of Police* and the Status of Public Oversight of the Police in Canada" (1998) 36 Alta. L.R. 1000; Randall, "Sex Discrimination, Accountability of Public Authorities and the Public/Private Divide in Tort Law: An Analysis of *Doe v. Metropolitan Toronto (Municipality) Commissioners of Police*" (2001) 26 Queen's L.J. 451; and Hall, "Duty, Causation, and Third Party Perpetrators: The Bonnie Mooney Case" (2005) 50 McGill L.J. 597.

8. American courts are very unlikely to impose liability for police failure to prevent crime. Police or other officials can only be found liable where they worsen the plaintiff's situation by creating the danger, making the plaintiff more vulnerable, or deterring alternative assistance. See for example *DeShaney v. Winnebago County Department of Social Services*, 489 U.S. 189 (1989); *Ross v. United States*, 910 F.2d 1422 (7th Cir. 1990); and *Schieber v. City of Philadelphia*, 156 F.Supp.2d 451 (E.D. Pa. 2001). See Juthani, "Police Treatment of Domestic Violence and Sexual Abuse: Affirmative Duty to Protect vs. Fourth Amendment Privacy" (2003) 59 N.Y.U. Ann. Surv. Am. L. 51.

A particularly horrific case is *Estate of Sinthasamphone v. City of Milwaukee*, 785 F.Supp. 1343 (E.D. Wis. 1992). A 14-year-old Laotian boy was found lying on the street, drugged, naked and bleeding, by two women. Unknown to the women, the boy had escaped from the apartment of serial murderer Jeffrey Dahmer (who had then been convicted of sexual assault but was not as notorious as he later became). The women called the police but, when they arrived, the police refused to listen to them and threatened to arrest them if they tried to assist the boy. When Dahmer came to the scene, the police returned the boy to his custody, allegedly believing that he was Dahmer's homosexual partner. On return to the apartment, Dahmer killed the boy. His family sued the police not for failing to protect him, but for preventing others from providing assistance and for delivering him into the hands of someone who was not his legal guardian. Based on this affirmative conduct that worsened the boy's circumstances, the court allowed the claim to proceed to trial.

9. The courts have also begun to impose affirmative duties on private citizens to prevent crime. Landlords have been held liable to their tenants for injuries caused by attackers who gained access because of inadequate security. See *Allison v. Rank City Wall Can. Ltd.* (1984), 29 C.C.L.T. 50 (Ont. H.C.); *Q. v. Minto Management Ltd.* (1985), 49 O.R. (2d) 531 (H.C.), aff'd (1986), 57 O.R. (2d) 781 (C.A.); Merril, "Landlord Liability for Crimes Committed By Third Parties Against Tenants on the Premises" (1985) 38 Vand. L. Rev. 431; and Glesner, "Landlords as Cops: Tort, Nuisance and Forfeiture Standards Imposing Liability on Landlords for Crime on the Premises" (1992) 42 Case W. Res .L. Rev. 679. But see *Shultz v. Miki* (2006), 223 B.C.A.C. 248 (C.A.), where the defendant landlord was absolved of liability for the sexual assault committed by his cousin, whom the landlord had hired to perform carpentry work in the plaintiff's apartment.

See also *Rendall v. Ewart* (1989), 38 B.C.L.R. (2d) 1 (C.A.); *H.(M.) v. Bederman* (1995), 27 C.C.L.T. (2d) 152 (Ont. Gen. Div.); *Robertson v. Stang* (1997) 38 C.C.L.T. (2d) 62 (B.C.S.C.); *Coueslan v. Canadian Mini-Warehouse Properties Ltd. (c.o.b. Public Storage Canadian)*, 2000 BCPC 137 (CanLII); and *G.A. v. McGregor* (2003), 347 A.R. 376 (Q.B.).

10. Should drivers who leave their keys in their cars be held liable if their vehicles are stolen and involved in car accidents? See *Hollett v. Coca-Cola Ltd.* (1980), 11 C.C.L.T. 281 (B.C.S.C.); *Spagnolo v. Margesson's Sports Ltd.* (1983), 41 O.R. (2d) 65 (C.A.); *Moore v. Fanning* (1987), 60 O.R. (2d) 225 (H.C.); *Werbeniuk v. Maynard* (1994), 93 Man. R. (2d) 318 (Q.B.); and *Tong v. Bedwell* (2002), 311 A.R. 174 (Q.B.).

11. In *Okanagan Exteriors Inc. v. Perth Developments Inc.* (2002), 98 B.C.L.R. (3d) 274 (C.A.), the defendant owned an abandoned construction site that neighboured the plaintiff's greenhouse. The defendant knew that its site was frequented by children, transients and alcoholics, and that some of those individuals occasionally set fires. The defendant nevertheless did not take effective steps to control the actions of those third parties. The plaintiff suffered property damage when a fire that started on the defendant's property spread. The court held that, in the circumstances, the defendant owed a duty of care to the plaintiff. Liability followed. But see *Smith v. Littlewoods Organisation Ltd.*, [1987] 1 All E.R. 710 (H.L.), where a derelict cinema was set on fire by vandals and the fire spread to neighbouring properties. The House of Lords refused to impose liability on the owners of the cinema. *Littlewoods* can be distinguished because the defendants had insufficient knowledge of the presence of trespassers.

12. There has been a flood of cases concerning the duty to protect children from physical and sexual abuse. See *Lyth v. Dagg* (1988), 46 C.C.L.T. 25 (B.C.S.C.) (school);

G.(A.) v. British Columbia (Superintendent of Family & Child Services) (1989), 38 B.C.L.R. (2d) 215 (C.A.); *J.(L.A.) v. J.(H.)* (1993), 13 O.R. (3d) 306 (Gen. Div.) (claim against mother for failing to protect daughter from father); *Police Complaints Commissioner v. Dunlop* (1995), 26 O.R. (3d) 582 (Gen. Div.) (police officer); *C.(D.) v. Newfoundland (Minister of Social Services)* (1996), 137 Nfld. & P.E.I.R. 206 (Nfld. T.D.) (youth and social workers); *Brown (Next Friend of) v. University of Alberta Hospital* (1997), 197 A.R. 237 (Q.B.) (radiologist); and *K.(K.) v. G.(K.W.)* (2006), 40 C.C.L.T. (3d) 139 (Ont. S.C.J.) (claim against mother for failing to protect daughter from father). See Reaume & Van Praagh, "Family Matters: Mothers as Secondary Defendants in Child Sexual Abuse Actions" in Beaulac, Pitel & Schulz, eds., *The Joy of Torts* (2002) 179.

Many of the recent cases deal with abuse suffered years earlier in residential schools or in association with religious orders. See for example *Re Indian Residential Schools* (2000), 183 D.L.R. (4th) 552 (Alta. Q.B.); *Penney v. John Doe* (2002), 215 Nfld. & P.E.I.R. 310 (Nfld. C.A.) (claim against bishop, diocese and others); and *John Doe v. Bennett*, [2004] 1 S.C.R. 436 (claim against diocese).

Children who are physically and sexually abused suffer a broad range of serious psychological and other problems, including an increased likelihood of abusing others. In *Rumley v. British Columbia* (1999), 72 B.C.L.R. (3d) 1 (C.A.), aff'd [2001] 3 S.C.R. 184, the court indicated that claims from "secondary-abuse victims" should not be included in any class actions because they raise difficult issues of duty and foreseeability, as well as plaintiff-specific issues of proximity. On the broader issue, is there any legal or policy reason to limit the claims of "secondary-abuse victims?"

Within the context of child abuse cases, it is important to appreciate that liability may also be imposed in negligence or defamation with respect to unfounded or unwarranted allegations of abuse. See for example, *B.(D.) v. Children's Aid Society of Durham (Region)* (1996), 92 O.A.C. 60 (C.A.); *G.(R.) v. Christison* (1996), 150 Sask. R. 1 (Q.B.); *D. v. East Berkshire Community NHS Trust*, [2005] 2 A.C. 373 (H.L.); *Young v. Bella*, [2006] 1 S.C.R. 108; and *B.D. v. Halton Region Children's Aid Society* (2006), 79 O.R. (3d) 45 (C.A.).

13. What obligations do counsellors, therapists and health professionals have to protect their patients and those endangered by their patients? What impact should the fact that the information was obtained in confidence have on these duties?

In *Tarasoff v. Regents of the University of California*, 17 Cal. Rptr.3d 425 (U.S. 1976), a patient told his psychologist at the University Hospital that he intended to kill his former girlfriend when she returned from her vacation. The psychologist concluded that the patient was dangerous, and contacted the campus police. The patient was picked up, briefly detained and then released. Neither the woman nor her family were warned of the potential danger. When the woman returned, the patient killed her. The family sued the psychologist for failing to warn. The court acknowledged the psychologist's arguments about the difficulty of predicting dangerousness, but indicated that this was not the issue. The psychologist was not being sued because he had negligently assessed his patient. Rather, he was being sued because he had concluded that the patient was dangerous and yet failed to warn the intended victim. The psychologist argued that there should be no duty to warn because it would necessitate breaching confidentiality. In rejecting this argument, the court emphasized that the confidentiality obligation to the patient ends when the public peril begins. Consequently, the judge rejected the psychologist's request to dismiss the family's claim and sent the case to trial. The psychologist and the University settled out of court before the trial.

14. The dilemma posed by *Tarasoff* is not limited to violent crime. For example, what should a therapist do if an extremely intoxicated patient attempts to leave a treatment session with car keys in hand? Even if the therapist is willing to breach confidence by calling the police, will this do any good? Should the therapist attempt or threaten to physically restrain the patient? What if a patient poses only a risk to him or herself?

Should an addictions counsellor have any legal duty to control the conduct of an alcohol or drug-dependant patient who is currently employed in a safety-sensitive position?

15. *Tarasoff* has generated substantial academic interest in both the legal and treatment communities. See for example Twerski, "Affirmative Duty After *Tarasoff*" (1983) 11 Hofstra L. Rev. 1013; Givelber, Bowers & Blitch, "*Tarasoff*, Myth and Reality: An Empirical Study of Private Law in Action" [1984] Wisc. L. Rev. 433; Bednar, "The Psychotherapist's Calamity: Emerging Trends in the *Tarasoff* Doctrine" [1989] B.Y.U.L. Rev. 261; Egley, "Defining the *Tarasoff* Duty" (1991) 19 J. Psych & Law 19; Rosenhan *et al.*, "Warning Third Parties: The Ripple Effects of *Tarasoff*" (1993) 24 Pac. L.J. 1165; Lake, "Revisiting *Tarasoff*" (1994) 58 Albany L. Rev. 97; Smith, "*Wenden v. Trikha* and Third Party Liability of Doctors and Hospitals: What's Been Happening to *Tarasoff*?" (1995) 4 Health L. Rev. 12; and Ferris *et al.*, "Defining the Physician's Duty to Warn: Consensus Statement of Ontario's Medical Expert Panel on Duty to Inform" (1998) 158 C.M.A.J. 1473; Grant, "Psychiatrists Have No Duty to Warn Third Parties of Patient's Threats" (2001) 7 Tex. Wesleyan L. Rev. 157; Van Exan, "The Legal and Ethical Issues Surrounding the Duty to Warn in the Practice of Psychology" (2004) 18 W.R.S.L.I. 123; and Ginsberg, "*Tarasoff* at Thirty: Victim's Knowledge Shrinks the Psychotherapist's Duty to Warn and Protect" (2004) 21 J. Contemp. Health L. & Pol'y 1.

16. The issues raised in *Tarasoff* have never been squarely addressed by the Canadian courts, although the decision has been referred to approvingly. See for example *Tanner v. Norys*, [1980] 4 W.W.R. 33 (Alta. C.A.); and *Wenden v. Trikha* (1993), 14 C.C.L.T. (2d) 225 (Alta. C.A.). In *Smith v. Jones* (1999), 169 D.L.R. (4th) 385 (S.C.C.), the *Tarasoff* decision was again referred to approvingly. However, *Smith* did not deal with a therapist's common law duty to warn in negligence. Rather, the majority of the Supreme Court of Canada ruled that a therapist could choose to breach solicitor-client privilege in the public interest to avert a clear risk of imminent death or serious injury to an identifiable person or group. What are the implications of *Smith* in terms of a therapist's duty to warn?

REVIEW PROBLEMS

1. John, the owner of a local variety store, sold one dollar's worth of firecrackers and three packages of matches to Billy, a 10-year-old. Billy was severely burned while he was playing alone with the firecrackers. Would John owe Billy a common law duty of care in these circumstances? How would your analysis differ if: (a) Billy's mother had told John not to sell Billy any firecrackers, (b) Billy had told John that he was taking the firecrackers home to light with his 17-year-old brother, (c) Billy had always appeared to be a polite, well-behaved child, or (d) John had received complaints from some parents about selling their children matches, cigarettes and firecrackers?

2. Mr. Green pulled into a plaza and ran into a store, leaving the engine of the car running and the door unlocked. As he emerged a minute later, he saw a teenager pulling

away in his car. He had noticed some teenagers milling about in front of the store, but had thought nothing of it. An hour later, Green was contacted by the police, who informed him that the driver had lost control of the car and had slammed into a bus. The driver of his car and several passengers in the bus were severely injured. Would Mr. Green owe a common law duty of care to the thief or the passengers?

3. Mandy, a drug addict who is HIV-positive, told her doctor that she had no intention of practising safe sex or informing her partner. The doctor contacted the medical officer of health but did not inform Mandy's partner. Fourteen months later, Mandy's partner tested HIV-positive and now wants to sue the doctor for not warning him of the risk. Did the doctor owe the partner a duty of care? Would it make a difference if: (a) the local medical officer of health had adopted a policy of not contacting sexual partners, (b) Mandy had many sexual partners, or (c) the partner was also one of the doctor's patients?

5. The Duty to Perform Gratuitous Undertakings

In keeping with the distinction between misfeasance and nonfeasance, the common law did not generally require an individual to honour a gratuitous promise. The failure to fulfil such a promise was characterized as a nonfeasance and the remedy, if any, was in contract and not in tort. In the classic case of *Thorne v. Deas* (1809), 4 Johns. 84 (N.Y.), the defendant twice assured the plaintiffs that he would obtain insurance on a boat they jointly owned. Relying on these promises, the plaintiffs did nothing further on the matter. When the boat was wrecked and the plaintiffs learned that it had not been insured, they sued the defendant in tort for their loss. In dismissing their action, the court stated that "by the common law . . . one who undertakes to do an act for another without reward, is not answerable for omitting to do the act, and is only responsible when he attempts to do it, and does it amiss."

Once the defendant begins to perform a gratuitous undertaking, he or she may be held liable in negligence for positively injuring the plaintiff. However, defendants generally are not subject to a common law duty to complete the task itself, or to otherwise act for the plaintiff's benefit. A different rule applies only if the defendant somehow worsened the plaintiff's original position. That may be true, for instance, if the defendant lulled the plaintiff into a false sense of security, denied the plaintiff other opportunities for aid, or put the plaintiff in a more precarious physical position. The courts have held that those principles may apply if the defendant withdrew a gratuitous service that he or she had customarily provided.

Although the rule in *Thorne* has been criticized, it has rarely been rejected – partially because its impact can often be avoided. First, the courts may skirt the issue in *Thorne* by classifying the defendant's conduct as misfeasance, rather than nonfeasance. Second, tort and contract have developed since 1809 to cover many of the situations in which *Thorne* initially denied relief. For example, if the parties are in a contractual relationship, the courts may now invoke the concept of promissory estoppel to enforce some gratuitous promises. Furthermore, liability may be imposed in tort for pure economic losses caused by fraudulent misrepresentations, negligent or innocent misrepresentations made in fiduciary relationships, and negligent misrepresentations made in the special circumstances defined in *Hedley Byrne & Co. v. Heller & Partners Ltd.*, [1964] A.C. 465 (H.L.). A defendant may also be held liable in tort for making a negligent statement that creates a foreseeable risk of physical injury. Recent changes in the common law governing the duties of builders, occupiers, manufacturers, suppliers, and public authorities have further expanded the situations in which the failure to fulfil a gratuitous undertaking may give rise to tort liability. In the end, while the principle in *Thorne* has not been directly rejected, it has been very significantly eroded by the growing number of exceptions to it.

NOTES AND QUESTIONS

1. The principles governing the performance of gratuitous promises appear to have been established in *Coggs v. Bernard* (1703), 92 E.R. 107 (Q.B.), but they were more clearly stated in *Thorne*. One of the first Canadian cases in which these issues were addressed, *Baxter & Co. v. Jones* (1903), 6 O.L.R. 360 (C.A.), cited both *Coggs* and *Thorne* as authority. Thereafter, the Canadian courts have typically cited *Baxter*, rather than either *Coggs* or *Thorne*, in support of these principles.

2. What is the rationale for refusing to impose liability in tort for injuries or losses resulting from a defendant's failure to fulfil a gratuitous promise?

3. It is interesting to contrast *Thorne* with the subsequent cases in which individuals have been held liable for failing to honour a gratuitous promise to obtain insurance. In *Baxter & Co. v. Jones, supra*, and *Menna v. Guglietti* (1969), 10 D.L.R. (3d) 132 (Ont. H.C.), the courts characterized the agents' conduct in filling out the application form and taking down information as misfeasance and imposed liability in negligence. See also *Ferland v. Keith* (1958), 15 D.L.R. (2d) 472 (Ont. C.A.) (liability for breach of an independent or collateral contract); *Northwestern Mut. Ins. Co. v. J.T. O'Bryan & Co.* (1974), 51 D.L.R. (3d) 693 (B.C.C.A.) (liability in tort for negligent misrepresentation); and *Fine's Flowers Ltd. v. Gen. Accident Assur. Co.* (1977), 81 D.L.R. (3d) 139 (Ont. C.A.) (liability for breach of contract, and liability in tort for negligent misrepresentation and breach of a fiduciary duty). But see *Mason v. Morrow's Moving & Storage Ltd.* (1978), 5 C.C.L.T. 59 (B.C.C.A.); *Maxey v. Can. Perm. Trust Co.*, [1984] 2 W.W.R. 469 (Man. C.A.); and *Fletcher v. Manitoba Public Insurance Co.* (1990), 74 D.L.R. (4th) 636 (S.C.C.).

4. The rule in *Thorne* also conflicts with a growing body of case law in which defendants have been held liable for economic losses resulting from the negligent performance of, or failure to perform, gratuitous business or professional services. What makes these cases unique is that a duty is imposed even though there is no contractual relationship between the parties and the defendant makes no representation to the plaintiff. A typical case of this kind involves beneficiaries who lose their inheritance due to the negligence of the deceased's lawyer in drafting the will. For the modern law, see *Whittingham v. Crease & Co.* (1978), 6 C.C.L.T. 1 (B.C.S.C.); *White v. Jones*, [1995] 2 A.C. 207 (H.L.); and *Earl v. Wilhelm* (2000), 1 C.C.L.T. (3d) 215 (Sask. C.A.). See also Benson, "Should *White v. Jones* Represent Canadian Law? A Return to First Principles" in Neyers, Chamberlain & Pitel, eds., *Emerging Issues in Tort Law* (2007), ch. 6. This topic is considered further in Chapter 14.

5. The American Law Institute has identified a number of situations in which it favours imposing tort liability for the negligent performance of a gratuitous undertaking. See *Restatement of the Law, Third, Torts: Liability for Physical Harm* (Proposed Final

Draft No. 1) (2005) at §44. This appears to include the mere failure to perform a gratuitous promise, as long as the defendant induced the plaintiff to rely on the promise and the plaintiff suffered detriment as a result (see comment (f)). The drafters of the proposed *Restatement* reasoned that, if a promise supported by reliance was sufficient to give rise to promissory estoppel in the law of contract, it could also give rise to liability in tort, at least if it causes personal injury or property damage.

SMITH v. RAE

(1919), 51 D.L.R. 323 (Ont. C.A.)

MIDDLETON J.A.: – The action was brought by a married woman against a practising physician and surgeon residing in the city of Toronto. The plaintiff, expecting confinement, called, with her husband, upon the defendant, who undertook and agreed to attend her.

Upon the facts there can be no doubt that the contract was made with the plaintiff's husband. The confinement, which was expected to take place about the middle of November, did not take place until the 2nd December, 1918. The defendant did not attend the plaintiff, and the child died during delivery. The action is against the defendant for his alleged breach of duty in failing to attend at the time of the confinement.

[The court held that the appellant doctor had not been negligent in failing to attend the birth, given his other responsibilities and the information that he had received.]

Quite apart from this, there is, I think, a serious difficulty in the plaintiff's way. The contract was with the husband. The action is by the wife. She cannot sue on the contract, and her claim must, therefore, be based upon tort. Had there been actual misfeasance in anything done to the plaintiff, she could undoubtedly recover for the tort, but where the action is for damages for failure to attend, then it must be based on a breach of a contract to attend.

ZELENKO v. GIMBEL BROS., INC.

287 N.Y.S. 134 (S.C. 1936)

LAUER J.: – The general proposition of the law is that if a defendant owes a plaintiff no duty, then refusal to act is not negligence. . . . But there are many ways that a defendant's duty to act may arise. Plaintiff's intestate was taken ill in defendant's store. We will assume the defendant owed her no duty at all; the defendant could have let her be and die. But if a defendant undertakes a task, even if under no duty to undertake it, the defendant must not omit to do what an ordinary man would do in performing the task.

Here the defendant undertook to render medical aid to the plaintiff's intestate. Plaintiff says that defendant kept his intestate for six hours in an infirmary without any medical care. If the defendant had left plaintiff's intestate alone, beyond doubt some bystander, who would be influenced more by charity than by legalistic duty, would have summoned an ambulance. Defendant segregated this plaintiff's intestate where such aid could not be given and then left her alone.

The plaintiff is wrong in thinking that the duty of a common carrier of passengers is the same as the duty of this defendant. The common carrier assumes its duty by its contract of carriage. This defendant assumed its duty by meddling in matters with which legalistically it had no concern. The plaintiff is right in arguing that when the duty arose, the same type of neglect is actionable in both cases.

[Affirmed without reasons 287 N.Y.S. 136 (1936).]

SOULSBY v. TORONTO

(1907), 15 O.L.R. 13 (H.C.)

BRITTON J.: – On the 30th October, 1906, the plaintiff was employed as the driver of a baker's delivery wagon, and was delivering bread to customers in the western part of the city. On that day the plaintiff entered High Park, and drove along the road through the park, which leads out of the park, across the tracks of the Grand Trunk Railway and to the Lake Shore road. Within the park and near the railway crossing, the city has erected gates, and during the season when the park is most frequented, the city keeps a watchman at the gate nearest the crossing, keeping it open for users of the road when there is no danger from passing trains, and closing it when trains are approaching this crossing. The statement of claim alleges that the plaintiff on the day mentioned was approaching the crossing along the road in High Park, intending to proceed to the Lake Shore road. When he arrived at the crossing, he found the gate open, and, relying upon that fact as notice to him that no train was approaching, he proceeded to cross the tracks, and while so crossing was struck by a train and seriously injured.

At the close of the evidence, counsel for the defendants asked that the action be dismissed, on the grounds that no actionable negligence had been shewn, and that the plaintiff was guilty of contributory negligence. It was then agreed that the only thing to be left to the jury was the assessment of damages, and that I should dispose of all other questions, subject to the rights of parties to appeal. . . .

The case of *Stapley v. London, Brighton, and South Coast R.W. Co.* (1865), L.R. 1 Ex. 21, was relied upon by the plaintiff. That case is clearly distinguishable. "At the time of the accident, *contrary to the provisions*, by *statute* and by the *defendants' rules*, for the safety of carriage-traffic, the gates on one side of the line were partially open, and there was no gatekeeper." It was held that there was evidence of negligence, inasmuch as by neglecting the required precautions "the defendants might be considered to have intimated that their line might safely be traversed by foot passengers."

It was argued that even if the defendants were not compelled to establish the gate and employ the watchman, having undertaken it, the plaintiff was entitled to rely upon its continuance, at least until notice, actual or constructive, to the contrary.

Skelton v. London and North Western R.W. Co. (1867), L.R. 2 C.P. 631, is against the plaintiff's contention. In that case a railway, consisting of several lines, crossed a public footpath on a level, at a point near a station. On each side of the railway was a gate, as required by statute. The railway company, by way of extra precaution, usually, but not invariably, fastened the gates when a train was approaching. S., wishing to cross the railway, found the gate unfastened, and a coal train standing immediately in front of it. He waited until the coal train had moved off, and then, without looking up or down the line, commenced crossing the railway, and was killed by a passing train. If he had looked up the line, he would have seen the train in time to stop and avoid the accident. It was held that S. contributed to the accident by his negligence, and could not recover. And it was also held by Willes, J., "that the mere failure to perform a self-imposed duty is not actionable negligence; that the omission to fasten the gate did not amount to an invitation to S. to come on the line; and that, therefore, even if S. was not guilty of contributory negligence, the company were not liable."

Here the plaintiff found the gate open, but did not see the watchman. That in itself should have suggested to the plaintiff the possibility at least that the gate was open, not as an intimation that there was no danger, but that the watchman had been withdrawn – that there was no watchman in fact. No inquiry was made. The plaintiff thought the watchman was in his cabin – if so, he was not attending to the gate. The plaintiff knew of the railway, that this road led across it, and he knew of the ordinary danger at any railway crossing, and had these all in mind, so there was nothing to relieve the plaintiff of the duty of taking care and using caution when the crossing was reached, unless that care and caution were unnecessary by the fact of the gate being open.

The plaintiff relied upon *Baxter & Co. v. Jones* (1903), 6 O.L.R. 360, and upon cases cited in Anson on Contracts, 10th ed., p. 98. One case is where a person undertook gratuitously to effect insurance upon another person's house, and, having failed to do so, was held liable. These cases, which are cases of mandate, and nothing of the kind exists here, are said to rest upon this broad ground, as stated by Willes, J., in the *Skelton* case, that if a person undertake to perform a voluntary act, he is liable if he performs it improperly, but not if he neglects to perform it. The charge here is that a watchman employed did not do his duty properly. He was not at the gate at all. He was, as to the plaintiff and the public, when this accident happened, the same as during the night time – or during the rest of the year after October – when withdrawn from the gate.

I do not think the defendants are liable for merely leaving the gate open, as there is not, in my opinion, any duty to keep the gate closed at the time of approaching or passing trains.

NOTES AND QUESTIONS

1. What was the basis upon which the judge resolved the duty issue in *Smith*? Did the doctor deny the plaintiff an opportunity to obtain another doctor by agreeing to attend the birth? Assuming that he had, would this have given rise to a duty to fulfil his promise to attend? See also *Hurley v. Eddingfield* 59 N.E. 1058 (Ind. 1901). How would the courts resolve this issue now?

2. What was the basis upon which the judge resolved the duty issue in *Zelenko*? If the store's employees had attended to the plaintiff without moving her, but after a few minutes discontinued their efforts, would they have been liable in negligence? Can you reconcile the decision in *Smith* with that in *Zelenko*? Is the decision in *Zelenko* compatible with the principles in *Thorne*? See *Dudley v. Victor Lynn Lines Inc.* 138 A.2d 53 (N.J. 1958); and *Barnett v. Chelsea & Kensington Hosp. Mgmt. Committee*, [1969] 1 Q.B. 428.

3. In *Ross v. United States*, 910 F.2d 1422 (7th Cir. 1990), the plaintiff's estate claimed against the defendant county for "forcing" its gratuitous services upon him. The deceased was a 12-year-old boy who fell off a deteriorating breakwater and immediately sank below the surface. Several municipal rescue professionals and two civilian scuba divers appeared on the scene and wished to attempt a rescue. However, the municipality had recently made an agreement with the county that rescue efforts on the lake were the responsibility of the county alone. The county's Deputy Sheriff arrived in a patrol boat and informed the would-be rescuers that all rescues were to be performed by the county. He verbally and physically prevented the would-be rescuers from proceeding, even when they offered to perform the rescue at their own risk. He threatened to arrest them if they persisted. By the time the county divers arrived (some 20-30 minutes later), the boy had

died. His estate's claim against the county was allowed to proceed not because the county had failed to rescue him, but because its policy of being the sole provider of rescue services prevented the plaintiff from receiving alternative assistance.

4. What was the basis of the plaintiff's argument in *Soulsby*? Is Britton J. suggesting that an individual can never be held liable for discontinuing a gratuitous service? Do you think that the case would have been decided the same way if the watchman had been present and knew of the train's imminent arrival, but chose not to lower the gate or otherwise warn the plaintiff? Can you distinguish *Soulsby* from *Zelenko*?

5. In *Mercer v. South Eastern & Chatham Ry. Co.'s Managing Committee*, [1922] 2 K.B. 549, the court held that the defendant's regular practice of closing the gate when a train approached constituted a tacit invitation to cross the tracks when the gate was up. The defendant was held liable for the injuries sustained by the plaintiff when he acted upon this invitation and was struck by a train. Can you reconcile *Soulsby* and *Mercer*? What factors would lead to the recognition of a duty of care? Which case is preferable? See also *Erie Ry. Co. v. Stewart*, 40 F.2d 855 (6th Cir. 1930).

6. What must an individual do to notify the public that he or she is withdrawing a gratuitous service? Would it be sufficient for a railroad company to post a sign at the crossing a month before it withdraws its gatekeeper? In such a case, would the company owe a duty of care to an illiterate pedestrian who still expected a gatekeeper to be present at the crossing? Would the company have to post a notice prior to changing a gatekeeper's hours? Do the same principles apply to a municipality that wishes to withdraw a lifeguard from a public beach, a supervisor from a playground or a crossing guard from a school crossing? See generally *Wilmington Gen. Hosp. v. Manlove*, 174 A.2d 135 (Del. 1961); *Hendricks v. R.*, [1970] S.C.R. 237; *R. v. Nord-Deutsche Versicherungs-Gesellschaft*, [1971] S.C.R. 849; and *County of Parkland No. 31 v. Stetar; County of Parkland No. 31 v. Woodrow*, [1975] 2 S.C.R. 884.

7. An insurance company that has previously sent renewal reminders to its clients prior to the expiry of their policies may be under a duty of care in tort to continue this practice until it notifies the policyholders of its contrary intention. See *Morash v. Lockhart & Ritchie Ltd.* (1978), 48 A.P.R. 180 (N.B.C.A.); and *Grove Services Ltd. v. Lenhart Agencies Ltd.* (1979), 10 C.C.L.T. 101 (B.C.S.C.). But see *Vienneau Assur. Ltée v. Roy* (1986), 67 N.B.R. (2d) 16 (C.A.); and *Bijeau v. Pelletier* (1996), 176 N.B.R. (2d) 241 (C.A.).

8. Section 217 of the *Criminal Code* imposes a criminal law duty on an individual who "undertakes to do an act" to complete it, if an omission to do so is or may be dangerous to life. Although the section's origins can be traced to Canada's first *Criminal Code* in 1892, these provisions have generated little comment. Nevertheless, it is interesting to note that one's criminal liability for discontinuing a gratuitous undertaking appears to be far broader than one's civil liability.

9. See generally Seavey, "Reliance Upon Gratuitous Promises or Other Conduct" (1951) 64 Harv. L. Rev. 913; and Gregory, "Gratuitous Undertakings and the Duty of Care" (1951) 1 De Paul L. Rev. 30.

REVIEW PROBLEMS

1. Bill had told John that he would give him a ride to the university to write the LSAT. On the morning of the examination, Bill drove halfway to John's house before he realized that he had left his identification card at home. In his rush and nervousness, Bill forgot about his promise to John. As a result, John missed the last sitting of the LSAT for the next academic year. Discuss whether Bill owed John a duty of care to perform his promise. See *Université Laval v. Carriere* (1987), 38 D.L.R. (4th) 503 (Qc. C.A.).

2. The Vista Credit Card Company had widely advertised that it would provide $100,000 flight insurance free of charge to any cardholder who purchased an airline ticket with the card. The plan was quietly dropped six months after it was initiated, because Vista's market researchers indicated that the free insurance offer was having little impact on sales. Under what circumstances would Vista owe a duty of care to notify a cardholder that it was withdrawing this service?

3. The Marvel Bleach Company marketed its highly toxic household bleach in a childproof jug for ten years. In an attempt to reduce costs, Marvel planned to replace the expensive childproof top with an identical looking, but easy-to-open spout. Since it had never advertised that the jug was childproof, Marvel decided to switch tops without advertising this change. You have been asked to advise Marvel on the potential tort consequences of this decision.

12

SPECIAL DUTIES OF CARE: MISCELLANEOUS CATEGORIES

1. Introduction
2. The Duty of Care Owed to Rescuers
3. Duties Owed to the Unborn
4. Nervous Shock
5. A Health Professional's Duty to Inform
6. A Manufacturer's and Supplier's Duty to Warn
7. Duty of Care Owed by a Barrister

1. Introduction

As previously explained, in the past, Canadian courts occasionally used *Anns/Kamloops* as a general test for the recognition of a duty of care. That trend raised questions as to whether *Anns/Kamloops* should replace the unique duty of care principles that historically developed in each of the special categories of negligence discussed in this chapter. Previous editions of this casebook suggested that it would be "premature to jettison the customized analytical frameworks that evolved in these categories for the open-ended principles in *Anns*." Indeed, it was partly that sentiment that led the British and Australian courts to reject the *Anns* test (see *Anns v. Merton London Borough Council*, [1977] 2 All E.R. 492 (H.L.)).

In *Cooper v. Hobart*, [2001] 3 S.C.R. 537, which was excerpted in Chapter 10, the Supreme Court of Canada reiterated its support for *Anns*, but also stressed the need to consider the discrete policy issues that arise in a variety of special circumstances. It is therefore to be expected that, when confronted with one of the special categories discussed in this chapter, courts will refer to the older, more finely tuned duty principles rather than apply a generalized conception of *Anns/Cooper*.

Each of the special duties examined in this chapter evolved independently on the basis of distinct principles. The first part of this chapter examines the special duties of care that may arise in connection with three categories of claimants: (i) rescuers, (ii) unborn children, and (iii) those who suffer nervous shock. The second part of this chapter examines the special duties of care that may arise in connection with three categories of defendants: (i) health care professionals who are in a position to inform patients of the risks associated with treatment or care, (ii) manufacturers and suppliers who are in a position to warn consumers of the risks associated with dangerous products, and (iii) barristers.

2. The Duty of Care Owed to Rescuers

In *Matthews v. MacLaren* (1969), 4 D.L.R. (3d) 557 (Ont. H.C.), which was excerpted in the previous chapter, the question was whether MacLaren, as captain of *The*

Ogopogo, owed a duty of care to rescue Matthews, a gratuitous passenger who had fallen overboard. That question was answered in the affirmative. In the case that follows, the question is whether MacLaren also owed a duty of care to Horsley, another gratuitous passenger, who died while attempting to rescue Matthews.

HORSLEY v. MACLAREN

(1972), 22 D.L.R. (3d) 545 (S.C.C.)

RITCHIE J.: – I have had the opportunity of reading the reasons for judgment of my brother Laskin and I agree with him that . . . a duty rested upon the respondent MacLaren in his capacity as a host and as the owner and operator of the "Ogopogo", to do the best he could to effect the rescue of one of his guests [Matthews] who had accidentally fallen overboard.

. . .

The duty, if any, owing to the late Mr. Horsley stands on an entirely different footing. If, upon Matthews falling overboard, Horsley had immediately dived to his rescue and lost his life, as he ultimately did upon contact with the icy water, then I can see no conceivable basis on which the respondent could have been held responsible for his death.

There is, however, no suggestion that there was any negligence in the rescue of Horsley and if [MacLaren is to be held liable for Horsley's death] such liability must in my view stem from a finding that the situation of peril brought about by Matthews falling into the water was thereafter, within the next three or four minutes, so aggravated by the negligence of MacLaren in attempting his rescue as to induce Horsley to risk his life by diving in after him.

I think that the best description of the circumstances giving rise to the liability to a second rescuer such as Horsley is contained in the reasons for judgment of Lord Denning, M.R., in *Videan v. British Transport Commission*, [1963] 2 Q.B. 650, where he said, at p. 669:

> It seems to me that, if a person *by his fault* creates a situation of peril, he must answer for it to any person who attempts to rescue the person who is in danger. He owes a duty to such a person above all others. The rescuer may act instinctively out of humanity or deliberately out of courage. But whichever it is, so long as it is not wanton interference, if the rescuer is killed or injured in the attempt, he can recover damages *from the one whose fault has been the cause of it.*

The italics are my own.

In the present case a situation of peril was created when Matthews fell overboard, but it was not created by any fault on the part of MacLaren, and before MacLaren can be found to have been in any way responsible for Horsley's death, it must be found that there was such negligence in his method of rescue as to place Matthews in an apparent position of increased danger subsequent to and distinct from the danger to which he had been initially exposed by his accidental fall. In other words, any duty owing to Horsley must stem from the fact that a new situation of peril was created by MacLaren's negligence which induced Horsley to act as he did . . . .

In assessing MacLaren's conduct in attempting to rescue Matthews, I think it should be recognized that he was not under a duty to do more than take all reasonable steps which would have been likely to effect the rescue of a man who was alive and could take some action to assist himself . . . .

Reconstructing the events from the evidence of those who were actually at the scene, it appears to me that MacLaren was first alerted to Matthews' fall when the body was only about a boat-length and a half behind him. He put the engines momentarily in neutral and as soon as he saw the body he reversed, almost immediately after which Jones threw a life-ring within 10 ft. of the man in the water. . . .

Just before the gust of wind carried the boat to port, Marck had the pike pole within Matthews' reach if he had been able to grab it. . . .

I am satisfied that Matthews' body had been in the water for a little less than two minutes when Marck first had the pike pole within his grasp and a life-jacket thrown by Jones was within six inches of him.

The finding of the learned trial Judge that MacLaren was negligent in the rescue of Matthews is really twofold. On the one hand he finds that there was a failure to comply with the "man overboard" rescue procedure recommended by two experts called for the plaintiff, and on the other hand he concludes that MacLaren "was unable to exercise proper judgment in the emergency created because of his excessive consumption of alcohol." In the course of his reasons for judgment in the Court of Appeal, Mr. Justice Schroeder expressly found that there was nothing in the evidence to support the view that MacLaren was incapable of proper management and control owing to the consumption of liquor, the question was not seriously argued in this Court, and like my brother Laskin, I do not think there is any ground for saying that intoxicants had anything to do with the fatal occurrences. . . .

The procedure recommended by the experts in such circumstances was to bring the boat bow on towards the body and the witness Mumford, who had written a "boating course" for the Canadian Boating Federation and had considerable experience in small boats, testified that "it would take about two minutes to turn the boat around and come back on him and have him along side, and possibly another twenty-five, thirty seconds to get him on the boat". The other expert, Livingstone, took the view that by using the bow-on procedure it would take a maximum of two minutes to effect the rescue. . . .

As I have indicated, the evidence discloses that the boat was first brought to a stop in a maximum of two minutes after the body was sighted and at that time there was not only a life-jacket but a pike pole within Matthews' grasp had he been conscious.

In the present case, however, although the procedure followed by MacLaren was not the most highly recommended one, I do not think that the evidence justifies the finding that any fault of his induced Horsley to risk his life by diving as he did. In this regard I adopt the conclusion reached by Mr. Justice Schroeder in the penultimate paragraph of his reasons for judgment where he says [at 287]:

> . . . if the appellant erred in backing instead of turning the cruiser and proceeding towards Matthews "bow on", the error was one of judgment and not negligence, and in the existing circumstances of emergency ought fairly to be excused.

I think it should be made clear that, in my opinion, the duty to rescue a man who has fallen accidentally overboard is a common law duty, the existence of which is in no way dependent upon the provisions of s. 526(1) of the *Canada Shipping Act*, R.S.C. 1952, c. 29 [now R.S.C. 1985, c. S-9, s. 451].

I should also say that, unlike Jessup, J.A., the failure of Horsley to heed MacLaren's warning to remain in the cockpit or cabin plays no part in my reasoning.

For all these reasons I would dismiss this appeal with costs.

LASKIN J. (dissenting): – . . . In this Court, counsel . . . relied on three alternative bases of liability. There was, first, the submission that in going to the aid of Matthews, as he did, MacLaren came under a duty to carry out the rescue with due care in the circumstances, and his failure to employ standard rescue procedures foreseeably brought Horsley into the picture with the ensuing fatal result. The second basis of liability was doubly found as resting (a) on the common law duty of care of a private carrier to his passengers, involving a duty to come to the aid of a passenger who has accidentally fallen overboard, or (b) on a statutory duty under s. 526(1) of the *Canada Shipping Act*, R.S.C. 1952, c. 29 [now R.S.C. 1985, c. S-9, s. 451], to come to the aid of a passenger who has fallen overboard. There was failure, so the allegation was, to act reasonably in carrying out these duties or either of them, with the foreseeable consequence of Horsley's encounter of danger. The third contention was the broadest, to the effect that where a situation of peril, albeit not brought about originally by the defendant's negligence, arises by reason of the defendant's attempt at rescue, he is liable to a second rescuer for ensuing damage on the ground that the latter's intervention is reasonably foreseeable.

None of the bases of liability advanced by the appellants is strictly within the original principle on which the "rescue" cases were founded. That was the recognition of a duty by a negligent defendant to a rescuer coming to the aid of the person imperilled by the defendant's negligence. The evolution of the law on this subject, originating in the moral approbation of assistance to a person in peril, involved a break with the "mind your own business" philosophy. Legal protection is now afforded to one who risks injury to himself in going to the rescue of another who has been foreseeably exposed to danger by the unreasonable conduct of a third person. The latter is now subject to liability at the suit of the rescuer as well as at the suit of the imperilled person, provided, in the case of the rescuer, that his intervention was not so utterly foolhardy as to be outside of any accountable risk and thus beyond even contributory negligence.

Moreover, the liability to the rescuer, although founded on the concept of duty, is now seen as stemming from an independent and not a derivative duty of the negligent person. As *Fleming on Torts*, 3rd ed. (1965), has put it (at p. 166), the cause of action of the rescuer in arising out of the defendant's negligence, is based "not in its tendency to imperil the person rescued, but in its tendency to induce the rescuer to encounter the danger. Thus viewed, the duty to the rescuer is clearly independent. . .". This explanation of principle was put forward as early as 1924 by Professor Bohlen (see his *Studies in the Law of Torts*, at p. 569) in recognition of the difficulty of straining the notion of foreseeability to embrace a rescuer of a person imperilled by another's negligence. Under this explanation of the basis of liability, it is immaterial that the imperilled person does not in fact suffer any injury or that, as it turns out, the negligent person was under no liability to him either because the injury was not caused by the negligence or the damage was outside the foreseeable risk of harm to him: *cf. Videan v. British Transport Commission*, [1963] 2 Q.B. 650. It is a further consequence of the recognition of an independent duty that a person who imperils himself by his carelessness may be as fully liable to a rescuer as a third person would be who imperils another. In my opinion, therefore, *Dupuis v. New Regina Trading Co. Ltd.*, [1943] 4 D.L.R. 275, [1943] 2 W.W.R. 593, ought no longer to be taken as a statement of the common law in Canada in so far as it denies recovery because the rescuer was injured in going to the aid of a person who imperilled himself. . . .

I realize that this statement of the law invites the conclusion that Horsley's estate might succeed against that of Matthews if it was proved that Matthews acted without proper care for his own safety so that Horsley was prompted to come to his rescue. This issue does not, however, have to be canvassed in these proceedings since the estate of Matthews was not joined as a co-defendant. . . .

MacLaren was not a random rescuer. As owner and operator of a boat on which he was carrying invited guests, he was under a legal duty to take reasonable care for their safety. This was a duty which did not depend on the existence of a contract of carriage, nor on whether he was a common carrier or private carrier of passengers. Having brought his guests into a relationship with him as passengers on his boat, albeit as social or gratuitous passengers, he was obliged to exercise reasonable care for their safety. That obligation extends, in my opinion, to rescue from perils of the sea where this is consistent with his duty to see to the safety of his other passengers and with concern for his own safety. The duty exists whether the passenger falls overboard accidentally or by reason of his own carelessness.

. . .

On the view that I take of the issues in this case and, having regard to the facts, the appellants cannot succeed on the first of the alternative submissions on liability if they cannot succeed on the second ground of an existing common law duty of care. Their third contention was not clearly anchored in any original or supervening duty of care and breach of that duty; and, if that be so, I do not see how their counsel's submission on the foreseeability of a second rescuer, even if accepted, can saddle a non-negligent first rescuer with liability either to the rescuee or to a second rescuer. Encouragement by the common law of the rescue of persons in danger would, in my opinion, go beyond reasonable bounds if it involved liability of one rescuer to a succeeding one where the former has not been guilty of any fault which could be said to have induced a second rescue attempt. . . .

The present case is thus reduced to the question of liability on the basis of (1) an alleged breach of a duty of care originating in the relationship of carrier and passenger; (2) whether the breach, if there was one, could be said to have prompted Horsley to go to Matthews' rescue; and (3) whether Horsley's conduct, if not so rash in the circumstances as to be unforeseeable, none the less exhibited want of care so as to make him guilty of contributory negligence.

Whether MacLaren was in breach of his duty of care to Matthews was a question of fact on which the trial Judge's affirmative finding is entitled to considerable weight. That finding was, of course, essential to the further question of a consequential duty to Horsley. Lacourciere J., came to his conclusion of fact on the evidence, after putting to himself the following question: "What would the reasonable boat operator do in the circumstances, attributing to such person the reasonable skill and experience required of the master of a cabin cruiser who is responsible for the safety and rescue of his passengers?" (see 4 D.L.R. (3d) 557 at p. 564. . .). It was the trial Judge's finding that MacLaren, as he himself admitted, had adopted the wrong procedure for rescuing a passenger who had fallen overboard. He knew the proper procedure and had practised it. Coming bow on to effect a rescue was the standard procedure and was taught as such. . . .

I do not see how it can be said that the trial Judge's finding against MacLaren on the issue of breach of duty is untenable. In relation to Horsley's intervention, the finding stands unembarrassed by any question of causation in relation to Matthews. . .

I turn to the question whether the breach of duty to Matthews could properly be regarded in this case as prompting Horsley to attempt a rescue. Like the trial Judge, I am content to adopt and apply analogically on this point the reasoning of Cardozo, J., as he then was, in *Wagner v. International R. Co.* (1921), 133 N.E. 437, and of Lord Denning, M.R., in *Videan v. British Transport Commission,* supra. To use Judge Cardozo's phrase, Horsley's conduct in the circumstances was "within the range of the natural and probable." The fact, moreover, that Horsley's sacrifice was futile is no more a disabling ground here than it was in the *Wagner* case, where the passenger thrown off the train was dead when the plaintiff went to help him, unless it be the case that the rescuer acted wantonly. . .

In responding as he did, and in circumstances where only hindsight made it doubtful that Matthews could be saved, Horsley was not wanton or foolhardy. Like the trial Judge, I do not think that his action passed the point of brave acceptance of a serious risk and became a futile exhibition of recklessness for which there can be no recourse. There is, however, the question whether Horsley was guilty of contributory negligence. This was an alternative plea of the respondent based *inter alia,* on Horsley's failure to put on a life-jacket or secure himself to the boat by a rope or call on the other passengers to stand by, especially in the light of the difficulties of Matthews in the cold water. The trial Judge rejected the contentions of contributory negligence, holding that although "Wearing a life-jacket or securing himself to a lifeline would have been more prudent . . . Horsley's impulsive act without such precautions was the result of the excitement, haste and confusion of the moment, and cannot be said to constitute contributory negligence" (see 4 D.L.R. (3d) at p. 569). In view of its conclusions on the main issue of MacLaren's liability, the Ontario Court of Appeal did not canvass the question of contributory negligence.

The matter is not free from difficulty. About two minutes passed after Matthews had fallen overboard and MacLaren made his first abortive attempt at rescue by proceeding astern. Two life-jackets had been successively thrown towards Matthews without any visible effort on his part to seize them. Then came the second attempt at rescue by backing the boat, and it was in progress when Horsley dived in. Horsley had come on deck at the shout of "Roly's overboard" and was at the stern during MacLaren's first attempt at rescue, and must have been there when the life-jackets were thrown towards Matthews. However, in the concern of the occasion, and having regard to MacLaren's breach of duty, I do not think that Horsley can be charged with contributory negligence in diving to the rescue of Matthews as he did. I point out as well that the evidence does not indicate that the failure to put on a life-jacket or secure himself to a lifeline played any part in Horsley's death.

. . .

[Judson J. and Spence J. concurred with Ritchie J., and Hall J. concurred with Laskin J.]

NOTES AND QUESTIONS

1. Both the majority and dissent in *Horsley* refer to Denning M.R.'s judgment in *Videan v. British Transport Comm.*, [1963] 2 All E.R. 860 (C.A.). In *Videan*, the stationmaster's young son wandered onto the tracks and the stationmaster attempted to rescue him from an approaching trolley. The driver, who was not keeping a proper look-out, could not stop. The stationmaster was killed and his son was badly injured. The child's claim was dismissed because, as a trespasser, his presence was unforeseeable. Nevertheless, Denning M.R. held that the driver ought to have foreseen that his conduct might create an emergency of some kind. Consequently, the stationmaster's presence as

a rescuer was foreseeable and he was owed a duty of care. Is Denning M.R.'s analysis compelling?

2. Cardozo J. had adopted a similar position in *Wagner v. Int. Ry. Co.*, 133 N.E. 437 at 437 (N.Y. 1921). His statement that "danger invites rescue" is now generally accepted. Given this broad test of foreseeability, under what circumstances would a rescuer be denied recovery as an unforeseeable plaintiff? How is the foreseeable plaintiff test applied differently in rescue cases than in other negligence cases? Is this appropriate? See Linden, "Down with Foreseeability! Of Thin Skulls and Rescuers" (1969) 47 Can. Bar Rev. 545 at 558-70; and Smith, "The Mystery of Duty" in Klar, ed., *Studies in Canadian Tort Law* (1977) 1 at 30-32.

3. In *Horsley*, Ritchie J. also quotes Denning M.R.'s statement "if a man by his fault creates a situation of peril, he must answer for it to any person who attempts to rescue the person who is in danger." What does this mean?

According to Ritchie J., what had to be established to prove that MacLaren owed Horsley a duty of care? What is the test for breaching the standard of care? Based on the expert evidence, was MacLaren's use of the reverse, rather than the bow-on method, a causal factor in inducing Horsley's rescue attempt? Why did Ritchie J. dismiss Horsley's claim?

4. What was the basis upon which Laskin J. held that MacLaren owed Horsley a duty of care? How did Laskin J.'s analysis relate to the appellant's three alternative bases of liability? What was the basis upon which Laskin J. concluded that MacLaren breached the standard of care? Do you agree with Laskin J.'s analysis of the causation or contributory negligence issue? Assuming Horsley realized that Matthews was dead, would he have been contributorily negligent in jumping overboard to recover the body?

5. Although the courts have occasionally held rescuers to be contributorily negligent, such findings are rare. Rescuers confronting a sudden emergency are not held to the same standard of care as those acting in less extreme circumstances. See *Sayers v. Harlow Urban Dist. Council*, [1958] 2 All E.R. 342 (C.A.); *Corothers v. Slobodian*, [1975] 2 S.C.R. 633; *Toy v. Argenti*, [1980] 3 W.W.R. 276 (B.C.S.C.); and *Cleary v. Hansen* (1981), 18 C.C.L.T. 147 (Ont. H.C.). See also Binchy, "Torts – Rescuers – Foreseeability – Contributory Negligence" (1974) 52 Can. Bar Rev. 292; and Voechting, "Negligence – Rescuer Doctrine – Liability of a Tortfeasor for Injuries to Rescuers Extended" (1976) 7 Man. L.J. 87.

In *Meyer v. Parker* (1995), 7 B.C.L.R. (3d) 131 (S.C.), the plaintiff went to a convenience store after receiving an allegedly "distraught" call from a friend working at the store. On arrival, he found three youths arguing with his friend. After a heated verbal exchange, the plaintiff convinced the youths to leave the store. However, the plaintiff then followed the youths outside and told his friend to lock the store's doors. He was subsequently beaten by the youths and lost his left eye. The plaintiff's attempt to rely on the rescuer doctrine failed because he had left a place of safety and deliberately put himself at risk by confronting the youths outside. The court found that he had not taken reasonable care for his own safety, and his claim was dismissed.

6. The defence of voluntary assumption of risk has been all but eliminated in rescue cases. In *Urbanski v. Patel* (1978), 84 D.L.R. (3d) 650 (Man. Q.B.), the plaintiff donated

a kidney to his daughter after the defendant surgeon had negligently removed her only kidney. The plaintiff claimed that the loss of his donated kidney had been caused by the defendant's negligence in injuring his daughter. The court found for the plaintiff, concluding that his act was a reasonably foreseeable result of the defendant's negligence. The defence of voluntary assumption of risk was dismissed with a statement to the effect that the defence is inapplicable where the plaintiff consciously faces a risk in an attempt to rescue another who has been imperilled by the defendant's negligence. In light of *Urbanski*, can you suggest a situation in which a rescuer might be denied recovery on the basis of voluntary assumption of risk? See Robertson, "A New Application of the Rescue Principle" (1980) 96 L.Q.R. 19.

Is the treatment of voluntary assumption of risk in rescue cases consistent with the common law's refusal to impose a duty to rescue (see Chapter 11)? If there is no legal obligation to rescue, then why do the courts not find that rescuers have voluntarily assumed the risks associated with their conduct? Is the decision to risk one's life in a rescue attempt not a conscious assumption of risk?

7. In many jurisdictions in the United States, police officers, firefighters and other professional rescuers are denied recovery from tortfeasors for injuries sustained in their rescue efforts. The "fireman's rule," as it is called, is based in part on voluntary assumption of risk. See generally "Assumption of the Risk and the Fireman's Rule" (1981) 7 Wm. Mitchell L. Rev. 749; Riley, "The Fireman's Rule: Defining its Scope Using the Cost-Spreading Rationale" (1983) 71 Cal. L. Rev. 218; Werner, "*Berko v. Freda*: The Fireman's Rule Burns Police Officers" (1984) 37 Rutgers L. Rev. 195; Palumbo, "Equal Protection and the Fireman's Rule in Ohio" (1987) 38 Case W.L. Rev. 123; and Scholz, "*Rosa v. Dunkin' Donuts*: The Fireman's Rule Revisited" (1992) 44 Rutgers L. Rev. 405.

In *Ogwo v. Taylor*, [1987] 3 All E.R. 961 (H.L.), the House of Lords stated that the rule had no place in English law. This principle was affirmed in *White v. Chief Constable of South Yorkshire*, [1999] 1 All E.R. 1 (H.L.). In Canada, it also appears that firefighters and other professional rescuers can recover for the injuries they sustain in rescue attempts. What argument would you make in favour of the "fireman's rule?" See Dreiman, "Extending the Fireman's Rule to Great Britain: Protecting British Citizens from Tort Liability for Firefighters' Line-of-Duty Injuries" (1998) 8 Ind. Int'l & Comp. L. Rev. 381.

8. Since the rescuer's claim is independent of that of the person being rescued, a rescuer may recover for injuries sustained in assisting those who have negligently imperilled themselves. See *Chapman v. Hearse* (1961), 106 C.L.R. 112 (H.C.A.); *Corothers v. Slobodian, supra*; *C.N.R. v. Bakty* (1977), 18 O.R. (2d) 481 (Co. Ct.); *Roberts v. Morana* (1997), 38 C.C.L.T. (2d) 1 (Ont. Gen. Div.); and *Bridge v. Jo* (1998), [1999] 3 W.W.R. 167 (B.C.S.C.). But see *Clyke v. Clyke* (1987), 80 N.S.R. (2d) 149 (T.D.), aff'd (1988), 83 N.S.R. (2d) 79 (C.A.); and *Smith v. Tucker*, 2007 CarswellBC 709 (S.C.) (WLeC) . See also *Dufault v. Excelsior Mortgage Corp.* (2002), 310 A.R. 117 (Q.B.), aff'd (2003), 20 Alta. L.R. (4th) 220 (C.A.), where the plaintiff was injured while trying to protect a night clerk at the defendant's hotel from a gang of aggressive youths. The hotel was found liable for having inadequate security measures in place to protect its night staff. The court found that it was foreseeable that staff might become threatened and that patrons would step in to assist.

9. The general principles governing rescuers also apply to cases in which plaintiffs are injured while attempting to save themselves or their own property. See *Prescott v. Connell* (1893), 22 S.C.R. 147; *Hutterly v. Imperial Oil Ltd.* (1956), 3 D.L.R. (2d) 719 (Ont. H.C.); *Sayers v. Harlow Urban District Council, supra*; *Zervobeakos v. Zervobeakos* (1969), 8 D.L.R. (3d) 377 (N.S.C.A.); and *Toy v. Argenti, supra.*

A duty of care may be refused, however, if the plaintiff was attempting to protect a purely economic interest. In *Saccone v. Fandrakis* (2002), 11 C.C.L.T. (3d) 151 (B.C.S.C.), the plaintiff saw, from a distance of half a city block, the aftermath of an accident in which his van had been damaged. He ran toward his vehicle because he was concerned that the defendant, who he correctly believed was responsible for the accident, would leave the scene. The plaintiff feared that this would affect his insurance claim. In running to the scene, he slipped and hurt himself. The court applied *Cooper v. Hobart* and held that the defendant did not owe a duty of care with respect to the plaintiff's injuries. While accepting that it "might . . . be reasonably foreseeable that the plaintiff in such a situation would be injured while sprinting . . . to the scene," Catliff J. held that there was insufficient proximity between the parties and, further, that policy considerations militated against the recognition of a duty of care. It was one thing to recognize a duty of care where the plaintiff, pressed by exigency, came to the rescue of person or property; quite another to recognize a duty where, in the absence of an emergency, the plaintiff tried to protect a purely economic interest. Does this decision seem fair to you? How would you have responded to the accident if you had been in the plaintiff's position?

10. One unresolved issue in *Horsley* is whether the general principles governing the discontinuance of a gratuitous undertaking apply to rescue cases. The majority of the Court of Appeal indicated that an individual who has voluntarily begun a rescue attempt is under no duty to continue it unless he or she has worsened the victim's original position. The Court of Appeal cited *East Suffolk Rivers Catchment Bd. v. Kent*, [1941] A.C. 74 (H.L.) as authority, even though that case concerned the liability of public authorities for property damage arising from negligence in exercising their statutory powers. Why did the Supreme Court of Canada not find it necessary to address the gratuitous rescue issue? Laskin J. suggested that *East Suffolk* should not govern liability for the discontinuance of rescue attempts when human lives are at stake. Should there be a duty to continue a voluntary rescue attempt in such circumstances?

11. The courts have taken a relatively broad approach to the definition of "rescuer." See for example *Urbanski v. Patel, supra* (kidney donor); *Bridge v. Jo, supra* (911 caller); and *Emerson v. Insurance Corporation of British Columbia* (2003), 123 A.C.W.S. (3d) 1169 (B.C.S.C.) (woman who helped an elderly couple get out of their car after it left the road). However, in *Joudrey v. Swissair Transport Company*, (2004) 225 N.S.R. (2d) 156 (S.C.), the court denied the claim of a member of the armed forces for the nervous shock he suffered after attending to the wreckage of Swissair Flight 111, which crashed off the coast of Halifax. Because it quickly became clear that there would be no survivors, the plaintiff was not involved in a "rescue" operation but in a "recovery" operation. The court stressed at para. 35 that, in order to qualify as a "rescuer," the plaintiff "must have been engaged in the process of attempting to save someone who is in danger at the time of the purported rescue."

For a discussion of the policy considerations behind the generous recovery obtained by rescuers, see Klar, "The Role of Fault and Policy in Negligence Law" (1996) 35 Alta. L. Rev. 24.

12. As indicated in the previous chapter, s. 217 of the *Criminal Code*, R.S.C. 1985, c. C-46, requires an individual who undertakes an act to complete it if an omission to do so is, or may be, dangerous to life. There are few reported cases, but presumably the section should apply to an individual who, having undertaken a voluntary rescue attempt, abandons the victim in a life-threatening situation. Based on this criminal law provision, what argument would you make for recognizing a parallel common law duty in negligence?

In *R. v. Browne* (1997), 33 O.R. (3d) 775 (C.A.), the defendant and the deceased were drug dealers. The deceased swallowed a bag of cocaine in order to avoid detection by police. She was unable to throw up the bag, and began to exhibit symptoms of narcotics poisoning. The defendant told the deceased that he would take her to the hospital. He called a taxi to take her to the hospital but she died shortly after her arrival. At trial, the defendant was convicted of criminal negligence causing death for failing to complete the "undertaking" that he had assumed under s. 217 to take the deceased to the hospital. The trial judge found that calling a taxi, rather than 911, constituted wanton and reckless disregard for the deceased's life. The conviction was reversed by the Court of Appeal for Ontario, which found that the offer to take the deceased to the hospital did not constitute an "undertaking" under s. 217. Abella J.A. (as she then was), speaking for the court, wrote that "[t]he mere expression of words indicating a willingness to do an act cannot trigger the legal duty."

REVIEW PROBLEMS

1. The Apex Corporation was shooting a gangster film in downtown Toronto. One of the scenes depicted two thugs beating a police officer just outside of the Toronto Art Gallery. Apex had obtained permission to film the scene on the Gallery's property, cordoned off the outside area and staged the scene behind the Gallery away from possible intermeddlers. During the middle of the scene, a patron in the Art Gallery burst through a fire door and lunged at the two thugs. He had lost his way in the basement of the Gallery. All he could see through the small window beside the fire door was the officer on the ground being kicked. Believing the officer to be in danger, he opened the fire door, hoping to set off the alarm and scare off the thugs. Unfortunately, in lunging at the thugs, he slipped and broke his leg. You have been asked to advise the patron on his prospects of recovering from the Apex Corporation.

2. Several weeks after he was informed that he had terminal cancer, Mr. Smith decided to commit suicide. However, when he stepped out on the ledge of his fourth floor apartment window, he began to have second thoughts. While he was deliberating, a bystander called the police and fire departments. Within minutes, two emergency rescue teams arrived on the scene. By this time, Smith had changed his mind and had re-entered his apartment. Smith died of natural causes shortly thereafter. Advise the rescue teams who wish to sue Smith's estate for their expenses in coming to the scene.

3. Duties Owed to the Unborn

The courts increasingly are being asked to resolve complex issues surrounding injuries associated with birth. For analytical purposes, it is helpful to divide the cases into discrete categories and to focus on the unique considerations that arise in each. We will consider four such categories: (i) pre-conception wrongs, (ii) wrongful birth and wrongful life, (iii) wrongful pregnancy, and (iv) pre-natal injuries. Within the various categories, claims sometimes are made by a parent or a child or both. It is therefore important to distinguish between the different types of losses that may be involved, including the mother's pain and suffering, the parents' increased financial burdens, and the child's loss of potential earnings. It is also important to consider the legal status of unborn children: the common law does not ascribe the status of "person" until a child is born alive.

In the materials that follow, the text provides a general outline, while further details are presented in the notes.

(a) PRE-CONCEPTION WRONGS

A pre-conception wrong occurs when the defendant carelessly causes a parent to suffer an injury that detrimentally affects a subsequently conceived child. For example, a mother or father may have been exposed to hazardous chemicals that caused injury to her ova or his sperm. That defect is later passed on to a child through conception and becomes manifest upon birth. Aside from very complex problems of causation, these cases often raise policy issues regarding the scope of a defendant's potential liability. It may be necessary to ask, for instance, whether a parent's knowledge of the potential genetic problems has any bearing on the defendant's liability.

Moreover, there is debate regarding what steps a potential defendant may take to avoid harm to the plaintiff's reproductive system. In the American case of *U.A.W. v. Johnson Controls*, 499 U.S. 187 (1991), employees at the defendant's battery factory were exposed to lead levels that posed a risk to foetal health in women planning to have children. Fearing claims for pre-conception harms, the defendant required all women under 70 who worked at the factory to provide medical documentation of their sterility or lose their jobs. The United States Supreme Court ultimately found that this policy was discriminatory against women, and that women should be free to decide whether to expose themselves to the risk. *Johnson Controls* illustrates the delicate balancing of interests involved in protecting the health of potential children against the autonomy rights of their mothers.

NOTES AND QUESTIONS

1. What limits should be placed on recovery for pre-conception torts? Assume that a child suffers injuries during delivery because of his or her mother's misshapen pelvis. Assume as well that the mother's pelvis was misshapen because she was run over by a negligent driver 15 years ago. What claim, if any, should the child have against the driver? What policy objections can be raised concerning such claims? Should those policy concerns be addressed in connection with the duty of care, or at some other stage in the negligence analysis?

2. Should different considerations apply in pre-conception cases involving workplace exposures to hazardous products? Should the employer's obligation be limited to: (a) fully informing all potential employees, (b) complying with workplace health and safety legislation, (c) complying with industry safety norms, or (d) obtaining a waiver of liability from the employees? Should employers be free to deny jobs or limit placements to women of child-bearing age? What other less discriminatory options were available to the employer in *Johnson Controls*? One author has suggested that employers may be able to argue that a discriminatory plan is warranted given the potential for ruinous foetal tort liability. See Grover, "The Employer's Fetal Injury Quandary After *Johnson Controls*" (1992-93) 81 Kentucky L.J. 639.

3. In *Paxton v. Ramji*, 2006 CarswellOnt 1844 (S.C.J.) (WLeC), the infant plaintiff suffered severe disabilities because her mother took a prescription acne drug prior to the plaintiff's conception and during the ensuing pregnancy. The effects of the drug on a foetus were known to the prescribing doctor, but the mother's partner had had a vasectomy and the doctor did not expect her to become pregnant. The plaintiff claimed that the doctor was negligent in failing to recommend extra birth control to the mother. The court found that, due to the known effects of the drug, the doctor owed a duty of care to the potential child of a woman who was taking it. However, due to her partner's vasectomy and her extreme concern about her acne, the court concluded that the doctor had not fallen below the standard of care.

4. For more general discussion about balancing women's rights against the health of the foetus, see Katz Rothman, *Recreating Motherhood: Ideology and Technology in a Patriarchal Society* (1989); Daniels, *At Women's Expense: State Power and the Politics of Fetal Rights* (1993); Merrick & Blank, eds., *The Politics of Pregnancy: Policy Dilemmas in the Maternal-Fetal Relationship* (1993); and Roth, *Making Women Pay: The Hidden Costs of Fetal Rights* (2000).

(b) WRONGFUL BIRTH AND WRONGFUL LIFE

A physician may carelessly fail to inform a woman that she faces an unusually high risk of giving birth to a child with a disability, or may negligently perform tests that are designed to detect foetal abnormalities. Because of this negligence or failure to inform, the woman may continue a pregnancy that she otherwise would have terminated. In such circumstances, the defendant physician does not positively cause an injury to the child. Instead, the physician has merely deprived the child's mother of an opportunity to make an informed decision regarding abortion. Nevertheless, the defendant may be faced with a claim by the mother, the child, or both. A claim brought by a parent is said to be for "wrongful birth." A claim brought by a child is said to be for "wrongful life."

The mother's claim is, in large part, based on fairly straightforward principles governing a physician's duty to inform a patient of medical risks. That issue is discussed in greater detail later in this chapter. The child's claim, in contrast, is much more problematic. Its gist is that, but for the defendant's carelessness, the child would not have been born and therefore would not have been required to struggle through life with a disability. In essence, the claim suggests that it would have been better if the child had not been born at all. Not surprisingly, the courts have struggled with questions concerning the sanctity of life and the quantification of damages. These issues remain largely unresolved in Canadian law.

NOTES AND QUESTIONS

1. For many years, the leading Commonwealth authority on this topic was *McKay v. Essex Area Health Authority*, [1982] 2 All E.R. 771 (C.A.). The plaintiff contracted German measles early in her pregnancy, but the infection was not diagnosed in the blood tests that were done. As a result of the disease, her child was born severely disabled. The mother and child sued the doctor and health authority for failing to treat the infection and for failing to advise the mother of the desirability of an abortion. The court struck out the child's claim as not showing any reasonable cause of action. The child's claim could succeed only if one accepted that the child had a right not to be born. The court stated that such a claim for wrongful life was contrary to public policy as a violation of the sanctity of human life. Do you agree? Moreover, the court stated that it was impossible to assess damages by comparing the value of non-existence to the value of existence in a disabled state. Is this an appropriate test for assessing the child's losses?

2. The High Court of Australia recently decided two cases on the issue of wrongful life: *Harriton v. Stephens*, [2006] HCA 15; and *Waller v. James; Waller v. Hoolahan*, [2006] HCA 16. The court affirmed that damages for wrongful life are not available at common law. Among the reasons given by the court were that: it is impossible to compare a life with disabilities to non-existence; broader public policy favoured equal treatment to those with disabilities, and their lives would be devalued by a decision that disabled life is worse than no life at all; and complex decisions of this nature ought to be decided, if at all, by legislators.

3. These issues are unsettled in Canada. In *Arndt v. Smith* (1994), 93 B.C.L.R. (2d) 220 (S.C.), a mother gave birth to a severely disabled child as a result of contracting chicken pox during pregnancy. Although such disabilities rarely result from chicken pox, the physician was found to be negligent for failing to inform the mother of these risks and offer her the option of an abortion. The court commented favourably on the dropping of the child's claim for wrongful life, stating that no viable action could be brought on that basis in British Columbia. The father's claim to recover the costs of supporting the child was dismissed. The court accepted that the mother could claim for the additional expenses of rearing a disabled child, but held that her action failed on the issue of causation. The plaintiff could not prove that a reasonable woman in her position would have had an abortion if informed of the very small risks of serious birth defects. The British Columbia Court of Appeal ordered a new trial on the issue of causation, but the Supreme Court of Canada restored the trial judgment: *Arndt v. Smith* (1995), 6 B.C.L.R. (3d) 201 (C.A.), rev'd [1997] 2 S.C.R. 539.

In *H.(R.) v. Hunter* (1996), 32 C.C.L.T. (2d) 44 (Ont. Gen. Div.), the parents of two disabled children were awarded approximately $3,000,000 for the additional costs they would incur in raising the children. The defendant doctors were held negligent in not referring the mother for additional genetic counselling.

In *Krangle (Guardian ad litem of) v. Brisco* (1997), 55 B.C.L.R. (3d) 23 (S.C.), aff'd on point (2000), 76 B.C.L.R. (3d) 1 (C.A.), rev'd on other grounds [2002] 1 S.C.R. 205, a child was born with Down's Syndrome. The defendant physician had carelessly failed to inform the mother about the availability of an amniocentesis test that would have detected that condition during pregnancy. The evidence indicated that, if so informed, the woman would have had an abortion. The court held that, while the child did not have a cause of action against the physician for wrongful life, the parents were entitled to damages regarding the expenses associated with his care.

In *Jones (Guardian ad litem of) v. Rostvig* (1999), 44 C.C.L.T. (3d) 313 (B.C.S.C.), the courts struck out a wrongful life claim by a child on the basis that it disclosed no cause of action. The court held that, while a physician owes a duty of care to a child regarding pre-natal injuries that become manifest on birth, a physician does not owe a duty of care to a child to provide its mother with information that would lead to an abortion. See also *Lacroix (Litigation Guardian of) v. Dominique* (2001), 156 Man. R. (2d) 262 (C.A.). However, in *Petkovic (Litigation Guardian of) v. Olupona* (2002), 11 C.C.L.T. (3d) 91 (Ont. S.C.J.), aff'd (2002), 30 C.C.L.T. (3d) 266 (Ont. Div. Ct.), the court refused to strike out a similar claim.

4. Presumably, as medical technology improves and more abnormalities become detectable during pregnancy, claims for wrongful birth will increase. Should parents be able to make a claim if the child suffers from a relatively mild disability? What if the child will suffer from a condition that is easily treatable by medication, but the parents do not want the hassle or expense? What if doctors can only predict that the child might, sometime in the future, develop a certain medical condition? What test of causation should be used in such actions? Should the parents have to prove that reasonable parents in their position would decide to terminate the pregnancy? See Sonnenburg, "A Preference for Nonexistence: Wrongful Life and a Proposed Tort of Genetic Malpractice" (1982) 55 S. Cal. L. Rev. 477; Jankowski, "Wrongful Birth and Wrongful Life Actions Arising from Negligent Counselling: The Need for Legislation Supporting Reproductive Choice" (1989) 17 Fordham Urb. L.J. 27; Shapira, "'Wrongful life' lawsuits for faulty genetic counselling: should the impaired newborn be entitled to sue?" (1998) 24 J. Med. Ethics 369; and Pattinson, "Wrongful Life Actions as a Means of Regulating Use of Genetic and Reproductive Technologies" (1999) 7 Health L.J. 19.

In *Bovingdon (Litigation Guardian of) v. Hergott* (2006), 83 O.R. (3d) 465 (S.C.J.), the defendant doctor prescribed a fertility drug to the plaintiffs' mother. The defendant failed to inform the mother that the drug would increase the chance of multiple pregnancy. The mother became pregnant with the plaintiffs, who are twins. The plaintiffs suffered disabilities due to being born prematurely. The defendant conceded that the drug caused the twin pregnancy, which in turn caused the premature delivery and the ensuing disabilities. The plaintiffs' parents were successful in their action for the costs of raising the disabled children, arguing that the mother would not have taken the fertility drug if properly informed. The plaintiffs' action for compensation for their disabilities was also successful. The judge characterized their claim as involving prenatal injury: the plaintiffs would not be disabled but for the defendant's negligent failure to inform their mother about the risks of the fertility drug. The judge stressed that this was not a case of wrongful life, and avoided the more controversial issues involved in such actions. Is the judge's characterization correct? If the defendant had not been negligent, would the plaintiffs have been born at all? Was it wise for the defendant to concede the issue of causation?

(c) WRONGFUL PREGNANCY

The third category is based on general principles of medical negligence. It arises when parents have taken medical steps to prevent pregnancy or childbirth but, due to the negligence of a medical professional, a pregnancy occurs or continues. Suppose, for example, that a physician carelessly performed an abortion with the result that a pregnancy was not terminated. The woman may claim economic loss, pain and suffering, and emotional harm from having to undergo a second abortion. Similarly, if a physician negligently performs a sterilization procedure, the woman may claim damages for having to terminate a pregnancy that she was specifically trying to avoid.

The situation is more complicated, however, if the woman does not terminate the unwanted pregnancy but instead gives birth to the child. Over the years, the courts have responded to these circumstances in different ways. As summarized by Justice Kirby in the Australian case of *Cattanach v. Melchior* (2003), 77 A.L.J.R. 1312 (H.C.A.) at para. 138, the court may decide any of the following:

> (1) That no damages may be recovered where the child is born healthy and without disability or impairment;
>
> (2) That damages may be recovered but confined to the immediate damage to the mother (and loss of consortium for the father) together with any expenses and loss of earnings immediately consequential on the pregnancy and delivery but excluding the costs of upkeep until self-reliance of a healthy child;
>
> (3) That damages may be recovered but confined to the foregoing together with any additional costs of rearing a child born with a disability or born to a parent or parents with a disability;
>
> (4) That damages may be recovered in full for the reasonable costs of rearing an unplanned child to the age when that child might be expected to be economically self-reliant, whether the child is "healthy" or "disabled" or "impaired" but with a deduction from the amount of such damages for the joy and benefits received, and the potential economic support derived, from the child; and
>
> (5) That full damages against the tortfeasor for the cost of rearing the child may be allowed, subject to the ordinary limitations of reasonable foreseeability and remoteness, with no discount for joys, benefits and support, leaving restrictions upon such recovery to such limitations as may be enacted by a Parliament with authority to do so.

Traditionally, the Canadian and Commonwealth courts have chosen option (3). Parents who give birth to an unwanted child may claim damages for the expenses associated with the unwanted pregnancy and childbirth, and the mother may claim damages for the related pain and suffering. Further, if the child is disabled, the parents may claim for the extra costs associated with raising a disabled child. However, if the parents give birth to a healthy child, they cannot claim damages for the ordinary costs of raising that child to maturity. The courts have generally adopted the view that a healthy child is a "blessing" and its birth cannot be treated as a legal harm.

More recently, the courts have been more receptive to claims for the expenses of raising a healthy child. Significantly, in *Cattanach* the High Court of Australia rejected earlier authorities and, by a decision of four to three, decided to award damages to a couple for the costs of raising a healthy child. The court was persuaded by the fact that the parents had decided to limit the size of their family and had undergone a sterilization procedure specifically to prevent further pregnancy. Although the unplanned child was welcomed into the family, its birth inevitably led to lifestyle changes and required the parents to forsake other opportunities. The defendant had negligently performed a service, and the unplanned pregnancy was a foreseeable result of that negligence. The High Court decided that there were no longer any convincing policy reasons to grant physicians "immunity" from liability for the foreseeable consequences of their negligence. In the United Kingdom, the House of Lords recently affirmed its position that the costs of raising healthy children should not be compensated, but devised the unique solution of providing a "conventional award" of £15,000 in wrongful pregnancy cases to compensate parents for the violation of their right to choose the size of their family. See *Rees v. Darlington Memorial NHS Trust*, [2004] 1 A.C. 309 (H.L.).

The Canadian courts have also been moving toward greater recovery for the costs of rearing an unplanned child. First, in *Suite v. Cooke* (1993), 15 C.C.L.T. (2d) 15 (Qc. S.C.), aff'd [1995] R.J.Q. No. 2765 (C.A.), the Quebec Court of Appeal found that pecuniary damages for the costs of raising a healthy child were recoverable, but also that they had to be set off against the emotional benefits and burdens that the child would bring to its parents. Next, damages for child-rearing costs were awarded without lengthy discussion in *Joshi v. Wooley* (1995), 4 B.C.L.R. (3d) 208 (S.C.), a case that has not been extensively followed. Finally, in a more influential judgment, *Kealey v. Berezowski* (1996), 136 D.L.R. (4th) 708 (Ont. Gen. Div.), Lax J. rejected the argument that claims for child-rearing costs should be universally denied as a matter of public policy. Nevertheless, Lax J. characterized such claims as a form of pure economic loss, and concluded that they could only be recovered where the plaintiffs' primary motivation for wanting to limit the size of their family was financial. This did not apply on the facts of the case, so damages for child-rearing costs were not recoverable. The Canadian law in this area remains unsettled.

NOTES AND QUESTIONS

1. What policy considerations would lead a court to deny claims for the costs of rearing a healthy child? See *Doiron v. Orr* (1978), 20 O.R. (2d) 71 (H.C.J.); *Udale v. Bloomsbury Area Health Authority*, [1983] 2 All E.R. 522 (Q.B.); *McFarlane v. Tayside Health Board (Scotland)*, [1999] 4 All E.R. 961 (H.L.); and *Cattanach v. Melchior* (2003), 77 A.L.J.R. 1312 (H.C.A.). See also Symmons, "Policy Factors in Actions for Wrongful Birth" (1987) 50 Mod. L. Rev. 269; Cameron-Perry, "Return of the burden of the blessing" (1999) 149 N.L.J. 1887; Mason, "Unwanted pregnancy: a case of retroversion?" (2000) 4 Edin. L.R. 191; Weir, "The Unwanted Child" [2000] C.L.J. 238; and Elvin, "Are Healthy Children Always a Blessing?" [2002] C.L.J. 516.

2. For cases awarding damages for the costs of rearing a disabled child, see *Emeh v. Kensington and Chelsea and Westminster Area Health Authority*, [1985] 1 Q.B. 1012 (C.A.); *Cherry v. Borsman* (1990), 75 D.L.R. (4th) 668 (B.C.S.C.), varied (1992), 70 B.C.L.R. (2d) 273 (C.A.); and *Parkinson v. St. James and Seacroft University Hospital NHS Trust*, [2002] Q.B. 266 (C.A.). Is there any legal or policy reason for allowing claims for the additional costs of raising a disabled child, but not the general costs of raising a healthy, but unplanned, child? See Kerr, "Indemnity for the Costs of Raising Unwanted Children from Unwanted Pregnancies" (1998) 6 Tort L. Rev. 121.

What principles should apply if an unplanned child is born healthy, but subsequently develops a disability? See *Groom v. Selby*, [2001] E.W.C.A. Civ. 1522, where the plaintiff's baby developed salmonella meningitis a few weeks after birth. The mother's claim for the extra costs of raising a disabled child was allowed.

3. In *Roe v. Dabbs* (2004), 31 B.C.L.R. (4th) 158 (S.C.), Parrett J. surveyed the existing options in wrongful pregnancy cases and found them all to be inadequate. Due to the difficulties in weighing the financial and emotional benefits and burdens of raising a healthy, but unplanned, child, Parrett J. concluded that the damages should be considered as non-pecuniary. The plaintiff in that case was awarded $55,000 in non-pecuniary damages for her distress on discovering that her abortion attempt had failed, and for the limitations on her lifestyle and activities due to the birth of an unplanned child. See also *Fredette v. Wiebe* (1986), 4 B.C.L.R. (2d) 184 (S.C.), where the plaintiff was awarded non-pecuniary damages for the distress caused by having twins as a young, single mother.

4. What is the legal significance of the parents' choice not to terminate an unplanned pregnancy or put a child up for adoption? Is this a break in the chain of causation, contributory negligence, or a failure to mitigate damages? The courts have typically held that the parents' decision to keep the unplanned child does not affect their claim against a negligent medical professional, since the decision not to abort or put a child up for adoption is reasonable, particularly within the confines of marriage. See *McFarlane, supra.* Nevertheless, in *C.E.S. v Superclinics (Australia) Pty. Ltd.* (1995), 38 N.S.W.L.R. 47 (C.A.), the court found that the cause of the plaintiff's child-rearing costs was her own decision to keep the unplanned child, and consequently denied her claim. See also *Emeh, supra*, where the trial judge found the mother's decision not to undergo abortion was a *novus actus interveniens*. This decision was reversed on appeal.

Is it fair for a negligent physician to be saddled with all the costs of raising a healthy child that the parents have welcomed into their family? Do the parents receive a windfall in such cases, *i.e.*, they have the emotional benefits of a child, while having its upkeep paid for by a negligent physician? See *Keats v. Pearce* (1984), 48 Nfld. & P.E.I.R. 102 (Nfld. S.C.T.D.).

5. What should be included in the "ordinary costs" of raising a healthy child? These obviously include food and clothing, but what about birthday presents, music lessons, participation in sports, or higher education? If wealthy parents decide to spend more money on their children, should they receive greater compensation for having an unplanned child? See the discussion in *Bevilacqua v. Altenkirk* (2004), 35 B.C.L.R. (4th) 281 (S.C.). See also *Benarr v. Kettering Health Authority*, [1988] N.L.J. 179 (Q.B.), where the judge awarded the costs of private education because that was what the child could expect in that particular family.

6. In *Kealey v. Berezowski* (1996), 136 D.L.R. (4th) 708 (Ont. Gen. Div.), discussed above, Lax J. concluded that child-rearing costs should only be recoverable if the primary motivation for wanting to limit the size of one's family were financial. Are the parents' motives really relevant? Will this tempt plaintiffs to slant their evidence? What about cases where there are mixed reasons for not wanting to become pregnant, or where the father and mother have differing views? See *McFarlane, supra*; and *M.S. v. Baker* (2001), 309 A.R. 1 (Q.B.).

Should courts be more likely to award damages for child-rearing costs if the family's financial resources are already limited? One author has argued that the effects of denying claims for child-rearing costs are disproportionately borne by poor, single mothers: Adjin-Tettey, "Claims for Involuntary Parenthood: Why the Resistance?" in Neyers, Chamberlain & Pitel, eds., *Emerging Issues in Tort Law* (2007).

7. While there has been some willingness to award damages for the costs of raising a healthy child, there are still numerous instances of courts denying such claims. See for example *Mummery v. Olsson*, 2001 CarswellOnt 151 (S.C.J.) (WLeC); *M.Y. v. Boutros* (2002), 313 A.R. 1 (Q.B.); and *Bevilacqua*, *supra*. Thus, the Canadian law in this area remains unsettled.

8. Is there a legally significant difference between claims for wrongful birth and claims for wrongful pregnancy? In either situation, the parents are left to care for a child who, but for the defendant's negligence, would not exist. Should it matter whether the parents were attempting to avoid pregnancy altogether, or whether they were only attempting to avoid having a disabled child? See Hoyano, "Misconceptions about Wrongful Conception" (2002) 65 Mod. L. Rev. 883; and Mason, "Wrongful Pregnancy, Wrongful Birth and Wrongful Terminology" (2002) 6 Edin. L.R. 46.

9. The decision in *Cattanach* was greeted by political and public disdain, and its effects have been largely abrogated by statute in three Australian states. While the legislation still allows claims for the extra costs associated with raising disabled children, no claims are permitted for the costs of raising healthy children. See the discussion in Hirsch, "Rights and Responsibilities in Wrongful Birth and Wrongful Life Cases" (2006) 29 U.N.S.W.L.J. 233.

10. For general commentary on recent developments in the Commonwealth, see Vranken, "Damages for 'Wrongful Birth': Where to After *Cattanach*?" (2003) 24 Adel. L. Rev. 243; Fordham, "Blessing or Burden? Recent Developments in Actions in Wrongful Conception and Wrongful Birth in the U.K. and Australia" [2004] Sing. J. Legal Stud. 462; Todd, "Wrongful Conception, Wrongful Birth and Wrongful Life" (2005) 27 Syd. L. Rev. 525; and Stretton, "Birth Torts: Damages for Wrongful Birth and Wrongful Life" (2005) 10 Deakin L. Rev. 319.

(d) PRE-NATAL INJURIES

The final category may be the most significant in terms of frequency of claims. The basic question is whether a child can sue in negligence for injuries sustained *in utero*. The answer to that question begins with the proposition that, unless the child is subsequently born with an injury, no cause of action arises. As indicated above, a foetus is not recognized in Canadian law as a person and therefore has no standing to sue. If, however, the child is subsequently born with a disability, then a claim in negligence may be possible. The courts have long recognized that a person may owe a duty of care to avoid careless actions before birth that may result in a loss upon birth. See *Duval v. Seguin* (1972), 26 D.L.R. (3d) 418 (Ont. H.C.), aff'd (1973), 40 D.L.R. (3d) 666 (Ont. C.A.); and *Montreal Tramways Co. v. Léveillé*, [1933] S.C.R. 456. In *Dobson (Litigation Guardian of) v. Dobson* (1999), 174 D.L.R. (4th) 1 (S.C.C.), however, the Supreme Court of Canada held that a different rule applied with respect to the child's mother.

The facts in *Dobson* were simple. A woman who was 27 weeks pregnant carelessly caused an automobile accident that inflicted damage upon her unborn child. The child was delivered by Caesarean section later the same day with severe and permanent disabilities. By way of a litigation guardian, he subsequently sued his mother in negligence. That action was, in effect, "friendly." Its real purpose was not to recover damages from the mother, but rather from her insurer. Ironically, then, despite being the nominal defendant, the mother was anxious for her son's claim to succeed. Without recourse to insurance benefits, the financial burden associated with his disabilities would fall much more heavily on her personally.

Although the lower courts found in favour of the plaintiff, the Supreme Court of Canada held that liability was impossible because the defendant did not owe a duty of care to her son prior to his birth. Cory J.'s majority decision demonstrates the extent to which policy considerations affect the tort of negligence. He began by assuming that a *prima facie* duty of care arose under the first branch of the *Anns/Kamloops* test. He found that it was reasonably foreseeable that the mother's carelessness could adversely affect her foetus, and that the relationship between the parties could not possibly have been any closer or more proximate. Under the second branch of the *Anns/Kamloops* test, however, Cory J. found policy considerations that negated the prima facie duty:

> [F]or reasons of public policy, the Court should not impose a duty of care upon a pregnant woman towards her foetus or subsequently born child. To do so would result in very extensive and unacceptable intrusions into the bodily integrity, privacy and autonomy rights of women.
>
> . . .
>
> The unique relationship between a pregnant woman and her foetus is so very different from the relationship with third parties. Everything the pregnant woman does or fails to do may have a potentially detrimental impact on her foetus. Everything the pregnant woman eats or drinks, and every physical action she takes, may affect the foetus. Indeed, the foetus is entirely dependent upon its mother-to-be. Although the imposition of tort liability on a third party for prenatal negligence advances the interests of both mother and child, it does not significantly impair the right of third parties to control their own lives. In contrast to the third-party defendant, a pregnant woman's every waking and sleeping moment, in essence, her entire existence, is connected to the foetus she may potentially harm. If a mother were to be held liable for prenatal negligence, this could render the most mundane decision taken in the course of her daily life as a pregnant woman subject to the scrutiny of the courts.
>
> . . .
>
> First, the recognition of a duty of care owed by a pregnant woman to her foetus has a very real potential to intrude upon that woman's fundamental rights. Any intervention may create a conflict between a pregnant woman as an autonomous decision-maker and the foetus she carries. Second, the judicial definition of an appropriate standard of care is fraught with insoluble problems due to the difficulty of distinguishing tortious and non-tortious behaviour in the daily life of an expectant woman. Third, certain so-called lifestyle "choices" such as alcoholism and drug addiction may be beyond the control of the pregnant woman, and hence the deterrent value of the imposition of a duty of care may be non-existent. Lastly, the imposition of a duty of care upon a pregnant woman towards her foetus could increase, to an unwarranted degree, the level of external scrutiny focused upon her.

. . .

> [Under a general duty of care] a mother could be held liable in tort for . . . the careless performance of household activities – such as preparing meals, carrying loads of laundry, or shovelling. . .. A mother who injured her foetus in a careless fall, or who had an unreasonable lapse of attention in the home, at work or on the roadways, could potentially be held liable in tort for the damages suffered by her born alive child. The imposition of tort liability in those circumstances would significantly undermine the privacy and autonomy rights of women.
>
> . . .
>
> Moreover, the imposition of tort liability in this context would carry psychological and emotional repercussions for a mother who is sued in tort by her newborn child. To impose tort liability on a mother for an unreasonable lapse of prenatal care could have devastating consequences for the future relationship between the mother and her born alive child. In essence, the judicial recognition of a cause of action for maternal prenatal negligence is an inappropriate response to the pressing social issue of caring for children with special needs. Putting a mother through the trauma of a public trial to determine whether she was at fault for the injury suffered by her child can only add emotional and psychological trauma to an already tragic situation.
>
> . . .
>
> Such litigation would, in all probability, have detrimental consequences, not only for the relationship between mother and child, but also for the relationship between the child and his or her family. Yet, family harmony will be particularly important for the creation of a caring and nurturing environment for the injured child, who will undoubtedly require much loving attention. It seems clear that the well-being of such a child cannot be readily severed from the interests of his or her family. In short, neither the best interests of the injured child, nor those of the remainder of the family, would be served by the judicial recognition of the suggested cause of action.
>
> . .
>
> The primary purposes of tort law are to provide compensation to the injured and deterrence to the tortfeasor. In the ordinary course of events, the imposition of tort liability on a mother for prenatal negligence would provide neither compensation nor deterrence. The pressing societal issue at the heart of this appeal is the lack of financial support currently available for the care of children with special needs. The imposition of a legal duty of care on a pregnant woman towards her foetus or subsequently born child will not solve this problem. If anything, attempting to address this social problem in a litigious setting would merely exacerbate the pain and trauma of a tragic situation. It may well be that carefully considered legislation could create a fund to compensate children with prenatally inflicted injuries. Alternatively, amendments to the motor vehicle insurance laws could achieve the same result in a more limited context. If, as a society, Canadians believe that children who sustain damages as a result of maternal prenatal negligence should be financially compensated, then the solution should be formulated, after careful study and debate, by the legislature.

In a dissenting opinion, Major J. (Bastarache J. concurring) recognized that it was necessary to mediate a compromise between the child's interest in recovering damages for carelessly inflicted injuries and the mother's interest in being free from unreasonable restraint during pregnancy. He believed, however, that that tension was best resolved by adopting a limited duty of care, rather than by staking a position at either extreme. Like

Cory J., he rejected the imposition of a general duty of care upon pregnant women for fear that it would entail judicial scrutiny of "lifestyle choices," such as "smoking, drinking, and dietary and health-care decisions." But, in contrast to the majority, he stressed that those types of policy concerns should not be determinative in circumstances where they do not actually arise. Major J. therefore preferred to impose a duty of care upon a pregnant woman toward her foetus where she already owed a similar duty of care toward other parties. On the facts, the defendant owed a duty of care, while driving, to other motorists. The burdens associated with that obligation would not be increased if it was extended to her unborn child.

NOTES AND QUESTIONS

1. In *Dobson*, Cory J. presented several policy reasons for denying the existence of any duty of care between a pregnant woman and her unborn child. Do you find those reasons persuasive, either individually or collectively?

2. Does the issue of maternal tort liability truly lie beyond judicial competence, such that any solution must be devised by the legislature? If so, should courts similarly refuse to extend the duty of care in other complex situations, such as those involving nervous shock?

Are there truly insuperable difficulties in formulating a standard of care that would sufficiently respect a woman's autonomy? How do the courts approach the question of breach in other circumstances? Is it realistic to believe that a court would ever find that an expectant mother had breached the standard of care by "preparing meals [or] carrying loads of laundry?"

3. Is it appropriate to refuse recognition of a duty of care for fear of causing tension within the family unit? How did Mrs. Dobson feel about her son's claim? If concerns regarding familial harmony are compelling, should a duty of care similarly be rejected as between a father and an unborn child, or as between a mother and a child that is already alive?

Is it true that "[i]n the ordinary course of events" the recognition of a duty of care "for prenatal negligence would [not] provide compensation"? What evidence did Cory J. have for that proposition? Would a child typically sue its mother unless the real purpose was to secure access to her insurer? In any event, should the courts be influenced by such matters?

4. In *Dobson*, Cory J. suggested that it would be appropriate for the legislators to enact, subject to the provisions of the *Charter*, a statutory cause of action for children who suffer pre-natal injuries caused by their mothers. In Ontario, s. 66 of the *Family Law Act*, R.S.O. 1990, c. F.3, provides that no person is disentitled from recovering damages simply because the injuries were incurred before birth. However, it has been held that s. 66 does not override the maternal immunity outlined in *Dobson*: *Hall (Litigation Guardian of) v. Kellar* (2002) 23 C.C.L.T. (3d) 40 (Ont. S.C.J.). Given Cory J.'s emphasis on women's autonomy rights, would any statutory imposition of maternal tort liability survive a *Charter* challenge?

In 2005, Alberta enacted the *Maternal Tort Liability Act*, S.A. 2005, c. M-75, which creates a limited exception to the common law immunity of mothers that was established in *Dobson*. The Alberta legislation allows born alive children to sue their mothers for injuries suffered *in utero* only if they resulted from the mother's operation of an automobile, and only if the mother was covered by automobile insurance. Does this legislation adequately resolve the problems posed by the decision in *Dobson*?

5. Is it sound public policy to leave a child born with serious preventable disabilities without any common law action against the person who carelessly caused those injuries, just because that person happens to be the child's mother?

Australian courts have imposed liability in cases like *Dobson* on the basis that road accident victims should all be compensated and vehicle owners should all contribute, through insurance, to redressing the cost of traffic-related injuries. See *Lynch v. Lynch* (1991), 25 N.S.W.L.R. 411 (C.A.). In *Dobson*, Cory J. rejected this insurance rationale as being an inappropriate basis for making policy decisions. Do you agree?

6. For comments on the implications of *Dobson*, see McInnes, "Pre-Natal Injuries in the Supreme Court of Canada" (2000) 116 L.Q.R. 26; Nelson, "One of These Things is Not Like The Other: Maternal Legal Duties and the Supreme Court of Canada" (2000) 12 S.C.L.R. 31; Rafferty, "Developments in Contract and Tort: The 1999-2000 Term" (2000) 13 S.C.L.R. 125; and Malkin, "A Mother's Duty of Care to Her Foetus While Driving" (2001) 9 Torts L.J. 109. See also Johnsen, "The Creation of Fetal Rights: Conflicts with Women's Constitutional Rights to Liberty, Privacy, and Equal Protection" (1986) 95 Yale L.J. 599; and Kerr, "Pre-Natal Fictions and Post-Partum Actions" (1998) 20 Dal. L.J. 237.

7. Although a pregnant woman does not owe a duty of care to her unborn child, a born alive child can sue other parties for injuries suffered *in utero*. Thus, notwithstanding *Dobson*, claims for pre-natal negligence continue to be heard. See for example *Oliver (Guardian ad litem of) v. Ellison*, [2001] 7 W.W.R. 677 (B.C.C.A.); *Keys v. Mistahia Regional Health Authority* (2001), 291 A.R. 97 (Q.B.), aff'd (2002), 320 A.R. 87 (C.A.); and *Pozdzik (Next friend of) v. Wilson* (2002), 11 C.C.L.T. (3d) 96 (Alta. Q.B.).

8. Pregnancy and the cause of birth defects were largely a mystery to medical professionals for many years, making the causation issue in prenatal injury cases difficult. See generally Oakley, *The Captured Womb: A History of the medical care of pregnant women* (1984); and McLaren, *Reproductive Rituals* (1984). Concerns regarding pre-natal injuries came to prominence during the 1960s as a result of a worldwide measles epidemic and the litigation stemming from birth defects caused by the drug thalidomide. See Hindell & Simms, *Abortion Law Reformed* (1971); Sarvis & Roman, *The Abortion Controversy*, 2d. ed. (1974); and Sunday Times Insight Team, *Suffer the Children: The Story of Thalidomide* (1979).

Modern advances in the medical sciences have made it easier to prove that drugs, chemicals, radiation, and other substances can cause birth defects. For example, in *Sindell v. Abbott Laboratories*, 607 P.2d 924 (Cal. 1980), a mother's use of a prescription drug, DES, during pregnancy was proven to cause a particular form of deadly cancer in female children a minimum of 10 to 12 years after birth.

For a general discussion of pre-natal injuries, see Winfield, "The Unborn Child" (1942-44) 8 C.L.J. 76; Law Commission, *Report on Injuries to Unborn Children* (1974)

(Law Com. No. 60); Weiler & Catton, "The Unborn Child in Canadian Law" (1976) 14 Osgoode Hall L.J. 643; and Pace, "Civil Liability For Pre-Natal Injuries" (1977) 40 Mod. L. Rev. 141.

9. Are civil claims likely to have any beneficial effect on foetal health? Can you suggest other means of addressing this issue? Should the state have the power to intervene to protect foetal health? Would legislation be any more effective than civil liability? What constitutional arguments would be raised in challenging such laws? How would these challenges be resolved?

Both English and Canadian courts have held that there is no common law authority to impose treatment or restraint upon a pregnant woman for the benefit of a foetus. See *Winnipeg Child & Family Services (Northwest Area) v. G.(D.F.)* (1997), 152 D.L.R. (4th) 193 (S.C.C.); and *St. George's Healthcare NHS Trust v. S.*, [1998] 3 All E.R. 673 (C.A.). See also Kirman, "Four Dialogues on Fetal Protection" (1993) 2(2) Health L. Rev. 31.

The issue is much more controversial in the United States, where there have been several high-profile cases of doctors applying to the courts to force pregnant women to undergo caesarean sections or other medical treatments the doctors believe necessary for the health of the foetus. For instance, Angela Carder, who was 25 weeks pregnant, was diagnosed with terminal lung cancer in 1987 and given only weeks to live. Although she agreed to treatments that would improve the survival prospects of her child, she refused consent to an immediate caesarean section. She believed that the foetus was not likely to survive at that age, and that the procedure would likely shorten her own life. Her doctors applied to a court, which ordered that she undergo the caesarean section. The child died within two hours and Angela died two days later. The trial judge's decision on the forced caesarean was reversed by the Court of Appeal in 1990, too late to help Angela. See *In re A.C.*, 573 A.2d 1235 (D.C. App. 1990). For a more thorough discussion of the issue, see Daniels, *At Women's Expense: State Power and the Politics of Fetal Rights* (1993).

10. In Canada, damages are not awarded for the death of a foetus; rather, the child must be born alive. See *Davey v. Victoria General Hospital* (1995), 106 Man. R. (2d) 81 (Q.B.); and *Gibbons v. Port Hope & District Hospital* (1998), 44 C.C.L.T. (2d) 198 (Ont. Gen. Div.), rev'd on a different point (1999), 46 C.C.L.T. (2d) 266 (C.A.). This position is consistent with the Supreme Court of Canada's position concerning criminal liability: see *R. v. Sullivan*, [1991] 1 S.C.R. 489.

Some American jurisdictions have modified the "born alive" rule in tort actions, allowing the parents to claim for the loss of companionship and comfort of a foetus that would have, but for the defendant's negligence, been born alive. These jurisdictions recognize the anomaly that a defendant who negligently kills a foetus escapes liability, while a negligent defendant who inflicts less serious injury is held accountable. See *O'Grady v. Brown*, 654 S.W.2d 904 (Mo. S.C. 1983). Should the "born alive" rule be retained in negligence?

11. Having now reviewed the law on the various pre-natal torts, what recommendations would you make to a provincial law reform commission on improving and rationalizing this branch of negligence law?

4. Nervous Shock

The law relating to the negligent infliction of nervous shock is notoriously confusing. Unfortunately, the Supreme Court of Canada has not addressed this issue in some time. While there has been a great deal of activity in the House of Lords, the resulting judgments are both perplexing and unprincipled. Nevertheless, despite those shortcomings, the English cases are instructive insofar as they highlight the policy concerns inherent in this area. Consequently, it will be useful, following a brief introduction, to consider the English position in some detail.

(a) INTRODUCTION

In medical terms, the phrase "nervous shock" is an anachronism. It is both overly broad, because it encompasses many different species of psychiatric illness, and inaccurate, because it suggests that a condition must arise in a sudden or "shocking" manner. Nevertheless, the older phrase continues to be heard in the courts, and the requirement of sudden shock has been relatively persistent. The legal meaning of nervous shock has evolved only gradually, and is not as sophisticated or advanced as medical science might allow. The situation is one of "[l]aw marching with medicine, but in the rear and limping a little": See *Mount Isa Mines Ltd. v. Pusey* (1970), 125 C.L.R. 383 at 395 (H.C.A.).

Although the law has slowly become more nuanced and more receptive to the basic idea of recovery for psychiatric injury, there are some respects in which the definition of "nervous shock" has remained constant. It has never encompassed many of the day-to-day emotional upsets (*e.g.* anger, disappointment, frustration, disgust) that are natural incidents of modern life. Nor, more significantly, does the legal concept of nervous shock encompass the feelings of grief and sorrow that inevitably follow upon the death or serious injury of a loved one. As a general rule, something more, by way of a "recognized psychiatric illness," is required for the purposes of liability. Interestingly, the medical profession has far less confidence in its ability to distinguish psychiatric illness from grief.

The courts traditionally were loath to impose liability for the careless infliction of nervous shock. Various reasons were provided in defence of that position. Judges were worried that, as compared with physical illness, nervous shock was easy to feign. X-rays can prove the existence of a broken bone, but there (still) is no similarly conclusive test for the existence of a psychiatric illness. The assessment of damages for psychiatric illness was also thought to be particularly difficult. And within the hierarchy of harms, there was a sense that damage to one's psyche was less worthy of protection than damage to one's body. The common law's conception of the "reasonable man" did not include someone who would complain about emotional upset. Perhaps most significantly, however, the courts have always been worried about opening the floodgates of liability. Whereas the agents of physical harm are usually limited in both time and space, the potential triggering mechanisms for nervous shock are much more far-ranging. The litigation arising from the Hillsborough disaster, discussed below, is illustrative.

NOTES AND QUESTIONS

1. English and most Canadian courts have defined "nervous shock" narrowly in an attempt to exclude claims for minor emotional upsets. In effect, the plaintiff has been

required to prove that the nervous shock manifested itself in some form of physical, psychiatric or psychological disorder. See *Hinz v. Berry*, [1970] 1 All E.R. 1074 (C.A.); *Beaulieu v. Sutherland* (1986), 35 C.C.L.T. 237 (B.C.S.C.); *Heighington v. Ontario* (1987), 60 O.R. (2d) 641 (H.C.), additional reasons at (1987), 41 C.C.L.T. 230 (Ont. H.C.), aff'd (1989), 69 O.R. (2d) 484 (C.A.); *Cox v. Fleming* (1993), 13 C.C.L.T. (2d) 305 (S.C.), aff'd (1995), 15 B.C.L.R. (3d) 201 (C.A); *McLoughlin v. Arbor Memorial Services Inc.* (2004), 36 C.C.L.T. (3d) 158 (Ont. S.C.J.); *Anderson v. Excel Collection Services Ltd.* (2005), 260 D.L.R. (4th) 367 (Ont. S.C.J.); *Knife (Litigation Guardian of) v. Charles* (2005), 272 Sask. R. 111 (Q.B.); and *Satara Farms Inc. v. Parrish & Heimbecker, Ltd. (c.o.b. New-Life Feeds)* (2006), 280 Sask. R. 44 (Q.B.). But see *Mason v. Westside Cemeteries Ltd.* (1996), 135 D.L.R. (4th) 361 (Ont. Gen. Div.); *Anderson v. Wilson* (1999), 44 O.R. (3d) 673 (C.A.); *Bastien v. Ottawa Hospital (General Campus)* (2001), 56 O.R. (3d) 397 (S.C.J.); and *Philip v. Whitecourt General Hospital* (2004), 359 A.R. 259 (Q.B.).

2. Is it possible to draw a meaningful distinction between nervous shock, which is recoverable, and grief and sorrow, which are not recoverable? See *Mathison v. Hofer*, [1984] 3 W.W.R. 343 (Man. Q.B.); *Beecham v. Hughes* (1988), 27 B.C.L.R. (2d) 1 (C.A.); *Cox v. Fleming* (1993), 13 C.C.L.T. (2d) 305 (B.C.S.C.), varied on other grounds (1995), 15 B.C.L.R. (3d) 201 (C.A.); and *Dube (Litigation Guardian of) v. Penlon Ltd.* (1994), 21 C.C.L.T. (2d) 268 (Ont. Gen. Div.).

3. The courts have also limited recovery for nervous shock by requiring claimants to be "of reasonable fortitude and robustness" or "customary phlegm." Hypersensitive individuals are not reasonably foreseeable. See *Hay (or Bourhill) v. Young*, [1942] 2 All E.R. 396 (H.L.); *Duwyn v. Kaprelian* (1978), 22 O.R. (2d) 736 (C.A.); *Vanek v. Great Atlantic & Pacific Co. of Canada* (1999), 48 O.R. (3d) 228 (C.A.); *White v. Chief Constable of South Yorkshire Police*, [1999] 2 A.C. 455 (H.L.); and *Mustapha v. Culligan Canada Ltd.* (2006), 43 C.C.L.T. (3d) 27 (Ont. C.A.), excerpted later in this chapter. But see *Sant v. Jack Andrews Kirkfield Pharmach Ltd.* (2002), 161 Man. R. (2d) 121 (Q.B.), where the court stated that the requirement of reasonable fortitude only applied to claims by bystanders.

In *Clark v. Scotiabank* (2004), 25 C.C.L.T. (3d) 109 (Ont. S.C.J.), the plaintiff suffered depression after he was denied a loan based on a negligent report of his credit status by the defendant. While the court acknowledged that he suffered a recognizable psychiatric illness, it found that a person of reasonable fortitude would not have suffered such illness as the result of an erroneous credit report. Therefore, his illness was not reasonably foreseeable.

4. In *Greatorex v. Greatorex*, [2000] 4 All E.R. 769 (Q.B.), a young man was seriously injured in an automobile accident that he had carelessly caused. Because he was trapped inside his vehicle, firefighters were called to rescue him. One of the firefighters was his father. As a result of the incident, the father suffered a psychiatric disorder. The issue before the court was whether the victim of a self-inflicted injury owed a duty of care to not thereby cause nervous shock to a third party. The court answered that question in the negative. It held that recognition of such a duty would impose a significant restraint on a person's freedom of choice, and would open the doors to a particularly undesirable form of intra-familial litigation.

5. See generally Wheat, *Napier and Wheat's Recovering Damages for Psychiatric Injury*, 2d ed. (2002); and Handford, *Mullany & Handford's Tort Liability for Psychiatric Damage*, 2d ed. (2006).

(b) COMMONWEALTH DEVELOPMENTS

Because of the concerns mentioned above, the Commonwealth courts have historically sought to create rules to limit liability. This began with the idea that a plaintiff could not recover unless the nervous shock was precipitated by some physical impact. This developed out of *Victoria Railways Commissioner v. Coultas* (1888), 13 App. Cas. 222 (P.C.). The plaintiff suffered severe shock when, as a result of the defendant's carelessness in raising a gate, she was nearly hit by a train. The lower courts imposed liability, but the Privy Council disagreed:

> Damages arising from mere sudden terror unaccompanied by any actual physical injury, but occasioning a nervous or mental shock, cannot . . . be considered a consequence which, in the ordinary course of things, would flow from the negligence of the gate-keeper. . . .
>
> Not only in such a case as the present, but in every case where an accident caused by negligence had given a person a serious nervous shock, there might be a claim for damage on account of mental injury. The difficulty which now often exists in cases of alleged physical injuries of determining whether they were caused by the negligent act would be greatly increased, and a wide field opened for imaginary claims.

Accordingly, for many years the courts held that liability for nervous shock was available only if the plaintiff had suffered some physical injury or at least a physical impact. Over time, the artificiality of the so-called "impact rule" became unsustainable. In *Dulieu v. White & Sons*, [1901] 2 K.B. 699 (C.A.), the plaintiff suffered nervous shock when the defendant crashed his horse-drawn carriage into the public house in which she was working. She was allowed to recover even though she had not suffered any actual impact, because her nervous shock was triggered by "a reasonable fear of immediate personal injury to [herself]." However, *Dulieu* replaced the impact rule with a new restriction on liability: the plaintiff must suffer shock as a result of fear of injury to him or herself. If the plaintiff was not in physical danger, or the plaintiff suffered shock due to fear for injury to someone else, he or she could not recover.

This restriction was also modified, in turn, two decades later. In *Hambrook v. Stokes Brothers* (1924), [1925] 1 K.B. 141 (C.A.), a woman suffered nervous shock when she saw a runaway truck speeding down a hill toward the place where she had left her children to walk to school. She rushed to the scene of the crash, and was told that a girl matching her daughter's description had been injured. She suffered nervous shock, subsequently gave birth to a stillborn child, and died a few months later. Her husband's claim under fatal accidents legislation was questionable because his wife had not been in any physical danger and she had not feared that she would suffer personal injury. However, rejecting the rule from *Dulieu*, the court held that liability was possible if "the shock was due to a reasonable fear of immediate personal injury either to herself or to her children." See also *Horne v. New Glasgow (Town)* (1953), [1954] 1 D.L.R. 832 (N.S.S.C.); and *Hinz v. Berry*, [1970] 2 Q.B. 40 (C.A.). Nevertheless, the court in *Hambrook* was careful to limit recovery to situations where the shock occurred because of something the claimant "either saw or realized from her own unaided senses, and not from something which someone told her." This created a new limitation on recovery: the plaintiff had to witness the shocking incident with his or her own senses; it was not sufficient if the plaintiff heard about the accident from someone else.

In time, even this limitation was rejected. The high water mark for recovery in nervous shock came in *McLoughlin v. O'Brian*, [1982] 2 All E.R. 298 (H.L.). The plaintiff was married with three children. The defendant carelessly caused a traffic accident that killed one of those children and seriously injured the other two, as well as the plaintiff's husband. Having been told of the incident two hours later, the plaintiff went to the hospital where she received details of the tragedy. Thus, the plaintiff's shock was not due to physical impact, fear for her own safety or for the safety of her family, or even her presence at the scene of an accident. Nevertheless, the House of Lords imposed liability largely on the basis that the plaintiff's psychiatric injury was, in all of the circumstances of the case, reasonably foreseeable. Although she was not present at the scene of the accident, she attended to its "aftermath" and saw her injured family with her own eyes. It was foreseeable that a mother in this situation would suffer psychiatric injury.

However, the judges in *McLoughlin* were divided on the need for other limiting factors. Lord Bridge found no reason to continue distinguishing psychiatric injury from physical injury, and argued that reasonable foreseeability would be enough to impose a duty of care. Nevertheless, Lord Wilberforce's leading opinion held that, as a matter of policy, some boundaries on recovery had to be drawn. Lord Wilberforce found (at 422) three considerations to be particularly important: "the class of persons whose claims should be recognised; the proximity of such persons to the accident; and the means by which the shock is caused."

These three criteria were discussed at length in *Alcock v. Chief Constable of South Yorkshire Police*, [1991] 4 All E.R. 907 (H.L.), excerpted below. The case arose out of the Hillsborough disaster of 1989, in which, as a result of police carelessness, a soccer stadium became dangerously overcrowded. As millions watched on television and listened on radio, over 90 fans were crushed to death and many more were seriously injured. Actions were brought by several categories of claimants. *Alcock* involved 16 plaintiffs, representing approximately 150 others, who allegedly suffered nervous shock after fearing for the safety of loved ones who were in the Hillsborough Stadium. Some of those plaintiffs were themselves in the stands, others saw the events live on television or heard them live on the radio, and still others saw or heard news reports afterwards. Among the plaintiffs were wives, parents, grandparents, brothers, sisters, uncles, brothers-in-law, fiancés and friends of the (potential) victims. Another case, *White v. Chief Constable of South Yorkshire Police*, [1999] 2 A.C. 455 (H.L.), involved claims by the police officers who were present at the stadium and assisted with the rescue and recovery operation. That case is discussed in the notes and questions that follow.

ALCOCK v. CHIEF CONSTABLE OF SOUTH YORKSHIRE POLICE

[1991] 4 All E.R. 907 (H.L.)

LORD ACKNER: – My Lords, if sympathy alone were to be the determining factor in these claims, then they would never have been contested. It has been stressed throughout the judgments in the courts below and I would emphasise it yet again in your Lordships' House that the human tragedy which occurred on the afternoon of 15 April 1989 at the Hillsborough Stadium when 95 people were killed and more than 400 others received injuries from being crushed necessitating hospital treatment, remains an utterly appalling one.

It is, however, trite law that the defendant, the Chief Constable of South Yorkshire, is not an insurer against psychiatric illness occasioned by the shock sustained by the relatives or friends of those who died or were injured, or were believed to have died or to have been injured. This is, of course, fully recognised by the appellants, the plaintiffs in these actions, whose claims for damages to compensate them for their psychiatric illnesses are based upon the allegation that it was the defendant's negligence, that is to say his breach of his duty of care owed to them as well as to those who died or were injured in controlling the crowds at the stadium, which caused them to suffer their illnesses. The defendant, for the purposes of these actions, has admitted that he owed a duty of care only to those who died or were injured and that he was in breach of only that duty. He has further accepted that each of the plaintiffs has suffered some psychiatric illness. Moreover for the purpose of deciding whether the defendant is liable to pay damages to the plaintiffs in respect of their illnesses, the trial judge, Hidden J., made the assumption that the illnesses were caused by the shocks sustained by the plaintiffs by reason of their awareness of the events at Hillsborough. The defendant has throughout contested liability on the ground that, in all the circumstances, he was not in breach of any duty of care owed to the plaintiffs.

Since the decision of your Lordships' House in *McLoughlin v. O'Brian* [*supra*], if not earlier, it is established law that (1) a claim for damages for psychiatric illness resulting from shock caused by negligence can be made without the necessity of the plaintiff establishing that he was himself injured or was in fear of personal injury; (2) a claim for damages for such illness can be made when the shock results: (a) from death or injury to the plaintiff's spouse or child or the fear of such death or injury and (b) the shock has come about through the sight or hearing of the event, or its immediate aftermath.

To succeed in the present appeals the plaintiffs seek to extend the boundaries of this cause of action by: (1) removing any restrictions on the categories of persons who may sue; (2) extending the means by which the shock is caused, so that it includes viewing the simultaneous broadcast on television of the incident which caused the shock; (3) modifying the present requirement that the aftermath must be "immediate."

A recital of the cases over the last century shows that the extent of the liability for shock-induced psychiatric illness has been greatly expanded. This has largely been due to a better understanding of mental illness and its relation to shock. The extension of the scope of this cause of action sought in these appeals is not on any such ground but, so it is contended, by the application of established legal principles.

. . .

The nature of the cause of action

In *Bourhill v. Young* [1943] A.C. 92, 103, Lord Macmillan said:

> "in the case of mental shock there are elements of greater subtlety than in the case of an ordinary physical injury and these elements may give rise to debate as to the precise scope of the legal liability."

It is now generally accepted that an analysis of the reported cases of nervous shock establishes that it is a type of claim in a category of its own. Shock is no longer a variant of physical injury but a separate kind of damage. Whatever may be the pattern of the future development of the law in relation to this cause of action, the following propositions illustrate that the application *simpliciter* of the reasonable foreseeability test is, today, far from being operative.

[His Lordship summarized the existing principles of law on nervous shock.]

I do not find it surprising that in this particular area of the tort of negligence, the reasonable foreseeability test is not given a free rein. As Lord Reid said in *McKew v. Holland & Hannen & Cubitts (Scotland) Ltd.* [1969] 3 All E.R. 1621, 1623:

> A defender is not liable for a consequence of a kind which is not foreseeable. But it does not follow that he is liable for every consequence which a reasonable man could foresee.

. . .

Although it is a vital step towards the establishment of liability, the satisfaction of the test of reasonable foreseeability does not, in my judgment, *ipso facto* satisfy Lord Atkin's well known neighbourhood principle enunciated in *Donoghue v. Stevenson* [1932] A.C. 562, 580. For him to have been reasonably in contemplation by a defendant he must be:

> so closely and directly affected by my act that I ought reasonably to have them in contemplation as being so affected when I am directing my mind to the acts or omissions which are called in question.

The requirement contained in the words "so closely and directly affected . . . that" constitutes a control upon the test of reasonable foreseeability of injury. Lord Atkin was at pains to stress, at pp. 580-582, that the formulation of a duty of care, merely in the general terms of reasonable foreseeability, would be too wide unless it were "limited by the notion of proximity" which was embodied in the restriction of the duty of care to one's "neighbour."

The three elements

Because "shock" in its nature is capable of affecting such a wide range of persons, Lord Wilberforce in *McLoughlin v. O'Brian* [*supra*], 422, concluded that there was a real need for the law to place some limitation upon the extent of admissible claims and in this context he considered that there were three elements inherent in any claim. It is common ground that such elements do exist and are required to be considered in connection with all these claims. The fundamental difference in approach is that on behalf of the plaintiffs it is contended that the consideration of these three elements is merely part of the process of deciding whether, as a matter of fact, the reasonable foreseeability test has been satisfied. On behalf of the defendant it is contended that these elements operate as a control or limitation on the mere application of the reasonable foreseeability test. They introduce the requirement of "proximity" as conditioning the duty of care.

The three elements are (1) the class of persons whose claims should be recognised; (2) the proximity of such persons to the accident - in time and space; (3) the means by which the shock has been caused.

I will deal with those three elements seriatim.

(1) The class of persons whose claim should be recognised

When dealing with the possible range of the class of persons who might sue, Lord Wilberforce. . . contrasted the closest of family ties - parent and child and husband and wife - with that of the ordinary bystander. He said that while existing law recognises the claims of the first, it denied that of the second, either on the basis that such persons must be assumed to be possessed with fortitude sufficient to enable them to endure the calamities of modern life, or that defendants cannot be expected to compensate the world at large. He considered that these positions were justified, that other cases involving less close relationships must be very carefully considered, adding, at p. 422:

> "The closer the tie (not merely in relationship, but in care) the greater the claim for consideration. The claim, in any case, has to be judged in the light of the other factors, such as proximity to the scene in time and place, and the nature of the accident."

I respectfully share the difficulty expressed by Atkin L.J. in *Hambrook v. Stokes Brothers*. . . - how do you explain why the duty is confined to the case of parent or guardian and child and does not extend to other relations of life also involving intimate associations; and why does it not eventually extend to bystanders? As regards the latter category, while it may be very difficult to envisage a case of a stranger, who is not actively and foreseeably involved in a disaster or its aftermath, other than in the role of rescuer, suffering shock-induced psychiatric injury by the mere observation of apprehended or actual injury of a third person in circumstances that could be considered reasonably foreseeable, I see no reason in principle why he should not, if in the circumstances, a reasonably strong-nerved person would have been so shocked. In the course of argument your Lordships were given, by way of an example, that of a petrol tanker careering out of control into a school in session and bursting into flames. I would not be prepared to rule out a potential claim by a passer-by so shocked by the scene as to suffer psychiatric illness.

As regards claims by those in the close family relationships referred to by Lord Wilberforce, the justification for admitting such claims is the presumption, which I would accept as being rebuttable, that the love and affection normally associated with persons in those relationships is such that a defendant ought reasonably to contemplate that they may be so closely and directly affected by his conduct as to suffer shock resulting in psychiatric illness. While as a generalisation more remote relatives and, *a fortiori*, friends, can reasonably be expected not to suffer illness from the shock, there can well be relatives and friends whose relationship is so close and intimate that their love and affection for the victim is comparable to that of the normal parent, spouse or child of the victim and should for the purpose of this cause of action be so treated. This was the opinion of Stocker L.J. in the instant appeal, *ante*, p. 376E-G, and also that of Nolan L.J. who thus expressed himself, *ante*, pp. 384-385:

> For my part, I would accept at once that no general definition is possible. But I see no difficulty in principle in requiring a defendant to contemplate that the person physically injured or threatened by his negligence may have relatives or friends whose love for him is like that of a normal parent or spouse, and who in consequence may similarly be closely and directly affected by nervous shock . . . The identification of the particular individuals who come within that category, like that of the parents and spouses themselves, could only be carried out *ex post facto*, and would depend upon evidence of the 'relationship' in the broad sense which gave rise to the love and affection.

. . .

Whether the degree of love and affection in any given relationship, be it that of relative or friend, is such that the defendant, in the light of the plaintiff's proximity to the scene of the accident in time and space and its nature, should reasonably have foreseen the shock-induced psychiatric illness, has to be decided on a case by case basis. As Deane J. observed in *Jaensch v. Coffey*, 155 C.L.R. 549, 601:

> While it must now be accepted that any realistic assessment of the reasonably foreseeable consequences of an accident involving actual or threatened serious bodily injury must, in an appropriate case, include the possibility of injury in the form of nervous shock being sustained by a wide range of persons not physically injured in the accident, the outer limits of reasonable foreseeability of mere psychiatric injury cannot be identified in the abstract or in advance. Much may depend upon the nature of the negligent act or omission, on the gravity or apparent gravity of any actual or apprehended injury and on any expert evidence about the nature and explanation of the particular psychiatric injury which the plaintiff has sustained.

(2) The proximity of the plaintiff to the accident

It is accepted that the proximity to the accident must be close both in time and space. Direct and immediate sight or hearing of the accident is not required. It is reasonably foreseeable that injury by shock can be caused to a plaintiff, not only through the sight or hearing of the event, but of its immediate aftermath.

Only two of the plaintiffs before us were at the ground. However, it is clear from *McLoughlin v. O'Brian*. . . that there may be liability where subsequent identification can be regarded as part of the "immediate aftermath" of the accident. Mr. Alcock identified his brother-in-law in a bad condition in the mortuary at about midnight, that is some eight hours after the accident. This was the earliest of the identification cases. Even if this identification could be described as part of the "aftermath," it could not in my judgment be described as part of the immediate aftermath. McLoughlin's case was described by Lord Wilberforce as being upon the margin of what the process of logical progression from case to case would allow. Mrs. McLoughlin had arrived at the hospital within an hour or so after the accident. Accordingly in the post-accident identification cases before your Lordships there was not sufficient proximity in time and space to the accident.

(3) The means by which the shock is caused

Lord Wilberforce concluded that the shock must come through sight or hearing of the event or its immediate aftermath but specifically left for later consideration whether some equivalent of sight or hearing, *e.g.* through simultaneous television, would suffice: see p. 423. Of course it is common ground that it was clearly foreseeable by the defendant that the scenes at Hillsborough would be broadcast live and that amongst those who would be watching would be parents and spouses and other relatives and friends of those in the pens behind the goal at the Leppings Lane end. However he would also know of the code of ethics which the television authorities televising this event could be expected to follow, namely that they would not show pictures of suffering by recognisable individuals. Had they done so, Mr. Hytner accepted that this would have been a "*novus actus*" breaking the chain of causation between the defendant's alleged breach of duty and the psychiatric illness. As the defendant was reasonably entitled to expect to be the case, there were no such pictures. Although the television pictures certainly gave rise to feelings of the deepest anxiety and distress, in the circumstances of this case the simultaneous television broadcasts of what occurred cannot be equated with the "sight or hearing of the event or its immediate aftermath." Accordingly shocks sustained by reason of these broadcasts cannot found a claim. I agree, however, with Nolan L.J. that simultaneous broadcasts of a disaster cannot in all cases be ruled out as providing the equivalent of the actual sight or hearing of the event or its immediate aftermath. Nolan L.J. gave, *ante*, pp. 386G-387A, an example of a situation where it was reasonable to anticipate that the television cameras, whilst filming and transmitting pictures of a special event of children travelling in a balloon, in which there was media interest, particularly amongst the parents, showed the balloon suddenly bursting into flames. Many other such situations could be imagined where the impact of the simultaneous television pictures would be as great, if not greater, than the actual sight of the accident.

Conclusion

Only one of the plaintiffs, who succeeded before Hidden J., namely Brian Harrison, was at the ground. His relatives who died were his two brothers. The quality of brotherly love is well known to differ widely - from Cain and Abel to David and Jonathan. I assume that Mr. Harrison's relationship with his brothers was not an abnormal one. His claim was not presented upon the basis that there was such a close and intimate relationship between them, as gave rise to that very special bond of affection which would make his shock-induced psychiatric illness reasonably foreseeable by the defendant. Accordingly, the judge did not carry out the requisite close scrutiny of their relationship. Thus there was no evidence to establish the necessary proximity which would make his claim reasonably foreseeable and, subject to the other factors, to which I have referred, a valid one. The other plaintiff who was present at the ground, Robert Alcock, lost a brother-in-law. He was not, in my judgment, reasonably foreseeable as a potential sufferer from shock-induced psychiatric illness, in default of very special facts and none was established. Accordingly their claims must fail, as must those of the other plaintiffs who only learned of the disaster by watching simultaneous television. I, too, would therefore dismiss these appeals.

NOTES AND QUESTIONS

1. How does Lord Ackner define the element of sudden "shock?" Why should claims be limited to those induced by shock, rather than a more gradual onset of psychiatric illness? The High Court of Australia has rejected the requirement of sudden shock: *Tame v. New South Wales; Annetts v. Australian Stations Pty. Ltd.* (2002), 191 A.L.R. 449 (H.C.A.).

2. How does Lord Ackner define the class of persons whose claims ought to be recognized? How is this related to the concept of foreseeability? What does it mean for claims of bystanders who do not know the accident victims?

3. Why was Brian Harrison's claim denied? How can a plaintiff go about proving close ties of love and affection? If Harrison suffered nervous shock due to the tragic death of his brother, does it seem "fair, just and reasonable" to deny his claim because he did not legally prove a sufficiently intimate relationship with his brother?

4. How does Lord Ackner define the scope of "aftermath?" Is this compelling? Plaintiffs who witness the immediate consequences at the scene of a serious accident have generally been allowed to recover for nervous shock. For example in *Vernon v. Bosley (No.1)*, [1997] 1 All E.R. 577 (C.A.), the plaintiff was allowed to recover for the nervous shock he suffered in witnessing the police attempt to pull the vehicle containing his two drowned children from a fast flowing river.

There are indications that the strict definition of "aftermath" may be relaxed. In *W. v. Essex County Council*, [2000] 2 All E.R. 237 (H.L.), the plaintiffs were parents of four young children. They also accepted foster children into their home. They expressly told the local authority, however, that they were not willing to accept a foster child who posed a risk of sexual abuse. The local authority knowingly disregarded that request and secretly placed into their care a boy of 15 who had been accused of sexual abuse in the past. Once in the home, the boy allegedly assaulted the plaintiffs' children, with the result that the plaintiffs suffered psychiatric illnesses. The defendant's motion to strike the statement of claim was granted at first instance on the ground that the plaintiffs' had not, with their own unaided senses, witnessed the alleged assaults or their immediate aftermath. That decision was affirmed in the Court of Appeal, but reversed in the House of Lords. In the course of judgment, Lord Slynn suggested that:

> the concept of "the immediate aftermath" of the incident has to be assessed in the particular factual situation. I am not persuaded that in a situation like the present the parents must come across the abuser or the abused "immediately" after the sexual incident has terminated. All the incidents here happened in the period of four weeks before the parents learned of them.

In some Canadian cases, the plaintiffs have been allowed to recover for the nervous shock suffered in seeing their deceased loved ones at the hospital. See *Grzywacz v. Vanderheide*, [1992] O.J. No. 2856 (Gen. Div.) (QL); *Cox v. Fleming* (1995), 15 B.C.L.R. (3d) 201 (C.A.); and *Yu v. Yu* (1999), 48 M.V.R. (3d) 285 (B.C.S.C.). But see *Devji v. Burnaby (District)* (1998), 158 D.L.R. (4th) 747 (B.C.S.C.), aff'd (1999), 70 B.C.L.R. (3d) 42 (C.A.), where recovery was denied because the plaintiffs, who were parents and siblings of the deceased, saw her body in the hospital four hours after the fatal traffic accident occurred.

5. In *White v. Chief Constable of South Yorkshire Police*, [1999] 1 All E.R. 1 (H.L.), the plaintiffs were police officers who witnessed the Hillsborough tragedy first-hand and subsequently developed psychiatric illnesses as a result of being involved in the gruesome events. While addressing the issue of duty of care, Lord Hoffman candidly stated that "in this area, the search for principle was called off in *Alcock*." There was a perceived need to limit the scope of liability, but also recognition that the line-drawing exercise was, perhaps inevitably, arbitrary. On the facts, the court applied the *Alcock* test and denied liability on the ground that the claimants had not shared a close relationship with the victims. In doing so, however, it narrowly, and somewhat unconvincingly, distinguished older authorities that appeared to create special rules for rescuers within the area of nervous shock. According to those earlier decisions, a rescuer might be entitled to relief even if he or she had not been exposed to physical danger and even if he or she had not been closely connected to any of the victims. See *Chadwick v. British Railways Commission*, [1967] 2 All E.R. 945 (Q.B.). See also *Bechard v. Haliburton*

Estate (1991), 5 O.R. (3d) 512 (C.A.); and *Fullowka v. Royal Oak Ventures Inc.*, [2005] 5 W.W.R. 420 (N.W.T.S.C.).

6. In *Page v. Smith*, [1995] 2 All E.R. 736 (H.L.), the defendant carelessly caused a traffic accident with the plaintiff. No one suffered any physical injury. Nevertheless, as a result of the incident, the plaintiff relapsed into chronic fatigue syndrome, a condition from which he had previously suffered. The court drew a distinction between "primary victims" (*i.e.* people placed in physical danger) and "secondary victims" (*i.e.* people not placed in physical danger). Although the details are complicated in some respects, the general significance of that distinction can be quickly explained. With respect to primary victims, liability for *psychiatric injury* is possible as long as it was reasonably foreseeable that the plaintiff might suffer a *physical injury* as a result of the defendant's carelessness. That is true even if, as in *Page* itself, the foreseeable physical injury never materialized, and even if the psychiatric injury that did materialize was not itself reasonably foreseeable. In contrast, a secondary victim cannot recover for the careless infliction of nervous shock unless psychiatric illness itself was reasonably foreseeable and *Alcock*'s three-part test of proximity is satisfied.

The distinction drawn in *Page v. Smith* between primary and secondary victims has been trenchantly criticized by academics. See especially Hilson, "Nervous Shock and the Categorisation of Victims" (1998) 6 Tort L. Rev. 37; and Mullany, "English Psychiatric Injury Law – Chronically Depressing" (1999) 115 L.Q.R. 30. Its authority in Canada has been doubtful, and was explicitly rejected by the Court of Appeal for Ontario in *Mustapha v. Culligan Canada Ltd.* (2006), 43 C.C.L.T. (3d) 27 (Ont. C.A.).

(c) THE CANADIAN POSITION

The preceding materials were intended to outline, in general terms, the evolution of the duty of care for nervous shock in England. The lesson to be drawn from that overview is three-fold: (i) the scope of the duty of care is apt to shift from time to time in response to the judicially perceived need to expand or limit the scope of liability, (ii) there is always some need to impose restrictions on the application of general negligence principles, and (iii) the formulation of such restrictions tends to be, perhaps inevitably, arbitrary.

There have been relatively few appellate level decisions on the negligent infliction of nervous shock in Canada, so it is difficult to gauge the Canadian position in this area of the law. Nevertheless, there will come a time when the Canadian courts will have to resolve the same policy issues that have vexed English courts in the past 15 years. In *Mustapha v. Culligan Canada Ltd.* (2006), 43 C.C.L.T. (3d) 27 (Ont. C.A.), the Court of Appeal for Ontario took the opportunity to comment on the English jurisprudence.

MUSTAPHA v. CULLIGAN CANADA LTD.

(2006), 43 C.C.L.T. (3d) 27 (Ont. C.A.)

R.A. BLAIR J.A.:—

OVERVIEW

The Mustaphas maintain a spotless home. Cleanliness and hygiene are matters of utmost importance to them. On November 21, 2001, an incident occurred that offended their sense of sanctity in the purity of their home, and shattered Mr. Mustapha's life. In the course of replacing an empty bottle of Culligan water on the dispenser provided by Culligan, he and his wife saw a dead fly, and part of another dead fly, in the fresh, unopened, replacement bottle.

Neither Mr. Mustapha nor any member of his family drank from the bottle. He became obsessed, however, with thoughts about the dead fly in the water and about the potential implications for his family's health of their having possibly been drinking unpurified water supplied in the past.

The trial judge accepted the medical evidence that Mr. Mustapha suffers from a major depressive disorder, with associated phobia and anxiety – all triggered by the fly-in-the-bottle incident. In the result, Mr. Mustapha recovered judgment at trial in the total amount of $341,775, plus pre-judgment interest, for psychiatric injuries suffered because of the incident.

Culligan of Canada Ltd. appeals the finding of liability against it and, in the alternative, seeks to reduce the amount of damages awarded.

For the reasons that follow, I would allow the appeal and set aside the judgment below.

FACTS

Mr. Mustapha emigrated from Lebanon to Canada in 1976 at the age of sixteen. After schooling and training as a hair stylist, he opened a business as Martin's Coiffure in 1986. By all accounts the business did well, expanding ultimately to two outlets – one in the Radisson Hotel in Windsor, and a second at Casino Windsor. He married Mrs. Mustapha in 1984. They have two daughters, Amanda and Martina, aged seven and three at the time of trial. Mrs. Mustapha was seven-months pregnant with Martina when the fly-in-the-bottle incident occurred.

The Mustaphas had been using bottled Culligan water for personal consumption in their home since a Culligan representative persuaded Mr. Mustapha to adopt its use at his hair salon shortly after it opened in 1986. Based on Culligan's representations about the purity and healthy quality of Culligan water, including how it would benefit pregnant women and children, and how much better it was for someone than city water, Mr. Mustapha installed Culligan dispensers both in his salon and at home. He and his family used nothing but bottled Culligan water for consumption thereafter. Culligan regularly delivered jugs of water to their home and picked up the empty jugs.

On November 21, 2001, Mr. Mustapha was replacing the bottle in the home dispenser at his wife's request. They were both present. As she always did, Mrs. Mustapha washed the neck of the new bottle to ensure there were no germs on the outside of it before the bottle was placed on the dispenser. As she was doing so, Mr. Mustapha observed something dark in the bottle. On closer examination, they both realized that what they were looking at was a dead fly. Mrs. Mustapha vomited immediately and afterwards held her stomach and complained of cramps and pain. Although Mr. Mustapha felt nauseous, he did not vomit at the time (he did so later). He also felt abdominal pain.

Both Mr. and Mrs. Mustapha experienced ill effects as a result of this incident. The trial judge dismissed Mrs. Mustapha's claim because he was not satisfied that her reaction rose to the level of nervous shock or psychiatric illness sufficient to found a claim in negligence. He found, however, that Mr. Mustapha – unlike his wife – became afflicted with a "recognizable psychological injury" as a result of the incident.

The evidence established that Mr. Mustapha could not get the fly in the bottle out of his mind in the aftermath of the incident. He became anxious over the possible effects on his family of drinking water that he no longer trusted to have been pure. Indeed, he became obsessed, believing that his health and that of his family had been compromised and that his trust in Culligan water had been betrayed.

. . .

Mr. Mustapha's self description is that he could not get the fly in the bottle out of his mind, he had nightmares, he was only sleeping four hours or so a night, he has been unable to drink water since the incident, he has lost his sense of humour and instead become argumentative and edgy, he has been constipated, is bothered by revolting mental images of flies on feces etc., can no longer take long and enjoyable showers and instead, after lengthy treatment, can only take perfunctory showers with his head down so the water does not strike his face. It took lengthy treatment before he could drink coffee made with water. He has to take a variety of medications which he says leave him feeling that he is not in full control and draggy. He can't get up and get off to work in the mornings as he always used to. He has lost clients because of the changes in his personality and mood and also because of the reduction in his previous skills as a hairstylist. He has lost interest in, and ability to perform sexually. He had initial complaints of nausea and present complaints of constant, unexplained abdominal pain or discomfort.

The trial judge accepted Mr. Mustapha's evidence. In addition, the expert medical testimony amply supports his finding that Mr. Mustapha developed a psychiatric/psychological illness – often referred to in legal parlance as "nervous shock" – sufficient to support a claim in negligence, namely a major depressive disorder, with associated phobia and anxiety. Culligan does not contest the finding that the fly-in-the-bottle incident was a contributing cause of Mr. Mustapha's resulting illness.

The trial judge also concluded that the psychiatric effect of the fly-in-the-bottle incident was due to Mr. Mustapha's particular sensibilities to such an event. Acknowledging that Mr. Mustapha's reaction was "objectively bizarre", the trial judge found that his background in the Middle East, "where the devotion to and concern for the family is at a higher level than is found in North America," combined with "the higher level of cleanliness and avoidance of insects practised by this family than is usual", predisposed the respondent to react as he did.

. . .

ANALYSIS AND LAW

A. Liability in Tort

On the findings made by the trial judge, it is apparent that Mr. Mustapha suffered significant and lingering psychiatric injury as a result of the fly-in-the-bottle incident. Nothing I say in these reasons is intended to minimize or belittle the difficulties he has experienced.

The trial judge also found, however, that "[t]he reaction of Mr. Mustapha to seeing a dead fly, and part of another, in a bottle of Culligan water was certainly, *and objectively* bizarre." [Emphasis added.] He concluded that this reaction, and the psychiatric injuries the appellant sustained, were a function of Mr. Mustapha's specific cultural background and personal sensibilities, and the particular circumstances of this case.

The issue of tort law raised on this appeal is whether a defendant may be liable for damages for psychiatric harm where the harm, by any objective measurement, consists of an exaggerated reaction by an obsessive person of particular sensibilities to what, in reality, is a relatively minor or trivial incident – the sight of a dead fly in a bottle of consumer water. In my view, the answer to this question is no.

The Evolution of Liability for Psychiatric Injury

. . .

In the United Kingdom, at least, the common law has divided the types of cases in which damages may be recovered for nervous shock or psychiatric injury into two broad categories: "those cases in which the injured plaintiff was involved, either mediately or immediately, as a participant, and those in which the plaintiff was no more than the passive and unwilling witness of injury caused to others": *Alcock v. Chief Constable of South Yorkshire Police*, [1992] 1 A.C. 310 at 407 (H.L.), per Lord Oliver. The former type of case is referred to as a "primary victim" case, whereas the latter is known as a "secondary victim" or "bystander" case.

This distinction was crystallized in *Page v. Smith*, [1996] A.C. 155 (H.L.), and is important for the different test of foreseeability that applies, depending upon the category in which the plaintiff's case is found to fall. In *Page*, the House of Lords held that in primary victim cases a plaintiff seeking damages for psychiatric harm need only establish reasonable foreseeability of physical injury in order to recover; reasonably foreseeable psychiatric injury of some form is not necessary in such situations, even where there has been no actual physical harm. In secondary victim or bystander cases, on the other hand, a plaintiff seeking damages for psychiatric harm must show that some form of psychiatric illness in a person of normal fortitude was reasonably foreseeable before being entitled to recover.

The distinction between primary and secondary victim cases – and the different tests for liability for psychiatric injury flowing from it – has not yet been adopted in Canada. Whether it should be is an issue on this appeal, because Mr. Pape submits on behalf of Mr. Mustapha that he is not a bystander and, therefore, that the requirement of foreseeability of psychiatric harm has no relevance for the disposition of this case. I shall return to the primary victim/secondary victim dichotomy after completing this brief overview of the jurisprudence respecting liability for psychiatric injury.

[Blair J.A. reviewed the debate among courts and academics whether liability for psychiatric harm is based on the notion of reasonable foreseeability alone, or whether additional control mechanisms are required.]

In the United Kingdom the debate on this question has been settled by the decision of the House of Lords in *White v. Chief Constable of South Yorkshire*, [1999] 2 A.C. 455 (H.L.), following on its earlier ruling in *Alcock*, *supra*. Reasonable foreseeability plus policy carried the day. *White* confirmed that in addition to reasonable foreseeability of psychiatric injury in a person of normal fortitude, it was necessary for a plaintiff seeking damages for psychiatric illness to establish a relationship of proximity between the plaintiff and defendant. The House of Lords acknowledged that the requirement of proximity was a "control mechanism" designed to limit the ambit of the remedy in such cases. Where the plaintiff was personally involved in the incident – a primary victim case – the majority said, proximity is easily demonstrated. Where psychiatric injury is caused out of fear for the safety of someone else, however – a "bystander" case –

foreseeability of injury by shock is insufficient. Rather, the law in the United Kingdom requires the following proximity indicators – factors intended to control the spectre of indeterminate liability in tort – be satisfied: (i) close ties of love and affection must exist between the plaintiff and the victim (called "relational proximity"); (ii) the plaintiff must have been present at the accident or its immediate aftermath (called "locational proximity"); and (iii) the psychiatric injury must have been caused by direct perception of the accident or its immediate aftermath, and not after hearing about it from someone else (called "temporal proximity").

The Canadian and Ontario Experience

Until *Alcock*, *Page*, and *White*, Canadian courts generally had followed the English evolution in terms of granting relief for psychiatric injury in negligence. . ..

No provincial appellate court in Canada has considered or approved the primary victim/secondary victim distinction established in *Page, supra*. Nor has the Supreme Court of Canada. Canadian courts have not explicitly adopted the reasonable foreseeability plus proximity paradigm prescribed in *Alcock* and *White* either, although various decisions have alluded to the notion of resorting to policy considerations to place some boundaries on the foreseeability rule:. . ..

In Ontario – within the context of bystander situations, but without overtly referring to the dichotomy between primary victim and bystander cases – this Court has stated clearly that "reasonable foresight of nervous shock to the plaintiff is the touchstone of liability" for damages for nervous shock: *Haliburton Estate*, *supra*, at p. 518. See also *Duwyn*, *supra*, at pp. 754-755; *Nespolon*, *supra*, at pp. 364-366; and *Vanek*, *supra*.

. . .

Foreseeable consequences, however, as noted in *Vanek* at para. 45, are consequences that the "event and its aftermath might engender *in the reasonable person*." [Emphasis in original.] At para. 58, MacPherson J.A. adopted the following passage from the speech of Lord Griffiths in *White*, *supra*, at pp. 462-463, as "a particularly succinct and useful statement on the foreseeability issue in this type of case":

> There is a further requirement in the bystander case and that is that psychiatric injury was reasonably foreseeable as a likely consequence of exposure to the trauma of the accident or its immediate aftermath. *The law expects reasonable fortitude and robustness of its citizens and will not impose liability for the exceptional frailty of certain individuals.* This is not to be confused with the "eggshell skull" situation, where as a result of a breach of duty the damage inflicted proves to be more serious than expected. It is a threshold test of breach of duty; before a defendant will be held in breach of duty to a bystander he must have exposed them to a situation in which it is reasonably foreseeable that a person of reasonable robustness and fortitude would be likely to suffer psychiatric injury. [Emphasis added.]

Vanek is close to the case at bar in a factual sense, although it is clearly a "bystander" case. Mr. and Mrs. Vanek's eleven-year old child drank a small amount from a juice bottle containing toxic fluids at school. She noticed the drink had a foul taste and regurgitated some of it, although she did not vomit or lose consciousness. The parents were called to the school, and took the child to the hospital. At the hospital, the child was examined and the parents were assured that she had not been poisoned and would suffer no long-term effects. The parents subsequently received the same assurances from different government and health authorities. The child showed no further symptoms from the incident and returned to her normal life. The parents, however, became obsessed with the possibility that the child might suffer harm in the future. They sued the distributor of the drink and its manufacturer. At trial, they recovered moderate damages for anxiety and distress.

The judgment was reversed on appeal. Writing for the Court, MacPherson J.A. concluded that the parents' reaction to what was, in effect, a minor mishap of the type that frequently occurs in schools and in family life, was not that of an average concerned parent. He further found that the defendants could not have reasonably foreseen the parents' highly unusual reaction and the psychiatric damages engendered by it. After noting the passage from the speech of Lord Griffiths in *White*, cited above, and observing that the actual event witnessed by the Vaneks was neither "distressing in the extreme" (*McLoughlin, supra*) nor "horrifying or gruesome" (*Haliburton Estate, supra*) – the same may be said in the case at bar – MacPherson J.A. determined as follows at para. 60:

> In conclusion, the juice incident on June 16, 1993 was the type of incident that happens, in schools and in family life, every day. A minor mishap occurs.. . . Life goes on. Unfortunately, for the Vaneks normal life did not go on. They became obsessed with the incident. In doing so, they were not acting like the average concerned parent. They were displaying a "particular hypersensitivity" (*Duwyn v. Kaprielian*); they lacked the "reasonable fortitude and robustness" (*White v. Chief Constable of South Yorkshire* [*Police*]) that the law expects of all its citizens, including concerned parents.

Why should the same principles not apply to the claim of Mr. Mustapha? Mr. Pape says: because Mr. Mustapha was not a bystander but a primary participant and this rendered reasonable foreseeability of psychiatric harm unnecessary. He submits that it was reasonably foreseeable that a purchaser or consumer of Culligan water would be injured in some fashion if Culligan distributed contaminated bottled water, and that this foreseeability is sufficient for the purpose of Mr. Mustapha's claim.

I do not accept that argument.

"Primary Victims" vs. "Secondary Victims": Should the Distinction be Adopted in Ontario?

For the reasons that follow, I would not adopt the distinction between primary victim and secondary victim or bystander cases, articulated in *Page, supra*, or the different tests for foreseeability emerging from that distinction, as part of the law of Ontario.

The *Page v. Smith* dichotomy has been the subject of considerable criticism, both in the House of Lords and by academics. . ..

Essentially, the criticisms are threefold. First, removal of the requirement for foreseeability of the type of harm incurred, in relation to the primary victim cases, runs contrary to the fundamental principle of tort law as established in *The Wagon Mound No. 1* and *The Wagon Mound No. 2* (the particular type of injury must be foreseeable). In Lord Goff's view, in *White, supra*, at pp. 474-475, "Lord Lloyd [in *Page*] dethroned foreseeability of psychiatric injury from its central position as the unifying feature of this branch of the law." Secondly, the distinction between primary victims and secondary victims is an artificial one that camouflages the policy choices that have to be made and moreover, is problematic in application. The case at bar is a good example of this problem, as I shall explore in a moment. As Bélanger-Hardy, *supra*, at p. 564, notes, the distinction "allows artificial criteria to display the more natural question: should the defendant be liable to the plaintiff in all the circumstances?" Finally, the critics observe that the majority in *Page* have misunderstood the thinskull plaintiff principle, which relates only to quantum of damages once liability has already been established. As Lord Wright explained in *Bourhill v. Young*, [1943] A.C. 92 (H.L.) – a seminal nervous shock case – at 109-110:

> No doubt, it has long ago been stated and often restated that if the wrong is established the wrongdoer must take the victim as he finds him. That, however, is only true . . . on the condition that the wrong has been established or admitted. The question of liability is anterior to the question of the measure of the consequences which go with the liability.

I find these criticisms persuasive. In particular, the view that the *Page v. Smith* distinction is artificial and not always easy to apply resonates in this case. Is Mr. Mustapha indeed a "primary victim", or is he a bystander or "secondary victim"? Is he both? Or neither? An argument can be made that he falls into any of these four categories.

. . .

Why should it matter in principle? I can see no convincing rationale for concluding that the test for foreseeability in a psychiatric harm case should depend upon the outcome of the exercise of determining whether the plaintiff is a primary or secondary victim. Instead, I prefer the reasoning of the dissenting opinions in *Page* rejecting the distinction between primary and secondary victims, and concluding that even a plaintiff who was involved in the incident must demonstrate reasonable foreseeability of psychiatric illness in order to recover in tort. . ..

. . .

It seems to me that the primary victim/secondary victim distinction is another example of a mechanism constructed and deployed by the courts to put limits, for policy reasons, on the scope of recovery in psychiatric harm cases. This objective is accomplished in other ways in Canada.

Although I would not apply the *Page v. Smith* dichotomy to the determination of liability for psychiatric harm, I nonetheless accept that the authorities support an approach to liability in such cases that involves a consideration of policy issues in addition to reasonable foreseeability alone. This is consistent with the two-part *Anns* test as adopted in *Kamloops*, *supra*, namely, (i) whether there is a sufficiently close relationship of proximity or neighbourhood between the parties, such that in the reasonable contemplation of the alleged wrongdoer, carelessness on his or her part may be likely to cause damage to the defendant; and, if so (ii) whether there are any considerations which ought to negative or limit (a) the scope of the duty and (b) the class of persons to whom it is owed or (c) the damages to which a breach of it may give rise. This test clearly imports both the notion of reasonable foreseeability and policy limitations on the scope of liability even where the harm was foreseeable.

Whether – and, if so, to what extent – the control mechanisms of relational, locational and temporal proximity, as outlined in *Alcock* and *White*, are integral to the *Anns* approach, as adopted in Canada, is not a question that needs to be decided on the facts of this case. Canadian courts have resorted to all of them, in some fashion, on occasion. It is clear that Mr. Mustapha satisfies those criteria in any event. The concerns driving his obsession about the dead fly in the bottle were centred on the possible impact the consumption of contaminated water had, or might have in the future, on his family (relational proximity), and he was present at the event itself and witnessed the fly in the bottle (locational and temporal proximity).

The policy consideration that applies in this case, however, is the following: what is the ambit of liability in psychiatric harm cases where the harm suffered (a) is significantly disproportionate to the relatively inconsequential nature of the incident in question, and (b) is a function of the particular sensibilities of the plaintiff rather than a function of the sensibilities that a person of normal fortitude would demonstrate? This concern is accommodated, in my view, by factoring the "person of normal fortitude and robustness" principle into the reasonable foreseeability equation, as this Court did in *Vanek*.

The Test in Ontario

Reasonable foreseeability of harm is the hallmark of tort liability. In my opinion, the test for the existence of a duty of care – and, therefore, for liability – in cases of psychiatric harm is whether it is reasonably foreseeable that a person of normal fortitude or sensibility is likely to suffer some type of psychiatric harm as a consequence of the defendant's careless conduct. That is what reasonable foreseeability means. This test, which is the foreseeability test enunciated in *Vanek*, applies regardless of the distinction between "primary victim" and "secondary victim" cases.

Application of the Test in this Case

[Blair J.A. summarized and quoted from the trial judge's decision.]

These paragraphs represent the nub of the trial judge's reasoning respecting foreseeability on the facts of the case. It is apparent that he was focused primarily, if not exclusively, on the peculiar impact seeing the dead fly in the bottle had on Mr. Mustapha arising from "his previous history", his "unusually high concern over the health and well being of his family", the "unusually clean home" maintained by Mrs. Mustapha, and his concerns over the risks of her pregnancy. The trial judge's comment that it was foreseeable to Culligan "that if it supplied a water bottle with dead flies floating around in it, Mr. Mustapha, and other customers like him, would suffer 'some degree' of nervous shock", must be viewed in that light. The reference to "other customers *like him*" turns the analysis right back to the subjective specific sensibilities of Mr. Mustapha.

All of the medical evidence characterized Mr. Mustapha's reaction in individualistic terms and, in varying ways, as unique and strange. Dr. Chung said, "[H]e had never seen anything quite like the symptomatology described by Mr. Mustapha, and he felt it was highly unusual." Dr. Rai testified that the appellant's fear was "a rational fear *for that particular individual*" [emphasis added]. Dr. Litman said that Mr. Mustapha displayed a "very individual response, depending on the vulnerabilities of the particular individual." The experts were not asked to comment on the objective component of the *Vanek* test, namely, whether a person of normal fortitude would be likely to suffer psychiatric injury from having seen a dead fly in a bottle of water from which no water had been consumed.

Moreover, the trial judge made no finding – nor was there evidence to support one – that Culligan was made aware of, or ought to have known, anything about the particular sensibilities of Mr. Mustapha and his family. The appellant's reaction to the fly-in-the-bottle incident was "abnormal", a product of his "particular hypersensitivity" (*Duwyn*); it was not the response of the "average sensitive" person (*Haliburton Estate*); nor was it the response of a person of "reasonable fortitude and robustness" (*White* and *Vanek*). These objective elements are essential to the psychiatric harm analysis. Respectfully, the trial judge erred in failing to take into account the objective component of the test for reasonable foreseeability in such circumstances, focusing entirely, instead, on the individual characteristics and vulnerabilities of the appellant.

I am satisfied, as well, that the trial judge erred in considering, as illustrated in para. 240 of his reasons, whether there was a foreseeable "*possibility* of damage, including psychological damage" [Emphasis added] arising as a result of seeing the dead fly in the bottle of water, rather than considering whether there was a foreseeable "probability" of such damage. As Abella J.A. observed, in *Nespolon, supra*, at pp. 363-364:

> A duty of care will only be found where the resultant harm is reasonably foreseeable. In order to determine whether the harm was or ought to have been foreseeable, one examines the proximity of the relationship between the parties and the probability of the harm actually occurring [citations omitted by Blair J.A.].
>
> In his text *The Law of Torts in Canada*, Professor G.H.L. Fridman confirms this nexus as follows: "Foreseeability of harm is a necessary ingredient of a relationship that is apt to give rise to a duty of care" (vol. 1 (Toronto: Carswell, 1989) at p. 235). Foreseeability, in other words, arises where the harm resulting from the conduct of the defendant was, or ought to have been contemplated by the alleged wrongdoer as a *probable consequence* of his or her actions (at p. 238).
>
> As characterized by Fridman, "[o]nly if what happened is considered to be a natural and *probable* result of what the defendant did or omitted to do will the defendant be regarded as having behaved so unreasonably as to be guilty of negligence, *i.e.* of conduct falling short of the standards of the ordinary reasonable man" [citations omitted]. . .. [Emphasis added.]

I would therefore give effect to this ground of appeal.

NOTES AND QUESTIONS

1. Why does Blair J.A. reject the dichotomy between primary and secondary victims? Is there any justification for treating bystanders differently from those directly involved in the incident? Are there alternative ways to limit recovery by bystanders?

2. After you have read Chapter 17, return to this chapter and explain how the test of reasonable robustness and fortitude is distinguished from the thin-skull principle in remoteness. Why does one principle allow recovery and the other one deny it?

3. Another leading Canadian case on recovery for nervous shock in negligence is *Rhodes v. Canadian National Railway* (1990), 50 B.C.L.R. (2d) 273 (C.A.). The plaintiff's son was killed in a train crash negligently caused by the defendant. She heard about the crash on the radio, and travelled from her home on Vancouver Island to Hinton, Alberta to see if her son had been killed. The defendant's employees denied her access to the crash site for eight days. She realized after several days that her son must have been killed, but she never saw his body because it was consumed by fire in the crash. Her claim to recover for her psychiatric injury was denied because it was not a foreseeable consequence of the defendant's negligence. Although she had close ties of love and affection with her son, she had not witnessed the accident or its aftermath with her own unaided senses.

4. Although most cases involve serious automobile, industrial and household accidents, nervous shock claims have arisen in a broad range of fact situations. See for

example *Curll v. Robin Hood Multifoods Ltd.* (1974), 56 D.L.R. (3d) 129 (N.S.T.D.); *Taylor v. Weston Bakeries Ltd.* (1976), 1 C.C.L.T. 158 (Sask. Dist. Ct.) (involving contaminated food products); *Guay v. Sun Publishing Co.*, [1953] 2 S.C.R. 216 (false newspaper report of husband's and children's deaths); *Cook v. S.*, [1967] 1 All E.R. 299 (C.A.) (solicitor's negligence in divorce proceedings); *Dietelbach v. British Columbia (Public Trustee)* (1973), 37 D.L.R. (3d) 621 (B.C.S.C.); *Pratt & Goldsmith v. Pratt*, [1975] V.R. 378 (S.C.) (involving trauma of adjusting to the injuries of close relatives); and *McMullin v. F.W. Woolworth Co.* (1974), 9 N.B.R. (2d) 214 (Q.B.) (diseased turtle infecting plaintiff's children). Except in the food products cases, the courts held that the plaintiffs were not owed a duty of care because nervous shock was unforeseeable. But see *Boudreau v. Benaiah* (2000), 46 O.R. (3d) 737 (C.A.) (offender awarded damages for mental distress due to his defence counsellors' negligence in arranging a plea bargain).

5. Having read the authorities, do you think that the distinction between recovery for nervous shock and physical injuries can still be justified? Do nervous shock claims pose any unique concerns about false or trivial claims, problems of proof or indeterminate liability? Are nervous shock claims less important or worthy of protection than physical injury or property loss claims?

6. If a distinction is to be made for nervous shock claims, should the duty be defined in terms of the specific fact situation, rather than the open-ended tests of foreseeability and proximity, which have yielded such a perplexing body of jurisprudence?

7. Recovery for nervous shock in Australia is considerably broader than recovery in Canada or England. See generally Vines, "Proximity as Principle or Category: Nervous Shock in Australia and England" (1993) 16 U.N.S.W.L.J. 458; Mullany, "Fear for the Future: Liability for Infliction of Psychiatric Disorder" in Mullany, ed., *Torts in the Nineties* (1997) 101; and Mullany, "Negligently Inflicted Psychiatric Injury and the Means of Communication of Trauma – Should it Matter?" in Mullany & Linden, eds., *Torts Tomorrow: A Tribute to John Fleming* (1998) 162.

8. For further commentary on Commonwealth developments in negligent nervous shock, see Teff, "Liability for Negligently Inflicted Psychiatric Harm: Justification and Boundaries" [1998] C.L.J. 91; Teff, "Liability for Psychiatric Illness: Advancing Cautiously" (1998) Mod. L. Rev. 849; Witting, "A Primer on the Modern Law of 'Nervous Shock'" (1998) 22 Melb. U. L. Rev. 62; Bélanger-Hardy, "Nervous Shock, Nervous Courts: The *Anns/Kamloops* Test to the Rescue?" (1999) 37 Alta. L. Rev. 553; and Mackenzie, "Oh, What a Tangled Web We Weave: Liability in Negligence for Nervous Shock" in Beaulac, Pitel & Schulz, eds., *The Joy of Torts* (2003) 125.

REVIEW PROBLEM

John Smith fell asleep at the wheel of his truck, crashed through a barrier and struck an oncoming car. The driver of the car, Mike Berry, was killed and his wife, Helen, was injured. Although Helen's physical injuries healed quickly, she was unable to cope with the shock of the accident and her husband's death. It was only after 15 months of intensive psychiatric care that Helen was able to return to work and a relatively normal lifestyle. Steven Finch, the other passenger in the Berry car, was uninjured. Unfortunately, David

Finch, his father, had been following the Berry car and suffered severe shock on witnessing the collision, as did Mrs. Pewter, an old friend who was travelling in the Finch car. As a result of his attempts to assist the accident victims, Melvin, a bystander, suffered recurring nightmares. The gruesome scene triggered Melvin's memories of a childhood accident in which his younger brother had been killed. As Sarah Berry drove past the scene she recognized the demolished car of her brother, Mike Berry. By the time she stopped and ran back to the scene, all of the accident victims had been taken to the hospital. She fought back her tears long enough to ask one of the officers what had happened. All he was able to tell her was that the accident had been a serious one involving several members of the Berry family. Sarah was overwhelmed and passed out. She was informed of her brother's death when she regained consciousness in the hospital. Lastly, Mike Berry's mother suffered a heart attack when she heard of her son's death in a radio broadcast.

You have been consulted by John Smith for advice concerning his possible liability for the negligent infliction of nervous shock.

5. A Health Professional's Duty to Inform

As discussed in Chapter 6, the Supreme Court of Canada decided in *Reibl v. Hughes*, [1980] 2 S.C.R. 880 to limit a doctor's liability in battery to cases in which the patient did not consent at all, the consent was exceeded, or the consent was obtained fraudulently. Once the patient is aware of the general nature of the proposed treatment and consents to it, the doctor's failure to inform will not vitiate the consent and give rise to liability in battery. Rather, the Supreme Court of Canada indicated that the doctor may be held liable in negligence for breaching an affirmative duty to disclose the risks of the proposed treatment. This duty is a special duty of care that arises independently of doctors' general duty to exercise reasonable care in treating patients.

The court focused on the information that a reasonable patient in the plaintiff's position would want. More specifically, the court stated that doctors must disclose all material risks of the proposed treatment. A "material risk" includes a low percentage risk of a serious consequence. In *Reibl*, it was held that a 4% chance of death and a 10% chance of paralysis constituted material risks. A relatively minor consequence of high probability may also constitute a material risk. As well, doctors have an obligation to disclose non-material risks that they know, or ought to know, would be of particular concern to the patient. For example, a doctor may not have to disclose a 5% risk of minor residual stiffness in the shoulder to a patient who is an accountant, but would have to disclose this risk to a patient who is a professional tennis player.

Patients may choose to rely on their doctors' judgment and decide that they do not wish to be informed of the risks. However, the decision not to be fully informed is the patient's to make, and he or she must clearly communicate this to the doctor. All questions must be answered honestly and fully, even if they relate to minor matters or if the answers might be upsetting.

Doctors who do not meet these disclosure requirements will be held to have breached the requisite standard of care. However, patients must also establish that this failure to inform was a cause of their loss. In effect, patients must prove that, had they been adequately informed, they would not have proceeded with the treatment. In *Reibl*, the Supreme Court of Canada rejected the general common law test of causation and adopted a special objective/subjective test of causation. The plaintiff must prove that a reasonable person in the plaintiff's position would have refused the procedure if properly informed.

As the following case and the accompanying notes and questions illustrate, the courts have broadened the duty to inform considerably since it was first established in *Reibl*. The duty is no longer limited to warning patients of the risks of the specific procedure; rather, the doctor is required to provide the patient with sufficient information to make an informed decision. The definition of a material risk has been broadened to include very remote risks of death or serious injury. The courts are far less willing to give doctors discretion to withhold information because doctors believe it will be disconcerting to the patient. Finally, the principles governing the duty to inform now appear to apply to all health professionals and care givers.

HAUGHIAN v. PAINE

(1987), 37 D.L.R. (4th) 624 (Sask. C.A.)

[The plaintiff underwent disc surgery that left him paralyzed. A second operation partially alleviated the paralysis. The plaintiff's action against the defendant surgeon for failing to obtain an informed consent was dismissed at trial. The plaintiff appealed.]

SHERSTOBITOFF J.A.: – [The judge quoted from *Videto v. Kennedy* (1981), 33 O.R. (2d) 497 (C.A.), a summary of the Supreme Court of Canada's conclusions from *Reibl* and *Hopp v. Lepp*, [1980] 2 S.C.R. 192.]

I would add to the principles outlined above a matter which was not under direct consideration in the foregoing cases: In order to enable a patient to give informed consent, a surgeon must also, where the circumstances require it, explain to the patient the consequences of leaving the ailment untreated, and alternative means of treatment and their risks.

. . .

In my respectful view, the trial Judge erred in failing to give any weight, under the aspect of informed consent, to the duty of the respondent in this case to advise the appellant of the consequences of leaving the ailment untreated and the duty to advise of alternate means of treatment. A careful examination of the evidence . . . under the head of negligence indicates that there was no adequate discussion, if any at all, of the consequences of leaving the ailment untreated or of undergoing conservative management, and that the consequences were, at worst, a continuation of pain and discomfort and possible need for surgery in the future. The appellant was not told that the prospect was that the condition might, in a matter of months, very well improve, albeit with the prospect of recurrence from time to time. If the condition deteriorated, surgery was always an option in the future. In the absence of such information having been given to the appellant, he was not in a position to give informed consent.

It makes no difference that the respondent may have been under a misconception that the appellant had had conservative management. If that was the case it was due to the respondent's negligence in failure to take an adequate history, or to consider it.

The other aspect of the informed consent is the failure of the respondent to warn the appellant of the possibility of total paralysis, the risk which in fact materialized. Although no exact statistics were given, a consensus seems to have arisen amongst the neurosurgeons giving evidence that the risk of paralysis in surgery such as under consideration here is not more than one in five hundred. The respondent's practice was not to give any warning if the risk was less than one in one hundred.

. . .

The trial Judge made reference to the similarity of facts in *Hopp v. Lepp* and this case: both involve disc surgery. He commented that the doctor was found not liable in *Hopp v. Lepp* and he told the patient less of the risks than the respondent did in this case. However, a careful reading of *Hopp v. Lepp* does not disclose that any alternative such as conservative management was available in that case. It was certainly not an issue. That is sufficient to distinguish it, on the facts, from this case.

Finally, I touch upon an argument advanced by the respondent. His position is that statistically the risk of paralysis is less than one in five hundred, a risk so insignificant that it could not be considered material. In my respectful view, the issue of materiality cannot be reduced to numbers for all cases. Statistics are but one factor to be taken into account.

In my respectful view, the disclosure made by the respondent was not adequate to enable the appellant to give informed consent. On the principles laid down above which I have quoted from *Hopp v. Lepp*, *Reibl v. Hughes*, *Canterbury v. Spence*, and the dissenting opinion of Lord Scarman in *Sidaway v. Bethlem Royal Hospital Governors*, the following deficiencies in disclosure are apparent in this case:

1. A failure to advise adequately, or at all, of the available options of no treatment, or conservative management. While it may have been open to the respondent not to recommend these options by way of treatment, the patient was entitled to be advised that these alternatives were open to him.

2. A failure to advise of the risk of paralysis. Admittedly, the risk was small, but given that alternative non-surgical treatment was available, with lack of risk, a significant chance of success, and the paucity of evidence that the condition disabled the appellant significantly, disclosure should have been made.

A significant factor is that the trial Judge considered failure to warn of risk of paralysis, and failure to advise of alternatives to surgery, independently of, and in isolation from, each other. These two elements of informed consent have, on the facts of this case, a strong bearing on each other. One cannot make an informed decision to undertake a risk without knowing the alternatives to undergoing the risk.

There is no suggestion here that the respondent withheld the information because of "therapeutic privilege". There was no suggestion that disclosure would have unduly frightened the appellant, caused him psychological harm or deterred him from taking treatment essential to his health. The respondent's position was simply that it was not his practice to warn of this risk.

[Appeal allowed; judgment for the plaintiff.]

NOTES AND QUESTIONS

1. How does *Haughian* expand the principles in *Reibl*? What role did the alternative treatments play in the judge's conclusion in *Haughian* that a 1 in 500 chance of paralysis was a material risk? See also *Coughlin v. Kuntz* (1989), 2 C.C.L.T. (2d) 42 (B.C.C.A.); *Van Mol (Guardian ad litem of) v. Ashmore* (1999), 168 D.L.R. (4th) 637 (Alta. C.A.); *Thibault v. Fewer*, [2002] 1 W.W.R. 204 (Man. Q.B.); and *Groves v. Morton* (2006), 44 C.C.L.T. (3d) 108 (Ont. S.C.J.).

2. In *Reibl* and *Haughian*, the courts suggest that a health professional has a limited "therapeutic privilege" to withhold information if its disclosure would unduly frighten or deter the patient. However, in *Hopp v. Lepp*, [1980] 2 S.C.R. 192, the court suggested that the privilege no longer existed. In *Meyer Estate v. Rogers* (1991), 2 O.R. (3d) 356 (Gen. Div.), the judge stated that the doctrine was no longer part of the law. In *Pittman Estate v. Bain* (1994), 112 D.L.R. (4th) 257 (Ont. Gen. Div.), the court acknowledged that the privilege existed, but defined it narrowly (*i.e.*, the doctor may choose how to present the information and what aspects to emphasize). In what circumstances, if any, should the courts recognize a privilege to withhold information?

3. The scope of what constitutes a material risk has been progressively broadened since *Reibl*. See for example *Buchan v. Ortho Pharmaceutical (Canada) Ltd.* (1986), 25 D.L.R. (4th) 658 (Ont. C.A.) (very rare chance of a stroke as a result of taking oral contraceptives); *Feist v. Gordon* (1989), 67 Alta. L.R. (2d) 283 (Q.B.), aff'd (1990), 76 Alta. L.R. (2d) 234 (C.A.) (1 in 40,000 risk of puncturing eyeball with cortisone treatment); *Rolof v. Morris* (1990), 109 A.R. 128 (Q.B.) (1 in 1,000 risk of an intra-uterine contraceptive device leaving the uterus and requiring surgical removal); *Meyer Estate v. Rogers*, *supra* (1 in 40,000 to 1 in 100,000 chance of death as a result of a severe reaction to a diagnostic dye); *Leung v. Campbell* (1995), 24 C.C.L.T. (2d) 63 (Ont. Gen. Div.) (rare risk of stroke during neck manipulation by a chiropractor); *Martin v. Inglis*, [2002] 9 W.W.R. 500 (Sask. Q.B.) (a mere possibility of stomach perforation and death from gastric surgery); and *Brock v. Anderson* (2003), 20 C.C.L.T. (3d) 70 (B.C.S.C.) (very small likelihood of damaging a major blood vessel which, if it occurred, posed a significant risk of death). But see *DeFerrari v. Neville* (1998), 42 C.C.L.T. (2d) 327 (Ont. Gen. Div.) (1 in 800,000 chance of permanent numbness arising from dental anaesthetic found not to be a material risk); and *Munir v. Jackson*, 2006 CarswellOnt 2518 (S.C.J.) (WLeC) (3 in 10,000 chance of permanent tracheotomy found not to be a material risk).

4. Disclosing some material risks, while not disclosing others, is insufficient: see *Tremblay v. McLauchlan* (2001), 6 C.C.L.T. (3d) 238 (B.C.C.A.).

5. A doctor does not have to inform patients that he or she will be assisted by a resident or other treatment professional. It is less clear, however, if a patient must be informed that an intern or resident, rather than the specialist, will be performing the procedure or a major part of it. For example, failing to inform the patient that a resident, as opposed to a fully-qualified specialist, would be performing a cardiac catheterization was held to be a material risk that had to be disclosed in *Currie v. Blundell* (1992), 10 C.C.L.T. (2d) 288 at 290 (Qc. S.C.). But see *Bezusko v. Waterfall* (1997), 45 O.T.C. 241 (Gen. Div.), which reached the opposite conclusion. In what circumstances should a doctor be required to inform a patient that a resident or intern will be involved in the proposed procedure? See also *Marcoux v. Bouchard*, [2001] 2 S.C.R. 726.

6. Must a health practitioner inform patients that his or her success rate is lower than average? Should the seriousness of the risks involved in the procedure be a factor in resolving this issue? Is the fact that a health professional is being sued for malpractice or investigated by the governing professional body a material risk? See *Turner v. Bederman* (1996), 2 O.T.C. 215 (Gen. Div.), where the court found that there was no duty

to disclose the health professional's experience with the procedure or pending lawsuits. See also *Stiles v. Hatfield*, 2003 CarswellOnt 2241 (S.C.J.) (WLeC).

7. Is the fact that a doctor or dentist is HIV-positive a material risk that must be disclosed? One difficulty in resolving this issue is the divergent estimates of the risks of infection from doctor to patient. Aside from one unresolved incident in Florida, there have been no documented reports of HIV-positive health practitioners infecting their patients in the course of providing treatment.

In *Halkyard v. Mathew* (1998), 43 C.C.L.T. (2d) 171 (Alta. Q.B.), aff'd (2001), 4 C.C.L.T. (3d) 271 (Alta. C.A.), it was held that practitioners need not disclose personal medical conditions that do not affect their capacity to provide the proposed treatment. The doctor in that case was epileptic. For a discussion of the need to balance the right to make informed consent against the privacy rights of physician and protection from unwarranted discrimination, see Johnson, "Recent Decision: Must Doctors Disclose Their Own Personal Risk Factors? *Halkyard v. Mathew*" (2001) 10 Health L. Rev. 18.

Do you agree with this principle and would it govern an HIV-positive surgeon? See Spielman, "Expanding the boundaries of informed consent: disclosing alcoholism and HIV status to patients" (1992) 93 Am. J. Med. 216; Flanagan, "AIDS-Related Risks in the Health Care Setting: HIV Testing of Health Care Workers and Patients" (1993) 18 Queen's L.J. 71; Canadian Medical Association, "HIV Infection in the Workplace" (1994) 3 Health L. Rev. 27; and DeVille, "Nothing to fear but fear itself: HIV-infected physicians and the law of informed consent" (1994) 22 J. Law Med. Ethics 163.

8. Even if the risks discussed in notes 5 and 6 are held not to be material, should they be viewed as special risks if the patient has expressed concern about them?

In *Martin v. Capital Health Authority*, 2007 CarswellAlta 513 (Q.B.) (WLeC) the plaintiff was advised to have surgery to remove a brain tumour. The tumour was not debilitating, and the plaintiff was able to walk and talk. The plaintiff told the defendant neurosurgeon that his daughter was getting married and that he wanted to actively participate in the wedding. The defendant advised the plaintiff to go ahead with the surgery and did not adequately inform the plaintiff of the risk of stroke. The defendant was held liable when the surgery left the plaintiff confined to a wheelchair and with difficulty speaking, such that he could not participate in his daughter's wedding. The court found that, had the plaintiff been properly informed of the risks, he would have postponed the surgery until after the wedding.

9. It has been held that a health professional must answer a patient's questions fully, even if they relate to minor aspects of the procedure. See *Sinclaire v. Boulton* (1985), 33 C.C.L.T. 125 (B.C.S.C.); and *Hartjes v. Carmen* (2003), 20 C.C.L.T. (3d) 31 (Ont. S.C.J.). However, the courts have not defined the range of questions that a health professional must answer.

10. The preceding questions involve issues that are at least potentially relevant to treatment. Does a health professional have to answer questions that are unrelated to the patient's treatment? For example, are doctors required to answer questions about their religion, position on abortion, or ethnic background?

11. There are numerous situations in tort law in which the plaintiff's claim turns on proving that he or she relied upon the defendant's advice, yet in these cases no special

causation test is adopted. Are there any unique factors that warrant adopting a special causation test in cases involving a doctor's duty to inform? Given the test of causation, can a patient ever succeed on the issue of causation in cases of non-elective surgery?

In *Arndt v. Smith* (1997), 35 C.C.L.T. (2d) 233 (S.C.C.), three of the nine justices rejected the objective/subjective test of causation in informed consent cases in favour of the subjective test of causation that generally applies in negligence.

In *Chappel v. Hart* (1998), 156 A.L.R. 517 (H.C.A.), the court held that the subjective test of causation should be applied in medical duty to inform cases. This is consistent with the earlier Australian cases and the position of the English courts. See also McInnes, "Failure to Warn in Medical Negligence – A Cautionary Note From Canada: *Arndt v. Smith*" (1998) 6 Tort L. Rev. 135; and Nelson & Caulfield, "You Can't Get There From Here: A Case Comment on *Arndt v. Smith*" (1998) 32 U.B.C.L. Rev. 353. Nevertheless, the Canadian courts continue to apply the objective/subjective test of causation. See for example *Brito (Guardian ad litem of) v. Wooley* (2003), 16 B.C.L.R. (4th) 220 (C.A.); and *Van Dyke v. Grey Bruce Regional Health Centre* (2005), 255 D.L.R. (4th) 397 (Ont. C.A.).

Given the difficulties with *Arndt*, and the English and Australian position, should the Canadian courts adopt a subjective test of causation for duty to inform cases?

12. The *Health Care Consent Act, 1996*, S.O. 1996, c. 2, s. 1, provides that, for consent to be valid, it must be "informed." The section then defines "informed" consent in terms very similar to the preceding common law principles. However, the statute is silent on the civil liability consequences of providing treatment without an informed consent. Will a health professional's failure to obtain an informed consent now give rise to a battery action in any case involving a physical contact? What legal implications flow from framing the action in battery? Are there any circumstances in which a patient would want to proceed in negligence? See Robertson, "Ontario's New Informed Consent Law: Codification or Radical Change?" (1994) 2 Health L.J. 88.

13. The obligation to inform patients is applied more vigorously in the case of medical research and experimental or unconventional therapies. See for example *Weiss v. Solomon* (1989), 48 C.C.L.T. 280 (S.C. Qc.); and *Coughlin v. Kuntz, supra*. For discussion of this issue, see Côté, "Adequate Protection for the Autonomous Research Subject? The Disclosure of Sources of Funding and Commercialisation in Genetic Research Trials" (2002) 28 Man. L.J. 347.

14. For an analysis of the effects of the *Reibl* decision on claims based on lack of informed consent, see Robertson, "Informed Consent 20 Years Later" (2003) (unnumbered special ed.) Health L.J. 153. For a general discussion of informed consent, see Picard & Robertson, *Legal Liability of Doctors and Hospitals*, 3d ed. (1996) at 109-72; Englard, "Informed Consent – The Double-Faced Doctrine" in Mullany & Linden, eds., *Torts Tomorrow: A Tribute to John Fleming* (1998) 152; and Dickens, "Informed Consent" in Downie, Caulfield & Flood, eds., *Canadian Health Law and Policy* (1999) 117.

REVIEW PROBLEM

Andrew distrusts all doctors and has a morbid fear of hospitals and operations. He was understandably upset when informed that he required an operation to repair a weak blood vessel in his brain. He was told that it was a serious operation and that, without it, he would live only eight to ten years. The general mortality rate for this procedure was 10%, although one surgeon in London, Ontario had a mortality rate of less than 5%. Dr. Baker, Andrew's surgeon, had lost 15% of her patients, but this was due in part to the large number of high-risk patients in her practice. Dr. Baker informed Andrew of the general mortality rate of 10%, but did not mention her own record or that of the very successful surgeon. In addition to the risk of mortality, there was a 5% risk of partial paralysis, and a 1% risk of infection, which is common to all operations. Because of Andrew's general anxiety and the effect that this information might have on his condition, Dr. Baker thought it best not to trouble him with this additional information.

Andrew consented to the operation. Regrettably, the operation left him partially paralyzed, and an infection set in, hindering his recovery. It had been Andrew's lifelong dream to fly a balloon solo across the Atlantic, but this is now impossible. Dr. Baker knew nothing of the planned flight, which she dismisses as the unreasonable desire of an eccentric personality. Nonetheless, prior to the operation, Andrew had acquired the sponsorship of a major brewery for what Dr. Baker calls "his flight of fantasy." Andrew is in the depths of depression. He now says that, had he known about these other risks, Dr. Baker's personal record and that of the London surgeon, he would have postponed the operation, made his flight and then gone to the surgeon in London. Advise Andrew on suing Dr. Baker for breaching her duty to inform.

6. A Manufacturer's and Supplier's Duty to Warn

HOLLIS v. DOW CORNING CORP.

(1995), 129 D.L.R. (4th) 609 (S.C.C.)

[The plaintiff underwent breast implant surgery in 1983. The implants had been manufactured by the defendant, Dow Corning. After 17 months, one of the implants ruptured and the plaintiff was required to undergo several operations to remove silicone gel and implant coverings. The literature accompanying the product warned of the risk of rupture during surgery, but not of any risks of post-surgical rupturing "from ordinary, non-traumatic, human activities." The plaintiff sued both the surgeon and Dow Corning. At trial, the claim against the surgeon was dismissed because the risk of injury that in fact materialized was not well-known among surgeons at the time or extensively discussed in the literature. However, Dow Corning was held liable on the basis that the implant had been negligently manufactured.

The British Columbia Court of Appeal granted the plaintiff's appeal and ordered a new trial on the surgeon's liability. The court held Dow Corning liable, but not on the basis that the implant had been negligently manufactured. Rather, it was held liable because it had failed to warn of the risks of post-surgery rupture, even though it had received about 50 reports of ruptures by 1983. Dow Corning appealed to the Supreme Court of Canada.]

LA FOREST J. (L'HEUREUX-DUBÉ, GONTHIER, CORY and IACOBUCCI JJ. concurring): –

. . .

The sole issue raised in this appeal is whether the Court of Appeal erred in finding Dow liable to the respondent Ms Hollis for failing adequately to warn the implanting surgeon, Dr. Birch, of the risk of a post-surgical implant rupture inside Ms Hollis' body.

The appellant Dow does not contest Bouck J.'s factual finding that Ms Hollis' seven-year surgical ordeal caused her great physical and psychological pain, residual scarring on her breasts, and a loss of past and future income. However, Dow submits that it was not responsible for Ms Hollis' injuries. In support of this submission, Dow argues, first, that the warning it gave Dr. Birch was adequate and sufficient to satisfy its duty to Ms Hollis, and second, that even if it did breach its duty to warn Ms Hollis, this breach was not the proximate cause of her injuries.

For the reasons that follow, it is my view that the Court of Appeal reached the correct conclusion and that the appeal should be dismissed.

. . .

It is well-established in Canadian law that a manufacturer of a product has a duty in tort to warn consumers of dangers inherent in the use of its product of which it has knowledge or ought to have knowledge. This principle was enunciated by Laskin J. (as he then was), for the court, in *Lambert v. Lastoplex Chemicals Co.* (1971), 25 D.L.R. (3d) 121 at pp. 124-5, [1972] S.C.R. 569.

. . .

The duty to warn is a continuing duty, requiring manufacturers to warn not only of dangers known at the time of sale, but also of dangers discovered after the product has been sold and delivered: see *Rivtow Marine Ltd. v. Washington Iron Works* (1973), 40 D.L.R. (3d) 530 at pp. 536-7, [1974] S.C.R. 1189, [1973] 6 W.W.R. 692, *per* Ritchie J. All warnings must be reasonably communicated, and must clearly describe any specific dangers that arise from the ordinary use of the product:

. . .

The rationale for the manufacturer's duty to warn can be traced to the "neighbour principle", which lies at the heart of the law of negligence, and was set down in its classic form by Lord Atkin in *Donoghue v. Stevenson*, [1932] A.C. 562 (H.L.). When manufacturers place products into the flow of commerce, they create a relationship of reliance with consumers, who have far less knowledge than the manufacturers concerning the dangers inherent in the use of the products, and are therefore put at risk if the product is not safe. The duty to warn serves to correct the knowledge imbalance between manufacturers and consumers by alerting consumers to any dangers and allowing them to make informed decisions concerning the safe use of the product.

The nature and scope of the manufacturer's duty to warn varies with the level of danger entailed by the ordinary use of the product. Where significant dangers are entailed by the ordinary use of the product, it will rarely be sufficient for manufacturers to give general warnings concerning those dangers; the warnings must be sufficiently detailed to give the consumer a full indication of each of the specific dangers arising from the use of the product. This was made clear by Laskin J. in *Lambert*, *supra*, where this court imposed liability on the manufacturer of a fast-drying lacquer sealer who failed to warn of the danger of using the highly explosive product in the vicinity of a furnace pilot light. The manufacturer in *Lambert* had placed three different labels on its containers warning of the danger of inflammability. The plaintiff, an engineer, had read the warnings before he began to lacquer his basement floor and, in accordance with the warnings, had turned down the thermostat to prevent the furnace from turning on. However, he did not turn off the pilot light, which caused the resulting fire and explosion. Laskin J. found the manufacturer liable for failing to provide an adequate warning, deciding that none of the three warnings was sufficient in that none of them warned specifically against leaving pilot lights on near the working area. . . .

In the case of medical products such as the breast implants at issue in this appeal, the standard of care to be met by manufacturers in ensuring that consumers are properly warned is necessarily high. Medical products are often designed for bodily ingestion or implantation, and the risks created by their improper use are obviously substantial. The courts in this country have long recognized that manufacturers of products that are ingested, consumed or otherwise placed in the body, and thereby have a great capacity to cause injury to consumers, are subject to a correspondingly high standard of care under the law of negligence.

. . .

Given the intimate relationship between medical products and the consumer's body, and the resulting risk created to the consumer, there will almost always be a heavy onus on manufacturers of medical products to provide clear, complete and current information concerning the dangers inherent in the ordinary use of their product.

. . .

As a general rule, the duty to warn is owed directly by the manufacturer to the ultimate consumer. However, in exceptional circumstances, a manufacturer may satisfy its informational duty to the consumer by providing a warning to what the American courts have, in recent years, termed a "learned intermediary".

. . .

Generally, the rule is applicable either where a product is highly technical in nature and is intended to be used only under the supervision of experts, or where the nature of the product is such that the consumer will not realistically receive a direct warning from the manufacturer before using the product. In such cases, where an intermediate inspection of the product is anticipated or where a consumer is placing primary reliance on the judgment of a "learned intermediary" and not the manufacturer, a warning to the ultimate consumer may not be necessary and the manufacturer may satisfy its duty to warn the ultimate consumer by warning the learned intermediary of the risks inherent in the use of the product.

However, it is important to keep in mind that the "learned intermediary" rule is merely an exception to the general manufacturer's duty to warn the consumer. The rule operates to discharge the manufacturer's duty not to the learned intermediary, but to the ultimate consumer, who has a right to full and current information about any risks inherent in the ordinary use of the product. Thus, the rule presumes that the intermediary is "learned", that is to say, fully apprised of the risks associated with the use of the product. Accordingly, the manufacturer can only be said to have discharged its duty to the consumer when the intermediary's knowledge approximates that of the manufacturer. To allow manufacturers to claim the benefit of the rule where they have not fully warned the physician would undermine the policy rationale for the duty to warn, which is to ensure that the consumer is fully informed of all risks.

[I]t is my view that the "learned intermediary" rule is applicable in this context, and that Dow was entitled to warn Dr. Birch concerning the risk of rupture without warning Ms Hollis directly. A breast implant is distinct from most manufactured goods in that neither the implant nor its packaging are placed directly into the hands of the ultimate consumer. It is the surgeon, not the consumer, who obtains the implant from the manufacturer and who is therefore in the best position to read any warnings contained in the product packaging.

. . .

Although Bouck J. declined to rule on this issue, a majority of the Court of Appeal found that Dow's warning to Dr. Birch was inadequate. In my view, the Court of Appeal was correct in reaching this conclusion. . . .

It is significant that the only reference in the 1976 and 1979 warnings to a risk of post-surgical rupture was the statement that "abnormal squeezing or trauma" might rupture the implants. There is no reference in these warnings to the possibility of rupture arising from normal squeezing or non-traumatic, everyday activity. This is significant because, in 1985, Dow began warning physicians of the possibility of rupture due to normal, non-traumatic activity in the product insert for the Silastic II implant, a new breast implant developed in the early 1980s with a thicker envelope and greater durability than the earlier Silastic I model. . . .

It is clear from a comparison of the 1985 warning with the earlier warnings that the 1985 warning is far more explicit, both with respect to the potential causes of post-surgical implant rupture and the potential effects. Of particular significance, in my view, is the statement in the 1985 warning that rupture can be caused by "excessive stresses or manipulation as may be experienced during normal living experiences" such as "vigorous exercise, athletics, and intimate physical contact". There is, without question, a substantial difference between "trauma", on the one hand, and the "stresses" and "manipulation" of "everyday living experiences", on the other hand. The difference is that, while the earlier warnings implied that rupture would occur only in extreme cases of violent impact, the 1985 warning made it clear that a patient who received an implant would have to consider altering her lifestyle to avoid rupture. The difference between the 1985 warning and the earlier warnings was significant to a woman in Ms Hollis' position because, subsequent to her surgery, she decided to enrol in a baker's course, which involved regular and heavy upper body movements. While a baker's course may not cause "trauma" to an implant, it would certainly create a risk of "excessive stresses or manipulation". Thus, a more accurate warning could quite reasonably have affected her choice of profession and her resulting exposure to unnecessary risk.

This is not to say, of course, that the standard of care to which Dow must be held for its warning practices in 1983 should be measured according to its knowledge of the risks of implant rupture in 1985. In light of the significant differences between the 1985 warning and the earlier warnings, the crucial next question is whether Dow knew or should have known of the risks referred to in the 1985 warning when Ms Hollis had her implantation surgery in 1983. In my view, there was sufficient evidence adduced at trial to establish that Dow did have such knowledge.

. . .

[I]t is apparent that, by late 1983, Dow had already received between 48 and 61 of the 78 unexplained rupture reports it received before issuing its revised 1985 warning. Counsel for Dow conceded that the nature and quantity of the information available to Dow did not change significantly between late 1983 and early 1985. Thus, although the reports were admitted into evidence at trial for the purpose of establishing their existence and not as to the truth of their contents, the mere fact that Dow had these reports in their possession demonstrates that, in 1983, Dow had notice that ruptures were occurring that were not directly attributable to abnormal squeezing or trauma. Counsel for Dow was unable to explain why it took Dow more than two years to convey the information concerning the unexplained ruptures to either the medical community or the consumers.

A similar lag time can be discerned with respect to Dow's warnings concerning the effects of implant ruptures on the body. The evidence indicates that, prior to 1983, and even as early as 1979, Dow was aware that implant ruptures could cause adverse reactions in the body arising from loose gel. . . .

In my view, Dow had a duty to convey its findings concerning both the "unexplained" rupture phenomenon and the possible harm caused by loose gel inside the body to the medical community much sooner than it did. In light of the fact that implants are surgically placed inside the human body, and that any defects in these products will obviously have a highly injurious effect on the user, the onus on Dow to be forthcoming with information was extremely high throughout the relevant period. Despite this fact, for over six years Dow took no action to express its concerns to the medical community. Given Dow's knowledge of the potential harm caused by loose gel in the body, this lag time is simply unacceptable. The duty to warn is a continuing one and manufacturers of potentially hazardous products have an obligation to keep doctors abreast of developments even if they do not consider those developments to be conclusive. As Robins J.A. noted in *Buchan*, supra, at p. 678:

> . . . where medical evidence exists which tends to show a serious danger inherent in the use of a drug, the manufacturer is not entitled to ignore or discount that information in its warning because it finds it to be unconvincing; the manufacturer is obliged to be forthright and to tell the whole story.

. . .

I conclude, therefore, that the Court of Appeal made no error in ruling that Dow did not discharge its duty to Ms Hollis by properly warning Dr. Birch concerning the risk of post-surgical implant rupture.

2. *Did Dow's breach of the duty to warn cause Ms Hollis' injury?*

Dow raises two distinct causation issues in this appeal. The first is whether Ms Hollis would have elected to have the operation if she had been properly warned of the risk by Dr. Birch. Dow submits that a reasonable woman in Ms Hollis' position would have consented to the surgery despite the risk and, on this basis, argues that its failure to warn was not the proximate cause of Ms Hollis' injury. The second issue Dow raises is whether Dr. Birch would have warned Ms Hollis if he had been properly warned by Dow of the risk. Dow submits that Ms Hollis had the onus of establishing that Dr. Birch would not have warned Ms Hollis even if fully apprised by Dow of the risk and, once again, argues that its failure to warn cannot be the proximate cause of her injuries. Counsel for Ms Hollis sought to meet the first issue on a factual basis alone. As to the second issue, however, he contested as well the underpinnings of Dow's argument, which as will appear raises more substantial legal issues. I shall accordingly approach the issues on that basis.

(a) *Would Ms Hollis have consented to the operation if properly warned of the risk?*

(i) *The appropriate test*

In determining whether Ms Hollis would have consented to the operation had she been properly warned by Dr. Birch of the risk of rupture, Prowse J.A. applied the modified objective test developed by this court in *Reibl*, *supra*, which involved a negligence action by a patient against a surgeon for failing to warn him of the risk of paralysis entailed in elective surgery performed by that surgeon. The test applied by Prowse J.A. was as follows: would a reasonable woman in Ms Hollis' particular circumstances have consented to the surgery if she had known all the material risks? I note, however, that in *Buchan*, *supra*, at pp. 685-7, Robins J.A. found the *Reibl* test to be inapplicable to products liability cases, and instead applied a subjective test. . . .

As Robins J.A. intimated in *Buchan*, the duty of the doctor is to give the best medical advice and service he or she can give to a particular patient in a specific context. It is by no means coterminous with that of the manufacturer of products used in rendering that service. The manufacturer, on the other hand, can be expected to act in a more self-interested manner. In the case of a manufacturer, therefore, there is a greater likelihood that the value of a product will be overemphasized and the risk underemphasized. It is, therefore, highly desirable from a policy perspective to hold the manufacturer to a strict standard of warning consumers of dangerous side-effects to these products. There is no reason, as in the case of a doctor, to modify the usual approach to causation followed in other tortious actions. Indeed the imbalance of resources and information between the manufacturer and the patient, and even the doctor, weighs in the opposite direction. Moreover, it is important to remember that many product liability cases of this nature will arise in a context where no negligence can be attributed to a doctor. It would appear ill-advised, then, to distort the rule that is appropriate for claims against a manufacturer simply because of an apparent anomaly that results in cases where a doctor is also alleged to have been negligent.

(ii) *The application of the test to the facts of the case at bar*

In my view, there was sufficient evidence adduced at trial to satisfy the subjective *Buchan* test. Ms Hollis testified quite clearly at trial that, had she been properly warned by Dr. Birch of the risk of rupture, she would not have had the surgery.

. . .

The second causation issue *raised by Dow* is whether Dr. Birch would have warned Ms Hollis of the risk of rupture if Dow had properly warned Dr. Birch about that risk. Dow argues that there is no direct causal link between its breach of the duty to warn and Ms Hollis' injury because, in 1983, Dr. Birch was aware of the risk of implant rupture but did not make a habit of warning his patients about that risk. In support of this argument, Dow relies on Dr. Birch's testimony at trial that, in 1983, he was warning only 20% to 30% of his patients of implant rupture, and that, in determining the nature and scope of his warnings to patients, he relied more on the articles he read in medical journals than on manufacturers' warnings.

It is right to say, however, that the trial judge found that in 1983 the average plastic surgeon in British Columbia did not in fact know about the possibility that rupture of Silastic implants could be a factor of any significance. This finding is supported and amplified by the fact that after Dow began circulating its more extensive 1985 warning and knowledge of the risk of rupture in the medical community became more prevalent, Dr. Birch adapted his practice accordingly, and by 1989 he was warning all his patients of the risk of rupture.

I do not propose to enter further into or assess these factors. I say this because, while Dow is correct in submitting that there was some ambiguity at trial concerning Dr. Birch's warning practices in 1983, Dow's argument is based upon the assumption that to succeed in her claim against Dow Ms Hollis must prove that Dr. Birch would have warned her if Dow had properly warned Dr. Birch. I do not think this assumption is well founded. Ms Hollis, it will be remembered, demonstrated that Dow had breached its duty to warn her of the risk of rupture, that she would not have undergone the medical procedure if she had been fully informed of the risks, and that she suffered injury from the rupture. Had Dr. Birch been adequately warned but had not passed on the information to Ms Hollis, Dow would, it is true, have been absolved of liability by virtue of the learned intermediary doctrine. But I fail to see how one can reason from this that, for Dow to be liable, Ms Hollis must now establish that Dr. Birch would have informed her if he had known. To require her to do so would be to ask her to prove a hypothetical situation relating to her doctor's conduct, one, moreover, brought about by Dow's failure to perform its duty. While the legal and persuasive onus in a negligence case generally falls on the plaintiff, I do not see how this can require the plaintiff to prove a hypothetical situation of this kind.

. . .

Simply put, I do not think a manufacturer should be able to escape liability for failing to give a warning it was under a duty to give, by simply presenting evidence tending to establish that even if the doctor had been given the warning, he or she would not have passed it on to the patient, let alone putting an onus on the plaintiff to do so. Adopting such a rule would, in some cases, run the risk of leaving the plaintiff with no compensation for her injuries. She would not be able to recover against a doctor who had not been negligent with respect to the information that he or she *did* have; yet she also would not be able to recover against a manufacturer who, despite having failed in its duty to warn, could escape liability on the basis that, had the doctor been appropriately warned, he or she still would not have passed the information on to the plaintiff. Our tort law should not be held to contemplate such an anomalous result.

. . .

Conclusion

On the basis of the foregoing, it is my view that Dow breached its duty to warn Dr. Birch concerning the risks of post-surgical rupture in the Silastic implant and because of this failure to warn is liable to Ms Hollis for her injuries. Accordingly, I would dismiss the appeal.

[Sopinka J., with McLachlin J. concurring, dissented. Sopinka J. held that the plaintiff was not entitled to succeed unless she could establish that a reasonable person would have refused the implant if properly warned and that her surgeon would have passed the warning on to her if he had been properly informed.]

NOTES AND QUESTIONS

1. Based on *Hollis*, define a manufacturer's duty to inform consumers of the risks inherent in the use of its products. Did the court impose a unique standard of care on manufacturers of pharmaceuticals and medical products?

2. In what circumstances can a manufacturer rely on the learned intermediary rule? According to *Hollis*, what information must a manufacturer disclose to a learned intermediary to meet its duty to warn? What obligation, if any, does a manufacturer have after it has adequately informed a learned intermediary to ensure that the information is passed on to the consumer?

3. Given Dow Corning's knowledge of the unexplained ruptures and the accompanying risks, was it negligent in continuing to market the implant in 1983? Had the plaintiff's case proceeded on this basis, would the adequacy of the warning have been relevant?

4. What was La Forest J.'s rationale for adopting the subjective test of causation in *Hollis*? Was it compelling? If it was, is there any justification for continuing to use the special objective/subjective test in cases involving health professionals' duty to inform?

Sopinka J., in dissent, stated that the subjective approach fails to address the inherent unreliability of the plaintiff's "self-serving assertions" or the fact that the plaintiff's opinion is likely to be coloured by the injury he or she has suffered. Is there anything unique about the credibility issues in this area that would warrant special rules of causation? See Black & Klimchuk, "Torts–Negligent Failure to Warn – Learned Intermediary Rule – Causation – Appellate Court Powers – *Hollis v. Dow Corning Corp.*" (1996) 75 Can. Bar Rev. 355; Lewans, "Subjective Tests and Implied Warranties: Prescriptions for *Hollis v. Dow Corning* and *ter Neuzen v. Korn*" (1996) 60 Sask. L. Rev. 209; Boivin, "Factual Causation in the Law of Manufacturer Failure to Warn" (1998) 30 Ottawa L. Rev. 47; McInnes, "Causation in Tort Law: A Decade in the Supreme Court of Canada" (2000) 63 Sask. L. Rev. 445; McInnes, "Common Sense and Constructive Reasoning: Causal Policy in the Supreme Court of Canada" in *Special Lectures of the Law Society of Upper Canada 1998: Personal Injury* (2000) 422; and Black "Decision Causation: Pandora's Tool-Box" in Neyers, Chamberlain & Pitel, eds., *Emerging Issues in Tort Law* (2007).

5. Why did the court reject the defendant's argument that its failure to inform Dr. Birch played no causal role in the plaintiff's injuries, because Dr. Birch would not have informed her in any event? Could it be argued that the defendant's failure to inform Dr. Birch has caused the plaintiff a loss, namely, the opportunity to sue him for failing to obtain an informed consent to the procedure?

6. What assumptions can a manufacturer make about the people who are likely to use its products? What impact should such considerations have on the standard of care and its breach? In *Austin v. 3M Canada Ltd.* (1974), 54 D.L.R. (3d) 656 (Ont. Co. Ct.) the plaintiff, who professed to be an auto-body repairman, was injured by the defendant's grinding disc which disintegrated while being used at 9,200 rpm. No warnings were provided about the speeds at which the discs should be used. However, the court found that any reasonably competent repairman would have known that it was hazardous to use the discs at more than 8,000 rpm. The court held that the defendant was not negligent in failing to warn the plaintiff of this danger. Would the result have been the same if a neighbour, inexperienced in auto-body repair, borrowed an unopened package of discs and suffered injury while using them at an excessive speed? See also *Murphy v. St.*

Catharines Gen. Hosp. (1963), 41 D.L.R. (2d) 697 (Ont. H.C.); and *Park v. B & B Electronics Ltd.* (2003), 340 A.R. 246 (Q.B.). See generally Downs, "Duty to Warn and the Sophisticated User Defense in Products Liability Cases" (1986) 15 U. Balt. L. Rev. 276.

The duty to warn is specific to the primary user of the product. Therefore, a manufacturer must be careful not to assume that a risk is obvious in circumstances where a child or young person is likely to be the primary consumer. See *Amin (Litigation Guardian of) v. Klironomos*, [1996] O.J. No. 826 (Gen. Div.) (QL).

7. Given that the plaintiff in *Lambert v. Lastoplex Chemicals Co.* (1971), 25 D.L.R. (3d) 121 (S.C.C.), cited in *Hollis*, was aware of the danger of working with the product near an open flame, should he have been held contributorily negligent for not turning off the pilot light? In *Labrecque v. Saskatchewan Wheat Pool* (1980), 110 D.L.R. (3d) 686 (Sask. C.A.), an experienced farmer was held contributorily negligent because he should have been aware of certain dangers, despite the defendant manufacturer's inadequate warning. Can you reconcile *Lastoplex* and *Labrecque*?

8. In *Cominco Ltd. v. Westinghouse Can. Ltd.* (1981), 127 D.L.R. (3d) 544 (B.C.S.C.), varied on other grounds (1983), 147 D.L.R. (3d) 279 (B.C.C.A.), it was held that a manufacturer who hears of a new risk after its product is distributed has a duty to warn users as soon as possible. The plaintiff did not have to prove that the manufacturer had actual knowledge, provided the manufacturer ought to have been aware of the new risk. See also *Rivtow Marine Ltd. v. Washington Iron Works*, [1974] S.C.R. 1189; *Nicholson v. John Deere Ltd.* (1986), 58 O.R. (2d) 53 (H.C.); *Vlchek v. Koshel* (1988), 44 C.C.L.T. 314 (B.C.S.C.); and *Walford (Litigation Guardian of) v. Jacuzzi Canada*, 2005 CarswellOnt 1392 (S.C.J.) (WLeC).

9. In *Hollis*, the Supreme Court of Canada indicated that manufacturers have a broad obligation to inform learned intermediaries of new research findings of adverse consequences, even if those findings are speculative or inconclusive. Does this principle create potential problems? At what point would a manufacturer be required to inform learned intermediaries? Would that obligation have arisen after Dow Corning received 20, 10 or 5 reports of unexplained ruptures? Are such isolated, adverse findings of practical use to the learned intermediary? Is there a risk of overloading the intermediaries and consumers with reports of isolated, unanalyzed adverse findings?

10. In recent years, pharmacies have taken on greater responsibility by inquiring about patients' drug allergies, keeping a record of prescriptions, and providing independent summaries of potential side effects. What implications do these actions have for the application of the learned intermediary doctrine? Can a pharmaceutical manufacturer that provides an inadequate warning be absolved of liability because the pharmacy independently provided a sufficient warning? See Garbutt & Hofmann, "Recent Developments in Pharmaceutical Products Liability Law: Failure to Warn, the Learned Intermediary Defense, and Other Issues in the New Millenium" (2003) 58 Food & Drug L.J. 269.

What are the implications of the increase in direct-to-consumer advertising by pharmaceutical companies (*e.g.* on television or via the internet)? Does such advertising weaken the manufacturers' argument that they cannot communicate directly with the consumer? Should a manufacturer who advertises on television be permitted to rely on the learned intermediary doctrine?

11. In *Beshada v. Johns-Manville Products Corp.*, 447 A.2d 539 (N.J. 1982), the defendant was held liable for failing to warn of asbestos-related illness, despite the medical community's "presumed unawareness" of such risks at the time. The court stated at 549:

> The burden of illness from dangerous products such as asbestos should be placed upon those who profit from its production and, more generally, upon society at large, which reaps the benefits of the various products our economy manufactures. That burden should not be imposed exclusively on the innocent victim. Although victims must in any case suffer the pain involved, they should be spared the burdensome financial consequences of unfit products. At the same time, we believe this position will serve the salutary goals of increasing product safety research and simplifying tort trials.
>
> Defendants have argued that it is unreasonable to impose a duty on them to warn of the unknowable. Failure to warn of a risk which one could not have known existed is not unreasonable conduct. But this argument is based on negligence principles. We are not saying what defendants should have done. That is negligence. We are saying that defendants' products were not reasonably safe because they did not have a warning. Without a warning, users of the product were unaware of its hazards and could not protect themselves from injury. We impose strict liability because it is unfair for the distributors of a defective product not to compensate its victims. As between those innocent victims and the distributors, it is the distributors – and the public which consumes their products – which should bear the unforeseen costs of the product.

Is this an appropriate solution to the allocation of losses arising from hazardous products? Is there something unique about manufacturers, as opposed to other defendants, that justifies imposing liability on them in the absence of negligence? Are the courts an appropriate institution for deciding how to allocate such losses? See Berry, "*Beshada v. Johns-Manville Products Corp.*: Revolution – Or Aberration – in Products' Liability Law" (1984) 52 Fordham L. Rev. 786; Boivin, "Negligence, Strict Liability, and Manufacturer Failure to Warn: On Fitting Round Pegs in a Square Hole" (1993) 16 Dal. L.J. 299; and *Hunt v. T&N plc.* (1990), 4 C.C.L.T. (2d) 1 (S.C.C.).

It is interesting to contrast the approach in *Beshada* with that adopted by the Supreme Court of Canada in *Lapierre v. A.G. Que.* (1985), 16 D.L.R. (4th) 554 (S.C.C.). In *Lapierre*, the court refused to impose strict liability on the government for a measles vaccine that caused the infant plaintiff to suffer a severe attack of encephalitis. See also *Davidson v. Connaught Laboratories* (1980), 14 C.C.L.T. 251 (Ont. H.C.); and *Rothwell v. Raes* (1988), 66 O.R. (2d) 449 (H.C.), aff'd (1990), 2 O.R. (3d) 332 (C.A.). *Lapierre* led to the introduction of a provincial compensation system, based on no-fault principles, for those suffering serious injuries as a result of vaccinations in Québec: see now the *Public Health Act*, R.S.Q. c. S-2.2, s. 71. See generally Kutlesa, "Creating a Sustainable Immunization System in Canada – The Case for a Vaccine-Related Injury Compensation Scheme" (2004) 12 Health L.J. 201.

12. A supplier's duty to warn of risks in the use of its products is largely the same as that of a manufacturer. Suppliers are required to warn of risks of which they know or ought to know. See *Allard v. Manahan* (1974), 46 D.L.R. (3d) 614 (B.C.S.C.); *Lem v. Borotto Sports Ltd.* (1976), 69 D.L.R. (3d) 276 (Alta. C.A.); and *Rozenhart v. Skier's*

Sport Shop (Edmonton) Ltd. (2002), 12 Alta. L.R. (4th) 263 (Q.B.), aff'd (2004), 28 Alta. L.R. (4th) 44 (C.A.).

Although the courts increasingly require manufacturers to be experts in their field and to undertake research or at least keep current with the scientific, academic and industry literature, suppliers would not be expected to have the same level of expertise. Can you suggest a situation in which the manufacturer would be held liable for failing to warn, but the supplier would not? See also *Buchan v. Ortho Pharmaceutical (Can.) Ltd.* (1986), 35 C.C.L.T. 1 (Ont. C.A.). The courts have extended the duty to warn to installers and repairers. See *Bow Valley Husky (Bermuda) Ltd. v. Saint John Shipbuilding Ltd.* (1997), 153 D.L.R. (4th) 385 (S.C.C.).

13. Should the way in which a supplier markets a product affect its duty or standard of care? Should a greater obligation be imposed on a specialty store that waits on customers than on a department store, self-service shop or mail-order house?

14. To what extent can a manufacturer or supplier discharge its obligation to warn by providing instructions and cautions in printed material accompanying the product? In *Lem v. Borotto Sports Ltd., supra*, the court denied the plaintiff's claim on the assumption that the plaintiff was aware of the warnings in the instruction booklet, even though he had not read it. The product in question, a shotgun shell re-loader, did not appear to be particularly difficult to use, provided the step-by-step instructions were followed. However, in *O'Fallan v. Inecto Rapid (Can.) Ltd.*, [1939] 1 D.L.R. 805 (B.C.S.C.), aff'd [1940] 4 D.L.R. 276 (B.C.C.A.), it was held that the manufacturer should have put a warning on the container of its hair dye because the warning provided in the separate accompanying literature might not come to the user's attention. Can you reconcile these two cases?

15. In determining if consumers have been adequately informed, the courts will examine the totality of the manufacturer's marketing and promotional activities. In addition to the actual warnings provided, the court may consider any countervailing messages, or advertising, marketing or promotional activities. A manufacturer may be held liable, despite providing an adequate warning, if that warning has been obscured or undermined. See *Buchan v. Ortho Pharmaceutical (Can.) Ltd., supra*; *Siemens v. Pfizer C. & G. Inc.* (1988), 51 Man. R. (2d) 252 (C.A.); and *Moran v. Wyeth-Ayerst Canada Inc. (c.o.b. Cyanamid Crop Protection)* (2004), 369 A.R. 145 (Q.B.). See also Klar, "Recent Developments in Canadian Law: Tort Law" (1991) 23 Ottawa L. Rev. 177; and Howells, *Comparative Product Liability* (1993) at 262.

16. Another important issue raised by *Lem v. Borotto Sports Ltd., supra*, is the manufacturer's and supplier's duty to warn of risks arising from the misuse of a product. The court noted:

> In respect of such dangers the duty . . . is to give adequate warning, that is to say explicit warning, not only as to such that would arise out of the contemplated proper use of the product, but also as to such that might arise out of reasonably foreseeable fault on the part of the purchaser in its contemplated use . . . The duty . . . grows more exacting with the degree of danger . . . arising from its misuse, and accordingly the reach of foreseeability is extended further as the circumstances may reasonably require . . . On the other side of the scale, the dangers of use or misuse may be sufficiently apparent or well

known to the ordinary prudent person that a warning in respect of them should be taken to be unnecessary in law. An example would be a sharp knife; another, the effect of electricity at high voltage on the human body.

The issue of what constitutes an obvious risk has generated considerable litigation. See *Austin v. 3M Canada Ltd.*, *supra* (grinding disc will shatter at excessive rpm); *Schulz v. Leaside Devs.* (1978), 6 C.C.L.T. 248 (B.C.C.A.) (dangerous to ride in the bow of a small motor boat); *Kirby v. Canadian Tire* (1989), 57 Man. R. (2d) 207 (Q.B.) (blade on food processor will cut); *Deshane v. Deere & Co.* (1993), 15 O.R. (3d) 225 (C.A.) (forage harvester poses danger to those coming into contact with feed rolls); *Godin v. Wilson Laboratories Inc.* (1994), 145 N.B.R. (2d) 29 (Q.B.) (rat poison will kill rats, which will then begin to smell); and *Rozenhart v. Skier's Sport Shop (Edmonton) Ltd.*, *supra* (novice in-line skater is likely to fall).

17. What obligations should tobacco companies have to warn consumers of the dangers of smoking? How should the following facts influence the manufacturer's duty to warn: (a) smoking is by far the largest preventable cause of death and illness in Canada (estimated at more than 40,000 deaths per year), (b) smoking is addictive, (c) most smokers become addicted before the age of 18, (d) the sale of cigarettes to minors is a federal and provincial offence, and (e) emerging evidence indicates that the tobacco manufacturers were aware of the highly addictive and potentially addictive properties of their products for decades and yet publicly denied that smoking was harmful. For a review see Ashley, *The Health Effects of Tobacco Use* (1995).

In *Létourneau v. Imperial Tobacco Ltd.* (1998), 162 D.L.R. (4th) 734 (C.Q.), the court found that the defendant did not have a duty to warn of its products' addictiveness in 1964, the year the plaintiff began smoking. Moreover, the court held that, even if such a duty existed, the plaintiff could not prove that its breach caused her loss. Do you agree with this analysis? Are there other bases for imposing liability in tort? See also Cunningham, "Tobacco Products Liability in Common Law Canada" (1990) 11 Health Law in Canada 43; Nolan, "Passive Smoking Litigation in Australia and America" (1993) 9 J. Contemp. Health L. & Pol'y 563; and Smith, "'Counterblastes' to Tobacco: Five Decades of North American Tobacco Litigation" (2002) 14 W.R.S.L.I. 1.

18. It should be noted that a manufacturer who complies with federal or provincial warning legislation may still be held liable for failing to adequately inform. See *Buchan, supra*; *Smithson v. Saskem Chemicals Ltd.* (1985), 43 Sask. R. 1 (Q.B.); and Waddams, *Products Liability*, 4th ed. (2002) at 58.

19. In *Good-Wear Treaders v. D. & B. Holdings Ltd.* (1979), 98 D.L.R. (3d) 59 (N.S.C.A.), the appellant supplier warned a purchaser that the re-treaded tires he wanted were unsuitable for the front wheels of a heavy gravel truck. Although the appellant knew that the purchaser was going to ignore the warning, he completed the sale. One of these tires failed and the truck crossed the centre line, demolishing an oncoming car. The driver of the car and his two children were killed, and his widow sued both the purchaser and supplier. She succeeded at trial. The supplier appealed, claiming that he had not breached his duty. The court indicated that the warnings absolved the supplier of liability to the purchaser, but not to third parties. The supplier should not have sold the tires to someone he knew would misuse them and thereby endanger other users of the road.

Should this obligation extend to cases in which a supplier merely suspects that a purchaser will misuse a product? Must the misuse of a product pose an obvious risk of injury to third parties? Is the *Good-Wear* case based on a supplier's and manufacturer's duty to warn or on an individual's obligation to control the conduct of others?

20. For additional academic commentary, see Logie, "Affirmative Action in the Law of Tort: The Case of the Duty to Warn" [1989] C.L.J. 115; Peppin, "Drug/Vaccine Risks: Patient Decision-Making and Harm Reduction in the Pharmaceutical Company Duty to Warn Action" (1991) 70 Can. Bar Rev. 473; Roccamo, "Medical Implants and Other Health Care Products: Theories of Liability and Modern Trends" (1994) 16 Adv. Q. 421; and Richmond, "Expanding Products Liability: Manufacturers' Post-Sale Duties to Warn, Retrofit and Recall" (1999) 36 Idaho L. Rev. 7.

REVIEW PROBLEMS

1. Acme Company manufactures special gauges and valves with built-in warning devices for use in the chemical industry. Acme sells gauges to distributors, who in turn resell them to chemical companies. In June 1996, Acme discovered that about one-tenth of its K12 valves were defective in that they were prone to emit false warning signals. Acme had stopped making K12 valves in 1990. To the best of Acme's knowledge, its distributors had sold only four valves in 1990 and none in the years since then. Acme was in the midst of a major advertising campaign, focusing on the reliability of its new valves and gauges. Consequently, it was most reluctant to issue a general recall of its K12 valves. It has sought your advice concerning its potential liability if it were to simply ignore this defect in its K12 valves.

2. Mark, an avid amateur repairman, enjoyed fixing his car. When Mark realized that his brakes were becoming worn he decided to replace them. He went to the local Apex Auto Store and purchased a set of very complicated brake drums. The salesman asked Mark if he was having the job done by the Apex service department or whether he was going to take it to another garage. Mark replied that he would install the brakes himself. The salesman asked Mark if he was a certified automobile mechanic. Mark responded that he was not, but that he enjoyed maintaining his own car. This struck the salesman as being odd because these brakes were extremely difficult to install. The salesman knew that it was highly unlikely that anyone other than a certified mechanic could properly install these brakes. Indeed, he knew that many mechanics refused such work and that they referred it to mechanics who specialized in brake work. Nevertheless, the salesman handed the brakes to Mark without another word or providing any warning as to the difficulty of installing them.

Mark went home and installed the brakes. Unfortunately, he had not installed them properly. While driving in busy traffic, the brakes failed and he ran over Mrs. Winter. Mrs. Winter has sought your advice about suing the Apex Auto Store in negligence for the injuries that she has suffered.

7. Duty of Care Owed by a Barrister

The final area for discussion in this chapter concerns the duty of care owed by a barrister. It is important to place this topic into context. A lawyer undoubtedly owes a general obligation to a client to act competently. That is true in both tort and contract. In limited circumstances, a lawyer may also be held liable in negligence to a third party. See *Whittingham v. Crease & Co.* (1978), 88 D.L.R. (3d) 353 (B.C.S.C.); *White v. Jones*, [1995] 2 A.C. 207 (H.L.). The more specific question addressed here pertains to a lawyer's liability to a client for errors made, as a barrister, in the course of litigation. Under the *Anns/Cooper* test, it certainly is reasonably foreseeable that careless litigation may expose a client to loss. Over time, however, Anglo-Canadian courts have vacillated on the significance of policy considerations that are thought to militate against the recognition of a duty of care. Traditionally, Canadian barristers did not enjoy any immunity from liability: see *Leslie v. Ball* (1863), 22 U.C.Q.B. 522; and *Wade v. Ball* (1870), 20 U.C.C.P. 302. As the next extract demonstrates, that continues to be true. By contrast, the House of Lords held in *Rondel v. Worsley*, [1969] 1 A.C. 191 (H.L.) that, in English law, a barrister could not be sued in negligence for the careless handling of a file. However, the House of Lords has since over-ruled *Rondel v. Worsley* and abandoned the concept of "barristers immunity" in *Arthur J.S. Hall & Co. v. Simons*, [2000] 3 W.L.R. 543 (H.L.).

DEMARCO v. UNGARO

(1979), 95 D.L.R. (3d) 385 (Ont. H.C.)

KREVER J.: – In Ontario is a lawyer immune from action at the suit of a client for negligence in the conduct of the client's civil case in Court? That is the important question of substantive law that, to paraphrase Maine weakly, is secreted interstitially by this procedural motion relating to the adequacy of pleadings.

[Krever J. explained that England "has a divided profession" in which "the barrister enters into no contract with the client and is not entitled to sue for his or her fee." In Ontario, in contrast, "lawyers are both barristers and solicitors" and "the lawyer conducting litigation contracts directly with the client and is entitled to sue for his or her fee."]

For my purposes it will be sufficient to summarize the grounds on which it was held in *Rondel v. Worsley* [*supra*] that public policy requires immunity of the barrister. I shall limit myself to four of these grounds.

The first ground related to the duty, which, in interest of proper administration of justice, every counsel must discharge to the Court, a duty which was said to be higher than and, in some cases, in conflict with, the duty owed to the client. . . . Clearly related to the duty owed by a barrister to the Court was the expressed risk that, in the absence of the barrister's immunity, counsel, out of fear of a potential action for negligence by his or her client, would prolong proceedings, contrary to his or her best judgment, in effect, to prevent the client from complaining.

. . .

The second ground was the harm to the public interest that would result for relitigating the original issue in the negligence action against the client's counsel.

. . .

The third consideration related to the obligation of a barrister to accept any client, however difficult, who sought his or her services, an obligation on which the very freedom of the subject was said to depend.

. . .

The final consideration to which I intend to refer is the anomaly that would result from the absence of barristers' immunity in the light of the absolute privilege all participants in a proceeding in Court enjoy with respect to what is said by them in Court.

. . .

I have come to the conclusion that the public interest (another phrase used in the speeches of *Rondel v. Worsley*) in Ontario does not require that our Courts recognize an immunity of a lawyer from action for negligence at the suit of his or her former client by reason of the conduct of a civil case in Court. It has not been, is not now, and should not be, public policy in Ontario to confer exclusively on lawyers engaged in Court work an immunity possessed by no other professional person. Public policy and the public interest do not exist in a vacuum. They must be examined against the background of a host of sociological facts of the society concerned. Nor are they lawyers' values as opposed to the values shared by the rest of the community. In the light of recent developments in the law of professional negligence and the rising incidence of "malpractice" actions against physicians (and especially surgeons who may be thought to be to physicians what barristers are to solicitors), I do not believe that enlightened, non-legally trained members of the community would agree with me if I were to hold that the public interest requires that litigation lawyers be immune from actions for negligence. I emphasize again that I am not concerned with the question whether the conduct complained about amounts to negligence. Indeed, I find it difficult to believe that a decision made by a lawyer in the conduct of a case will be held to be negligence as opposed to a mere error of judgment. But there may be cases in which the error is so egregious that a Court will conclude that it is negligence. The only issue I am addressing is whether the client is entitled to ask a Court to rule upon the matter.

Many of the sociological facts that are related to public policy and the public interest may be judicially noticed. The population of Ontario is approximately eight and a quarter million people. In 1978 there were approximately 12,300 lawyers licensed by the Law Society of Upper Canada to practise law in Ontario. All of them have a right of audience in any Court in Ontario as well as in the Federal Court of Canada and the Supreme Court of Canada. The vast majority of these lawyers are in private practice and, as such, are required to carry liability insurance in respect of negligence in the conduct of their clients' affairs. No distinction is made in this respect between those exclusively involved in litigation and all other lawyers. The current rate of increase in the size of the profession is approximately 1,000 lawyers annually. It is widely recognized that a graduating class of that size places such an enormous strain on the resources of the profession that the articling experience of students-at-law is extremely variable. Only a small percentage of lawyers newly called to the Bar can be expected to have had the advantage of working with or observing experienced and competent counsel. Yet very many of those recently qualified lawyers will be appearing in Court on behalf of clients. To deprive these clients of recourse if their cases are negligently dealt with will not, to most residents of this Province, appear to be consistent with the public interest.

It is with a great sense of deference that I offer a few brief remarks on the grounds and consideration which formed the basis of the public policy as expressed by the House of Lords in *Rondel v. Worsley*. I am only concerned with the applicability of those considerations to Ontario conditions and have no hesitation in accepting them as entirely valid for England. With respect to the duty of counsel to the Court and the risk that, in the absence of immunity, counsel will be tempted to prefer the interest of the client to the duty to the Court and will thereby prolong trials, it is my respectful view that there is no empirical evidence that the risk is so serious that an aggrieved client should be rendered remediless. Between the dates of the decisions in *Leslie v. Ball*, 1863, and *Rondel v. Worsley*, 1967, immunity of counsel was not recognized in Ontario and negligence actions against lawyers respecting their conduct of Court cases did not attain serious proportions. Indeed, apart from the cases I have cited, I know of no case in which a lawyer was sued for negligence by his or her client in the conduct of a case in Court. A very similar argument is advanced in many discussions of the law of professional negligence as it applies to surgeons. Surgeons, it is claimed, are deterred from using their best judgment out of fear that the consequence will be an action by the patient in the event of an unfavourable result. This claim has not given rise to an immunity for surgeons. As to the second ground – the prospect of relitigating an issue already tried, it is my view that the undesirability of that event does not justify the recognition of lawyers' immunity in Ontario. It is not a contingency that does not already exist in our law and seems to me to be inherently involved in the concept of *res judicata* in the recognition that a party, in an action *in personam*, is only precluded from relitigating the same matter against a person who was a party to the earlier action. I can find no fault with the way in which Hagarty, C.J., dealt with this consideration in *Wade v. Ball et al.* (1870), 20 U.C.C.P. 302 at p. 304: "Practically, such a suit as the present may involve the trying over again of *Wade v. Hoyt*. This cannot be avoided." Better that than that the client should be without recourse.

The third consideration related to the obligation of a lawyer to accept any client. Whether that has ever been the universally accepted understanding of a lawyer's duty in Ontario is doubtful. In any event, I do not believe that such a duty exists in the practice of civil litigation and that is the kind of litigation with which I am now concerned. Indeed, as I understand the speech of Lord Diplock in *Saif Ali v. Sidney Mitchell & Co. (a firm) et al.*, [1978] 3 W.L.R. 849, that learned Law Lord was not persuaded of the validity of this ground. . . .

The last consideration to be dealt with is the perceived anomaly related to the absolute privilege enjoyed in respect of anything said in Court by a lawyer. I confess that I am unable to appreciate why it should follow from the existence of that privilege that a lawyer may not be sued by his or her client for the negligent performance of the conduct of the client's case in court. The privilege, a fundamental aspect of the law of slander, is not concerned with relationships among persons. It relates to legal proceedings in open Court. The special relationship of lawyer and client is not involved as it is, of course, when one is considering the law of negligence.

. . .

It may, in conclusion, be of interest, from a comparative point of view that, in the United States, the Courts have not granted immunity to an attorney in the conduct of litigation: "an attorney must exercise reasonable care, skill and knowledge in the conduct of litigation . . . and must be properly diligent in the prosecution of the case" (see 7 C.J.S. pp. 982-4, §146).

To sum up, for the reasons I have given, in Ontario, a lawyer is not immune from action at the suit of a client for negligence in the conduct of the client's civil case in

Court. The defendants' motion, in effect, for a determination that a lawyer does enjoy such immunity is, therefore, dismissed with costs to the plaintiff in the cause.

NOTES AND QUESTIONS

1. Analyze Krever J.'s reasons in light of *Cooper v. Hobart*. Would the policy arguments presented in favour of a barrister's immunity fall under the first branch or the second branch of the *Anns/Cooper* test?

2. What role did the early case law play in Krever J.'s analysis?

3. What were the bases upon which Krever J. rejected the House of Lords' policy considerations in *Rondel v. Worsley*, [1969] 1 A.C.. 191 (H.L.)? What considerations did he rely on in concluding that lawyers engaged in litigation ought to owe their clients a duty of care? On balance, would the differences in the legal profession and practice in England and Ontario warrant imposing a duty in one jurisdiction, but not in the other?

4. As indicated in the text above, England finally abolished barristers' immunity in *Arthur J.S. Hall & Co. v. Simons*, [2000] 3 W.L.R. 543 (H.L.). More recently, New Zealand also abolished the immunity in *Chamberlains v. Lai*, [2006] NZSC 70. Australia remains the main Commonwealth holdout, having affirmed barristers' immunity in *D'Orta-Ekenaike v. Victoria Legal Aid* (2005), 214 A.L.R. 92 (H.C.A.), largely based on the need to maintain the integrity of the legal system and the finality of proceedings. See Tobin, "An Uncommon Common Law: Barristers' Immunity in New Zealand" (2006), 14 Torts L.J. 224.

5. Krever J. makes only passing reference to the issues that courts will have to resolve in imposing liability on lawyers engaged in litigation. For example, what effect should a successful action have on the original case? Would it make a difference if the original case were criminal or civil?

6. Given the nature of litigation, it may be difficult for plaintiffs to establish that their lawyers were negligent. In *Karpenko v. Paroian, Courey, Cohen & Houston* (1980), 117 D.L.R. (3d) 383 (Ont. H.C.), the court held that a lawyer could only be found negligent for recommending a settlement of a civil claim prior to trial if he or she made some "egregious error." The judge noted that it was in the public interest to discourage litigation, that lawyers should not be unduly inhibited in encouraging settlements and that the lawyer's decision to recommend acceptance or rejection of a settlement involved various factors. In *Wechsel v. Stutz* (1980), 15 C.C.L.T. 132 (Ont. Co. Ct.), the court rejected the plaintiff's claim that his former lawyer had been negligent in conducting the cross-examination at trial. The judge stated that the method of cross-examination had to be left to the judgment of counsel.

Nevertheless, in *Folland v. Reardon* (2005), 74 O.R. (3d) 688 (C.A.), the "egregious error" standard was rejected by the Court of Appeal for Ontario. Doherty J.A., for the court, commented at para. 41 that the "judgment calls made by lawyers are no more difficult than those made by other professionals." Thus, there was no justification for departing from a standard of reasonableness. See also *Wernikowski v. Kirkland, Murphy*

& Ain (1999), 50 O.R. (3d) 124 (C.A.); *Boudreau v. Benaiah* (2000), 46 O.R. (3d) 737 (C.A.); and *Ristimaki v. Cooper* (2006), 79 O.R. (3d) 648 (C.A.).

7. In *German v. Major* (1985), 20 D.L.R. (4th) 703 (Alta. C.A.), the defendant had been the prosecuting attorney in a tax evasion case against the plaintiff. After the acquittal, the plaintiff sued the defendant in negligence for "failure to investigate" and to "take care." The court held that a prosecutor does not owe an accused any duty of care in negligence, except possibly in cases of bad faith. In dismissing the action, the court stated at 718, "If this suit were permitted, every convict could have his case retried in a civil case." Should prosecutors be subject to different liability principles than other counsel in litigation? Did the judge's concern about re-litigation warrant limiting prosecutors' potential liability in negligence? See also *Munro v. Canada* (1993), 110 D.L.R. (4th) 580 (Ont. Div. Ct.), where the court found that, while the Attorney General and Crown attorneys can be subject to liability for malicious prosecution or conspiracy to injure, they remained immune to liability in negligence.

In *Milgaard v. Kujawa*, [1994] 9 W.W.R. 305 (Sask. C.A.), the plaintiff had served 22 years of a life sentence for murder when it was revealed that the prosecutor had failed to disclose information received during the original appeal period that tended to incriminate another person. The Saskatchewan Court of Appeal refused to strike out Milgaard's claim against the prosecutor. The court stated that the allegations, if true, constituted a form of abuse that should not be protected by prosecutorial immunity. See also *Curry v. Vancouver (City)* (1996), 62 A.C.W.S. (3d) 45 (B.C.S.C.); and *Ramsay v. Saskatchewan* (2003), 234 Sask. R. 172 (Q.B.).

See also *Nelles v. Ontario* (1989), 60 D.L.R. (4th) 609 (S.C.C.), and the section on malicious prosecution in Chapter 3 for a discussion of the limits of prosecutorial immunity.

8. As indicated in the text above, lawyers do not owe a duty of care to third parties except in special circumstances. In *Mantella v. Mantella* (2006), 80 O.R. (3d) 270 (S.C.J.), a husband and wife had signed a separation agreement, but the wife later challenged the agreement on the basis of undue influence, unconscionability and inadequate financial disclosure. The husband then brought a claim against the lawyer who had provided his wife with independent legal advice on the agreement. The court found that the wife's lawyer owed no duty of care to the husband, commenting that there is insufficient proximity between a party to an agreement and the other party's lawyer. The court also suggested that policy considerations would negative any *prima facie* duty of care, particularly in the highly personalized context of family law litigation.

9. In *Calvert v. Law Society of Upper Canada* (1981), 32 O.R. (2d) 176 (H.C.), it was held that the Law Society could not be held liable for negligently admitting or failing to disbar a lawyer. The court stated that such decisions were quasi-judicial in nature and could not be reviewed by a court unless it was shown that the Law Society acted maliciously. Is the result in *Calvert* consistent with the policy underlying *Demarco*? See also *Birchard v. Alberta Securities Commission* (1987), 82 A.R. 273 (Q.B.); and *755165 Ontario Inc. v. Parsons* (2006), 259 Nfld. & P.E.I.R. 82 (N.L.S.C.(T.D.)).

10. For a discussion of a barrister's liability, see Hutchinson, "Negligence – Barrister" (1979) 57 Can. Bar Rev. 339; Bogart, "Immunity of Advocates From Suit: The

Unresolved Issue" (1980) 29 U.N.B.L.J. 27; and Baynham & Baldwin, "Barristers' Immunity" (1985) 43 The Advocate 611.

13

SPECIAL DUTIES OF CARE: NEGLIGENT MISREPRESENTATION

1. Introduction
2. Negligent Misrepresentation Causing Pure Economic Loss
3. Negligent Misrepresentation and Contract

1. Introduction

The preceding chapters focussed on the concept of a duty of care as it pertains to physical actions or omissions. This chapter, in contrast, focuses on the duty of care that may arise with respect to written or oral communications. Common examples include inaccurate or incomplete advice or information provided by financial advisers, business consultants, lawyers, stockbrokers and bankers.

Actions differ from statements in several important respects. One difference is that people tend to be more careful about actions. Because the potential for damage is usually more apparent in the case of physical conduct, the need for caution is often relatively clear. In contrast, because the possibility of harm resulting from statements is often less obvious, people are less cautious in their choice of words. Particularly on social occasions, there can be a tendency to speak using loose rather than careful language.

A more significant difference between actions and statements was noted by Lord Pearce in the leading case of *Hedley Byrne & Co. v. Heller & Partners Ltd.*, [1963] 2 All E.R. 575 (H.L.) at 602. He stated: "Words are more volatile than deeds. They travel fast and far afield. They are used without being expended and take effect in combination with innumerable facts and other words." In most instances, physical actions become a spent force shortly after occurrence; unless injury arises immediately and in close physical proximity, it is unlikely to arise at all. In contrast, statements have greater durability and portability. They more easily may cause damage long after and far removed from where and when they were made. For the same reasons, careless actions tend to trigger injuries only once; negligent words, in contrast, may repeatedly inflict harm.

The volatility of words has led to a judicial concern that recognition of a duty of care with respect to negligent misrepresentations can lead to "liability in an indeterminate amount for an indeterminate time to an indeterminate class": *Ultramares Corp. v. Touche*, 255 N.Y. 170 (C.A. 1931). A written report, for example, may be republished after many years to a massive audience that the author never contemplated. Consequently, the desirability of awarding compensation to people who sustain losses as a result of careless statements must be carefully balanced against the desirability of limiting the potential scope of liability. In some circumstances, it may be appropriate to formulate the rules governing negligent misrepresentations more narrowly than the rules governing negligent actions.

In addition, freedom of speech is a core value of our legal system. It is enshrined, as freedom of "thought, belief, opinion and expression," in the *Canadian Charter of*

Rights and Freedoms, Part I of the *Constitution Act, 1982*, being Schedule B to the *Canada Act 1982* (U.K.), 1982, c. 11. Imposing liability in tort for statements has the potential to undercut this important value.

To this point, we have focused on a distinction based on the nature of the defendant's carelessness: actions on the one hand, and words on the other. However, we must also draw a further distinction based on the nature of the plaintiff's loss: physical injury on the one hand, and pure economic loss on the other. The term "physical injury" broadly covers cases in which the plaintiff or the plaintiff's property is damaged or destroyed. The term "pure economic loss" covers cases in which the plaintiff does not sustain any personal injury or property damage but nonetheless suffers an economic loss. A common example arises when the plaintiff loses money on an investment as a result of relying on the defendant's erroneous advice.

It is certainly possible for a negligent misrepresentation to result in widespread physical injury. For example, as Lord Asquith noted in *Candler v. Crane, Christmas & Co.*, [1951] 2 K.B. 164 (C.A.) at 195, a defective marine map could take a heavy toll on property and human life. For the most part, however, the scope of physical injury is naturally limited whether the defendant's carelessness consists of careless words or careless actions. For that reason, while the cases are somewhat ambiguous, the preferred view is that liability for physical injury resulting from careless statements has long fallen under the basic approach articulated in *Donoghue v. Stevenson*, [1932] A.C. 562 (H.L.). In other words, with respect to personal injury and property damage, no substantial distinction is drawn between negligent actions and negligent words. For example, in *Robson v. Chrysler Canada Ltd.* (1962), 32 D.L.R. (2d) 49 (Alta. C.A.) the defendant instructed the plaintiff, a model, to take a step back while on a stage. When she did so, she fell from the stage and sustained physical injury. The court imposed liability on the basis of the defendant's careless advice. See also *Gertsen v. Metropolitan Toronto* (1973), 2 O.R. (2d) 1 (H.C.); *Manitoba Sausage Manufacturing Ltd. v. Winnipeg (City)* (1976), 1 C.C.L.T. 221 (Man. C.A.); *Hendrick v. DeMarsh* (1984), 45 O.R. (2d) 243 (H.C.); *Kripps v. Touche Ross & Co.* (1992), 94 D.L.R. (4th) 284 (B.C.C.A.); and *Rozenhart v. Skier's Sport Shop (Edmonton) Ltd.* (2004), 28 Alta. L.R. (4th) 44 (C.A.).

In contrast, the courts have always taken a more restricted view when carelessness causes pure economic loss. This is especially true if the carelessness in question consists of a negligent misrepresentation. Traditionally, the law simply refused to recognize a duty of care in such circumstances. Consequently, the defendant was not liable unless the plaintiff was able to prove that the defendant's words amounted to a breach of fiduciary duty, a breach of contract or, as discussed in Chapter 26, deceit under *Derry v. Peek* (1889), 14 A.C. 337 (H.L.): see *Candler v. Crane, Christmas & Co., supra.* However, in 1963 the House of Lords signalled a new approach in *Hedley Byrne & Co. v. Heller & Partners Ltd., supra.*

The plaintiff in *Hedley Byrne*, a firm of advertising agents, wanted to know whether it would be advisable to extend credit to Easipower, a customer. To that end, the plaintiff's bankers asked the defendant, who was Easipower's banker, to provide a credit rating. The defendant was unaware of the plaintiff's identity, but it did know that the inquiry pertained to an advertising contract. The defendant responded by stating that Easipower was "quite good for the arrangements." In reliance on that information, the plaintiff extended credit to Easipower. In time, however, Easipower went into liquidation, without having reimbursed the plaintiff for the expenses that it had incurred in connection with the advertising contract. The plaintiff then brought an action against the defendant, claiming that it had suffered a pure economic loss as a result of a negligent misrepresentation. The lower courts dismissed the action on the basis that, in light of the precedents on point, no duty of care arose on the facts. The House of Lords ultimately denied liability, but it did so on the basis that the defendant had expressly given its advice "without responsibility." In *obiter dicta*, the court held that, but for the disclaimer, recovery was possible in certain circumstances. Significantly, then, the House of Lords recognized that a duty of care can arise with respect to careless statements that cause pure economic loss.

Although *Hedley Byrne* recognized the possibility of a duty of care, it left many questions and issues unresolved. Since 1963 the courts have struggled to articulate a principled justification for liability and to delineate a satisfactory set of rules. While it is now accepted that careless statements resulting in pure economic loss can trigger liability, the precise circumstances in which they will do so remains somewhat uncertain and controversial. As you read through the cases in this chapter, determine whether the factors that the courts consider in connection with the duty of care for negligent statements fall under the first branch or the second branch of the *Anns/Kamloops* test as interpreted in *Cooper v. Hobart*, [2001] 3 S.C.R. 537.

In this chapter we will consider the Supreme Court of Canada's most recent judgments pertaining to negligent misrepresentations and pure economic loss. We will also consider the issue of "concurrent liability" in tort and contract. While concurrent liability may arise in several contexts, it frequently arises under the *Hedley Byrne* rubric for the simple reason that careless statements are often made in the context of contractual relationships. When that occurs, the plaintiff may wish to sue in both negligence and contract.

NOTES AND QUESTIONS

1. *Hedley Byrne* has been applied against members of various businesses and professions. See for example *Chand v. Sabo Brothers Realty Ltd.* (1979), 96 D.L.R. (3d) 445 (Alta. C.A.); *Betker v. Williams*, [1992] 2 W.W.R. 534 (B.C.C.A.); and *Johnston v. Re/max Real Estate (Edmonton) Ltd.* (2004), 30 Alta. L.R. (4th) 52 (Q.B.) (real estate agent); *Fine's Flowers Ltd. v. General Accident Assurance Co.* (1977), 81 D.L.R. (3d) 139 (Ont. C.A.); *General Motors Acceptance Corp. of Canada v. Fulton Insurance Agencies Ltd.* (1978), 24 N.S.R. (2d) 114 (C.A.); and *Fletcher v. M.P.I.C.*, [1990] 3 S.C.R. 191 (insurance agent); *Farish v. National Trust Co.* (1974), 54 D.L.R. (3d) 426 (B.C.S.C.) (trust company); *Elderkin v. Merrill Lynch, Royal Securities Ltd.* (1977), 80 D.L.R. (3d) 313 (N.S.C.A.); and *Wynberg v. Daley*, 2006 CarswellOnt 4533 (Sm. Cl. Ct.) (WLeC) (investment dealer); *Central B.C. Planers Ltd. v. Hocker* (1970), 10 D.L.R. (3d) 689 (B.C.C.A.), aff'd (1971), 16 D.L.R. (3d) 368n (S.C.C.) (security salesman); *Bank of Montreal v. Young* (1969), [1970] S.C.R. 328; and *Raypath Resources Ltd. v. Toronto Dominion Bank* (1996), 184 A.R. 125 (C.A.) (banker); *Haig v. Bamford* (1976), [1977] 1 S.C.R. 466; and *Kripps v. Touche Ross & Co.* (1997), 33 B.C.L.R. (3d) 254 (C.A.) (accountant); *Tracy v. Atkins* (1979), 105 D.L.R. (3d) 632 (B.C.C.A.); and *347671 B.C. Ltd. v. Heenan Blaikie* (2002), 98 B.C.L.R. (3d) 205 (C.A.) (lawyer); *Sealand of Pac. Ltd. v. Robert C. McHaffe Ltd.* (1974), 51 D.L.R. (3d) 702 (B.C.C.A.); and *British Columbia v. R.B.O. Architecture Inc.* (1994), 94 B.C.L.R. (2d) 96 (C.A.) (architect); *Toronto-Dominion Bank v. Leigh Investments Ltd. (Trustee of)* (1999), 178 D.L.R. (4th) 634 (Ont. C.A.) (parent company providing "comfort letter" about a subsidiary); *Kelly*

v. Lundgard (2001), 202 D.L.R. (4th) 385 (Alta. C.A.) (physician); *Ismail v. Treats Inc.* (2004), 220 N.S.R. (2d) 151 (S.C.) (franchisor); *York v. Alderney Consultants Ltd.* (2000), 187 N.S.R. (2d) 383 (S.C.) (surveyor); and *Treaty Group Inc. (c.o.b. as Leather Treaty) v. Drake International Inc.* (2005), 15 B.L.R. (4th) 83 (Ont. S.C.J.) (placement agency).

2. Following *Hedley Byrne*, Canadian courts typically said that a duty of care could not be imposed with respect to a negligent misrepresentation causing pure economic loss unless a "special relationship" existed between the parties. Does this concept have clear boundaries? For examples of judicial interpretations of the special relationship concept see *Central B.C. Planers Ltd. v. Hocker, supra*; *Elderkin v. Merrill Lynch, Royal Securities Ltd., supra*; *Sodd Corp. v. Tessis* (1977), 79 D.L.R. (3d) 632 (Ont. C.A.); *V.K. Mason Construction Ltd. v. Bank of Nova Scotia*, [1985] 1 S.C.R. 271; and *Gallant v. Central Credit Union Ltd.* (1994), 22 C.C.L.T. (2d) 251 (P.E.I.T.D.). This concept will be further explained in the remaining sections of this chapter.

3. Although the disclaimer clause in *Hedley Byrne* was effective, such provisions are interpreted narrowly and, in the event of ambiguity, against their drafter. Consequently, they may not preclude liability.

In *Keith Plumbing & Heating Co. v. Newport City Club Ltd.* (2000), 184 D.L.R. (4th) 75 (B.C.C.A.) the defendant bank was involved in the financing of a development project. The plaintiff contractor, worried about receiving payment on the project, asked the bank if sufficient funds were available. The bank sent a letter that carelessly answered that question in the affirmative. The letter also contained a disclaimer clause stipulating that the information was provided "without any responsibility on the bank and its signing officers." Some time later, the contractor contacted the bank after a payment had been missed under the project. The bank then carelessly gave its oral assurance that sufficient funds were indeed available. The project subsequently collapsed and the contractor was not paid for its work. It sued the bank for negligent misrepresentation. Despite a vigorous dissent by Ryan J.A., the majority of the Court of Appeal held that the disclaimer clause did not apply with respect to the initial written communication because: (i) it "was not well calculated to convey any clear meaning to persons not versed in the mysteries of banking practice," (ii) the plaintiff had no other means by which to check the developer's financial condition, and (iii) in the circumstances, including trade practice, it was reasonable for the plaintiff to rely upon the defendant's statement. Moreover, the disclaimer clause was held to not apply with respect to the second representation that the bank gave orally. What more could the bank have done to disclaim responsibility for its statements? Should it have refused to give any statement at all? If so, would the project have gone ahead?

4. A court may refuse to recognize a duty of care if it was not reasonably foreseeable that the plaintiff would rely on the representation. In *Border Enterprises Ltd. v. Beazer East Inc.* (2002), 216 D.L.R. (4th) 107 (B.C.C.A.) a corporation held a lease over environmentally contaminated land. After a clean-up effort, the government represented to the corporation that the site was clean. The plaintiff bought shares in the corporation. Some time later, the government issued an order requiring the corporation to undertake a further costly clean-up. The plaintiff alleged that it thereby suffered a financial loss as a result of acting in reliance on the government's initial representation. The Court of

Appeal held that the plaintiff's claim in negligence should be struck out on the ground that a duty of care did not arise in the circumstances. The plaintiff was not a reasonably foreseeable victim of the defendant's allegedly careless statement. See also *Toronto Dominion Bank v. Forsythe* (2000), 47 O.R. (3d) 321 (C.A.); and *Gross v. Great-West Life Assurance Co.*, [2002] 4 W.W.R. 421 (Alta. C.A.).

5. Alternatively, the plaintiff in a negligent misrepresentation case may establish a duty of care but fail to prove some other element of the tort. For example in *Roncato v. Caverly* (1991), 5 O.R. (3d) 714 (C.A.) the court held that the defendant owed the plaintiff a duty of care and breached the standard of care but dismissed the action because the plaintiff failed to prove that the misrepresentation had caused his loss. In *Auto Concrete Curb Ltd. v. South Nation River Conservation Authority* (1993), 105 D.L.R. (4th) 382 (S.C.C.) the court found that the defendant engineers owed the plaintiff a duty of care but had not breached the standard of care. See also *Wynberg v. Daley, supra.*

6. A controversial modification to *Hedley Byrne* was suggested by the Privy Council in *Mutual Life & Citizens' Assurance Co. v. Evatt* (1970), [1971] 1 All E.R. 150 (P.C.). The court reviewed the plaintiff's pleadings in which he alleged that he had received negligent financial advice from the defendant, his own insurance company, about the financial affairs of a subsidiary company of the defendant. The Privy Council held that no valid cause of action had been pleaded. Some courts interpreted this decision to mean that a negligent misrepresentation claim could only be maintained against defendants who were in the business or profession of giving the relevant advice. Other courts took the view that being in the business was merely the usual, but not the only, manner of holding out that one was undertaking responsibility for the advice, and that the claim in *Evatt* had failed because the plaintiff had not pleaded any other way in which the defendant had undertaken responsibility.

In *Queen v. Cognos Inc.* (1993), 99 D.L.R. (4th) 626 (S.C.C.), an extract of which appears below, Iacobucci J. expressly rejected the "restrictive approach" that confined the duty of care to "professionals." While accepting that the defendant's status as a professional adviser provided evidence of a "special relationship," he denied that it was invariably necessary.

7. Another frequently contentious issue concerns the reasonableness of the plaintiff's reliance on the defendant's negligent misstatement. See for example *Dutton v. Bognor Regis United Building Co.*, [1972] 1 All E.R. 562 (C.A.); *Burman's Beauty Supplies Ltd. v. Kempster* (1974), 48 D.L.R. (3d) 682 (Ont. Co. Ct.); and *Gordelli Management Ltd. v. Turk* (1991), 6 O.R. (3d) 521 (Gen. Div.). In *Conversions By Vantasy Ltd. v. General Motors of Canada Ltd.* (2006), 205 Man. R. (2d) 131 (C.A.) the court held that the plaintiff's own knowledge of the defendant's operations and the fact that three years had passed since the statements were made by the defendant's employees meant that it was not reasonable for the plaintiff to have relied on them.

8. The courts recognize the defence of contributory negligence, discussed in Chapter 19, in negligent misrepresentation cases. How can the courts base the duty on reliance but then apportion the loss because the reliance was negligent? In *Grand Restaurants of Canada Ltd. v. Toronto (City)* (1981), 32 O.R. (2d) 757 (H.C.), aff'd (1982), 39 O.R. (2d) 752 (C.A.) Trainor J. stated at 775: "there is a distinction at law between reasonable

reliance as a necessary prerequisite to ground liability, to constitute the cause of action under *Hedley Bryne*, and reliance in the context of contributory negligence as simply a factor going to the extent of the damage suffered." This approach was confirmed in *Avco Financial Services Realty Ltd. v. Norman* (2003), 64 O.R. (3d) 239 (C.A.). The court held at 251 that "a finding that the tort of negligent misrepresentation has been made out is not inherently inconsistent with a finding of contributory negligence because the test that underlies each finding is different." It also observed at 254 that "an approach that allows for the apportionment of fault in cases of negligent misrepresentation is not only consistent with the approach in other negligence cases, it is also consistent with the principle underlying the very concept of contributory negligence. This principle is rooted in a concern to do justice as between the parties." See also *Chapeskie v. Canadian Imperial Bank of Commerce* (2004), 197 B.C.A.C. 22 (C.A.); Roth, "Liability for Loose Lips" (1987) 51 Sask. L. Rev. 317 at 325-26; and Feldthusen, *Economic Negligence*, 4th ed. (2000) at 113-15.

9. It is common for a claim in negligent misrepresentation to be pleaded alongside a claim in fraud, deceit or breach of fiduciary duty. In each instance, the plaintiff's complaint is that the defendant somehow was less than accurate and forthright. The courts carefully approach such claims and insist on clear proof under each cause of action. See *Toronto-Dominion Bank v. Forsythe, supra*; *H.(V.A.) v. Lynch* (2000), [2001] 1 W.W.R. 83 (Alta. C.A.); and *Crown West Steel Fabricators v. Capri Insurance Services Ltd.*, [2002] 8 W.W.R. 18 (B.C.C.A.).

2. Negligent Misrepresentation Causing Pure Economic Loss

HERCULES MANAGEMENTS LTD. v. ERNST & YOUNG

(1997), 146 D.L.R. (4th) 577 (S.C.C.)

[The respondents, who were accountants, prepared audited financial statements for two companies, NGA and NGH. Those statements were required by statute. The appellants, who were shareholders in NGA and NGH, claimed that the respondents had acted carelessly in preparing the statements. The appellants further alleged that as a result of that carelessness they (i) suffered economic losses as a result of relying upon the statements in deciding to make additional investments in the companies, and (ii) suffered economic losses based on their existing shareholdings. The respondents successfully brought an application for summary dismissal on the basis that the appellants were not owed a duty of care. The Manitoba Court of Appeal affirmed that judgment. The appellants then appealed to the Supreme Court of Canada.]

LA FOREST J. [for the court] —

. . .

Issue 1: Whether the Respondents owe the Appellants a Duty of Care

(i) *Introduction*

It is now well established in Canadian law that the existence of a duty of care in tort is to be determined through an application of the two-part test first enunciated by Lord Wilberforce in *Anns v. Merton London Borough Council*, [1978] A.C. 728 (H.L.). . .

[T]his two-stage approach has been applied by this Court in the context of various types of negligence actions, including actions involving claims for different forms of economic loss. . . .

I see no reason in principle why the same approach should not be taken in the present case. Indeed, to create a "pocket" of negligent misrepresentation cases . . . in which the existence of a duty of care is determined differently from other negligence cases would, in my view, be incorrect. . . This is not to say, of course, that negligent misrepresentation cases do not involve special considerations stemming from the fact that recovery is allowed for pure economic loss as opposed to physical damage. Rather, it is simply to posit that the same general framework ought to be used in approaching the duty of care question in both types of case. Whether the respondents owe the appellants a duty of care for their allegedly negligent preparation of the 1980-82 audit reports, then, will depend on (a) whether a *prima facie* duty of care is owed, and (b) whether that duty, if it exists, is negatived or limited by policy considerations. Before analysing the merits of this case, it will be useful to set out in greater detail the principles governing this appeal.

(ii) *The Prima Facie Duty of Care*

The first branch of the *Anns/Kamloops* test demands an inquiry into whether there is a sufficiently close relationship between the plaintiff and the defendant that in the reasonable contemplation of the latter, carelessness on its part may cause damage to the former. The existence of such a relationship – which has come to be known as a relationship of "neighbourhood" or "proximity" – distinguishes those circumstances in which the defendant owes a *prima facie* duty of care to the plaintiff from those where no such duty exists. In the context of a negligent misrepresentation action, then, deciding whether or not a *prima facie* duty of care exists necessitates an investigation into whether the defendant-representor and the plaintiff-representee can be said to be in a relationship of proximity or neighbourhood.

What constitutes a "relationship of proximity" in the context of negligent misrepresentation actions? . . . I would begin by reiterating . . . that the term "proximity" itself is nothing more than a label expressing a result, judgment or conclusion; it does not, in and of itself, provide a principled basis on which to make a legal determination. . . In order to render "proximity" a useful tool in defining when a duty of care exists in negligent misrepresentation cases, therefore, it is necessary to infuse that term with some meaning. In other words, it is necessary to set out the basis upon which one may properly reach the conclusion that proximity inheres between a representor and a representee.

This can be done most clearly as follows. The label "proximity", as it was used by Lord Wilberforce in *Anns*, *supra*, was clearly intended to connote that the circumstances of the relationship inhering between the plaintiff and the defendant are of such a nature that the defendant may be said to be under an obligation to be mindful of the plaintiff's legitimate interests in conducting his or her affairs. Indeed, this idea lies at the very heart of the concept of a "duty of care", as articulated most memorably by Lord Atkin in *Donoghue v. Stevenson*. . . . In cases of negligent misrepresentation, the relationship between the plaintiff and the defendant arises through reliance by the plaintiff on the defendant's words. Thus, if "proximity" is meant to distinguish the cases where the defendant has a responsibility to take reasonable care of the plaintiff from those where he or she has no such responsibility, then in negligent misrepresentation cases, it must pertain to some aspect of the relationship of reliance. To my mind, proximity can be seen to inhere between a defendant-representor and a plaintiff-representee when two criteria relating to reliance may be said to exist on the facts: (a) the defendant ought reasonably to foresee that the plaintiff will rely on his or her representation; and (b) reliance by the plaintiff would, in the particular circumstances of the case, be reasonable. . .

I should pause here to explain that, in my view, to look to whether or not reliance by the plaintiff on the defendant's representation would be reasonable in determining whether or not a *prima facie* duty of care exists in negligent misrepresentation cases as opposed to looking at reasonable foreseeability alone is not, as might first appear, to abandon the basic tenets underlying the first branch of the *Anns/Kamloops* formula. The purpose behind the *Anns/Kamloops* test is simply to ensure that enquiries into the existence of a duty of care in negligence cases is conducted in two parts: The first involves discerning whether, in a given situation, a duty of care would be imposed by law; the second demands an investigation into whether the legal duty, if found, ought to be negatived or ousted by policy considerations. In the context of actions based on negligence causing physical damage, determining whether harm to the plaintiff was reasonably foreseeable to the defendant is alone a sufficient criterion for deciding proximity or neighbourhood under the first branch of the *Anns/Kamloops* test because the law has come to recognize (even if only implicitly) that, absent a voluntary assumption of risk by him or her, it is always reasonable for a plaintiff to expect that a defendant will take reasonable care of the plaintiff's person and property. The duty of care inquiry in such cases, therefore, will always be conducted under the assumption that the plaintiff's expectations of the defendant are reasonable.

In negligent misrepresentation actions, however, the plaintiff's claim stems from his or her detrimental reliance on the defendant's (negligent) statement, and it is abundantly clear that reliance on the statement or representation of another will not, in all circumstances, be reasonable. The assumption that always inheres in physical damage cases concerning the reasonableness of the plaintiff's expectations cannot, therefore, be said to inhere in reliance cases. In order to ensure that the same factors are taken into account in determining the existence of a duty of care in both instances, then, the reasonableness of the plaintiff's reliance must be considered in negligent misrepresentation actions. Only by doing so will the first branch of the *Kamloops* test be applied consistently in both contexts.

As should be evident from its very terms, the reasonable foreseeability/reasonable reliance test for determining a *prima facie* duty of care is somewhat broader than the tests used both in the cases decided before *Anns*, *supra*, and in those that have rejected the *Anns* approach. Rather than stipulating simply that a duty of care will be found in any case where reasonable foreseeability and reasonable reliance inhere, those cases typically require (a) that the defendant know the identity of either the plaintiff or the class of plaintiffs who will rely on the statement, and (b) that the reliance losses claimed by the plaintiff stem from the particular transaction in respect of which the statement at issue was made. This narrower approach to defining the duty can be seen in a number of the more prominent English decisions dealing either with auditors' liability specifically or with liability for negligent misstatements generally. . . . It is also evident in the approach taken by this Court in *Haig v. Bamford*, [1977] 1 S.C.R. 466.

While I would not question the conclusions reached in any of these judgments, I am of the view that inquiring into such matters as whether the defendant had knowledge of the plaintiff (or class of plaintiffs) and whether the plaintiff used the statements at issue for the particular transaction for which they were provided is, in reality, nothing more than a means by which to circumscribe – for reasons of policy – the scope of a representor's potentially infinite liability. As I have already tried to explain, determining whether "proximity" exists on a given set of facts consists in an attempt to discern whether, as a matter of simple justice, the defendant may be said to have had an obligation to be mindful of the plaintiff's interests in going about his or her business. Requiring, in addition to proximity, that the defendant know the identity of the plaintiff (or class of plaintiffs) and that the plaintiff use the statements in question for the specific purpose for which they were prepared amounts, in my opinion, to a tacit recognition that considerations of basic fairness may sometimes give way to other pressing concerns. Plainly stated, adding further requirements to the duty of care test provides a means by which policy concerns that are extrinsic to simple justice – but that are, nevertheless, fundamentally important – may be taken into account in assessing whether the defendant should be compelled to compensate the plaintiff for losses suffered.

. . .

In light of this Court's endorsement of the *Anns/Kamloops* test, however, enquiries concerning (a) the defendant's knowledge of the identity of the plaintiff (or of the class of plaintiffs) and (b) the use to which the statements at issue are put may now quite properly be conducted in the second branch of that test when deciding whether or not policy considerations ought to negate or limit a *prima facie* duty that has already been found to exist. In other words, criteria that in other cases have been used to define the legal test for the duty of care can now be recognized for what they really are – policy-based means by which to curtail liability – and they can appropriately be considered under the policy branch of the *Anns/Kamloops* test. To understand exactly how this may be done and how these criteria are pertinent to the case at bar, it will first be useful to set out the prevailing policy concerns in some detail.

(iii) *Policy Considerations*

As Cardozo C.J. explained in *Ultramares Corp. v. Touche*, 174 N.E. 441 (N.Y.C.A. 1931), at p. 444, the fundamental policy consideration that must be addressed in negligent misrepresentation actions centres around the possibility that the defendant might be exposed to "liability in an indeterminate amount for an indeterminate time to an indeterminate class". This potential problem can be seen quite vividly within the framework of the *Anns/Kamloops* test. Indeed, while the criteria of reasonable foreseeability and reasonable reliance serve to distinguish cases where a *prima facie* duty is owed from those where it is not, it is nevertheless true that in certain types of situations these criteria can, quite easily, be satisfied and absent some means by which to circumscribe the ambit of the duty, the prospect of limitless liability will loom.

The general area of auditors' liability is a case in point. In modern commercial society, the fact that audit reports will be relied on by many different people (e.g., shareholders, creditors, potential takeover bidders, investors, etc.) for a wide variety of purposes will almost always be reasonably foreseeable to auditors themselves. Similarly, the very nature of audited financial statements – produced, as they are, by professionals whose reputations (and, thereby, whose livelihoods) are at stake – will very often mean that any of those people would act wholly reasonably in placing their reliance on such statements in conducting their affairs. These observations are consistent with the following remarks of Dickson J. in *Haig*, *supra*, at pp. 475-76, with respect to the accounting profession generally:

> The increasing growth and changing role of corporations in modern society has been attended by a new perception of the societal role of the profession of accounting. The day when the accountant served only the owner-manager of a company and was answerable to him alone has passed. The complexities of modern industry combined with the effects of specialization, the impact of taxation, urbanization, the separation of ownership from management, the rise of professional corporate managers, and a host of other factors, have led to marked changes in the role and responsibilities of the accountant, and in the reliance which the public must place upon his work. The financial statements of the corporations upon which he reports can affect the economic interests of the general public as well as of shareholders and potential shareholders.

In light of these considerations, the reasonable foreseeability/reasonable reliance test for ascertaining a prima facie duty of care may well be satisfied in many (even if not all) negligent misstatement suits against auditors and, consequently, the problem of indeterminate liability will often arise.

Certain authors have argued that imposing broad duties of care on auditors would give rise to significant economic and social benefits in so far as the spectre of tort liability would act as an incentive to auditors to produce accurate (i.e., non-negligent) reports. . . . I would agree that deterrence of negligent conduct is an important policy consideration with respect to auditors' liability. Nevertheless, I am of the view that, in the final analysis, it is outweighed by the socially undesirable consequences to which the imposition of indeterminate liability on auditors might lead. Indeed, while indeterminate liability is problematic in and of itself inasmuch as it would mean that successful negligence actions against auditors could, at least potentially, be limitless, it is also problematic in light of certain related problems to which it might give rise.

Some of the more significant of these problems are thus set out in Brian R. Cheffins, "Auditors' Liability in the House of Lords: A Signal Canadian Courts Should Follow" (1991), 18 C.B.L.J. 118, at pp. 125-27:

> In addition to providing only limited benefits, imposing widely drawn duties of care on auditors would probably generate substantial costs. . . .
>
> One reason [for this] is that auditors would expend more resources trying to protect themselves from liability. For example, insurance premiums would probably rise since insurers would anticipate more frequent claims. Also, auditors would probably incur higher costs since they would try to rely more heavily on exclusion clauses. Hiring lawyers to draft such clauses might be expensive because only the most carefully constructed provisions would be likely to pass judicial scrutiny. . . .
>
> Finally, auditors' opportunity costs would increase. Whenever members of an accounting firm have to spend time and effort preparing for litigation, they forego revenue generating accounting activity. More trials would mean that this would occur with greater frequency.
>
> . . .
>
> The higher costs auditors would face as a result of broad duties of care could have a widespread impact. For example, the supply of accounting services would probably be reduced since some marginal firms would be driven to the wall. Also, because the market for accounting services is protected by barriers to entry imposed by the profession, the surviving firms would pass [*sic*] at least some of the increased costs to their clients.

. . .

I should, at this point, explain that I am aware of the arguments put forth by certain scholars and judges to the effect that concerns over indeterminate liability have sometimes been overstated. . . Arguments to this effect rest essentially on the premise that actual *liability* will be limited in so far as a plaintiff will not be successful unless both negligence and reliance are established in addition to a duty of care. While it is true that damages will not be owing by the defendant unless these other elements of the cause of action are proved, neither the difficulty of proving negligence nor that of proving reliance will preclude a disgruntled plaintiff from bringing an action against an auditor and such actions would, we may assume, be all the more common were the establishment of a duty of care in any given case to amount to nothing more than a mere matter of course. This eventuality could pose serious problems both for auditors, whose legal costs would inevitably swell, and for courts, which, no doubt, would feel the pressure of increased litigation. Thus, the prospect of burgeoning negligence suits raises serious concerns, even if we assume that the arguments positing proof of negligence and reliance as a barrier to liability are correct. In my view, therefore, it makes more sense to circumscribe the ambit of the duty of care than to assume that difficulties in proving negligence and reliance will afford sufficient protection to auditors, since this approach avoids both "indeterminate liability" and "indeterminate litigation".

As I have thus far attempted to demonstrate, the possible repercussions of exposing auditors to indeterminate liability are significant. In applying the two-stage *Anns/Kamloops* test to negligent misrepresentation actions against auditors, therefore, policy considerations reflecting those repercussions should be taken into account. In the general run of auditors' cases, concerns over indeterminate liability will serve to negate a *prima facie* duty of care. But while such concerns may exist in most such cases, there may be particular situations where they do not. In other words, the specific factual matrix of a given case may render it an "exception" to the general class of cases in that while (as in most auditors' liability cases) considerations of proximity under the first branch of the *Anns/Kamloops* test might militate in favour of finding that a duty of care inheres, the typical concerns surrounding indeterminate liability do *not* arise. This needs to be explained.

As discussed earlier, looking to factors such as "knowledge of the plaintiff (or an identifiable class of plaintiffs) on the part of the defendant" and "use of the statements at issue for the precise purpose or transaction for which they were prepared" really amounts to an attempt to limit or constrain the scope of the duty of care owed by the defendants. If the purpose of the *Anns/Kamloops* test is to determine (a) whether or not a *prima facie* duty of care exists and then (b) whether or not that duty ought to be negated or limited, then factors such as these ought properly to be considered in the second branch of the test once the first branch concerning "proximity" has been found to be satisfied. To my mind, the presence of such factors in a given situation will mean that worries stemming from indeterminacy should not arise, since the scope of potential liability is sufficiently delimited. . . .

. . .

The foregoing analysis should render the following points clear. A *prima facie* duty of care will arise on the part of a defendant in a negligent misrepresentation action when it can be said (a) that the defendant ought reasonably to have foreseen that the plaintiff would rely on his representation and (b) that reliance by the plaintiff, in the circumstances, would be reasonable. Even though, in the context of auditors' liability cases, such a duty will often (even if not always) be found to exist, the problem of indeterminate liability will frequently result in the duty being negated by the kinds of policy considerations already discussed. Where, however, indeterminate liability can be shown not to be a concern on the facts of a particular case, a duty of care will be found to exist.

. . .

(iv) *Application to the Facts*

In my view, there can be no question that a *prima facie* duty of care was owed to the appellants by the respondents on the facts of this case. As regards the criterion of reasonable foreseeability, the possibility that the appellants would rely on the audited financial statements in conducting their affairs and that they may suffer harm if the reports were negligently prepared must have been reasonably foreseeable to the respondents. This is confirmed simply by the fact that shareholders generally will often choose to rely on audited financial statements for a wide variety of purposes.

. . .

Similarly, I would find that reliance on the audited statements by the appellant shareholders would, on the facts of this case, be reasonable. Professor Feldthusen [*Economic Negligence*, 3d ed. (1994)] (at pp. 62-63) sets out five general *indicia* of reasonable reliance; namely:

(1) The defendant had a direct or indirect financial interest in the transaction in respect of which the representation was made.

(2) The defendant was a professional or someone who possessed special skill, judgment, or knowledge.

(3) The advice or information was provided in the course of the defendant's business.

(4) The information or advice was given deliberately, and not on a social occasion.

(5) The information or advice was given in response to a specific enquiry or request.

While these *indicia* should not be understood to be a strict "test" of reasonableness, they do help to distinguish those situations where reliance on a statement is reasonable from those where it is not. On the facts here, the first four of these indicia clearly inhere. To my mind, then, this aspect of the *prima facie* duty is unquestionably satisfied on the facts.

Having found a *prima facie* duty to exist, then, the second branch of the *Anns/Kamloops* test remains to be considered.

. . .

At first blush, it may seem that no problems of indeterminate liability are implicated here and that this case can easily be likened to . . . *Hedley Byrne*. . . . After all, the respondents knew the very identity of all the appellant shareholders who claim to have relied on the audited financial statements through having acted as NGA's and NGH's auditors for nearly 10 years by the time the first of the audit reports at issue in this appeal was prepared. It would seem plausible to argue on this basis that because the identity of the plaintiffs was known to the respondents at the time of preparing the 1980-82 reports, no concerns over indeterminate liability arise.

To arrive at this conclusion without further analysis, however, would be to move too quickly. While knowledge of the plaintiff (or of a limited class of plaintiffs) is undoubtedly a significant factor serving to obviate concerns over indeterminate liability, it is not, alone, sufficient to do so. In my discussion of . . . *Hedley Byrne*, *supra*, and *Haig*, *supra*, I explained that indeterminate liability did not inhere on the specific facts of those cases not only because the defendant knew the identity of the plaintiff (or the class of plaintiffs) who would rely on the statement at issue, but also because the statement itself was used by the plaintiff *for precisely the purpose or transaction for which it was prepared*. The crucial importance of this additional criterion can clearly be seen when one considers that even if the specific identity or class of potential plaintiffs is known to a defendant, use of the defendant's statement for a purpose or transaction other than that for which it was prepared could still lead to indeterminate liability.

For example, if an audit report which was prepared for a corporate client for the express purpose of attracting a $10,000 investment in the corporation from a known class of third parties was instead used as the basis for attracting a $1,000,000 investment or as the basis for inducing one of the members of the class to become a director or officer of the corporation or, again, as the basis for encouraging him or her to enter into some business venture with the corporation itself, it would appear that the auditors would be exposed to a form of indeterminate liability, even if they knew precisely the identity or class of potential plaintiffs to whom their report would be given. With respect to the present case, then, the central question is whether or not the appellants can be said to have used the 1980-82 audit reports for the specific purpose for which they were prepared. The answer to this question will determine whether or not policy considerations surrounding indeterminate liability ought to negate the *prima facie* duty of care owed by the respondents.

What, then, is the purpose for which the respondents' audit statements were prepared?

. . .

[T]he purpose for which the audit reports were prepared in this case was the standard statutory one of allowing shareholders, *as a group*, to supervise management and to take decisions with respect to matters concerning the proper overall administration *of the corporations*. In other words, it was . . . to permit the shareholders to exercise their role, *as a class*, of overseeing the *corporations'* affairs at their annual general meetings. . . . On the appellants' argument, however, the purpose to which the 1980-82 reports were ostensibly put was not that of allowing the shareholders as a class to take decisions in respect of the overall running of the corporation, but rather to allow them, as *individuals*, to monitor management so as to oversee and protect their own personal investments. Indeed, the nature of the appellants' claims (i.e. personal tort claims) *requires* that they assert reliance on the auditors' reports *qua* individual shareholders if they are to recover any personal damages.

. . .

Conclusion

In light of the foregoing, I would find that even though the respondents owed the appellants (*qua* individual claimants) a *prima facie* duty of care both with respect to the 1982-83 investments made [by the appellants] and with respect to the losses they incurred through the devaluation of their existing shareholdings, such *prima facie* duties are negated by policy considerations which are not obviated by the facts of the case. Indeed, to come to the opposite conclusion on these facts would be to expose auditors to the possibility of indeterminate liability, since such a finding would imply that auditors owe a duty of care to any known class of potential plaintiffs regardless of the purpose to which they put the auditors' reports. This would amount to an unacceptably broad expansion of the bounds of liability.

NOTES AND QUESTIONS

1. According to LaForest J.'s judgment in *Hercules*, when will a duty of care be imposed on auditors? On what basis will the first branch of the *Anns/Kamloops* test be satisfied? What considerations fall under the second branch of the test? Do you agree with LaForest J.'s approach to the *Anns/Kamloops* test? Is it necessary to reconsider LaForest J.'s classification of the various policy issues in light of the Supreme Court of Canada's judgment in *Cooper v. Hobart*, which was discussed in Chapter 10?

2. List the policy considerations that LaForest J. said warranted a restricted duty of care. Do you agree with his assessment? Are any of his concerns overstated or misplaced? Are "floodgates" arguments ever convincing? Are the rules that he articulated sufficiently sensitive or do they involve broad propositions that occasionally will produce unjust results?

3. While LaForest J. focussed on reasons why a duty of care should not be recognized in some situations, it might be equally enlightening to ask why a duty of care should ever be recognized with respect to negligent misrepresentations that cause pure economic loss. Why should society be concerned with protecting people from loss in such circumstances? Would such circumstances be better addressed on the basis of first-party insurance?

B. Feldthusen has argued that recognition of a duty of care in misrepresentation cases often improperly allows a plaintiff to "unilaterally appropriate" the services of the defendant in so far as the plaintiff is entitled to compensation if the defendant's negligent statements cause pure economic loss. He therefore argues that recognition of a duty of care should be carefully confined to circumstances in which the defendant voluntarily assumed responsibility toward the plaintiff. On that view, while absence of reasonable reliance may justify the negation of a duty of care, it cannot justify the imposition of a duty of care: only assumption of responsibility can serve that role. See Feldthusen, "Liability for Pure Economic Loss: Yes, But Why?" (1999) 28 U.W.A.L. Rev. 84. How does that proposal differ from LaForest J.'s opinion in *Hercules*? Which approach is preferable? See also Hollyman, "*Hercules Managements* and the Duty of Care in Negligent Misstatement: How Dispensable is Reliance?" (2001) 34 U.B.C.L. Rev. 515.

4. American and Commonwealth courts have used various tests to control the ambit of liability. They have emphasized the defendant's knowledge of the class of potential plaintiffs, knowledge of the contemplated use of the information, or both. However, most of the cases are consistent with a fairly simple rule, derived from *Glanzer v. Shepard*, 135 N.E. 275 at 277 (N.Y.C.A. 1922). In *Glanzer* the court held the defendant liable for losses which he knew or ought to have known were related to the "end and aim" of the

transaction giving rise to the misrepresentation. In *Caparo Industries plc. v. Dickman*, [1990] 2 W.L.R. 358 (H.L.) the House of Lords observed that advice is tendered with a specific purpose in mind and that liability must be restricted to losses incurred in transactions related to that purpose. See also *Esanda Finance Corp. v. Peat Marwick Hungerfords (Reg)* (1997), 142 A.L.R. 750 (H.C.A.); *Boyd Knight v. Purdue*, [1999] 2 N.Z.L.R. 278 (C.A.); and *Price Waterhouse v. Kwan* (1999), [2000] 3 N.Z.L.R. 39 (C.A.).

5. As noted in the introduction to this chapter, in *Ultramares* Cardozo C.J. expressed concern that the application of the ordinary rules of negligence law might expose accountants to "liability in an indeterminate amount for an indeterminate time to an indeterminate class." Generally, the courts have shared Cardozo C.J.'s concern about the indeterminate amount and have regarded indeterminate time and class as indirect indicators of this issue. However, each factor may have independent significance.

The issue of potentially indeterminate time was raised in *Williams v. Polgar*, 215 N.W.2d 149 (S.C. Mich. 1974). An abstract of a land title was negligently issued in 1926. The defect was not discovered until 1959, when the plaintiffs relied upon the abstract to their detriment. The court held that the defendant's duty ran to any successor in title who relied on the abstract. Whereas the limitation period in contract had long expired, the tort period had not begun to run until the plaintiffs discovered the negligence. Does this decision violate the policy underlying statutory limitations periods?

The problem of a potentially indeterminate class raises the issue of whether there is a sufficient relationship between the plaintiff and defendant to warrant imposing liability, regardless of the amount of the potential loss. In *Beebe v. Robb* (1977), 81 D.L.R. (3d) 349 (B.C.S.C.) a boat owner commissioned the defendant, a marine surveyor, to evaluate his boat in order to assist him in obtaining a bank loan. Unknown to the defendant, the owner showed the assessment to the plaintiff, a prospective purchaser, who relied upon it to his detriment. The plaintiff alleged that the defendant had been negligent and sued under the principles in *Hedley Byrne*. Clearly the defendant knew about the amount at risk. Nevertheless, the court held that the relationship between the parties was insufficient to justify recognizing a duty of care. A similar result was reached in *Le Lievre v. Gould*, [1893] 1 Q.B. 491 (C.A.). In *Gordon v. Moen*, [1971] N.Z.L.R. 526 (S.C.), a case virtually identical to *Beebe*, the court held the defendant liable. Which line of cases is preferable?

6. *Hercules* has been applied in a variety of circumstances. In *Deraps v. Coia* (1999), 179 D.L.R. (4th) 168 (Ont. C.A.) a woman and her gravely ill husband sought advice from a benefits counsellor employed by the husband's trade union. Because of a careless omission by the counsellor, the woman did not realize that, by signing a certain waiver, she would lose all of her benefits when her husband died. She signed the waiver and, when her husband passed away eight months later, learned that she no longer enjoyed any benefits. In affirming the imposition of liability, the Court of Appeal for Ontario held that the failure to divulge information may be just as actionable as the providing of positively misleading advice.

See also *Lakefield (Village) v. Black* (1998), 41 O.R. (3d) 741 (C.A.); *NBD Bank, Canada v. Dofasco Inc.* (1999), 46 O.R. (3d) 514 (C.A.); *Toronto-Dominion Bank v. Forsythe* (2000), 47 O.R. (3d) 321 (C.A.); and *Apex Mountain Resort Ltd. v. British Columbia* (2001), 6 C.C.L.T. (3d) 157 (B.C.C.A.). For a discussion of the decision in

Hercules, see Deturbide, "Liability of Auditors – *Hercules Managements Ltd. et al. v. Ernst and Young et al.*" (1998) 77 Can. Bar Rev. 260.

7. In the wake of recent high-profile corporate and accounting scandals such as those involving Enron, WorldCom and Nortel, the issue of auditor liability has become a very important tort law topic. See for example Khoury, "The Liability of Auditors beyond Their Clients: A Comparative Study" (2001) 46 McGill L.J. 413; Hession, "Auditor Independence and Liability in Canada: Are We Ready for Third Party Liability?" (2003) 36 U.B.C.L. Rev. 575; and Trakman & Trainor, "The Rights and Responsibilities of Auditors to Third Parties: A Call for a Principled Approach" (2005) 31 Queen's L. Rev. 148.

8. In *Premakumaran v. Canada* (2006), 270 D.L.R. (4th) 440 (F.C.A.) the plaintiff alleged that the government had negligently misrepresented to potential immigrants the extent to which accountants could get work in Canada. The plaintiff had come to Canada but had been unable to find work as an accountant. On a motion by the defendant for summary judgment, the court dismissed the claim. It held that there was no special relationship of proximity or reliance between the parties, and that the information provided by the government was "merely general material" for potential immigrants to consider. The court also held that it was far from clear that the statements were negligent or that the plaintiff had actually relied on them.

9. In *Baldwin v. Daubney* (2006), 216 O.A.C. 72 (C.A.) the plaintiffs wanted to supplement their income but had limited financial resources. They consulted financial advisors, who referred them to a program which allowed them to borrow money to use for investments. The investments decreased significantly in value and the plaintiffs sued both the advisors and the lenders that had loaned them the money. The plaintiffs argued that the providing of the loans was a direct cause of their financial losses. However, the court held that they had no claim against the lenders. The lenders had not provided any advice, only the money. Further, there was no basis for finding a special relationship between the plaintiffs and the lenders.

10. The same set of facts could be analyzed as involving a negligent misrepresentation, the negligent performance of a service, or a more novel way of causing pure economic loss. As a result, it is not always easy to categorize a case. When you read the next chapter, consider how *Haskett v. Equifax Canada Inc.* (2003), 63 O.R. (3d) 577 (C.A.) and *Lowe v. Guarantee Co. of North America* (2005), 200 O.A.C. 236 (C.A.) might be analyzed as negligent misrepresentation cases. See also *Baldwin*, *supra*.

3. Negligent Misrepresentation and Contract

The rules governing tortious liability for negligent misrepresentations are further complicated if the statement arises in a contractual context. Contract is the primary means by which parties allocate benefits, burdens and risks among themselves. For that reason, there traditionally was strong support for the view that if the parties' relationship was governed by contract, tort law should have little, if any, role to play.

This raises the question of *concurrent liability*: can the defendant incur liability in both contract and tort on the basis of essentially the same event? The answer to that question often has considerable practical significance. While there is no possibility of double recovery, the plaintiff may see some advantage to suing in tort rather than contract.

Assuming that concurrent liability is theoretically possible, it then becomes necessary to determine the extent to which the terms of a contract may nevertheless oust or negate a duty of care that would otherwise arise in negligence.

The interplay of contract and tort also raises the question of whether negligence principles should be allowed to operate with respect to the period of negotiation that precedes the formation of a contract. This issue can be further subdivided. This chapter concludes with an examination of *Queen v. Cognos Inc.* (1993), 99 D.L.R. (4th) 626 (S.C.C.), in which the Supreme Court of Canada addressed the existence of a duty of care to avoid negligent misrepresentations during pre-contractual negotiations. The next chapter opens with an examination of *Martel Building Ltd. v. Canada* (2000), 193 D.L.R. (4th) 1 (S.C.C.), in which the Supreme Court of Canada addressed several other issues, including the existence of a duty of care to otherwise conduct pre-contractual negotiations in such a way as to avoid inflicting pure economic loss.

(a) CONCURRENT LIABILITY IN TORT AND CONTRACT

BG CHECO INTERNATIONAL LTD. v. B.C. HYDRO & POWER AUTHORITY

(1993), 99 D.L.R. (4th) 577 (S.C.C.)

[Hydro called for tenders for a contract to erect transmission towers and string transmission lines. Checo had a representative inspect the area by helicopter before it submitted a tender. The representative noted that a right-of-way had been partially cleared, and also noted evidence of ongoing clearing activity. He assumed that there would be further clearing prior to the commencement of Checo's work. Hydro accepted Checo's tender and the parties entered into a written contract. The tender documents, which were subsequently incorporated into the contract, stated that clearing of the right-of-way would be done by others and formed no part of the work to be performed by Checo. They also stated that it was Checo's responsibility to inform itself of all aspects of the work and that, should any errors appear in the tender documents, or should Checo note any conditions conflicting with the letter or spirit of the tender documents, it was Checo's responsibility to obtain clarification before submitting its tender. The tender documents also provided that Checo would satisfy itself as to all site conditions and the correctness and sufficiency of the tender for the work and the stipulated prices. In fact, no further clearing of the right-of-way ever took place, and the inadequate clearing caused Checo difficulties in completing its work.

Checo sued Hydro for negligent misrepresentation and breach of contract. The evidence at trial indicated that Hydro had contracted the clearing of the right-of-way to another company, and that, to Hydro's knowledge, the work was not done adequately. There was no direct discussion between the representatives of Checo and Hydro concerning this issue. During the trial, Checo amended its statement of claim to include a claim in fraud. The trial judge found that Hydro had acted fraudulently in its dealings with Checo and awarded damages representing "the total loss suffered by [Checo] as a result of being fraudulently induced to enter into this contract." Hydro appealed to the British Columbia Court of Appeal, which rejected the finding of fraud but found that there had been a negligent misrepresentation which induced Checo to enter into the contract. The Court of Appeal awarded damages for the misrepresentation but reduced the trial judge's damage award, and referred the question of breach of contract back to the trial court. Hydro appealed, and Checo cross-appealed, to the Supreme Court of Canada.]

IACOBUCCI J. (dissenting in part) (SOPINKA J. concurring): — The narrow question raised by this appeal is what remedy should be available for pre-contractual representations made during the tendering process. This question also raises a more general and more important issue. . . [C]an a plaintiff who is in a contractual relationship with the defendant sue the defendant in tort if the duty relied upon by the plaintiff in tort is also made a contractual duty by an express term of the contract?

. . .

As a general rule, the existence of a contract between two parties does not preclude the existence of a common law duty of care. Subject to the substantive and procedural differences that exist between an action in contract and an action in tort, both the duty of care and the liability may be concurrent in contract and tort. In such circumstances, it is for the plaintiff to select the cause of action most advantageous to him or her. That was the position adopted by Le Dain J. in *Central & Eastern Trust v. Rafuse* [(1986), 31 D.L.R. (4th) 481 (S.C.C.)].

. . .

In my opinion, the [rule formulated] by Le Dain J. is an appropriate one. If the parties to a contract choose to define a specific duty as an express term of the contract, then the consequences of a breach of that duty ought to be determined by the law of contract, not by tort law. Whether or not an implied term of a contract can define a duty of care in such a way that a plaintiff is confined to a remedy in contract is not at issue in this case. I leave that determination to another day. While the rule articulated by Le Dain J. is a rule of law which does not depend on the presumed or actual intention of the parties, the intention which can be inferred from the fact that the parties have made the duty an express term of the contract provides policy support for the rule. If a duty is an express term of the contract, it can be inferred that the parties wish the law of the contract to govern with respect to that duty. This is of particular significance given that the result of a breach of a contractual duty may be different from that of a breach of a duty in tort. As Wilson J.A. noted in *Dominion Chain Co.*, supra, a plaintiff's substantive rights may be different in contract and in tort (at p. 409):

> His cause of action may arise later in tort resulting in a later expiry of the limitation period. His damage may be greater in quantum and different in kind if he sues in tort. On the other hand his action in contract may survive him or be the subject of a set-off or counterclaim, neither of which would be so if his action were framed in tort.

The fact that damages may be assessed differently in contract from in tort was recently affirmed by this Court in *Rainbow Industrial Caterers Ltd. v. Canadian National Railway Co.*, [1991] 3 S.C.R. 3.

A further policy rationale for the rule advanced by Le Dain J. is that contracts have become, particularly in commercial contexts, increasingly complex. Commercial contracts allocate risks and fix the mutual duties and obligations of the parties. Where there is an express term creating a contractual duty, it is appropriate that the parties be held to the bargain which they have made.

. . .

However, I do not believe that the rule advanced by Le Dain J. that forecloses a claim in tort is absolute in all circumstances. In this respect, I would favour a contextual approach which takes into account the context in which the contract is made, and the position of the parties with respect to one another, in assessing whether a claim in tort is foreclosed by the terms of a contract. The policy reasons in favour of the rule advanced by Le Dain J. are strongest where the contractual context is commercial and the parties are of equal bargaining power. There was no question of unconscionability or inequality of bargaining power in *Central & Eastern Trust v. Rafuse*, supra, as there is no such question in this case. If such issues, or others analogous to them, were to arise, however, a court should be wary not to exclude too rapidly a duty of care in tort on the basis of an express term of the contract, especially if the end result for the plaintiff would be a wrong without a remedy.

. . .

LA FOREST and MCLACHLIN JJ. (L'HEUREUX-DUBÉ and GONTHIER JJ. concurring): — We have had the advantage of reading the reasons of our colleague Justice Iacobucci. We agree with his conclusion that Hydro is liable to Checo for breach of contract. We disagree, however, with his conclusion that the contract precludes Checo from suing in tort. In our view, our colleague's approach would have the effect of eliminating much of the rationalizing thrust behind the movement towards concurrency in tort and contract. Rather than attempting to establish new barriers in tort liability in contractual contexts, the law should move towards the elimination of unjustified differences between the remedial rules applicable to the two actions, thereby reducing the significance of the existence of the two different forms of action and allowing a person who has suffered a wrong full access to all relevant legal remedies.

. . .

[Having concluded that Hydro was liable to Checo for breach of contract, the court went on to discuss the claim in tort.]

The Claim in Tort

The Theory of Concurrency

The first question is whether the contract precludes Checo from suing in tort.

Iacobucci J. concludes that a contract between the parties may preclude the possibility of suing in tort for a given wrong where there is an express term in the contract dealing with the matter. We would phrase the applicable principle somewhat more narrowly. As we see it, the right to sue in tort is not taken away by the contract in such a case, although the contract, by limiting the scope of the tort duty or waiving the right to sue in tort, may limit or negate tort liability.

In our view, the general rule emerging from this Court's decision in *Central & Eastern Trust v. Rafuse*, [1986] 2 S.C.R. 147, is that where a given wrong prima facie supports an action in contract and in tort, the party may sue in either or both, except where the contract indicates that the parties intended to limit or negative the right to sue in tort. This limitation on the general rule of concurrency arises because it is always open to parties to limit or waive the duties which the common law would impose on them for negligence. This principle is of great importance in preserving a sphere of individual liberty and commercial flexibility. Thus if a person wishes to engage in a dangerous sport, the person may stipulate in advance that he or she waives any right of action against the person who operates the sport facility: *Dyck v. Manitoba Snowmobile Assn. Inc.*, [1985] 1 S.C.R. 589. Similarly, if two business firms agree that a particular risk should lie on a party who would not ordinarily bear that risk at common law they may do so. So a plaintiff may sue either in contract or tort, subject to any limit the parties themselves have placed on that right by their contract. The mere fact that the parties have dealt with a matter expressly in their contract does not mean that they intended to exclude the right to sue in tort. It all depends on *how* they have dealt with it.

Viewed thus, the only limit on the right to choose one's action is the principle of primacy of private ordering — the right of individuals to arrange their affairs and assume risks in a different way than would be done by the law of tort. It is only to the extent that this private ordering contradicts the tort duty that the tort duty is diminished. The rule is not that one cannot sue concurrently in contract and tort where the contract limits or contradicts the tort duty. It is rather that the tort duty, a general duty imputed by the law in all the relevant circumstances, must yield to the parties' superior right to arrange their rights and duties in a different way. In so far as the tort duty is not contradicted by the contract, it remains intact and may be sued upon. For example, where the contractual limitation on the tort duty is partial, a tort action founded on the modified duty might lie. The tort duty as modified by the contractual agreement between the parties might be raised in a case where the limitation period for an action for breach of contract has expired but the limitation period for a tort action has not. If one says categorically, as we understand Iacobucci J. to say, that where the contract deals with a matter expressly, the right to sue in tort vanishes altogether, then the latter two possibilities vanish.

This is illustrated by consideration of the three situations that may arise when contract and tort are applied to the same wrong. The first class of case arises where the contract stipulates a more stringent obligation than the general law of tort would impose. In that case, the parties are hardly likely to sue in tort, since they could not recover in tort for the higher contractual duty. The vast majority of commercial transactions fall into this class. The right to sue in tort is not extinguished, however, and may remain important, as where suit in contract is barred by expiry of a limitation period.

The second class of case arises where the contract stipulates a lower duty than that which would be presumed by the law of tort in similar circumstances. This occurs when the parties by their contract indicate their intention that the usual liability imposed by the law of tort is not to bind them. The most common means by which such an intention is indicated is the inclusion of a clause of exemption or exclusion of liability in the contract. Generally, the duty imposed by the law of tort can be nullified only by clear terms. We do not rule out, however, the possibility that cases may arise in which merely inconsistent contract terms could negative or limit a duty in tort, an issue that may be left to a case in which it arises. The issue raises difficult policy considerations, viz., an assessment of the circumstances in which contracting parties should be permitted to agree to contractual duties that would subtract from their general obligations under the law of tort. These important questions are best left to a case in which the proper factual foundation is available, so as to provide an appropriate context for the decision. In the second class of case, as in the first, there is usually little point in suing in tort since the duty in tort and consequently any tort liability is limited by the specific limitation to which the parties have agreed. An exception might arise where the contract does not entirely negate tort liability (e.g., the exemption clause applies only above a certain amount) and the plaintiff wishes to sue in tort to avail itself of a more generous limitation period or some other procedural advantage offered by tort.

The third class of case arises where the duty in contract and the common law duty in tort are co-extensive. In this class of case, like the others, the plaintiff may seek to sue concurrently or alternatively in tort to secure some advantage peculiar to the law of tort, such as a more generous limitation period. The contract may expressly provide for a duty that is the same as that imposed by the common law. Or the contractual duty may be implied. The common calling cases, which have long permitted concurrent actions in contract and tort, generally fall into this class. There is a contract. But the obligation under that contract is typically defined by implied terms, i.e., by the courts. Thus there is no issue of private ordering as opposed to publicly imposed liability. Whether the action is styled in contract or tort, its source is an objective expectation, defined by the courts, of the appropriate obligation and the correlative right.

The case at bar, as we see it, falls into this third category of case. The contract, read as we have proposed, did not negate Hydro's common law duty not to negligently misrepresent that it would have the right-of-way cleared by others. Had Checo known the truth, it would have bid for a higher amount. That duty is not excluded by the contract, which confirmed Hydro's obligation to clear the right-of-way. Accordingly, Checo may sue in tort.

We conclude that actions in contract and tort may be concurrently pursued unless the parties by a valid contractual provision indicate that they intended otherwise. This excludes, of course, cases where the contractual limitation is invalid, as by fraud, mistake or unconscionability. Similarly, a contractual limitation may not apply where the tort is independent of the contract in the sense of falling outside the scope of the contract, as the example given in *Elder, Dempster & Co. v. Paterson, Zochonis & Co.*, [1924] A.C. 522 (H.L.), of the captain of a vessel falling asleep and starting a fire in relation to a claim for cargo damage.

The Express-Implied Distinction

Our colleague asserts that where the parties deal with a matter expressly in their contract, all right to sue in tort is lost. We have suggested, with great respect, that this proposition is unnecessarily Draconian. The converse of this proposition is that implied terms of contracts do not oust tort liability.

Although Iacobucci J. states . . . that he is leaving open the question of "Whether or not an implied term of a contract can define a duty of care in such a way that a plaintiff is confined to a remedy in contract", the distinction between implied and express terms figures in his discussion of the effect of contract terms on tort liability. For example, . . . our colleague states:

> The compromise position adopted by Le Dain J. was that any duty arising in tort will be concurrent with duties arising under the contract, *unless the duty which the plaintiff seeks to rely on in tort is also a duty defined by an express term of the contract.* [The emphasis is Iacobucci J.'s.]

It would seem to follow from this statement that concurrent duties in contract and tort would lie where the contract duty is defined by an *implied* term of the contract, but not where the term is express. In these circumstances, it is not amiss to consider the utility of the distinction between express and implied terms of the contract as a basis for determining when a contract term may affect tort liability.

In our view, using the express-implied distinction as a basis for determining whether there is a right to sue in tort poses a number of problems. The law has always treated express and implied contract terms as being equivalent in effect. Breach of an implied term is just as serious as breach of an express term. Moreover, it is difficult to distinguish between them in some cases. Implied terms may arise from custom, for example, or from the conduct of the parties. In some cases words and conduct intermingle. Why should parties who were so certain in their obligations that they did not take the trouble to spell them out find themselves able to sue in tort, while parties who put the same matters in writing cannot?

Nor is it evident to us that if parties to a contract choose to include an express term in the contract dealing with a particular duty relevant to the contract, they intended to oust the availability of tort remedies in respect of that duty. In such cases, the intention may more likely be:

(a) To make it clear that the parties understand particular contractual duties to exist as between them, rather than having the more uncertain situation of not knowing whether a court will imply a particular duty under the contract; and/or

(b) To prevent litigation (for breach of contract) in the event of disputes arising — the more certain the parties' respective rights and obligations (as is usually the case when those rights and obligations are set out in express contractual terms), the more likely it will be that disputes between the parties can be settled.

While the tort duty may be limited by the contractual terms so as to be no broader than the contract duty, there is no reason to suppose that merely by stipulating a duty in the contract, the parties intended to negate all possibility of suing in tort.

Indeed, a little further on in his reasons, our colleague appears to concede that the ouster of recourse to tort law must depend on more than the fact the contract has expressly dealt with the matter. He indicates . . . that whether the parties will be held to have intended to oust tort remedies in favour of contract remedies will depend on the context, including:

(a) whether the contract is commercial or non-commercial;

(b) whether the parties were of equal bargaining power;

(c) whether the court is of the view that to find such an intention will lead to an unjust result in the court action.

Thus the question of whether a concurrent action in tort lies would depend not only on whether the contract expressly deals with the matter, but also on the elastic distinctions between commercial and non-commercial contracts, the court's perception of relative bargaining power, and finally, whether the court sees the result as just or unjust. We do not agree that parties contracting in a commercial context should be presumed to be more desirous of ousting the availability of tort remedies than parties contracting in a non-commercial context. If there are particular commercial relationships in which the parties wish remedies for disputes between them to be in contract only, then they may be expected to indicate this intention by including an express clause in the contract waiving the right to sue in tort. As for equality of bargaining power and the court's view of whether the result would be just or unjust, we fear they would introduce too great a measure of uncertainty. Parties should be able to predict in advance whether their remedies are confined to contract or whether they can sue concurrently in tort and contract. Finally, it seems to us that Iacobucci J.'s test for determining when concurrent liability is precluded will be difficult to apply in situations where the express contractual term does not exactly overlap a tort duty. In the present case, the contractual term was identical to the negligent misrepresentation, but that is not often to be expected.

. . .

Summary

We conclude that neither principle, the authorities nor the needs of contracting parties, support the conclusion that dealing with a matter by an express contract term will, in itself, categorically exclude the right to sue in tort. The parties may by their contract limit the duty one owes to the other or waive the right to sue in tort. But subject to this, the right to sue concurrently in tort and contract remains.

In the case at bar, the contract did not limit the duty of care owed by Hydro to Checo. Nor did Checo waive its common law right to bring such tort actions as might be open to it. It follows that Checo was entitled to claim against Hydro in tort.

NOTES AND QUESTIONS

1. What is meant by the term "concurrency?" Why was it relevant in *BG Checo*?

2. Can a tort claim be barred by a prior or subsequent contract between the parties? What is the key question in determining the effect of a contract?

3. On what point did Iacobucci and Sopinka JJ. dissent from the majority? What policy considerations divided the court? Whose reasoning is the most persuasive?

4. In traditional contract law, an innocent misrepresentation that induces a contract may support rescission but not damages. Alternatively, the court might view the misrepresentation as the basis of a collateral contract, holding that the plaintiff entered into the main contract in return for the promise in the misrepresentation: see *Shanklin Pier Ltd. v. Detel Products Ltd.*, [1951] 2 K.B. 854. Finally, the court may hold that a misrepresentation which induces a contract is a term of the contract: see *Mendelssohn v. Normand Ltd.*, [1970] 1 Q.B. 177 (C.A.); and *Esso Petroleum Co. v. Mardon*, [1976] 2 All E.R. 5 (C.A.).

5. Concurrent liability in negligent misrepresentation and contract was recognized in England in *Esso Petroleum Co. v. Mardon, ibid.* However, the English courts remain more sympathetic to the contractual approach reflected in Iacobucci and Sopinka JJ.'s dissent in *BG Checo*: see for example *National Bank of Greece S.A. v. Pinios Shipping Co. (No. 1)* (1988), [1989] 1 All E.R. 213 (C.A.), rev'd on other grounds (1989), [1990] 1 A.C. 637 (H.L.); and *Pacific Associates Inc. v. Baxter*, [1989] 2 All E.R. 159 (C.A.).

6. For an authoritative discussion of damages in tort and contract, see the majority judgment in *BG Checo*.

7. For commentary on *BG Checo*, see Sim, "Negligent Misrepresentation in a Pre-Contractual Setting" (1993) 15 Adv. Q. 238; and Blom, "Contract and Tort – Negligent

Misstatement Inducing Contract – Concurrent Liability – Effect of Contractual Terms" (1994) 73 Can. Bar Rev. 243.

(b) PRE-CONTRACTUAL MISREPRESENTATIONS

QUEEN v. COGNOS INC.

(1993), 99 D.L.R. (4th) 626 (S.C.C.)

[The respondent, a computer software company based in Ottawa, advertised an accounting position. At the time, the appellant was a chartered accountant who held a well-paying and secure position with a company in Calgary. He applied for the position with the respondent company and was granted an interview. During the interview, a manager of the company made several representations regarding the nature of the employment opportunity on offer. He further stated that the advertised position was associated with the "Multiview project," a major project that would be developed over a two-year period, and that the prospects for employment after that time were very positive. He did not, however, reveal that funding for the proposed two-year project had not yet been secured.

The appellant accepted the respondent's offer of a contract and moved his family from Calgary to Ottawa. Shortly after the appellant's arrival in April 1983, however, the company decided to substantially reduce the scope of the proposed project. Eighteen months later, the respondent terminated the appellant's employment. The appellant sued the company, alleging that the respondent's manager had made negligent misrepresentations during the job interview and that he had suffered economic loss as a result.]

LA FOREST J. (L'HEUREUX-DUBÉ and GONTHIER JJ. concurring) — Subject to what I said in *BG Checo International Ltd. v. British Columbia Hydro and Power Authority* . . . I agree with Justices Iacobucci and McLachlin, and would dispose of the appeal in the manner proposed by them. Though Iacobucci repeats the essence of his analysis in *Checo*, the present case is not one of concurrency at all. It is sufficient for me to say that the tort here was independent of the contract and the liability was not limited by an exclusion clause in the contract.

[McLachlin J. substantially agreed with Iacobucci J., subject, *inter alia*, to her position in *BG Checo*.]

IACOBUCCI J. (SOPINKA J. concurring): — . . . Some have suggested that it is inappropriate to extend the application of *Hedley Byrne*, *supra*, to representations made by an employer to a prospective employee in the course of an interview because it places a heavy burden on employers. As will be apparent from my reasons herein, I disagree in principle with this view.

. . .

The required elements for a successful *Hedley Byrne* claim have been stated in many authorities, sometimes in varying forms. The decisions of this court cited above suggest five general requirements: (1) there must be a duty of care based on a "special relationship" between the representor and the representee; (2) the representation in question must be untrue, inaccurate, or misleading; (3) the representor must have acted negligently in making said misrepresentation; (4) the representee must have relied, in a reasonable manner, on said negligent misrepresentation; and (5) the reliance must have been detrimental to the representee in the sense that damages resulted. In the case at bar, the trial judge found that all elements were present and allowed the appellant's claim.

In particular, [the trial judge] found, as a fact, that the respondent's representative, Mr. Johnston, had misrepresented the nature and existence of the employment opportunity for which the appellant had applied, and that the appellant had relied to his detriment on those misrepresentations. These findings of fact were undisturbed by the Court of Appeal and . . . the respondent does not challenge them before this court. Thus, the second, fourth, and fifth requirements are not in question here.

The only issues before this court deal with the duty of care owed to the appellant in the circumstances of this case and the alleged breach of this duty (*i.e.*, the alleged negligence). The respondent concedes that a "special relationship" existed between itself (through its representative) and the appellant so as to give rise to a duty of care. However, it argues that this duty is negated by a disclaimer contained in the employment contract signed by the appellant more than two weeks after the interview. Furthermore, the respondent argues that any misrepresentations made during the hiring interview were not made in a negligent manner. For reasons that follow, it is my view that both submissions fail.

However, before turning to these issues, I intend to deal with a preliminary matter not directly raised in argument. This appeal was argued before this Court in close proximity to the case *BG Checo International Ltd. v. British Columbia Hydro and Power Authority*. . . That case involved circumstances somewhat similar to those in the present appeal in that it also dealt with a claim for damages based on an alleged negligent misrepresentation stemming from pre-contractual negotiations. Generally speaking, in *BG Checo* as in the case at bar, it was argued that certain representations made in a pre-contractual setting did not correspond with the post-agreement reality and were made in a negligent manner. In both cases, the defendants relied on the contract signed by the parties subsequent to the alleged negligent misrepresentation in order to bar the plaintiffs' claim in tort. As my conclusion in *BG Checo* is opposite from the one I take herein, I believe it is useful at the outset to explain why this case is clearly distinguishable from *BG Checo*. In doing so, my hope is to clarify some of the confusion which currently exists with respect to pre-contractual negligent misrepresentations.

B. *Preliminary observations on the effect of the employment agreement on this appeal*

There lies, in my view, [a] fundamental difference between the present appeal and *BG Checo, supra*. In the latter case, the alleged pre-contractual misrepresentation had been incorporated verbatim as an express term of the subsequent contract. As such, the common law duty of care relied on by the plaintiff in its tort action was co-extensive with a duty imposed on the defendant in contract by an express term of their agreement. Thus, it was my view that the plaintiff was barred from exercising a concurrent action in tort for the alleged breach of said duty, and this view was reinforced by the commercial context in which the transaction occurred. In the case at bar, however, there is no such concurrency. The employment agreement signed by the appellant . . . does not contain any express contractual obligation co-extensive with the duty of care the respondent is alleged to have breached. The provisions most relevant to this appeal (clauses 13 and 14) contain contractual duties clearly different from, not co-extensive with, the common law duty invoked by the appellant in his tort action.

Had the appellant's action been based on pre-contractual representations concerning the length of his involvement on the Multiview project or his "job security", as characterized by the Court of Appeal, the concurrency question might be resolved differently in light of the termination and reassignment provisions of the contract. However, it is clear that the appellant's claim was *not* that Mr. Johnston negligently misrepresented the amount of time he would be working on Multiview or the conditions under which his employment could be terminated. In other words, he did not argue that the respondent, through its representative, breached a common law duty of care by negligently misrepresenting his security of employment with Cognos. Rather, the appellant argued that Mr. Johnston negligently misrepresented the nature and existence of the employment opportunity being offered. It is the existence, or reality, of the job being interviewed for, not the extent of the appellant's involvement therein, which is at the heart of this tort action. A close reading of the employment agreement reveals that it contains no express provisions dealing with the respondent's obligations with respect to the nature and existence of the Multiview project. Accordingly, the ratio decidendi of my reasons in *BG Checo* is inapplicable to the present appeal. While both cases involve pre-contractual negligent misrepresentations, only *BG Checo* involved an impermissible concurrent liability in tort and contract; an exception to the general rule of concurrency. . . . The case at bar does not involve concurrency at all, let alone an exception thereto.

Having said this, it does not follow that the employment agreement is irrelevant to the disposition of this appeal. As I mentioned earlier, even if the tort claim is not barred altogether by the contract as in *BG Checo*, the duty or liability of the representor in tort may be limited or excluded by a term of the subsequent contract. In this respect, the respondent submits that the Court of Appeal was correct in finding that clauses 13 and 14 of the employment agreement represent a valid disclaimer for the misrepresentations allegedly made during the hiring interview, thereby negating any duty of care. I shall return to this issue [below]. I prefer to deal next with the questions of whether the respondent or its representative owed a duty of care to the appellant during the pre-employment interview and, if so, whether there was a breach of this duty in all the circumstances of this case.

C. *The duty of care owed to the appellant*

The respondent concedes that it itself and its representative, Mr. Johnston, owed a duty of care towards the six job applicants being interviewed, including the appellant, not to make negligent misrepresentations as to Cognos and the nature and permanence of the job being offered. In so doing, it accepts as correct the findings of both the trial judge and the Court of Appeal that there existed between the parties a "special relationship" within the meaning of *Hedley Byrne, supra.*

In my view, this concession is a sensible one. Without a doubt, when all the circumstances of this case are taken into account, the respondent and Mr. Johnston were under an obligation to exercise due diligence throughout the hiring interview with respect to the representations made to the appellant about Cognos and the nature and existence of the employment opportunity.

. . .

It was foreseeable that the appellant would be relying on the information given during the hiring interview in order to make his career decision. It was reasonable for the appellant to rely on said representations. There is nothing before this court that suggests that the respondent was not, at the time of the interview or shortly thereafter, assuming responsibility for what was being represented to the appellant by Mr. Johnston. As noted by the trial judge, Mr. Johnston discussed the . . . project in an unqualified manner, without making any relevant caveats. The alleged disclaimers of responsibility are provisions of a contract signed more than two weeks after the interview. . . [T]hese provisions are not valid disclaimers. They do not negate the duty of care owed to the appellant or prevent it from arising as in *Hedley Byrne*. . . It was foreseeable to the respondent and its representative that the appellant would sustain damages should the representations relied on prove to be false and negligently made. There was, undoubtedly, a relationship of proximity between the parties at all material times. Finally, it is not unreasonable to impose a duty of care in all the circumstances of this case; quite the contrary, it would be unreasonable *not* to impose such a duty. In short, therefore, there existed between the parties a "special relationship" at the time of the interview. The respondent and its representative Mr. Johnston were under a duty of care during the pre-employment interview to exercise reasonable care and diligence in making representations as to the employer and the employment opportunity being offered.

[Iacobucci J. then addressed the issue of standard of care. He held that the applicable standard was the reasonable person test, which does not require a person to guarantee the accuracy of statements but does require a person to exercise such care as is reasonable in the circumstances. On that basis, Iacobucci J. concluded that the trial judge had not erred in holding that the respondent's manager had acted carelessly in making statements during the appellant's job interview.]

NOTES AND QUESTIONS

1. How is the analysis of the duty of care issue in *Queen* different from that in the more recent decision in *Hercules Managements*? Why is the additional element of a special relationship required in negligent misrepresentation cases? How is a special relationship identified?

2. What was the difference between the contracts in *Queen* and *BG Checo*?

3. Having failed to attract majority support in *BG Checo*, why did Iacobucci J. persist in his analysis in *Queen*?

4. Why did the contractual disclaimer clause in *Queen* not have the effect of negating the duty of care in tort law? How does *Queen* differ from *Hedley Byrne* in that respect? See also *Intrawest Corp. v. No. 2002 Taurus Ventures Ltd.* (2006), 54 B.C.L.R. (4th) 173 (S.C.) in which the defendant sought to avoid liability for certain pre-contractual statements. The defendant failed, for three reasons: the contractual disclaimer did not expressly refer to pre-contractual statements, the statements were made well before the contract was signed, and the plaintiff had no opportunity to verify the accuracy of the statements. Compare with *Mariani v. Lemstra* (2004), 246 D.L.R. (4th) 489 (Ont. C.A.) where the court indicated that an express "entire agreement" clause in a standard-form agreement of purchase and sale, coupled with the buyer's opportunity to inspect the property, would exclude liability for negligent misrepresentation.

5. If the defendant in *Queen* did not want to be held liable with respect to its pre-contractual statements, how could it have effectively disclaimed responsibility?

6. For further reading on the relationship between tort and contract, see Blom, "Fictions and Frictions on the Interface Between Tort and Contract" in Burns & Lyon, eds., *Donoghue v. Stevenson and the Modern Law of Negligence* (1991) at 139-90; Blom, "Tort Recovery for Economic Loss and the Intersection Between Tort and Contract" (1996) 54 The Advocate 367; and Whittaker, "The Application of the 'Broad Principle of *Hedley Byrne*' as Between Parties to a Contract" (1997) 17 L.S. 169.

7. In *Queen* the court suggested that "only representations of existing facts, and not those relating to future occurrences, can give rise to actionable negligence." See also *Smith v. Union of Icelandic Fish Producers Ltd.* (2005), 238 N.S.R. (2d) 145 (C.A.); and *Conversions By Vantasy Ltd. v. General Motors of Canada Ltd.* (2006), 205 Man. R. (2d) 131 (C.A.). Should a forecast as to the future, or a prediction of events to come, ever lead to liability for negligent misrepresentation?

In *Ismail v. Treats Inc.* (2004), 220 N.S.R. (2d) 151 (S.C.) the court stated that "while the pro forma [financial] statements are future predictions, they contain the implicit assertion of fact that they are based on actual operational experience. That assertion may form the basis of a misrepresentation claim." Is this reasoning consistent with the above cases?

REVIEW PROBLEM

Alice, a resident of the City of Milbury, suffered a serious heart attack one morning while walking to work. Two nearby pedestrians wrapped Alice in warm clothing while a third went to call the police on the central emergency number.

The City had just installed a new central switchboard system designed to handle all calls for the police, fire department and ambulance services. Ideally, the calls would be handled by specially trained operators who would prioritize the emergency and dispatch the appropriate service. The pedestrian tried for over an hour to get through on the central emergency number, but to no avail. When he returned to the scene of the accident, he learned that Alice had just died.

A subsequent investigation indicated that the system's shortcomings were due to inferior equipment supplied by Sonar. Experts in the field indicated that the Sonar equipment was notoriously unreliable and that all those knowledgeable about this type of electrical equipment knew it.

The City had hired Panamar to design the new system, and all parties agree that its design was quite satisfactory. Panamar originally recommended that the equipment be purchased from a Japanese company.

After Panamar completed its contractual obligations and was paid, it kept in touch with the City. Ralph, Panamar's President, had called the appropriate City officials and offered, free of charge, to provide whatever advice he could. The City engineer responsible for implementing the plan took the President up on his gracious offer several times and was favourably impressed by his helpful suggestions.

As a result of labour unrest in Japan, the City fell behind schedule in installing the system. Ralph indicated that the City could get exactly the same equipment immediately for the same price from Sonar. When the City engineer mentioned the unreliability of the Sonar equipment, Ralph stated: "I may not be a certified expert, but rumours about Sonar are fuelled by foreign competitors playing on Canadians' sense of inferiority." Despite the trade reports to the contrary, Ralph stated that the Sonar equipment was as reliable as any produced in the world. Ralph had used Sonar's products in several jobs 15 years ago, but he had no experience with the new product lines in question and he failed to mention this to the City. The City ultimately took Ralph's advice and purchased $500,000 worth of Sonar equipment for its new system.

The equipment never functioned properly and complaints began to mount as the system continually broke down. Alice's death was the last straw. The City was forced to take out all the Sonar equipment and replace it at a cost of $600,000.

Discuss Panamar's liability to Alice's estate and to the City in negligent misrepresentation.

14

SPECIAL DUTIES OF CARE: RECOVERY OF PURE ECONOMIC LOSS IN NEGLIGENCE

1. Introduction
2. New Categories of Pure Economic Loss
3. Negligent Performance of a Service
4. Negligent Supply of Shoddy Goods or Structures
5. Relational Economic Loss

1. Introduction

As suggested in the previous chapter, liability for pure economic loss – economic loss that does not flow from personal injury or property damage – presents considerable difficulties. Most obviously, it raises the risk of indeterminate liability. Moreover, it extends legal protection to interests that most people would agree are less important than does liability for personal injury and property damage. The loss of a life and the destruction of a house, for example, warrant more attention than the mere loss of money. Given the scarcity of judicial resources, it may not be appropriate to use them on the resolution of disputes arising from the mere loss of money. Finally, it is often more efficient for pure economic losses to be borne by the victim. That party, typically a business entity, is usually better positioned to assess the prospect of such losses and to arrange insurance coverage beforehand.

Historically, such difficulties were generally resolved on the basis of a broad rule that excluded liability for such losses: see *Cattle v. Stockton Waterworks Co.* (1874), L.R. 10 Q.B. 453. More recently, however, the Supreme Court of Canada has moved to a more sophisticated, sensitive and liberal approach. In a series of decisions it has adopted a taxonomy developed by B. Feldthusen (see *Economic Negligence: The Recovery of Pure Economic Loss*, 4th ed. (2000)) that classifies pure economic loss claims into five categories:

1. negligent misrepresentation,
2. independent liability of statutory public authorities,
3. negligent performance of a service,
4. negligent supply of shoddy goods or structures, and
5. relational economic loss.

This classification is important insofar as it reveals the court's recognition that, while unified by the common theme of pure economic loss, the different categories of cases involve different policy considerations. The reasons for imposing or denying liability in one situation may not properly apply in another situation.

The five categories of pure economic loss cases will be addressed separately. The first category, negligent misrepresentation, was considered in the previous chapter. Policy considerations pertaining to the second category, liability of statutory public authorities, will be considered in Chapter 21. The bulk of this chapter will be devoted to: (i) the negligent performance of services, (ii) the supply of shoddy goods or structures, and (iii) relational economic loss.

NOTE

1. The issue of tort liability for pure economic loss has spawned a large amount of academic comment. See Feldthusen, "The Recovery of Pure Economic Loss in Canada: Proximity, Justice, Rationality, and Chaos" (1996) 24 Man. L.J. 1; Feldthusen, "Liability for Pure Economic Loss: Yes, But Why?" (1999) 28 U.W.A.L. Rev. 84; Cherniak & How, "Policy and Predictability: Pure Economic Loss in the Supreme Court of Canada" (1999) 31 C.B.L.J. 209; Klar, "Judicial Activism in Private Law" (2001) 80 Can. Bar Rev. 215; Blom, "Tort, Contract and the Allocation of Risk" in Beaulac, Pitel & Schulz, eds., *The Joy of Torts* (2003) 289; and Brown, "Still Crazy After All These Years: *Anns, Cooper v. Hobart* and Pure Economic Loss" (2003) 36 U.B.C.L. Rev. 159.

2. New Categories of Pure Economic Loss

It is important to understand that the categories of recoverable pure economic loss, like the categories of negligence generally, are not closed. It is open for the courts, from time to time, to recognize a duty of care in a new type of situation, outside the five categories mentioned above. In doing so, they will use the *Anns/Kamloops* test, as interpreted in *Cooper v. Hobart*, [2001] 3 S.C.R. 537. As you read through the next case, consider how you would now classify the policy factors that influenced Iacobucci and Major JJ. Do they properly fall under the first branch or the second branch of the test?

MARTEL BUILDING LTD. v. CANADA
(2000), 193 D.L.R. (4th) 1 (S.C.C.)

[The plaintiff leased a building to the defendant. When that lease was about to expire, the parties entered into negotiations for a renewal. The defendant led the plaintiff to believe that it would be amenable to renewing the lease on certain terms. However, when the plaintiff formally extended an offer on those terms, the defendant rejected the proposal and issued a call for tenders. In general terms, a call for tenders consists of an invitation to receive contractual offers, on a competitive basis, from several parties – in this case, building owners willing to lease space to the defendant. The defendant eventually accepted a tender from another party and therefore did not renew its lease with the plaintiff.

The plaintiff sued on several grounds. For present purposes, the relevant claim was that the defendant had breached a duty of care to negotiate in such a way as to avoid causing the plaintiff pure economic loss (the loss of the opportunity to renew the original lease). The defendant allegedly did so by, for example, repeatedly delaying matters, breaking appointments, ignoring requests, and failing to put the plaintiff into contact with the appropriate personnel.]

IACOBUCCI AND MAJOR JJ: This appeal calls for an extension of the tort of negligence to include a duty of care on parties during negotiations, during the preparation of calls for tender and during the evaluation of bids submitted in response to such calls. In each instance the respondent sought damages for pure economic loss.

. . .

Analysis

1. *Given that one owes a duty of care not to harm those who might foreseeably suffer damage, does a duty of care exist to that same group with respect to negotiations? Does the tort of negligence extend to damages for pure economic loss arising out of the conduct of pre-contractual negotiations?*

. . .

The appellant submitted that to extend the tort of negligence into the conduct of commercial negotiations would be an unnecessary and unsound invasion of the marketplace. It argued that this case involves business risks inherent in commercial negotiation, risks which should be borne by parties and not be re-allocated through the imposition of a duty of care.

A breach of a duty of care in negotiations would, in this case, result in the loss of an opportunity to negotiate a lease renewal. This is a claim for damages not accompanied by physical injury or property damage. What is left is a claim for pure economic loss. . . .

As a cause of action, claims concerning the recovery of economic loss are identical to any other claim in negligence in that the plaintiff must establish a duty, a breach, damage and causation. Nevertheless, as a result of the common law's historical treatment of economic loss, the threshold question of whether or not to recognize a duty of care receives added scrutiny relative to other claims in negligence.

An historical review of the common law treatment of recovery for economic loss has been undertaken by this Court on several occasions. . . . Rather than re-canvassing the jurisprudential genealogy reviewed in these cases, it is enough to say that the common law traditionally did not allow recovery of economic loss where a plaintiff had suffered neither physical harm nor property damage. . . .

Over time, the traditional rule was reconsidered. . . . [I]t has been recognized that in limited circumstances damages for economic loss absent physical or proprietary harm may be recovered. The circumstances in which such damages have been awarded to date are few. To a large extent, this caution derives from the same policy rationale that supported the traditional approach not to recognize the claim at all. First, economic interests are viewed as less compelling of protection than bodily security or proprietary interests. Second, an unbridled recognition of economic loss raises the spectre of indeterminate liability. Third, economic losses often arise in a commercial context, where they are often an inherent business risk best guarded against by the party on whom they fall through such means as insurance. Finally, allowing the recovery of economic loss through tort has been seen to encourage a multiplicity of inappropriate lawsuits. . . .

[Iacobucci and Major JJ. then referred to the five recognized categories of recovery for pure economic loss.]

The allegation of negligence in the conduct of negotiations does not fall within any of these classifications. Thus, Martel's claim is novel when weighed against the prior jurisprudence of this Court. That by itself should not preclude the claim. The question is whether the numbered categories ought to be enlarged or some other method identified to include a new head of economic loss. To answer this question it is useful to set out a framework for the recognition of new categories such as that advanced by Martel.

. . .

Canadian jurisprudence has consistently applied the flexible two-stage analysis of *Anns v. Merton London Borough Council*, [1978] A.C. 728 (H.L.), originally adopted in *Kamloops*, *supra*, in determining whether to extend a duty of care in a given case.

. . .

This analysis begins with the oft-repeated question: Was there a sufficiently close relationship between Martel and the Department so that, in the reasonable contemplation of the Department, carelessness on its part might cause damage to a party such as Martel with whom it negotiated?

. . .

So as to infuse the term "proximity" with greater meaning, the courts take into account a variety of factors in ascertaining whether the relationship between two parties gives rise to a prima facie duty of care.

. . .

It may be foreseeable that carelessness on the part of one negotiating party may cause an opposite negotiating party economic loss. Generally, negotiation is undertaken with a view to obtaining mutual economic gain. Given the bilateral nature of most negotiations, such gains are sometimes obtained at the other party's expense. Although negotiations often provide synergistic effects for all concerned, the prospect of causing deprivation by economic loss is implicit in the negotiating environment. The causal relationship in contractual negotiations is usually significant for a finding of proximity. In the circumstances of this appeal, the appellant's pre-existing contractual arrangement with Martel is an impressive indicator of proximity.

Both the pre-existing lease arrangement and the communications between the appellant and respondent here are indicators of proximity. That does not mean that any exchange loosely viewed as a negotiation will necessarily give rise to a proximate relationship. The expression of interest does not automatically create proximity absent some evidence of genuine and mutual contracting intent. We are satisfied that the parties in this appeal evidenced such an intent. The communications between the appellant and Martel disclose a readiness to arrive at an agreement despite the fact one was never reached.

We conclude that the circumstances of this case satisfy the first stage of *Anns* and raise a prima facie duty of care.

. . .

In the wake of a finding of proximity, the second question in *Anns* arises: Are there any policy considerations that serve to negative or limit (a) the scope of the prima facie duty of care (b) the class of persons to whom it is owed or (c) the damages to which a breach of it may give rise?

Notwithstanding our finding of proximity above, there are compelling policy reasons to conclude that one commercial party should not have to be mindful of another commercial party's legitimate interests in an arm's length negotiation.

. . .

The scope of indeterminate liability remains a significant concern underlying any analysis of whether to extend the sphere of recovery for economic loss. In this appeal, however, the inherent nature of negotiations in this case place definable limits on the ultimate extent of liability so that concerns of indeterminacy are not determinative in this appeal.

Here, the class of potential claimants is limited to those persons that the Department directly negotiated with.

. . .

In addition, although the quantum of damages arising out of failed negotiations may be quite high, it is limited by the nature of the transaction being negotiated. . . . Martel's claim is clearly restricted to the loss of an opportunity to conclude a 10-year lease renewal. While there are serious difficulties in valuing a lost opportunity, the extent of the loss has definable limits.

However, simply addressing indeterminacy does not represent the sole hurdle to extending a duty of care.

. . .

In light of the diverse array of factual circumstances that can fall under the moniker of pure economic loss, unique policy considerations may infuse the analysis of any given case. Indeed, notwithstanding the fact that indeterminacy does not rear its head sufficiently in this appeal, there are a number of ancillary policy considerations that necessitate precluding the extension of the tort of negligence into commercial negotiations. Even in the absence of any serious potential for indeterminate liability, these factors are sufficient to deny recovery notwithstanding the finding of proximity. What we have identified as ancillary policy considerations weighing against recovery are defined by the following five illustrations.

First, the very object of negotiation works against recovery. The primary goal of any economically rational actor engaged in commercial negotiation is to achieve the most advantageous financial bargain. As noted above, in the context of bilateral negotiation, such gains are realized at the expense of the other negotiating party. From an economic perspective, some authors describe negotiation as a zero-sum game involving a transference rather than loss of wealth.

. . .

Perhaps following the traditional view that, at least in some circumstances, economic losses are less worthy of protection than physical or proprietary harm, it has been noted that the absence of net harm on a social scale is a factor weighing against the extension of liability for pure economic loss. That is to say, negotiation merely transfers wealth between parties. Although one party may suffer, another often gains. Thus, as an economic whole, society is not worse off.

. . .

Second, . . . to extend a duty of care to pre contractual commercial negotiations could deter socially and economically useful conduct. The encouragement of economically efficient conduct can be a valid concern in favour of the extension of liability for pure economic loss. . . . Equally, in other circumstances, this goal may be a valid rationale against extending liability.

In essence, Martel claims that the appellant was negligent in not providing it with adequate information concerning the appellant's bargaining position or its readiness to conclude a renewal. The appellant's conduct in negotiating with Martel might be construed as "hard bargaining". The Department's agents displayed casual contempt towards Martel and its personnel as illustrated by broken appointments and general disregard of the minimal courtesy Martel could have reasonably expected. However indifferent the agents of the Department appear from the record, that by itself does not create a cause of action. Doubtless, the appellant's ability to assume such a position in relation to Martel was due to its dominant position in the Ottawa leasing market. The foregoing all point to the advantages enjoyed by the Crown, but do not point to liability.

In many if not most commercial negotiations, an advantageous bargaining position is derived from the industrious generation of information not possessed by the opposite party as opposed to its market position as here. Helpful information is often a by-product of one party expending resources on due diligence, research or other information gathering activities. It is apparent that successful negotiating is the product of that kind of industry.

It would defeat the essence of negotiation and hobble the marketplace to extend a duty of care to the conduct of negotiations, and to label a party's failure to disclose its bottom line, its motives or its final position as negligent. Such a conclusion would of necessity force the disclosure of privately acquired information and the dissipation of any competitive advantage derived from it, all of which is incompatible with the activity of negotiating and bargaining.

Third, to impose a duty in the circumstances of this appeal could interject tort law as after-the-fact insurance against failures to act with due diligence or to hedge the risk of failed negotiations through the pursuit of alternative strategies or opportunities. . . .

Notwithstanding Martel's hope that the negotiations would produce a favourable outcome, it could at any point have concluded that the Department was not serious or interested in concluding a renewal of the Martel Building lease, but simply delaying for an undisclosed reason and seeking other potential landlords. While Martel may have suffered from its innocence and optimism, at least some of the responsibility for the delays in communication evident in this appeal can be attributed to it. The retention of self-vigilance is a necessary ingredient of commerce.

Fourth, to extend the tort of negligence into the conduct of commercial negotiations would introduce the courts to a significant regulatory function, scrutinizing the minutiae of pre-contractual conduct. It is undesirable to place further scrutiny upon commercial parties when other causes of action already provide remedies for many forms of conduct. Notably, the doctrines of undue influence, economic duress and unconscionability provide redress against bargains obtained as a result of improper negotiation. As well, negligent misrepresentation, fraud and the tort of deceit cover many aspects of negotiation which do not culminate in an agreement.

A concluding but not conclusive fifth consideration is the extent to which needless litigation should be discouraged. To extend negligence into the conduct of negotiations could encourage a multiplicity of lawsuits. Given the number of negotiations that do not culminate in agreement, the potential for increased litigation in place of allowing market forces to operate seems obvious.

For these reasons we are of the opinion that, in the circumstances of this case, any prima facie duty is significantly outweighed by the deleterious effects that would be occasioned through an extension of a duty of care into the conduct of negotiations. We conclude then that, as a general proposition, no duty of care arises in conducting negotiations. While there may well be a set of circumstances in which a duty of care may be found, it has not yet arisen.

NOTES AND QUESTIONS

1. On what basis did Iacobucci and Major JJ. reject the recognition of a duty of care? Was the plaintiff's loss reasonably foreseeable? Was there a relationship of sufficient proximity between the parties? What policy considerations influenced the court? Do you agree with the court's decision?

2. Within the law of contract, the tendering process involves an interesting series of events. *Martel* was a typical case.

By issuing the call for tenders after negotiations with the plaintiff broke down, the defendant did two things. First, it issued an "invitation to treat" that indicated its willingness to receive contractual offers from interested parties. In doing so, the defendant incurred no obligations. It merely indicated that it might, in the future, accept one of the tenders and thereby enter into a new lease with the winning bidder. That lease would constitute what is known as "Contract B." Second, however, by issuing the call for tenders, the defendant also extended its own offer, to every potential tenderer, to enter into something called "Contract A." The purpose of "Contract A" is to ensure fairness in the tender process. For instance, it would be unfair, or at least disruptive, if, while the defendant was considering the various tenders that it had received, one of the bidders withdrew its offer. Likewise, it would be unfair if the defendant exercised its choice among the various tenders on the basis of some illegitimate or capricious criterion. "Contract A" therefore typically imposes obligations on both parties to abide by a certain set of rules. A different "Contract A" is created every time that a party submits a tender. Consequently, in *Martel*, there were as many instances of "Contract A" as there were bidders. There was, in contrast, only one "Contract B," and because the defendant had chosen an offer from another tender, that contract did not involve the plaintiff.

In *Martel*, the plaintiff's primary claim was that the defendant breached a duty of care pertaining to the negotiation process. That action failed. However, the plaintiff also brought two other claims in negligence that pertained to the tendering process.

First, the plaintiff argued that it had suffered a loss because the defendant had breached a duty of care when it carelessly drafted its call for tenders. In that regard, the plaintiff stressed that it had made certain assumptions based on its prior negotiations with the defendant. The Supreme Court of Canada rejected that argument. It held that there was no duty of care:

> Assuming without deciding that sufficient proximity existed between the parties, any prima facie duty of care would be negated by policy considerations. Indeed, considerations unique to the tendering process nullify any duty of care sought by Martel. First and foremost, we agree with the Department that it would call into question the integrity of the tender process if, by reason of a past relationship with, or special knowledge of, a potential bidder, there could be an enforceable obligation to take the interests of that particular bidder into account. . .
>
> A party calling for tenders has the discretion to set out its own specifications and requirements. This includes the discretion to change its mind with respect to the terms or preferences that were discussed in the course of non-committal negotiations. Tender

> requirements are not negotiable. To decide otherwise would in fact force the party making the call for tenders to continue in its negotiations with one potential bidder even after those negotiations have proven unfruitful.

Second, the plaintiff claimed that the defendant had breached a duty of care in tort law by failing to fairly evaluate the bids that it had received. Having previously found that the defendant had not breached any of the contractual obligations that it owed to the plaintiff under "Contract A," the Supreme Court of Canada rejected the negligence argument as well:

> [W]e acknowledge that . . . an action in tort may lie notwithstanding the existence of a contract. . . . However, in the circumstances of this case, regardless of whether there exists a coextensive duty in tort to treat tenderers fairly and equally in evaluating the bids, Martel's tort claim cannot succeed for the same reasons that a contractual claim would fail. The duty of care alleged in tort in the case at bar is the same as the duty which is implied as a term of Contract A; this is not a case where Martel is suing in tort to avail itself of a more generous limitation period, or some other advantage offered only by tort law.

3. For a discussion of *Martel*, see Rafferty, "Developments in Contract and Tort Law: The 2000-2001 Term" (2001) 15 S.C.L.R. (2d) 173; and Wallace, "Tender Call Obligations in Canada" (2001) 117 L.Q.R. 351.

4. The Supreme Court of Canada was unwilling to recognize a new category of recoverable pure economic loss in *Martel*, as were the appellate courts in *Blacklaws v. 470433 Alberta Ltd.* (2000), 261 A.R. 28 (C.A.); *Fraser v. Westminer Canada Ltd.* (2003), 215 N.S.R. (2d) 377 (C.A.); and *Esser v. Brown* (2004), 242 D.L.R. (4th) 112 (B.C.C.A.). However, the prospect has received more favourable treatment in some other cases. In *Haskett v. Equifax Canada Inc.* (2003), 63 O.R. (3d) 577 (C.A.), additional reasons at 2003 CarswellOnt 1295 (C.A.), the plaintiff was discharged from bankruptcy in 1996. Nevertheless, despite being current on all of his debts and annually earning more than $75,000, he was consistently denied commercial credit. He claimed that his poor credit rating was caused by an inaccurate report that the defendant company, a credit reporting agency, had carelessly prepared and made available to potential creditors. The plaintiff sued in negligence for his alleged losses. The defendant brought a motion to strike out the claim on the basis that it did not disclose a cause of action. More specifically, the defendant argued that since the plaintiff's claim pertained to a pure economic loss, and since it did not fit within any of the five existing categories, it must fail. The judge who heard the motion agreed, but that decision was overturned on appeal. The Court of Appeal for Ontario held that the plaintiff's claim should proceed to trial because either (i) the situation fell by analogy into the established category of negligent misrepresentation, or (ii) it was possible for the trial judge to recognize a new category of recoverable pure economic loss. See also *Clark v. Scotiabank* (2004), 25 C.C.L.T. (3d) 109 (Ont. S.C.J.); and *Neil v. Equifax Canada Inc.* (2005), 271 Sask. R. 160 (Prov. Ct.), reversed (2006), 277 Sask. R. 275 (Q.B.).

5. Because the court can create new categories, there may be less concern to fit any particular case into an existing category. In *Haskett* the court only briefly discussed whether the case could fit into the negligent misrepresentation category. In *Lowe v.*

Guarantee Co. of North America (2005), 200 O.A.C. 236 (C.A.), additional reasons at (2005), 23 M.V.R. (5th) 161 (Ont. C.A.) the plaintiffs were examined by the defendant, a Designated Assessment Centre under Ontario's scheme for no-fault auto accident benefits. The plaintiffs were denied benefits and as a result sued the defendant in negligence. Rather than consider the case as involving the negligent performance of a service, the court relied on the more general test in *Cooper*. Could the test in *Cooper* lead to a breakdown of the categories? Should the categories be maintained? See *Heinicke v. Cooper Rankin Ltd.*, [2007] 2 W.W.R. 112 (Man. Q.B.).

6. In *Customs and Excise Commissioners v. Barclays Bank plc.*, [2006] 4 All E.R. 256 (H.L.) the novel issue was whether a third party, such as a bank, that holds the assets of a defendant whose assets have been frozen by court order, and that carelessly allows the defendant to transfer the assets despite the order, owes a duty of care to the plaintiff who obtained the order. Lord Bingham noted:

> the authorities disclose three tests which have been used in deciding whether a defendant sued as causing pure economic loss to a claimant owed him a duty of care in tort. The first is whether the defendant assumed responsibility for what he said and did vis-à-vis the claimant, or is to be treated by the law as having done so. The second is commonly known as the threefold test: whether loss to the claimant was a reasonably foreseeable consequence of what the defendant did or failed to do; whether the relationship between the parties was one of sufficient proximity; and whether in all the circumstances it is fair, just and reasonable to impose a duty of care on the defendant towards the claimant. . . Third is the incremental test, based on the observation of Brennan J in *Sutherland Shire Council v Heyman* (1985) 60 ALR 1 at 43-44, (1985) 157 CLR 424 at 481, approved by Lord Bridge of Harwich in *Caparo Industries plc v Dickman* [1990] 1 All ER 568 at 576, [1990] 2 AC 605 at 618, that: "It is preferable in my view, that the law should develop novel categories of negligence incrementally and by analogy with established categories, rather than by a massive extension of a prima facie duty of care restrained only by indefinable 'considerations which ought to negative, or to reduce or limit the scope of the duty or the class of person to whom it is owed'."

The House of Lords refused to impose a duty of care. In response to this diversity of tests in English law, in *United Project Consultants Pte Ltd. v. Leong Kwok Onn*, [2005] 4 S.L.R. 214 (C.A.) the Singapore Court of Appeal stated:

> While the learned authors of *Clerk & Lindsell on Torts* (Sweet & Maxwell, 18th Ed, 2000) may find this approach useful in that each test may be used to check the provisional conclusion reached by the application of the other tests, we found ourselves unable to agree with this state of affairs. The laws of any country must be sufficiently clear and capable of guiding parties in the regulation of their affairs. While a measure of uncertainty will always be present, for that is the consequence of any jurisdiction that founds its laws upon previously decided cases, it would be undesirable for a court to refrain from coming down in favour of any particular test when faced with various alternative approaches. . .

See on this uncertainty Mitchell & Mitchell, "Negligence Liability for Pure Economic Loss" (2005) 121 L.Q.R. 194; and Barker, "Wielding Occam's Razor: Pruning Strategies for Economic Loss" (2006) 26 O.J.L.S. 289.

Consider the extent to which the cases in this chapter make use of one or more of the three tests outlined by Lord Bingham, and consider also whether the Canadian approach is "sufficiently clear." Should there be only one test for recovery of pure economic loss?

7. In *Young v. Bella*, [2006] 1 S.C.R. 108 the plaintiff was negligently reported as a potential child abuser by the defendant university. In finding that the defendant owed the plaintiff a duty of care the court applied the analysis from *Martel* and *Cooper*. However, the plaintiff's claim was for both personal injury and economic loss, and the court did not analyze the case as one about pure economic loss. If the plaintiff had not suffered anxiety, embarrassment, insomnia, paranoia and depression as a result of the allegations against her, and had only suffered economic loss due to an inability to find work, how should the duty issue have been analyzed?

3. Negligent Performance of a Service

There are no recent decisions by the Supreme Court of Canada pertaining to liability for pure economic loss caused by the negligent performance of a service. As the following extract reveals, however, the applicable principles closely mirror the rules that govern liability for negligent misrepresentations. That is hardly surprising – in many situations, there is a fine line between services and representations. As one commentator notes, "Advice is a particular form of business service, and in many representation cases the negligence lies in the performance of an underlying service rather than in the representation itself": Feldthusen, "Economic Loss in the Supreme Court of Canada: Yesterday and Tomorrow" (1991) 17 C.B.L.J. 356 at 366. For an example of a case on the borderline see *Edgeworth Construction Ltd. v. N.D. Lea & Associates Ltd.*, [1993] 3 S.C.R. 206.

B.D.C. LTD. v. HOFSTRAND FARMS LTD.

(1986), 26 D.L.R. (4th) 1 (S.C.C.)

[The appellant, a courier company, contracted with the Province of British Columbia to deliver an envelope from a government office in Victoria to the Land Registry Office in Prince George. Unknown to the appellant, the envelope contained a Crown grant in favour of the respondent. The respondent was anxious for the grant to be registered before December 31, 1976: if it was not, the respondent would lose the ability to bind a third party to a contract for the sale of certain land. The appellant delivered the envelope late, with the result that the third party refused to complete the contemplated contract with the respondent. The respondent accordingly suffered an economic loss.

The respondent sued the appellant. The trial judge dismissed the claim on the basis that the courier company was unaware of the envelope's contents and was not informed of the need for timely delivery. The Court of Appeal came to the opposite conclusion. The courier company appealed to the Supreme Court of Canada.]

ESTEY J.:

[Estey J. reviewed the two-stage test that Lord Wilberforce developed in *Anns v. Merton London Borough Council*, [1978] A.C. 728, regarding the recognition of a duty of care.]

Despite this expansion of the principles governing tort liability, however, the courts have remained conscious throughout of the need for reasonable limitations. Nowhere is this need more urgent than in cases involving purely economic losses, many of which, in the words of Cardozo C.J. in *Ultramares Corp. v. Touche*, 255 N.Y. 170 (1931), may involve the possibility of liability "in an indeterminate amount for an indeterminate time to an indeterminate class."

There are various ways of circumscribing, in pure economic loss cases, what otherwise might be an unending chain of liability in an incalculable amount. As Lord Pearce said in *Hedley Byrne*, at p. 615:

> How wide the sphere of the duty of care in negligence is to be laid depends ultimately on the courts' assessment of the demands of society for protection from the carelessness of others.

. . .

Application of the two tests laid out in *Anns* is sufficient to dispose of this appeal. The first test to be met is that there be shown to exist a relationship of proximity or neighbourhood "such that in a reasonable contemplation" of the actor, his carelessness may likely damage the plaintiff. The second test, once the first has been met, is whether there are present any circumstances which would negate or reduce (a) the scope of the duty, or (b) the class of persons to whom such a duty is owed, or (c) the damage seen in law to flow from breach of the duty.

. . .

On the facts as revealed by the evidence before the Court in this appeal, the appellant courier had no knowledge of the existence of the respondent, nor, because of the Crown practice of not disclosing the nature of the documents being forwarded, could it reasonably have known of the existence of a class of persons whose interests depended upon timely transmission of the envelope. There was, therefore, no actual or constructive knowledge in the courier that the rights of a third party could in any way be affected by the transmission or lack of transmission of the envelope in question. If a person in the position of the respondent is included in a class considered to be reasonably within the contemplation of the appellant, there is no logical point of breaking off so as to put a reasonable practical limitation on the courier's range of liability. It is a stretching of concept to conclude that anyone who might conceivably be affected by a failure by the Province of British Columbia to register a Crown grant within the calendar year, constitutes a "limited class", the existence of which is known to a courier employed to deliver the Crown grant to a registry office. In the words of Lord Reid in *Hedley Byrne*, *supra*, ". . . it would be going very far to say that [the defendant] owes a duty to every ultimate 'consumer' . . . ."

Another aspect of proximity which was stressed in *Hedley Byrne*, *supra*, . . . is reliance by the plaintiff upon the undertaking or representation made by the defendant.

. . .

What was the reliance here by the respondent? There was none. The respondent was, by the time of the appellant's engagement by the Crown, in a position of risk through no act of its own. The situation of risk, in which a delay would be fatal to the respondent's interests, was created by the terms of the respondent's contract with the third party, in conjunction with the Crown's refusal to allow a representative of the respondent to carry the documents to Prince George himself. There was no assumption of risk in reliance upon the appellant's undertaking to deliver the documents. The respondent did not rely on the appellant in any way prior to the creation of this risk. The respondent did not permit the engagement of the appellant or reject the idea of engaging another courier by reason of any representation made by the appellant. Nor was the decision not to use the facilities of the Post Office motivated by any act or statement by the appellant.

In sum, the requirements of proximity contained in the principles enunciated in *Hedley Byrne*, *supra*, and confirmed in *Anns*, *supra*, are not met on the facts of this appeal. As I have concluded that the respondent did not come within a limited class in the reasonable contemplation of a person in the position of the appellant, it is unnecessary to proceed to the second stage or test set out by Lord Wilberforce in *Anns*, *supra*.

JAMES v. BRITISH COLUMBIA

(2005), 38 B.C.L.R. (4th) 263 (C.A.)

[The plaintiff's employer held a tree farm licence from the province of British Columbia which contained a provision that would have prevented the employer's sawmill from being closed by the employer without the approval of the Minister of Forests. On a renewal of the license, the Minister inadvertently omitted the protective clause and the employer later closed the mill. The plaintiff launched a class action against the government, alleging that its negligence had caused him and others similarly situated to suffer a loss of employment income. The government alleged that the claim was unfounded in law.]

ESSON J.A.: . . .

The Crown's submission that the plaintiff cannot succeed without pleading and proving "detrimental reliance" finds support in some cases and some academic writing but, with respect, appears to be based on a misapprehension of the extent of the "new law" propounded in *Hedley Byrne & Co. v. Heller & Partners Ltd.* (1963), [1964] A.C. 465 (U.K. H.L.). Because that case overruled the longstanding rule that there could be no recovery in tort for pure economic loss, and because it was held that detrimental reliance was an essential element of the cause of action, it seems to have been assumed by some that the requirement of proving detrimental reliance applies to all actions seeking recovery of damages for pure economic loss.

That requirement, however, was "old law". It flowed, not from the decision to change the law with respect to claims for pecuniary loss, but from the fact that *Hedley Byrne* was a claim in misrepresentation. In such an action, it was always incumbent upon the plaintiff to plead and prove reliance upon the false representation. With respect to that issue, there is no logical reason to distinguish between fraudulent misrepresentation and negligent misrepresentation. In either case, proof of reliance is essential to establish causation.

On the facts alleged here, the causal relationship established by reliance in a misrepresentation case is arguably covered by the finding of foreseeability and proximity. The essential feature of each concept is the "something more" which the Supreme Court, in *Cooper*, held must be demonstrated in order to establish that the plaintiff and the defendant were in a sufficiently close relationship. . . .

In this case, it would be unrealistic to impose upon the plaintiffs a burden to establish detrimental reliance. That is not their case. However, the facts may demonstrate a different form of reliance. The employees can be said to have relied upon the Minister to exercise reasonable care to retain Clause 7 in the licence unless and until he reached a decision on policy grounds to remove it. That view of the matter can be inferred from the facts alleged. It does not support the view that the law requires these plaintiffs to prove detrimental reliance.

Perhaps the best known cases in the negligent service category are those brought by a disappointed beneficiary. The earliest such case was the decision of Mr. Justice Aikins (later J.A.) in *Whittingham v. Crease & Co.* (1978), 88 D.L.R. (3d) 353. . .

It is regrettable that the decision of Aikins J., which exhibited the thorough and careful reasoning characteristic of the decisions of that learned judge, has been ignored for so long. To return to the present issue, I would adopt his analysis of the relationship between reliance and liability in cases of this kind, which is the clearest exposition of the issue which has come to my attention. I quote from pp. 373-74:

> The facts in the present case differ in one particular and troublesome aspect from those in the general run of cases in which *Hedley Byrne* has been successfully invoked. I have not been referred to a case, nor have I been able to find one, in which the principle of *Hedley Byrne* has been applied where the plaintiff had not acted on the strength of the representation made by the defendant and it was the plaintiff's own act which was the *immediate* cause of the loss.
>
> In this case the plaintiff has suffered a loss but without his having done anything in reliance on the implied representation made by [the solicitor]. In my opinion there are two reasons, linked to each other, which enable the plaintiff to succeed in this case, notwithstanding that he remained passive and did nothing, relying on [the solicitor's] implied representation. First, it was unnecessary for the plaintiff to act at all on the implied representation in order to attract the loss which he has suffered; second, [the solicitor] could reasonably foresee that if he, in the performance of his duty, failed to see to it that the will was properly witnessed, then that neglect would cause the very loss the plaintiff has suffered, without the plaintiff doing anything at all. Granted that there was an implied duty on the part of [the solicitor] to the plaintiff and that the plaintiff relied on [the solicitor] fulfilling that duty, it seems to me on principle that it is immaterial that the plaintiff himself did nothing in reliance on the implied representation made by [the solicitor] which brought about his loss. This is so because the negligence of the solicitor caused the loss without there having to be any intervening act by the plaintiff to perfect the chain of causation. . . .

In the reasons of Megarry V.-C. in *Ross v. Caunters* [[1979] 3 All E.R. 580 (Ch.)] and in the speeches of the majority in *White v. Jones* [[1995] 2 A.C. 207], the absence of reliance was held not to preclude recovery because its place was taken by the voluntary assumption of responsibility by the solicitor. I agree with the chambers judge that that approach may be properly applicable to the position of the Minister in this case.

NOTES AND QUESTIONS

1. While the court refused to recognize a duty of care in *B.D.C.*, it did outline the situations in which a duty would be recognized with respect to pure economic losses resulting from the careless provision of services. Summarize the relevant rules.

2. As mentioned in *James*, the issue of liability for pure economic loss resulting from negligent services commonly arises in the context of carelessly prepared wills.

Although the Supreme Court of Canada has yet to resolve the issue, it is generally accepted that a solicitor may be held liable to a disappointed beneficiary who is deprived of a bequest because of the lawyer's negligence. See *Whittingham v. Crease & Co.* (1978), 88 D.L.R. (3d) 353 (B.C.S.C.); *Ross v. Caunters*, [1979] 3 All E.R. 580 (Ch.); *Gartside v. Sheffield, Young & Ellis*, [1983] N.Z.L.R. 37 (C.A.); *White v. Jones*, [1995] 2 A.C. 207 (H.L.); *Hill v. Van Erp* (1997), 142 A.L.R. 687 (H.C.A.); *Wilhelm v. Hickson* (2000), 189 Sask. R. 71 (C.A.); and *Hall v. Bennett Estate* (2003), 64 O.R. (3d) 191 (C.A.). See also McJannet, "*Wilhelm v. Hickson*: The Canadian Tort Approach to the Disappointed Beneficiary and the Negligent Solicitor" (2001) 64 Sask. L.R. 113; and Benson, "Should *White v Jones* Represent Canadian Law: A Return to First Principles" in Neyers, Chamberlain & Pitel, eds., *Emerging Issues in Tort Law* (2007), ch. 6.

In the absence of any contractual relationship between the solicitor and the disappointed beneficiary, and perhaps in the absence of any reliance by the latter, is there any convincing reason to impose liability in such circumstances? Should the plaintiff essentially be entitled to the defendant's services without paying for them? See Klar, "Downsizing Torts" in Mullany & Linden, eds., *Torts Tomorrow: A Tribute to John Fleming* (1998), ch. 16.

3. Is the analysis in *James* consistent with *B.D.C.*? Should the courts adopt an "assumption of responsibility" test rather than focusing on reliance by the plaintiff?

4. In *Hughes v. Sunbeam Corp. (Canada) Ltd.* (2002), 61 O.R. (3d) 433 (C.A.) the plaintiffs sued the Underwriters' Laboratories of Canada for negligently endorsing a smoke detector. ULC was neither a statutory regulator nor an institution akin to a statutory regulator. It was a private corporation which undertook to examine and certify the safety of products. The Court of Appeal, relying on *Cooper*, reasoned that no duty was owed by ULC to the plaintiffs. The service offered by ULC was meant to provide a benefit to the public as a whole by encouraging manufacturers to ensure that their products met certain standards. Further, the plaintiffs had not paid ULC for the service. Do you agree with this reasoning?

5. If a doctor negligently fails to perform an abortion and the baby is born, and the biological father is compelled to pay child support to the mother, should the father be able to sue the doctor? Is this a claim for pure economic loss resulting from the negligent performance of a service, or should it be characterized differently? See *Freeman v. Sutter* (1996), 110 Man. R. (2d) 23 (C.A.).

4. Negligent Supply of Shoddy Goods or Structures

Liability clearly will lie in tort with respect to personal injuries and property damage that the plaintiff suffers as a result of the defendant's supply of shoddy goods or structures. Indeed, the law on products liability is a significant part of negligence law: see Linden & Feldthusen, *Canadian Tort Law*, 8th ed. (2006), ch. 16. The defendant will also be held liable in breach of contract for pure economic losses that the plaintiff suffers if the plaintiff is able to establish the requisite agreement. Problems arise, however, if the plaintiff suffers pure economic losses as a result of the defendant's carelessness but is unable to establish privity of contract. Historically, such losses were generally not recoverable. More recently, however, the Supreme Court of Canada has adopted a more liberal approach.

WINNIPEG CONDOMINIUM CORP. NO. 36 v. BIRD CONSTRUCTION CO.

(1995), 121 D.L.R. (4th) 193 (S.C.C.)

[A land developer contracted with the respondent to construct an apartment building. Some years later, the building was converted into a condominium when the appellant became the registered owner of the land and building. In 1982, the appellant's directors became concerned about the masonry work on the exterior of the building. They retained architects and a firm of consulting engineers to inspect the building. The architects and engineers offered the opinion that the building was structurally sound. In 1989, a section of the exterior cladding fell from the ninth storey of the building. The appellant had further inspections undertaken which revealed structural defects in the masonry work. Following these inspections, the entire cladding was replaced at the appellant's expense.

The appellant brought an action in negligence against several parties, including the respondent. The statement of claim alleged inadequacies in design and workmanship, without assigning specific blame to one defendant or another. The respondent moved for summary judgment and to strike out the claim as disclosing no reasonable cause of action. Both motions were dismissed. The respondent appealed to the Manitoba Court of Appeal. The appeal was dismissed with respect to the motion for summary judgment but allowed with respect to the motion to strike out, and the statement of claim was therefore struck out as against the respondent. The appellant appealed to the Supreme Court of Canada.]

LA FOREST J. [for the court] — May a general contractor responsible for the construction of a building be held tortiously liable for negligence to a subsequent purchaser of the building, who is not in contractual privity with the contractor, for the cost of repairing defects in the building arising out of negligence in its construction?

. . .

Analysis

This case gives this Court the opportunity once again to address the question of recoverability in tort for economic loss. In *Norsk, supra*, at p. 1049, I made reference to an article by Professor Feldthusen in which he outlined five different categories of cases where the question of recoverability in tort for economic loss has arisen ("Economic Loss in the Supreme Court of Canada: Yesterday and Tomorrow" (1990-91), 17 C.B.L.J. 356, at pp. 357-58), namely:

1. The Independent Liability of Statutory Public Authorities;
2. Negligent Misrepresentation;
3. Negligent Performance of a Service;
4. Negligent Supply of Shoddy Goods or Structures;
5. Relational Economic Loss.

I stressed in *Norsk* that the question of recoverability for economic loss must be approached with reference to the unique and distinct policy issues raised in each of these categories. That is because ultimately the issues concerning recovery for economic loss are concerned with determining the proper ambit of the law of tort, an exercise that must take account of the various situations where that question may arise. This case raises issues different from that in *Norsk*, which fell within the fifth category. The present case, which involves the alleged negligent construction of a building, falls partially within the fourth category, although subject to an important *caveat*. The negligently supplied structure in this case was not merely shoddy; it was dangerous. In my view, this is important because the degree of danger to persons and other property created by the negligent construction of a building is a cornerstone of the policy analysis that must take place in determining whether the cost of repair of the building is recoverable in tort. As I will attempt to show, a distinction can be drawn on a policy level between "dangerous" defects in buildings and merely "shoddy" construction in buildings and that, at least with respect to dangerous defects, compelling policy reasons exist for the imposition upon contractors of tortious liability for the cost of repair of these defects.

Traditionally, the courts have characterized the costs incurred by a plaintiff in repairing a defective chattel or building as "economic loss" on the grounds that costs of those repairs do not arise from injury to persons or damage to property apart from the defective chattel or building itself; see *Rivtow Marine Ltd. v. Washington Iron Works*, [1974] S.C.R. 1189, at p. 1207. For my part, I would find it more congenial to deal directly with the policy considerations underlying that classification. . . . However, I am content to deal with the issues in the terms in which the arguments were formulated. Adopting this traditional characterization as a convenient starting point for my analysis, I observe that the losses claimed by the Condominium Corporation in the present case fall quite clearly under the category of economic loss. In their statement of claim, the Condominium Corporation claim damages in excess of $1.5 million from the respondent Bird, the subcontractor Kornovski & Keller and the architects Smith Carter, representing the cost of repairing the building subsequent to the collapse of the exterior cladding on May 8, 1989. The Condominium Corporation is not claiming that anyone was injured by the collapsing exterior cladding or that the collapsing cladding damaged any of its other property. Rather, its claim is simply for the cost of repairing the allegedly defective masonry and putting the exterior of the building back into safe working condition.

. . .

In my view, where a contractor (or any other person) is negligent in planning or constructing a building, and where that building is found to contain defects resulting from that negligence which pose a real and substantial danger to the occupants of the building, the reasonable cost of repairing the defects and putting the building back into a non-dangerous state are recoverable in tort by the occupants. The underlying rationale for this conclusion is that a person who participates in the construction of a large and permanent structure which, if negligently constructed, has the capacity to cause serious damage to other persons and property in the community, should be held to a reasonable standard of care.

. . .

Was There a Sufficiently Close Relationship Between the Parties so that, in the Reasonable Contemplation of Bird, Carelessness on its Part Might Cause Damage to a Subsequent Purchaser of the Building such as the Condominium Corporation?

In my view, it is reasonably foreseeable to contractors that, if they design or construct a building negligently and if that building contains latent defects as a result of that negligence, subsequent purchasers of the building may suffer personal injury or damage to other property when those defects manifest themselves. A lack of contractual privity between the contractor and the inhabitants at the time the defect becomes manifest does not make the potential for injury any less foreseeable. Buildings are permanent structures that are commonly inhabited by many different persons over their useful life. By constructing the building negligently, contractors (or any other person responsible for the design and construction of a building) create a foreseeable danger that will threaten not only the original owner, but every inhabitant during the useful life of the building. . . .

In my view, the reasonable likelihood that a defect in a building will cause injury to its inhabitants is also sufficient to ground a contractor's duty in tort to subsequent purchasers of the building for the cost of repairing the defect if that defect is discovered prior to any injury and if it poses a real and substantial danger to the inhabitants of the building. In coming to this conclusion, I adopt the reasoning of Laskin J. in *Rivtow*, which I find highly persuasive. If a contractor can be held liable in tort where he or she constructs a building negligently and, as a result of that negligence, the building causes damage to persons or property, it follows that the contractor should also be held liable in cases where the dangerous defect is discovered and the owner of the building wishes to mitigate the danger by fixing the defect and putting the building back into a non-dangerous state. In both cases, the duty in tort serves to protect the bodily integrity and property interests of the inhabitants of the building . . . .

Apart from the logical force of holding contractors liable for the cost of repair of dangerous defects, there is also a strong underlying policy justification for imposing liability in these cases . . . . Allowing recovery against contractors in tort for the cost of repair of dangerous defects thus serves an important preventative function by encouraging socially responsible behaviour.

This conclusion is borne out by the facts of the present case, which fall squarely within the category of what I would define as a "real and substantial danger" . . . . Had this cladding landed on a person or on other property, it would unquestionably have caused serious injury or damage. Indeed, it was only by chance that the cladding fell in the middle of the night and caused no harm. In this light, I believe that the Condominium Corporation behaved responsibly, and as a reasonable home owner should, in having the building inspected and repaired immediately. Bird should not be insulated from liability simply because the current owner of the building acted quickly to alleviate the danger that Bird itself may well have helped to create . . . .

Given the clear presence of a real and substantial danger in this case, I do not find it necessary to consider whether contractors should also in principle be held to owe a duty to subsequent purchasers for the cost of repairing non-dangerous defects in buildings . . . .

Without entering into this question, I note that the present case is distinguishable on a policy level from cases where the workmanship is merely shoddy or substandard but not dangerously defective. In the latter class of cases, tort law serves to encourage the repair of dangerous defects and thereby to protect the bodily integrity of inhabitants of buildings. By contrast, the former class of cases bring into play the questions of quality of workmanship and fitness for purpose . . . .

Are There Any Considerations that Ought to Negate (a) the Scope of the Duty and (b) the Class of Persons to Whom it is Owed or (c) the Damages to which a Breach of it May Give Rise?

There are two primary and interrelated concerns raised by the recognition of a contractor's duty in tort to subsequent purchasers of buildings for the cost of repairing dangerous defects. The first is that warranties respecting quality of construction are primarily contractual in nature and cannot easily be defined or limited in tort. . . .

The second concern is that the recognition of . . . a duty interferes with the doctrine of *caveat emptor* which, as this Court affirmed in *Fraser-Reid v. Droumtsekas*, [[1980] 1 S.C.R. 720 at 723], "has lost little of its pristine force in the sale of land". The doctrine of *caveat emptor* dictates that, in the absence of an express warranty, there is no implied warranty of fitness for human habitation upon the purchase of a house already completed at the time of sale. Huband J.A. of the Manitoba Court of Appeal relied on this doctrine in concluding that no duty in tort could be owed to subsequent purchasers of a building. . .

In my view, these concerns are . . . merely versions of the more general and traditional concern that allowing recovery for economic loss in tort will subject a defendant to what Cardozo C.J. in *Ultramares Corp. v. Touche*, 174 N.E. 441 (N.Y.C.A. 1931), at p. 444, called "liability in an indeterminate amount for an indeterminate time to an indeterminate class." In light of the fact that most buildings have a relatively long useful life, the concern is that a contractor will be subject potentially to an indeterminate amount of liability to an indeterminate number of successive owners over an indeterminate time period. The doctrines of privity of contract and *caveat emptor* provide courts with a useful mechanism for limiting liability in tort. But the problem, as I will now attempt to demonstrate, is that it is difficult to justify the employment of these doctrines in the tort context in any principled manner apart from their utility as mechanisms for limiting liability.

The Concern with Overlap Between Tort and Contract Duties

Turning to the first concern, a duty on the part of contractors to take reasonable care in the construction of buildings can, in my view, be conceptualized in the absence of contract and will not result in indeterminate liability to the contractor. As I mentioned earlier, this Court has recognized that a tort duty can arise concurrently with a contractual duty, so long as that tort duty arises independently of the contractual duty. . . . As I see it, the duty to construct a building according to reasonable standards and without dangerous defects arises independently of the contractual stipulations between the original owner and the contractor because it arises from a duty to create the building safely and not merely according to contractual standards of quality. It must be remembered that we are speaking here of a duty to construct the building according to reasonable standards of safety in such a manner that it does not contain *dangerous* defects. As this duty arises independently of any contract, there is no logical reason for allowing the contractor to rely upon a contract made with the original owner to shield him or her from liability to subsequent purchasers arising from a dangerously constructed building. . . .

The tort duty to construct a building safely is thus a circumscribed duty that is not parasitic upon any contractual duties between the contractor and the original owner. Seen in this way, no serious risk of indeterminate liability arises with respect to this tort duty.

In the first place, there is no risk of liability to an indeterminate class because the potential class of claimants is limited to the very persons for whom the building is constructed: the inhabitants of the building. The fact that the class of claimants may include successors in title who have no contractual relationship with the contractors does not, in my view, render the class of potential claimants indeterminate. . . .

Secondly, there is no risk of liability in an indeterminate amount because the amount of liability will always be limited by the reasonable cost of repairing the dangerous defect in the building and restoring that building to a non-dangerous state. Counsel for Bird advanced the argument that the cost of repairs claimed for averting a danger caused by a defect in construction could, in some cases, be disproportionate to the actual damage to persons or property that might be caused if that defect were not repaired. For example, he expressed concern that a given plaintiff could claim thousands of dollars in damage for a defect which, if left unrepaired, would cause only a few dollars damage to that plaintiff's other property. However, in my view, any danger of indeterminacy in damages is averted by the requirement that the defect for which the costs of repair are claimed must constitute a real and substantial danger to the inhabitants of the building, and the fact that the inhabitants of the building can only claim the reasonable cost of repairing the defect and mitigating the danger. The burden of proof will always fall on the plaintiff to demonstrate that there is a serious risk to safety, that the risk was caused by the contractor's negligence, and that the repairs are required to alleviate the risk.

Finally, there is little risk of liability for an indeterminate time because the contractor will only be liable for the cost of repair of dangerous defects during the useful life of the building. Practically speaking, I believe that the period in which the contractor may be exposed to liability for negligence will be much shorter than the full useful life of the building. With the passage of time, it will become increasingly difficult for owners of a building to prove at trial that any deterioration in the building is attributable to the initial negligence of the contractor and not simply to the inevitable wear and tear suffered by every building. . . .

The Caveat Emptor Concern

Turning to the second concern, *caveat emptor* cannot, in my view, serve as a complete shield to tort liability for the contractors of a building. In *Fraser-Reid*, *supra*, this Court relied on the doctrine of *caveat emptor* in rejecting a claim by a buyer of a house for the recognition of an implied warranty of fitness for human habitation. However, the Court explicitly declined to address the question of whether *caveat emptor* serves to negate a duty in tort. . . . Accordingly, the question remains at large in Canadian law and must be resolved on the level of principle.

In *Fraser-Reid*, Dickson J. (as he then was) observed that the doctrine of *caveat emptor* stems from the *laissez-faire* attitudes of the eighteenth and nineteenth centuries and the notion that purchasers must fend for themselves in seeking protection by express warranty or by independent examination of the premises. . . . The assumption underlying the doctrine is that the purchaser of a building is better placed than the seller or builder to inspect the building and to bear the risk that latent defects will emerge necessitating repair costs. However, in my view, this is an assumption which (if ever valid) is simply not responsive to the realities of the modern housing market. . . . [C]ontractors and builders, because of their knowledge, skill and expertise, are in the best position to ensure the reasonable structural integrity of buildings and their freedom from latent defect. In this respect, the imposition of liability on builders provides an important incentive for care in the construction of buildings and a deterrent against poor workmanship.

My conclusion that a subsequent purchaser is not the best placed to bear the risk of the emergence of latent defects is borne out by the facts of this case. It is significant that, when cracking first appeared in the mortar of the building in 1982, the Condominium Corporation actually hired Smith Carter, the original architect of the building, along with a firm of structural engineers, to assess the condition of the mortar work and exterior cladding. These experts failed to detect the latent defects that appear to have caused the cladding to fall in 1989. Thus, although it is clear that the Condominium Corporation acted with diligence in seeking to detect hidden defects in the building, they were nonetheless unable to detect the defects or to foresee the collapse of the cladding in 1989. This, in my view, illustrates the unreality of the assumption that the purchaser is better placed to detect and bear the risk of hidden defects. For this Court to apply the doctrine of *caveat emptor* to negate Bird's duty in tort would be to apply a rule that has become completely divorced, in this context at least, from its underlying rationale.

Conclusion

I conclude, then, that no adequate policy considerations exist to negate a contractor's duty in tort to subsequent purchasers of a building to take reasonable care in constructing the building, and to ensure that the building does not contain defects that pose foreseeable and substantial danger to the health and safety of the occupants. In my view, the Manitoba Court of Appeal erred in deciding that Bird could not, in principle, be held liable in tort to the Condominium Corporation for the reasonable cost of repairing the defects and putting the building back into a non-dangerous state. These costs are recoverable economic loss under the law of tort in Canada.

NOTES AND QUESTIONS

1. What policy rationale motivated La Forest J.'s decision? Does that rationale outweigh the concerns that traditionally led courts to deny recovery in such cases?

2. Although the plaintiff's primary argument was that it had suffered a pure economic loss, it also argued, in the alternative, that it had suffered property damage. That claim was based on a passage in *D&F Estates Ltd. v. Church Commissioners for England*, [1989] A.C. 177 (H.L.) in which Lord Bridge had suggested that:

> . . .it may well be arguable that in the case of complex structures . . . one element of the structure should be regarded for the purpose of the application of the principles under discussion as distinct from another element, so that damage to one part of the structure caused by a hidden defect in another part may qualify to be treated as damage to "other property".

Along those lines, the plaintiff in *Winnipeg Condominium* claimed that the collapsed cladding was *property damage* that had been caused by the defendant's negligent installation of metal ties, and since the action pertained to property damage, there was no need for the unusually restrictive approach that applies in cases of *pure economic loss.*

La Forest J. rejected that argument. As he observed, Lord Bridge had subsequently retreated from his observations in *D&F Estates*. In *Murphy v. Brentwood District Council* (1990), [1991] 1 A.C. 398 (H.L.) he said:

> The reality is that the structural elements in any building form a single indivisible unit of which the different parts are essentially interdependent. To the extent that there is any defect in one part of the structure it must to a greater or lesser degree necessarily affect all other parts of the structure. Therefore any defect in the structure is a defect in the quality of the whole and it is quite artificial, in order to impose a legal liability which the law would not otherwise impose, to treat a defect in an integral structure, so far as it weakens the structure, as a dangerous defect liable to cause damage to 'other property'.
> A critical distinction must be drawn here between some part of a complex structure which is said to be a 'danger' only because it does not perform its proper function in sustaining the other parts and some distinct item incorporated in the structure which positively malfunctions so as to inflict positive damage on the structure in which it is incorporated. Thus, if a defective central heating boiler explodes and damages a house or a defective electrical installation malfunctions and sets the house on fire, I see no reason to doubt that the owner of the house, if he can prove that the damage was due to the negligence of the boiler manufacturer in the one case or the electrical contractor in the other, can recover damages in tort on *Donoghue v. Stevenson* principles.
> For these reasons the complex structure theory offers no escape from the conclusion that damage to a house itself which is attributable to a defect in the structure of the house is not recoverable in tort on *Donoghue v. Stevenson* principles, but represents purely economic loss which is only recoverable in contract or in tort by reason of some special relationship of proximity which imposes on the tortfeasor a duty of care to protect against economic loss.

La Forest J. agreed with those observations and added that in "cases involving the recoverability of economic loss in tort, it is preferable for the courts to weigh the relevant policy issues openly." In his view, the "complex structure" theory merely tends to "circumvent and obscure the underlying policy questions."

3. As a general rule, the plaintiff cannot establish the required property damage simply by pointing to the defective product itself. For example, a plaintiff who has purchased an appliance that does not work has not suffered property damage. See for example *Edmonton (City) v. Lovat Tunnel Equipment Inc.* (2000), 279 A.R. 1 (Q.B.); and *Zidaric v. Toshiba of Canada Ltd.* (2001), 5 C.C.L.T. (3d) 61 (Ont. S.C.J.). Consider, in the cases below, how rigidly the courts uphold this general rule.

4. What arguments did La Forest J. consider in *Winnipeg Condominium* with respect to the possible negation of a duty of care? Are you satisfied with his disposition of those arguments?

5. Architects and engineers involved in the construction of defective structures are engaged in performing a service, which could blur the line between these two categories of pure economic loss. However, *Bird* indicates that the principles it develops regarding defective structures apply not only to contractors (or subcontractors) but also to architects and engineers. See *Heinicke v. Cooper Rankin Ltd.*, [2007] 2 W.W.R. 112 (Man. Q.B.).

6. La Forest J. carefully confined his decision to cases in which the defendant's carelessness results in shoddy goods or structures that pose a "real and substantial

danger." That rule was applied in *M. Hasegawa & Co. v. Pepsi Bottling Group (Canada) Co.* (2002), 1 B.C.L.R. (4th) 209 (C.A.). The plaintiff purchased bottled glacial water from a third party. The third party had contracted with the defendant to bottle the water. Because the defendant had not sanitized the bottle caps, the water developed "mould flocs." Although that problem meant the water could not be sold, it had not caused physical injury or property damage and it did not pose a health risk to potential consumers. The Court of Appeal therefore held that a duty of care did not arise.

7. Questions sometimes arise as to the scope of the "real and substantial danger" requirement. For example in *Roy v. Thiessen* (2005), 257 Sask. R. 239 (C.A.) the defendant argued that the defect in the plaintiff's house had to create an "imminent" danger. The court disagreed, stating: "The policy goal must be to encourage homeowners to make any necessary repairs as soon as possible in order to mitigate potential losses; they should not have to delay such repairs until there is an imminent danger of harm." See also *Mariani v. Lemstra* (2004), 246 D.L.R. (4th) 489 (Ont. C.A.).

In *Hughes v. Sunbeam Corp. (Canada)* (2002), 61 O.R. (3d) 433 (C.A.) the plaintiff purchased an allegedly defective smoke alarm manufactured by the defendant. Although the alleged defect had not caused any additional damage, the plaintiff sued in negligence for the recovery of the pure economic loss that he suffered as a result of replacing the unit. At first instance, the defendant succeeded in having the claim struck out on the ground that it did not disclose a cause of action. The motions judge held that since a defective smoke alarm is not dangerous in itself, the case fell outside the scope of the rule formulated in *Winnipeg Condominium*. On appeal, however, the claim was allowed to stand. Laskin J.A. agreed that "under the current state of the law," the claim "would likely fail." However, he also insisted that on a motion to strike out, "causes of action should not be barred simply because they are novel." He considered at 443 the possibility that the scope of *Winnipeg Condominium* should be extended:

> A smoke detector that does not detect fires . . . is not itself dangerous, but relying on it is. The occupants are lulled into a false sense of security. . . . Safety justified compensating the owner of the apartment building in *Winnipeg Condominium* to eliminate the dangerously defective cladding. Safety may also justify compensating the owner of a defective smoke alarm to eliminate dangerous reliance on it.

8. In *Winnipeg Condominium* La Forest J. expressly refrained from formulating a rule that would be applicable to cases in which the defendant's carelessness does not create a real and substantial danger. Should a duty of care arise if a defect in a building is non-threatening? An early English decision answered in the affirmative. In *Junior Books Ltd. v. Veitchi*, [1982] 3 W.L.R. 477 (C.A.) the defendant subcontractor carelessly installed a floor in the plaintiff's building. Although that floor developed cracks, the defect did not pose any danger to person or property. The plaintiff brought an action in negligence to recover costs associated with replacing the floor, which a majority of the House of Lords allowed. In delivering judgment, Lord Roskill explained that the defendant knew that the plaintiff relied upon its expertise and described the parties' relationship as being "as close as it could be short of actual privity of contract." However, while *Junior Books* has not been directly overruled, it has been carefully confined to its unique facts in more recent decisions: *D&F Estates Ltd. v. Church Commissioners for England, supra*; and *Murphy v. Brentwood District Council, supra.* The status of *Junior Books* in Canada is uncertain. La Forest J. did not address it in *Winnipeg Condominium*. In

Kamloops v. Neilson, [1984] 2 S.C.R. 2 at 32 Wilson J. referred to *Junior Books* as representing "a significant step forward." Some lower courts have followed the English decision, while others have confined it to its special facts: *University of Regina v. Pettick* (1986), 38 C.C.L.T. 230 (Sask. Q.B.); *Buthmann v. Balzer*, [1983] 4 W.W.R. 695 (Alta. Q.B.); *Logan Lake (Dist.) v. Rivtow Industries Ltd.* (1990), 71 D.L.R. (4th) 333 (B.C.C.A.); and *M. Hasegawa & Co. v. Pepsi Bottling Group (Canada) Co.*, *supra*.

9. The High Court of Australia has held that a duty of care could be recognized even if the defect caused by the defendant's carelessness is non-threatening: *Bryan v. Maloney* (1995), 182 C.L.R. 609. In that case, the defendant built a house for his sister. The property passed through another set of hands before being acquired by the plaintiff. Six months after the purchase cracks appeared in the walls. The plaintiff then discovered that the house had been built with footings that were inadequate to withstand seasonal changes in the soil. The defect required costly repairs but did not pose any danger. A majority of the High Court affirmed the trial judge's decision in the plaintiff's favour. See Wallace, "The *Murphy* Saga in Australia: *Bryan* in Difficulties?" (1997) 113 L.Q.R. 355; Wallace, "*Bryan v. Maloney* Revisited in Victoria" (1997) 5 Tort L. Rev. 152; and Brooking, "*Bryan v. Maloney* – Its Scope and Future" in Mullany & Linden, eds., *Torts Tomorrow: A Tribute to John Fleming* (1998), ch. 4. The majority judgment in *Bryan* rested largely on the proposition that the defendant had assumed responsibility toward the reliant plaintiff. Is such a relationship truly likely to arise between a builder and a remote owner?

Bryan was subsequently limited solely to residential housing by the High Court in *Woolcock Street Investments Pty. Ltd. v. C.D.G. Pty. Ltd.* (2004), 205 A.L.R. 522 (H.C.). For a similar limiting view see *66295 Manitoba Ltd. v. Imperial Oil Ltd.* (2002), 165 Man. R. (2d) 29 (Q.B.).

In light of all of these cases, it is unclear whether Canadian courts will extend recovery to cases involving non-dangerous defects. See the recent analysis of many of the key cases in *Sable Offshore Energy Inc. v. Ameron International Corp.* (2006), 249 N.S.R. (2d) 122 (S.C.).

10. Claims for economic loss caused by defective products are also governed by legislation in all of the Canadian provinces. Many provinces have statutory warranties of merchantability which cannot be excluded in consumer transactions, and some abolish the privity requirement for claims against the manufacturer. There is also federal and provincial legislation prohibiting false and misleading advertising.

11. Claims involving defective products can be analyzed in different ways. In *Plas-Tex Canada Ltd. v. Dow Chemical of Canada Ltd.* (2004), 357 A.R. 139 (C.A.) the defendant supplied defective resin. The case was analyzed as involving a duty to warn. In *Serhan v. Johnson & Johnson* (2006), 213 O.A.C. 298 (Div. Ct.) the defendants manufactured defective blood glucose monitors. A majority of the court considered the claim to be based on "waiver of tort" and allowed it to proceed. Could these cases have been decided using the analysis in *Hughes*, *supra*?

12. For academic analysis of this category of pure economic loss see Rafferty, "Case Comment: *Winnipeg Condominium v. Bird Construction* - Recovery of Purely Economic Loss in the Tort of Negligence: Liability of Builders to Subsequent Purchasers

for Construction Defects" (1996) 34 Alta. L. Rev. 472; Neyers, "*Donoghue v. Stevenson* and the Rescue Doctrine: A Public Justification of Recovery in Situations Involving the Negligent Supply of Dangerous Structures" (1999) 49 U.T.L.J. 475; Quill, "Consumer Protection in Respect of Defective Buildings" (2006) 14 Tort L. Rev. 105; and Todd, "Policy Issues in Defective Property Cases" in Neyers, Chamberlain & Pitel, eds., *Emerging Issues in Tort Law* (2007), ch. 8.

REVIEW PROBLEMS

1. In a construction contract between Owner and Contractor, there is a clause which exculpates Contractor from liability for any losses other than repair costs if the work or materials provided under the contract prove to be substandard. There is no similar clause in the subcontract between Contractor and SubContractor. Should SubContractor be held directly liable to Owner in negligence for business losses consequent on the subcontractor's installation of faulty materials? Does it matter whether the defect is dangerous or merely shoddy? Would your conclusion change if the exculpatory clause was in the subcontract but not in the main contract?

2. The plaintiff purchased carpet from the defendant. The carpet began to wear badly after one year. Is the carpet defective? What further information would assist you in your answer? Does this suggest whether negligence or sales law is best suited to deal with claims about shoddy goods?

5. Relational Economic Loss

The most difficult pure economic loss cases are those involving "relational economic losses." That phrase refers to situations in which the defendant, as a result of negligently damaging property belonging to a third party, also causes a pure economic loss to the plaintiff with whom the third party had a relationship. Suppose, for example, that a construction company carelessly cuts a power line belonging to a municipality. Clearly, the construction company may be liable for losses sustained by the municipality. However, should the company also be liable to a factory that receives its supply of electricity from the municipality and that was forced to temporarily shut down as a result of the accident? What if the defendant's carelessness caused an entire city to lose power for an hour, a day or a week?

As the potential for "indeterminate liability" is particularly pronounced in such circumstances, the courts have been required to strike a balance between allowing victims to recover compensation for their losses and protecting defendants from the prospect of crushing liability. The courts have also recognized the need to consider the manner in which, from a societal perspective, the costs associated with such accidents should be distributed.

The Supreme Court of Canada has addressed the issue of relational economic loss in three key cases: *Canadian National Railway Co. v. Norsk Pacific Steamship Co.*, [1992] 1 S.C.R. 1021, *D'Amato v. Badger*, [1996] 2 S.C.R. 1071 and *Bow Valley Husky (Bermuda) Ltd. v. Saint John Shipbuilding Ltd.*, [1997] 3 S.C.R. 1210. An extract from the most recent decision appears below. The other two cases are discussed in the notes that follow.

BOW VALLEY HUSKY (BERMUDA) LTD. v. SAINT JOHN SHIPBUILDING LTD.

(1997), 153 D.L.R. (4th) 385 (S.C.C.)

[Husky Oil Operations Ltd. ("HOOL") and Bow Valley Industries Ltd. ("BVI") made arrangements to have an off-shore oil drilling rig constructed by Saint John Shipbuilding Limited ("SJSL"). In order to take advantage of government financing, HOOL and BVI incorporated an offshore company, Bow Valley Husky (Bermuda) Ltd. ("BVHB"). Before construction began, ownership of the rig and the construction contract with SJSL were transferred to BVHB. HOOL and BVI entered into contracts with BVHB for the hire of the rig to conduct drilling operations at sites chosen by HOOL and BVI. These contracts provided that HOOL and BVI would continue to pay "day rates" to BVHB even if the rig was out of service.

A heat trace system was required in order to prevent the rig's pipes from freezing during the winter. BVHB directed SJSL to use a system manufactured by Raychem. That system used Thermaclad wrap to keep moisture away from the insulation and heat trace wire. However, a fire broke out on the rig as a result of the flammability of the Thermaclad wrap. The evidence indicated that neither Raychem nor SJSL warned any of the plaintiffs that Thermaclad wrap was flammable under certain circumstances. The evidence also indicated that the fire was caused in part by BVHB's misuse of the heat trace system.

As a result of the fire damage, the rig had to be towed to port for repairs and was out of service for several months. BVHB, HOOL and BVI sued SJSL for breach of contract and negligence and sued Raychem for negligence. BVHB claimed both for the cost of the repairs to the rig and for the revenue lost as a result of the rig being out of service for several months. HOOL and BVI sought to recover economic losses that they suffered during the repair period, including the day rates that they were contractually required to pay to BVHB.

The trial judge reached four important conclusions. First, he found that the defendant SJSL had, *inter alia*, breached a tort law duty to warn of the flammability of Thermaclad wrap. Second, he similarly held that Raychem had breached a tort law duty to warn. Third, he found that BVHB was primarily at fault for the accident because it had carelessly operated the heat tracing system. Responsibility was apportioned 60% to BVHB and 40% to SJSL and Raychem. Fourth, the trial judge ultimately dismissed the plaintiffs' claims on the basis that the case arose from negligence at sea, and therefore was governed by maritime law, in which contributory negligence constitutes a complete defence.

The Court of Appeal allowed an appeal by BVHB, but not by HOOL and BVI. It held that since the loss suffered by HOOL and BVI was purely economic, it was not recoverable. In contrast to the trial judge, however, it held that either (i) the provincial contributory negligence legislation applied on the facts, or (ii) contributory negligence no longer constituted a complete bar to recovery in maritime law. In either event, it held that BVHB was entitled to 40% of its damages from SJSL and Raychem. Further appeals proceeded to the Supreme Court of Canada.]

The reasons of La Forest and McLachlin JJ. were delivered by

MCLACHLIN J. (dissenting in part):

[McLachlin J. held that: (i) SJSL and Raychem owed a duty to warn BVHB of the flammability of Thermaclad wrap, (ii) SJSL's duty of care to BVHB was not negated by the terms of their contract, (iii) a sufficient causal relationship existed between the defendants' failure to warn and the loss sustained by BVHB, (iv) the trial judge's assessment of BVHB's contributory negligence was appropriate, and (v) BVHB's contributory negligence did not constitute a complete bar to recovery.]

. . .

F. *Did SJSL and Raychem Owe BVI and HOOL a Duty to Warn? (Recovery of Contractual Relational Economic Loss)*

(1) The Law

The plaintiffs HOOL and BVI had contracts with BVHB for the use of the rig owned by BVHB. They seek damages for economic loss incurred as a result of the shutdown of the drilling rig during the period it was being repaired. In other words, the plaintiffs HOOL and BVI seek to recover the economic loss they suffered as a result of damage to the property of a third party. This sort of loss is often called "contractual relational economic loss." The issue is whether the loss suffered by HOOL and BVI is recoverable.

The issue arises because common law courts have traditionally regarded many types of contractual relational economic loss as irrecoverable.

. . .

In England the situation is clear – no relational economic loss can ever be recovered: *Murphy v. Brentwood District Council*, [1991] 1 A.C. 398 (H.L.). Although *Murphy* concerned the liability of a public authority for approval of a negligently constructed building, not relational economic loss, the House of Lords stipulated that pure economic loss is recoverable only where there is actual physical damage to property of the plaintiff, thus excluding recovery for relational economic loss. In the civil law jurisdictions of Quebec and France, by contrast, the law does not distinguish between loss arising from damage of one's own property and loss arising from damage to the property of another. If civil law judges restrict recovery, it is not as a matter of law, but on the basis of the facts and causal connection. The law in the common law provinces of Canada falls somewhere between these two extremes. While treating recovery in tort of contractual relational economic loss as exceptional, it is accepted in Canadian jurisprudence that there may be cases where it may be recovered.

The foregoing suggests the need for a rule to distinguish between cases where contractual relational economic loss can be recovered and cases where it cannot be recovered. Such a rule, as I wrote in *Canadian National Railway Co. v. Norsk Pacific Steamship Co.*, [1992] 1 S.C.R. 1021, should be morally and economically defensible and provide a logical basis upon which individuals can predicate their conduct and courts can decide future cases. . . . Although this Court attempted to formulate such a rule in *Norsk*, a split decision prevented the emergence of a clear rule. Given the commercial importance of the issue, it is important that the rule be settled. It is therefore necessary for this Court to revisit the issue.

The differences between the reasons of La Forest J. and myself in *Norsk* are of two orders: difference in result and difference in methodology. The difference in result, taken at its narrowest, is a difference in the definition of what constitutes a "joint venture" for the purposes of determining whether recovery for contractual relational economic loss should be allowed. We both agreed that if the plaintiff is in a joint venture with the person whose property is damaged, the plaintiff may claim consequential economic loss related to that property. We parted company because La Forest J. took a stricter view of what constituted a joint venture than I did.

The difference in methodology is not, on close analysis, as great as might be supposed. Broadly put, La Forest J. started from a general exclusionary rule and proceeded to articulate exceptions to that rule where recovery would be permitted. I, by contrast, stressed the two-step test for when recovery would be available, based on the general principles of recovery in tort as set out in *Anns v. Merton London Borough Council*, [1978] A.C. 728 (H.L.), and *Kamloops (City of) v. Nielsen*, [1984] 2 S.C.R. 2: (1) whether the relationship between the plaintiff and defendant was sufficiently proximate to give rise to a *prima facie* duty of care; and (2) whether, if such a *prima facie* duty existed, it was negated for policy reasons and recovery should be denied.

Despite this difference in approach, La Forest J. and I agreed on several important propositions: (1) relational economic loss is recoverable only in special circumstances where the appropriate conditions are met; (2) these circumstances can be defined by reference to categories, which will make the law generally predictable; (3) the categories are not closed. La Forest J. identified the categories of recovery of relational economic loss defined to date as: (1) cases where the claimant has a possessory or proprietary interest in the damaged property; (2) general average cases; and (3) cases where the relationship between the claimant and property owner constitutes a joint venture.

The case at bar does not fall into any of the above three categories. The plaintiffs here had no possessory or proprietary interest in the rig and the case is not one of general averaging. While related contractually, the Court of Appeal correctly held that the plaintiff and the property owner cannot, on any view of the term, be viewed as joint venturers.

However, that is not the end of the matter. The categories of recoverable contractual relational economic loss in tort are not closed. Where a case does not fall within a recognized category the court may go on to consider whether the situation is one where the right to recover contractual relational economic loss should nevertheless be recognized. This is in accordance with *Norsk*, *per* La Forest J., at p. 1134:

> Thus I do not say that the right to recovery in all cases of contractual relational economic loss depends exclusively on the terms of the contract. Rather, I note that such is the tenor of the exclusionary rule and that *departures from that rule should be justified on defensible policy grounds*. [Emphasis added.]

More particularly, La Forest J. suggested that the general rule against recovery for policy-based reasons might be relaxed where the deterrent effect of potential liability to the property owner is low, or, despite a degree of indeterminate liability, where the claimant's opportunity to allocate the risk by contract is slight, either because of the type of transaction or an inequality of bargaining power. I agreed with La Forest J. that policy considerations relating to increased costs of processing claims and contractual allocation of the risk are important. . . . I concluded that the test for recovery "should be flexible enough to meet the complexities of commercial reality and to permit the recognition of new situations in which liability ought, in justice, to lie as such situations arise" (p. 1166). It thus appears that new categories of recoverable contractual relational economic loss may be recognized where justified by policy considerations and required by justice. At the same time, courts should not assiduously seek new categories; what is required is a clear rule predicting when recovery is available.

More recently, in *Hercules Managements Ltd. v. Ernst & Young*,. . . this Court described the general approach that should be followed in determining when tort recovery for economic loss is appropriate.

. . .

La Forest J. set out the methodology that courts should follow in determining whether a tort action lies for relational economic loss. He held that the two-part methodology of *Anns*, *supra*, adopted by this Court in *Kamloops*, *supra*, should be followed: (1) whether a *prima facie* duty of care is owed; and (2) whether that duty, if it exists, is negated or limited by policy considerations. In applying the second step, La Forest J. wrote that while policy considerations will sometimes result in the *prima facie* duty being negated, in certain categories of cases such considerations may give way to other overriding policy considerations.

La Forest J. held that the existence of a relationship of "neighbourhood" or "proximity" distinguishes those circumstances in which the defendant owes a *prima facie* duty of care to the plaintiff from those where no such duty exists. The term "proximity" is a label expressing the fact of a relationship of neighbourhood sufficient to attract a *prima facie* legal duty. Whether the duty arises depends on the nature of the case and its facts. Policy concerns are best dealt with under the second branch of the test. Criteria that in other cases have been used to define the legal test for the duty of care can now be recognized as policy-based ways by which to curtail indeterminate or inappropriate recovery.

. . .

The same approach may be applied to the contractual relational economic loss at stake in the case at bar. The first step is to inquire whether the relationship of neighbourhood or proximity necessary to found a *prima facie* duty of care is present. If so, one moves to the second step of inquiring whether the policy concerns that usually preclude recovery of contractual relational economic loss, such as indeterminacy, are overridden.

(2) Application of the Law

. . .

I return to the question of whether, on the approach articulated in *Hercules*, *supra*, the plaintiffs' claim for contractual relational economic loss is actionable. The Newfoundland Court of Appeal, without the benefit of *Hercules*, essentially followed the two-step process outlined in that case. It held that the defendants owed a *prima facie* duty of care to BVI and HOOL. The duty arose because BVI and HOOL's economic interests could foreseeably have been affected by a failure to warn BVHB of the danger of fire resulting from the use of products supplied by the defendants. The Court of Appeal went on to hold that there should be no recovery for other reasons. It held that it would be totally impractical to warn every person who could foreseeably suffer economic loss arising from the shutdown of the drilling rig. If there was a duty to warn BVI and HOOL, then there would also be a duty to warn other potential investors in the project, such as Mobil Oil Canada Ltd. and Petro Canada, as well as a host of other persons who stood to gain from the uninterrupted operation of the drilling rig, including employees and suppliers of the rig. In these circumstances, in the Court of Appeal's view, the only duty on the defendants was to warn the person in control and possession of the rig of the dangers of fire associated with the use of Thermaclad.

As in *Hercules*, the decision as to whether a *prima facie* duty of care exists requires an investigation into whether the defendant and the plaintiff can be said to be in a relationship of proximity or neighbourhood. Proximity exists on a given set of facts if the defendant may be said to be under an obligation to be mindful of the plaintiff's legitimate interests in conducting his or her affairs. . . . On the facts of this case, I agree with the Court of Appeal that a *prima facie* duty of care arises.

. . .

Where a duty to warn is alleged, the issue is not reliance (there being nothing to rely upon), but whether the defendants ought reasonably to have foreseen that the plaintiffs might suffer loss as a result of use of the product about which the warning should have been made. I have already found that [the defendants owed a duty to warn to BVHB with respect to the flammability of Thermaclad]. The question is, however, whether [that duty] extended as far as HOOL and BVI. The facts establish that this was the case. The defendants knew of the existence of the plaintiffs and others like them and knew or ought to have known that they stood to lose money if the drilling rig was shut down.

The next question is whether this *prima facie* duty of care is negatived by policy considerations. In my view, it is. The most serious problem is that seized on by the Court of Appeal – the problem of indeterminate liability. If the defendants owed a duty to warn the plaintiffs, it is difficult to see why they would not owe a similar duty to a host of other persons who would foreseeably lose money if the rig was shut down as a result of being damaged. Other investors in the project are the most obvious persons who would also be owed a duty, although the list could arguably be extended to additional classes of persons. What has been referred to as the ripple effect is present in this case. A number of investment companies which contracted with HOOL are making claims against it, as has BVI.

No sound reason to permit the plaintiffs to recover while denying recovery to these other persons emerges. To hold otherwise would pose problems for defendants, who would face liability in an indeterminate amount for an indeterminate time to an indeterminate class. It also would pose problems for potential plaintiffs. Which of all the potential plaintiffs can expect and anticipate they will succeed? Why should one type of contractual relationship, that of HOOL, be treated as more worthy than another, e.g., that of the employees on the rig? In this state, what contractual and insurance arrangements should potential plaintiffs make against future loss?

The plaintiffs propose a number of solutions to the problem of indeterminacy. None of them succeeds, in my respectful view. The first proposal is to confine liability to persons whose *identity* was known to the defendants. This is a reversion to the "known plaintiff" test. . . . As commentators have pointed out, the fact that the defendant knew the identity of the plaintiff should not in logic or justice determine recovery. On such a test, the notorious would recover, the private would lose. . . . The problem of indeterminate liability cannot be avoided by arbitrary distinctions for which there is no legal or social justification. . . . There must be something which, for policy reasons, permits the court to say this category of person can recover and that category cannot, something which justifies the line being drawn at one point rather than another.

Second, and in a similar vein, the plaintiffs argue that determinacy can be achieved by restricting recovery to the users of the rig, a class which they say is analogous in time and extent to the owners and occupiers of the building in *Winnipeg Condominium Corporation No. 36 v. Bird Construction Co.*, [1995] 1 S.C.R. 85. This argument fails for the same reasons as the known plaintiff test. There is no logical reason for drawing the line at users rather than somewhere else.

Third, the plaintiffs attempt to distinguish themselves from other potential claimants through the concept of reliance. The defendants correctly answer this argument by pointing out that any person who is contractually dependent on a product or a structure owned by another "relies" on the manufacturer or builder to supply a safe product.

Finally, the plaintiffs argue that a finding of a duty to warn negates the specter of indeterminate liability as the duty to warn does not extend to everyone in any way connected to the manufactured product. This argument begs the question. The duty to warn found to this point is only a *prima facie* duty to warn in accordance with the first requirement of *Anns*, *supra*, that there be sufficient proximity or neighbourhood to found a duty of care. It is not circumscribed and imports no limits on liability. Considerations of indeterminate liability arise in the second step of the *Anns* analysis. Hence the *prima facie* duty of care, by itself, cannot resolve the problem of indeterminate liability.

The problem of indeterminate liability constitutes a policy consideration tending to negative a duty of care for contractual relational economic loss. However, the courts have recognized positive policy considerations tending to support the imposition of such a duty of care. One of these, discussed by La Forest J. in *Norsk*, is the need to provide additional deterrence against negligence. The potential liability to the owner of the damaged property usually satisfies the goal of encouraging persons to exercise due care not to damage the property. However, situations may arise where this is not the case. In such a case, the additional deterrent of liability to others might be justified. The facts in the case at bar do not support liability to the plaintiffs on this basis. BVHB, the owner of the drilling rig, suffered property damage in excess of five million dollars. This is a significant sum. It is not apparent that increasing the defendants' potential liability would have led to different behaviour and avoidance of the loss.

Another situation which may support imposition of liability for contractual relational economic loss, recognized by La Forest J. in *Norsk*, is the case where the plaintiff's ability to allocate the risk to the property owner by contract is slight, either because of the type of the transaction or inequality of bargaining power. Again, this does not assist the plaintiffs in this case. BVI and HOOL not only had the ability to allocate their risks; they did just that. It cannot be said that BVI and HOOL suffered from inequality of bargaining power with BVHB, the very company they created. Moreover, the record shows they exercised that power. The risk of loss caused by down-time of the rig was specifically allocated under the Drilling Contracts between BVI, HOOL and BVHB. The contracts provided for day rate payments to BVHB and/ or termination rights in the event of lost or diminished use of the rig. The parties also set out in the contracts their liability to each other and made provision for third party claims arising out of rig operations. Finally, the contracts contained provisions related to the purchase and maintenance of insurance.

I conclude that the policy considerations relevant to the case at bar negative the *prima facie* duty of care to BVI and HOOL.

. . .

The judgment of Gonthier, Cory, Iacobucci and Major JJ. was delivered by

IACOBUCCI J.: — I have had the advantage of reading the lucid reasons of my colleague, Justice McLachlin. At the outset, I wish to commend my colleague for her treatment of the approaches taken by her and La Forest J. in [*Norsk*]. In that respect, I simply wish to add one comment regarding the issue of contractual relational economic loss.

I understand my colleague's discussion of this matter to mean that she has adopted the general exclusionary rule and categorical exceptions approach set forth by La Forest J. in *Norsk*. My colleague has found that the circumstances of the present case do not fall within any of the three exceptions identified in that case. She points out that both her reasons and those of La Forest J. in *Norsk* recognize that the categories of recoverable contractual relational economic loss are not closed and that whether or not a new category ought to be created is determined on a case-by-case basis. In that connection, I approve of her analysis of the facts of this case and applaud the approach she has taken to meld her reasoning in *Norsk* with that of La Forest J. in this very difficult area of the law.

[Iacobucci J., however, held that the contract between BVHB and SJSL did, contrary to McLachlin J.'s opinion, negate the duty to warn that SJSL owed to BVHB. In the final result, HOOL and BVI failed in their actions in negligence. BVHB failed in its negligence action against SJSL, but succeeded against Raychem. Damages against Raychem were, however, reduced to 40% on account of BVHB's contributory negligence.]

NOTES AND QUESTIONS

1. In light of *Bow Valley*, describe the circumstances in which a duty of care will be owed with respect to relational pure economic losses. Why did HOOL and BVI fail in their claims? Why was it unnecessary for BVHB to rely on the law on relational economic loss? For more on *Bow Valley* see Wallace, "Contractual Relational Loss in Canada" (1998) 114 L.Q.R. 370.

2. Traditionally, recovery did not lie for relational pure economic losses. Rather, the courts followed a general exclusionary rule in circumstances in which the plaintiff sustained neither personal injury nor property damage: see *Cattle v. Stockton Waterworks Co.* (1875), L.R. 10 Q.B. 453. As McLachlin J. noted in *Bow Valley*, the general exclusionary approach governs in England: see *Murphy v. Brentwood District Council*, [1991] 1 A.C. 398 (H.L.).

3. In *Canadian National Railway Co. v. Norsk Pacific Steamship Co.*, [1992] 1 S.C.R. 1021 the plaintiff company entered into a contract for the use of a bridge owned by the government. The defendant carelessly damaged that bridge and as a result the plaintiff sustained considerable economic losses due to the disruption of its services. The Supreme Court of Canada allowed the claim, but was split in doing so.

McLachlin J., writing for herself, L'Heureux-Dubé and Cory JJ., rejected the traditional exclusionary rule, preferring instead an incremental approach in which the courts develop, on a case-by-case basis, a list of categories of situations in which a duty may be recognized. She believed that this task was best achieved through the two-stage test formulated in *Anns* and *Kamloops*. At the first stage of that test, she referred to foreseeability and stressed the concept of proximity, which was said to encompass the existence of a relationship between the parties, physical propinquity, assumed or imposed obligations, and close causal connection. At the second stage of the *Anns/Kamloops* test, she considered factors that might negate a *prima facie* duty of care that arose under the first stage. On her analysis, a duty of care was owed by the defendant to the plaintiff in *Norsk*. A *prima facie* duty arose under the first stage of the *Anns/Kamloops* test, largely because, given the close contractual relationship between the plaintiff and the government, those parties essentially were in a "joint venture" with respect to the bridge. Consequently, a sufficient degree of proximity existed between the plaintiff and the defendant. McLachlin J. further held that, in the circumstances, the spectre of indeterminate liability did not arise and that there was no policy reason to negate the existence of a duty of care.

Stevenson J. agreed that a duty of care existed on the facts, but he reached that conclusion on much narrower reasoning. In his view, a duty of care could arise in a case of relational economic loss only with respect to specific individuals that the defendant could have reasonably foreseen would suffer economic losses. All of the other justices expressly rejected this "notorious plaintiff" test.

In a forceful dissent, La Forest J., writing for himself, Sopinka and Iacobucci JJ., held that a general exclusionary rule should apply except where clear policy considerations demand otherwise. Accordingly, in cases of relational economic loss, he would recognize a duty of care only if: (i) the plaintiff held a proprietary or possessory interest in the damaged property, (ii) the concept of general average (a maritime law concept applied for example among various cargo owners to share in paying for cargo thrown overboard in a storm in order to save the rest of the cargo) applied, or (iii) the plaintiff and the owner of the damaged property were parties in a joint venture. On the facts, it was clear that neither the first nor the second exception applied. Moreover, contrary to McLachlin J., he refused to accept that CNR's contractual relationship with the government gave rise to a joint venture with respect to the damaged bridge. Finally, while recognizing that the general exclusionary rule "excludes recovery by people who have undeniably suffered losses as a result of an accident" and "is not attractive in itself," La Forest J. defended it because it reduces the incidence of litigation, relieves the courts of the need to draw fine lines, and efficiently indicates which parties should purchase insurance coverage.

Interestingly, La Forest J. joined McLachlin J.'s opinion in *Bow Valley*. How were the two able to reconcile the differences between them in *Norsk*? Did McLachlin J. limit the seemingly broad concept of proximity that she favoured in the earlier decision? Does her judgment in *Bow Valley* provide greater certainty and predictability than her judgment in *Norsk*? Did La Forest J. agree to open up the general exclusionary rule he previously recognized? Which judge's definition of "joint venture" eventually prevailed? See Feldthusen, "Dynamic Change to Maritime Law – Gracious Retreat on Relational Economic Loss" (1998) 6 Tort L. Rev. 164.

For further discussion of the court's judgment in *Norsk*, see Feldthusen & Palmer, "Economic Loss and the Supreme Court of Canada: An Economic Critique of *Norsk Steamship* and *Bird Construction*" (1997) 74 Can. Bar Rev. 427; Mactavish, "Tort Recovery for Economic Loss: Recent Developments" (1993) 21 C.B.L.J. 395; McInnes, "Contractual Relational Economic Loss" [1993] C.L.J. 12; Fleming, "Economic Loss in Canada" (1993) 1 Tort L. Rev. 68; and Waddams, "Further Reflections on Economic Loss" (1994) 2 Tort L. Rev. 116.

4. In *D'Amato v. Badger*, [1996] 2 S.C.R. 1071 a person who owned a 50% share in a company was injured by the defendant's carelessness. As a result of that accident, the injured party was unable to continue performing services for the company, which consequently was required to hire a new employee. Several claims were brought against

the defendant, including one by the company for relational economic loss: the company argued that the cost of hiring a new employee constituted a pure economic loss that arose because of the company's relationship with the injured party. That claim was allowed at trial, but rejected by both the British Columbia Court of Appeal and the Supreme Court of Canada. In a unanimous judgment, Major J. refused to choose between the approaches developed by La Forest J. and McLachlin J. in *Norsk*. He stated that those approaches usually produce the same result, as was true on the facts before him. The claim did not fall within any of the exceptions that La Forest J. recognized with respect to the general exclusionary rule. Likewise, a duty of care did not arise under McLachlin J.'s *Anns/Kamloops* approach because the company's loss was neither foreseeable nor sufficiently proximate to the defendant's act of negligence to warrant recovery. Moreover, even if a *prima facie* duty did arise under the first stage of the *Anns/Kamloops* test, it was negated under the second stage. If a company was allowed to recover pure economic loss arising from the loss of a key shareholder and employee, the problem of indeterminacy would arise.

There is a long history of debate over the recovery of economic losses suffered as a result of personal injuries sustained by a third party. Some of the cases are based on the old common law action *per quod servitium amisit* under which an employer could sue for the loss of services which would have been provided by an employee. See the discussion in Klar, *Tort Law*, 3d ed. (2003) at 248-53.

5. In the area of relational pure economic loss, as in other areas of pure economic loss, it may sometimes be difficult to determine whether the plaintiff suffered property damage or pure economic loss. Is computer data property? See *Seaboard Life Insurance Co. v. Babich*, [1995] 10 W.W.R. 756 (B.C.S.C.).

6. The courts have been reluctant to expand the situations in which relational pure economic loss is recoverable, making this arguably the most certain of the categories of pure economic loss cases: see Feldthusen, "The *Anns/Cooper* Approach to Duty of Care for Pure Economic Loss: The Emperor has no Clothes" (2003) 18 C.L.R. (3d) 67 at 71; and *Livingstone v. Canada (Attorney General)* (2004), 357 A.R. 3 (C.A.). For arguments that recovery in this category should be extended, see Brown, "Justifying the Impossibility of Recoverable Relational Economic Loss" (2005) 5 O.U.C.L.J. 155.

15

THE STANDARD OF CARE

1. Introduction
2. The Common Law Standard of Care: The Reasonable Person Test
3. Factors Considered in Determining Breach of the Standard of Care
4. An Economic Analysis of the Standard of Care
5. Special Standards of Care
6. Degrees of Negligence
7. Custom

1. Introduction

Although there is some disagreement concerning the elements of a negligence action and their correct analysis, most judges recognize a distinction between the concepts of duty and standard of care. The *duty of care* analysis is generally understood to be an inquiry into the existence, nature and scope of the legal relationship between the plaintiff and the defendant. As we have seen, the duty of care concept is the legal foundation of the tort of negligence. It involves a combination of legal and public policy analyses regarding the boundaries of legal responsibility in the particular factual circumstances of a case.

Once it is established that the defendant owed a duty of care to the plaintiff, it then becomes necessary to formulate the *standard of care* and to determine whether that standard was *breached*. Broadly stated, the standard of care determines how the defendant should have acted. A breach occurs if he or she acted without that requisite degree of care.

The issues of standard of care and breach sometimes are referred to as the "negligence issues." Judges occasionally say that a defendant was "negligent" if he or she breached the standard of care. There is, however, a potential problem with that practice. "Negligence" has two meanings: one narrow and one broad. The narrow meaning refers only to the questions of standard and breach. The defendant was "negligent" in that sense as long as he or she acted without sufficient care. The broader meaning of "negligence" refers, in contrast, to the cause of action as a whole. The defendant was "negligent" in that sense only if, in addition to proving a breach of the standard of care, the plaintiff proved the other elements of the tort (such as causation). As noted at the outset of Chapter 9, one way to avoid possible confusion between these two meanings is to confine the term "negligence" to the cause of action as a whole and to use the term "carelessness" to describe the fact that the defendant breached the standard of care.

The duty of care is a legal issue that is therefore resolved by the judge. In contrast, the issues of standard of care and breach raise questions of both law and fact. It is for the judge, who resolves questions of law, to formulate the standard of care and determine the factors that need to be considered. It is then for the jury (or judge, if there is no jury), as the trier of fact, to apply those factors to the case and to determine whether the defendant met the standard. In other words, it is for the jury to translate the general into the specific. See *Des Brisay v. Canadian Government Merchant Marine Ltd.*, [1941] 2 D.L.R. 209 (S.C.C.); and Fleming, *The Law of Torts*, 9th ed. (1998) at 118.

The distinction between questions of law and questions of fact sometimes causes confusion: see *Galaske v. O'Donnell* (1994), 112 D.L.R. (4th) 109 (S.C.C.). The distinction nevertheless is important even if a judge sits alone, rather than with a jury. Although such a judge will answer both types of questions, an appellate court will treat the answers differently. With respect to a question of law, the appellate court is entitled to substitute its view for that of the trial judge, so long as it is satisfied that he or she committed an error. In contrast, with respect to a question of fact, an appellate court is entitled to overturn the trial judge only if it is convinced that he or she committed a "palpable and overriding error" or reached a conclusion that could not be supported by the evidence: see *Housen v. Nikolaisen* (2002), 211 D.L.R. (4th) 577 (S.C.C.); *Bannon v. Thunder Bay (City)* (2002), 210 D.L.R. (4th) 62 (S.C.C.); *Allen (Next friend of) v. University Hospitals Board* (2002), 13 C.C.L.T. (3d) 95 (Alta. C.A.); and *H.L. v. Canada (Attorney General)*, [2005] 1 S.C.R. 401.

The issues of standard of care and breach also raise another recurring difficulty. As the cases and notes below illustrate, judges and jurors struggle to reach decisions that are both fair and consistent. The question of carelessness, perhaps inevitably, is substantially open-ended. Canadian courts have resisted attempts to reduce the issue to systematic mathematical or economic formulae. In the final analysis, it therefore may be necessary to be content with the vagaries of human judgment.

2. The Common Law Standard of Care: The Reasonable Person Test

ARLAND v. TAYLOR

[1955] 3 D.L.R. 358 (Ont. C.A.)

[The plaintiff was injured in a motor vehicle accident. At trial, the jury held that the defendant had not breached the requisite standard of care. The plaintiff appealed, objecting to the trial judge's charge to the jury.]

LAIDLAW J.A.: . . . The second ground of appeal arises from the following passage, in particular, in the charge to the jury:

> First of all you will consider his [the respondent's] negligence. I suggest that you put yourself in the driver's seat of his car. After you have determined the weather and the conditions that existed, ask yourself — "Would I have done that? Was that reasonable for him to do? What precautions would I have taken that he did not? Would I have gone over that hill at the same speed that he did? Would I have reduced my speed?", especially if you decide that as he approached he could not have seen over that hill.

I extract another passage of the charge in which the learned judge said: ". . . having put yourself in the driver's seat and asked yourself whether he satisfied you under the circumstances, then we go on to the next question . . ." The learned trial judge told the jury in more than one part of his charge that ten of them "set the standard of what is reasonable under a given set of circumstances."

The learned trial judge was in error in those instructions to the jury, and this manner of leaving the case to the jury was the subject of disapproval in *Kralj v. Murray*, [[1954]

1 D.L.R. 781 (Ont. C.A.)]. The standard of care by which a jury is to judge the conduct of parties in a case of the kind under consideration is the care that would have been taken in the circumstances by "a reasonable and prudent man". I shall not attempt to formulate a comprehensive definition of "a reasonable man" of whom we speak so frequently in negligence cases. I simply say he is a mythical creature of the law whose conduct is the standard by which the Courts measure the conduct of all other persons and find it to be proper or improper in particular circumstances as they may exist from time to time. He is not an extraordinary or unusual creature; he is not superhuman; he is not required to display the highest skill of which anyone is capable; he is not a genius who can perform uncommon feats, nor is he possessed of unusual powers of foresight. He is a person of normal intelligence who makes prudence a guide to his conduct. He does nothing that a prudent man would not do and does not omit to do anything a prudent man would do. He acts in accord with general and approved practice. His conduct is guided by considerations which ordinarily regulate the conduct of human affairs. His conduct is the standard "adopted in the community by persons of ordinary intelligence and prudence." See *Blyth v. Birmingham Waterworks Co.* (1856), 11 Exch. 781, 156 E.R. 1047, and Mazengarb, *Negligence on the Highway*, 2nd ed. 1952, p. 15.

In *Glasgow Corporation v. Muir et al.*, [1943] A.C. 448, [1943] 2 All E.R. 44, Lord Macmillan at p. 457 said:

> The standard of foresight of the reasonable man is, in one sense, an impersonal test. It eliminates the personal equation and is independent of the idiosyncracies of the particular person whose conduct is in question. Some persons are by nature unduly timorous and imagine every path beset with lions. Others, of more robust temperament, fail to foresee or nonchalantly disregard even the most obvious dangers. The reasonable man is presumed to be free both from over-apprehension and from over-confidence, but there is a sense in which the standard of care of the reasonable man involves in its application a subjective element. It is still left to the judge to decide what, in the circumstances of the particular case, the reasonable man would have had in contemplation, and what, accordingly, the party sought to be made liable ought to have foreseen. Here there is room for diversity of view . . . What to one judge may seem far-fetched may seem to another both natural and probable.

In Mazengarb, *op. cit.*, p. 18, the learned author says:

> In fixing responsibility, the law has adopted an external standard of care. It realizes that care is a matter of degree, and therefore it has set a standard which is neither too high nor too low. It seeks safety without at the same time unduly hampering transport and transit. It does not require the highest degree of care of which mankind is capable.

And I quote further from p. 20:

> The legal standard of care always remains the same in the sense that it is what a reasonably prudent man would have done in like circumstances. But although this legal standard is fixed and immutable, the factual standard changes from time to time and from place to place.

It will be plain from the statements I have quoted that it is improper for a juryman to judge the conduct of a person in given circumstances by considering, after the event, what he would or would not have done in the circumstances.

In *Eyres v. Gillis & Warren Ltd.*, 48 Man. R. 164 at 170, [1940] 3 W.W.R. 390, [1940] 4 D.L.R. 747, Trueman J.A., delivering the unanimous judgment of the Court of

Appeal of Manitoba, referred to the definition of negligence as given by Baron Alderson in *Blyth v. Birmingham Waterworks Co.*, *supra*, and then said:

> In determining the standard of duty so defined a Judge must not interpose himself, for, the accident having happened, his point of view may be warped by extraneous or subjective considerations, however much he may think he is free from bias. It is for this reason that a jury must not be instructed by the Judge or counsel to put themselves in the place of a defendant in a negligence action when called upon to pronounce upon his conduct.

. . .

[Although Laidlaw J.A. felt that there had been a misdirection, he held that there was no substantial wrong caused by the misdirection in this case and so dismissed the appeal.]

NOTES AND QUESTIONS

1. What is the common law standard of care? Is the reasonable person test objective, subjective or a combination of both?

2. The degree to which the perception of "reasonable" conduct is influenced by factors such as the trier of fact's sex, race, social class and ethnic background is a subject of debate among academics and lawyers. Assume that A and B were involved in a traffic accident late at night in a dangerous neighbourhood. A's injuries would have been much less severe if B had stopped to provide assistance. B did not do so, however, for fear of being attacked by a third party. If A sues B for negligence, should the content of the standard of care be influenced by the fact that B is a woman and that several other women had recently been attacked in the area? In the same circumstances, would it be reasonable to expect more of a male driver than a female driver if it could be shown that male drivers were generally not at risk of attack? For an introduction to a feminist analysis of the standard of care, see generally Bender, "An Overview of Feminist Torts Scholarship" (1993) 78 Cornell L. Rev. 575. See also Schlanger, "Gender Matters: Teaching a Reasonable Woman Standard in Personal Injury Law" (2001) 45 St. Louis L.J. 769. For a critical response see Schwartz, "Feminist Approaches to Tort Law" (2001) 2 Theor. Inq. L. 175.

3. As *Arland* indicates, the reasonable person test is not a standard of perfection. A court therefore may draw a distinction between a non-tortious mistake, referred to as an error of judgment, and actionable carelessness. Examples of cases involving errors of judgment are *Graham v. Persyko* (1986), 55 O.R. (2d) 10 (C.A.); *Smith v. B.C. (A.G.)* (1988), 30 B.C.L.R. (2d) 356 (C.A.); *Edgar v. Richmond (Township)* (1991), 6 C.C.L.T. (2d) 241 (B.C.S.C.); *Gros v. Victoria General Hospital* (2000), 151 Man R. (2d) 111 (Q.B.), aff'd (2001), 160 Man. R. (2d) 7 (C.A.); and *Pelletier v. Stewart*, 2005 CarswellAlta 897 (Q.B.) (WLeC).

4. If the prospect of the plaintiff suffering injury is virtually unforeseeable to the reasonable person, should the plaintiff's claim be resolved at the duty stage or the standard of care stage?

5. Why did the Court of Appeal conclude in *Arland* that the trial judge's charge to the jury constituted a misdirection? Why did the judge not order a new trial?

6. Although most negligence cases are governed by the reasonable person test, more specific rules have developed in connection with some commonly litigated activities. In a motor vehicle negligence case, for example, it may be helpful to consult the case law to determine whether the type of conduct in issue has previously been held to have breached the standard of care.

7. In *Ryan v. Victoria (City)*, [1999] 1 S.C.R. 201 at 222 the court summarized the standard of care as follows:

> Conduct is negligent if it creates an objectively unreasonable risk of harm. To avoid liability, a person must exercise the standard of care that would be expected of an ordinary, reasonable and prudent person in the same circumstances. The measure of what is reasonable depends on the facts of each case, including the likelihood of a known or foreseeable harm, the gravity of that harm, and the burden or cost which would be incurred to prevent the injury. In addition, one may look to external indicators of reasonable conduct, such as custom, industry practice, and statutory or regulatory standards.

Most of the elements mentioned by the court in *Ryan* are considered in this chapter. The role of statutory standards is considered in Chapter 22.

8. For examples of an analysis of the common law standard of care from different times over the past century see Seavey, "Negligence — Subjective or Objective" (1927) 41 Harv. L. Rev. 1; James, "The Qualities of the Reasonable Man in Negligence Cases" (1951) 16 Mod. L. Rev. 1; Green, "The Reasonable Man — Legal Fiction or Psychological Reality?" (1968) 2 Law & Society Rev. 241; and Linden & Feldthusen, *Canadian Tort Law*, 8th ed. (2006) at 129-51.

9. For a detailed analysis of problems with the reasonable person standard see Moran, *Rethinking the Reasonable Person* (2003). She argues in her conclusion that "adopting some ideal person as a standard of behaviour creates an almost irresistible opening to endow that imaginary person with all sorts of qualities that are not in fact prudential." See also Horder, "Can the Law Do Without the Reasonable Person?" (2005) 55 U.T.L.J. 253.

3. Factors Considered in Determining Breach of the Standard of Care

Judges consider, or direct the jury to consider, several factors in determining whether the defendant breached the standard of care. The two most important factors are (i) the probability of injury and (ii) the potential severity of injury. Those considerations are balanced against the private and social costs that would have been associated with avoiding the risk and the social utility of the defendant's conduct.

It is important to understand that these various considerations must be assessed at the time of the alleged breach, rather than in hindsight. After the fact, it may be obvious that the defendant should have acted more carefully. The real question, however, is how a reasonable person in the defendant's circumstances would have acted at the relevant time. *Roe v. Minister of Health*, [1954] 2 All E.R. 131 (C.A.) is illustrative. The defendant ran a hospital. It stored spinal anaesthetic in glass ampoules, which were placed into liquid phenol for the purpose of sterilization. The plaintiff, who had undergone an operation, suffered spastic paraplegia because the anaesthetic that he received had been contaminated by phenol. The contamination occurred because phenol had seeped into the anaesthetic through imperceptibly small cracks in the glass ampoules. The medical community recognized that risk by the time of trial in 1954. At the time of the plaintiff's operation in 1947, however, the risk was unknown and not reasonably foreseeable. Liability consequently was denied. Denning L.J. stressed that "We must not look at the 1947 accident with 1954 spectacles." See also *Desautels v. Katimavik* (2003), 175 O.A.C. 201 (C.A.).

Is such reasoning ever inappropriate? Consider the following situation. During the 1950s, a respectable body of medical opinion favoured the sterilization of "mental defectives," a class of people that was broadly defined. Acting on the basis of that view, a province enacted legislation under which it sterilized a woman. The authorizing legislation was repealed during the 1970s and the woman sued for negligence in the 1990s. By that time, the practice of sterilization had been thoroughly discredited. Should the province be held liable? Did it breach the standard of care? See, on stronger facts, *Muir v. Alberta* (1996), 132 D.L.R. (4th) 695 (Alta. Q.B.). See also *Mack v. Canada (Attorney General)* (2002), 217 D.L.R. (4th) 583 (Ont. C.A.). For more on the problem of hindsight and how it can affect the standard of care analysis see Rachlinski, "A Positive Psychological Theory of Judging in Hindsight" (1998) 65 U. Chicago L. Rev. 571.

(a) PROBABILITY AND SEVERITY OF THE HARM

BOLTON v. STONE
[1951] A.C. 850 (H.L.)

[The plaintiff was walking on a road adjacent to a cricket ground when she was struck and injured by a ball that had been hit out of the ground.]

LORD REID: — My Lords, it was readily foreseeable that an accident such as befell the respondent might possibly occur during one of the appellants' cricket matches. Balls had been driven into the public road from time to time, and it was obvious that if a person happened to be where a ball fell that person would receive injuries which might or might not be serious. On the other hand, it was plain that the chance of that happening was small. The exact number of times a ball has been driven into the road is not known, but it is not proved that this has happened more than about six times in about thirty years. If I assume that it has happened on the average once in three seasons I shall be doing no injustice to the respondent's case. Then there has to be considered the chance of a person being hit by a ball falling in the road. The road appears to be an ordinary side road giving access to a number of private houses, and there is no evidence to suggest that the traffic on this road is other than what one might expect on such a road. On the whole of that part of the road where a ball could fall there would often be nobody and seldom any great number of people. It follows that the chance of a person ever being struck even in a long period of years was very small.

This case, therefore, raises sharply the question what is the nature and extent of the duty of a person who promotes on his land operations which may cause damage to persons on an adjoining highway. Is it that he must not carry out or permit an operation which he knows or ought to know clearly can cause such damage, however improbable that result may be, or is it that he is only bound to take into account the possibility of such damage if such damage is a likely or probable consequence of what he does or permits, or if the risk of damage is such that a reasonable man, careful of the safety of his neighbour, would regard that risk as material? I do not know of any case where this question has had to be decided or even where it has been fully discussed. Of course there are many cases in which somewhat similar questions have arisen, but, generally speaking, if injury to another person from the defendants' acts is reasonably foreseeable the chance that injury will result is substantial and it does not matter in which way the duty is stated. In such cases I do not think that much assistance is to be got from analysing the language which a judge has used. More assistance is to be got from cases where judges have clearly chosen their language with care in setting out a principle, but even so, statements of the law must be read in light of the facts of the particular case. Nevertheless, making all allowances for this, I do find at least a tendency to base duty rather on the likelihood of damage to others than on its foreseeability alone.

The definition of negligence which has, perhaps, been most often quoted is that of Alderson, B., in *Blyth v. Birmingham Waterworks Co.* [(1856), 11 Ex. 781]. . .:

> Negligence is the omission to do something which a reasonable man, guided upon those considerations which ordinarily regulate the conduct of human affairs, would do, or doing something which a prudent and reasonable man would not do.

I think that reasonable men do, in fact, take into account the degree of risk and do not act on a bare possibility as they would if the risk were more substantial.

. . .

Counsel for the respondent in the present case had to put his case so high as to say that, at least as soon as one ball had been driven into the road in the ordinary course of a match, the appellants could and should have realised that that might happen again, and that, if it did, someone might be injured, and that that was enough to put on the appellants a duty to take steps to prevent such an occurrence. If the true test is foreseeability alone I think that must be so. Once a ball has been driven on to a road without there being anything extraordinary to account for the fact, there is clearly a risk that another will follow and if it does there is clearly a chance, small though it may be, that somebody may be injured. On the theory that it is foreseeability alone that matters it would be irrelevant to consider how often a ball might be expected to land in the road and it would not matter whether the road was the busiest street or the quietest country lane. The only difference between these cases is in the degree of risk. It would take a good deal to make me believe that the law has departed so far from the standards which guide ordinary careful people in ordinary life. In the crowded conditions of modern life even the most careful person cannot avoid creating some risks and accepting others. What a man must not do, and what I think a careful man tries not to do, is to create a risk which is substantial. Of course, there are numerous cases where special circumstances require that a higher standard shall be observed and where that is recognized by the law, but I do not think that this case comes within any such special category. In my judgment, the test to be applied here is whether the risk of damage to a person on the road was so small that a reasonable man in the position of the appellants, considering the matter from the point of view of safety, would have thought it right to refrain from taking steps to prevent the danger. In considering that matter I think that it would be right to take into account, not only how remote is the chance that a person might be struck, but also how serious the consequences are likely to be if a person is struck, but I do not think that it would be right to take into account the difficulty of remedial measures. If cricket cannot be played on a ground without creating a substantial risk, then it should not be played there at all. I think that this is in substance the test which Oliver, J., applied in this case. He considered whether the appellants' ground was large enough to be safe for all practical purposes and held that it was. This is a question, not of law, but of fact and degree. It is not an easy question, and it is one on which opinions may well differ. I can only say that, having given the whole matter repeated and anxious consideration, I find myself unable to decide this question in favour of the respondent. I think, however, that this case is not far from the border-line. If this appeal is allowed, that does not, in my judgment, mean that in every case where cricket has been played on a ground for a number of years without accident or complaint those who organise matches there are safe to go on in reliance on past immunity. I would have reached a different conclusion if I had thought that the risk here had been other than extremely small because I do not think that a reasonable man, considering the matter from the point of view of safety, would or should disregard any risk unless it is extremely small.

. . .

[Lord Reid allowed the appeal. Lords Porter, Normand, Oaksey and Radcliffe delivered separate concurring speeches.]

PARIS v. STEPNEY BOROUGH COUNCIL
[1951] A.C. 367 (H.L.)

LORD OAKSEY: — My Lords, I agree entirely with the opinion just delivered by my noble and learned friend Lord Normand.

The duty of an employer towards his servant is to take reasonable care for the servant's safety in all the circumstances of the case. The fact that the servant has only one eye, if that fact is known to the employer, and that if he loses it he will be blind, is one of the circumstances which must be considered by the employer in determining what precautions if any shall be taken for the servant's safety. The standard of care which the law demands is the care which an ordinarily prudent employer would take in all the circumstances. As the circumstances may vary infinitely it is often impossible to adduce evidence of what care an ordinarily prudent employer would take. In some cases, of course, it is possible to prove that it is the ordinary practice for employers to take or not to take a certain precaution, but in such a case as the present, where a one-eyed man has been injured, it is unlikely that such evidence can be adduced. The court has, therefore, to form its own opinion of what precautions the notional ordinarily prudent employer would take. In the present case the question is whether an ordinarily prudent employer would supply goggles to a one-eyed workman whose job was to knock bolts out of a chassis with a steel hammer while the chassis was elevated on a ramp so that the workman's eye was close to and under the bolt. In my opinion Lynskey, J., was entitled to hold that an ordinarily prudent employer would take that precaution. The question was not whether the precaution ought to have been taken with ordinary two-eyed workmen and it was not necessary, in my opinion, that Lynskey, J., should decide that question

— nor did he purport to decide it, although it is true that he stated the question in one sentence too broadly as "whether the employers in adopting this system and not providing or requiring the use of goggles for the workers on this system were taking reasonable care to provide a suitable system of work and to provide a suitable plant."

The risk of splinters of steel breaking off a bolt and injuring a workman's eye or eyes may be and, I think, is slight and it is true that the damage to a two-eyed workman if struck by a splinter in the eye or eyes may be serious, but it is for the judge at the trial to weigh up the risk of injury and the extent of the damage and to decide whether, in all the circumstances, including the fact that the workman was known to be one-eyed and might become a blind man if his eye was struck, an ordinarily prudent employer would supply such a workman with goggles. It is a simple and inexpensive precaution to take to supply goggles, and a one-eyed man would not be likely, as a two-eyed man might be, to refuse to wear the goggles. Lynskey, J., appears to me to have weighed the extent of the risk and of the damage to a one-eyed man and I am of opinion that his judgment should be restored.

. . .

LORD MORTON OF HENRYTON (dissenting): — My Lords, it cannot be doubted that there are occupations in which the possibility of an accident occurring to any workman is extremely remote, while there are other occupations in which there is constant risk of accident to the workmen. Similarly, there are occupations in which, if an accident occurs, it is likely to be of a trivial nature, while there are other occupations in which, if an accident occurs, the results to the workman may well be fatal. Whether one is considering the likelihood of an accident occurring, or the gravity of the consequences if an accident happens, there is in each case a gradually ascending scale between the two extremes which I have already mentioned.

In considering generally the precautions which an employer ought to take for the protection of his workmen it must, in my view, be right to take into account both elements, the likelihood of an accident happening and the gravity of the consequences. I take as an example two occupations in which the risk of an accident taking place is exactly equal; if an accident does occur in the one occupation, the consequences to the workman will be comparatively trivial; if an accident occurs in the other occupation the consequences to the workman will be death or mutilation. Can it be said that the precautions which it is the duty of an employer to take for the safety of his workmen are exactly the same in each of these occupations? My Lords, that is not my view. I think that the more serious the damage which will happen if an accident occurs, the more thorough are the precautions which an employer must take.

If I am right as to this general principle, I think it follows logically that if A and B, who are engaged on the same work, run precisely the same risk of an accident happening, but if the results of an accident will be more serious to A than to B, precautions which are adequate in the case of B may not be adequate in the case of A, and it is a duty of the employer to take such additional precautions for the safety of A as may be reasonable. The duty to take reasonable precautions against injury is one which is owed by the employer to every individual workman.

In the present case it is submitted by counsel for the appellant that although the appellant ran no greater risk of injury than the other workmen engaged in the maintenance work, he ran a risk of greater injury. Counsel points out that an accident to one eye might transform the appellant into a blind man, and this event in fact happened. A similar accident to one of his comrades would transform that comrade into a one-eyed man, a serious consequence indeed but not so serious as the results have been to the appellant.

My Lords, the Court of Appeal thought that the one-eyed condition of the appellant, known to his employers, was wholly irrelevant in determining the question whether the employer did or did not take reasonable precautions to avoid an accident of this kind. I do not agree. Applying the general principle which I have endeavoured to state, I agree with your Lordships and with Lynskey, J., that the condition of the appellant was a relevant fact to be taken into account.

There still remains, however, the question whether the judge rightly came to the conclusion that there was, "so far as this particular plaintiff was concerned, a duty upon the employers to provide goggles and require the use of goggles as part of their system." He thought, as I read his judgment, and as the Court of Appeal read it, that there was no duty upon the employers to provide goggles for two-eyed men who were employed on the same work as the appellant. With this latter view the Court of Appeal agreed, and I take the same view. The evidence given at the trial has already been analysed by my noble and learned friend on the woolsack, and I shall only add that, although Captain Paterson had knowledge of about half-a-dozen eye injuries in the course of thirty-two years' experience, he did not say whether any of them was of a serious nature. The only other eye injury deposed to was that of Mr. Seeley. He was asked by the judge "Were you off work at all with your eye?", and he answered "Oh no". "Just that something got into your eye?" said the judge. "Yes, and I got it out," replied the witness.

My Lords, is it really possible to draw a distinction, on the facts of the present case, between a two-eyed man and a one-eyed man? If the employers were not negligent in failing to provide goggles for two-eyed men doing this work, during all the years prior to this accident, did they become negligent, so far as regards the appellant alone, as from July 22, 1946, when Mr. Boden, their public cleansing officer, became aware for the first time that the appellant had practically no vision in his left eye? The loss of an eye is a most serious injury to any man, and I can only see two alternatives in this case: (a) that the employers were negligent throughout in failing to provide goggles and insist on their use by all men employed in this type of work; or (b) that the risk of an eye injury to any man was so remote that no employer could be found negligent in failing to take these precautions.

My Lords, I think the first alternative must be rejected. Applying the test laid down by Lord Dunedin in *Morton v. William Dixon* [[1909] S.C. 807] already quoted by my noble and learned friend Lord Normand, I cannot find that the provision of goggles "was a thing which was commonly done by other persons in like circumstances." The evidence is conclusive to the contrary. Nor does the evidence support the view that it was "a thing which was so obviously wanted that it would be folly in anyone to neglect to provide it." Although I recognize that the one-eyed condition of the appellant was a factor to be taken into account, I think alternative (b) is correct. I cannot reach the conclusion that a one-eyed man, but not a two-eyed man, has a remedy against the employer for so serious an injury. I think it must be both or neither, and on the facts of the present case I agree with the conclusion of the Court of Appeal, that the evidence does not establish any negligence on the part of the respondents.

I would dismiss the appeal.

[Lords Normand and MacDermott delivered separate concurring speeches. Lord Simonds dissented for reasons similar to those of Lord Morton of Henryton.]

NOTES AND QUESTIONS

1. In *Bolton*, what factors did Lord Reid consider in determining whether the defendant breached the standard of care? Do you think the defendant would have been absolved of liability if: (a) balls were hit out of the club an average of two times a year; (b) the club was surrounded by busy roadways; or (c) the risk factors were the same, but the last time a ball was hit out it seriously injured a pedestrian walking on the quiet street?

2. *Bolton v. Stone* is often contrasted with *Miller v. Jackson*, [1977] 1 Q.B. 966 (C.A.). In *Miller*, a new subdivision was built on the edge of a cricket ground that had been in operation for many years. Fewer than ten times a year, cricket balls left the grounds, cleared a protective fence and landed in someone's backyard. The plaintiff, who owned one of the affected houses, sued in negligence and nuisance and asked for both damages and injunctive relief. The defendant admitted that it could not entirely eliminate the possibility of damage unless it stopped holding cricket matches. Lord Denning M.R. held a strong view on the matter:

> In summer time, village cricket is the delight of everyone. Nearly every village has its own cricket field where the young men play and the old men watch. In the village of Lintz in County Durham they have their own ground where they have played these last 70 years. They tend it well. The wicket area is well rolled and mown. . . . The village team plays there on Saturdays and Sundays. . . . Yet now after 70 years a judge of a High Court has ordered that they must not play there any more. He has issued an injunction to stop them. He has done it at the instance of a newcomer who is no lover of cricket. The newcomer has built, or has had built for him, a house on the edge of the cricket green which four years ago was a field where cattle grazed. The animals did not mind the cricket. But now this adjoining field has been turned into a housing estate. The newcomer bought one of the houses on the edge of the cricket ground. . . . Now he complains that when a batsman hits a six, the ball has been known to land in his garden or near his house. His wife got so upset about it that they always go out at weekends. They say that this is intolerable. So they asked the judge to stop the cricket being played, and the judge, much against his will, has felt he must order the cricket to be stopped, with the consequence, I suppose, that the Lintz Cricket Club will disappear. The cricket ground will be turned to some other use. I expect for more houses or a factory. The young men will turn to other things instead of cricket. The whole village will be much the poorer. And all this because of a newcomer who has just bought a house next to the cricket ground.

Lord Denning M.R. referred to *Bolton v. Stone*, but rejected Lord Reid's suggestion that "If cricket cannot be played on a ground without creating a substantial risk, then it should not be played there at all." While accepting that the defendant was liable if "by a million-to-one chance a cricket ball does go out of the ground and causes damage," he refused to impose an injunction to prevent the games from being played.

In the majority judgment in *Miller*, Lane L.J. agreed with Cumming-Bruce L.J. that the risk of property damage was both foreseeable and foreseen by the defendants. Lane L.J. further decided that the plaintiffs had no obligation "to protect themselves in their own home" from the threat presented by the defendants' activities. While both judges agreed that the defendants were liable in nuisance and negligence, only Lane L.J. was prepared to grant an injunction.

In the end result, the plaintiff was awarded £400 in damages, but was not granted an injunction. Should the factors that Lord Denning M.R. cited in *Miller* be relevant to the formulation of the standard of care?

3. The defendant need only take precautions against "reasonably foreseeable" risks. That concept is difficult to define with any precision. There are, however, some well-accepted propositions. A risk may be reasonably foreseeable even if it is not "probable," in the sense of being greater than 50% or more likely than not. An unusual, even remarkable, event may be sufficiently foreseeable in some circumstances. In *Bolton v. Stone*, for instance, the risk was sufficiently foreseeable even though only a half dozen balls had been hit onto the road in the preceding thirty years. At the same time, however, the defendant need not guard against dangers that are fanciful or far-fetched. In the final analysis, the concept of reasonable foreseeability creates a generous amount of leeway and discretion for the trier of fact. See generally Fleming, *The Law of Torts*, 9th ed. (1998) at 128.

4. Explain the difference between Lord Oaksey's and Lord Morton's assessment of the risk factors in *Paris*. Would Lord Oaksey have reached the same decision if the plaintiff had possessed normal vision? Would Lord Morton have reached the same conclusion if there had been a previous accident involving a worker with two eyes? See also *Shilson v. Northern Ont. Light & Power Co.* (1919), 59 S.C.R. 443 and *Gloster v. Toronto Electric Light Co.* (1906), 38 S.C.R. 27 in which the court considered the probability of children coming into contact with exposed electric wires.

5. Consider the possible practical effect of the decision in *Paris*. If presented with two applicants for a job, one with one eye and one with two eyes, which would an economically rational employer choose? Would the temptation to (improperly) hire the latter be sufficiently negated by the obligations that exist under human rights legislation?

(b) COST OF RISK AVOIDANCE

VAUGHN v. HALIFAX-DARTMOUTH BRIDGE COMM.

(1961), 29 D.L.R. (2d) 523 (N.S.S.C.)

[A bridge operated and maintained by the defendant was painted. Flecks of paint were blown by the wind onto nearby cars. The owner of one of those cars sued in negligence. The defendant argued that it had taken all necessary and proper measures to prevent or to minimize injury to the plaintiff from paint dripping from the bridge, so that it was not careless.]

MACDONALD J.: . . . We must take it that no amount of ordinary care would prevent the dripping paint nor the likelihood of its being carried by the wind varying distances up to some hundreds of feet, to various parts of the dockyard (including the parking lot in question) when the painting operations were carried on in the general area of the bridge adjacent thereto. Thus we may conclude that it was inevitable that paint should fall on the cars in the parking lot in question and during the painting operations in early July. The duty of the defendant was to take all reasonable measures to prevent that result or to minimize damage from falling paint.

The usual horrific argument was made as to the impracticability of any effective steps to do so except at prohibitive cost, particularly because of the large area of affection, say 300-400 ft. of the dockyard north of the bridge to which paint might come from an extent of the bridge 500 ft. long. The answer is that the season of such painting did not exceed a month; and that we are only concerned with precautions in respect of one parking lot relatively close to the bridge. Moreover, no policy was established of warning car owners or the dockyard authorities in advance of painting operations, though the defendant well knew of the danger to them implicit in such operations. On occasion, however, when complaints did come, as they did from time to time, the defendant did bestir itself by advising the Security Officer of the dockyard of painting operations, with the result that certain cars were moved to safer parts of the dockyard. These instances suggest the feasibility of such a practice which if adopted would have obviated damage in this case. Nor can it be said that the defendant could not have asked for permission to post warning signs at the parking lot (or other parts of the dockyard) or communicated *via* press or radio similar warnings of danger from painting expected to be done in the neighbourhood of that lot. If it be said that neglect in this regard was overcome by the provision of a man in the dockyard charged with the duty of wiping fallen paint from the parked cars, the answer is that this method depended upon the wiping operation being done promptly; and that during such a painting season as that in question such provision was clearly inadequate in point of number of men, as is illustrated by the employment of four or more on other occasions. It is notable that precautions in either of these regards would have entailed relatively little expense in view of the shortness of the painting season and would in all probability have prevented or at least minimized the plaintiff's damage.

[Currie J. and Patterson J. also concluded that the defendant was negligent. Ilsley C.J. did not address this issue.]

LAW ESTATE v. SIMICE

(1994), 21 C.C.L.T. (2d) 228 (B.C.S.C.)

[The plaintiff sued the defendant doctors in negligence, claiming that her husband died because of their failure to provide timely, appropriate and skillful emergency care. Among other things, they had not initially taken a CT scan of the patient. The case dramatically raised the issue of the allocation of limited and costly medical resources.]

SPENCER J.: . . . I must observe that throughout this case there were a number of times when doctors testified that they feel constrained by the British Columbia Medical Insurance Plan and by the British Columbia Medical Association standards to restrict their requests for CT scans as diagnostic tools. No doubt such sophisticated equipment is limited and costly to use. No doubt there are budgetary restraints on them. But this is a case where, in my opinion, those constraints worked against the patient's interest by inhibiting the doctors in their judgment of what should be done for him. That is to be deplored. I understand that there are budgetary problems confronting the health care system. I raise it in passing only to point out that there were a number of references to the effect of financial restraint on the treatment of this patient. I respectfully say it is something to be carefully considered by those who are responsible for financing it. I also say that if it comes to a choice between a physician's responsibility to his or her individual patient and his or her responsibility to the medicare system overall, the former must take precedence in a case such as this. The severity of the harm that may occur to the patient who is permitted to go undiagnosed is far greater than the financial harm that will occur to the medicare system if one more CT scan procedure only shows the patient is not suffering from a serious medical condition.

[Several of the doctors who had treated the patient were held liable in negligence.]

NOTES AND QUESTIONS

1. In *Vaughn*, what factors did the court consider in determining that the defendant had breached the standard of care? Would the result have been the same if it had been proven that the accident prevention costs exceeded the total damages?

2. Is a patient entitled to the best available, or to merely the most affordable, medical care? Did the court in *Law Estate* apply an appropriate perspective in assessing the physician's reluctance to order a CT scan? If health professionals have no role to play as financial gatekeepers or allocators of scarce resources, who should play these roles? Has the court adequately considered that ordering a CT scan or booking an operation in one case may result in delays or denials of treatment in other cases?

3. In *Bateman v. Doiron* (1991), 8 C.C.L.T. (2d) 284 (N.B.Q.B.), aff'd (1993), 18 C.C.L.T. (2d) 1 (N.B.C.A.) the court accepted that a Moncton hospital had no choice but to grant privileges to general practitioners in order to fully staff its emergency department. The court acknowledged that this practice resulted in physicians with limited skill and experience staffing the emergency room. However, the court stated at 292 that:

> to suggest that the defendant Moncton Hospital might be reasonably expected by the community to staff its emergency department with physicians qualified as expert in the management of critically ill patients does not meet the test of reality, nor is it a reasonably expected community standard. The non-availability of trained and experienced personnel, to say nothing of the problems of collateral resource allocation, simply makes this standard unrealistic, albeit desirable.

The majority of the Court of Appeal did not address this issue, but Justice Rice wrote a scathing dissent, criticizing the staffing and administrative practices of the emergency department.

Should hospitals be held liable in negligence because they cannot afford to adequately staff emergency rooms? Are inadequately staffed emergency rooms preferable to no emergency rooms? Can or should a hospital be held liable in negligence for not allocating sufficient resources to its emergency department? What role, if any, should courts play in reviewing resource allocation and other hospital management decisions?

4. How should courts assess the cost of avoidance issues in dealing with limited health resources? Should the same approach be adopted in analyzing public agencies, such as the police and child welfare departments, which do not have adequate resources to respond to all the demands for service?

5. In *De Vos v. Robertson* (2000), 48 C.C.L.T. (2d) 172 (Ont. S.C.J.) Lofchik J. used language that is almost identical to the extract above from *Law Estate*. He observed that:

> it was suggested that the time pressures involved in day surgery require that the most expedient form of anaesthesia be used so as not to upset the routine of those involved in the process. No doubt there are budgetary and time constraints involved in scheduling day surgeries such as those undergone by the plaintiff but, in my view, this is a case where those constraints worked against the patient's interest. . . It is difficult in this case to resist the observation that the patient's problems were at least in part related to what might be described as "*production line medicine*" in that the procedures which were followed and the standard of disclosure applied might be considered acceptable in the vast majority of cases being handled, but this patient did not fit the mould. . . [emphasis in original]

The court held that the anaesthetist breached the standard of care. For an American case raising similar considerations see *Wickline v. California*, 228 Cal. Rptr. 661 (Cal. App. 2 Dist. 1986).

6. Cases like *Law Estate* consider these cost issues in the context of a negligence claim brought by an injured plaintiff. Similar considerations can arise in a different context: administrative proceedings brought by members of the public against the government challenging broader health care resource allocation decisions, such as a decision to close a hospital or discontinue a procedure. See for example *Eldridge v. British Columbia (Attorney General)*, [1997] 3 S.C.R. 624; *Auton (Guardian ad litem of) v. British Columbia (Attorney General)*, [2004] 3 S.C.R. 657; and *Chaoulli v.Quebec (Attorney General)*, [2005] 1 S.C.R. 791.

7. As suggested in *Vaughn* and *Law Estate*, the plaintiff must prove that there was a reasonably practicable precaution that the defendant failed to adopt. In those cases, the precautions were fairly obvious. See also *Ware's Taxi Ltd. v. Gilliham*, [1949] S.C.R. 637. In other situations, however, the issue may be more difficult. In *Neill v. New South Wales Fresh Food & Ice Pty. Ltd.* (1963), 108 C.L.R. 362 (H.C.A.) the defendant employed the plaintiff for the purpose of washing out a large cylindrical tank that it used for transporting milk. The combination of milk residue and soapy water made the tank very slick. The plaintiff was injured when he slipped and fell. At trial, the jury found that the defendant had breached the standard of care. That decision was reversed on appeal, however, because the plaintiff had not adduced sufficient evidence of a practical solution (such as a handrail inside the tank or non-slip boots). Consequently, there was no basis in evidence upon which the jury could find that the defendant had breached the standard of care. See also *Whelan v. Parsons & Sons Transportation Ltd.* (2005), 250 Nfld. & P.E.I.R. 23 (N.L.C.A.).

(c) SOCIAL UTILITY

WATT v. HERTFORDSHIRE COUNTY COUNCIL

[1954] 1 W.L.R. 835 (C.A.)

[The plaintiff, a fireman, responded to an emergency call requiring the use of a special jack. The jack had been used only once in the last 15 years. The truck that was fitted for carrying the jack was unavailable and consequently the jack was loaded in the rear of another vehicle. When the driver braked suddenly, the jack became dislodged and seriously injured the plaintiff.]

. . .

The plaintiff claimed that the defendants, his employers, were negligent in that they (a) failed to load or secure the jack in such a way that it could not become dislodged; (b) loaded the jack in such a way that they knew or ought to have known it was likely that if the lorry pulled up suddenly the jack would become dislodged and cause injuries to any person riding on the back of the lorry; (c) permitted and/ or caused the plaintiff to ride on the back of the lorry on to which the jack had been loaded; (d) caused or permitted the jack to be transported on the lorry which, as the defendants knew or ought to have known, was not provided with clips, straps, or other suitable means to secure it; (e) failed to provide any or any adequate supervision of the loading of the jack on to the lorry; and it was claimed that the plaintiff's accident was due to negligence and that he was entitled to recover damages against the defendants.

. . .

DENNING L.J.: — It is well settled that in measuring due care you must balance the risk against the measures necessary to eliminate the risk. To that proposition there ought to be added this: you must balance the risk against the end to be achieved. If this accident had occurred in a commercial enterprise without any emergency there could be no doubt that the servant would succeed. But the commercial end to make profit is very different from the human end to save life or limb. The saving of life or limb justifies taking considerable risk, and I am glad to say that there have never been wanting in this country men of courage ready to take those risks, notably in the fire service.

In this case the risk involved in sending out the lorry was not so great as to prohibit the attempt to save life. I quite agree that fire engines, ambulances and doctors' cars should not shoot past the traffic lights when they show a red light. That is because the risk is too great to warrant the incurring of the danger. It is always a question of balancing the risk against the end. I agree that this appeal should be dismissed.

[Singleton and Morris L.JJ. gave separate concurring judgments dismissing the fireman's claim.]

NOTES AND QUESTIONS

1. In *Watt* would the defendant have been held liable if the emergency call had involved only property damage? Would the case have been decided differently if the plaintiff had been a volunteer? See *Hammond v. Wabana (Town)* (1998), 170 Nfld. & P.E.I.R. 97 (N.L.C.A.); and *Killip's Television Service Ltd. v. Stony Plain (Town)* (2000), 257 A.R. 92 (Q.B.).

2. Police high-speed chases pose controversial social utility issues. Should the police be subject to a reduced standard of care because they are attempting to apprehend a fleeing suspect? What effect, if any, should the alleged offence have on the assessment of the officer's conduct?

In *Priestman v. Colangelo* (1959), 19 D.L.R. (2d) 1 (S.C.C.) the defendant police officers had attempted several times to stop a suspected car thief. While travelling at high speeds, the officer in the front passenger seat leaned out the window and fired at the rear tire of the suspect's car in an attempt to stop it as it approached a busy intersection. The bullet hit the car frame, ricocheted and struck the driver, rendering him unconscious.

The car went out of control, mounted the curb, hit a hydro pole, and struck and killed two pedestrians. The court reasoned that the officers were under an affirmative duty to apprehend suspects and were justified by what is now s. 25(4) of the *Criminal Code*, R.S.C. 1985, c. C-46 in using as much force as was necessary to prevent their escape. Do you think that the officer was careless in shooting at the vehicle? What impact should the fact that the officer was under a statutory duty to apprehend the suspect have on the issues of standard of care and breach? See also *Miller v. Wolbaum* (1986), 47 M.V.R. 162 (Sask. Q.B.); *Moore v. Fanning* (1987), 41 C.C.L.T. 67 (Ont. H.C.); and *Hill v. Hurst* (2001), 203 D.L.R. (4th) 749 (B.C.S.C.).

3. Would a claim based on the facts in *Priestman* be decided differently now? How have public and judicial attitudes toward policing and police changed in the past 25 years? See *Patenaude c. Roy* (1994), 26 C.C.L.T. (2d) 237 (Qc. C.A.). In the 1980s most police departments in Canada adopted strict rules to govern both high-speed chases and the use of firearms. For example, a directive of the Ontario Solicitor General limited police pursuits to a "measure of last resort." The directive listed 11 factors to be considered by police, including the seriousness of the offence, the presence of bystanders and traffic, and the age of the fleeing driver. High-speed chases continued to claim the lives of police officers, fleeing suspects and bystanders. For example, there were 33 chase-related deaths in Ontario from 1991 to 1997. See St. Amand, "Police Settle Lawsuit with Victims of Crash" *Toronto Star* (1 November 1993) A9; French, "Woman Killed as Truck Rams Bus" *The Globe and Mail* (28 June 1996) A5; and Appleby, "Police-Chase Deaths Prompt Call for Action" *The Globe and Mail* (24 March 1999) A3.

A report by the Commission for Public Complaints Against the RCMP, *Police Reports and Public Safety* (1999) criticized police policy on vehicle pursuits as "vague and confusing." It recommended police pursuit only for serious offences and only by officers with sufficient training.

See also *Criminal Code*, R.S.C. 1985, c. C-46, s. 249.1 which makes it a criminal offence for a driver to fail to stop his or her vehicle when being pursued by a police officer.

In *Burbank v. Bolton*, 2007 CarswellBC 762 (C.A.) (WLeC) an R.C.M.P. constable pursued what turned out to be a 15-year-old unlicensed driver, impaired by methadone, in a stolen car. The driver ran a stop sign and hit another car, killing one person and injuring four others. The victims sued the driver and the constable. The court reviewed the regulations and R.C.M.P. policies governing police pursuit. It held that while the driver was 85% responsible, the constable was 15% responsible. With respect to the latter, the court concluded that the pursuit "should never have started" and that the constable was in breach of the standard of care. Newbury J.A. dissented, concerned that the majority's approach left little room for police pursuit in any circumstances.

4. Generally the courts only consider the social utility of the defendant's conduct if he or she is a public officer or is employed by a public authority. Should the social utility of a private citizen's conduct also be considered in determining whether he or she acted carelessly? What problems would arise from this approach? How could this apply to the conduct of the rescuers in *Horsley v. MacLaren* (1972), 22 D.L.R. (3d) 545 (S.C.C.), extracts of which are found in Chapters 11 and 12? See Griffiths, "The Standard of Care Expected of a First-aid Volunteer" (1990) 53 Mod. L. Rev. 255.

4. An Economic Analysis of the Standard of Care

UNITED STATES v. CARROLL TOWING CO.

159 F.2d 169 (2d Cir. 1947)

L. HAND, Circuit Judge: . . . It appears . . . that there is no general rule to determine when the absence of a bargee or other attendant will make the owner of the barge liable for injuries to other vessels if she breaks away from her mooring. However, in any cases where he would be so liable for injuries to others, obviously he must reduce his damages proportionately, if the injury is to his own barge. It becomes apparent why there can be no such general rule, when we consider the grounds for such a liability. Since there are occasions when every vessel will break from her moorings, and since, if she does, she becomes a menace to those about her; the owner's duty, as in other similar situations, to provide against resulting injuries is a function of three variables: (1) the probability that she will break away; (2) the gravity of the resulting injury, if she does; (3) the burden of adequate precautions. Possibly it serves to bring this notion into relief to state it in algebraic terms: if the probability be called P; the injury, L; and the burden, B; liability depends upon whether B is less than L multiplied by P: i.e., whether B is less than PL. Applied to the situation at bar, the likelihood that a barge will break from her fasts and the damage she will do, vary with the place and time; for example, if a storm threatens, the danger is greater; so it is, if she is in a crowded harbor where moored barges are constantly being shifted about. On the other hand, the barge must not be the bargee's prison, even though he lives aboard; he must go ashore at times. We need not say whether, even in such crowded waters as New York Harbor a bargee must be aboard at night at all; it may be that the custom is otherwise, as Ward, J., supposed in "*The Kathryn B. Guinan*. . .". . .; and that, if so, the situation is one where custom should control. We leave that question open; but we hold that it is not in all cases a sufficient answer to a bargee's absence without excuse, during working hours, that he has properly made fast his barge to the pier, when he leaves her. In the case at bar the bargee left at five o'clock in the afternoon of January 3rd, and the flotilla broke away at about two o'clock in the afternoon of the following day, twenty-one hours afterwards. The bargee had been away all the time, and we hold that his fabricated story was affirmative evidence that he had no excuse for his absence. At the locus in quo — especially during the short January days and in the full tide of war activity — barges were being constantly "drilled" in and out. Certainly it was not beyond reasonable expectation that, with the inevitable haste and bustle, the work might not be done with adequate care. In such circumstances we hold — and it is all that we do hold — that it was a fair requirement that the Connors Company should have a bargee aboard (unless he had some excuse for his absence), during the working hours of daylight.

Judgment accordingly.

In "A Theory of Negligence" (1972) 1 J. Legal Stud. 29 at 32-33, R. Posner (later Judge Posner) revisited "the Hand formula":

> It is time to take a fresh look at the social function of liability for negligent acts. The essential clue, I believe, is provided by Judge Learned Hand's famous formulation of the negligence standard – one of the few attempts to give content to the deceptively simple concept of ordinary care. . . . In a negligence case, Hand said, the judge (or jury) should attempt to measure three things: the magnitude of the loss if an accident occurs; the probability of the accident's occurring; and the burden of taking precautions that

> would avert it. If the product of the first two terms exceeds the burden of precautions, the failure to take those precautions is negligence. Hand was adumbrating, perhaps unwittingly, an economic meaning of negligence. Discounting (multiplying) the cost of an accident if it occurs by the probability of occurrence yields a measure of economic benefit to be anticipated from incurring the costs necessary to prevent the accident. The cost of prevention is what Hand meant by the burden of taking precautions against the accident. It may be the cost of installing safety equipment or otherwise making the activity safer, or the benefit foregone by curtailing or eliminating the activity. If the cost of safety measures or of curtailment — whichever cost is lower — exceeds the benefit in accident avoidance to be gained by incurring that cost, society would be better off, in economic terms, to forego accident prevention. A rule making the enterprise liable for the accidents that occur in such cases cannot be justified on the grounds that it will induce the enterprise to increase the safety of its operations. When the cost of accidents is less than the cost of prevention, a rational profit-maximizing enterprise will pay tort judgments to the accident victims rather than incur the larger cost of avoiding liability. Furthermore, overall economic value or welfare would be diminished rather than increased by incurring a higher accident-prevention cost in order to avoid a lower accident cost. If, on the other hand, the benefits in accident avoidance exceed the costs of prevention, society is better off if those costs are incurred and the accident averted, and so in this case the enterprise is made liable, in the expectation that self-interest will lead it to adopt the precautions in order to avoid a greater cost in tort judgments.
>
> One misses any reference to accident avoidance by the victim. If the accident could be prevented by the installation of safety equipment or the curtailment or discontinuance of the underlying activity by the victim at lower cost than any measure taken by the injurer would involve, it would be uneconomical to adopt a rule of liability that placed the burden of accident prevention on the injurer. Although not an explicit part of the Hand formula this qualification. . . is implicit in the administration of the negligence standard.
>
> Perhaps, then, the dominant function of the fault system is to generate rules of liability that if followed will bring about, at least approximately, the efficient—the cost-justified—level of accidents and safety. Under this view, damages are assessed against the defendant as a way of measuring the costs of accidents, and the damages so assessed are paid over to the plaintiff (to be divided with his lawyer) as the price of enlisting their participation in the operation of the system. Because we do not like to see resources squandered, a judgment of negligence has inescapable overtones of moral disapproval, for it implies that there was a cheaper alternative to the accident. Conversely, there is no moral indignation in the case in which the cost of prevention would have exceeded the cost of the accident. Where the measures necessary to avert the accident would have consumed excessive resources, there is no occasion to condemn the defendant for not having taken them.
>
> If indignation has its roots in inefficiency, we do not have to decide whether regulation, or compensation, or retribution, or some mixture of these best describes the dominant purpose of negligence law. In any case, the judgment of liability depends ultimately on a weighing of costs and benefits.

The economic analysis is not, however, without its critics. J. Fleming states in *The Law of Torts*, 9th ed. (1998) at 131-2:

> The negligence concept, with its complex balance just described, has a decidedly utilitarian flavour. Indeed, it has been forcibly argued that the negligence matrix reflects norms of economic efficiency, tending to maximise wealth and minimise costs, by encouraging cost justified accident prevention while discouraging excessive investment in safety. If the loss caused by a given activity to the actor and his victim is greater than

its benefit, the activity should be (and is) discouraged by being labelled negligent and requiring the actor to compensate the victim; if the balance is the other way, the actor may go ahead scot-free.

But negligence cannot be reduced to a purely economic equation. True, economic factors are given weight, especially regarding the value of the defendant's activity and the cost of eliminating the risk. In a few situations, allowance for the defendant's limited financial resources has been expressly sanctioned. But in general, judicial opinions do not make much of the cost factor, and for good reasons. For one thing, our legal tradition in torts has strong roots in an individualistic morality with its focus primarily on interpersonal equity rather than broader social policy. The infusion of economic criteria like insurability, loss distribution and efficient resource allocation has so far remained largely unsystematic, interstitial and controversial. Secondly, the calculus of negligence includes some important non-economic values, like health and life, freedom and privacy, which defy comparison with competing economic values. Negligence is not just a matter of calculating the point at which the cost of injury to victims (that is the damages payable) exceeds that of providing safety precautions. The reasonable man is by no means a caricature cold blooded, calculating Economic Man. Lastly, courts remain sceptical as to their ability, let alone that of juries, to pursue economic analyses.

NOTES AND QUESTIONS

1. What factors did Judge Hand consider in *Carroll Towing Co.* when determining whether the defendant had breached the standard of care? What did he mean by the phrase "the burden of adequate precautions?"

2. Notwithstanding his judgment in *Carroll Towing Co.*, Judge Hand later warned against placing too much emphasis on an "economic" approach: *Conway v. O'Brien*, 111 F.2d 611 at 612 (2d Cir. 1940). He also observed that, in some cases, the cost of avoiding the risk may be very difficult to calculate. See *Moisan v. Loftus*, 178 F.2d 148 (2d. Cir. 1949). See also Englard, "The System Builders: A Critical Appraisal of Modern American Tort Theory" (1980) 9 J. Legal Stud. 27 at 54.

Likewise, in *McCarty v. Pheasant Run Inc.*, 826 F.2d 1554 at 1557 (7th Cir. 1987), Judge Posner stated:

> Ordinarily, and here, the parties do give the jury the information required to quantify the variables that the Hand Formula picks outs as relevant. That is why the formula has greater analytic than operational significance. Conceptual as well as factual difficulties in monetizing personal injuries may continue to frustrate efforts to measure expected accident costs with the precision that is possible, in principle at least, in measuring the other side of the equation — the cost or burden of precaution.

What impact does such certainty have on the viability of the cost-benefit approach?

3. Apply the formula suggested by Judge Hand in *Carroll Towing Co.* to the facts of *Paris*. What does the formula indicate?

4. How would Judge Posner determine whether a defendant had breached the standard of care? According to him, what is the purpose of tort law? Would you agree with his assumption that most actors are rational profit-maximizers who are amenable to deterrence? Does Judge Posner use the formula in the same way that Judge Hand does?

5. Are J. Fleming's concerns about the economic analysis of tort law warranted? More specifically, does an economic approach exclude "non-economic values, like health and life, freedom and privacy?" Do such values "defy comparison with competing economic values?" See Veljanovski, "Economic Theorizing About Tort" [1985] Curr. Legal Probs. 117; Englard, "Law and Economics in American Tort Cases: A Critical Assessment of the Theory's Impact on Courts" (1991) 41 U.T.L.J. 359; and Saks, "Do We Really Know Anything About the Behavior of the Tort Litigation System — And Why Not" (1992) 140 U. Penn. L. Rev. 1147.

6. Many otherwise valid tort claims fail on technical grounds and others are settled for far less than the full loss. Moreover, the law of damages does not permit the plaintiff to recover for certain losses, such as grief, and has limited recovery for other types of injuries, such as nervous shock. Consequently, a tortfeasor's accident liability costs may be far less than the actual social costs of his or her conduct. Does Judge Posner's approach adequately address these features of the tort system? See Epstein, "A Theory of Strict Liability" (1973) 2 J. Legal Stud. 151; Grady, "A New Positive Economic Theory of Negligence" (1983) 92 Yale L.J. 799; and Williams, "Second Best: The Soft Underbelly of Deterrence Theory in Tort" (1993) 106 Harv. L. Rev. 932.

7. E. Weinrib has indicated that the Hand formulation may be adopted on moral rather than economic grounds. One must first assume that this test provides a standard that a rational actor would use in deciding whether to take a risk of personal injury or loss. An actor who breaches the standard and injures another is held liable in negligence for imposing upon others a risk which he or she would not have taken. Thus, the Hand test is used to impose liability on those who have acted in a morally impermissible manner in failing to extend equal consideration to others: Weinrib, "Toward a Moral Theory of Negligence Law" (1983) 2 Law and Phil. 37 at 49-52. See also Abel, "A Critique of Torts" (1994) 2 Tort L. Rev. 99; and Weinrib, *The Idea of Private Law* (1995).

5. Special Standards of Care

(a) THE STANDARD OF CARE EXPECTED OF THE DISABLED

FIALA v. CECHMANEK
(2001), 201 D.L.R. (4th) 680 (Alta. C.A.)

WITTMANN J.A.: . . .

Facts

On the morning of March 11, 1995, Robert John MacDonald ("MacDonald") went for a run. During his run, he experienced a severe manic episode, diagnosed later, but never previously, as bipolar disorder, type 1. He believed he was God and had a plan to save the world. Hoping to inform others of his ideas, MacDonald asked several individuals for their telephone or fax numbers.

Still on his run, MacDonald approached a car, which was stopped at an intersection. MacDonald walked around the car and beat on both its driver-side window and roof. While yelling obscenities at Katalin Cechmanek ("Cechmanek"), the owner and operator of the car, he jumped on the car's trunk and roof. He then broke through the sunroof of the car and began choking Cechmanek. Cechmanek involuntarily hit the gas pedal and accelerated into the intersection, striking another car, owned and operated by the appellant Jana Fiala and carrying as a passenger, her daughter, the appellant Lenka Fiala. The Fialas were injured by the collision.

After the collision, MacDonald continued to threaten and yell obscenities at Cechmanek. He also approached the Fialas and shouted sexually explicit statements at 17-year-old Lenka Fiala. Clearly agitated, he flailed his arms wildly, darted back and forth between individuals who had surrounded the accident scene, and ran down the middle of the road. Despite MacDonald's relatively small stature, it took two policemen and two EMS attendants to forcibly restrain him.

[Wittman J.A. reviewed the evidence of the psychiatrists who had examined MacDonald and continued.]

Trial Decision

The trial judge was satisfied that MacDonald was in the midst of a severe manic episode at the time of the attack and was not in control of his mind. The trial judge held that MacDonald had no control over his behaviour and was incapable of appreciating either the nature or quality of his actions. . . .

The trial judge determined that MacDonald [had proved] that he had no reason to foresee any danger that he might be on the verge of a manic episode. Without warning or notice, there was a sudden, absolute change in MacDonald's condition and, as a result, MacDonald had no ability to reason or to appreciate his duty of care to others.

The trial judge noted that, unlike the facts of *Wenden v. Trikha* (1991), 116 A.R. 81 (Q.B.), affirmed 135 A.R. 382 (C.A.), where the defendant was aware of his mental illness before causing the collision that injured the plaintiff, MacDonald was not aware of his mental illness before the alleged tort occurred. He had not been warned, as had Mr. Trikha, of the dangers associated with his illness.

Analysis

The action against MacDonald was pleaded in negligence even though his conduct may more easily fit within the legal framework associated with the intentional tort of battery.

While there has been much debate about the liability of the mentally ill in the context of tort law, considerable uncertainty still abounds: see G.B. Robertson, *Mental Disability and the Law in Canada*, 2nd ed. (Toronto: Carswell, 1994) at 239. A review of the opinions expressed on the topic exemplifies the confusion that has plagued this area of the law.

In A.M. Linden, *Canadian Tort Law*, 6th ed. (Toronto: Butterworths, 1997) at 142, the author states:

> Persons suffering from mental illness may not have to comply with the reasonable person standard, the theory being that it is unfair to hold people liable for accidents they are incapable of avoiding. No allowance is made, however, for those who are merely deficient intellectually and therefore cannot live up to the objective standard. Nor is any mercy shown to defendants whose minds are clouded because of drugs or drunkenness. It is only when the inadequacy amounts to a serious mental illness that the excuse is countenanced.

Linden's approach suggests that the objective reasonable person standard is properly relaxed in instances where a defendant's mental illness prevents him or her from meeting the standard of care normally required. Arguably, this position emphasizes the "fault" requirement underlying tort liability.

In contrast, several authors have stated that the compensatory nature of tort law is of paramount concern and, therefore, those suffering from mental illness should not be allowed a lower standard. Robertson states at 240 that the function of negligence law is to compensate the victim rather than punish the wrongdoer.

Those who support holding the mentally ill to the higher objective standard make similar arguments. First, they suggest that when two innocent persons are involved in an accident, the person who caused the accident should be liable for the resulting damage. According to this view, victim compensation is the primary aim of tort law.

Second, they argue that, unlike instances where the defendant is a child or is afflicted with a physical disability, the practical difficulties associated with determining the extent of a person's mental illness and the person's ability to act in a reasonable manner would create such confusion that the courts would be vulnerable to those feigning mental illness for the purpose of avoiding liability. Courts would be unable to draw a line between incapacitating mental illness and variations of temperament.

Third, they submit that holding the severely mentally ill to the higher standard would encourage their caregivers to take adequate precautions, which is especially important in this de-institutionalization era. It is argued that relieving the mentally ill of liability will result in their increased isolation, as community members will avoid contact with them for fear of harm without compensation.

Finally, those who support holding the mentally ill to an objective standard argue that any consideration of a defendant's mental illness will erode the objective standard to such an extent that it will no longer be of consequence. This concern was encapsulated long ago by Chief Justice Tindal in *Vaughan v. Menlove* (1837), 132 E.R. 490 (C.P.) at 493:

> Instead, therefore, of saying that the liability for negligence should be co-extensive with the judgment of each individual, which would be as variable as the length of the foot of each individual, we ought rather to adhere to the rule which requires in all cases a regard to caution such as a man of ordinary prudence would observe.

While some of these arguments appear valid on their face, a closer analysis reveals weakness.

When two "innocent" persons are involved in an accident, presumably the element of fault is absent. Although the term "innocent" may refer to an absence of moral culpability, negligence law is concerned with fault associated with falling below the requisite standard of care in the circumstances. If a person is suffering from a mental illness such that it is impossible to attribute fault to him, holding him liable for his actions would create a strict liability regime. Although compensation of victims of tort is very important, the statement begs the question: what is a tort? For the most part, fault is still an essential element of Canadian tort law. Strict liability has been imposed in only limited areas of tort law such as conversion, defamation, and non-natural use of land that results in an escape of a harmful substance. But strict liability has not been extended to product liability as it has in the United States, nor to cases like this.

In "The Role of Fault and Policy in Negligence Law" (1996), 35 Alta. L. Rev. 24, Professor Klar describes as misguided the recent emphasis on the compensatory role of tort law. At p. 29, he states:

> Negligence law is about wrongdoing. While this is admittedly an imprecise notion, there ought to be an element of moral blame in all conduct which tort law deems as negligent and hence liable for damages. The elements of the negligence action ought to conform and be interpreted by courts according to this notion of fault and the goal of correcting wrongs. Loss distribution by liability insurance, compensating the disabled, deterring wrongful conduct, regulating and educating professionals and industry, or achieving other public policy objectives, although frequently advanced through negligence law, ought to remain as the consequences of the tort action and not be seen as the purposes of the tort action. In this way, society can maintain a strong system of civil justice while recognizing the limitations to a system of civil justice. These limitations and gaps can then be best accommodated by non-tort schemes which are designed to accomplish these other objectives in an efficient and effective manner.

If compensating the injured is the overriding goal of tort law, the legal process becomes rife with fictions leading to the application of legal principles in a results-oriented manner, thereby compromising tort law as a system of corrective justice. According to Professor Klar, tort law should refocus on a system of corrective justice where fault is a key consideration when determining or apportioning liability. Such a system could be supplemented by programs designed to achieve such policy goals as compensation of victims, punishment of wrongdoers, deterrence and accident prevention — programs that would be more efficient than legal process. . . .

The "innocent" victim argument also falters when one considers how tort law has treated children and those who are suddenly physically disabled. Children of tender years are presumed to be incapable of negligence because they lack sufficient judgment to exercise reasonable care. . . . Unless engaging in adult activities, older children are held to a standard of a reasonable child of the same age, intelligence, and experience. . . . With respect to physically disabled defendants, courts routinely inquire into the voluntariness of their actions, whether the onset of the incapacity to control their actions could have been anticipated, and whether the damage could have been avoided. . . .

Given increased understanding of the biological or physiological roots of mental illness, a distinction between those who are suddenly physically incapacitated due to such conditions as epilepsy or diabetic shock and those who are incapacitated as a result of mental illness seems wholly unjustified. Such a distinction risks legitimizing physical illness while reinforcing negative stereotypes concerning mental illness. Concerns about the erosion of the objective reasonable person standard have not prevented courts from taking age or physical disability into consideration. Therefore, such concern should not prevent consideration of a defendant's mental illness.

Nor should the practical difficulties associated with assessing mental illness and the related lack of control of a defendant's behaviour prevent courts from crafting a test for a mental illness defence in tort actions. When this argument was originally made, an assessment of the capacity of a mentally ill defendant may not have been possible. However, there have been significant advancements in the study of mental illness. Courts can hear the testimony of experts with respect to myriad issues that arise in negligence actions. These experts may provide comprehensive and detailed information. . . .

The need to encourage caregivers of the mentally ill to take adequate precautions is not met effectively by imposing liability on the mentally ill. Rather than using tort law to ensure appropriate care, it seems more reasonable to impose liability directly on caregivers for failing in their duties. In any event, those who advocate adopting a strict liability stance in order to encourage caregivers to adequately care for the mentally ill perhaps assume wrongly that caregivers recognize the legal ramifications of a failure to properly execute their duties.

While several writers suggest that allowing the mentally ill a lower standard will reinforce the stereotype that the mentally ill are dangerous and should be isolated . . . the failure to acknowledge the impact of mental illness risks undermining the legitimacy of such disorders. . . . Arguably, an increased understanding of mental illness will allow the public to distinguish between the real risks associated with the integration of the mentally ill and fears that are mired in ignorance. If mentally ill individuals still have the capacity to conform to the objective standard, they will not be relieved of liability. . . . However, holding the mentally ill to the strict objective standard would essentially create a no-fault regime. . . .

Although Canadian courts have acknowledged that some consideration must be given to a defendant's mental illness, the case law offers a wide range of possible tests.

In *Buckley and T.T.C. v. Smith Transport Ltd.*, [1946] O.R. 798, [1946] 4 D.L.R. 721, the Ontario Court of Appeal held that a defendant who, by reason of mental disorder was either incapable of appreciating the duty to take care or incapable of discharging that duty, would not be liable in negligence. Unlike the test used in criminal law, the determination of whether the plaintiff could appreciate the duty of care owed and whether he could discharge that duty would not involve an assessment of whether the defendant could understand that his actions were "wrong". The Court held that a driver suffering from an insane delusion that his truck was being powered by a remote control was not liable for the collision he caused, as his insanity prevented him from discharging his duty. . . .

In *Canada (Attorney General) v. Connolly* (1989), 41 B.C.L.R. (2d) 162, 64 D.L.R. (4th) 84, the British Columbia Supreme Court held that there could be no liability in the absence of foreseeable harm. Therefore, because the defendant's bipolar disorder prevented him from foreseeing the injury that could result from driving his car at a high rate of speed while the plaintiff's arm was pinned inside the car, he could not be held liable. An essential element of the tort of negligence was absent.

. . .

While it could be argued that *Connolly* and *Buckley* apply a subjective standard and ignore the edict that an inability to meet the reasonable person test is no defence, it is clear that they import an exception to the general rule. In light of the exceptions granted to children, and the physically disabled, such an exception is not unreasonable. However, any such exception must be narrowly defined. As noted by Linden, supra: "It is only when the inadequacy amounts to a serious mental illness that the excuse [will be] countenanced."

The case law and academic literature reveal that there has been judicial recognition in Canada of the need to relieve the mentally ill of tort liability in certain circumstances. While the compensation of victims is still a worthy goal, that should not compromise the basic tenets of tort law. To find negligence, the act causing damage must have been voluntary and the defendant must have possessed the capacity to commit the tort. The burden of showing the absence of either falls on the defendant. If the defendant understood the duty of care he owed and was able to discharge that duty, his actions would be voluntary and the requisite capacity would exist.

In order to be relieved of tort liability when a defendant is afflicted suddenly and without warning with a mental illness, that defendant must show either of the following on a balance of probabilities:

(1) As a result of his or her mental illness, the defendant had no capacity to understand or appreciate the duty of care owed at the relevant time; or

(2) As a result of mental illness, the defendant was unable to discharge his duty of care as he had no meaningful control over his actions at the time the relevant conduct fell below the objective standard of care.

This test will not erode the objective reasonable person standard to such a degree that the courts will be imposing a standard "as variable as the length of the foot". It will preserve the notion that a defendant must have acted voluntarily and must have had the capacity to be liable. Fault will still be an essential element of tort law.

On the facts of this case, the expert evidence . . . clearly indicated that MacDonald was afflicted suddenly, and without prior warning, with a condition that left him with no meaningful control of his behaviour and an inability to appreciate the duty of care he owed to Cechmanek and others, including the Fialas. His mental illness was manifestly incapacitating.

Unlike the defendant in *Wenden*. . ., MacDonald was unaware of his mental illness until after the accident. He was not driving a vehicle at the time and there was no way he could have foreseen the onset of his manic episode or taken preventative measures to avoid its result. His fault was no greater than Cechmanek's or the Fialas'; there was no fault.

If a strict liability regime is to apply to the acts of the mentally ill, the Legislature must give such direction. If the courts favour the compensatory goal of tort law by treating like any other person those suddenly afflicted with a serious and debilitating mental illness, the historical roots of tort law would be submerged and fault would become irrelevant. The result would be to taunt the tort.

On the facts found by the trial judge, MacDonald has satisfied the onus of showing that not one, but both of the tests to relieve him of tort liability are met.

NOTES AND QUESTIONS

1. Did the court apply a subjective or an objective standard of care in *Fiala*?

2. What arguments did the plaintiff make in favour of adopting a relatively unforgiving standard of care? How did Wittmann J.A. respond to those arguments? Do you agree with his decision?

3. The American Law Institute in the *Restatement (Second) of the Law of Torts* (1965) at para. 283B states that: "Unless the actor is a child, his insanity or other mental deficiency does not relieve the actor from liability for conduct which does not conform to the standard of the reasonable man under the circumstances." The position in England appears to be similar. In *Roberts v. Ramsbottom*, [1980] 1 All E.R. 7 (Q.B.), the court held that mental impairment short of automatism would not relieve the defendant from complying with the objective standard of care. Can you reconcile the American and English positions with the principle of no liability without fault? See generally Picher,

"The Tortious Liability of the Insane in Canada" (1975) 13 Osgoode Hall L.J. 1983; Coleman, "Mental Abnormality, Personal Responsibility and Tort Liability" in Brody & Englehardt, eds., *Mental Illness: Law and Public Policy* (1980) 107; Splane, "Tort Liability of the Mentally Ill in Negligence Actions" (1983) 93 Yale L.J. 153; and Light, "Rejecting the Logic of Confinement: Care Relationships and the Mentally Disabled under Tort Law" (1999) 109 Yale L.J. 381.

The English position may be changing. In *Mansfield v. Weetabix*, [1998] 1 W.L.R. 1263 (C.A.) a driver's brain functions became impaired when his blood sugar dropped. The court held that he was not liable for the accidents he caused. Leggatt L.J. stated "the standard of care. . . was that which is to be expected of a reasonably competent driver unaware that he is or may be suffering from a condition that impairs his ability to drive." The court noted that to not take into account the driver's condition would be to impose strict liability rather than a negligence standard.

4. The question of who should bear the risks posed by the mentally ill remains a contentious legal and policy issue. See Klar, *Tort Law*, 3d ed. (2003) at 308-309. For example in *Hutchings v. Nevin* (1992), 9 O.R. (3d) 776 (Gen. Div.) the defendant, who was having psychotic delusions, caused a car accident, injuring his passenger. While acknowledging the general authority of *Buckley v. Smith Transport Ltd.*, [1946] O.R. 798 (C.A.), the plaintiff's counsel argued that Ontario's compulsory automobile insurance legislation had shifted the risk of mentally ill drivers onto the defendant's insurer. The judge rejected this argument and held that the defendant was not liable.

5. It is well established that the physically disabled are required to meet only the standard of care of a reasonable person with a similar disability. This principle is reflected in the case law dealing with the blind. See *Carroll v. Chicken Palace Ltd.*, [1955] 3 D.L.R. 681 (Ont. C.A.); *Haley v. London Electric Board*, [1965] A.C. 778 (H.L.); *Crawford v. Halifax* (1977), 81 D.L.R. (3d) 316 (N.S.S.C.); and *Strickland v. St. John's* (1982), 37 Nfld. & P.E.I.R. 208 (Nfld. Dist. Ct.). See also Lowry, "The Blind and the Law of Tort: The Position of a Blind Person as Plaintiff in Negligence" (1972) 20 Chitty's L.J. 253; ten Broek, "The Right to Live in the World: The Disabled in the Law of Torts" (1966) 54 Cal. L. Rev. 841; and Milani, "Living in the World: A New Look at the Disabled in the Law of Torts" (1999) 48 Cath. U.L. Rev. 323.

6. What standard of care should be expected of automobile drivers who have heart disease or other similar illnesses? What factors should be taken into account to determine whether this standard has been breached? What weight should the court give to the argument that such people should attempt to live as normally as possible? See *Gootson v. R.*, [1948] 4 D.L.R. 33 (S.C.C.) (epileptic seizure); *Boomer v. Penn* (1965), 52 D.L.R. (2d) 673 (Ont. H.C.) (insulin reaction); *Gordon v. Wallace* (1973), 42 D.L.R. (3d) 342 (Ont. H.C.); and *Dobbs v. Mayer* (1985), 32 C.C.L.T. 191 (Ont. Dist. Ct.) (heart attack); and *Calgary (City) v. Thomas* (1995), 173 A.R. 51 (Prov. Ct.) (low blood sugar). See also Blalock, "Liability of the Unconscious Defendant" (1970) 6(2) Trial 29; and Smith, "Automatism — A Defence to Negligence?" [1980] New L.J. 1111.

(b) THE STANDARD OF CARE EXPECTED OF CHILDREN

JOYAL v. BARSBY

(1965), 55 D.L.R. (2d) 38 (Man. C.A.)

MILLER C.J.M. (dissenting): . . . The real point to be decided in this appeal is whether the infant was guilty of contributory negligence. Negligence on the part of the defendant is not disputed and is not in issue on this appeal.

. . .

The infant admittedly ran out onto this busy highway into the side of defendant's motor vehicle and suffered grievous injuries. Her home was between this highway and a railway track, and she and two younger brothers had left their home to cross the highway and enter a park on the opposite side. The infant was aged six years and two months, and both her brothers were younger than she. This is a busy highway and the infant, according to the evidence of the father and the evidence of the infant plaintiff, had been thoroughly instructed in the dangers of crossing this highway and the lesson to "Stop, Look, and Listen" had been thoroughly drilled into her by the father and learned by the infant. There is no question that the evidence established that the infant plaintiff was conscious of the traffic danger inherent on this busy highway.

One of the two younger brothers ran across the highway at a time when it appears to have been dangerous to do so, as a big semi-trailer transport truck was approaching from the north. The truck driver sounded a siren ("fog-horn" as it was called in the evidence) to warn either the boy running across the highway or the children generally. Hearing the "fog-horn", the infant plaintiff and her other brother apparently thought better of following the first venturesome brother across, so they stepped back onto the shoulder of the road and stood there about two feet east of the pavement.

A motorist by the name of Despins was about 100 yards ahead of the defendant's motor vehicle, and, seeing the one boy on the west side of the highway as well as the girl and her other brother on the east side of the highway, he took his foot off the accelerator and by doing so decreased his speed to about 35 m.p.h. He apparently was nervous lest the sister and her other brother should follow the first brother across the highway, but he did not apply his brakes and was satisfied to reduce speed by compression. He saw the girl make a motion to cross the road as he approached and was passing her. Presumably this was just about the time the truck horn sounded, which caused the girl to step back onto the shoulder. She and her brother continued to stand motionless on the shoulder about two feet off the hard surface after Despins had passed. Despins and the defendant were both proceeding north on the east side of the highway. Despins said he first saw the children on the side of the road when he was a considerable distance south, so they must have stood motionless for some little while to let traffic pass. The defendant saw the two children on the east side but concluded — and with some cause — that they had realized traffic was on the highway, were waiting for it to pass, and would stay where they were until he passed them. Apparently he was not close enough to see, or in any event did not see, the one boy run across the highway. Nevertheless, he did as Despins did — took his foot off the accelerator and let the compression decrease his speed from 60 m.p.h. to 38 or 40 m.p.h. When the defendant was less than a car length away from her, the infant plaintiff suddenly started to run across the highway from east to west. She took only four or five steps, and then collided with the rear door of the defendant's vehicle. She was apparently struck by the door handle and sustained severe injuries.

. . .

The defendant's counsel accepted the principle that his client was guilty of some negligence but, as intimated above, conducted his appeal on the ground that the infant was guilty of contributory negligence. This involves first of all the question "Could this six-year old infant be guilty of contributory negligence?"

A binding authority is the decision of the Supreme Court of Canada in *McEllistrum v. Etches*, 6 D.L.R. (2d) 1 at pp. 6-7, [1956] S.C.R. 787, where it is stated:

> It should now be laid down that where the age is not such as to make a discussion of contributory negligence absurd, it is a question for the jury in each case whether the infant exercised the care to be expected from a child of like age, intelligence and experience.

. . .

The learned trial Judge said she was not more heedless than other children of her age, intelligence and experience, which expression is analogous to the words used in the *Etches* case, *supra*. The sad fact remains that she was heedless, careless, and negligent, despite her training and traffic experience. It appears to me the learned trial Judge found that, as she was no more heedless than other similar children, she could not be guilty of contributory negligence and consequently was not so guilty.

I think the infant plaintiff was partly responsible for this regrettable accident. She was thoroughly trained on the dangers of the highway, had experience with the traffic thereon, and, without first looking, had suddenly left a place of safety for a place of danger. There was still traffic proceeding along the highway, including the defendant's vehicle, which, had she looked, she could not help seeing and have thus avoided the accident. If contributory negligence cannot be found in an instance such as this, against a child with such training and experience, then it would be rare indeed that this doctrine could be invoked against a child.

. . .

On the undisputed facts, I feel justified in holding that the infant plaintiff's negligence contributed to the accident and that she can properly be adjudged liable for contributory negligence to the extent of 40%.

I would allow the appeal and vary the judgment of the learned trial Judge by charging the plaintiffs with 40% liability. The plaintiffs will therefore recover 60% of the damages rather than the 100% awarded by the trial Judge, but will still have their costs in the Court below.

The defendant is entitled to his costs in this Court.

. . .

FREEDMAN J.A., concurs with MONNIN J.A.

MONNIN J.A.: . . . The learned trial Judge applied this standard to the case at bar in the manner following. He said:

> The age of the infant plaintiff was six years and two months and she appeared to me not to be of above average intelligence. Living near a fairly busy highway she would know of the danger from passing cars and admitted that her father had warned her of this danger; but she would have had far less experience than a city child of her age. I believe she acted as a normal child of her age and experience could be expected to act. She was momentarily stopped from crossing the highway by the blare of the truck siren, but this

> terrifying warning completely absorbed her attention. When the truck had passed she did not think of other traffic but darted forward as both Mr. Despins and the defendant anticipated she might do. In doing this she was not more heedless than any other child of her age, intelligence and experience. I do not consider that she was guilty of contributory negligence. The defendant must be held solely responsible.

The learned trial Judge considered the conduct of the child in the context of the situation which confronted her. This, of course, was the proper thing to do, since negligence is always a want of care in the particular circumstances. The learned trial Judge does not say that this child of six years and two months was incapable of being guilty of contributory negligence. He says that her behaviour in the specific situation should not be categorized as contributorily negligent. Faced with the approach of this large truck with its horn blaring, she riveted her attention upon it. That necessarily made her inattentive, for the moment, to traffic approaching from the other direction. But the learned trial Judge finds that the ordinary child of her age, intelligence and experience would have responded to the situation in the same way. Hence he refused to stamp her conduct with the label of negligence. I am not prepared to say he was wrong.

. . .

The appeal is therefore dismissed with costs. The cross-appeal is also dismissed with costs fixed at $50; the costs on the cross-appeal to be set off against the other costs.

NOTES AND QUESTIONS

1. What is the standard of care expected of a child? Is this test objective or subjective? Do you think the plaintiff in *Joyal* was contributorily negligent? See in comparison *Dao v. Sabatino* (1996), 24 B.C.L.R. (3d) 29 (C.A.). In *McEllistrum v. Etches*, [1956] S.C.R. 787, a case referred to by both the majority and dissent in *Joyal*, the court indicated that there is an age below which a child cannot be held liable in negligence. Can you suggest an appropriate test of capacity for children?

2. A child involved in an adult activity, such as driving a car, snowmobiling, golfing or hunting, is required to meet the standard of care expected of a reasonable adult. What is the rationale for imposing a higher standard of care in these situations? See *Ryan v. Hickson* (1974), 55 D.L.R. (3d) 196 (Ont. H.C.); *Dellwo v. Pearson*, 107 N.W.2d 859 (Minn. S.C. 1961); and *McErlean v. Sarel* (1987), 42 C.C.L.T. 78 (Ont. C.A.). But see *Chaisson v. Hebert* (1986), 187 A.P.R. 105 (N.B.Q.B.).

This raises the question of what will be found to be an adult activity. See *Pope v. R.G.C. Management Inc.* (2002), 8 Alta. L.R. (4th) 143 (Q.B.), a case about playing golf.

3. For other examples of the standard of care expected of children see *Ottosen v. Kasper* (1986), 37 C.C.L.T. 270 (B.C.C.A.); *Laviolette v. C.N.R.* (1987), 40 C.C.L.T. 138 (N.B.C.A.); *Bajkov v. Canil* (1990), 66 D.L.R. (4th) 572 (B.C.C.A.); and *Nespolon v. Alford* (1998), 40 O.R. (3d) 355 (C.A.). See also Bohlen, "Liability in Tort of Infants and Insane Persons" (1924) 23 Mich. L. Rev. 9; Dunlop, "Torts Relating to Infants" (1966) 5 U.W.O.L. Rev. 116; and Alexander, "Tort Liability of Children and Their Parents" in Mendes da Costa, ed., *Studies In Canadian Family Law* (1975) 845.

4. If the law is prepared to relax the standard of care based on youth, should it also do so based on old age? Why or why not? See Barrett, "Negligence and the Elderly: A

Proposal for a Relaxed Standard of Care" (1984) 17 J. Marshall L. Rev. 873. Should such a relaxed standard apply to activities like driving? See *McKee (Guardian ad litem of) v. McCoy* (2001), 9 C.C.L.T. (3d) 294 (B.C.S.C.).

5. Although parents, guardians and others who supervise children are not held vicariously liable when a child commits a tort, they can be held liable if they have carelessly failed to monitor or control the child's conduct. As discussed in Chapter 3, such liability can also be imposed under legislation such as the *Parental Responsibility Act, 2000*, S.O. 2000, c. 4. The courts have defined the requisite standard of care in terms of a "reasonable parent of ordinary prudence." See *Myers v. Peel County Board of Education*, [1981] 2 S.C.R. 21; and *Thomas v. Hamilton (City) Board of Education* (1994), 20 O.R. (2d) 598 (C.A.). Is it appropriate to use this parental standard in assessing the behaviour of educators, daycare workers and others who are not parents or guardians?

In *LaPlante (Guardian ad litem of) v. LaPlante* (1995), 26 C.C.L.T. (2d) 32 (B.C.C.A.) the defendant father was held liable in negligence for permitting his 16-year-old son, who had recently obtained his licence, to drive in traffic at highway speeds under icy conditions. The court held that a reasonable parent of ordinary prudence would not have let the son drive in those conditions.

In *C.S. (Next friend of) v. Miller* (2002), 306 A.R. 289 (Q.B.) a five-year-old child was sexually molested by Miller, a friend of the child's parents, while the two of them were visiting a Boy Scout Camp. The Camp Chief, who was a volunteer, witnessed the sexual assault but took no action to stop it or to prevent any further assaults while the child was at the camp. The child's mother sued the Boy Scouts for the assaults on her daughter. The court held that, even though she was a volunteer, the Camp Chief was liable in negligence. She had willingly and knowingly entered into a relationship of supervisory care and control over the children at the camp. This imposed on the Camp Chief an obligation to take appropriate steps to protect the victim, despite the fact that she was a visitor and not a registered camper and that she was accompanied by Miller, who had parental authority over the victim. The Boy Scouts were vicariously liable for the volunteer Camp Chief's negligence.

(c) THE STANDARD OF CARE EXPECTED OF PROFESSIONALS

At one time, only those involved in a limited number of public callings, such as innkeepers and common carriers, were held to special standards of care. The courts have now developed modified standards of care to govern not only professionals but also most skilled trades and occupations. The following materials focus on medical cases, but the courts' approach applies across many professions and trades.

WHITE v. TURNER

(1981), 31 O.R. (2d) 773 (H.C.)
aff'd (1982), 12 D.L.R. (3d) 319 (Ont. C.A.)

[The defendant plastic surgeon, Dr. Turner, performed a breast reduction operation on the plaintiff. The plaintiff suffered several post-operative complications and her breasts were scarred and poorly shaped. The plaintiff sued the defendant, claiming that he had been negligent both in performing the operation and in not properly disclosing the risks of the surgery. The following excerpt addresses only the first allegations of negligence.]

LINDEN J.: — Needless to say, a mere error in judgment by a professional person is not by itself negligence. The Courts recognize that professionals may make mistakes during the course of their practice, which do not bespeak negligence. Sometimes medical operations do not succeed. Sometimes lawyers lose cases. The mere fact of a poor result does not mean that there has been negligence. In order to succeed in an action against a professional person, a plaintiff must prove, on the balance of probabilities, not only that there has been a bad result, but that this was brought about by negligent conduct.

Before liability can be imposed for the operation itself, therefore, the plaintiff must prove that the defendant performed the surgery in such a way that a reasonable plastic surgeon would consider it to have been less than satisfactory. . . . In other words, unless it is established on a balance of probabilities that this mammoplasty was done in a substandard way by the defendant, he cannot be held liable in negligence.

Plastic surgery is a specialty that has its own standards — standards which are unique to that specialty. If the work of a plastic surgeon falls below the accepted practices of his colleagues, he will be held civilly liable for any damage resulting. But if his work complies with the custom of his confrères he will normally escape civil liability for his conduct, even where the result of the surgery is less than satisfactory.

[The plaintiff alleged that the defendant had breached the standard of care in three respects. The first two concerned: (i) the defendant's choice of "the Strombeck procedure" and (ii) his planning for the operation. Both of those allegations were rejected on the evidence, some of which had been given by two experts, Dr. Birch and Dr. Robertson.]

The third area of complaint is with the actual execution of the surgery. Although Dr. Birch testified that a similar result to this could occur without the plastic surgeon being negligent, I find that the evidence, on the whole, supports a finding that the poor result obtained in the mammoplasty performed on Mrs. White was the result of Dr. Turner's negligent execution of the surgery.

The reason for the bad result here was that insufficient tissue was removed by Dr. Turner. . . .

There were two reasons why Dr. Turner did not remove sufficient tissue, both of which I find were negligence in the circumstances: (1) the operation was done too quickly, and (2) the suturing was started before a proper check was made of whether enough tissue had been removed.

As for the length of time taken to perform the operation, the evidence is clear that the usual time required is between two and four hours. Dr. Birch said that the Strombeck procedure took an average of two and a half hours to do. Dr. Robertson testified that more than three hours is required to perform a Strombeck properly. If he has only a junior intern assisting him, he normally requires about four hours to do a Strombeck. If he has an expert assistant, he can do it properly in three and a half hours. He indicated that, when the doctors on his staff at the Toronto General Hospital booked only three hours operating-room time for a Strombeck, they often could not complete the operation in time and other doctors were kept waiting for the operating-room. Dr. Robertson advised his own staff, therefore, to book four hours operating-room time in order to perform a Strombeck.

I have found on the facts here that Dr. Turner did this Strombeck in approximately one hour, 35 minutes. This was described by Dr. Birch as "very fast". He said that the operation was "very rapidly done". Dr. Turner must have seen no "hitches" to go at that speed, he concluded. Dr. Robertson was less charitable than Dr. Birch. He testified that even Dr. Turner's estimate of two and a half to two and three-quarters hours was a "pretty short" time for the Strombeck operation. Dr. Robertson could not imagine that a Strombeck could be properly done in one hour and 35 minutes. To him, it was "almost incredible" that it could. He thought it would take one hour just to close up. A simple mastectomy took one hour and 35 minutes to do. This mammoplasty by Dr. Turner was a "very rapid operation", he opined. "Detail takes time", he said and, consequently, the necessary attention to detail, which required some stepping back, was not done in this case. "When one is in a hurry, expediency rather than art comes into play", he suggested. In such a short time, thought Dr. Robertson, all the considerations could not be taken into account. The more time that is taken, the less likely is an undesirable result, he said. In the time Dr. Turner took to perform this operation, Dr. Robertson testified that he could not look back. Dr. Robertson concluded by saying that, although he hated to talk that way, he felt he had to: the patient was entitled to expect more than she received on this occasion.

I hold, therefore, that Dr. Turner did this operation too quickly. This resulted in his not removing enough tissue, which in turn caused the incisions to open, leading to the substandard result. This was actionable negligence.

As for the failure to make a check of the amount of tissue removed before closing, Dr. Birch testified that it was standard practice, at the conclusion of the cutting, to tack the flaps of skin together with a few sutures and make a judgment about the bulk of the breast. He said that some doctors do not do any actual stitching at this stage, but that all plastic surgeons put the pieces together and take a look before proceeding to close up. I find on the basis of this evidence that this was the standard practice of plastic surgeons.

There is no evidence that Dr. Turner did this standard check. It is not mentioned in his notes of the operation, but this is not controlling, according to Dr. Birch, who said that he did not usually make any notes about doing the check, although he invariably did it. Dr. Turner did not say that he made such a check. He did not even indicate that he was aware that it was standard practice. Actually, even though Dr. Turner did not do this check, he admitted that, when he went to close up, he actually noticed more tension on the flaps than usual, but he did nothing about it. He explained this by observing that there was always "quite a bit of tension". This extra tension should have served as a warning to him that insufficient tissue had been removed. But he was too much in a hurry to do anything about it. Moreover, Dr. Turner's written report stated that he had removed 800 gr., although, in fact, he had taken out only 705 gr. He was fully aware that the removal of only 705 gr. of tissue was less than the usual amount removed in such cases. Dr. Turner agreed that he probably should have taken out an additional 300 gr. of tissue. Dr. Robertson, in correcting the result, removed about 350 gr. (or three-quarter pound), an additional 50% of tissue, which demonstrates that this was no small error. If Dr. Turner had paused to do a proper check, he would have learned that he had removed only 705 gr., that this was less than usual, and that there was too much tension on the flaps. This would have revealed his error to him and permitted him to take the necessary corrective measures before closing. This, in turn, would have avoided the bad result. I find, therefore, that this failure to do the customary check was actionable negligence.

NOTES AND QUESTIONS

1. What allegations of breach were made against the defendant? How did the court define the standard of care expected of the defendant? Do you agree with the reasoning in *White*?

2. What is the standard of care that should be imposed on doctors to keep up with new drugs, surgical procedures and treatment programs? See *Dhalla v. Jodrey* (1985), 16 D.L.R. (4th) 732 (N.S.C.A.); *Sigouin (Guardian ad litem of) v. Wong* (1991), 10 C.C.L.T. (2d) 236 (B.C.S.C.); and *ter Neuzen v. Korn* (1995), 127 D.L.R. (4th) 577 (S.C.C.).

3. In *ter Neuzen v. Korn*, *ibid.*, Justice Sopinka noted that "physicians have a duty to conduct their practice in accordance with the conduct of a prudent and diligent doctor in the same circumstances." General practitioners are thus required to exercise the standard of care of a reasonable, competent general practitioner. This includes knowing their limits and when to refer patients to a specialist. In *Layden v. Cope* (1984), 28 C.C.L.T. 140 (Alta. Q.B.) the plaintiff, who had previously suffered from gout, went to two general practitioners in a small town. They both concluded that he had gout and prescribed medication. The doctors continued treating him for gout, even though his condition deteriorated and the hospital nurses expressed concern. After nine days, the plaintiff was referred to a specialist, who immediately diagnosed cellulitis with possible secondary infection. The plaintiff's condition deteriorated and his leg had to be amputated. In holding the general practitioners liable, the court stated that the standard of care expected of a general practitioner in a small town is not significantly different from that of general practitioners in a city. They should have considered other diagnoses when the plaintiff's condition did not improve and referred him to a specialist much sooner. See also *Dillon v. LeRoux*, [1994] 6 W.W.R. 280 (B.C.C.A.); and *Crawford (Litigation guardian of) v. Penney* (2003), 14 C.C.L.T. (3d) 60 (Ont. S.C.J.), aff'd (2004), 26 C.C.L.T. (3d) 246 (Ont. C.A.).

4. The standard of care expected of an intern is that of a reasonably competent intern in the circumstances. Although interns have completed medical school and passed their licensing examinations, they are not qualified to practice on their own. Rather, interns are required to work under the supervision of a fully qualified doctor. Consequently, the standard of care expected of interns is lower than that required of general practitioners. See *Vancouver General Hospital v. Fraser Estate*, [1952] 2 S.C.R. 36; and *Aldana v. March* (1999), 44 C.C.L.T. (2d) 164 (B.C.S.C.). In contrast, residents are fully qualified doctors who seek additional training in a specialty. As a result, even a junior resident would be held to the standard of care expected of a general practitioner. A more senior resident would be expected to have advanced skills in his or her specialty consistent with a resident of comparable training, but would not be expected to have the skills of a fully qualified specialist. See *Dale v. Munthali* (1978), 21 O.R. (2d) 554 (C.A.); *Boulay v. Charbonneau* (1988), 46 C.C.L.T. 16 (Qc. C.A.); *Wills v. Saunders*, [1989] 2 W.W.R. 715 (Alta. Q.B.); *Brown (Next friend of) v. University of Alberta Hospital* (1997), 197 A.R. 237 (Q.B.); *Miles v. Judges* (1997), 37 C.C.L.T. (2d) 160 (Ont. Gen. Div.); *Chow (Litigation guardian of) v. Wellesley Hospital*, 1999 CarswellOnt 349 (Gen. Div.) (WLeC); and *Adair (Litigation administrator of) v. Hamilton Health Sciences Corp.* (2005), 32 C.C.L.T. (3d) 283 (Ont. S.C.J.).

On the standard of care for nurses see *Latin v. Hospital for Sick Children*, 2007 CarswellOnt 19 (S.C.J.) (WLeC).

5. The growing volunteer movement, the recognition of the value of peer counselling, and efforts to reduce costs have resulted in greater use of non-professionals in

various health and care situations. Although these individuals would not be expected to meet a professional standard of care, they would be required to have the skills and training necessary to do their assigned tasks competently. They would also be expected to know their own limits and when they should get professional assistance. Agencies that use non-professionals are required to adequately screen, train, place and supervise these workers. For example, an agency might be held liable in negligence for using inadequately trained volunteers to staff a suicide crisis line.

On the standard of care expected of a volunteer (as opposed to professional) fire-fighter, see *Killip's Television Services Ltd. v. Stony Plain (Town)* (2000), 257 A.R. 92 (Q.B.).

6. Individuals may be held to a professional standard of care if they implicitly or explicitly suggest that they have the skills and training of a professional. By holding themselves out as counsellors or therapists, individuals may be seen as explicitly suggesting that they have professional qualifications and training. Indeed, merely offering to provide a particular service, such as marriage counselling, might reasonably create the impression that one has special training and skills.

By the same token, however, a person practising in a secondary or related field will not be held liable simply because he or she failed to satisfy the standard expected in the primary field. For example in *Shakoor v. Situ*, [2000] 4 All E.R. 181 (Q.B.) the court held that a practitioner of traditional Chinese herbal medicine, who did not hold himself out as an "orthodox" physician, was only required to meet the standard of care appropriate to his "art." A similar analysis has been applied to midwives: *Carere v. Cressman* (2002), 12 C.C.L.T. (3d) 217 (Ont. S.C.J.).

7. For additional examples of medical malpractice see *Davies v. Gabel Estate*, [1995] 2 W.W.R. 35 (Sask. Q.B.); *Briffet v. Gander & District Hospital Board* (1996), 29 C.C.L.T. (2d) 251 (Nfld. C.A.); *Strichen v. Stewart* (2005), 367 A.R. 18(C.A.); *Barker v. Montfort Hospital*, 2007 CarswellOnt 2202 (C.A.) (WLeC); and *Taylor v. Morrison* (2006), 41 C.C.L.T. (3d) 79 (Ont. S.C.J.) (diagnosis); *Eady v. Tenderenda*, [1975] 2 S.C.R. 599; *Cherry (Guardian ad litem of) v. Borsman* (1991), 75 D.L.R. (4th) 668 (B.C.S.C.), aff'd on liability for procedure (1992), 94 D.L.R. (4th) 487 (B.C.C.A.); *Lyne v. McClarty* (2003), 170 Man. R. (2d) 161 (C.A.); and *Chasse v. Evenson* (2006), 59 Alta. L.R. (4th) 159 (Q.B.) (surgical procedure); *Joseph Brant Memorial Hospital v. Koziol* (1977), 77 D.L.R. (3d) 161 (S.C.C.); *Pittman Estate v. Bain* (1994), 19 C.C.L.T. (2d) 1 (Ont. Gen. Div.); and *Aristorenas v. Comcare Health Services* (2006), 216 O.A.C. 161 (C.A.) (post-operative care); *Champigny v. Ste-Marie* (1993), 19 C.C.L.T. (2d) 307 (Qc. S.C.) and *Pierre (Next Friend of) v. Marshall*, [1994] 8 W.W.R. 478 (Alta. Q.B.) (treatment); *Mustafic v. Smith (G.)* (1988), 55 Man. R. (2d) 188 (C.A.); and *Wenden v. Trikha* (1993), 14 C.C.L.T. (2d) 225 (Alta. C.A.) (psychiatric care); and *Rupert v. Toth* (2006), 38 C.C.L.T. (3d) 261 (Ont. S.C.J.) (patient management).

8. In *Meyers (Next friend of) v. Moscovitz* (2005), 363 A.R. 262 (C.A.), the court found that the trial judge had erred in defining the standard of care expected of a reasonable doctor in the management of a birth. Instead of framing the standard in terms of the overall management of the birth, the judge focussed on a single aspect of the woman's care: the monitoring of her temperature for infection. The court noted that in

some situations the breach of a single element of the standard of care could warrant a finding that the standard has been breached, but this was not such a case.

9. The current system for resolving allegations of medical malpractice has been roundly criticized by both patients' rights groups and the medical profession. For a discussion of alternatives to the existing fault-based adversarial approach see Sharpe, "Alternatives to the Court Process for Resolving Medical Malpractice Claims" (1981) 26 McGill L.J. 1036; Mitchell & McDiarmid, "Medical Malpractice: A Challenge to Alternative Dispute Resolution" (1988) 3 Can. J.L. & Society 227; Chapman, "Controlling the Costs of Medical Malpractice: An Argument for Strict Hospital Liability" (1990) 28 Osgoode Hall L.J. 523; and Abraham & Weiler, "Enterprise Medical Liability and the Evolution of the American Health Care System" (1994) 108 Harv. L. Rev. 381.

10. For a discussion of the standard of care expected of lawyers see *Brumer v. Gunn* (1982), 18 Man. R. (2d) 155 (Q.B.); *Jacks v. Davis* (1982), 141 D.L.R. (3d) 355 (B.C.C.A.); *Pound v. Nakonechny* (1983), 27 C.C.L.T. 146 (Sask. C.A.); *Central Trust Co. v. Rafuse* (1986), 31 D.L.R. (4th) 481 (S.C.C.); *Harela v. Powell* (1998), 163 D.L.R. (4th) 365 (Ont. Gen. Div.); *Wilcox v. Johnston* (2001), 238 N.B.R. (2d) 325 (Q.B.); and *Hagblom v. Henderson* (2003), 232 Sask. R. 81 (C.A.). See also Mahoney, "Lawyers — Negligence — Standard of Care" (1985) 63 Can. Bar Rev. 221; Lundy, MacKenzie & Newbury, *Barristers and Solicitors in Practice* (1998); Klar, *Tort Law*, 3d ed. (2003) at 359-369; and Flenley & Leech, *Solicitors' Negligence*, 2d ed. (2006). On the standard of care for paralegals see *Elliot v. Chiarelli* (2006), 83 O.R. (3d) 226 (S.C.J.).

11. For examples of other special standards of care see: *Dabous v. Zuliani* (1976), 68 D.L.R. (3d) 414 (Ont. C.A.); and *Trizec Equities Ltd. v. Ellis-Don Management Services Ltd.* (1998), [1999] 5 W.W.R. 1 (Alta. Q.B.) (architects); *Auto Concrete Curb Ltd. v. South Nation River Conservation Authority*, [1993] 3 S.C.R. 201; and Rochester, "Professional Engineers: Does a Higher Risk Imply a Higher Standard of Care?" (2000) 50 C.L.R. (2d) 199 (engineers); *Smith v. B.C. (A.G.)* (1988), 30 B.C.L.R. (2d) 356 (C.A.); and *Hill v. Hamilton-Wentworth Regional Police Services Board* (2005), 76 O.R. (3d) 481 (C.A.) (police officers); *Myers v. Peel County Board of Education*, [1981] 2 S.C.R. 21; *Fraser v. Board of School Trustees of School District No. 72 (Campbell River)* (1988), 54 D.L.R. (4th) 563 (B.C.C.A.); *MacCabe v. Westlock Roman Catholic Separate School District No. 110* (2001), 96 Alta. L.R. 217 (C.A.); and *Young v. Bella*, [2006] 1 S.C.R. 108 (teachers); *Hofstrand Farms Ltd. v. B.D.C. Ltd.*, [1986] 1 S.C.R. 228; and *Visanji v. Eaton* (2006), 39 C.C.L.T. (3d) 150 (B.C.S.C.) (common carriers); *Dom. Securities Ames Ltd. v. Deep* (1984), 4 O.A.C. 386 (C.A.); *Varcoe v. Sterling* (1992), 7 O.R. (3d) 204 (Gen. Div.), aff'd (1992), 7 O.R. (3d) 204 (C.A.); and *Refco Futures (Canada) Ltd. – Refco v. SYB Holdings Corp.* (2004), 23 B.C.L.R. (4th) 309 (C.A.) (stockbrokers); *Spiewak v. 251268 Ont. Ltd.* (1987), 61 O.R. (2d) 655 (H.C.) (real estate agents); *Haig v. Bamford*, [1977] 1 S.C.R. 466 (auditors); *Sceptre Resources Ltd. v. Deloitte Haskins & Sells* (1988), 64 Alta. L.R. (2d) 48 (Q.B.); and *Bloor Italian Gifts Ltd. v. Dixon* (2000), 2 C.C.L.T. (3d) 73 (Ont. C.A.) (accountants); *Waldman's Fish Co. v. Anderson Ins. Ltd.* (1979), 25 N.B.R. (2d) 482 (C.A.) (insurance agents); *Graham v. Picot Gorman and A.E.S. Consultants Ltd.* (1985), 66 N.B.R. (2d) 434 (T.D.); and *Indian Head Credit Union Ltd. v. A. Hosie & Co.* (1992), 103 Sask. R. 213 (Q.B.), aff'd (1994), 120 Sask. R. 73 (C.A.) (real estate appraisers); *Smith v. Eric S. Bush (a firm)*, [1987] 3

All E.R. 179 (C.A.) (land surveyors); *R.(L.) v. Nyp* (1995), 25 C.C.L.T. (2d) 309 (Ont. Gen. Div.) (journalists); *Wheeler v. Muri* (1996), 32 C.C.L.T. (2d) 180 (Sask. Q.B.) (veterinarians); *B.(D.) v. Children's Aid Society of Durham (Region)* (1996), 30 C.C.L.T. (2d) 310 (Ont. C.A.) (social workers); *Hendrick v. De Marsh* (1984), 6 D.L.R. (4th) 713 (Ont. H.C.), aff'd (1986), 54 O.R. (2d) 185 (C.A.); and *D.N. v. Oak Bay (District)* (2005), 261 D.L.R. (4th) 692 (B.C.S.C.) (probation officers); and Schulz, "Mediator Liability in Canada: An Examination of Emerging American and Canadian Jurisprudence" (2001) 32 Ottawa L. Rev. 269; and Schulz, "Obstacles to Tortious Liability for Mediator Malpractice" in Beaulac, Pitel & Schulz, eds., *The Joy of Torts* (2003) 149 (mediators).

12. For the standard of care expected of professionals generally, see Campion, ed., *Professional Liability in Canada* (1994); and Jackson, *Jackson & Powell on Professional Negligence*, 5th ed. (2002).

6. Degrees of Negligence

The common law generally recognizes one standard of care in negligence – that of a reasonable person. Even the special standards of care focus on what is reasonable to expect of those with recognized disabilities or unique skills, education or training.

Occasionally, however, statutes restrict the scope of liability to injuries inflicted as a result of "gross negligence." The definition of that concept has always been something of a mystery. Baron Wolfe once described it as ordinary negligence "with the addition of a vituperative epithet": *Wilson v. Brett* (1843), 152 E.R. 737. It has also been sarcastically suggested that the differences between negligence, gross negligence and recklessness equate to the differences between a fool, a damned fool and a God-damned fool: Linden & Feldthusen, *Canadian Tort Law*, 8th ed. (2006) at 196. For practical purposes, it may suffice to say that gross negligence requires something less blameworthy than criminal negligence but something worse than ordinary tort negligence.

The idea of gross negligence tends to be confined to two types of statutes. The first concerns the liability of a municipality for injuries caused by snow or ice on sidewalks. Section 44 of the *Municipal Act, 2001*, S.O. 2001, c. 25, s. 44, is typical. It provides:

> (1) The municipality that has jurisdiction over a highway or bridge shall keep it in a state of repair that is reasonable in the circumstances, including the character and location of the highway or bridge.
>
> . . .
>
> (9) Except in case of gross negligence, a municipality is not liable for a personal injury caused by snow or ice on a sidewalk.

The second type of statute concerns the liability of medical professionals who provide medical assistance during emergencies. Section 2 of the *Good Samaritan Act, 2001*, S.O. 2001, c. 2, is typical, providing:

> *Protection from liability*
>
> (1) Despite the rules of common law, a person described in subsection (2) who voluntarily and without reasonable expectation of compensation or reward provides the services described in that subsection is not liable for damages that result from the person's negligence in acting or failing to act while providing the services, unless it is established that the damages were caused by the gross negligence of the person.

Persons covered

(2) Subsection (1) applies to,

(a) a health care professional who provides emergency health care services or first aid assistance to a person who is ill, injured or unconscious as a result of an accident or other emergency, if the health care professional does not provide the services or assistance at a hospital or other place having appropriate health care facilities and equipment for that purpose; and

(b) an individual, other than a health care professional described in clause (a), who provides emergency first aid assistance to a person who is ill, injured or unconscious as a result of an accident or other emergency, if the individual provides the assistance at the immediate scene of the accident or emergency.

A more specialized example is *Sabrina's Law, 2005*, S.O. 2005, c. 7, s. 3(4) which applies to emergency responses to anaphylactic reactions suffered by students in schools.

Beyond these two types, there are other statutes that use this standard of care. For example, it applies to police conduct under the *Police Act*, R.S.B.C. 1996, c. 367, s. 21 and to trustees in bankruptcy and receivers in several sections of the *Environmental Protection Act*, R.S.O. 1990, c. E.19.

NOTES AND QUESTIONS

1. What is the rationale for legislation that protects municipalities from liability in negligence for slippery sidewalks? See *Dorschell v. Cambridge (City)* (1980), 30 O.R. (2d) 714 (C.A.); and *Mete v. Mississauga*, [1984] O.J. No. 1139 (H.C.) (QL).

2. Good Samaritan statutes are intended to encourage emergency intervention by reducing the threat of liability for those who intervene. It is, however, doubtful that they have much effect. See McInnes, "Good Samaritan Statutes: A Summary and Analysis" (1992) 26 U.B.C.L. Rev. 239. There have been few cases in Canada brought against those who intervened in an emergency situation.

3. The ordinary standard of care requires the defendant to act as the reasonable person would have acted in similar circumstances. In light of this focus on the circumstances, courts recognize the "sudden peril" doctrine, under which conduct that normally would be considered careless is exempted from liability if, in the context of an emergency, it nevertheless was reasonable. Reasonable people make reasonable mistakes under pressure: see *Canadian Pacific Ltd. v. Gill* (1973), 37 D.L.R. (3d) 229 (S.C.C.). In light of that doctrine, how low is the standard of care under Good Samaritan legislation?

4. Under what circumstances does Ontario's *Good Samaritan Act, 2001* apply? Should it apply more broadly? Are there situations in which some types of individuals should not be encouraged to intervene?

5. Under a third type of legislation that previously existed in some provinces, a driver of a non-commercial vehicle could be held liable for injuries sustained by a passenger only if an accident was caused by the driver's gross negligence. The courts were generally suspicious of such provisions and often found gross negligence in conduct that looked remarkably like regular negligence. For an excellent example of the problems

of interpreting the guest passenger legislation see *Engler v. Rossignol* (1975), 10 O.R. (2d) 721 (C.A.). See also *Levesque v. Wedge* (1977), 13 Nfld. & P.E.I.R. 283 (P.E.I.C.A.); *Cheevers v. Van Norden* (1980), 42 N.S.R. (2d) 337 (T.D.); and *McIntyre v. Sawatsky* (1982), 18 Sask. R. 406 (Q.B.).

Guest passenger statutes were roundly criticized. See Gibson, "Let's Abolish Guest Passenger Legislation" (1965) 35 Man. Bar News 274. They have now been abolished.

7. Custom

TER NEUZEN v. KORN

(1995), 127 D.L.R. (4th) 577 (S.C.C.)

[The plaintiff contracted HIV as a result of artificial insemination in January 1985. The risk of such infection was not widely known in North America when the procedure was performed. The defendant doctor was responsible for screening semen donors. Expert evidence established that the physician had adopted standard medical practices in this regard. The jury nevertheless found him liable. One of the issues on appeal was whether it was open to the jury to find that the standard practice itself fell short of the standard of care.]

SOPINKA J.: –

. . .

1. *Standard of care and evidence of standard practice*

It is well-settled that physicians have a duty to conduct their practice in accordance with the conduct of a prudent and diligent doctor in the same circumstances. In the case of a specialist, such as a gynaecologist and obstetrician, the doctor's behaviour must be assessed in light of the conduct of other ordinary specialists, who possess a reasonable level of knowledge, competence and skill expected of professionals in Canada, in that field. A specialist, such as the respondent, who holds himself out as possessing a special degree of skill and knowledge, must exercise the degree of skill of an average specialist in his field.

. . .

It is also particularly important to emphasize, in the context of this case, that the conduct of physicians must be judged in the light of the knowledge that ought to have been reasonably possessed at the time of the alleged act of negligence. . . .

No issue is taken with this proposition which was applied both in the trial judge's charge to the jury and by the Court of Appeal.

The Court of Appeal, after a thorough review of the evidence, held that it was not possible for a jury acting judicially to have found that, in 1985, the respondent ought to have known of the risk. . . . I agree with this finding and can find no basis upon which it can be questioned. Indeed my review of the evidence leads to the same conclusion. The evidence of standard practice . . . was based entirely on the state of knowledge required of the reasonable practitioner in 1985 and it would have been . . . impossible for a jury acting judicially to have found that, given the state of knowledge, the reasonable practitioner ought to either have discontinued AI or warned the patients of the risk. . . .

The appellant, therefore, can only support a favourable finding on this aspect of the case on the basis that the jury was entitled to find that the standard established by the evidence itself departed from that of a prudent and diligent physician and that the respondent, in failing to conform with a higher standard, was guilty of negligence. . . .

It is generally accepted that when a doctor acts in accordance with a recognized and respectable practice of the profession, he or she will not be found to be negligent. This is because courts do not ordinarily have the expertise to tell professionals that they are not behaving appropriately in their field. In a sense, the medical profession as a whole is assumed to have adopted procedures which are in the best interests of patients and are not inherently negligent. As L'Heureux-Dubé J. stated in [*Lapointe v. Hôpital Le Gardeur*, [1992] 1 S.C.R. 351], in the context of the Quebec *Civil Code*. . .:

> Given the number of available methods of treatment from which medical professionals must at times choose, and the distinction between error and fault, *a doctor will not be found liable if the diagnosis and treatment given to a patient correspond to those recognized by medical science at the time, even in the face of competing theories.* As expressed more eloquently by André Nadeau in "La responsabilité médicale" (1946), 6 R. du B. 153 at p. 155:
> "[TRANSLATION] The courts do not have jurisdiction to settle scientific disputes or to choose among divergent opinions of physicians on certain subjects. *They may only make a finding of fault where a violation of universally accepted rules of medicine has occurred. The courts should not involve themselves in controversial questions of assessment having to do with diagnosis or the treatment of preference.*"

(Emphasis added.)

In *The Law of Torts*, 7th ed. (Sydney: Law Book Co., 1987), Professor John G. Fleming observed the following with respect to the role of standard practice, at p. 109:

> *Conformity* with general practice, on the other hand, usually dispels a charge of negligence. It tends to show what others in the same "business" considered sufficient, not that the defendant could not have learnt how to avoid the accident by the example of others, that most probably no other practical precautions could have been taken, and that the impact of an adverse judgment (especially in cases involving industry or a profession) will be industry-wide and thus assume the function of a "test case". *Finally, it underlines the need for caution against passing too cavalierly upon the conduct and decision of experts.*
> All the same, even a common practice may itself be condemned as negligent *if fraught with obvious risks.*

(Emphasis added.)

With respect to the medical profession in particular, Professor Fleming noted, at p. 110:

> Common practice plays a conspicuous role in medical negligence actions. Conscious at once of the layman's ignorance of medical science and apprehensive of the impact of jury bias on a peculiarly vulnerable profession, courts have resorted to the safeguard of insisting that negligence in diagnosis and treatment (including disclosure of risks) cannot ordinarily be established without the aid of expert testimony or in the teeth of conformity with accepted medical practice. *However there is no categorical rule. Thus an accepted practice is open to censure by a jury (no expert testimony required) at any rate in matters not involving diagnostic or clinical skills, on which an ordinary person may presume to*

> *pass judgment sensibly, like omission to inform the patient of risks, failure to remove a sponge, an explosion set off by an admixture of ether vapour and oxygen or injury to a patient's body outside the area of treatment.*

(Emphasis added. Footnotes omitted.)

It is evident from the foregoing passage that while conformity with common practice will generally exonerate physicians of any complaint of negligence, there are certain situations where the standard practice itself may be found to be negligent. However, this will only be where the standard practice is "fraught with obvious risks" such that anyone is capable of finding it negligent, without the necessity of judging matters requiring diagnostic or clinical expertise.

. . .

As was observed in *Lapointe*, courts should not involve themselves in resolving scientific disputes which require the expertise of the profession. Courts and juries do not have the necessary expertise to assess technical matters relating to the diagnosis or treatment of patients. Where a common and accepted course of conduct is adopted based on the specialized and technical expertise of professionals, it is unsatisfactory for a finder of fact to conclude that such a standard was inherently negligent. On the other hand, matters falling within the ordinary common sense of juries can be judged to be negligent. For example, where there are obvious existing alternatives which any reasonable person would utilize in order to avoid risk, one could conclude that the failure to adopt such measures is negligent notwithstanding that it is the prevailing practice among practitioners in that area.

. . .

I conclude from the foregoing that, as a general rule, where a procedure involves difficult or uncertain questions of medical treatment or complex, scientific or highly technical matters that are beyond the ordinary experience and understanding of a judge or jury, it will not be open to find a standard medical practice negligent. On the other hand, as an exception to the general rule, if a standard practice fails to adopt obvious and reasonable precautions which are readily apparent to the ordinary finder of fact, then it is no excuse for a practitioner to claim that he or she was merely conforming to such a negligent common practice.

The question as to whether the trier of fact can find that a standard practice is itself negligent is a question of law to be determined by the trial judge irrespective of the mode of trial. It is, of course, for the jury to determine on the evidence what the standard practice is. If the evidence is conflicting on this issue, the jury will have to resolve the conflict. If, as in this case, the evidence is virtually conclusive, the trial judge should instruct the jury that failure to accept the evidence may very well result in an unreasonable verdict which will be set aside. Moreover, unless the nature of the issue is of a kind to bring it within the exception to the general rule, the jury should be instructed that once they have determined on the evidence what the standard is, the only remaining issue is whether the defendant conformed to the standard. On the other hand, if the case is one coming within the exception so that the jury can fix the standard on the basis of common sense and the ordinary understanding of the jury without the assistance of expert testimony, the trial judge must instruct the jury accordingly.

[The plaintiff had alleged that the defendant breached the standard of care in two respects: (i) with respect to his screening of potential donors for HIV specifically, and (ii) with respect to his screening of donors for sexually transmitted infections generally.

The court held that there should not be a new trial on the first allegation. At the time of treatment, the defendant had complied with a standard practice that was beyond the understanding of a lay person and that was not so obviously fraught with danger that it could be declared careless in itself. A properly instructed jury consequently could not find the defendant liable on that basis.

In contrast, the court held that a new trial should be ordered with respect to the second allegation. HIV falls within a more general class of sexually transmitted infections. The defendant might be held liable for the transmission of HIV if he could have been held liable for the transmission of one of those other infections. There was, however, insufficient evidence regarding the existence of a standard practice for the screening for those infections. The matter was consequently sent back to trial to determine whether there was such a practice. If there was not, then the jury could, without relying upon expert evidence, find that the defendant had been careless.]

NOTES AND QUESTIONS

1. The party relying on either compliance with or breach of custom has the burden of proving that such a custom exists. The courts will only accept that an act, approach or pattern of conduct constitutes a custom if it is a well-established and recognized practice that has been widely accepted in a trade, industry or profession. See generally *Heeney v. Best* (1979), 11 C.C.L.T. 66 (Ont. C.A.); and *Goodwin v. McCully* (1989), 101 N.B.R. (2d) 289 (Q.B.(T.D.)).

2. Prior to *ter Neuzen* it was generally accepted that compliance with custom provided evidence of reasonableness and breach of custom provided evidence of negligence. How has the decision in *ter Neuzen* changed the impact of compliance with or breach of custom? Is *ter Neuzen* limited to customary practice in highly technical fields?

3. How was the customary practice established in *ter Neuzen*? What was the nature of the dispute over the role of the jury? How did Sopinka J. resolve it? Did Sopinka J. concede too much authority to professionals to dictate the standards of negligence in their fields?

In *ter Neuzen*, the court referred to North American practices in artificial insemination. How should the courts address the standard of care if the Canadian and American medical practices differ? In *Walker Estate v. York-Finch General Hospital* (1999), 169 D.L.R. (4th) 689 (Ont. C.A.), aff'd (2001), 198 D.L.R. (4th) 193 (S.C.C.) the blood-donor screening practices of the Canadian Red Cross were held to be negligent, given the more specific and detailed screening practices in the United States. What concerns, if any, does this reliance on American practices raise?

4. It is important to understand that *ter Neuzen* does not require deference to expert opinion in every medical case. In *Walker Estate v. York-Finch General Hospital* (2001), 198 D.L.R. (4th) 193 (S.C.C.) the plaintiffs contracted HIV as a result of receiving tainted blood through transfusions. In each instance, the donor was a homosexual male. The plaintiffs claimed that the defendant was liable insofar as it had failed to properly screen

potential donors for the risk of HIV. In contrast to its American counterpart, which had used a screening procedure that involved very specific information, the defendant's screening procedure was of a much more general nature. Only two experts gave evidence at trial and both agreed that the defendant's approach, while less specific than the American, was adequate and appropriate.

Despite that evidence, the trial judge held that the defendant had breached the standard of care. The Court of Appeal and the Supreme Court of Canada agreed. Major J. explained that "the trial judge was not asked to assess complex or highly scientific matters. Simply, the issue was whether the general health question was sufficient to deter the infected donor from donating blood. The issue is not how an expert would respond to the donor screening questions in the questionnaire, but how a lay person would respond." See also *Comeau v. Saint John Regional Hospital* (2001), 9 C.C.L.T. (3d) 223 (N.B.C.A.); and *Kelly v. Lundgard* (2001), 202 D.L.R. (4th) 385 (Alta. C.A.).

5. For other judicial discussions of custom see *Vancouver Gen. Hosp. v. McDaniel*, [1934] 4 D.L.R. 593 (P.C.); *Rothwell v. Raes* (1988), 66 O.R. (2d) 449 (H.C.), aff'd (1990), 2 O.R. (3d) 332 (C.A.); and *Emmonds v. Makarewicz* (2000), 81 B.C.L.R. (3d) 75 (C.A.) (doctors); *Moss v. Ferguson* (1979), 35 N.S.R. (2d) 181 (S.C.); and *Lowry v. Cdn. Mountain Holidays Ltd.* (1987), 40 C.C.L.T. 1 (B.C.C.A.) (industrial practices); and *Glivar v. Noble* (1985), 8 O.A.C. 60 (C.A.); and *Shute v. Premier Trust Co.* (1993), 35 R.P.R. (2d) 141 (Ont. Gen. Div.) (lawyers).

6. For a discussion of custom see Linden & Feldthusen, *Canadian Tort Law*, 8th ed. (2006) at 199-222; and American Law Institute, *Restatement (Second) of the Law of Torts* (1965) at para. 295A.

7. A doctor performs a neurological examination on a patient, using the standard practice. Part of the examination involves the doctor assessing the way the patient walks, watching from a few metres behind the patient. During the walking the patient falls and is injured. The patient wants to sue the doctor. Has the doctor breached the standard of care?

REVIEW PROBLEMS

1. Dr. Carver, a general practitioner, prescribed a strong buffering agent to Mr. Jones to treat his ulcer, despite the fact that some ulcer patients with certain allergies and 2% of ulcer patients without these allergies suffer serious reactions to it. There was another drug that was equally effective but three times more expensive. Since Mr. Jones was poor, Dr. Carver decided to prescribe the buffering agent, and carried out the customary tests used by most general practitioners to verify that Mr. Jones had none of the known allergies. Although Dr. Carver had heard of a new study which indicated ways of predicting whether an ulcer patient would react badly to the buffering agent, he had not had time to read it prior to treating Mr. Jones. Had Carver read the new study, he would have realized that there was a 25% chance that Mr. Jones would react badly to the buffering compound.

Unfortunately, Mr. Jones had a severe reaction to the buffering agent which necessitated his hospitalization. He is seeking your advice about suing Dr. Carver in negligence. Your preliminary investigation revealed that Dr. Carver had three years of special training in internal medicine and therefore should have known a great deal more about ulcers than an average general practitioner.

2. Mr. Smith was crossing an intersection on a green light one quiet Sunday morning when he was struck by an ambulance which was carrying a critically ill man to the emergency ward of a nearby hospital. Although the intersection was level, Mr. Smith's and the ambulance driver's views of each other were blocked by a large truck that had stopped in the right-hand lane for the red light. The ambulance driver had turned on his flashing beacon and loud siren and had slowed down from 100 to 20 kph when he entered the intersection against the red light. Mr. Smith did not see the ambulance's flashing light because of the truck and did not hear the siren because he was deaf. Discuss whether the ambulance driver, Mr. Smith or both were negligent.

16

CAUSATION

1. Introduction
2. The But-For Test
3. Established Exceptions to the But-For Test
4. Recent Attempts to Modify the But-For Test
5. Multiple Causes
6. Issues in Assessing the Plaintiff's Loss

1. Introduction

In some areas of tort law, the reported cases provide a relatively clear statement of the legal principles and guidance on the courts' likely approach. Since causation is not one such area, this chapter contains more background information, case summaries and commentary than most others. Causation may be seen as involving two subissues. First, what test of causation governs the situation? The general test of causation in negligence is the but-for test, although this is subject to modifications and exceptions. Second, based on the facts, can the plaintiff prove on the balance of probabilities that the defendant's breach of the standard of care was a cause of his or her loss? This second subissue is often referred to as the cause-in-fact test.

Causation is the element of a negligence action that links the defendant's breach of the standard of care to the plaintiff's loss. Consequently, it is important to state with precision the alleged breach of the standard of care and the specific injury in issue. The plaintiff may have two or more distinct injuries or sets of injuries, each of which must be separately analyzed in terms of causation. For example, assume that defendant A negligently shoots the plaintiff in the arm, defendant B negligently shoots the plaintiff in the leg, and that the combined blood loss results in the plaintiff's death. The plaintiff has suffered three distinct losses: the bullet wound in the arm caused by A, the bullet wound in the leg caused by B, and death caused by A and B.

In order to facilitate analysis, it is helpful to focus initially on each distinct loss or category of losses suffered by the plaintiff and determine if it is attributable to a single tortfeasor or to two or more tortfeasors. The term "divisible loss" is typically used to refer to a loss that, as a practical matter, is attributable to the conduct of a single tortfeasor. The term "indivisible loss" is used to refer to a loss that, as a practical matter, is attributable to the conduct of more than one tortfeasor. If a plaintiff suffers a series of distinct injuries occurring in rapid succession, such as multiple whiplash injuries in a 15-vehicle chain reaction crash, the courts will likely treat the plaintiff's injuries as a single indivisible loss caused by all of the at-fault drivers. In the example in the previous paragraph, the arm wound and leg wound are each divisible injuries, and the plaintiff's death is an indivisible injury.

Some courts and commentators refer to a divisible loss as requiring a "single cause" approach and an indivisible loss as requiring a "multiple cause" approach. Traditionally, the courts have used a single cause analysis where, in addition to a negligent defendant, there has been an absconding tortfeasor, a contributorily negligent plaintiff, or an innocent, pre-existing or naturally occurring contributory cause. This approach is compatible with the view that a divisible injury should be defined narrowly, as one that is attributable to a single tortfeasor who is before the courts. In some cases, the courts may acknowledge that there is more than one cause, but explain that this other cause is not relevant to the tortfeasor's liability.

The plaintiff need not prove that the defendant's negligence was the sole, immediate, direct, or even the most important cause of his or her loss. Rather, the plaintiff only has to establish that the defendant's negligence was a cause. Moreover, the plaintiff is not required to prove causation to the standard of scientific certainty or beyond a reasonable doubt. Instead, the plaintiff need only establish causation on a balance of probabilities. The courts have modified the accepted burden and standard of proof in causation in narrow categories of cases to prevent a perceived unfairness or to achieve a public policy goal. While some courts have provided a compelling or plausible justification for modifying the accepted principles, others have not.

Some courts have failed to distinguish between causation and remoteness of damages, which is discussed in the next chapter. Even if the defendant negligently caused the plaintiff's loss, the defendant will not be held liable if that loss is too far removed from, or too remote a consequence of, his or her negligence. Remoteness of damages is a legal issue that governs the extent of the defendant's liability for the losses that he or she has negligently caused. Unlike in intentional torts, defendants in negligence actions are generally held liable for only the foreseeable injuries that they have caused. The American and some Canadian courts have used the term "proximate cause" as a convenient means of glossing over the distinct issues of causation and remoteness of damages. If a court concludes that a defendant's negligence was not a proximate cause, does it mean that the negligence was not a cause, that the negligence was a cause but the loss was too remote to be recoverable, or that the negligence was not a cause and that in any event the loss was too remote?

2. The But-For Test

The standard test of factual causation is the but-for test. If the plaintiff's injury would not have occurred but for the defendant's negligent act, then that act is a cause of the injury. In such circumstances, a court or commentator may state that the defendant's negligence was "causally effective." If the plaintiff's injury would have occurred regardless of the defendant's negligent act, then that act will generally not be held to be a cause.

KAUFFMAN v. TORONTO TRANSIT COMMISSION

(1959), 18 D.L.R. (2d) 204 (Ont. C.A.), aff'd [1960] S.C.R. 251

MORDEN J.A.: —The defendant appeals from the judgment of McLennan J., dated June 3, 1958, upon the findings of a jury, awarding the plaintiff the sum of $25,000 damages for injuries suffered by her following a fall on an escalator in the defendant's St. Clair Ave. subway station. The defendant's counsel on the appeal argued that the jury's findings were against the evidence, were perverse and did not state any ground of actionable negligence for which the defendant could be held liable.

Late in the evening of February 11, 1955, the plaintiff and a friend, a Mrs. Mathewson, after travelling on a northbound subway train alighted at the St. Clair station. . . The plaintiff stepped upon the escalator followed by Mrs. Mathewson. Immediately ahead of the plaintiff was a man and ahead of him two youths. The youths began scuffling and fell back against the man who in turn lost his balance and fell back upon the plaintiff. The plaintiff fell upon the escalator steps with these two or three people on top of her. As a result of her fall and of the continuing movement upwards of the escalator, the plaintiff sustained very severe and permanent injuries. The defendant's appeal against the amount of the damages was abandoned at the hearing of the appeal.

. . .

The jury found the defendant negligent specifically as follows:

"1. The defendant, in acquiring an escalator of radical departure in hand-rail design, did not sufficiently test or cause to be tested by a qualified expert the coefficient of friction and contour of the Peelle Motor Stair Handrail."

. . .

The theory advanced by the plaintiff's counsel to quote his own words was that "in the operation of an escalator, particularly in a public transit system where large crowds are to be expected, if a person near the top falls backward (for whatever reason) against the person behind him, each person will fall against the other knocking him down in much the same fashion as a row of dominoes". But there was a total absence of evidence that the man immediately ahead of the plaintiff or the two reckless and irresponsible youths ahead of him were grasping or attempted to grasp the hand rail before or in the course of the scuffle and consequent falling. Nor was there any evidence that in the circumstances the plaintiff would not have fallen if her hands had been grasping a rubber oval hand rail. In my opinion, there was no evidence to justify a finding that the type of hand rail in use at the St. Clair Ave. station was a contributing cause of the plaintiff's unfortunate and serious accident. It is a fundamental principle that the causal relation between the alleged negligence and the injury must be made out by the evidence and not left to the conjecture of the jury .... The first finding of negligence in view of the evidence in this case does not justify a verdict against the defendant.

. . .

The appeal must be allowed and the action dismissed, both with costs, if demanded.

BARNETT v. CHELSEA & KENSINGTON HOSPITAL MANAGEMENT COMMITTEE

[1969] 1 Q.B. 428

[Three men went to the defendant hospital complaining about vomiting for several hours after drinking tea. The nurse on duty called the medical casualty officer, who instructed the nurse to tell them to go home to bed and call their own doctors. One of the men died of arsenic poisoning about five hours later. The judge held that the doctor's dismissal of the deceased's complaints without even seeing or examining him breached the standard of care. The judge then turned to the issue of whether the doctor's negligence was a cause of the man's death.]

NEILD J.: . . . There has been put before me a timetable which I think is of much importance. The deceased attended at the casualty department at five or 10 minutes past eight in the morning. If the casualty officer had got up and dressed and come to see [him] and examined [him] and decided to admit [him], the deceased . . . could not have been in bed in a ward before 11 a.m. I accept Dr. Goulding's evidence that an intravenous drip would not have been set up before 12 noon, and if potassium loss was suspected it could not have been discovered until 12.30 p.m. Dr. Lockett, dealing with this, said: "If [the deceased] had not been treated until after 12 noon the chances of survival were not good."

Without going in detail into the considerable volume of technical evidence which has been put before me, it seems to me to be the case that when death results from arsenical poisoning it is brought about by two conditions; on the one hand dehydration and on the other disturbance of the enzyme processes. If the principal condition is one of enzyme disruption — as I am of the view it was here — then the only method of treatment which is likely to succeed is the use of the specific antidote which is commonly called B.A.L. Dr. Goulding said in the course of his evidence:

> "The only way to deal with this is to use the specific B.A.L. I see no reasonable prospect of the deceased being given B.A.L. before the time at which he died" – and at a later point in his evidence – "I feel that even if fluid loss had been discovered death would have been caused by the enzyme disturbance. Death might have occurred later."

I regard that evidence as very moderate, and it might be a true assessment of the situation to say that there was no chance of B.A.L. being administered before the death of the deceased.

For those reasons, I find that the plaintiff has failed to establish, on the balance of probabilities, that the defendants' negligence caused the death of the deceased.

NOTES AND QUESTIONS

1. Why did the plaintiff's claim in *Kauffman* fail? What kind of evidence should the plaintiff have introduced to support her allegation that the handrail on the escalator played a causal role in her injuries? The plaintiff also argued that the TTC was liable for failing to prevent the boys from fighting. Although the TTC's failure in this regard clearly played a causal role in the plaintiff's injuries, the court rejected her argument. On what basis do you think the court reached this conclusion?

2. Was the result in *Barnett* fair? Given that most patients are at a distinct disadvantage in understanding medical evidence, accessing medical records, obtaining expert witnesses, and financing litigation, should the standard test of causation, and the burden and standard of proof be modified in medical malpractice cases? Are there any other factors that warrant modifying the established principles in malpractice cases?

3. For recent discussions of causation in malpractice cases, see *Phillip v. Whitecourt General Hospital* (2004), 359 A.R. 259 (Q.B.) (negligent management of hypoglycaemic crisis in newborn); *Meyers v. Stanley* (2005), 363 A.R. 262 (C.A.) (management of early labour); *Arruda v. Scarborough Hospital*, 2005 CarswellOnt 3181 (S.C.J.) (WLeC) (failure to order ECG and heart enzyme test); *Aristorenas v. Comcare Health Services* (2006), 216 O.A.C. 161 (C.A.) (delay in treating wound and development of necrotizing

fasciitis (flesh-eating disease)); and *Ahmed v. Stefaniu* (2006), 216 O.A.C. 323 (C.A.) (release of a psychiatric patient who subsequently murdered his sister).

4. In *Qualcast (Wolverhampton) Ltd. v. Haynes*, [1959] A.C. 743 (H.L.), an experienced foundry worker was injured when a ladle slipped and splashed molten metal on his foot. The defendant company had protective spats which, if worn, would have prevented the injury. However, the company had not ordered the worker to wear the spats, and he had not asked to use them. After recuperating, the worker returned to the job and still did not wear the spats. The House of Lords held that the defendant had not been careless. Lord Denning stated that, in any event, the plaintiff's claim would have failed on causation. Do you agree? Would Lord Denning have reached the same conclusion if the worker had framed the allegation of negligence in terms of the defendant's failure to ensure that he wore spats?

5. In *Richard v. C.N.R.* (1970), 15 D.L.R. (3d) 732 (P.E.I.S.C.), the plaintiff was asleep in his car aboard a ferry when he was awakened by someone shouting "we're here!" Believing that an attendant had made the statement, the plaintiff started his car and backed it off the ferry. Unfortunately, the boat had not yet docked and the car landed in the Gulf of St. Lawrence. The plaintiff sued and alleged, among other things, that the defendant had been negligent in untying the nylon rope across the end of the ferry before it docked. The court concluded that the "sole, direct, proximate and effective cause" of the accident was the plaintiff's rash act of backing off the boat, contrary to the warning signs and the crew's attempts to stop him. Do you agree that the removal of the rope was not a cause of the plaintiff's loss? If, as the plaintiff believed, a ferry employee had shouted, "we're here!" would his act have been a cause of the plaintiff's loss? Would the result have been the same if the plaintiff had alleged that the defendant was negligent in failing to provide an adequate restraining barrier?

6. *Kauffman*, *Qualcast* and *Richard* illustrate the importance of carefully analyzing the relationship between the allegation of negligence and causation. The negligence allegation must be carefully drafted to ensure that it is a cause of the plaintiff's loss.

7. The but-for test has been subject to volumes of criticism and comment. For example one author states "Its affinity for absurd hypotheticals should suggest that the 'but-for' test should be abandoned even as a tentative account of the concept of causation": Epstein, "A Theory of Strict Liability"(1973) 2 J. Legal Stud. 151 at 161. For a sampling of the commentaries see Malone, "Ruminations on Cause-in-Fact" (1956-57) 9 Stanford L. Rev. 60; Wright, "Causation in Tort Law" (1985) 73 Cal. L. Rev. 1735; Goldberg, *Causation and Risk in the Law of Torts* (1999); McInnes, "Causation in Tort Law: A Decade in the Supreme Court of Canada" (2000) 63 Sask. L. Rev. 445; Beever, "Cause-in-Fact: Two Steps Out Of The Mire" (2001) 51 U.T.L.J. 327; and Wright, "Acts and Omissions as Positive and Negative Causes" and Black, "Decision Causation: Pandora's Tool-Box" in Neyers, Chamberlain & Pitel, eds., *Emerging Issues in Tort Law* (2007), ch. 11 and ch. 12.

3. Established Exceptions to the But-For Test

Numerous efforts have been made over the years to rework the but-for test of causation with varying degrees of success. The most widely accepted modifications involve limited exceptions that apply to relatively narrow categories of cases. This section briefly reviews three established exceptions to the but-for test: the multiple negligent defendants rule, the learned intermediary rule, and the objective/subjective test in informed consent cases. The first exception is reviewed in greater detail in chapter 20 and the second two exceptions are discussed in chapter 12.

(a) THE MULTIPLE NEGLIGENT DEFENDANTS RULE

In *Cook v. Lewis*, [1951] S.C.R. 830, the plaintiff was shot in the face by one of two negligent hunters who had fired at the same time. Each hunter denied that he had aimed in the plaintiff's direction, and the plaintiff could not prove on the balance of probabilities which one had shot him. The court held that if the plaintiff could prove that the two defendants were negligent, one had to have caused his loss, and it was impossible to prove which one, then the burden of proving causation would shift to the defendants. Each defendant would be held to be negligent in causing the loss unless he could disprove causation on the balance of probabilities.

In Canada, the multiple negligent defendants rule appears to be limited to cases involving two negligent defendants. As will be discussed later in this chapter, United Kingdom courts and some American courts have applied a variation of this principle to cases involving more than two negligent defendants.

(b) THE LEARNED INTERMEDIARY RULE

Manufacturers of products that are not directly available to the public, such as prescription drugs, may discharge their duty to inform consumers by adequately disclosing information to a learned intermediary. In *Hollis v. Dow Corning Corp.*, [1995] 4 S.C.R. 634, the plaintiff was injured when one of Dow's breast implants ruptured inside her. Dow, which had negligently failed to inform the plaintiff's surgeon of this risk, argued that it had to be absolved of liability on the basis of causation. The plaintiff could not prove that her doctor would have warned her, even if Dow had adequately informed him.

The court rejected this argument because it would create an anomalous situation in which the negligently injured plaintiff would have no cause of action. Her claim against the doctor would fail because he was not negligent, as he had never been informed of the risks. According to Dow, her claim against it would fail on the issue of causation. The court stated that Dow could not use the learned intermediary rule to shield itself from claims arising from its own negligence. The court also noted that the plaintiff would not have had the procedure had she been adequately informed of the risks of non-traumatic rupture. The court exempted these cases from the but-for rule and held Dow liable for the plaintiff's injuries.

(c) INFORMED CONSENT

In *Hopp v. Lepp*, [1980] 2 S.C.R. 192 and *Reibl v. Hughes*, [1980] 2 S.C.R. 880, the court held that healthcare professionals have a duty to put patients in a position to make informed decisions about whether to consent to proposed treatment. The court then adopted a special objective/subjective test of causation, framed in terms of whether a reasonable person in the plaintiff's position would have consented if adequately informed. The great majority of informed consent cases appear to fail on this unique pro-defendant test of causation. The court did not provide a compelling rationale for why the credibility issues in informed consent cases warranted altering the standard test of causation.

The majority in *Arndt v. Smith*, [1997] 2 S.C.R. 539 defended the objective/subjective approach on the basis that a purely subjective test would: require the court to hypothesize about how the patient would have reacted if properly informed; result in the patient's testimony being coloured by hindsight and bitterness; and leave the causation issue to be determined solely on the patient's testimony on how he or she would have acted if properly informed. In contrast, the three dissenting justices applied the standard subjective test of causation. Despite the split in *Arndt*, the Canadian courts continue to apply the objective/subjective test in informed cases without comment.

NOTES AND QUESTIONS

1. Do you agree with the decision in *Cook*? If so, what is the rationale for adopting a special rule in *Cook* when other plaintiffs who fall just short of proving causation on a balance of probabilities are denied recovery?

2. Do you agree with the court's approach to causation in *Hollis*? Did Dow's failure to inform the doctor cause the plaintiff a loss, namely the opportunity to sue her doctor for negligently failing to inform her of the risks of the implant procedure?

3. Do you find the majority's reasons in *Arndt* compelling? If so, why do the courts continue to apply a subjective test of causation in manufacturer's duty to warn and other cases in which plaintiffs may be required to testify about how they would have reacted had the defendant not breached the standard of care? Can you suggest other policy factors that would warrant adopting an objective/subjective test of causation in duty to inform cases?

For a discussion of the approach in the United Kingdom and Australia, see *Chester v. Afshar*, [2004] 3 W.L.R. 927 (H.L.); *Chappel v. Hart* (1998), 195 C.L.R. 232 (H.C.A.); and *Naxakis v. West General Hospital* (1999), 197 C.L.R. 269 (H.C.A.). See generally McInnes, "Failure to Warn in Medical Negligence – A Cautionary Note From Canada" (1998) 6 Torts L.J. 135; Gunson, "Turbulent Causal Waters: The High Court, Causation and Medical Negligence" (2001) 9 Tort L. Rev. 53; and Stevens, "An Opportunity to Reflect" (2005) 121 L.Q.R. 189.

4. Recent Attempts to Modify the But-For Test

This section examines evolving modifications or exceptions to the but-for test in three situations: material contribution, materially increased risk, and proportionate cause and loss of chance. There is a measure of uncertainty with each of these tests. As will be discussed, it was never clear how the material contribution test differed from the but-for test or when the material contribution test was to be applied. Fortunately, in *Hanke v. Resurfice Corp.* (2007), 357 N.R. 175 (S.C.C.), the court addressed some of the confusion generated by the material contribution test and outlined the narrow circumstances in which it might be available.

The current Canadian approach to the materially increased risk test parallels the but-for test, albeit in different words. However, the House of Lords has taken a far broader approach to this test, at least in regard to employment-related diseases. Finally, the loss of chance test continues to be raised on a regular basis, even though it has yet to be adopted by the Canadian courts.

Although these tests currently have a relatively limited impact on the analysis of causation, students need to be familiar with their basic principles. These tests come in and out of favour with some regularity, and the process of attempting to modify the but-for test is unlikely to abate in the foreseeable future.

(a) MATERIAL CONTRIBUTION

WALKER ESTATE v. YORK FINCH GENERAL HOSPITAL
[2001] 1 S.C.R. 647

[Alma Walker was one of the three plaintiffs who contracted HIV from tainted blood products supplied by the Canadian Red Cross Society (CRCS). The plaintiffs claimed that the CRCS was negligent in screening potential blood donors and that its negligence resulted in their becoming infected. Only the Walker claim is discussed below. The blood that Walker received was donated by Robert M on September 12, 1983, when relatively little was known about HIV. At that time, there was no test for determining if a blood donation was infected. Consequently, donor screening was the only means of reducing the risk of receiving infected donations, and pamphlets were used for this purpose in both Canada and the United States. The following three pamphlets were relevant to the Walker claim.

> *American Red Cross 1983*: In March 1983, the American Red Cross (ARC) began using a pamphlet that contained three important features. First, it expressly said that a person may "feel in excellent health" but nevertheless be infected. Second, it listed possible symptoms of AIDS. Third, it specifically identified "homosexual or bisexual men with multiple partners" as having an increased risk of infection. High-risk donors were told to refrain from donating.
>
> *CRCS 1983*: In April 1983, the CRCS began using a pamphlet that simply told potential donors that "it is important for you to be in good health." It did not refer to possible symptoms of AIDS. Moreover, the CRCS decided not to follow the ARC practice of identifying homosexual and bisexual men as high-risk donors because it was concerned about stigmatizing them.
>
> *CRCS 1984*: In May 1984, the CRCS adopted a new pamphlet which, like the ARC pamphlet, specifically referred to "homosexual and bisexual males who have multiple partners" as being at risk, and directed them to refrain from donating. However, unlike the ARC model, the CRCS 1984 pamphlet did not expressly inform potential donors that they may be infected even though they feel healthy. Nor did it list the possible symptoms of AIDS.

The trial judge held that the CRCS was negligent in using the vague 1983 pamphlet, given what was known in September 1983. The CRCS should have been using a pamphlet in September 1983 that contained the more specific information in its 1984 pamphlet. However, the evidence established that Robert M continued to donate blood until he was told to stop in January 1987, well after he would have seen the CRCS 1984 pamphlet. Accordingly, the trial judge held that even if the CRCS had met its standard of care,

Robert M would have still donated the blood that infected Walker. Consequently, the trial judge concluded that Walker could not prove that the CRCS's negligence was a cause of her loss.

The Court of Appeal for Ontario reversed the trial decision, finding that causation could be established on the basis of the "*Hollis* test." The CRCS appealed. As will be discussed in the notes, the Supreme Court of Canada held that *Hollis*, discussed above in the context of the learned intermediary rule, did not apply and rejected the Court of Appeal's analysis of causation. The following excerpt focuses on the Supreme Court of Canada's discussion of the standard of care and adoption of a unique causal analysis in support of the plaintiff's claim.]

MAJOR J:

. . .

With respect to negligent donor screening, the plaintiffs must establish the duty of care and the standard of care owed to them by the CRCS. The plaintiffs must also prove that the CRCS caused their injuries. The unique difficulties in proving causation make this area of negligence atypical. The general test for causation in cases where a single cause can be attributed to a harm is the "but-for" test. However, the but-for test is unworkable in some situations, particularly where multiple independent causes may bring about a single harm.

In cases of negligent donor screening, it may be difficult or impossible to prove hypothetically what the donor would have done had he or she been properly screened by the CRCS. The added element of donor conduct in these cases means that the but-for test could operate unfairly, highlighting the possibility of leaving legitimate plaintiffs uncompensated. Thus, the question in cases of negligent donor screening should not be whether the CRCS's conduct was a necessary condition for the plaintiffs' injuries using the "but-for" test, but whether that conduct was a sufficient condition. The proper test for causation in cases of negligent donor screening is whether the defendant's negligence "materially contributed" to the occurrence of the injury. In the present case, it is clear that it did. "A contributing factor is material if it falls outside the *de minimis* range" (see *Athey v. Leonati*, [1996] 3 S.C.R. 458, at para. 15). As such, the plaintiff retains the burden of proving that the failure of the CRCS to screen donors with tainted blood materially contributed to Walker contracting HIV from the tainted blood.

The trial judge found that the *Walker* action failed on causation because Robert M. was not deterred from donating blood when the CRCS May 1984 pamphlet was in existence. . . .

. . .

With respect, the trial judge asked himself the wrong question. Rather than asking whether Robert M. would have self-deferred or been excluded from donating blood on September 12, 1983 if he had seen the *CRCS May 1984 pamphlet*, he should have asked whether Robert M. would have self-deferred or been excluded if the CRCS had followed the appropriate standard of care as represented by the *ARC March 1983 pamphlet*. It is my opinion that the ARC March 1983 pamphlet represented the appropriate standard of care for a professional voluntary blood bank in North America at that time.

Borins J. [the trial judge] noted the primacy of the ARC March 1983 pamphlet over the CRCS May 1984 pamphlet during a discussion of the standard of care to be used in the *Osborne* case. He noted that both pamphlets make reference to the newly described condition known as AIDS. However, the CRCS May 1984 pamphlet states that it is important that a donor be in "good health" and cautions the prospective donor to "be sure that you are feeling generally well". However, the CRCS May 1984 pamphlet does not mention any signs or symptoms of AIDS. On the other hand, the ARC March 1983 pamphlet points out that although "some persons may feel in excellent health", they may have viruses or infectious agents in their blood and informs donors that the ARC must rely on donors' health histories to exclude individuals whose blood might contain AIDS. "The ARC then includes among the high risk groups those persons 'with signs and symptoms suggestive of AIDS', and lists the signs and symptoms. . .." (para. 143).

Listing the signs and symptoms of AIDS in the CRCS May 1984 pamphlet (as was done in the ARC 1983 pamphlet) would not have excluded Robert M. as he had no signs or symptoms of AIDS on any occasion that he donated blood. Therefore, it is not surprising that the trial judge concluded . . . that a donor screening programme which focussed on symptom-specific questions would not have deterred Robert M. from donating blood.

However, the true problem with the CRCS May 1984 pamphlet is the focus on being in "good health", a focus which Borins J. found to be inadequate in the *Osborne* case. Borins J. found that Robert M. likely would have donated blood because he believed that he was in good health and believed that his blood would be tested. . . . The earlier ARC 1983 pamphlet makes it clear that some persons may feel in excellent health but may be carrying viruses.

Another important difference is that, according to the trial judge, while the ARC 1983 pamphlet is clearly focussed on the AIDS problem, the CRCS May 1984 pamphlet is not.

. . .

. . . As stated above, the proper test for causation in negligent donor screening cases is whether the defendant's negligence materially contributed to the plaintiff's harm. Even using the strict but-for test, which is not required in these types of cases, causation is proved on the facts. The trial judge concluded, in response to a hypothetical question, that Robert M. would not have been deferred or excluded from donating blood on September 12, 1983 had he seen the CRCS May 1, 1984 pamphlet. That would not have been the case had Robert M. seen the ARC 1983 pamphlet. Robert M. told the trial judge that had he seen, or been given, information on AIDS and the . . . high risk categories of people who were requested not to donate blood, he would have raised the issue with a nurse, since he fit into one of the risk groups — homosexual males who have multiple partners. The trial judge disbelieved him, expressing the thought that Robert M. did not raise the issue because he considered himself to be in good health. This was the very misconception which the CRCS's May 1, 1984 pamphlet failed to warn against, while the ARC 1983 pamphlet did so expressly.

As a result, the CRCS's appeal in the *Walker* action should be dismissed. . . . When the proper standard of care is applied in this appeal (that is, the requirements of the ARC pamphlet of March 1983) the causal link is established.

NOTES AND QUESTIONS

1. Explain in your own words the disagreement between the trial judge and Major J. on what constituted a reasonable standard of disclosure in September 1983. How did

their differing views of the standard of care affect their analysis of causation? Given all of the information about Robert M, do you agree with Major J. that he would have refrained from giving blood in September 1983 had the CRCS used the ARC pamphlet?

2. Major J.'s discussion of the material contribution test of causation is troubling. He first rejects the but-for test in cases of negligent donor screening because it could unfairly leave "legitimate plaintiffs" uncompensated. He then states that the material contribution test should be used in these circumstances. However, he concludes his judgment by saying that the plaintiff would have recovered in this case, even if the but-for test had been used.

3. Major J. first introduced the material contribution test in *Athey v. Leonati*, [1996] 3 S.C.R. 458. Like *Walker*, *Athey* does little to explain the material contribution test or the circumstances in which it is to be used. Despite considerable effort, academic commentators have not been able to discern a difference between the but-for and material contribution tests. See Demeyere, "The 'Material Contribution' Test: An Immaterial Contribution to Tort Law: A Comment on *Briglio v. Faulkner*" (2000) 34 U.B.C.L. Rev. 317; Black, "A Farewell to Cause: Canadian Red Cross Society v. Walker Estate" (2001) 24 Adv. Q. 478; and Rafferty, "Developments in Contract and Tort Law: The 2000-2001 Term" (2001) 15 S.C.L.R. (2d) 173.

4. In *Walker*, the Court of Appeal relied on *Hollis* to establish causation. It held that an irrefutable presumption of causation arose once the plaintiff established that the CRCS did not have adequate screening procedures in place when Robert M donated the blood that proved fatal to Walker. Major J. rejected this analysis on the basis that *Walker* did not involve a learned intermediary. Consequently, no rebuttable presumption of causation arose in *Walker* and a different test of causation was required. Was Major J.'s decision to exclude the "learned intermediary rule" in *Walker* appropriate? What was the most salient difference between the facts in *Walker* and *Hollis*?

5. In *Hanke v. Resurfice Corp.* (2007), 357 N.R. 175 (S.C.C.), the court addressed some of the confusion generated by the material contribution test. It criticized the routine application of the material contribution test in cases involving multiple causes. The court expressly affirmed that the but-for test is the standard test for causation for cases involving either a single cause or multiple causes. The material contribution test can only be applied if two requirements are met. First, the plaintiff must establish that it is impossible to prove causation using the but-for test and that this impossibility results from factors beyond the plaintiff's control, such as the current limits of scientific knowledge. Second, the plaintiff must establish that the defendant breached the standard of care and that his or her injuries fell within the ambit of the risk created by the defendant's breach. The court stated that the material contribution test has to be applied in these circumstances, because denying the plaintiff recovery pursuant to the but-for test would be unfair and unjust.

The court refrained from reviewing the jurisprudence and cited two examples that it said demonstrated the requirements for invoking the material contribution test. The first example was drawn from *Cook v. Lewis*, [1951] S.C.R. 830 and the second from *Walker*. The court did, however, acknowledge that on the particular facts of *Walker* there was no need to resort to the material contribution test.

While *Hanke* has clarified when the material contribution test applies, has it helped to explain what the test means? Do you agree with the court that it would be unfair and unjust to apply the but-for test in circumstances in which the two requirements of the material contribution test are met? What do you think the court means by "unfair and unjust" in this context? Is the material contribution terminology relevant, helpful or accurate in characterizing the types of situations created by *Cook* and *Walker*?

The material contribution test in *Hanke* was discussed in *Jackson v. Kelowna*, 2007 CarswellBC 394 (C.A.) (WLeC); *Hutchings v. Dow*, 2007 CarswellBC 512 (C.A.) (WLeC); *Bohun v. Sennewald*, 2007 CarswellBC 424 (S.C.) (WLeC); and *Greenall v. MacDougall*, 2007 CarswellBC 514 (S.C.) (WLeC). These cases have not clarified what the material contribution test means or when it is "unfair and unjust" to apply the but-for test.

(b) MATERIALLY INCREASED RISK

Scientific advances have made it possible to establish that certain events and exposures to substances, even 10 to 15 years in the past, increase the risk that a person will develop a disease or disability. Under the but-for test, the increased risk must be such as to make it more probable than not that the defendant's negligent act was a cause of the plaintiff's loss. Traditionally, if the plaintiff could not prove that the increased risk met the but-for test, his or her claim would fail. Some courts have been willing to abandon the but-for test in these cases.

The discussion begins with *McGhee v. National Coal Board*, [1972] 3 All E.R. 1008 (H.L.). The defendant employed the plaintiff to clean out brick kilns. The working conditions were such that by the end of the day, the plaintiff was covered in sweat and dust. In breach of the requisite standard of care, the defendant failed to provide shower facilities at the work site, and the plaintiff was required to cycle home while still filthy. The plaintiff developed dermatitis and sued the defendant. The expert witnesses indicated that the defendant's failure to provide showers materially increased the risk of the plaintiff developing this condition. However, they were unable to say that the absence of showers was more likely than not to have been a cause of the plaintiff's dermatitis. The dermatitis might have arisen innocently. The House of Lords found for the plaintiff. Lord Reid held that if a defendant's negligence materially increases the risk of a particular kind of injury occurring and that very injury befalls the plaintiff, then the defendant will be deemed to be a cause. In contrast, Lord Wilberforce held that in such circumstances the burden of proving causation should shift from the plaintiff to the defendant, who must then disprove causation on a balance of probabilities. Lord Wilberforce limited this principle to cases in which sound policy warranted making an exception to the standard test of causation.

Several Canadian courts adopted *McGhee*, but almost all focused on Lord Wilberforce's approach. Moreover, the Canadian courts often applied *McGhee* well beyond the confines of workplace health and safety issues, and rarely referred to any special policy considerations that warranted deviating from the accepted principles of causation and proof. The status of *McGhee* was further complicated by *Wilsher v. Essex Area Health Authority*, [1988] A.C. 1074 (H.L.). In this case, the House of Lords "reinterpreted" *McGhee* in a way that essentially overruled it. This was the backdrop against which the Supreme Court of Canada addressed the materially increased risk test in the case below.

SNELL v. FARRELL
[1990] 2 S.C.R. 311

[Dr. Farrell performed a cataract operation on Mrs. Snell. After injecting a local anaesthetic into the retrobulbar muscles behind the eyeball, Dr. Farrell noticed a slight discolouration, which he stated on discovery was due to a very small retrobulbar bleed. However, on further examination, he found no other signs of bleeding. After waiting 30 minutes, he proceeded with the operation. Following the surgery, there was blood in the eye. It cleared nine months later, but the optic nerve had atrophied, resulting in blindness in that eye.

The damage to the optic nerve could have occurred naturally or been the result of continuing the operation. Neither expert witness was willing to state with certainty the cause or when the damage occurred. The trial judge accepted the expert testimony that Dr. Farrell was negligent in continuing the operation after noticing the discolouration. Relying on *McGhee*, the trial judge concluded that Mrs. Snell had established a *prima facie* case of causation and the burden shifted to Dr. Farrell to disprove causation. Since Dr. Farrell could not discharge this burden, he was held liable. The Court of Appeal dismissed Dr. Farrell's appeal. He then appealed to the Supreme Court of Canada.]

The judgment of the Court was delivered by

SOPINKA J. — The issue of law in this case is whether the plaintiff in a malpractice suit must prove causation in accordance with traditional principles or whether recent developments in the law justify a finding of liability on the basis of some less onerous standard. . . .

. . .

Causation — Principles

Both the trial judge and the Court of Appeal relied on *McGhee*, which (subject to its re-interpretation in the House of Lords in *Wilsher*) purports to depart from traditional principles in the law of torts that the plaintiff must prove on a balance of probabilities that, but for the tortious conduct of the defendant, the plaintiff would not have sustained the injury complained of. In view of the fact that *McGhee* has been applied by a number of courts in Canada to reverse the ordinary burden of proof with respect to causation, it is important to examine recent developments in the law relating to causation and to determine whether a departure from well-established principles is necessary for the resolution of this appeal.

The traditional approach to causation has come under attack in a number of cases in which there is concern that due to the complexities of proof, the probable victim of tortious conduct will be deprived of relief. This concern is strongest in circumstances in which, on the basis of some percentage of statistical probability, the plaintiff is the likely victim of the combined tortious conduct of a number of defendants, but cannot prove causation against a specific defendant or defendants on the basis of particularized evidence in accordance with traditional principles. The challenge to the traditional approach has manifested itself in cases dealing with non-traumatic injuries such as man-made diseases resulting from the widespread diffusion of chemical products, including product liability cases in which a product which can cause injury is widely manufactured and marketed by a large number of corporations. . . .

Although, to date, these developments have had little impact in other common law countries, it has long been recognized that the allocation of the burden of proof is not immutable. The legal or ultimate burden of proof is determined by the substantive law "upon broad reasons of experience and fairness": 9 *Wigmore on Evidence*, § 2486, at p. 292. In a civil case, the two broad principles are:

1. that the onus is on the party who asserts a proposition, usually the plaintiff;
2. that where the subject matter of the allegation lies particularly within the knowledge of one party, that party may be required to prove it.

This Court has not hesitated to alter the incidence of the ultimate burden of proof when the underlying rationale for its allocation is absent in a particular case: see *National Trust Co. v. Wong Aviation Ltd.*, [1969] S.C.R. 481. This flexibility extends to the issue of causation. . . .

Proof of causation in medical malpractice cases is often difficult for the patient. The physician is usually in a better position to know the cause of the injury than the patient. On the basis of the second basic principle referred to above, there is an argument that the burden of proof should be allocated to the defendant. . . .

This brings me to the *McGhee* case and its influence on subsequent cases, particularly in the medical malpractice field. . . .

. . .

Two theories of causation emerge from an analysis of the speeches of the Lords in this case. The first, firmly espoused by Lord Wilberforce, is that the plaintiff need only prove that the defendant created a risk of harm and that the injury occurred within the area of the risk. The second is that in these circumstances, an inference of causation was warranted in that there is no practical difference between materially contributing to the risk of harm and materially contributing to the harm itself.

The speeches were subjected to a careful examination and interpretation in *Wilsher v. Essex Area Health Authority* . . . by Lord Bridge when some fifteen years later, the House of Lords revisited the issue. The plaintiff claimed damages from the defendant health authority for negligence in medical treatment which resulted in a condition of the eyes leading to blindness. A likely cause of the condition but not a definite one, in the opinion of medical experts, was too much oxygen. The plaintiff proved that for a period of time he was supersaturated with oxygen. A number of different factors other than excessive oxygen could have caused or contributed to the injury. The expert evidence was conflicting. The trial judge applied *McGhee* and held the defendant liable since it had failed to prove that the plaintiff's condition had not resulted from its negligence. The Court of Appeal dismissed the appeal by a majority judgment with the Vice-Chancellor dissenting. The House of Lords allowed the appeal and directed a new trial. Lord Bridge, delivering the unanimous judgment of the court, reaffirmed the principle that the burden of proving causation rested on the plaintiff. Since the trial judge had not made the relevant finding of fact to sort out the conflicting evidence, a new trial was directed on this basis. Lord Bridge interpreted *McGhee* as espousing no new principle. Instead, *McGhee* was explained as promoting a robust and pragmatic approach to the facts to enable an inference of negligence to be drawn even though medical or scientific expertise cannot arrive at a definitive conclusion. . . .

. . .

Lord Bridge concluded with a caution at p. 571:

> But, whether we like it or not, the law, which only Parliament can change, requires proof of fault causing damage as the basis of liability in tort. We should do society nothing but disservice if we made the forensic process still more unpredictable and hazardous by distorting the law to accommodate the exigencies of what may seem hard cases.

Canadian cases decided after *McGhee* but before *Wilsher* tended to follow *McGhee* by adopting either the reversal of onus or the inference interpretation. Which interpretation was adopted made no practical difference because even when the latter approach was applied, the creation of the risk by the defendant's breach of duty was deemed to have established a prima facie case, thus shifting the onus to the defendant. . . .

Decisions in Canada after *Wilsher* accept its interpretation of *McGhee*. In the circumstances in which *McGhee* had been previously interpreted to support a reversal of the burden of proof, an inference was now permissible to find causation, notwithstanding that causation was not proved by positive evidence. . . .

The question that this Court must decide is whether the traditional approach to causation is no longer satisfactory in that plaintiffs in malpractice cases are being deprived of compensation because they cannot prove causation where it in fact exists.

. . . If I were convinced that defendants who have a substantial connection to the injury were escaping liability because plaintiffs cannot prove causation under currently applied principles, I would not hesitate to adopt one of [the *McGhee*] alternatives. In my opinion, however, properly applied, the principles relating to causation are adequate to the task. Adoption of either of the proposed alternatives would have the effect of compensating plaintiffs where a substantial connection between the injury and the defendant's conduct is absent. Reversing the burden of proof may be justified where two defendants negligently fire in the direction of the plaintiff and then by their tortious conduct destroy the means of proof at his disposal. In such a case it is clear that the injury was not caused by neutral conduct. It is quite a different matter to compensate a plaintiff by reversing the burden of proof for an injury that may very well be due to factors unconnected to the defendant and not the fault of anyone.

[Sopinka J. then discussed how the liberalization of the recovery principles in the United States contributed to their malpractice crises of the 1970s. He noted that a British Royal Commission specifically rejected the proposal to shift the burden of proof in malpractice cases.]

I am of the opinion that the dissatisfaction with the traditional approach to causation stems to a large extent from its too rigid application by the courts in many cases. Causation need not be determined by scientific precision. It is, as stated by Lord Salmon in *Alphacell Ltd. v. Woodward*, [1972] 2 All E.R. 475 [(H.L.)], at p. 490,

> . . . essentially a practical question of fact which can best be answered by ordinary common sense rather than abstract metaphysical theory.

Furthermore, as I observed earlier, the allocation of the burden of proof is not immutable. Both the burden and the standard of proof are flexible concepts. In *Blatch v. Archer* (1774), 1 Cowp. 63, 98 E.R. 969, Lord Mansfield stated at p. 970:

> It is certainly a maxim that all evidence is to be weighed according to the proof which it was in the power of one side to have produced, and in the power of the other to have contradicted.

In many malpractice cases, the facts lie particularly within the knowledge of the defendant. In these circumstances, very little affirmative evidence on the part of the plaintiff will justify the drawing of an inference of causation in the absence of evidence to the contrary. . . .

. . .

The legal or ultimate burden remains with the plaintiff, but in the absence of evidence to the contrary adduced by the defendant, an inference of causation may be drawn although positive or scientific proof of causation has not been adduced. If some evidence to the contrary is adduced by the defendant, the trial judge is entitled to take account of Lord Mansfield's famous precept. This is, I believe, what Lord Bridge had in mind in *Wilsher* when he referred to a "robust and pragmatic approach to the . . . facts" (p. 569).

It is not therefore essential that the medical experts provide a firm opinion supporting the plaintiff's theory of causation. Medical experts ordinarily determine causation in terms of certainties whereas a lesser standard is demanded by the law. . . .

[Sopinka J. stated that part of the problem stems from the reluctance of doctors to express an opinion unless they are 100% certain. The law does not require certainty but rather a balance of probabilities (*i.e.* 51%). It is in this sense that the plaintiff's case need not be based on a firm medical opinion.

He then reviewed the evidence, emphasizing that Dr. Farrell was negligent in continuing the operation. While the blindness could have resulted from natural causes, Sopinka J. quoted the expert testimony and it indicated that the continuation of the operation was more likely to have been the cause.]

The appellant was present during the operation and was in a better position to observe what occurred. Furthermore, he was able to interpret from a medical standpoint what he saw. In addition, by continuing the operation which has been found to constitute negligence, he made it impossible for the respondent or anyone else to detect the bleeding which is alleged to have caused the injury. In these circumstances, it was open to the trial judge to draw the inference that the injury was caused by the retrobulbar bleeding. There was no evidence to rebut this inference. The fact that testing the eye for hardness did not disclose bleeding is insufficient for this purpose. If there was any rebutting evidence it was weak, and it was open to the trial judge to find causation, applying the principles to which I have referred.

I am confident that had the trial judge not stated that "I cannot go beyond this since neither [expert witness] did and I should not speculate", he would have drawn the necessary inference. In stating the above, he failed to appreciate that it is not essential to have a positive medical opinion to support a finding of causation. Furthermore, it is not speculation but the application of common sense to draw such an inference where, as here, the circumstances, other than a positive medical opinion, permit.

While this Court does not ordinarily make findings of fact, this course is fully justified in this case. First, I am of the opinion that the trial judge either made the necessary finding or would have but for error of law. Second, it would be a disservice to all to send this case back for a new trial when the evidence is not essentially in conflict. I note that in *Wilsher*, the House of Lords refrained from deciding the case only because the evidence of the experts was seriously in conflict. That is not the case here.

In the result, I would dismiss the appeal with costs.

NOTES AND QUESTIONS

1. Prior to *Snell, McGhee* generated considerable confusion and debate. See for example *Nowsco Well Service Ltd. v. Canadian Propane Gas & Oil Ltd.* (1981), 122 D.L.R. (3d) 228 (Sask. C.A.); *Letnik v. Metropolitan Toronto (Municipality)*, [1988] 2 F.C. 399 (C.A.); *Haag v. Marshall* (1989), 1 C.C.L.T. (2d) 99 (B.C.C.A.); and *Belknap v. Meakes* (1989), 1 C.C.L.T. (2d) 192 (B.C.C.A.). See also Weinrib, "A Step Forward in Factual Causation" (1975) 38 Mod. L. Rev. 518.

2. According to Sopinka J., was Mrs. Snell able to prove on the balance of probabilities that Dr. Farrell's negligence was a cause of her loss? What test of causation did Sopinka J. apply?

3. Sopinka J. stated that the burden of proving causation was not immutable, but could be shifted where reasons of "experience and fairness" made it appropriate to do so. The examples cited were situations in which the evidence of causation lay exclusively in the defendant's hands and cases in which the negligent conduct of two defendants destroyed the means of proving causation. However, in *Snell* Sopinka J. refused to shift the burden of proof to Dr. Farrell, even though his negligence made it impossible to prove causation. Sopinka J. explained that it would be inappropriate to shift the burden of proof for "any injury that may very well be due to factors unconnected to the defendant and not the fault of anyone." What are the implications of this statement?

4. What are the limits of Sopinka J.'s suggestion that, in some circumstances, it may be possible for a trier of fact to rely on common sense pragmatism to fill in an evidentiary void? See *Meloche v. Hotel Dieu Grace Hospital/Villa Marie* (1999), 179 D.L.R. (4th) 77 (Ont. C.A.); and *Mathura v. Scarborough General Hospital*, 1999 CarswellOnt 43 (Gen. Div.) (WLeC), aff'd 2000 CarswellOnt 3320 (C.A.) (WLeC).

5. Even a "robust and pragmatic approach to the facts" may not help the plaintiff. In *Bigcharles v. Dawson Creek & District Health Care Society* (2001), 5 C.C.L.T. (3d) 157 (B.C.C.A.), the plaintiff was in a car crash and taken to the hospital while unconscious. Based on cervical spine x-rays, the plaintiff was removed from immobilizing equipment to a bed, and then turned and moved regularly. When the plaintiff's legs remained unresponsive, thoracic x-rays were taken that revealed a spinal fracture and spinal cord damage. The doctor acknowledged that he was negligent in moving the plaintiff and not taking the thoracic x-rays earlier. However, the doctor claimed that his negligence was irrelevant as the plaintiff's spinal cord injuries were "complete" at the scene of the crash. The plaintiff argued that the doctor's negligence caused or contributed to his paralysis. The trial judge found the conflicting medical evidence to be equally balanced and dismissed the plaintiff's claim because the plaintiff failed to proved causation on the balance of probabilities. The Court of Appeal upheld the trial court decision. See also *Egedebo v. Windermere District Hospital Assn.* (1993), 78 B.C.L.R. (2d) 63 (C.A.); and *Aristorenas v. Comcare Health Services* (2006), 216 O.A.C. 161 (C.A.).

6. In *Fairchild v. Glenhaven Funeral Services Ltd.*, [2002] 3 W.L.R. 89 (H.L.), *McGhee* made a remarkable comeback in an altered guise. In *Fairchild*, the plaintiff contracted mesothelioma, a fatal disease which is caused by the inhalation of a single

fibre of asbestos. The previous and subsequent inhalation of other fibres is causally irrelevant, and the disease may lie dormant for decades after the causative fibre has taken effect. The plaintiff had been negligently exposed to asbestos by several employers over the years and had no means of proving which one had exposed him to the single fibre that caused his disease. The House of Lords again reinterpreted Lord Reid's judgment in *McGhee*, relying on it for the proposition "that a breach of duty which materially increased the risk should be treated as if it had materially contributed to the disease." Several judges provided differing analyses and accordingly the precise scope of *Fairchild* is unclear. However, in the end result, all of the employers were held jointly and severally liable for the plaintiff's mesothelioma.

Is the result in *Fairchild* fair to the defendants? Although negligent, all but one of the defendants were held liable for an injury which they did not cause and to which they did not contribute. Rather than further muddying the causation analysis, should the House of Lords have expressly acknowledged that it was holding employers strictly liable for negligently exposing workers to the risk of a serious industrial disease?

The Canadian courts have not yet addressed the causation issues posed by cases like *Fairchild.* While *Hunt v. Carey Canada Inc.*, [1990] 2 S.C.R. 959 involved a mesothelioma claim, the judgment dealt with the tort of conspiracy and the striking out of claims, but not causation. Not surprisingly, much academic ink has been spilled over *Fairchild.* See for example Weir, "Making It More Likely v. Making It Happen" [2002] C.L.J. 519; Woods, "Establishing Causation in Negligence: The House of Lords Speaks Again" (2003) 26 Adv. Q. 471; Stapleton, "'Lords a Leaping' Evidentiary Gaps" (2002) 10 Torts L.J. 276; and Morgan, "Lost Causes in the House of Lords: *Fairchild v. Glenhaven Funeral Services*" (2003) 66 Mod. L. Rev. 277.

7. In *Holtby v. Brigham & Cowan (Hull) Ltd.*, [2000] 3 All E.R. 421 (C.A.), the plaintiff developed asbestosis after working as a marine pipe fitter for nearly 40 years. He was negligently exposed to asbestos fibres for about 20 years, during half of which he worked for the defendant. Unlike mesothelioma, asbestosis results from the cumulative inhalation of fibres and becomes more severe as more fibres are inhaled. The court held the defendant liable, but for only 25% of the plaintiff's losses, reflecting the proportion of time that he had worked for the defendant. Should the plaintiff have been allowed full recovery against the defendant, which could then seek contribution from the other negligent employers? Can you reconcile *Holtby* and *Fairchild*?

See also *Barker v. Saint Gobain Pipelines plc*, [2005] 3 All E.R. 661 (C.A.); Hedley, "Employer's Liability - Assessment of Damages - Reduction to Reflect Fault of Other Parties" [2000] C.L.J. 435; Gullifer, "One Cause After Another" (2001) 117 L.Q.R. 403; Cassels & Jones, "Rethinking Ends and Means in Mass Tort: Probabilistic Causation and Risk-Based Mass Tort Claims After *Fairchild v. Glenhaven Funeral Services*" (2003) 82 Can. Bar Rev. 597; Porat & Stein, "Indeterminate Causation and Apportionment of Damages: An Essay on *Holtby, Allen*, and *Fairchild*" (2003) Oxford J. Legal. Stud. 667; and Kramer, "Smoothing the Rough Justice of the Fairchild Principle" (2006) 122 L.Q.R. 547.

8. In *Sindell v. Abbott Laboratories*, 26 Cal.3d 588 (Sup. Ct. 1980), the plaintiff developed a deadly cancer caused by a drug called DES which her mother had taken while pregnant. The cancer had a minimum latency period of 10 to 12 years. About 200 pharmaceutical companies had manufactured DES but there were no significant differ-

ences in the brands. The plaintiff sued several of the larger manufacturers. The court held that all of the companies had been negligent in marketing DES because they knew or ought to have known of its risks at that time. Even though the plaintiff could not prove which company had produced the DES her mother had taken, the court held all of the defendants liable in proportion to their individual market share. Thus, a company which had 20% of the DES market when the plaintiff's mother was pregnant was held liable for 20% of the plaintiff's losses. See also *In re "Agent Orange" Product Liability Litigation*, 597 F.Supp. 740 (N.Y. Dist. Ct. 1984), which involved numerous manufacturers and plaintiffs in a large class action.

Can you distinguish the causal role of the defendants in *Sindell* from that in *Fairchild* and *Holtby*? Is the market share approach to liability in *Sindell* preferable to the approach in *Fairchild*?

9. The Canadian courts have not adopted the approaches in *Fairchild*, *Holtby* or *Sindell*. Rather, pursuant to *Snell*, the plaintiff must prove that the defendant's negligence increased the risk to the extent that the negligence was more likely than not to have been a cause of the loss in issue. Are the Canadian courts simply applying the but-for test, albeit in different terms?

10. Is the common law the appropriate vehicle for addressing the policy issues that appear to underlie the causation analysis in the preceding cases? Would it be simpler, clearer and more intellectually candid to enact specific workplace, healthcare, products liability, and other legislation to promote well-defined policy priorities?

For example, several provinces have enacted legislation making it far easier for the government to sue tobacco manufacturers for the public health costs of tobacco-related illnesses and disabilities in their jurisdiction. The legislation typically authorizes the government to sue the tobacco companies to recover its costs, permits the admissibility of general epidemiological and statistical data to prove causation, and allows the government to claim damages on an aggregate basis. In *British Columbia v. Imperial Tobacco Canada Ltd.*, [2005] 2 S.C.R. 473, the court upheld the constitutionality of the *Tobacco Damages and Health Care Costs Recovery Act*, S.B.C. 2000, c. 30.

(c) PROPORTIONATE CAUSE AND LOSS OF CHANCE

In several of the preceding cases, the major problem appears to be the all-or-nothing approach to losses occurring prior to trial. If there is only a 49% chance that the defendant's negligence was a cause, the plaintiff's claim fails; whereas if there is a 51% chance, the plaintiff's claim succeeds and he or she recovers 100% of the loss. If, as in *Sindell v. Abbott Laboratories*, 26 Cal.3d 588 (Sup. Ct. 1980), a proportionate approach is adopted, a plaintiff would recover based on a possibility that the defendant was a cause. Therefore, if there was a 30% chance that the defendant's negligence was a cause, the plaintiff would recover 30% of his or her loss from that defendant.

The loss of chance cases typically arise when the defendant's negligence has denied the plaintiff a possibility of avoiding a loss. Assume that, following their son's death, a family learns that there would have been a 25% chance for a full recovery had the doctor not negligently delayed their son's cancer treatment. The Canadian and English courts have denied recovery in these cases because the plaintiff cannot prove on a balance of probabilities that the defendant's negligence was a cause of his or her loss.

NOTES AND QUESTIONS

1. Would you favour abandoning the all-or-nothing approach to losses occurring prior to trial? What problems, if any, would result from adopting a proportionate cause approach? Would this approach necessitate limiting a plaintiff's recovery to 60%, if causation was only established to this probability?

2. The Canadian courts apply a different standard of proof for losses that may occur after trial. If the plaintiff can establish a substantial or reasonable possibility that the defendant's negligence will cause a future loss, the plaintiff can recover for a percentage of that loss. For example, assume there is a 40% chance that the defendant's negligence will cause the plaintiff to go blind and that this injury, if it occurs, will result in $100,000 in damages. Pursuant to *Janiak v. Ippolito*, [1985] 1 S.C.R. 146, the plaintiff would be awarded 40% of $100,000 as compensation for this possibility.

3. Can you suggest a justification for treating the loss of chance cases differently from other proportionate cause situations? Do loss of chance cases pose unique emotional harms?

4. See *Smith v. Moscovich* (1989), 40 B.C.L.R. (2d) 49 (S.C.); *Laferrière v. Lawson*, [1991] 1 S.C.R. 541; *Sellars v. Adelaide Petroleum NL* (1994), 179 C.L.R. 332 (H.C.A.); *Hotson v. East Berkshire Area Health Authority*, [1987] 2 All E.R. 417 (H.L.); and *Gregg v. Scott*, [2005] 2 A.C. 176 (H.L.).

See also Fleming, "Probabilistic Causation in Tort Law" (1989) 68 Can. Bar Rev. 661; Waddams, "The Valuation of Chances" (1998) 30 C.B.L.J. 86; Black, "Not a Chance: Comments on Waddams, The Valuation of Chances" (1998) 30 C.B.L.J. 96; and Black, "Ghost of a Chance: Gregg v. Scott in the House of Lords" (2005) 14 Health L. Rev. 38.

REVIEW PROBLEM

Assume that the incidence of a particular kind of cancer is 6 per 100,000 in the general population, but 10 per 100,000 in populations exposed to PCBs. Assume as well that Helen contracted this type of cancer after the defendant negligently exposed her to PCBs. Finally, assume that PCB-induced cancer cases cannot be distinguished from naturally occurring cancer cases.

(a) Would the principles of causation in *McGhee* (Lord Reid), *McGhee* (Lord Wilberforce), *Snell*, *Fairchild*, *Holtby*, *Sindell* or *Hanke*, all discussed above, be applicable to the causation issue in Helen's claim against the defendant?

(b) What result would be reached in Helen's case based on the principles in the applicable cases?

(c) Answer the preceding questions again, this time based on the assumption that incidence of this cancer is 4 per 100,000 in the general population, and 10 per 100,000 in populations exposed to PCBs.

5. Multiple Causes

The issue of causation becomes more complex when the plaintiff's injuries are brought about by two or more causes. As indicated at the outset of this chapter, it must first be determined if the injuries are divisible. In other words, can the injuries be divided into distinct losses that are each readily attributable to the conduct of a particular tortfeasor? If the plaintiff's injuries are divisible, he or she will have a separate cause of action against each tortfeasor.

This situation must be distinguished from one in which two or more tortfeasors cause a single indivisible harm. It may be useful to divide these multiple cause cases into two categories: those involving independent insufficient causes and those involving independent sufficient causes. As the following cases illustrate, the but-for test adequately addresses the causation issues posed by independent insufficient causes, but produces what are generally viewed as anomalous results when applied to independent sufficient causes.

Finally, it is important to distinguish situations in which the defendants are independent tortfeasors from those in which they are joint tortfeasors. An independent tortfeasor can only be held liable for the injuries he or she causes or contributes to bringing about. In contrast, a joint tortfeasor is held liable for the torts committed by his or her fellow tortfeasors, even if he or she did not cause or contribute to the plaintiff's loss. In *Cook v. Lewis*, [1951] S.C.R. 830, the court recognized three situations in which defendants will be held to be joint tortfeasors: an agent committing a tort while acting on his or her principal's behalf; an employee committing a tort while acting on his or her employer's behalf; and two or more individuals agreeing to act in concert to bring about a common end which is illegal, inherently dangerous, or one in which negligence can be anticipated. The issue of whether the defendants are joint or independent tortfeasors should be considered prior to analyzing the other elements of the cause of action. If the defendants are joint tortfeasors, the plaintiff need only prove that one of them was a negligent cause. Thus, the determination that the defendants are joint tortfeasors alters the subsequent analysis of the remaining issues.

NOTES AND QUESTIONS

1. Identify a situation in which the defendants are (a) both joint tortfeasors and multiple causes, and (b) joint tortfeasors but not multiple causes.

2. The third category recognized in *Cook* has generated considerable judicial attention. For example, in *Newcastle (Town) v. Mattatall* (1987), 78 N.B.R. (2d) 236 (Q.B.), aff'd (1988), 87 N.B.R. (2d) 238 (C.A.), three intoxicated youths broke into the town rink with the intent of stealing whatever they could find. One of the youths negligently caused a fire that resulted in substantial property damage. Although the other two were not negligent or even with the youth when he started the fire, all three were held to be joint tortfeasors and equally liable. The court stated that the fire was caused in pursuit of the three youths' common wrongful intention. Do you agree? See also *Raywalt Construction Co. v. Bencic* (2005), 386 A.R. 230 (Q.B.).

3. Should the defendants in the following situations be considered joint tortfeasors?

(a) A was driving a truck towing B's disabled van with B sitting in its driver's seat. While attempting to pass, the plaintiff was forced off the road by A, who had begun a left turn. The plaintiff could not see the truck's turn signal and the van's signal was not working. See *Harpe v. Lefebvre* (1976), 1 C.C.L.T. 331 (Alta. Dist. Ct.); and Klar, "Annotation" (1976), 1 C.C.L.T. 332.

(b) A and B each threw a handful of sand at a school bus. Some of the sand hit the plaintiff in the eye, but it was impossible to determine whether A or B had thrown that sand. See *Beecham v. Henderson*, [1951] 1 D.L.R. 628 (B.C.S.C.).

(c) A, B and C set out together for a night of heavy drinking. They took turns driving to different bars. All three were impaired, but B was driving when he caused an accident, seriously injuring the plaintiff. See generally *Hague v. Billings* (1989), 68 O.R. (2d) 321 (H.C.); and *Pizzolon v. Pedrosa* (1988), 46 C.C.L.T. 243 (B.C.S.C.).

4. At common law there was no apportionment among joint tortfeasors. While the negligence statutes now permit contribution and apportionment among joint tortfeasors, the common law principle that a release of one joint tortfeasor extinguishes the plaintiff's right to sue the other joint tortfeasors remains. To avoid this problem, the plaintiff may agree in a settlement not to sue one of the joint tortfeasors, but not provide a release. Since the settlement is not viewed as a release, the plaintiff is free to seek redress from the remaining joint tortfeasors. See *Tucker (Public Trustee of) v. Asleson*, [1993] 6 W.W.R. 45 (B.C.C.A.); *Bransfield v. Fletcher* (2003), 264 N.B.R. (2d) 366 (C.A.); and Ontario Law Reform Commission, *Report on Contribution Among Wrongdoers and Contributory Negligence* (1988).

(a) INDEPENDENT INSUFFICIENT CAUSES

In this category of cases, several factors combine to cause the plaintiff's loss. Each factor is individually necessary, as the loss would not have occurred without it. However, no factor is individually sufficient to have caused the loss, in the absence of the other factor. In *Athey v. Leonati*, [1996] 3 S.C.R. 458, the plaintiff's injury was caused by a non-culpable factor (his pre-existing back condition) and a culpable factor (the defendant's negligent driving). In contrast, *Nowlan v. Brunswick Construction Ltee.* (1972), 5 N.B.R. (2d) 529 (C.A.), aff'd [1975] 2 S.C.R. 523, addresses the causal role of two negligent parties in damaging the plaintiff's house.

ATHEY v. LEONATI
[1996] 3 S.C.R. 458

[The plaintiff, who had a pre-existing back condition, suffered neck and back injuries in a traffic crash that the defendant negligently caused. On his doctor's advice, the plaintiff began an exercise program at Fitness World. One day, during warm-up stretches, he felt a "pop" in his back and sustained a herniated disc. The incident resulted in a permanent partial disability that required him to leave his job as an auto body worker and take a less demanding job at lower pay. The trial judge accepted that the crash causally contributed to the onset of the disability, but reduced the plaintiff's damages by 75% to reflect the greater causal role played by his pre-existing back condition. The British Columbia Court of Appeal upheld the trial decision, and the plaintiff appealed.]

MAJOR J.: . . .It is not now necessary, nor has it ever been, for the plaintiff to establish that the defendant's negligence was the *sole cause* of the injury. There will frequently be a myriad of other background events which were necessary preconditions to the injury occurring. . . . As long as a defendant is *part* of the cause of an injury, the defendant is liable, even though his act alone was not enough to create the injury. There is no basis for a reduction of liability because of the existence of other preconditions: defendants remain liable for all injuries caused or contributed to by their negligence.

. . .

The respondents submitted that apportionment is permitted where the injuries caused by two defendants are divisible (for example, one injuring the plaintiff's foot and the other the plaintiff's arm). . . . Separation of distinct and divisible injuries is not truly apportionment; it is simply making each defendant liable only for the injury he or she has caused, according to the usual rule. The respondents are correct that separation is also permitted where some of the injuries have tortious causes and some of the injuries have non-tortious causes. . . . Again, such cases merely recognize that the defendant is not liable for injuries which were not caused by his or her negligence.

In the present case, there is a single indivisible injury, the disc herniation, so division is neither possible nor appropriate. The disc herniation and its consequences are one injury, and any defendant found to have negligently caused or contributed to the injury will be fully liable for it.

. . .

The Thin Skull and "Crumbling Skull" Doctrines

The respondents argued that the plaintiff was predisposed to disc herniation and that this is therefore a case where the "crumbling skull" rule applies. The "crumbling skull" doctrine is an awkward label for a fairly simple idea. It is named after the well-known "thin skull" rule, which makes the tortfeasor liable for the plaintiff's injuries even if the injuries are unexpectedly severe owing to a pre-existing condition. The tortfeasor must take his or her victim as the tortfeasor finds the victim, and is therefore liable even though the plaintiff's losses are more dramatic than they would be for the average person. [The thin-skull rule is examined in the next chapter, which deals with the issue of remoteness.]

The so-called "crumbling skull" rule simply recognizes that the pre-existing condition was inherent in the plaintiff's "original position". The defendant need not put the plaintiff in a position *better* than his or her original position. The defendant is liable for the injuries caused, even if they are extreme, but need not compensate the plaintiff for any debilitating effects of the pre-existing condition which the plaintiff would have experienced anyway. The defendant is liable for the additional damage but not the pre-existing damage. . . . Likewise, if there is a measurable risk that the pre-existing condition would have detrimentally affected the plaintiff in the future, regardless of the defendant's negligence, then this can be taken into account in reducing the overall award. . . . This is consistent with the general rule that the plaintiff must be returned to the position he would have been in, with all of its attendant risks and shortcomings, and not a better position.

The "crumbling skull" argument is the respondents' strongest submission, but in my view it does not succeed on the facts as found by the trial judge. There was no finding of any measurable risk that the disc herniation would have occurred without the accident, and there was therefore no basis to reduce the award to take into account any such risk.

. . .

Application of Principles to Facts

A matter to be resolved is the identification of the competing causes. Some of the trial judge's comments suggest that the "Fitness World incident" was a possible cause of the herniation. The "Fitness World incident" was not a cause; it was the *effect*. It was the injury. Mere stretching alone was not sufficient to cause disc herniation in the absence of some latent disposition or previous injuries. There was no suggestion that it was negligent of the appellant to attempt to exercise or that he exercised in a negligent manner.

Some latent weakness spontaneously manifested itself during the stretching, and the issue is whether the weakness was because of the accidents or a pre-existing condition. The reasons of the trial judge show that she understood this. She referred to the appellant's poor spinal health, his history of back problems, and to the fact that there had been no herniation or injury to the disc prior to the accidents. The competing causes in this case were the injuries sustained in the accidents and a pre-existing disposition to back problems.

The applicable principles can be summarized as follows. If the injuries sustained in the motor vehicle accidents caused or contributed to the disc herniation, then the defendants are fully liable for the damages flowing from the herniation. The plaintiff must prove causation by meeting the "but for" or material contribution test. Future or hypothetical events can be factored into the calculation of damages according to degrees of probability, but causation of the injury must be determined to be proven or not proven. This has the following ramifications:

1. If the disc herniation would likely have occurred at the same time, without the injuries sustained in the accident, then causation is not proven.

2. If it was necessary to have *both* the accidents *and* the pre-existing back condition for the herniation to occur, then causation is proven, since the herniation would not have occurred but for the accidents. Even if the accidents played a minor role, the defendant would be fully liable because the accidents were still a *necessary* contributing cause.

3. If the accidents alone could have been a sufficient cause, and the pre-existing back condition alone could have been a sufficient cause, then it is unclear which was the cause-in-fact of the disc herniation. The trial judge must determine, on a balance of probabilities, whether the defendant's negligence materially contributed to the injury.

The findings of the trial judge are slightly ambiguous. She awarded only 25 percent of the global damages because she held that the accidents were a "causation factor" of 25 percent. Taken out of context, this could be read as meaning that there was a 25 percent chance that the injury was caused by the accidents, and a 75 percent chance that it was caused by the pre-existing condition. In that case, causation would simply not be proven. However, it is clear from the reasons for judgment that this is not what the trial judge concluded.

The findings of the trial judge indicate that it was necessary to have *both* the pre-existing condition *and* the injuries from the accidents to cause the disc herniation in this case. She made a positive finding that the accidents contributed to the injury, but that the injuries suffered in the two accidents were "not the sole cause" of the herniation. She expressly found that "the herniation was not unrelated to the accidents" and that the accidents "contributed to some degree" to the subsequent herniation. She concluded that the injuries in the accidents "played some causative role, albeit a minor one". These findings indicate that it was the combination of the pre-existing condition and the injuries sustained in the accidents which caused the herniation. Although the accidents played a lesser role than the pre-existing problems, the accidents were nevertheless a necessary ingredient in bringing about the herniation.

The trial judge's conclusion on the evidence was that "[i]n my view, the plaintiff has proven, on a balance of probabilities, that the injuries suffered in the two earlier accidents contributed to some degree to the subsequent disc herniation". She assessed this contribution at 25 percent. This falls outside the *de minimis* range and is therefore a material contribution. . . . This finding of material contribution was sufficient to render the defendant fully liable for the damages flowing from the disc herniation.

[The appeal was allowed and the plaintiff was entitled to recover 100% of his damages.]

NOWLAN v. BRUNSWICK CONSTRUCTION LTEE

(1972), 5 N.B.R. (2d) 529 (C.A.), aff'd [1975] 2 S.C.R. 523

[The defendant contractor had been negligent in constructing the plaintiff's house, which suffered extensive rot due to leaks in the structure. However, the defendant argued that no damage would have occurred, but for the architect's poor design which had not provided for proper ventilation.]

LIMERICK J.A.: . . . While structural design particularly in lack of ventilation contributed greatly to the damage occasioned to the building, the poor workmanship of the defendant and poor quality of materials used also contributed.

This is a case of poor design on the part of the architect, as well as poor workmanship and materials contributing to the same damage.

If the design had provided proper ventilation there would have been no dry rot even though leaks occurred due to poor workmanship. Even though the design was poor there would have been no dry rot if the roof had been impervious to water and a proper drain installed and proper vapour barriers and insulation installed and windows had been properly constructed according to the plan.

Where there are concurrent torts, breaches of contract or a breach of contract and a concurrent tort both contributing to the same damage, whether or not the damage would have occurred in the absence of either cause, the liability is a joint and several liability and either party causing or contributing to the damage is liable for the whole damage to the person aggrieved. . . .

The defendant is a concurrent wrongdoer and the fact that the damage might not have occurred but for the poor design of the building does not excuse him from the liability arising out of his poor workmanship and inadequate material supplied by him.

The appeal is allowed. The judgment of the trial Judge is set aside. The plaintiffs, appellants shall have judgment against the defendant for the amount of $36,068.48 determined by the trial Judge and costs of trial and appeal.

[Hughes C.J.N.B. concurred with Limerick J.A., and Bugold J.A. wrote a separate concurring judgment.]

NOTES AND QUESTIONS

1. The plaintiff's pre-existing condition is generally not discussed when analyzing the causal role of the defendant's negligence. Why was it raised in *Athey*?

2. In *Athey* why did the court reject the defendant's arguments on divisible injuries, the crumbling skull doctrine and causation? What did Major J. mean by the statement that although the plaintiff's pre-existing condition does not diminish the causal relevance of the defendant's carelessness, it might reduce the plaintiff's damage award?

3. As indicated earlier, in *Hanke* the Supreme Court of Canada has significantly narrowed the material contribution test that Major J. introduced in *Athey* and has affirmed the but-for test for both divisible and indivisible injuries.

4. In *Arneil v. Paterson*, [1931] A.C. 560 (H.L.), several of the plaintiff's sheep were killed and injured when two dogs, separately belonging to the two defendants, chased, mauled and bit the sheep. The court held each defendant liable for the entire loss, because it was impossible to determine which dog had caused which injuries to which sheep. The loss was viewed as being indivisible, and both dog owners were held liable for the entire loss. It may also be difficult to disentangle the causal roles of two or more negligent acts if they follow one another closely in time. Chain reaction, multi-vehicle car crashes are perhaps the best example of this type of problem.

5. As *Athey* illustrates, once the defendant has been found to be a cause of the plaintiff's loss, the defendant will be held liable for the entire loss even if there were other causal factors.

6. As in *Nowlan*, if two or more negligent defendants cause or contribute to an indivisible injury, each defendant will be held jointly and severally liable for the entire loss. The plaintiff may choose to sue each defendant separately for the whole loss or, as is more often the case, may sue the defendants in the same action. If the plaintiff chooses the latter option and is successful, he or she may enforce the judgment against any one of the defendants.

7. At common law, there was no contribution among tortfeasors. Thus, a defendant who played a relatively minor role in causing the plaintiff's loss could be held fully liable, and yet have no redress against other tortfeasors who may have been primarily at fault. The provincial negligence statutes now provide that one tortfeasor may obtain contribution from his or her fellow tortfeasors, based upon their respective degrees of fault. See for example *Negligence Act*, R.S.O. 1990, c. N.1, ss. 1-2; and *Negligence Act*, R.S.B.C. 1996, c. 333, s. 4. Apportionment issues are discussed in more detail in chapter 19. For a general text on the treatment of multiple tortfeasors in various jurisdictions see Rogers, ed., *Unification of Tort Law: Multiple Tortfeasors* (2004).

(b) INDEPENDENT SUFFICIENT CAUSES

The previous section considered cases in which the plaintiff's indivisible loss was brought about by several necessary, but individually insufficient, causal factors. This section addresses the more difficult issues posed when the plaintiff's indivisible loss results from two or more sufficient causes. For example, assume that two negligent hunters fire fatal shots that simultaneously strike the plaintiff or that two negligent companies each permit toxins to escape into a river at levels fatal to the plaintiff's cattle.

Under the but-for test, each tortfeasor would be absolved of liability, because the plaintiff would have suffered the same loss regardless of any individual tortfeasor's negligence.

In order to avoid this obvious inequity, the courts have applied a significant or substantial factor test of causation in such situations. In light of *Hanke*, the Canadian courts may reframe the significant or substantial factor test in terms of a material contribution test.

LAMBTON v. MELLISH

[1894] 3 Ch. 163

The Defendants *Mellish* and *Cox* were rival refreshment contractors who catered for visitors and excursionists to the common, and both the Defendants had merry-go-rounds on their premises, and were in the habit of using organs as an accompaniment to the amusements.

It appeared from the evidence that these organs were for three months or more in the summer continuously being played together from 10 or 11 a.m. till 6 or 7 p.m., and that the noise caused by the two organs was "maddening".

The organs used by *Mellish* had been changed, and it was alleged by him that the organ in use when the motion was made was a small portable hand-organ making comparatively little noise. That used by *Cox* was a much larger one provided with trumpet stops and emitting sounds which could be heard at the distance of one mile.

The Plaintiff now moved against the Defendant in each action for an injunction restraining him from playing any organs so as to cause a nuisance or injury to the Plaintiff or his family, or other occupiers of the Plaintiff's property.

. . .

CHITTY J.: – Notwithstanding the conflict of evidence, I am of opinion that the Plaintiff is entitled to the injunction he asks for as against the Defendant in each action.

A man may tolerate a nuisance for a short period. A passer-by or a by-stander would not find any nuisance in these organs; but the case is very different when the noise has to be continuously endured: under such circumstances it is scarcely an exaggeration to term it "maddening", going on, as it does, hour after hour, day after day, and month after month. I consider that the noise made by each Defendant, taken separately, amounts to a nuisance. But I go further. It was said for the Defendant *Mellish* that two rights cannot make a wrong – by that it was meant that if one man makes a noise not of a kind, duration, or degree sufficient to constitute a nuisance, and another man, not acting in concert with the first, makes a similar noise at the same time, each is responsible only for the noise made by himself, and not also for that made by the other. If the two agreed and acted in combination each would be a wrongdoer. If a man shouts outside a house for most of the day, and another man, who is his rival (for it is to be remembered that these Defendants are rivals), does the same, has the inhabitant of the house no remedy? It is said that that is only so much the worse for the inhabitant. On the ground of common sense it must be the other way. Each of the men is making a noise and each is adding his quantum until the whole constitutes a nuisance. Each hears the other, and is adding to the sum which makes up the nuisance. In my opinion each is separately liable, and I think it would be contrary to good sense, and, indeed, contrary to law, to hold otherwise. It would be contrary to common sense that the inhabitants of the house should be left without remedy at law.

. . .

The Defendants here are both responsible for the noise as a whole so far as it constitutes a nuisance affecting the Plaintiff, and each must be restrained in respect of his own share in making the noise. I therefore grant an interim injunction in both the actions in the terms of the notices of motion.

NOTES AND QUESTIONS

1. Did the judge in *Lambton* view the case as one involving independent sufficient causes or independent insufficient causes? How did the defendant attempt to characterize the case? Would the result have been different had the judge accepted the defendant's characterization?

2. The significant or substantial factor test is also used when an independent sufficient cause and one or more independent insufficient causes bring about an indivisible loss. Depending on the facts, using the but-for test might result in exonerating some or all of the negligent parties. For example, assume that a fatal level of a toxin is 20 units, and that A negligently releases 21 units and B negligently releases 19. Under the but-for test, A would be held liable and B would be exonerated. However, if A was responsible for 21 units, B was responsible for 19 and C was responsible for 17, the but-for test would absolve all three of liability.

3. Some authors have recommended replacing the existing causation tests with the NESS test, which has been described as a more complete casual inquiry. A defendant's tortious act would be a cause-in-fact if it was a necessary element of a set of antecedent actual conditions that were sufficient for the occurrence of the plaintiff's loss. Canadian courts have yet to analyze the NESS test in detail. See for example Wright, "Causation in Tort Law" (1985) 73 Cal. L. Rev. 1735; and Wright, "Causation, Responsibility, Risk, Probability, Naked Statistics, and Proof: Pruning the Bramble Bush by Clarifying the Concepts" (1988) 73 Iowa L. Rev. 1001.

REVIEW PROBLEMS

1. Assume that 20 decibels of noise constitute a nuisance and that noises from different sources have a simple cumulative effect. Based on these assumptions, analyze the causal roles of the parties in the following situations:

(a) Allen causes 21 decibels, Barry causes 19 and Carl causes 5.
(b) Allen and Barry each independently cause 21 decibels.
(c) Allen causes 10 decibels, Barry causes 9.9 and Carl causes 0.2.
(d) Allen, Barry and Carl each cause 6 decibels and the plaintiff causes 3.

2. Allan and Bob were showing each other their favourite revolvers in a basement recreation room when they were called upstairs to meet Carol. They left their revolvers on the coffee table and came upstairs. As they talked, Carol's four-year-old son went off to explore the house. He eventually found the revolvers and shot himself with Bob's gun. Allan's gun was also loaded, but the child had not touched it. Carol has sued both Bob and Allan in negligence.

(a) Allan has sought your advice about his potential liability.

(b) Answer the same question, but assume that only Allan's gun would have been visible to the boy when he walked down the basement hall and looked into the recreation room.

6. Issues in Assessing the Plaintiff's Loss

(a) SUCCESSIVE CAUSES OF PARALLEL INJURY

This section deals with the extent of the original tortfeasor's liability when the plaintiff suffers an independent successive parallel injury prior to the trial on the first injury. This type of issue arises relatively infrequently, because once the trial and appeal period for the first injury has expired, the plaintiff's subsequent fate is irrelevant to the original tortfeasor.

PENNER v. MITCHELL
(1978), 10 A.R. 555 (C.A.)

PROWSE J.A.:

. . .

In the present case the trial Judge awarded the respondent special damages for loss of income for a period of thirteen (13) months following the date of the accident which gave rise to the respondent's cause of action. During that 13 month period the respondent would have been unable to work for a period of three months, even if the accident had not occurred, as she suffered from a heart condition which was unrelated to the accident.

The appellant's submission was that the respondent's award of special damages should not have included compensation for loss of wages during that three month period.

. . .

As the respondent relies on obiter dictum in the judgment of Lord Reid, in *Baker v. Willoughby*, [1970] A.C. 467 at 494 . . . (H.L.), I should first consider that case.

There the plaintiff, while crossing a road, sustained injuries to his left leg when he was struck by a motor vehicle operated by the defendant. Shortly before the trial he was shot in the left leg by a robber during the course of robbery. This later injury necessitated the immediate amputation of his left leg. The issue dealt with by Lord Reid was whether the first tortfeasor could call in aid the second tort to reduce the damages he should be made to pay on the ground that the disability the plaintiff suffered in his left leg resulting from the first tort ceased to be an effective cause of further loss after that leg was amputated as a result of the second tort.

[Reid L.J. concluded that original tortfeasors could only take into account a successive culpable parallel injury if it reduced the plaintiff's disability or shortened the period of time that he or she would suffer it.]

. . .

The issue on the present appeal is whether the rule applied in the *Baker* case, which resulted in treating the injury arising from the second event as irrelevant in assessing damages against the first tortfeasor, should be applied in the present case when the second event, the heart problem, arose in non-culpable circumstances. Lord Reid in the *Baker* case suggested that it should. . . .

In the *Andrews* case, in dealing with prospective loss of income and the effect thereon of contingencies of life, Mr. Justice Dickson stated: "It is a general practice to take account of contingencies which might have affected future earnings such as unemployment, illness, accidents and business depression.". . . . It will be noted that the nature of the contingencies of unemployment, illness, and business depression is such that a person who suffers a loss as a result of their occurrence does not have a cause of action against a wrongdoer as a consequence thereof. If the word "accident" is given its ordinary meaning, then its occurrence also arises in non-culpable circumstances. In my view the contingencies taken into account in assessing prospective loss of income should only include those that occur in non-culpable circumstances, that is, in circumstances that do not give rise to a cause of action. The rule applied in the *Baker* case should be applied only to those contingencies which arise from culpable circumstances.

My reason for concluding that future contingencies arising in culpable circumstances should not be taken into account in assessing damages such as prospective loss of income, is, because if that were done, the plaintiff would receive less than full compensation from the two wrongdoers. This would follow as there would be a deduction from the first loss because of the contingency that the second culpable event might occur and there would be a deduction from the second claim as the first culpable incident had occurred. The result of both deductions would produce a result the *Baker* case sought to avoid. Such a result would infringe the dominant rule applied in assessing damages as the injured person would then receive less than full compensation for the injuries he had sustained.

On the other hand not to take into account future contingencies arising in non-culpable circumstances would result in an injured person being overcompensated. For example not to make some allowance for early retirement which might arise for any number of reasons including health, non-culpable accidents, technological changes, or business depression, would result in the plaintiff being overcompensated in the event such contingency occurred.

The same reasoning applies if the contingency in fact is realized before trial. For example if the claimant was a carpenter and massive unemployment arose before the date of the trial then, to afford him compensation by way of special damages for loss of income, which he could not have earned, would result in him being overcompensated.

. . .

In conclusion, I am of the opinion that the learned trial Judge erred in awarding the respondent damages for the three month period she was disabled as a result of her heart condition. To include in her award damages for that three month period would result in her being overcompensated for the injuries caused by the appellant and the award would then infringe what I have referred to above as the dominant rule in assessment of damages for personal injuries. To include in the award damages for the three month period would have the result of including in the award a sum she would not have earned even if the motor accident had not occurred.

In the result I would set aside the award of special damages in the sum of $12,000 for loss of income and substitute therefor an award of $9,230.

NOTES AND QUESTIONS

1. In *Baker*, what injuries did the defendant cause, and were they divisible from those caused by the robbers? For what damages would the robbers have been held liable if they had been caught? Based on *Baker*, state the principles that govern the assessment of damages in cases of successive parallel injuries where (a) both causes are culpable, and (b) the first cause is culpable and the second is innocent.

2. Did Prowse J.A. agree with the *ratio* in *Baker*? What were the bases upon which he disagreed with Lord Reid? Based on *Penner*, state the principles that govern the assessment of damages in cases of successive parallel injuries where (a) both causes are culpable, and (b) the first cause is culpable and the second is innocent. See McInnes, "Causation in Tort Law: Back to Basics at the Supreme Court of Canada" (1997) 35 Alta. L. Rev. 1013.

3. For cases considering *Penner* see *Paziuk v. Ewbank*, [1987] 2 W.W.R. 317 (Man. Q.B.), aff'd [1987] 5 W.W.R. 307 (Man. C.A.); and *Sczebel v. Silvertson* (1988), 85 A.R. 293 (Q.B.). See also *Lankenau v. Dutton* (1988), 46 C.C.L.T. 256 (B.C.S.C.), aff'd (1991), 79 D.L.R. (4th) 705 (B.C.C.A.); and *DNM Mining Pty. Ltd. v. Barwick*, [2004] NSWCA 137 (AustLII).

In *Sunrise Co. v. Lake Winnipeg (The)*, [1991] 1 S.C.R. 3, the defendant's ship negligently caused the plaintiff's ship to run aground, which necessitated 27 days of repairs. In an unrelated incident, the plaintiff's ship sustained damages requiring 14 days of repairs, which were carried out within the 27-day period. Based solely on shipping cases, the majority found the defendant liable for 27 days of lost income. The dissent, based on general negligence principles, found the defendant liable for only 13 days of lost income. Which reasoning do you prefer?

4. The British courts have adopted a similar position to *Penner* in regard to non-culpable supervening causes. However, the House of Lords appears to have left open the issue of whether a culpable supervening cause might also be taken into account to reduce the first tortfeasor's liability. See *Jobling v. Associated Dairies Ltd.*, [1981] 2 All E.R. 752 (H.L.).

(b) DEVALUING THE PLAINTIFF'S LOSS

DILLON v. TWIN STATE GAS AND ELEC. CO.

163 A. 111 (N.H. 1932)

The defendant maintained wires to carry electric current over a public bridge in Berlin. In the construction of the bridge there were two spans of girders on each side between the roadway and footway. In each span the girders at each end sloped upwards towards each other from the floor of the bridge until connected by horizontal girders about nineteen feet above the floor.

The wires were carried above the framework of the bridge between the two rows of girders. To light the footway of the bridge at its center a lamp was hung from a bracket just outside of one of the horizontal girders and crossing over the end of the girder near its connection with a sloping girder. Wires ran from a post obliquely downward to the lamp and crossed the horizontal girder a foot or more above it. The construction of the wire lines over and upon the bridge is termed aerial. The wires were insulated for weather protection but not against contact.

The decedent and other boys had been accustomed for a number of years to play on the bridge in the daytime, habitually climbing the sloping girders to the horizontal ones, on which they walked and sat and from which they sometimes dived into the river. No current passed through the wires in the daytime except by chance.

The decedent, while sitting on a horizontal girder at a point where the wires from the post to the lamp were in front of him or at his side, and while facing outwards from the side of the bridge, leaned over, lost his balance, instinctively threw out his arm, and took hold of one of the wires with his right hand to save himself from falling. The wires happened to be charged with a high voltage current at the time and he was electrocuted.

. . .

ALLEN J.: — The circumstances of the decedent's death give rise to an unusual issue of its cause. In leaning over from the girder and losing his balance he was entitled to no protection from the defendant to keep from falling. Its only liability was in exposing him to the danger of charged wires. If but for the current in the wires he would have fallen down on the floor of the bridge or into the river, he would without doubt have been either killed or seriously injured. Although he died from electrocution, yet, if by reason of his preceding loss of balance he was bound to fall except for the intervention of the current, he either did not have long to live or was to be maimed. In such an outcome of his loss of balance, the defendant deprived him, not of a life of normal expectancy, but of one too short to be given pecuniary allowance, in one alternative, and not of normal, but of limited, earning capacity, in the other.

If it were found that he would have thus fallen with death probably resulting, the defendant would not be liable, unless for conscious suffering found to have been sustained from the shock. In that situation his life or earning capacity had no value. To constitute actionable negligence there must be damage, and damage is limited to those elements the statute prescribes.

If it should be found that but for the current he would have fallen with serious injury, then the loss of life or earning capacity resulting from the electrocution would be measured by its value in such injured condition. Evidence that he would be crippled would be taken into account in the same manner as though he had already been crippled.

His probable future but for the current thus bears on liability as well as damages. Whether the shock from the current threw him back on the girder or whether he would have recovered his balance, with or without the aid of the wire he took hold of, if it had not been charged, are issues of fact, as to which the evidence as it stands may lead to different conclusions.

NOTES AND QUESTIONS

1. Do the facts of *Dillon* materially differ from those in *Penner*? Is there a material difference between the situations in which (i) a victim would have been killed by one causal factor if he or she had not been killed by another, and (ii) a victim was affected by two causal factors, either of which alone would have been sufficient to cause death? See McInnes, "Causation in Tort Law: Back to Basics at the Supreme Court of Canada" (1997) 35 Alta. L. Rev. 1013.

2. What was the cause of the boy's death in *Dillon*? How did the court calculate the value of his loss? Is the court's approach consistent with the general principles for assessing damages in tort law?

3. It has been argued that an impending devaluing factor should only be taken into account to reduce the plaintiff's claim if (a) the impending factor is innocent in nature, and (b) an objective observer would say that, at the time of the defendant's tortious act, that the impending factor was certain to come to pass. Thus in *Dillon*, even if there had been a slight chance that the boy would have fallen into a small, deep pocket of water and escaped injury, the defendant would have been held fully liable for his death. Is it not more appropriate to discount the defendant's liability according to the likelihood of such possibilities? See Peaslee, "Multiple Causation and Damage" (1934) 47 Harv. L. Rev. 1127 at 1138-41; and Keeton *et al.*, *Prosser and Keeton on The Law of Torts*, 5th ed. (1984) at 353-54.

4. Assume that the plaintiff's $100,000 house is situated in the path of a forest fire negligently started by A. Before the flames reach the plaintiff's property, B negligently demolishes the house while cutting down a massive tree. How would you distinguish this case from *Dillon*? What is the cause of the plaintiff's loss and how would you calculate it? It is generally agreed that the plaintiff's loss would not be devalued in this situation. What is the rationale for this position?

REVIEW PROBLEMS

1. Jack and Harvey, two friends from Fairview University, were attending a football game at Midwest University. After the game they, along with about 50 other Fairview students, rushed onto the field and attempted to pull down the goal posts. Jack and Harvey were the first students to jump to the crossbar and they urged others to do the same. When the crossbar broke, either Jack or Harvey fell onto Lloyd, a member of the student police who was attempting to protect the goal posts. As Lloyd was clutching his broken arm, Clarkson, another Fairview student who had been hanging from the crossbar, fell onto Lloyd, fracturing Lloyd's leg. Discuss Lloyd's potential causes of action against Jack, Harvey and Clarkson.

2. John designed a cottage consisting of three bedrooms, a kitchen, a bathroom, and a living-room. Morris, who had contracted to build the living-room, unwittingly used rotten wooden beams. There was no doubt that the living-room would collapse within two years and that its collapse would not damage the other rooms. Ralph was the contractor for the bathroom and the three bedrooms. He had noticed that the timbers were rotten, but he decided to take a chance in using them. It is clear that the bathroom and bedrooms would suffer the same fate as the living-room. Ernie, the landscape contractor, was levelling the grounds after the cottage was completed. While distracted, he drove the bulldozer into the back of the cottage, destroying the bedrooms and the living-room. The next day Desmond, John's neighbour, chopped down a tree which unfortunately landed in the middle of the kitchen. Only the bathroom of John's cottage remained standing.

Ralph, Ernie and Desmond concede that they were negligent, but Morris has been absolved of liability. Discuss the liability of Ralph, Ernie and Desmond.

3. The Cruise Drug Company maintained a research laboratory which was developing a treatment for breast cancer. Lila and the other 47 researchers were required to handle toxic chemicals in the course of their research. Six months after beginning her employment at Cruise, Lila became pregnant. In due course, she gave birth to David, who unfortunately was born with a cognitive disability. Although he will be able to live in a home setting, David will require special education and full-time adult supervision for the rest of his life. It is agreed that David's total damages are $2.5 million.

At the time that Lila began working for Cruise, the company had known about an American study of a similar research project. That study revealed a greater incidence of birth defects among the children of female employees who worked with such chemicals during pregnancy. The rate of such birth defects is 6% in the general female population, but 9% among female researchers engaged in the American project. Cruise also knew that an elaborate ventilation system would most likely remove the dangerous chemical fumes from the laboratory. The company chose not to install the ventilation system because it found the $400,000 price tag prohibitive. Nor did it bother to inform its employees of the risks because it thought such knowledge would be bad for morale.

Discuss David's possible claim against the Cruise Drug Company.

17

REMOTENESS OF DAMAGES

1. Introduction
2. Directness Versus Foreseeability
3. Modifications to the Foreseeability Test
4. Intervening Causes

1. Introduction

Even if the defendant breached the standard of care in a way that caused the plaintiff to suffer a loss, liability will be denied if the connection between the breach and the loss was too "remote." Remoteness is a rule of fairness. In some circumstances, the law relieves the defendant of responsibility for an injury that he or she carelessly caused.

The concept can be dramatically illustrated by a passage in Benjamin Franklin's *Poor Richard's Almanac* (1757):

For the want of a nail the shoe was lost,
For the want of a shoe the horse was lost,
For the want of a horse the rider was lost,
For the want of a rider the battle was lost,
For the want of a battle the kingdom was lost,
And all for the want of a horseshoe nail.

If "the want of a nail" was caused by a blacksmith's carelessness, the question would be whether the blacksmith should be held responsible for the loss of the kingdom. Despite the causal connection between the initial breach and the ultimate loss, the answer seems obvious. As a matter of fairness, the blacksmith must not be liable for the loss of the kingdom.

The blacksmith's case is an easy one. Very often, however, the issue of remoteness is far more contentious. As the cases in this chapter reveal, the courts have struggled to develop a test that strikes an appropriate balance between the desirability of holding the defendant responsible for a loss that he or she carelessly inflicted on the plaintiff and the desirability of relieving the defendant of an unreasonable burden.

There is a close relationship between the issues of remoteness and causation. Causation is concerned with the *factual* connection between the defendant's breach and the plaintiff's loss. Remoteness is concerned with the *legal* connection between the defendant's breach and the plaintiff's loss. For that reason, remoteness is sometimes referred to as "legal causation" or "proximate causation."

There is, however, an important difference between causation and remoteness. Causation is, for the most part, an exercise in hard facts and logic. Even if the law is set aside, it remains possible to sensibly ask the question "did D's conduct cause P's loss?" A question concerning remoteness, however, only really makes sense in a legal context. This is because, as Andrews J. explained in *Palsgraf v. Long Island Railway Co.*, 248 N.Y. 339 at 352 (1928), "This is not logic. It is practical politics." Indeed, the whole purpose of the remoteness principle is to cut off the logical inquiry at some point. Moreover, that cut-off point will necessarily be somewhat arbitrary, because it is based on policy rather than logic.

In that respect, the concept of remoteness is similar to the concept of duty of care. Both are means by which the courts, for practical policy reasons, control the scope of liability. Not surprisingly, in each instance the content of the applicable rule has tended to vary from time to time, and from place to place, as judicial perceptions of societal values have shifted.

2. Directness Versus Foreseeability

(a) THE DIRECTNESS TEST

In *Re Polemis and Furness, Withy & Co.*, [1921] 3 K.B. 560, the Court of Appeal established "directness" as the test for remoteness. The test stated that the plaintiff's loss would not be too remote to be recoverable if it was a direct result of the defendant's carelessness. For the purpose of that test, "directness" was defined in terms of a close temporal and spatial connection between the defendant's breach and the plaintiff's loss.

In *Re Polemis*, the defendant's servants carelessly dropped a plank into the hold of the plaintiff's ship, which contained a cargo of benzene. The plank struck something and caused a spark that ignited the benzene fumes. The plaintiff's ship was destroyed by the ensuing explosion. The court held that this sequence of events was not reasonably foreseeable. It nevertheless imposed liability on the basis that there was a direct connection between the defendant's breach and the plaintiff's loss.

NOTES AND QUESTIONS

1. The Canadian courts applied the directness test prior to and after *Re Polemis*. See *Toronto Ry. Co. v. Grinstead* (1895), 24 S.C.R. 570; *Winnipeg Elec. Ry. Co. v. Can. Nor. Ry.* (1919), 59 S.C.R. 352; *Duce v. Rourke; Pearce v. Rourke* (1951), 1 W.W.R. (N.S.) 305 (Alta. S.C.); and *Simms v. Butt* (1975), 8 Nfld. & P.E.I.R. 14 (Nfld. C.A.).

2. The directness test has been criticized as being unworkable, unfair, illogical, too pro-plaintiff and theoretically unsound. Do you agree? Much of the criticism is based on the fact that the directness test does not relate the degree of the defendant's fault to the extent of his or her liability. See Seavey, "Mr. Justice Cardozo and the Law of Torts" (1939) 52 Harv. L. Rev. 372 at 381-91; Wright, "The Law of Torts: 1923-1947" (1948) 26 Can. Bar Rev. 46 at 56-58; and Goodhart, "The Imaginary Necktie and the Rule in *Re Polemis*" (1952) 68 L.Q.R. 515.

(b) THE FORESEEABILITY TEST

THE WAGON MOUND (NO. 1); OVERSEAS TANKSHIP (U.K.) LTD. v. MORTS DOCK & ENGINEERING CO.

[1961] A.C. 388 (P.C.)

[The appellants, charterers of the Wagon Mound (a ship), carelessly permitted oil to spill into Sydney Harbour while taking on fuel. The oil, which continued to escape for over a day, was carried by the wind and tide under the respondent's wharf. The respondent's employees were using welding equipment. Some molten metal fell, igniting a rag that was floating on some debris. The burning debris either directly ignited the floating oil or ignited it after first setting the oil-soaked pilings of the wharf ablaze. The respondent's wharf and some of its equipment were severely damaged in the ensuing fire.]

VISCOUNT SIMMONDS: — . . . The trial judge also made the all-important finding, which must be set out in his own words:

> The raison d'être of furnace oil is, of course, that it shall burn, but I find the defendant did not know and could not reasonably be expected to have known that it was capable of being set afire when spread on water.

. . .

One other finding must be mentioned. The judge held that apart from the damage by fire the respondents had suffered some damage from the spillage of oil in that it had got upon their slipways and congealed upon them and interfered with their use of the slips. He said:

> The evidence of this damage is slight and no claim for compensation is made in respect of it. Nevertheless it does establish some damage, which may be insignificant in comparison with the magnitude of the damage by fire, but which nevertheless is damage which, beyond question, was a direct result of the escape of the oil.

It is upon this footing that their Lordships will consider the question whether the appellants are liable for the fire damage.

. . .

It is inevitable that first consideration should be given to the case of *Re Polemis*. . . For it was avowedly in deference to that decision and to decisions of the Court of Appeal that followed it that the Full Court was constrained to decide the present case in favour of the respondents. In doing so Manning J., after a full examination of that case, said:

> To say that the problems, doubts and difficulties which I have expressed above render it difficult for me to apply the decision in *In re Polemis* with any degree of confidence to a particular set of facts would be a grave understatement. I can only express the hope that, if not in this case, then in some other case in the near future, the subject will be pronounced upon by the House of Lords or the Privy Council in terms which, even if beyond my capacity fully to understand, will facilitate, for those placed as I am, its everyday application to current problems.

This cri de coeur would in any case be irresistible, but in the years that have passed since its decision *Polemis* has been so much discussed and qualified that it cannot claim, as counsel for the respondents urged for it, the status of a decision of such long standing that it should not be reviewed.

Enough has been said to show that the authority of *Polemis* has been severely shaken though lip-service has from time to time been paid to it. In their Lordships' opinion it should no longer be regarded as good law. It is not probable that many cases will for that reason have a different result, though it is hoped that the law will be thereby simplified, and that in some cases, at least, palpable injustice will be avoided. For it does not seem consonant with current ideas of justice or morality that for an act of negligence, however slight or venial, which results in some trivial foreseeable damage the actor should be liable for all consequences however unforeseeable and however grave, so long as they can be said to be "direct". It is a principle of civil liability, subject only to qualifications which have no present relevance, that a man must be considered to be responsible for the probable consequences of his act. To demand more of him is too harsh a rule, to demand less is to ignore that civilised order requires the observance of a minimum standard of behaviour.

This concept applied to the slowly developing law of negligence has led to a great variety of expressions which can, as it appears to their Lordships, be harmonised with little difficulty with the single exception of the so-called rule in *Polemis*. For, if it is asked why a man should be responsible for the natural or necessary or probable consequences of his act (or any other similar description of them) the answer is that it is not because they are natural or necessary or probable, but because, since they have this quality, it is judged by the standard of the reasonable man that he ought to have foreseen them. Thus it is that over and over again it has happened that in different judgments in the same case, and sometimes in a single judgment, liability for a consequence has been imposed on the ground that it was reasonably foreseeable or, alternatively, on the ground that it was natural or necessary or probable. The two grounds have been treated as coterminous, and so they largely are. But, where they are not, the question arises to which the wrong answer was given in *Polemis*. For, if some limitation must be imposed upon the consequences for which the negligent actor is to be held responsible — and all are agreed that some limitation there must be — why should that test (reasonable foreseeability) be rejected which, since he is judged by what the reasonable man ought to foresee, corresponds with the common conscience of mankind, and a test (the "direct" consequence) be substituted which leads to nowhere but the never-ending and insoluble problems of causation. "The lawyer," said Sir Frederick Pollock, "cannot afford to adventure himself with philosophers in the logical and metaphysical controversies that beset the idea of cause." Yet this is just what he has most unfortunately done and must continue to do if the rule in *Polemis* is to prevail.

. . .

Their Lordships conclude this part of the case with some general observations. They have been concerned primarily to displace the proposition that unforeseeability is irrelevant if damage is "direct." In doing so they have inevitably insisted that the essential factor in determining liability is whether the damage is of such a kind as the reasonable man should have foreseen. This accords with the general view thus stated by Lord Atkin in *M'Alister (or Donoghue) v. Stevenson*:

> The liability for negligence, whether you style it such or treat it as in other systems as a species of "culpa", is no doubt based upon a general public sentiment of moral wrong-doing for which the offender must pay.

It is a departure from this sovereign principle if liability is made to depend solely on the damage being the "direct" or "natural" consequence of the precedent act. Who knows or can be assumed to know all the processes of nature? But if it would be wrong that a man should be held liable for damage unpredictable by a reasonable man because it was "direct" or "natural", equally it would be wrong that he should escape liability, however "indirect" the damage, if he foresaw or could reasonably foresee the intervening events which led to its being done. . . . Thus foreseeability becomes the effective test.

. . .

Their Lordships will humbly advise Her Majesty that this appeal should be allowed, and the respondents' action so far as it related to damage caused by the negligence of the appellants be dismissed with costs, but that the action so far as it related to damage caused by nuisance should be remitted to the Full Court to be dealt with as that court may think fit. The respondents must pay the costs of the appellants of this appeal and in the courts below.

NOTES AND QUESTIONS

1. Explain the test of remoteness adopted by the court.

2. Why did the court reject the directness test of remoteness? Were the court's criticisms of this test equally applicable to the foreseeability test? Were the arguments in favour of the foreseeability test persuasive?

3. The concept of reasonable foreseeability is used in connection with three elements of the negligence analysis: duty of care, standard of care and remoteness. Is the test precisely the same in each instance? If so, what purpose is served by the repetition? And if not, how does the test differ as between duty, breach and remoteness?

In attempting to answer these questions, it is worth re-examining (from Chapter 10) how the different manifestations of reasonable foreseeability were addressed in the Australian case of *Minister Administering the Environmental Planning and Assessment Act 1979 v. San Sebastien Pty. Ltd.*, [1983] 2 N.S.W.L.R. 268 at 295-96 (C.A.) (emphasis in original):

> [A] recognition has emerged that the foreseeability inquiry at the duty, breach and remoteness stages raises different issues which progressively decline from the general to the particular. The proximity upon which a *Donoghue* type duty rests depends upon proof that the defendant and plaintiff are so placed in relation to each other that it is reasonably foreseeable as a possibility that careless conduct of *any kind* on the part of the former may result in damage of *some kind* to the person or property of the latter. . . The breach question requires proof that it was reasonably foreseeable as a possibility that *the kind* of carelessness charged against the defendant might cause damage of *some kind* to the plaintiff's person or property. . . The remoteness test is only passed if the plaintiff proves that *the kind* of damage suffered by him was foreseeable as. . . [an] outcome of the kind of carelessness charged against the defendant.

Does it help to understand the different uses of foreseeability to think in terms of a funnel, wide at one end and narrow at the other, through which the plaintiff's claim must pass?

4. The court in *Wagon Mound (No. 1)* proceeded on the basis that the plaintiff's losses were directly caused but not foreseeable. Do you agree with these assumptions?

5. Like *Polemis*, the decision in *Wagon Mound (No. 1)* generated considerable academic debate. See Fleming, "The Passing of Polemis" (1961) 39 Can. Bar Rev. 489; Gibson, "The Wagon Mound in Canadian Courts" (1963) 2 Osgoode Hall L.J. 416;

Smith, "Requiem for Polemis" (1965) 2 U.B.C.L. Rev. 159; and Davies, "The Road From Morocco: *Polemis* through *Donoghue* to No-Fault" (1982) 45 Mod. L. Rev. 534.

6. It has been argued that neither directness nor foreseeability provides an appropriate test of remoteness. See Green, "Foreseeability in Negligence Law" (1961) 61 Columbia L. Rev. 1401; Smith, "The Mystery of Duty" in Klar, ed., *Studies in Canadian Tort Law* (1977) 1 at 15; and Rizzo, "The Imputation Theory of Proximate Cause: An Economic Framework" (1981) 15 Ga. L. Rev. 1007. See also Chiu, "A Just and Fair Principle of Compensation? Rethinking the Remoteness of Damage Rule in Wagon Mound" (2004) 12 Tort L. Rev. 147.

7. It is often difficult to determine which test or tests of remoteness the Canadian courts are applying. For example in *Richard v. C.N.R.* (1970), 15 D.L.R. (3d) 732 (P.E.I.S.C.) the judge concluded at 739 that the plaintiff was "the sole, direct, proximate and effective cause" of his own injuries. See also *Jones v. Wabigwan* (1969), 8 D.L.R. (3d) 424 (Ont. C.A.); and *Hunter v. Briere* (1989), 49 C.C.L.T. 93 (Man. Q.B.).

Most of the courts in Canada have followed *Wagon Mound (No. 1)*. See McLaren, "Negligence and Remoteness — The Aftermath of Wagon Mound" (1967) 32 Sask. L. Rev. 45; and Linden & Feldthusen, *Canadian Tort Law*, 8th ed. (2006) at 362-64.

REVIEW PROBLEMS

Analyze the following situations and determine whether the plaintiff's damages are too remote under each of the directness and foreseeability tests.

(a) The defendant negligently drove into a fire hydrant, causing a heavy flow of water which forced open the basement window of the plaintiff's building. The basement was flooded in several feet of water and the plaintiff sued for the damage done to his supplies. See *Weiner v. Zoratti* (1970), 11 D.L.R. (3d) 598 (Man. Q.B.); and *Kennedy v. Hughes Drug (1969) Inc.* (1974), 47 D.L.R. (3d) 277 (P.E.I.S.C.).

(b) The defendant negligently lit his house on fire while using a blowtorch to burn off the paint under the eaves. A fireman suffered burns, despite wearing protective clothing, while attempting to put out the fire. See *Ogwo v. Taylor*, [1987] 3 All E.R. 961 (H.L.).

(c) The defendant negligently drove into the plaintiff's fence causing metal fence staples to be scattered onto the plaintiff's pasture. Several months later, several of the plaintiff's cattle died as a result of ingesting the staples. The plaintiff sued the defendant for the loss of his cattle. See *Falkenham v. Zwicker* (1978), 93 D.L.R. (3d) 289 (N.S.S.C.).

(d) The defendant took the plaintiff's car without consent and the plaintiff gave chase in another vehicle. As a result of his negligence, the defendant knocked down a hydro pole and ended up in a field. The plaintiff stopped and ran into the field, where he stepped on a downed, live hydro wire. The plaintiff was severely burned and his leg had to be amputated. He sued the defendant for his personal injuries. See *Jones v. Wabigwan* (1969), 8 D.L.R. (3d) 424 (Ont. C.A.).

(e) The defendant negligently polluted the plaintiff's well, which in turn resulted in damage to his crops. The plaintiff claimed damages for developing a new water supply, for the loss of his crop and for the heart attack he suffered as a result of the strain caused by the incident. See *Connery v. Gov't. of Man.* (1970), 15 D.L.R. (3d) 303 (Man. Q.B.).

(f) The defendant ambulance attendants allowed the plaintiff, a paranoid schizophrenic, to sit in the front seat while being transported to hospital for treatment. The plaintiff suddenly grabbed the steering wheel and caused a serious accident. The plaintiff, who was injured in the crash, sued the defendants in negligence for allowing him to sit in the front seat. See *Shackleton v. Knittle* (1999), 46 C.C.L.T. (2d) 300 (Alta. Q.B.).

3. Modifications to the Foreseeability Test

(a) THE KIND OF INJURY

HUGHES v. LORD ADVOCATE

[1963] A.C. 837 (H.L.)

[The defendant's employees left a paraffin lamp and open manhole unattended. An eight-year-old boy knocked the lamp into the manhole and the vaporized paraffin that escaped from the broken lamp caused an explosion. The boy then fell into the manhole and was badly burned.]

LORD REID: — My Lords, I have had an opportunity of reading the speech which my noble and learned friend, Lord Guest, is about to deliver. I agree with him that this appeal should be allowed and I shall only add some general observations. I am satisfied that the Post Office workmen were in fault in leaving this open manhole unattended and it is clear that if they had done as they ought to have done this accident would not have happened. It cannot be said that they owed no duty to the appellant. But it has been held that the appellant cannot recover damages.

It was argued that the appellant cannot recover because the damage which he suffered was of a kind which was not foreseeable. That was not the ground of judgment of the First Division or of the Lord Ordinary and the facts proved do not, in my judgment, support that argument. The appellant's injuries were mainly caused by burns, and it cannot be said that injuries from burns was unforeseeable. As a warning to traffic the workmen had set lighted red lamps around the tent which covered the manhole, and if boys did enter the dark tent it was very likely that they would take one of these lamps with them. If the lamp fell and broke it was not at all unlikely that the boy would be burned and the burns might well be serious. No doubt it was not to be expected that the injuries would be as serious as those which the appellant in fact sustained. But a defender is liable, although the damage may be a good deal greater in extent than was foreseeable.

So we have (first) a duty owed by the workmen, (secondly) the fact that if they had done as they ought to have done there would have been no accident, and (thirdly) the fact that the injuries suffered by the appellant, though perhaps different in degree, did not differ in kind from injuries which might have resulted from an accident of a foreseeable nature. The ground on which this case has been decided against the appellant is that the accident was of an unforeseeable type. Of course, the pursuer has to prove that the defender's fault caused the accident, and there could be a case where the intrusion of a new and unexpected factor could be regarded as the cause of the accident rather than the fault of the defender. But that is not this case. The cause of this accident was a known source of danger, the lamp, but it behaved in an unpredictable way.

The explanation of the accident which has been accepted, and which I would not seek to question, is that, when the lamp fell down the manhole and was broken, some paraffin escaped, and enough was vaporised to create an explosive mixture which was detonated by the naked light of the lamp. The experts agree that no one would have expected that to happen: it was so unlikely as to be unforeseeable. The explosion caused the boy to fall into the manhole: whether his injuries were directly caused by the explosion or aggravated by fire which started in the manhole is not at all clear. The essential step in the respondent's argument is that the explosion was the real cause of the injuries and that the explosion was unforeseeable. He can only escape liability if the damage can be regarded as differing in kind from what was foreseeable.

. . .

This accident was caused by a known source of danger, but caused in a way which could not have been foreseen, and, in my judgment, that affords no defence. I would therefore allow the appeal.

LORD GUEST: . . . Concentration has been placed in the courts below on the explosion which, it was said, could not have been foreseen because it was caused in a unique fashion by the paraffin forming into vapour and being ignited by the naked flame of the wick. But this, in my opinion, is to concentrate on what is really a non-essential element in the dangerous situation created by the allurement. The test might better be put thus: Was the igniting of paraffin outside the lamp by the flame a foreseeable consequence of the breach of duty? In the circumstances, there was a combination of potentially dangerous circumstances against which the Post Office had to protect the appellant. If these formed an allurement to children it might have been foreseen that they would play with the lamp, that it might tip over, that it might be broken, and that when broken the paraffin might spill and be ignited by the flame. All these steps in the chain of causation seem to have been accepted by all the judges in the courts below as foreseeable. But because the explosion was the agent which caused the burning and was unforeseeable, therefore the accident, according to them, was not reasonably foreseeable. In my opinion, this reasoning is fallacious. An explosion is only one way in which burning can be caused. Burning can also be caused by the contact between liquid paraffin and a naked flame. In the one case paraffin vapour and in the other case liquid paraffin is ignited by fire. I cannot see that these are two different types of accident. They are both burning accidents and in both cases the injuries would be burning injuries. Upon this view the explosion was an immaterial event in the chain of causation. It was simply one way in which burning might be caused by the potentially dangerous paraffin lamp. . . .

[Lords Jenkins, Morris of Borth-Y-Gest and Pearce gave concurring speeches holding that the damage was not too remote.]

NOTES AND QUESTIONS

1. Explain the test of remoteness that was applied in *Hughes*. Do you agree with how the test was applied to the facts?

2. The impact of the test in *Hughes* depends on how broadly or narrowly one characterizes the kind of injury that the plaintiff has suffered. In *Doughty v. Turner Mfg. Co.*, [1964] 1 Q.B. 518 (C.A.) an employee in a metal treatment plant was injured when

an asbestos cover slid into the treatment vat. The cover reacted chemically with the contents of the vat, causing an eruption of molten liquid that burned the employee. The covers had been used for 20 years but this chemical reaction had never been observed. The man sued his employer, arguing that the injury was foreseeable. The court held for the defendant because it characterized the injury as one caused by a chemical reaction that was not foreseeable. Do you agree? Would it have made a difference if the injury had been characterized as a burn? For a criticism of *Doughty* see Dworkin, "Risk and Remoteness — Causation Worse Confounded?" (1964) Mod. L. Rev. 344. See also Linden & Feldthusen, *Canadian Tort Law*, 8th ed. (2006) at 368-69.

3. The characterization of the plaintiff's injury played a critical role in *Tremain v. Pike*, [1969] 3 All E.R. 1303. The defendant carelessly failed to control the rat population on his farm. The plaintiff, a farmhand, contracted Weil's disease after coming into contact with rat urine. Liability was denied. The court held that while it was reasonably foreseeable that the defendant's breach might lead to injury through, say, rat *bites*, it was not reasonably foreseeable that rat *urine* would prove problematic. Do you agree with that assessment? If you were inclined to impose liability, could you convincingly set out a description of the relevant risk so as to facilitate recovery?

4. The characterization of the plaintiff's injury again played a critical role in *Jolley v. Sutton London B.C.*, [1998] 1 W.L.R. 1546 (C.A.), rev'd [2000] 1 W.L.R. 1082 (H.L.). A dangerously decrepit boat was located on property under the defendant's authority. The defendant made a decision to remove the boat for safety reasons, but because of administrative dithering failed to perform the task. The plaintiff and his friend, both aged 14, found the boat. They decided to repair it and sail "to Cornwall because that was where the pirates were to be found!" In order to fix the hull, they hoisted the boat up on a car jack. The jack gave way, the boat fell and the plaintiff was rendered a paraplegic. The trial judge imposed liability, subject to a reduction of 25% for contributory negligence.

The Court of Appeal reversed that decision on the basis of remoteness. Taking a narrow view of both *The Wagon Mound (No. 1)* and *Hughes*, it said that the accident was "of a different type and kind from anything which the council could have reasonably foreseen." According to the Court of Appeal, while it was reasonably foreseeable that children might be hurt while "playing" on the abandoned boat, it was not reasonably foreseeable that they would be hurt while engaged in the "adult activity" of trying to repair it. See O'Sullivan, "Remoteness of Damage in Negligence: A Rotten Structure Collapses" [1999] 58 C.L.J. 12.

On further appeal to the House of Lords, the trial judgment was restored. Lord Steyn characterized the relevant risk as "the collapse of the propped up boat." He also stressed that when considering the foreseeability of risk to children, it is necessary to bear in mind that "play can take the form of mimicking adult behaviour." Likewise, Lord Hoffmann said that it was reasonably foreseeable that children would "meddle with the boat at some risk of physical injury." By phrasing the relevant risk more broadly, the House of Lords imposed liability where the Court of Appeal had not. See Williams, "Remoteness: Some Unexpected Mischief" (2001) 117 L.Q.R. 30.

Do you agree with the Court of Appeal or the House of Lords? Was the plaintiff's injury reasonably foreseeable? If so, are there nevertheless any policy considerations that would justify denying liability, and if so, how would these change the analysis?

5. In *Lauritzan v. Barstead* (1965), 53 D.L.R. (2d) 267 (Alta. S.C.) the defendant's negligence resulted in his car becoming stuck in the snow during a bad storm on a relatively unused portion of a rural highway. The plaintiff and defendant were forced by the wind and cold to stay in the vehicle for 36 hours. When the weather broke, the plaintiff went for help. The plaintiff was eventually found by a farmer but, as a result of frostbite, parts of both his feet had to be amputated. The plaintiff's wife of 26 years apparently left him because she did not want to live with a disabled man. While the court held that the plaintiff's physical injuries were not too remote, it held that his claim for loss of *consortium* was not a foreseeable kind of injury and denied this claim. Do you agree with the court's analysis? See also *Antell v. Simons*, [1976] 6 W.W.R. 202 (B.C.S.C.).

6. In *Trevison v. Springman*, [1996] 4 W.W.R. 760 (B.C.S.C.) the defendants had been entrusted with the plaintiff's house key. The defendants' son stole the house key and set fire to the plaintiff's house in order to cover up a series of thefts. The court held that losses due to the fire were too remote from the defendants' negligent failure to supervise and control their frequently delinquent son. The defendants were held liable for only the plaintiff's losses due to theft. What argument would you make on behalf of the plaintiff to recover for the arson?

7. For other judicial discussions of the principle in *Hughes* see *Williams v. St. John (City)* (1985), 34 C.C.L.T. 299 (N.B.C.A.); *C.N.R. Co. v. Sask. Wheat Pool*, [1986] 4 W.W.R. 371 (Sask. Q.B.); *Smith v. Littlewoods Organisation Ltd.*, [1987] 1 All E.R. 710 (H.L.); *Belzile v. Dumais* (1986), 69 N.B.R. (2d) 142 (Q.B.); and *Jebson v. Ministry of Defence*, [2000] 1 W.L.R. 2055 (C.A.).

(b) THE THIN-SKULLED PLAINTIFF RULE

SMITH v. LEECH BRAIN & CO.

[1962] 2 Q.B. 405

[The plaintiff's husband was a galvanizer employed by the defendants. The articles to be galvanized were lowered into a tank containing molten metallic zinc and flux. The method used depended on the size of the article. All articles were first dipped in hydrochloric acid and the larger articles were then lowered into the tank, using an overhead crane, by an operator behind a sheet of corrugated iron. On August 15, 1950, the plaintiff's husband was operating the overhead crane, using the corrugated iron sheet supplied, when a piece of molten metal or flux struck and burned his lower lip. The burn was treated at the time and he thought nothing of it. Some time later, the spot where he had been burned began to ulcerate and get larger. His general practitioner sent him to the hospital, where he was diagnosed with cancer. Treatment destroyed the primary growth but the cancer spread. Despite several operations, the worker died of cancer on October 14, 1953.

Lord Parker C.J. found that the defendants were negligent, that there had been no contributory negligence and that the burn promoted the cancer in tissues which already had a pre-malignant condition as a result of the employee's exposure to tar or tar vapours from 1926 to 1935.

The case is reported only on the question of remoteness of damage.]

LORD PARKER, C.J.: I am confronted with the recent decision of the Privy Council in . . . *The Wagon Mound*. But for *The Wagon Mound*, it seems to me perfectly clear that, assuming negligence proved, assuming that the burn caused in whole or in part the cancer and the death, this plaintiff would be entitled to recover.

. . .

For my part, I am quite satisfied that the Judicial Committee in *The Wagon Mound* did not have what I may call, loosely, the "thin skull" cases in mind. It has always been the law of this country that a tortfeasor takes his victim as he finds him. It is unnecessary to do more than refer to the short passage in the decision of Kennedy, J., in *Dulieu v. White & Sons*, [[1901] 2 K.B. 669] where he said:

> If a man is negligently run over or otherwise negligently injured in his body, it is no answer to the sufferer's claim for damages that he would have suffered less injury, or no injury at all, if he had not an unusually thin skull or an unusually weak heart.

. . . But quite apart from those . . . references, as is well known, the work of the courts for years and years has gone on on that basis. There is not a day that goes by where some trial judge does not adopt that principle, that the tortfeasor takes his victim as he finds him. If the Judicial Committee had any intention of making an inroad into that doctrine, I am quite satisfied that they would have said so.

. . .

In those circumstances, it seems to me that this is plainly a case which comes within the old principle. The test is not whether these defendants could reasonably have foreseen that a burn would cause cancer and that Mr. Smith would die. The question is whether these defendants could reasonably foresee the type of injury which he suffered, namely, the burn. What, in the particular case, is the amount of damage which he suffers as a result of that burn, depends on the characteristics and constitution of the victim. Accordingly, I find that the damages which the plaintiff claims are damages for which these defendants are liable.

MARCONATO v. FRANKLIN
[1974] 6 W.W.R. 676 (B.C.S.C.)

[The female plaintiff suffered relatively minor physical injuries in a car accident caused by the defendant's negligence. Following the accident, she developed symptoms of pain and stiffness for which there was no physical explanation. She became depressed, hostile and anxious. Although the psychiatric evidence indicated that she had paranoid tendencies before the accident, she had been "a good homemaker." The accident triggered a major personality change.]

AIKINS J.: — I turn to the question of causation. One would not ordinarily anticipate, using reasonable foresight, that a moderate cervical strain with soft tissue damage would give rise to the consequences which followed for Mrs. Marconato. These arose, however, because of her pre-existing personality traits. She had a peculiar susceptibility or vulnerability to suffer much greater consequences from a moderate physical injury than the average person. The consequences for Mrs. Marconato could no more be foreseen than it could be foreseen by a tortfeasor that his victim was thin-skulled and that a minor blow to the head would cause a very serious injury. It is plain enough that the defendant could foresee the probability of physical injury. It is implicit, however, in the principle that a wrongdoer takes his victim as he finds him, that he takes his victim with all the victim's peculiar susceptibilities and vulnerabilities. The consequences of Mrs. Marconato's injuries were unusual but arose involuntarily. Granted her type of personality they arose as night follows day because of the injury and the circumstances in which she found herself because of the injury.

As to the argument that the damage suffered is too remote because not reasonably foreseeable, I refer first to an English case, *Smith v. Leech Brain & Co. Ltd.*. . . . In this case the plaintiff widow claimed damages for the death of her husband under the Fatal Accidents Acts. The defendant was the deceased's employer. The deceased suffered a burn on his lip; as a result cancer developed at that site, from which the injured man died some three years later. Remoteness on the ground of lack of foreseeability was argued. I cite two passages from the judgment of Lord Parker C.J. The first is at p. 414:

> For my part, I am quite satisfied that the Judicial Committee in *Overseas Tankship (U.K.) v. Morts Dock & Engineering Co. (The Wagon Mound) . . . did not have what I may call, loosely, the thin skull cases in mind. It has always been the law of this country that a tortfeasor takes his victim as he finds him.*

. . .

> The second passage is at p. 415:

> The test is not whether these employers could reasonably have foreseen that a burn would cause cancer and that he would die. The question is whether these employers could reasonably foresee the type of injury he suffered, namely, the burn. What, in the particular case, is the amount of damage which he suffers as a result of that burn, depends upon the characteristics and constitution of the victim.

I also refer to the judgment of McIntyre J. (now J.A.) in *Elloway v. Boomars* (1968), 69 D.L.R. (2d) 605 (B.C.). In *Elloway* the plaintiff developed schizophrenia following injury in a motor accident. At p. 606, McIntyre J. said:

> . . . As I understand the law . . . a schizophrenic condition caused by the wrongful conduct of a defendant may be a basis of compensation as may be a schizophrenia caused by the aggravation of a latent condition but always provided that it can be shown that the cause of the condition was the accident.

> At p. 607 McIntyre J. said:

> I find the plaintiff's present condition was caused by the accident. He suffered from a pre-existing condition which predisposed him to a schizophrenic illness and the accident, operating upon this predisposition, brought about the full schizophrenic illness and it is therefore a proper basis for compensation.

What I have cited might well be transposed in the present case to go as follows: Mrs. Marconato was predisposed by her personality to suffer the consequences which she did suffer as a result of the modest physical injury caused by the accident and it was that predisposition which brought on the unusual consequences of the injury. The defendant must pay damages for all the consequences of her negligence.

NOTES AND QUESTIONS

1. Explain what is meant by the "thin-skulled plaintiff rule." What is the relationship between the foreseeability test of remoteness and the thin-skulled plaintiff rule?

The thin-skull rule is captured by the phrase "in for a buck, in for a bundle." If it was not reasonably foreseeable that the defendant's carelessness would cause any injury of a particular type, then the plaintiff cannot recover even if, because of a peculiar vulnerability, he or she actually suffered a great deal. However, if it was reasonably foreseeable that the defendant's carelessness would cause *some* injury of a particular type, then the plaintiff can recover in full even if, because of a special vulnerability, he or she suffered to a greater extent than could have been reasonably foreseen.

2. What would have been the result in *Smith* if the deceased had not had a pre-existing susceptibility to cancer but nevertheless developed cancer at the site of the burn and died of the disease? What would have been the result if the burn had increased the deceased's risk of getting cancer and he developed cancer at the site of the burn and died? See also *Pesonen v. Melnyk* (1993), 17 C.C.L.T. (2d) 66 (B.C.C.A.); *Hunter v. Manning*, [1993] 5 W.W.R. 738 (Sask. Q.B.); *Hooiveld v. Van Biert*, [1994] 4 W.W.R. 143 (B.C.C.A.); and *Buteikis v. Adams*, [1994] 7 W.W.R. 119 (B.C.S.C.).

3. Sarah negligently closes a door on Andrew's hand, permanently disabling it. Unknown to Sarah, Andrew is a baseball infielder with the Ithaca Rangers who has lost future earnings of $25 million as a result of the injury. Are these losses too remote?

4. According to *Marconato*, what application does the thin-skulled plaintiff rule have to a plaintiff with an "eggshell" personality? Is the damage award in *Marconato* compatible with the argument that there should be some reasonable relationship between the degree of the defendant's fault and the extent of his or her liability? See *Price v. Garcha* (1988), 44 C.C.L.T. 1 (B.C.S.C.), aff'd (1989), 2 C.C.L.T. (2d) 265 (B.C.C.A.); *Graham v. Rourke* (1988), 43 C.C.L.T. 119 (Ont. H.C.), varied on damages (1990), 75 O.R. (2d) 622 (C.A.); and *Dushynski v. Rumsey* (2001), 94 Alta. L.R. (3d) 26 (Q.B.), varied (2003), 16 Alta. L.R. (4th) 237 (C.A.).

5. In *Swami v. Lo*, [1980] 1 W.W.R. 379 (B.C.S.C.) the plaintiff's husband committed suicide 14 months after he had been seriously injured in a car accident caused by the defendant's carelessness. The constant pain forced the husband to give up work and he began to drink heavily. Although the deceased became very depressed, there was no allegation that he was either criminally or civilly insane. The judge concluded that *Smith* did not apply to the facts of the case and dismissed the plaintiff's claim as being too remote. Given the serious physical injuries that the husband suffered in the car accident, was it foreseeable that he would suffer emotional injuries of some kind as a result? If such injuries were foreseeable, should damages for the husband's suicide have been recoverable under the kind-of-injury test in *Hughes*? See also *Wright Estate v. Davidson*, [1992] 3 W.W.R. 611 (B.C.C.A.) where the court held that the deceased's suicide following a minor car accident was too remote. Were *Swami* and *Wright Estate* rightly decided?

See also *Gray v. Cotic* (1983), 26 C.C.L.T. 163 (S.C.C.) where the plaintiff recovered damages for her husband's suicide following a car accident because he had a pre-existing mental health problem. See also *Costello v. Blakeson*, [1993] 2 W.W.R. 562 (B.C.S.C.); *Hauk Estate v. Hudson* (1997), 50 C.C.L.I. (2d) 159 (Ont. Gen. Div.); and *Corr v. IBC Vehicles*, [2006] 2 All E.R. 929 (C.A.).

6. As in *Marconato* and *Swami*, a plaintiff may raise the thin-skulled plaintiff rule to establish that an emotional harm stemming from a physical injury is not too remote to be recoverable. This issue frequently arises in sexual battery cases. See for example *K.(W.) v. Pornbacher* (1997), 34 C.C.L.T. (2d) 174 (B.C.S.C.); and *D.(P.A.) v. H.(A.E.)* (1998), [1999] 2 W.W.R. 139 (B.C.S.C.). These cases must be distinguished from claims for the negligent infliction of nervous shock. As discussed in Chapter 12, these latter claims are not consequent on any physical injury to the plaintiff. The careless infliction of nervous shock is analyzed under special duty of care principles: see *Bechard v. Haliburton Estate* (1991), 10 C.C.L.T. (2d) 156 (Ont. C.A.).

7. In *Kavanagh v. Akhtar* (1998), 45 N.S.W.L.R. 588 (C.A.) the plaintiff was injured when a heavy box fell on her at the defendant's store. As a result of physical injuries to her left shoulder and arm she was unable to care for her very long hair. Months after the accident she had her hair cut short. Her husband, a devout Muslim, reacted very badly to her decision to cut her hair short, which he perceived "as defiance of his scripturally-based right of control over his wife as well as her defiance of religious injunctions about women cutting their hair without permission of their husband." He withdrew immediately from her and ultimately the haircut led to the breakdown of the marriage. She sued the defendant for psychiatric injury suffered as a result. Is this injury too remote? What arguments would you make for each party?

8. The thin-skull rule must be distinguished from the "crumbling skull" rule that Major J. discussed in the extract of *Athey v. Leonati* (1996), 140 D.L.R. (4th) 235 (S.C.C.) in the previous chapter.

Although a plaintiff with a thin skull is unusually vulnerable to harm, he or she was not doomed at the outset. By leading a careful life, he or she might have been able to avoid injury. The legal question therefore is whether the defendant should be held responsible for carelessly cracking a skull that, while weak, might otherwise have survived.

The position of a plaintiff with a crumbling skull is significantly different. His or her skull was not only thin, but doomed to damage. The legal question therefore is whether the defendant should be held responsible for hastening the onset of an injury that eventually would have occurred in any event. The answer is that damages are available, but only to the extent that the defendant worsened the plaintiff's condition. If, for instance, the breach caused the plaintiff's skull to crumble two years earlier than expected, then the defendant's liability is limited to that period. On the difference between a thin skull and a crumbling skull see *Lam v. Sorochan Estate* (2000), 259 A.R. 270 (Q.B.); *T.W.N.A. v. Clarke* (2003), 20 C.C.L.T. (3d) 165 (B.C.C.A.); *Zacharias v. Leys* (2005), 36 C.C.L.T. (3d) 93 (B.C.C.A.); and *Blackwater v. Plint*, [2005] 3 S.C.R. 3. For a recent discussion of the key cases on the crumbling skull rule see *Lyne v. McClarty* (2003), 170 Man. R. (2d) 161 (C.A.).

9. The thin-skull rule can also be contrasted with the "thin wallet" rule. The latter asks whether the defendant should be held liable for damages that were exacerbated by the fact that the plaintiff had limited financial resources and therefore was unusually vulnerable to financial harm.

This question was traditionally answered in the negative. In *Dredger Liesbosch v. Steamship Edison*, [1933] A.C. 449 (H.L.) the plaintiff's ship was sunk and lost due to the defendant's carelessness. The plaintiff was obviously entitled to damages representing the value of its ship. However, it also claimed damages under another head. Before the accident, the plaintiff had contractually promised to use the ship to provide certain services to a third party. As a result of the accident, however, the ship was not available for this purpose. Furthermore, because of the plaintiff's generally strained financial situation, it was unable to buy a replacement ship immediately. Consequently, it was required to rent another ship for the purpose of fulfilling the contractual obligation. The plaintiff claimed that it was entitled to damages representing the additional cost that it incurred as a result of being required to rent the other ship. The House of Lords rejected that claim on the ground that the defendant was not responsible for the plaintiff's impecuniosity. This decision established the proposition that a plaintiff cannot claim additional damages that flow from the fact that it had a "thin wallet" and therefore was unusually susceptible to economic harm.

The modern approach, however, rejects any such blanket rule in favour of a test of reasonable foreseeability. *Alcoa Minerals of Jamaica v. Broderick*, [2000] 3 W.L.R. 23 (P.C.) is illustrative. The defendant committed the tort of nuisance by operating a smelting plant in Jamaica that emitted corrosive materials. Those materials caused substantial damage to the roof of the plaintiff's house. The plaintiff commenced an action in 1989, at which time the cost of repairing the roof was $211,000. In the following years, the Jamaican economy suffered through a recession and inflation increased markedly. By 1994, when the matter was decided at trial, the cost of repairing the plaintiff's roof was $938,000. The trial judge awarded damages in that amount. The defendant eventually appealed to the Privy Council on the ground that the plaintiff was limited, by the decision in *Liesbosch*, to the initial value of its loss. The defendant argued that the plaintiff should have repaired the roof immediately and that the increased cost of repair was due to the plaintiff's own impecuniosity in being unable to afford immediate repairs.

The Privy Council found in favour of the plaintiff and affirmed the trial judge's decision to award damages of $938,000. The court said that there is no absolute rule that requires damages to be assessed at the date of the initial damage. It also said that there is no absolute rule to the effect that the plaintiff cannot recover the full value of a loss that was exacerbated by its own impecuniosity. The availability of damages in such circumstances is determined by an application of the usual test of reasonable foreseeability. On the facts of the case, it was reasonably foreseeable that a person in the plaintiff's position might not be able to afford to immediately repair the damage caused by the defendant's nuisance and that economic factors would render later repairs more costly. See also *Amar Cloth House Ltd. v. LA Van & Co.* (1997), 35 C.C.L.T. (2d) 99 (B.C.S.C.); and *Lagden v. O'Connor*, [2004] 1 All E.R. 277 (H.L.) in which the House of Lords expressly overruled *Liesbosch*.

10. If the plaintiff suffers a pure economic loss – an economic loss that is not consequent on injury to the plaintiff's person or property – then special duty principles

are applied. Those principles were discussed at length in Chapter 14. However, if the plaintiff's economic loss results from injuries to his person or property, the issue is dealt with under the remoteness of damages principles.

(c) THE POSSIBILITY OF INJURY

THE WAGON MOUND (NO. 2); OVERSEAS TANKSHIP (U.K.) LTD. v. MILLER STEAMSHIP CO. PTY.

[1967] 1 A.C. 617 (P.C.)

[This case arose from the same incident as the *Wagon Mound (No. 1)*, extracted earlier in this chapter. The plaintiffs in this action, however, were the owners of two boats that were damaged in the harbour fire. At trial the plaintiffs succeeded in nuisance. However, their action in negligence was dismissed because their damages were not reasonably foreseeable and thus too remote to be recoverable. The defendant appealed and the plaintiffs cross-appealed. Only the court's discussion of the negligence issue is reproduced below.]

LORD REID: . . . It is now necessary to turn to the respondents' submission that the trial judge was wrong in holding that damage from fire was not reasonably foreseeable. In *Wagon Mound (No. 1)* the finding on which the Board proceeded was that of the trial judge:

> . . . [the appellants] did not know and could not reasonably be expected to have known that [the oil] was capable of being set afire when spread on water.

In the present case the evidence led was substantially different from the evidence led in *Wagon Mound (No. 1)* and the findings of Walsh J., are significantly different. That is not due to there having been any failure by the plaintiffs in *Wagon Mound (No. 1)* in preparing and presenting their case. The plaintiffs there were no doubt embarrassed by a difficulty which does not affect the present plaintiffs. The outbreak of the fire was consequent on the act of the manager of the plaintiffs in *Wagon Mound (No. 1)* in resuming oxy-acetylene welding and cutting while the wharf was surrounded by this oil. So if the plaintiffs in the former case had set out to prove that it was foreseeable by the engineers of the Wagon Mound that this oil could be set alight, they might have had difficulty in parrying the reply that then this must also have been foreseeable by their manager. Then there would have been contributory negligence and at that time contributory negligence was a complete defence in New South Wales.

The crucial finding of Walsh, J., in this case is in finding (v): that the damage was "not reasonably foreseeable by those for whose acts the defendant would be responsible." That is not a primary finding of fact but an inference from the other findings, and it is clear from the learned judge's judgment that in drawing this inference he was to a large extent influenced by his view of the law. The vital parts of the findings of fact which have already been set out in full are (i) that the officers of the Wagon Mound "would regard furnace oil as very difficult to ignite on water" — not that they would regard this as impossible, (ii) that their experience would probably have been "that this had very rarely happened" — not that they would never have heard of a case where it had happened, and (iii) that they would have regarded it as a "possibility, but one which could become an actuality only in very exceptional circumstances" — not, as in *Wagon Mound (No. 1)*, that they could not reasonably be expected to have known that this oil was capable of being set afire when spread on water. The question which must now be determined is whether these differences between the findings in the two cases do or do not lead to different results in law.

In *Wagon Mound (No. 1)* the Board were not concerned with degrees of foreseeability because the finding was that the fire was not foreseeable at all. So Viscount Simonds had no cause to amplify the statement that the "essential factor in determining liability is whether the damage is of such a kind as the reasonable man should have foreseen." Here the findings show, however, that some risk of fire would have been present to the mind of a reasonable man in the shoes of the ship's chief engineer. So the first question must be what is the precise meaning to be attached in this context to the words "foreseeable" and "reasonably foreseeable".

Before *Bolton v. Stone* [[1951] 1 All E.R. 1078], the cases had fallen into two classes: (i) those where, before the event, the risk of its happening would have been regarded as unreal either because the event would have been thought to be physically impossible or because the possibility of its happening would have been regarded as so fantastic or far-fetched that no reasonable man would have paid any attention to it — "a mere possibility which would never occur to the mind of a reasonable man" (per Lord Dunedin in *Fardon v. Harcourt-Rivington* [[1932] All E.R. Rep. 81]) — or (ii) those where there was a real and substantial risk or chance that something like the event which happens might occur and then the reasonable man would have taken the steps necessary to eliminate the risk.

Bolton v. Stone posed a new problem. There a member of a visiting team drove a cricket ball out of the ground on to an unfrequented adjacent public road and it struck and severely injured a lady who happened to be standing in the road. That it might happen that a ball would be driven on to this road could not have been said to be a fantastic or far-fetched possibility: according to the evidence it had happened about six times in twenty-eight years. Moreover it could not have been said to be a far-fetched or fantastic possibility that such a ball would strike someone in the road: people did pass along the road from time to time. So it could not have been said that, on any ordinary meaning of the words, the fact that a ball might strike a person in the road was not foreseeable or reasonably foreseeable. It was plainly foreseeable; but the chance of its happening in the foreseeable future was infinitesimal. A mathematician given the data could have worked out that it was only likely to happen once in so many thousand years. The House of Lords held that the risk was so small that in the circumstances a reasonable man would have been justified in disregarding it and taking no steps to eliminate it.

It does not follow that, no matter what the circumstances may be, it is justifiable to neglect a risk of such a small magnitude. A reasonable man would only neglect such a risk if he had some valid reason for doing so: e.g., that it would involve considerable expense to eliminate the risk. He would weigh the risk against the difficulty of eliminating it. If the activity which caused the injury to Miss Stone had been an unlawful activity there can be little doubt but that *Bolton v. Stone* would have been decided differently. In their Lordships' judgment *Bolton v. Stone* did not alter the general principle that a person must be regarded as negligent if he does not take steps to eliminate a risk which he knows or ought to know is a real risk and not a mere possibility which would never influence the mind of a reasonable man. What that decision did was to recognise and give effect to the qualification that it is justifiable not to take steps to eliminate a real risk if it is small and if the circumstances are such that a reasonable man, careful of the safety of his neighbour, would think it right to neglect it.

In the present case there was no justification whatever for discharging the oil into Sydney Harbour. Not only was it an offence to do so, but also it involved considerable loss financially. If the ship's engineer had thought about the matter there could have been no question of balancing the advantages and disadvantages. From every point of view it was both his duty and his interest to stop the discharge immediately.

It follows that in their Lordships' view the only question is whether a reasonable man having the knowledge and experience to be expected of the chief engineer of the Wagon Mound would have known that there was a real risk of the oil on the water catching fire in some way: if it did, serious damage to ships or other property was not only foreseeable but very likely. Their Lordships do not dissent from the view of the trial judge that the possibilities of damage "must be significant enough in a practical sense to require a reasonable man to guard against them", but they think that he may have misdirected himself in saying

> there does seem to be a real practical difficulty, assuming that some risk of fire damage was foreseeable, but not a high one, in making a factual judgment as to whether this risk was sufficient to attract liability if damage should occur.

In this difficult chapter of the law decisions are not infrequently taken to apply to circumstances far removed from the facts which give rise to them, and it would seem that here too much reliance has been placed on some observations in *Bolton v. Stone* and similar observations in other cases.

In their Lordships' view a properly qualified and alert chief engineer would have realised there was a real risk here, and they do not understand Walsh, J., to deny that; but he appears to have held that, if a real risk can properly be described as remote, it must then be held to be not reasonably foreseeable. That is a possible interpretation of some of the authorities; but this is still an open question and on principle their Lordships cannot accept this view. If a real risk is one which would occur to the mind of a reasonable man in the position of the defendant's servant and which he would not brush aside as far-fetched, and if the criterion is to be what that reasonable man would have done in the circumstances, then surely he would not neglect such a risk if action to eliminate it presented no difficulty, involved no disadvantage and required no expense.

In the present case the evidence shows that the discharge of so much oil on to the water must have taken a considerable time, and a vigilant ship's engineer would have noticed the discharge at an early stage. The findings show that he ought to have known that it is possible to ignite this kind of oil on water, and that the ship's engineer probably ought to have known that this had in fact happened before. The most that can be said to justify inaction is that he would have known that this could only happen in very exceptional circumstances; but that does not mean that a reasonable man would dismiss such risk from his mind and do nothing when it was so easy to prevent it. If it is clear that the reasonable man would have realised or foreseen and prevented the risk, then it must follow that the appellants are liable in damages. The learned judge found this a difficult case: he said that this matter is "one on which different minds would come to different conclusions." Taking a rather different view of the law from that of the learned judge, their Lordships must hold that the respondents are entitled to succeed on this issue.

. . .

NOTES AND QUESTIONS

1. Why was the plaintiff in *Wagon Mound (No. 2)* able to provide evidence that it was foreseeable that the furnace oil would burn, when the court in *Wagon Mound (No. 1)* reached the opposite conclusion? How did the court define foreseeability and what did it mean by the term "real risk?" What did the court mean by the term "justified?" Does *Wagon Mound (No. 2)* apply only to those cases in which the defendant's conduct is without social value? If not, can you distinguish between Lord Reid's test of remoteness and the test used to determine whether the standard of care has been breached?

2. What impact does the rule in *Wagon Mound (No. 2)* have on the scope of recovery in negligence? H. Glasbeek contends that *Wagon Mound (No. 2)* has, for "all practical purposes," restored the *Re Polemis* test, "for surely all direct consequences must be regarded as possible if the ordinary man is not required to foresee how they are to eventuate." J. Smith has written that *Wagon Mound (No. 2)* broadened the test of foreseeability of damages from one based upon probability of damages to one based upon a possibility of damages. See Glasbeek, "Wagon Mound II — Re Polemis Revived: Nuisance Revised" (1967) 6 U.W.O.L. Rev. 192 at 200; and Smith, "The Limits of Tort Liability in Canada: Remoteness, Foreseeability and Proximate Cause" in Linden, ed., *Studies in Canadian Tort Law* (1968) 102. Do you agree with Glasbeek's or Smith's assessment of *Wagon Mound (No. 2)*?

ASSINIBOINE SOUTH SCHOOL DIVISION, NO. 3 v. GREATER WINNIPEG GAS CO.

(1971), 21 D.L.R. (3d) 608 (Man. C.A.)
aff'd (1973), 40 D.L.R. (3d) 480 (S.C.C.)

DICKSON J.A.: — The facts giving rise to this case lie in a compact compass and are not in dispute. At approximately 12:00 noon, 25th February 1968 a Ski Daddler auto toboggan owned by Ephraim Hoffer and operated by his son Michael Hoffer ran out of control at a speed of approximately 30 m.p.h., over a snowbank and across a parking lot, for some 100 yards, and struck a gas-riser pipe servicing Laidlaw School in Tuxedo, Manitoba. The pipe was fractured below the pressure regulator and shut-off valve, with the result that gas under high pressure escaped and, being lighter than air, rose and entered the boiler room of the school through a fresh-air inlet duct situate in the wall of the school immediately above the gas-riser pipe and beneath a wide overhanging eave. In the boiler room the gas reached an explosive mixture and was ignited by the naked flame of the pilot light, or the flames of the gas furnace. An explosion and fire occurred, causing extensive damage to the school. Deniset J. . . . allowed damages of $50,739.90 to the School Division of Assiniboine South No. 3, owners of the school, against Ephraim Hoffer and Michael Hoffer as well as against the Greater Winnipeg Gas Company. The Gas Company was responsible for the installation of the gas-riser pipe. The damages were apportioned 50 per cent to Michael Hoffer and Ephraim Hoffer and 50 per cent to the Gas Company. All defendants have appealed.

[Dickson J.A. explained that Ephraim Hoffer had specially altered the machine to allow his 11-year-old son to start it. These changes required that the machine be started in high gear. The father advised his son to put up the kickstand when starting the machine. The son forgot to do this and the machine got away from him. Dickson J.A. held that it was probable that a young boy would forget to use the kickstand and "almost inevitable that in such event the machine would get out of control and run away." Dickson J.A. concluded that both the father and son had breached the standard of care.]

The second question is whether the damage done by them was reasonably foreseeable and therefore recoverable within the principles stated in [*The Wagon Mound (No. 1)*]. This question is not without difficulty. Denning L.J. said in *King v. Phillips*, [1953] 1 Q.B. 429, [1953] 1 All E.R. 617 at 623: "there can be no doubt since *Hay (Bourhill) v. Young*, [1942] 2 All E.R. 396, that the test of *liability for shock* is foreseeability of *injury by shock*". (The italics are mine.) In *The Wagon Mound (No. 1)* Viscount Simonds substituted the word "fire" for "shock" and indorsed this statement of the law. Liability depends upon whether the damage is of such a kind as a reasonable man should have foreseen.

It might well be argued that damage by impact is to be expected when a machine runs amok but not damage by fire and explosion. Their Lordships in *The Wagon Mound (No. 1)* were clearly of the opinion that the Court of Appeal erred in *Re Polemis and Furness, Withy & Co. Ltd.* . . ., in allowing recovery in respect of damage from fire and explosion which followed the impact of a plank dropped into the hold of a ship.

In *The Wagon Mound (No. 1)* damage to plaintiffs' wharf by oil fouling was foreseeable when defendants carelessly allowed a large quantity of bunkering oil to spill into Morts Bay but damage by fire was unforeseeable and recovery denied. Vital to the decision was the finding of fact that defendants did not know, and could not reasonably have been expected to know, that furnace oil was capable of being set afire when spread on water.

The force of *The Wagon Mound (No. 1)* was somewhat dissipated by *Hughes v. Lord Advocate*, [1963] 1 All E.R. 705, per Lord Jenkins at p. 710:

> "It is true that the duty of care expected in cases of this sort is confined to reasonably foreseeable dangers, but it does not necessarily follow that liability is escaped because the danger actually materialising is not identical with the danger reasonably foreseen and guarded against."

One need not envisage "the precise concatenation of circumstances which led up to the accident": p. 712.

In [*The Wagon Mound (No. 2)*], the Privy Council, on different findings of fact, reached a conclusion different from that in *The Wagon Mound (No. 1)*. . . Lord Reid said at p. 717:

> "The vital parts of the findings of fact which have already been set out in full are (i) that the officers of the Wagon Mound 'would regard furnace oil as very difficult to ignite on water' — not that they would regard this as impossible, (ii) that their experience would probably have been 'that this had very rarely happened' — not that they would never have heard of a case where it had happened, and (iii) that they would have regarded it as a "possibility, but one which could become an actuality only in very exceptional circumstances' — not, as in *Wagon Mound* (No. 1), that they could not reasonably be expected to have known that this oil was capable of being set afire when spread on water".

These words would suggest that recovery may be had, provided the event giving rise to the damage is not regarded as "impossible", and even though it "very rarely happened . . . only in very exceptional circumstances". The test of foreseeability of damage becomes a question of what is possible rather than what is probable.

. . .

It is enough to fix liability if one could foresee in a general way the sort of thing that happened. The extent of the damage and its manner of incidence need not be foreseeable if physical damage of the kind which in fact ensues is foreseeable. In the case at bar I would hold that the damage was of the *type* or *kind* which any reasonable person might foresee. Gas-riser pipes on the outside of Tuxedo buildings are common. Damage to such a pipe is not of a kind that no one could anticipate. When one permits a power toboggan to run at large, or when one fires a rifle blindly down a city street, one must not define narrowly the outer limits of reasonable prevision. The ambit of foreseeable damage is indeed broad.

. . .

Counsel for Michael Hoffer concedes that the boy was negligent and that the type of damage that resulted was reasonably foreseeable by him as by any other rational person. Counsel submits, however, that the causation chain, the first link of which was forged by his failure to put the machine on the kick stand before starting it, ended when the riser pipe had been broken and the gas began to escape. I cannot accept this argument. Since *The Wagon Mound (No. 1)* the "scholastic theories of causation and their ugly and barely intelligent jargon", have taken a back place to foreseeability. It is now settled that foresight is the test both for duty and for remoteness. Accepting that the "chain of causation" can be broken by a "nova causa" or "novus actus interveniens", it is clear that the state of affairs created by the Gas Company several years prior to the accident could not be considered a novus actus. Where a state of affairs has already occurred at the time of the wrongful act, that act is regarded as the cause of the damage in the absence of subsequent intervening factors.

It is manifest that Michael's culpable conduct was a causally relevant factor. His failure to exercise due care was the "cause" of the damage in the proper sense of the term. If one applies the "but for" test it is readily apparent that the plaintiff's harm would not have occurred but for Michael's fault. Michael cannot escape liability for the consequences of that fault merely because other causal factors for which he is not responsible also contributed to the damage which resulted. He was *a* cause, though not the *sole* cause of the harm. His fault was a cause-in-fact.

. . .

I agree with the finding of Deniset J. that Ephraim Hoffer and Michael Hoffer are joint tortfeasors.

Liability of Greater Winnipeg Gas Company Limited

I am also of the opinion that Greater Winnipeg Gas Company Limited is liable to the plaintiff on the ground that the installation of the gas service was negligently constructed in the sense that it was constructed in such place and manner as to make likely the type of damage which ensued. The Gas Company was responsible for the construction of the service line leading from the street, the service riser, and attached equipment and meter. It is difficult to conceive of any person, conscious of the explosive properties of natural gas, designing and installing a service so patently dangerous. Gas escaping from any fracture of the pipe below the regulator would assuredly find its way into the boiler room. The Gas Company ought to have reasonably foreseen damage to the gas-riser pipe. It is true that persons are not bound to take extravagant precautions but they must weigh the probability of injury resulting and the probable seriousness of the injury. Although the probability of the gas-riser pipe being struck by an automobile, a motorcyle or an auto toboggan was not great, the pipe being tucked into the corner of the building, the probable seriousness of any injury was very great. Against this must be weighed the cost and difficulty of the precautions which could have been taken. Protective pipes could have been installed at small cost and little difficulty. The duty to take protective measures increases in direct proportion to the risk. In these circumstances, the Gas Company failed to exercise reasonable care where there was a duty to exercise a high degree of care.

NOTES AND QUESTIONS

1. Do you agree with (a) Dickson J.A.'s interpretation of the various foreseeability tests and (b) his application of them to the facts? Does the test in *Assiniboine* establish an appropriate relationship between the nature of the defendant's negligent act and the scope of his liability?

2. *Assiniboine* has been widely followed in Canada. See for example *Belzile v. Dumais* (1986), 69 N.B.R. (2d) 142 (Q.B.); and *Monkman v. Singh* (1989), 62 Man. R. (2d) 277 (Q.B.).

3. Critical of the existing law, Justice Linden has suggested that the courts ought to adopt a "new approach" to the issue of the remoteness of damages. In Linden & Feldthusen, *Canadian Tort Law*, 8th ed. (2006) the authors state at 376-77:

> It would also be helpful if the courts would approach these remoteness cases with the attitude that a person found to have been negligent should only be relieved of liability if the result of the negligence was truly "freakish", "one in a million", "fantastic or highly improbable". In other words, there should be an assumption of liability unless the court is convinced that the harm is so unrelated to the negligent conduct that it would be too harsh a result for a defendant in the circumstances. [footnotes omitted]

Will Linden's approach alleviate the difficulties that exist in this area? What new problems, if any, would it create? See also Coval, Smith & Rush, "'Out of the Maze': Towards a 'Clear Understanding' of the Test for Remoteness of Damages in Negligence" (1983) 61 Can. Bar Rev. 561.

4. Should the principles of remoteness be applied in the same way in personal injury and property damage cases? See *Stephenson v. Waite Tileman*, [1973] 1 N.Z.L.R. 152 (C.A.).

4. Intervening Causes

To this point, we have discussed situations in which the defendant's careless act was the sole cause of the plaintiff's loss. We will now examine cases in which the plaintiff's loss was caused by the defendant's breach and a subsequent intervening act. An intervening act is one that causes or contributes to the plaintiff's loss after the original defendant's breach has taken effect. For example, assume that a defendant contractor carelessly blocked a sidewalk, forcing pedestrians to walk on the road, and that one of the pedestrians was struck by a negligent driver. Both the contractor and the negligent driver causally contributed to the situation that resulted in the plaintiff's injuries. However, should the contractor be held liable for the injuries that were caused by the negligent driver?

Traditionally, the original tortfeasor was relieved of liability because the causal link between his or her breach and the plaintiff's loss was considered to have been severed by the intervening cause. The issue was framed in various ways: some courts talked about the second act breaking the chain of causation and other courts labelled the act as a *novus actus interveniens* ("a new intervening act"). No matter how it was described, the last wrongdoer was held solely responsible for the plaintiff's loss, even if his or her conduct was a relatively minor cause of the injury.

As the courts developed more complex notions of causation, the "last wrongdoer" doctrine was replaced. The courts divided intervening acts into three categories based on their nature and moral blameworthiness. Cases in the first category, intervening acts that were naturally occurring or non-culpable, were generally held not to break the chain of causation. For example, a contractor could not escape liability merely because its shoddy work resulted in property damage following an unusually severe storm. Cases in the second category, negligent intervening acts, were generally held to break the chain of causation, thereby absolving the original tortfeasor of liability. For example, a careless driver would not be held liable if the plaintiff that he or she injured died in hospital as a result of being negligently given the wrong drug. Cases in the third category of intervening acts, deliberately wrongful or illegal acts, invariably broke the chain of causation unless the original tortfeasor had a specific duty to prevent the act. Thus, a careless driver would not be held liable for the fact that the pedestrian that he or she ran down was robbed while lying by the side of the road. In contrast, an armed guard who carelessly left his or her truck unlocked would be held liable if a thief walked off with several bags of money.

In turn, this elaborate categorization has been replaced, at least in theory, by a more general principle: the "within the scope of the risk" test. As the following cases illustrate, the application of that test can create difficulties. Some courts analyze the issue in terms of whether the *loss* caused by the intervening act was within the scope of the risk created by the original tortfeasor. Other courts ask whether the *intervening act* itself was within the scope of the risk created by the original tortfeasor. While focusing on the relationship between the plaintiff's specific injuries and the original tortfeasor's careless act is more consistent with the purpose of the remoteness principles, this issue requires further clarification.

BRADFORD v. KANELLOS

(1973), 40 D.L.R. (3d) 578 (S.C.C.)

MARTLAND J.: — On the morning of April 12, 1967, the appellants, who are husband and wife, were customers in the respondents' restaurant, in the City of Kingston. While seated at the counter in the restaurant, a flash fire occurred in the grill used for cooking purposes. The grill was equipped with an automatic fire extinguisher system, of an approved type, which, when it became operative, discharged carbon dioxide on to the heated area to extinguish the fire.

Shortly after the start of the fire the fire extinguisher was activated, manually, and the fire was extinguished almost immediately. The fire was not a cause of concern to the appellants. No damage was done by the fire because the fire was of very short duration and all that burned was grease that had accumulated in the grill and a rag or rags which had been thrown on the fire when it broke out in an effort to extinguish it.

The fire extinguisher made a hissing or popping noise when it operated. This caused an unidentified patron in the restaurant to shout that gas was escaping and that there was going to be an explosion. The result of these words was to cause a panic in the restaurant. While people ran from the restaurant the appellant wife was pushed or fell from her seat at the counter and sustained injury.

The appellants brought action against the respondents, the appellant wife claiming general damages and the appellant husband claiming special damages for expenses incurred as a result of his wife's injuries.

The trial Judge awarded damages in the amounts of $3,582.43 to the appellant husband and $6,400 to the appellant wife. He found there had been negligence involved in the flash fire because the grill had not been cleaned as efficiently as it should have been, and said: "Therefore while the negligence may be small, it pinpoints this as negligence."

He did not find that the fire, in itself, had caused the panic, but ascribed it to the noise caused by the fire extinguisher. He said:

> As the result of this hissing explosive noise, or whatever it was, some rather foolish people in the restaurant called out that it might explode. For this reason it appears that some considerable panic ensued and there was a rushing for the door.

His conclusion was that, while the act of yelling out almost qualified as that of an "idiotic person", the panic could have been foreseen.

By unanimous decision, the Court of Appeal allowed the appeal of the present respondents. Schroeder, J.A., who delivered the judgment of the Court, said. . .:

> The practical and sensible view to be taken of the facts here leads fairly to the conclusion that it should not be held that the person guilty of the original negligence resulting in the flash fire on the grill ought reasonably to have anticipated the subsequent intervening act or acts which were the direct cause of the injuries and damages suffered by the plaintiffs.

From this judgment the present appeal has, with leave, been brought to this Court.

I agree with the decision of the Court of Appeal. The judgment at trial found the respondents to be liable because there had been negligence in failing to clean the grill efficiently, which resulted in the flash fire. But it was to guard against the consequences of a flash fire that the grill was equipped with a fire extinguisher system. This system was described by the Chief of the Kingston Fire Department, who was called as a witness by the appellants, as, not only an approved installation, but one of the best.

This system, when activated, following the flash fire, fulfilled its function and put out the fire. This was accomplished by the application of carbon dioxide on the fire. In so doing, there was a hissing noise and it was on hearing this that one of the customers exclaimed that gas was escaping and that there was danger of an explosion, following which the panic occurred, the appellant wife was injured.

On these facts it is apparent that her injuries resulted from the hysterical conduct of a customer which occurred when the safety appliance properly fulfilled its function. Was that consequence fairly to be regarded as within the risk created by the respondent's negligence in permitting an undue quantity of grease to accumulate on the grill? The Court of Appeal has found that it was not and I agree with that finding.

In my opinion, the appeal should be dismissed with costs.

Judson and Ritchie, JJ., concur with Martland, J.

SPENCE J. (dissenting): — . . . I am of the opinion that in the particular circumstances of this case, "the person guilty of the original negligence ought reasonably to have anticipated such subsequent intervening negligence and to have foreseen that if it occurred the result would be that his negligence would lead to loss or damage." Upon the evidence, the owners and proprietors, the respondents here, did anticipate that such negligence as leaving the grill in a dirty and greasy condition would cause a fire and frequently warned the cook of such fact, and requiring the cook not once but on several occasions to clean up the grill. The grill was midway down the length of the restaurant. There was seating for many patrons to the rear of the grill so that the grill intervened between them and the only entrance or exit at the front of the restaurant and the space between the grill and the other restaurant equipment through which the said patrons would have to pass was narrow.

The proprietors knew of the fire extinguisher and its action. Such action was described by the witness Warren Gibson, the Chief of Police of Kingston, as being a very rapid expansion of carbon dioxide that makes a hissing noise which explodes rather rapidly as it expands.

I am of the opinion that any reasonable person knew that a greasy grill might well take fire and that in such event a CO^2 fire extinguisher is put into action either automatically or manually and that such fire extinguisher makes a hissing and popping sound and he could not fail to anticipate that a panic might well result. The panic did result and on the evidence the whole affair from beginning to end was almost instantaneous. The plaintiff Elizabeth Bradford described it variously in the words "no, it was quick": Again, that she had been watching the fire approximately a minute when the man next to her called out "gas" and that thereupon there was an immediate panic.

. . .

I am not of the opinion that the persons who shouted the warning of what they were certain was an impending explosion were negligent. I am, on the other hand, of the opinion that they acted in a very human and usual way and that their actions, as I have said, were utterly foreseeable and were part of the natural consequence of events leading inevitably to the plaintiff's injury. I here quote and adopt Fleming, *Law of Torts*, 4th ed. (1971), at pp. 192-3:

> Nowadays it is no longer open to serious question that the operation of an intervening force will not ordinarily clear a defendant from further responsibility, if it can fairly be considered a not abnormal incident of the risk created by him — if, as sometimes expressed, it is "part of the ordinary course of things." Nor is there room any longer for any categorical distinction in this regard between forces of nature, like rain or ice, on the one hand, and the action of human beings even when consciously controlled, on the other.
>
> Least difficult are instances of just normal and reasonable response to the stimulus of the hazard engendered by the defendant's negligence. . . . A time-honoured illustration is the famous *Squib Case*: *Scott v. Shepherd* (1773) 2 W.Bl. 892 [[1558-1774] All E.R. 295 (C.P.)], where a wag threw a lighted fire-work into a market whence it was tossed

from one stall to another in order to save the wares until it eventually exploded in the plaintiff's face. Yet it was held that *trespass* lay because "all that was done subsequent to the original throwing was a continuation of the first force and first act and continued until the squib was spent by bursting."

Even if the actions of those who called out "gas" and "it is going to explode" were negligent and, as I have said, I do not think it was, then I am of the opinion that the plaintiffs would still have a right of action against the defendants, here respondents, or against such persons or against both.

. . .

For these reasons, I would allow the appeal and restore the judgment at trial. The appellants are entitled to their costs here and in the Court of Appeal.

Laskin, J., concurs with Spence, J.

NOTES AND QUESTIONS

1. Did Martland and Spence JJ. disagree on the test of remoteness governing the original tortfeasor's liability for intervening causes, or on its application to the specific facts? Which judgment do you find more compelling? Based on *Bradford*, define the test of remoteness governing the original tortfeasor's liability for intervening causes. Should this same test be applied whether the intervening cause is a naturally occurring phenomenon, the negligent act of a second tortfeasor, a patently reckless act, a deliberate illegal act or the plaintiff's own contributorily negligent act?

2. In *Oke v. Weide Tpt. Ltd.* (1963), 41 D.L.R. (3d) 53 (Man. C.A.) the defendant knocked down a traffic sign on a gravel strip separating the eastbound and westbound lanes of traffic. The defendant stopped and removed some debris, but was unable to move the sign post, which was left projecting upwards. Although he informed a garage attendant of the incident, the defendant did not contact the police or highway authorities. The next day a driver, while attempting to pass illegally on the gravel strip, was killed when the post came up through the car's floor and pierced his chest. The majority stated that even if the defendant had been careless in not reporting the incident, he could not be held liable because the deceased's intervening act of driving on the gravel strip and its consequences could not have been foreseen. The dissent concluded that the defendant had been negligent and that an accident of some kind was a foreseeable consequence of his failure to report the hazardous situation that he had created. Thus, the defendant should be held liable even though the exact way in which the accident occurred and its severity may not have been foreseeable. Do you agree with the dissenting or the majority analysis of remoteness? Would the case have been resolved the same way if the deceased had been pulling over to fix a flat tire?

3. In subsequent cases, the Canadian courts have adopted a broad interpretation of foreseeability. See for example *R. v. Cote* (1974), 51 D.L.R. (3d) 244 (S.C.C.); *Hendrick v. De Marsh* (1984), 45 O.R. (2d) 463 (H.C.), aff'd (1986), 54 O.R. (2d) 185 (C.A.); *Funk v. Clapp* (1986), 68 D.L.R. (4th) 229 (B.C.C.A.); *Smith v. B.C. (A.G.)* (1988), 30 B.C.L.R. (2d) 356 (C.A.); and *Werbeniuk v. Maynard*, [1994] 7 W.W.R. 704 (Man. Q.B.).

4. A question sometimes arises as to whether the plaintiff's own contributory negligence constitutes an intervening act that severs the chain of causation flowing from the defendant's breach.

The issue arose in *Jolley v. Sutton London B.C.*, [1998] 1 W.L.R. 1546 (C.A.), rev'd [2000] 1 W.L.R. 1082 (H.L.). As explained in a previous note in this chapter, a dangerously decrepit boat was located on property under the defendant's authority. The defendant made a decision to remove the boat for safety reasons, but because of administrative dithering failed to perform the task. The plaintiff and his friend, both aged 14, found the boat. They decided to repair it and sail "to Cornwall because that was where the pirates were to be found!" In order to fix the hull, they hoisted the boat up on a car jack. The jack gave way, the boat fell and the plaintiff was rendered a paraplegic.

The trial judge imposed liability, subject to a reduction of 25% for contributory negligence. However, a majority in the Court of Appeal held that the plaintiff's losses were too remote because the boys' actions were "unforeseen" and "extraneous." This was a dubious decision. As J. O'Sullivan has noted, the plaintiff's own carelessness generally does not sever the chain of causation unless it satisfies a very high threshold of being unwarranted or extraneous. Ordinary contributory negligence normally just has the effect of reducing the amount of damages: O'Sullivan, "Remoteness of Damage in Negligence: A Rotten Structure Collapses" [1999] C.L.J. 12.

On further appeal, the House of Lords reinstated the trial decision and held that the plaintiff's losses were not too remote and, more specifically, that the boys' conduct did not sever the chain of causation.

PRICE v. MILAWSKI

(1977), 82 D.L.R. (3d) 130 (Ont. C.A.)

[The plaintiff injured his right ankle playing soccer and went to the emergency department of a hospital to have it examined. He told the defendant, Dr. Murray, that he heard his ankle crack and thought it was broken. Dr. Murray sent the plaintiff for x-rays but instructed the technicians to x-ray his right foot, not his right ankle. After examining the x-rays, Dr. Murray informed the plaintiff that there was no fracture and that his ankle was only sprained. In fact, the ankle was broken.

After a series of visits to his family doctor, the plaintiff was eventually referred to Dr. Carbin, an orthopaedic surgeon, because the ankle remained painful and swollen. Dr. Carbin telephoned the hospital and discovered that the plaintiff's x-ray results were negative. Despite the plaintiff's complaints, Dr. Carbin did not order new x-rays, even though he had a machine in his office and a technician available to him. He diagnosed the plaintiff's injury as a strained ligament and applied a cast. When the cast was removed four weeks later, the ankle began to swell. Following some further delays, the plaintiff eventually went to another orthopaedic surgeon who took new x-rays and discovered the fractured ankle. As a result of delays in properly treating the fracture, the plaintiff suffered some permanent disabilities.

At trial, both Dr. Murray and Dr. Carbin were found liable in negligence and were held equally at fault for the plaintiff's permanent injury. Both defendants appealed the finding of negligence and the quantum of damages.

On appeal, Arnup J.A., for the court, affirmed that both defendants had been negligent. Only that portion of his judgment dealing with Dr. Murray's liability for Dr. Carbin's intervening act is reproduced below.]

ARNUP J.A.:

. . .

The "foreseeability" argument

As stated in Part III, it was submitted on behalf of Dr. Murray that it was not foreseeable by him that such dire consequences would flow from his initial acts of negligence.

We are concerned here with what one may properly call an intervening act of negligence (*i.e.*, by Dr. Carbin). In *Bradford et al. v. Kanellos et al.*, [1974] 1 S.C.R. 409 at pp. 412-3. . ., the majority, *per* Martland, J., referring to the hysterical act of a restaurant customer who shouted out "gas!" and that there was going to be an explosion, resulting in a panic which caused injuries to the plaintiff, said:

> Was that consequence fairly to be regarded as within the risk created by the respondents' negligence in permitting an undue quantity of grease to accumulate on the grill [in the restaurant]?

A set of facts having some analogy to the present case arose in *Mercer v. Gray*, [1941] O.R. 127, [1941] 3 D.L.R. 564, where it was held that if reasonable care has been used by the plaintiff to employ a competent physician or surgeon to treat personal injuries wrongfully inflicted by a defendant, the results of the treatment are a proper head of damages, even though through an error in treatment, it is unsuccessful.

In *"Wagon Mound" (No. 2), supra*, Lord Reid, referring to cases "based purely on negligence" states. . .:

> It has now been established by *The Wagon Mound (No. 1) supra*, and by *Hughes v. Lord Advocate, supra*, that in such cases damages can only be recovered if the injury complained of was not only caused by the alleged negligence but was also an injury of a class or character foreseeable as a possible result of it.

Applying these principles to a case in which there are negligent acts by two persons in succession, I would hold that a person doing a negligent act may, in circumstances lending themselves to that conclusion, be held liable for future damages arising in part from the subsequent negligent act of another, and in part from his own negligence, where such subsequent negligence and consequent damage were reasonably foreseeable as a possible result of his own negligence.

It was reasonably foreseeable by Dr. Murray that once the information generated by his negligent error got into the hospital records, other doctors subsequently treating the plaintiff might well rely on the accuracy of that information, *i.e.*, that the x-ray showed no fracture of the ankle. It was also foreseeable that some doctor might do so without checking, even though to do so in the circumstances might itself be a negligent act. The history is always one factor in a subsequent diagnosis and the consequent treatment. Such a possibility was not a risk which a reasonable man (in the position of Dr. Murray) would brush aside as far-fetched — see *"Wagon Mound" (No. 2)*. . . .

The later negligence of Dr. Carbin compounded the effects of the earlier negligence of Dr. Murray. It did not put a halt to the consequences of the first act and attract liability for all damage from that point forward. In my view the trial Judge was correct in holding that each of the appellants was liable to the plaintiff and that it was not possible to try to apportion the extent to which each was responsible for the plaintiff's subsequent operation and his permanent disability.

NOTES AND QUESTIONS

1. Is there a significant difference between the "foreseeable as possible" test in *Price* and the test in *Bradford*? Had the latter test been applied in *Price*, would the result have been the same?

2. Did Arnup J.A. properly interpret and apply *Wagon Mound (No. 2)*? Can you suggest a way of distinguishing *Wagon Mound (No. 2)* and *Price*?

3. Can you distinguish *Price* from *Mercer v. Gray*, [1941] 3 D.L.R. 564 (Ont. C.A.)? See also *Mercer v. South Eastern & Chatham Ry. Co.'s Managing Committee*, [1922] 2 K.B. 549.

4. In *Papp v. Leclerc* (1977), 16 O.R. (2d) 158 (C.A.), a case decided in the same year as *Price*, Lacourcière J.A., speaking for the court, stated at 161:

> Every tortfeasor causing injury to a person placing him in the position of seeking medical or hospital help, must assume the inherent risks of complications, *bona fide* medical error or misadventure, if they are reasonably foreseeable and not too remote. . . It is for the defendant to prove that some new act rendering another person liable has broken the chain of causation. This was not done in the present case. I must, therefore, rule against the appellant on this first contention based on lack of foreseeability and *novus actus*.

Is this statement compatible with the decision in *Price*? Is there any reason to treat an intervening act of medical negligence differently than any other negligent intervening act? See also *Thompson v. Toorenburgh* (1973), 50 D.L.R. (3d) 717 (B.C.C.A.), aff'd [1973] S.C.R. vii; *Robinson v. Post Office*, [1974] 2 All E.R. 737 (C.A.); *David v. Toronto Transit Comm.* (1976), 77 D.L.R. (3d) 717 (Ont. H.C.); *Katzman v. Yaeck* (1982), 37 O.R. (2d) 500 (C.A.); and *Rahman v. Arearose Ltd.*, [2001] Q.B. 351 (C.A.).

5. In what circumstances should the defendant be held liable for injuries that the plaintiff sustains while recovering? In *Block v. Martin*, [1951] 4 D.L.R. 121 (Alta. S.C.) the defendant negligently ran over the plaintiff, causing a slight fracture of his leg. The plaintiff followed his doctor's orders and continued to walk. Six months after the accident, the plaintiff slipped while fishing and completely fractured his leg. It was held that the original injury was a contributing cause of the second fracture and that the plaintiff's conduct in going fishing was not a *novus actus interveniens*. The defendant was held liable for the plaintiff's entire loss. See also *Boss v. Robert Simpson Eastern Ltd.* (1968), 2 D.L.R. (3d) 114 (N.S.S.C.); *Wieland v. Cyril Lord Carpets Ltd.*, [1969] 3 All E.R. 1006 (Q.B.); *Saccardo v. Hamilton* (1971), 18 D.L.R. (3d) 271 (Ont. H.C.); *Pauluik v. Paraiso*, [1996] 2 W.W.R. 57 (Man. C.A.); and *Athey v. Leonati* (1996), 31 C.C.L.T. (2d) 113 (S.C.C.).

6. Should the original tortfeasor be absolved of liability for an injury the plaintiff sustains while recuperating if the plaintiff has been contributorily negligent? The courts

have occasionally answered this question in the affirmative. See *McKew v. Holland*, [1969] 3 All E.R. 1621 (H.L.); *Goldhawke v. Harder* (1976), 74 D.L.R. (3d) 721 (B.C.S.C.); *Brushett v. Cowan* (1990), 69 D.L.R. (4th) 743 (Nfld. C.A.); and *Dudek v. Li*, [2000] 6 W.W.R. 209 (B.C.C.A.). Is there any reason to treat the plaintiff's contributory negligence in these cases differently from any other intervening cause? Is this approach consistent with *Bradford* or *Price*?

7. Should the original tortfeasor be held liable for the additional losses a plaintiff suffers as a result of failing to undergo a needed operation? What if the operation posed a small risk of death, was very painful or had only a 70% chance of success? Would it make any difference if the plaintiff had a pre-existing fear of surgery? Is it appropriate to deal with this as a question of remoteness, as an issue of mitigation of loss or as contributory negligence? The Supreme Court of Canada addressed these questions in *Janiak v. Ippolito* (1985), 16 D.L.R. (4th) 1 (S.C.C.). See also *Couillard v. Waschulewski Estate* (1988), 44 C.C.L.T. 113 (Alta. Q.B.); *Tomizza v. Fraser* (1990), 71 O.R. (2d) 705 (H.C.); *Wills v. Doe* (1992), 90 D.L.R. (4th) 164 (B.C.S.C.); and *Engel v. Kam-Ppelle Holdings Ltd.*, [1993] 1 S.C.R. 306.

In *Bourgoin v. Leamington (Municipality)* (2006), 39 C.C.L.T. (3d) 41 (Ont. S.C.J.) the plaintiff suffered an ankle injury while walking on an uneven sidewalk. She developed chronic intractable pain, identified as Complex Regional Pain Syndrome. The defendant municipality argued that she had failed to reduce her damages from the pain by refusing to undergo the treatment recommended by her physiatrist, 95% likely to eliminate the pain, which was to have her leg amputated below the knee. How should the court have resolved this issue?

8. Should a negligent defendant who causes a car accident be held liable for the additional costs associated with the negligent repair of the plaintiff's car? See *Russell v. Esson (M.F.) & Sons Ltd.* (1986), 72 N.B.R. (2d) 55 (Q.B.).

9. In what circumstances should the original tortfeasor be held liable for the additional damages that result from the victim's suicide? See *Swami v. Lo*, [1980] 1 W.W.R. 379 (B.C.S.C.); *Gray v. Cotic* (1983), 26 C.C.L.T. 163 (S.C.C.); and *Wright Estate v. Davidson* (1992), 88 D.L.R. (4th) 698 (B.C.C.A.).

HEWSON v. RED DEER

(1976), 63 D.L.R. (3d) 168 (Alta. T.D.)

KIRBY J.: . . . The plaintiff claims damages against the City of Red Deer (hereinafter referred to as "the City"), sustained on May 15, 1973, when a tractor owned by the City crashed into the plaintiff's dwelling-house.

The tractor, a "crawler type" weighing approximately 25 tons, was being used to level and stockpile gravel in an open area approximately two and a half city blocks' distance to the south of the Hewson residence. The gravel was brought to the site by trucks from a crushing plant located elsewhere in the City. Loading at the plant was suspended from 12:00 midnight until 1:00 a.m., the last load before this break generally arriving at the stockpile at about 12:15 a.m. The trucks took the loads of gravel up an inclined roadway built for that purpose to the top of the existing pile of gravel which on the day in question had attained a considerable height.

Following the arrival of the last load before the midnight break, Weisenburger, an employee of the City operating the crawler tractor, left the tractor at the top of the stockpile facing in the direction of the inclined roadway and departed from the site in a city truck for coffee and cigarettes. Before leaving, he lowered the blade, adjusted the throttle to idle gear, turned off the ignition but did not remove the key or close and lock the cab to which he had a key.

Weisenburger impressed me as a credible witness and I accept his account as to the precautions he took before leaving the site.

On his return, which he said was about 12:45 a.m. the tractor was gone. He looked for it around the site thinking some fellow employee may have moved it as a joke. Not finding it, he looked for its tracks and found them leading down the inclined roadway and going to the north. In due course he found the tractor crashed into the Hewson residence. The engine was still running and was in high gear. The blade was up. The time at which the crash took place is established by an electric clock in the residence, serviced by wires severed by the tractor. It had stopped at 12:03 a.m.

In the company of police, Weisenburger closely examined the stockpile in the immediate vicinity of where he had left the tractor. Tracks were found indicating that a motor vehicle had turned around on the top of the stockpile. Two footprints consistent with a person having jumped out of the cab of the tractor were found.

I am satisfied and find that the tractor was set in motion by an unknown person, who raised the blade, turned on the ignition and put the engine into high gear causing it to move from the top of the stockpile, down the inclined roadway, across the open space lying to the north, continuing in its course until it crashed into the Hewson residence.

. . .

It is argued, however, that if there was negligence upon the part of Weisenburger or the City, the damages that occurred were too remote to be attributed to them and that the defence of *novus actus interveniens* is applicable.

[The judge then quoted several cases to the effect that the "defence" was not available if the defendant failed to guard against the very thing that was likely to occur.]

. . .

The maxim was not considered applicable by the Supreme Court of Canada in *Booth et al. v. St. Catharines et al.*, [1948] 4 D.L.R. 686, [1948] S.C.R. 564. This case involved an action against the city following an accident which occurred in a city park when a number of boys climbed a flagpole to watch a fireworks exhibit — the pole fell, injuring one plaintiff and killing the daughter of the other plaintiffs. A great deal of the case deals with the question of the duty of care owed by a licensor towards licensees on his property, but the other major issue concerns foreseeability and the *novus actus* doctrine.

Kerwin, J., said at p. 690 D.L.R., p. 569 S.C.R.:

> The maxim *novus actus interveniens* has no application because while the structure was sufficient for its purpose as a flag tower, in view of the great concourse of people and of the fireworks, the presence of boys upon the tower, even though unauthorized, was the very thing that should have been anticipated.

Rand, J., at p. 693 D.L.R., p. 573 S.C.R., observed:

> On the basis of prudent foresight, it must have been anticipated as natural and probable that boys of all ages would climb the tower to get a better view of what was going on.

. . .

In the instant case, however, as has been pointed out, the tractor could be set in motion by any person opening the door of the cab, turning the ignition key and raising the blade. This might have been prevented by taking the elementary precautions of removing the ignition key, engaging the safety lever and locking the cab door, none of which was done.

The stockpile was located in an open field approximately two city blocks from the nearest residential building, two and a half to three city blocks' distance from Red Deer College which was then in session, about 50 ft. from 32nd St. which was surfaced with rough gravel, connecting with a road allowance which in turn intersected with provincial Highway 2.

The stockpile being so located was accessible to persons living in the residences referred to, students and staff at the college and to persons using 32nd St. or the road allowance.

It seems to me that it was reasonably foreseeable that any one of such persons might become aware that the tractor was being left at the stockpile unattended and might be tempted to put it in motion. The elementary precautions referred to above were not taken to prevent this happening. I am of the view, therefore, that the maxim *novus actus interveniens* is not applicable. Accordingly, the plaintiff is entitled to damages against the City.

NOTES AND QUESTIONS

1. Do you agree with Kirby J. that it was reasonably foreseeable that someone would put the bulldozer in motion? Would the result have been the same if: (a) the bulldozer had been parked in a rural, rather than an urban, area, (b) the defendant had taken the keys and the intruder started the bulldozer by hot-wiring it, and (c) the defendant had left for only five minutes? Do you think that Kirby J. would have reached the same conclusion if the intruder had been caught? See *Wright v. McCrea*, [1965] 1 O.R. 300 (C.A.); and *Moss v. Ferguson* (1979), 35 N.S.R. (2d) 181 (S.C.).

2. Should a driver who leaves the keys in his or her car be held liable if the car is stolen and the thief negligently causes a car accident? Would the police be able to recover against the driver if they were injured while attempting to catch the car thief? See *Hollett v. Coca-Cola Ltd.* (1980), 37 N.S.R. (2d) 695 (S.C.); *Spagnolo v. Margesson's Sports Ltd.* (1983), 145 D.L.R. (3d) 381 (Ont. C.A.); *Moore v. Fanning* (1987), 60 O.R. (2d) 225 (H.C.); and *Werbeniuk v. Maynard*, [1994] 7 W.W.R. 704 (Man. Q.B.).

In *Tong v. Bedwell*, [2002] 6 W.W.R. 327 (Alta. Q.B.) the defendant was stopped at an intersection. A hoodlum smashed the windshield of his car. The defendant ran after the hoodlum, leaving the keys in his car. He later returned to find that his car had been stolen. Moreover, he later discovered that the thief had crashed his car into the plaintiff's vehicle. The plaintiff sued the defendant in negligence for the cost of repairs. The court held that while it was reasonably foreseeable that the defendant's car would be stolen if he left the keys in it, it was not reasonably foreseeable that the thief would drive in such a manner as to cause damage. In reaching that conclusion, the court stressed that there were apparently no witnesses to the theft, whose presence would have made the thief drive in a nervous or panicky manner. Do you agree with the court's decision? Is it reasonably foreseeable that a car thief will drive without sufficient care? Consider the possible reasons why a thief may steal a car.

3. If a worker leaves without locking the plaintiff's house, should he or she be held liable for losses caused by theft? See *Stansbie v. Troman*, [1948] 2 K.B. 48 (C.A.); *Thiele v. Rod Service (Ottawa) Ltd.* (1962), 45 D.L.R. (2d) 503 (Ont. C.A.); and *Ward v. Cannock Chase Dist. Council*, [1985] 3 All E.R. 537 (Ch. Div.).

4. Assume that a defendant driver negligently runs over the plaintiff and that during the ensuing commotion someone steals the plaintiff's wallet. Should the defendant be held liable for the theft? See *Brauer v. New York Cent. & H.R.R. Co.*, 103 A. 166 (N.J.C.A. 1918); *Patten v. Silberschein*, [1936] 3 W.W.R. 169 (B.C.S.C.); *Duce v. Rourke* (1951), 1 W.W.R. (N.S.) 305 (Alta. C.A.); *Abbott v. Kasza* (1974), [1975] 3 W.W.R. 163 (Alta. S.C.), varied [1976] 4 W.W.R. 20 (Alta. C.A.).

5. In *Lamb v. London Borough of Camden*, [1981] 2 All E.R. 408 (C.A.) the three judges agreed that the reasonable foreseeability test is not always appropriate for cases involving deliberate intervening acts of third parties. They were concerned that the test would extend the defendant's liability "beyond all reason" and lead to "bizarre and ludicrous" results. However, the judges each adopted a different test to govern these situations. But see *P Perl (Exporters) Ltd. v. Camden London Borough Council*, [1983] 3 All E.R. 161 (C.A.); *Smith v. Littlewoods Organisation Ltd.*, [1987] 1 All E.R. 710 (H.L.); and *Okanagan Exteriors Inc. v. Perth Developments Inc.*, [2002] 3 W.W.R. 224 (B.C.C.A.). See also Lee & Merkin, "Human Action as Novus Actus Interveniens" [1981] New L.J. 965; and Highley, "Comment on *P Perl (Exporters) Ltd. v. Camden London Borough Council*" (1985) 43 U.T. Fac. L. Rev. 136.

6. Some studies show that young sexual assault victims are more likely to subsequently commit crimes and spend time in jail. In a claim against the defendant for the sexual assault, can the victim recover for loss of earnings during any time spent in jail? Can the victim establish that the defendant caused those losses? Is the crime, intentionally committed by the victim, a *novus actus*? Even if the victim can clear these hurdles, should the courts as a matter of policy be awarding such damages? See *H.L. v. Canada (Attorney General)*, [2005] 1 S.C.R. 401; and *X. v. R.D.M.* (2006), 225 B.C.A.C. 191 (C.A.).

7. A difficult remoteness question can arise in cases of secondary child abuse. If studies establish that an abused child is more likely to go on to abuse his or her own children, then should an abusive parent be liable to his or her grandchildren if they are in turn abused? For a factual situation raising similar issues see *Rumley v. British Columbia* (1999), 180 D.L.R. (4th) 639 (B.C.C.A.), aff'd [2001] 3 S.C.R. 184.

REVIEW PROBLEM

As a child, Mrs. Adams had been overprotected by her parents. Since they considered bicycles to be dangerous, she had never learned to ride one. In an attempt to overcome her fears, Mrs. Adams purchased a bicycle, which she rode to and from work. While riding on a quiet street, Mrs. Adams witnessed a car accident right in front of her. Mr.

Jones had gone through a stop sign and struck Mr. King's vehicle. Neither the drivers nor their passengers were hurt. However, the accident startled Mrs. Adams, who veered into the curb and fell, striking her head on the pavement. Her physical injuries were relatively minor and her bike was undamaged, but she became increasingly afraid to leave her house except to go shopping and to work. Her family doctor suggested that she enter therapy to deal with her fear of going outside. Through no fault of the therapist, Mrs. Adams had a very unusual and extremely severe reaction to the treatment and has become a complete shut-in. She now refuses to work or to leave the house for any reason. To make matters worse, her husband has left her because he is incapable of dealing with her "paranoia."

After the collision, Mr. King attempted to drive his car to his usual service station. He signalled left at an intersection and stopped for the oncoming traffic. Unfortunately, Mr. King's rear left signal light was no longer working because of the first accident, and his car was struck from behind by Mr. Smith. As a result of this collision, Mr. King's arm was fractured and he had to be taken to hospital in an ambulance. His arm was put in a cast and he was told not to use the arm until the cast came off. Mr. King was still able to run his plumbing store and initially he followed his doctor's orders. However, in a rush to fill a large order for a very important customer, who had already complained about delays, Mr. King tried to assist. As his doctor feared, in attempting to steady a heavy sink with his broken arm, King fractured the bone again. He had to undergo surgery, was hospitalized for four weeks and was prohibited from returning to work for an additional two months.

You have been contacted by Mrs. Adams and Mr. King. Mrs. Adams wishes to sue Mr. Jones for all of her physical injuries, the deterioration in her mental health, her financial losses due to her inability to work, and the break-up of her marriage. Mr. King is seeking damages from both Mr. Jones and Mr. Smith. Your initial investigations have established that Mr. King's car sustained $1,600 worth of damage in the first collision and an additional $4,400 worth of damage in the second collision. Mr. King has brought it to your attention that his tool chests worth $1,000 were stolen at the scene of the second accident.

18

THE ASSESSMENT OF DAMAGES

1. Introduction
2. Damages for Personal Injuries
3. Survival of Actions and Dependants' Claims
4. Damages for Property Loss
5. Collateral Benefits

1. Introduction

In this chapter we introduce the legal principles governing the assessment of damages in Canada. While some of these principles apply equally to intentional tort claims and claims in negligence, our focus here, as in the preceding and subsequent chapters, is on negligence. Some general principles are explained in this introduction, and more specific principles are discussed in the remaining sections. For example, we examine the principles relating to personal injury claims and analyze some of the more technical rules governing their assessment. This detailed discussion is intended to illustrate the complexities of applying the general principles to specific cases. Space limitations do not permit us to provide a similar analysis of other types of damage claims.

(a) THE PURPOSES OF DAMAGE AWARDS IN NEGLIGENCE

As noted in Chapter 2, damages may be classified according to the purpose for which they are awarded. In this functional classification system, damages are traditionally divided into three categories: nominal, compensatory and punitive.

Nominal damages are generally awarded to vindicate the plaintiff's rights in situations in which he or she has suffered no injuries. Since the plaintiff must establish loss or injury as one of the elements of a negligence claim, nominal damages are not available in negligence actions.

With rare exceptions, negligence actions are brought to recover compensatory damages. In negligence, as in the intentional torts, the purpose of compensatory damages is to put the plaintiff in the position that he or she would have been in had the tort not been committed. As will become apparent in the material below, this principle is easy to understand but often extremely difficult to apply in even moderately complicated personal injury or property damage cases.

Unlike their English counterparts, Canadian courts have not defined punitive damages narrowly or restricted them to specific categories of cases. Rather, Canadian courts have held that punitive damages may be awarded for one of the following four purposes: punishment, deterrence, denunciation and to relieve a wrongdoer of profits made from the wrong: see *Whiten v. Pilot Insurance Co.*, [2002] 1 S.C.R. 595. Canadian courts have accepted that punitive damages can be awarded in those negligence cases in which the defendant has acted with an arrogant, high-handed or blatant disregard for the plaintiff's safety or other interests. However, the courts remain reluctant to award punitive damages in negligence. In large measure this is because the vast majority of negligence cases involve simple carelessness, and thus punitive damages are rarely appropriate. The same reluctance can be seen in awarding aggravated damages. As noted in Chapter 2, the courts distinguish between punitive and aggravated damages. The latter are not intended as punishment, but rather are designed to compensate for intangible injuries like humiliation or distress caused as a result of how the defendant committed the tort. Again, these will rarely be appropriate in cases of simple carelessness.

NOTES AND QUESTIONS

1. For a discussion of nominal damages see *The Mediana*, [1900] A.C. 113 (H.L.), which is extracted in Chapter 2, and Waddams, *The Law of Damages*, 4th ed. (2004) at 10.10-10.30. In contrast to the orthodox view, Cooper-Stephenson, *Personal Injury Damages in Canada*, 2d ed. (1996) at 100 states that "where the plaintiff can provide evidence of quantum but unreasonably omits to do so, the reward may be nominal damages." See also *Fisher v. Knibbe* (1992), 125 A.R. 219 (C.A.) where the plaintiff was awarded $100 in nominal damages against the defendant solicitor who missed a limitation period. The court awarded nominal damages because the original action would not have succeeded in any event. What purpose would such an award serve?

2. *Robitaille v. Vancouver Hockey Club Ltd.* (1979), 19 B.C.L.R. 158 (S.C.), aff'd (1981), 124 D.L.R. (3d) 228 (B.C.C.A.) is one of the few negligence cases in which punitive damages have been awarded. The trial judge held that the defendant's medical staff had consciously ignored the plaintiff's complaints about a serious injury. As a result, the plaintiff suffered a permanent disabling injury when he was forced to play hockey in an injured condition. He also acquired a reputation as a malingerer. The judge characterized the defendant's conduct as "high-handed, arrogant and displaying a reckless disregard for the rights of the plaintiff" and awarded the plaintiff $35,000 in punitive damages. Do you agree with the court's application of punitive damages to the facts? *Robitaille* was approved by the Supreme Court of Canada in *Vorvis v. Insurance Corporation of B.C.*, [1989] 4 W.W.R. 218 (S.C.C.).

3. In *Kraft (Next friend of) v. Oshawa General Hospital*, [1985] O.J. No. 1085 (H.C.) (QL), varied on other grounds, [1986] O.J. No. 838 (C.A.) (QL), the plaintiff, a healthy woman, suffered severe brain damage following a cardiac arrest during a relatively safe and simple surgical procedure. The cardiac arrest was precipitated by the failure of the defendant anaesthetist to properly ventilate the plaintiff or monitor her vital signs for a period of at least four minutes. Rather than attending to the plaintiff, the anaesthetist was apparently doing a crossword puzzle that he had clipped to the plaintiff's chart. In dismissing the plaintiff's claim for punitive damages, the judge stated:

> I am unable to find in the defendant's conduct maliciousness, intent to harm, or that disregard of every principle of decency which is the foundation for an award of punitive damages. It is my view that punitive damages should be awarded only on rare occasions and I am not persuaded that they should be awarded in the circumstances of this case.

Do you agree with the court's statement of the circumstances in which punitive damages may be awarded or the application of this principle to the facts? Is the defendant's conduct in this case any less morally blameworthy than the conduct that gives rise to punitive damages in intentional tort cases? Can you reconcile *Kraft* and *Robitaille*? See also *Rumsey v. R.*, [1984] 5 W.W.R. 585 (Fed. T.D.).

4. In *Vlchek v. Koshel* (1988), 44 C.C.L.T. 314 (B.C.S.C.) the plaintiff was seriously injured when she was thrown from an all-terrain vehicle. She sued the manufacturer for failing to recall or redesign the vehicle despite numerous similar accidents. On a motion to determine a question of law, the court concluded that punitive damages could be awarded even if the defendant's act was not directed toward the plaintiff, as long as it was malicious or reckless enough to indicate a complete indifference to the welfare and safety of others.

5. What principles should apply to a defendant who drives while impaired? In both *Nelson v. Welsh* (1985), 70 N.S.R. (2d) 422 (S.C.) and *Wilson v. Lind* (1985), 35 C.C.L.T. 95 (Ont. H.C.) punitive damages were denied because criminal law provides a mechanism for punishing impaired drivers. However, there was no evidence that either driver had been criminally prosecuted. See also Whitehill, "*Taylor v. Superior Court*: Punitive Damages for Nondeliberate Torts: The Drunk Driving Context" (1980) 68 Cal. L. Rev. 911. Can you suggest other types of negligence cases in which punitive damages might be appropriate? When should a criminal conviction, or the possibility of a criminal conviction, preclude punitive damages? See *Daniels v. Thompson*, [1998] 3 N.Z.L.R. 22 (C.A.); and Waters, "Multiple Punishment: The Effect of a Prior Criminal Conviction on an Award of Punitive Damages" (1996) 18 Adv. Q. 34.

6. In *McIntyre v. Grigg* (2006), 83 O.R. (3d) 161 (C.A.) an impaired driver sped through a stop sign and struck a pedestrian. The defendant initially faced criminal charges but these were withdrawn because the police had not advised him of his right to counsel, making key evidence inadmissible. He pled guilty to careless driving and was fined $500. He was sued by the pedestrian, who suffered serious physical and psychological injuries. In addition to compensatory damages, an Ontario jury awarded $100,000 in aggravated damages and $100,000 in punitive damages. The Court of Appeal overturned the award of aggravated damages, holding that the expert medical evidence did not establish that the plaintiff's psychological injuries were increased as a result of the driver's intoxication. As to the punitive damages, it held by a majority that (at para. 57):

> By making the deliberate choice to drink excessively and then drive, Andrew Grigg's misconduct was more than mere negligence. It demonstrated a conscious and reckless disregard for the lives and safety of others. There was evidence he was two to three times over the legal limit for alcohol consumption and was speeding and driving recklessly. In our view, this was sufficient evidence for the jury to find that an award of punitive damages was warranted. . . . Grigg also argued an award of punitive damages would be inappropriate and unnecessary given that [he] had already been punished, *i.e.* a $500 fine for careless driving. In our view, analyzing the principles articulated by the Supreme Court of Canada in *Whiten*, and given the fact that the misconduct in question was much more serious than careless driving, it was open to the jury to find that punitive damages did not amount to double punishment, that others would not be deterred by the fine imposed on Andrew Grigg, and that punitive damages were appropriate.

However, the court nonetheless reduced the amount of the punitive damages to $20,000. In dissent, Justice R.A. Blair would have overturned the punitive damage award altogether. He stated (at para. 134): "I think there can be no doubt, however, that if punitive damages are found to be available in this case, they will be found to be available – and will be awarded – in many other personal injury or fatal accident cases arising out of alcohol-related motor vehicle accidents." In his view, such awards had to be confined to truly exceptional cases. Do you agree with the majority or the dissent?

7. A few cases have apparently allowed punitive damages for inadvertent negligence. See for example *Rowland's Transport Ltd. v. Nasby Sales & Services Ltd.* (1978), 16 A.R. 192 (S.C. (T.D.)). The better view is that only advertent negligence, such as in *Robitaille, supra*, will support a punitive damage award.

8. For other cases involving punitive damages in negligence, see *Heighington v. Ontario* (1987), 60 O.R. (2d) 641 (H.C.), additional reasons at (1987), 60 O.R. (2d) 655 (H.C.), aff'd (1989), 69 O.R. (2d) 484 (C.A.); *Coughlin v. Kuntz* (1987), 42 C.C.L.T. 142 (B.C.S.C.), aff'd (1989), 2 C.C.L.T. (2d) 42 (B.C.C.A.); *MacDonald v. Sebastian* (1987), 81 N.S.R. (2d) 189 (S.C.); *Augustus v. Gosset* (1995), 27 C.C.L.T. (2d) 161 (Qc. C.A.), rev'd (1996), 34 C.C.L.T. (2d) 111 (S.C.C.); and *Shobridge v. Thomas* (1999), 47 C.C.L.T. (2d) 73 (B.C.S.C.).

9. What is the purpose of punitive damages? Although Canadian courts often speak of "punishment and deterrence," those goals are not necessarily consistent or mutually compatible. Suggest situations in which an award of punitive damages would be appropriate for one goal but not the other. For a discussion on that point, and for a general overview of punitive damages, see Polinsky & Shavell, "Punitive Damages: An Economic Analysis" (1998) 111 Harv. L. Rev. 869.

(b) PRELIMINARY ISSUES

There are several preliminary issues that must be addressed before turning to the specific principles governing different types of damage claims. These include the burden and standard of proof in damages, mitigation of damages, the set-off of parallel expenditures, the use of lump sum payments and the roles of juries, judges and appellate courts.

The plaintiff has the burden of proving that he or she has suffered a type of loss that is recognized as being recoverable in tort law. For example, no one doubts that grief and sorrow may be debilitating, but unless they cause nervous shock they are not recognized heads of damage in a common law tort action. The plaintiff also bears the burden of proving the quantum of the damages that are claimed.

The standard of proof for losses that have occurred prior to trial is relatively straightforward. The plaintiff must prove the existence and quantum of such losses on the balance of probabilities. If the plaintiff meets this standard, he or she is entitled to recover 100% of the claim; if not, he or she recovers nothing. The standard of proof for losses that may occur after trial is more complicated. There are two possible approaches. An earlier line of authority in Canada employed a balance of probabilities test. If the plaintiff established on the balance of probabilities that a future loss would occur, he or she recovered the entire amount. However, if he or she could not meet this test, the claim was denied. A more recent line of authorities is based on a reasonable or substantial possibility test. Once the plaintiff establishes that there is a substantial or reasonable possibility of injury, he or she is entitled to recover for this loss, but subject to the likelihood of it occurring. Pursuant to this second line of cases, a plaintiff who establishes that there is a 35% chance of suffering blindness in the future is entitled to 35% of the damages that such blindness would cause.

The plaintiff is under an obligation to act reasonably in all of the circumstances of the case to mitigate his or her loss. The defendant has the burden of proving that the plaintiff failed to do so. McGregor, *McGregor on Damages*, 17th ed. (2003) at 216-17 outlines three related principles of mitigation. First, the plaintiff must take all reasonable steps to avoid or minimize the loss. Second, the plaintiff may recover for losses incurred in taking such reasonable steps. Third, the plaintiff cannot recover for losses that have been successfully avoided, even if he or she was not required to have avoided them under the first rule. These principles are generally applied more rigorously to claims for property damages and business losses than to claims for personal injuries. Although relatively easy to state, these principles are often very difficult to apply in specific fact situations. See also Cooper-Stephenson, *Personal Injury Damages in Canada*, 2d ed. (1996) at 862-92.

A defendant is allowed to set-off against the plaintiff's damage claim any parallel expenditures that the plaintiff would have incurred had the tort not been committed. For example, if the plaintiff is claiming the full cost of nursing home care which includes food, the defendant may be permitted to reduce this claim by the amount the plaintiff would have spent anyway on food during this period. As a general rule, set-off is only permitted if the defendant can establish that the two items in issue are truly parallel in nature and that their values are readily calculable.

At common law, damages are awarded in a one-time lump sum to compensate the plaintiff for all the losses he or she has suffered and will likely suffer in the future. Under the lump-sum payment system the trier of fact is forced to speculate on a range of issues including the future condition of the injured plaintiff, the probable increases in health care and nursing costs, and the impact of inflation on the purchasing power of the damage award. If a loss turns out to be far greater or smaller than that calculated at trial, there is no means of re-assessment. As we shall discuss, the inadequacies of this system have been widely criticized by both commentators and judges.

In a jury trial, it is the jury's responsibility to assess damages and the law does not allow counsel or the judge to provide much assistance. With respect to *special damages*, that situation creates relatively few difficulties. Special damages consist of pre-trial pecuniary losses, such as expenses incurred and income lost prior to trial. Because such damages must be specifically pleaded and proved by the plaintiff on a balance of probabilities, the jury is provided with considerable guidance for the purposes of quantification. In contrast, juries are provided with relatively little guidance with respect to *general damages*. General damages consist of pre-trial non-pecuniary losses and all post-trial losses, such as pain and suffering, future expenses and loss of income. Traditionally, counsel and judges were not permitted to suggest appropriate amounts or to inform jurors of the usual range of non-pecuniary awards. However, that attitude is changing and the courts are increasingly willing to apprise jurors of suitable ranges and rough upper limits: see *ter Neuzen v. Korn*, [1995] 3 S.C.R. 674; and *Foreman v. Foster* (2001), 84 B.C.L.R. (3d) 184 (C.A.). However, see *Brisson v. Brisson* (2002), 11 C.C.L.T. (3d) 197 (B.C.C.A.); and *Yin v. Lewin* (2006), 61 Alta. L.R. (4th) 138 (Q.B.).

At common law counsel and the trial judge are precluded from referring the jury to awards that have been made in similar cases, although counsel may refer to such information on appeal. The problems of inconsistency are further heightened by the general rule that appellate courts are not to interfere with a jury's assessment of damages unless there is a clear error in law or the amount is so grossly out of line that it is a "wholly erroneous" estimate of the damages.

NOTES AND QUESTIONS

1. Because of a delay between the trial of an action and the court rendering its judgment, hypothetical future facts may become past actual facts. In assessing damages, the court should adjust its calculations accordingly. In *Monahan v. Nelson* (2000), 186 D.L.R. (4th) 193 (B.C.C.A.) the defendant negligently injured the plaintiff. The trial judge heard evidence under several heads of damage, including loss of future income, cost of future care and future non-pecuniary losses (like pain and suffering). The plaintiff then died, for reasons unrelated to the defendant's tort, before the trial judge rendered judgment. Relying upon the *Estate Administration Act*, R.S.B.C. 1996, c. 122, s. 59, the trial judge nevertheless proceeded to award damages as if the plaintiff were still alive. The British Columbia Court of Appeal reduced the damages, insisting that recovery reflect actual losses to the extent possible. See also *Strachan (Guardian ad litem of) v. Reynolds* (2006), 39 C.C.L.T. (3d) 79 (B.C.S.C.).

2. It is often difficult to distinguish issues pertaining to the existence of liability from those pertaining to the extent of liability. The courts often take different approaches to these issues and use different terminology. For example, is it most appropriate to state that there is no duty to avoid causing grief and sorrow, that grief and sorrow are too remote or that grief and sorrow are not recognized heads of damage?

3. For cases supporting the balance of probabilities test for future losses see *B.C. Electric Ry. Co. v. Clarke*, [1950] 3 D.L.R. 161 (S.C.C.); *Turenne v. Chung* (1962), 36 D.L.R. (2d) 197 (Man. C.A.); *Corrie v. Gilbert*, [1965] S.C.R. 457; and *Conklin v. Smith* (1978), 5 C.C.L.T. 113 (S.C.C.). For cases supporting the reasonable possibility test see *Davies v. Taylor*, [1972] 3 All E.R. 836 (H.L.); *Schrump v. Koot* (1977), 18 O.R. (2d) 337 (C.A.); *Hearndon v. Rondeau* (1984), 29 C.C.L.T. 149 (B.C.C.A.); *Janiak v. Ippolito* (1985), 16 D.L.R. (4th) 1 (S.C.C.); *Steenblok v. Funk*, [1990] 5 W.W.R. 365 (B.C.C.A.); *Bachalo v. Robson* (1998), 129 Man. R. (2d) 1 (C.A.); *Hornick v. Kochinsky* (2005), 22 C.C.L.I. (4th) 29 (Ont. S.C.J.); and *Haile v. Johns* (2005), 50 B.C.L.R. (4th) 241 (C.A.).

Although the Canadian courts may now simply follow the reasonable possibility test set out in *Janiak*, this decision did not address the conflicting line of cases. Can you provide an example in which the result would be the same regardless of which test was used? Provide an example in which the tests would produce different results. Which test is more in keeping with the purpose of compensatory damage awards? For a discussion of these issues see Kirkham, "Proof of Future Loss: Probabilities and Possibilities" (1984) 24 The Advocate 21; Cooper-Stephenson, *Personal Injury Damages in Canada*, 2d ed. (1996) at 754-61; and Waddams, *The Law of Damages*, 4th ed. (2004) at 13.260-13.370.

4. It may be difficult to determine whether the plaintiff's conduct should be raised under remoteness, contributory negligence, mitigation or all three issues. Moreover, some courts deal with the question of set-off of parallel expenditures as an issue of mitigation. For a comprehensive review of the principles of mitigation, see Cooper-Stephenson, *supra*, at 862-92; and Waddams, *supra*, ch. 15.

5. In *Janiak v. Ippolito, supra*, the defendant negligently caused the plaintiff's serious back injury. The plaintiff was informed that if he had corrective surgery there was a 70 to 75% chance of complete recovery which would allow him to return to work. The chance of a "poor result" was 10%, including a 1% risk of quadriplegia and a 0.1% risk of death. The plaintiff refused to have the operation. The court had to decide if his refusal constituted an unreasonable failure to mitigate. The court held that this issue was to be resolved by the trier of fact and depended upon the risks of surgery, the consequences of refusing surgery, and its potential benefits. The court concluded that the trial judge was correct in finding that the plaintiff unreasonably failed to mitigate his loss by refusing surgery. Do you agree? See also *Souto v. Anderson*, [1996] 5 W.W.R. 394 (B.C.C.A.); and *Kozak v. Funk*, [1996] 1 W.W.R. 79 (Sask. Q.B.).

In *Janiak* the court also stated that a plaintiff's pre-existing fear of surgery does not justify an unreasonable failure to have an operation unless he or she suffers from a psychological infirmity that precludes rational decision-making. Is this proposition consistent with the general principles governing the thin-skulled plaintiff rule? Should these same principles apply if the surgical procedure violates the plaintiff's religious beliefs? Should the same principles apply to recommended psychiatric treatment, even if participation would stigmatize the plaintiff? See *Brian v. Mador* (1985), 32 C.C.L.T. 157 (Ont. C.A.); *Engel v. Kam-Ppelle Holdings Ltd.* (1993), 15 C.C.L.T. (2d) 245 (S.C.C.); and *Gray v. Gill* (1993), 18 C.C.L.T. (2d) 120 (B.C.S.C.). See also Kemp, "Mitigation of Damage — Plaintiff's Refusal to Undergo Operation — Onus of Proof" (1983) 99 L.Q.R. 497.

6. For a discussion of mitigation in a personal injury context see *Parypa v. Wickware* (1999), 169 D.L.R. (4th) 661 (B.C.C.A.); *Kern v. Steele* (2003), 220 N.S.R. (2d) 51 (C.A.); and *Morel v. Bryden* (2006), 246 N.S.R. (2d) 43 (S.C.). For a discussion in commercial and property damage situations, see respectively *Hongkong Bank of Canada v. Richardson Greenshields of Canada Ltd.* (1990), 72 D.L.R. (4th) 161 (B.C.C.A.); and *University of Regina v. Pettick* (1991), 77 D.L.R. (4th) 615 (Sask. C.A.).

7. For a discussion of the set-off of parallel expenditures see *Shearman v. Folland*, [1950] 1 All E.R. 976 (C.A.); *Andrews v. Grand & Toy Alberta Ltd.* (1978), 83 D.L.R. (3d) 452 (S.C.C.); and Cooper-Stephenson, *supra*, at 533-62.

8. For a discussion of the role of the judge and jury see Schroeder, "The Charge to the Jury" in *Special Lectures of the Law Society of Upper Canada 1959* (1959) 311. In *Howes v. Crosby* (1984), 6 D.L.R. (4th) 698 (Ont. C.A.) the court noted that it would not be an error for a trial judge to inform the jury of the Supreme Court of Canada's limits on awards for non-pecuniary loss (discussed below). However, in *Baurose v. Hart* (1990), 44 C.P.C. (2d) 283 (Ont. Gen. Div.) the court stated that the upper limit should only be mentioned in cases of catastrophic injury. In Ontario the *Courts of Justice Act*, R.S.O. 1990, c. C.43, s. 118 now allows the parties and the judge to inform the jury about general damage awards.

9. Although the principles governing an appellate review of a damage award are well established, it is often difficult to reconcile the cases. For a comprehensive review, see Waddams, *supra*, at 13.420-13.480. See also *Cody v. Leonard*, [1996] 4 W.W.R. 96 (B.C.C.A.); and *Stafford v. Motomochi*, [1997] 3 W.W.R. 571 (B.C.C.A.).

10. Traditionally, the courts held that the defendant would have grounds for appeal if the jury was informed that the defendant had liability insurance: *Theakston v. Bowley*, [1950] 3 D.L.R. 804 (Ont. C.A.). However, the Supreme Court of Canada has held that there is no absolute rule regarding the effect of disclosing such information to the jury: *Hamstra (Guardian ad litem of) v. British Columbia Rugby Union*, [1997] 1 S.C.R. 1092. Rather, the trial judge should determine whether, in all of the circumstances of the case, the disclosure of such information was prejudicial to the parties. If so, the trial judge should fashion an appropriate solution. The jury might be dismissed, a new trial might be ordered, or the jury might simply be directed to disregard the information in question.

11. Do the rules governing judges, juries and appeals make sense given the complexity of the law of damages? J. Fleming has argued that the inconsistency and apparent arbitrariness of damage awards has led more than anything else to the restricted use of juries in civil actions: Fleming, "Damages For Non-Material Loss" in *Special Lectures of the Law Society of Upper Canada 1973* (1973) 1 at 5-10. Should the assessment of damages be left to the judge in jury cases? If not, how would you modify the existing rules?

12. The recovery of prejudgment and post-judgment interest on the plaintiff's losses raises extremely complex issues that are increasingly governed by legislation. See for example *Courts of Justice Act*, R.S.O. 1990, c. C.43, ss. 127-130. See Bowles & Whelan, "The Law of Interest: Dawn of a New Era?" (1986) 64 Can. Bar Rev. 142; and Waddams, *supra*, at 7.330-7.1000.

2. Damages for Personal Injuries

(a) INTRODUCTION

Until the late 1970s Canadian courts used a "global approach" in assessing damages, which involved selecting a single figure to compensate the plaintiff for all of his or her injuries. The governing principles were very general and meaningful appellate review was difficult. Moreover, there was no effective means of addressing the large variations in awards for apparently similar injuries. The global approach typically resulted in very low damage awards. For example in *Clarke v. Penny* (1975), 10 Nfld. & P.E.I.R. 220 (Nfld. T.D.) a five-year-old girl who sustained severe brain damage was awarded $180,000 for her loss of earning capacity, future care costs, pain and suffering, and loss of enjoyment of life.

In the late 1970s the Supreme Court of Canada rejected the global assessment approach in favour of the separate assessment of each head of recovery that has been proved by the plaintiff: *Andrews v. Grand & Toy Alberta Ltd.*, [1978] 2 S.C.R. 229; *Arnold v. Teno*, [1978] 2 S.C.R. 287; and *Thornton (Next friend of) v. Prince George School District No. 57*, [1978] 2 S.C.R. 267. The "trilogy," as those cases came to be known, established a framework for quantifying general damages under the following headings:

(1) Pecuniary loss
- (a) Future loss
- (b) Lost earning capacity

(c) Considerations relevant to both heads of pecuniary loss

(2) Non-pecuniary loss

Perhaps the most striking consequence of the damages trilogy has been the increase in the size of damage awards. The courts' efforts to rationalize damage assessments have led to inflation adjustments, home care awards, the increasing (grossing up) of future care costs to offset the impact of taxes, and awards to hire professional financial managers. Million-dollar awards, unheard of in Canada before the late 1970s, were commonplace by the mid-1980s. The jury's award in *Sandhu (Litigation Guardian of) v. Wellington Place Apartments*, 2006 CarswellOnt 3668 (S.C.J.) (WLeC) to a two-year-old plaintiff who suffered a frontal lobe brain injury was almost $14 million. In *Gordon v. Greig*, 2007 CarswellOnt 343 (S.C.J.) (WLeC) a car accident left one plaintiff with severe brain injuries and the other plaintiff a paraplegic. Both men were in their early 20s. The judge awarded the former over $11 million and the latter over $12 million, the vast majority of which was in each case for the cost of future care.

In this section, we will examine the current Canadian framework for assessing personal injury claims using the relevant portions of Dickson J.'s judgment in *Andrews*. The first excerpt introduces some of the underlying concepts.

ANDREWS v. GRAND & TOY ALBERTA LTD.

(1978), 83 D.L.R. (3d) 452 (S.C.C.)

DICKSON J. — This is a negligence action for personal injury involving a young man rendered a quadriplegic in a traffic accident for which the respondent Anderson and his employer, Grand & Toy Alberta Ltd., have been found partially liable. Leave to appeal to this Court was granted on the question whether the Appellate Division of the Supreme Court of Alberta erred in law in the assessment of damages. At trial Mr. Justice Kirby awarded $1,022,477.48 . . . : the Appellate Division reduced that sum to $516,544.48. . . .

Let me say in introduction what has been said many times before, that no appellate Court is justified in substituting a figure of its own for that awarded at trial simply because it would have awarded a different figure if it had tried the case at first instance. It must be satisfied that a wrong principle of law was applied, or that the overall amount is a wholly erroneous estimate of the damage. . . .

The method of assessing general damages in separate amounts, as has been done in this case, in my opinion, is a sound one. It is the only way in which any meaningful review of the award is possible on appeal and the only way of affording reasonable guidance in future cases. Equally important, it discloses to the litigants and their advisers the components of the overall award, assuring them thereby that each of the various heads of damage going to make up the claim has been given thoughtful consideration.

The subject of damages for personal injury is an area of the law which cries out for legislative reform. The expenditure of time and money in the determination of fault and of damage is prodigal. The disparity resulting from lack of provision for victims who cannot establish fault must be disturbing. When it is determined that compensation is to be made, it is highly irrational to be tied to a lump-sum system and a once-and-for-all award.

The lump-sum award presents problems of great importance. It is subject to inflation, it is subject to fluctuation on investment, income from it is subject to tax. After judgment new needs of the plaintiff arise and the present needs are extinguished; yet, our law of damages knows nothing of periodic payment. The difficulties are greatest where there is a continuing need for intensive and expensive care and a long-term loss of earning capacity. It should be possible to devise some system whereby payments would be subject to periodic review and variation in the light of the continuing needs of the injured person and the cost of meeting those needs. In making this comment I am not unaware of the negative recommendation of the British Law Commission (Law Com. 56 — *Report on Personal Injury Litigation — Assessment of Damages*) following strong opposition from insurance interests and the plaintiffs' bar.

The apparent reliability of assessments provided by modern actuarial practice is largely illusionary, for actuarial science deals with probabilities, not actualities. This is in no way to denigrate a respected profession, but it is obvious that the validity of the answers given by the actuarial witness, as with a computer, depends upon the soundness of the postulates from which he proceeds. Although a useful aid, and a sharper tool than the "multiplier-multiplicand" approach favoured in some jurisdictions, actuarial evidence speaks in terms of group experience. It cannot, and does not purport to, speak as to the individual sufferer. So long as we are tied to lump-sum awards, however, we are tied also to actuarial calculations as the best available means of determining amount.

In spite of these severe difficulties with the present law of personal injury compensation, the positive administrative machinery required for a system of reviewable periodic payments, and the need to hear all interested parties in order to fashion a more enlightened system, both dictate that the appropriate body to act must be the Legislature, rather than the Courts. Until such time as the Legislature acts, the Courts must proceed on established principles to award damages which compensate accident victims with justice and humanity for the losses they may suffer.

I proceed now to a brief recital of the injuries sustained by the appellant James Andrews in the present case. He suffered a fracture with dislocation of the cervical spine between the fifth and sixth cervical vertebrae, causing functional transection of the spinal cord, but leaving some continuity; compound fracture of the left tibia and left humerus; fracture of the left patella. The left radial nerve was damaged. The lesion of the spinal cord left Andrews with paralysis involving most of the upper limbs, spine and lower limbs. He has lost the use of his legs, his trunk, essentially his left arm and most of his right arm. To add to the misery, he does not have normal bladder, bowel and sex functions. He suffers from spasticity in both upper and lower limbs. He has difficulty turning in bed and must be re-positioned every two hours. He needs regular physiotherapy and should have someone in close association with him at all times, such as a trained male orderly. The only functioning muscles of respiration are those of the diaphragm and shoulders. There is much more in the evidence but it need not be recited. Andrews is severely, if not totally disabled. Dr. Weir, a specialist in neurosurgery, said of Andrews' condition that "there is no hope of functional improvement." For the rest of his life he will be dependent on others for dressing, personal hygiene, feeding, and, indeed, for his very survival. But, of utmost important, he is not a vegetable or a piece of cordwood. He is a man of above average intelligence and his mind is unimpaired. He can see, hear and speak as before. He has partial use of his right arm and hand. With the aid of a wheelchair he is mobile. With a specially designed van he can go out in the evening to visit friends, or to the movies, or to a pub. He is taking driving lessons and proving to be an apt pupil. He wants to live as other human beings live. Since May 31, 1974, he has resided in his own apartment with private attendant care. The medical long-term care required is not at a sophisticated level but rather at a practical care level.

Andrews was 21 years of age and unmarried on the date of the accident. On that date he was an apprentice carman employed by the Canadian National Railways in the City of Edmonton.

I turn now to consider assessment of the damages to which Andrews is entitled.

. . .

NOTES AND QUESTIONS

1. What criticisms did Dickson J. make of the fault system and of lump-sum awards? Dickson J. elaborated on his concerns about lump-sum awards in "The Role and Function of Judges" (1980) 14 L.S.U.C. Gazette 138. Although subsequent events may reveal a lump sum to be grossly inadequate, the courts stress the need for finality and refuse to revisit the assessment of damages: *Tsaoussis (Litigation Guardian of) v. Baetz* (1998), 165 D.L.R. (4th) 268 (Ont. C.A.).

2. There are two types of periodic payment schemes. In one, the payment schedule is fixed in advance and cannot be varied to reflect changes in circumstances. In the other, variable periodic payments may be adjusted as circumstances change. Which type of periodic payment scheme best addresses Dickson J.'s concerns?

3. What extra costs would be incurred with variable periodic payments? Are victims more likely to malinger under such a scheme? Is the case for periodic payments paternalistic? The limited research on how plaintiffs fare after receiving lump-sum damage awards is not encouraging. See Keeton & O'Connell, *Basic Protection for the Traffic Victim* (1965) at 353-54; Fleming, "Damages: Capital or Rent?" (1969) 19 U.T.L.J. 295 at 299-300; Kretzner, "No-Fault Comes to Israel: The Compensation for Victims of Road Accidents Law, 1975" (1976) 11 Isr. L.R. 288 at 306; and Bale, "Encouraging the Hearse Horse Not to Snicker: A Tort Fund Providing Variable Periodic Payments for Pecuniary Loss" in Steel & Rogers-Magnet, eds., *Issues in Tort Law* (1983) 91.

4. Periodic payments are a central feature of the increasing number of structured settlements being reached by parties. Typically, a structured settlement includes a sum for expenses already incurred, followed by a series of periodic payments to cover future losses. In most cases the defendant's insurer purchases an annuity designed to generate periodic payments for the plaintiff's life. The payments may, and usually do, vary over the term of the settlement. For example, cost-of-living increases are built into the schedule and balloon payments may be included to meet projected occasional needs such as the cost of a child's university education. Thus, a structured settlement may be tailored to the individual plaintiff's needs. Such settlements protect plaintiffs who might otherwise squander or inefficiently manage the lump-sum award. However, the conditions for variation are established at the time of settlement and no adjustment for unanticipated changes in circumstances are possible.

5. The main advantage of a structured settlement is that the periodic payments which are generated are not taxable. Although a lump-sum award is not taxable either, any interest it generates is taxable. This tax savings with structured settlements thus becomes a matter for negotiation, which may be mutually beneficial. The defendant will

be able to purchase an annuity for less than the lump sum that would have been awarded, and yet the plaintiff's periodic payments will exceed the after-tax income he or she would have obtained from the interest on the lump sum. See *Yepremian v. Scarborough Gen. Hosp.* (1981), 120 D.L.R. (3d) 341 (Ont. H.C.), in which a judicially approved structured settlement is set out; Weir, *Structured Settlement* (1984); Holland, "Structured Settlements in Injury and Wrongful Death Cases" (1987) 8 Adv. Q. 185; and Watkin, "The New Method of Structuring Settlement Agreements" (1992) 71 Can. Bar Rev. 27.

6. The tax savings in a structured settlement would also occur in a structured judgment. However, in *Watkins v. Olafson* (1989), 61 D.L.R. (4th) 577 (S.C.C.) the court held that the courts lacked jurisdiction to impose judgment in a structured form. Canadian legislatures have been very reluctant to authorize the imposition of structured judgments, although this was recommended by Osborne J. in the *Report of Inquiry into Motor Vehicle Compensation in Ontario* (1988) and by the Law Reform Commission of Saskatchewan in *Proposals for a Structured Judgments Act* (1993). Under the *Insurance (Motor Vehicle) Act*, R.S.B.C. 1996, c. 231, s. 55(1)(a) the court is required to order periodic payments when the damages in a motor vehicle action exceed $100,000 and the court considers the payments to be in the plaintiff's best interests.

7. The *Courts of Justice Act*, R.S.O. 1990, c. C.43, s. 116, reads as follows:

Periodic payment and review of damages

(1) In a proceeding where damages are claimed for personal injuries or under Part V of the *Family Law Act* for loss resulting from the injury to or death of a person, the court,

(a) if all affected parties consent, may order the defendant to pay all or part of the award for damages periodically on such terms as the court considers just; and

(b) if the plaintiff requests that an amount be included in the award to offset any liability for income tax on income from the investment of the award, shall order the defendant to pay all or part of the award periodically on such terms as the court considers just.

No order

(2) An order under clause (1) (b) shall not be made if the parties otherwise consent or if the court is of the opinion that the order would not be in the best interests of the plaintiff, having regard to all the circumstances of the case.

Best interests

(3) In considering the best interests of the plaintiff, the court shall take into account,

(a) whether the defendant has sufficient means to fund an adequate scheme of periodic payments;

(b) whether the plaintiff has a plan or a method of payment that is better able to meet the interests of the plaintiff than periodic payments by the defendant; and

(c) whether a scheme of periodic payments is practicable having regard to all the circumstances of the case.

Future review

(4) In an order made under this section, the court may, with the consent of all the affected parties, order that the award be subject to future review and revision in such circumstances and on such terms as the court considers just.

Amount to offset liability for income tax

(5) If the court does not make an order for periodic payment under subsection (1), it shall make an award for damages that shall include an amount to offset liability for income tax on income from investment of the award.

In *Wilson v. Martinello* (1995), 23 O.R. (3d) 417 (C.A.) the court considered an earlier wording of s. 116(1)(b). Resolving ambiguities in the "very badly drafted" earlier wording, it held that where a plaintiff seeks a lump-sum award including a gross up, and the defendant proposes a structured award with periodic payments, s. 116 requires the court to impose a structured award unless the plaintiff can prove that it would not be in his or her best interests. In 1996, in accordance with the reasoning in *Wilson*, the legislature amended s. 116(1)(b) to its present form. See also *Chesher v. Monaghan* (2000), 186 D.L.R. (4th) 595 (Ont. C.A.) where the Court of Appeal rejected the defendant's request for a structured award because it was not in the plaintiff's best interests.

8. Ontario has recently enacted s. 116.1 of the *Courts of Justice Act*. It goes beyond s. 116 to expand the mandatory use of court-ordered periodic payments for future care costs in medical malpractice cases. Why might the legislature have enacted this section?

9. See generally Ontario Law Reform Commission, *Report on Compensation for Personal Injuries and Death* (1987); and Dufays, "Introducing Provisional Damages for Personal Injuries in Canada" (1997) 6 Dal. J. Leg. Stud. 1. For an analysis of the recent English experience with court-ordered periodic payment awards see Lewis, "Tort Law in Practice: Appearance and Reality in Reforming Periodical Payments of Damages" in Neyers, Chamberlain & Pitel, eds., *Emerging Issues in Tort Law* (2007), ch. 19.

10. Three useful reference works on a wide range of issues relating to personal injury damages are Cooper-Stephenson, *Personal Injury Damages in Canada*, 2d ed. (1996); Brown, *Damages: Estimating Pecuniary Loss* (2001); and Bruce, *Assessment of Personal Injury Damages*, 4th ed. (2004).

(b) PECUNIARY LOSS: FUTURE CARE

ANDREWS v. GRAND & TOY ALBERTA LTD.

(1978), 83 D.L.R. (3d) 452 (S.C.C.)

DICKSON J.: . . . In theory a claim for the cost of future care is a pecuniary claim for the amount which may reasonably be expected to be expended in putting the injured party in the position he would have been in if he had not sustained the injury. Obviously, a plaintiff who has been gravely and permanently impaired can never be put in the position he would have been in if the tort had not been committed. To this extent, *restitutio in integrum* is not possible. Money is a barren substitute for health and personal happiness, but to the extent, within reason, that money can be used to sustain or improve the mental or physical health of the injured person it may properly form part of a claim.

Contrary to the view expressed in the Appellate Division of Alberta, there is no duty to mitigate, in the sense of being forced to accept less than real loss. There is a duty to be reasonable. There cannot be "complete" or "perfect" compensation. An award must be moderate, and fair to both parties. Clearly, compensation must not be determined on the basis of sympathy, or compassion for the plight of the injured person. What is being sought is compensation not retribution. But, in a case like the present, where both Courts have favoured a home environment, "reasonable" means reasonableness in what is to be provided in that home environment. It does not mean that Andrews must languish in an institution which on all evidence is inappropriate for him.

The reasons for judgment of the Appellate Division embodied three observations which are worthy of brief comment. The first:

> . . . it is the choice of the respondent to live in a home of his own, and from the point of view of advancing a claim for damages, it is a most salutary choice, because it is vastly the most expensive.

I am not entirely certain as to what is meant by this observation. If the import is that the appellant claimed a home life for the sole purpose of inflating his claim, then I think the implication is both unfair and unsupported by evidence. There is no doubt upon the medical and other evidence that a home environment would be salutary to the health of the appellant and productive of good effects. It cannot be unreasonable for a person to want to live in a home of his own.

The next observation:

> Secondly, it should be observed that in many cases, particularly in Alberta where damages have been awarded, the persons injured were going to live with their families. Here, the evidence (in spite of the fact that the respondent's mother advanced a claim for $237 which represented a towing charge for the motor-cycle and parking, taxis and bus fare expended on visits to her son in the hospital for approximately a nine-month period prior to the issue of the statement of claim) is that the respondent and his mother were not close before the accident, and matters proceeded on the footing that the mother's natural love and affection should have no part in Andrews' future. Again, this situation is the most expensive from the point of view of the respondent.

The evidence showed that the mother of the appellant James Andrews was living alone, in a second-floor apartment and that relations between Andrews and his mother were strained at times. This should have no bearing in minimizing Andrews' damages. Even if his mother had been able to look after Andrews in her own home, there is now ample authority for saying that dedicated wives or mothers who choose to devote their lives to looking after infirm husbands or sons are not expected to do so on a gratuitous basis. The second observation is irrelevant.

The third observation was in these words:

> Thirdly, it should be observed that the learned trial Judge has referred with approval to the English authorities which held that full compensation for pecuniary loss must be given. It does not, however, follow that every conceivable expense which a plaintiff may conjure up is a pecuniary loss. On the evidence, then, should this Court consider that Andrews should live in a home of his own for the next 45 years at the expense of the appellant?

I agree that a plaintiff cannot "conjure up" "every conceivable expense". I do not think that a request for home care falls under that rubric.

Each of the three observations seems to look at the matter solely from the point of view of the respondents and the expense to them. An award must be fair to both parties but the ability of the defendant to pay has never been regarded as a relevant consideration in the assessment of damages at common law. The focus should be on the injuries of the innocent party. Fairness to the other party is achieved by assuring that the claims raised against him are legitimate and justifiable.

. . .

With respect to Andrews' disinclination to live in an institution, the Court commented:

> He might equally say that he would not live in Alberta, as he did not wish to face old friends, or for any other reasons, and that he wished to live in Switzerland or the Bahamas.

Andrews is not asking for a life in Europe or in the Caribbean. He asks that he be permitted to continue to live in Alberta and to see his old friends, but in his own home or apartment, not in an institution.

The Court then expressed the view that the standard accepted by the trial Judge was the equivalent of supplying a private hospital. The phrase "private hospital" is both pejorative and misleading. It suggests an extravagant standard of care. The standard sought by the appellant is simply practical nursing in the home. The amount Andrews is seeking is, without question, very substantial, but essentially it means providing two orderlies and a housekeeper. The amount is large because the victim is young and because life is long. He has 45 years ahead. That is a long time.

In reducing the monthly payment to $1,000 the Appellate Division purported to apply a "final test" which was expressed in terms of the expenses that reasonably-minded people would incur, assuming sufficient means to bear such expense. It seems to me difficult to conceive of any reasonably-minded person of ample means who would not be ready to incur the expense of home care, rather than institutional care, for himself or for someone in the condition of Andrews for whom he was responsible. No other conclusion is open upon the evidence adduced in this case. If the test enunciated by the Appellate Division is simply a plea for moderation then, of course, no one would question it. If the test was intended to suggest that reasonably-minded people would refuse to bear the expense of home care, there is simply no evidence to support that conclusion.

The Appellate Division, seeking to give some meaning to the test, said that it should be open to consider "standards of society as a whole as they presently exist." As instances of such standards the Court selected the daily allowances provided under the *Workmen's Compensation Act* . . ., and the federal *Pension Act* . . .. The standard of care expected in our society in physical injury cases is an elusive concept. What a Legislature sees fit to provide in the cases of veterans and in the cases of injured workers and the elderly is only of marginal assistance. The standard to be applied to Andrews is not merely "provision", but "compensation", *i.e.*, what is the proper compensation for a person who would have been able to care for himself and live in a home environment if he had not been injured? The answer must surely be home care. If there were severe mental impairment, or in the case of an immobile quadriplegic the results might well be different; but, where the victim is mobile and still in full control of his mental faculties, as Andrews is, it cannot be said that institutionalization in an auxiliary hospital represents proper compensation for his loss. Justice requires something better.

. . .

Is it reasonable for Andrews to ask for $4,135 per month for home care? Part of the difficulty of this case is that 24-hour orderly care was not directly challenged. Counsel never really engaged in consideration of whether, assuming home care, such care could be provided at lesser expense. Counsel wants the Court, rather, to choose between home care and auxiliary hospital care. There are unanimous findings below that home care is better. Although home care is expensive, auxiliary hospital care is so utterly unattractive and so utterly in conflict with the principle of proper compensation that this Court is offered no middle ground.

The basic argument, indeed the only argument, against home care is that the social cost is too high. In these days the cost is distributed through insurance premiums. In this respect, I would adopt what was said by Salmon, L.J., in *Fletcher v. Autocare & Transporters, Ltd.*, [1968] 1 All E.R. 726 at 750, where he stated:

> Today, however, virtually all defendants in accident cases are insured. This certainly does not mean compensation should be extravagant, but there is no reason why it should not be realistic . . . It might result in some moderate increase in premium rates, which none would relish, but of which no-one, in my view, could justly complain. It would be monstrous to keep down premiums by depressing damages below their proper level, i.e., a level which ordinary men would regard as fair — unprejudiced by its impact on their own pockets.

I do not think the area of future care is one in which the argument of the social burden of the expense should be controlling, particularly in a case like the present, where the consequences of acceding to it would be to fail in large measure to compensate the victim for his loss. Greater weight might be given to this consideration where the choice with respect to future care is not so stark as between home care and an auxiliary hospital. Minimizing the social burden of expense may be a factor influencing a choice between acceptable alternatives. It should never compel the choice of the unacceptable.

(ii) *Life expectancy*. At trial, figures were introduced which showed that the life expectancy of 23-year-old persons in general is 50 years. As Chief Justice McGillivray said in the Appellate Division, it would be more useful to use statistics on the expectation of life of quadriplegics. A statistical average is helpful only if the appropriate group is used. At trial, Dr. Weir and Dr. Gingras testified that possibly five years less than normal would be a reasonable expectation of life for a quadriplegic. The Appellate Division accepted this figure. On the evidence I am willing to accept it.

(iii) *Contingencies of life*. The trial Judge did, however, allow a 20% discount for "contingencies and hazards of life". The Appellate Division allowed a further 10% discount. It characterized the trial Judge's discount as being for "life expectancy" or "duration of life", and said that this ignored the contingency of "duration of expense", *i.e.*, that despite any wishes to the contrary, Andrews in the years to come may be obliged to spend a great deal of time in hospital for medical reasons or because of the difficulty of obtaining help. With respect, the Appellate Division appears to have misunderstood what the trial Judge did. The figure of 20% as a discount for contingencies was arrived at first under the heading of "Prospective Loss of Earnings" and then simply transferred to the calculation of "Costs of Future Care". It was not an allowance for a decreased life expectancy, for this had already been taken into account by reducing the normal 50-year expectancy to 45 years. The "contingencies and hazards of life" in the context of future care are distinct. They relate essentially to duration of expense and are different from those which might affect future earnings, such as unemployment, accident, illness. They are not merely to be added to the latter so as to achieve a cumulative result. Thus, so far as the action taken by the Appellate Division is concerned, in my opinion, it was an error to increase by an extra 10% the contingency allowance of the trial Judge.

This whole question of contingencies is fraught with difficulty, for it is in large measure pure speculation. It is a small element of the illogical practice of awarding lump-sum payments for expenses and losses projected to continue over long periods of time. To vary an award by the value of the chance that certain contingencies may occur is to assure either over-compensation or under-compensation, depending on whether or not the event occurs. In light of the considerations I have mentioned, I think it would be reasonable to allow a discount for contingencies in the amount of 20%, in accordance with the decision of the trial Judge.

. . .

(v) *Cost of special equipment.* In addition to his anticipated expenses, Andrews requires an initial capital amount for special equipment. Both Courts below held that $14,200 was an appropriate figure for the cost of this equipment. In my opinion, this assessment is correct in principle, and I would therefore accept it.

. . .

NOTES AND QUESTIONS

1. Why, in Dickson J.'s opinion, is the level of care provided to injured persons under legislation irrelevant in the case of a tort victim? Do you agree?

2. Do you agree with Dickson J. that the plaintiff in *Andrews* should be entitled to be cared for in his own home? What type of evidence must the plaintiff adduce to obtain an award for home care? See *Rayner v. Knickle* (1988), 47 C.C.L.T. 141 (P.E.I.S.C.). The victim's stated preference for home care is not sufficient to justify an award on that basis. See for example *MacDonald v. Alderson* (1982), 20 C.C.L.T. 64 (Man. C.A.). In *Arce (Guardian ad litem of) v. Simon Fraser Health Region* (2003), 17 C.C.L.T. (3d) 97 (B.C.S.C.) the court concluded on the evidence that home care for a 79-year-old medically fragile plaintiff with quadriplegia was not reasonable or medically justifiable.

3. How does the court calculate the duration of the future care period? The insurance industry relies on actuarial tables of "impaired life expectancy" for particular injuries when computing the cost of an annuity for a structured settlement. The courts tend to estimate a longer expectancy period than the tables, which is another factor that makes structured awards less expensive than lump-sum awards. Should the courts use the actuarial tables? What are the limitations of applying actuarial evidence to individual cases? See generally Boyle & Murray, "Assessment of Damages: Economic and Actuarial Evidence" (1981) 19 Osgoode Hall L.J. 1; and Anderson, *Actuarial Evidence*, 2d ed. (1986).

4. What is the purpose of the contingency deduction in future care awards? How was the contingency figure determined in *Andrews*? The court seemed to assume that the contingencies would occur at regular intervals, which is most unlikely. If Andrews

were to spend the first 20% of his projected lifespan in an institution, thus using less capital than he would if he was at home, he would be over-compensated. However, if he was institutionalized for the last 20% of his life, he would have to spend more of his capital early in his projected lifespan and would be under-compensated.

The same issue arose in *Krangle (Guardian ad litem of) v. Brisco* (1997), 55 B.C.L.R. (3d) 23 (S.C.), rev'd (2000), 76 B.C.L.R. (3d) 1 (C.A.), rev'd [2002] 1 S.C.R. 205. A child was born with Down's syndrome. The defendant physician negligently failed to detect the condition during pregnancy, thereby depriving the mother of the opportunity to abort. The defendant was therefore liable to the parents for the cost of the child's care. The evidence indicated that the boy would leave his parents' home to live in an institution at the age of 19. At the time of trial, the existing legislation provided that, in such circumstances, the state would pay the associated expenses. However, the trial judge also found that there was a 5% chance that by the time the child actually turned 19 the legislation would no longer provide such benefits. The parents therefore were awarded $80,000, representing 5% of the total cost of future care that they had requested. That sum was either $80,000 too much or 95% too little. If the existing legislative scheme continued to operate throughout the child's adult life, then his parents did not require *any* money for that cost of care. In contrast, if the legislative scheme was altered so as to shift that cost of care onto the parents of a disabled adult child, then the plaintiffs received 95% less than required.

5. The lump-sum award is quantified on the assumption that the plaintiff will invest the sum prudently and that the income from the self-extinguishing fund will be sufficient to meet the projected care costs. Although the lump sum itself is not taxable, the interest it generates is taxable. Thus, after the trilogy, the Ontario courts increased the future care award by the estimated future tax liability to ensure that the fund would generate sufficient after-tax income to meet the cost of care. This increase is known as the "gross up." The Supreme Court of Canada has confirmed that it is appropriate to gross up the future care award: see *Watkins v. Olafson* (1989), 61 D.L.R. (4th) 577 (S.C.C.); and *Scarff v. Wilson* (1989), 61 D.L.R. (4th) 749 (S.C.C.).

6. Although the gross up is sound in principle, it is notoriously difficult and expensive to estimate future taxation in individual cases. The Ontario Law Reform Commission, *Report on Compensation for Personal Injuries and Death* (1987) at 139-47 has recommended revisions to the tax laws or standardized assumptions to alleviate these difficulties.

7. The amount for gross up is significant. A gross up in excess of 50% of the future care award has been approved by the courts. See for example *Giannone v. Weinberg* (1989), 68 O.R. (2d) 767 (C.A.); *Tronrud v. French* (1991), 84 D.L.R. (4th) 275 (Man. C.A.); and *MacDonald (Guardian ad litem of) v. Neufeld* (1993), 17 C.C.L.T. (2d) 201 (B.C.C.A.). If the gross up is greater than the expected taxes, as some believe is often the case, plaintiffs will not sacrifice the gross up by consenting to a structured judgment. See Feldthusen, "Mandatory Structured Judgments" (1989) 1 C.I.L. Rev. 1.

8. In *Townsend v. Kroppmanns*, [2004] 1 S.C.R. 315 the defendants argued that since the plaintiff intended to spend some of the lump-sum award immediately, to buy a house, the gross up should only be on the remaining amount, since only that lesser

amount would actually be invested. The court rejected this argument and confirmed that the gross up was on the full lump sum for future care. It stated at 324, "In assessing damages, courts do not take into consideration what victims actually do with the award." Relying on *Andrews*, the court noted at 325 that "The plaintiff is free to do whatever he or she wants with the sum of money awarded." In part this decision was based on concern that reducing the gross up would adversely affect impecunious plaintiffs, who are more likely to have to spend some of the lump sum immediately than are plaintiffs who are able to invest the whole award. Do you agree with this reasoning?

9. After the trilogy, it has been held that the award may include a sum to enable the plaintiff to hire a financial manager "if the plaintiff's level of intelligence is such that he is either unable to manage his affairs or lacks the acumen to invest funds awarded for future care so as to produce the requisite rate of return": *Insurance Corp. of British Columbia v. Mandzuk*, [1988] 2 S.C.R. 650 at 651; *Townsend, supra*. See also *Watkins, supra*. How many people do you think have the necessary acumen?

In the most serious cases the plaintiff's needs in this area will be even greater. In *Sandhu (Litigation guardian of) v. Wellington Place Apartments*, 2006 CarswellOnt 3668 (S.C.J.) (WLeC) a two-year-old suffered a severe brain injury. The jury awarded almost $11 million for the cost of future care. The court acknowledged that, in light of the size of the award, the plaintiff would need both a personal guardian, likely a relative, and a corporate guardian. The court awarded the plaintiff $1,795,800 to cover the costs, including legal fees, of these guardians.

10. In a typical case the plaintiff claims on his or her own behalf for the cost of future care. In some cases, like *Krangle, supra*, the future care claim is made by the parents of an injured child. Does this raise concerns about double recovery? Are these concerns resolved by the duty of care analysis? As noted in Chapter 12, in *Krangle* the defendant owed a duty of care to the parents but not to the child. Compare this result with *Bovingdon (Litigation guardian of) v. Hergott*, 2006 CarswellOnt 6237 (S.C.J.) (WLeC), additional reasons at (2006), 83 O.R. (3d) 465 (S.C.J.).

(c) PECUNIARY LOSS: LOST EARNING CAPACITY

ANDREWS v. GRAND & TOY ALBERTA LTD.

(1978), 83 D.L.R. (3d) 452 (S.C.C.)

DICKSON J.: . . . We must now gaze more deeply into the crystal ball. What sort of a career would the accident victim have had? What were his prospects and potential prior to the accident? It is not loss of earnings but, rather, loss of earning capacity for which compensation must be made. . . . A capital asset has been lost: what was its value?

(i) *Level of earnings*. The trial Judge fixed the projected level of earnings of Andrews at $830 per month, which would have been his earnings on January 1, 1973. The Appellate Division raised this to $1,200 per month, a figure between his present salary and the maximum for his type of work of $1,750 per month. Without doubt the value of Andrews' earning capacity over his working life is higher than his earnings at the time of the accident. Although I am inclined to view even that figure as somewhat conservative, I would affirm the holding of the Appellate Division that $1,200 per month represents a reasonable estimate of Andrews' future average level of earnings.

(ii) *Length of working life.* Counsel for the appellants object to the use of 55 rather than 65 as the projected retirement age for Andrews. It is agreed that he could retire on full pension at 55 if he stayed with his present employer, Canadian National Railways. I think it is reasonable to assume that he would, in fact, retire as soon as it was open for him to do so on full pension.

One must then turn to the mortality tables to determine the working life expectancy for the appellant over the period between the ages of 23 and 55. The controversial question immediately arises whether the capitalization of future earning capacity should be based on the expected working life span prior to the accident, or the shortened life expectancy. Does one give credit for the "lost years"? When viewed as the loss of a capital asset consisting of income-earning capacity rather than a loss of income, the answer is apparent; it must be the loss of that capacity which existed prior to the accident. This is the figure which best fulfils the principle of compensating the plaintiff for what he has lost. . . . I would accept . . . that Andrews had a working life expectancy of 30.81 years.

(iii) *Contingencies.* It is a general practice to take account of contingencies which might have affected future earnings, such as unemployment, illness, accidents and business depression. In the *Bisson* case, which also concerned a young quadriplegic, an allowance of 20% was made. There is much support for this view that such a discount for contingencies should be made. . . . There are, however, a number of qualifications which should be made. First, in many respects, these contingencies implicitly are already contained in an assessment of the projected average level of earnings of the injured person, for one must assume that this figure is a projection with respect to the real world of work, vicissitudes and all. Second, not all contingencies are adverse, as the above list would appear to indicate. As is said in *Bresatz v. Przibilla* (1962), 108 C.L.R. 541, in the Australian High Court, at p. 544: "Why count the possible buffets and ignore the rewards of fortune?" Finally, in a modern society there are many public and private schemes which cushion the individual against adverse contingencies. Clearly, the percentage deduction which is proper will depend on the facts of the individual case, particularly the nature of the plaintiff's occupation, but generally it will be small. . . .

In reducing Andrews' award by 20% Mr. Justice Kirby gives no reasons. The Appellate Division also applied a 20% reduction. It seems to me that actuarial evidence could be of great help here. Contingencies are susceptible to more exact calculation than is usually apparent in the cases. . . . In my view, some degree of specificity, supported by the evidence, ought to be forthcoming at trial.

The figure used to take account of contingencies is obviously an arbitrary one. The figure of 20% which was used in the lower Courts (and in many other cases), although not entirely satisfactory, should, I think, be accepted.

. . .

(iv) *Duplication with compensation for loss of future earnings.* It is clear that a plaintiff cannot recover for the expense of providing for basic necessities as part of the cost of future care while still recovering fully for prospective loss of earnings. Without the accident, expenses for such items as food, clothing and accommodation would have been paid for out of earnings. They are not an additional type of expense occasioned by the accident.

When calculating the damage award, however, there are two possible methods of proceeding. One method is to give the injured party an award for future care which makes no deduction in respect of the basic necessities for which he would have had to pay in any event. A deduction must then be made for the cost of such basic necessities when computing the award for loss of prospective earnings, *i.e.*, the award is on the basis of net earnings and not gross earnings. The alternative method is the reverse, *i.e.*, to deduct the cost of basic necessities when computing the award for future care and then to compute the earnings award on the basis of gross earnings.

The trial judge took the first approach, reducing loss of future earnings by 53%. The Appellate Division took the second. In my opinion, the approach of the trial Judge is to be preferred. This is in accordance with the principle which I believe should underlie the whole consideration of damages for personal injuries; that proper future care is the paramount goal of such damages. To determine accurately the needs and costs in respect of future care, basic living expenses should be included. The costs of necessaries when in an infirm state may well be different from those when in a state of health. Thus, while the types of expenses would have been incurred in any event, the level of expenses for the victim may be seen as attributable to the accident. In my opinion, the projected cost of necessities should, therefore, be included in calculating the cost of future care, and a percentage attributable to the necessities of a person in a normal state should be reduced from the award for future earnings.

. . .

NOTES AND QUESTIONS

1. How did Dickson J. determine the base figure that he used to calculate lost earning capacity? How accurate is this approach?

2. In *Arnold v. Teno* (1978), 83 D.L.R. (3d) 609 (S.C.C.), a case in which a four-year-old child was totally disabled, Spence J. arbitrarily selected $7,500 as an "equitable" yearly income for calculating the child's lost earning capacity. He stated that $5,000 was too low because that would relegate the child to poverty and that $10,000, the figure used by the Court of Appeal, was too high. Can such awards be properly made in the absence of actuarial or other expert evidence?

The damages trilogy helped to identify issues, such as future income, that required expert evidence. Lawyers now rely heavily on expert evidence in establishing base figures and contingencies in the calculation of both future care and earning capacity. Unlike *Teno*, the courts are no longer put in the position of having to make such unsubstantiated estimates.

What types of expert evidence would have been useful in *Teno*? Injured children now fare far better than the plaintiff in *Teno*. See Bruce, "The Calculation of an Infant's Lost Earnings: *Houle v. Calgary*" (1984) 22 Alta. L. Rev. 291; Sutherland, "Predicting a Child's Future Wage Loss" (1984) 42 The Advocate 169; and *O'Hara v. Belanger* (1989), 98 A.R. 86 (Q.B.).

3. Earning capacity is also difficult to estimate when the plaintiff is not a member of the paid labour force, as in the cases of students and homemakers. Many believe that the value of homemaking services, usually provided by women, is grossly undervalued by the courts. How should the lost earning capacity of a person who has decided to work in the home be calculated? See *Fobel v. Dean* (1991), 9 C.C.L.T. (2d) 87 (Sask. C.A.);

Benstead v. Murphy (1994), 22 C.C.L.T. (2d) 271 (Alta. C.A.); *Toneguzzo-Norvell (Guardian ad litem of) v. Burnaby Hospital* (1994), 110 D.L.R. (4th) 289 (S.C.C.); *Kroeker v. Jansen* (1995), 24 C.C.L.T. (2d) 113 (B.C.C.A.); and *McTavish v. MacGillivray*, [2000] 5 W.W.R. 554 (B.C.C.A.). See also Cassels, "Damages for Lost Earning Capacity: Women and Children Last!" (1992) 71 Can. Bar Rev. 445; Fast & Munro, "Toward Eliminating Gender Bias in Personal Injury Awards: Contributions from Family Economics" (1994) 32 Alta. L. Rev. 1; and Brown, "Exposing and Remedying Vexing Problems in Household Claims for Personal Injury and Wrongful Death Cases: An Economist's View" (1998) 19 Adv. Q. 83.

The courts have also recognized that damages may be available to reflect the fact that an injury has reduced the plaintiff's chances of entering into a (financially advantageous) "permanent interdependent relationship." See *Reekie v. Messervey* (1989), 59 D.L.R. (4th) 481 (B.C.C.A.); *Belyea v. Hammond* (2000), 231 N.B.R. (2d) 305 (C.A.); and *Walker v. Ritchie* (2005), 197 O.A.C. 81 (C.A.), varied (2006), 43 C.C.L.T. (3d) 1 (S.C.C.).

4. If a highly successful lawyer retired at age 40 to pursue a passion for sailing and was then rendered totally unable to work or sail, how should his or her lost earning capacity be calculated? See generally Reaume, "Rethinking Personal Injury Damages: Compensation For Lost Capacities" (1988) 67 Can. Bar Rev. 82.

In *Rowe v. Bobell Express Ltd.* (2005), 39 B.C.L.R. (4th) 185 (C.A.) the 73-year-old plaintiff was seriously injured in a car accident. At the time he was running a company which he predominantly owned, but he was not being paid by it. The court stated at para. 34, "Mr. Rowe was neither a wage-earner nor a salaried employee, nor did he receive remuneration for his work in the form of the profits of a closely-held company through which he carried on business. However, it is not disputed that, by reason of his injuries, he was unable to do many things that, but for his injuries, he could have done to earn income." As a postscript to the case, Justice Southin posed the following question: "Suppose a comparatively young man or woman with a private income who devotes his or her considerable time and talents without remuneration to charitable endeavours is so severely injured as to no longer be able to do so? Is it open to the tortfeasor to say to the plaintiff, 'You have suffered and will suffer no financial loss. The loss is that of the charities for whom you worked and would have continued to work. . .'." How would you answer this question?

5. How does the court estimate the length of time used in calculating the victim's earning capacity? Contrast this to the length of time used to calculate future care awards. What approach should the courts adopt if the plaintiff dies after trial but before an appeal? See *Bifolchi v. Sherar* (1998), 38 O.R. (3d) 772 (C.A.).

6. What is the purpose of the contingency deduction under lost earning capacity? Distinguish it from the contingency deduction under future care. How did the court arrive at the deduction in *Andrews*? Expert evidence now plays a much greater role and often suggests that positive and negative contingencies tend to cancel one another out. Positive contingencies include private and public plans which cushion the impact of unemployment. See *Fenn v. Peterborough* (1979), 104 D.L.R. (3d) 174 (Ont. C.A.); and *Graham v. Rourke* (1990), 75 O.R. (2d) 622 (C.A.). In *Herring v. England (Ministry of Defence)*

(2003), [2004] 1 All E.R. 44 (C.A.) Potter L.J. observed that the courts have historically overestimated negative contingencies in their awards.

7. Explain the problem of potential duplication between the future care and lost earning capacity awards. Outline the two approaches that Dickson J. identifies to address the duplication problem. The *Andrews* approach generally favours the plaintiff, especially when the unadjusted future care award is grossed up. Which approach is more consistent with the basic principle of damage quantification? See Feldthusen, "Duplication In Personal Injury Damage Awards" (1987) 66 Can. Bar Rev. 784.

8. The damages trilogy involved catastrophic injuries. In less serious cases different types of problems may arise, particularly in calculating damages for partial or temporary loss of earning capacity. See for example *Lan v. Wu* (1980), 14 C.C.L.T. 282 (B.C.C.A.); and *Engel v. Kam-Ppelle Holdings Ltd.* (1993), 99 D.L.R. (4th) 401 (S.C.C.). See also Westcott, "Calculating Loss of Opportunity for Career Advancement: Clearing the Clouds in the Crystal Ball" (1983) 4 Adv. Q. 268; and Wunder, "Compensation for the Plaintiff's Competitive Position on the Labour Market Being Compromised: The Concept and the Law" (1984) 28 C.C.L.T. 117.

9. Given that damages are intended to place the plaintiff in the position that he or she would have been in if the tort had not been committed, the measure of relief awarded with respect to lost earning capacity depends upon the plaintiff's pre-accident employment prospects. It has been argued, however, that those prospects are often subject to discriminatory forces. On average, women earn approximately 64% of what men earn. Consequently, if an infant female suffers permanent and disabling injuries, she is apt to receive considerably less in damages than a similarly injured infant male. The same pattern emerges between aboriginal and non-aboriginal plaintiffs and between disabled and non-disabled plaintiffs. In several cases the courts have been asked to disregard the effect of discriminatory societal forces and to assess damages for injured females on the basis of male income statistics: *Tucker (Guardian ad litem of) v. Asleson* (1993), 102 D.L.R. (4th) 518 (B.C.C.A.); *Toneguzzo-Norvell (Guardian ad litem of) v. Burnaby Hospital, supra*; *MacCabe v. Westlock Roman Catholic Separate School District No. 110* (1998), 226 A.R. 1 (Q.B.), rev'd [2002] 1 W.W.R. 610 (Alta. C.A.); and *Walker v. Ritchie, supra*.

Is this approach compatible with the fundamental aim of tort damages? What are the theoretical and practical implications of this approach? See Gibson, "The Gendered Wage Dilemma" in Cooper-Stephenson & Gibson, eds., *Tort Theory* (1993); and McInnes, "The Gendered Earnings Proposal in Tort Law" (1998) 77 Can. Bar Rev. 153. See also Cassels, "(In)Equality and the Law of Tort: Gender, Race and the Assessment of Damages" (1995) 17 Adv. Q. 158.; Adjin-Tettey, "Contemporary Approaches to Compensating Female Tort Victims for Incapacity to Work" (2000) 38 Alta. L. Rev. 504; Cooper-Stephenson, "Sliding Doors: Alternative Life Patterns in Personal Injury Damages" in Beaulac, Pitel & Schulz, eds., *The Joy of Torts* (2003) 315; and Adjin-Tettey, "Replicating and Perpetuating Inequalities in Personal Injury Claims Through Female-Specific Contingencies" (2004) 49 McGill L.J. 309.

(d) CONSIDERATIONS RELEVANT TO BOTH HEADS OF PECUNIARY LOSS

ANDREWS v. GRAND & TOY ALBERTA LTD.

(1978), 83 D.L.R. (3d) 452 (S.C.C.)

DICKSON J.: . . . (i) *Capitalization rate: allowance for inflation and the rate of return on investments*. What rate of return should the Court assume the appellant will be able to obtain on his investment of the award? How should the Court recognize future inflation? Together these considerations will determine the discount rate to use in actuarially calculating the lump-sum award.

The approach at trial was to take as a rate of return the rental value of money which might exist during periods of economic stability, and consequently to ignore inflation. This approach is widely referred to as the Lord Diplock approach, as he lent it his support in *Mallett v. McMonagle*, [1970] A.C. 166. Although this method of proceeding has found favour in several jurisdictions in this country and elsewhere, it has an air of unreality. Stable, non-inflationary economic conditions do not exist at present, nor did they exist in the recent past, nor are they to be expected in the foreseeable future. In my opinion, it would be better to proceed from what known factors are available rather than to ignore economic reality. Analytically, the alternate approach to assuming a stable economy is to use existing interest rates and then make an allowance for the long-term expected rate of inflation. At trial the expert actuary, Mr. Grindley, testified as follows:

> Yes, as I mentioned yesterday, I was comfortable with that assumption 5% interest because it produces the same result as for example 8% interest and 3% inflation.
>
> . . .
>
> I would be happy to use either of the following two packages of assumption, either an 8% interest rate combined with provision for amounts which would increase 3% in every year in the future or a 5% interest rate and level amount, level amounts, that is no allowance for inflation.

One thing is abundantly clear; present interest rates should not be used with no allowance for future inflation. To do so would be patently unfair to the plaintiff. It is not, however, the level of inflation in the short term for which allowance must be made, but that predicted over the long term. It is this expectation which is built into present interest rates for long-term investments. It is also this level of inflation which may at present be predicted to operate over the lifetime of the plaintiff to increase the cost of care for him at the level accepted by the Court, and to erode the value of the sum provided for lost earning capacity.

. . .

The approach which I would adopt, therefore, is to use present rates of return on long-term investments and to make some allowance for the effects of future inflation. Once this approach is adopted, the result, in my opinion, is different from the 5% discount figure accepted by the trial Judge. While there was much debate at trial over a difference of a half to one percentage point, I think it is clear from the evidence that high quality long-term investments were available at time of trial at rates of return in excess of 10%. On the other hand, evidence was specifically introduced that the former head of the Economic Council of Canada, Dr. Deutsch, had recently forecast a rate of inflation of

3.5% over the long-term future. These figures must all be viewed flexibly. In my opinion, they indicate that the appropriate discount rate is approximately 7%. I would adopt that figure. It appears to me to be the correct result of the approach I have adopted, *i.e.*, having regard to present investment market conditions and making an appropriate allowance for future inflation. I would, accordingly, vary to 7% the discount rate to be used in calculating the present value of the awards for future care and loss of earnings in this case. The result in future cases will depend upon the evidence adduced in those cases.

(ii) *Allowance for tax.* In *The Queen v. Jennings* [(1966), 57 D.L.R. (2d) 654 (S.C.C.)], this Court held that an award for prospective income should be calculated with no deduction for tax which might have been attracted had it been earned over the working life of the plaintiff. This results from the fact that it is earning capacity and not lost earnings which is the subject of compensation. For the same reason, no consideration should be taken of the amount by which the income from the award will be reduced by payment of taxes on the interest, dividends, or capital gain. A capital sum is appropriate to replace the lost capital asset of earning capacity. Tax on income is irrelevant either to decrease the sum for taxes the victim would have paid on income from his job, or to increase it for taxes he will now have to pay on income from the award.

In contrast with the situation in personal injury cases, awards under the *Fatal Accident Act*, R.S.A. 1970, c. 138, should reflect tax considerations, since they are to compensate dependants for the loss of support payments made by the deceased. These support payments could only come out of take-home pay, and the payments from the award will only be received net of taxes: see the contemporaneous decision of this Court in *Keizer v. Hanna et al.* (1978), 82 D.L.R. (3d) 449.

The impact of taxation upon the income from the capital sum for future care is mitigated by . . . the *Income Tax Act*. . . ., in respect of the deduction of medical expenses, which provides that medical expenses in excess of 3% of the taxpayer's income includes "remuneration for one full-time attendant upon an individual who was a taxpayer . . . in a self-contained domestic establishment in which the cared for person lived." This exemption, I should think, permits a deduction for the payment of one full-time attendant for seven days a week, regardless of whether this attendance is provided by several attendants working over 24-hour periods, or one person working 24-hour shifts seven days a week.

The exact tax burden is extremely difficult to predict, as the rate and coverage of taxes swing with the political winds. What concerns us here is whether some allowance must be made to adjust the amount assessed for future care in light of the reduction from taxation. No such allowance was made by the Courts below. Elaborate calculations were provided by the appellant to give an illusion of accuracy to this aspect of the wholly speculative projection of future costs. Because of the provision made in the *Income Tax Act* and because of the position taken in the Alberta Courts, I would make no allowance for that item. The Legislature might well consider a more generous income tax treatment of cases where a fund is established by judicial decision and the sole purpose of the fund is to provide treatment or care of an accident victim.

One subsidiary point should be affirmed with respect to the determination of the present value of the cost of future care. The calculations should provide for a self-extinguishing sum. To allow a residual capital amount would be to over-compensate the injured person by creating an estate for him. This point was accepted by the lower Courts and not challenged by the parties.

. . .

NOTES AND QUESTIONS

1. What is the purpose of the discount or capitalization rate? A 7% discount rate, as adopted in *Andrews*, means that the lump sum will be quantified on the assumption that if prudently invested it will generate real earnings (net of inflation) of 7% per year.

2. The 7% discount rate has been subjected to severe criticism. Experience indicates that in the long run the gap between the rate of interest and the rate of inflation will be in the vicinity of 2 to 2.5%. See Feldthusen & McNair, "General Damages in Personal Injury Suits: The Supreme Court's Trilogy" (1978) 28 U.T.L.J. 381; Rea, "Inflation and the Law of Contracts and Torts" (1982) 14 Ottawa L. Rev. 465; and Bale, "Adding Insult to Injury: The Inappropriate Use of Discount Rates to Determine Damage Awards" (1983) 28 McGill L.J. 1015.

3. It is now clear that the calculation of the discount rate is a factual issue to be determined in individual cases. In *Lewis v. Todd* (1980), 115 D.L.R. (3d) 257 (S.C.C.) the court indicated that it lacked the authority to "legislate" a fixed discount rate and that even if it had such authority it was not sufficiently certain of the issues to exercise it.

The costs of litigating the appropriate discount rate on a case-by-case basis are substantial and most Canadian jurisdictions have passed legislation to address this problem. See for example the Ontario Rules of Civil Procedure, R.R.O. 1990, Reg. 194, R. 53.09. Fixed legislative rates are between 2.5 and 3.5%, considerably lower than that used in the trilogy.

It is possible for the courts, in some situations, to depart from the legislated discount rate. See *Ligate v. Abick* (1996), 28 O.R. (3d) 1 (C.A.). In *Walker v. Ritchie* (2005), 197 O.A.C. 81 (C.A.), varied (2006), 43 C.C.L.T. (3d) 1 (S.C.C.) the Court of Appeal stated that "evidence called before the trial judge established that the costs of professional services are increasing faster than the rate of inflation, thus justifying the variation to a 1.5% discount rate." In *Warriner v. Warriner* (2002), [2003] 3 All E.R. 447 (C.A.) the court noted that in the interests of certainty departures from the established rate should be rare.

For a legislative summary and discussion, see The Ontario Law Reform Commission, *Report on Compensation for Personal Injuries and Death* (1987) at 218-25.

4. Why does the court not consider the taxes that the plaintiff would have paid in calculating lost earning capacity? This failure to consider taxes would appear to overcompensate the plaintiff. This is offset, albeit not perfectly, by the fact that the plaintiff will pay tax on the investment earnings from the earning capacity award, which is not grossed up.

5. Why should the calculation of the future care award provide for a self-extinguishing sum? Why is the same not true of the earning capacity head?

6. In *Townsend v. Kroppmanns*, [2004] 1 S.C.R. 315 the defendants argued that because the plaintiff was being awarded the cost of paying a financial manager, a higher discount rate should be used because with professional assistance the plaintiff would

achieve a higher rate of return. The court rejected this argument, in part on the basis that to accept it would defeat the point of having the discount rate set by statute or regulation.

(e) NON-PECUNIARY LOSS

ANDREWS v. GRAND & TOY ALBERTA LTD.

(1978), 83 D.L.R. (3d) 452 (S.C.C.)

DICKSON J.: . . . Andrews used to be a healthy young man, athletically active and socially congenial. Now he is a cripple, deprived of many of life's pleasures and subjected to pain and disability. For this, he is entitled to compensation. But the problem here is qualitatively different from that of pecuniary losses. There is no medium of exchange for happiness. There is no market for expectation of life. The monetary evaluation of non-pecuniary losses is a philosophical and policy exercise more than a legal or logical one. The award must be fair and reasonable, fairness being gauged by earlier decisions; but the award must also of necessity be arbitrary or conventional. No money can provide true restitution. Money can provide for proper care: this is the reason that I think the paramount concern of the Courts when awarding damages for personal injuries should be to assure that there will be adequate future care.

However, if the principle of the paramountcy of care is accepted, then it follows that there is more room for the consideration of other policy factors in the assessment of damages for non-pecuniary losses. In particular, this is the area where the social burden of large awards deserves considerable weight. The sheer fact is that there is no objective yardstick for translating non-pecuniary losses, such as pain and suffering and loss of amenities, into monetary terms. This area is open to widely extravagant claims. It is in this area that awards in the United States have soared to dramatically high levels in recent years. Statistically, it is the area where the danger of excessive burden of expense is greatest.

It is also the area where there is the clearest justification for moderation. As one English commentator has suggested, there are three theoretical approaches to the problem of non-pecuniary loss (A.J. Ogus, "Damages for Lost Amenities: For a Foot, a Feeling or a Function?", 35 Mod. L. Rev. 1 (1972)). The first, the "conceptual" approach, treats each faculty as a proprietary asset with an objective value, independent of the individual's own use or enjoyment of it. This was the ancient "bot", or tariff system, which prevailed in the days of King Alfred, when a thumb was worth 30 shillings. Our law has long since thought such a solution unsubtle. The second, the "personal" approach, values the injury in terms of the loss of human happiness by the particular victim. The third, or "functional" approach, accepts the personal premise of the second, but rather than attempting to set a value on lost happiness, it attempts to assess the compensation required to provide the injured person "with reasonable solace for his misfortune." "Solace" in this sense is taken to mean physical arrangements which can make his life more endurable rather than "solace" in the sense of sympathy. To my mind, this last approach has much to commend it, as it provides a rationale as to why money is considered compensation for non-pecuniary losses such as loss of amenities, pain and suffering, and loss of expectation of life. Money is awarded because it will serve a useful function in making up for what has been lost in the only way possible, accepting that what has been lost is incapable of being replaced in any direct way. As Windeyer, J., said in *Skelton v. Collins* [(1966), 115 C.L.R. 94 (H.C.A.)]:

> . . .he is, I do not doubt, entitled to compensation for what he suffers. Money may be compensation for him if having it can give him pleasure or satisfaction. . .But the money is not then a recompense for a loss of something having a money value. It is given as some consolation or solace for the distress that is the consequence of a loss on which no monetary value can be put.

If damages for non-pecuniary loss are viewed from a functional perspective, it is reasonable that large amounts should not be awarded once a person is properly provided for in terms of future care for his injuries and disabilities. The money for future care is to provide physical arrangements for assistance, equipment and facilities directly related to the injuries. Additional money to make life more endurable should then be seen as providing more general physical arrangements above and beyond those relating directly to the injuries. The result is a coordinated and interlocking basis for compensation, and a more rational justification for non-pecuniary loss compensation.

However one may view such awards in a theoretical perspective, the amounts are still largely arbitrary or conventional. As Lord Denning, M.R., said in *Ward v. James*, [1965] 1 All E.R. 563, there is a great need in this area for assessability, uniformity and predictability. In my opinion, this does not mean that the courts should not have regard to the individual situation of the victim. On the contrary, they must do so to determine what has been lost. For example, the loss of a finger would be a greater loss of amenities for an amateur pianist than for a person not engaged in such an activity. Greater compensation would be required to provide things and activities which would function to make up for this loss. But there should be guidelines for the translation into monetary terms of what has been lost. There must be an exchange rate, albeit conventional. In *Warren v. King, supra*, at p. 528 the following *dictum* of Harman, L.J., appears, which I would adopt, in respect of the assessment of non-pecuniary loss for a living plaintiff:

> It seems to me that the first element in assessing such compensation is not to add up items as loss of pleasures, of earnings, of marriage prospects, of children and so on, but to consider the matter from the other side, what can be done to alleviate the disaster to the victim, what will it cost to enable her to live as tolerably as may be in the circumstances.

Cases like the present enable the Court to establish a rough upper parameter on these awards. It is difficult to conceive of a person of his age losing more than Andrews has lost. Of course, the figures must be viewed flexibly in future cases in recognition of the inevitable differences in injuries, the situation of the victim, and changing economic conditions.

The amounts of such awards should not vary greatly from one part of the country to another. Everyone in Canada, wherever he may reside, is entitled to a more or less equal measure of compensation for similar non-pecuniary loss. Variation should be made for what a particular individual has lost in the way of amenities and enjoyment of life, and for what will function to make up for this loss, but variation should not be made merely for the Province in which he happens to live.

There has been a significant increase in the size of awards under this head in recent years. As Moir, J.A., of the Appellate Division of the Alberta Supreme Court, has warned: "To my mind, damages under the head of loss of amenities will go up and up until they are stabilized by the Supreme Court of Canada": *Hamel et al. v. Prather et al.* (1976), 66 D.L.R. (3d) 109 at p. 127. . ., In my opinion, this time has come.

It is customary to set only one figure for all non-pecuniary loss, including such factors as pain and suffering, loss of amenities, and loss of expectation of life. This is a sound practice. Although these elements are analytically distinct, they overlap and merge at the edges and in practice. To suffer pain is surely to lose an amenity of a happy life at that time. To lose years of one's expectation of life is to lose all amenities for the lost period, and to cause mental pain and suffering in the contemplation of this prospect. These problems, as well as the fact that these losses have the common trait of irreplaceability, favour a composite award for all non-pecuniary losses.

There is an extensive review of authorities in the Court of Appeal judgment in this case as well as in the *Thornton* and *Teno* cases, *supra*, to which I have referred. I need not review these past authorities. What is important is the general picture. It is clear that until very recently damages for non-pecuniary losses, even from very serious injuries such as quadriplegia, were substantially below \$100,000. Recently, though, the figures have increased markedly. In *Jackson v. Millar et al.* (1975), 59 D.L.R. (3d) 246. . ., this Court affirmed a figure of \$150,000 for non-pecuniary loss in an Ontario case of a paraplegic. However, this was done essentially on the principle of non-interference with awards allowed by provincial Courts of Appeal. The need for a general assessment with respect to damages for non-pecuniary loss, which is now apparent, was not as evident at that time. Even in Ontario, prior to these recent cases, general damages allocable for non-pecuniary loss, such as pain and suffering and loss of amenities, were well below \$100,000.

In the present case, \$150,000 was awarded at trial, but this amount was reduced to \$100,000 by the Appellate Division. In *Thornton* and *Teno* \$200,000 was awarded in each case, unchanged in the provincial Courts of Appeal.

I would adopt as the appropriate award in the case of a young adult quadriplegic like Andrews the amount of \$100,000. Save in exceptional circumstances, this should be regarded as an upper limit of non-pecuniary loss in cases of this nature.

NOTES AND QUESTIONS

1. What is the purpose of an award for non-pecuniary loss? What are the differences among the three methods of assessing non-pecuniary loss according to the article by A.J. Ogus cited in *Andrews*? Which approach do you prefer? See Klar, "The Assessment of Damages for Non-Pecuniary Losses" (1978) 5 C.C.L.T. 262; and Ritchie, "Non-pecuniary Damages" in *Special Lectures of the Law Society of Upper Canada: Law of Remedies* (1995). In *Lindal v. Lindal* (1981), 129 D.L.R. (3d) 263 (S.C.C.) the court affirmed the functional approach and elaborated on how that approach should be applied. *Lindal* also approved adjusting the \$100,000 figure for inflation.

2. The Supreme Court of Canada has indicated that a plaintiff can recover damages in excess of the upper limit if he or she can prove exceptional circumstances in which a larger award is necessary to provide solace. Nevertheless, the courts have rarely granted such awards. See *Fenn v. Peterborough* (1979), 104 D.L.R. (3d) 174 (S.C.C).

3. By the late 1990s the upper limit was approximately \$260,000: see *Roberts v. Morana* (1997), 38 C.C.L.T. (2d) 1 (Ont. Gen. Div.). It had further increased to between \$290,000 and \$300,000 by the middle of the current decade: see *Lee v. Dawson* (2006),

51 B.C.L.R. (4th) 221 (C.A.); and *McIntyre v. Grigg* (2006), 83 O.R. (3d) 161 (C.A.). In *Sandhu (Litigation guardian of) v. Wellington Place Apartments*, 2006 CarswellOnt 3668 (S.C.J.) (WLeC) the court awarded $311,000.

4. In *ter Neuzen v. Korn*, [1995] 3 S.C.R. 674 the court held that a non-pecuniary award of $460,000 was inappropriate and ordered that the jury in the new trial be instructed on the approximate upper limit for such damages. But in *Hill v. Church of Scientology of Toronto* (1995), 126 D.L.R. (4th) 129 (S.C.C.) the court approved a $300,000 non-pecuniary general damage award in addition to awards of $500,000 in aggravated and $800,000 in punitive damages. The court said that the cap on non-pecuniary awards does not apply to defamation. Is such a distinction justifiable?

In *Young v. Bella*, [2006] 1 S.C.R. 108 a woman who was negligently reported as a suspected sexual abuser of children was awarded $430,000 in non-pecuniary damages by a jury. On appeal the defendants argued that this exceeded the upper limit. The court, drawing on *Hill*, held at para. 65 that it was "not established why the policy considerations which arise from negligence causing catastrophic personal injuries, in the contexts of accident and medical malpractice, should be extended to cap a jury award in a case such as the present." What is the rationale for the upper limit? Why does it not apply in cases like *Hill* and *Young*?

5. In *Andrews* Dickson J. stated that non-pecuniary loss "is the area where the social burden of large awards deserves considerable weight." Is the justification he provides compelling? Why should this burden fall on the victims of catastrophic personal injuries and not on those who are defamed or those who would otherwise receive punitive damages?

Assume that a homemaker with no intention of joining the paid workforce is badly burned and suffers severe ongoing pain and permanent disfigurement. How would his or her damages be assessed under *Andrews*? Does the so-called functional approach result in an injustice in cases such as these?

6. Prior to *Andrews*, non-pecuniary losses were divided into claims for pain and suffering, loss of amenities and loss of expectation of life. Traditionally, the award for pain and suffering was assessed on a subjective basis, in terms of the actual pain and suffering the plaintiff experienced. The loss of amenities was assessed objectively in terms of how a reasonable person in the plaintiff's position would have valued the loss of enjoyment of life. Although the courts stated that awards for loss of expectation of life were not simply conventional sums, these awards were limited to several thousand dollars. S. Waddams suggests that these categories governing non-pecuniary loss may no longer apply because *Andrews* requires a "functional approach": Waddams, *The Law of Damages*, 4th ed. (2004) at 3.650-3.690.

See *Knutson v. Farr* (1984), 30 C.C.L.T. 8 (B.C.C.A.) which clearly supports Waddams' view. *Knutson* indicated that the functional approach meant that an unconscious plaintiff was not entitled to compensation under this head. See also Mew, "Comment" (1986) 64 Can. Bar Rev. 562; and Waddams, "Compensation for Non-Pecuniary Loss: Is There a Case for Legislative Intervention?" (1985) 63 Can. Bar Rev. 734.

7. The cap has come under increasing scrutiny, particularly in British Columbia. See the critical comments in *Boyd v. Harris* (2004), 24 B.C.L.R. (4th) 155 (C.A.); *Dilello*

v. Montgomery (2005), 37 B.C.L.R. (4th) 72 (C.A.); and *Courdin v. Meyers* (2005), 37 B.C.L.R. (4th) 222 (C.A.). In *Dilello*, the Court of Appeal stated that "the attempt by this and other courts to fit juries' damage awards for personal injuries into a grid or tariff system with an upper limit of any amount (that has not been enacted by a legislature) is an unjustified interference with the function of the jury as finders of fact, and a fettering of the proper principles of appellate review." In *Lee v. Dawson, supra*, the jury awarded non-pecuniary damages of $2 million. This was reduced to $292,000 by the trial judge to comply with the cap. The Court of Appeal thought that "the time may have come for the rationalization or conceptual underpinning for having a rough upper limit on non-pecuniary damages to be re-examined," but felt bound to follow *Andrews* as binding authority. The Supreme Court of Canada refused leave to appeal: 2006 CarswellBC 2594.

Even if the cap remains in place, what impact could these sentiments have on the size of awards?

8. Some commentators have argued for the abolition of non-pecuniary damages. See O'Connell & Simon, *Payment for Pain & Suffering: Who Wants What When and Why?* (1972); Fleming, "Damages for Non-Material Loss" in Law Society of Upper Canada, *Special Lectures on New Developments in the Law of Torts* (1973) 1; Ontario Law Reform Commission, *Report on Motor Vehicle Accident Compensation* (1973); Woodhouse, *The Report of the National Committee of Inquiry on Compensation and Rehabilitation in Australia* (1974); and Pearson, *The Report of the Royal Commission on Civil Liability and Compensation for Personal Injury* (1978). See more recently Avraham, "Should Pain-and-Suffering Damages Be Abolished from Tort Law? More Experimental Evidence" (2005) 55 U.T.L.J. 941. One argument for retaining non-pecuniary damages proceeds from what is called the "*ex ante* insurance perspective," which is based on the view that rational people would not insure themselves against non-pecuniary loss because money cannot compensate for such loss. See generally The Ontario Law Reform Commission, *Report on Compensation for Personal Injuries and Death* (1987) at 79-114 which supports the present law. For the approach in England see *Heil v. Rankin*, [2001] Q.B. 272 (C.A.).

9. There is some debate about whether the cap on non-pecuniary damages includes any amount awarded as aggravated damages. This is rarely in issue in negligence cases because they rarely trigger aggravated damages. But the issue can arise in intentional tort cases: see *Bob v. Bellerose* (2003), 227 D.L.R. (4th) 602 (B.C.C.A.).

3. Survival of Actions and Dependants' Claims

(a) SURVIVAL OF ACTIONS

At common law when an individual died all outstanding or potential causes of action that could have otherwise been brought by or against the deceased were extinguished. Legislation has been enacted in England and all Canadian jurisdictions to nullify this common law rule. The statutes, which vary from jurisdiction to jurisdiction, allow the deceased's estate to maintain legal actions that the deceased could have otherwise brought. These statutes also allow actions to be brought against the deceased's estate that could have been brought against the deceased. Typically, however, the legislation excludes specified causes of action, such as defamation, malicious prosecution and false imprisonment. Most jurisdictions also exclude certain types of damages, such as non-pecuniary and punitive damages. The following provisions of the Alberta and Ontario legislation illustrate some common features of the survival of action statutes.

SURVIVAL OF ACTIONS ACT

R.S.A. 2000, c. S-27

2 A cause of action vested in a person who dies after January 1, 1979 survives for the benefit of the person's estate.

3 A cause of action existing against a person who dies after January 1, 1979 survives against the person's estate.

4 If a cause of action for damages suffered by reason of an act or omission would have existed against a person had that person not died at or before the time the damage was suffered, the cause of action is deemed to have existed against the person before the person's death.

5 (1) If a cause of action survives under section 2, only those damages that resulted in actual financial loss to the deceased or the deceased's estate are recoverable.

(2) Without restricting the generality of subsection (1), the following are not recoverable:

(a) punitive or exemplary damages;

(b damages for loss of expectation of life, pain and suffering, physical disfigurement or loss of amenities;

(c) damages in relation to future earnings, including damages for loss of earning capacity, ability to earn or chance of future earnings.

(3) Subsection (2)(c) applies only to causes of action that arise after the coming into force of this section.

6 If the death of a person was caused by an act or omission that gives rise to a cause of action, the damages shall be calculated without reference to a loss or gain to the person's estate as a result of the person's death, but reasonable expenses of the funeral and the disposal of the body of the deceased may be included in the damages awarded, if the expenses were, or liability for them was, incurred by the estate.

7 A cause of action that survives under this Act and a judgment or order on it or relating to the costs of it is an asset or liability, as the case may be, of the estate to which the cause of action relates.

TRUSTEE ACT

R.S.O. 1990, c. T.23

38(1) Except in cases of libel and slander, the executor or administrator of any deceased person may maintain an action for all torts or injuries to the person or to the property of the deceased in the same manner and with the same rights and remedies as the deceased would, if living, have been entitled to do, and the damages when recovered shall form part of the personal estate of the deceased but if death results from such injuries no damages shall be allowed for the death or for the loss of the expectation of life, but this proviso is not in derogation of any rights conferred by Part V of the *Family Law Act*.

(2) Except in cases of libel and slander, if a deceased person committed or is by law liable for a wrong to another in respect of his or her person or to another person's property, the person wronged may maintain an action against the executor or administrator of the person who committed or is by law liable for the wrong.

(3) An action under this section shall not be brought after the expiration of two years from the death of the deceased.

(b) FATAL ACCIDENTS LEGISLATION

It was established in *Baker v. Bolton* (1808), 1 Camp. 493 (H.L.) that an individual has no common law cause of action for losses that he or she suffers as a result of the death of another person. This common law rule has been superseded by fatal accidents legislation which is designed to compensate the deceased's dependants for the losses they suffer as a result of the death. Generally the purpose of this legislation is to put the dependants in the position they would have been in had the victim not been wrongfully killed. Most of the provincial legislation is modelled after the 1846 English legislation, commonly referred to as *Lord Campbell's Act*. The Nova Scotia legislation illustrates many of the common features of the provincial statutes. We have also included the Ontario provision which provides for far broader recovery.

FATAL INJURIES ACT
R.S.N.S. 1989, c. 163

Liability

3 Where the death of a person has been caused by such wrongful act, neglect or default of another as would, if death had not ensued, have entitled the person injured to maintain an action and recover damages in respect thereto, in such case, the person who would have been liable if death had not ensued shall be liable to an action of damages, notwithstanding the death of the person injured, and although the death has been caused under such circumstances as amount in law to a crime.

Damages

5 (1) Every action brought under this Act shall be for the benefit of the wife, husband, parent, or child of such deceased person and the jury may give such damages as they think proportioned to the injury resulting from such death to the persons respectively for whose benefit such action was brought, and the amount so recovered, after deducting the costs not recovered, if any, from the defendant, shall be divided among such persons in such shares as the jury by their verdict find and direct.

(2) In subsection (1), "damages" means pecuniary and non-pecuniary damages and, without restricting the generality of this definition, includes

(a) out-of-pocket expenses reasonably incurred for the benefit of the deceased;

(b) a reasonable allowance for travel expenses incurred in visiting the deceased between the time of the injury and the death;

(c) where, as a result of the injury, a person for whose benefit the action is brought provided nursing, housekeeping or other services for the deceased between the time of the injury and the death, a reasonable allowance for loss of income or the value of the services; and

(d) an amount to compensate for the loss of guidance, care and companionship that a person for whose benefit the action is brought might reasonably have expected to receive from the deceased if the death had not occurred.

(3) In assessing the damage in any action there shall not be taken into account any sum paid or payable on the death of the deceased, whether by way of pension or proceeds of insurance, or any future premiums payable under any contract of assurance or insurance.

(4) In an action brought under this Act where funeral expenses have been incurred by the parties for whose benefit the action is brought, damages may be awarded for reasonable necessary expenses of the burial of the deceased, including transportation and things supplied and services rendered in connection therewith.

Statement of Claim

6 In every action the plaintiff on the record shall set forth, in his statement of claim, or deliver therewith to the defendant, or his solicitor, full particulars of the person or persons for and on behalf of whom such action was brought and of the nature of the claim in respect to which damages are sought to be recovered.

Apportionment by Judge

9 In all cases where for any reason the compensation is not apportioned among the several persons entitled under this Act, a judge may apportion the same and dispose of the costs of the application and inquiry as he thinks just.

Limitation of Action

10 Not more than one action shall lie for and in respect to the same subject-matter of complaint and every such action shall be commenced within twelve months after the death of the deceased person.

FAMILY LAW ACT

R.S.O. 1990, c. F.3

Dependants' Claim for Damages

61. (1) If a person is injured or killed by the fault or neglect of another under circumstances where the person is entitled to recover damages, or would have been entitled if not killed, the spouse, as defined in Part III (Support Obligations), children, grandchildren, parents, grandparents, brothers and sisters of the person are entitled to recover their pecuniary loss resulting from the injury or death from the person from whom the person injured or killed is entitled to recover or would have been entitled if not killed, and to maintain an action for the purpose in a court of competent jurisdiction.

(2) The damages recoverable in a claim under subsection (1) may include,

(a) actual expenses reasonably incurred for the benefit of the person injured or killed;

(b) actual funeral expenses reasonably incurred;

(c) a reasonable allowance for travel expenses actually incurred in visiting the person during his or her treatment or recovery;

(d) where, as a result of the injury, the claimant provides nursing, housekeeping or other services for the person, a reasonable allowance for loss of income or the value of the services; and

(e) an amount to compensate for the loss of guidance, care and companionship that the claimant might reasonably have expected to receive from the person if the injury or death had not occurred.

NOTES AND QUESTIONS

1. What is the rationale for restricting the applicable actions and kinds of damages under the provincial survival legislation and the provincial fatal accident legislation? For a discussion of this legislation see *Duncan Estate v. Baddeley* (2000), 266 A.R. 323 (C.A.); *Macartney v. Warner* (2000), 46 O.R. (3d) 641 (C.A.); *MacLean v. MacDonald* (2002), 11 C.C.L.T. (3d) 57 (N.S.C.A.); and *MacKay Estate v. Smith* (2003), 230 Nfld. & P.E.I.R. 178 (P.E.I.C.A.). See also Cooper-Stephenson, *Personal Injury Damages in Canada*, 2d ed. (1996) at 721-46; Brown, "*Duncan v. Baddeley*: Reconciling the 'Lost Years' Deduction with Fatal Accident Cases" (1997) 35 Alta. L. Rev. 1108; and Waddams, *The Law of Damages*, 4th ed. (2004), ch. 12. Note that at the time *Duncan* was decided, s. 5 of the Alberta *Survival of Actions Act* had not yet been amended to exclude claims for loss of earning capacity or future earnings.

2. How does the purpose of the survival legislation differ from that of the fatal accidents legislation? What parties are allowed to recover under each type of legislation? Is there a potential for double recovery because of the overlapping benefits? Generally the actions are brought together to reduce this problem: see *Balkos v. Cook* (1990), 75 O.R. (2d) 593 (C.A.). For a discussion of how the two types of legislation might be combined see Waddams, "Damages For Wrongful Death: Has Lord Campbell's Act Outlived Its Usefulness?" (1984) 47 Mod. L. Rev. 437.

3. In what specific ways is the scope of the Ontario *Family Law Act* broader than that of the Nova Scotia *Fatal Injuries Act*? How do you suppose Nova Scotia deals with these claims in the absence of a statutory right such as that in the Ontario statute? What are the advantages of each approach?

4. Dependants' claims under the Ontario *Family Law Act* have generated considerable litigation and controversy. One of the interesting issues is the status of claims brought in respect of, or on behalf of, persons who acquire dependency status by sub-

sequent birth or marriage. The authorities are reviewed in *Garland v. Rowsell* (1990), 73 O.R. (2d) 280 (Dist. Ct.). Another interesting issue is the scope of non-pecuniary damages available under s. 61(2)(e) (compare with s. 5(2)(d) in Nova Scotia). It has been held that a dependant is entitled to damages under s. 61(2)(e) for loss of care, guidance and companionship in cases of both death and injury. See generally *Mason v. Peters* (1982), 39 O.R. (2d) 27 (C.A.); *Wessell v. Kinsmen Club of Sault Ste. Marie Ont. Inc.* (1982), 37 O.R. (2d) 481 (H.C.); *Reidy v. McLeod* (1984), 30 C.C.L.T. 183 (Ont. H.C.); *Gervais v. Richard* (1984), 48 O.R. (2d) 191 (H.C.); *Seede v. Camco Inc.* (1985), 50 O.R. (2d) 218 (S.C.); and *Nielsen v. Kaufmann* (1986), 54 O.R. (2d) 188 (C.A.). See also *Macartney v. Warner* (2000), 46 O.R. (3d) 641 (C.A.).

5. Grief and sorrow are not recoverable under s. 61(2)(e) of Ontario's *Family Law Act*. However, some other provincial statutes permit a separate award for grief, as opposed to loss of guidance, care and companionship. See for example *Fatal Accidents Act*, R.S.N.B. 1973, c. F-7, s. 3(4). Grief and sorrow are discussed in van Praagh, "Who Lost What? Relationship and Relational Loss" in Beaulac, Pitel & Schulz, eds., *The Joy of Torts* (2003) 269.

6. The Court of Appeal for Ontario has held that s. 61 of the *Family Law Act* precludes an estate from recovering either punitive or aggravated damages: *Lord (Litigation Guardian of) v. Downer* (1999), 179 D.L.R. (4th) 430 (Ont. C.A.).

7. The specific wording of the statute is highly important. Under the *Fatal Accidents Act*, R.S.N.W.T. 1988, c. F-3 and the *Trustee Act*, R.S.N.W.T. 1988, c. T-8, s. 31(1), unlike in several provinces, a deceased's estate can claim for both loss of "expectation of life" (a non-pecuniary head of damages compensating for the lost prospect of a predominantly enjoyable life) and loss of future earnings: see *Caron Estate v. Paneak Estate* (2006), 42 C.C.L.T. (3d) 48 (Nu. C.A.).

(i) *The Death of the Family Provider*

KEIZER v. HANNA

[1978] 2 S.C.R. 342

[Mr. Keizer died as a result of the injuries he sustained in an automobile collision. The defendant admitted that the collision was due solely to his negligence.]

DICKSON J.: — I have had the advantage of reading the reasons for judgment prepared by Mr. Justice Spence and Mr. Justice de Grandpré in this appeal. There are two issues: (i) the deductibility of income tax in arriving at an award of damages; (ii) quantum. . . .

[Dickson J. briefly addressed the taxation issue and continued.]

On point (ii), however, "quantum", I have come to a conclusion other than that arrived at by my brother de Grandpré. I would allow the appeal, and like my brother Spence, award the amount of $100,000 claimed in the statement of claim but deduct therefrom the amount of $6,500 insurance benefits already received by the appellant under the accident and death benefits provision found in . . . the deceased's insurance policy. In the result, the award of general damages would amount to $93,500.

The accident in which Mr. Keizer was killed occurred on July 16, 1973. At that date he was 33 years of age with a life expectancy of 38.55 years. He was a tool-room foreman for the Town of Renfrew, capable, conscientious, industrious and in good health. He had been married for nine years to the appellant who, at the date of his death was 27 years of age with a life expectancy of 49.60 years. Mr. and Mrs. Keizer had one child, an infant of six months.

The trial Judge projected average earnings of $15,000 for a working expectancy of 31 years. From this figure he deducted $3,200 for income tax, $1,800 for personal use, and $3,000 for personal support leaving disposable income for dependants in the amount of $7,000. The Judge made a deduction for income tax with which the Court of Appeal agreed and which, in my view, was proper. The Court of Appeal did not question the Judge's finding that the deceased would expend $1,800 for his personal use and $3,000 for his personal support. Thus, as a result, $7,000 would be available as disposable income for dependants. The evidence was that he contributed his pay cheque weekly to his family reserving only nominal sums and odd-job earnings for his own use. Having concluded that $7,000 per year would have been available to the appellant and her child each year, the Judge said. . .:

> Actuarial tables filed as ex. 1 herein at 9% and 10% compound interest show the present value of $1 to age 65 for the male as $9.9375 and $9.1381 respectively. I believe a more realistic interest rate would be the approximate amount of 6.5% which would materially inflate these figures; for example, at 4% the factor is 18.66461. One must consider income tax as a reality of modern life and its depreciating impact along with the contingencies hereinbefore alluded to is reflected in my assessment. Under the provisions of the *Fatal Accidents Act* I award the plaintiff the sum of $120,000, of which sum I apportion $17,500 for the infant Mitchel Stephen.

It is difficult, if not impossible, to know what use, if any, the trial Judge made of actuarial tables to which he was referred. It would seem, however, that he proceeded on an exhausting fund basis, with a discount rate of approximately 6.5%. He made an allowance in respect of the income tax which the deceased would have had to pay on his earnings, had he lived, and he further reduced the award by a contingency allowance. He referred to the contingencies which might bear on assessment, as follows:

> (a) Possibility of remarriage;
>
> (b) Possibility of widow's death before expiry of joint expectancy period;
>
> (c) Possibility of deceased's dying under other circumstances prior to expiry of said joint expectancy period;
>
> (d) Possibility of deceased husband's retiring before expiry of joint expectancy period;
>
> (e) Acceleration of inheritance to widow — bearing in mind likelihood of increased inheritance in event death had not occurred;
>
> (f) Possibility the infant child may not be a burden to the father or require additional benefits for the full period of his calculated working life.

On the question of prospects of remarriage, the judge adopted the apt comments of Phillimore J. in *Buckley v. John Allen & Ford (Oxford), Ltd.*, [1967] 1 All E.R. 539, including the statement that Judges should act on evidence rather than guesswork and, there being no evidence of any existing interest or attachment, concluded: "I therefore accord no material significance to this prospect by way of deduction." He does not say that he is according no weight to the contingency.

As to the possibility of the early demise of either husband or wife, the Judge said:

> All of the evidence indicates excellent health prospects and I rule that relatively little real significance can be attached to this contingency by way of reduction.

Again, it is not a question of refusing to consider a particular contingency. The judge considered the contingency, but decided it merited little significance. I do not think he can be faulted on this account.

With respect to the possibility of acceleration of the inheritance to the appellant, the Judge had this to say:

> So far as the acceleration of her inheritance is concerned, I am readily satisfied that the same should have no reducing effect as in these circumstances. I am assured it is more than offset by the substantial loss she has suffered in future realization from this source.

Finally, the possibility that the infant child might not be a burden during his father's working life. On this point, the Judge said that he would give this fact material consideration in considering his award. These are his words:

> Unquestionably, there is the probability that the child Mitchel Stephen would not have been a burden to his father for anything like the 30 years or so of his working expectancy and I give this fact material consideration in considering this award.

The quantum of the award came before the Court of Appeal for Ontario. In that Court, reference was made by Mr. Justice Arnup, for the Court, to the six contingencies to which the trial Judge referred. Mr. Justice Arnup observed that the trial Judge might have added "possibility of incapacity to earn, occasioned by industrial or other accident, or by illness." He then continued. . .:

> Having listed these contingencies, the trial Judge decided he should make no deduction for any of them. In so doing, he erred. A contingency, in the context of damages under the *Fatal Accidents Act*, is obviously an event that may or may not happen. A defendant is entitled to have contingencies taken into account by way of reduction from the result that would be reached if every contingency turned out favourably to the dependants, although due weight must be given in each case to the probability, or otherwise, of the contingent event actually happening.

I have been unable to find in the trial judgment any statement by the trial Judge that he had decided he should not make any deduction for any of the contingencies. The evidence, as I read it, is to the contrary. It is true that the trial Judge might have considered the possibility of the deceased husband becoming unable to earn, but I do not think it can be said that failure to express himself on this point amounts to reversible error. The award of $120,000 exceeded the amount claimed of $100,000 but that does not preclude an award of $100,000.

In making a gross award of $65,000 the Court of Appeal was content with the following cryptic statement:

> In my view, the appropriate award of general damages in all of the circumstances of this case, as disclosed by the evidence, would have been $65,000.

The judgment does not assist us, or the parties, by explaining why $65,000 should be considered to be the appropriate award. From this amount the Court of Appeal deducted the $6,500 to which I have referred and directed that $10,000 be paid into Court for the infant. In the result, the widow would receive from the defendants for her support and maintenance for the next fifty years the sum of $48,500. This, plus $6,500 already received, totals $55,000.

It is, of course, true that a trial Judge must consider contingencies tending to reduce the ultimate award and give those contingencies more or less weight. It is equally true there are contingencies tending to increase the award to which a Judge must give due weight. At the end of the day the only question of importance is whether, in all the circumstances, the final award is fair and adequate. Past experience should make one realize that if there is to be error in the amount of an award it is likely to be one of inadequacy.

In my opinion, in the circumstances of this case, an award of $55,000 to the appellant can only be described as niggardly. The appellant is entitled to an award of such amount as will assure her the comforts and station in life which she would have enjoyed but for the untimely death of her husband. If one is speaking of contingencies, I think it is not unreasonable to give primary attention to the contingencies, and they are many, the occurrence of which would result in making the award, in the light of events, entirely inadequate. An assessment must be neither punitive nor influenced by sentimentality. It is largely an exercise of business judgment. The question is whether a stated amount of capital will provide, during the period in question, having regard to contingencies tending to increase or decrease the award, a monthly sum at least equal to that which might reasonably have been expected during the continued life of the deceased.

The proper method of calculating the amount of a damage award under the *Fatal Accidents Act* is similar to that used in calculating the amount of an award for loss of future earnings, or for future care, in cases of serious personal injury. In each, the Court is faced with the task of determining the present value of a lump sum which, if invested, would provided payments of the appropriate size over a given number of years in the future, extinguishing the fund in the process. This matter has been discussed in detail in the decisions of this Court in *Andrews v. Grand & Toy Alberta Ltd.*; *Thornton v. Prince George Board of Education*; and *Arnold v. Teno*, which are being delivered with the decision in the present case.

The object here is to award a sum which will replace present-day payments of $7,000 per year for a future period of 31 years, with some reduction for contingencies. The trial Judge used a discount rate of 6.5% without explaining this choice except to say that it was a "more realistic" rate than 9% or 10%. As I have said in *Andrews* and *Thornton*, in my opinion the discount rate should be calculated on the basis of present rates of return on long-term investments with an allowance for the effects of future inflation. Evidence on these matters was not introduced at trial in the present case. However, the 6.52% chosen by the Judge can be tested by the fact that present-day investment rates reach about 10.5%, and Dr. Deutsch of the Economic Council of Canada forecasted an inflation rate of about 3.5% over the long-term future. These two figures suggest that an appropriate discount rate is approximately 7%. This is only marginally different from the rate used by the trial Judge. Ignoring, for the moment, the other factors to be taken into consideration, the sum required to produce $7,000 per year for 31 years, payable monthly, discounted at 6.5%, is slightly less than $95,000. The award should be reduced somewhat to account for contingencies although, as I have mentioned, this amount will probably not be large. On the other hand, in order to yield the sum required net of taxes a greater sum would obviously be called for. The resulting amount would not reach the figure of $120,000 which the trial Judge chose. The sum of $100,000, the amount claimed, can be justified, however, with reasonable allowance made for income tax impact and contingency deduction.

I would allow the appeal, set aside the judgment of the Court of Appeal and direct that the appellant recover from the defendants the sum of $93,500. Out of that sum there should be paid to Marilyn E. Keizer the sum of $78,500 and there should be paid into Court to the credit of the infant, Mitchel Stephen Keizer, the sum of $15,000, to be paid out to the said infant when he attains the age of 18 years, or upon further order of a Judge of the County Court of the County of Renfrew. The appellant is also entitled to her award of $1,600 under the provisions of the *Trustee Act*, R.S.O. 1970, c. 470, in respect of funeral expenses and the value of an automobile.

I would allow the appellant her costs at trial against both defendants and her costs in this Court and in the Court of Appeal against the defendant Buch.

[Laskin C.J.C., Martland, Ritchie, Pigeon and Beetz JJ. concurred. Spence J. dissented in part, holding that income tax should not be taken into account in calculating the value of the deceased's support. De Grandpré J., with whom Judson J. agreed, dissented in part, holding that the Supreme Court of Canada ought not to interfere unless it was convinced the Court of Appeal had erred in principle.]

NOTES AND QUESTIONS

1. According to Dickson J., what basic principle should govern the appellant's claim?

2. What is the purpose of reducing the award by the amounts that the deceased would have spent for his own personal use and support? Do these deductions violate the basic principle identified above?

3. What is the "joint expectancy" period and why is it used in fatal accident cases? Is the possibility of the widow's death before the expiry of that period a relevant contingency?

4. What rationale underlies the other contingency deductions in the case? Do you agree with them? Are there other contingencies, positive or negative, which the court should have considered?

5. What adjustment is made in *Keizer* to reflect the income tax the deceased would have paid? Is it appropriate to make such a deduction here but not in the personal injury cases? See *Lewis v. Todd* (1980), 115 D.L.R. (3d) 257 (S.C.C.). Note that awards for pecuniary loss in fatal accident cases are now "grossed up" for the same purpose and in the same manner as in the personal injury cases. See generally *O'Hara v. Belanger*, [1990] 1 W.W.R. 214 (Alta. Q.B.); and *Oleschak Estate v. Wilganowski* (1991), 70 Man. R. (2d) 149 (C.A.). See also Feldthusen & McNair, "General Damages in Personal Injury Suits: The Supreme Court's Trilogy" (1978) 28 U.T.L.J. 381 at 401-403; and Rea, "Inflation, Taxation and Damage Assessment" (1980) 58 Can. Bar Rev. 280.

6. Why is evidence about the deceased's former prospects so important in a fatal accident case? What evidence would you adduce on behalf of a dependant on this issue?

7. In *Beljanski (Guardian ad litem of) v. Smithwick* (2006), 56 B.C.L.R. (4th) 99 (C.A.) the dependant children of a "career criminal" brought a claim when their father was killed negligently. The case raised difficult valuation questions. For reasons discussed in the next chapter, the court refused to base an award on any illegal income the deceased would have made through criminal activities. The trial judge concluded that the deceased would have provided no care or guidance to his children nor left them any inheritance. The appeal court disagreed, based on the possibility that the deceased might have reformed later in life, and concluded that the children should recover $15,000 each.

8. How would you assess the damages for dependant children if both parents were killed by a negligent tortfeasor? See *Clement v. Leslies Storage Ltd.* (1979), 97 D.L.R. (3d) 667 (Man. C.A.); *McDermott v. Ramadanovic Estate* (1988), 44 C.C.L.T. 249 (B.C.S.C.); and *Coe Estate v. Tennant* (1990), 46 B.C.L.R. (2d) 62 (C.A.).

9. It is impossible to provide a typical example of a fatal accident case because quantification depends heavily on the specific attributes of the deceased and the relevant relationships. For a comprehensive review of the case law, see Klar *et al.*, *Damages and Remedies in Tort* (1995) at 27-122.28 to 27-146.

(ii) *The Death of a Dependant Family Member*

Actions are usually brought under fatal accidents legislation as a result of the death of a family's primary earner. However, the legislation also extends to other family members, so it is possible for a plaintiff to bring an action as a result of an accident that resulted in the death of his or her dependant spouse or child: see *Alaffe v. Kennedy* (1973), 40 D.L.R. (3d) 429 (N.S.T.D.). Since the fatal accidents legislation is generally intended to provide compensation for pecuniary losses only, the measure of relief awarded with respect to the death of such individuals is often considerably less than the measure of relief awarded with respect to the death of a family provider. Another reason for the relatively low value of awards arising from the death of dependant family members may be that the courts continue to substantially undervalue the services provided within the home.

NOTES AND QUESTIONS

1. When a young child dies, it is typically very difficult to accurately assess the pecuniary loss suffered by a parent. Not only must the court speculate as to how the child would have fared economically in life, it must also speculate about the extent to which the parent would have benefited from the child's economic fortunes. Is there any way for a parent's lawyer to overcome these difficulties? In this sort of case, what kind of evidence would you present on a parent's behalf? See Sutherland, "Predicting a Child's Future Wage Loss" (1984) 42 The Advocate 169; Bruce, "Measure of Damages for the Wrongful Death of a Child" (1987) 66 Can. Bar Rev. 344; and Smith, Merchant & Killback, "Risible Compensation for the Dead Child" (1996) 7 M.V.L.R. 125.

2. In *Mason v. Peters* (1980), 30 O.R. (2d) 409 (H.C.), aff'd (1982), 39 O.R. (2d) 27 (C.A.) the trial judge awarded the unusually large sum of $45,000 to a disabled, single mother for the death of her 11-year-old son. This exceptional award was the result of the unusually close bond between the mother and her son and the probability that he would have provided her with emotional and financial support throughout her life.

3. Should the damages awarded for the death of a child be reduced to take into account the parents' expenses in rearing the child? In *Mason v. Peters*, *ibid.*, Robins J.A. noted that except in rare circumstances the cost of raising and educating children greatly exceeds the pecuniary benefits that they provide to their parents. However, in *Lai v. Gill*, [1980] 1 S.C.R. 431 the court accepted that Chinese traditions encouraging the supporting of one's parents justified a pecuniary award of $25,000 for the parents of a deceased 14-year-old girl. Similar reasoning led at trial to a pecuniary award of $180,000 in *Lian v. Money*, [1994] 8 W.W.R. 463 (B.C.S.C.), rev'd [1996] 4 W.W.R. 263 (B.C.C.A.). This award was reversed on appeal on the grounds that the trial judge failed to consider the contribution that the deceased's older sister would make to the parents' welfare.

4. In *To v. Toronto (City) Board of Education* (2001), 55 O.R. (3d) 641 (C.A.) a 14-year-old boy was killed as a result of the defendant's negligence. He had been an excellent student. Moreover, because neither of his parents spoke English, he had helped them a great deal with their business and personal correspondence. He was described as a "trusted companion and advisor to his father." Finally, his relationship with his sister was described as "almost paternal." The family was devastated by his death. The jury awarded $100,000 to each of his parents and $50,000 to his sister under the *Family Law Act*. The Court of Appeal found that the awards to the parents were higher than usual, but not so inordinately high as to be reversible. The court did, however, reduce the sibling's award by half, partially on the ground that while she had suffered a terrible loss, she was likely to become independent and have a family of her own. See also *Osman v. 629256 Ontario Ltd.*, 2005 CarswellOnt 2728 (S.C.J.) (WLeC) in which the parents of a 16-year-old boy who was stabbed as a result of the defendants' negligence were each awarded $80,000 and his ten siblings were each awarded $20,000.

5. The assessment of pecuniary losses resulting from the death of a dependant spouse is also very difficult. In *Nielsen v. Kaufmann* (1984), 28 C.C.L.T. 54 (Ont. H.C.) the value of the deceased's household services was valued in "cold commercial terms" at $8,840 a year. This amount was reduced significantly on appeal: (1986), 54 O.R. (2d) 188 (C.A.). See also *Frawley v. Asselstine* (1990), 73 O.R. (2d) 525 (H.C.); and *Skelding (Guardian ad litem of) v. Skelding*, [1994] 9 W.W.R. 538 (B.C.C.A.). Many people believe that the courts have grossly undervalued these services in the past. See Yale, "The Valuation of Household Services in Wrongful Death Actions" (1984) 34 U.T.L.J. 283; Quah, "Compensation for Loss of Household Services" (1986) 24 Osgoode Hall L.J. 467; and Cooper-Stephenson, *Personal Injury Damages in Canada*, 2d ed. (1996) at 319-22.

More recently, in *McVea (Guardian ad litem of) v. T.B.* (2002), 5 B.C.L.R. (4th) 367 (S.C.) the victim was killed when a 14-year-old driving a stolen car and pursued by police crashed into her. She was the principal provider of household services and child care but also worked outside the home. Her husband and children were awarded $261,000 for loss of past and future support, $207,900 for loss of past and future services, $60,000 for loss of care, guidance and affection, and $20,000 for loss of inheritance.

6. In *Bjornson v. McDonald*, 2005 CarswellBC 1457 (S.C.) (WLeC) both parents of a 38-year-old single mother of three children were killed in a car accident. The plaintiff recovered $125,000 for loss of child care and household services, loss of financial support, and loss of love, guidance and affection. The court accepted the evidence of the close relationship between the plaintiff and her parents, especially since her divorce.

7. Although awards under fatal accidents legislation have generally been limited to pecuniary losses, as in *Vana v. Tosta*, [1968] S.C.R. 71; and *Bianco v. Fromow* (1998), 161 D.L.R. (4th) 765 (B.C.C.A.), some statutes specifically allow awards for grief and anguish. For example, the Alberta *Fatal Accidents Act*, R.S.A. 2000, c. F-8, s. 8(2) allows a claim for "grief and loss of guidance, care and companionship," up to a maximum of $75,000 to a parent or spouse of the deceased and up to $45,000 to a child. The New Brunswick *Fatal Accidents Act*, R.S.N.B. 1973, c. F-7, ss. 3(4) and (5) allows recovery for grief suffered by the parents of a deceased minor: see *Nightingale v. Mazerall* (1991), 9 C.C.L.T. (2d) 186 (N.B.C.A.). A similar provision in the Manitoba *Fatal Accidents Act* was repealed: S.M. 2002, c. 13, s. 3.

8. It is impossible to provide a typical example of a dependant's fatal accident case because quantification depends heavily on the specific attributes of the deceased and the relevant relationships. For a comprehensive review of the case law, see Klar *et al.*, *Damages and Remedies in Tort* (1995) at 27-122.28 to 27-146.

4. Damages for Property Loss

The general principles governing the assessment of compensatory damages in personal injury cases apply to claims for damage to property. For analytical purposes, we have divided our discussion of damages for property loss into three issues: the assessment of the damages to the property itself, the assessment of the economic losses consequent on the damage to the property and the plaintiff's obligation to mitigate.

(a) THE ASSESSMENT OF THE DAMAGE TO THE PROPERTY ITSELF

As J. Fleming has stated, "whether the property be damaged or destroyed, the plaintiff is in the first instance entitled to restitution for the loss of its value to him": Fleming, *The Law of Torts*, 9th ed. (1998) at 282. This principle is often difficult to apply because there are several different ways of assessing the loss in value, including the cost of repair, the cost of replacement and the decrease in the value of the property. The method chosen for assessing the damage may well affect the size of the award.

In a case of damage to a chattel, it is necessary to determine whether the property in question is commonplace or unique. In the former situation, the plaintiff generally receives the lesser of the amount by which the thing has decreased in value, the cost of repair or the cost of replacement. Essentially, then, the plaintiff is entitled to be restored to his or her former position by the least expensive means possible. In contrast, if the chattel in question is unique or of great sentimental value, the courts recognize that true restoration may require greater expenditure. In that respect, the courts take account of the plaintiff's subjective valuation of property. Consequently, for example, if a family heirloom is damaged by the defendant's carelessness, the plaintiff may be awarded the cost of repair, even if that amount exceeds the market value of a replacement item. Regardless of market value, a replacement item would be an inadequate substitute for the damaged heirloom.

Similar principles apply in cases involving damage to real property. In general terms, the plaintiff is also entitled to the lesser of the amount by which the thing has decreased in value, the cost of repair or the cost of replacement. However, just as the measure of relief may be higher if a damaged chattel holds special value for the plaintiff, so too the general approach is displaced if the plaintiff uses the land for residential purposes or would find it difficult to relocate a business that is operated on the property. In those situations, the plaintiff is more apt to be awarded the cost of repair.

It is not settled whether the defendant's liability should be reduced if a repaired or replaced chattel or real property is more valuable than the original. To deny the deduction would place the plaintiff in a better position than he or she would have been in had the tort not been committed. However, to allow the deduction in effect would force the plaintiff to pay for the unplanned upgrading of his or her chattel or real property. The courts will usually allow for a betterment deduction if it is established that the new chattel or real property would be worth more to the plaintiff than the original.

(b) THE ASSESSMENT OF ECONOMIC LOSSES CONSEQUENT ON THE DAMAGE TO THE PROPERTY

Particularly in the case of business assets, the plaintiff will often suffer economic losses consequent on the damage to his or her property. The principles governing the recovery of consequential economic loss are largely the same as in personal injury and property loss cases. However, the House of Lords originally indicated in *Dredger Liesbosch v. S.S. Edison (Owners)*, [1933] A.C. 448 (H.L.) that these principles should be applied more strictly in claims for property loss. In that case, the defendants negligently destroyed the plaintiffs' vessel, which could have been replaced quickly at a reasonable price if the plaintiffs had possessed the necessary funds. Unfortunately, the plaintiffs were in financial difficulties and were forced to incur far greater costs in replacing their vessel. The defendants were absolved of liability for this additional economic loss, which was attributable to the plaintiffs' impecuniosity.

More recently, however, the law has moved toward a more relaxed approach. *Liesbosch* was frequently criticized by courts. See for example *Dodd Properties (Kent) Ltd. v. Canterbury C.C.*, [1980] 1 All E.R. 928 (C.A.); and *Rollinson v. R.* (1994), 20 C.C.L.T. (2d) 92 (Fed. T.D.). Moreover, as explained in the previous chapter, the Privy Council has now rejected a blanket rule denying recovery of losses attributable to the plaintiff's "thin wallet." Instead, it has stressed that the general principles of foreseeability and remoteness should govern recovery. See *Alcoa Minerals of Jamaica v. Broderick*, [2000] 3 W.L.R. 23 (P.C.); and *Lagden v. O'Connor*, [2004] 1 A.C. 1067 (H.L.) in which the House of Lords expressly overruled *Liesbosch*.

(c) THE PLAINTIFF'S OBLIGATION TO MITIGATE

It is generally accepted that the principles of mitigation are applied more rigorously in claims for property loss than in claims for personal injury. In property loss cases the courts appear to demand that the plaintiff act reasonably in a business sense. As in so many other areas of damages, the principle is relatively straightforward but is often difficult to apply in specific cases. For example, it may be reasonable to purchase a replacement machine at an inflated price if waiting for a damaged chattel to be repaired would generate even greater consequential economic losses.

NOTES AND QUESTIONS

1. In some situations it is very difficult to accurately assess the loss suffered by the plaintiff as a result of loss or damage to property. In *Mason v. Westside Cemeteries Ltd.* (1996), 29 C.C.L.T. (2d) 125 (Ont. Gen. Div.) the defendant carelessly lost the ashes of the plaintiff's deceased parents. The plaintiff had intended to have those ashes buried near his own grave. How would you assess his loss?

2. In *Darbishire v. Warren*, [1963] 3 All E.R. 310 (C.A.) the defendant negligently damaged the plaintiff's well-maintained used car. Although the car had a market value of only £85, the plaintiff spent £192 repairing it because he felt he could not get a reliable replacement vehicle for less than the cost of repair. The Court of Appeal limited the plaintiff's award to the market value. Harman L.J. stated at 314: "this was not an irreplaceable article, and, therefore, as the cost of repairs greatly exceeded the value, the car should be treated as a constructive total loss and the measure of damages is its value." Pearson L.J. held that the plaintiff had not acted reasonably in mitigating his loss because he had not made an effort to find a reliable replacement. Although this case is consistent with the general principles, is the result fair to the plaintiff? This case illustrates the problem of assessing damages for certain kinds of property. See also *Pac. Blasting Ltd. v. D.J. Byrne Const. Ltd.*, [1977] 2 W.W.R. 505 (B.C.S.C.); *Chappell v. Baratti* (1984), 30 C.C.L.T. 137 (Ont. S.C.); *Scobie v. Wing* (1992), 63 B.C.L.R. (2d) 76 (C.A.); and *Kevington Building Corp. v. Lee* (1998), 36 C.L.R. (2d) 293 (B.C.S.C.).

3. In *N.B. Telephone Co. v. Wright* (1982), 140 D.L.R. (3d) 188 (N.B.Q.B.) the plaintiff was able to replace the vehicle damaged by the defendant with one of its other vehicles which it was not using. Nevertheless, the plaintiff was able to recover the amount it would have cost to rent a replacement. Although this decision is generally accepted as correct, is the result fair to the defendant? Is it consistent with the basic principles of compensatory damages? For other discussions of damages for loss of use see *Pac. Elevators Ltd. v. C.P.R. Co.* (1973), 41 D.L.R. (3d) 608 (S.C.C.); *Municipal Spraying & Contracting Ltd. v. J. Harris & Sons. Ltd.* (1979), 35 N.S.R. (2d) 237 (S.C.); *Hefferman v. Elizabeth Irving Service Centre* (1980), 29 Nfld. & P.E.I.R. 470 (Nfld. T.D.); *Blair's Plumbing & Heating Ltd. v. McGraw* (1981), 35 N.B.R. (2d) 501 (Q.B.); and *Pembina Resources Ltd. v. ULS International Inc.*, [1990] 1 F.C. 666 (T.D.).

4. In *Harbutt's Plasticine v. Wayne Tank & Pump Co.*, [1970] 1 All E.R. 225 (C.A.) the plaintiffs could not repair their old premises and therefore built a new factory. The

issue was whether the plaintiffs were entitled to the cost of replacement even though it exceeded the decrease in the value of the old building. Lord Denning stated at 236:

> The destruction of a building is different from the destruction of a chattel. If a secondhand car is destroyed, the owner only gets its value, because he can go into the market and get another secondhand car to replace it. He cannot charge the other party with the cost of replacing it with a new car. But, when this mill was destroyed the plaintiffs had no choice. They were bound to replace it as soon as they could, not only to keep their business going, but also to mitigate the loss of profit (for which they would be able to charge the defendants). They replaced it in the only possible way, without adding any extras. I think they should be allowed the cost of replacement. True it is they got new for old, but I do not think the wrongdoer can diminish the claim on that account. If they had added extra accommodation or made extra improvements, they would have to give credit. But that is not this case.

Did the plaintiffs have to rebuild to mitigate their loss? Could they have mitigated by choosing another business investment? Does the fact that they did rebuild indicate that they thought a new factory was a wise business investment? If so, should the defendant have to bear the full cost? See also *James Street Hardware and Furniture Co. v. Spizziri* (1987), 62 O.R. (2d) 385 (C.A.); *Nan v. Black Pine Manufacturing Ltd.*, [1991] 5 W.W.R. 172 (B.C.C.A.); and *Canada (Attorney General) v. Clorey* (1996), 144 Nfld. & P.E.I.R. 132 (P.E.I.S.C. (T.D.)). See Berryman, "Betterment Before Canadian Common Law Courts" (1993) 72 Can. Bar Rev. 54.

5. In *Waterloo Warehousing & Storage Ltd. v. Swenco Mfg. Ltd.* (1975), 58 D.L.R. (3d) 180 (Ont. H.C.) the plaintiff's building was destroyed in a fire caused by the defendant's negligence. Prior to the fire, the plaintiff had entered into a contract to sell the land and building. Since the purchaser intended to demolish the building and construct an apartment building in its place, the purchase price remained the same after the fire. The court denied the plaintiff's claim for the amount which it would have cost to replace the building.

In *Jens v. Mannix Co. Ltd.* (1978), 89 D.L.R. (3d) 351 (B.C.S.C.), varied (1979), 30 D.L.R. (4th) 260 (B.C.C.A.) a house was effectively destroyed because of the defendant's negligence. The property had recently been zoned for commercial use, resulting in an increase in its resale value regardless of whether there were buildings on the property. However, because the plaintiff reasonably planned to keep living there, and had received planning approval to rebuild, he was entitled to recover the cost of replacing his home.

Can you reconcile *Jens* and *Darbishire v. Warren*, *supra*? Can you reconcile *Jens* and *Waterloo Warehousing & Storage Ltd.*? See also, as concerns chattels, *The Maersk Colombo*, [2001] 2 Lloyd's Rep. 275 (C.A.).

6. In *Tridan Developments Ltd. v. Shell Canada Products Ltd.* (2002), 57 O.R. (3d) 503 (C.A.) the defendant owned a service station. It negligently allowed 9,000 litres of gas to leak onto the plaintiff's neighbouring property. A clean-up could be performed to one of two standards: "pristine condition" or a condition that would have satisfied guidelines established by the Ministry of the Environment. The former was more expensive by $250,000. The trial judge nevertheless held that the plaintiff was entitled to the higher amount. The Court of Appeal agreed even though the plaintiff's property would probably never be used for residential purposes. It reasoned that "[w]here a product that

may cause mischief escapes to a neighbour's property, there is 'responsibility for all the damage which is the natural consequence of the escape'." The trial judge also awarded: (i) $350,000 for loss of property value due to the stigma of an environmental hazard and (ii) an injunction requiring the defendant to install an environmental barrier between the properties, or, failing that, additional damages of $85,000. The Court of Appeal, however, eliminated the $350,000 award on the basis that there would be no residual stigma if the land was cleaned up to a pristine condition. It further held that while the plaintiff was entitled to $85,000, representing the cost of an environmental barrier, there was no basis for linking that award to injunctive relief. See van Rensburg, "Deconstructing *Tridan*: A Litigator's Perspective" (2004) 15 J. Envtl. L & Prac. 85.

7. In *British Columbia v. Canadian Forest Products Ltd.*, [2004] 2 S.C.R. 74 the defendants were 70% responsible for a negligently caused forest fire. The province had in place a sophisticated timber pricing system that raised its "stumpage" revenues in other forested areas when revenues in one or more areas fell. After the fire the province sued for loss of revenue from trees that, but for the fire, would have been harvested, and for loss of trees set aside in environmentally-sensitive areas. The defendants argued that because of the revenue increases from other areas under the pricing system, and because the set-aside trees were never to be harvested, the province had suffered no financial loss. The trial judge agreed with the defendants. The Court of Appeal agreed with respect to the harvestable trees but awarded the province 33% of the commercial value of the set-aside trees. A majority of the Supreme Court of Canada reinstated the decision of the trial judge, while the dissent held that the province should recover for both the harvestable and set-aside trees. The case illustrates several different approaches to calculating damages for property loss. See Elgie & Lintner, "The Supreme Court's *Canfor* Decision: Losing the Battle but Winning the War for Environmental Damages" (2005) 38 U.B.C.L. Rev. 223.

8. For a comprehensive review of the issues raised by *Dredger Liesbosch* see Phillips, "Compensation For Losses Flowing from an Injured Party's Impecuniosity" (1982) 20 Osgoode Hall L.J. 18; Wexler, "The Impecunious Plaintiff: Liesbosch Reconsidered" (1987) 66 Can. Bar Rev. 129; David *et al.*, "Impecuniosity and the Duty to Mitigate: *Dredger Liesbosch (Owners) v. The Edison (Owners)*" (1998) 20 Adv. Q. 366; and Coote "Damages, *The Liesbosch* and Impecuniosity" [2001] C.L.J. 511. Cases like *Geld v. Dehavilland Aircraft of Can. Ltd.*, [1983] 6 W.W.R. 229 (B.C.S.C.); *A.G. Ont. v. Fatehi* (1984), 31 C.C.L.T. 1 (S.C.C.); and *Armak Chemicals Ltd. v. Canadian National Railway Co.* (1991), 3 O.R. (3d) 1 (C.A.) also raise interesting issues relating to economic loss consequent upon damage to property.

9. The principles of contributory negligence and mitigation of loss overlap in some cases. For example in *Indust. Teletype Electronics Corp. v. Montreal* (1976), 10 N.R. 517 (S.C.C.) the plaintiff considered his flood-damaged inventory to be a total loss and claimed damages for the full replacement cost. The plaintiff offered all of the inventory to the defendant, who declined to take it. Beetz J. stated at 524:

> Finally, according to a defence expert the damages could have been substantially reduced and some new parts still considered as such after the flood, had a cleaning and drying operation that was simple and inexpensive been diligently carried out. The parts exposed to water remained at the risk of appellants who continued to have custody and ownership

> of them. If this expert's opinion is accurate, surely the offer made by appellants cannot exempt them from mitigating their damages, as would a reasonable man. Indeed, to allow a plaintiff to rid himself of this obligation by means of such an offer, and allow him the replacement value of the merchandise, would be equivalent to treating as an insurer the perpetrator of the damage. I do not believe that this is the state of our law. This aspect of the case is obviously such as to affect the quantum of the damages, but it goes beyond the question of quantum; it concerns the causal relationship between the fault of the city and the loss sustained by appellants. Thus, the claim of the latter could be reduced to the extent that their own negligence after the flood contributed to increase the damage.

Do you agree with Beetz J. that the plaintiff's conduct should be considered as an issue of contributory negligence rather than as a question of mitigation? Does it make any difference which approach is adopted? For other illustrations of mitigation of loss see *Can. Western Natural Gas Co. v. Pathfinder Surveys Ltd.* (1980), 21 A.R. 459 (C.A.); *John Maryon Int. Ltd. v. N.B. Telephone Co.* (1982), 24 C.C.L.T. 146 (N.B.C.A.); *Galantiuk v. Regina*, [1984] 6 W.W.R. 262 (Sask. Q.B.); *Miller Dredging Ltd. v. Dorothy Mackenzie (The)* (1994), 119 D.L.R. (4th) 63 (B.C.C.A.); and *Wiebe v. Gunderson* (2004), 32 B.C.L.R. (4th) 230 (C.A.).

5. Collateral Benefits

To this point it has been assumed that the defendant is the plaintiff's sole source of compensation. However, in most cases the plaintiff will also receive compensation in various forms from collateral sources such as government health insurance, private insurance or employment benefits. Should the defendant's liability be reduced to reflect the benefit that the plaintiff has received from such collateral sources?

In the absence of a statutory or contractual provision to the contrary, certain types of collateral benefits need not be deducted from the plaintiff's damages. These include private insurance benefits, charitable or benevolent gifts, and pension benefits. Moreover, the deductibility of many other types of collateral benefits is largely governed by statute. These include provincial health insurance, workers' compensation and automobile insurance. For a recent example involving the latter see *Gurniak v. Nordquist*, [2003] 2 S.C.R. 652. See also *Walker v. Ritchie* (2005), 197 O.A.C. 81 (C.A.), varied (2006), 43 C.C.L.T. (3d) 1 (S.C.C.).

In the past courts have held that public welfare benefits like social assistance are not deducted from the damage award. But in *M.B. v. British Columbia*, [2003] 2 S.C.R. 477 the court held that social assistance is intended as a form of wage replacement and is not akin to private charitable donations. In line with the views of several leading tort scholars, and in accordance with a general trend towards deducting collateral benefits, the court held that social assistance payments were to be deducted from the award. See also *Krangle (Guardian ad litem of) v. Brisco*, [2002] 1 S.C.R. 205; and *H.L. v. Canada (Attorney General)*, [2005] 1 S.C.R. 401. In England see *Lincoln v. Hayman*, [1982] 2 All E.R. 819 (C.A.); and *Hodgson v. Trapp*, [1989] 1 A.C. 807 (H.L.).

The issue of collateral benefits has been particularly significant in the context of employee benefits. In normal circumstances, if a plaintiff is required to miss work as a result of injuries sustained through the defendant's negligence, the lost income is compensable. The situation is more complicated, however, if, as often occurs under employment contracts, the employer continues to pay the employee for the lost days. The proper resolution of that situation has been the subject of considerable controversy.

In *Ratych v. Bloomer* (1990), 69 D.L.R. (4th) 25 (S.C.C.) a police officer continued to receive payment from his employer while recuperating. The Supreme Court of Canada held that the defendant was able to deduct those payments from the damages that were payable. The basic facts of *Cunningham v. Wheeler* (1994), 113 D.L.R. (4th) 1 (S.C.C.) were similar. A railway employee continued to receive payment from his employer during a period of convalescence. In contrast to *Ratych*, however, a majority of the Supreme Court of Canada held that the defendant was not permitted to deduct those payments from the damages that were payable.

As Cory J. explained in *Cunningham*, the difference between the two cases was attributable to the evidence of proof of loss. In *Ratych* the plaintiff failed to prove that he had in any way "paid" for the disability benefits that he received from his employer. Moreover, the evidence indicated that the police officer did not lose any accumulated "sick days" as a result of missing work. In contrast, the plaintiff in *Cunningham* proved that while he did not pay for the disability benefits by way of pay cheque deductions, he and his fellow employees effectively purchased the right to receive such benefits during labour negotiations. The employer had agreed to provide the employees with a global package of benefits – if the employees had not chosen to receive part of that package in the form of disability benefits, they would have received higher hourly wages. On that basis, Cory J. reasoned that the disability benefits in *Cunningham* were indistinguishable from the benefits acquired under private insurance, which are not deductible. He therefore concluded that it would be "unjust to deprive the employees of benefits which, through prudence and thrift, they had purchased for themselves."

Perhaps not surprisingly, McLachlin J., who wrote the judgment in *Ratych*, dissented in *Cunningham*. Whereas the majority in *Cunningham* was concerned primarily with the injustice of allowing the defendant to derive a benefit from the fact that the plaintiff purchased disability protection, McLachlin J.'s reasoning was primarily motivated by the desire to prevent a claimant from enjoying "double recovery" for the same loss. "The watchword," she wrote, "is restoration; what is required to restore the plaintiff to his or her pre-accident position." She accordingly held that employment benefits should be subject to deductibility "except where it is established that a right of subrogation will be exercised." The concept of subrogation is considered in the next section.

(a) THE DOCTRINE OF SUBROGATION

The doctrine of subrogation originated in equity, but the right to subrogation may also be created by contract or legislation. At the risk of oversimplification, the effect of subrogation is that a party who has provided an indemnity payment to another is entitled to recover any excess compensation received by that other party for that same loss. For example, assume that a fire insurance company pays the full value of $250,000 for the loss of a negligently destroyed home, and the insured then recovers $250,000 from the tortfeasor. Under the doctrine of subrogation, the insured will be required to refund $250,000 to the insurance company. If the insured is awarded $250,000 but only recovers $100,000 from the tortfeasor, he or she need only refund $100,000 to the insurance company.

Any party who honours a legal obligation to indemnify another has an equitable right to subrogation. Thus if an employer compensates an injured employee under the provisions of a collective bargaining agreement, the employer can seek recovery from the negligent defendant who caused the injury. However, many employers find it too expensive to pursue subrogated claims and some have abandoned the right in their collective agreements, leaving employees free to attempt to obtain double recovery.

Whenever the right of subrogation is enforced, the collateral source rule becomes a matter of indifference to the plaintiff. Anything the plaintiff recovers from the tortfeasor for which he or she has already been indemnified by the collateral source has to be refunded to the collateral source.

NOTES AND QUESTIONS

1. What is the impact of the majority decision in *Cunningham* on the principle established in *Bloomer*? Based on the facts, did the plaintiff in *Cunningham* make a sufficient contribution to the benefit to justify not having it deducted from his damage award?

2. What impact do you think McLachlin J.'s position in *Cunningham* would have had on collective bargaining had she been in the majority?

3. Despite the theoretical justifications provided, does the split in the court simply reflect the justices' pro-plaintiff or pro-defendant leanings? In other words, do the theoretical justifications compel a decision in favour of either position?

4. As McLachlin J. noted in her dissenting judgment in *Cunningham*, one of the primary justifications for the private insurance exception is that such insurers have a statutory right of subrogation. When the insurer exercises this right, double recovery is avoided. However, as indicated, it may be expensive to exercise this subrogation right and it is frequently abandoned. It has been argued that double recovery could be more effectively prevented by making all collateral benefits deductible from the defendant's liability. See Cooper, "A Collateral Benefits Principle" (1971) 49 Can. Bar Rev. 501. Legislation governing some public benefits has adopted this approach. See as an historical example the *Insurance Act*, R.S.O. 1990, c. I.8, s. 267(1); and generally Brown & Menezes, *Insurance Law in Canada*, 2d ed. (1991) at 315-42.

5. For a discussion of Canadian pension and unemployment benefits see *Can. Pac. Ltd. v. Gill*, [1973] S.C.R. 654; *Guy v. Trizec Equities Ltd.*, [1979] 2 S.C.R. 756; and *Jack Cewe Ltd. v. Jorgenson*, [1980] 4 W.W.R. 494 (S.C.C.).

6. The prevailing view is that health benefits received by the plaintiff will not reduce the defendant's liability. For example in *McLeod v. Palardy* (1981), 124 D.L.R. (3d) 506 (Man. C.A.) the court awarded the plaintiff future care costs even though such care was provided free of charge under the provincial health plan. The contrary position was taken in *Wipfli v. Britten* (1984), 29 C.C.L.T. 240 (B.C.C.A.). In reference to cases similar to *McLeod*, Taggart J.A. stated at 270: "I remain unconvinced that they have application to the case of a claimant protected by a universal hospital plan for which he paid nothing in the past (i.e., no premiums or user fee) and is unlikely to be called on to pay anything in the future." Which view is supported by the decision in *Cunningham*?

7. In Ontario, plaintiffs are required to advance a claim against the defendant on behalf of the Ontario Health Insurance Plan for costs already borne by the OHIP in

treating the plaintiff. This avoids the OHIP having to bring its own claim against the tortfeasor. See *Health Insurance Act*, R.S.O. 1990, c. H.6, s. 31(1).

8. If the defendant is not permitted to reduce his or her liability to reflect a collateral benefit that has been received by the plaintiff, should the plaintiff be required to return the excess amount to the collateral source? The courts have generally held that the plaintiff is entitled to retain both the damage award and the collateral benefit unless precluded from doing so by contract or statute.

9. In *Gaca v. Pirelli General plc.*, [2004] 3 All E.R. 348 (C.A.) the plaintiff was injured at work and his employers were responsible. They voluntarily paid him an "ill health gratuity." While in general charitable or benevolent gifts are not deductible from a damage award, the court held that this principle should not apply to a gratuity paid by the defendant rather than by others, and deducted the payment from the subsequent damage award.

10. For a detailed discussion of collateral benefits see Cooper-Stephenson, *Personal Injury Damages in Canada*, 2d ed. (1996), ch. 9. For a detailed discussion of subrogation see Mitchell, *The Law of Subrogation* (1994).

11. Suppose the government establishes an in-home assistance program for tort victims. Suppose also that it has the discretion to stop the assistance if the victim recovers damages from the tortfeasor to cover in-home care. Should the court award the plaintiff the cost of in-home care? See *Fullerton (Guardian ad litem of) v. Delair* (2006), 55 B.C.L.R. (4th) 252 (C.A.).

REVIEW PROBLEMS

1. By all appearances, Helen and Bob were the ideal young couple. Prior to marriage, they carefully made future plans. First, Bob would go to law school while Helen worked and supported him; then Helen would go to law school and Bob would support her. Thereafter, they planned to have two children, one right after the other. Helen would take care of the children until they entered kindergarten. At that time, Helen would join Bob in the law practice.

Things went exactly as planned for the happy young couple until a week before Helen's first-year law school exams, when she was seriously injured in a grease fire at a local restaurant. Her face was badly scarred, and even after three painful operations she remained badly disfigured. Moreover, in spite of the doctor's initial optimism, an operation to restore her sight was unsuccessful and it is now clear that Helen will be permanently blind. Not surprisingly, the accident also caused acute personality changes in Helen. She refuses to have anything whatsoever to do with her family or friends and sits for hours alone in her room playing classical music. After a year, the marriage was ruined. Although Bob still maintains a home for the two of them and provides for Helen's normal needs, he has lost all interest in the marriage.

(a) Assume Helen has a 50% chance of establishing liability and securing damages from the restaurant's liability insurance company within two years. Prepare Helen's claim for general damages in her tort action. Organize and itemize the claims, and indicate the type of evidence that you would adduce to secure the greatest possible award for Helen.

(b) What factors would you consider, and what demands would you make if the insurance company were interested in settling Helen's claim before trial?

2. Albert Sweet was injured when his car was struck by a negligently driven Ace Transport truck. Liability is admitted by Ace Transport and the sole issue at trial is the quantum of damages. At the time of the accident, Albert was 23 years old and had just graduated from law school. He was about to start an articling job at an annual salary of $50,000. His pre-accident life expectancy was 52 years, but the doctors now estimate he will die within 20 years. Albert suffered brain damage and now has the intellectual capabilities of a five-year-old child.

Between the time of the accident and the trial, Albert and his wife Miriam have been supported by her wealthy parents. The proceeds of a small insurance policy have covered all medical expenses and have paid for a nurse for Albert, but these funds are almost exhausted.

You have been contacted by Miriam to assess the possible damage claim that can be brought on behalf of Albert, her parents and herself against Ace Transport.

3. Mr. and Mrs. Troup were an elderly childless couple. Both were actively engaged in the work force throughout their 40-year marriage. Mr. Troup is a famous medical doctor and Mrs. Troup was a university professor until July 1, 2002. At that time, she was compelled to retire from the university and was granted a pension worth 80% of her salary for the remainder of her life. The individual income of either Mr. or Mrs. Troup had always been sufficient to meet their joint expenditures, and the Troups had pooled their funds, accumulating a sizeable surplus during their married years.

The only significant quarrel in their lengthy marriage involved Mrs. Troup's nephew. Out of a sense of moral duty to her late sister, Mrs. Troup undertook in 2005 to house and support her nephew for four years while he attended university. Mr. Troup disliked the nephew, whom he regarded as a leech.

Upon retiring, Mrs. Troup became a famous author of historical novels. Her second novel, allegedly fiction, recounted a story which closely resembled the life of a leading Canadian politician. On July 1, 2007, her home-town newspaper, *The Press*, carried a story announcing that the politician had begun a defamation action based on the book. National sales of Mrs. Troup's books began to increase dramatically in response to the publicity.

Later that day Mrs. Troup was shopping in the city when she walked past a construction site. Unfortunately, the cable securing a load of concrete failed. Some of the blocks fell on Mrs. Troup, causing her severe injuries. The incident also destroyed the $10,000 gold watch that Mrs. Troup was wearing. Mrs. Troup went into a coma and was taken to the intensive care unit at the hospital. Some 80% of her hospital bills were borne by government medical insurance and the remaining 20% were paid by Mrs. Troup's private Blue Cross plan. Mrs. Troup died ten days later without ever regaining consciousness. She was 67. Mr. Troup was named the sole beneficiary and executor under his wife's will. He was also named the sole beneficiary of her $100,000 life insurance policy.

Mr. Troup now seeks your advice with respect to a possible legal action against the construction company that owned and operated the crane. The company has admitted negligence. Based upon the relevant legislation in your province, what damages will flow from the action, to whom will damages be awarded, and how will damages be divided among the possible claimants?

19

DEFENCES IN NEGLIGENCE

1. Introduction
2. Contributory Negligence
3. Voluntary Assumption of Risk
4. Participation in a Criminal or Immoral Act
5. Inevitable Accident

1. Introduction

Even if the plaintiff proves that he or she was negligently injured by the defendant, damages may be reduced or denied on the basis of a defence. The first three defences that we discuss – contributory negligence, voluntary assumption of risk and participation in a criminal or immoral act – pertain to the plaintiff's own behaviour. The fourth defence, inevitable accident, is concerned with the factual circumstances surrounding the defendant's conduct and can be seen as a special denial of negligence.

For each defence, the burden of proof is on the defendant. The defendant may be able to plead and prove more than one defence.

2. Contributory Negligence

(a) THE DEVELOPMENT OF THE DEFENCE

At common law the plaintiff traditionally was denied recovery if his or her negligent conduct contributed to the injury. There was no apportionment of loss between the defendant and plaintiff, even if the plaintiff's negligence was a relatively insignificant cause. To avoid this inequity, the courts developed what became known as the "last clear chance" or "last opportunity" rule. This doctrine permitted the plaintiff to recover, despite his or her contributory negligence, if the defendant had the last clear chance to avoid the accident and negligently failed to take it. While the doctrine clearly benefited the plaintiff, it perpetuated the existing all-or-nothing approach by placing the entire loss on the defendant. With the acceptance of more complex theories of causation and liability the doctrine came under severe criticism. Fleming, *The Law of Torts*, 9th ed. (1998) states at 305:

> Over the century of its sway, the last opportunity doctrine developed into a plastic instrument for allocating the loss to either plaintiff or defendant in accordance with the court's view of whose was the disproportionately greater share of responsibility . . . . The resulting casuistry tended to make the task of appellate review a veritable farce and eventually prompted a retreat.

Legislation permitting the apportionment of liability was not enacted until well into the 20th century. By allowing the dividing of liability according to the parties' relative degrees of fault, the legislation tempered the harshness of the common law's all-or-nothing approach.

NOTES AND QUESTIONS

1. The courts first dealt with contributory negligence as a question of legal causation rather than as a defence: see *Butterfield v. Forrester* (1809), 103 E.R. 926 (K.B.); and *Davies v. Mann* (1842), 152 E.R. 588 (Exch.). What are the advantages and disadvantages of this approach?

2. Once the courts recognized that there could be more than one legal cause of an accident, was there any justification for continuing to treat contributory negligence as a complete bar to recovery? See Bohlen, "Contributory Negligence" (1908) 21 Harv. L. Rev. 233; Malone, "The Formative Period of Contributory Negligence" (1946) 41 Ill. L. Rev. 151; James, "Contributory Negligence" (1953) 62 Yale L. Rev. 691; and Fleming, "Forward: Comparative Negligence at Last - by Judicial Choice" (1976) 64 Cal. L. Rev. 239.

3. *Davies v. Mann, supra*, was the first case in which the last clear chance doctrine was clearly articulated. For Canadian applications of the doctrine see *Long v. Toronto Ry. Co.* (1914), 50 S.C.R. 224; *B.C. Elec. Ry. Co. v. Loach*, [1916] 1 A.C. 719 (P.C.); *Boulay v. Rousselle* (1984), 30 C.C.L.T. 149 (N.B.Q.B.); and *Hunter v. Briere* (1989), 49 C.C.L.T. 93 (Man. Q.B.). See also MacIntyre, "The Rationale of Last Clear Chance" (1940) 18 Can. Bar Rev. 665; Williams, *Joint Torts and Contributory Negligence* (1951) at 223-55; and Casswell, "Avoiding Last Clear Chance" (1990) 69 Can. Bar Rev. 129.

4. In what circumstances did the last clear chance doctrine work to the defendant's advantage? As we shall later discuss, the apportionment legislation did not eliminate the last clear chance doctrine. Following the enactment of apportionment legislation, in what circumstances would the last clear chance doctrine benefit the defendant?

5. The patent unfairness of the common law rule led the Supreme Court of Canada to abolish it even in the absence of contributory negligence legislation. In *Bow Valley Husky (Bermuda) Ltd. v. Saint John Shipbuilding Ltd.* (1997), 153 D.L.R. (4th) 385 (S.C.C.) McLachlin J. held that Newfoundland and Labrador's *Contributory Negligence Act*, R.S.N.L. 1990, c. C-33 did not apply to a claim arising in maritime law. Nevertheless, she held:

> The considerations on which the contributory negligence bar was based no longer comport with the modern view of fairness and justice. Tort law no longer accepts the traditional theory underpinning the contributory negligence bar – that the injured party cannot prove that the tortfeasor "caused" the damage. The contributory negligence bar results in manifest unfairness, particularly where the negligence of the injured party is slight in comparison with the negligence of others. Nor does the contributory negligence bar further the goal of modern tort law of encouraging care and vigilance. So long as an injured party can be shown to be marginally at fault, a tortfeasor's conduct, no matter how egregious, goes unpunished.

Accordingly, she held that claims in maritime law should be subject to a rule of joint and several liability, together with a right of contribution.

(b) CONDUCT CONSTITUTING CONTRIBUTORY NEGLIGENCE

Contributory negligence can take many forms. The plaintiff may carelessly enter into a dangerous situation, such as a sober passenger negligently accepting a ride from a drunk driver who later crashes into a wall. Or the plaintiff may carelessly contribute to the creation of an accident, such as a passenger engaging a driver in horseplay that results in an accident. Or the plaintiff may carelessly contribute not to the creation of an accident but rather to the resulting harm, such as a passenger negligently failing to wear a seat belt and consequently suffering additional injuries. The cases in this section provide further illustrations.

WALLS v. MUSSENS LTD.
(1969), 11 D.L.R. (3d) 245 (N.B.C.A.)

HUGHES J.A.: – In the afternoon of January 18, 1968, the defendant Morrison, a serviceman and mechanic in the employ of the defendant Mussens Limited, drove a machine used in logging operations called a timberjack, belonging to one Murdock Hallihan, to the plaintiff's service station premises where he obtained permission to repair the front drive shaft of the timberjack in one of the bays of the service station. Shortly after 6:30 p.m. while Morrison and Hallihan were working on the machine, a propane gas torch being used by Morrison ignited a pool containing gasoline on the floor beneath the machine.

The learned trial Judge found that the gasoline on the floor had leaked from a tube leading from the gas tank to the engine of the timberjack and that the fire was caused by the negligence of Morrison in the use of the propane gas torch while acting in the course of his employment with Mussens Ltd. There is no appeal against these findings.

When the fire started the plaintiff was at home for his evening meal, having left Terry Hambrook, a 17-year-old high school boy employed by him to tend the gas tanks, change tires and do other such work, in charge of the service station. Hambrook, who was in the office talking with two boys, heard someone call out: "Fire – come on out and bring a fire extinguisher" – but, instead of bringing one of the available extinguishers, Hambrook and others including Morrison, Hallihan and probably the two boys attempted to smother the fire by throwing snow on it. Hallihan says he also tried to extinguish it with water from a hose.

When the plaintiff, who was told of the fire by Hambrook, arrived at the service station the flame was about 18 inches in height and two feet in diameter. The plaintiff joined the others in shovelling snow onto the fire but in the excitement of the emergency the five fire extinguishers which were on the premises were not thought of. Morrison testified that when he realized the snow would not smother the fire he ran out of the building, drove his truck to the door, and tried to tow the timberjack from the building but was unable to do so as his truck was too light to move it. The fire spread quickly and the service station and most of the contents were destroyed.

Alpha D. Curl, an expert in the production, design and use theory of fire prevention equipment, expressed an opinion, which the learned trial Judge accepted, that had the available fire extinguishers been used when the plaintiff arrived at the service station the fire could probably have been extinguished. In their defence the defendants alleged that the damage suffered by the plaintiff was caused wholly by the negligence or breach of duty by the plaintiff, his workmen, licensees, servants and agents. The learned trial Judge carefully considered the evidence and found that the failure of the plaintiff to use the fire extinguishers in the prevailing excitement did not constitute contributory negligence even though his failure to do so may have deprived those present of the chance of minimizing the loss, and he held the negligence of Morrison was the sole cause of the plaintiff's damage.

I have read the evidence with respect to the frantic efforts of all concerned, including the plaintiff, to extinguish the fire, and I agree that the conclusions reached by the learned trial Judge are amply supported by the evidence.

No portion of the responsibility for starting the fire can be attributed to the plaintiff. There was no antecedent negligence on his part and he had no part in the repair work which was carried out by Morrison. The emergency was created solely by the negligence of Morrison for whose acts and omissions Mussens Ltd. is vicariously liable. While it may be unfortunate the plaintiff did not have the presence of mind in the emergency to use the fire extinguishers which were available, and notwithstanding his participation in throwing snow on the fire may have aggravated the situation, I think the plaintiff is entitled to invoke the "agony of the moment" rule as an answer to the allegation of contributory negligence made against him.

The Law of Torts, 3rd ed., by J.G. Fleming, contains the following statement at p. 247:

> On the other hand, a person's conduct, in the face of a sudden emergency, cannot be judged from the standpoint of what would have been reasonable behaviour in the light of hind-knowledge and in a calmer atmosphere conducive to a nice evaluation of alternatives. A certain latitude is allowed when "in the agony of the moment" he seeks to extricate himself from an emergency not created by his own antecedent negligence. The degree of judgment and presence of mind expected of the plaintiff is what would have been reasonable conduct in such a situation, and he will not be adjudged guilty of contributory negligence merely because, as it turns out, he unwittingly took the wrong course.

. . .

The test to be applied in circumstances such as those as in the case at bar is, in my opinion, not whether the plaintiff exercised a careful and prudent judgment in doing what he did, but whether what he did was something an ordinarily prudent man might reasonably have done under the stress of the emergency.

In my opinion it might well have appeared to an ordinarily prudent man in the emergency with which the plaintiff was confronted that shovelling snow on the fire was the most effective way to extinguish it, although in fact it was not, and may actually have tended to spread the fire. It is now apparent that the fire could not have been smothered as it was being fed by gasoline leaking from the fuel line of the timberjack and it is most improbable the plaintiff had any knowledge of that fact until the cause of the fire was investigated. The plaintiff's reaction to the emergency was merely to do what the others were doing and I cannot say that it was something an ordinarily prudent man might not reasonably have done in the circumstances.

In my opinion the appeal on this ground should fail.

NOTES AND QUESTIONS

1. What criteria did the court in *Walls* use in determining whether the plaintiff had breached the standard of care expected of him? Should the test be applied in exactly the

same way in assessing the defendant's carelessness and the plaintiff's contributory negligence? See also *Zervobeakos v. Zervobeakos* (1969), 8 D.L.R. (3d) 377 (N.S.C.A.); and *Neufeld v. Landry* (1975), 55 D.L.R. (3d) 296 (Man. C.A.). It has been suggested that while the same principles theoretically apply to both parties, judges and especially juries tend to be relatively more reluctant to find contributory negligence than negligence: Fleming, *The Law of Torts*, 9th ed. (1998) at 320. What factors do you suspect underlie that tendency?

2. In *A.G. Ont. v. Keller* (1978), 94 D.L.R. (3d) 632 (Ont. C.A.) the plaintiff was a police officer who was injured in a high-speed chase when his cruiser went out of control and struck a pole. The officer was driving at about 85 miles per hour on icy roads within 100 to 150 feet of the defendant. The court held that the officer was not contributorily negligent because his actions were "no more than was reasonably necessary to carry out his statutory duty." Nevertheless, given the risks involved in high-speed chases, did the officer act reasonably? Should the police officer in *Keller* have been held to a higher standard of care than the average driver? Would the court have found the officer negligent if he had hit a pedestrian? Should it make any difference? See *Priestman v. Colangelo*, [1959] S.C.R. 615; *Roberge v. R.* (1983), 147 D.L.R. (3d) 493 (S.C.C.); *Miller v. Wolbaum* (1986), 47 M.V.R. 162 (Sask. Q.B.); and *Moore v. Fanning* (1987), 41 C.C.L.T. 67 (Ont. H.C.).

The issue of a police officer's negligence will also arise if he or she injures a third party while pursuing a suspect. In such circumstances, however, the victim's damages may be reduced if he or she carelessly failed to see or hear the oncoming police car: see *Hill v. Hurst* (2001), 203 D.L.R. (4th) 749 (B.C.C.A.).

3. In *Lewis v. Todd* (1980), 115 D.L.R. (3d) 257 (S.C.C.) a police officer was killed by a driver while investigating a traffic accident. Working alone and ignoring the traffic, Constable Lewis apparently relied on the warnings given by several flashing lights. The Supreme Court of Canada rejected the argument that Lewis was contributorily negligent for not keeping a proper lookout. It stated that his conduct had to be judged according to the standard of care expected of a police officer investigating an accident and not the standard of an ordinary pedestrian. According to *Lewis* and *Keller*, how would you characterize a police officer's standard of care: is it higher or lower than that of the average citizen?

4. In *Heeney v. Best* (1979), 108 D.L.R. (3d) 366 (Ont. C.A.) the plaintiff's chickens died of asphyxiation when the defendant negligently cut off the power supply to the plaintiff's barns. An alarm system that would have warned of a power failure had inexplicably not been plugged in on the night of the incident. Since only 25 to 50% of local poultry farmers had alarm systems, the plaintiff argued that it was the custom not to have an alarm system. Therefore, the plaintiff contended, he could not be found contributorily negligent for having a non-operating alarm. Nevertheless, the plaintiff was found to have been contributorily negligent for failing to take reasonable care of his own property. Would the court have reached the same conclusion if the plaintiff had not installed an alarm system? Should compliance with and breach of a custom have the same effect in establishing contributory negligence as they do in negligence?

Heeney raises the issue of the precautions that an individual must take to protect against the tortious or illegal conduct of others. Should a homeowner be held contributorily negligent for failing to install a fire alarm if its absence contributed to his or her fire losses? Would a homeowner be contributorily negligent for failing to replace an existing fire alarm with a more modern and reliable device? Would a homeowner be held contributorily negligent for not purchasing a burglar alarm and other security devices? Would your answers be affected by the costs of the devices? See also the discussion of the duty to control the conduct of others in Chapter 11.

5. The standard of care imposed in contributory negligence is affected by the age, disabilities and professional training of the plaintiff. For example, a child is required to meet the standard of care of a reasonable child of like age, intelligence and experience. See *Myers v. Peel County Bd. of Ed.* (1981), 123 D.L.R. (3d) 1 (S.C.C.); *Laviolette v. C.N.R.* (1987), 40 C.C.L.T. 138 (N.B.C.A.); *Bajkov v. Canil* (1990), 66 D.L.R. (4th) 572 (B.C.C.A.); and *Lee (Guardian ad litem of) v. Barker*, [1992] 5 W.W.R. 256 (B.C.C.A.).

6. By virtue of the doctrine of identification, the common law attributed the negligence of one party to the conduct of another if a special relationship existed between them. Thus at one time the negligence of a child's supervisor or parent was imputed to the child, thereby reducing the child's claim against the negligent defendant. Although this principle has been eliminated in the parent and child relationship, it still applies in certain situations involving (i) a master and servant and (ii) a car owner and driver. See *Ducharme v. Davies*, [1984] 1 W.W.R. 699 (Sask. C.A.); *Alliance & Leicester Building Society v. Edgestop Ltd.*, [1994] 2 All E.R. 38 (Ch.); *Galaske v. O'Donnell* (1994), 112 D.L.R. (4th) 109 (S.C.C.); and Fleming, *The Law of Torts*, 9th ed. (1998) at 323.

7. As with negligence, the issue of contributory negligence turns on the specific facts of the case. For a discussion of contributory negligence see *Wells v. Parsons* (1970), 1 Nfld. & P.E.I.R. 513 (Nfld. C.A.); *Comeau v. Laliberte* (1986), 69 N.B.R. (2d) 87 (Q.B.); *Lee v. O'Farrell* (1988), 43 C.C.L.T. 269 (B.C.S.C.); *McEvoy v. Capital Motors* (1992), 88 D.L.R. (4th) 358 (B.C.C.A.); *Findley v. Driver* (1992), 7 O.R. (3d) 48 (C.A.); *Hutchings v. Nevin* (1992), 12 C.C.L.T. (2d) 259 (Ont. Gen. Div.); and *Fortey (Guardian ad litem of) v. Canada (Attorney General)* (1999), 46 C.C.L.T (2d) 271 (B.C.C.A.).

8. As noted in Chapter 13, there is some concern about allowing contributory negligence to be raised as a defence to a claim of negligent misrepresentation, since that cause of action requires the plaintiff's reliance to be reasonable. The courts have generally allowed the defence to be raised: see *Grand Restaurants of Canada Ltd. v. Toronto (City)* (1981), 32 O.R. (2d) 757 (H.C.), aff'd (1982), 39 O.R. (2d) 752 (C.A.); and *Avco Financial Services Realty Ltd. v. Norman* (2003), 64 O.R. (3d) 239 (C.A.).

GAGNON v. BEAULIEU

[1977] 1 W.W.R. 702 (B.C.S.C.)

FULTON J.: – The plaintiff was injured in a collision which took place on 31st August 1974 on Highway 401 near Chilliwack, British Columbia, when a 1972 Vega "Hatchback", owned and driven by the defendant Beaulieu and in which the plaintiff was riding as a front seat passenger, ran into the rear end of a pick-up truck which was stopped at a railroad crossing waiting for a train to pass by. Liability of the defendant driver is admitted – the main issue in this connection is whether or not the plaintiff was wearing a seat belt and, if not, whether this constituted negligence contributing to the nature and extent of his injuries.

The plaintiff suffered vertical lacerations of the right forehead and scalp, a deep horizontal laceration running across the right lower eyelid and upper right cheek and into the right temple. The cheek was fractured and crushed, and the right eye was damaged. The injuries are consistent with the plaintiff having been thrown forward by the impact, striking the windshield and/ or dashboard of the car with his forehead and face. The defendant maintains that the plaintiff was not wearing a seat belt apparatus provided for the passenger, consisting of a lap belt and shoulder harness, and that if the plaintiff had been wearing this apparatus, he would not have suffered those head and facial injuries.

. . .

For the plaintiff it was contended that failure to wear a seat belt is not per se negligence, and that it is not negligence in any circumstances if the person concerned is not convinced of the efficacy of seat belts and/ or believes that the wearing of a seat belt, including particularly the shoulder strap, may in certain circumstances create the hazard of greater injury or damage than if it were not worn – that if, for instance, the car were to overturn, the wearer might be trapped between the seat and the roof. There was evidence that the plaintiff had this opinion.

. . .

The leading case in British Columbia is *Yuan v. Farstad,* supra, a decision of this court.

. . .

What Munro J. [the judge in *Yuan*] seems to me to have clearly said is this: that in the light of modern-day knowledge of the benefits and reduction of danger of injury flowing from the use of seat belts, an occupant of a motor vehicle in which such apparatus is provided for his use who nevertheless fails to wear it is negligent in that he has failed to take reasonable precautions for his own safety. If in those circumstances he is injured in a collision, and if it is established as a fact that in the circumstances of that collision the wearing of the seat belt provided would have prevented or lessened the injuries he sustained, then his negligence in failing to wear it has contributed to the extent of his injuries and becomes contributory negligence. If, of course, it is not shown in connection with the particular circumstances of the accident in question that the wearing of the seat belt would have prevented or lessened the injuries, then the failure to wear it, while negligent in itself, does not constitute negligence contributing to the injuries or to the extent thereof.

. . .

[O]n the basis of the authorities which I believe to be binding on me, and which, with respect, I believe also to be the logical and sensible application to the situation of facts of which judges, as rational human beings, do have knowledge, I am of opinion that the law in British Columbia on this subject is as follows:

(a) Failure, while travelling in a motor vehicle on a street or highway, to wear a seat belt or any part thereof as provided in a vehicle in accordance with the safety standards from time to time applicable is failure to take a step which a person knows or ought to know to be reasonably necessary for his own safety.

(b) If in such circumstances he suffers injury as the result of the vehicle being involved in an accident, and if it appears from the evidence that if the seat belt had been worn the injuries would have been prevented or the severity thereof lessened, then the failure to wear a seat belt is negligence which has contributed to the nature and extent of those injuries.

(c) In the case of this particular form of contributory negligence, the onus is on the defendant to satisfy the court, in accordance with the usual standard of proof, not only that the seat belt was not worn but also that the injuries would have been prevented or lessened if the seat belt had been worn. The courts should not find the second of these facts merely by inference from the first, even if that has been established.

. . .

Before reviewing the evidence as to the facts of this case to which these propositions apply, I should refer to the argument addressed that people may in fact be unconvinced of the efficacy, or desirability, of wearing seat belts, as was urged on behalf of the plaintiff here. This argument was carefully reviewed by Lord Denning M.R., in the English Court of Appeal, in the recent case of *Froom v. Butcher*, [1975] 3 All E.R. 520. At p. 526 he said:

> Quite a lot of people, however, think differently about seat belts. Some are like Mr. Froom here. They think that they would be less likely to be injured if they were thrown clear than if they were strapped in. They would be wrong. The chances of injury are four times as great. Yet they believe it honestly and firmly. On this account Nield J. thought they should not bear any responsibility. He recognized that such persons are in a minority, but he thought that proper respect should be paid to the minority view. He said:
>
>> ". . . I do not feel that the courts are justified in invading the freedom of choice of the motorist by holding it to be negligence, lack of care or fault to act on an opinion firmly and honestly held and shared by many other sensible people."
>
> I am afraid I do not agree. In determining responsibility, the law eliminates the personal equation. It takes no notice of the views of the particular individual; or of others like him. It requires everyone to exercise all such precautions as a man of ordinary prudence would observe.
>
> . . .

I agree with counsel for the plaintiff that I am not bound by this English case, and need not apply it in the case before me. However, I say at once that I do respectfully agree with the reasoning expressed in that judgment, and consider that it is entirely applicable to the facts established by the evidence before me, which I now review.

The evidence is that the defendant's car was equipped with seat belts consisting of a lap belt and a cross-over shoulder harness on the passenger side, in good working order. The plaintiff does not remember whether he was wearing either part of this equipment: as a result of the blow to his head, his recollection of the circumstances of the accident itself is entirely blank.

. . .

Expert evidence as to the protection afforded by seat belts was given by Mr. A.C.

Shiels, director of traffic safety programs for the province of Saskatchewan. Mr. Shiels has done extensive research into the whole question of the protection of occupants of automobiles from injury in accidents, including the measurement of the relative effectiveness of various safety devices and the measurement of the relative severity of collisions and the type and extent of injury which may be expected in collisions of differing degrees of severity as between occupants who wear seat belts with shoulder harnesses and those who do not. His evidence was of considerable help in this regard.

He testified that from the degree of crushing of the front of the car as shown in the photographs Exs. 18 and 19, and from the description of the items in and on the car which were damaged, he rated the severity of the collision as class 2. In a collision of this type he would expect that a passenger in the front seat not wearing any seat belt apparatus would suffer injuries consisting of bumps and bruises, some undetermined degree of head injuries consisting of lacerations, including lacerations to the eyelids and to the face, and possible damage to the eyeball itself. For a passenger wearing properly adjusted seat belt apparatus including the shoulder harness, he said it would be virtually impossible to contact the windshield or dashboard with his head in a collision of this class and that there would probably be minor bruises and tenderness at the points where the restraining harness had taken the load of the body on impact. Here the evidence is that the windshield was struck and shattered; in the opinion of the expert it was struck by a round object such as the head, and the evidence is equally consistent with its having been struck from inside as from outside. The plaintiff received head and facial injuries of the type said to be expected to be incurred in a collision of this type, by a person not wearing a restraining apparatus, and there is no evidence of any marks or bruising on his body such as would be expected if he had been restrained by a lap and/ or shoulder belt.

. . .

On the whole of the evidence I am satisfied that the plaintiff knew or ought to have known that the wearing of the seat belt provided, including the shoulder harness, would reduce the possibility of his being injured in a collision, that at the time of this accident he was not wearing the seat belt equipment provided and that, had he been wearing it, and particularly the shoulder harness, his injuries would have been less severe, if not prevented altogether. I consider that the expert, Mr. Shiels, was not merely speculating as to this result, but had a sound basis for his opinion. Applying the law which I have held to be applicable to these circumstances in this province, I find it to have been established that the plaintiff was negligent and that his negligence contributed to the nature and extent of his injuries.

There will be judgment accordingly.

NOTES AND QUESTIONS

1. Why were the plaintiff's beliefs about the safety value of seat belts considered irrelevant? Would the result have been the same if the plaintiff had refused to wear the seat belt because it was physically uncomfortable for him to do so, or because he had a morbid fear of being trapped in a burning vehicle which made wearing a seat belt emotionally traumatic? See *Froom v. Butcher*, [1975] 3 All E.R. 520 (C.A.); *Davis v. Anderson* (1980), 15 C.C.L.T. 192 (B.C.C.A.); and *Shaw v. Roemer* (1982), 134 D.L.R. (3d) 590 (N.S.C.A.).

2. Based on *Gagnon*, would a driver and owner of a car be negligent for: (a) failing to equip a car with seat belts, (b) failing to make passengers aware of the presence of seat belts, or (c) permitting a passenger to remain in the car without wearing a seat belt? See *Pasternack v. Poulton*, [1973] 2 All E.R. 74 (Q.B.); *Haley v. Richardson; McCrae v. Richardson* (1975), 60 D.L.R. (3d) 480 (N.B.C.A.); and *Heller v. Martens*, [2002] 9 W.W.R. 71 (Alta. C.A.). In *Galaske v. O'Donnell*, [1994] 1 S.C.R. 670 the court held that the defendant had a duty to ensure that an eight-year-old passenger wore a seat belt. The fact that the boy's father was also a passenger in the car and may have been negligent did not negate the defendant's duty.

3. In *Rewcastle v. Sieben* (2003), 20 Alta. L.R. (4th) 17 (C.A.) the court found that the plaintiff was not contributorily negligent for not wearing a seat belt. The vehicle had four seat belts but the plaintiff was one of six people in the car. The plaintiff asked to sit in the front seat but was refused. She then sat on the lap of a person in the back seat. At the time the plaintiff was 16 years old. It was close to midnight, she was 7.5 km from home, and she had a cell phone and credit card. The car crashed and the plaintiff was killed. The court held that her decision to ride in the car without a seat belt was reasonable. Do you agree?

4. What evidence did the court in *Gagnon* rely on in concluding that the plaintiff's failure to wear his seat belt contributed to his losses? Was the court's approach consistent with the general principles that govern causation? See *Lucas v. Antoniak* (1978), 7 C.C.L.T. 209 (B.C.S.C.), aff'd (1980), 15 C.C.L.T. 195 (B.C.C.A.); and *Snushall v. Fulsang* (2005), 78 O.R. (3d) 142 (C.A.). For examples in which the plaintiff's failure to wear a seatbelt was held to be causally irrelevant to his injuries see *Madge v. Meyer*, [2002] 5 W.W.R. 50 (Alta. C.A.); and *Claiter v. Rose*, 2004 CarswellBC 59 (S.C.) (WLeC).

5. Would a passenger in a boat who failed to wear a life jacket, a motorcyclist or bicyclist who failed to wear a crash helmet, an airline passenger who failed to wear a seat belt, or a hockey player who failed to wear a helmet be treated the same way as someone who failed to wear a seat belt while driving? Is there any justification for treating the seat belt cases differently from other contributory negligence cases?

6. All of the provinces have enacted legislation requiring occupants of motor vehicles to wear seat belts in most situations. See for example the *Highway Traffic Act*, R.S.O. 1990, c. H.8, s. 106. Should the existence of a statutory duty affect the analysis of the seat belt defence? See *Genik v. Ewanylo* (1980), 12 C.C.L.T. 121 (Man. C.A.); *Shkwarchuk v. Hansen* (1984), 30 C.C.L.T. 121 (Sask. Q.B.); and *Gray v. Macklin* (2000), 4 C.C.L.T. (3d) 13 (Ont. S.C.J.). But see *Webber v. Crawford* (1988), 46 C.C.L.T. 1. (B.C.S.C.); and *Wallace v. Berrigan* (1988), 47 D.L.R. (4th) 752 (N.S.C.A.). See also Wakeling, "Seat Belt Legislation: An End to Cruel and Unusual Punishment" (1977) 42 Sask. L. Rev. 105.

7. Do you think that the court's recognition of the seat belt defence has significantly affected the patterns of seat belt use? Can you suggest alternative means of inducing people to wear seat belts?

8. For an academic discussion of this issue see Hicks, "Seat Belts and Crash Helmets" (1974) 37 Mod. L. Rev. 308; and Slatter, "Seat Belts and Contributory Negligence" (1977) 4 Dal. L.J. 96.

(c) APPORTIONMENT OF LOSS

In 1924 Ontario enacted Canada's first apportionment legislation and the remaining common law provinces soon followed suit. Although the form of the legislation varies, there are few substantial differences in the operation of the provincial statutes. The legislation permits the court to divide responsibility for damages between the parties according to their relative degrees of fault.

NEGLIGENCE ACT

R.S.O. 1990, c. N.1

. . .

Extent of liability, remedy over

1. Where damages have been caused or contributed to by the fault or neglect of two or more persons, the court shall determine the degree in which each of such persons is at fault or negligent, and, where two or more persons are found at fault or negligent, they are jointly and severally liable to the person suffering loss or damage for such fault or negligence, but as between themselves, in the absence of any contract express or implied, each is liable to make contribution and indemnify each other in the degree in which they are respectively found to be at fault or negligent.

Recovery as between tortfeasors

2. A tortfeasor may recover contribution or indemnity from any other tortfeasor who is, or would if sued have been, liable in respect of the damage to any person suffering damage as a result of a tort by settling with the person suffering such damage, and thereafter commencing or continuing action against such other tortfeasor, in which event the tortfeasor settling the damage shall satisfy the court that the amount of the settlement was reasonable, and in the event that the court finds the amount of the settlement was excessive it may fix the amount at which the claim should have been settled.

Plaintiff guilty of contributory negligence

3. In any action for damages that is founded upon the fault or negligence of the defendant if fault or negligence is found on the part of the plaintiff that contributed to the damages, the court shall apportion the damages in proportion to the degree of fault or negligence found against the parties respectively.

Where parties to be deemed equally at fault

4. If it is not practicable to determine the respective degree of fault or negligence as between any parties to an action, such parties shall be deemed to be equally at fault or negligent.

Adding parties

5. Wherever it appears that a person not already a party to an action is or may be wholly or partly responsible for the damages claimed, such person may be added as a party defendant to the action upon such terms as are considered just or may be made a

third party to the action in the manner prescribed by the rules of court for adding third parties.

Jury to determine degrees of negligence of parties

6. In any action tried with a jury, the degree of fault or negligence of the respective parties is a question of fact for the jury.

When plaintiff may be liable for costs

7. Where the damages are occasioned by the fault or negligence of more than one party, the court has power to direct that the plaintiff shall bear some portion of the costs if the circumstances render this just.

NOTES AND QUESTIONS

1. Alberta, Nova Scotia and New Brunswick deal with apportionment between the plaintiff and defendant in one statute and contribution among tortfeasors in another. The other common law provinces deal with both issues in the same legislation. For a comparison see the Institute of Law Research and Reform, *Contributory Negligence and Concurrent Wrongdoers* (1979) at 2-7. See Cheifetz, *Apportionment of Fault in Tort* (1981), who provides a detailed section-by-section analysis of the Ontario legislation followed by a brief reference to the other provincial statutes. See also Ontario Law Reform Commission, *Report on Contribution Among Wrongdoers and Contributory Negligence* (1988); and Law Reform Commission of British Columbia, *Report on Apportionment of Costs and Contributory Negligence: Section 3 of the Negligence Act* (1993).

2. In *Pilon v. Janveaux* (2005), 203 O.A.C. 345 (C.A.), additional reasons (2006), 211 O.A.C. 19 (C.A.) the plaintiff was injured as a passenger in a car driven by an impaired driver. The driver, the owner of the car and the bar where the driver had been drinking all admitted liability for causing the accident. The judge told the jury to determine the plaintiff's degree of contributory negligence but, apparently because of the admission, not to apportion liability among the defendants. The jury found the plaintiff, who was also intoxicated, 35.5% responsible for accepting a ride from an impaired driver and failing to wear a seat belt. The jury's verdict did not make clear the bar's degree of liability, and in particular did not address its responsibility for the plaintiff's intoxication. The Court of Appeal held that under s. 3 of the *Negligence Act* the court was required to apportion liability, so that the jury verdict could not stand. It held that "the jury should have been asked to apportion responsibility for the [plaintiff's] damages in four parts: (1) to the driver (and owner) of the vehicle; (2) to the injured passenger for his contributory negligence; (3) to the tavern for over-serving the driver; and (4) to the tavern for over-serving the passenger." Under the fourth of these parts, the Court of Appeal found the bar responsible for 40% of the plaintiff's 35.5% liability, so that the plaintiff was only 21.3% responsible.

3. There is an ongoing debate as to whether the apportionment legislation applies only to negligence or to all torts. The Court of Appeal for Ontario has overruled an earlier decision, *Hollebone v. Barnard*, [1954] O.R. 236 (H.C.), and held that "fault" in s. 1 incorporates all intentional wrongdoing "as well as other types of substandard conduct": *Bell Canada v. Cope (Sarnia) Ltd.* (1980), 11 C.C.L.T. 170 (H.C.), aff'd 119 D.L.R.

(3d) 254 (C.A.). See also *Brown v. Cole* (1995), 14 B.C.L.R. (3d) 53 (C.A.); *Berntt v. Vancouver (City)*, [1997] 4 W.W.R. 505 (B.C.S.C.), rev'd on other grounds (1999), 46 C.C.L.T. (2d) 139 (B.C.C.A.); and *Gerling Global General Insurance Co. v. Siskind, Cromarty, Ivey & Dowler* (2004), 12 C.C.L.I. (4th) 278 (Ont. S.C.J.). In contrast, the courts of Saskatchewan have held that the comparable provision in that jurisdiction applies only to negligence: *Chernesky v. Armadale Publishers Ltd.* (1974), 53 D.L.R. (3d) 79 (Sask. C.A.); and *Trends Holdings Ltd. (Trustee of) v. Tilson* (2006), 25 C.B.R. (5th) 239 (Sask. Q.B.).

As a matter of statutory interpretation, which line of analysis do you prefer? In principle, is there any reason to limit contributory negligence and the statutory right to seek contribution to negligence cases? See Kutner, "Contribution Among Tortfeasors: Liability Issues in Contribution Law" (1985) 63 Can. Bar Rev. 1; and Law Reform Commission of British Columbia, *Report on Shared Liability* (1986).

4. The Supreme Court of Canada has stated "as a matter of principle that contributory negligence would not be available in the context of a strict liability tort . . . . While this argument would be available in an action for negligence, the notion of strict liability involved in an action for conversion is *prima facie* antithetical to the concept of contributory negligence": *Boma Manufacturing Ltd. v. C.I.B.C.* (1996), 140 D.L.R. (4th) 463 (S.C.C.). The issue in *Boma* arose in the context of an action for conversion of cheques. It is not clear whether the court intended to preclude application of apportionment legislation to other strict liability torts as well. Given that conversion requires intent, would you agree with characterizing the action as involving strict liability?

In *Cowles v. Balac* (2006), 83 O.R. (3d) 660 (C.A.) the plaintiffs were attacked by Bengal tigers at the defendant's drive-through safari zoo. At para. 216 Justice Borins said of *Boma*: "In my respectful view, in stating contributory negligence is not available in the context of a strict liability tort, Iacobucci J. was not intending to state a general principle. Rather, he was referring to the law of bills of exchange." After a detailed review of the cases and academic views, he concluded that contributory negligence should be a defence to strict liability torts. In *Cowles* Justice Borins was in dissent. The majority held that on the facts the plaintiffs were not contributorily negligent and so did not address this issue.

5. Depending on the tort involved, it may not matter whether a provincial apportionment statute applies more broadly than to negligence because the courts have indicated that liability for some torts can be apportioned at common law. See *Bow Valley Husky (Bermuda) Ltd. v. Saint John Shipbuilding Ltd.*, [1997] 3 S.C.R. 1210. In *Blackwater v. Plint*, [2005] 3 S.C.R. 3 the court apportioned liability 75-25% between two defendants who were each vicariously liable for the sexual assaults by a dormitory supervisor at a residential school.

6. It has been suggested that the apportionment legislation encompasses not only torts but other branches of the law as well. See *Giffels Associates Ltd v. Eastern Const. Co.* (1978), 84 D.L.R. (3d) 344 (S.C.C.); *Can. Western Nat. Gas Co. v. Pathfinder Surveys Ltd.* (1980), 12 C.C.L.T. 211 (Alta. C.A.); *Tompkins Hardware Ltd. v. North West Flying Services Ltd.* (1982), 139 D.L.R. (3d) 329 (Ont. H.C.); and *Crown West Steel Fabricators v. Capri Insurance Services Ltd.* (2002), 214 D.L.R. (4th) 577 (B.C.C.A.). See also Weinrib, "Contribution in a Contractual Setting" (1976) 54 Can.

Bar Rev. 338; Klar, "Developments In Tort Law: The 1979-80 Term" (1981) 2 S.C.L.R. 325 at 340-54; and Ontario Law Reform Commission, *Report on Contribution Among Wrongdoers and Contributory Negligence* (1988) at 65-83.

7. The apportionment legislation eliminated the rationale for the last clear chance doctrine. Initially, however, many Canadian courts continued to apply the doctrine, while others interpreted it narrowly or avoided the issue. See Bowker, "Ten More Years Under Contributory Negligence Acts" (1964) 2 U.B.C.L. Rev. 198; and Casswell, "Avoiding Last Clear Chance" (1990) 69 Can. Bar Rev. 129.

See also *Hartman v. Fisette* (1976), 66 D.L.R. (3d) 516 (S.C.C.); *MacKay v. MacLellan* (1976), 1 C.C.L.T. 310 (N.S.C.A.); *Poitras v. Goulet* (1987), 46 Man. R. (2d) 87 (C.A.); *Hunter v. Briere* (1989), 49 C.C.L.T. 93 (Man. Q.B.); *Fillier v. Whittom* (1995), 171 N.B.R. (2d) 92 (C.A.); and *Wickberg v. Patterson*, [1997] 4 W.W.R. 591 (Alta. C.A.).

The Ontario statute, like the legislation in Manitoba, New Brunswick and Nova Scotia, makes no reference to the doctrine, whereas the Alberta, British Columbia and Prince Edward Island statutes have specifically abolished it. Newfoundland and Labrador and Saskatchewan have attempted to define the doctrine's scope in their apportionment legislation. See Fridman, *The Law of Torts in Canada*, 2d ed. (2002) at 476-78. For a case applying the doctrine see *French v. Harbour Grace (Town)* (2001), 203 Nfld. & P.E.I.R. 290 (Nfld. S.C. (T.D.).

8. As s. 4 of the Ontario statute indicates, the parties are deemed to be equally negligent if it is impossible or impractical on the evidence to determine their respective degrees of fault. Although the courts try to accurately assess matters, they sometimes have no choice but to use this default position. See *Nice v. John Doe* (2000), 190 D.L.R. (4th) 402 (Alta. C.A.); *Alberta Wheat Pool v. Northwest Pile Driving Ltd.* (2000), 2 C.C.L.T. (3d) 53 (B.C.C.A.). Compare *Martin v. Listowel Memorial Hospital* (2000), 192 D.L.R. (4th) 250 (Ont. C.A.); and *J.M. v. W.B.* (2004), 71 O.R. (3d) 171 (C.A.).

MORTIMER v. CAMERON

(1994), 17 O.R. (3d) 1 (C.A.)

ROBINS J.A.: – On the afternoon of July 17, 1987, following an accounting examination, Stephen Mortimer attended a party at the apartment of a classmate, Sandra Hunt. The apartment was on the second floor of a house owned by Stingray Holdings Limited in the City of London. Those present were drinking and relaxing; no one was boisterous or unruly. By all accounts, the mood was convivial but subdued. At some point late in the afternoon, Mortimer engaged John Cameron, another classmate, in friendly conversation while they were standing at the top of a short stairway in the apartment. They had both been drinking beer and Mortimer was "mildly intoxicated". Neither of them was angry or hostile.

While they were "joking around" with one another, Mortimer made a motion so as to indicate that he was going to pour beer on Cameron. This led to some good-natured horseplay. They began to push each other back and forth and, while doing so, moved down the stairs to the interior landing leading to the front door of the apartment. The door was open at the time. When they reached the interior landing, Mortimer, who was moving backwards, tripped over the raised threshold to the apartment and fell backwards. As he did so, he grabbed Cameron and pulled him towards him. Together, they tumbled onto the exterior landing at the top of the enclosed exterior stairway leading to street level, and came in contact with the exterior wall. Even though they hit the wall with "minimal" or "little" force, it gave way and the two of them plunged to the ground 10 feet below.

Fortunately, Cameron was unhurt. Mortimer, however, suffered a devastating injury. His spinal cord was permanently fractured at the C4-5 or neck level. As a result, Mortimer is a complete quadriplegic without any motor function or sensation below the site of the injury.

The issue here is whether the trial judge erred in holding that the plaintiff's injuries were not proximately caused by his own conduct or by the conduct of the defendant Cameron. The conduct in question is the "horseplay" to which I referred earlier. The city and Stingray contend that, by engaging in this kind of conduct, the plaintiff was guilty of contributory negligence and the defendant Cameron was guilty of negligence. Their negligence, it is contended, contributed in some degree to the loss and should have been taken into account in apportioning liability.

. . .

The trial judge specifically found that Cameron breached his duty of care to Mortimer when he pushed Mortimer at the interior landing by the threshold. He also can be taken to have found that Mortimer, in initiating and participating in the horseplay, was in breach of the duty not to harm himself. The trial judge concluded, however, that their conduct did not constitute a proximate cause of Mortimer's injuries and that no liability should attach to them. In his view, the accident was not within the realm of their reasonable foreseeability.

There is no basis for disturbing this conclusion. On the findings made by the trial judge, which are adequately supported by the evidence, the conduct of Mortimer and Cameron cannot be treated as a proximate or effective cause of Mortimer's injuries. It is, of course, true that "but for" the condition created by the horseplay Mortimer and Cameron would not have fallen from the upper landing of the enclosed exterior stairway to the ground below. However, a defendant's negligence is actionable only with respect to harm that is within the scope of the risk that makes the offending conduct actionable. Similarly, a plaintiff's contributory negligence will not limit his recovery unless it is a proximate cause of his injury.

Here, neither Cameron's negligence nor Mortimer's contributory negligence entailed an unreasonable or foreseeable likelihood of the risk or hazard that actually befell Mortimer. It was reasonable for them to assume that what purported and appeared to be a properly constructed wall was in fact a properly constructed wall. In regulating their conduct and having regard for their own safety, they were entitled to rely on the wall providing them reasonable protection. The risk to which they exposed themselves was the risk of being injured by falling down the stairs or onto the exterior landing or by hitting the exterior wall. The risk that materialized was of a different nature. They had no reason to think that the state of the wall was such that it would give way to the modest degree of lateral force that they were found to have applied to it. The risk of falling to the ground through a defectively constructed and unprotected wall was beyond their reasonable contemplation. This risk was not one to which they can be said to have unreasonably exposed themselves or one another. . ..

These parties were not found to have charged the wall with the force of their combined weight, as the city and Stingray have suggested. Had the wall been properly constructed or a 2 x 4 stud properly installed to eliminate the unprotected gap, and the same sequence of events had occurred, on the findings of the trial judge, the wall could have withstood the minimal force that caused the plywood panel to "pop out". The accident that in fact occurred was, in sum, beyond the reasonable contemplation of these parties; it was not within the scope of the risk created by their horseplay, no matter how imprudent that conduct may be considered.

4. *The Apportionment of Liability*

The issue here is whether the trial judge erred in apportioning liability as between the city and Stingray at 80 per cent and 20 per cent respectively. In the city's submission, this apportionment is inconsistent with the findings upon which the liability of these parties was based and disproportionate to their relative degrees of culpability.

I agree with this submission. In my respectful opinion, the trial judge reached his findings of relative culpability without proper regard to the facts in this case. In particular, he failed to take into account or give proper weight to the specific findings which he made in holding Stingray liable to the plaintiffs.

The city was held responsible for a far larger proportion of liability than Stingray essentially because the trial judge was of the view that its conduct represented "a marked departure" from the applicable standard of care. The marked departure consisted of its "egregious" failure to comply with the Building Code requirements and good building practice and its having permitted a "particularly insidious condition" to be created by failing to provide the protection to be expected of a wall. In apportioning liability, however, the trial judge did not mention the particulars of Stingray's breach of the duty towards the plaintiff. Nor did he provide any reason why, given his findings, this tortfeasor's negligence was comparatively less egregious or less marked a departure from the applicable standard of care than the city's.

Stingray, it will be recalled, had the "primary burden" for maintaining the stairway in a reasonably safe condition. It was under a legal obligation to take reasonable care to see that persons coming onto the premises were safe while on the premises. In breach of that duty, Stingray failed to conduct a reasonable inspection to determine the soundness of this exterior wooden structure and thus permitted the "particularly insidious condition" to which the trial judge referred to be maintained. It failed to have this inspection notwithstanding the obvious deterioration of the structure. The unsafe condition of the upper landing would have been discovered if a proper inspection had been made, and the plainly foreseeable risk of harm would have been eliminated. Furthermore, Stingray's failure to comply with the building by-law in 1985 resulted in "the continuance of the hazardous condition" that would have been discovered had the required permit been obtained.

In my opinion, a substantially greater degree of fault ought to have been attributed to Stingray for its departures from the standard of care exacted by the law. This company was under an "ongoing duty" to properly inspect these premises. The circumstances were such as to require affirmative action on its part as occupier to see that its premises were reasonably safe for persons in the position of the plaintiff. Its failure to discharge this statutory duty over the many years of its ownership of the property constituted a more proximate or current cause of the accident than did the city's negligence.

Following its final inspection, the city had no reason or opportunity to conduct any further inspection of the premises. The negligence of its inspectors in 1972 when the exterior stairway was constructed, in so far as it was concerned, was undiscoverable.

While, as I have said, that negligence remained operative notwithstanding the passage of time, the fact is that had Stingray fulfilled its legal duty the risk created by the city's negligence would have been removed. Stingray cannot, and indeed does not, rely on the inspection made years earlier by the city as an excuse for non-compliance with its primary burden to maintain the safety of the premises. Taking into account Stingray's ongoing breach of the duty of care imposed on it by law, I am of the opinion that the apportionment was disproportionate to the respective degrees of culpability of these parties. Stingray should bear a significantly larger share of responsibility than that fixed by the trial judge.

While I appreciate that an appellate court should rarely interfere with a trial judge's apportionment of liability (*Sparks v. Thompson*, [1975] 1 S.C.R. 618, 46 D.L.R. (3d) 225), I am satisfied that there are sufficiently strong and exceptional circumstances here to warrant doing so. In reaching his conclusion as to relative fault, the trial judge failed to have proper regard to the totality of circumstances and the findings upon which he held Stingray liable. In my opinion, the comparative blameworthiness of these tortfeasors is such that liability for this accident should be apportioned 60 per cent against Stingray and 40 per cent against the city.

NOTES AND QUESTIONS

1. The trial judge held that both Mortimer and Cameron were negligent and that their combined negligence was a cause of Mortimer's devastating injuries. Why was Cameron not held liable to Mortimer and why was Mortimer not found contributorily negligent? Why did the Court of Appeal uphold this aspect of the trial judgment? Do you agree with the trial judge's and Court of Appeal's analysis?

2. Would the courts' analysis of these issues have been the same if the horseplay had not been in fun, if Cameron had been a well-insured corporate defendant, or if Mortimer had suffered only a broken leg and several thousand dollars of economic loss?

3. The Ontario *Negligence Act* indicates that damages are to be apportioned in relation to the parties' respective degrees of fault or negligence. Does this test relate to the parties' relative causal contributions or relative blameworthiness? How does the Court of Appeal resolve this issue? See *Heller v. Martens*, (2002) 303 A.R. 84 (C.A.) in which Fruman J.A. adopted a comparative blameworthiness approach. See also *Snushall v. Fulsang*, *infra*.

4. On what basis did the Court of Appeal interfere with the trial judge's apportionment of damages? Do you agree with its decision to intervene and its apportionment decision? See also *Taylor v. Asody*, [1975] 2 S.C.R. 414; *Rabideau v. Maddocks* (1992), 12 O.R. (3d) 83 (Gen. Div.); and *Hall v. Hebert* (1993), 101 D.L.R. (4th) 129 (S.C.C.).

In *Ryan v. Victoria (City)* (1999), 168 D.L.R. (4th) 513 (S.C.C.) the plaintiff was injured after the front tire of his motorcycle became caught in a railway track that ran within a city street. The trial judge held the defendant, who was responsible for the street, liable in negligence. However, the British Columbia Court of Appeal held that the plaintiff had been equally responsible for the accident and reduced recovery by 50%. On further appeal, the Supreme Court of Canada disagreed. Major J. stressed that the issue raised a question of fact and wrote:

In *Stein v. Kathy K (The Ship)* [(1976), 62 D.L.R. (3d) 1], it was held that while findings of fact with regard to the allocation of fault are not immutable, they should not be reversed by an appellate court "unless it can be established that the learned trial judge made some palpable and overriding error which affected his assessment of the facts". The record reveals no such errors by the trial judge, and the Court of Appeal ought not to have interfered with his findings on the issue of contributory negligence. Accordingly, the assessment of liability against the appellant for 50% of his damages is set aside.

5. In *Chamberland v. Fleming* (1984), 29 C.C.L.T. 213 (Alta. Q.B.) the court suggested that a rough upper limit of 25% should be established for contributory negligence if the plaintiff's negligence did not cause the incident but merely affected the extent of the loss. Chamberland, a non-swimmer and inexperienced canoeist, drowned when the defendant negligently approached in his motor boat and caused a wave to overturn the canoe. The deceased had declined to wear a life jacket that would have saved his life. Do you agree with the court's apportionment of loss in this case? What test did the court use to apportion the loss? Do you think that it is appropriate to establish fixed apportionment ratios for specific kinds of cases? See Irvine, "Annotation" (1984) 29 C.C.L.T. 213.

6. In *Snushall v. Fulsang* (2005), 78 O.R. (3d) 142 (C.A.) the trial judge found the plaintiff 35% contributorily negligent for her injuries in a car accident because she had failed to wear her shoulder belt, although she had worn her lap belt. The Court of Appeal reduced this to 5%. It held that "The relationship of the failure to wear a seatbelt to the injuries is different because the accident would have occurred whether or not a seatbelt was worn. . . . The failure to wear a seatbelt may be said to be a "cause" of the plaintiff's injuries only in the sense that it contributes to the extent of the injuries suffered." The court held that the range of contributory negligence for failure to wear a seat belt should always be between 5% and 25%, with 25% appropriate in cases where wearing a proper seat belt would have, as a matter of causation, prevented 100% of the injuries. See also *Fowler v. Schneider National Carriers Ltd.* (2001), 193 N.S.R. (2d) 206 (C.A.); and *Chae v. Min* (2005), 43 Alta. L.R. (4th) 1 (C.A.).

REVIEW PROBLEM

1. Edward, Ralph and Harry operated a window-washing business in Ontario. Ralph was responsible for checking the equipment and setting up the scaffold. Edward and Harry washed the windows. While the scaffold was at the third storey a frayed rope snapped, tilting the scaffold at a sharp angle. Harry was prevented from falling by his safety line. Edward had forgotten to attach his line and fell onto the roof of Bill's new car.

(a) Edward has sued Ralph in negligence. Ralph concedes that he was negligent, but alleges that Edward was contributorily negligent. Discuss Ralph's defence of contributory negligence and the possible apportionment of liability.

(b) Bill has sued both Edward and Ralph in negligence to recover the damages to his car. Advise Edward as to whether he is likely to be held liable to Bill and, if so, to what extent. Assuming that Bill can recover from Edward, what recourse does Edward have against Ralph?

3. Voluntary Assumption of Risk

With the introduction of modern apportionment legislation Canadian courts have become reluctant to apply the defence of voluntary assumption of risk. The reason is not difficult to see. Unlike contributory negligence, which now leads to a reduction in damages, voluntary assumption of risk remains a complete defence. If established, it precludes recovery altogether, notwithstanding the fact that the defendant negligently caused the plaintiff's injury. The inflexibility of such an all-or-nothing approach can easily lead to injustice. Consequently, while the defence is theoretically available in any negligence action, it tends to be confined to certain situations such as those involving participation in sports. Even in those situations it tends to be interpreted narrowly. An excellent illustration was seen in the extract of *Crocker v. Sundance Northwest Resorts Ltd.* (1988), 51 D.L.R. (4th) 321 (S.C.C.) in Chapter 11. In that case, the defence was rejected even though the event ("tubing") was obviously fraught with danger and even though the plaintiff had signed a waiver form.

DUBE v. LABAR

(1986), 27 D.L.R. (4th) 653 (S.C.C.)

ESTEY J.: – The appellant (plaintiff) and respondent (defendant), co-workers at a construction site, became acquainted shortly before the car accident giving rise to the action occurred. The night before the accident, the parties had participated in an evening of drinking and partying in Haines Junction, a town close to the construction camp where both lived. The morning of the accident, drinking was resumed early. The parties decided to retrieve the respondent's car, which had become stuck on the way home the night before, and then drive into Haines Junction to retrieve the appellant's eyeglasses and to try to find two young women they had met the previous night. On their arrival in Haines Junction, the appellant and respondent each consumed more alcohol. They left the bar, found the two women, and drove them approximately 50 or 60 miles toward Whitehorse at their request. Having dropped the women off, the parties started back to Haines Junction. The appellant had been driving throughout. The respondent, while a passenger, had apparently been drinking beer in the car. At some point on the return trip, the parties passed two hitchhikers, and decided to stop to pick them up. When the appellant tried to start the car again, he was unable to do so, and the respondent got into the driver's seat and started the car. At about this time, the appellant saw some friends passing in another vehicle, and, when they stopped, went to talk to them. He returned to the car and went to the driver's side, but the respondent was still in the driver's seat. In a short exchange, the respondent said that he was capable of driving. The appellant then got into the car as a passenger.

The accident occurred very shortly thereafter. The respondent, while driving, turned to speak to the hitchhiker sitting in the back seat. As he did so, the car veered to the right. The appellant, according to the testimony of the other hitchhiker who was seated on the front seat between the appellant and the respondent, attempted to grab the wheel and straighten out the car's course. The respondent's attempts at correction resulted, eventually, in the car's overturning on the righthand embankment, causing personal injuries to the appellant. Samples of the respondent's breath later registered at .25 and .24 in tests administered by the police.

At trial, without objection from the parties, only two defences, *volenti non fit injuria* and contributory negligence, were put to the jury. The trial judge, after summarizing the evidence, charged the jury on the *volenti* defence as follows:

> One of the defences of the defendant in this case is the maxim *volenti non fit injuria*. Translated, that means "to one who is willing no harm is done".
>
> The burden is on the defendant, in each case, to prove that the plaintiff, expressly or by necessary implication, agreed to exempt the defendant from liability for any damage suffered by the plaintiff, occasioned by the defendant's negligence. In every case, the question is whether the plaintiff gave an express or implied consent to accept or assume the risk without compensation. In other words, did the plaintiff really consent to absolve the defendant from his common-law duty of care, saying or implying, in effect, "I am prepared to take the risk of your negligence and if I am injured you will not be legally responsible for my damages." The question is not simply whether the plaintiff knew of the risk but whether the circumstances were such as necessarily to lead to the conclusion that the whole risk was intentionally incurred by the plaintiff.
>
> . . .
>
> If you find that there is evidence of an initial common design which would, as a matter of common sense, entail the risk of injury, you might think that the appropriate inference may be not that the defendant undertook to exercise due care throughout, but that the plaintiff agreed to take upon himself the obvious risk of harm. The burden lies upon the defendant of proving that the plaintiff, expressly or by necessary implication, agreed to exempt the defendant from liability.
> Therefore your test is not simply whether the plaintiff knew of the risk, but whether the circumstances are such as necessarily to lead to the conclusion that the whole risk was voluntarily incurred by the plaintiff.

Immediately after his discussion of the *volenti* defence, the trial judge said:

> Having earlier discussed negligence [which was done in an earlier general part of the charge just before volenti was discussed], I want to turn to the allied and associated matter of contributory negligence. . . If you are satisfied by a preponderance of evidence that Dube's conduct amounted to a breach of that duty to take reasonable care for his own safety, then you would be justified in ascribing to him a portion of the blame for his injuries . . .

The judge charged the jury that contributory negligence could arise in two ways, "firstly, from the plaintiff's active conduct in grasping the steering wheel . . . secondly, you may find that the plaintiff was negligent about his own safety, when he remained in the vehicle after the defendant took over the driving, knowing what he knew of the defendant's condition at that time".

. . .

[The jury found that the plaintiff had been contributorily negligent and that he voluntarily assumed the risk. On the basis of the latter, they held for the defendant.]

The plaintiff's appeal to this Court was argued on the basis that the defence of *volenti* is inapplicable to a case involving negligence on the highways. This submission is plainly inconsistent with four decisions of this Court: *Car & General Ins. Corp. Ltd v. Seymour et al.* (1956), 2 D.L.R. (2d) 369. . .; *Miller v. Decker* (1957), 9 D.L.R. (2d) 1. . .; *Lehnert v. Stein* (1962), 36 D.L.R. (2d) 159. . ., and *Eid v. Dumas, Hatherly v. Dumas* (1969), 5 D.L.R. (3d) 561. . . . However, while acknowledging that *volenti* is in principle available to a defendant driver, these cases establish that the defence will only be made out in unusual circumstances. The test has been variously described. . . .

Abbott J., dissenting in the *Miller* case [stated]:

> [F]or a negligent driver to be completely relieved from liability, the plaintiff must have agreed expressly or by implication to exempt the defendant from liability for damages suffered by the plaintiff and occasioned by the negligence of the defendant during the carrying out of the latter's undertaking. In other words, to constitute a defence there must have been an express or implied bargain between the parties whereby the plaintiff gave up his right of action for negligence. As was pointed out by Kellock J. . . ., the question in each particular case is, in the language of Lindley L.J. in *Yarmouth v. France* (1887), 19 Q.B.D. 647 at p. 660, "not simply whether the plaintiff knew of the risk but whether the circumstances are such as necessarily to lead to the conclusion that the whole risk was voluntarily incurred by the plaintiff".

Finally, in *Lehnert v. Stein, supra*, Cartwright J. held . . . that:

> [W]here a driver of a motor vehicle invokes the maxim *volenti non fit injuria* as a defence to an action for damages for injuries caused by his negligence to a passenger, the burden lies upon the defendant of proving that the plaintiff, expressly or by necessary implication, agreed to exempt the defendant from liability for any damage suffered by the plaintiff occasioned by that negligence, and that, as stated in *Salmond on Torts*, 13th ed., p. 44:
>
>> "The true question in every case is: did the plaintiff give a real consent to the assumption of the risk without compensation; did the consent really absolve the defendant from the duty to take care?"

Thus, *volenti* will arise only where the circumstances are such that it is clear that the plaintiff, knowing of the virtually certain risk of harm, in essence bargained away his right to sue for injuries incurred as a result of any negligence on the defendant's part. The acceptance of risk may be express or may arise by necessary implication from the conduct of the parties, but it will arise, in cases such as the present, only where there can truly be said to be an understanding on the part of both parties that the defendant assumed no responsibility to take due care for the safety of the plaintiff, and that the plaintiff did not expect him to.

Common sense dictates that only rarely will a plaintiff genuinely consent to accept the risk of the defendant's negligence.

. . .

The defence of *volenti* will, furthermore, necessarily be inapplicable in the great majority of drunken driver-willing passenger cases. It requires an awareness of the circumstances and the consequences of action that are rarely present on the facts of such cases at the relevant time.

. . .

Prior to the enactment of legislation allowing for apportionment of damages in cases where the plaintiff's own negligence had contributed to his injuries. . ., drawing a distinction between the defences of *volenti* and contributory negligence was unnecessary. Both had the same drastic effect of denying completely compensation to the plaintiff.

This is no longer the case. Apportionment permits a sensible distribution of the financial burden of negligent conduct. It is a more flexible and more appropriate response in the great majority of cases in which negligent conduct of the plaintiff is argued to support a *volenti* defence. Thus, it is of great importance to keep the two defences distinct. . . .

. . .

The jury's conclusion that the plaintiff consented to bear the legal risk when he entered the car as passenger, knowing of the defendant's state of impairment, is doubtless one that not every jury would have reached. It does not have the character of unreasonableness, however, that must be apparent on the face of a jury verdict before an appellate court can upset it . . . .

I therefore would dismiss the appeal with costs to the respondent.

MCINTYRE and CHOUINARD JJ. concur with ESTEY J.

[Wilson J. wrote a concurring judgment.]

NOTES AND QUESTIONS

1. How did the court define the elements of voluntary assumption of risk? What policy reasons were given for narrowly interpreting this defence?

2. The courts have been divided on the issue of whether the defence of *volenti* applies to willing passengers of drunk drivers. Estey J. states that the defence will be inapplicable in the great majority of cases.

What do you think prompted the jury to conclude that Dube voluntarily assumed the risk? Based on the factual record, do you agree with its conclusion? Given that Estey J. did not agree with the jury, why did he deny the appeal?

Estey J. suggests that contributory negligence may be the more appropriate defence in these circumstances. Consider the *Motor Accidents Act 1988* (NSW), s. 74(2)(b)(ii) which requires a finding of contributory negligence where the plaintiff is a "voluntary passenger," the driver was impaired by drugs or alcohol, and the plaintiff was, or ought to have been, aware of the impairment: see *Joslyn v. Berryman; Wentworth Shire Council v. Berryman* (2003), 198 A.L.R. 137 (H.C.A.). See also *Pilon v. Janveaux* (2005), 203 O.A.C. 345 (C.A.), additional reasons (2006), 211 O.A.C. 19 (C.A.); and *Robinson v. Williams Estate* (2005), 34 C.C.L.T. (3d) 131 (Alta. Q.B.), aff'd (2007), 44 C.C.L.T. (3d) 1 (Alta. C.A.).

3. The courts may find that the plaintiff voluntarily assumed the risk if he or she encouraged the defendant to be careless. See *Allen v. Lucas* (1971), 25 D.L.R. (3d) 218 (Sask. C.A.); *Conrad v. Crawford*, [1972] 1 O.R. 134 (H.C.); and *Cherrey v. Steinke* (1980), 13 C.C.L.T. 50 (Man. C.A.). But see *Eid v. Dumas*, [1969] S.C.R. 668; and *Betts v. Sanderson Estate* (1988), 53 D.L.R. (4th) 675 (B.C.C.A.).

4. As a matter of policy, what principles should govern the legal position of a passenger who accepts a ride from an intoxicated driver? What role does the fact that the driver will most likely be insured have on your analysis? See generally Skene, "Voluntary Assumption of Risk and the Gratuitous Passenger" (1974) 1 Dal. L.J. 605; Harpum, "Contributory Negligence Defences for the Drunken Driver" (1977) 40 Mod.

L. Rev. 350; and Koressis, "Injured Passenger Actions Against Intoxicated Drivers - Volenti or Contributory Negligence" (1983) 4 Adv. Q. 297.

5. The debate over the scope of voluntary assumption of risk has also arisen in the context of intoxicated patrons of drinking establishments. See *Jordan House Ltd. v. Menow* (1974), 38 D.L.R. (3d) 105 (S.C.C.); and *Crocker v. Sundance Northwest Resorts Ltd.* (1988), 51 D.L.R. (4th) 321 (S.C.C.). See the discussion in Chapter 11.

6. Is there an age below which children lack the capacity to assess the physical risks of injury and to accept legal responsibility for injuries that may befall them? Should the principles of voluntary assumption of risk be applied the same way in cases involving adults and children? See *Savard v. Urbano* (1977), 85 D.L.R. (3d) 33 (Qc. C.A.); *Doiron v. Brideau* (1979), 28 N.B.R. (2d) 520 (C.A.); *McGinlay v. British Railway Bd.*, [1983] 1 W.L.R. 1427 (H.L.); and *Laviolette v. C.N.R.* (1987), 40 C.C.L.T. 138 (N.B.C.A.).

7. What risks should a participant in a sport be held to have voluntarily assumed? Should it matter whether the participant is experienced or a novice? See *Hanson v. St. John Horticultural Assn.*, [1974] S.C.R. 354; *Delaney v. Cascade River Holidays Ltd.* (1983), 24 C.C.L.T. 6 (B.C.C.A.); *Temple v. Hallem*, [1989] 5 W.W.R. 669 (Man. C.A.); *Potvin v. Stipetic* (1989), 50 C.C.L.T. 233 (Qc. C.A.); *Scurfield v. Cariboo Helicopter Skiing Ltd.*, [1993] 3 W.W.R. 418 (B.C.C.A.); *Dyck v. Laidlaw* (2000), 263 A.R. 241 (Q.B.); *Johnson v. Webb* (2002), 162 Man. R. (2d) 48 (Q.B.), aff'd (2002), 170 Man. R. (2d) 58 (C.A.); and *Matharu v. Nam* (2006), 57 B.C.L.R. (4th) 374 (S.C.). See generally Yeo, "Accepted Inherent Risks Among Sporting Participants" (2001) 9 Tort L. Rev. 114. Some Canadian courts have been unwilling to apply voluntary assumption of risk even in the context of violent sports: see *Unruh (Guardian ad litem of) v. Webber* (1994), 112 D.L.R. (4th) 83 (B.C.C.A.); and *Zapf v. Muckalt* (1995), 26 C.C.L.T. (2d) 61 (B.C.S.C.), varied (1996), 31 C.C.L.T. (2d) 201 (B.C.C.A.).

8. What risks should a spectator at a sporting event be held to have voluntarily assumed? See *Payne v. Maple Leaf Gardens Ltd.*, [1949] 1 D.L.R. 369 (Ont. C.A.); *White v. Blackmore*, [1972] 2 Q.B. 651 (C.A.); and *Carson v. Thunder Bay* (1985), 52 O.R. (2d) 173 (Dist. Ct.). See generally Kligman, "Tort Liability for Sports Injuries" (1989) 1 C.I.L. Rev. 153.

9. In the cases discussed to this point the defence of voluntary assumption of risk has been established by drawing an inference from the plaintiff's conduct. The defence may also be established by express agreement. The meaning and effect given such agreements is essentially governed by the law of contract. See *Dyck v. Man. Snowmobile Assn.* (1985), 18 D.L.R. (4th) 635 (S.C.C.); *ITO – International Terminal Operators Ltd. v. Miida Electronics Inc.* (1986), 28 D.L.R. (4th) 641 (S.C.C.); *Crocker v. Sundance Northwest Resort Ltd.*, *supra*; *London Drugs Ltd. v. Kuehne & Nagel International Ltd.* (1992), 97 D.L.R. (4th) 261 (S.C.C.); *Ocsko v. Cypress Bowl Recreations Ltd.* (1992), 95 D.L.R. (4th) 701 (B.C.C.A.); *Greeven v. Blackcomb Skiing Enterprises Ltd.* (1994), 22 C.C.L.T. (2d) 265 (B.C.S.C.); *Fraser Jewellers v. Dominion Electric* (1997), 35 C.C.L.T. (2d) 298 (Ont. C.A.); *Air Nova v. Messier-Dowty Ltd.* (2000), 128 O.A.C. 11 (C.A.); *Cudmore v. Home Chec Canada Ltd.* (2000), 174 Man. R. (2d) 30 (Q.B.); and *Dixon v. British Columbia Snowmobile Federation* (2003), 180 B.C.A.C. 99 (C.A.). See

also Neumann, "Disclaimer Clauses and Personal Injury" (1991) 55 Sask. L. Rev. 312; and Tomlinson & Machum, "The contractual waiver of liability in ski resort negligence claims" (1997) 15 Can. J. Ins. L. 49.

10. In *Cowles v. Balac* (2005), 29 C.C.L.T. (3d) 284 (Ont. S.C.J.), aff'd (2006), 83 O.R. (3d) 660 (C.A.) the plaintiffs were attacked by tigers while driving through the defendant's wildlife park. Signs at the entry to the park stated "All visitors enter the park at their own risk. No responsibility for damage to vehicle or person however caused is accepted." The brochure given to the plaintiffs contained similar language. Should the defence of voluntary assumption of risk apply?

11. For a general discussion of voluntary assumption of risk see Hertz, "Volenti Non Fit Injuria: A Guide" in Klar, ed., *Studies in Canadian Tort Law* (1977) 101 at 119-26; Jaffey, "Volenti Non Fit Injuria" [1985] C.L.J. 87; Simons, "Assumption of Risk and Consent in the Law of Torts: A Theory of Full Preference" (1987) 67 B.U.L. Rev. 213; and Sugarman, "Assumption of Risk" (1997) 31 Val. U.L. Rev. 833.

4. Participation in a Criminal or Immoral Act

The defence of *ex turpi causa non oritur actio* was raised in Chapter 6 in relation to intentional torts. The application of the principle is essentially the same in negligence. Significantly, like voluntary assumption of risk, and unlike contributory negligence, the *ex turpi* defence does not merely lead to a reduction in damages: it precludes recovery altogether. As a result, it too has been narrowly interpreted in modern times.

HALL v. HEBERT

(1993), 101 D.L.R. (4th) 129 (S.C.C.)

[The plaintiff and the defendant got "quite and equally drunk" at a party. While driving home, the defendant stalled his "souped-up muscle" car on a steep, unlit gravel road that sharply dropped away on one side. The defendant agreed to allow the plaintiff to drive. The plaintiff attempted a "rolling start" but lost control almost immediately and flipped the vehicle down the embankment. The plaintiff was severely injured and sued the defendant for allowing him to drive in his intoxicated condition.

The major issue on appeal to the Supreme Court of Canada was whether the defendant could raise the defence of *ex turpi causa non oritur actio* to negate the plaintiff's cause of action.]

MCLACHLIN J.: . . . My colleague Cory J. suggests that the defence of ex turpi causa non oritur actio should be eliminated. In its place, he suggests that the courts should be granted the power to disallow a plaintiff's claim, on account of the plaintiff's wrongful conduct, by finding that no duty of care arises. This power is to be exercised under the second branch of the test articulated in *Anns v. Merton London Borough Council*, [1978] A.C. 728, as approved and reformulated in this Court in *Kamloops (City) v. Nielsen*, [1984] 2 S.C.R. 2. On this view, the plaintiff's illegal or immoral conduct may constitute a policy reason for holding that the defendant owed the plaintiff no duty of care.

A variant of this approach has been adopted in Australia, *Gala v. Preston* [(1991), 172 C.L.R. 342] and by the English Court of Appeal, *Pitts v. Hunt* [[1991] 1 Q.B. 24].

This view holds that no duty should be postulated where it is either *impossible* or *improper* for the courts to establish a standard of care to govern the conduct in issue. It is recognized that there is no a priori reason in law why a duty cannot subsist between criminals or wrongdoers. However, some cases raise such "special and exceptional" circumstances that a court cannot, or cannot in good conscience, enquire into the standard of care needed to ground the duty of care in a particular situation. Unlike the view espoused by Cory J., the very possibility of a duty arising is not denied; rather the court declines to enter into the question of whether a duty exists.

With great respect, I am not sure that much is gained by replacing the defence of ex turpi causa non oritur actio with a judicial discretion to negate, or to refuse to consider, the duty of care. Shifting the analysis to the issue of duty provides no new insight into the fundamental question of when the courts should be entitled to deny recovery in tort to a plaintiff on the ground of the plaintiff's immoral or illegal conduct. Moreover, it introduces a series of new problems. In the end I fear that it would prove more problematic than has the defence of ex turpi causa non oritur actio.

I begin by noting that the duty approach, as expressed by Cory J., does not fully capture what we mean when we invoke the principle of ex turpi causa. If what I have said above is correct, the ex turpi causa principle operates most naturally as a defence because its purpose is to frustrate what would be, had ex turpi causa no role, a complete cause of action. Liability for tort arises out of the relationship between the alleged tortfeasor and the injured claimant. The power of the court to deny recovery where it would undermine the coherence of the legal system, on the other hand, represents concerns independent of this relationship. It is important, if only for the purposes of conceptual clarity, that ex turpi causa operate, on those rare occasions where its operation is justified, as a defence to frustrate tort claims which could otherwise be fully made out, because this best expresses what is in fact decided. The courts make it clear that the defendant has acted wrongly in negligently causing harm. They also make it clear that responsibility for this wrong is suspended only because concern for the integrity of the legal system trumps the concern that the defendant be responsible.

Donoghue v. Stevenson, [1932] A.C. 562 (H.L.), the source of our modern law of negligence and of the concept of duty upon which it is founded, requires that a person exercise reasonable care toward all his neighbours. It does not say that the duty is owed only to neighbours who have acted morally and legally. Tort, unlike equity which requires that the plaintiff come with clean hands, does not require a plaintiff to have a certain moral character in order to bring an action before the court. The duty of care is owed to *all* persons who may reasonably be foreseen to be injured by the negligent conduct.

Policy concerns unrelated to the legal rules which govern the relationship between the parties to an action have not generally been considered in determining whether a duty [of] care lies. This follows from the fact that the justice which tort law seeks to accomplish is justice between the parties to the particular action; the court acts at the instance of the wronged party to rectify the damage caused by a particular defendant: see Ernest J. Weinrib, "The Special Morality of Tort Law" (1989) 34 McGill L.J. 403, at p. 408.

The relationship between plaintiff and defendant which gives rise to their respective entitlement and liability arises from a duty predicated on foreseeable consequences of harm. This being the concern, the legality or morality of the plaintiff's conduct is an extrinsic consideration. In the rare cases where concerns for the administration of justice require that the extrinsic consideration of the character of the plaintiff's conduct be considered, it seems to me that this is better done by way of defence than by distorting the notion of the duty of care owed by the defendant to the plaintiff.

It can be argued that the Australian rule avoids these doctrinal problems by recognizing that, while a duty of care might otherwise lie, it cannot be raised because the parties, by their conduct, have made it impossible or improper to consider the claim. In other words, that a duty could arise from the relationship between the parties is not denied - plaintiff is simply barred from relying on it. Thus the Australian High Court formally avoids conflict with the principle it has articulated in earlier judgments: that no person becomes a caput lupinum, or an outlaw, in the eyes of the civil law merely because that person was engaged in some unlawful act. . .. On analysis, however, this notion that the courts cannot, in certain circumstances, consider whether a duty of care arises has the practical effect of denying a duty which would otherwise arise, and hence, in substance, of violating the very principle against making certain parties outlaws to which the court seeks to adhere.

Beyond this, a more practical objection can be raised: why is it necessary to take the rather novel step of positing judicial "inability" to investigate the appropriate standard of care, instead of using the concept by which the law has traditionally recognized considerations that prevent otherwise valid claims from succeeding, that is, the concept of a defence to the action?

The law of tort recognizes many types of defence. Some go to the relationship between the parties; for example, the defence of volenti non fit injuria, the plaintiff's assumption of risk. But others go to matters unrelated to that relationship. Limitation periods, for example, are raised by way of defence. I see no reason to treat ex turpi causa differently. Like a lapsed limitation period, it represents a reason why a cause of action, which might otherwise be fully made out, should not succeed.

The debate is not purely academic. There are practical reasons for finding that it is proper to view ex turpi causa as a defence. I mention three. If the ex turpi causa principle arises in the course of the investigation into whether there exists a duty of care, the onus will lie on the plaintiff to show why he or she should not be disentitled by way of his or her conduct. It is well established that the plaintiff bears the onus of establishing a valid cause of action; if not, the plaintiff faces non-suit. Thus a plaintiff whose conduct is alleged to be immoral or illegal might be bound to disprove the illegality or immorality in order to proceed with her action and avoid non-suit. On the other hand, if the matter is left as a defence, the onus rests on the defendant. As I have indicated, the power to preclude recovery on the basis of the plaintiff's immoral or illegal conduct is an *exceptional* power, operating in derogation of the general principles of tort applicable to all persons in our society. As such, it seems to me appropriate that the onus of establishing the exceptional circumstances should rest with the defendant. The plaintiff should not be required to *disprove* the existence and relevance of his or her illegal or immoral conduct; rather it should be for the defendant to establish it.

Second, the duty of care approach is an all or nothing approach, and cannot be applied selectively to discreet [*sic*] heads of damage. As discussed above, cases may arise in which a particular damage claim, e.g., for exemplary damages, or for damages for loss of future earnings, might be seen as claim to profit from an illegal act. Another damage claim in the same action, e.g., one for compensation for personal injuries, could not be so regarded. If the ex turpi causa principle operates as a defence it is possible to distinguish between such claims. If it operates as a factor negating a duty of care, on the other hand, it is not possible to treat an action in the selective manner that justice seems to require.

Finally, consideration of illegal or immoral conduct at the stage of determining the duty of care raises procedural problems. A plaintiff may sue in both tort and contract. If the approach suggested by Cory J. is adopted, in the contract claim, the plaintiff's illegal or immoral conduct would be raised as a defence to the claim; in the tort, the same conduct would be an element of the enquiry into the duty of care. In other words, in contract the onus would be on the defendant to prove the relevance of the plaintiff's conduct; in tort, the onus would be on the plaintiff to disprove the relevance of the conduct. The resulting confusion would unnecessarily complicate the task of the trial judge and the parties.

These considerations lead me to conclude that the important but limited power of the court to prevent tort recovery on the ground of the plaintiff's illegal or immoral conduct is better viewed as a defence than as a factor going to the existence of a duty of care.

II. Application to These Facts

The doctrine of ex turpi causa non oritur actio properly applies in tort where it will be necessary to invoke the doctrine in order to maintain the internal consistency of the law. Most commonly, this concern will arise where a given plaintiff genuinely seeks to profit from his or her illegal conduct, or where the claimed compensation would amount to an evasion of a criminal sanction. This appellant need not be denied recovery since these grounds are not relevant to his claim. The compensation sought by this appellant is for injuries received. This compensation can be reduced to the extent of the appellant's contributory negligence, but cannot be wholly denied by reason of his disreputable or criminal conduct.

[La Forest, L'Heureux-Dubé and Iacobucci JJ. concurred with McLachlin J. Cory J. concurred in the result, but indicated that the defence of *ex turpi causa* should be eliminated. Gonthier J. concurred in the result. While he agreed that *ex turpi causa* had to be limited, he did not accept that it should be limited to the narrow categories that McLachlin J. set out. Sopinka J. agreed that *ex turpi causa* did not apply on the facts but held that the plaintiff's claim should be dismissed because the defendant did not owe the plaintiff any duty of care.]

NOTES AND QUESTIONS

1. The Canadian courts consistently narrowed *ex turpi causa* in a series of often conflicting cases. While few judges liked the defence, they could not agree on the purpose it should serve. This chequered history is discussed in more detail in Chapter 6.

2. McLachlin J. stated in *Hall* that the purpose of the *ex turpi causa* doctrine is to protect "the integrity of the legal system." In her view, the plaintiff's illegal or immoral conduct would only rarely be relevant if the plaintiff was seeking compensation for actual physical injuries or losses. She distinguished these claims from those in which the plaintiff was seeking to profit from his or her wrongdoing.

Do you agree with McLachlin J. that the doctrine's goal should be to protect the integrity of the legal system? Assuming that this is an appropriate goal, does it follow that the doctrine would only rarely apply to claims for actual physical injuries?

3. McLachlin J. raised three "practical reasons" why *ex turpi causa* should be treated as a defence and not dealt with at the duty stage. Are these reasons compelling?

4. All seven justices appear to agree on the goal of the doctrine, the need to limit it and its inapplicability to the facts in *Hall*. What are the implications of the fact that, despite this agreement, there are four judgments?

The complexity of the legal and policy issues generated by the doctrine is reflected by the range of approaches that have been taken by other Commonwealth courts. See *Pitts v. Hunt*, [1990] 3 All E.R. 344 (C.A.); *Gala v. Preston* (1991), 172 C.L.R. 243 (H.C.A.); and *Brown v. Dunsmuir*, [1994] 3 N.Z.L.R. 485 (H.C.).

5. In *John Bead Corp. v. Soni* (2002), 10 C.C.L.T. (3d) 318 (Ont. C.A.) the court commented on the effect of *Hall*. The plaintiff claimed that the defendant had stolen $1,600,000 from the plaintiff's company. The defendant denied the allegation and further pleaded *ex turpi causa* on the basis that the plaintiff had also illegally taken money from the company. The issue was whether that defence should be struck from the pleadings. The Court of Appeal answered in the affirmative. It held, first, that the defence does not apply merely because the plaintiff was engaged in an illegal activity that was unrelated to the facts underlying the plaintiff's claim. That is true even if both parties were separately engaged in similar forms of illegal activity (like stealing money from a company). Second, the court offered two examples of when damages will be refused in order to prevent the plaintiff from profiting from his or her own wrongdoing: (i) "where one wrongdoer claims in tort against another for financial loss arising from an illegal activity," and (ii) "where the plaintiff claims as a head of damage suffered in a personal injury claim, loss of earnings from an illegal activity."

6. It is generally accepted that the police owe some duty of care to those in their custody after an arrest. In *Vellino v. Chief Constable of Greater Manchester Police*, [2002] 1 W.L.R. 218 (C.A.) the plaintiff was injured while jumping from a window to escape from police custody. The court denied the claim, in part on the basis that in attempting to escape the plaintiff was committing a criminal offence and could not sue for the injuries sustained while doing so. Do you agree with this reasoning? How else might the case have been decided against the plaintiff?

7. In *Beljanski (Guardian ad litem of) v. Smithwick* (2006), 56 B.C.L.R. (4th) 99 (C.A.) the dependant children of a "career criminal" brought a claim when their father was killed negligently. The court relied on *ex turpi causa* in refusing to base any part of the award on any illegal income the deceased would have made through criminal activities.

8. For a recent judicial analysis of the defence see *Zastowny v. MacDougall* (2006), 269 D.L.R. (4th) 510 (B.C.C.A.). For academic commentary see MacDoughall, "*Ex Turpi Causa*: Should a Defence Arise from a Base Cause?" (1991) 55 Sask. L. Rev. 1; McInnes, "Ex Turpi Causa and Tort: A Canadian Perspective" [1993] C.L.J. 378; Klar,

"Negligence Defences - Ex Turpi Causa Non Oritur Actio - Volenti Non Fit Injuria - The Purpose of Negligent Accident Law: *Hall v. Herbert*" (1993) 72 Can. Bar Rev. 553; Kostal, "Currents in the Counter-Reformation: Illegality and Duty of Care in Canada and Australia" (1995) 3 Tort L. Rev. 100; Fordham, "The Role of Ex Turpi Causa in Tort Law" [1998] Sing. J.L.S. 238; and Glofcheski, "Plaintiff's Illegality as a Bar to Recovery of Personal Injury Damages" (1999) 19 L.S. 6.

5. Inevitable Accident

RINTOUL v. X-RAY AND RADIUM INDUST. LTD.
[1956] S.C.R. 674

CARTWRIGHT J.: – The facts as deposed to by Ouellette were as follows. On April 13, 1954, at about 8:50 a.m. Ouellette was driving a 1952 Dodge motor vehicle owned by his employer, the respondent X-Ray and Radium Industries Limited, easterly on Wellington Street in the city of Ottawa. He stopped at the intersection of Bayview Avenue for a traffic-light and his service brakes worked properly. From the time that he had left his home up to this point he had applied his service brakes five times and on each occasion they had worked properly. The traffic-light having changed he proceeded across Bayview Avenue and saw that the line of traffic ahead of him was at a standstill. The appellant's car was at the rear of this line of traffic. When Ouellette was about 150 feet away from the appellant's car he took his foot off the accelerator and applied his service brakes. At this moment he was proceeding uphill at a speed of not more than twelve miles per hour; he found that the brakes did not work; the brake pedal went down to the floor of the car without his feeling any braking action; he allowed the pedal to rise and pressed it down again, still without getting any braking action. Thinking that the service brakes had become useless, he applied his hand brakes; at the moment of this application his car was between 50 and 75 feet from that of the appellant. The application of the hand brakes reduced the speed of his car but did not stop it and it was still moving at about 6 miles per hour when it struck the rear of the appellant's vehicle.

. . .

The defence relied on at the trial and before us was pleaded in the Statement of Defence as follows:–

> (4) The Defendants allege and the fact is that at the time and place referred to in the Statement of Claim the brakes of the Defendant motor vehicle suddenly and without warning failed and it was in the circumstances impossible for the Defendant driver to avoid the collision.
> (5) The Defendants allege and the fact is that they had taken all reasonable and proper precaution in the care of the brakes on the said motor vehicle and plead that the said collision was an inevitable or an unavoidable accident.

There can be no doubt that, generally speaking, when a car, in broad daylight, runs into the rear of another which is stationary on the highway and which has not come to a sudden stop, the fault is in the driving of the moving car, and the driver of such car must satisfy the Court that the collision did not occur as a result of his negligence. The learned trial judge regarded this principle as applicable to the case at bar but was of the view that the unexpected failure of the service brakes placed Ouellette in a situation of emergency in which he acted without negligence and that the collision was the result of an inevitable accident.

The defence of inevitable accident has been discussed in many decisions. A leading case in Ontario is *McIntosh v. Bell* [[1932] O.R. 179 (C.A.)], which was approved by this Court in *Claxton v. Grandy* [[1934] 4 D.L.R. 257 (S.C.C.) at 263]. At page 187 of the report of *McIntosh v. Bell*, Hodgins J.A. adopts the words of Lord Esher M.R. in *The Schwan* [[1892] P. 419 at 429], as follows:

> . . . In my opinion, a person relying on inevitable accident must show that something happened over which he had no control, and the effect of which could not have been avoided by the greatest care and skill.

In my view, in the case at bar the respondents have failed to prove two matters both of which were essential to the establishment of the defence of inevitable accident. These matters are (i) that the alleged failure of the service brakes could not have been prevented by the exercise of reasonable care on their part, and (ii) that, assuming that such failure occurred without negligence on the part of the respondents, Ouellette could not, by the exercise of reasonable care, have avoided the collision which he claims was the effect of such failure.

As to the first matter, assuming that the service brakes failed suddenly, the onus resting on the respondents was to show that such failure could not have been prevented by the exercise of reasonable care. In Halsbury, 2nd Edition, Volume 23, page 640, section 901, the learned author says:

> Driving with defective apparatus if the defect might reasonably have been discovered . . . (and other matters) . . . are negligent acts which render a defendant liable for injuries of which they are the effective cause.

This passage has been approved by McCardie J. in *Phillips v. Brittania Hygienic Laundry Co.* [[1923] 1 K.B. 539 at 551] and by Hogg J.A. in *Grise v. Rankin et al.* [[1951] O.W.N. 21 (C.A.) at 22], and, in my opinion, correctly states the law.

In the case at bar the respondents have made no attempt to prove that the sudden failure could not have been prevented by reasonable care on their part and particularly by adequate inspection. They called no witness to explain the extraordinary fact that the service brakes which were working properly immediately before and immediately after the accident and passed satisfactorily the test prescribed in the regulations failed momentarily at the time of the accident. Without going so far as to say that such a story appears to be intrinsically impossible, it is clear that its nature was such as to cast upon the defendants the burden of furnishing a clear and satisfactory explanation of so unusual an occurrence.

Furthermore, the respondents have made no attempt to show that the defect, whatever it was, could not reasonably have been discovered. The evidence is that the respondents' car was a 1952 Dodge. There is no evidence: (*a*) as to when it was purchased, or (*b*) whether it was purchased new or second-hand, or (*c*) how far it had been driven, or (*d*) how often, if ever, the service brakes had been inspected, or (*e*) how often, if ever, the hand brakes had been inspected. The only evidence touching the point at all is Ouellette's statement quoted above that there "was work done on the brakes" the day before the accident. There is nothing to indicate whether the brakes referred to in this statement were the service brakes or the hand brakes although in argument it seemed to be assumed that the reference was to the service brakes. No evidence was given as to what instructions were given to the third party, or as to what work was done by him, or as to what report, if any, was made by the third party when the car was delivered, or as to whether the third party was competent to inspect or repair brakes. The onus resting on the respondents in this regard is not discharged by the bald statement that on the day before the accident there was work (unspecified) done on the brakes.

. . .

In my opinion, on the evidence the respondents have not only failed to show that the alleged failure of the service brakes was inevitable, they have also failed to show that after such failure occurred Ouellette could not by the exercise of reasonable care have avoided the collision. It follows that the appeal of the plaintiff should be allowed.

NOTES AND QUESTIONS

1. What must the defendant establish to invoke the defence of inevitable accident? According to Cartwright J. what standard of care is the defendant required to meet? Is this consistent with Lord Esher's statement in *The Schwan*, [1892] P. 419 which Cartwright J. quotes with approval?

2. What is the effect of the defendant's plea of inevitable accident on the burden of proof? Given its impact in Canada, why would the defendant raise the defence?

3. The Canadian courts have generally applied *Rintoul*. The majority of cases involve sudden mechanical failures and other emergency situations. See *Levesque v. Day & Ross Ltd.* (1976), 15 N.B.R. (2d) 500 (C.A.); *Blackwood v. Butler* (1984), 48 Nfld. & P.E.I.R. 110 (Nfld. C.A.); *Dobbs v. Mayer* (1985), 32 C.C.L.T. 191 (Ont. S.C.); *White v. Sheaves* (1987), 194 A.P.R. 290 (Nfld. S.C.); and *Basra v. Gill*, [1995] 2 W.W.R. 213 (B.C.C.A.).

However, see *Graham v. Hodgkinson* (1983), 40 O.R. (2d) 697 (C.A.); and *Boutcher v. Stewart* (1989), 50 C.C.L.T. 77 (N.B.C.A.) in which it was indicated that inevitable accident was no more than a denial of negligence and that it did not alter either the plaintiff's or the defendant's case.

4. In *Barron v. Barron* (2003), 214 N.S.R. (2d) 76 (S.C.) the defendant was drinking coffee while driving. He had a sudden choking fit and fainted. He had frequently experienced similar choking fits but had never lost consciousness. This time he crashed, injuring the plaintiff passenger. The court stated that it was more difficult to make out the defence of inevitable accident based on factors "internal" to the defendant rather than "external" factors like icy roads or faulty brakes. The court rejected the defence, concluding that given his history the defendant should have refrained from drinking coffee while driving. See also *Codner v. Gosse* (2003), 227 Nfld. & P.E.I.R. 132 (N.L.S.C. (T.D.)).

5. Is there any reason to treat inevitable accident as a defence? See Klar, "Annotation" (1977) 1 C.C.L.T. 273; Smith, "Automatism - A Defence to Negligence?" [1980] New L.J. 1111; Kligman, "Inevitable Accident and the Infirm Driver: What You Don't Know Can Kill You" (1987) 8 Adv. Q. 311; Gilles, "Inevitable Accident in Classical English Tort Law" (1993) 43 Emory L.J. 575; and Currie, "Affirmative defence *redux*

or night of the living dead doctrines? Putting 'Inevitable Accident' To Rest" (2003) 16 C.C.L.T. (3d) 171.

REVIEW PROBLEM

David Carling and Randy Jones, two 15-year-old students, had several very strong drinks at David's house while his parents were out of town. Randy suggested that they take Mr. Carling's car for a drive and pick up their girlfriends, Carol and Mary. Although neither Randy nor David had a driver's licence, David agreed to the plan despite his parents' explicit prohibition against driving. Carol agreed to accompany them and asked them to bring along some liquor for her. Mary also agreed to go for a ride, but she was unaware that they had been drinking. Carol knew that the boys had taken the car without consent, but Mary did not.

During the drive, they picked up Louise, who was hitchhiking to work. She soon realized that David was drunk and very tired. She twice asked him to slow down. She thought about getting out of the car, but she was late for work. As a result of his speeding and intoxication, David lost control of the car and hit Mr. Crown's parked car. The car was parked illegally, partially blocking the roadway. Had David not panicked, however, he could easily have avoided the car. Both cars were badly damaged and all the occupants of Mr. Carling's vehicle were injured.

Mr. Crown, Louise, Mary, Carol and Randy have sued David in negligence. You have been retained to research the possible defences that David might raise and their impact on his liability.

20

PROOF OF NEGLIGENCE

1. The Burden of Proof in a Negligence Action
2. Exceptions to the General Principles Governing the Burden of Proof
3. *Res Ipsa Loquitur*

1. The Burden of Proof in a Negligence Action

It is important at the outset to distinguish between legal and evidentiary burdens of proof. The legal burden of proof in a civil action is the burden of proving an issue on the balance of probabilities. In other words, after both sides have been heard, the party who bears the legal burden will lose the issue unless he or she has convinced the judge or jury to this requisite degree of certainty. While the balance of probabilities test is clearly less onerous than the criminal standard of proof beyond a reasonable doubt, it is difficult to define precisely. Fleming, *The Law of Torts*, 9th ed. (1998) at 352 explains the civil standard in the following terms: "[It] requires more than a mere mechanical comparison of probabilities independently of any belief in its reality; the tribunal must feel an actual persuasion based on a preponderance of probability. Thus a merely mathematical or statistical probability of barely 51 per cent is not sufficient because it carries no conviction that the case falls within the 51 rather than the 49." The plaintiff usually bears the legal burden of proving all of the elements of a negligence action, and the defendant has the legal burden of proving any defence.

The legal burden generally remains on the same party throughout the trial. In contrast, the evidentiary burden may shift back and forth between the parties as evidence is introduced during the course of the trial. The evidentiary burden relates to the practical desirability of adducing evidence in support of one's position, and its placement is determined at any particular time by the cumulative weight of the evidence that has been presented. Thus, the plaintiff, who is required to present his or her case first, is subject to two burdens at the outset. First, he or she bears the obligation of ultimately proving the elements of the case on a balance of probabilities. This obligation arises from the legal burden and is assessed at the end of the entire trial. Second, he or she also bears the obligation of immediately adducing sufficient evidence to establish a *prima facie* case. This obligation arises from the evidentiary burden. If, after the plaintiff has presented his or her case, but before the defendant has presented its case, the judge does not believe that the plaintiff's evidence, considered on its own, could possibly support the imposition of liability, a nonsuit will be ordered. In other words, the trial will end immediately and the defendant will not be required to present its case.

In most situations, however, the plaintiff is able to discharge the evidentiary burden, establish a *prima facie* case and avoid a nonsuit. In that situation, the evidentiary burden then shifts to the defendant. The legal burden remains on the plaintiff; the defendant is not required to prove, on a balance of probabilities, that it was not negligent. However, if it wishes to avoid the risk of liability, it should adduce sufficient evidence to rebut the plaintiff's *prima facie* case against it. In other words, the defendant should introduce evidence that prevents the trier of fact from concluding that the plaintiff has established his or her case on a balance of probabilities.

In theory, the plaintiff may fail to discharge the legal burden of proof even though he or she has discharged the evidentiary burden and the defendant has not introduced any evidence. For example, while a judge might refuse to order a nonsuit because the evidence at the end of the plaintiff's case, considered on its own, *could* support a finding of negligence, the jury (assuming that there is one) might in the end conclude that on the balance of probabilities it in fact does not do so. Obviously, however, it is advisable for the defendant to present evidence in support of its position.

WAKELIN v. LONDON & SOUTH WESTERN RY. CO.

(1886), 12 A.C. 41 (H.L.)

The action was brought by the administratrix of Henry Wakelin on behalf of herself and her children under Lord Campbell's Act, 9 & 10 Vict. c. 93.

The statement of claim alleged that the defendant's line between Chiswick Station and Chiswick Junction crossed a public footway, and that on the 1st of May 1882 the defendants so negligently and unskilfully drove a train on the line across the footpath and so neglected to take precautions in respect of the train and the crossing that the train struck and killed one Henry Wakelin the plaintiff's husband whilst lawfully on the footpath.

The statement of defence admitted that on that day the plaintiff's husband whilst on or near the footpath was struck by a train of the defendants, and so injured that he died, but denied the alleged negligence; did not admit that the deceased was lawfully crossing the line at the time in question; and alleged that his death was caused by his own negligence and that he might by the exercise of reasonable caution have seen the train approaching and avoided the accident.

Oral evidence was given that from the cottage where the deceased lived it would take about ten minutes to walk to the crossing; that he left his cottage on the evening of the 1st of May after tea, and that he was never seen again till his body was found the same night on the down line near the crossing. There was no evidence as to the circumstances under which he got on to the line. Witnesses for the plaintiff gave evidence (not very intelligible) as to the limited number of yards at which an approaching train could be seen from the crossing, and as to obstructions to the view.

The defendants called no witnesses, and submitted that there was no case. Manisty J. left the case to the jury who returned a verdict for the plaintiff for £800. The Divisional Court (Grove J. Huddleston B. and Hawkins J.) set aside the verdict and entered judgment for the defendants. The Court of Appeal (Brett M.R. Bowen and Fry L.JJ.) on the 16th day of May 1884 affirmed this decision. In the course of his judgment Brett M.R. said that in his opinion the plaintiff in this case was not only bound to give evidence of negligence on the part of the defendants which was a cause of the death of the deceased, but was also bound to give prima facie evidence that the deceased was not guilty of negligence contributing to the accident; and that by reason of the plaintiff having been unable to give any evidence of the circumstances of the accident she had failed in giving evidence of that necessary part of her prima facie case.

From this decision the plaintiff appealed.

. . .

LORD HALSBURY L.C.: — My Lords, it is incumbent upon the plaintiff in this case to establish by proof that her husband's death has been caused by some negligence of the defendants, some negligent act, or some negligent omission, to which the injury complained of in this case, the death of the husband, is attributable. That is the fact to be proved. If that fact is not proved the plaintiff fails, and if in the absence of direct proof the circumstances which are established are equally consistent with the allegation of the plaintiff as with the denial of the defendants, the plaintiff fails, for the very simple reason that the plaintiff is bound to establish the affirmative of the proposition.

. . .

If the simple proposition with which I started is accurate, it is manifest that the plaintiff, who gives evidence of a state of facts which is equally consistent with the wrong of which she complains having been caused by - in this sense that it could not have occurred without - her husband's own negligence as by the negligence of the defendants, does not prove that it was caused by the defendants' negligence. She may indeed establish that the event has occurred through the joint negligence of both, but if that is the state of the evidence the plaintiff fails . . . It is true that the onus of proof may shift from time to time as matter of evidence, but still the question must ultimately arise whether the person who is bound to prove the affirmative of the issue, i.e., in this case the negligent act done, has discharged herself of that burden. I am of opinion that the plaintiff does not do this unless she proves that the defendants have caused the injury in the sense which I have explained.

In this case I am unable to see any evidence of how this unfortunate calamity occurred. One may surmise, and it is but surmise and not evidence, that the unfortunate man was knocked down by a passing train while on the level crossing; but assuming in the plaintiff's favour that fact to be established, is there anything to shew that the train ran over the man rather than that the man ran against the train?

. . .

Again, is there any legal presumption that people are careful and look before them on crossing a railway, or even when they do see the approach of a train that they never cross when the train is dangerously near? And yet if one of these hypotheses were established the plaintiff must fail, while on the other side it would be extremely difficult to lay down as a matter of law that precautions which the legislature has not enjoined should be observed by a railway company in the ordinary conduct of their traffic. Railway companies are permitted to establish their undertakings for the express purpose of running trains at high speed along their lines. Rightly or wrongly the legislature have permitted the railways to cross roadways on a level, and it must be taken that the legislature, wherever they have given that authority, and without requiring special measures of precaution, have left to the railway company the discretion of using their lines in a reasonable and proper fashion. I can understand that circumstances might exist which might call upon the railway company to take unusual precautions, though not prescribed by statute, but the peculiarity about this case is that no one knows what the circumstances were. The body of the deceased man was found in the neighbourhood of the level crossing on the down line, but neither by direct evidence nor by reasonable inference can any conclusion be arrived at as to the circumstances causing his death.

It has been argued before your Lordships that we must take the facts as found by the jury. I do not know what facts the jury are supposed to have found, nor is it, perhaps, very material to inquire, because if they have found that the defendants' negligence caused the death of the plaintiff's husband, they have found it without a fragment of evidence to justify such a finding.

Under these circumstances, I move that the judgment appealed from be affirmed, and the appeal dismissed.

LORD WATSON: . . . It appears to me that in all such cases the liability of the defendant company must rest upon these facts - in the first place that there was some negligent act or omission on the part of the company or their servants which materially contributed to the injury or death complained of, and, in the second place, that there was no contributory negligence on the part of the injured or deceased person. But it does not, in my opinion, necessarily follow that the whole burden of proof is cast upon the plaintiff. That it lies with the plaintiff to prove the first of these propositions does not admit of dispute. Mere allegation or proof that the company was guilty of negligence is altogether irrelevant; they might be guilty of many negligent acts or omissions, which might possibly have occasioned injury to somebody, but had no connection whatever with the injury for which redress is sought, and therefore the plaintiff must allege and prove, not merely that they were negligent, but that their negligence caused or materially contributed to the injury.

I am of opinion that the onus of proving affirmatively that there was contributory negligence on the part of the person injured rests, in the first instance, upon the defendants, and that in the absence of evidence tending to that conclusion, the plaintiff is not bound to prove the negative in order to entitle her to a verdict in her favour . . . .

The difficulty of dealing with the question of onus in cases like the present arises from the fact that in most cases it is well nigh impossible for the plaintiff to lay his evidence before a jury or the Court without disclosing circumstances which either point to or tend to rebut the conclusion that the injured party was guilty of contributory negligence. If the plaintiff's evidence were sufficient to shew that the negligence of the defendants did materially contribute to the injury, and threw no light upon the question of the injured party's negligence, then I should be of opinion that, in the absence of any counter-evidence from the defendants, it ought to be presumed that, in point of fact, there was no such contributory negligence. Even if the plaintiff's evidence did disclose facts and circumstances bearing upon that question, which were neither sufficient per se to prove such contributory negligence, nor to cast the onus of disproving it on the plaintiff, I should remain of the same opinion. Of course a plaintiff who comes into Court with an unfounded action may have to submit to the inconvenience of having his adversary's defence proved by his own witnesses; but that cannot affect the question upon whom the onus lies in the first instance . . . .

In the present case, I think the appellant must fail, because no attempt has been made to bring evidence in support of her allegations up to the point at which the question of contributory negligence becomes material. The evidence appears to me to shew that the injuries which caused the death of Henry Wakelin were occasioned by contact with an engine or a train belonging to the respondents, and I am willing to assume, although I am by no means satisfied, that it has also been proved that they were in certain respects negligent. The evidence goes no further. It affords ample materials for conjecturing that the death may possibly have been occasioned by that negligence, but it furnishes no data from which an inference can be reasonably drawn that as a matter of fact it was so occasioned.

I am accordingly of opinion that the order appealed from must be affirmed.

[Lord Blackburn concurred with Lord Watson, and Lord Fitzgerald gave a concurring speech.]

NOTES AND QUESTIONS

1. Should the plaintiff have been nonsuited at trial? If, as Lord Halsbury indicates, there was not a fragment of evidence to justify the jury's finding, what factors induced the jury to find for the plaintiff?

2. Does *Wakelin* add support to those who would abolish civil jury trials? What arguments can be made in favour of jury trials in civil matters? Although civil jury trials have become infrequent in parts of the Commonwealth, they remain important in several Canadian provinces. See Sommers & Firestone, "In Defence of the Civil Jury Trial in Personal Injury Actions" (1987) 7 Adv. Q. 492; and MacIntyre, Manes & McGrenere, "More in Defence of the Civil Jury Trial in Personal Injury Actions" (1987) 8 Adv. Q. 109.

In *Hunt (Litigation guardian of) v. Sutton Group Incentive Realty Inc.* (2002), 60 O.R. (3d) 665 (C.A.) the court stated that "the right to trial by jury is a substantial right and one which is not to be taken away lightly. The onus is upon a party moving to discharge a jury and that onus must also be substantial." The court held that the trial judge erred in exercising his discretion to discharge the jury on the grounds that the issues in the case were too complex for it to resolve, and it ordered a new trial. Compare with *Cowles v. Balac* (2006), 83 O.R. (3d) 660 (C.A.), where the court held that the trial judge had correctly struck out a jury notice on grounds of complexity.

3. What was the basis on which Lord Halsbury dismissed the plaintiff's case? What did Lord Halsbury mean by the following statement: "It is true that the onus of proof may shift from time to time as a matter of evidence, but still the question must ultimately arise whether the person who is bound to prove the affirmative of the issue . . . has discharged herself of that burden?" For a Canadian case on point see *Prinse v. Fraser Valley Foods Ltd.*, [1994] 2 W.W.R. 331 (B.C.C.A.).

4. At the time of *Wakelin* contributory negligence was a complete defence to an action in negligence. What effect did this have on the plaintiff's case? Lord Watson clearly disagreed with Brett M.R. as to who bears the burden of proving contributory negligence. With whom would Lord Halsbury agree?

5. Would the result have been the same if the defendant had the legal and evidentiary burden of disproving negligence?

6. For a discussion of the legal and evidentiary burdens of proof see Tapper, *Cross and Tapper on Evidence*, 8th ed. (1995) at 119-75; Fleming, *The Law of Torts*, 9th ed. (1998) at 345-53; Redmayne, "Standards of Proof in Civil Litigation" (1999) 62 Mod.

L. Rev. 167; Fridman, *The Law of Torts in Canada*, 2d ed. (2002) at 403-405; and Klar, *Tort Law*, 3d ed. (2003) at 503-505.

2. Exceptions to the General Principles Governing the Burden of Proof

(a) STATUTES AND SHIFTING BURDENS OF PROOF

MACDONALD v. WOODARD

(1974), 43 D.L.R. (3d) 182 (Ont. Co. Ct.)

MATHESON CO. CT. J.: — The plaintiff, a service station proprietor, was struck while standing in front of the automobile of the defendant Donald Woodard just after the plaintiff had given a boost to Woodard's battery from his own stationwagon which had been conveniently positioned nose to nose facing the Woodard automobile.

. . .

What, in the circumstances, does the plaintiff have to establish in order to succeed against the defendant Donald Woodard? Because Angus MacDonald was on his feet, in the process of disengaging the starter cables when the Woodard vehicle crushed him, this is a case where the provisions of s. 133 of the *Highway Traffic Act*, R.S.O. 1970, c. 202, must be considered.

Section 133 reads as follows:

> 133(1) When loss or damage is sustained by any person by reason of a motor vehicle on a highway, the onus of proof that the loss or damage did not arise through the negligence or improper conduct of the owner or driver of the motor vehicle is upon the owner or driver.
> (2) This section does not apply in case of a collision between motor vehicles or between motor vehicles and cars of electric or steam railways or other motor vehicles running only on stationary rails on the highway nor to an action brought by a passenger in a motor vehicle in respect of any injuries sustained by him while a passenger.

. . .

This section was enacted in order to overcome difficulties experienced by plaintiffs in obtaining and presenting sufficient evidence of a motorist's negligence to avoid a non-suit at the close of their case. Knowledge of relevant acts and circumstances leading up to an accident might be in the possession only of the defendant and injustice might result if a plaintiff was unable to overcome the initial obstacle of a *prima facie* case and to avoid having his case determined before all the evidence was before the Court. Hence the introduction of a type of statutory *res ipsa loquitur* doctrine under which the owner or driver is *prima facie* liable for damage caused by his motor vehicle unless he satisfied the Court on a preponderance of evidence that he was not in fact negligent.

A plaintiff must therefore show, in order that the section may apply, that his damages were occasioned by the presence of a motor vehicle on the highway.

This does not mean that before the onus begins to operate, the plaintiff must first prove that the effective cause of the collision was the conduct of the driver; he need only show that the collision — not the conduct of the driver — was the cause of the damage. . . .

The plaintiff has satisfied me that the damage to his knee was occasioned by the presence of the defendant Woodard's motor vehicle on the highway. The onus thus begins to operate. But specifically what is the nature of this statutory onus now upon the defendant Woodard?

The leading authority on the interpretation of this section is *Winnipeg Electric Co. v. Geel,* [1932] 4 D.L.R. 51. . . . In the Supreme Court of Canada, Duff, J., stated. . .:

> The statute creates, as against the owners and drivers of motor vehicles . . . a rebuttable presumption of negligence. The onus of disproving negligence remains throughout the proceedings. If, at the conclusion of the evidence, it is too meagre or too evenly balanced to enable the tribunal to determine this issue, as a question of fact, then, by force of the statute, the plaintiff is entitled to succeed.

This statement was approved by the Privy Council where Lord Wright further said. . .:

> But the onus which the section places on the defendant is not in law a shifting or transitory onus: it cannot be displaced merely by the defendant giving some evidence that he was not negligent, if that evidence however credible is not sufficient reasonably to satisfy the jury that he was not negligent: the burden remains on the defendant until the very end of the case, when the question must be determined whether or not the defendant has sufficiently shown that he did not in fact cause the accident by his negligence.

It is accordingly upon the whole of the evidence submitted at the trial, including all the circumstances and inferences to be drawn therefrom that the defendant must satisfy the jury that the accident was not in fact caused by his negligence. . .. And once the onus is placed on the defendant it will not be discharged unless he satisfied the Court not merely that the damages were in fact sustained without such negligence. . .. Thus, it is not necessary to find any specific act of negligence against the defendant in order that liability may attach to him, and if any doubt remains on a consideration of all the evidence as to whether or not the defendant was negligent, the plaintiff is entitled to the verdict.

The plaintiff throughout this trial has remained virtually mute concerning the cause of the accident, allowing the defendants to fight it out between themselves. Indeed with his meagre information he is scarcely in a position to do otherwise.

. . .

In light of the extreme confusion of Donald Woodard's own testimony in so many particulars and areas, and his inability personally or through his witnesses, who gave mechanical evidence, to suggest how this automobile, if properly operated, could "leap" or "lurch" forward at the time in question, I am compelled to find that Woodard has failed to satisfy the onus which s. 133(1) has imposed upon him.

NOTES AND QUESTIONS

1. What must the plaintiff establish in order to invoke s. 133 (now R.S.O. 1990, c. H.8, s. 193(1))? Explain the effect of s. 133 on the burden of proof in a negligence action.

2. What must the defendant prove to discharge the burden of proof placed on him or her? See *Angelopoulos v. Machen* (1992), 7 O.R. (3d) 45 (C.A.).

3. In *A.G. Ont. v. Keller* (1978), 94 D.L.R. (3d) 632 (Ont. C.A.) a police officer was seriously injured when his car went out of control and struck a pole during a high-speed chase. The fleeing driver knew he was being pursued and was attempting to escape. At no time did the two vehicles collide. The Court of Appeal held that the reverse onus provision applied to the escaping driver. Do you agree? Would the result have been the same if the provision had not been applied? See also *Marks v. Campbell* (1977), 76 D.L.R. (3d) 715 (N.S.S.C.); *De Gurse v. Henry* (1984), 47 O.R. (2d) 172 (H.C.); *Moore v. Fanning* (1987), 60 O.R. (2d) 225 (H.C.); and *Crew v. Nicholson* (1989), 68 O.R. (2d) 232 (C.A.).

4. For a discussion of comparable provisions in other provincial legislation see *Feener v. McKenzie* (1971), 25 D.L.R. (3d) 283 (S.C.C.); *Homer v. Comeau* (1988), 88 N.S.R. (2d) 295 (S.C.); *Hilderman v. Rattray* (1988), 93 A.R. 217 (Q.B.); *Melnychuk v. Moore* (1989), 57 Man. R. (2d) 174 (C.A.); *Doem v. Phillips Estate*, [1995] 4 W.W.R. 1 (B.C.S.C.); *Nice v. John Doe* (2000), 190 D.L.R. (4th) 402 (Alta. C.A.); and *Cardinal v. Loo*, [2003] 5 W.W.R. 719 (Alta. Q.B.), varied (2006), 384 A.R. 200 (C.A.).

(b) DIRECTLY CAUSED INJURY: UNINTENDED TRESPASS

DAHLBERG v. NAYDIUK

(1969), 10 D.L.R. (3d) 319 (Man. C.A.)

[The defendant fired at a deer, but missed. The bullet carried 250 to 300 yards and struck the plaintiff, who was working on his farm. The defendant had obtained consent to hunt from the owner of the land on which he was situated, but he had not sought the plaintiff's permission to fire over, or hunt on, the farm.]

DICKSON, J.A.:

. . .

Trespass or negligence

Mr. Dahlberg's action was framed both in negligence and in trespass. This gives rise to one of those strange anomalies of the law. It is this. If Mr. Dahlberg relies on negligence the onus rests upon him to prove Mr. Naydiuk was negligent. This follows the normal evidentiary rule that he who asserts must prove. However, if Mr. Dahlberg relies upon trespass, (i) Mr. Naydiuk is entitled to judgment only "if he satisfies the onus of establishing the absence of both intention and negligence on his part" [*Cook v. Lewis*, [1952] 1 D.L.R. 1 (S.C.C.)] that is to say the onus rests upon him to disprove negligence, and (ii) the question arises whether such "negligence" means "a negligent *(i.e.*, careless) trespass or something which would give rise to an action on negligence": Street, *The Law of Torts*, 4th ed., p. 14.

As Clyne, J., said in *Walmsley v. Humenick,* [1954] 2 D.L.R. 232 at p. 244:

> It seems to be equally curious that since the passing of the Judicature Acts a situation should arise where on the same facts the plaintiffs' action must fail if it is framed in negligence, but might succeed if it is brought in trespass.

Two English cases, decided since *Cook v. Lewis*, *supra*, might be mentioned. In *Fowler v. Lanning*, [1959] 1 Q.B. 426 . . ., Diplock, J. (as he then was), in the course of a lengthy judgment, held that the onus of proving negligence, where the trespass is not intentional, lies upon the plaintiff, whether the action be framed in trespass or in negligence. Lord Denning, M.R., took the matter one step further in *Letang v. Cooper*, [1964] 2 All E.R. 929 at p. 932:

> If he does not inflict injury intentionally, but only unintentionally, the plaintiff has no cause of action in trespass. His only cause of action is in negligence, and then only on proof of want of reasonable care.

The late Dean C. A. Wright has referred (Linden, *Studies in Canadian Tort Law*, at p. 44) to "this irrational and unnecessary exception of trespass", expressing the hope that some Canadian Court would "put an end to the possibility of a difference in burden of proof depending solely on the direct or indirect application of the force." If such a change is to be made in the law it must be made by a Court higher than this. In the present case we, as we must, reached our decision in accord with the dictates of *Cook v. Lewis, supra.*

Finding

It remains to apply the principles enunciated above to the facts before us.

The Judge found that Mr. Naydiuk failed in his duty to take care, and I agree. He failed to prove he was not negligent. In my view of the matter he was negligent in two respects:

(1) In firing in the direction of farm buildings.

. . .

(2) In failing to obtain permission from Mr. Dahlberg before hunting his land or firing across his land.

. . .

Hunters must recognize that firing over land without permission of the owner constitutes a trespass to land and if injury to person results, trespass to person. A hunter who fires in the direction in which he knows or ought to know farm buildings are located must accept full responsibility for resultant damage to person or property. It is no answer to say he thought the buildings were unoccupied. There are vast areas of western Canada in which deer abound and where no farming activities are carried on. Even in farming areas there are often hills from which one can fire at game in the valley below without risk of injury to others. If a hunter chooses to hunt in a farming area he must do so in full awareness of the paramount right of the farmer to carry on his lawful occupation without risk of injury from stray bullets.

NOTES AND QUESTIONS

1. Did the plaintiff succeed in negligence or in trespass? Given the evidence adduced at trial, was it possible for the plaintiff to succeed in either cause of action? When will it be advantageous for a plaintiff to plead one cause of action rather than the other?

2. Dickson J.A. felt compelled to follow the Supreme Court of Canada's judgment in *Cook v. Lewis*, [1951] S.C.R. 830 on the question of proof of carelessness in the context of an action in trespass. As seen in the following extract, the judgment in *Cook*

also addresses the issue of proof of causation. What must a plaintiff establish in order to invoke the rule in *Cook* as it pertains to proof of negligence? If the bullet fired from Naydiuk's gun hit a tree and ricocheted before striking Dahlberg, would the rule in *Cook* have applied?

3. Explain the impact of the rule in *Cook* on the burden of proof. Do you agree with the way in which the rule was applied in *Dahlberg*?

4. Do you agree with Dickson J.A.'s criticism of the rule? If not, can you suggest a rationale for its continued use? See *Bell Canada v. Cope (Sarnia) Ltd.* (1980), 11 C.C.L.T. 170 (Ont. H.C.), aff'd (1981), 119 D.L.R. (3d) 254 (Ont. C.A.). See also Tindale, "The Burden of Proof in Actions for Negligent Trespass in Canada" (1971) 49 Can. Bar Rev. 612; Sharp, "Negligent Trespass in Canada: A Persistent Source of Embarrassment" (1978) 1 Adv. Q. 311; and Sullivan, "Trespass to the Person in Canada: A Defence of the Traditional Approach" (1987) 19 Ottawa L. Rev. 533.

(c) MULTIPLE NEGLIGENT DEFENDANTS

COOK v. LEWIS

[1952] 1 D.L.R. 1 (S.C.C.)

[The plaintiff, Lewis, was hit in the face by bird-shot when the defendants, Cook and Akenhead, fired simultaneously at different birds which had flown in the plaintiff's direction. The jury found that the plaintiff had been shot by one of the two hunters, but was unable to say which one. It also found that the injuries were not caused by the negligence of either. The Court of Appeal set aside the jury's finding on the negligence issue and ordered a new trial. This judgment was upheld by the Supreme Court of Canada, with Locke J. dissenting.]

RAND J.: — I agree with the Court of Appeal . . . that the finding of the jury exculpating both defendants from negligence was perverse and it is unnecessary to examine the facts on which that conclusion is based.

There remains the answer that, although shots from one of the two guns struck the respondent, the jury could not determine from which they came. This is open to at least four interpretations: first, believing that only one discharge could have inflicted the injuries, they found it difficult to decide which testimony, whether that of Cook or Akenhead, was to be accepted, the evidence of each, taken at its face, excluding guilt; or that the shots from both guns having been fired so nearly at the same time and to have been aimed so nearly at the same target, it was impossible for them to say which struck the eye: or that they were unable to say whether the situation was either of those two alternatives: or finally, that they were not unanimous on any one or more of these views.

It will be seen that there is one feature common to the first three: having found that either A or B had been the cause of injury to C, the jury declare that C has not satisfied them which of the two it was. It is then a problem in proof and must be considered from that standpoint.

. . .

What, then, the culpable actor has done by his initial negligent act is, first, to have set in motion a dangerous force which embraces the injured person within the scope of its probable mischief; and next, in conjunction with circumstances which he must be held to contemplate, to have made more difficult if not impossible the means of proving the possible damaging results of his own act or the similar results of the act of another. He has violated not only the victim's substantive right to security, but he has also culpably impaired the latter's remedial right of establishing liability. By confusing his act with environmental conditions, he has, in effect, destroyed the victim's power of proof.

The legal consequence of that is, I should say, that the onus is then shifted to the wrongdoer to exculpate himself; it becomes in fact a question of proof between him and the other and innocent member of the alternatives, the burden of which he must bear. The onus attaches to culpability, and if both acts bear that taint, the onus or prima facie transmission of responsibility attaches to both, and the question of the sole responsibility of one is a matter between them.

. . .

The risks arising from these sporting activities by increased numbers of participants and diminishing opportunity for their safe exercise, as the facts here indicate, require appropriate refinement in foresight. Against the private and public interests at stake, is the privilege of the individual to engage in a sport not inherently objectionable. As yet, certainly, the community is not ready to assume the burden of such a mishap. The question is whether a victim is to be told that such a risk, not only in substantive right but in remedy, is one he must assume. When we have reached the point where, as here, shots are considered spent at a distance of between 150 feet and 200 feet and the woods are "full" of hunters, a somewhat stringent regard to conduct seems to me to be obvious. It would be a strange commentary on its concern toward personal safety, that the law, although forbidding the victim any other mode of redress, was powerless to accord him any in its own form of relief. I am unable to assent to the view that there is any such helplessness.

. . .

Assuming, then, that the jury have found one or both of the defendants here negligent, as on the evidence I think they must have, and at the same time have found that the consequences of the two shots, whether from a confusion in time or in area, cannot be segregated, the onus on the guilty person arises. This is a case where each hunter would know of or expect the shooting by the other and the negligent actor has culpably participated in the proof-destroying fact, the multiple shooting and its consequences. No liability will, in any event attach to an innocent act of shooting, but the culpable actor, as against innocence, must bear the burden of exculpation.

These views of the law were not as adequately presented to the jury as I think they should have been.

I would, therefore, dismiss the appeal with costs. The motion to quash for want of jurisdiction is dismissed with costs.

The judgment of Estey, Cartwright and Fauteux JJ. was delivered by

CARTWRIGHT J. . . . It is argued, however, that *Summers v. Tice* [33 Cal.2d 80 (S.C. 1948)] should be followed and that under the principles stated in that judgment the jury might properly have found both Akenhead and Cook liable for the plaintiff's injury if in their view of the evidence both of them fired in the direction of the clump of trees in which the plaintiff in fact was, under such circumstances that the conduct of each constituted a breach of duty to the plaintiff. I have not been able to find any case in the courts of this country, or of England in which consideration has been given to certain propositions of law laid down in *Summers v. Tice*. The underlying reason for the decision appears to me to be found in the following quotation from the case of *Oliver v. Miles* [144 Miss. 852 (S.C. 1926)]:

> . . . We think that . . . each is liable for the resulting injury to the boy, although no one can say definitely who actually shot him. To *hold otherwise would be to exonerate both from liability, although each was negligent, and the injury resulted from such negligence.*

The judgment in *Summers v. Tice* reads in part as follows:

> . . . When we consider the relative position of the parties and the results that would flow if plaintiff was required to pin the injury on one of the defendants only, a requirement that the burden of proof on that subject be shifted to defendants becomes manifest. They are both wrongdoers - both negligent toward plaintiff. They brought about a situation where the negligence of one of them injured the plaintiff, hence, it should rest with them each to absolve himself if he can. The injured party has been placed by defendants in the unfair position of pointing to which defendant caused the harm. If one can escape the other may also and plaintiff is remediless. Ordinarily defendants are in a far better position to offer evidence to determine which one caused the injury. This reasoning has recently found favour in this Court.

I do not think it necessary to decide whether all that was said in *Summers v. Tice* should be accepted as stating the law of British Columbia, but I am of opinion, for the reasons given in that case, that if under the circumstances of the case at bar the jury, having decided that the plaintiff was shot by either Cook or Akenhead, found themselves unable to decide which of the two shot him because in their opinion both shot negligently in his direction, both defendants should have been found liable. I think that the learned trial judge should have sent the jury back to consider the matter further with a direction to the above effect. . . .

NOTES AND QUESTIONS

1. According to Rand J., what must the plaintiff establish to shift the burden of proof regarding causation to the defendants? Is his analysis dependent on there being more than one defendant? What would the defendants have to establish to discharge the burden of proof cast upon them? Answer these same questions based on Cartwright J.'s judgment.

2. In *Joseph Brant Memorial Hosp. v. Koziol* (1976), 12 O.R. (2d) 142 (C.A.), aff'd (1977), [1978] 1 S.C.R. 491 a nurse's negligence in failing to maintain adequate records made it impossible to determine the exact circumstances surrounding a patient's death. The Court of Appeal for Ontario, quoting from Rand J.'s judgment, held that the burden of disproving causation should be on the nurse. The Supreme Court of Canada rejected this proposition, noting that the "destruction of evidence" rationale had been adopted by only Rand J. and formed no part of the majority judgment. Was Rand J.'s rationale for shifting the burden of proof any less compelling than that of the majority?

3. As in *Koziol, ibid.*, a patient is often unable to identify the person responsible for a negligent act that occurs during or immediately after surgery. Some courts have aided such plaintiffs by shifting the burden of proof regarding causation to the defendant

doctors. For example in *Ybarra v. Spangard*, 154 P.2d 687 (Cal. S.C. 1944) the court inferred negligence against an entire surgical team of doctors and nurses even though only one of them may have caused the plaintiff's injury.

Denning L.J. adopted a similar position in *Roe v. Min. of Health*, [1954] 2 All E.R. 131 (C.A.) at 136-37:

> Each of these plaintiffs is entitled to say to the hospital: "While I was in your hands something has been done to me which has wrecked my life. Please explain how it has come to pass". . . I do not think that the hospital authorities and Dr. Graham can both avoid giving an explanation by the simple expedient of each throwing responsibility on the other. If an injured person shows that one or other or both of two persons injured him, but cannot say which of them it was, then he is not defeated altogether. He can call on each of them for an explanation.

Unfortunately, Denning L.J. did not elaborate. Given the majority judgment in *Cook* and the decision in *Koziol*, is Denning L.J.'s approach likely to be followed in Canada?

4. Do the problems of establishing causation in medical malpractice cases warrant the creation of special rules concerning the burden of proof? If so, how would you state these rules? In *Snell v. Farrell* (1990), 72 D.L.R. (4th) 289 (S.C.C.) the court stated in *obiter dicta* that the burden of proof was not immutable and suggested that where the facts were within the defendant's knowledge and not accessible to the plaintiff, the burden of proof may be shifted. Unfortunately, the court did not elaborate on the issue. See Roth, "Causation and the Burden of Proof: An Age Old Dilemma and a New Age Approach" (1992) 14 Adv. Q. 70.

5. *Cook v. Lewis* involved a situation in which each of two defendants acted carelessly but only one actually caused the plaintiff's injury. A different approach may be adopted when the potential causal factors include the defendant's carelessness and the plaintiff's carelessness. In *Leaman v. Rea*, [1954] 4 D.L.R. 423 (N.B.C.A.) there was a collision between two cars, both of which had been driving in the middle of a highway. The trial judge dismissed a claim and counterclaim on the basis that he could not determine on a balance of probabilities how the accident had occurred or which party was at fault. However, the New Brunswick Court of Appeal held that both parties were equally to blame and apportioned the damages accordingly. Would it have made any practical difference to the parties if the Court of Appeal had simply dismissed both claims as the trial judge had done?

The *Leaman* approach is applied in limited circumstances. In *Wotta v. Haliburton Oil Well Cementing Co.*, [1955] S.C.R. 377 the Supreme Court of Canada explained *Leaman* as a case in which the facts supported an inference of carelessness against *both* parties. The court further held that *Leaman* was inapplicable to situations in which *either* the defendant *or* the plaintiff was negligently responsible but the facts did not point to one or both parties as being the probable cause of the accident. In that situation, *neither* party is able to recover any damages. See also *Bray v. Palmer*, [1953] 2 All E.R. 1449 (C.A.); *Barton v. Weaver* (1981), 36 N.B.R. (2d) 483 (C.A.); *Host v. Bassett* (1983), 48 A.L.R. 404 (H.C.A.); and *Stamp v. R. in Right of Ontario* (1984), 47 O.R. (2d) 214 (C.A.). Compare on highly similar facts *Martin v. Murray Estate*, 1995 CarswellOnt 2463 (Gen. Div.) (WLeC) where the court was able to identify, from the totality of the evidence, the lane in which the accident occurred.

Consider the following situation. Two cars collide in circumstances in which one driver or the other, but not both, is carelessly responsible for the accident. Both drivers suffer injuries that render them incapable of remembering the events in question. A passenger who was asleep in one of the cars at the time of the accident sues both drivers for the injuries that he or she sustained in the collision. How would a court resolve the issues of carelessness and causation? Would both drivers be held liable to the passenger? Would both actions fail according to the decision in *Wotta*? See *Baker v. Market Harborough; Wallace v. Richards*, [1953] 1 W.L.R. 1472 (C.A.).

6. As discussed in Chapter 16, English and American courts have adopted a broader approach to the problems posed in cases like *Cook v. Lewis*. In *McGhee v. National Coal Board*, [1972] 3 All E.R. 1008 (H.L.) Lord Wilberforce stated that the burden of proving causation should shift from the plaintiff to the defendant if the defendant's negligence materially increased the risk of injury and that very injury befell the plaintiff. Lord Wilberforce limited his analysis to cases in which it was impossible to determine the cause of the plaintiff's loss and "policy and justice" warranted imposing liability on the defendant as the creator of a risk. In reaching his conclusion, Lord Wilberforce emphasized that this was an industrial disease case involving an employee's claim against his employer. The other members of the court did not accept Lord Wilberforce's suggestion that the burden of proof should be shifted. However, they did find for the plaintiff on the basis that carelessness that materially increases the risk of injury can be taken to have caused or materially contributed to the occurrence of actual injuries that fall within the scope of risk, thereby discharging the plaintiff's burden.

As explained in Chapter 16, *McGhee*'s legacy has yet to be settled. In *Wilsher v. Essex Area Health Authority*, [1988] A.C. 1074 (H.L.) Lord Bridge "re-interpreted" *McGhee* to simply mean that, in certain circumstances, the court may take a robust and pragmatic approach to drawing an inference of causation. Likewise, in *Snell v. Farrell*, *supra*, which appears in Chapter 16, the court reiterated that the plaintiff bears the legal burden of proving causation on a balance of probabilities and held that evidence of conduct that materially increased the risk of injury does not *per se* constitute sufficient proof. However, it also stressed that questions of causation should be resolved on the basis of common sense and recognized that where the facts are particularly within the knowledge of one party, an inference of causation may be drawn on the basis of very little evidence. See Pardy, "Risk, Cause and Toxic Torts: A Theory for a Standard of Proof" (1989) 10 Adv. Q. 277; Fleming, "Probabilistic Causation in Tort Law" (1989) 68 Can. Bar Rev. 661; and Fleming, "Probabilistic Causation in Tort Law: A Postscript" (1991) 70 Can. Bar Rev. 136.

The House of Lords revisited the issue again in *Fairchild v. Glenhaven Funeral Services Ltd.*, [2002] 3 W.L.R. 89 (H.L.). That decision is explained at length in Chapter 16. While continuing to reject Lord Wilberforce's theory of a reversed burden of proof, it endorsed Lord Reid's suggestion in *McGhee* that there "is no substantial difference between saying that what the [defendants] did materially increased the risk of injury to the [plaintiff] and that what [they] did made a material contribution to his injury." In *Fairchild*, the House of Lords read that statement to mean that "a breach of duty which materially increased the risk should be treated as if it had materially contributed to the disease." See Weir, "Making It More Likely v. Making It Happen" [2002] C.L.J. 519; Stapleton, "'Lords a Leaping' Evidentiary Gaps" (2002) 10 Torts L.J. 276; Woods, "Establishing Causation in Negligence: The House of Lords Speaks Again" (2003) 26

Adv. Q. 471; Klar, *Tort Law*, 3d ed. (2003) at 401; Stapleton, "Cause-in-Fact and the Scope of Liability for Consequences" (2003) 119 L.Q.R. 388; Morgan, "Lost Causes in the House of Lords: *Fairchild v. Glenhaven Funeral Services*" (2003) 66 Mod. L. Rev. 277; and Kramer, "Smoothing the Rough Justice of the Fairchild Principle" (2006) 122 L.Q.R. 547.

7. The issues posed by cases like *McGhee*, *Wilsher*, *Snell* and *Fairchild* are becoming more important. Advances in the medical sciences now make it possible to prove that exposure to toxic chemicals, radiation and other substances may have serious long-term consequences that do not manifest themselves for 20 or 30 years. By the time the plaintiff becomes ill or disabled, he or she may not be able to isolate the impact of this exposure from other possible risk factors. The plaintiff's evidence may take the form of extrapolations from animal studies, epidemiological data and other statistical information. In the past, such evidence was often dismissed as being "speculative." The more recent cases, however, while somewhat inconsistent in approach, indicate greater judicial willingness to overcome evidentiary hurdles, at least in cases where the nature of the defendant's conduct makes it difficult to prove causation. See also *Holtby v. Brigham & Cowan (Hull) Ltd.*, [2000] 3 All E.R. 421 (C.A.). See generally Mulcahy, "Proving Causation in Toxic Tort Litigation" (1983) 11 Hofstra L. Rev. 1299; and Brennan, "Causal Chains and Statistical Links" (1989) 73 Cornell L. Rev. 469.

8. In *Sindell v. Abbott Laboratories*, 607 P.2d 924 (Cal. S.C. 1980) the plaintiff was a cancer victim whose mother had taken diethylstilbestrol (DES) during pregnancy. DES was manufactured by approximately 200 pharmaceutical companies, but there were no significant differences in the product between manufacturers. The drug had been prescribed to prevent miscarriages but eventually proved ineffective and was found to pose a risk of causing a particular kind of cancer in female children. This cancer was deadly once it manifested itself, but it had a minimum latency period of 10 to 12 years. The plaintiff could prove that her cancer was caused by DES, but she could not establish which company had produced the DES that her mother had taken. The plaintiff sued all of the major manufacturers, arguing that they had been negligent in continuing to market DES when they knew or ought to have known that it was ineffective and carcinogenic. The court found the defendants negligent and held each liable in proportion to its share of the DES market, unless it could prove that it had not produced the DES that caused the plaintiff's cancer. The court acknowledged that there was a 10% chance that the DES in question had been manufactured by one of the approximately 195 smaller producers which had not been sued.

Would the plaintiff have been able to prove causation based on the general principles governing proof in a negligence action? Would the plaintiff have been able to prove causation based on the multiple negligent defendants rule in *Cook v. Lewis*? Do you agree with the result on the causation issue in *Sindell*? Can you derive a general principle from *Sindell* to deal with similar causation cases? Could this approach be used to establish causation in tobacco litigation?

9. What would have been the result of applying the established principles of apportionment to the defendants in *Sindell*? Do you agree with the court's resolution of the apportionment issue? What changes would have to be made in the apportionment legislation to accommodate the approach in *Sindell*? See Delgado, "Beyond Sindell: Relax-

ation of Cause-In-Fact Rules for Indeterminate Plaintiffs" (1982) 70 Cal. L. Rev. 880; Black, "Epidemiological Proof in Toxic Tort Litigation" (1984) 52 Fordham L. Rev. 732; Legum, "Increased Risk of Cancer as an Actionable Injury" (1984) 18 Ga. L. Rev. 563; Farber, "Toxic Causation" (1987) 71 Minn. L. Rev. 1219; Goldberg, "Fungible? New Uses for Sindell" (1992) 78 A.B.A.J. 73; and Wiechmann, "Standard of Proof for Increased Risk of Disease or Injury" (1994) 61 Defence Counsel J. 59.

10. By way of review, succinctly state the manner in which the courts addressed the issue of proof of causation in each of the following cases: (i) *Cook v. Lewis*, (ii) Lord Wilberforce's judgment in *McGhee v. National Coal Board*, (iii) Lord Reid's judgment in *McGhee*, (iv) *Wilsher v. Essex Area Health Authority*, (v) *Snell v. Farrell*, (vi) *Fairchild v. Glenhaven Funeral Services Ltd.*, (vii) *Sindell v. Abbott Industries* and (viii) *Leaman v. Rea*. How do those various theories relate to the but-for test of causation? See also *Hanke v. Resurfice Corp.* (2007), 357 N.R. 175 (S.C.C.), which is discussed in Chapter 16.

11. A plaintiff may find it difficult to adduce proof on the balance of probabilities because the defendant intentionally destroyed evidence. In several cases, plaintiffs have argued that such conduct constitutes the independent tort of spoliation. The courts have generally rejected that proposal, preferring instead to redress such conduct at the evidentiary level by drawing a rebuttable presumption that the destroyed evidence was unfavorable to the party who destroyed it: *St. Louis v. R.* (1895), 25 S.C.R. 649; *Robb Estate v. St. Joseph's Health Care Centre* (1998), 43 C.C.L.T. (2d) 296 (Ont. Div. Ct.); and *Endean v. Canadian Red Cross Society* (1998), 157 D.L.R. (4th) 465 (B.C.C.A.). See Jones, "The Spoliation Doctrine and Expert Evidence in Civil Trials" (1998) 32 U.B.C. L. Rev. 293; Wilhoit, "Spoliation of Evidence: The Viability of Four Emerging Torts" (1998) 46 U.C.L.A.L. Rev. 631; and Sommers & Siebert, "Intentional Destruction of Evidence: Why Procedural Remedies are Insufficient" (1999) 78 Can. Bar Rev. 38. More recently, however, the Court of Appeal for Ontario left open the possibility that spoliation might provide a grounds for compensation in itself: *Spasic Estate v. Imperial Tobacco Ltd.* (2000), 188 D.L.R. (4th) 577 (Ont. C.A.). For Australia see Witzleb, "Spoliation of Evidence – A New Tort for Australia?" (2003) 11 Tort L. Rev. 135.

3. *Res Ipsa Loquitur*

In some cases, the plaintiff must rely on circumstantial evidence to prove that the defendant was the negligent party who injured him or her. The term "circumstantial evidence" is used to refer to evidence from which an inference may be drawn to reach a conclusion. For example, Carol's testimony that she saw Bob shoot Carl is direct evidence that Bob shot Carl. However, Carol's testimony that she found Bob's fingerprints on the murder weapon is circumstantial evidence. It provides a step in the process of logical inference.

Traditionally, Canadian courts used the Latin maxim *res ipsa loquitur* ("the thing speaks for itself") to describe the circumstances in which the occurrence of an accident provided circumstantial evidence that the plaintiff's injury was caused by the defendant's carelessness. For example, in the classic case of *Byrne v. Boadle* (1863), 159 E.R. 299

(Ex.) the plaintiff was walking on a sidewalk when he was struck by a barrel of flour that had fallen from a window of the defendant's warehouse. The court applied the maxim *res ipsa loquitur* to infer that the barrel fell as a result of the defendant's carelessness. In subsequent cases, the maxim was said to consist of the following elements. First, the occurrence must have been one that does not, in the ordinary course of events, happen without carelessness. Otherwise, it would not be possible to draw an inference of *carelessness* against the defendant. Second, the instrumentality of harm must have been under the sole management and control of the defendant or someone for whom the defendant was responsible. Otherwise, it would not be possible to draw an inference of carelessness against the *defendant* as opposed to some other party. Third, there must not have been any direct evidence as to how or why the accident occurred. Otherwise, the court would resolve the legal issues on the basis of that evidence, rather than the inferences supported by *res ipsa loquitur*. See *Scott v. London and St. Katherine Docks Co.* (1865), 159 E.R. 665; *Hellenius v. Lees*, [1972] S.C.R. 165; and *Jackson v. Millar*, [1976] 1 S.C.R. 225.

One of the most difficult issues pertaining to *res ipsa loquitur* concerned its effect. There were at least three views. The first approach, which was favoured historically, held that successful invocation of the maxim reversed the legal burden of proof such that the defendant was required to prove on a balance of probabilities that his or her carelessness did not cause the plaintiff's injury. See *Barkway v. South Wales Transport Co.*, [1948] 2 All E.R. 460 (per Lord Asquith); and *Bartlett v. Children's Hospital Corp.* (1983), 40 Nfld. & P.E.I.R. 88 (Nfld. C.A.). The second, more conservative approach held that while successful invocation of the maxim did not reverse the legal burden of proof, it did require the defendant to adduce evidence that was sufficient to raise an inference of proper care that was at least as strong as the inference of negligence that had been raised by the plaintiff. See *Erison v. Higgins* (1974), 4 O.R. (2d) 631 (C.A.); and *Ng Chun Pui v. Lee Chuen Tat*, [1988] R.T.R. 298 (P.C.). The third and most conservative approach held that successful invocation of the maxim merely provided a basis upon which *some* inference of negligence *might* be drawn. On that view, the trier of fact was entitled, but not required, to draw an inference. Moreover, if an inference was drawn, it might or might not be sufficient to tip the balance of probabilities in the plaintiff's favour. For that reason, even if the maxim was applied, the defendant might avoid liability without even attempting to rebut the plaintiff's inference. See *Easson v. L.N.E. Rwy. Co.*, [1944] K.B. 421 (per Du Parq L.J.); and *Widdowson v. Newgate Meat Corp.* (1997), [1998] P.I.Q.R. P138 (C.A.).

In England, the result of *res ipsa loquitur* remains somewhat unsettled. In Canada, however, the existence and effect of the maxim was clarified in the following case.

FONTAINE v. BRITISH COLUMBIA (OFFICIAL ADMINISTRATOR)

(1997), 156 D.L.R. (4th) 577 (S.C.C.)

[Edwin Fontaine and Larry Loewen went missing during a weekend hunting trip. Three months later their truck was discovered in a river bed at the bottom of a steep embankment. Loewen's body was buckled behind the steering wheel and Fontaine's body was in the passenger seat. There was no direct evidence regarding the events that resulted in their deaths. The circumstantial evidence indicated that that area had been subject to torrential rain on the weekend when they were presumed to have died. A police officer's report also indicated that there was a swale, or dip, in the road where their truck was believed to have left the road. Finally, the physical evidence revealed that the truck left the road with sufficient speed to cut a path through a patch of small trees.

Fontaine's widow brought an action under the *Family Compensation Act* with respect to her husband's death and sought to prove her claim on the basis of the doctrine of *res ipsa loquitur*. She argued that the mere occurrence of the accident sufficiently established that her husband's death was attributable to Loewen's carelessness. The trial judge disagreed on the basis that the widow had not shown that, in the ordinary course of events, the accident would not have occurred without negligence by the driver. The British Columbia Court of Appeal agreed and the widow brought a further appeal to the Supreme Court of Canada.]

MAJOR J. — This appeal provides another opportunity to consider the so-called maxim of *res ipsa loquitur*. What is it? When does it arise? And what effect does its application have?

. . .

Analysis

A. *When does res ipsa loquitur apply?*

[Major J. set out the traditional rules governing the applicability of the maxim.]

. . .

For *res ipsa loquitur* to arise, the circumstances of the occurrence must permit an inference of negligence attributable to the defendant. The strength or weakness of that inference will depend on the factual circumstances of the case. As described in *Canadian Tort Law* (5th ed. 1993), by Allen M. Linden, at p. 233, "[t]here are situations where the facts merely whisper negligence, but there are other circumstances where they shout it aloud."

As the application of *res ipsa loquitur* is highly dependent upon the circumstances proved in evidence, it is not possible to identify in advance the types of situations in which *res ipsa loquitur* will arise. The application of *res ipsa loquitur* in previous decisions may provide some guidance as to when an inference of negligence may be drawn, but it does not serve to establish definitive categories of when *res ipsa loquitur* will apply. It has been held on numerous occasions that evidence of a vehicle leaving the roadway gives rise to an inference of negligence. Whether that will be so in any given case, however, can only be determined after considering the relevant circumstances of the particular case.

B. Effect of the application of res ipsa loquitur

As in any negligence case, the plaintiff bears the burden of proving on a balance of probabilities that negligence on the part of the defendant caused the plaintiff's injuries. The invocation of *res ipsa loquitur* does not shift the burden of proof to the defendant. Rather, the effect of the application of *res ipsa loquitur* is as described in *The Law of Evidence in Canada* (1992), by John Sopinka, Sidney N. Lederman and Alan W. Bryant, at p. 81:

> Res ipsa loquitur, correctly understood, means that circumstantial evidence constitutes reasonable evidence of negligence. Accordingly, the plaintiff is able to overcome a motion for a non-suit and the trial judge is required to instruct the jury on the issue of negligence. The jury may, but need not, find negligence: a permissible fact inference. If, at the conclusion of the case, it would be equally reasonable to infer negligence or no negligence, the plaintiff will lose since he or she bears the legal burden on this issue. Under this construction, the maxim is superfluous. It can be treated simply as a case of circumstantial evidence.

Should the trier of fact choose to draw an inference of negligence from the circumstances, that will be a factor in the plaintiff's favour. Whether that will be sufficient for the plaintiff to succeed will depend on the strength of the inference drawn and any explanation offered by the defendant to negate that inference. If the defendant produces a reasonable explanation that is as consistent with no negligence as the *res ipsa loquitur* inference is with negligence, this will effectively neutralize the inference of negligence and the plaintiff's case must fail. Thus, the strength of the explanation that the defendant must provide will vary in accordance with the strength of the inference sought to be drawn by the plaintiff.

The procedural effect of *res ipsa loquitur* was lucidly described by Cecil A. Wright in "Res Ipsa Loquitur" (*Special Lectures of the Law Society of Upper Canada (1955), Evidence*, pp. 103-36), and more recently summarized by Klar in *Tort Law*, [2d ed. (1996)] at pp. 423-24:

> If the plaintiff has no direct or positive evidence which can explain the occurrence and prove that the defendant was negligent, appropriate circumstantial evidence, as defined by the maxim *res ipsa loquitur*, may be introduced. Should the defendant, at this stage of the proceeding, move for a nonsuit, on the basis that the plaintiff's evidence has not even made out a *prima facie* case for it to answer, the practical effect of the maxim will come into play. The court will be required to judge whether a reasonable trier of fact could, from the evidence introduced, find an inference of the defendant's negligence. That is, could a reasonable jury find that on these facts the maxim *res ipsa loquitur* applies? If it could so find, the motion for a nonsuit must be dismissed. If such an inference could not reasonably be made, the motion must be granted. In other words, the maxim, at the least, will get the plaintiff past a nonsuit.
>
> This, however, does not end the matter. What, if anything, must the defendant do at this point? In theory, where the case is being tried by a judge and jury, the defendant still need not do anything. Although the judge has decided that as a matter of law it would not be an error for the trier of fact to find for the plaintiff on the basis of the circumstantial evidence which has been introduced, it is still up to the jury to decide whether it has been sufficiently persuaded by such evidence. In other words, the judge has decided that as a matter of law, the maxim can apply. Whether as a question of fact it does, is up to the jury. The jury may decide, therefore, that even despite the defendant's failure to call evidence, the circumstantial evidence ought not to be given sufficient weight to discharge the plaintiff's onus. Thus, even if a defendant has decided not to introduce evidence, a trial judge should not, in an action tried by judge and jury, either take the case from the jury and enter judgment for the plaintiff, or direct the jury to return a verdict in favour of the plaintiff. It is up to the trial judge to determine whether the maxim can apply, but up to the jury to decide whether it does apply.

Whatever value *res ipsa loquitur* may have once provided is gone. Various attempts to apply the so-called doctrine have been more confusing than helpful. Its use has been restricted to cases where the facts permitted an inference of negligence and there was no other reasonable explanation for the accident. Given its limited use it is somewhat meaningless to refer to that use as a doctrine of law.

It would appear that the law would be better served if the maxim was treated as expired and no longer used as a separate component in negligence actions. After all, it was nothing more than an attempt to deal with circumstantial evidence. That evidence is more sensibly dealt with by the trier of fact, who should weigh the circumstantial evidence with the direct evidence, if any, to determine whether the plaintiff has established on a balance of probabilities a *prima facie* case of negligence against the defendant. Once the plaintiff has done so, the defendant must present evidence negating that of the plaintiff or necessarily the plaintiff will succeed.

C. Application to this case

In this appeal, the trial judge had to consider whether there was direct evidence from which the cause of the accident could be determined, or, failing that, whether there was circumstantial evidence from which it could be inferred that the accident was caused by negligence attributable to Loewen.

The trial judge found that the only potential evidence of negligence on Loewen's part concerned the fact that the vehicle left the roadway and was travelling with sufficient momentum to break a path through some small trees. She concluded that, when taken together with other evidence concerning the road and weather conditions, this was no more than neutral evidence and did not point to any negligence on Loewen's part. That conclusion was not unreasonable in light of the evidence, which at most established that the vehicle was moving in a forward direction at the time of the accident, with no indication that it was travelling at an excessive rate of speed.

. . .

There are a number of reasons why the circumstantial evidence in this case does not discharge the plaintiff's onus. Many of the circumstances of the accident, including the date, time and precise location, are not known. Although this case has proceeded on the basis that the accident likely occurred during the weekend of November 9, 1990, that is only an assumption. There are minimal if any evidentiary foundations from which any inference of negligence could be drawn.

As well, there was evidence before the trial judge that a severe wind and rainstorm was raging at the presumed time of the accident. While it is true that such weather conditions impose a higher standard of care on drivers to take increased precautions, human experience confirms that severe weather conditions are more likely to produce situations where accidents occur and vehicles leave the roadway regardless of the degree of care taken. In these circumstances, it should not be concluded that the accident would ordinarily not have occurred in the absence of negligence.

If an inference of negligence might be drawn in these circumstances, it would be modest. The trial judge found that the defence had succeeded in producing alternative explanations of how the accident may have occurred without negligence on Loewen's part. Most of the explanations offered by the defendants were grounded in the evidence and were adequate to neutralize whatever inference the circumstantial evidence could permit to be drawn. The trial judge's finding was not unreasonable and should not be interfered with on appeal.

. . .

The appellant submitted that an inference of negligence should be drawn whenever a vehicle leaves the roadway in a single-vehicle accident. This bald proposition ignores the fact that whether an inference of negligence can be drawn is highly dependent upon the circumstances of each case: see *Gauthier & Co.* [[1945] S.C.R. 143 at 150]. The position advanced by the appellant would virtually subject the defendant to strict liability in cases such as the present one.

[The appeal was dismissed and the widow's claim was denied.]

NOTES AND QUESTIONS

1. Major J. stated the maxim of *res ipsa loquitur* should be treated as "expired." Has the law been changed in any substantive sense? Consider *Robb Estate v. Canadian Red Cross Society* (2001), 9 C.C.L.T. (3d) 131 (Ont. C.A.); and *Newfoundland Light and Power Co. v. Furlong Estate* (2005), 247 Nfld. & P.E.I.R. 65 (N.L.S.C. (C.A.)).

2. If the plaintiff adduces evidence that is sufficient to raise a presumption of negligence against the defendant, what, if anything, must the defendant do to avoid liability? On the traditional approach, if the maxim was invoked, was it ever possible for the defendant to win despite failing to present any evidence at all? Has the answer been changed by *Fontaine*?

3. Regardless of the technical effect of *Fontaine*, will Major J.'s decision lead lower courts to be more or less inclined to draw inferences on the basis of circumstantial evidence? Are there any reasons to lament the expiry of *res ipsa loquitur*?

4. *Res ipsa loquitur* has long been criticized by Canadian commentators and its expiry has been applauded: *M. v. Sinclair* (1980), 15 C.C.L.T. 57 (Ont. H.C.J.); McInnes, "The Death of *Res Ipsa Loquitur* in Canada" (1998) 114 L.Q.R. 547; and Sopinka, Lederman & Bryant, *The Law of Evidence in Canada*, 2d ed. (1999) at 78-79.

5. The High Court of Australia refused to abolish *res ipsa loquitur*: *Schellenberg v. Tunnel Holdings Pty. Ltd.* (2000), 200 C.L.R. 121 (H.C.A.). See McInnes, "Res Ipsa Loquitur in the High Court of Australia: A Missed Opportunity" (2000) 8 Tort L. Rev. 162. See also Witting, "*Res Ipsa Loquitur*: Some Last Words?" (2001) 117 L.Q.R. 392.

6. In *Mustapha v. Culligan of Canada Ltd.* (2005), 32 C.C.L.T. (3d) 123 (Ont. S.C.J.), rev'd on other grounds (2006), 43 C.C.L.T. (3d) 27 (Ont. C.A.), the plaintiff became ill on seeing a dead fly in a sealed bottle of water. The court stated "where an injurious substance is in the product when it left the manufacturer, there is a presumption of negligence on the part of the manufacturer and a burden upon him to disprove negligence to the satisfaction of the jury. Here that presumption would exist, it was not disproved, and, in fact, the manager indicated that it would be possible for a fly to get into one of the bottles." Can you reconcile this reasoning with the abolition of *res ipsa loquitur*?

7. Benny and Bjorn, who are both smokers, stay in a room at the Wanderers' Inn. They have no guests during the evening. During the evening a fire starts in their room, caused by careless smoking, which seriously damages the Inn and kills Benny and Bjorn. The Inn wants to sue their estates for the damage. Could it prove negligence using the principle of *res ipsa loquitur* or otherwise?

8. In *Visanji v. Eaton* (2006), 39 C.C.L.T. (3d) 150 (B.C.S.C.) the plaintiff slipped and fell on a wet bus floor. As noted in Chapter 15, historically common carriers, like the bus company, were held to a high standard of care: *Day v. Toronto Transit Commission*, [1940] S.C.R. 433. This sometimes involved shifting the onus of proof on the standard of care issue to the defendant. In light of the decision in *Fontaine*, the court in *Visanji* stated at 157 that "Whether the burden upon a public carrier in cases of injury or accident sustained by a passenger can be referred to as the shifting of the burden as in *Day*, or a matter of inferences to be drawn from the evidence once the plaintiff has established a *prima facie* case of negligence against the defendant carrier as articulated in *Fontaine*, it is for the defendant to present evidence to answer, or be found negligent." See also *Nice v. Calgary (City)* (2000), 83 Alta. L.R. (3d) 1 (C.A.). In *Visanji* the court held that the defendant had fallen short of presenting sufficient evidence to negate the plaintiff's case.

REVIEW PROBLEMS

Analyze the following facts and discuss the burden of proof. Does the abolition of *res ipsa loquitur* affect your answers?

(a) Ann went to a race track to photograph racing cars. She found a secluded spot near a sharp curve. As she was photographing one car, she was hit from behind by another car that had left the track and travelled 100 metres. She regained consciousness in the hospital and remembered nothing about the accident. She has sought your legal advice about suing the driver of the car.

(b) Bill set out from his farm at 8 a.m. An hour later, Bill's body was found in a ditch beside his overturned jeep. The road was flat and straight and the weather was warm and sunny. There were no skid marks, but there were signs that the car had veered off the highway and onto the gravel shoulder twice, before finally leaving the road and overturning in the ditch. A mechanical check of the jeep revealed that all four bolts in the steering mechanism were sheared off. A month earlier, a mechanic had replaced the bolts. Bill's wife has contacted you about suing the mechanic. You have found an expert witness who is willing to testify that the bolts could be sheared off in such a manner if they had been tightened improperly.

(c) Mr. James underwent surgery performed by Dr. Reed and Dr. Lang. Dr. Reed, who performed the first part of the operation, took longer than anticipated. In order to make up this lost time, the second surgeon, Dr. Lang, took several shortcuts. Both doctors left the operating room several times to consult with lab technicians and radiologists. During these periods, surgical assistants, operating nurses and medical students explored the incision. When the operation was finished, a nurse indicated that all of the sponges were accounted for. Dr. Lang then closed the incision. Mr. James died two days later because a sponge had been left in his abdomen. What legal recourse does the James family have?

(d) Becky has an oil furnace in the basement of her house. It has been regularly serviced by HeatCo for the past eight years. Becky never services, or even touches, the furnace. One week after a twice-yearly servicing the furnace exploded and Becky's house was severely damaged. If it is impossible to determine why the furnace exploded, can Becky sue HeatCo in negligence?

21

THE TORT LIABILITY OF PUBLIC AUTHORITIES

1. Introduction
2. Special Rules for Public Authorities
3. The Negligence Liability of Public Authorities
4. Misfeasance in a Public Office
5. Other Torts

1. Introduction

In the previous chapter, we completed our basic examination of the cause of action in negligence. Before entirely leaving that tort, however, it is necessary to consider various other situations in which the negligence principle plays a significant role, either directly or indirectly. This and the next two chapters therefore address the tort liability of public authorities (Chapter 21), statutory provisions and tort liability (Chapter 22) and occupiers' liability (Chapter 23).

We begin with the tort liability of public authorities. Although most tort actions involve private actors, claims increasingly are being brought against public officials. That is hardly surprising. Government intervention has reached the point where the typical citizen's day-to-day life is profoundly affected by the decisions and operations of public officials. Of course, in public life, as in private life, accidents are inevitable. And when an accident does occur, the victim may well try to affix responsibility to the government. Indeed, in at least one respect, a public authority presents a very attractive target. In comparison to many types of tortfeasors, a public body is relatively more likely to be solvent and capable of satisfying any judgment issued against it.

The fact that judgment will be satisfied from public funds does, however, create controversy. We sometimes fall into the naive belief that public resources, if not infinite, at least are outside the concern of the average citizen. The truth, of course, is that public authority liability affects us all. Money spent satisfying tort judgments must either be drawn away from other uses (*e.g.* health care and education) or generated through higher taxes. Consequently, there are, broadly speaking, two schools of thought. Some commentators insist that public officials should be subject to the same rules as private actors and that, by extension, the financial burden of misadventure should be borne by society as a whole, rather than by individual victims. Other commentators emphasize the tremendous extent to which modern government, by its very nature, is exposed to potential liability, and therefore insist upon special exemptions. As you read through this chapter, ask yourself how the legal system should resolve that debate. Also ask yourself if and when judges should second-guess decisions made by elected officials and their delegates. Is it legitimate for the courts to perform such a task? And even if so, do the courts have sufficient information upon which to pass judgment on social policies?

This chapter is divided into two sections. The first section outlines a number of special rules that currently exist to protect public authorities from liability. The second section then considers bases upon which public authorities may be held liable in tort. The focus will be on the tort of negligence, but reference will also be made to misfeasance in a public office and other intentional torts.

2. Special Rules for Public Authorities

(a) LEGISLATIVE AND JUDICIAL FUNCTIONS

The term "public authorities" is very broad. It obviously encompasses governments and elected officials. However, it also encompasses bodies to which many of the day-to-day functions of government are legislatively delegated. Examples include marketing, licensing and professional boards, regulatory agencies, investigatory commissions, prison administrations, police agencies, labour arbitrators, and municipal governments.

In Canada, public authorities, including those who exercise delegated authority, perform a broad range of functions. First, public authorities that are empowered to enact rules or regulations may exercise a *legislative* function. That is clearly true of Parliament, but it is also true of, say, a municipal government when passing a by-law. Second, public authorities that are empowered to resolve disputes may exercise a *judicial* or *quasi-judicial* function. The courts provide the most obvious example, but again, many bodies exercising delegated authority also fall under the same rubric. In some situations, those bodies closely adhere to normal judicial practices by, for example, hearing submissions from counsel and receiving evidence under oath. In other situations, they employ far less formal procedures. An example of a quasi-judicial function occurs when a labour arbitrator interprets labour relations legislation governing a union-management dispute. Finally, public authorities that are empowered to perform administrative acts may exercise *administrative* functions. Administrative functions involve the establishment and application of policies that affect the public. For example, a liquor licensing board performs an administrative function when it decides to prohibit the sale of alcoholic beverages at sporting events.

It is important to appreciate that a given body may be capable of exercising more than one type of function. For example, while a liquor licensing board may commonly perform an administrative function (as explained in the last paragraph), it may also perform a quasi-judicial function. It will do so, for example, if it evaluates a complaint against a tavern owner and decides to revoke the tavern owner's licence.

For analytical purposes, it is necessary to classify the nature of the function being performed, rather than the nature of the body performing it. The distinction between different types of functions is significant because the Supreme Court of Canada has held that public authorities generally cannot be held liable in tort for actions taken in the performance of legislative, judicial or quasi-judicial functions: *Welbridge Hldg. Ltd. v. Winnipeg* (1970), 22 D.L.R. (3d) 470 (S.C.C.). Accordingly, the tort liability of public authorities generally arises in the context of administrative actions.

The reasons for those limitations are not difficult to discern. With respect to legislative functions, the courts recognize that, given the theory of separation of powers that lies at the heart of the Canadian constitutional system, it is generally inappropriate for them to pass judgment on decisions reached by elected officials and their delegates. Judges also recognize that, given the limited range of information that is disclosed in the course of adversarial litigation, they are ill-equipped to undertake the sorts of policy analyses that are required in order to properly mediate compromises between competing social interests. Similar reasons underlie the immunity enjoyed by public authorities with respect to the exercise of judicial and quasi-judicial functions.

BRADLEY v. FISHER
80 U.S. 646 (1872)

[The plaintiff was a member of the Bar of the Supreme Court in the District of Columbia, and the defendant was a judge of the Criminal Court in that jurisdiction. As a result of the plaintiff's contemptuous language and conduct, the defendant directed an order striking the plaintiff's name from the roll of attorneys practicing in the Criminal Court. This was subsequently interpreted as also striking the plaintiff from the rolls of the Supreme Court. A judge of the Criminal Court had no jurisdiction to strike an attorney from the rolls of the Supreme Court, and the plaintiff sued to recover the damages he suffered because he was unable to practice in the Supreme Court. The United States Supreme Court held that the defendant was not responsible for that error. The court then went on to consider the defendant's plea of judicial immunity. The judgment of the majority was delivered by Field J.]

. . .

FIELD J.: — For it is a general principle of the highest importance to the proper administration of justice that a judicial officer, in exercising the authority vested in him, shall be free to act upon his own convictions, without apprehension of personal consequence to himself. Liability to answer to everyone who might feel himself aggrieved by the action of the judge, would be inconsistent with the possession of this freedom, and would destroy that independence without which no judiciary can be either respectable or useful. As observed by a distinguished English judge, it would establish the weakness of the judicial authority in a degrading responsibility. *Taaffe v. Downes*, 3 Moore, P.C. 41, n.

The principle, therefore, which exempts judges of courts of superior or general authority from liability in a civil action for acts done by them in the exercise of their judicial functions, obtains in all countries where there is any well-ordered system of jurisprudence. It has been the settled doctrine of the English courts for many centuries, and has never been denied, that we are aware of, in the courts of this country.

It has, as Chancellor Kent observes, "a deep root in the common law." *Yates v. Lansing*, 5 Johns, 291.

Nor can this exemption of the judges from civil liability be affected by the motives with which their judicial acts are performed. The purity of their motives cannot in this way be the subject of judicial inquiry. This was adjudged in the case of *Floyd and Barker*, reported by Coke, in 1608 (12 Coke, 25) where it was laid down that the judges of the realm could not be drawn in question for any supposed corruption impeaching the verity of their records, except before the King himself, and it was observed that if they were required to answer otherwise, it would "tend to the scandal and subversion of all justice, and those who are the most sincere, would not be free from continual calumniations."

The truth of this latter observation is manifest to all persons having much experience with judicial proceedings in the superior courts. Controversies involving not merely great pecuniary interests, but the liberty and character of the parties and, consequently, exciting deepest feelings, are being constantly determined in those courts, in which there is a great conflict in the evidence and great doubt as to the law which should govern their decision. It is this class of cases which imposes upon the judge the severest labor, and often creates in his mind a painful sense of responsibility. Yet it is precisely in this class of cases that the losing party feels most keenly the decision against him, and most readily accepts anything but the soundness of the decision in explanation of the action of the judge. Just in proportion to the strength of his convictions of the correctness of his own view of the case is he apt to complain of the judgment against him, and from complaints of the judgment to pass to the ascription of improper motives to the judge. When the controversy involves questions affecting large amounts of property or relates to a matter of general public concern, or touches the interests of numerous parties, the disappointment occasioned by an adverse decision, often finds vent in imputations of this character, and from the imperfection of human nature this is hardly a subject of wonder. If civil actions could be maintained in such cases against the judge, because the losing party should see fit to allege in his complaint that the acts of the judge were done with partiality, or maliciously or corruptly, the protection essential to judicial independence would be entirely swept away. Few persons sufficiently irritated to institute an action against a judge for his judicial acts would hesitate to ascribe any character to the acts which would be essential to the maintenance of the action.

If upon such allegations a judge could be compelled to answer in a civil action for his judicial acts, not only would his office be degraded and his usefulness destroyed, but he would be subjected for his protection to the necessity of preserving a complete record of all the evidence produced before him in every litigated case, and of the authorities cited and arguments presented, in order that he might be able to show to the judge before whom he might be summoned by the losing party — and that judge perhaps one of an inferior jurisdiction — that he had decided as he did with judicial integrity; and the second judge would be subjected to a similar burden, as he in his turn might also be held amenable by the losing party.

NOTES AND QUESTIONS

1. The privileges of legislators are at least partially governed by statutes in all Canadian jurisdictions. See for example *Parliament of Canada Act*, R.S.C. 1985, c. P-1, s. 4; *Legislative Assembly Act*, R.S.O. 1990, c. L.10, s. 37; and *Legislative Assembly Privilege Act*, R.S.B.C. 1996, c. 259, s. 1. See also *Roman Corp. v. Hudson's Bay Oil & Gas Co.* (1973), 36 D.L.R. (3d) 413 (S.C.C.); McKay, ed., *May's Parliamentary Practice*, 23rd ed. (2004), ch. 5; and Chisholm, "Cautionary tales for actions against Cabinet" *Ont. Lawyers Weekly* (8 November 1985) 1.

2. The immunity enjoyed by members of legislatures extends only to actions that are directly or indirectly related to legislative activities. Other actions may be the subject of tort liability. See *George v. Beaubien* (1998), 166 D.L.R. (4th) 185 (Ont. Gen. Div.); and *Decock v. Alberta* (2000), 186 D.L.R. (4th) 265 (Alta. C.A.).

3. *Welbridge Hldg. v. Winnipeg* was reaffirmed by the Supreme Court of Canada in *Enterprises Sibeca Inc. v. Frelighsburg (Municipality)*, [2004] 3 S.C.R. 304. Deschamps J., for the majority, found that a municipality cannot be held liable in negligence for adopting, amending or repealing a by-law, even if such actions cause foreseeable

economic loss to landowners. The majority reasoned (at 315) that "[a] municipality has a margin of legitimate error" and will not be liable "for the exercise of its regulatory power if it acts in good faith or if the exercise of this power cannot be characterized as irrational." Deschamps J. was careful, however, to distinguish immunity in a civil action from judicial review of a by-law's validity. See also *Birch Builders v. Esquimalt (Township)* (1992), 66 B.C.L.R. (2d) 208 (C.A.); and *Woestenburg v. Kamloops (City)* (2001), 18 M.P.L.R. (3d) 257 (B.C.S.C.).

4. There are relatively few actions brought against judicial officers. The older case law is very complex. See generally Thompson, "Judicial Immunity and the Protection of Justices" (1958) 21 Mod. L. Rev. 517; Rubenstein, "Liability in Tort of Judicial Officers" (1964) 15 U.T.L.J. 317; Brazier, "Judicial Immunity and the Independence of the Judiciary" [1976] Pub. Law 397; Sadler, "Judicial and Quasi-Judicial Immunities: A Remedy Denied" (1982) 13 Melb. U.L. Rev. 508; Rosenberg, "Whatever Happened to Absolute Judicial Immunity?" (1984) 21 Hous. L. Rev. 875; Law, "A Tale of Two Immunities: Judicial and Prosecutorial Immunities in Canada" (1990) 28 Alta. L.R. 468; and Gibson, "Monitoring Arbitrary Government Authority: *Charter* Scrutiny of Legislative, Executive and Judicial Privilege" (1998) 61 Sask. L.Rev. 297.

5. There has been a longstanding debate as to whether judicial immunity should be limited to judges of superior courts, extended to judges of any court of record, or applied to all judges and even justices of the peace. In *Sirros v. Moore*, [1974] 3 All E.R. 776 (C.A.), Lord Denning indicated that the immunity rule ought to cover all judges and justices. However, he failed to consider the *Justices Protection Act*, 1848 (11 & 12 Vict.), c. 44 which specifically governs the liability of justices of the peace. Do you agree with Denning L.J. that the immunity granted to judges should not vary according to the level of court? It would now appear that immunity extends to any court of record. See *McC v. Mullan*, [1984] 3 All E.R. 908 (H.L.).

6. Legislation in Canada's common law jurisdictions typically provides for the immunity of judges at all levels, including masters, justices of the peace, and judges of small claims courts. See for example *Courts of Justice Act*, R.S.O. 1990, c. C-43, s. 82; *Court of Queen's Bench Act*, R.S.A. 2000, c. C-31, s. 14; and *Provincial Court Act*, R.S.B.C. 1996, c. 379, s. 42. See also *Morier v. Rivard*, [1985] 2 S.C.R. 716, where the statutory immunity was extended to commissioners of a provincial commission of inquiry.

7. Legislation regarding judicial immunity typically provides that a judge can only be held liable in tort if the plaintiff can establish that he or she acted maliciously and without reasonable and probable grounds. See for example *Provincial Court Act*, C.C.S.M. c. C275, s. 71. See also *Foran v. Tatangello* (1976), 73 D.L.R. (3d) 126 (Ont. H.C.); *Organ v. Newfoundland and Labrador (Minister of Social Services)*, 2007 CarswellNfld 81 (T.D.) (WLeC); and Feldthusen, "Judicial Immunity: In Search of an Appropriate Limiting Formula" (1980) 29 U.N.B.L.J. 73 at 80. However, the limitation regarding malice or absence of reasonable and probable grounds was excluded from the most recent consolidation of Ontario's judicial immunity legislation, suggesting that judges might enjoy immunity even when acting maliciously. Similarly, in *Prefontaine v. Gosman* (2000), 270 A.R. 97 (Q.B.), aff'd (2002), 317 A.R. 160 (C.A.), Jones J. stated

at para. 39 that "a judge acting in her or his judicial capacity will not be liable civilly for any actions done in such judicial capacity whether the judge was acting within or outside of her or his jurisdiction, and even if the judge was acting out of hatred, envy or malice, if the judge believed that he or she was acting with jurisdiction and in the course of his or her judicial duties." Is such broad immunity more likely to foster or hinder public confidence in the judicial system? Can a judge who is acting out of hatred truly be said to be acting in his or her "judicial capacity?"

8. The *Criminal Code*, R.S.C. 1985, c. C-46, s. 783, permits a reviewing court, upon quashing a conviction, order or other proceeding of a provincial court judge or justice of the peace, to issue an order protecting the original judge from tort liability. The reviewing court can also issue a "protection order," as it is called, for anyone acting in accordance with the order (*e.g.* a peace officer who has complied with a warrant or held someone in custody). Similar legislation exists in the provinces. In *Mayrand v. Cronier* (1981), 63 C.C.C. (2d) 561 (Qc. C.A.), the Quebec Court of Appeal held that, although these orders should not be made automatically, they should generally be made in the absence of malice, misconduct or ulterior motive by the inferior court judge. See also *Re Royal Can. Legion Branch 177* (1964), 48 D.L.R. (2d) 164 (B.C.S.C.); *Re Yoner* (1969), 7 D.L.R. (3d) 185 (B.C.S.C.); and Johnson, "Tort Liability: Search Warrant Quashed: Protection Order Denied: Magistrate Negligent" (1971) 4 Ottawa L. Rev. 627.

9. In *Nelles v. Ont.* (1989), 60 D.L.R. (4th) 609 (S.C.C.), an extract of which appears in Chapter 3, the court held that the Crown was protected by statute from civil claims based on how it discharged its judicial responsibilities. However, it denied immunity to the Attorney General and Crown Attorneys personally. The court reviewed the rationale and authority for judicial as well as prosecutorial immunity. L'Heureux-Dubé J., dissenting in part, objected to personal liability for acts done in the furtherance of public functions. See also *Proulx v. Quebec (Attorney General)* (2001), 206 D.L.R. (4th) 1 (S.C.C.); *MacAlpine v. H.(T.)* (1991), 7 C.C.L.T. (2d) 113 (B.C.C.A.); *Prete v. Ontario* (1993), 16 O.R. (3d) 161 (C.A.); *Milgaard v. Kujawa*, [1994] 1 W.W.R. 338 (Sask. Q.B.), aff'd [1994] 9 W.W.R. 305 (C.A.); and *Hawley v. Bapoo* (2000), 187 D.L.R. (4th) 533 (Ont. Div. Ct.). Prosecutorial immunity was also extended to the municipal prosecutor in *Little v. Ottawa (City)* (2004), 49 M.P.L.R. (3d) 115 (Ont. S.C.J.). See generally Roach, "The Attorney General and the *Charter* Revisited" (2000) 50 U.T.L.J. 1.

10. In *MacKeigan v. Hickman* (1989), 61 D.L.R. (4th) 688 (S.C.C.), the court affirmed judicial immunity from being compelled to testify about the decision-making process or composition of the court in a particular case. This immunity principle is grounded in constitutional theory about the independence of the judiciary from legislative control. The decision summarized much of the relevant background to the Donald Marshall Inquiry in Nova Scotia.

11. The courts have extended judicial immunity to public authorities other than judges who perform quasi-judicial functions. However, no clear position has emerged to determine which boards, tribunals and officials will be granted immunity. See *Everett v. Griffiths*, [1921] 1 A.C. 631 (H.L.); *Calvert v. Law Soc. of Upper Can.* (1981), 121 D.L.R. (3d) 169 (Ont. H.C.); *Howarth v. The Queen* (1984), 29 C.C.L.T. 157 (F.C.T.D.),

aff'd (1985), 13 Admin. L.R. 189 (F.C.A.); *Lonrho plc. v. Tebbit*, [1991] 4 All E.R. 973 (Ch.); *Harrington (Public Trustee of) v. Pappachristos* (1992), 5 Admin. L.R. (2d) 130 (B.C.S.C.), aff'd 75 B.C.L.R. (2d) 121 (S.C.); *Reynen v. Canada* (1993), 70 F.T.R. 158 (T.D.), rev'd (1995), 184 N.R. 350 (Fed. C.A.); and *Al's Steak House & Tavern Inc. v. Deloitte & Touche* (1994), 20 O.R. (3d) 673 (Gen. Div.). See also Rubinstein, "Liability in Tort of Judicial Officers" (1964) 15 U.T.L.J. 317; Brazier, "Judicial Immunity and the Independence of the Judiciary" [1976] Pub. Law 397; and Sadler, "Judicial and Quasi-Judicial Immunities: A Remedy Denied" (1982) 4 Melb. U.L. Rev. 508.

12. Are the arguments for limiting the liability of judicial officers compelling? Which types of judicial decisions should be immune from liability? Answer these same questions in relation to Attorneys General, crown counsel, and quasi-judicial decision makers.

13. Should judicial immunity also apply to mediators? Does it make a difference if the mediators are legal practitioners? Does it make a difference if mediation is compulsory or optional in the jurisdiction? See generally Schulz, "Mediator Liability in Canada: An Examination of Emerging American and Canadian Jurisprudence" (2000-2001) 32 Ottawa L. Rev. 269.

(b) CROWN IMMUNITY

Another type of difficulty may arise if the public authority is a Crown agent. At common law, the courts did not have power to sanction the Crown. The guiding principle was that "the King can do no wrong." The only way for citizens to sue the Crown was by petition of right, which did not apply to most tort actions. Thus, the Crown was effectively immune from tort liability. Various reforms were passed over the 19th and early 20th centuries to address this situation, but it was not until 1947 that the British *Crown Proceedings Act* allowed the Crown to be sued in tort as if it were a person. Canada followed suit with the *Crown Liability Act* in 1952. Now part of the *Crown Liability and Proceedings Act*, R.S.C. 1985, c. C-50, the relevant provisions are as follows:

> 3. The Crown is liable for the damages for which, if it were a person, it would be liable. . .
>
> (b) . . .in respect of
>
> (i) a tort committed by a servant of the Crown, or
>
> (ii) a breach of duty attaching to the ownership, occupation, possession or control of property.

Similar legislation exists in every Canadian jurisdiction, most of it based on a model statute prepared by the Conference of Commissioners on Uniformity of Legislation in Canada in 1950. However, the statutes are complex and, in many respects, a trap for the unwary. Still, it remains true today that the Crown is subject to liability only to the extent that it voluntarily submits itself to judicial authority through such legislation.

Not all public authorities are Crown agents – only those over which the Crown exercises a significant degree of actual or potential control are characterized as such. The Crown includes the executive governments of Canada and the provinces, their ministries, departments, corporations and boards, as well as "servants or agents" thereof. The Crown can be sued directly or, as occurs more frequently, vicariously for torts committed by its servants or agents. It is worthwhile to note here that municipalities are not considered to be part of the Crown, but are covered by other legislative provisions.

* municipalities → not considered to be part of crown.

NOTES AND QUESTIONS

1. For a general discussion of Crown liability, see Hogg & Monahan, *Liability of the Crown*, 3d ed. (2000). Examples of provincial legislation include: *Proceedings Against the Crown Act*, R.S.O. 1990, c. P.27, s. 5; *Proceedings against the Crown Act*, R.S.N.S. 1989, c. 360, s. 5; and *Crown Proceeding Act*, R.S.B.C. 1996, c. 89, s. 2.

2. For an excellent discussion of the Ontario legislation that deals with suing the Crown, see Goldenberg, "Tort Actions Against the Crown in Ontario" in Law Society of Upper Canada, *Special Lectures on New Developments in the Law of Torts* (1973) 341.

3. In some situations, it may be difficult to sue a public authority that does not enjoy the status of either a natural person or a corporation. Marketing boards provide a common example. The enabling legislation may address the issue, but often is silent on the point. No clear guidelines have yet developed and the courts continue to struggle with the issue. See *MacLean v. Liquor Lic. Bd. of Ontario* (1975), 51 D.L.R. (3d) 64 (Ont. H.C.J.), rev'd in part (1975), 61 D.L.R. (3d) 237 (Ont. Div. Ct.). *MacLean* also dealt with the issue of whether the Board was a Crown agent.

4. The issue of Crown immunity arose in *Black v. Chrétien* (2001), 199 D.L.R. (4th) 228 (Ont. C.A.). Conrad Black sued the Prime Minister for negligence, abuse of power, and misfeasance in public office. The Prime Minister brought a motion to have the statement of claim struck out on the basis that it did not disclose a cause of action.

Black, a Canadian, wished to receive a peerage from the Queen and to sit in the House of Lords. The Canadian government initially indicated that it would not object to the honour, as long as Black held dual citizenship and did not use his title in Canada. Subsequently, the Prime Minister had a change of heart and announced his opposition. That decision was ostensibly based on the Nickel Resolution, passed by the Canadian Parliament in 1918, which asked the King "to refrain hereafter from conferring any title or honour or titular distinction upon any of your subjects domiciled or ordinarily resident in Canada." Black alleged, however, that the real reason for the Prime Minister's position was personal animosity.

The Court of Appeal for Ontario upheld LeSage C.J.S.C.'s decision that the matter was non-justiciable and that the statement of claim should be struck out. Laskin J.A. found that the issue of honours and titles fell within the scope of the Prime Minister's Crown prerogative, which he defined as "the residue of discretionary or arbitrary authority, which at any given time is legally left in the hands of the Crown" (quoting Dicey, *Introduction to the Study of the Law of the Constitution*, 10th ed. (1959) at 424). Laskin J.A. agreed that the exercise of the Crown prerogative was amenable to challenge under the *Canadian Charter of Rights and Freedoms*, Part I of the *Constitution Act, 1982*, being Schedule B to the *Canada Act 1982* (U.K.), 1982, c. 11, but noted that Black had not made any such argument. Laskin J.A. also held that Crown prerogative is subject to judicial review if it affects the rights or legitimate expectations of an individual. On the facts, however, Black had neither a right to a peerage, nor a reasonable expectation of receiving one. In the final analysis, then, the dispute was purely political. The Court of Appeal consequently saw no basis for a claim in tort:

> Once Prime Minister Chrétien's exercise of the honours prerogative is found to be beyond review by the courts, how the Prime Minister exercised the prerogative is also beyond review. Even if [the Prime Minister's position] was wrong or careless or negligent, even if his motives were questionable, they cannot be challenged by judicial review.

Despite the setback that he suffered in the courts, Black received his peerage after renouncing his Canadian citizenship. He sits today as Lord Black of Crossharbour. It remains to be seen whether the felony charges laid against him in the United States in 2005 will affect his continued peerage.

5. A different manifestation of Crown prerogative arose in *Aleksic v. Canada (Attorney General)* (2002), 215 D.L.R. (4th) 720 (Ont. Div. Ct.). The plaintiffs sued the Attorney General of Canada in tort and for violations of ss. 7 and 15 of the *Charter*. Their claims arose in connection with Canada's participation in NATO's bombing of Yugoslavia. The plaintiffs alleged that the bombing campaign was illegal and that it had caused injury, death and property damage.

The defendant's motion to strike the statement of claim as disclosing no cause of action was granted. The tort claims were held to be non-justiciable because the decision regarding the bombing campaigns was akin to a declaration of war and hence pertained to a purely political matter. Moreover, even if the government's decision was justiciable, it was a matter of policy, rather than operation, and therefore, according to the decision in *Just v. British Columbia* (1989), 64 D.L.R. (4th) 689 (S.C.C.), an extract of which appears below, it did not give rise to a duty of care.

The court held that the plaintiffs' *Charter* claims were similarly futile. In theory, those claims were justiciable because the court had an obligation to determine whether the exercise of the Crown prerogative had violated an aggrieved individual's rights and freedoms. On the facts, however, those actions were doomed.

(c) LIMITATION PERIODS AND SPECIAL PROCEDURES

A tort action against a public authority may be complicated by the existence of special limitation periods. Invariably, these limitation periods are shorter than normal. They may be found not only in enabling legislation, but also in general legislation governing Crown agencies and public authorities. In addition, there may be other limiting provisions, such as a requirement that the public authority be notified prior to receiving a writ, a prohibition on jury trials in actions involving the Crown, or payment of security for costs.

NOTES AND QUESTIONS

1. For a review of limitation periods and other procedural rules applicable in actions against public authorities, see Mew, *The Law of Limitations*, 2d ed. (2004), ch. 17.

2. For examples of legislation imposing special limitation periods or other special procedural rules, see the *Proceedings Against the Crown Act*, R.S.N.L. 1990, c. P-26; *Public Authorities Protection Act*, R.S.O. 1990, c. P.38; and the *Protection of Persons Acting Under Statute Act*, R.S.N.B. 1973, c. P-20.

3. Ontario previously had a six month limitation period for actions against public authorities. However, it was replaced with the generally applicable "basic" two year limitation period under the *Limitations Act, 2002*, S.O. 2002, c. 24. See Krishna, ed., *The New Ontario Limitations Regime: Exposition and Analysis* (2005).

4. Special limitation periods and other procedural rules applying to claims against public authorities have been challenged under the *Charter* (usually s. 15). The results have varied. See for example *Colangelo v. Mississauga (City)* (1988), 53 D.L.R. (4th) 145 (Ont. C.A.), in which the relevant case law is reviewed; and *Mirhadizadeh v. Ontario* (1989), 69 O.R. (2d) 422 (C.A.). See also *Prete v. Ontario* (1993), 16 O.R. (3d) 161 (C.A.); *Bisoukis v. Brampton (City)* (1999), 46 O.R. (3d) 417 (C.A.); and *B. (K.L.) v. British Columbia* (1999), 46 C.C.L.T. (2d) 237 (B.C.C.A.).

5. Although the limitation periods tend to strongly favour public authorities, it sometimes is possible for the plaintiff to find relief. *Bannon v. Thunder Bay (City)* (2002), 210 D.L.R. (4th) 62 (S.C.C.) is illustrative. The plaintiff was injured after she slipped on an icy sidewalk. She was required, under s. 284(5) of the *Municipal Act*, R.S.O. 1990, c. M.45, to give the municipality notice of her intention to sue within seven days. She failed to do so. She nevertheless was permitted to pursue her action because her delay in giving notice was attributable to the narcotics that she was prescribed following the accident. The court applied s. 47 of the *Limitations Act*, R.S.O. 1990, c. L.15, which states: "Where a person entitled to bring an action . . . is at the time the cause of action accrues a minor, mental defective, mental incompetent or of unsound mind, the period within which the action may be brought shall be reckoned from the date when such person became of full age or of sound mind."

6. The harsh effect of an abbreviated limitation period was also avoided in *Berendsen v. Ontario* (2001), 204 D.L.R. (4th) 318 (S.C.C.). The Supreme Court of Canada found that the six month limitation period then applicable in Ontario under the *Public Authorities Protection Act, supra*, only applied to "public" duties performed by government authorities. However, operational decisions of a predominantly private nature were subject to the then six year general limitation period under the *Limitations Act*, R.S.O. 1990, c. L.15, s. 45(1)(g). The alleged wrong in *Berendsen* was the disposal of waste asphalt on private property, which was found to be "predominantly private" by the court. See also *Berardinelli v. Ontario Housing Corp.* (1978), [1979] 1 S.C.R. 275; *Des Champs v. Conseil des Écoles séparées catholiques de langue française de Prescott-Russell*, [1999] 3 S.C.R. 281; and *Gringmuth v. North Vancouver (District)* (2002), 98 B.C.L.R. (3d) 116 (C.A.).

3. The Negligence Liability of Public Authorities

(a) INTRODUCTION

A person aggrieved by the acts or omissions of a public authority may claim relief under several different types of actions, but by far the most common is the tort of negligence. In discussing a public authority's liability in negligence, it is important to distinguish between two issues. The first involves the doctrine of *vicarious liability*. Depending upon the circumstances, an employer may be vicariously liable for the torts of its employee. That is to say, if an employee commits a tort in the course of employment, responsibility may be imposed on the employee personally and on the employer vicariously. The victim may then recover damages from one, the other, or both. That is true even though the employer did not itself do anything wrong. Its responsibility arises merely by virtue of its relationship to the tortfeasor. The justifications for this rule are examined in Chapter 25. Needless to say, public authorities employ a great many people for whom they may be held vicariously liable.

The current discussion focuses on a different issue. The question is not whether a public authority can be held vicariously liable on the basis of an employee's tort, but rather whether it can be held directly liable for its own negligence.

Within that context, it is important to first determine whether the public authority was exercising a *statutory public duty* or a *statutory discretionary power*. If the enabling legislation required the public authority to pursue a particular course of action, the authority was exercising a statutory duty. In contrast, if the public authority had discretion, it was exercising a statutory power. Although liability in negligence may arise in either event, the governing principles differ.

In the case of a statutory *duty*, a public authority cannot be held liable for simply doing what it was required to do. Significantly, however, the existence of a duty (as opposed to a power) means that the court may be relatively less circumspect about imposing liability. Since the public authority was *required* to act in a particular manner, the judge need not be concerned about usurping the legislature's decision-making role. Consequently, liability may be imposed if the public authority performed its task *carelessly*, or if it *failed* to perform its duty at all.

The situation is more complex in a case involving a statutory *power*, where the public authority had the ability, but not the obligation, to act in a certain way. In that situation, the court must be concerned about substituting its choices for that of the legislature. The law therefore has developed a distinction between policy matters and operational matters. The nature of that distinction is explained in the next case, which was a turning point for public authority liability in Canada.

JUST v. BRITISH COLUMBIA

(1989), 64 D.L.R. (4th) 689 (S.C.C.)

The judgment of Dickson C.J. and Wilson, La Forest, L'Heureux-Dubé, Gonthier and Cory JJ. was delivered by

CORY J.: – This appeal puts in issue the approach that should be taken by courts when considering the liability of government agencies in tort actions.

Factual Background

On the morning of January 16, 1982, the appellant and his daughter set out, undoubtedly with high hopes and great expectations, for a day of skiing at Whistler Mountain. As a result of a heavy snow fall they were forced to stop in the northbound line of traffic on Highway 99. While they were waiting for the traffic to move forward a great boulder weighing more than a ton somehow worked loose from the wooded slopes above the highway and came crashing down upon the appellant's car. The impact killed the appellant's daughter and caused him very serious injuries. He then brought this action against the respondent contending that it had negligently failed to maintain the highway properly.

Highway 99 is a major commuter road between Vancouver and the major ski resorts located at Whistler Mountain. The appellant alleged that there had been earlier rock falls near the scene of the tragedy. As well it was said that the climatic conditions of freezing and thawing, coupled with a heavy build-up of snow in the trees and resulting tree damage created a great risk of rock falls. Trees were said to be a well-known factor in levering rocks loose. It was contended that inadequate attention had been given to all these factors by the respondent and that a reasonable inspection would have demonstrated that the rock constituted a danger to users of the highway.

At the time of the accident the Department of Highways had set up a system for inspection and remedial work upon rock slopes particularly along Highway 99. At the apex of the organization was a Mr. Eastman, the regional geotechnical material engineer. He is a specialist in rock slope maintenance and together with another engineer was responsible for inspecting rock slopes and making recommendations regarding their stability.

. . .

Was the Decision of the Rockwork Section as to the Quantity and Quality of Inspections a "Policy" Decision Exempting the Respondent from Liability?

The respondent placed great reliance on the decision of this Court in *Barratt v. District of North Vancouver*, [1980] 2 S.C.R. 418. In the *Barratt* case injury occurred as a result of a pothole on the road. It was established that the City of North Vancouver had a policy of inspecting its roads for potholes every two weeks. Indeed it had inspected the road where the accident occurred one week earlier and found no pothole. It was found that the inspection policy established by the municipality was a reasonable and proper one. However, Justice Martland in giving the reasons for this Court went on to express an opinion that the municipality could not be held negligent for formulating one inspection policy rather than another. He put it this way at pp. 427-28:

> In essence, he [the trial judge] is finding that the Municipality should have instituted a system of continuous inspection to ensure that no possible damage could occur and holds that, in the absence of such a system, if damage occurs, the Municipality must be held liable.
>
> In my opinion, no such duty existed. The Municipality, a public authority, exercised its power to maintain Marine Drive. It was under no statutory duty to do so. Its method of exercising its power was a matter of policy to be determined by the Municipality itself. If, in the implementation of its policy its servants acted negligently, causing damage, liability could arise, but the Municipality cannot be held to be negligent because it formulated one policy of operation rather than another.

This statement was not necessary to the decision as it had already been determined that the system of inspection established by the municipality was eminently reasonable. Neither was there any serious question raised that there had been any negligence in carrying out the system of inspection. The finding that a reasonable system of inspection had been established and carried out without negligence constituted the basis for the conclusion reached by the Court in that case. With the greatest respect, I am of the view that the portion of the reasons relied on by the respondent went farther than was necessary to the decision or appropriate as a statement of principle. For example, the Court would not have approved as "policy" a system that called for the inspection of the roads in a large urban municipality once every five years. Once a policy to inspect is established then it must be open to a litigant to attack the system as not having been adopted in a *bona fide* exercise of discretion and to demonstrate that in all the circumstances, including budgetary restraints, it is appropriate for a court to make a finding on the issue.

The functions of government and government agencies have multiplied enormously in this century. Often government agencies were and continue to be the best suited entities and indeed the only organizations which could protect the public in the diverse and difficult situations arising in so many fields. They may encompass such matters as the manufacture and distribution of food and drug products, energy production, environmental protection, transportation and tourism, fire prevention and building developments. The increasing complexities of life involve agencies of government in almost every aspect of daily living. Over the passage of time the increased government activities gave rise to incidents that would have led to tortious liability if they had occurred between private citizens. The early governmental immunity from tortious liability became intolerable. This led to the enactment of legislation which in general imposed liability on the Crown for its acts as though it were a person. However, the Crown is not a person and must be free to govern and make true policy decisions without becoming subject to tort liability as a result of those decisions. On the other hand, complete Crown immunity should not be restored by having every government decision designated as one of "policy". Thus the dilemma giving rise to the continuing judicial struggle to differentiate between "policy" and "operation". Particularly difficult decisions will arise in situations where governmental inspections may be expected.

The dividing line between "policy" and "operation" is difficult to fix, yet it is essential that it be done. The need for drawing the line was expressed with great clarity by Becker J. of the United States District Court, in *Blessing v. United States*, 447 F.S. 1160. The case required him to deal with a claim under the *Federal Tort Claims Act*, 28 U.S.C. § 2680 which provides:

> The provisions of this chapter and section 1346(b) of this title shall not apply to –
> (a) Any claim based upon an act or omission of an employee of the Government, exercising due care, in the execution of a statute or regulation, whether or not such statute or regulation be valid, or based upon the exercise or performance or the failure to exercise or perform a discretionary function or duty on the part of a federal agency or an employee of the Government, whether or not the discretion involved be abused.

He wrote at p. 1170:

> Read as a whole and with an eye to discerning a policy behind this provision, it seems to us only to articulate a policy of preventing tort actions from becoming a vehicle for judicial interference with decisionmaking that is properly exercised by other branches of the government and of protecting "the Government from liability that would seriously handicap efficient government operations," *United States v. Muniz*, 374 U.S. 150, 163,

> 83 S.Ct. 1850, 1858, 10 L.Ed.2d 805 (1963). Statutes, regulations, and discretionary functions, the subject matter of § 2680(a), are, as a rule, manifestations of policy judgments made by the political branches. In our tripartite governmental structure, the courts generally have no substantive part to play in such decisions. Rather, the judiciary confines itself – or, under laws such as the FTCA's discretionary function exception, is confined – to adjudication of facts based on discernible objective standards of law. In the context of tort actions, with which we are here concerned, these objective standards are notably lacking when the question is not negligence but social wisdom, not due care but political practicability, not reasonableness but economic expediency. Tort law simply furnishes an inadequate crucible for testing the merits of social, political or economic decisions.

The duty of care should apply to a public authority unless there is a valid basis for its exclusion. A true policy decision undertaken by a government agency constitutes such a valid basis for exclusion. What constitutes a policy decision may vary infinitely and may be made at different levels although usually at a high level.

The decisions in *Anns v. Merton London Borough Council* [[1978] A.C. 728 (H.L.)] and *City of Kamloops v. Nielsen* [[1984] 2 S.C.R. 2] indicate that a government agency in reaching a decision pertaining to inspection must act in a reasonable manner which constitutes a *bona fide* exercise of discretion. To do so they must specifically consider whether to inspect and if so, the system of inspection must be a reasonable one in all the circumstances.

For example, at a high level there may be a policy decision made concerning the inspection of lighthouses. If the policy decision is made that there is such a pressing need to maintain air safety by the construction of additional airport facilities with the result that no funds can be made available for lighthouse inspection, then this would constitute a *bona fide* exercise of discretion that would be unassailable. Should then a lighthouse beacon be extinguished as a result of the lack of inspection and a shipwreck ensue no liability can be placed upon the government agency. The result would be the same if a policy decision were made to increase the funds for job retraining and reduce the funds for lighthouse inspection so that a beacon could only be inspected every second year and as a result the light was extinguished. Once again this would constitute the *bona fide* exercise of discretion. Thus a decision either not to inspect at all or to reduce the number of inspections may be an unassailable policy decision. This is so provided it constitutes a reasonable exercise of *bona fide* discretion based, for example, upon the availability of funds.

On the other hand, if a decision is made to inspect lighthouse facilities the system of inspections must be reasonable and they must be made properly. See *Indian Towing Co.*, 350 U.S. 61 (1955). Thus once the policy decision to inspect has been made, the Court may review the scheme of inspection to ensure it is reasonable and has been reasonably carried out in light of all the circumstances, including the availability of funds, to determine whether the government agency has met the requisite standard of care.

At a lower level, government aircraft inspectors checking on the quality of manufactured aircraft parts at a factory may make a policy decision to make a spot check of manufactured items throughout the day as opposed to checking every item manufactured in the course of one hour of the day. Such a choice as to how the inspection was to be undertaken could well be necessitated by the lack of both trained personnel and funds to provide such inspection personnel. In those circumstances the policy decision that a spot check inspection would be made could not be attacked. . . .

Thus a true policy decision may be made at a lower level provided that the government agency establishes that it was a reasonable decision in light of the surrounding circumstances.

The consideration of the duty of care that may be owed must be kept separate and distinct from the consideration of the standard of care that should be maintained by the government agency involved.

Let us assume a case where a duty of care is clearly owed by a governmental agency to an individual that is not exempted either by a statutory provision or because it was a true policy decision. In those circumstances the duty of care owed by the government agency would be the same as that owed by one person to another. Nevertheless the standard of care imposed upon the Crown may not be the same as that owed by an individual. An individual is expected to maintain his or her sidewalk or driveway reasonably, while a government agency such as the respondent may be responsible for the maintenance of hundreds of miles of highway. The frequency and the nature of inspection required of the individual may well be different from that required of the Crown. In each case the frequency and method must be reasonable in light of all the surrounding circumstances. The governmental agency should be entitled to demonstrate that balanced against the nature and quantity of the risk involved, its system of inspection was reasonable in light of all the circumstances including budgetary limits, the personnel and equipment available to it and that it had met the standard duty of care imposed upon it.

It may be convenient at this stage to summarize what I consider to be the principles applicable and the manner of proceeding in cases of this kind. As a general rule, the traditional tort law duty of care will apply to a government agency in the same way that it will apply to an individual. In determining whether a duty of care exists the first question to be resolved is whether the parties are in a relationship of sufficient proximity to warrant the imposition of such a duty. In the case of a government agency, exemption from this imposition of duty may occur as a result of an explicit statutory exemption. Alternatively, the exemption may arise as a result of the nature of the decision made by the government agency. That is, a government agency will be exempt from the imposition of a duty of care in situations which arise from its pure policy decisions.

In determining what constitutes such a policy decision, it should be borne in mind that such decisions are generally made by persons of a high level of authority in the agency, but may also properly be made by persons of a lower level of authority. The characterization of such a decision rests on the nature of the decision and not on the identity of the actors. As a general rule, decisions concerning budgetary allotments for departments or government agencies will be classified as policy decisions. Further, it must be recalled that a policy decision is open to challenge on the basis that it is not made in the *bona fide* exercise of discretion. If after due consideration it is found that a duty of care is owed by the government agency and no exemption by way of statute or policy decision-making is found to exist, a traditional torts analysis ensues and the issue of standard of care required of the government agency must next be considered.

The manner and quality of an inspection system is clearly part of the operational aspect of a governmental activity and falls to be assessed in the consideration of the standard of care issue. At this stage, the requisite standard of care to be applied to the particular operation must be assessed in light of all the surrounding circumstances including, for example, budgetary restraints and the availability of qualified personnel and equipment.

Turning to the case at bar it is now appropriate to . . . determine whether the decision or decisions of the government agency were policy decisions exempting the province from liability. Here what was challenged was the manner in which the inspections were carried out, their frequency or infrequency and how and when trees above the rock cut should have been inspected, and the manner in which the cutting and scaling operations should have been carried out. In short, the public authority had settled on a plan which called upon it to inspect all slopes visually and then conduct further inspections of those slopes where the taking of additional safety measures was warranted. Those matters are all part and parcel of what [may be] described as "the product of administrative direction, expert or professional opinion, technical standards or general standards of care". They were not decisions that could be designated as policy decisions. Rather they were manifestations of the implementation of the policy decision to inspect and were operational in nature. As such, they were subject to review by the Court to determine whether the respondent had been negligent or had satisfied the appropriate standard of care.

At trial the conclusion was reached that the number and frequency of inspections, of scaling and other remedial measures were matters of policy; as a result no findings of fact were made on the issues bearing on the standard of care. Since the matter was one of operation the respondent was not immune from suit and the negligence issue had to be canvassed in its entirety. The appellant was therefore entitled to a finding of fact on these questions and a new trial should be directed to accomplish this.

. . .

SOPINKA J. (dissenting) – My colleague's reasons are based essentially on an attack on the policy of the respondent with respect to the extent and manner of the inspection program. In my opinion, absent evidence that a policy was adopted for some ulterior motive and not for a municipal purpose, it is *not* open to a litigant to attack it, nor is it appropriate for a court to pass upon it. As stated by Lord du Parcq in *Kent v. East Suffolk Rivers Catchment Board*, [1940] 1 K.B. 319, at p. 338:

> . . . it must be remembered that when Parliament has left it to a public authority to decide which of its powers it shall exercise, and when and to what extent it shall exercise them, there would be some inconvenience in submitting to the subsequent decision of a jury, or judge of fact, the question whether the authority had acted reasonably, a question involving the consideration of matters of policy and sometimes the striking of a just balance between the rival claims of efficiency and thrift.

This statement was approved by Lord Wilberforce in *Anns v. Merton London Borough Council*, [1978] A.C. 728, at p. 754.

If a court assumes the power to review a policy decision which is made in accordance with the statute, this amounts to a usurpation by the court of a power committed by statute to the designated body. As pointed out by Wilson J. in *City of Kamloops v. Nielsen*, *supra*, at pp. 9-10:

> It is for the local authority to decide what resources it should make available to carry out its role in supervising and controlling the activities of builders. For example, budgetary considerations may dictate how many inspectors should be hired for this purpose, what their qualifications should be, and how often inspections should be made. He approved the statement of du Parcq L.J. in *Kent v. East Suffolk Rivers Catchment Board* . . . that public authorities have to strike a balance between the claims of efficiency and thrift and whether they get the right balance can only be decided through the ballot box and not in the courts.

In *Anns v. Merton London Borough Council*, *supra*, Lord Wilberforce was of the opinion that although the exercise by a public authority of discretionary power was not entirely immune from attack, it was open to challenge only if no consideration was given to whether to exercise the power which, there as here, was whether to inspect and the manner of the inspection, *supra*, at p. 755. He did not elaborate as to whether such a challenge could be by way of a claim for damages by a person injured by the failure to inspect. Lord Salmon, however, was of the view that an improper exercise of discretion could only be corrected by *certiorari* or mandamus, and did not give rise to an action for damages, *supra*, at p. 762.

In the following passage, at p. 755, Lord Wilberforce makes it clear that a decision to inspect, and the time, manner and techniques of inspection, may all be within the discretionary power:

> There may be a discretionary element in its exercise – discretionary as to the time and manner of inspection, and the techniques to be used. A plaintiff complaining of negligence must prove, the burden being on him, that action taken was not within the limits of a discretion bona fide exercised, before he can begin to rely upon a common law duty of care. But if he can do this, he should, in principle, be able to sue.

If, as here, the statute creates no duty to inspect at all, but simply confers a power to do so, it follows logically that a decision to inspect and the extent and manner thereof are all discretionary powers of the authority.

It is not suggested here that the respondent failed to consider whether to inspect or the manner of inspections. The trial judge and the Court of Appeal found that a policy decision was made that inspections would be carried out by a crew of men called the Rockwork Section. In view of the fact that the crew had responsibility for the inspection of the slopes of all highways, the extent and manner of the inspection was delegated to the Rockwork Section. While it might be suggested that guidelines for inspection should have been laid down for the guidance of the crew, this would be second guessing the policy decision and not a matter for the Court. The appellant's attack on the conduct of the respondent and its employees is an attack on the manner in which they carried out the inspection and scaling of the mountain. The Rockwork Section had decided it could not closely monitor all slopes at all times. Some slopes would only be visually inspected from the highway. The appellant contended that the slopes above manmade cuts should have been closely inspected and that the trees should have been removed within ten feet of a cut slope. The trial judge made the following important findings concerning the decision of the respondent as to the extent and manner of the inspection program:

> The question in the case at bar is thus whether the failure of the Crown to take the steps which the plaintiff says it should have taken to prevent the rock fall was a matter of policy or operational. In order to answer it, it is necessary to consider the nature of the decisions here in question. The Crown had never established as a matter of policy that all slopes above highways must be inspected for potential rock fall. Nor had it laid out specific guidelines for dealing with problems if danger was perceived. What it had done was to establish a small crew of men (the rock scaling crew) to deal with problems arising on cliff faces throughout the Province. This crew responded to specific requests from various highway districts for inspection and scaling. For the most part, however, it developed and followed its own program. Given that it was responsible for inspection of slopes and appropriate remedial measures for all the highways in the Province, it could not closely monitor all slopes at all times. The slope here in question was visually inspected from the highway on a number of occasions. However, there had never been

scaling or close inspection of the area above the cut because the rock scaling crew did not deem that work to be a priority.

In stating that the authority "must specifically consider whether to inspect and if so the system must be a reasonable one in all the circumstances", my colleague is extending liability beyond what was decided in *Anns v. Merton London Borough Council, Barratt v. District of North Vancouver*, and *City of Kamloops v. Nielsen, supra*. The system would include the time, manner and technique of inspection. On this analysis it is difficult to determine what aspect of a policy decision would be immune from review. All that is left is the decision to inspect. It can hardly be suggested that all the learning that has been expended on the difference between policy and operational was expended to immunize the decision of a public body that something will be done but not the content of what will be done. It seems to me that a decision to inspect rather than not inspect hardly needs protection from review. The concern that has resulted in extending immunity from review in respect of policy decisions is that those entrusted with the exercise of the statutory powers make the decision to expend public resources. It is not engaged by a decision simply to do something. It is the decision as to what is to be done that will entail the taxation of the public purse. Lord Wilberforce underscores this concern when he states, at p. 754:

> Let us examine the Public Health Act 1936 in the light of this. Undoubtedly it lays out a wide area of policy. It is for the local authority, a public and elected body, to decide upon the scale of resources which it can make available in order to carry out its functions under Part II of the Act – how many inspectors, with what expert qualifications, it should recruit, how often inspections are to be made, what tests are to be carried out, must be for its decision. It is no accident that the Act is drafted in terms of functions and powers rather than in terms of positive duty. As was well said, public authorities have to strike a balance between the claims of efficiency and thrift (du Parcq L.J. in *Kent v. East Suffolk Rivers Catchment Board* [1940] 1 K.B. 319, 338): whether they get the balance right can only be decided through the ballot box, not in the courts.

In this case, the extent of the inspection program was delegated to the Rockwork Section. The respondent acted within its statutory discretion in making that decision. It was a decision that inspections should be done and the manner in which they should be done. In order for a private duty to arise, it would have to be shown that the Rockwork Section acted outside its delegated discretion to determine whether to inspect and the manner in which the inspection is to be made.

NOTES AND QUESTIONS

1. What is the purpose of immunizing policy decisions? Do you agree? Why is this purpose not relevant in the operational sphere? Which definition of the operational sphere in *Just* makes better sense if one accepts the purpose of policy immunity?

2. What special consideration does Cory J. extend to public authorities on the question of the standard of care? Why is the standard not the same as for private defendants? At this point, are the courts not usurping the public authorities' decision on how to allocate their budgets? Are courts institutionally competent to make such determinations?

3. A useful illustration of the policy/operational distinction can be found in *Ingles v. Tutkaluk Construction Ltd.*, [2000] 1 S.C.R. 298, which involved a claim of negligent building inspection. The municipality was not obligated to institute a building inspection system, and the decision whether to do so was a matter of policy that was not reviewable by the courts unless made in bad faith. However, once the city had decided to institute an inspection system, the implementation of that system was an operational function that was subject to the standard of reasonable care, *i.e.*, the inspection had to be carried out reasonably.

4. The first articulation of the policy/operational distinction in the Commonwealth came in *Anns v. Merton London Borough Council*, [1978] A.C. 728 (H.L.) which built upon the decision in *Dorset Yacht Co. v. Home Office*, [1970] A.C. 1004 (H.L.). There are many similarities between *Anns* and the decision in *Welbridge Holdings Ltd. v. Greater Winnipeg* (1970), 22 D.L.R. (3d) 470 (S.C.C.), where the court immunized legislative functions of municipal governments from negligence liability. See also *Comeau's Sea Foods Ltd. v. Canada (Minister of Fisheries & Oceans)* (1997), 142 D.L.R. (4th) 193 (S.C.C.).

5. Prior to *Just*, the leading Canadian authority on the negligence liability of public authorities was *Kamloops v. Nielsen* (1984), 10 D.L.R. (4th) 641 (S.C.C.). As in *Just*, the majority and minority disagreed on the boundary between the policy and operational spheres. See Irvine, "Case Comment: *Kamloops v. Nielsen*" (1985) 29 C.C.L.T. 185; Gibson, "Tort Law" (1985) 7 S.C.L.R. 387 at 400-18; and Feldthusen, "*City of Kamloops v. Nielsen*: A Comment on the Supreme Court's Modest Clarification of Colonial Tort Law" (1985) 30 McGill L.J. 539.

6. For a variety of applications of *Just* and *Kamloops*, see *Lewis v. Prince Edward Island* (1998), 160 Nfld. & P.E.I.R. 183 (P.E.I.C.A.); *Atlantic Leasing Ltd. v. Newfoundland* (1998), 164 Nfld. & P.E.I.R. 119 (Nfld. C.A.); *Tottrup v. Lund* (2000), 255 A.R. 204 (C.A.); *Gobin (Guardian ad litem of) v. British Columbia* (2002), 214 D.L.R. (4th) 328 (B.C.C.A.); *Neuman v. Parkland County* (2004), 355 A.R. 169 (Prov. Ct.); *Bowes v. Edmonton (City)* (2005) 49 Alta. L.R. (4th) 50 (Q.B.); and *Wynberg v. Ontario* (2006), 213 O.A.C. 48 (C.A.).

7. The distinction between policy and operational functions is notoriously difficult to make. Compare *Just* with *Swinamer v. Nova Scotia (Attorney General)*, [1994] 1 S.C.R. 445. The plaintiff in *Swinamer* was injured when a diseased tree growing along the highway fell onto his truck. The province had instituted a program to identify and remove dangerous trees, and the plaintiff alleged that this program was subject to review by the courts. The trial judge, relying on *Just*, found that the implementation of the program was an operational function, and found the defendant negligent. However, the Supreme Court of Canada concluded that the tree removal program was a matter of policy that could not be reviewed. See also *Brown v. British Columbia (Minister of Transportation and Highways)*, [1994] 1 S.C.R. 420.

8. The following activities have been found to be operational: the failure to erect higher median barriers on a highway in a timely manner (*Malat v. Bjornson (No. 2)* (1978), 6 C.C.L.T. 142 (B.C.S.C.), aff'd (1980), 14 C.C.L.T. 206 (B.C.C.A.)); a munic-

ipality's decision to issue a building permit and its failure to identify construction defects (*Mortimer v. Cameron* (1994), 111 D.L.R. (4th) 428 (Ont. C.A.), excerpted in Chapter 19); the Crown's failure to inspect and maintain a highway (*Lewis (Guardian ad litem of) v. British Columbia*, [1997] 3 S.C.R. 1145); the denial of a crabbing licence by the Ministry of Fisheries and Oceans on account of an Officer's negligent measurement of the plaintiff's boat (*Keeping v. Canada (Minister of Fisheries and Oceans)* (2003), 224 Nfld. & P.E.I.R. 234 (N.L.C.A.)); and the failure to anticipate "freeze-up" and apply salt to highways in a timely manner (*Benoit v. Farrell Estate* (2004), 27 B.C.L.R. (4th) 226 (C.A.)).

9. The following activities have been found to involve policy decisions: the maintenance of municipal manhole covers (*Wegren v. Prince Albert (City)* (2004), 251 Sask. R. 313 (Prov. Ct.)); the adoption of a particular system for clearing snow and ice from municipal sidewalks (*Knodell v. New Westminster (City)* (2005), 14 M.P.L.R. (4th) 258 (B.C.S.C.)); a municipality's decision not to reduce the speed limit in a school area (*Potts v. Heutink*, 2006 CarswellBC 2702 (S.C.) (WLeC)); and the refusal to enter into an agreement with parents to provide for the needs of a special needs child (*A.L. v. Ontario (Minister of Community and Social Services)* (2006), 83 O.R. (3d) 512 (C.A.). Can any of these be meaningfully distinguished from the operational functions listed in note 8?

10. J.A. Smillie has argued that public authorities should be under a duty of care whenever the same conduct would attract a duty if the defendant were a private citizen. See "Liability of Public Authorities For Negligence" (1985) 23 U.W.O.L. Rev. 213. Can a meaningful analogy be drawn to private conduct leading to the duty of care in *Just*? In contrast, D. Cohen and J.C. Smith emphasize the unique public authority aspects of cases such as *Just*, where the plaintiff's claim rests on the failure to obtain a public benefit. See "Entitlement and the Body Politic: Rethinking Negligence in Public Law" (1986) 64 Can. Bar Rev. 1. B. Feldthusen has argued that there should be total immunity from liability in negligence with respect to the exercise of public discretion. See "Failure to Confer Discretionary Public Benefits: The Case for Complete Negligence Immunity" (1997) 5 Tort L. Rev. 17.

11. The policy/operational distinction has been endorsed throughout the Commonwealth, but there is considerable divergence in how it is interpreted within and among the different jurisdictions, and it has been undermined to varying extents. See for example *Sutherland Shire Council v. Heyman* (1985), 60 A.L.R. 1 (H.C.A.); *X (Minors) v. Bedfordshire Country Council*, [1995] 2 A.C. 633 (H.L.); and *Stovin v. Wise*, [1996] A.C. 923 (H.L.). See also Bailey & Bowman, "The Policy/operational Dichotomy – a Cuckoo in the Nest" [1986] C.L.J. 430; and Deegan, "The Public/Private Dichotomy and Its Relationship With The Policy/Operational Factors In Negligence Law" (2001) 1 Queensland U. Tech. L. & Just. J. 241.

12. The scholarly literature on the negligence liability of public authorities is voluminous. See for example Klar, "The Supreme Court of Canada: Extending the Tort Liability of Public Authorities" (1990) 28 Alta. L. Rev. 648; Woodall, "Private Law Liability of Public Authorities for Negligent Inspection and Regulation" (1991-1992) 37 McGill L.J. 83; Cohen, "Government Liability for Economic Losses: The Case of Regulatory Failure" (1992) 20 C.B.L.J. 215; Cohen & Finkle, "Crown Liability in Canada:

Developing Compensation Policies for Regulatory Failure" (1994) 37 Can. Pub. Admin. 79; Perell, "Negligence Claims Against Public Authorities" (1994) 16 Adv. Q. 48; Sopinka, "The Liability of Public Authorities: Drawing the Line" (1994) 1 Tort L. Rev. 123; Hilson & Rogers, "*X v Bedfordshire County Council*: Tort Law and Statutory Functions – Probably not the End of the Story" (1995) 3 Torts L.J. 221; Davies, "Common Law Liability of Statutory Authorities" (1997) U.W.A.L. Rev. 21; Brodie, "Public Authorities – Negligence Actions – Control Devices" (1998) 18 L.S. 1; Kneebone, *Tort Liability of Public Authorities* (1998); Doyle & Redwood, "The Common Law Liability of Public Authorities: The Interface Between Public and Private Law" (1999) 7 Tort L. Rev. 30; Feldthusen, *Economic Negligence*, 4th ed. (2000), ch. 6; and Bailey & Bowman, "Public Authority Negligence Revisited" [2000] C.L.J. 85.

13. As discussed in Chapter 14, tort law often struggles when the plaintiff's injury takes the form of pure economic loss. However, in the context of claims against public authorities, the Supreme Court of Canada draws no distinction between cases involving physical damage and those involving pure economic loss. Accordingly, once a court recognizes a duty of care and formulates the standard of care applicable to a public authority, the defendant is liable for either type of loss. See *Ingles v. Tutkaluk Construction Ltd.*, *supra*; and Brown, "Still Crazy After All These Years: *Anns*, *Cooper v. Hobart* and Pure Economic Loss" (2003) 36 U.B.C.L. Rev. 159.

(b) THE EFFECT OF *COOPER v. HOBART*

As discussed in Chapter 10, the Supreme Court of Canada reformulated its analysis of the duty of care in *Cooper v. Hobart*, [2001] 3 S.C.R. 537. The decision in *Cooper* has affected negligence analysis relating to public authorities in four main ways.

First, it has become necessary to situate the policy/operational distinction within the framework provided in *Cooper*. Recall that the first stage of the *Cooper* test involves an analysis of (i) whether the harm was foreseeable and (ii) whether there was a proximate relationship between the parties. The second stage involves a consideration of "residual" policy considerations that might serve to negative or limit the scope of the duty of care. The policy/operational dichotomy falls within this second stage of the *Cooper* analysis. That is, even if harm was foreseeable and the parties were in a relationship of proximity, a court could still decline to find a duty of care because the public authority was exercising its policy or planning functions, rather than its operational functions.

Second, the decision in *Cooper* placed greater emphasis on the element of proximity than had previous decisions in Canada. This means that many cases that would previously have been decided on the issue of policy and operational functions may now be decided based on the question of proximity. However, this does not necessarily make the determination any easier: proximity is notoriously difficult to define, and the considerations are similar to those involved in a policy/operational analysis. For instance, if the relevant conduct involved planning, budgetary considerations and a balancing of competing interests at a ministerial level, a court could conclude either that the decision was one of policy or that the plaintiff was not in a sufficiently proximate relationship with the relevant government authority.

Third, since *Cooper*, the interaction of statutory duties and the common law duty of care has become more complex. Recall that in *Cooper* the Supreme Court of Canada examined the *Mortgage Brokers Act*, R.S.B.C. 1996, c. 313, to determine whether the

Registrar of Mortgage Brokers owed a common law duty of care to the plaintiffs. The court described the statute as "the only source of [the defendant's] duties, private or public." This approach essentially conflates statutory and common law duties. This is contrary to historical jurisprudence, which suggests that the common law duty of care must be determined independently from statute, and may arise in addition to any statutory duties. The approach in *Cooper* is also, arguably, contrary to the Supreme Court of Canada's decision in *R. v. Saskatchewan Wheat Pool*, [1983] 1 S.C.R. 205, which is excerpted in the next chapter. That case decided that breach of statutory duty is not a nominate tort in Canada: a plaintiff cannot succeed unless there existed a common law duty of care. While the statute may be relevant to the issue of common law duty, it is not determinative. Unfortunately, as thoroughly discussed by L. Klar in "Breach of Statute and Tort Law" in Neyers, Chamberlain & Pitel, eds., *Emerging Issues in Tort Law* (2007), the approach in *Cooper* has been copied and expanded in subsequent cases, such that breach of statutory duty is sometimes equated with breach of a common law duty of care. In any event, the effect of *Cooper* has been to increase the importance of the statutory framework when deciding whether a public authority owed a duty of care in the circumstances of the case. See Klar, "The Tort Liability of the Crown: Back to Canada v. Saskatchewan Wheat Pool" (2007) 32 Adv. Q. 293.

Finally, on a broader level, the decision in *Cooper* seems to reflect a more restrictive attitude toward public authority liability in Canada. While the 1970s and 1980s can be characterized as an era of expansion for public authority liability, the new millennium can be characterized by a more conservative attitude. The Canadian courts now seem somewhat more reluctant to impose a duty of care on public authorities. See for example *Holland v. Saskatchewan (Minister of Agriculture, Food and Rural Revitalization)*, 2007 CarswellSask 120 (C.A.) (WLeC).

NOTES AND QUESTIONS

1. *Williams v. Canada (Attorney-General)* (2005), 76 O.R. (3d) 763 (S.C.J.) involved a class action against the Crown in connection with the SARS outbreak in Toronto in 2003. The plaintiff alleged against the federal Crown, *inter alia*, that it had breached its duty to prevent the spread of diseases in Canada, including surveillance, analysis and testing in relation to the monitoring of new diseases. In particular, the plaintiff alleged that the Attorney General had failed to co-ordinate its response to the SARS crisis with the Ontario Ministry of Health and Long-Term Care, failed to translate a Chinese report regarding a flu outbreak in China, and denied the continuation of the outbreak. Cullity J. struck out the claim against the federal Crown because the element of proximity was not satisfied. In particular, there was no "close and direct causal connection" between the alleged omissions and the harms suffered by members of the class, and the relevant statutory duties were framed in terms of the general public. Could Cullity J. have just as easily struck out the claim as being based on government policy decisions? See also *Eliopoulos (Litigation Trustee of) v. Ontario (Minister of Health and Long-Term Care)* (2006), 82 O.R. (3d) 321 (C.A.) (claim against the government in connection with the West Nile Virus struck out as disclosing no reasonable cause of action); *Lowe v. The Guarantee Company of North America* (2005), 80 O.R. (3d) 222 (C.A.); and *Klein v. American Medical Systems, Inc.* (2006), 44 C.C.L.T. (3d) 47 (Ont. Div. Ct.).

2. In *Holtslag v. Alberta* (2006), 55 Alta. L.R. (4th) 214 (C.A.), the plaintiffs sued the provincial Director of Building Standards for issuing a product listing authorizing

the use of untreated pine shakes on residential homes. The shakes rotted within five years of installation, and the plaintiffs claimed for the costs of replacing their roofs and the decreased value of their homes. The Alberta Court of Appeal rejected the claim on the basis that the plaintiffs lacked proximity with the Director. However, in deciding the issue of proximity, the court made extensive reference to case law on the policy/operational dichotomy. *Holtslag* therefore shows the difficulty separating the two determinations. See also *Bagnell v. Taser International, Inc.* (2006), 44 C.C.L.T. (3d) 293 (B.C.S.C.), where both the proximity and policy/operational tests were resolved in the plaintiff's favour.

3. For commentary on the relative reluctance to impose a duty of care on public authorities since *Cooper*, see Klar, "New horizons emerge in the ever evolving area of tort law" *The Lawyers Weekly* (18 August 2006).

4. Misfeasance in a Public Office

(a) INTRODUCTION

Another uniquely public tort is misfeasance in a public office, sometimes called abuse of office or abuse of power. This is an intentional tort, and historically involved malicious conduct by a public officer that was directly aimed at a particular individual. For instance, one of its seminal cases, *Ashby v. White* (1703), 92 E.R. 126 (K.B.), involved a claim that an electoral officer had wrongfully denied the plaintiff the right to vote in an effort to prejudice the candidate for whom the plaintiff wished to vote. However, as will be discussed below, the misfeasance tort has now expanded to include conduct that is less obviously malicious or abusive.

For many years, the leading Canadian case on misfeasance in a public office was *Roncarelli v. Duplessis* (1959), 16 D.L.R. (2d) 689 (S.C.C.). *Roncarelli* is an example of a clear abuse of power deliberately intended to injure a particular individual.

RONCARELLI v. DUPLESSIS
(1959), 16 D.L.R. (2d) 689 (S.C.C.)

[The plaintiff was the proprietor of a restaurant in Montreal which had held a liquor licence for 34 years. He was also a member of the Witnesses of Jehovah, a religious sect whose printed works had been provoking considerable social unrest in the primarily Roman Catholic province of Quebec. Starting in 1945, the provincial authorities had arrested large numbers of the Witnesses of Jehovah in an effort to end what they considered to be the group's insulting and offensive conduct. The plaintiff had provided bail for approximately 380 Jehovah's Witnesses. Beyond that, the plaintiff had not engaged in behaviour which the provincial government found objectionable.

Mr. Archambault, the Liquor Commissioner, notified Mr. Duplessis, the Attorney General and Premier of Quebec, of the plaintiff's conduct. Duplessis, feeling that his position in the provincial government required him to do so, directed Mr. Archambault to refuse to renew the plaintiff's liquor licence. The plaintiff sued Mr. Duplessis for his loss of profits stemming from the government's refusal to renew the restaurant's liquor licence.

The relevant legislation gave Mr. Archambault the sole authority to grant or cancel liquor licences, and specified that the "Commission may cancel any permit at its discretion."

In a six-three judgment, the defendant was held liable, and the plaintiff was awarded approximately $33,000. Mr. Justice Martland, with whom Kerwin C.J. and Locke J. agreed, wrote one majority judgment. Mr. Justice Rand, with whom Judson J. agreed, wrote another, and Abbott J. wrote a third. Justices Taschereau, Cartwright and Fauteaux wrote separate dissenting judgments. Only a brief excerpt of Rand J.'s judgment is reprinted below.]

RAND J.: . . . The field of licensed occupations and businesses of this nature is steadily becoming of greater concern to citizens generally. It is a matter of vital importance that a public administration that can refuse to allow a person to enter or continue a calling which, in the absence of regulation, would be free and legitimate, should be conducted with complete impartiality and integrity; and that the grounds for refusing or cancelling a permit should unquestionably be such and such only as are incompatible with the purposes envisaged by the statute: the duty of a Commission is to serve those purposes and those only. A decision to deny or cancel such a privilege lies within the "discretion" of the Commission; but that means that decision is to be based upon a weighing of considerations pertinent to the object of the administration.

In public regulation of this sort there is no such thing as absolute and untrammelled "discretion", that is that action can be taken on any ground or for any reason that can be suggested to the mind of the administrator; no legislative Act can, without express language, be taken to contemplate an unlimited arbitrary power, exercisable for any purpose, however capricious or irrelevant, regardless of the nature or purpose of the statute. Fraud and corruption in the Commission may not be mentioned in such statutes but they are always implied as exceptions. "Discretion" necessarily implies good faith in discharging public duty; there is always a perspective within which a statute is intended to operate; and any clear departure from its lines or objects is just as objectionable as fraud or corruption. Could an applicant be refused a permit because he had been born in another Province, or because of the colour of his hair? The ordinary language of the Legislature cannot be so distorted.

To deny or revoke a permit because a citizen exercises an unchallengeable right totally irrelevant to the sale of liquor in a restaurant is equally beyond the scope of the discretion conferred. There was here not only revocation of the existing permit but a declaration of a future, definitive disqualification of the appellant to obtain one: it was to be "forever". This purports to divest his citizenship status of its incident of membership in the class of those of the public to whom such a privilege could be extended. Under the statutory language here, that is not competent to the Commission and *a fortiori* to the Government or the respondent: *McGillivray v. Kimber* (1915), 26 D.L.R. 164, 52 S.C.R. 146. There is here an administrative tribunal which, in certain respects, is to act in a judicial manner; and even on the view of the dissenting Justices in *McGillivray*, there is liability: what could be more malicious than to punish this licensee for having done what he had an absolute right to do in a matter utterly irrelevant to the *Alcoholic Liquor Act*? Malice in the proper sense is simply acting for a reason or purpose knowingly foreign to the administration, to which was added here the element of intentional punishment by what was virtually vocation outlawry.

It may be difficult if not impossible in cases generally to demonstrate a breach of this public duty in the illegal purpose served; there may be no means, even if proceedings against the Commission were permitted by the Attorney-General, as here they were refused, of compelling the Commission to justify a refusal or revocation or to give reasons for its actions; on these questions I make no observation; but in the case before us that difficulty is not present: the reasons are openly avowed.

The act of the respondent through the instrumentality of the Commission brought about a breach of an implied public statutory duty toward the appellant; it was a gross abuse of legal power expressly intended to punish him for an act wholly irrelevant to the statute, a punishment which inflicted on him, as it was intended to do, the destruction of his economic life as a restaurant keeper within the Province. Whatever may be the immunity of the Commission or its member from an action for damages, there is none in the respondent. He was under no duty in relation to the appellant and his act was an intrusion upon the functions of a statutory body. The injury done by him was a fault engaging liability within the principles of the underlying public law of Quebec: *Mostyn v. Fabrigas* (1774), 1 Cowp. 161, 98 E.R. 1021, and under art. 1053 of the *Civil Code*. That, in the presence of expanding administrative regulation of economic activities, such a step and its consequences are to be suffered by the victim without recourse or remedy, that an administration according to law is to be superseded by action dictated by and according to the arbitrary likes, dislikes and irrelevant purposes of public officers acting beyond their duty, would signalize the beginning of disintegration of the rule of law as a fundamental postulate of our constitutional structure. An administration of licences on the highest level of fair and impartial treatment to all may be forced to follow the practice of "first come, first served", which makes the strictest observance of equal responsibility to all of even greater importance; at this stage of developing government it would be a danger of high consequence to tolerate such a departure from good faith in executing the legislative purpose. It should be added, however, that that principle is not, by this language, intended to be extended to ordinary governmental employment: with that we are not here concerned.

It was urged by Mr. Beaulieu that the respondent, as the incumbent of an office of state, so long as he was proceeding in "good faith", was free to act in a matter of this kind virtually as he pleased. The office of Attorney-General traditionally and by statute carries duties that relate to advising the Executive, including here, administrative bodies, enforcing the public law and directing the administration of justice. In any decision of the statutory body in this case, he had no part to play beyond giving advice on legal questions arising. In that role this action should have been limited to advice on the validity of a revocation for such a reason or purpose and what that advice should have been does not seem to me to admit of any doubt. To pass from this limited scope of action to that of bringing about a step by the Commission beyond the bounds prescribed by the Legislature for its exclusive action converted what was done into his personal act.

"Good faith" in this context, applicable both to the respondent and the General Manager, means carrying out the statute according to its intent and for its purpose; it means good faith in acting with a rational appreciation of that intent and purpose and not with an improper intent or for an alien purpose; it does not mean for the purposes of punishing a person for exercising an unchallengeable right; it does not mean arbitrarily and illegally attempting to divest a citizen of an incident of his civil status.

NOTES AND QUESTIONS

1. *Roncarelli* was an action brought under article 1053 of the Quebec Civil Code. How would you have framed this case if it had been brought in a common law jurisdiction? Would the result have been different if the case had been brought in a common

law court? Would any of the common law legislative immunity rules have protected Duplessis?

2. How does Rand J. define malice and good faith?

3. What is the basis for Rand J.'s finding of liability? Is liability predicated on intentional excess of jurisdiction, excess of jurisdiction independent of any intent, improper purpose, or a combination of these factors?

4. Fauteaux and Taschereau JJ. dissented on the basis that Roncarelli had failed to give Duplessis adequate notice in breach of article 88 of the Code of Civil Procedure, which reads: "No public officer or other person fulfilling any public function or duty can be sued for damages by reason of any act done by him in the exercise of his functions . . . unless notice of such action has been given him at least one month before the issue of the writ of summons. . .." How do you think the majority avoided the effect of this section?

5. Cartwright J. wrote a separate dissenting judgment in *Roncarelli*. He held that the defendant was exercising an administrative discretion which should not be reviewed by the courts. Alternatively, if the defendant was exercising a quasi-judicial function, Cartwright J. argued that he should be protected by judicial immunity. Do you agree that judicial immunity should be extended to those performing quasi-judicial functions? Even if the principles of judicial immunity applied, would they have protected Duplessis given the facts of the case? Is there any justification for absolving public authorities of liability if they abuse their powers?

(b) MODERN DEVELOPMENTS

The tort of misfeasance in a public office was litigated infrequently during most of the 20th century, largely because of the dominance of negligence during that period. However, there has been a resurgence of the misfeasance tort during the last few decades, and the elements of the tort have been substantially redefined. These developments are discussed in the Supreme Court of Canada's decision in *Odhavji Estate v. Woodhouse*, [2003] 3 S.C.R. 263, which sets out the modern Canadian position.

ODHAVJI ESTATE v. WOODHOUSE
[2003] 3 S.C.R. 263

The judgment of the Court was delivered by

IACOBUCCI J.: . . .. On September 26, 1997, Manish Odhavji was fatally shot by officers of the Metropolitan Toronto Police Service while running from his vehicle subsequent to a bank robbery. Within 25 minutes of the shooting, an assistant to Metropolitan Toronto Chief of Police David Boothby (the "Chief") notified the Special Investigations Unit of the Ministry of the Solicitor General (the "SIU") of the incident.

The SIU is a civilian agency statutorily mandated to conduct independent investigations of police conduct in cases of death or serious injury caused by the police. The SIU began its investigation immediately. It requested that the defendant officers remain segregated, that they make themselves available for same-day interviews, and that they provide their shift notes, on-duty clothing, and blood samples. Under s. 113(9) of the *Police Services Act*, R.S.O. 1990, c. P.15, members of the force are under a statutory obligation to cooperate with members of the SIU in the conduct of the investigation. Under s. 41(1) of the *Police Services Act*, a chief of police is required to ensure that members of the force carry out their duties in accordance with the provisions of the Act.

The estate of Mr. Odhavji and the members of his immediate family (the "plaintiffs") allege that the defendant officers intentionally breached their statutory obligation to cooperate fully with the SIU investigation. In particular, the plaintiffs allege that the defendant officers did not attend for interviews with the SIU until September 30, that they did not comply with the request to remain segregated, and that they failed to comply with the request for shift notes, on-duty clothing, and blood samples in a timely manner – and that when statements were eventually given to the SIU, they were both inaccurate and misleading. In the plaintiffs' statement of claim, the lack of a thorough investigation into the shooting incident has caused the plaintiffs to suffer mental distress, anger, depression and anxiety. The plaintiffs further allege that these damages are consequences that the defendant officers and the Chief knew or ought to have known would result from an inadequate investigation into the shooting incident.

The actions at issue in this appeal are not related to the allegedly wrongful death of Mr. Odhavji, but, rather, to the defendant officers' alleged failure to cooperate with the SIU. It is the plaintiffs' submission that the foregoing facts give rise to an action for misfeasance in a public office against the defendant officers and the Chief, and actions for negligence against the Chief, the Metropolitan Toronto Police Services Board (the "Board") and Her Majesty the Queen in Right of Ontario (the "Province").

(1) action for misfesance in public office against defendant officers.

(1) *The Defining Elements of the Tort*

The origins of the tort of misfeasance in a public office can be traced to *Ashby v. White* (1703), 2 Ld. Raym. 938, 92 E.R. 126, in which Holt C.J. found that a cause of action lay against an elections officer who maliciously and fraudulently deprived Mr. White of the right to vote. Although the defendant possessed the power to deprive certain persons from participating in the election, he did not have the power to do so for an improper purpose. Although the original judgment suggests that he was simply applying the principle *ubi jus ibi remedium*, Holt C.J. produced a revised form of the judgment in which he stated that it was because fraud and malice were proven that the action lay: J. W. Smith, *A Selection of Leading Cases on Various Branches of the Law* (13th ed. 1929), at p. 282. Thus, in its earliest form it is arguable that misfeasance in a public office was limited to circumstances in which a public officer abused a power actually possessed.

Subsequent cases, however, have made clear that the ambit of the tort is not restricted in this manner. In *Roncarelli v. Duplessis*, [1959] S.C.R. 121, this Court found the defendant Premier of Quebec liable for directing the manager of the Quebec Liquor Commission to revoke the plaintiff's liquor licence. Although Roncarelli was decided at least in part on the basis of the Quebec civil law of delictual responsibility, it is widely regarded as having established that misfeasance in a public office is a recognized tort in Canada. . .. In *Roncarelli*, the Premier was authorized to give advice to the Commission in respect of any legal questions that might arise, but had no authority to involve himself in a decision to revoke a particular licence. As Abbott J. observed, at p. 184, Mr. Duplessis "was given no statutory power to interfere in the administration or direction of the Quebec Liquor Commission". Martland J. made a similar observation, at p. 158, stating that Mr. Duplessis' conduct involved "the exercise of powers which, in law, he did not possess at all". From this, it is clear that the tort is not restricted to the abuse of a statutory or prerogative power actually held. If that were the case, there would have been no grounds on which to find Mr. Duplessis liable.

This understanding of the tort is consistent with the widespread consensus in other common law jurisdictions that there is a broad range of misconduct that can found an action for misfeasance in a public office. For example, in *Northern Territory of Australia v. Mengel* (1995), 129 A.L.R. 1 (H.C.), Brennan J. wrote as follows, at p. 25:

> The tort is not limited to an abuse of office by exercise of a statutory power. *Henly v. Mayor of Lyme* [(1828), 5 Bing. 91, 130 E.R. 995] was not a case arising from an impugned exercise of a statutory power. It arose from an alleged failure to maintain a sea wall or bank, the maintenance of which was a condition of the grant to the corporation of Lyme of the sea wall or bank and the appurtenant right to tolls. *Any act or omission done or made by a public official in the purported performance of the functions of the office can found an action for misfeasance in public office.* [Emphasis added.]
>
> In *Garrett v. Attorney-General*, [1997] 2 N.Z.L.R. 332, the Court of Appeal for New Zealand considered an allegation that a sergeant failed to investigate properly the plaintiff's claim that she had been sexually assaulted by a police constable. Blanchard J. concluded, at p. 344, that the tort can be committed "by an official who acts or omits to act in breach of duty knowing about the breach and also knowing harm or loss is thereby likely to be occasioned to the plaintiff".

The House of Lords reached the same conclusion in *Three Rivers District Council v. Bank of England (No. 3)*, [2000] 2 W.L.R. 1220. In *Three Rivers*, the plaintiffs alleged that officers with the Bank of England improperly issued a licence to the Bank of Credit and Commerce International and then failed to close the bank once it became evident that such action was necessary. Forced to consider whether the tort could apply in the case of omissions, the House of Lords concluded that "the tort can be constituted by an omission by a public officer as well as by acts on his part" (*per* Lord Hutton, at p. 1267). In Australia, New Zealand and the United Kingdom, it is equally clear that the tort of misfeasance is not limited to the unlawful exercise of a statutory or prerogative power actually held.

What then are the essential ingredients of the tort, at least insofar as it is necessary to determine the issues that arise on the pleadings in this case? In *Three Rivers*, the House of Lords held that the tort of misfeasance in a public office can arise in one of two ways, what I shall call Category A and Category B. Category A involves conduct that is specifically intended to injure a person or class of persons. Category B involves a public officer who acts with knowledge both that she or he has no power to do the act complained of and that the act is likely to injure the plaintiff. This understanding of the tort has been endorsed by a number of Canadian courts. . . .. It is important, however, to recall that the two categories merely represent two different ways in which a public officer can commit the tort; in each instance, the plaintiff must prove each of the tort's constituent elements. It is thus necessary to consider the elements that are common to each form of the tort.

In my view, there are two such elements. First, the public officer must have engaged in deliberate and unlawful conduct in his or her capacity as a public officer. Second, the public officer must have been aware both that his or her conduct was unlawful and that it was likely to harm the plaintiff. What distinguishes one form of misfeasance in a public office from the other is the manner in which the plaintiff proves each ingredient of the tort. In Category B, the plaintiff must prove the two ingredients of the tort independently of one another. In Category A, the fact that the public officer has acted for the express purpose of harming the plaintiff is sufficient to satisfy each ingredient of the tort, owing to the fact that a public officer does not have the authority to exercise his or her powers for an improper purpose, such as deliberately harming a member of the public. In each instance, the tort involves deliberate disregard of official duty coupled with knowledge that the misconduct is likely to injure the plaintiff.

Insofar as the nature of the misconduct is concerned, the essential question to be determined is not whether the officer has unlawfully exercised a power actually possessed, but whether the alleged misconduct is deliberate and unlawful. As Lord Hobhouse wrote in *Three Rivers*, *supra*, at p. 1269:

> The relevant act (or omission, in the sense described) must be unlawful. This may arise from a straightforward breach of the relevant statutory provisions or from acting in excess of the powers granted or for an improper purpose.

Lord Millett reached a similar conclusion, namely, that a failure to act can amount to misfeasance in a public office, but only in those circumstances in which the public officer is under a legal obligation to act. Lord Hobhouse stated the principle in the following terms, at p. 1269: "If there is a legal duty to act and the decision not to act amounts to an unlawful breach of that legal duty, the omission can amount to misfeasance [in a public office]." . . . So, in the United Kingdom, a failure to act can constitute misfeasance in a public office, but only if the failure to act constitutes a deliberate breach of official duty.

Canadian courts also have made a deliberate unlawful act a focal point of the inquiry. In *Alberta (Minister of Public Works, Supply and Services) v. Nilsson* (1999), 70 Alta. L.R. (3d) 267, 1999 ABQB 440, at para. 108, the Court of Queen's Bench stated that the essential question to be determined is whether there has been deliberate misconduct on the part of a public official. Deliberate misconduct, on this view, consists of: (i) an intentional illegal act; and (ii) an intent to harm an individual or class of individuals. See also *Uni-Jet Industrial Pipe Ltd. v. Canada (Attorney General)* (2001), 156 Man. R. (2d) 14, 2001 MBCA 40, in which Kroft J.A. adopted the same test. In *Powder Mountain Resorts*, *supra*, Newbury J.A. described the tort in similar terms, at para. 7:

> . . . it may, I think, now be accepted that the tort of abuse of public office will be made out in Canada where a public official is shown either to have exercised power for the specific purpose of injuring the plaintiff (i.e., to have acted in "bad faith in the sense of the exercise of public power for an improper or ulterior motive") or to have acted "unlawfully with a mind of reckless indifference to the illegality of his act" and to the probability of injury to the plaintiff. (See Lord Steyn in *Three Rivers*, at [1231].) Thus there remains what in theory at least is a clear line between this tort on the one hand, and what on the other hand may be called negligent excess of power – i.e., an act committed without knowledge of (or *subjective* recklessness as to) its unlawfulness and the probable consequences for the plaintiff. [Emphasis in original.]

Under this view, the ambit of the tort is limited not by the requirement that the defendant must have been engaged in a particular type of unlawful conduct, but by the requirement that the unlawful conduct must have been deliberate and the defendant must have been aware that the unlawful conduct was likely to harm the plaintiff.

As is often the case, there are a number of phrases that might be used to describe the essence of the tort. In *Garrett*, *supra*, Blanchard J. stated, at p. 350, that "[t]he purpose behind the imposition of this form of tortious liability is to prevent the deliberate injuring of members of the public by deliberate disregard of official duty." In *Three Rivers*, *supra*, Lord Steyn stated, at p. 1230, that "[t]he rationale of the tort is that in a legal system based on the rule of law executive or administrative power 'may be exercised only for the public good' and not for ulterior and improper purposes." As each passage makes clear, misfeasance in a public office is not directed at a public officer who inadvertently or negligently fails adequately to discharge the obligations of his or her office: see *Three Rivers*, at p. 1273, *per* Lord Millett. Nor is the tort directed at a public officer who fails adequately to discharge the obligations of the office as a consequence of budgetary constraints or other factors beyond his or her control. A public officer who cannot adequately discharge his or her duties because of budgetary constraints has not deliberately disregarded his or her official duties. The tort is not directed at a public officer who is *unable* to discharge his or her obligations because of factors beyond his or her control but, rather, at a public officer who *could* have discharged his or her public obligations, yet wilfully chose to do otherwise.

Another factor that may remove an official's conduct from the scope of the tort of misfeasance in a public office is a conflict with the officer's statutory obligations and his or her constitutionally protected rights, such as the right against self-incrimination. Should such circumstances arise, a public officer's decision not to comply with his or her statutory obligation may not amount to misfeasance in a public office. I need not decide that question here except that it could be argued. A public officer who properly insists on asserting his or her constitutional rights cannot accurately be said to have deliberately disregarded the legal obligations of his or her office. Under this argument, an obligation inconsistent with the officer's constitutional rights is not itself lawful.

As a matter of policy, I do not believe that it is necessary to place any further restrictions on the ambit of the tort. The requirement that the defendant must have been aware that his or her conduct was unlawful reflects the well-established principle that misfeasance in a public office requires an element of "bad faith" or "dishonesty". In a democracy, public officers must retain the authority to make decisions that, where appropriate, are adverse to the interests of certain citizens. Knowledge of harm is thus an insufficient basis on which to conclude that the defendant has acted in bad faith or dishonestly. A public officer may in good faith make a decision that she or he knows to be adverse to interests of certain members of the public. In order for the conduct to fall within the scope of the tort, the officer must deliberately engage in conduct that he or she knows to be inconsistent with the obligations of the office.

The requirement that the defendant must have been aware that his or her unlawful conduct would harm the plaintiff further restricts the ambit of the tort. Liability does not attach to each officer who blatantly disregards his or her official duty, but only to a public officer who, in addition, demonstrates a conscious disregard for the interests of those who will be affected by the misconduct in question. This requirement establishes the required nexus between the parties. Unlawful conduct in the exercise of public functions is a public wrong, but absent some awareness of harm there is no basis on which to conclude that the defendant has breached an obligation that she or he owes to the plaintiff, *as an individual*. And absent the breach of an obligation that the defendant owes to the plaintiff, there can be no liability in tort.

In sum, I believe that the underlying purpose of the tort is to protect each citizen's reasonable expectation that a public officer will not intentionally injure a member of the public through deliberate and unlawful conduct in the exercise of public functions. Once these requirements have been satisfied, it is unclear why the tort would be restricted to a public officer who engaged in the unlawful exercise of a statutory power that she or he actually possesses. If the tort were restricted in this manner, the tort would not extend to a public officer, such as Mr. Duplessis, who intentionally *exceeded* his powers for the express purpose of interfering with a citizen's economic interests. Nor would it extend to a public officer who breached a statutory obligation for the same purpose. But there is no principled reason, in my view, why a public officer who wilfully injures a member of the public through intentional *abuse* of a statutory power would be liable, but not a public officer who wilfully injures a member of the public through an intentional *excess* of power or a deliberate failure to discharge a statutory duty. In each instance, the alleged misconduct is equally inconsistent with the obligation of a public officer not to intentionally injure a member of the public through deliberate and unlawful conduct in the exercise of public functions.

. . . .

(2) *Application to the Case at Hand*

As outlined earlier, on a motion to strike on the basis that the statement of claim discloses no reasonable cause of action, the facts are taken as pleaded. Consequently, the primary question that arises on this appeal is whether the statement of claim pleads each of the constituent elements of the tort.

In respect of the first constituent element, namely, unlawful conduct in the exercise of public functions, the statement of claim alleges that the defendant officers did not cooperate with the SIU investigation, but, rather, took positive steps to frustrate the investigation. As described above, police officers are under a statutory obligation to cooperate fully with members of the SIU in the conduct of investigations, pursuant to s. 113(9) of the *Police Services Act*. On the face of it, the decision not to cooperate with an investigation constitutes an unlawful breach of statutory duty. Similarly, the alleged failure of the Chief to ensure that the defendant officers cooperated with the investigation also would seem to constitute an unlawful breach of duty. Under s. 41(1)(b) of the *Police Services Act*, the duties of a chief of police include ensuring that members of the police force carry out their duties in accordance with the Act. A decision not to ensure that police officers cooperate with the SIU is inconsistent with the statutory obligations of the office.

. . . .

Insofar as the second requirement is concerned, the statement of claim alleges that the acts and omissions of the defendant officers "represented intentional breaches of their legal duties as police officers". This plainly satisfies the requirement that the officers were aware that the alleged failure to cooperate with the investigation was unlawful. The allegation is not simply that the officers failed to comply with s. 113(9) of the *Police Services Act*, but that the failure to comply was intentional and deliberate. Insofar as the Chief is concerned, the statement of claim alleges as follows:

(i) Chief Boothby, through his legal counsel, was directed by S.I.U. officers to segregate the defendant officers and he deliberately failed to do so;

(ii) Chief Boothby failed to ensure that defendant police officers produced timely and complete notes;

(iii) Chief Boothby failed to ensure that the defendant police officers attended for requested interviews by S.I.U. in a timely manner; and

(iv) Chief Boothby failed to ensure that the defendant police officers gave accurate and complete accounts of the specifics of the shooting incident.

Although the allegation that the Chief *deliberately* failed to segregate the officers satisfies the requirement that the Chief *intentionally* breached his legal obligation to ensure compliance with the *Police Services Act*, the same cannot be said of his alleged failure to ensure that the defendant officers produced timely and complete notes, attended for interviews in a timely manner, and provided accurate and complete accounts of the incident. As above, inadvertence or negligence will not suffice; a mere failure to discharge the obligations of the office cannot constitute misfeasance in a public office. In light of the allegation that the Chief's failure to segregate the officers was deliberate, this is not a sufficient basis on which to strike the pleading. Suffice it to say, the failure to issue orders for the purpose of ensuring that the defendant officers cooperated with the investigation will only constitute misfeasance in a public office if the plaintiffs prove that the Chief deliberately failed to comply with the standard established by s. 41(1)(b) of the *Police Services Act*.

The statement of claim also alleges that the defendant officers and the Chief "knew or ought to have known" that the alleged misconduct would cause the plaintiffs to suffer physically, psychologically and emotionally. Although the allegation that the defendants *knew* that a failure to cooperate with the investigation would injure the plaintiffs satisfies the requirement that the alleged misconduct was likely to injure the plaintiffs, misfeasance in a public office is an intentional tort that requires subjective awareness that harm to the plaintiff is a likely consequence of the alleged misconduct. At the very least, according to a number of cases, the defendant must have been subjectively reckless or wilfully blind as to the possibility that harm was a likely consequence of the alleged misconduct. . .. This, again, is not a sufficient basis on which to strike the pleading. It is clear, however, that the phrase "or ought to have known" must be struck from the statement of claim.

The final factor to be considered is whether the damages that the plaintiffs claim to have suffered as a consequence of the aforementioned misconduct are compensable. In the defendant officers' submission, the alleged damages are non-compensable. Consequently, it is their submission that even if the plaintiffs could prove the other elements of the tort, it still would be plain and obvious that the actions for misfeasance in a public office must fail.

[Iacobucci J. comments that, while emotional distress alone is not compensable in Canadian tort law, the plaintiffs might be successful if they could prove a recognizable psychiatric illness. He concludes that, at this stage of the proceedings, it is too early to determine whether the plaintiffs could meet this burden. Therefore, it would be premature to strike out their cause of action.]

. . . .

In the final analysis, I would allow the appeal in respect of the actions for misfeasance in a public office. If the facts are taken as pleaded, it is not plain and obvious that the actions for misfeasance in a public office against the defendant officers and the Chief must fail. The plaintiffs may well face an uphill battle, but they should not be deprived of the opportunity to prove each of the constituent elements of the tort.

NOTES AND QUESTIONS

1. Describe the elements of a claim for misfeasance in a public office. How does Iacobucci J. distinguish the two branches of the tort?

2. Compare the tort of misfeasance in a public office with the tort of negligence. Which tort is easier to prove? Would the plaintiffs in *Odhavji* have a successful negligence claim against the officers involved in the shooting? Does the relevant section of the *Police Services Act*, R.S.O. 1990, c. P.15, give rise to a duty of care? Are there policy reasons to negate that duty?

3. The leading Commonwealth decision on misfeasance in a public office is *Three Rivers District Council v. Governor and Company of the Bank of England (No. 3)*, [2003] 2 A.C. 1 (H.L.). In Lord Steyn's leading opinion, he sets out the "ingredients" of the tort as follows: (i) public office, (ii) the exercise of power as a public officer, (iii) the state of mind of the defendant, (iv) duty to the plaintiff, (v) causation, and (vi) damages and remoteness.

4. For cases illustrating the modern revival and expansion of misfeasance in a public office in the Commonwealth, see for example *Dunlop v. Woollahra District Council* (1981), 33 A.L.R. 621 (P.C.); *Bourgoin v. Ministry of Agriculture, Fisheries and Food*, [1986] Q.B. 716 (C.A.); *Calveley v. Chief Constable of Merseyside*, [1989] A.C. 1228 (H.L.); *Jones v. Swansea City Council*, [1989] 3 All E.R. 162 (C.A.), rev'd on other grounds [1990] 3 All E.R. 737 (H.L.); *Racz v. Home Office*, [1994] 2 A.C. 45 (H.L.); *Northern Territory v. Mengel* (1995), 185 C.L.R. 307 (H.C.A.); *Garrett v. Attorney General*, [1997] 2 N.Z.L.R. 332 (C.A.); *Kuddus v. Chief Constable of Leicestershire Constabulary*, [2001] 2 W.L.R. 1789 (H.L.); *Akenzua v. Secretary of State for the Home Department*, [2003] 1 All E.R. 35 (C.A.); and *Watkins v. Home Office*, [2006] UKHL 17.

5. Canada has also experienced an increase in claims for misfeasance in a public office. See for example *Longley v. Canada* (2000), 73 B.C.L.R. (3d) 222 (C.A.); *Wiche v. Ontario* (2001), 9 C.C.L.T. (3d) 72 (Ont. S.C.J.); *Powder Mountain Resorts Ltd. v. British Columbia* (2001), 94 B.C.L.R. (3d) 14 (C.A.); *First National Properties Ltd. v. Highlands (District)* (2001), 88 B.C.L.R. (3d) 125 (C.A.); *Uni-Jet Industrial Pipe Ltd v. Canada* (2001), 198 D.L.R. (4th) 577 (Man. C.A.); *LeBlanc v. Canada* (2005), 339 N.R. 244 (F.C.A.); and *Freeman-Maloy v. Marsden* (2006), 79 O.R. (3d) 401 (C.A.).

6. The expansion of the misfeasance tort has been accompanied by an expansion in the relevant scholarly literature. See Evans, "Damages for Unlawful Administrative

Action: The Remedy for Misfeasance in Public Office" (1982) 31 I.C.L.Q. 640; Sadler, "Liability for Misfeasance in a Public Office" (1992) 14 Syd. L.R. 137; Kneebone, "Misfeasance in a Public Office After Mengel's Case: A 'Special' Tort No More?" (1996) 4 Tort L.R. 111; Allott, "EC Directives and Misfeasance in Public Office" [2001] C.L.J. 4; Irvine, "Misfeasance in Public Office: Reflections on Some Recent Developments" (2001) 9 C.C.L.T. (3d) 26; and Mason & Laurie, "Misfeasance in Public Office: An Emerging Medical Law Tort" (2003) 11 Med. L. Rev. 194.

5. Other Torts

Although the action in negligence dominates, and the misfeasance tort is expanding, there are still other bases upon which a public authority may be held liable in tort. Most torts apply equally to both private and public actors. That is true, for instance, of intentional torts (*e.g.* false imprisonment and trespass) and nuisance. Nevertheless, it is important to appreciate that differences do occasionally arise. Perhaps most significantly, a public official is often able to plead the defence of statutory authority. Briefly stated, that defence precludes recovery with respect to a loss that was the inevitable result of the defendant's performance of a statutorily authorized act. This defence is considered in greater detail in Chapter 24.

Some types of claims, however, arise uniquely in connection with public authorities. That is true of *Charter* "torts," which were previously discussed in Chapters 3, 8 and 11, and which will be further examined in the next chapter. By virtue of s. 32, the *Charter* applies only to government and government agencies – not to purely private actors. Moreover, most *Charter* violations are addressed through public law remedies (*e.g.* invalidation of offending legislation). Nevertheless, s. 24(1) entitles the victim of a *Charter* violation to "such remedy as the court considers appropriate and just in the circumstances." Although the governing principles remain somewhat under-developed, the range of remedies clearly includes an award of damages.

NOTES AND QUESTIONS

1. For an example of the application of the intentional economic torts to public authorities, see *Gershman v. Man. Vegetable Producers' Marketing Bd.* (1976), 69 D.L.R. (3d) 114 (Man. C.A.).

2. As discussed in Chapter 11, a leading case on *Charter* torts is *Jane Doe v. Metropolitan Toronto (Municipality) Commissioners of Police* (1998), 39 O.R. (3d) 487 (Gen. Div.). The plaintiff was sexually assaulted by a serial rapist. Although the police knew that the plaintiff was a member of a group of potential victims, they did not warn her of that danger. The plaintiff argued that they used her as "bait" in their attempts to apprehend the perpetrator. The trial judge found that the officers' decision to not issue a warning was based on their belief that, if alerted, potential victims would become "hysterical" and thereby jeopardize the investigation. The plaintiff's action succeeded in both negligence and under the *Charter*. As to the former, the trial judge held that the police officers failed to discharge the duty of care that they owed to the plaintiff. As to the latter, the trial judge held that the police officers' conduct: (i) violated s. 7 of the *Charter* in so far as it deprived the plaintiff of security of the person, and (ii) violated s. 15 of the *Charter* in so far as it was based on discriminatory stereotypes regarding the

behaviour of women. Damages were assessed on the same basis for both negligence and *Charter* violations.

3. Civil liability of public authorities arising from *Charter* violations is increasing. See *Crossman v. R.*, [1984] 1 F.C. 681 (T.D.); *Chrispen v. Kalinowski* (1997), 156 Sask. R. 58 (Q.B.); and *Krznaric v. Chevrette* (1997), 154 D.L.R. (4th) 527 (Ont. Gen. Div.).

4. For a discussion of trends in liability for police conduct, see Childs & Ceyssens, "*Doe v. Metropolitan Toronto Board of Commissioners of Police* and the Status of Public Oversight of the Police in Canada" (1998) 36 Alta. L. Rev. 1000.

REVIEW PROBLEM

Harold is a fruit farmer who owns a number of peach and apple orchards in the Niagara peninsula. His orchards are next to a major provincial highway which receives the highest level of winter maintenance from the Works Department. As part of the maintenance program, the Department spreads large quantities of road salt on the highway whenever conditions are icy. The Department does not use sand for this purpose.

Harold can prove that, when the Department's trucks pass his orchard applying road salt, some of the salt bounces onto his land. In addition, when the Department plows the roads, additional quantities of salt mixed with snow are pushed onto his orchards. However, the majority of the salt on his orchards is carried by water when the roadside snowbanks melt.

Over the years, a sufficient quantity of salt has accumulated on Harold's orchards to render a 30-foot strip of his land adjoining the highway useless for fruit production. The peach trees in this strip have withered and died, and the apple trees produce virtually no fruit.

The pertinent legislation is the *Highway Maintenance Act*. There is only one relevant section which reads: "The Provincial Works Department shall maintain all public highways and take all reasonable steps to ensure that motorists may obtain safe passage thereon at any time."

Is Harold likely to succeed in a tort suit against the Department in: (a) trespass, (b) negligence, (c) nuisance, or (d) under the rule in *Rylands v. Fletcher*? First, analyze these issues assuming that the Department is not a Crown agency. Second, analyze these issues assuming that the Department is a Crown agency, governed by the relevant legislation in your province. This problem is based on the case of *R. in Right of Ont. v. Schenck* ;*R. in Right of Ont. v. Rokeby* (1984), 15 D.L.R. (4th) 320 (Ont. C.A.), aff'd [1987] 2 S.C.R. 289.

22

STATUTORY PROVISIONS AND TORT LIABILITY

1. Introduction
2. Express Statutory Causes of Action
3. The Use of Statutes in Common Law Negligence
4. A Note on the *Canadian Charter of Rights and Freedoms*

1. Introduction

Tort often is said to be a prime example of a "common law" subject. This certainly is true, but in the interests of clarity, it is important to define the operative phrase. There are at least three possibilities.

- *Systems of Law*: At the broadest level, "common law" refers to a *system of law* that was derived from England. In that respect, "common law" can be contrasted with, say, civil law (as applied, for instance, in Quebec, Louisiana, and most of Europe), Jewish law, Islamic law, or Aboriginal law. Although every legal system has some means of redressing private wrongs, the body of rules considered in this book comprise a common law subject insofar as it has English roots.

- *Sources of Law*: On a more specific level, within our legal system as a whole, the phrase "common law" can be used, within any given area of law, to denote rules that were created by judges as opposed to legislators. Some subjects are governed almost entirely by legislation. This is true, for instance, of crime and income tax. The *Criminal Code of Canada*, R.S.C. 1985, c. C-46 and the *Income Tax Act*, R.S.C. 1985, c. 1 (5th Supp.) cover pretty much all of the relevant territory. Judges obviously play an interpretive role, but the governing rules are set by Parliament. Tort, in contrast, is very largely a common law subject. For the most part, legislators have left the area to judicial development.

- *Courts of Law*: Finally, at the most specific level, the term "common law" can be used to distinguish the body of rules historically created in the courts of law, as opposed to the courts of equity or chancery. This distinction was explained in Chapter 1. Tort law has always been classified as a common law subject in this respect as well. It may be questioned, however, whether there remain any compelling reasons for treating some species of private wrongs (*e.g.* negligence) separately from others (*e.g.* breach of fiduciary duty) simply because the former originated in one set of courts and the latter in another. Indeed, there are signs that Canadian courts are becoming less interested in pedigree and more interested in substance. See for example *Cadbury Schweppes Inc. v. FBI Foods Ltd.*, [1999] 1 S.C.R. 142, where the court refused to classify the action in breach of confidence as an exclusively equitable wrong.

For the purposes of this chapter, the most important distinction is the second one. Tort law generally is a "common law" subject because most of its rules were developed by judges rather than legislators. There nevertheless are circumstances in which statutory provisions affect the availability of relief in tort law. We already have encountered several examples. In the previous chapter, for instance, we saw that legislated limitation periods often protect public authorities from liability. In this chapter, we examine two other ways in which statutory provisions may be relevant.

- *Statutory Cause of Action*: Legislation may create a statutory cause of action that is distinct from any judicially developed claim. Quite often, such legislation will addresses specific aspects of the statutory claim, such as the standard of care and the quantum of relief. In such circumstances, the judiciary's role is interpretive, rather than creative. In such circumstances, tort law is not "common law" at its *source*.
- *Statutes in Common Law Torts*: Even if a particular piece of legislation does not create an independent statutory cause of action, it may affect the court's analysis of the common law (*i.e.* judicially created) claim in negligence. For example, a regulatory statute may prohibit a certain type of conduct and impose a fine for non-compliance, but remain silent on the issue of civil liability. A judge nevertheless may decide, as a matter of principle and policy, that the regulatory scheme supports the recognition of a duty of care in negligence. Likewise, in determining the standard of care under the action in negligence, a judge may be influenced by the provisions of a health and safety statute that Parliament drafted with the assistance of expert advice. In either event, it is important to understand that it is the court, rather than the legislature, that bears ultimate responsibility. In other words, notwithstanding judicial reliance upon statute, tort law is, at its source, "common law."

NOTE

1. Until 1983, Canadian courts occasionally used statutes in a third way. Even if a piece of legislation did not expressly create a statutory cause of action, a judge might *infer* such a claim. Unfortunately, despite numerous attempts to establish guidelines for such inferences, the jurisprudence remained confused. In *R. in Right of Can. v. Sask. Wheat Pool* (1983), 143 D.L.R. (3d) 9 (S.C.C.), an extract of which appears below, the Supreme Court of Canada eliminated the problem by declaring that the courts cannot create implied statutory causes of action. See also Fridman, *The Law of Torts in Canada*, 2d ed. (2002) at 624-33; and Linden & Feldthusen, *Canadian Tort Law*, 8th ed. (2006) at 224-31.

2. Express Statutory Causes of Action

TRESPASS TO PROPERTY ACT
R.S.O. 1990, c. T.21

2. (1) Every person who is not acting under a right or authority conferred by law and who,

(*a*) without the express permission of the occupier, the proof of which rests on the defendant,

(i) enters on premises when entry is prohibited under this Act, or

(ii) engages in an activity on premises when the activity is prohibited under this Act; or

(*b*) does not leave the premises immediately after he or she is directed to do so by the occupier of the premises or a person authorized by the occupier,

is guilty of an offence and on conviction is liable to a fine of not more than $2,000.

(2) It is a defence to a charge under subsection (1) in respect of premises that is land that the person charged reasonably believed that he or she had title to or an interest in the land that entitled him or her to do the act complained of.

. . .

12. (1) Where a person is convicted of an offence under section 2, and a person has suffered damage caused by the person convicted during the commission of the offence, the court shall, on the request of the prosecutor and with the consent of the person who suffered the damage, determine the damages and shall make a judgment for damages against the person convicted in favour of the person who suffered the damage, but no judgment shall be for an amount in excess of $1,000.

(2) Where a prosecution under section 2 is conducted by a private prosecutor, and the defendant is convicted, unless the court is of the opinion that the prosecution was not necessary for the protection of the occupier or the occupier's interests, the court shall determine the actual costs reasonably incurred in conducting the prosecution and, despite section 60 of the *Provincial Offences Act*, shall order those costs to be paid by the defendant to the prosecutor.

(3) A judgment for damages under subsection (1), or an award of costs under subsection (2), shall be in addition to any fine that is imposed under this Act.

(4) A judgment for damages under subsection (1) extinguishes the right of the person in whose favour the judgment is made to bring a civil action for damages against the person convicted arising out of the same facts.

(5) The failure to request or refusal to grant a judgment for damages under subsection (1) does not affect a right to bring a civil action for damages arising out of the same facts.

(6) The judgment for damages under subsection (1), and the award for costs under subsection (2), may be filed in the Small Claims Court and shall be deemed to be a judgment or order of that court for the purposes of enforcement.

COMPETITION ACT

R.S.C. 1985, c. C-34

36. (1) Any person who has suffered loss or damage as a result of

(*a*) conduct that is contrary to any provision of Part VI, or

(*b*) the failure of any person to comply with an order of the Tribunal or another court under this Act, may, in any court of competent jurisdiction, sue for and recover from the person who engaged in the conduct or failed to comply with the order an amount equal to the loss or damage proved to have been suffered by him, together with any additional amount that the court may allow not exceeding the full cost to him of any investigation in connection with the matter and of proceedings under this section.

. . .

PART VI
OFFENCES IN RELATION TO COMPETITION

45. (1) Every one who conspires, combines, agrees or arranges with another person

(*a*) to limit unduly the facilities for transporting, producing, manufacturing, supplying, storing or dealing in any product,

(*b*) to prevent, limit or lessen, unduly, the manufacture or production of a product or to enhance unreasonably the price thereof,

(*c*) to prevent or lessen, unduly, competition in the production, manufacture, purchase, barter, sale, storage, rental, transportation or supply of a product, or in the price of insurance on persons or property, or

(*d*) to otherwise restrain or injure competition unduly,

is guilty of an indictable offence and liable to imprisonment for a term not exceeding five years or to a fine not exceeding ten million dollars or to both.

NOTES AND QUESTIONS

1. Most violations of s. 2(1) of the *Trespass to Property Act* will also give rise to a common law action for trespass to land. What is the rationale for s. 12? Why is the statutory defence in s. 2(2) broader than the common law defence?

2. One purpose of s. 36 of the *Competition Act* is to encourage private citizens to participate in the enforcement of the criminal law in this field. Similar provisions in the United States provide treble damages to successful private litigants. See for example the *Clayton Act*, 15 U.S.C. §26. What other functions are served by s. 36 of the *Competition Act*? Why is private law enforcement necessary or desirable in this field? Is there any reason why the public enforcement agency cannot adequately protect the public interest? Is a private litigant's interest necessarily similar to the public interest? For further consideration of these issues see Pitel, ed., *Litigating Conspiracy* (2006).

3. The statutory action in s. 36 of the *Competition Act* is similar to the common law tort action for conspiracy. If the plaintiff is unsuccessful under s. 36, should it be possible to bring a common law conspiracy action on the same facts?

4. In *Burgess (Litigation Guardian of) v. Canadian National Railway* (2005), 78 O.R. (3d) 209 (S.C.J.), aff'd (2006), 41 C.C.L.T. (3d) 10 (Ont. C.A.), a young child was seriously injured after being struck by the defendant's train. The gist of the plaintiff's action was that the defendant was responsible because it failed to install a pedestrian

crossing system. The action failed. The court held that the situation was governed by the *Railway Safety Act*, R.S.C. 1985, c. 32 (4th Supp.). However, the court also held that Parliament intended to create obligations to benefit the public generally, rather than any given person individually. The court further held that notwithstanding the existence of that public obligation, the parties did not share a relationship of sufficient proximity so as to trigger an independent duty of care under the tort of negligence.

5. The sections reproduced above are but two of the many statutory provisions that expressly govern civil liability. Such provisions are especially common in statutes concerning government and public enterprises. There is no such thing as a typical provision, and care must be taken to search for and interpret relevant legislation on a case-by-case basis.

TRACHSLER v. HALTON

[1955] O.W.N. 909 (H.C.)

KING J. [orally, after stating the nature of the actions]: . . . The duty of a municipality is to keep its highways in such condition that travellers using them with ordinary care may do so in safety. Section 453(1) of The Municipal Act [now R.S.O. 1990, c. M.45, s. 284(1)] to which I have referred says:

> Every highway and every bridge shall be kept in repair by the corporation the council of which has jurisdiction over it, or upon which the duty of repairing it is imposed by this Act, and in case of default the corporation shall, subject to the provisions of *The Negligence Act*, be liable for all damages sustained by any person by reason of such default.

It will be noticed that the word used in the subsection, and used twice, is "default" and not merely failure to repair.

The question whether a highway is in repair is a question of fact. The duty to repair a highway may be described generally as a duty to do all things that may be reasonably necessary in the way of repairs to keep it fit for the lawful traffic over it. Notice of need of repair is not an ingredient of the duty to repair, but it may be a controlling factor in the question whether that duty has been performed.

When a highway is put out of repair without any fault of those whose duty it is to repair it, then that duty is reasonably performed if the repair is made within a reasonable time after they are informed, know or should have acquired knowledge of the need of repair.

In *Trueman v. The King; Dewan v. The King*, [1932] O.R. 703 at 708-9. . ., Riddell J.A. says:

> In cases against a municipality for damages for injury due to a want of repair, the law of this Province has long been settled, and is not disputed. On the occurrence of a want of repair, the municipality is not liable unless, after such occurrence, the municipality has had an opportunity to repair the defect, either by notice or knowledge, or by the lapse of such time as should have enabled it to have discovered the defect.

. . .

The system of inspecting the highways by the defendant County appeared to me to be adequate. No reasonable inspection of the highways could have led to faster action than occurred on this occasion. I do not say, for example, that the police of Trafalgar Township might not have proceeded at once to the place where the upheaval had been reported, but this does not fix any liability upon the defendant County, in my opinion.

It appears to me that by s. 453(1) of The Municipal Act the Legislature aimed at securing for the public reasonably easy and convenient avenues of communication and, as far as might be done by the exercise of corporate diligence, the safety of persons using the highways, but stopped short of providing an accident policy or indemnity against loss without regard to the effort of the corporation to comply with the statute.

On the evidence it appears to me that with respect to any circumstances that might have prevented the accident with which we are concerned, the defendant did all that might be reasonably expected of it in discharge of its duty under The Municipal Act. I believe that the defendant has shown that it was not in default with respect to its obligations imposed by the statute . . .

I do not find, on the evidence, that there is any liability on the defendant municipality.

[King J. dismissed the plaintiffs' actions. A subsequent appeal by one of the plaintiffs was dismissed by the Ontario Court of Appeal: [1955] O.W.N. 912 (C.A.).]

NOTES AND QUESTIONS

1. The terms "statutory duty" and "statutory standard" are used inconsistently. The term "duty," as used in this chapter, refers to the obligation itself. Thus, in *Trachsler* there was a duty keep the highway in a state of repair. The term "standard" refers to the degree of care that the defendant must exercise to meet this duty. What standard of care did King J. impose? Did he simply adopt the common law standard or did he derive the standard from the statutory language? How should the standard be determined? See also *R. v. Jennings*, [1966] S.C.R. 532; *Allan v. Saskatoon* (1971), 21 D.L.R. (3d) 338 (Sask. C.A.); *Millette v. Kalogeropoulos* (1974), 51 D.L.R. (3d) 244 (S.C.C.); *O'Rourke v. Schacht* (1976), 55 D.L.R. (3d) 96 (S.C.C.); and *Rydzik v. Edwards* (1982), 38 O.R. (2d) 486 (H.C.).

2. The current common law obligation of a municipality is similar to the obligation in *Trachsler*. However, at that time, the courts were reluctant to impose affirmative common law duties on statutory public authorities. Thus, the express statutory duty in the *Municipal Act* may have been the sole basis for bringing the action in *Trachsler*.

3. Some statutes will specifically define the required standard of care. See for example the Alberta *Municipal Government Act*, R.S.A. 2000, c. M-26, s. 532. The predecessor to the current section was discussed in *Parkland No. 31 v. Stetar* (1974), 50 D.L.R. (3d) 376 (S.C.C.); and *Berezowski v. Edmonton* (1986), 45 Alta. L.R. (2d) 247 (C.A.).

4. This chapter examines statutory provisions that affect liability in tort. It is, however, important to remember the notion of *alternative analysis* that was explained in Chapter 1. A single set of facts may be analyzed from different perspectives in order to support various causes of action. The most common overlap occurs between tort and breach of contract. Moreover, just as legislation may affect a tort claim, so too it may affect a claim in contract. For example, many contracts fall within the scope of the statutes about the sale of goods that exist in every province and territory. When that

occurs, the statute automatically inserts a number of provisions into the parties' agreement (though the parties generally are free to exclude such provisions). Accordingly, a sale of goods often presumptively carries terms by which the vendor promises that the goods are, among other things, of merchantable quality and fit for their intended purposes. Consequently, a purchaser who suffers a loss or injury may be entitled to sue for both negligence and breach of contract. Notice, however, that the latter claims are available only to a *party* to the contract and not to every consumer. See generally *Grant v. Australian Knitting Mills Ltd.*, [1935] All E.R. Rep. 209 (P.C.). For a recent example of contractual liability arising from statutorily supplied terms see *Satara Farms Inc. v. Parrish & Heimbecker Ltd.* (2006), 280 Sask. R. 44 (Q.B.).

REVIEW PROBLEM

Answer the following questions based on s. 51 of the *Marine Liability Act*, S.C. 2001, c. 6.

PART 6: LIABILITY AND COMPENSATION FOR POLLUTION
DIVISION 1: CIVIL LIABILITY FOR POLLUTION

Liability for pollution and related costs
(1) Subject to the other provisions of this Part, the owner of a ship is liable
(a) for oil pollution damage from the ship;
(b) for costs and expenses incurred by
(i) the Minister of Fisheries and Oceans,
(ii) a response organization within the meaning of section 654 of the *Canada Shipping Act*,
(iii) any other person in Canada, or
(iv) any person in a state, other than Canada, that is a party to the Civil Liability Convention,
in respect of measures taken to prevent, repair, remedy or minimize oil pollution damage from the ship, including measures taken in anticipation of a discharge of oil from the ship, to the extent that the measures taken and the costs and expenses are reasonable, and for any loss or damage caused by those measures; and
(c) for costs and expenses incurred
(i) by the Minister of Fisheries and Oceans in respect of measures taken under paragraph 678(1)(a) of the *Canada Shipping Act*, in respect of any monitoring under paragraph 678(1)(b) of that Act or in relation to any direction given under paragraph 678(1)(c) of that Act, or
(ii) by any other person in respect of measures the person was directed to take or prohibited from taking under paragraph 678(1)(c) of the *Canada Shipping Act*,
to the extent that the measures taken and the costs and expenses are reasonable, and for any loss or damage caused by those measures.

Liability for environmental damage
(2) If oil pollution damage from a ship results in impairment to the environment, the owner of the ship is liable for the costs of reasonable measures of reinstatement actually undertaken or to be undertaken.

Strict liability subject to certain defences
(3) The owner's liability under subsection (1) does not depend on proof of fault or negligence, but the owner is not liable under that subsection if the owner establishes that the occurrence

(a) resulted from an act of war, hostilities, civil war or insurrection or from a natural phenomenon of an exceptional, inevitable and irresistible character;
(b) was wholly caused by an act or omission of a third party with intent to cause damage; or
(c) was wholly caused by the negligence or other wrongful act of any government or other authority responsible for the maintenance of lights or other navigational aids, in the exercise of that function.

. . .

Limitation period
(6) No action lies in respect of a matter referred to in subsection (1) unless it is commenced

(a) if pollution damage occurred, before the earlier of
(i) three years after the day on which the pollution damage occurred, and
(ii) six years after the occurrence that caused the pollution damage or, if the pollution damage was caused by more than one occurrence having the same origin, six years after the first of the occurrences; or
(b) if no pollution damage occurred, within six years after the occurrence.

1. Explain the duty of care that is created by s. 51 of the *Marine Liability Act*. Who owes the duty? To whom is the duty owed?

2. Explain the standard of care that applies under the provision. Will a claim be defeated by proof of reasonable care? Assume that a ship owner knew that a disgruntled ex-crew member was planning to damage the ship, but did nothing to stop the attack. According to the terms of s. 51(3), is the ship owner liable for the resulting pollution? Was the damage "wholly caused" by the vandal's intentional act?

3. What losses are compensable under the statutory action contained in s. 51? Assume that, as a result of an oil spill from the defendant's ship, the plaintiff suffered several losses and injuries, as follows: (1) $25,000 already has been spent to eliminate the pollution, (2) at least $10,000 more will be required for the same purpose in the foreseeable future, (3) as a result of coming into contact with the pollutant, the plaintiff suffers from a physical condition that causes great discomfort, but does not prevent the plaintiff from working, (4) the pollution has destroyed a natural clam bed that the plaintiff regularly harvested for an annual net profit of $15,000, and (5) the pollution has ruined the aesthetic value of the beach attached to the plaintiff's land, thereby diminishing the property's market value by $50,000. How much is the plaintiff entitled to recover from the defendant under section 51?

4. The *Marine Liability Act* was enacted in 2001. Has s. 51 received judicial comment or interpretation? If so, what is the effect of those decisions?

3. The Use of Statutes in Common Law Negligence

R. IN RIGHT OF CAN. v. SASK. WHEAT POOL

(1983), 143 D.L.R. (3d) 9 (S.C.C.)

[The Saskatchewan Wheat Pool delivered infested wheat to the Canadian Wheat Board in violation of s. 86(c) of the *Canada Grain Act*, S.C. 1970-71-72, c. 7. The statute made no reference to the issue of civil liability for breach of its provisions. The Board made no claim in common law negligence, but rather sought damages based solely on the Pool's breach of s. 86(c).]

The judgment of the court was delivered by

DICKSON J.: — This case raises the difficult issue of the relation of a breach of a statutory duty to a civil cause of action. Where "A" has breached a statutory duty causing injury to "B", does "B" have a civil cause of action against "A"? If so, is "A's" liability absolute, in the sense that it exists independently of fault, or is "A" free from liability if the failure to perform the duty is through no fault of his?

. . .

III

STATUTORY BREACH GIVING RISE TO A CIVIL CAUSE OF ACTION

(a) *General*

The uncertainty and confusion in relation between breach of statute and a civil cause of action for damages arising from the breach is of long standing. The commentators have little but harsh words for the unhappy state of affairs, but arriving at a solution, from the disarray of cases, is extraordinarily difficult. It is doubtful that any general principle or rationale can be found in the authorities to resolve all of the issues or even those which are transcendent.

There does seem to be general agreement that the breach of a statutory provision which causes damage to an individual should in some way be pertinent to recovery of compensation for the damage. Two very different forces, however, have been acting in opposite directions. In the United States the civil consequences of breach of statute have been subsumed in the law of negligence. On the other hand, we have witnessed in England the painful emergence of a new nominate tort of statutory breach. . . . It is now imperative for this court to choose.

(b) *The English position*

In 1948 in the case of *London Passenger Transport Board v. Upson*, [1949] A.C. 155. . ., the House of Lords affirmed the existence of a tort of statutory breach distinct from any issue of negligence. The statute prescribes the duty owed to the plaintiff who need only show (i) breach of the statute, and (ii) damage caused by the breach.

Legitimacy for this civil action for breach of statute has been sought in the *Statute of Westminster II*, 1285, 9 Edw. I, c. 50, which provided for a private remedy by action on the case to those affected by the breach of statutory duties. However, "old though it may be, the action upon the statute has rarely been the subject of careful scrutiny in English law, and its precise judicial character remains a thing of some obscurity": Fricke, "The Juridical Nature of the Action upon the Statute", 76 L.Q.R. 240 (1960). As the gap widened between "public" and "private" law with the passing centuries this broad general right of action, enigmatic as it was, became hedged. Where a public law penalty was provided for in the statute a private civil cause of action would not automatically arise. The oft-quoted formulation of this principle was found in *Doe d. Rochester v. Bridges* (1831), 1 B. & Ad. 847 at p. 857, 109 E.R. 1001:

> And where an Act creates an obligation, and enforces the performance in a specified manner, we take it to be a general rule that performance cannot be enforced in any other manner.

Although taken out of context, the dictum served the purpose of limiting the multiplication of suits of dubious value. "With the vast increase in legislative activity of modern times, if the old rule were still law it might lead to unjust, not to say absurd, results in creating liabilities wider than the legislature can possibly have intended" (Winfield & Jolowicz, *Tort*, 11th ed. (1979), at p. 154). By the end of the 19th century, however, the civil action on the statute began to revive as a response to industrial safety legislation. The statement of the doctrine propounded in *Doe d. Rochester v. Bridges* did not enjoy a long period of acceptance. *Couch v. Steel* (1854), 3 El. & Bl. 402, 118 E.R. 1193, marked the beginning of a new era of construction. Lord Campbell C.J., relying on statements in Comyn's Digest, concluded that the injured party has a common law right to maintain an action for special damage arising from the breach of a public duty. *Couch v. Steel* was questioned some twenty years later in *Atkinson v. Newcastle & Gateshead Waterworks Co.* (1877), 2 Ex. D. 441. Lord Cairns L.C., dealing with the matter apart from authority, concluded that the private remedy had been excluded. He expressed "grave doubts" whether the authorities cited by Lord Campbell in *Couch v. Steel* justified the broad general rule there laid down. Lord Cockburn C.J. agreed that the correctness of *Couch v. Steel* was "open to grave doubts", while Brett L.J. entertained the "strongest doubt" as to the correctness of the broad general rule enunciated in *Couch v. Steel.*

As Street puts it "The effect of the leading cases in the nineteenth century (which remain important authorities) however, was to make the cause of action rest on proof that the legislature intended that violation of the right or interest conferred by the statute was to be treated as tortious" (Street, *Law of Torts*, 2nd ed., p. 273). Fricke pointed out (76 L.Q.R., at p. 260) that that doctrine leads to many difficulties. In the first place it is not clear what the *prima facie* rule or presumption should be. Some of the cases suggest that *prima facie* an action is given by the statement of a statutory duty, and that it exists unless it can be said to be taken away by any provisions to be found in the Act. Other authorities suggest the *prima facie* rule is that the specific statement of a certain manner of enforcement excluded any other means of enforcement. Sometimes the courts jump one way, sometimes the other. Fricke concludes (pp. 263-4) that as a matter of pure statutory construction the law went wrong with the decision in 1854 in *Couch v. Steel*: "If one is concerned with the intrinsic question of interpreting the legislative will as reflected within the four corners of a document which made express provision of a fine, but makes no mention of a civil remedy, one is compelled to the conclusion that a civil remedy was not intended."

. . .

This fragmentation of approach has given rise to some theoretical, and some not-so-theoretical, difficulties. The pretence of seeking what has been called a "will o' the wisp", a non-existent intention of Parliament to create a civil cause of action, has been harshly criticized. It is capricious and arbitrary, "judicial legislation" at its very worst.

> Not only does it involve an unnecessary fiction, but it may lead to decisions being made on the basis of insignificant details of phraseology instead of matters of substance. If the question whether a person injured by breach of a statutory obligation is to have a

> right of action for damages is in truth a question to be decided by the court, let it be acknowledged as such and some useful principles of law developed.

Winfield & Jolowicz, *supra*, at p. 159. It is a "bare faced fiction" at odds with accepted canons of statutory interpretation: "the legislature's silence on the question of civil liability rather points to the conclusion that it either did not have it in mind or deliberately omitted to provide for it" (Fleming, *The Law of Torts*, 5th ed. (1977), at p. 123). Glanville Williams is now of the opinion that the "irresolute course" of the judicial decisions "reflect no credit on our jurisprudence" and with respect, I agree. He writes:

> The failure of the judges to develop a governing attitude means that it is almost impossible to predict, outside the decided authorities, when the courts will regard a civil duty as impliedly created. In effect the judge can do what he likes, and then select one of the conflicting principles stated by his predecessors in order to justify his decision.

"The Effect of Penal Legislation in the Law of Tort", *supra*, at p. 246. . ..

The door to a civil cause of action arising from breach of statute had swung closed at the beginning of the 19th century with the proliferation of written legislation and swung open again, for reasons of policy and convenience, to accommodate the rising incidence of industrial accidents at the end of the 19th century. But the proposition that every statutory breach gave rise to a private right of action was still untenable, as it is today. The courts looked for a screening mechanism which would determine the cases to which an action should be limited.

Various presumptions or guidelines sprang up. "Thus, it has often been tediously repeated that the crucial test is whether the duty created by the statute is owed primarily to the State, and only incidentally to the individual, or vice versa" (Fleming, *supra*, at p. 125). A duty to all the public (ratepayers, for example) does not give rise to a private cause of action whereas a duty to an individual (an injured worker, for example) may. The purpose of the statute must be the protection of a certain "class" of individuals of whom the plaintiff is one and the injury suffered must be of a kind which it was the object of the legislation to prevent. Both requirements have, in the past, been fairly narrowly construed and fairly heavily criticized.

Although "[i]t is doubtful, indeed, if any general principle can be found to explain all the cases on the subject" (*Salmond on Torts*, 7th ed. (1977), at p. 243) several justifications are given for the tort of statutory breach. It provides fixed standards of negligence and replaces the judgment of amateurs (the jury) with that of professionals in highly technical areas. In effect, it provides for absolute liability in fields where this has been found desirable such as industrial safety. Laudable as these effects are, the state of the law remains extremely unsatisfactory.

. . .

(c) *The American position*

Professor Fleming prefers the American approach which has assimilated civil responsibility for statutory breach into the general law of negligence (*The Law of Torts*, *supra*, at p. 124):

> Intellectually more acceptable, because less arcane, is the prevailing American theory which frankly disclaims that the civil action is in any sure sense a creature of the statute, for the simple enough reason that the statute just does not contemplate, much less

> provide, a civil remedy. Any recovery of damages for injury due to its violation must, therefore, rest on common law principles. But though the penal statute does not create civil liability the court may think it proper to adopt the legislative formulation of a specific standard in place of the unformulated standard of reasonable conduct, in much the same manner as when it rules peremtorily [*sic*] that certain acts or omissions constitute negligence of the law.

There are, however, differing views of the effect of this assimilation: at one end of the spectrum, breach of a statutory duty may constitute negligence *per se* or, at the other, it may merely be evidence of negligence.

. . .

The majority view in the United States has been that statutory breach constitutes negligence *per se* — in certain circumstances (Prosser, *The Law of Torts, supra*, at p. 200):

> Once the statute is determined to be applicable — which is to say, once it is interpreted as designed to protect the class of persons in which the plaintiff is included, against the risk of the type of harm which had in fact occurred as a result of its violation — the great majority of the courts hold that an unexcused violation is conclusive on the issue of negligence, and that the court must so direct the jury. The standard of conduct is taken over by the court from that fixed by the legislature, and "jurors have no dispensing power by which to relax it", except in so far as the court may recognize the possibility of a valid excuse for disobedience of the law. This usually is expressed by saying that the unexcused violation is negligence "per se", or in itself. The effect of such a rule is to stamp the defendant's conduct as negligence, with all of the effects of common law negligence, but with no greater effect.

. . .

The American courts have not broken away from a consideration of the purpose or intent of the legislature; the *Restatement, Torts, Second*, sets out the circumstances in which the court may adopt a legislative enactment as embodying the standard of care applicable in the circumstances:

> 286. When Standards of Conduct Defined by Legislation or Regulations Will be Adopted
> The court may adopt as the standard of conduct of a reasonable man the requirements of a legislative enactment or an administrative regulation whose purpose is found to be exclusively or in part
>
> (a) to protect a class of persons which includes the one whose interest is invaded, and
> (b) to protect the particular interest which is invaded, and
> (c) to protect that interest against the kind of harm which has resulted, and
> (d) to protect that interest the particular hazard from which the harm results.

The so-called "minority view" in the United States considers breach of a statute to be merely evidence of negligence. There are, however, varying degrees of evidence. Statutory breach may be considered totally irrelevant, merely relevant, or *prima facie* evidence of negligence having the effect of reversing the onus of proof . . . .

The major criticism of the negligence *per se* approach has been the inflexible application of the legislature's criminal standard of conduct to a civil case. I agree with this criticism. The defendant in a civil case does not benefit from the technical defences or protection offered by the criminal law; the civil consequences may easily outweigh any penal consequences attaching to the breach of statute; and finally the purposes served by the imposition of criminal as opposed to civil liability are radically different. The compensatory aspect of tort liability has won out over the deterrent and punitive aspect; the perceptible evolution in the use of civil liability as a mechanism of loss shifting to that of loss distribution has only accentuated this change. And so "[t]he doctrine of negligence *per se* is, therefore, not fitted for relentless use, nor is it so used" (Morris, "The Relation of Criminal Statutes to Tort Liability", 46 Harv. L.R. 453 (1932-33), at p. 460). Thus the guidelines in the *Restatement, Torts, Second.*

(d) *The Canadian position*

Professor Linden has said that the "Canadian courts appear to oscillate between the English and American positions without even recognizing this fact": "Comment, *Sterling Trusts Corporation v. Postma*", 45 Can. Bar Rev. 121 (1967), at p. 126. The most widely used approach, however, has been that stated in *Sterling Trusts Corp. v. Postma, supra.* The breach of a statutory provision is "*prima facie* evidence of negligence". There is some difficulty in the terminology used. "*Prima facie* evidence of negligence" in the *Sterling Trusts* case is used seemingly interchangeably with the expression "*prima facie* liable". In a later case in the Ontario Court of Appeal, *Queensway Tank Lines Ltd. v. Moise* (1969), 9 D.L.R. (3d) 30. . ., MacKay J.A. assumes *prima facie* evidence of negligence to be a presumption of negligence with concomitant shift in the onus of proof to the defendant.

The use of breach of statute as evidence of negligence as opposed to recognition of a nominate tort of statutory breach is, as Professor Fleming has put it, more intellectually acceptable. It avoids, to a certain extent, the fictitious hunt for legislative intent to create a civil cause of action which has been so criticized in England. It also avoids the inflexible application of the legislature's criminal standard of conduct to a civil case. Glanville Williams is of the opinion, with which I am in agreement, that where there is no duty of care at common law, breach of non-industrial penal legislation should not affect civil liability unless the statute provides for it. As I have indicated above, industrial legislation historically has enjoyed special consideration. Recognition of the doctrine of absolute liability under some industrial statutes does not justify extension of such doctrine to other fields, particularly when one considers the jejune reasoning supporting the juristic invention.

. . .

Tort law itself has undergone a major transformation in this century with nominate torts being eclipsed by negligence, the closest the common law has come to a general theory of civil responsibility. The concept of duty of care, embodied in the neighbour principle has expanded into areas hitherto untouched by tort law.

One of the main reasons for shifting a loss to a defendant is that he has been at fault, that he has done some act which should be discouraged. There is then good reason for taking money from the defendant as well as a reason for giving it to the plaintiff who has suffered from the fault of the defendant. But there seems little in the way of defensible policy for holding a defendant who breached a statutory duty unwittingly to be negligent and obligated to pay even though not at fault. The legislature has imposed a penalty on a strictly admonitory basis and there seems little justification to add civil liability when such liability would tend to produce liability without fault. The legislature has determined the proper penalty for the defendant's wrong but if tort admonition of liability without fault is to be added, the financial consequences will be measured, not by the amount of the penalty, but by the amount of money which is required to compensate the plaintiff. Minimum fault may subject the defendant to heavy liability. Inconsequential violations should not subject the violator to any civil liability at all but should be left to the criminal courts for enforcement of a fine.

In this case the Board contends that the duty imposed by the Act is absolute, that is to say, the Pool is liable, even in absence of fault, and all that is requisite to prove a breach of duty is to show that the requirements of the statute have not, in fact, been complied with; it is not necessary to show how the failure to comply arose or that the Pool was guilty of any failure to take reasonable care to comply.

The tendency of the law of recent times is to ameliorate the rigours of absolute rules and absolute duty in the sense indicated, as contrary to natural justice. "Sound policy lets losses lie where they fall except where a special reason can be shown for interference": Holmes, *The Common Law*, p. 50. In the case at bar the evidence is that substantially all of the grain entering the terminal of the Pool at Thunder Bay came from agents of the Board. The imposition of heavy financial burden as in this case without fault on the part of the Pool does not incline one to interfere. It is better that the loss lies where it falls, upon the Board.

For all of the above reasons I would be adverse to the recognition in Canada of a nominate tort of statutory breach. Breach of statute, where it has an effect upon civil liability, should be considered in the context of the general law of negligence. Negligence and its common law duty of care have become pervasive enough to serve the purpose invoked for the existence of the action for statutory breach.

It must not be forgotten that the other elements of tortious responsibility equally apply to situations involving statutory breach, *i.e.*, principles of causation and damages. To be relevant at all, the statutory breach must have caused the damage of which the plaintiff complains. Should this be so, the violation of the statute should be evidence of negligence on the part of the defendant.

. . .

In sum I conclude that:

1. Civil consequences of breach of statute should be subsumed in the law of negligence.
2. The notion of a nominate tort of statutory breach giving a right to recovery merely on proof of breach and damages should be rejected, as should the view that unexcused breach constitutes negligence *per se* giving rise to absolute liability.
3. Proof of statutory breach, causative of damages, may be evidence of negligence.
4. The statutory formulation of the duty may afford a specific, and useful, standard of reasonable conduct.
5. In the case at bar negligence is neither pleaded nor proven. The action must fail.

I would dismiss the appeal with costs.

NOTES AND QUESTIONS

1. What is the English position on the use of statutes in tort actions? What criticisms does Dickson J. make of that case law? Do you agree with his criticisms? For a review of the English law, see Stanton, *Breach of Statutory Duty in Tort* (1986); Heuston & Buckley, *Salmond and Heuston on the Law of Torts*, 21st ed. (1996) at 247-57; Rogers, *Winfield and Jolowicz on Tort*, 17th ed. (2006) at 337-58; and Buckley, "Liability in Tort for Breach of Statutory Duty" (1984) 100 L.Q.R. 204.

2. What is the majority position in the United States and how has it been modified by the *Restatement (Second) of Torts* (1965) at §288B and §286? What is the American minority position? Which position is preferable and which one does Dickson J. favour?

3. Explain the Canadian approach to the use of statutes prior to *Sask. Wheat Pool.* Summarize the principles of law that now govern the use of statutes based on *Sask. Wheat Pool.* Has Dickson J. adequately dealt with the problems in the English, American, and prior Canadian positions?

4. Dickson J. indicated that industrial safety statutes have been treated differently than other types of legislation. What is the rationale for this practice? What principles of law now govern the use of industrial safety statutes in Canadian tort actions?

5. Given the Supreme Court of Canada's rejection of implied statutory causes of action, what impact should strict liability in a regulatory statute have on a common law cause of action?

6. For a more detailed discussion of *Sask. Wheat Pool*, see Alexander, "Legislation and Civil Liability: Public Policy and 'Equity of the Statute' " (1984) 30 McGill L.J. 1; Fridman, "Civil Liability for Criminal Conduct" (1984) 16 Ottawa L. Rev. 34; Brudner, "Tort — Civil Liability For Breach of Statutory Duty Abolished" (1984) 62 Can. Bar Rev. 668; and Rogers, "Rusty Beetles in the Elevator" [1984] C.L.J. 23.

HORSLEY v. MACLAREN
(1972), 22 D.L.R. (3d) 545 (S.C.C.)

[A lengthy extract of this case was reproduced in Chapter 11. In the following passage, Laskin J., dissenting, briefly discusses the relationship between the common law duty of care and the *Canada Shipping Act*, R.S.C. 1952, c. 29, a statute that governs commercial shipping. More specifically, he examines the basis upon which the operator of a non-commercial passenger boat owes a duty to rescue to an invited guest who has fallen overboard through no fault of the operator.]

LASKIN J.: . . . I do not rest the duty to which I would hold MacLaren in this case on s. 526(1) of the *Canada Shipping Act*, even assuming that its terms are broad enough to embrace the facts herein. That provision, a penal one, is as follows:

> 526(1) The master or person in charge of a vessel shall, so far as he can do so without serious danger to his own vessel, her crew and passengers, if any, render assistance to

> every person, even if that person be a subject of a foreign state at war with Her Majesty, who is found at sea and in danger of being lost, and if he fails to do so he is liable to a fine not exceeding one thousand dollars.

I do not find it necessary in this case to consider whether s. 526(1), taken alone, entails civil consequences for failure to perform a statutory duty; or, even, whether it fixes a standard of conduct upon which the common law may operate to found liability. There is an independent basis for a common law duty of care in the relationship of carrier to passenger, but the legislative declaration of policy in s. 526(1) is a fortifying element in the recognition of that duty, being in harmony with it in a comparable situation.

. . .

[Ritchie J., who rendered the majority judgment, also held that the defendant was under a common law duty to rescue, but he stated that it was "in no way dependent upon the provisions of s. 526(1)." Unlike Laskin J., the majority concluded that the defendant had not breached the common law standard of care.]

NOTES AND QUESTIONS

1. Do you think that Laskin J. would have resolved the duty issue differently in the absence of the statutory duty? See also *Jordan House Ltd. v. Menow* (1973), 38 D.L.R. (3d) 105 (S.C.C.); and *O'Rourke v. Schacht* (1974), 55 D.L.R. (3d) 96 (S.C.C.).

2. In *Bhadauria v. Board of Governors of Seneca College* (1979), 105 D.L.R. (3d) 707 (Ont. C.A.), Wilson J.A. stated that the Ontario *Human Rights Code*, R.S.O. 1990, c. H.19, expressed "the public policy of this Province respecting fundamental human rights." She then referred to *Ashby v. White* (1703), 92 E.R. 126 (K.B.) in support of the proposition that if there is a right, there must be a remedy. She recognized a new common law tort of discrimination on that basis. The Supreme Court of Canada rejected her approach, distinguishing *Ashby* as a case that granted a remedy for a pre-existing right. The court concluded that the *Human Rights Code*'s remedial provisions were the only remedy available to the plaintiff: *Bhadauria v. Board of Governors of Seneca College* (1981), 124 D.L.R. (3d) 193 (S.C.C.). Is the Supreme Court of Canada's decision in *Bhadauria* consistent with its decision in *Sask. Wheat Pool*?

RINTOUL v. X-RAY AND RADIUM INDUST.

[1956] S.C.R. 674

[A claim was made in connection with a motor vehicle collision. The defendant attempted to escape liability by arguing that his foot brake had failed. One of the issues before the court was whether the defendant could have avoided the accident by applying his hand brake. The judgment of the court was delivered by Cartwright J.]

. . .

Accepting the evidence of Ouellette as to the speed and position of his car at the instant he actually applied the hand brakes, it is obvious that if they had been in the state of efficiency prescribed by the regulations he could have stopped his car before the collision occurred, even if the car had not been, as it was, proceeding uphill. It is unnecessary to consider whether the effect of the statute and regulations was to cast an absolute duty on the respondents to have the hand brakes in the prescribed condition, for, at the least, the unexplained failure to comply with the regulation was evidence of a breach of the common law duty to take reasonable care to have the motor vehicle fit for the road. Apart from statute there must obviously be a common law duty on anyone who drives a motor vehicle on a highway to have it equipped with brakes, and the regulations may well be taken as the expression of the Legislature's view as to what constitutes a reasonable braking system.

In my opinion, on the evidence the respondents have not only failed to show that the alleged failure of the service brakes was inevitable, they have also failed to show that after such failure occurred Ouellette could not by the exercise of reasonable care have avoided the collision. It follows that the appeal of the plaintiff should be allowed.

QUESTIONS

1. How does Cartwright J.'s use of the statute in *Rintoul* differ from Laskin J.'s use of the statute in *Horsley*?

2. Could the defendant in *Rintoul* have succeeded by proving that he had a reasonable braking system on his car, despite the fact that the system did not comply with the legislative requirements?

3. What advantage does the legislature have over the court in defining the standard of reasonable care?

GALASKE v. O'DONNELL

[1994] 1 S.C.R. 670

[The eight-year-old plaintiff and his father were passengers in a truck being driven by the defendant. Because he assumed that the plaintiff's father was responsible for the boy's safety, the defendant did not take steps to ensure that the plaintiff was wearing a seat belt.

Cory J. found the existence of a duty of care between the parties. He then explained that damages arising from motor vehicle accidents may be reduced on the basis of contributory negligence if the relevant injuries were attributable not only to the defendant's carelessness but also to the claimant's failure to wear a seat belt. Cory J. then turned to the question of the defendant's standard of care on the facts before him.]

CORY J.: . . . There is therefore a duty of care owed by an occupant of a car to wear a seat belt. This duty is based upon the sensible recognition of the safety provided by seatbelts and the foreseeability of harm resulting from the failure to wear them. What then of children in a car? Children under 16, although they may contest it, do require guidance and direction from parents and older persons. This has always been recognized by society. That guidance and protection must extend to ensuring that those under 16 properly wear their seatbelts. To the question of who should assume that duty, the answer must be that there may be two or more people who bear that responsibility. However, one of those responsible must always be the driver of the car.

A driver taking children as passengers must accept some responsibility for the safety of those children. The driving of a motor vehicle is neither a God-given nor a constitutional right. It is a licensed activity that is subject to a number of conditions, including the demonstration of a minimum standard of skill and knowledge pertaining to driving. Obligations and responsibilities flow from the right to drive. Those responsibilities must include some regard for the safety of young passengers. Children, as a result of their immaturity, may be unable to properly consider and provide for their own safety. The driver must take reasonable steps to see that young passengers wear their seatbelts. This is so since it is foreseeable that harm can result from the failure to wear a seatbelt, and since frequently, a child will, for any number of reasons, fail to secure the seatbelt.

The driver of a car is in a position of control. The control may not be quite as great as that of the master of a vessel or the pilot of an aircraft. Nevertheless it exists. Coexistent with the right to drive and control a car is the responsibility of the driver to take reasonable steps to provide for the safety of passengers. Those reasonable steps must include not only the duty to drive carefully but also to see that seatbelts are worn by young passengers who may not be responsible for ensuring their own safety.

In my view, quite apart from any statutory provisions, drivers must accept the responsibility of taking all reasonable steps to ensure that passengers under 16 years of age are in fact wearing their seat-belts. The general public knowledge of the vital importance of seat-belts as a safety factor requires a driver to ensure that young people make use of them. . . . The statutory provisions pertaining to seat-belts must now be considered.

The effect of the Motor Vehicle Act

Section 217(6) of the *Motor Vehicle Act* reads as follows:

> A person shall not drive on a highway a motor vehicle in which there is a passenger who has attained age 6 but is under age 16 and who occupies a seating position for which a seat belt assembly is provided unless that passenger is wearing the complete seat belt assembly in a properly adjusted and securely fastened manner.

In *The Queen in Right of Canada v. Saskatchewan Wheat Pool, supra*, the issue was whether a breach of the *Canada Grain Act*, S.C. 1970-71-72, c. 7, by delivery of infested grain out of a grain elevator, conferred upon the Canadian Wheat Board a civil right of action against the Saskatchewan Wheat Pool for damages. No allegation of negligence at common law was put forward. The notion of a nominate tort of statutory breach giving rise to recovery simply on proof of breach of the statute was rejected. So too was the argument that an unexcused breach of a statute constituted negligence *per se* which would lead to an automatic finding of liability. The Court, in the clear and convincing reasons delivered by Dickson J. (as he then was), took the position that proof of a statutory breach which causes damages *may* be evidence of negligence. Further, it was held that the statutory formulation of the duty *may*, but not necessarily will, afford a specific or useful standard of reasonable conduct.

It follows that the statutory requirement pertaining to seatbelts is subsumed in the general law of negligence. However, the statute can, I think, be taken as a public indication that the failure of a driver to ensure that children in the vehicle are wearing seatbelts constitutes unreasonable conduct. Further, it may be taken as indicating that such a failure on the part of the driver demonstrates conduct which falls below the standard required by the community and is thus negligent. In this case, the legislation is simply another factor which can be taken into account by the court in the course of determining whether the failure to ensure children in the car are wearing seatbelts constituted negligent behaviour on the part of a driver.

It is clear that the breach of a statutory provision is not conclusive of liability. Yet the existence of the section does provide further support for finding that a duty of care rests on the driver to take all reasonable steps to see that seat-belts are worn by children. The statute reflects the public importance placed on safety measures and a societal concern for promoting the safety of children. It is, as well, a public recognition that children often require the help and supervision of adults, particularly in ensuring that when they are passengers in a vehicle, they are made reasonably safe.

Is the Driver's Duty of Care Negated by the Presence of a Parent?

The duty of a driver to ensure that young passengers wear their seatbelts is well established. It then must be asked whether the presence of a parent in the car negates this duty of care owed by the driver. The trial judge and the Court of Appeal took the position that the presence of the parent in the car removed or terminated the duty of care owed by the driver. In my view, . . . there may be a joint responsibility or duty of care resting upon both a parent and a third party. The presence of a parent in the car may mean that the responsibility is shared but it cannot negate the duty owed by the driver to the passenger under the age of 16.

The driver of a car owes a duty of care to a child who is a passenger. For example, the driver must obey the rules of the road and drive carefully whether a parent is present or not. That duty of care is owed and continues to be owed by a driver to all child passengers, irrespective of their parents' presence. The relationship between driver and passenger is such that the driver's negligent actions or negligent failure to act can lead to injuries to the passengers. Further, it is well established and clearly foresee able that harm may well result from the failure to wear a seatbelt just as much as it may result from negligent driving.

Again, as I have said, the driver of a car is in a position of control. The driver's control remains even in the presence of a child passenger's parent. The responsibility of the driver to take reasonable steps to provide for the safety of passengers flows, in part, from this control and it includes not only a duty to drive carefully but also to take reasonable steps to ensure that seatbelts are worn by young passengers who may not be able to ensure their own safety.

In my view, there is a duty of care resting upon a driver of a motor vehicle to ensure that the seatbelts of young passengers are in place. That duty exists whether or not a parent of the child is in the car. The presence of the parent does no more than indicate that the duty of care or responsibility towards the child may be shared by both the parent and the driver. . . .

The trial judge and the Court of Appeal were in error in failing to recognize that the duty of care owed by the driver of the motor vehicle to young passengers continued to exist despite the presence of a parent in the vehicle. That is an error of law that can and should be corrected by an appellate court.

Standard of Care or the Extent of the Duty Owed by the Driver

The definition of the standard of care is a mixed question of law and fact. It will usually be for the trial judge to determine, in light of the circumstances of the case, what would constitute reasonable conduct on the part of the legendary reasonable man placed in the same circumstances. In some situations a simple reminder may suffice while in others, for example when a very young child is the passenger, the driver may have to put the seatbelt on the child himself. In this case, however, the driver took no steps whatsoever to ensure that the child passenger wore a seatbelt. It follows that the trial judge's decision on the issue amounted to a finding that there was no duty at all resting upon the driver. This was an error of law.

The extent of the duty owed by the driver of a vehicle to a child passenger when a parent is present will undoubtedly vary with the circumstances. Although the duty will always exist, the extent of it will vary infinitely. For example, a 17-year-old driving a car with an eight-year-old and his father, who is an old friend of the family, may well owe a much smaller duty of care to the child than the father. On the other hand, the driver of a motor vehicle who is driving home a mother who is an employee and her child may have a significantly higher degree of responsibility for the child. The difference in degree of responsibility will vary widely, depending on the circumstances of each case. That degree of responsibility will have to be determined in this case.

[A majority of the Supreme Court of Canada held that the defendant was liable for the plaintiff's injuries.]

RYAN v. VICTORIA (CITY)

(1999), 168 D.L.R. (4th) 513 (S.C.C.)

[The plaintiff was injured after the front wheel of his motorcycle became caught in a "flangeway" that comprised part of a railway track that ran through the city's street. The plaintiff alleged that the railway was negligent in failing to take precautions against such an occurrence. The defendant resisted liability by arguing that it had complied with all of the relevant statutory regulations.

A duty of care was found to exist between the parties. For present purposes, the crucial question was whether the defendant had met its standard of care.]

MAJOR J.: . . .

Standard of Care

Conduct is negligent if it creates an objectively unreasonable risk of harm. To avoid liability, a person must exercise the standard of care that would be expected of an ordinary, reasonable and prudent person in the same circumstances. The measure of what is reasonable depends on the facts of each case, including the likelihood of a known or foreseeable harm, the gravity of that harm, and the burden or cost which would be incurred to prevent the injury. In addition, one may look to external indicators of reasonable conduct, such as custom, industry practice, and statutory or regulatory standards.

Legislative standards are relevant to the common law standard of care, but the two are not necessarily co-extensive. The fact that a statute prescribes or prohibits certain activities may constitute evidence of reasonable conduct in a given situation, but it does not extinguish the underlying obligation of reasonableness. . . . By the same token, mere compliance with a statute does not, in and of itself, preclude a finding of civil liability. . . . Statutory standards can, however, be highly relevant to the assessment of reasonable conduct in a particular case, and in fact may render reasonable an act or omission which would otherwise appear to be negligent. This allows courts to consider the legislative framework in which people and companies must operate, while at the same time recognizing that one cannot avoid the underlying obligation of reasonable care simply by discharging statutory duties.

. . .

Compliance with a statutory standard of care does not abrogate or supersede the obligation to comply with the common law standard of care. The requirements are concurrent, and each carries its own penalty for breach. However, in appropriate circumstances, compliance with statutory standards may entirely satisfy the common law standard of care and thus absolve a defendant of liability in negligence. . ..

This approach is consistent with the holding in *Canadian National Railway Co. v. Vincent, [1979] 1 S.C.R. 364, 93 D.L.R. (3d) 663.* Although *Vincent* arose in the context of Quebec civil law, the reasoning of Pratte J. in that case is instructive, particularly since the common law standard of care is analogous to the requirement of reasonable prudence under the *Civil Code*. The facts in *Vincent* were straightforward. A child was struck by a train while riding her bicycle on a railway crossing in a densely populated area. It was undisputed that the railway had complied with all relevant safety measures prescribed by statute and regulations. The issue was whether the railways should have taken additional precautions in the circumstances of the case. Pratte J. stated at pp. 372-73:

> It must be said at the outset that, under the verdict, appellant is not held liable by reason of any breach of the *Railway Act* . . . or of the regulations of the Canadian Transport Commission. The issue is rather whether appellant can be found guilty of negligence under . . . [the *Civil Code*] although it complied with all the special statutory and regulatory provisions to which it is subject. The special provisions governing appellant certainly do not have the effect of exempting it from the ordinary law of civil liability. . .
> .

Additional support for this view can be found in s. 367(4) of the *Railway Act* which provides:

> 367(4) No inspection under or by the authority of this Act . . . and nothing in this Act . . . and nothing done, ordered, directed, required or provided for, or omitted to be done . . . under or by virtue of this Act . . . shall, except in so far as a compliance with the Act in question or with the order, direction, requirement or provision constitutes a justification for what would otherwise be wrongful, relieve . . . any company of or from, or in any way diminish or affect, any liability or responsibility resting on it by law . . . for anything done or omitted to be done by that company, or for any wrongful act, negligence or default, misfeasance, malfeasance or nonfeasance of that company.

Section 367(4) confirms that compliance with statutory standards does not normally exhaust a railway's obligations under principles of negligence. . . . A railway is presumptively bound by the common law, subject only to those situations where compliance with the statute or regulations provides "a justification for what would otherwise be wrongful". Like any exculpatory provision limiting common law rights, that passage should be narrowly construed. In the absence of a clear indication to the contrary, compliance with statutory standards should not be viewed as excusing a railway's obligation to take whatever precautions are reasonably required in the circumstances.

The weight to be accorded to statutory compliance in the overall assessment of reasonableness depends on the nature of the statute and the circumstances of the case. It should be determined whether the legislative standards are necessarily applicable to the facts of the case. Statutory compliance will have more relevance in "ordinary" cases — i.e. cases clearly within the intended scope of the statute—than in cases involving special or unusual circumstances. . . . It should also be determined whether the legislative standards are specific or general, and whether they allow for discretion in the manner of performance. It is a well-established principle that an action will lie against any party, public or private, "for doing that which the legislature has authorized, if it be done negligently." . . . It follows that a party acting under statutory authority must still take such precautions as are reasonable within the range of that authority to minimize the risks which may result from its actions. See *Tock*, supra (applying similar principles in the nuisance context).

Where a statute authorizes certain activities and strictly defines the manner of performance and the precautions to be taken, it is more likely to be found that compliance with the statute constitutes reasonable care and that no additional measures are required. By contrast, where a statute is general or permits discretion as to the manner of performance, or where unusual circumstances exist which are not clearly within the scope of the statute, mere compliance is unlikely to exhaust the standard of care. This approach strikes an appropriate balance among several important policies, including deference to legislative determinations on matters of railway safety, security for railways which comply with prescribed standards, and protection for those who may be injured as a result of unreasonable choices made by railways in the exercise of official authority.

Application to the Case at Bar

. . .

The standard of care required of the Railways was that of a prudent and reasonable person in the circumstances, having regard to all relevant factors including applicable statutes and regulations. It is undisputed that the Railways complied with certain safety standards prescribed in regulations and Board orders. The question is whether such compliance satisfied the requirement of objective reasonableness in this case and absolved the Railways of liability for the appellant's injury.

At the outset, it should be noted that the location of the Store Street tracks does not, by itself, give rise to liability. The construction of a branch line on an urban street inevitably creates a risk to the public. When a party is specifically authorized to create that risk, compliance with such authority cannot be negligent. There is negligence only if, in the performance of the authorized activity, the party creates a risk that is objectively unreasonable in the circumstances. The construction of the Store Street tracks was authorized by the Board in 1908 on the basis of a detailed plan and profile, and the location of the tracks was reapproved in 1927. Pursuant to s. 223 of the 1906 *Railway Act*, those orders could not have issued unless the Board was "satisfied that the branch line [was] necessary in the public interest or for the purpose of giving increased facilities to business". It cannot be said that it was unreasonable for the Railways to comply with those orders by constructing the tracks in the manner authorized.

The real issue is whether the Railways were negligent with respect to the dimensions of the flangeways on Store Street. In particular, it must be determined whether the Railways acted unreasonably by enlarging the flangeways to a width of nearly four inches in 1982, and by failing to install flange fillers at any time prior to the appellant's accident. This issue has to do with the minimization of risk, and is separate from the Railways' undisputed duty to warn the public of the inevitable hazard created by the tracks.

. . .

(iii) Application of the Common Law Standard of Care

The trial judge correctly held that the Railways were subject to the common law standard of care. In applying that standard, he noted that the Railways have been aware of the risks associated with the flangeways on Store Street for some time. In particular, he found that the Railways knew or should have known of at least three other accidents between 1982 and 1986 which involved the flangeways and two-wheeled vehicles. On the basis of all the evidence adduced, he concluded as follows (at pp. 197-98):

> In the case at bar, the defendant Railways ought to have built the flangeways either at the minimum allowable width or with some form of flange filler. It was not enough to proceed on the basis that so long as their flangeways were durable and did not exceed the maximum regulatory standards . . . their neighbours must endure the consequent injuries arising from their "preferred" construction choice.
>
> . . .
>
> Because of the hazard created and the remedial measures available to the defendant Railways, I find the defendant Railways were obliged to take precautions over and above those mandated by statute and regulation. This they failed to do.
> In the result, I find that the defendant Railways were negligent.

The trial judge's conclusion is consistent with the principles stated above. It was a proper exercise of his role as the finder of fact, and it should not have been disturbed by the Court of Appeal. Accordingly, the appeal is allowed with respect to the claim of negligence against the Railways.

[The court ultimately held that the defendant railway *prima facie* was liable for the plaintiff's injuries, and that damages should not be reduced or denied on the basis of any defence (*e.g.* contributory negligence).]

NOTES AND QUESTIONS

1. In what sense was compliance or non-compliance with a statutory obligation relevant in *Galaske* and in *Ryan*?

2. For other applications of the same principle, see for example *School Div. of Assiniboine South (No. 3) v. Hoffer* (1971), 21 D.L.R. (3d) 608 (Man. C.A.), aff'd (1973), 40 D.L.R. (3d) 480 (S.C.C.); and *Rinas v. Regina (City)* (1983), 26 Sask. R. 132 (Q.B.).

3. Leaving aside precedent, what impact *should* the breach of a statutory provision have in a common law action?

4. In *Varcoe v. Sterling* (1992), 7 O.R. (3d) 204 (Gen. Div.), aff'd (1992), 10 O.R. (3d) 574 (C.A.), an experienced investor lost a very large amount of money in the highly speculative futures market. The investor, who had not relied on his broker and who made

all of his own decisions, sued the broker for his losses. The court held the broker liable in negligence under common law principles, referring at length to the broker's violation of both statutory regulations and industry practice concerning margin calls, trading limits and the transfer of funds between the investor's various stock accounts.

5. Adherence to the common law duty and standard is not a defence to a statutory cause of action. For example, in *London Passenger Transport Board v. Upson*, [1949] A.C. 155 (H.L.), the defendant bus driver struck a pedestrian in a crosswalk. Lord Porter expressly held that the defendant had taken all reasonable care. Nevertheless, the defendant was liable for breach of a statutory provision which required a driver who was unable to see if a crosswalk was clear to proceed at a speed that would enable the vehicle to be stopped before entering it.

6. Some statutes address the relationship between the statutory and common law actions. See for example the *Trespass to Property Act*, R.S.O. 1990, c. T.21, discussed earlier in this chapter. Legislation may also eliminate a common law action and replace it with a statutory cause of action.

4. A Note on the *Canadian Charter of Rights and Freedoms*

Aside from specific torts statutes, the *Canadian Charter of Rights and Freedoms*, Part I of the *Constitution Act, 1982*, being Schedule B to the *Canada Act 1982* (U.K.), 1982, c. 11, will probably have as great an impact on civil liability as any single piece of federal or provincial legislation. There are two ways in which the *Charter* may affect tort liability. First, an individual whose *Charter* rights have been violated may have an express statutory cause of action under s. 24(1). Second, as part of the supreme law of Canada, the *Charter* may alter some existing common law causes of action and defences. In this section, we set out some of the most relevant *Charter* provisions and briefly illustrate how they may affect civil liability. The role of the *Charter* in tort law was also considered in Chapters 3, 8, 11, and 21.

CANADIAN CHARTER OF RIGHTS AND FREEDOMS

Part I of the Constitution Act, 1982

Schedule B to the *Canada Act 1982* (U.K.), 1982, c. 11

Rights and freedoms in Canada

1. The Canadian Charter of Rights and Freedoms guarantees the rights and freedoms set out in it subject only to such reasonable limits prescribed by law as can be demonstrably justified in a free and democratic society.

Fundamental freedoms

2. Everyone has the following fundamental freedoms:

(*a*) freedom of conscience and religion;
(*b*) freedom of thought, belief, opinion and expression, including freedom of the press and other media of communication;
(*c*) freedom of peaceful assembly; and
(*d*) freedom of association.

Life, liberty and security of person

7. Everyone has the right to life, liberty and security of the person and the right not to be deprived thereof except in accordance with the principles of fundamental justice.

Search or seizure

8. Everyone has the right to be secure against unreasonable search or seizure.

Detention or imprisonment

9. Everyone has the right not to be arbitrarily detained or imprisoned.

Arrest or detention

10. Everyone has the right on arrest or detention

(*a*) to be informed promptly of the reasons therefor;
(*b*) to retain and instruct counsel without delay and to be informed of that right; and
(*c*) to have the validity of the detention determined by way of *habeas corpus* and to be released if the detention is not lawful.

Equality before and under law and equal protection and benefit of law

15. (1) Every individual is equal before and under the law and has the right to the equal protection and equal benefit of the law without discrimination and, in particular, without discrimination based on race, national or ethnic origin, colour, religion, sex, age or mental or physical disability.

Enforcement of guaranteed rights and freedoms

24. (1) Anyone whose rights or freedoms, as guaranteed by this Charter, have been infringed or denied may apply to a court of competent jurisdiction to obtain such remedy as the court considers appropriate and just in the circumstances.

Application of Charter

32. (1) This Charter applies

(*a*) to the Parliament and government of Canada in respect of all matters within the authority of Parliament including all matters relating to the Yukon Territory and Northwest Territories; and
(*b*) to the legislature and government of each province in respect of all matters within the authority of the legislature of each province.

Primacy of Constitution of Canada

52. (1) The Constitution of Canada is the supreme law of Canada, and any law that is inconsistent with the provisions of the Constitution is, to the extent of the inconsistency, of no force or effect.

Section 24(1) creates an express statutory cause of action for individuals whose *Charter* rights have been violated. However, the plaintiff must first establish that the *Charter* applies to the situation. Two points are clear. First, by reason of s. 32(1), the *Charter* applies to federal and provincial laws, governments, and government agencies. Second, the *Charter* does *not* apply to litigation between private citizens. Difficult issues often arise, however, as to whether a particular person or institution fits into the first category. In that regard, the courts have resolved some questions.

- The *Charter* obviously applies to Parliament, provincial and territorial legislatures, and municipalities. It therefore governs statutes, regulations, by-laws, and the like.

- It also applies to the actions of government officials, including the police and Crown corporations. However, while the judiciary is sometimes classified as a branch of "government" (very broadly speaking), the Supreme Court of Canada in *R.W.D.S.U, Local 580 v. Dolphin Delivery Ltd.* (1986), 33 D.L.R. (4th) 174 (S.C.C.) rejected the suggestion that all judicial action is caught by the *Charter*. Since all laws must, in the final analysis, be interpreted and applied by judges, that view would intolerably subject *all* laws to *Charter* scrutiny.

- The *Charter* often applies to people, such as government-appointed adjudicators, who derive their power from legislation. In addition, it applies to bodies, such as law societies and colleges of surgeons, that exercise a regulatory power that has been delegated by government.

- Difficulty remains with respect to institutions that are "public" in a broad sense. The courts have said that the critical factor is the extent to which an institution is controlled by the government. Consequently, the *Charter* applies to community colleges, but not to universities. While both types of institution receive government funding, the government has relatively greater say in the day-to-day operations of the former. Universities, in contrast, generally are marked by a greater degree of independence.

- The *Charter* does not apply to private corporations, despite their statutory foundations. Like universities, private corporations are dependent upon government legislation for their existence. Once in existence, however, they take on an independent life of their own, substantially separate from government control.

If the *Charter* applies, the plaintiff must establish that the defendant violated a *Charter* right. Even if the plaintiff succeeds in doing so, relief will be denied under s. 1 if the defendant proves that the infringement was a "reasonable limit prescribed by law that can be demonstrably justified in a free and democratic society." Only unjustified *Charter* violations give an individual a right to seek a remedy under s. 24(1). The court has broad discretion to grant any remedy that it considers appropriate in the circumstances. Although damages, injunctions, and prohibitions have been awarded under s. 24(1), the plaintiff is not entitled to them as of right.

The *Charter* may also affect the existing common law causes of action and defences. Section 52 of the *Charter* provides that the *Charter* is the supreme law of Canada. Any law that is inconsistent with it consequently is, to the extent of the inconsistency, of no force or effect. Since the words "any law" include common law torts principles, the *Charter* may have a significant impact on existing causes of action. For example, an individual's freedoms of peaceful assembly and association in s. 2(c) and (d) may require some modifications in the common law principles governing trespass to Crown land.

The *Charter* can also be used to negate what would otherwise be a valid common law or statutory defence. Assume, for example, that a police officer searched the plaintiff at random pursuant to ss. 10 and 11 of the *Narcotic Control Act*, R.S.C. 1985, c. N-1. Assume as well that the plaintiff sued in battery and that the officer raised the *Narcotic Control Act* in defence. If the plaintiff established that this search power violated s. 8 of the *Charter*, which prohibits unreasonable search or seizure, and could not be justified under s. 1, then this section would be of no force or effect to the extent that it was inconsistent with s. 8. As a result, the officer's search would no longer be authorized by law and the defence of legal authority could fail.

Although the *Charter* came into force in 1982, the Supreme Court of Canada has as yet only begun to define the *Charter*'s impact on civil liability. It may be some time before its impact can be fully assessed.

NOTES AND QUESTIONS

1. As to the scope of s. 32(1), see generally Tassé, "Application of the Canadian Charter of Rights and Freedoms" in Beaudoin & Ratushny, eds., *The Canadian Charter of Rights and Freedoms*, 2d ed. (1989) at 65; and Hogg, *Constitutional Law of Canada—Student Edition 2005* (2005), ch. 34.

2. In *R.W.D.S.U, Local 580 v. Dolphin Delivery Ltd.* (1986), 33 D.L.R. (4th) 174 at 198 (S.C.C.), the Supreme Court of Canada held that the *Charter* does not apply to litigation between private citizens. However, the court also stated that "the judiciary ought to apply and develop the principles of the common law in a manner consistent with the fundamental values enshrined in the Constitution. . . . In this sense, then, the *Charter* is far from irrelevant to private litigants whose disputes fall to be decided at common law." This statement generated considerable academic comment. See for example Belobaba, "The Charter of Rights and Private Litigation: The Dilemma of *Dolphin Delivery*" in Finkelstein & Rogers, eds., *Charter Issues in Civil Cases* (1988) at 29. See also *Dobson (Litigation Guardian of) v. Dobson* (1999), 174 D.L.R. (4th) 1 (S.C.C.).

3. As noted above, difficult issues may arise if a party argues that the *Charter* applies to agencies and organizations that operate under statutory authority or are funded by a government. See *Lavigne v. O.P.S.E.U.* (1991), 81 D.L.R. (4th) 545 (S.C.C.); and *New Brunswick Broadcasting Co. v. Nova Scotia (Speaker of the House of Assembly)* (1993), 100 D.L.R. (4th) 212 (S.C.C.). It appears that the *Charter* will apply to an agency that is part of government. This determination is based on the form, function, and degree of government control and funding. Non-government agencies may also be subject to the *Charter* depending on the degree to which they are under government control. See *McKinney v. University of Guelph* (1990), 76 D.L.R. (4th) 545 (S.C.C.); *Douglas College v. Douglas/Kwantlen Faculty Assoc.* (1990), 77 D.L.R. (4th) 94 (S.C.C.); and *Vancouver General Hospital v. Stoffman* (1990), 76 D.L.R. (4th) 700 (S.C.C.).

4. For a discussion of s. 24(1) and express statutory causes of action, see Pilkington, "Monetary Redress for Charter Infringement" in Sharpe, ed., *Charter Litigation* (1987) 307; Morgan, "Charter Remedies: The Civil Side After the First Five Years" in Finkelstein & Rogers, *supra*, at 47; and Gibson & Gibson, "Enforcement of the Canadian Charter of Rights and Freedoms" in Beaudoin & Ratushny, eds., *The Canadian Charter of Rights and Freedoms*, 2d ed. (1989) 781. See also *Poirier v. Canada (Minister of Veterans Affairs)*, [1989] 3 F.C. 233 (C.A.).

5. For additional discussion of the *Charter*'s impact on common law causes of action and defences see Doody, "Freedom of the Press: The Canadian Charter of Rights and Freedoms, and a New Category of Qualified Privilege" (1983) 61 Can. Bar Rev. 124; Hutchinson & Petter, "Private Rights/ Public Wrongs: The Liberal Lie of the Charter" (1988) 38 U.T.L.J. 278; Weinrib, "Constitutional Values and Private Law in

Canada" in Friedmann & Barak-Erez, eds., *Human Rights in Private Law* (2002) 43. See also *Hill v. Church of Scientology of Toronto* (1995), 126 D.L.R. (4th) 129 (S.C.C.).

6. The *Charter* may apply to procedural matters. Special limitation periods and other procedural rules applying to claims against public authorities have been challenged under the *Charter*, usually under s. 15. See for example *Colangelo v. Mississauga (City)* (1988), 53 D.L.R. (4th) 283 (Ont. C.A.); *Mirhadizadeh v. Ontario* (1989), 69 O.R. (2d) 422 (C.A.); and *Canadian Assn. of Regulated Importers v. Canada (A.G.)* (1994), 17 Admin. L.R. (2d) 121 (F.C.A.).

REVIEW PROBLEMS

1. Assume that s. 15(1) of the *Charter* had been in force at the time of *Bhadauria v. Board of Governors of Seneca College* (1981), 124 D.L.R. (3d) 193 (S.C.C.), which was discussed in Chapter 3. What would the plaintiff have had to establish for an express statutory cause of action under the *Charter*? Would the *Charter* have assisted her claim at common law?

2. Assuming that the *Charter* had been in force, what impact would it have had on the majority and dissenting judgments in *Harrison v. Carswell* (1975), 62 D.L.R. (3d) 68 (S.C.C.), which is extracted in Chapter 5?

23

OCCUPIERS' LIABILITY

1. Introduction
2. The Common Law Principles of Occupiers' Liability
3. The Provincial Occupiers' Liability Statutes

1. Introduction

Occupiers' liability can be a difficult topic. The law has always recognized that an occupier of land owes at least *some obligation* to safeguard at least *some visitors*. The scope of that obligation, however, has varied significantly over time and place.

The early law was simple, but harsh. J. Fleming explained the situation in *The Law of Torts*, 7th ed. (1987) at 417:

> Until well into the midst of the 19th century, the prominent social value attached to landholding defied all serious challenge to the claim by occupiers to untrammelled use and enjoyment of their domain with least subordination to the interests of others. Qualified only by such concern for *neighbours* as was exacted by the law of nuisance and trespass, the landowner was virtually immune to demands for the safety of people who came *upon* his land, except not to injure them wilfully, set traps or use excessive force expelling trespassers. With respect to the condition of the premises, even a lawful visitor entered for all practical purposes at his own risk.

Over time, the law grew increasingly complex as the courts developed a range of rules that were intended to more sensitively address different situations. For that purpose, visitors were placed into four categories, each of which attracted a different standard of care. Although the cases that appear below provide greater detail, it is possible to quickly summarize the essential features of that scheme. Because the standards of care evolved over time, the table on the following page is merely intended to facilitate discussion. It is not intended to provide a authoritative statement of the law.

TYPE OF VISITOR	DESCRIPTION OF VISITOR	OCCUPIER'S STANDARD OF CARE
trespasser	person who does not have permission to be on property (*e.g.* burglar)	refrain from intentionally or recklessly injuring trespasser
licensee	person who has permission to be on property, but whose presence does not benefit occupier (*e.g.* house guest)	take reasonable care to protect licensee from unusual (or, historically, hidden) dangers about which occupier actually knows
invitee	person who has permission to be on property, and whose presence does benefit occupier (*e.g.* restaurant patron)	take reasonable care to protect invitee from unusual dangers about which occupier knows or ought to know
contractual entrant	person who entered contract to use premises, as opposed to receive services (*e.g.* hotel guest, but not restaurant patron)	take reasonable care to ensure that premises are fit for intended purpose

Not surprisingly, this scheme generates numerous difficulties. First, despite recognizing four categories of visitors, the common law scheme occasionally fails to sensitively distinguish between different types of people. Both the violent burglar and the curious child *prima facie* are trespassers. Yet it seems odd, if not offensive, that the occupier's obligation is the same in either instance. For that reason, courts often rely on fictions, such as the doctrine of allurement or the notion of implied licence, to upgrade a child's status from trespasser to licensee, and thereby to increase the standard of care. The results are certainly more palatable, but the reasoning leaves something to be desired: see *British Railways Board v. Herrington*, [1972] A.C. 877 (H.L.).

Second, it sometimes is difficult to determine a visitor's status. Is a person who uses a municipal library or a national park a licensee or an invitee? Does the occupier in each instance receive a sufficient benefit so as to attract the higher standard of care? See *Nickell v. City of Windsor* (1926), 59 O.L.R. 618 (H.C.); and *Coffyne v. Silver Lake Regional Park Authority* (1977), 75 D.L.R. (3d) 300 (Sask. Q.B.). What of a child who accompanies her father into a store? See *Gwynne v. Dominion Stores Ltd.* (1963), 43 D.L.R. (2d) 290 (Man. Q.B.); and *Kaplan v. Canada Safeway Ltd.* (1968), 68 D.L.R. (2d) 627 (Sask. Q.B.).

Third, a visitor's status may change from one moment to the next. If so, it may be difficult to determine the appropriate standard of care. In *Dunster v. Abbott*, [1953] 2 All E.R. 1572 at 1574 (C.A.), Lord Denning posed the following question.

> A canvasser who comes onto your premises without your consent is a trespasser. Once he has your consent, he is a licensee. Not until you do business with him is he an invitee. Even when you have done business with him, it seems rather strange that your duty towards him should be different when he comes to your front door than when he goes away. Does he change his colour in the middle of the conversation?

Fourth, questions may arise regarding the proper description of a given danger. Is an icy sidewalk in a Canadian winter an "unusual" or "hidden" risk against which an occupier must protect a licensee or invitee? See *Francis v. I.P.C.F. Properties Inc.* (1993), 136 N.B.R. (2d) 215 (Q.B.); and *Waldick v. Malcolm* (1991), 83 D.L.R. (4th) 114 (S.C.C.).

Fifth, the social conditions that historically supported the common law scheme have changed. The perceived desirability of protecting landowners from liability has diminished as the population has urbanized and as real property has lost its status as the primary source of wealth. The fiercely individualistic conception of Blackacre has given way to a model that more evenly balances rights and obligations. Moreover, attitudes toward public health and safety have grown much more generous.

Sixth, and perhaps most significantly, as modern tort law has come to focus on the action in negligence, the traditional rules governing occupiers' liability appear to be unnecessarily complex and inflexible.

For all of these reasons, the law of occupiers' liability has been subject to extensive revision. New Brunswick has simply replaced it with the general tort of negligence: *Law Reform Act*, S.N.B. 1993, c. L-1.2, s. 2; and *Jones v. Richard* (1998), 207 N.B.R. (2d) 265 (Q.B.), rev'd (2000), 226 N.B.R. (2d) 207 (C.A.). Several other jurisdictions (British Columbia, Alberta, Manitoba, Ontario, Nova Scotia and Prince Edward Island) have abandoned the common law rules in favour of a statutory regime. And while the common law tort of occupiers' liability continues to exist in the remaining jurisdictions, it has been modified so as to eliminate its more egregious defects.

This chapter will address the traditional common law scheme before turning to the statutory alternatives. In each instance, the case extracts and accompanying notes are intended to be illustrative, rather than exhaustive.

2. The Common Law Principles of Occupiers' Liability

(a) WHO IS AN OCCUPIER?

PALMER v. ST. JOHN

(1969), 3 D.L.R. (3d) 649 (N.B.C.A.)

[The plaintiff was injured when her toboggan went over a hump at the bottom of a hill and flew into the air before landing. A city work crew, in an attempt to make the hill safer, had inadvertently created the hump. The plaintiff sued both the Horticultural Association, which was responsible for maintaining the park, and the City. The trial judge held both defendants liable in occupiers' liability and further indicated that the City was vicariously liable for the negligence of its work crew. The defendants appealed.]

HUGHES J.A.: . . . The defendant, the Saint John Horticultural Association, hereinafter referred to as the Association, is a statutory corporation incorporated by 1893 (N.B.), c. 83, for the establishment and maintenance of public gardens and the encouraging of the cultivation of flowers and planting trees in the City of Saint John. Over a period of many years the Association acquired various parcels of land which now comprise Rockwood Park and has developed the Park for the enjoyment of the public. Near the shore of Lily Lake which is within the Park, the Association has constructed and operates a pavilion. In addition the Association maintains in the Park public gardens, greenhouses and camp sites and has developed recreational facilities for boating, swimming, skating, skiing, coasting and tobogganing.

. . .

The toboggan slide has been used by the public every season since being constructed, without supervision by the Association and without any charge to the public for its use.

The City of Saint John, hereinafter referred to as the City, has for many years made annual grants to the Association to be used to provide recreational facilities in the Park for citizens of the City. From time to time the City also assisted the Association by providing services of City work crews and personnel for maintenance and development of the Park, the cost of which was ordinarily charged by the City against the annual grants. There is no evidence that the City did any work on the slide other than snow plowing after 1934 until the autumn of 1965 when . . . a City works crew removed outcroppings of rock, cleared bushes and generally smoothened the hill to make it faster and safer for tobogganing and sliding. On the same occasion the crew placed gravel between the bank, which borders the paved roadway near the foot of the slide, and the edge of the Lake for the purpose of flattening out the slope in that area to make it safer for those using the slide. Again in November or December, 1966, works crews of the City under instructions of the Commissioner of Works placed and levelled fill across about three-quarters of the width of the slide at or near the shoreline of the Lake to lessen the severity of the drop from the bank to the edge of the Lake, in an effort to remove a hazardous condition for those using the slide.

. . .

I shall now turn to the question of the liability of the City to the plaintiffs.

The learned trial Judge has found that the City as well as the Association was an occupier of the sliding hill and held the City liable to the plaintiffs in that capacity. The question who is an occupier has been considered in a number of cases. In *Salmond on Torts*, 11th ed., p. 548, the author states:

> . . . The person responsible for the condition of the premises is he who is in actual occupation or possession of them for the time being, whether he is the owner of them or not. For it is he who has the immediate supervision and control and the power of permitting or prohibiting the entry of other persons. . .

. . .

In *Duncan v. Cammell Laird & Co. Ltd.*, [1943] 2 All E.R. 621 at p. 627, Wrottesley, J., said:

> It seems to me that the importance of establishing that the defendant who invites is the occupier of the premises lies in the fact that with occupation goes control. And the importance of control is that it affords the opportunity to know that the plaintiff is coming on to the premises, to know the premises, and to become aware of dangers whether concealed or not, and to remedy them, or at least to warn those that are invited on to the premises.

The evidence establishes that the City and the Association co-operated closely in efforts to provide recreational facilities at Rockwood Park. As previously stated the City made annual grants to the Association and from time to time used City work crews to perform work and services in the Park. Sometimes the work was performed after consultation with the Park's superintendent, but on other occasions work was done by City crews without consultation with the Association. On one occasion at least the City plowed the snow from the slide at the request of a private citizen. The City was not the owner of the Park at the time of the plaintiffs' accident and did not operate the slide or regulate its use. With all due deference to the learned trial Judge I am unable to agree that the evidence justifies a finding that the City was an occupier of the sliding hill so as to subject it to the duty of an occupier.

[However, Hughes J.A. agreed with the trial judge that the City was vicariously liable for the negligence of its work crew, and he dismissed the City's appeal on this basis.]

NOTES AND QUESTIONS

1. What test did the Court of Appeal use to determine if the City was an occupier of the hill? Do you agree with the court's application of that test to the facts? Assuming that both the City and the Association had been occupiers of the hill, would their liability as occupants necessarily have been the same?

2. In *Couch v. McCann; Ferguson v. McCann* (1977), 77 D.L.R. (3d) 387 (Ont. C.A.), the plaintiffs were injured when the barn floor collapsed at an auction they were attending. They sued Fry, the owner of the property, McCann, the person who had use of the barn, and Phifher and Coughlin, the auctioneers who had been hired by McCann to run the auction. At trial, the action against Fry was dismissed, and the remaining defendants were held liable in occupiers' liability. On appeal, the court held that since the auctioneers had invited the public to attend and had conducted the auction in the barn, they were joint occupants of the barn with McCann. Is this decision compatible with *Palmer*? Based on *Couch*, would a singer hired to perform in a concert hall be an occupier of the facility? Would it make any difference if the singer was responsible for advertising the event or if the singer's salary was based on a percentage of the seat sales? See *Haskett v. Univ. of Western Ont.*, [1955] 3 D.L.R. 234 (Ont. H.C.).

3. An occupier is responsible not only for the land and permanent structures, but also for moveable objects that are situated on the land, such as aircraft, trains, and scaffolding. See Di Castri, *Occupiers' Liability* (1981) at 12-14.

4. In the absence of fraud or contract, a landlord was under no common law duty to ensure that unfurnished premises were safe for tenants and visitors. What is the rationale for imposing fundamentally different obligations on owners and occupiers? It should be noted that the provincial statutes governing landlords and tenants now require landlords to maintain rented premises in a safe and habitable condition. See for example the *Tenant Protection Act*, S.O. 1997, c. 24, s. 24. See also *Allison v. Rank City Wall Can. Ltd.* (1984), 45 O.R. (2d) 141 (H.C.); and *Day v. Chaleur Developments Ltd.* (1985), 63 N.B.R. (2d) 313 (Q.B.).

Landlords also may owe a duty of care to tenants and their invitees under occupiers' liability legislation in certain circumstances. See for example *Stuart v. R. in Right of Can.*, [1988] 6 W.W.R. 211 (F.C.T.D.); and *Blake v. Kensche* (1990), 3 C.C.L.T. (2d) 189 (B.C.S.C.).

5. Simple ownership of a property will not constitute "occupation" for the purposes of occupiers' liability. An "occupier" is a person having direct control or physical

possession of particular premises. See *Wiley v. Tymar Management Inc.*, [1995] 3 W.W.R. 684 (B.C.S.C.); and *Murray v. Bitango*, [1995] 1 W.W.R. 79 (Alta. Q.B.).

(b) CATEGORIES OF ENTRANTS AND CORRESPONDING DUTIES

(i) *Contractual Entrants*

FINIGAN v. CALGARY

(1967), 65 D.L.R. (2d) 626 (Alta. C.A.)

CAIRNS J.A.: . . . The facts are that on May 23, 1966, the appellant accompanied by her husband entered the park and paid an admission fee of 25¢ to view the exhibits there installed. One of the series of exhibits consisted of a group of Indian teepees erected in a grove of trees. There was a pathway about 4 ft. in width cut through the trees to the entrance of one of the teepees. The pathway had been cleared of trees and roots and other debris but there was a root left on the edge of the pathway about 4 ft. from the entrance to the teepee which protruded about 2 ins. above the surface. Directly in front of the entrance in the middle of the pathway and about one foot from it the stump had been left which protruded about 2 ins. above the surrounding surface. The stump had been cut on a bias and the evidence was that it was difficult to see even if at the time in question, namely, 6:00 p.m., the light was good. In making the pathways the instructions were that all protruding root stumps were to be taken out. It is also a fact that the authorities inspected the grounds continuously and were in the habit of cutting down any obstructions which might be dangerous, but they had not noticed the stump prior to the accident.

The appellant walked down the pathway with the intention of entering the teepee and with her view on the entrance. She tripped on the exposed root and fell forward and was not able to recover her balance until she fell on the stump. . .. There is no doubt that it was the stump which caused her injuries.

The learned trial Judge was of the opinion that the case came within the principles governing the liability of an invitor to an invitee as laid down in *Indermaur v. Dames* (1867), L.R. 2 C.P. 311, and subsequent cases to the effect that the invitee using reasonable care for his own safety "is entitled to expect that the occupier shall on his part use reasonable care to prevent damage from unusual danger of which he knows or ought to know" [p. 313]. He therefore dismissed the action and must have been of the opinion, although he does not say so, that there was no unusual danger in all the circumstances.

In my view with great deference I think that the learned trial Judge was wrong in arriving at this decision and that even applying the principle he did he could not come to the conclusion that this was not an unusual danger. The facts are perfectly clear. We have a pathway leading to a teepee and in the middle of the entrance was a two-inch stump which was practically invisible and on which the appellant fell. Surely a person entering the teepee could expect not to encounter such an obstruction. There is no evidence that she was in any way negligent. Had the pathway been properly constructed the stump would not have been left there. In any event it should have been noticed by the respondent in one of the many inspections which were made to ensure the safety of the public.

For these reasons I am of the opinion that the respondents created or suffered to exist an unusual danger of which, if damage arose because of it as it did in this case, they are liable even on the principles enunciated in *Indermaur v. Dames*.

However, completely apart from the principles of the invitee cases it is my view that the respondents are liable on the basis of breach of contract.

Here the appellant paid an admission fee to view the exhibits and thereby entered into a contract with the respondents that she might enjoy those privileges provided she exercised prudence herself without risk of danger so far as reasonable care could make the premises safe. This principle was laid down by Rand, J., in *Brown and Brown v. B. & F. Theatres Ltd.*, [1947] 3 D.L.R. 593. . ., where the learned Judge, in giving the judgment of the Court excepting that of Kellock, J., who came to the same conclusion following *Francis v. Cockrell* (1870), L.R. 5 Q.B. 501, stated at p. 596:

> The case has been treated as raising the ordinary question of the duty owed by a proprietor of premises towards an invitee. I think, however, I should observe that this is not merely a case of such invitation as was present in *Indermaur v. Dames* (1867), L.R. 2 C.P. 311. Here, Mrs. Brown paid a consideration for the privileges of the theatre, including that of making use of the ladies' room. There was a contractual relation between her and the theatre management that exercising prudence herself she might enjoy those privileges without risk of danger so far as reasonable care could make the premises safe. Although the difference in the degree of care called for may not, in the circumstances here, be material, I think it desirable that the distinction between the two bases of responsibility be kept in mind: *Maclenan v. Segar*, [1917] 2 K.B. 325 following *Francis v. Cockrell* (1870), L.R. 5 Q.B. [501]. In *Cox. v. Coulson*, [1916] 2 K.B. 177 at p. 181, Swinfen Eady L.J. said: "The defendant must also be taken to have contracted to take due care that the premises should be reasonably safe for persons using them in the customary manner and with reasonable care", citing *Francis v. Cockrell* [(1870), L.R. 5 Q.B. 184].

. . .

The rule in *Francis v. Cockrell* was approved by Cartwright, J. in giving the majority judgment of the Court in *Carriss v. Buxton*, 13 D.L.R. (2d) 689 at pp. 713-4, [1958] S.C.R. 441, where he stated:

> The rule in *Francis v. Cockrell* is stated as follows in *Winfield on Tort*, 6th ed., p. 672: "Where A enters B's structure under a contract entitling him to do so, *it is an implied term in the contract that the structure shall be reasonably fit for the purpose for which it is intended; but this does not extend to any unknown defect incapable of being discovered by reasonable means.*"

There is no doubt therefore that there is a higher duty owed to a person who enters premises under a contract than that which is owed to an invitee under *Indermaur v. Dames*; as Rand, J., stated, *supra*, it is that anyone may enter "without risk of danger so far as reasonable care could make the premises safe" or at least under *Francis v. Cockrell* there is an implied warranty that the place is reasonably fit for the purposes for which it was intended.

In so far as this case is concerned it is immaterial whether there is a slight difference in the rule as to the liability to a contracting party. There is no doubt under either interpretation of the liability that the respondents did not discharge their obligations to see that the property was either "without risk of danger" or "reasonably fit for the purpose" in permitting the stump in question to obstruct the entrance to the teepee, and they are liable to the appellant in damages for such failure.

. . .

MCDERMID J.A.: – In *Maclenan v. Segar*, [1917] 2 K.B. 325 at p. 333, McCardie, J., in referring to the warranty implied, stated,

> The principle is basic and applies alike to premises and to vehicles. It matters not whether the subject be a race-stand, a theatre, or an inn; whether it be a taxicab, an omnibus, or

> a railway carriage. The warranty in each case is the same, and for a breach thereof an action will lie.

As the warranty is contractual I would like to reserve the question as to whether it is the same in respect of a park run for the benefit of the public as it would be in cases where the premises are being run to make a profit for the owner. It does seem odd to me that a public authority who is carrying on a park for the benefit and enjoyment of the public and not for profit has a greater duty than a departmental store which has invited the public onto its premises in order that the store may make a profit; however, such may be the case. In the case at bar the point does not have to be decided, for even if the warranty implied was the same, and I think it could not be less, as the duty imposed in respect of an invitee, there was still a breach of it. Subject to the foregoing comment, I concur in the judgment of my brother Cairns.

ALLEN, J.A., concurs with CAIRNS, J.A.

NOTES AND QUESTIONS

1. What duty of care does an occupier owe to contractual entrants? How does that duty differ from the duty owed to invitees? Do you agree with the court's application of these principles in *Finigan*? See also *Carriere v. Bd. of Gravelbourg School Dist. No. 2244 of Sask.* (1977), 79 D.L.R. (3d) 662 (Sask. C.A.); *Fanjoy v. Gaston* (1981), 127 D.L.R. (3d) 163 (N.B.C.A.); *McGivney v. Rustico Summer Haven* (1986), 197 A.P.R. 358 (P.E.I.C.A.); and *McGinty v. Cook* (1989), 59 D.L.R. (4th) 94 (Ont. H.C.), aff'd (1991), 79 D.L.R. (4th) 95 (Ont. C.A.).

2. Is McDermid J.A. suggesting that the courts should consider the occupier's motive in determining the nature of the implied contractual warranty? What are the advantages and disadvantages of such an approach? Should the contractual duty owed to a patron who paid $50 for a ticket to a boxing match be higher than that owed to a patron who paid $3?

3. Why was the City of Calgary held to be an occupier of the park in *Finigan*? Can you reconcile this case and *Palmer*?

4. Among other things, an occupier must protect a contractual entrant from dangers presented by other entrants. In *McGinty v. Cook*, *supra*, the defendant occupied a campsite. Because it failed to enforce its own rules regarding "quiet time" at night, the plaintiff was attacked and beaten by a number of other campers. The occupier was held liable for failing to prevent the attack.

An occupier is not, however, liable for every harm that befalls a contractual entrant. In *McTaggart v. Commonwealth Hospitality Ltd.* (1997), 159 Sask. R. 144 (Q.B.), vandals had removed a mirror from a wall and placed it between the inner and outer doors of an elevator. The plaintiff was injured when the door opened. The occupier was relieved of responsibility on the grounds that it had not received any report of rowdy behaviour and it had no reason to suspect the danger.

5. For a more detailed discussion of the duty owed to contractual entrants see Adair, "Occupier's Liability to the Contractual Visitor" (1979) 2 Adv. Q. 320; and Di Castri, *Occupiers' Liability* (1981) at 15-32.

(ii) *Invitees and Licensees*

McERLEAN v. SAREL

(1987), 42 D.L.R. (4th) 577 (Ont. C.A.)

[McErlean, who was almost 15 years old, and a friend were racing trail bikes on an old road in an abandoned gravel pit. McErlean was severely injured when he collided with Sarel, who also was riding a trail bike. At the time of the accident, Sarel was riding on the wrong side of the road and McErlean was emerging from a sharp corner that offered poor visibility.

The City of Brampton owned the gravel pit and planned to develop it as a park. Although City officials knew that trail bike riders used the pit, they made no attempt to stop or warn them. The trial judge attributed 75% of the responsibility to the City, 15% to Sarel and 10% to McErlean based on his contributory negligence. The City's liability was based on its status as an occupier.]

BY THE COURT: – This is an occupier's liability case. The appeal relates both to liability and damages. The occupier of the land at the relevant time was the appellant the Corporation of the City of Brampton. The trial judge found that the respondent Michael McErlean at the time of the accident was a licensee.

. . .

The first question to be asked is whether the respondent, Michael McErlean, was on the appellant's property as a trespasser or a licensee, it being common ground that he was not an invitee. In our opinion, the respondent must be categorized as a licensee and not a trespasser. A licence to enter or remain on property may be given by conduct which manifests consent or permission. Here, it is clear that the appellant made no effort to exclude pedestrians, bikers or others from its property by means of signs (except with respect to swimming) warning not to trespass, by the erection of adequate fencing, by supervision or by any other means. Their entry from time to time onto the lands over an appreciable period was readily ascertainable if not actually known. The owner's failure to object to their presence can reasonably be construed as tacit permission to their entry. Persons who, for instance, took short-cuts across this long-vacant piece of property or who came there to walk their dogs or ride their motorcycles or trail bikes cannot be treated as mere trespassers. The owner's inaction, while not amounting to an invitation to use the property, at least manifested a willingness to permit them entry and indicated its toleration of their presence. In these circumstances, the owner so conducted itself that it cannot be heard to say that it did not give permission. This is not a case in which an occupier unsuccessfully sought to prevent people from trespassing on its lands, nor is this a situation in which precautions against their intrusion would be unduly burdensome or expensive or, based on past experience, likely to be futile. Applying the common law approach, this respondent must, in our opinion, be treated as a licensee (albeit, on the authorities, a "bare licensee" or a "licensee without an interest") and the occupier's liability must be determined on the basis of that relationship. . . .

What then is the duty owed by an occupier of land to a licensee? Traditionally, it has been spoken of as a duty to warn of concealed dangers or traps of which the occupier had actual knowledge: *Hambourg v. T. Eaton Co. Ltd.*, [1935] 3 D.L.R. 305. . . . This is plainly a less stringent duty than the duty owed to an invitee which has long been expressed as a duty to take reasonable care to prevent damage from unusual danger of which the invitor knew or ought to have known: *Indermaur v. Dames* (1866), L.R. 1

C.P. 274; affirmed L.R. 2 C.P. 311. However, in 1974, the Supreme Court of Canada in *Mitchell et al. v. C.N.R. Co.* (1974), 46 D.L.R. (3d) 363. . ., a case involving a nine-year-old infant-licensee, abandoned the traditional requirement that the danger be concealed and held that mere knowledge of likely danger on the part of a licensee falling short of voluntary assumption of risk will not of itself exonerate the occupier. Later that same year, this court in *Bartlett et al. v. Weiche Apartments Ltd.* (1974), 55 D.L.R. (3d) 44, a case involving a three-year-old infant-licensee, thoroughly canvassed the then current law as to an occupier's liability to a licensee. Based on an analysis of the judgments of the Supreme Court of Canada in *Mitchell et al. v. C.N.R. Co., supra*, and in *Hanson et al. v. City of St. John et al.* (1973), 39 D.L.R. (3d) 417, Jessup J.A., speaking for the majority of the court . . . restated the general principle governing the liability of an occupier to a licensee in the following terms:

> It is to take reasonable care to avoid foreseeable risk of harm from any unusual danger on the occupier's premises of which the occupier actually has knowledge or of which he ought to have knowledge because he was aware of the circumstances. The licensee's knowledge of the danger goes only to the questions of contributory negligence or *volenti*.

That test has been applied by this court in other licensor-licensee situations. . . . It represents an accurate statement of the law in effect at the time of this accident, and liability in this case must be determined in accordance with the principles enunciated therein.

Applying this test, an occupier's liability is clearly limited to "unusual dangers" on his property and does not extend to every danger that might be found thereon. Thus, the first and most important question to be asked in this instance is whether at the time and place of the accident there was an "unusual danger" on the occupier's premises which created a foreseeable risk of harm.

Prior to the *Mitchell* case, the term "unusual danger" was applied to the duty owed by an occupier to an invitee, but not to the duty owed a licensee. The latter duty related only to "concealed dangers" or "traps". "Unusual danger" was defined by the House of Lords . . . in *London Graving Dock Co. Ltd. v. Horton*, [1951] A.C. 737 at p. 745, as follows:

> I think "*unusual*" *is used in an objective sense and means such danger as is not usually found in carrying out the task or fulfilling the function which the invitee has in hand, though what is unusual will, of course, vary with the reasons for which the invitee enters the premises*. Indeed, I do not think Phillimore, L.J., in *Norman v. Great Western Railway Co.*, [1915] 1 K.B. 584, 596, is speaking of individuals as individuals but of individuals as members of a type, e.g., that class of persons such as stevedores or seamen who are accustomed to negotiate the difficulties which their occupation presents. A tall chimney is not an unusual difficulty for a steeplejack though it would be for a motor mechanic. But I do not think a lofty chimney presents a danger less unusual for the last-named because he is particularly active or untroubled by dizziness.

(Emphasis added.)

This definition has been generally accepted and was specifically adopted by the Supreme Court of Canada in *Campbell v. Royal Bank of Canada* (1963), 43 D.L.R. (2d) 341, and in *City of Brandon v. Farley* (1968), 66 D.L.R. (2d) 289. In light of the fact that *Mitchell* has blurred the distinction between an occupier's duty to an invitee and his or her duty to a licensee, this definition of "unusual danger" can be applied by analogy also to the case of an occupier's duty to a licensee.

An occupier's duty is limited to "unusual dangers" on the theory that he or she is entitled to assume that ordinary reasonable people know and appreciate usual or common dangers and need not, therefore, be warned or otherwise protected against them. No list of dangers that categorically meet this concept of unusualness can be drawn up because, as Fleming points out . . ., "the quality of unusualness depends not only on the character of the danger itself, but also on the nature of the premises on which it is found and the range of experience with which the [entrant] may fairly be credited". In the final analysis, the issue of what is an unusual danger clearly must, like so many issues in the law of torts, depend on the facts and circumstances of the given case.

. . .

With the negligence of the respondent and Sarel established, the question remaining is whether the owner of the land upon which this unfortunate accident occurred bears any responsibility in law for the occurrence. A licensor is patently not a guarantor of a licensee's safety or an insurer against all injuries which may result from the condition of his or her property. As we have said, a licensor's duty at common law is limited to unusual dangers of which he or she was aware, ought to have known existed with respect to the property. The duty does not extend to usual or common dangers which ordinary reasonable persons can be expected to know and appreciate.

Accepting that the curve could be a danger and that the appellant-landowner should have known that its property was being used in the recreational operation of trail bikes, can it be said that this condition constituted an unusual danger? In our opinion, it cannot be so classified. The requisite quality of unusualness is not present in this case, and the circumstances adverted to by the trial judge in his brief reasons do not elevate the condition into one of unusual danger. We are concerned here with a country-type road on undeveloped private property running between a small lake on one side and dense bush on the other that can only be seen as commonplace and not out of the ordinary in this province. The existence and state of the one curve in this road was open to ordinary observation. It had been there for a long time. When travelled with due care and attention and at an appropriate speed, it was not dangerous. The curve had not been the subject of recent change nor the source of prior mishap. It was not concealed or hidden, nor was it unexpected. It could readily be seen at a considerable distance by persons approaching from either direction.

[Liability was apportioned equally between the plaintiff and the defendant Sarel.]

NOTES AND QUESTIONS

1. How have the courts distinguished between invitees and licensees? Why was the plaintiff not held to be a trespasser? Would the plaintiff have been considered a trespasser if the City had posted signs prohibiting entry and fenced the property?

2. What duty of care did an occupier traditionally owe to an invitee? How did the courts define the concept of an "unusual danger?"

3. What duty of care did an occupier owe to a licensee? How did the courts define the concept of "concealed danger or trap?"

4. How have *McErlean* and *Mitchell* (cited in *McErlean*) altered the traditional tests of an occupier's duty to invitees and licensees? Did these cases also change the definition of "unusual danger?"

5. Do you agree with the Court of Appeal's application of the current common law duty to the City's liability?

6. In *McErlean*, the Court of Appeal substantially collapsed the distinction between invitees and licensees. In *Stacey v. Anglican Church of Canada (Diocesan Synod of Eastern Newfoundland & Labrador)* (1999), 182 Nfld. & P.E.I.R. 1 (Nfld. C.A.), the Newfoundland Court of Appeal went even further. The defendant was the occupier of a cemetery. The plaintiff visited the cemetery during regular hours. There were several paths through the property. The plaintiff was injured when she chose instead to walk down an embankment. She had seen several other people doing so, despite a sign that said "do not walk" in the area. The plaintiff sued the defendant for occupiers' liability.

The court held that visitors no longer should be placed into different categories, each of which attracts a different standard of care. Instead, it formulated a new test that applied to all lawful visitors.

> An occupier's duty of care to a lawful visitor to his or her premises is to take such care as in all the circumstances is reasonable to see that the visitor will be reasonably safe in using the premises for the purposes for which he or she is invited or permitted by the occupier to be there or is permitted by law to be there.

Having regard to all of the circumstances, the court refused to impose liability. The defendant acted reasonably in providing various paths through the cemetery. It was not responsible for the plaintiff's decision to walk down an embankment despite a sign prohibiting her from doing so.

7. A more cautious approach can be seen in *Yelic v. Gimli (Town)* (1986), 33 D.L.R. (4th) 248 (Man. C.A.). Once again, the defendant was the occupier of a cemetery. The plaintiff wanted to visit a grave outside of the regular hours of operation. For that purpose, he climbed over a decorative fence that surrounded the premises. The fence, which was in a state of disrepair, collapsed and the plaintiff was injured. Because the Manitoba legislation had not yet been introduced, he sued the defendant under the common law rules for occupiers' liability.

The trial judge observed that under the common law rules, a licensee must be protected from dangers about which the occupier *actually knew*, while an invitee must be protected from dangers about which the occupier *knew or should have known*. Since the defendant actually knew of the defect and did nothing about it, the trial judge found it unnecessary to determine whether the categories of licensee and invitee should be merged. Liability would arise even on the higher threshold.

The Court of Appeal reversed the trial decision. It agreed in *obiter dicta* that there may still be a difference between licensees and invitees, insofar as the former must prove the occupier's *actual knowledge* whereas the latter may succeed on the basis of *constructive knowledge*. However, it also held that the plaintiff did not fall into either one of those categories. He was, rather, a trespasser and consequently was owed the lower standard of "common humanity" (as discussed in the next section). That standard did not require the repair of a decorative fence in the absence of evidence that the defendant knew that trespassers regularly climbed over the fence.

8. Occupiers also have a duty to protect invitees and licensees from other people who are allowed onto the premises and who pose a foreseeable risk of harm. This issue often arises after an intoxicated patron in a tavern becomes unruly or violent. The occupier may be found liable for failing to take reasonable steps to eject or restrain the patron. See for example *Duncan v. Braaten* (1980), 21 B.C.L.R. 369 (S.C.); *McGeough v. Don Enterprises Ltd.*, [1984] 1 W.W.R. 256 (Sask. Q.B.); *Jeffrey v. Commodore Cabaret Ltd.* (1995), 128 D.L.R. (4th) 535 (B.C.S.C.); *Mellanby v. Chapple*, 1995 CarswellOnt 5327 (Gen. Div.) (WLeC); and *Murphy v. Little Memphis Cabaret Ltd.* (1998), 167 D.L.R. (4th) 190 (Ont. C.A.).

A dramatic illustration of the possibility of liability in such circumstances occurred in *Fullowka v. Royal Oak Ventures Inc.*, [2005] 5 W.W.R. 420 (N.W.T.S.C.). The defendant was the occupier of an underground mine that was the subject of a heated labour dispute. As part of that dispute, Warren deliberately planted a bomb in a mine. The explosion killed nine replacement workers. Warren was convicted of nine counts of second degree murder. The victims' families then sued various parties, including the defendant. The court held the defendant liable on the basis that, because it was foreseeable that some such incident would occur, it was required to take reasonable steps to protect the deceased.

9. Canadian courts often take a broad view of the concept of "unusual danger." The following have been held to be "unusual dangers": *Houle v. S.S. Kresge Co.* (1974), 55 D.L.R. (3d) 52 (Ont. Dist. Ct.) (potholes in a parking lot); *Pajot v. Commonwealth Holiday Inns of Can. Ltd.* (1978), 86 D.L.R. (3d) 729 (Ont. H.C.) (unmarked glass door); *Lampert v. Simpson Sears Ltd.* (1986), 75 N.B.R. (2d) 128 (C.A.) (water on the floor of a department store); *Sandberg v. Steer Holdings Ltd.* (1987), 45 Man. R. (2d) 264 (Q.B.) (ice in a parking lot); *Vykysaly v. Jablowski* (1992), 8 O.R. (3d) 181 (Gen. Div.) (open stairwell at back of store); and *Ackerman v. Wascana Centre Authority* [1998] 2 W.W.R. 678 (Sask. Q.B.), aff'd [1999] 6 W.W.R. 167 (Sask. C.A.) (gaps between planks of a pier). But see *Monteith v. N.B. Command, Royal Can. Legion* (1973), 8 N.B.R. (2d) 438 (Q.B.) (no liability for slip caused by beer on floor of a tavern).

10. In most provinces, occupiers have statutory duties to keep their walkways free of slippery substances and hazardous obstructions. The central issue in these cases is not the legal duty, but rather the standard of care. For the purposes of these statutes, the common law distinction between an invitee and a licensee no longer is important. See *Preston v. Canadian Legion of British Empire Service League, Kingsway Branch No. 175* (1981), 123 D.L.R. (3d) 645 (Alta. C.A.).

In *Bongiardina v. York Regional Municipality* (1999), 46 O.R. (3d) 345 (S.C.J.), aff'd (2000), 49 O.R. (3d) 641 (C.A.) the court held that owners and occupiers of a dwelling adjacent to a municipal sidewalk, who are subject to a snow-clearing by-law, do not owe pedestrians a duty of care because the *Occupiers' Liability Act*, R.S.O. 1990, c. O.2, does not apply. Moreover, the by-law did not relieve the municipality of its duty to pedestrians under the *Municipal Act*, R.S.O. 1990, c. M.45. See also *Peterson v. Windsor (City)* (2006), 27 M.P.L.R. (4th) 129 (Ont. S.C.J.).

11. An occupier is under a positive duty to carry out periodic inspections of premises in order to maintain a reasonable degree of safety: see *Sauve v. Provost* (1990), 71 O.R. (2d) 774 (H.C.)

(iii) *Trespassers*

VEINOT v. KERR-ADDISON MINES LTD.

(1975), 51 D.L.R. (3d) 533 (S.C.C.)

DICKSON J.: – This is an occupiers' liability case. . . .Whether the entrant is a burglar or wandering child or irreproachable wayfarer, the general principles historically applied were those expressed in *Robert Addie & Sons (Collieries), Ltd. v. Dumbreck*, [1929] A.C. 358, by Lord Hailsham, L.C., at p. 365:

> Towards the trespasser the occupier has no duty to take reasonable care for his protection or even to protect him from concealed danger. The trespasser comes on to the premises at his own risk. An occupier is in such a case liable only where the injury is due to some wilful act involving something more than the absence of reasonable care. There must be some act done with deliberate intention of doing harm to the trespasser, or at least some act done with reckless disregard of the presence of the trespasser.

These rules, of course, perpetuated the traditional 19th century concern for the sanctity of landed property. The general principle was that a landowner could do as he wished with his land. He owed no duty to an intruder, however accidental or inadvertent the intrusion, other than to refrain from shooting him or otherwise recklessly and wantonly doing him harm. . . . As could be expected various inventions were employed from time to time to modify and ameliorate the harshness. In some of the cases the landowner's consent was implied or imputed, particularly in "children cases", the status of the intruder being elevated from that of trespasser, which he clearly was, to that of licensee, which he clearly was not. In other cases a generous meaning was given to the phrase "reckless disregard" or a tenuous distinction was drawn between land in a static condition and land upon which an operational activity was being conducted, productive of injury. In time, two distinct, not easy to reconcile, lines of jurisprudence emerged. One perpetuated the letter and spirit of *Addie*'s case. . . . The other gave effect to changing ideas of social responsibility and imposed upon the owner of land duties well beyond those in contemplation in *Addie*'s case. . . .

. . .

In [*British Railways Board v. Herrington*, [1972] A.C. 877 (U.K. H.L.)] their Lordships exhaustively considered the nature of the duty owed by occupiers to trespassers. Lord Reid applied a subjective test. He said (p. 899):

> So it appears to me that an occupier's duty to trespassers must vary according to his knowledge, ability and resources. It has often been said that trespassers must take the land as they find it. I would rather say that they must take the occupier as they find him.

and later on the same page:

> So the question whether an occupier is liable in respect of an accident to a trespasser on his land would depend on whether a conscientious humane man with his knowledge,

> skill and resources could reasonably have been expected to have done or refrained from doing before the accident something which would have avoided it. If he knew before the accident that there was a substantial probability that trespassers would come I think that most people would regard as culpable failure to give any thought to their safety. He might often reasonably think, weighing the seriousness of the danger and the degree of likelihood of trespassers coming against the burden he would have to incur in preventing their entry or making his premises safe, or curtailing his own activities on his land, that he could not fairly be expected to do anything. But if he could at small trouble and expense take some effective action, again I think that most people would think it inhumane and culpable not to do that. If some such principle is adopted there will no longer be any need to strive to imply a fictitious licence.

The test of common humanity was also applied by Lord Morris of Borth-y-Gest (p. 909):

> In my view, while it cannot be said that the railways board owed a common duty of care to the young boy in the present case they did owe to him at least the duty of acting with common humanity towards him.

. . .

Herrington's case was considered by the Court of Appeal of England in *Pannett v. McGuinness & Co. Ltd.*, [1972] 3 W.L.R. 387. The following excerpt from Lord Denning's judgment aptly expresses, in my opinion, the more salient points a Judge should have in mind when considering intrusion upon land [at pp. 390-1]:

> The long and short of it is that you have to take into account all the circumstances of the case and see then whether the occupier ought to have done more than he did. (1) You must apply your common sense. You must take into account the gravity and likelihood of the probable injury. Ultra-hazardous activities require a man to be ultra-cautious in carrying them out. The more dangerous the activity, the more he should take steps to see that no one is injured by it. (2) You must take into account also the character of the intrusion by the trespasser. A wandering child or a straying adult stands in a different position from a poacher or a burglar. You may expect a child when you may not expect a burglar. (3) You must also have regard to the nature of the place where the trespass occurs. An electrified railway line or a warehouse being demolished may require more precautions to be taken than a private house. (4) You must also take into account the knowledge which the defendant has, or ought to have, of the likelihood of trespassers being present. The more likely they are, the more precautions may have to be taken.

In the very recent case of *Southern Portland Cement Ltd. v. Cooper*, [1974] 1 All E.R. 87, the Privy Council considered the duty owed to a trespasser. Their Lordships rejected the argument that an occupier only comes under a duty to potential trespassers if he estimates or ought to estimate that the arrival of one or more trespassers on his land is "extremely likely". In the course of his speech Lord Reid said: "But in their Lordships' judgment it is now necessary to . . . abandon the limitation of extreme likelihood", and later [at p. 98]:

> If the occupier creates the danger when he knows that there is a chance that trespassers will come that way and will not see or realise the danger he may have to do more. There may be difficult cases where the occupier will be hampered in the conduct of his own affairs if he has to take elaborate precautions. But in the present case it would have been easy to prevent the development of the dangerous situation which caused the plaintiff's injuries.

And so we come to the facts of the present case. There is no need to labour them. The plaintiff, 37 years of age, and his wife, on one snowmobile, accompanied by another married couple on another snowmobile, set out from their home for an evening of healthful recreation through woods and across lakes of northern Ontario. They went along well-travelled snowmobile trails, from Larder Lake to Crosby Lake, along a creek to Beaver Lake, to Bear Lake, to a hydro right of way along which were many ski-doo trails, down an old logging road "which was well ski-doo packed", to a wide, hard-packed, well-ploughed road on which they travelled until the plaintiff, Mr. Veinot, on the leading snowmobile, struck a rusty pipe stretched across the road, at face-height, and sustained very serious injuries. The accident occurred on March 16, 1970. Mr. Veinot had owned snowmobiles since 1966. . . . The jury found that Mr. Veinot did not fail to take reasonable care for his own safety.

The pipe which Mr. Veinot struck was two inches in diameter, supported by unpainted posts located off the road, and invisible at night due to the background of trees. The pipe had been erected some 20 years earlier to prevent the movement of unauthorized vehicular traffic to the defendant company's powder magazine not far from the community of Virginiatown. No point can be made of the fact that the pipe had been there for 20 years without accident for the type of accident which occurred in this case could only have occurred after the advent of snowmobiles.

From the evidence there seems no doubt that during the winter there was a great deal of travel on snowmobiles in and around Virginiatown. . . . The defendant company permitted snowmobile traffic along the road as far as the iron pipe. Such traffic normally then turned to the right and continued north along the right of way until the intersecting east-west hydro right of way was reached which in turn led west to the lakes across which Mr. Veinot and his party had travelled. Generally, as I have indicated, the main ski-doo traffic was east of the iron pipe, but the defendant's security officer conceded that on a very few occasions he had seen ski-doo tracks in the winter of 1969-70 on the powder magazine side of the pipe. He did not report these discoveries to the mine manager and he did nothing about it.

The evidence is undisputed that there were "a lot of snowmobile tracks" on the road leading south from the east-west hydro power line to the ploughed road on which the unfortunate accident occurred. The ploughed road "seemed to be well travelled"; looked like a public road; and had no markings to indicate it was not a public road. Mr. Veinot had no idea he was on private property when he drove along the ploughed road and according to his evidence, which was not challenged, he would not have continued along it if he had known it was private property. Upon all of the evidence and following a charge by the trial Judge to which no objection has been, or could be, taken, the jury made certain findings: (1) That Mr. Veinot on the date of the accident was on the defendant's land with the implied permission of the defendant; (2) That his injuries were caused by a concealed or hidden danger or a trap of which the defendant had knowledge, described by the jury in its answers as "a rusty pipe approximately 2" in diameter suspended across the travelled portion of the road at a height of approximately 45 inches from the road"; (3) The defendant failed to take reasonable care to avoid injury to persons traversing the area, there being no distinguishing warnings of the location of the pipe across the roadway from either the east or west approach to the pipe or on the pipe itself; (4) The finding to which I have already referred, that plaintiff did not fail to take reasonable care for his own safety. At the close of the evidence presented by the plaintiff a motion was made for a nonsuit. The motion was renewed after the evidence for the defendant had been heard and again after the answers of the jury were received. The trial Judge, Houlden, J., dismissed the motion. He held that the finding of the jury that there was implied permission for the plaintiff to be on the land of the defendant could be substantiated on the evidence.

. . .

Whether or not there was an implied permission was a question of fact for the jury. The jury was properly instructed on the law and brought its finding. I do not think that finding should be disturbed.

. . .

Even if Mr. Veinot is regarded as a trespasser his appeal to this Court should succeed. If he was a trespasser, the inquiry must be as to whether his presence on the ploughed road could reasonably have been anticipated for, if so, the company owed him a duty and that duty was to treat him with ordinary humanity.

Although as a general rule a person is not bound to anticipate the presence of intruders on private property or to guard them from injury, a duty may arise if the owner of land knew of, or from all the surrounding circumstances ought reasonably to have foreseen, the presence of a trespasser. It appears to me that a person of good sense in the position of the defendant company, possessing the knowledge which its responsible officers possessed about snowmobiles and the degree of snowmobile travel in the area, the proclivity for travel by night, the ease by which the ploughed road could be reached by several old roads leading on to it would have been alerted, on a moment's reflection, to the probability of someone reaching the ploughed road as Mr. Veinot did. Stress was laid during argument upon the fact that the plaintiff came in by way of the back door, as it were, and that such avenue of approach could not reasonably have been anticipated. I do not agree. Snowmobiles are ubiquitous. They have an unusual and well-known capacity for travel on and off the beaten path. In an uncharted Canadian wilderness area, of forest, rivers and lakes, one could reasonably expect them to go in almost any direction, at least until such time as they reached *indicia* of private property. If there was a likelihood that someone would come upon the ploughed road on a snowmobile at night, and the evidence in my view supports such a likelihood, then I do not think there can be doubt that the company failed in the duty it owed to Mr. Veinot to treat him with common humanity. The ploughed road gave every appearance of being a public road. Mr. Veinot had good reason to believe that he might freely use it if he wished to do so. Acting on that belief he failed to see or appreciate the abeyant danger of the rusty pipe. The defendant company in my opinion erred in permitting the continuance of what should have been recognized by it as a covert peril, menacing the safety of anyone who came upon the road at night on a snowmobile. And it would have been so easy to have averted the accident, by painting the pipe white or by hanging a cloth or a sign from it.

I would allow the appeal, set aside the judgment of the Court of Appeal and restore the judgment of the trial Judge with costs throughout.

NOTES AND QUESTIONS

1. Do you agree with Dickson J. that the plaintiff was a licensee? In light of *Veinot* and the authorities discussed in it, have the courts rendered the concept of implied licence meaningless?

2. Based on *Herrington* (discussed in *Veinot*), define the duty of care that an occupier owes to a trespasser. Identify the various factors that a court should consider in determining whether this duty applies in a given case. How does this test of duty differ from that established in *Donoghue v. Stevenson*, [1932] A.C. 562 (H.L.)? How did the decisions in *Pannett* and *Southern Portland Cement* (both also discussed in *Veinot*) alter the common humanity test established in *Herrington*? Based on these three cases, define an occupier's common law duty of care to a trespasser. What criticisms would you make of this test?

3. Traditionally, the courts have distinguished between passive and active dangers on the defendant's land. An active danger generally has been governed by ordinary principles of negligence, whereas a passive danger, such as that in *Veinot*, generally has been governed by occupiers' liability. This distinction, like so many other aspects of occupiers' liability, has generated controversy and confusion. See for example *Wade v. C.N.R.* (1977), 80 D.L.R. (3d) 214 (S.C.C.); and Gibson, "Torts – Negligence and Occupiers' Liability – Role of Jury – Confusing Words from the Oracle" (1978) 58 Can. Bar Rev. 693.

4. For further discussion of an occupier's common law duty of care to a trespasser see Innes, "Recent Developments in the Law of Occupiers' Liability to Trespassers" (1975) 24 U.N.B.L.J. 39; Di Castri, *Occupiers' Liability* (1981) at 123-46; and Fleming, *The Law of Torts*, 9th ed. (1998) at 47-50.

5. In 1974, Ontario enacted legislation to resolve the conflicts between snowmobile operators and occupiers. See the *Motorized Snow Vehicles Act*, R.S.O. 1990, c. M.44; and *Cormack v. Mara (Township)* (1989), 59 D.L.R. (4th) 300 (Ont. C.A.).

3. The Provincial Occupiers' Liability Statutes

(a) INTRODUCTION

Because of problems associated with the common law regime, occupiers' liability now is governed by statute in British Columbia, Alberta, Manitoba, Ontario, Nova Scotia and Prince Edward Island. Although some differences exist, the legislation is much the same from province to province. By way of illustration, we present the Ontario *Occupiers' Liability Act*, R.S.O. 1990, c. O.2 and then consider its application in the leading case of *Waldick v. Malcolm* (1991), 83 D.L.R. (4th) 114 (S.C.C.).

(b) ONTARIO OCCUPIERS' LIABILITY ACT

OCCUPIERS' LIABILITY ACT
R.S.O. 1990, c. O.2

1. In this Act . . .

"occupier" includes,

(a) a person who is in physical possession of premises, or

(b) a person who has responsibility for and control over the condition of premises or the activities there carried on, or control over persons allowed to enter the premises,

despite the fact that there is more than one occupier of the same premises;

. . .

"premises" means lands and structures, or either of them, and includes,

(a) water,

(b) ships and vessels,

(c) trailers and portable structures designed or used for residence, business or shelter,

(d) trains, railway cars, vehicles and aircraft, except while in operation.

Common law duty of care superseded

2. Subject to section 9, this Act applies in place of the rules of the common law that determine the care that the occupier of premises at common law is required to show for the purpose of determining the occupier's liability in law in respect of dangers to persons entering on the premises or the property brought on the premises by those persons.

Occupier's duty

3. (1) An occupier of premises owes a duty to take such care as in all the circumstances of the case is reasonable to see that persons entering on the premises, and the property brought on the premises by those persons are reasonably safe while on the premises.

(2) The duty of care provided for in subsection (1) applies whether the danger is caused by the condition of the premises or by an activity carried on on the premises.

(3) The duty of care provided for in subsection (1) applies except in so far as the occupier of premises is free to and does restrict, modify or exclude the occupier's duty.

Risks willingly assumed

4. (1) The duty of care provided for in subsection 3(1) does not apply in respect of risks willingly assumed by the person who enters on the premises, but in that case the occupier owes a duty to the person to not create a danger with the deliberate intent of doing harm or damage to the person or his or her property and to not act with reckless disregard of the presence of the person or his or her property.

Criminal activity

(2) A person who is on premises with the intention of committing, or in the commission of, a criminal act shall be deemed to have willingly assumed all risks and is subject to the duty of care set out in subsection (1).

Trespass and permitted recreational activity

(3) A person who enters premises described in subsection (4) shall be deemed to have willingly assumed all risks and is subject to the duty of care set out in subsection (1),

(a) where the entry is prohibited under the Trespass to Property Act;

(b) where the occupier has posted no notice in respect of entry and has not otherwise expressly permitted entry; or

(c) where the entry is for the purpose of a recreational activity and,

(i) no fee is paid for the entry or activity of the person, other than a benefit or payment received from a government or government agency or a non-profit recreation club or association, and

(ii) the person is not being provided with living accommodation by the occupier.

(4) The premises referred to in subsection (3) are,

(a) a rural premises that is,

(i) used for agricultural purposes, including land under cultivation, orchards, pastures, woodlots and farm ponds,

(ii) vacant or undeveloped premises,

(iii) forested or wilderness premises;

(b) golf courses when not open for playing;

(c) utility rights-of-way and corridors, excluding structures located thereon;

(d) unopened road allowances;

(e) private roads reasonably marked by notice as such; and

(f) recreational trails reasonably marked by notice as such.

Restriction of duty or liability

5. (1) The duty of an occupier under this Act, or the occupier's liability for breach thereof, shall not be restricted or excluded by any contract to which the person to whom the duty is owed is not a party, whether or not the occupier is bound by the contract to permit such person to enter or use the premises.

Extension of liability by contract

(2) A contract shall not by virtue of this Act have the effect, unless it expressly so provides, of making an occupier who has taken reasonable care, liable to any person not a party to the contract, for dangers due to the faulty execution of any work of construction, maintenance or repair, or other like operation by persons other than the occupier, employees of the occupier and persons acting under the occupier's direction and control.

Reasonable steps to inform

(3) Where an occupier is free to restrict, modify or exclude the occupier's duty of care or the occupier's liability for breach thereof, the occupier shall take reasonable steps

to bring such restriction, modification or exclusion to the attention of the person to whom the duty is owed.

Liability where independent contractor

6. (1) Where damage to any person or his or her property is caused by the negligence of an independent contractor employed by the occupier, the occupier is not on that account liable if in all the circumstances the occupier had acted reasonably in entrusting the work to the independent contractor, if the occupier had taken such steps, if any, as the occupier reasonably ought in order to be satisfied that the contractor was competent and that the work had been properly done, and if it was reasonable that the work performed by the independent contractor should have been undertaken.

(2) Where there is more than one occupier of premises, any benefit accruing by reason of subsection (1) to the occupier who employed the independent contractor shall accrue to all occupiers of the premises.

(3) Nothing in this section affects any duty of the occupier that is non-delegable at common law or affects any provision in any other Act that provides that an occupier is liable for the negligence of an independent contractor.

Application of ss. 5 (1, 2), 6

7. In so far as subsections 5(1) and (2) prevent the duty of care owed by an occupier, or liability for breach thereof, from being restricted or excluded, they apply to contracts entered into both before and after the commencement of this Act, and in so far as section 6 enlarges the duty of care owed by an occupier, or liability for breach thereof, it applies only in respect of contracts entered into after the 8th day of September, 1980.

Obligations of landlord as occupier

8. (1) Where premises are occupied or used by virtue of a tenancy under which the landlord is responsible for the maintenance or repair of the premises, it is the duty of the landlord to show towards any person or the property brought on the premises by those persons, the same duty of care in respect of dangers arising from any failure on the landlord's part in carrying out the landlord's responsibility as is required by this Act to be shown by an occupier of the premises.

(2) For the purposes of this section, a landlord shall not be deemed to have made default in carrying out any obligation to a person unless the landlord's default is such as to be actionable at the suit of the person entitled to possession of the premises.

Definitions

(3) For the purposes of this section, obligations imposed by any enactment by virtue of a tenancy shall be treated as imposed by the tenancy, and "tenancy" includes a statutory tenancy, an implied tenancy and any contract conferring the right of occupation, and "landlord" shall be construed accordingly.

Application of section

(4) This section applies to all tenancies whether created before or after the commencement of this Act.

Preservation of higher obligations

9. (1) Nothing in this Act relieves an occupier of premises in any particular case from any higher liability or any duty to show a higher standard of care that in that case is incumbent on the occupier by virtue of any enactment or rule of law imposing special liability or standards of care on particular classes of persons including, but without restricting the generality of the foregoing, the obligations of,

(a) innkeepers, subject to the Innkeepers Act;

(b) common carriers;

(c) bailees.

Employer and employee relationships

(2) Nothing in this Act shall be construed to affect the rights, duties and liabilities resulting from an employer and employee relationship where it exists.

Application of Negligence Act

(3) The Negligence Act applies with respect to causes of action to which this Act applies.

Act binds Crown

10. (1) This Act binds the Crown, subject to the Proceedings Against the Crown Act.

Exception

(2) This Act does not apply to the Crown or to any municipal corporation, where the Crown or the municipal corporation is an occupier of a public highway or a public road.

NOTES AND QUESTIONS

1. How does the approach adopted in the Ontario statute differ from the common law approach? Does the statute require the courts to ignore the fact that different occupiers have different resources at their disposal? Can the courts consider the category of entrant in determining an occupier's liability under the statute? Do you think that the statute is significantly easier to interpret and apply than the common law?

2. Like the Ontario statute, the Nova Scotia, Manitoba and British Columbia statutes define an occupier's duty in terms of taking such care as is reasonable in the circumstances, without formally recognizing different types of occupiers and categories of entrants. See *Occupiers' Liability Act*, R.S.M. 1987, c. O8, s. 3(1); and *Occupiers' Liability Act*, R.S.B.C. 1996, c. 337.

The Alberta statute adopts a similar duty for lawful entrants, but provides a much more restricted duty for adult trespassers. It also contains a third set of principles governing an occupier's duty to trespassing children. See *Occupiers' Liability Act*, R.S.A. 2000, c. O-4, ss. 5, 12 and 13.

The Prince Edward Island statute also adopts a reasonable care test for lawful entrants. However, it restricts the duty for trespassers, criminals, and those engaging in recreational activities. See *Occupiers' Liability Act*, R.S.P.E.I. 1988, c. O-2, ss. 3 and 4.

3. As under the common law rules, the plaintiff must prove not only that an injury occurred on the defendant's premises, but also that the defendant breached the standard of care. Occupiers' liability is not strict: see *Desjardins v. Arcadian Restaurants Ltd.*, 2005 CarswellOnt 7549 (S.C.J.) (WLeC). However, the plaintiff need not identify the precise location where the accident and injury occurred: see *Kamin v. Kawartha Dairy Ltd.* (2006), 79 O.R. (3d) 284 (C.A.).

4. Given its special rules, it is important to distinguish occupiers' liability from other heads of liability. In *Kennedy v. Waterloo (County) Board of Education* (1999), 175 D.L.R. (4th) 106 (Ont. C.A.), the plaintiff was a student at the defendant's school. While leaving the premises on his motorcycle, he struck a barrier that the defendant had erected. The trial judge held the defendant could not be held liable because its decision regarding the placement of the barriers fell under the rubric of "policy" rather than "operational." The Court of Appeal reversed that decision. It held that while the distinction between policy and operational decisions was relevant to the common law action in negligence, it did not apply under the *Occupiers' Liability Act*. The appellate court accordingly imposed liability, but reduced damages by 75% to reflect the plaintiff's own carelessness.

5. Depending upon the circumstances, an occupier may be obliged to protect people from their own foolishness. *Stringer v. Ashley* (unreported, 1994, Ont. H.C.J.) provides a controversial illustration. The plaintiff attended a party at the defendant's house. The defendant warned the plaintiff to not dive into the backyard pool from the roof of the house. The plaintiff repeatedly ignored that warning and eventually was rendered paraplegic. The court held that, given the claimant's intoxicated condition, a mere warning was not sufficient. The defendant should have done more (*e.g.* lock doors or remove the plaintiff from the premises). Do you agree with this decision? See Simpson, "The Occupier's Responsibility to Protect Guests From Themselves: *Stringer v. Ashley*" (1995) 16 Adv. Q. 506; and *cf. Tomlinson v. Congleton Borough Council*, [2004] 1 A.C. 46 (H.L.).

6. The statute obviously does not render an occupier liable for every injury that occurs on the premises. In *Koperdak v. Wiesblatt*, 2006 CarswellBC 968 (S.C.) (WLeC) the defendant let his house sit empty for several years. To protect the property from damage, he enclosed it with a fence and double-locked the gate. The plaintiff nevertheless approached the house because she was interested in purchasing it. She was injured after a front stair collapsed and sent her tumbling. The court considered all of the circumstances and denied liability because (1) the defect in the stair was latent and not reasonably known to the defendant, and (2) the defendant clearly had revoked the implied licence for members of the public to approach the house.

7. Section 4 of the Ontario statute creates a special, reduced standard of care if a person is on a property for certain "recreational" activities. On the scope of that provision, see *Moloney v. Parry Sound (Town)* (2000), 184 D.L.R. (4th) 121 (Ont. C.A.). See also Alberta Law Reform Institute, *Occupiers' Liability: Recreational Use of Land* (2000).

8. Section 8 of the Ontario statute imposes obligations on landlords. The Nova Scotia, Manitoba and British Columbia legislation is similar. In *Zavaglia v. Maq Holdings*

Ltd. (1986), 6 B.C.L.R. (2d) 286 (C.A.), the defendant rented a house to a man named Ruggles. While visiting Ruggles, the plaintiff was injured after he fell in a stairwell that did not have a handrail. The Court of Appeal held that, at common law, the plaintiff could not have succeeded because the landlord was not an "occupier." The situation was different, however, under the statute.

9. Once liability is imposed under the statute, damages are calculated in the usual manner: *Traquair v. National Arts Centre Corp.*, [2004] O.J. No. 4198 (S.C.J.) (QL). The plaintiff was "a very talented trombone player" with the National Arts Centre Orchestra in Ottawa. He suffered a concussion and mild brain damage after falling from his chair during a rehearsal. The accident occurred because the leg of his chair was caught in a gap on the stage. The court held the defendant liable as an occupier. It held that it was reasonably foreseeable that musicians would adjust their seats while concentrating on either their music or the conductor. The court also held that the "gaps" in question could have been remedied at little cost.

Given his unique profession, the plaintiff received compensation under several heads: (1) $20,560 for past medical expenses because, as common for people in his position, he did not have medical insurance, (2) $44,362 for future medical expenses, (3) $75,000 for general damages – considerably more than usual – because his reduced capacity to attend social functions affected him to an unusual degree, (4) $21,089 for the fact that he no longer could teach at Queen's University, and (5) $424,956 (reduced to reflect his pre-accident prospect of success) for the loss of opportunity to secure a position with a superior orchestra.

WALDICK v. MALCOLM

(1991), 83 D.L.R. (4th) 114 (S.C.C.)

IACOBUCCI J. – The defendants, Marvin and Roberta Malcolm ("the Malcolms"), appeal from a judgment of the Ontario Court of Appeal dismissing their appeal from the judgment at trial finding the Malcolms liable for personal injuries suffered by the plaintiff, Norman Waldick ("Waldick").

The appeal involves the interpretation of the nature and extent of the duty of care under the Ontario *Occupiers' Liability Act*, R.S.O. 1980, c. 322 (the "Act"). In general terms, the Act sets out the duty of care owed by occupiers of premises to persons who come onto those premises and specifies certain exceptions to the prescribed duty of care. As this appeal is the first involving the Act to reach this Court and as several provinces have similar statutory regimes, it is important to clarify the scope of the duties owed by occupiers to their visitors.

Facts

On February 7, 1984, Waldick suffered a fractured skull when he fell on the icy parking area of the rural residential premises near Simcoe, Ontario which were occupied by the Malcolms. Waldick is Mrs. Malcolm's brother. Mrs. Malcolm worked as a hairdresser but she often cut hair at her home for friends and relatives without receiving any remuneration. The property, which consisted of a farmhouse and barn on approximately three acres of land, was owned by the other appellants, Betty Stainback and Harry Hill. The Malcolms rented the premises from them. Since they were not the occupiers of the farmhouse, the action and cross-claim against Stainback and Hill were dismissed on consent in June, 1986.

On the premises was a gravel laneway that ran for about 200 to 300 feet from the road, past the house, and to the barn. Opposite the house, the laneway widened to form a parking area which could accommodate three or four vehicles at any one time. The house had a small wooden porch with two steps. Leading from the steps toward the laneway was a walk made of cement slabs which was about six feet long but which did not reach the laneway. The rest of the distance between the walk and the laneway was grass-covered. The trial judge noted that there was "a perceptible grade downwards from the house to the parking area."

At the time of the injury, the porch and steps of the house had been shovelled and, while the walk and grassy area had also been shovelled, these were still snow-covered. The laneway had not been salted or sanded. The appellant, Roberta Malcolm, testified that she did not consider it necessary or reasonable to do so. She also testified that to her knowledge few of the residents in that rural region, including Waldick, salted or sanded their laneways in winter. Four days before the accident, the region had experienced an ice storm. Waldick was aware that the laneway was "slippery, very icy with a dusting of snow on it" and acknowledged that its condition could be seen without difficulty. Because of the ice, he took exceptional caution in driving up the laneway. He parked about 20 feet from where the gravel laneway met the grassy stretch, and entered the house, walking very carefully because of the ice. Some time later, he went out to his car to get a carton of U.S. cigarettes which he had purchased for his sister. He put on his winter boots, turned on the porch light, and got the cigarettes. As he was walking back to the house, he slipped on the ice, fell backwards in the parking area, and fractured his skull.

Waldick commenced an action in the Supreme Court of Ontario under the Act, alleging negligence on the part of the Malcolms and the owners of the premises; as noted above, the action against the owners was dismissed on consent. The trial judge found the Malcolms liable for the injuries sustained by Waldick and by agreement of the parties deferred the determination of damages.

Malcolms' appeal was dismissed by the Ontario Court of Appeal.

Analysis

1. Did the Court of Appeal of Ontario err in holding that the Malcolms breached the duty of care imposed by s. 3(1) of the Occupiers' Liability Act?

The courts below concluded that, in light of all the circumstances, the Malcolms breached the duty of care owed under s. 3(1) of the Act by doing nothing to render the parking area entrance to their house less slippery. While the Act in no way obliged them to salt or sand "every square inch of their parking area", Austin J. was of the view that doing nothing fell short of the reasonable care requirement. Blair J.A. agreed, noting the duty was limited only to salting or sanding that part of the parking area next to the entrance and adding that it was undeniable that the Malcolms knew this part would be used by visitors like Waldick.

Both Austin J. and Blair J.A. also stressed that sand and salt are not expensive and are readily available.

Counsel for the Malcolms submitted that the lower courts had reduced the statutory words "in all the circumstances of the case" to a consideration of only two factors:

foreseeability of an accident, and the *costs* of its avoidance. In counsel's view, this was an oversimplified "calculus of negligence" which constituted a reviewable error of law. More specifically, the Malcolms argued that the courts below should also have taken into account "the practices of persons in the same or similar situations as the person whose conduct is being judged", or in other words, local custom. This, it was argued, would inject an element of community standards into the negligence calculus, and would promote behaviour which better accords with the reasonable expectations of community members.

. . . In the instant appeal, the relevant local custom which the courts below allegedly neglected to consider was "not sanding or salting driveways".

I am unable to agree with the Malcolms' submissions for several reasons. First of all, I do not agree with the premise of their argument, viz., that the lower courts failed to consider local custom. In my view, both Austin J. and Blair J.A. gave ample consideration to all the factors which could enter into an assessment of what constitutes reasonable care, including the alleged custom in the rural community involved.

. . .

The mere fact that the alleged custom was not decisive of the negligence issue does not in any way support the conclusion that it was not considered. After all, the statutory duty on occupiers is framed quite generally, as indeed it must be. That duty is to take reasonable care in the circumstances to make the premises safe. That duty does not change but the factors which are relevant to an assessment of what constitutes reasonable care will necessarily be very specific to each fact situation – thus the proviso "such care as *in all circumstances of the case* is reasonable". One such circumstance is whether the nature of the premises is rural or urban. Another is local custom, which Blair J.A. explicitly mentions and I view his reasons as considering and rejecting the alleged custom.

Secondly, there are proof problems that complicate the Malcolms' argument in this regard. Acknowledging that custom can inform the courts' assessment of what is reasonable in any given set of circumstances, it is nevertheless beyond dispute that, in any case where an alleged custom is raised, the "party who relies on either his own compliance with custom or the other person's departure from general practice bears the onus of proof that the custom is in effect.". . . Only in the rarest and most patently obvious of cases will the courts take judicial notice of a custom. . . .

In the case at bar, there is nothing apart from the completely unsupported testimony of the appellant Mrs. Malcolm that tends to prove something that could qualify as custom.
. . .

Thirdly, even if there had been adequate evidence in the record of a general local custom of not salting or sanding driveways, I am not of the view that such a custom would necessarily be decisive against a determination of negligence in the case at bar. . . . [N]o amount of general community compliance will render negligent conduct "reasonable . . . in all the circumstances". . . . If, as the lower courts found, it is unreasonable to do absolutely nothing to one's driveway in the face of clearly treacherous conditions, it matters little that one's neighbours also act unreasonably. Presumably it is exactly this type of generalized negligence that the Act is meant to discourage.

. . .

2. In the event that the Court of Appeal of Ontario was correct that the Malcolms did not meet the duty of care, did Waldick willingly assume the risks of walking over the icy parking area, thus relieving them from liability, pursuant to s. 4(1) of the Act?

At issue under this ground of appeal is the scope of the defence which s. 4(1) offers to occupiers. They will be absolved of liability in those cases where the losses suffered by visitors on their premises come as a result of "risks willingly assumed" by those visitors. As Austin J. and Blair J.A. noted, there are two quite distinct and conflicting trends in the jurisprudence as to the proper interpretation of this term. In essence, they reflect two standards of what assuming a risk means: the first involves merely knowing of the risk that one is running, whereas the second involves not only knowledge of the risk, but also a consent to the legal risk, or in other words, a waiver of legal rights that may arise from the harm or loss that is being risked. The latter standard is captured by the maxim *volenti non fit injuria* (the *volenti* doctrine) whereas the former is sometimes referred to as "*sciens*", or in other words, mere "knowing" as opposed to actually "willing."

Counsel for the Malcolms argued that s. 4(1) should be interpreted as meaning something between mere knowledge and the strict *volenti* approach. He suggested that s. 4(1) would be met where it could be shown that the visitor had a knowledge *and* appreciation of the danger on the premises.

In my view, the reasons of Blair J.A. on this issue are also an admirably correct statement of the law. I have no doubt that s. 4(1) of the Act was intended to embody and preserve the *volenti* doctrine. This can be seen by looking at the statutory scheme that is imposed by the Act as a whole. It is clear the intention of the Act was to replace, refine and harmonize the common law *duty of care* owed by occupiers of premises to visitors on those premises. That much seems evident from the wording of s. 2 of the Act. . . .

I am of the view that the Act was *not* intended to effect a wholesale displacement of the common law defences to liability, and it is significant that no mention is made of common law defences in s. 2. Reinforcement of this view is found when one asks why this area of law should entail a defence other than *volenti* which is applicable to negligence actions generally. There does not appear to be anything special about occupiers' liability that warrants a departure from the widely accepted *volenti* doctrine.

. . .

The goals of the Act are to promote, and indeed, require where circumstances warrant, positive action on the part of occupiers to make their premises reasonably safe. The occupier may, however, wish to put part of his property "off limits" rather than to make it safe, and in certain circumstances that might be considered reasonable. Where no such effort has been made, as in the case at bar, the exceptions to the statutory duty of care will be few and narrow.

. . .

In my view, the legislature's intention in enacting s. 4(1) of the Act was to carve out a very narrow exception to the class of visitors to whom the occupier's statutory duty of care is owed. This exception shares the same logical basis as the premise that underlies *volenti*, i.e., that no wrong is done to one who consents. By agreeing to assume the risk the plaintiff absolves the defendant of all responsibility for it. Rare may be the case where a visitor who enters on premises will fully know of and accept the risks resulting from the occupier's non-compliance with the statute. To my mind, such an interpretation of s. 4(1) accords best with general principles of statutory interpretation, is more fully consonant with the legislative aims of the Act, and is consistent with tort theory generally.

Both Austin J. and Blair J.A. were of the view that Waldick did not consent to the legal risk or waive any legal rights that might arise from the negligence of the Malcolms. I agree with their disposition of this ground of appeal and conclude that Waldick is not barred from recovery by the operation of s. 4(1) of the Act.

Conclusion

For the foregoing reasons, I would dismiss the appeal with costs.

NOTES AND QUESTIONS

1. How would the case have been decided under the common law rules?

2. Prior to the decision in *Waldick*, there was considerable debate as to whether s. 4(1) of the Ontario statute essentially codified the common law defence of *volenti*. Do you agree with Iacobucci J.'s decision? For further discussion, see Tomlinson, Machum & Lyons, "The Contractual Waiver of Liability in Ski Resort Negligence Claims" (1997) 15 Can. J. Ins. L. 49.

3. For other decisions pertaining to occupiers' liability legislation, see *Olinski v. Johnson* (1997), 32 O.R. (3d) 653 (C.A.); *Slaferek v. TCG International Inc.* (1997), [1998] 3 W.W.R. 600 (Alta. Q.B.); *Pope v. Route 66 Clothing Inc.* (1997), 41 C.C.L.T. (2d) 72 (Ont. Gen. Div.); and *Bennett v. Kailua Estates Ltd.* (1997), 32 C.C.L.T. (2d) 217 (B.C.C.A.).

REVIEW PROBLEM

Florence rented part of an old house from Ranjit. Florence had possession of the ground floor and Ranjit kept possession of the basement apartment, which he used for storage and kept locked at all times. Neither Florence nor Ranjit used the stairs connecting the basement to the first floor. Florence had no reason or right to enter the basement apartment, and Ranjit always used the street entrance to his apartment.

Florence soon became friends with her neighbour, Lilly, although she disliked Lilly's boyfriend, Hugo. Late one night, some three weeks after Florence had moved in, Florence heard a commotion at Lilly's residence and became fearful for her friend's safety. Minutes later, Lilly arrived at Florence's front door. Lilly was crying and confided that Hugo was drunk and had threatened her. Suddenly Hugo arrived at her door and, ignoring Florence's protests, pushed his way into the house. Lilly ran down the stairs to the basement. Hugo followed her. Unfortunately, two steps were missing and both Lilly and Hugo fell. The missing stairs would have been noticed by anyone who was walking normally. Ranjit knew about the missing stairs but he did not bother to inform Florence, because he thought she would never use them.

Analyze the common law duty of care, if any, that Florence and Ranjit owe to Hugo and Lilly. Would they be held liable to Lilly and Hugo under the Ontario *Occupiers' Liability Act*?

24

NUISANCE

1. Introduction
2. Private Nuisance
3. Public Nuisance
4. Remedies

1. Introduction

In Chapter 5, we briefly compared the actions for private nuisance and trespass to land. In this chapter, we consider private nuisance in more detail. We also examine the private action for public nuisance.

Although the torts of trespass to land and private nuisance are closely related, they also are clearly distinct. Trespass to land provides a remedy for direct and intentional physical intrusions upon another's land. As we saw in Chapter 5, the concept of reasonableness is irrelevant to the inquiry. The tort originally was designed to ensure the inviolability of property rights and it remains true today that liability may be imposed even if the defendant acted with great care and even if the plaintiff suffered little or no harm.

The tort of nuisance is similar to trespass insofar as it was designed to protect the plaintiff's use and enjoyment of land. Consequently, relief may be granted against overhanging branches, seeping sewage, foul odours, barking dogs, bright lights, traffic vibrations, industrial pollution, subsidence of supporting soil, errant golf balls, and even unwanted telephone calls. Significantly, however, not every interference supports a right of action. Liability depends on proof of unreasonableness. The court must weigh the plaintiff's interest in being free from interference against the defendant's interest in carrying on the impugned activity, as well as society's interest in allowing some types of activities. Relief is available only if, having regard to all of the circumstances, the interference was unreasonable.

In that sense, nuisance might seem to have a great deal in common with the tort of negligence, which also relies on a theory of reasonableness. It therefore is important to draw a distinction. In negligence, the issue of reasonableness pertains primarily to the nature of the defendant's *conduct*. In nuisance, it pertains primarily to the *effect* that the defendant's conduct has on the plaintiff's enjoyment of land. One result of that distinction is that the defendant may be liable in nuisance despite acting reasonably.

Nuisance and negligence nevertheless do share at least one important feature. Whether it is used to assess the defendant's conduct or the plaintiff's interference, the concept of reasonableness necessarily imports a judicial discretion. The court cannot simply apply clear rules to hard facts. In addition, it must exercise a value judgment. It must strike a sensitive balance, on a case-by-case basis, between competing interests. Not surprisingly, the analysis is often both complex and contentious. Indeed, it has been suggested that "[t]here is no more impenetrable jungle in the entire law than that which surrounds the word 'nuisance'": Keeton *et al.*, *Prosser & Keeton on Torts*, 5th ed. (1984) at 616.

The tort of private nuisance must also be distinguished from the tort of public nuisance. That tort is linked to the criminal law concept of a "common nuisance." In addition to being criminally prosecuted for injuring society's interests, the defendant may be held civilly liable to those members of the community that suffered special injury.

2. Private Nuisance

340909 ONT. LTD. v. HURON STEEL PRODUCTS (WINDSOR) LTD.

(1990), 73 O.R. (2d) 641 (H.C.)

[The defendant's stamping plant had been in operation since 1947. In 1977, the plaintiff bought a nearby apartment building. In 1979, the defendant purchased an 880-tonne press and installed it across the street from the plaintiff's apartment building. The plaintiff complained of noise and vibrations. Although a second such press was installed in 1983, efforts were made to reduce noise and vibrations and the second press met Ministry of the Environment guidelines. The plaintiff brought an action for nuisance claiming loss of rental income and loss of the value of the building.]

POTTS J: – . . .

DOES THE PLAINTIFF HAVE A CAUSE OF ACTION IN NUISANCE?

Private nuisance can be defined as an unreasonable interference with the use and enjoyment of land. J.G. Fleming, in *The Law of Torts*, 4th ed. (Sydney: Law Book Co., 1971), states at p. 346 that the court goes through a balancing process to determine whether a nuisance exists or not:

The paramount problem in the law of nuisance is, therefore, to strike a tolerable balance between conflicting claims of landowners, each invoking the privilege to exploit the resources and enjoy the amenities of his property without undue subordination to the reciprocal interests of the other. Reconciliation has to be achieved by compromise, and the basis for adjustment is reasonable user. Legal intervention is warranted only when an excessive use of property causes inconvenience beyond what other occupiers in the vicinity can be expected to bear, having regard to the prevailing standard of comfort of the time and place. Reasonableness in this context is a two-sided affair. It is viewed not only from the standpoint of the defendant's convenience, but must also take into account the interest of the surrounding occupiers. It is not enough to ask: Is the defendant using his property in what would be a reasonable manner if he had no neighbour? The question is, Is he using it reasonably, having regard to the fact that he has a neighbour?

Furthermore, each case must be considered in light of the particular facts in question.

. . .

"Unreasonableness" in nuisance law is when the interference in question would not be tolerated by the ordinary occupier. What constitutes "unreasonable" interference is determined by considering a number of factors:

(1) the severity of the interference, having regard to its nature and duration and effect;

(2) the character of the locale;

(3) the utility of the defendant's conduct;

(4) the sensitivity of the use interfered with.

It is not necessary to deal with the sensitivity of the use interfered with, since the plaintiff's use of its property is not an unusually sensitive one. The remaining three factors will be discussed below.

(1) *The severity of the interference, having regard to its nature, duration and effect*

(a) *Nature of the interference*

The interference must be considered from the plaintiff company's point of view. However, the noise and vibration are allegedly disrupting the use and enjoyment by the tenants. This will ultimately affect the plaintiff as landlord, since the interference could be one reason why a tenant moves out. Therefore, the interference from the tenants' points of view is relevant, since it is *part of* the interference from the plaintiff's point of view.

. . .

Three expert witnesses testified in the area of sound and vibration assessment. I accept . . . that such evidence is helpful to confirm or disprove the evidence of other witnesses.

. . .

Kende made observations and took sound readings of the Huron Steel plant operations in December 1980. He testified that the #1 press was clearly audible and easily identifiable inside and outside the plant. The sound "was not a residential neighbourhood noise" and he "would not want to live with it".

. . .

He recorded an equivalent sound level (leq) of 69 dBA (not impulse) which exceeded the traffic level of 59 dBA and was in violation of the other guidelines the Ministry of the Environment uses.

. . .

Lightstone and Coulter both took impulse and sound and vibration measurements of Huron Steel plant operations. They agree that the impulse sound level at the apartment building is from 70-73 dBAI, with the Prince Road doors closed. Coulter also took indoor readings at the apartment with the window open and recorded about 60 dBAI. The *E.P.A.* guidelines are not meant for indoor readings. However, Lightstone agreed that this reading appears consistent with what he would expect, *i.e.*, 13-14 dBAI lower indoors. It should be mentioned that on cross-examination, Lightstone agreed that impulsive sounds are more intrusive than continuous ones.

Coulter and Lightstone agree that the #1 press is the source of the problem, although other sounds come from the plant as well. The press sound would be more noticeable at night, especially with the windows open, because the ambient levels are lower. Lightstone emphasizes the fact that many of the apartments facing the plant are equipped with air conditioners. The air conditioners, when running, would supposedly negate much of the sound from Huron Steel.

. . .

(b) *Duration*

The Huron Steel plant has been in operation since 1947. According to Mr. Andy Paonessa, who worked at Huron Steel from 1955 to 1978 and as plant manager from 1972, stamping occurred at the plant when he was there.

The number of shifts varied over the years. In 1974 or 1975, it was a three-shift operation, at which time it went to a one-shift, but when Morrison purchased the plant in 1977, it went to three shifts in three months. This continued after the #1 press was installed in 1979.

The major sound and vibration problems seem to occur when the #1 press is blanking heavy gauge material. This presumably would occur when orders had to be filled. Witnesses testified that, although the problem was not continuous, it was fairly regular. The press often operated during the night and on weekends, although there were periods of time when it did not run at all. The situation has continued since 1979, *i.e.*, ten years.

(c) *Effect*

To be successful, the plaintiff must show that the alleged nuisance has caused it damage. As discussed above, at least one of the plaintiff's tenants, Sbrocca, testified that he moved out primarily because of the noise and vibration coming from Huron Steel. Kenney testified that he received other tenant complaints about Huron Steel and that rents had not been increased and standards had been lowered in order to keep the vacancy rate down. Other property owners in the area testified as to the disruption they had experienced from the Huron Steel operations.

Mr. F.R. Jordan was put forward by the plaintiff as an expert in the value of real estate. He testified that he had examined the rent rolls of the plaintiff's apartment building for 1979-1987, in comparison with Canada Mortgage and Housing Corporation (C.M.H.C.) statistics. Based on a capitalized income approach, he concluded that the building lost revenue because of the comparatively high vacancy rate. Jordan stated that there was something abnormal about the property that caused the high vacancy rate and in his report he pointed to the disruptive Huron Steel operations as a probable cause. Jordan also concluded that there had been a loss in value of the building of about $71,000.

The defendant called two expert witnesses to discuss the effect the alleged nuisance had on the plaintiff. Mr. Glen Ladouceur is a business valuator. He examined Jordan's report and did his own study and concluded that the apartment as an income-producing asset did better than three similar buildings, worse than three and the same as one. He testified that he could not conclude that there was any loss in value based on these comparisons.

Mr. D. Rostant is an expert in chartered accountancy. He examined Jordan's report and the rent rolls. He concluded that it was not clear that the plaintiff suffered any loss of rental income over 1979-1988 because of Huron Steel operations.

I accept that the effect of the Huron Steel operations has been such as to cause some damage to the plaintiff.

(2) *Character of the locale*

Counsel for the plaintiff contends that technological advances have weakened the application of this type of "defence". Defendant's counsel places much greater emphasis on this aspect. Relatively recent cases continue to hold that this is an important factor and I accept it as such: In *Walker, supra*, Morden J. stated at p. 38 O.R.:

> The law makes it clear that the character of the locality is of importance in determining the standard of comfort which may reasonably be claimed by an occupier of land. "What would be a nuisance in Belgrave Square would not necessarily be so in Bermondsey": *Sturges v. Bridgman* (1879), 11 Ch.D 852 at p. 865.

The Huron Steel plant is bordered by Sandwich Street to the north (approximately), Peter Street to the south, Hill Avenue to the west and Prince Road to the east.

. . .

I find that the character of the locale is one of "mixed use". The area contains apartment buildings, houses, at least one school, and one church, commercial establishments, and factories.

The standard of comfort to be expected varies from area to area, depending on the character of the locale in question. According to Linden, *Canadian Tort Law*, p. 505, the standard to be expected in a predominantly residential area differs from that of an industrial or commercial one. However, "[t]he process of determining the proper standard becomes more difficult when the area is one of mixed or changing use".

. . .

First of all, it is well established that it is no defence to a nuisance action that the plaintiff moved to the nuisance. . .. Secondly, many of the witnesses testifed that although there was some noise coming from the Huron Steel plant prior to 1979, the problems with noise and vibration began when the #1 press was installed. *Rushmer v. Polsue & Afieri Ltd.*, [1906] 1 Ch. 234 (C.A.). . ., stands for the proposition that the addition of a fresh noise may give rise to a nuisance no matter what the character of the locale. In the Court of Appeal decision, Cozens-Hardy L.J. stated at pp. 250-51:

> A resident in such a neighbourhood must put up with a certain amount of noise. The standard of comfort differs according to the situation of the property and the class of people who inhabit it . . . But whatever the standard of comfort in a particular district may be, I think the addition of a fresh noise caused by the defendant's works may be so substantial as to create a legal nuisance. It does not follow that because I live, say, in the manufacturing part of Sheffield I cannot complain if a steam-hammer is introduced next door, and so worked as to render sleep at night almost impossible, although previously to its introduction my house was a reasonably comfortable abode, having regard to the local standard; and it would be no answer to say that the steam-hammer is of the most modern approved pattern and is reasonably worked. In short . . . it is no answer to say that the neighbourhood is noisy, and that the defendant's machinery is of first-class character.

(3) *The utility of the defendant's conduct*

The importance of the defendant's enterprise and its value to the community is a factor in determining if the defendant's conduct is unreasonable. However, this tends to go to the leniency of the remedy, rather than liability itself. Furthermore, the question whether the defendant took all reasonable precautions is relevant as to whether the interference is unreasonable.

Morrison and defendant's counsel mentioned that the Huron Steel plant is important to the community, since it employs about 200 people. Supposedly these jobs would be at risk if Huron Steel were required to make extensive structural changes to the plant to cut the noise and vibration from the #1 press.

. . .

I accept Mr. Morrison's contention that a lot of thought and effort went into the planning, purchase and installation of the #1 press. I also appreciate that the defendant has taken what it considers to be all reasonable and economically practical steps to alleviate the noise and vibration problem. However, the expert evidence indicates that improvements could be made to the building envelope that would ameliorate the situation.

. . .

CONCLUSION ON LIABILITY

The evidence indicates that the defendant's Huron Steel plant operations have caused and continue to cause an unreasonable interference with the plaintiff's use and enjoyment of its property.

. . .

Although this case has certainly not been clear cut, after considering all of the circumstances and factors set out above, I find that on balance of probabilities, the defendant's operations, and the #1 press in particular, do constitute an actionable nuisance.

[The plaintiff was awarded $14,927 for lost rental revenue and $56,500 for the reduction in value of the apartment building. The parties agreed to a remedial course of action and an injunction was granted incorporating the terms of the agreement.]

NOTES AND QUESTIONS

1. What were the plaintiff's allegations of nuisance? The judge considered four criteria in determining whether a nuisance had been committed. Explain in your own words the matters to be considered under each of the criteria. What evidence did the judge consider in assessing each of the criteria? Do you agree with the judge's application of the criteria to the facts?

2. Do you think the judge gave equal weight to all four criteria? Should he have done so?

3. Do you think the judge would have resolved this case the same way if:

(a) the #1 press was operating when the apartment building was constructed?

(b) the #1 press operated within Ministry guidelines with occasional violations?

(c) there was another factory on the other side of the apartment building which produced noise and vibrations equal to the #1 press?

(d) the defendant employed 1,000 workers and was the largest single employer in Windsor?

4. The judge in *Huron Steel* stated that a defendant cannot escape liability merely by proving that the plaintiff came to the nuisance. Nevertheless, such evidence can be

considered in determining whether the defendant's conduct constituted an unreasonable interference and, hence, a nuisance. See for example the extracts from *Miller v. Jackson*, [1977] Q.B. 966 (C.A.) and *Spur Industries Inc. v. Del E. Webb Development Co.*, 494 P.2d 700 (Ariz. S.C. 1972) that appear later in this chapter.

5. In *Kent v. Dom. Steel & Coal Corp. Ltd.* (1965), 49 D.L.R. (2d) 241 at 246 (Nfld. S.C.), the court stated:

> If I can adopt some other manner in the use of my land to achieve the same effect then it becomes all the more evident that I am using my land in an unreasonable way. To apply this to this case; Dosco could haul its ore across its land in such a way as to avoid the creation of a dust nuisance if it prepared its road of non-dust producing materials; if for example it paved the road, or if it did earlier what it did later, apply suitable dressing to the surface so as to eliminate the dust; or even more simply if it caused its trucks to drive at a slow rate of speed. It is clear that Dosco was unwilling to expend the money which paving would cost and perhaps the chemical dressing was not industriously sought by them; and as to moving the loads of ore at a low speed this would have reduced the rate of production at the mines and added to their costs. From its point of view these reasons – if in fact they were the reasons, for on this point I can only speculate – would have seemed reasonable to Dosco. But they would not provide much consolation to the plaintiff, nor could they be deemed reasonable to him. It would seem to me, though I am making no substantive finding on the point, that Dosco could have used its land in a way which would not have given the plaintiff any cause for complaint. But it did not do so, and I have no hesitation in rejecting Mr. Lewis' submission on this point.

Do you agree with the court? If it is cheaper for the plaintiff to avoid the harm than it is for the defendant to adopt an available alternative, is the defendant using its land in a reasonable way? See also *Renken v. Harvey Aluminum (Inc.)*, 226 F.Supp. 169 (D. Or. 1963); and *Cambridge Water Co. Ltd. v. Eastern Counties Leather plc*, [1994] 2 A.C. 264 (H.L.).

6. A nuisance may occur in a variety of ways. First, the clearest cases occur when the defendant's activity causes *physical damage* to the plaintiff's property. For instance, an industrial plant may emit chemical particles that drift on the wind and ruin the paint on the plaintiff's building, or heavy machinery may cause vibrations that crack the foundations of the plaintiff's house. Second, even if physical damage does not occur, a nuisance may arise if the defendant *impairs the enjoyment* of the plaintiff's property. For instance, a pig farm may cause an unbearable stench to waft over the plaintiff's outdoor café, or an all-night disco may produce a noise that prevents its neighbours from sleeping. Third, and exceptionally, a nuisance may occur even if the defendant's activity is entirely *non-intrusive*. For instance, the defendant's brothel may attract seedy characters into the plaintiff's neighbourhood, or the defendant may install a sewer system that drains water *away* from the plaintiff's land and thereby causes his land to collapse.

Although a nuisance may arise in various ways, the courts are much more likely to find the defendant's interference to be unreasonable if it causes physical damage to the plaintiff's property. Moreover, some courts have said that an interference that falls short of causing material damage must be continuous before it will constitute a nuisance. See for example *Andrews v. R A. Douglas* (1977), 17 N.S.R. (2d) 181 (C.A.); and *Chu v. Dawson* (1984), 31 C.C.L.T. 146 (B.C.C.A.). See also Fleming, *The Law of Torts*, 9th ed. (1998) at 460-62; and Keeton *et al.*, *Prosser and Keeton on Torts*, 5th ed. (1984) at 627-30.

7. It is often difficult to predict which interferences will be held to be nuisances. For example, in what circumstances should nuisance protect a landowner's interest in aesthetic scenery? See Noel, "Unaesthetics Sights as Nuisance" (1939) 25 Cornell L. Rev. 1. See also *Muirhead v. Timber Bros. Sand & Gravel Ltd.* (1977), 3 C.C.L.T. 1 (Ont. H.C.); *St. Pierre v. Ontario*, [1987] 1 S.C.R. 906; and *Zbarsky v. Lukashuk*, [1992] 1 W.W.R. 690 (B.C.C.A.).

P. Osborne lists eight factors that commonly affect the determination as to whether the defendant's conduct constitutes a nuisance – *i.e.* an unreasonable interference with the plaintiff's use and enjoyment of land: (1) the *character of the neighbourhood*, (2) the *intensity* of the interference, (3) the *duration* of the interference, (4) the *time* of day and *day* of the week, (5) the *zoning designation* of the neighbourhood, (6) the *utility* of the defendant's conduct, (7) the *nature* of the defendant's conduct, and (8) the *sensitivity* of the plaintiff: Osborne, *The Law of Torts*, 2d ed. (2003) at 346-49.

8. The categories of interests protected by nuisance have expanded to address new uses of property made possible by modern technology. One court, for instance, found that repeated and harassing phone calls constituted a nuisance: *Motherwell v. Motherwell* (1976), 1 A.R. 47 (C.A.). In contrast, a court refused to find a nuisance when the defendant carried on surveillance through the use of vehicles parked near the plaintiff's home: *K. (M.J.) v. M.(J.D.)* (1998), 167 D.L.R. (4th) 334 (Alta. Q.B.). See also *Khorasandjian v. Bush*, [1993] 3 All E.R. 669 (C.A.); and Cooke, "A Development in the Tort of Private Nuisance" (1994) 57 Mod. L. Rev. 289.

9. In *Nor-Video Services Ltd. v. Ontario Hydro* (1978), 84 D.L.R. (3d) 221 (Ont. H.C.), the defendant was held liable in nuisance because the location of its power lines disrupted the plaintiff's television broadcasts. The judge held that watching television was an important incident of ordinary enjoyment of property and an interest worthy of the law's protection and vindication. The defendant's conduct was held to be an unreasonable interference, even though it had acted in good faith in placing its lines in the most economically efficient location.

In *Hunter v. Canary Wharf Ltd.*, [1997] A.C. 655 (H.L.), the House of Lords held that the defendant's lawful construction of an enormous skyscraper, which interfered with the local residents' television reception, did not constitute a private nuisance. The defendant was free to build on its property any structure it wished, provided it did not violate the planning law. The House of Lords distinguished *Nor-Video* on the basis that, in *Hunter*, it was the mere presence of the structure, as opposed to an activity or something emanating from the land, that interfered with the reception.

Is the House of Lords' attempt to distinguish *Nor-Video* compelling? What other legal, economic and social factors might explain the results in these cases? Do you agree with the House of Lords that compliance with planning law should, in effect, immunize property developers from the tort of private nuisance? See generally O'Sullivan, "Nuisance in the House of Lords – Normal Service Resumed" [1997] C.L.J. 483.

10. *Hunter* also raised the issue of who has standing to sue in nuisance. The majority of the House of Lords ruled that only a person with a possessory interest in land can sue

in nuisance. Thus, a tenant can sue, but his or her spouse and children cannot. Similarly, a lodger occupying premises under a licence cannot maintain a nuisance action. See Rook, "Private Nuisance – A Proprietary Interest?" (1996) 4 Tort L. Rev. 181; and Cone, "What a Nuisance!" (1997) 113 L.Q.R. 515. But see *Pemberton v. Southwark London Borough Council*, [2000] 3 All E.R. 924 (C.A.); and *Dennis v. Ministry of Defence*, [2003] 2 E.G.L.R. 121 (Q.B.).

Standing to sue similarly was an issue in *Pemberton v. Southwark L.B.C.*, [2000] 1 W.L.R. 1672 (C.A.). The claimant occupied an apartment as a "tolerated trespasser." Although her lease had expired and she had been subject to an order for possession, the landlord chose not to enforce the order and allowed the claimant to remain. The premises subsequently were subject to a nuisance committed by the defendant. The Court of Appeal held that a tolerated trespasser has sufficient interest to support an action in nuisance.

11. Even if the defendant did not *create* a nuisance, liability may be imposed for *continuing* a nuisance. This is true if an occupier, despite actual or constructive knowledge of a nuisance, fails to take reasonable steps to abate it. A further question arose in *Delaware Mansions Ltd. v. Westminster City Council*, [2002] A.C. 321 (H.L.). Is relief available if the damage caused by the nuisance already existed *before* the claimant took possession of the adversely affected property? The House of Lords answered in the affirmative. On the facts, Lord Cooke of Thorndon addressed the issue from the perspective of "reasonableness between neighbours." In that respect, he emphasized the continuing nature of the damage and the need for remedial work. It also was significant that the price that the claimant paid for the property had not been reduced to reflect the existing damage. If it had been otherwise, damages would have constituted double recovery for the same loss, and consequently would have been denied. See generally Parker, "A Continued Nuisance" [2002] C.L.J. 260.

12. A typical nuisance case involves a dispute between neighbours. Strictly speaking, however, only the plaintiff needs to have a possessory interest in land. The defendant need not be a neighbour. It obviously is no defence to say, for instance, that an intolerable noise emanates from a vehicle parked on a public street rather than a nightclub located in a nearby building.

13. Liability in nuisance may be imposed if an occupier (a) knew, or ought to have known, of a hazard created by a third party or by nature, and (b) failed to take reasonable steps to protect neighbouring properties. Relief therefore was available when an occupier failed to abate a nuisance created after a trespasser's unauthorized drainage work caused flooding on the plaintiff's land: *Sedleigh-Denfield v. O'Callaghan*, [1940] A.C. 880 (H.L.). Likewise, while occupiers traditionally enjoyed immunity from an action in nuisance with respect to the natural condition of their property, the scope of liability has been expanded. In *Goldman v. Hargrave*, [1967] 1 A.C. 645 (P.C.) the plaintiff was entitled to compensation after his property was damaged by the spread of a fire that was started by lightning on the defendant's property.

The same principles were applied in *Lippiatt v. South Gloucestershire Council*, [1999] 4 All E.R. 149 (C.A.). The defendant allowed a group of "travellers" to reside on its property for three years. During that time, the travellers frequently trespassed onto the plaintiffs' neighbouring lands, dumping rubbish and excrement, and tethering animals. The court held that, in the circumstances, the defendants could be held liable for the damage done by the travellers who wandered onto the plaintiffs' properties. See also *Turner v. Delta Shelf Co. Ltd.* (1995), 24 C.C.L.T. (2d) 107 (B.C.S.C.); and *270233 Ontario Ltd. v. Weall & Cullen Nurseries Ltd.* (1993), 17 C.C.L.T. (2d) 176 (Ont. Gen. Div.), aff'd (1997), 41 C.C.L.T. (2d) 239 (Ont. C.A.).

14. Although the provincial limitation statutes generally provide that actions expire a fixed number of years (like two or six) after the cause of action arises, in nuisance a new cause of action arises each day the nuisance continues: see *Kerlenmar Holdings Ltd. v. Matsqui (District)* (1991), 81 D.L.R. (4th) 334 (B.C.C.A.).

15. For a discussion of the history of nuisance see Winfield, "Nuisance as a Tort" (1930-32) 4 C.L.J. 189; Loengard, "The Assize of Nuisance: Origins of an Action at Common Law" [1978] C.L.J. 144; McLaren, "Nuisance Law and the Industrial Revolution – Some Lessons from Social History" (1983) 3 O.J.L.S. 155; and Lewin, "Compensated Injunctions and the Evolution of Nuisance Law" (1986) 71 Iowa L. Rev. 775. For a review of contemporary developments, see Cross, "Does Only the Careless Polluter Pay? A Fresh Examination of the Nature of Private Nuisance" (1995) 111 L.Q.R. 445; and Lee, "What is Private Nuisance?" (2003) 119 L.Q.R. 298.

HOLLYWOOD SILVER FOX FARM LTD. v. EMMETT

[1936] 2 K.B. 468

[The plaintiff was a breeder of silver foxes. The sign that he had erected to advertise his business annoyed the defendant, who alleged that it was detrimental to his development of a building estate. When the plaintiff refused to move the sign, the defendant threatened to discharge guns near the fox pens during their breeding season in order to interfere with their whelping. When the defendant carried through with this threat, the plaintiff sued in nuisance.]

MACNAGHTEN J.: . . . Mr. Roche, who put the case for the defendant extremely well, argued that if the defendant had sent his son to shoot at the boundary of his land for the purpose of injuring the plaintiff and that if his conduct was malicious because he wanted to harm the plaintiff, nevertheless he had not committed any actionable wrong. The defendant was entitled to shoot on his own land. He might shoot there to keep down rabbits, or he might shoot for his own pleasure and if it pleased him to annoy his neighbour, although his conduct might be considered unneighbourly, he was entitled at law to do so. In the course of his argument, Mr. Roche relied upon the decision of the House of Lords in the case of *Bradford Corpn. v. Pickles* [[1895] A.C. 587]. In that case the Corporation of Bradford sought an injunction to restrain the defendant from sinking a shaft on land which belonged to him because, according to their view, his object in sinking the shaft was to draw away water which would otherwise become the property of the Corporation. Pickles was acting maliciously. His sole object in digging was to do harm to the Corporation. The House of Lords decided, once and for all, that in such a case the motive of the defendant is immaterial.

Mr. Roche contended that in this case the defendant had committed no nuisance at all in the legal sense of this case and he referred to *Robinson v. Kilvert* [(1889), 41 Ch. D. 88]. In that case complaint was made by the appellant that the brown paper which he kept on the ground floor of his premises suffered some damage from heat in the basement below, and it was held by the Court of Appeal that no actionable wrong was being committed by the defendant in that the heating was not of such a character as would interfere with the ordinary use of the rest of the house. He supplemented the argument, based on the consideration of that case, with the observations of Lord Robertson in *Eastern & South African Telegraph Co. v. Cape Town Tramways Cos.*, [[1902] A.C. 381], where Lord Robertson, delivering the judgment of the Privy Council, said, at page 393:

> A man cannot increase the liabilities of his neighbour by applying his own property to special uses, whether for business or pleasure.

It was argued that the keeping of a silver fox farm was not an ordinary use of land in the county of Kent, and what the defendant had done in discharging the bird-scaring cartridges would cause no alarm to the sheep or cattle which are usually to be found on Kentish farms. It was only because Captain Chalmers had brought these highly nervous animals – not natural to this country – that had caused the plaintiffs any loss and if silver foxes were brought to the county of Kent, one could not thereby restrict their neighbours in the matter of shooting. I am not satisfied that there is any substance in that argument. It is a perfectly lawful thing to keep a silver fox farm and I think the fact that the shooting took place intentionally for the purpose of injuring the plaintiffs made it actionable.

The authority for the view that in cases of alleged nuisance by noise, the intention of the person making the noise is not to be disregarded is to be found in the case of *Gaunt v. Fynney* [(1872), 8 Ch. App. 8]. Lord Selborne, L.C., delivered the judgment of the court, and he was dealing there with the question of nuisances, and he said this, at page 12:

> A nuisance by noise (supposing malice to be out of the question) is emphatically a question of degree.

It has been observed by high authority that Lord Selborne was always extremely careful in the use of language and that parenthetical statement "supposing malice to be out of the question" clearly indicates what his Lordship thought in the case of alleged nuisance by noise, where the noise was made maliciously. Different considerations would apply to cases where that ingredient was absent. Indeed, the matter is put beyond doubt by the decision of North, J., in *Christie v. Davey* [[1893] 1 Ch. 316]. The plaintiff and the defendant lived side by side in semi-detached houses in Brixton. The plaintiff was a teacher of music and he had a musical family. The result was that throughout clouds of music pervaded his house and were heard in the house of his neighbour. His neighbour did not like music to be heard and after writing rather an unfortunate letter of protest, he took to making noises himself by beating trays and rapping on the wall, and thereupon the music teacher brought an action for an injunction. The action came before North, J., and he delivered judgment in favour of the plaintiff and granted an injunction restraining the defendant from permitting any sounds or noises in his house so as to annoy the plaintiff or the occupiers of his house, and in the course of his judgment he said, at page 326:

> The result is that I think I am bound to interfere for the protection of the plaintiffs. In my opinion the noises which were made in the defendant's house were not of a legitimate kind. They were what, to use the language of Lord Selborne in *Gaunt v. Fynney* [above] "ought to be regarded as excessive and unreasonable." I am satisfied that they were made deliberately and maliciously for the purpose of annoying the plaintiffs. If what

> has taken place had occurred between two sets of persons, both perfectly innocent, I should have taken an entirely different view of the case. But I am persuaded that what was done by the defendant was done only for the purpose of annoyance, and in my opinion it was not a legitimate use of the defendant's house to use it for the purpose of vexing and annoying his neighbours.

. . .

In my opinion, the authorities to which I have referred support the view that a person who shoots on his own land, or makes other noises on his own land, for the purpose of annoying or injuring his neighbour, does, by the common law, commit the actionable wrong of nuisance for which he is liable in damages at common law and was liable to be restrained by an injunction in a court of equity before the Judicature Act. I think that the plaintiff is entitled to maintain this action and he has established the cause of action which he alleged.

. . .

[The plaintiff was awarded £250 in damages and granted an injunction which was limited to the breeding season.]

NOTES AND QUESTIONS

1. What is the relationship between the defendant's motive and the elements of a nuisance action? How did the court deal with this issue? See *A.G. Man. v. Campbell* (1985), 32 C.C.L.T. 57 (Man. C.A.).

2. In *Hollywood*, would the shooting have constituted a nuisance if it had been carried out for a legitimate purpose, such as destroying rodents on the defendant's land? See *Rattray v. Daniels* (1959), 17 D.L.R. (2d) 134 (Alta. C.A.).

3. How did the court in *Hollywood* deal with the defendant's contention that it could not be held liable due to the principles established in *Bradford Corp. v. Pickles*, [1895] A.C. 587 (H.L.)? Can you reconcile the decisions in *Hollywood* and *Bradford*? For conflicting interpretations of these two cases, see Fleming, *The Law of Torts*, 9th ed. (1998) at 471-72; and Heuston & Buckley, *Salmond and Heuston on the Law of Torts*, 21st ed. (1996) at 62.

4. It generally is accepted that an individual's ordinarily innocuous conduct will not constitute nuisance simply because the plaintiff is abnormally sensitive to that conduct. The defendant in *Hollywood* argued that the plaintiff only suffered loss because he had put his land to an extraordinary use that made him abnormally vulnerable to the sound of gun shots. How did the court address this argument? Do you agree with the court's analysis? For a criticism of that analysis, see Heuston & Buckley, *supra*, at 62. See also *Nor-Video Services Ltd. v. Ont. Hydro* (1978), 84 D.L.R. (3d) 221 (Ont. H.C.); *Devon Lumber Co. v. MacNeill* (1987), 42 C.C.L.T. 192 (N.B.C.A.); and *Ward v. Magna International Inc.* (1994), 21 C.C.L.T. (2d) 178 (Ont. Gen. Div.).

(a) DEFENCE OF STATUTORY AUTHORITY

TOCK v. ST. JOHN'S METROPOLITAN AREA BOARD
(1989), 64 D.L.R. (4th) 620 (S.C.C.)

LA FOREST J. (Dickson C.J. concurring): – In the early afternoon of October 10, 1981, a day of exceptionally heavy rainfall, the Tocks discovered that a large amount of water had entered their basement. They immediately notified the Board and attempted, in vain, to pump the water out themselves. Two employees of the Board came to inspect the storm sewer in the vicinity and determined that the sewer was blocked. A crew was summoned and by early evening it had located and removed the blockage. Within ten to fifteen minutes of the removal, the water drained from the basement which had, by this time, incurred substantial damage.

. . .

The trial judge, Adams C.J. Dist. Ct., held that the flooding was caused by the blockage and not by the exceptionally heavy rainfall. He went on to dismiss the claim in negligence, holding that the Board had not been negligent in the construction, maintenance or operation of the storm sewer. He did, however, hold that the escape of the water into the Tock's residence constituted a serious interference with their right of enjoyment of their property and, in consequence, allowed the claim in nuisance. In his opinion, the collection and drainage of water from rain or other sources constituted a non-natural user of land within the meaning of the rule in *Rylands v. Fletcher*. In the result, the trial judge awarded the Tocks a total of $13,456.11 in damages.

The Newfoundland Court of Appeal reversed this judgment. Gushue J.A., writing for a unanimous court, held that the rule in *Rylands v. Fletcher* had no application. In his view, the provisioning of an indispensable service such as a water and sewer system could not be held to constitute a non-natural user of land within the meaning of the rule.

On the question of nuisance, Gushue J.A. expressed the view that a claim in nuisance would not lie against a municipal corporation for damage resulting from a service provided under statutory authority if that body could establish that the occurrence complained of was inevitable in the sense that it could not have been avoided by the exercise of all reasonable and available expertise and care in the design, construction and operation of the service. On the facts, he concluded that the Board had satisfied the onus of demonstrating that it had done everything that could reasonably be expected to avoid the occurrence.

. . .

Turning to the question of inevitability, it seems to me that, in strict logic, most nuisances stemming from activities authorized by statute *are* in fact inevitable. Certainly, if one is to judge from the frequency with which storm drain and sewer cases occur in the reports, it would seem a safe conclusion that blockage of such systems is inevitable if one accepts this to mean that it is demonstrably impossible to operate these systems without such occurrences. But what escapes me is why any particular importance should be accorded this fact when weighing a nuisance claim against a statutory authority. The fact that the operation of a given system will inevitably visit random damage on certain unfortunate individuals among the pool of users of the system does not tell us why those individuals should be responsible for paying for that damage.

. . .

I would allow the appeal, set aside the judgment of the Court of Appeal and restore the judgment of the trial judge. The appellants are entitled to their costs throughout.

The judgment of Lamer, Wilson and L'Heureux-Dubé JJ. was delivered by

WILSON J. – I have had the benefit of reading the reasons for judgment of my colleague, Justice La Forest, and, while I agree with his proposed disposition of the appeal, I have reservations about his approach to the law of nuisance as it applies to public bodies acting under statutory authority. The facts are set out in detail by my colleague and I need not repeat them here.

I agree with my colleague's conclusion that the rule in *Rylands v. Fletcher* (1868), L.R. 3 H.L. 330, has no application to this case but that the appellants are entitled to recover from the respondent in nuisance. I agree with him also that the Court of Appeal erred in concluding that if the respondent could show that it had not been negligent, then it could not be liable in nuisance.

I do not, however, share La Forest J.'s view that this Court should, or indeed can, on this appeal virtually abolish the defence of statutory authority for policy reasons and treat municipalities exercising statutory authority in the same way as private individuals. Such a major departure from the current state of the law would, it seems to me, require the intervention of the legislature.

Moreover, I do not favour replacing the existing law in this area with a general test of whether it is reasonable or unreasonable in the circumstances of the case to award compensation. This test may, because of the high degree of judicial subjectivity involved in its application, make life easier for the judges but, in my respectful view, it will do nothing to assist public bodies to make a realistic assessment of their exposure in carrying out their statutory mandate. Nor will it provide much guidance to litigants in deciding whether or not to sue. It is altogether too uncertain. Nor can I, with respect, accept the proposition that a single individual suffering damage from an isolated nuisance should be dealt with differently from a group of people suffering damage from an ongoing nuisance. This seems to me to be quite incompatible with the concept of principled decision-making. Accordingly, while I agree with my colleague in the result he has reached in this case, I prefer to write my own concurring reasons.

I agree that the flooding of the appellants' basement constituted an unreasonable interference with the appellants' use and enjoyment of the property and that, had the parties been two private individuals, it clearly would have been an actionable nuisance. However, since the respondent is a municipality, the law dictates that different considerations apply. The crucial question is whether or not the respondent is able to rely on the defence of statutory authority in the circumstances of this case.

Since the availability of the defence of statutory authority depends on the language of the statute I set out the relevant provisions of *The Municipalities Act*, S.N. 1979, c. 33, on which the respondent must rely:

> 154. (1) The council may, subject to the provisions of *The Department of Consumer Affairs and Environment Act, 1973* and regulations made thereunder, construct, acquire, establish, own and operate
>
> (a) a public water supply system for the distribution of water within or, with the approval of the Minister, outside of the town,

(b) a public sewerage system, either independently of or in conjunction with a public water supply system, for the collection and disposal of sewerage within or, with the approval of the Minister, outside of the town, and

(c) a storm drainage system within or, with the approval of the Minister, outside of the town.

(2) For the purposes of subsection (1) the council may

(a) acquire any waters required for the purpose of providing a sufficient supply of water for the town, and

(b) acquire by purchase or expropriation any lands adjacent to such waters to prevent pollution of those waters.

(3) For the purpose of exercising its powers under subsection (1) the council may lay out, excavate, dig, make, build, maintain, repair, and improve all such drains, sewers, and water supply pipes as the council deems necessary.

There is no doubt that these provisions authorize the respondent to construct and continue to operate and maintain the sewage system in question. They are, however, permissive as opposed to mandatory. They confer a power; they do not impose a duty. Is this distinction relevant to the question of the respondent's liability in nuisance?

. . .

The principles to be derived from the . . . authorities would seem to be as follows:

(a) if the legislation imposes a duty and the nuisance is the inevitable consequence of discharging that duty, then the nuisance is itself authorized and there is no recovery in the absence of negligence;

(b) if the legislation, although it merely confers an authority, is specific as to the manner or location of doing the thing authorized and the nuisance is the inevitable consequence of doing the thing authorized in that way or in that location, then likewise the nuisance is itself authorized and there is no recovery absent negligence.

However:

(c) if the legislation confers an authority and also gives the public body a discretion, not only whether to do the thing authorized or not, but how to do it and in what location, then if it does decide to do the thing authorized, it must do it in a manner and at a location which will avoid the creation of a nuisance. If it does it in a way or at a location which gives rise to a nuisance, it will be liable therefor, whether there is negligence or not.

In other words, in the situations described in (a) and (b) above the inevitability doctrine is a good defence to the public body absent negligence. In situation (c) it is no defence at all and it is unnecessary for the plaintiff to prove negligence in order to recover.

In my view, these principles make a great deal of sense. The inevitability doctrine represents a happy judicial compromise between letting no one who has suffered damage as a consequence of the statutorily authorized activities of public bodies recover and letting everyone so suffering damage recover. Recovery will be allowed unless it is shown that the interference with the plaintiff's rights was permitted by either:

(1) express language in the statute such as a provision specifying that no action for nuisance may be brought for any damage caused. . .; or

(2) by necessary implication from the language of the statute coupled with a factual finding that the damage was the inevitable consequence of what the statute ordered or authorized the public body to do.

. . .

In my view, to the extent that some of the more recent cases are inconsistent with the early principles, they should not be followed. I find no acceptable rationale for the extension of the inevitable consequences doctrine to cases where the public body was perfectly free to exercise its statutory authority without violating private rights. It is only in cases where the public body has no choice as to the way in which or the place where it engages in the nuisance-causing activity that the inevitable consequences doctrine protects it. For only in such cases can it be said that the legislature has authorized any nuisance which is the inevitable consequence of the public body's carrying out its mandate.

. . .

The legislation in this case was purely permissive within the meaning of these cases. It authorized a sewage system to be constructed but did not specify how or where it was to be done. The respondent was accordingly obliged to construct and operate the system in strict conformity with private rights. It did not do so. The defence of statutory authority is not available to it and the appellants are entitled to recover.

SOPINKA J. . . . The burden of proof with respect to the defence of statutory authority is on the party advancing the defence. It is not an easy one. The courts strain against a conclusion that private rights are intended to be sacrificed for the common good. The defendant must negative that there are alternate methods of carrying out the work. The mere fact that one is considerably less expensive will not avail. If only one method is practically feasible, it must be established that it was practically impossible to avoid the nuisance. It is insufficient for the defendant to negative negligence. The standard is a higher one. While the defence gives rise to some factual difficulties, in view of the allocation of the burden of proof they will be resolved against the defendant.

If we are to depart from this state of the law, so recently confirmed by two decisions of this Court, there should be very strong ground for so doing. Moreover, there should be substantial unanimity. It is apparent from the reasons in this appeal that there is little unanimity as to whether we should retrench, advance or stay the same.

The change proposed by La Forest J. subsumes the defence of statutory authority within the test as to when it is reasonable to compensate the plaintiff. Trial judges will still have to grapple with the elements of the defence of statutory authority but in the context of a test of reasonableness. This will simply add uncertainty to any uncertainty which is said to exist.

Nor do I agree that it is logical or practical to distinguish between public works that are required and those that are permitted. While it was fashionable to require such works in the railway building age, mandatory public works are a feature of a by-gone era.

The disagreement with the result reached in the Court of Appeal is not because the law is defective but because it was incorrectly applied. As La Forest J. points out, the Court of Appeal exonerated the respondent from liability in nuisance on the basis that there was an absence of negligence. In my opinion, the heavier onus which must be discharged was not met in this case. The trial judge so found. I therefore would dispose of the appeal as proposed by my colleagues.

NOTES AND QUESTIONS

1. What is the major premise in each of the three judgments? With which judgment do you most agree?

2. A period of confusion followed *Tock* as lawyers and judges attempted to digest all three opinions. The situation was clarified, however, when the Supreme Court of Canada unanimously adopted Sopinka J.'s view in *Ryan v. Victoria (City)* (1999), 168 D.L.R. (4th) 513 (S.C.C.). Accordingly, the defence of statutory authority applies only if the defendant proves that it was practically impossible to avoid creating a nuisance. See Rafferty, "Tortious Liability of Railways: Defences of Statutory Compliance and Statutory Authority" (1999) 44 C.C.L.T. (2d) 55; and Rafferty, "Developments in Contract and Tort Law: The 1998-1999 Term" (2000) 11 S.C.L.R. 183. For applications of *Tock*, see *St. John's (City) v. Lake* (2000), 192 Nfld. & P.E.I.R. 84 (Nfld. C.A.); *Mandrake Management Consultants Ltd. v. Toronto Transit Commission* (1993), 102 D.L.R. (4th) 12 (Ont. C.A.); *Canada (A.G.) v. Ottawa Carleton (City)* (1991), 5 O.R. (3d) 11 (C.A.).

3. All of the judges in *Tock* agreed that the tort of nuisance will not be defeated by proof that the defendant neither intentionally nor carelessly caused the plaintiff's injury. In contrast, liability cannot be imposed under the general tort of negligence unless the defendant breached the standard of care. Why should the defendant be treated differently depending upon whether the plaintiff's injury arises from nuisance rather than negligence? What is so special about an infringement of the plaintiff's enjoyment of land? The courts' attempts to distinguish between the two torts has not always been helpful. See for example *Overseas Tankship (U.K.) Ltd. v. Miller S.S. Co. Pty.*, [1967] 1 A.C. 617 at 639-40 (P.C.). See also Newark, "The Boundaries of Nuisance" (1949) 65 L.Q.R. 480; and Fleming, *The Law of Torts*, 9th ed. (1998) at 473-74.

4. The defence of statutory authority was successfully invoked in *Sutherland v. Canada (Attorney General)* (2002), 215 D.L.R. (4th) 1 (B.C.C.A.). The plaintiffs proved that the noise generated by the operation of a new airport runway constituted a nuisance. The British Columbia Court of Appeal nevertheless denied their claim. It held that the noise was the inevitable product of a construction scheme that had been authorized. In doing so, it affirmed that the defence of statutory authority can be based not only on statutes, but also on subordinate legislation, such as orders-in-council and regulations. See also *St. John's (City) v. Lake*, *supra*.

In contrast, the defence was rejected in *Rideau Falls Generating Partnership v. Ottawa (City)* (1999), 174 D.L.R. (4th) 160 (Ont. C.A.). Pursuant to a legislative scheme, the defendant operated a system to prevent upstream flooding in the springtime. For that purpose, it broke up river ice and sent it over a set of falls. The plaintiff's property was located at the foot of the falls. It suffered flood damage as a result of the defendant's operations. The court held that the defence of statutory authority was inapplicable because the defendant had "fallen far short of establishing that it was practically impossible to avoid the nuisance."

5. Aside from the defence of *statutory authority*, the plaintiff may also be met by the defence of *statutory immunity*. Legislation may be enacted that expressly exempts certain forms of activity from liability. For instance, the Manitoba *Nuisance Act*, R.S.M. 1987, c. N.120 states:

> 2. A person who carries on a business and who, in respect of that business, does not violate
>
> (a) any land use control law; or
> (b) *The Public Health Act*; or

(c) any regulation under *The Public Health Act* that deals specifically with the carrying on of that class or type of business; or
(d) *The Clean Environment Act*; or
(e) an order of the Clean Environment Commission made under *The Clean Environment Act* in respect of the business; or
(f) any regulation under *The Clean Environment Act* that deals specifically with the carrying on of that class or type of business;

is not liable in nuisance to any person for any odour resulting from the business and shall not be prevented by injunction or other order of a court from carrying on the business because it causes or creates an odour that constitutes a nuisance.
3. Where a plaintiff or claimant in an action or proceeding against a person who carries on a business claims

(a) damages in nuisance for an odour resulting from the business; or
(b) an injunction or other order of a court preventing the carrying on of the business because it causes or creates an odour that constitutes a nuisance;

the onus of proving that the defendant violated any land use control law, or any Act, regulation or order mentioned in clause 2(b), (c), (d), (e) or (f) lies on the plaintiff or claimant.

It has been suggested that this legislation was a response to lobbying by hog farmers: Osborne, *The Law of Torts*, 2d ed. (2003) at 357-58. See also *Farm Practices Protection Act*, S.M. 1992, c. 41; *Farm Practices Protection (Right to Farm) Act*, R.S.B.C. 1996, c. 131, s. 2; *Farming and Food Protection Act*, S.O. 1998, c. 1, s. 2; and *Pyke v. TRI GRO Enterprises Ltd.* (2001), 204 D.L.R. (4th) 400 (Ont. C.A.). How does the defence of statutory immunity differ from the defence of statutory authority?

6. The tort of private nuisance may also be met by the defence of *public interest*. That possibility was recognized in *Dennis v. Ministry of Defence*, [2003] 2 E.G.L.R. 121 (Q.B.). The claimant's rural home was located near a property that the military used as a training base for pilots of Harrier jets (also known as "jump jets"). Harrier jets are unique insofar as they are capable of taking off and landing vertically, like a helicopter. Unfortunately for the claimant, the mechanical process required to achieve such feats produced a "particularly fearsome" noise. The flights, which occurred on weekdays, sometimes as late as 11:00 p.m., shook buildings, terrified children, and made conversation and thought impossible. The situation unsurprisingly adversely affected the value of the neighbouring properties. The claimant sought compensation and a declaration of his infringed rights. While the defendant was statutorily protected against injunctive relief, it had developed the practice of respecting such declarations by refraining from the impugned acts. The claimant in this case hoped for such a result.

The defendant resisted liability by arguing that "defence of the realm . . . was a public interest of a different and greater order altogether from commerce and other interests hitherto considered." It further argued that the training of Harrier pilots was essential to the public's interest in a state-of-the-art military. Buckley J. agreed that the circumstances called for special consideration, but denied that public interest was conclusive. He held instead that a determination as to whether a nuisance has been committed requires consideration of all of the facts. He further held that compensation generally is appropriate when the burdens associated with the public interest otherwise would fall heavily on a single person or a small group of individuals.

On the facts, Buckley J. accepted that the public interest demands the training of Harrier pilots and he therefore refused to issue a declaration. He nevertheless held that the defendant's actions constituted a nuisance and awarded £950,000 in damages. The compensatory award was intended to cover past losses and losses expected to accrue until 2012, when the Harrier training program was scheduled to end.

When, if ever, should public interest override a property owner's general right to be free of unreasonable interference? How does Buckley J.'s attitude regarding injunctive (or injunctive-like) relief compare to the courts' usual approach to such remedies? Would it ever be justifiable, for the sake of public interest, to deny both injunctive relief and compensation? See generally Elvin, "The Law of Nuisance and the Human Rights Act" [2003] C.L.J. 546; and Bagshaw, "Private Nuisance and the Defence of the Realm" (2004) 120 L.Q.R. 37.

7. A claim of nuisance may also be met by a number of other defences. Liability may be precluded if the plaintiff encouraged or clearly consented to the defendant's activities. Moreover, while seldom successfully invoked, the defence of contributory negligence may be used to reduce damages.

The defendant may also plead "prescription." After an uninterrupted period of 20 years, the defendant's conduct may become, in J. Fleming's words, "retrospectively legalised as if it had been authorized by a grant from the owner of the servient land": *The Law of Torts*, 9th ed. (1998) at 490. This defence can be invoked only if (a) the nature of the nuisance remains the same over the period, and (b) the plaintiff was aware of the nuisance. See *Sturges v. Bridgman* (1879), 11 Ch. D. 852 (C.A.); *Pilliterri v. Nor. Const. Co.* (1930), 66 O.L.R. 128 (T.D.); *Russell Transport Ltd. v. Ontario Malleable Iron Co.*, [1952] 4 D.L.R. 719 (Ont. H.C.); and *Schenck v. R.; Rokeby v. R.* (1981), 34 O.R. (2d) 595 (H.C.), aff'd, [1987] 2 S.C.R. 289.

8. *Marcic v. Thames Water Utilities Ltd.*, [2004] 2 A.C. 42 (H.L.) provides a recent English perspective on the concerns addressed in this section. In 1937 the defendant, a public authority, built an underground sewer system. At the time, that system was entirely adequate. Because of subsequent housing developments, however, the system had become inadequate by 1998. Every heavy rainfall resulted in the system overflowing into the claimant's backyard. The claimant sued in nuisance. The trial judge held that while liability otherwise would be imposed, the defendant was protected by a line of precedent that immunized public water authorities from liability in nuisance for flooding. The Court of Appeal reversed that decision on the basis that the traditional precedents no longer were good law. The House of Lords, however, reinstated the result at trial. It held that the Court of Appeal erred in (a) equating public authorities, like the defendant, with private entities, and (b) ignoring the *Water Industry Act 1991*, which creates a system for resolving complaints arising from overflowing sewers. The defendant's status as a public authority was significant insofar as it (a) could not deny access to its sewer system, and (b) could not charge users for the costs associated with upgrading the system. In the circumstances, the House of Lords held it would be inappropriate to hold the defendant to the standards applied to private entities. See generally O'Sullivan, "Nuisance, Human Rights and Sewage – Closing the Floodgates" [2004] C.L.J. 552; and Morgan, "Nuisance, Property and Human Rights" (2002) 118 L.Q.R. 27.

9. As the preceding cases and notes illustrate, the law of nuisance frequently is used to resolve conflicts between two lawful and socially useful activities. Traditionally,

the courts have assumed that the active party has caused the harm. Although the active party's interest in the use of land is considered, the law favours the passive user. That view was challenged by R. Coase in an influential article, "The Problem of Social Cost" (1960) 3 J.L. & Econ. 1. He argued that nuisance raises the issue of *reciprocity*. By preventing the defendant from interfering with the plaintiff's use of land, a court necessarily prevents the defendant from using its land for its desired lawful purpose. Coase argued that unless the law has a more important reason for favouring one party over another, it should resolve the issue in a manner which maximizes scarce social resources. Liability therefore should be imposed on the *cheapest cost avoider – i.e.* the party that can avoid the harm at the lowest cost. That calculation will favour the passive user in some cases and the active user in others.

Can Coase's analysis adequately take into account variables such as peace and quiet, clean air, and unpolluted water that have no easily ascertainable economic value? Do the courts have the ability or sufficient evidence to make determinations about the "cheapest cost avoider?" For a critique of Coase's analysis, see Simpson, "*Coase v. Pigou* Reexamined" (1996) 25 J. Legal Stud. 53; Fletcher, "Fairness and Utility in Tort Theory" (1972) 85 Harv. L. Rev. 537; Epstein, "A Theory of Strict Liability" (1973) 2 J. Legal Stud. 151; Gjerdingen, "The Coase Theorem and the Psychology of Common-Law Thought" (1983) 56 S. Cal. L. Rev. 711; and White, "Risk-Utility Analysis and the Learned Hand Formula: A Hand that Helps or a Hand that Hides?" (1990) 32 Ariz. L. Rev. 77.

3. Public Nuisance

The discussion to this point has considered the concept of *private nuisance*. It now is necessary to consider the distinct concept of *public nuisance*. A public nuisance may take one of two forms.

- *Common Interests*: A public nuisance may arise if the defendant's conduct unreasonably interferes with rights, resources, or interests that are common to the entire community. This may be true, for example, if the defendant blocks a public highway, pollutes a river, or operates a bawdy house.

- *Private Interests Combined*: A public nuisance may arise if the defendant's conduct unreasonably interferes, on a large scale, with the use and enjoyment of *private* property. This is true, for example, if the defendant's factory emits noxious fumes that cause damage to every nearby house. In this situation, two options exist. Each affected homeowner may sue individually in *private* nuisance and seek *private* remedies. Alternatively, the interests of the affected homeowners may be joined together in an action for *public* nuisance that seeks *public* remedies. It often is difficult, however, to determine whether the defendant's conduct adversely affects a sufficient number of *private* claimants so as to support a claim of *public* nuisance. The courts generally ask whether the individual claimants constitute a sufficient "class," and it appears that a public claim generally becomes available as membership in the class approaches ten.

Public nuisances usually are addressed through public law. Section 180(2) of the *Criminal Code*, R.S.C. 1985, c. C-46, defines the crime of "common nuisance":

> [E]very one commits a common nuisance who does an unlawful act or fails to discharge a legal duty and thereby
>
> (a) endangers the lives, safety, health, property or comfort of the public; or
> (b) obstructs the public in the exercise or enjoyment of any right that is common to all the subjects of Her Majesty in Canada.

If the defendant's conduct constitutes a criminal offence, the government may prosecute. The Attorney General, as the representative of the public, may also sue the defendant for damages and an injunction, or may consent to a *relator action* that allows a private citizen to seek relief in the Attorney General's name. The Attorney General has a virtually unfettered discretion in deciding whether to prosecute criminally, sue civilly, or consent to a relator action.

It occasionally is possible for a private person to sue in his or her own name, but only if that person has suffered some special injury, above and beyond the injury experienced by other members of the public. The development of that private action for public nuisance has generated considerable controversy.

In the following section, we focus on two main issues. First, how do the courts distinguish between private and public nuisance? Second, how do the courts determine which plaintiffs will be permitted to maintain private actions for public nuisance?

A.-G. ONT. v. ORANGE PRODUCTIONS LTD.

(1971), 21 D.L.R. (3d) 257 (Ont. H.C.)

[The Attorney-General sought an interim injunction to restrain the defendants from holding an outdoor rock concert, alleging that it would constitute a public nuisance. Evidence was given that there had been acts of trespass to private property, public sexual intercourse, and public consumption of alcohol and illicit drugs at one of the defendant's previous concerts.]

WELLS C.J.H.C.: – The law relating to public nuisance had its flowering in the late 18th Century and the early 19th Century. However, in 1957, a case, *A.-G. v. P.Y.A. Quarries, Ltd.*, [1957] 1 All E.R. 894, arising from the operation of a quarry in Wales, came before the Court of Appeal in England. A very strong Court consisting of Lord Justice Denning (as he then was), Lord Justice Parker (as he then was) and Lord Justice Romer considered the matter at some length. The principal judgment is that of Romer L.J. He went into the matter in great detail taking into account the various historical definitions of public nuisance over at last two centuries. I do not propose to set out this very detailed review he made but he went back to cases in the middle and late 18th Century and came down from the 19th Century up to the time he gave his judgment. . . . But it is of great assistance in dealing with the problem before me. His conclusions are found at p. 902 and are briefly set out as follows:

> The expression "the neighbourhood" has been regarded as sufficiently defining the area affected by a public nuisance in other cases also (see, for example, *A.-G. v. Stone* (1895), 60 J.P. 168; *A. G. v. Cole & Son*, [1901] 1 Ch. 205; and *A.-G. v. Corke*, [1933] Ch. 89). I do not propose to attempt a more precise definition of public nuisance than those which emerge from the textbooks and authorities to which I have referred. It is, however, clear, in my opinion, that any nuisance is "public" which materially affects the reasonable comfort and convenience of life of a class of Her Majesty's subjects. The sphere of nuisance may be described generally as "the neighbourhood"; but the question whether

> the local community within that sphere comprises a sufficient number of persons to constitute a class of the public is a question of fact in every case. It is not necessary, in my judgment, to prove that every member of the class has been injuriously affected; it is sufficient to show that a representative cross-section of the class has been so affected for an injunction to issue.

. . .

It was, of course, argued by the defendant quarry that this was in effect a private nuisance and that the action should not have been brought by the Attorney-General on behalf of the public generally, and at p. 906 Romer, L.J., made the following pertinent observations:

> Some public nuisances (for example, the pollution of rivers) can often be established without the necessity of calling a number of individual complainants as witnesses. In general, however, a public nuisance is proved by the cumulative effect which it is shown to have had on the people living within its sphere of influence. In other words, a normal and legitimate way of proving a public nuisance is to prove a sufficiently large collection of private nuisances. I am therefore of opinion that there was nothing improper or irregular in the statement of claim as originally delivered, or in the reception at the trial of evidence of the local residents' experiences.

It was also evident that, despite the strongly expressed public discontent with the operation of the quarry, the defendants had paid scant attention to the local residents or the representations of the local authorities and that they were slow to adopt the improvements suggested with reference to the escape of dust which was reasonable to the people living around the quarry. All these matters are found in the present case before me.

Before I part with the case I think I should deal with some of the observations of Lord Justice Denning (as he then was). At p. 908 he dealt with the question as to the distinction between public and private nuisance and he expressed himself as follows:

> The classic statement of the difference is that a public nuisance affects Her Majesty's subjects generally, whereas a private nuisance only affects particular individuals. But this does not help much. The question: when do a number of individuals become Her Majesty's subjects generally? is as difficult to answer as the question: when does a group of people become a crowd? Everyone has his own views. Even the answer "Two's company, three's a crowd" will not command the assent of those present unless they first agree on "which two". So here I decline to answer the question how many people are necessary to make up Her Majesty's subjects generally. I prefer to look to the reason of the thing and to say that a public nuisance is a nuisance which is so widespread in its range or so indiscriminate in its effect that it would not be reasonable to expect one person to take proceedings on his own responsibility to put a stop to it, but that it should be taken on the responsibility of the community at large. Take the blocking up of a public highway or the non-repair of it; it may be a footpath very little used except by one or two householders; nevertheless the obstruction affects everyone indiscriminately who may wish to walk along it. Take next a landowner who collects pestilential rubbish near a village or permits gypsies with filthy habits to encamp on the edge of a residential neighbourhood. The householders nearest to it suffer the most, but everyone in the neighbourhood suffers too. In such cases the Attorney-General can take proceedings for an injunction to restrain the nuisance: and when he does so he acts in defence of the public right, not for any sectional interest: see *A.-G. v. Bastow*, [1957] 1 All E.R. 497. When, however, the nuisance is so concentrated that only two or three property owners are affected by it, such as the three attornies in Clifford's Inn, then they ought to take

proceedings on their own account to stop it and not expect the community to do it for them; see *R. v. Lloyd* ((1802), 4 Esp. 200) and the precedent in *3 Chitty on Criminal Law* (1826), pp. 664, 665. Applying this test, I am clearly of opinion that the nuisance by stones, vibration and dust in this case was at the date of the writ so widespread in its range and so indiscriminate in its effect that it was a public nuisance.

. . .

In my opinion, the whole festival with the weight of numbers and the noise and dust, was a painful and troublesome experience for all those living in the neighbourhood and was, in fact, a social disaster to those who normally live there. Until proper sanitation has been installed in the park and some limitation put on the numbers attending, I do not think the festival should take place. It is unfair to the neighbourhood. It is actually unfair to those who attend it and it is operated at considerable risk as to health and well-being both of the guests of the park and those who live in the neighbourhood and who are entitled to quiet enjoyment of their property. The pressure on the neighbourhood when these festivals are held is, in my opinion, grossly excessive and is something that should be restrained.

[Interim injunction granted.]

HICKEY v. ELECTRICITY REDUCTION CO.

(1970), 21 D.L.R. (3d) 368 (Nfld. S.C.)

FURLONG C.J.: . . . The defendants by the discharge of poisonous waste from its phosphorus plant at Long Harbour, Placentia Bay, destroyed the fish life of the adjacent waters, and the plaintiffs, as all other fishermen in the area suffered in their livelihood. I have said "all other fishermen", but the resulting pollution created a nuisance to all persons – "all Her Majesty's subjects" – to use Stephen's phrase. It was not a nuisance peculiar to the plaintiffs, nor confined to their use of the waters of Placentia Bay. It was a nuisance committed against the public.

A somewhat similar occurrence happened at a fishing settlement in Labrador, at Little Grady Island, in 1927, when a whaling company erected a factory at Watering Cove on Big Grady Island and polluted the waters adjacent to the premises of a fishing establishment on the former island. In the event an action was taken by the fishery owners against the whaling company. The case was heard in this Court in 1929 by Kent, J., and his judgment has remained unchallenged. He found that amongst other things, that there was serious pollution of the fishing waters from the waste materials of the whale factory. The case is *McRae v. British Norwegian Whaling Co. Ltd.*, [1927-31] Nfld. L.R. 274. After declaring at p. 282 that:

> It is an established principle that the right to fish in the sea and public navigable waters is free and open to all. It is a public right that may be exercised by any of the King's subjects, and for any interference with it the usual remedies to vindicate a public right must be employed.

He proceeded to apply the principle to the facts before him at pp. 283-4:

> The plaintiffs in the present action must, therefore, in order to succeed on this cause of complaint, show that the injury inflicted upon them by the acts of the defendants, insofar as they affect the right of fishing in the public navigable waters in the vicinity of Little Grady Island, is, in regard to them, particular direct and substantial, over and above the

> injury thereby inflicted upon the public in general. It is not enough for the plaintiffs to show that their business is interrupted or interfered with, by the public nuisance, to enable them to maintain a private action against the defendants in respect thereof, for such interruption or interference is not a direct but merely a consequential damage resulting to them from the nuisance. Neither is it an injury peculiar to the plaintiffs themselves, but is suffered by them in common with everyone else whose right to fish in these public waters is affected by the nuisance. The plaintiff's right, as one of the public, to fish may be affected to a greater extent than that of others, but they have no ground of complaint different from anyone else who fishes or intends to fish in these waters. If the nuisance took the form of obstructing the right of the plaintiffs as adjacent land owners, of access from their land to the public navigable waters, the injury would be peculiar to themselves, not because it interrupted their right to fish in common with others in the public waters, but because it interrupted their right of access to these waters, which is an incident to the occupation of property adjacent to the sea and would therefore be an interference with a right peculiar to themselves and distinct from their right as one of the public to fish in the public waters. For these reasons I have come to the conclusion that the plaintiffs have failed to establish their right to maintain a private action in respect of the pollution by the defendants of these public navigable waters.

A somewhat similar situation arose in New Brunswick in 1934 in *Fillion v. New Brunswick International Paper Co.*, [1934] 3 D.L.R. 22, 8 M.P.R. 89. The waste from a paper mill into the Restigouche River in that Province polluted the waters of a bay where the plaintiff, with others, carried on smelt fishing. An action was taken in nuisance against the owners of the paper-mill and that part of the case was dismissed, Baxter, J., saying at p. 26:

> Assuming then, that the defendant's act constituted a public nuisance, and if it is wrongful I do not see how it can be anything else, the plaintiff has suffered differently from the rest of the public only in degree. That is not enough to entitle him to recover. Nearly all of the cases in which this principle has been invoked concern the obstruction of a highway, but *Ashby v. White*, 2 Ld. Raym. 938, at p. 955, 92 E.R. 126, *per* Holt, C.J., and the case of *Williams* in 5 Co. Rep. 72(b), 77 E.R. 163, show that the *ratio decidendi* is that it is inexpedient that there should be multiplicity of actions and that where a nuisance or injury is common to the whole public the remedy is by indictment but that no private right of action exists unless there is a special or particular injury to the plaintiff.

. . .

I think it is clear that the facts, as we have them, can only support the view that there has been pollution of the waters of this area of Placentia Bay which amounts to a public nuisance. If I am right in this view then the law is clear that a private action by the plaintiffs is not sustainable.

Counsel for the plaintiffs, Mr. Robert Wells, argued that when a public nuisance has been created anyone who suffers special damage, that is direct damage has a right of action. I am unable to agree to this rather wide application of Salmond's view that a public nuisance may become a tortious act. I think the right view is that any person who suffers peculiar damage has a right of action, but where the damage is common to all persons of the same class, then a personal right of action is not maintainable. Mr. Wells suggests that the plaintiff's right to outfit for the fishery and their right to fish is a particular right and this right having been interfered with they have a cause of action. This right which they enjoy is a right in common with all Her Majesty's subjects, an interference with which is the whole test of a public nuisance; a right which can only be vindicated by the appropriate means, which is an action by the Attorney-General, either with or without a relator, in the common interest of the public.

Rose et al. v. Miles, [1814-23] All E.R. Rep. 580, which has been cited is not in point, as the judgment of Lord Ellenborough, C.J., clearly shows [at 581], "This is something substantially more injurious to this person, than to the public at large," and Dampier, J., said "The present case admits of this distinction from most other cases, that here the plaintiff was interrupted in the actual enjoyment of the highway." With great respect I hold that view that that judgment was applicable only to the particular facts of that case, and can only support the general proposition that a peculiar and particular damage, distinct from that of the general public, is necessary to sustain an action.

NOTES AND QUESTIONS

1. How do Denning L.J.'s and Romer L.J.'s tests of public nuisance, both cited in *Orange Productions*, differ? Which test is more useful?

2. What is the rationale for the restrictive standing rule in public nuisance? In *Thorson v. A.G. Can.* (1974), 43 D.L.R. (3d) 1 at 10 (S.C.C.), Laskin J. stated that this rule was justified because "there is a clear way in which the public interest can be guarded through the intervention of the Attorney-General who would be sensitive to public complaints about the interference with public rights." Do you agree? See *Rosenburg v. Grand River Conservation Authority* (1975), 69 D.L.R. (3d) 384 (Ont. C.A.); and Estey, "Public Nuisance and Standing to Sue" (1972) 10 Osgoode Hall L.J. 563.

3. It has been held that as long as the requisite elements can be established, a nuisance may be simultaneously private and public. See *Stein v. Gonzales* (1984), 14 D.L.R. (4th) 263 (B.C.S.C.); and *Armstrong v. Langley (City)* (1992), 94 D.L.R. (4th) 21 (B.C.C.A.). In *Sutherland v. Canada (A.G.)* (2002), 215 D.L.R. (4th) 1 (B.C.C.A.), the defendant was responsible for an airport that was located near a residential area. The court held that the individual plaintiff had suffered a private nuisance and should not be deprived of a personal right of action merely because the defendant's conduct also adversely affected the public generally. Relief nevertheless was denied on the ground that the defendant's actions fell within the scope of the defence of statutory authority.

4. Had the Attorney-General not acted or consented to a relator action in *Orange Productions*, would the individuals in the vicinity have succeeded in private nuisance or in a private action for public nuisance?

5. In *A.G. N.S. v. Beaver* (1984), 31 C.C.L.T. 54 (N.S.S.C.), aff'd (1985), 32 C.C.L.T. 170 (N.S.C.A.), the plaintiff sought an injunction in public nuisance to prohibit prostitutes from soliciting. The trial judge dismissed the application. He stated that equitable remedies such as injunctions should not be used to suppress criminal conduct, thereby undermining the important procedural safeguards of criminal law. However, a similar action in *A.G.B.C. v. Couillard* (1984), 31 C.C.L.T. 26 (B.C.S.C.) succeeded. Apparently, this injunction resulted in the prostitutes moving to an adjacent area. The Attorney-General of British Columbia declined to bring a subsequent action at the request of this adjacent neighbourhood. When these individuals brought a private action, the

court dismissed their claim on the basis that the annoyance amounted to a public nuisance and they had no standing to sue: *Stein v. Gonzales, supra.*

These cases, and the associated academic commentary, demonstrate how difficult it is to define the tort of public nuisance and reconcile the precedents. See Klar, "Recent Developments in Canadian Tort Law" (1985) 17 Ottawa L. Rev. 325 at 386–88; and Cassels, "Prostitution and Public Nuisance: Desperate Measures and the Limits of Civil Adjudication" (1985) 63 Can. Bar Rev. 764.

6. The court in *Hickey* required the plaintiffs to prove that they had suffered injuries that were different in *kind* from those suffered by other members of the public. It was not enough that the *same* injuries were suffered to a different *degree*. Do you agree with the way the court applied this test to the facts? See also *A.G. Man. v. Adventure Flights Centre Ltd.* (1983), 25 C.C.L.T. 295 (Man. Q.B.); and *Bolton v. Forest Pest Management Institute* (1985), 21 D.L.R. (4th) 242 (B.C.C.A.).

A plaintiff in a private action for public nuisance must prove that he or she has suffered some "special damage" beyond that experienced by the general public. See Linden & Feldthusen, *Canadian Tort Law*, 8th ed. (2006) at 564-66; and Fleming, *The Law of Torts*, 9th ed. (1998) at 460-462.

7. Probably the largest single category of private actions for public nuisance involves plaintiffs injured on public sidewalks, highways, or waterways. F. Newark has identified this development as the major reason for the blurring of the boundaries of nuisance, a subject which is so "intractable to definition and analysis that it immediately betrays its mongrel origins": "The Boundaries of Nuisance" (1949) 65 L.Q.R. 480. J. Fleming is equally critical, stating that the cases have "saddled the law with a series of capricious distinctions which are difficult to justify on any rational basis": *The Law of Torts*, 9th ed. (1998) at 460. See also Laskin, "Torts – Nuisance or Negligence – Collisions On Highways With Standing Truck" (1944) 22 Can. Bar Rev. 468.

The Canadian case law reflects these difficulties. See for example *Lickoch v. Madu* (1973), 34 D.L.R. (3d) 569 (Alta. C.A.); *Goodwin v. Pine Point Park* (1974), 54 D.L.R. (3d) 498 (Ont. C.A.); and *Chessie v. J.D. Irvine Ltd.* (1982), 140 D.L.R. (3d) 501 (N.B.C.A.).

8. For a discussion of nuisance in the context of environmental concerns, see Silverman & Evans, "Aeronautical Noise in Canada" (1972) 10 Osgoode Hall L.J. 607; McLaren, "The Common Law Nuisance Actions And The Environmental Battle – Well Tempered Swords or Broken Reeds" (1972) 10 Osgoode Hall L.J. 505; McLaren, "The Law of Torts and Pollution" in *L.S.U.C. Special Lectures on New Developments in the Law of Torts* (1973) at 309; Jeffery, "Environmental Enforcement and Regulation in the 1980's" (1984) 10 Queen's L.J. 43; and Cross, "Does Only the Careless Polluter Pay? A Fresh Look at the Nature of Private Nuisance" (1995) 111 L.Q.R. 445.

4. Remedies

If the defendant has committed a nuisance, the plaintiff may be entitled to one or more remedies. The most common options, injunctive relief and damages, are discussed in the cases that follow. A third possibility, the self-help remedy of abatement, is discussed in the notes that follow.

Just as the threshold issue of liability requires the court to balance the plaintiff's interests against those of the defendant and the community as a whole, so too a judge may be required to weigh competing interests when fashioning a response to the tort. The choice between damages and an injunction is often quite difficult.

The principles underlying awards of damages were addressed in Chapter 18. For now, it will suffice to say a few words about injunctive relief. An *injunction* is a court order directing a person to act in a particular way. In the present context, it may be *prohibitory* or *mandatory*. The former compels the defendant to refrain from a certain act (*e.g.* stop dumping noxious substances into the plaintiff's pond), while the latter compels performance of a certain act (*e.g.* tear down a structure that hangs over the plaintiff's backyard). An injunction may be *interlocutory*, when a court temporarily restrains the defendant while the plaintiff attempts to establish a case for a permanent order. It may be *quia timet*, when a court grants an injunction in an effort to prevent an anticipated harm.

MENDEZ v. PALAZZI

(1976), 68 D.L.R. (3d) 582 (Ont. Co. Ct.)

HOLLINGWORTH CO. CT. J.: . . . The nub of this action is that roots from the poplar trees have allegedly ruined the plaintiffs' lawn, rock-garden and patio, and are allegedly threatening the septic tank, weeping tiles, and indeed the foundation of the plaintiffs' home and have gravely interfered with the enjoyment of their property.

. . .

What are the plaintiffs' remedies? It is necessary to decide whether damages are a proper remedy or whether a mandatory injunction shall issue or perhaps at the very least a *quia timet* injunction. The governing principles are set forth in the judgment of A.L. Smith, L.J., in *Shelfer v. London Electric Lighting Co.*, [1895] 1 Ch. 287 at pp. 322-3:

> (1.) If the injury to the plaintiff's legal rights is small,
> (2.) And is one which is capable of being estimated in money,
> (3.) And is one which can be adequately compensated by a small money payment,
> (4.) And the case is one in which it would be oppressive to the defendant to grant an injunction: –

. . .

I would hold in this case that paras. (2), (3) and (4) of A.L. Smith, L.J.'s dicta would be apposite. Is an injunction justified?

A careful review of the Canadian case law reveals no Canadian case in point. There are, however, English and Commonwealth authorities which are pertinent. In *Middleton v. Humphries* (1912), 47 I.L.T. 160, an Irish case before Ross, J., damage was caused to the plaintiff by the roots of a tree. The trial Judge had no trouble granting an injunction restraining the defendants from continuing to permit the injury and also awarded damages. Similarly, in *Butler v. Standard Telephones & Cables, Ltd.*, [1940] 1 K.B. 399, the plaintiff's house was damaged by Lombardy poplar roots burrowing under the house. Damages were awarded as apparently an injunction, although pleaded, was not asked for at trial.

In *McCombe v. Read et al.*, [1955] 2 All E.R. 458, again poplar roots damaged a house. Harman, J., granted damages and an injunction. In *Davey v. Harrow Corp.*, [1957]

2 All E.R. 305, the plaintiff obtained damages and an injunction when the roots "caused subsidence so that his house has been extensively damaged". Finally, in *Morgan v. Khyatt*, [1964] 1 W.L.R. 475, the Board, on Appeal from the Supreme Court of New Zealand, affirmed that Court's decision in granting damages and an injunction when the roots from four pohutukawa trees damaged a concrete wall and drains.

In order for an injunction to issue, as I read the cases, there must be two conditions precedent. First, there must be actual damage; second, that damage must be substantial. In the case at bar there is actual damage to the lawn, as I have found as a fact, but not that degree of substantial damage, for example, damage to the house foundation or the tile beds, to merit issuing a mandatory injunction. To order here a mandatory injunction would, in the words of A.L. Smith, L.J., be "oppressive to the defendant" but should a *quia timet* injunction issue? The principles governing the *quia timet* injunction have been cited by Pearson, J., in the case of *Fletcher v. Bealey* (1884), 28 Ch. D. 688. At p. 698 the learned Judge laid down the two necessary ingredients:

> [1] There must, if no actual damage is proved, be proof of *imminent danger*, and [2] there must also be proof that the apprehended damage will, if it comes, be very substantial.

[Emphasis added.] I would say it must be proved damage will be irreparable; if the danger is not proved to be so imminent that no one can doubt that if the remedy is delayed the damage will be suffered, I think it must be shown that, if the damage does occur at any time, it will come in such a way and under such circumstances, that it will be impossible for the plaintiffs to protect themselves against it if relief is denied to them in a *quia timet* injunction.

Here, there was no evidence at all that the roots had reached the tile bed. Although one root shoot was found near the house, there is no probative evidence before me that the basement has settled or has been damaged as a result of root action. Finally, although plaintiffs' counsel argued for a *quia timet* injunction, his pleadings are silent on this matter.

Therefore, a *quia timet* injunction shall not issue.

. . .

[The judge found damages to be the appropriate remedy and awarded the plaintiffs $500 special and general damages.]

NOTES AND QUESTIONS

1. Should the court have refused the injunction? What difference did it make to the plaintiff?

2. *Fletcher*, a case relied upon in *Mendez*, was reinterpreted in *Hooper v. Rogers*, [1975] Ch. 43 (C.A.). In *Hooper*, the court said that the requirement of "imminent danger" merely raised the issue of whether the plaintiff's request for an injunction was premature. Would *Mendez* have been decided differently using this approach?

3. As in *Mendez*, A.L. Smith L.J.'s comments in *Shelfer v. London Electric Lighting Co.*, [1895] 1 Ch. 287 are often cited by English and Canadian judges in determining whether the plaintiff should receive injunctive relief or merely damages. However, as

Sharpe J. notes in *Injunctions and Specific Performance*, 2d ed., looseleaf (1992) at paras. 4.60-4.240, the judicial attitudes toward those comments are very different in the two countries. In England, there is a strong presumption in favour of an injunction and judges are often unmoved by hardship to the defendant or the community, even if the plaintiff's loss is relatively small. In contrast, Canadian courts are much more inclined to flexibly balance the benefits and burdens associated with injunctive relief.

4. For additional Canadian cases involving the granting of injunctions, see *Palmer v. N.S. Forest Indust.* (1983), 2 D.L.R. (4th) 397 (N.S.S.C.); *Bolton v. Forest Pest Management Institute* (1985), 21 D.L.R. (4th) 242 (B.C.C.A.); *Banfai v. Formula Fun Centre Inc.* (1984), 34 C.C.L.T. 171 (Ont. H.C.); *A.G. N.S. v. Beaver* (1985), 32 C.C.L.T. 170 (N.S.C.A.); *Hynes v. Hynes* (1989), 3 R.P.R. (2d) 142 (Nfld. C.A.); *Nippa v. C.H. Lewis (Lucan) Ltd.* (1991), 82 D.L.R. (4th) 417 (Ont. Gen. Div.); and *Ward v. Magna International Inc.* (1994), 21 C.C.L.T. (2d) 178 (Ont. Gen. Div.).

MILLER v. JACKSON

[1977] Q.B. 966 (C.A.)

[The plaintiffs bought a house in a new subdivision which was adjacent to a small well-established cricket club. They sued the club in nuisance and negligence after several balls had been hit onto their property, causing minor damage to their house and garden. In an effort to prevent injury to the plaintiffs, the club erected a high fence and instructed players to keep their shots down. The club also offered to place a net over the plaintiffs' garden whenever there was a game, to install unbreakable glass windows, to provide shutters, and to pay for any damage. The plaintiffs rejected these offers and sought damages and an injunction. At trial, the plaintiffs succeeded in both nuisance and negligence, and were awarded damages and granted an injunction. The defendant appealed.

An excerpt from this case appears in the notes in Chapter 15. It may be helpful to read that excerpt before reading the following extract, which is limited to the issue of nuisance and the appropriate remedy.]

LORD DENNING M.R.: . . . In our present case, too, nuisance was pleaded as an alternative to negligence. The tort of nuisance in many cases overlaps the tort of negligence. . . . But there is at any rate one important distinction between them. It lies in the nature of the remedy sought. Is it damages? Or an injunction? If the plaintiff seeks a remedy in damages for injury done to him or his property, he can lay his claim either in *negligence* or *nuisance*. But, if he seeks an injunction to stop the playing of cricket altogether, I think he must make his claim in nuisance. The books are full of cases where an injunction has been granted to restrain the continuance of a nuisance. But there is no case, so far as I know, where it has been granted so as to stop a man being negligent. At any rate in a case of this kind, where an occupier of a house or land seeks to restrain his neighbour from doing something on his own land, the only appropriate cause of action, on which to base the remedy of an injunction is nuisance. . . . It is the very essence of a private nuisance that it is the unreasonable use by a man of his land to the detriment of his neighbour. He must have been guilty of the fault, not necessarily of negligence, but of the unreasonable use of the land. . . .

It has often been said in nuisance cases that the rule is *sic utere tuo ut alienum non laedas*. But that is a most misleading maxim. Lord Wright put it in its proper place in *Sedleigh-Denfield v. O'Callaghan*:

> [It] is not only lacking in definiteness but is also inaccurate. An occupier may make in many ways a use of his land which causes damage to the neighbouring landowners, yet be free from liability . . . a useful test is perhaps what is reasonable according to the ordinary usages of mankind living in society, or, more correctly, in a particular society.

I would, therefore, adopt this test: is the use by the cricket club of this ground for playing cricket a reasonable use of it. To my mind it is a most reasonable use. Just consider the circumstances. For over 70 years the game of cricket has been played on this ground to the great benefit of the community as a whole, and to the injury of none. No one could suggest that it was a nuisance to the neighbouring owners simply because an enthusiastic batsman occasionally hit a ball out of the ground for six to the approval of the admiring onlookers. Then I would ask: does it suddenly become a nuisance because one of the neighbours chooses to build a house on the very edge of the ground, in such a position that it may well be struck by the ball on the rare occasion when there is a hit for six? To my mind the answer is plainly No. The building of the house does not convert the playing of cricket into a nuisance when it was not so before. If and insofar as any damage is caused to the house or anyone in it, it is because of the position in which it was built.

. . .

In this case it is our task to balance the right of the cricket club to continue playing on their cricket ground, as against the right of the householder not to be interfered with. On taking the balance, I would give priority to the right of the cricket club to continue playing cricket on the ground, as they have done for the last 70 years. It takes precedence over the right of the newcomer to sit in his garden undisturbed. After all he bought the house four years ago in mid-summer when the cricket season was at its height. He might have guessed that there was a risk that a hit might possibly land on his property. If he finds that he does not like it, he ought, when cricket is played, to sit in the other side of the house or in the front garden, or go out; or take advantage of the offers the club have made to him of fitting unbreakable glass, and so forth. Or, if he does not like that, he ought to sell his house and move elsewhere. I expect there are many who would gladly buy it in order to be near the cricket field and open space. At any rate he ought not to be allowed to stop cricket being played on this ground.

This case is new. It should be approached on principles applicable to modern conditions. There is a contest here between the interests of the public at large and the interest of a private individual. The *public* interest lies in protecting the environment by preserving our playing fields in the face of mounting development, and by enabling our youth to enjoy all the benefits of outdoor games, such as cricket and football. The *private* interest lies in securing the privacy of his home and garden without intrusion or interference by anyone. In deciding between these two conflicting interests, it must be remembered that it is not a question of damages. If by a million to one chance a cricket ball does go out of the ground and cause damage, the cricket club will pay. There is no difficulty on that score. No, it is a question of an injunction. And in our law you will find it repeatedly affirmed that an injunction is a discretionary remedy. In a new situation like this, we have to think afresh as to how discretion should be exercised. On the one hand, Mrs. Miller is a very sensitive lady who has worked herself up into such a state that she exclaimed to the judge:

> I just want to be allowed to live in peace. Have we got to wait until someone is killed before anything can be done?

If she feels like that about it, it is quite plain that, for peace in the future, one or other has to move. Either the cricket club have to move, but goodness knows where. I do not suppose for a moment there is any field in Lintz to which they could move. Or Mrs. Miller must move elsewhere. As between their conflicting interests, I am of opinion that the public interest should prevail over the private interest. The cricket club should not be driven out. In my opinion the right exercise of discretion is to refuse an injunction; and, of course, to refuse damages in lieu of an injunction. Likewise as to the claim for past damages. The club were entitled to use this ground for cricket in the accustomed way. It was not a nuisance, nor was it negligence of them so to run it. Nor was the batsman negligent when he hit the ball for six. All were doing simply what they were entitled to do. So if the club had put it to the test, I would have dismissed the claim for damages also. But as the club very fairly say that they are willing to pay for any damage, I am content that there should be an award of £400 to cover any past or future damage.

. . .

I would allow the appeal, accordingly.

. . .

GEOFFREY LANE L.J.: . . . The only question is whether it is unreasonable. It is a truism to say that this is a matter of degree. What that means is this. A balance has to be maintained between on the one hand the rights of the individual to enjoy his house and garden without the threat of damage and on the other hand the rights of the public in general or a neighbour to engage in lawful pastimes. Difficult questions may sometimes arise when the defendants' activities are offensive to the senses, for example by way of noise. Where, as here, the damage or potential damage is physical the answer is more simple. There is, subject to what appears hereafter, no excuse I can see which exonerates the defendants from liability in nuisance for what they have done and what they threaten to do. It is true no one has yet been physically injured. That is probably due to a great extent to the fact that the householders in Brackenridge desert their gardens whilst cricket is in progress. The danger of injury is obvious and is not slight enough to be disregarded. There is here a real risk of serious injury.

There is, however, one obviously strong point in the defendants' favour. They or their predecessors have been playing cricket on this ground (and no doubt hitting sixes out of it) for 70 years or so. Can someone by building a house on the edge of the field in circumstances where it must have been obvious that balls might be hit over the fence, effectively stop cricket being played? Precedent apart, justice would seem to demand that the plaintiffs should be left to make the most of the site they have elected to occupy with all its obvious advantages and all its equally obvious disadvantages. It is pleasant to have an open space over which to look from your bedroom and sitting room windows, so far as it is possible to see over the concrete wall. Why should you complain of the obvious disadvantages which arise from the particular purpose to which the open space is being put? Put briefly, can the defendants take advantage of the fact that the plaintiffs have put themselves in such a position by coming to occupy a house on the edge of a small cricket field, with the result that what was not a nuisance in the past now becomes a nuisance? If the matter were *res integra*, I confess I should be inclined to find for the defendants. It does not seem just that a long-established activity, in itself innocuous, should be brought to an end because someone chooses to build a house nearby and so turn an innocent pastime into an actionable nuisance. Unfortunately, however, the question is not open. In *Sturges v. Bridgman* this very problem arose. The defendant had carried on a confectionery shop with a noisy pestle and mortar for more than 20 years. Although it was noisy, it was far enough away from neighbouring premises not to cause trouble to anyone, until the plaintiff, who was a physician, built a consulting-room on his own land but immediately adjoining the confectionery shop. The noise and vibrations seriously interfered with the consulting-room and became a nuisance to the physician. The defendant contended that he had acquired the right either at common law or under the Prescription Act 1832 by uninterrupted use for more than 20 years to impose the inconvenience. It was held by the Court of Appeal, affirming the judgment of Jessel MR, that use such as this which was, prior to the construction of the consulting-room, neither preventible nor actionable, could not found a prescriptive right. That decision involved the assumption, which so far as one can discover has never been questioned, that it is no answer to a claim in nuisance for the defendant to show that the plaintiff brought the trouble on his own head by building or coming to live in a house so close to the defendant's premises that he would inevitably be affected by the defendant's activities, where no one had been affected previously. See also *Bliss v. Hall.* It may be that this rule works injustice, it may be that one would decide the matter differently in the absence of authority. But we are bound by the decision in *Sturges v. Bridgman* and it is not for this court as I see it to alter a rule which has stood for so long.

Injunction

Given that the defendants are guilty of both negligence and nuisance, is it a case where the court should in its discretion give relief, or should the plaintiffs be left to their remedy in damages? There is no doubt that if cricket is played damage will be done to the plaintiffs' tiles or windows or both. There is not inconsiderable danger that if they or their son or their guests spend any time in the garden during the weekend afternoons in the summer they may be hit by a cricket ball. So long as this situation exists it seems to be that damages cannot be said to provide an adequate form of relief. Indeed, quite apart from the risk of physical injury, I can see no valid reason why the plaintiffs should have to submit to the inevitable breakage of tiles and/ or windows, even though the defendants have expressed their willingness to carry out any repairs at no cost to the plaintiffs. I would accordingly uphold the grant of the injunction to restrain the defendants from committing nuisance. However, I would postpone the operation of the injunction for 12 months to enable the defendants to look elsewhere for an alternative pitch.

. . .

CUMMING-BRUCE L.J.: . . . So on the facts of this case a court of equity must seek to strike a fair balance between the right of the plaintiffs to have quiet enjoyment of their house and garden without exposure to cricket balls occasionally falling like thunderbolts from the heavens, and the opportunity of the inhabitants of the village in which they live to continue to enjoy the manly sport which constitutes a summer recreation for adults and young persons, including one would hope and I expect the plaintiff's son. It is a relevant circumstance which a court of equity should take into account that the plaintiffs decided to buy a house which in June 1972 when completion took place was obviously on the boundary of a quite small cricket ground where cricket was played at weekends and sometimes on evenings during the working week. They selected a house with the benefit of an open space beside it. In February, when they first saw it, they did not think about the use of this open space. But before completion they must have realized it was the village cricket ground, and that balls would sometimes be knocked from the wicket into their garden, or even against the fabric of the house. If they did not realize it, they should have done. As it turns out, the female plaintiff has developed a somewhat obsessive attitude to the proximity of the cricket field and the cricketers who visit her to seek to recover their balls. The evidence discloses a hostility which goes beyond what is reasonable, although as the learned judge found she is reasonable in her fear that if the family use the garden while a match is in progress they will run the risk of serious injury if a great hit happens to drive a ball up to the skies and down into their garden. It is reasonable to decide that during matches the family must keep out of the garden. The risk of damage to the house can be dealt with in other ways, and is not such as to fortify significantly the case for an injunction stopping play on this ground.

With all respect, in my view the learned judge did not have regard sufficiently to these considerations. He does not appear to have had regard to the interest of the inhabitants of the village as a whole. Had he done so he would in my view have been led to the conclusion that the plaintiffs having accepted the benefit of the open space marching with their land should accept the restrictions on enjoyment of their garden which they may reasonably think necessary. That is the burden which they have to bear in order that the inhabitants of the village may not be deprived of their facilities for an innocent recreation which they have so long enjoyed on this ground. There are here special circumstances which should inhibit a court of equity from granting the injunction claimed.

. . .

[Appeal allowed. Past and future damages assessed at £400.]

NOTES AND QUESTIONS

1. Given that Lord Denning would have denied relief even if the defendants had refused to pay damages, which of the three suggested outcomes in *Miller* is preferable? Which approach maximizes social resources? What other factors should the court consider?

2. A determination as to whether a particular course of action constitutes a nuisance requires a consideration of all of the circumstances. While Canadians play much less cricket than do the English, they occasionally do hit golf balls onto neighbouring properties. Two recent cases demonstrate the significance of context. In each instance, the plaintiff sued over errant golf balls. In *Sammut v. Islington Golf Club Ltd.* (2005), 16 C.E.L.R. (3d) 66 (Ont. S.C.J.), the plaintiff's backyard was inundated by hundreds of balls, some of which cracked windows, dented stucco walls, and demolished ornamental statues. The court awarded $5,000 for the past nuisance, $9,000 for past damage, and enjoined the defendant from allowing golfers to play the hole in question until sufficient remedial measures were in place. In *Lakeview Gardens Ltd. v. Regina (City)*, [2005] 1 W.W.R. 651 (Sask. C.A.), 10 to 20 balls landed on the plaintiff's property each year. Windows had been smashed four or five times, but no person was ever injured. Given the layout of the defendant's course, the balls had to have been deliberately hit onto the plaintiff's land. The trial court ordered the defendant to employ a "monitor" to prevent future occurrences. The Court of Appeal, however, overturned that decision. Moreover, while allowing compensation of $73 for a broken window, it refused to award an

injunction. In reaching that decision, it stressed that the nuisance was "merely inconvenient or a minor discomfort," and was not an unreasonable threat to health or safety.

3. Under the tort of nuisance, an occupier generally is viewed as having merely an *interest*, rather than a *right*, in the reasonable use and enjoyment of the land. The tort of trespass, in contrast, is based on a *right* to uninterrupted possession of land. That difference is reflected in the fact that injunctive relief is available more readily in trespass than in nuisance. The nature of the interest underlying nuisance also explains the balancing exercise that occurred in *Miller*. Nevertheless, if a nuisance creates physical damage, and especially if it does so repeatedly, a court will likely recognize a nuisance and grant an injunction. This approach was adopted by Lane L.J. in *Miller*, and approved in *Kennaway v. Thompson*, [1980] 3 All E.R. 329 (C.A.). Does the fact that the interference is physical and repeated justify the granting of an injunction, virtually as of right?

SPUR INDUSTRIES INC. v. DEL E. WEBB DEVELOPMENT CO.

494 P.2d 700 (Ariz. S.C. 1972)

[For many years, the appellant operated a cattle feedlot in an exclusively agricultural area. In 1959, the respondent developed plans for a residential community. It purchased 20,000 acres of farmland near the appellant's operations. The price of that land was considerably lower than the price for land in nearby Phoenix. As the development expanded, the respondent discovered that smells and flies originating on the appellant's feedlot made it impossible to use certain plots of land. The respondent therefore sought injunctive relief on the basis of the nuisance allegedly created by the appellant's use of its property.]

CAMERON VICE C.J.: From a judgment permanently enjoining the defendant, Spur Industries, Inc. from operating a cattle feedlot near the plaintiff Del E. Webb Development Company's Sun City, Spur appeals. Webb cross-appeals. Although numerous issues are raised, we feel that it is necessary to answer only two questions. They are:

1. Where the operation of a business, such as a cattle feedlot is lawful in the first instance, but becomes a nuisance by reason of a nearby residential area, may the feedlot operation be enjoined in an action brought by the developer of the residential area?

2. Assuming that the nuisance may be enjoined, may the developer of a completely new town or urban area in a previously agricultural area be required to indemnify the operator of the feedlot who must move or cease operation because of the presence of the residential area created by the developer?

MAY SPUR BE ENJOINED?

The difference between a private nuisance and a public nuisance is generally one of degree. A private nuisance is one affecting a single individual or a definite small number of persons in the enjoyment of private rights not common to the public, while a public nuisance is one affecting the rights enjoyed by citizens as a part of the public. To constitute a public nuisance, the nuisance must affect a considerable number of people or an entire community or neighbourhood. . . .

Where the injury is slight, the remedy for minor inconveniences lies in an action for damages rather than in one for an injunction. . . . Moreover, some courts have held, in the "balancing of inconveniences" cases, that damages may be the sole remedy. . . .

Thus, it would appear from the admittedly incomplete record as developed in the trial court, that, at most, residents of Youngtown would be entitled to damages rather than injunctive relief.

We have no difficulty, however, in agreeing with the conclusion of the trial court that Spur's operation was an enjoinable public nuisance as far as the people in the southern portion of Del Webb's Sun City were concerned. . . .

Del Webb, having shown a special injury in the loss of sales, had a standing to bring suit to enjoin the nuisance. . . . The judgment of the trial court permanently enjoining the operation of the feedlot is affirmed.

MUST DEL WEBB INDEMNIFY SPUR?

A suit to enjoin a nuisance sounds in equity and the courts have long recognized a special responsibility to the public when acting as a court of equity.

In addition to protecting the public interest, however, courts of equity are concerned with protecting the operator of a lawfully, albeit noxious, business from the result of a knowing and wilful encroachment by others near his business.

In the so-called "coming to the nuisance" cases, the courts have held that the residential landowner may not have relief if he knowingly came into a neighbourhood reserved for industrial or agricultural endeavours and has been damaged thereby:

> Plaintiff chose to live in an area uncontrolled by zoning laws or restrictive covenants and remote from urban development. In such an area plaintiffs cannot complain that legitimate agricultural pursuits are being carried on in the vicinity, nor can plaintiffs, having chosen to build in an agricultural area, complain that the agricultural pursuits carried on in the area depreciate the value of their homes. The area being *primarily agricultural* any opinion reflecting the value of such property must take this factor into account. The standards affecting the value of residence property in an urban setting, subject to zoning controls and controlled planning techniques, cannot be the standards by which agricultural properties are judged.
>
> People employed in a city who build their homes in suburban areas of the county beyond the limits of a city and zoning regulations do so for a reason. Some do so to avoid the high taxation rate imposed by cities, or to avoid special assessments for street, sewer and water projects. They usually build on improved or hard surface highways, which have been built either at state or county expense and thereby avoid special assessments for these improvements. It may be that they desire to get away from the congestion of traffic, smoke, noise, foul air and the many other annoyances of city life. But with all these advantages in going beyond the area which is zoned and restricted to protect them in their homes, they must be prepared to take the disadvantages. [*Dill v. Excel Packing Company*, 183 Kan. 513, 525, 526 (1958).] . . .

And:

> . . . a party cannot justly call upon the law to make that place suitable for his residence which was not so when he selected it. . . [*Gilbert v. Showerman*, 23 Mich. 448 at 455 (1871)].

Were Webb the only party injured, we would feel justified in holding that the doctrine of "coming to the nuisance" would have been a bar to the relief asked by Webb, and, on the other hand, had Spur located the feedlot near the outskirts of a city and had the city grown toward the feedlot, Spur would have to suffer the cost of abating the nuisance as to those people locating within the growth pattern of the expanding city:

> The case affords, perhaps, an example where a business established at a place remote from population is gradually surrounded and becomes part of a populous center, so that a business which formerly was not an interference with the rights of others has become so by the encroachment of the population. . .. [*City of Ft. Smith v. Western Hide & Fur Co.*, 153 Ark. 99 at 103 (1922)].

> We agree, however, with the Massachusetts court that:

> The law of nuisance affords no rigid rule to be applied in all instances. It is elastic. It undertakes to require only that which is fair and reasonable under all the circumstances. In a commonwealth like this, which depends for its material prosperity so largely on the continued growth and enlargement of manufacturing of diverse varieties, "extreme rights" cannot be enforced. . . [*Stevens v. Rockport Granite Co.*, 216 Mass. 486 at 488 (1914).]

There was no indication in the instant case at the time Spur and its predecessors located in Western Maricopa County that a new city would spring up, full-blown, alongside the feeding operation and that the developer of that city would ask the court to order Spur to move because of the new city. Spur is required to move not because of any wrongdoing on the part of Spur, but because of a proper and legitimate regard of the courts for the rights and interests of the public.

Del Webb, on the other hand, is entitled to the relief prayed for (a permanent injunction), not because Webb is blameless, but because of the damage to the people who have been encouraged to purchase homes in Sun City. It does not equitably or legally follow, however, that Webb, being entitled to the injunction, is then free of any liability to Spur if Webb has in fact been the cause of the damage Spur has sustained. It does not seem harsh to require a developer, who has taken advantage of the lesser land values in a rural area as well as the availability of large tracts of land on which to build and develop a new town or city in the area, to indemnify those who are forced to leave as a result.

Having brought people to the nuisance to the foreseeable detriment of Spur, Webb must indemnify Spur for a reasonable amount of the cost of moving or shutting down. It should be noted that this relief to Spur is limited to a case wherein a developer has, with foreseeability, brought into a previously agricultural or industrial area the population which makes necessary the granting of an injunction against a lawful business and for which the business has no adequate relief.

It is therefore the decision of this court that the matter be remanded to the trial court for a hearing upon the damages sustained by the defendant Spur as a reasonable and direct result of the granting of the permanent injunction. Since the result of the appeal may appear novel and both sides have obtained a measure of relief, it is ordered that each side will bear its own costs.

NOTES AND QUESTIONS

1. On its facts, was *Miller v. Jackson* an appropriate case for the unusual remedy adopted in *Spur*?

2. Do you agree with the result in *Spur*? What factors should be considered in adopting this solution in other cases? What would have been the result in *Spur* if the court had found for the defendant?

3. Whatever its merits, the decision in *Spur* to grant a "compensated injunction" has not been followed in subsequent cases. Sharpe J. describes the possibility of indemnification as "mostly theoretical": *Injunctions and Specific Performance*, 2d ed., looseleaf (1992) at para. 4.310.

4. The court in *Spur* gave considerable weight to the interests of the people who had purchased units in the plaintiff's development. Assume that the defendant could not have relocated its feedlot within the same area and that many of its present staff would have lost their jobs if an injunction was granted. Should such considerations be relevant to the court's decision? See *Bottom v. Ont. Leaf Tobacco Co.*, [1935] O.R. 205 (C.A.). See generally Hawkins, "'In and Of Itself': Some Thoughts on the Assignment of Property Rights in Nuisance Cases" (1978) 36 U.T. Fac. L. Rev. 209; and Ogus & Richardson, "Economics and the Environment: A Study of Private Nuisance" [1977] C.L.J. 284. Should the same principles be applied in granting remedies in public and private nuisance? See *Boomer v. Atlantic Cement Co.*, 257 N.E.2d 870 (N.Y. 1970).

5. What role did the doctrine of "coming to the nuisance" play in the judge's analysis in *Spur*? The majority of the American cases do not recognize the fact that the plaintiff "came to the nuisance" as a defence, provided the plaintiff bought the land in good faith and not for the purpose of bringing a claim. Despite Lord Denning's view, the English authorities generally support the same principle. See Heuston & Buckley, *Salmond and Heuston on the Law of Torts*, 21st ed. (1996) at 70-71; Rogers, *Winfield and Jolowicz on Tort*, 17th ed. (2006) at 678-79; and Keeton *et al., Prosser and Keeton on Torts*, 5th ed. (1984) at 634-36.

6. The leading Commonwealth case on the issue of "coming to the nuisance" is *Sturges v. Bridgman* (1879), 11 Ch. D. 852 (C.A.). Frederick Bridgman lived on Wigmore Street. Dr. Octavius Sturges lived on Wimpole Street. Although there were no zoning or planning laws in operation in London at the relevant time, different streets tended to be put to different uses. Wigmore Street contained several premises that contained businesses similar to Bridgman's. Likewise, several physicians lived and worked on Wimpole Street, just like Dr. Sturges. Bridgman had lived in the same house on Wigmore Street for many years. During that time, he had always used his house for both domestic and commercial purposes. Because he was a confectioner, he used his kitchen to prepare his products. Among his equipment was a mortar, which was attached to the rear wall of his kitchen and which was used to grind up ingredients.

Bridgman had used his mortar for many years, with no complaints, before Dr. Sturges moved in. Dr. Sturges established a consulting room, for the purpose of seeing and advising patients, at the back of his house. It was the only room suitable for that purpose. Unfortunately, Wigmore Street and Wimpole Street were located such that Bridgman's house and Dr. Sturges' house shared a common wall. Even more unfortunately, the houses were arranged such that Bridgman's mortar was affixed to the same wall that closed Dr. Sturges' consulting room. The noise from the mortar unreasonably interfered with Dr. Sturges' ability to properly consult with his patients. The parties attempted to negotiate a solution, but those efforts failed.

Dr. Sturges sued for the tort of nuisance and requested an injunction ordering Bridgman to desist from the unreasonable racket. Bridgman's only defence was that he had, over the years, acquired a prescriptive right to operate his mortar. The court rejected that argument and imposed an injunction. In doing so, it recognized that the operative principle might occasionally create hardship. It nevertheless insisted that a contrary rule would lead to even more hardship, and moreover would inhibit the useful development of land. For a discussion of the story behind the case, see Simpson, "The Story of *Sturges v Bridgman*: The Resolution of Land Use Disputes Between Neighbours" in Korngold & Morriss, eds., *Property Stories* (2004) at 9.

7. G. Calabresi and D. Melamed provide an interesting analysis of nuisance remedies in "Property Rules, Liability Rules and Inalienability: One View of the Cathedral" (1972) 85 Harv. L. Rev. 1089. The authors suggest that the courts must first decide which party to *entitle* in a nuisance action, and then must decide whether to grant the entitled party *property rule protection* or *liability rule protection*. The authors distinguish between the rules in the following manner at 1092:

> An entitlement is protected by a property rule to the extent that someone who wishes to remove the entitlement from its holder must buy it from him in a voluntary transaction in which the value of the entitlement is agreed upon by the seller. It is the form of entitlement which gives rise to the least amount of state intervention: once the original entitlement is decided upon, the state does not try to decide its value. It lets each of the parties say how much the entitlement is worth to him. . .

Consider *Miller v Jackson* from the perspective suggested by the authors. Once the court found a nuisance, it had an option. On the one hand, by granting an injunction, the court would entitle the Millers to *property rule protection*. If the cricket club wanted to continue operations, it would be required to offer sufficient consideration in order to induce the Millers into relaxing their rights. For instance, the club might have purchased the Millers' home. On the other hand, by refusing to impose an injunction, and by confining the claimants to compensatory damages, the court provided the Millers with *liability rule protection*. In effect, the club would be entitled to purchase the right to commit a nuisance. It would be permitted to violate the Millers' interests as long as it was prepared to provide compensation. The following chart illustrates the authors' approach in reference to *Miller*.

	Entitle the Homeowner	*Entitle the Cricket Club*
Property Rule	Injunction to enjoin club	Neither injunction nor damages
Liability Rule	Damages for future interference, but no injunction	Allow injunction, but the plaintiff must pay to relocate the club

How do you think the authors would have resolved *Miller* and *Spur*? Can you suggest circumstances in which the property rule would be preferable to the liability rule and vice versa? Will the authors' approach likely produce different results than those produced by the existing doctrine?

See generally Thompson, "Injunction Negotiations: An Economic, Moral and Legal Analysis" (1975) 27 Stan. L. Rev. 1563; Polinsky, "Resolving Nuisance Disputes: The Simple Economics of Injunctive and Damage Remedies" (1980) 32 Stan. L. Rev. 1075;

and Prichard, "An Economic Analysis of *Miller v. Jackson*" in McArdle, ed., *The Cambridge Lectures, 1985* (1987) at 71. For an excellent discussion of *Spur*, see Morriss, "Cattle v. Retirees: Sun City and the Battle of *Spur Industries v. Del E. Webb Development Co.*" in Korngold & Morriss, eds., *Property Stories* (2004) at 259.

8. A common law alternative to seeking damages and an injunction is the remedy of *abatement of nuisance*. Like other self-help remedies, abatement can be traced to the early years of the common law. It provided an expedient, informal and inexpensive alternative to legal proceedings. However, it also entailed a potential for violence if the person against whom it was invoked chose to resist. This limitation, common to all self-help remedies, explains the modern trend toward restricting abatement. The case law is quite complex, particularly in regard to rights of entry. J. Wactor has provided a useful summary of the major principles governing abatement. He lists several factors the courts consider in upholding the defence of abatement: (1) Does the nuisance regularly manifest itself and require an immediate remedy? (2) Will the benefit of abatement be lost by waiting for a judicial remedy? (3) Can the abatement be effected without a breach of the peace or unnecessary damage? The defendant may be held civilly, and even criminally, liable for breaching the peace, causing damage, or trespassing without notice: see Wactor, "Self-Help: A Viable Remedy for Nuisance: A Guide for the Common Man's Lawyer" (1982) 24 Ariz. L. Rev. 83 at 98. See also Heuston & Buckley, *Salmond and Heuston on Tort*, 21st ed. (1996) at 574-76; and Keeton *et al.*, *Prosser and Keeton on Torts*, 5th ed. (1984) at 641-43.

REVIEW PROBLEM

Jonathan Bognor is the owner of a farm on which he had raised dairy cattle. When he purchased the farm in 1959, a steel mill owned by the National Steel Corporation, a company 50% owned by the federal government, was already operating on federal land about one mile from the farm. The steel mill is and was a visible source of air pollution because it relies on tall chimneys as a method of dispersing pollutants. This was a common approach to air pollution problems in 1959, but it is one that is no longer used in new plants. Technologies such as electrostatic precipitators now represent the state of the art in stationary source pollution control.

The price that Bognor paid for the farm was several thousand dollars less than the price of comparable properties situated further away from the mill. In the past, however, the pollutants had never had any serious discernible effect on Bognor's farm. The only possible apparent effect had been a slight browning of some grass, and Bognor had never been sure whether this was caused by the mill.

In 1978, dairy prices fell drastically. Foreseeing a difficult period ahead for dairy farmers, Bognor decided to diversify his farming activities in order to obtain greater security against future market fluctuations. After making extensive inquiries, he decided to grow blueberries, strawberries and other fruits.

The results of his first season's crop were disastrous. Most of the fruit was covered with brown speckles. A consultant advised Bognor that the brown speckles had been caused by sulphuric acid which, in turn, was caused by the emissions from the steel mill. The consultant also said that this acid caused the browning of the grass and that Bognor's new crops were much more sensitive to the acid. The consultant's report noted that it had not been known when the steel mill was established that sulphur from the coal fuel could mix with moisture in the atmosphere and produce sulphuric acid. In recent years, however, this connection had been clearly established and had been much discussed in the scientific literature.

Bognor is the only farmer in the area suffering such damage because he is the only one who has switched from dairy farming. It is also clear that the operators at the steel mill have no idea that they are harming Bognor's farming operations.

The steel mill was established by a federal statute which stated that the National Steel Corporation was authorized to erect a steel mill and to use the federal land for this purpose.

Bognor now wants to sue the National Steel Corporation for both damages and an injunction. Advise him.

25

STRICT AND VICARIOUS LIABILITY

1. Introduction
2. Strict Liability for Escape of Dangerous Substances: *Rylands v. Fletcher*
3. Strict Liability for Animals
4. Products Liability: Negligence or Strict Liability?
5. Vicarious Liability

1. Introduction

As a general rule, liability is imposed in tort law only if the defendant was at "fault." Fault, however, is a broad concept. To this point, we have focussed on situations in which the defendant intentionally or negligently caused the plaintiff's loss. As we saw in Chapter 3, however, "intention" is another frequently misleading term. In the context of the intentional torts, it is enough that the defendant intended to act in a certain way. The plaintiff need not prove that the defendant intended to act unlawfully. Consequently, for example, the "innocent" purchaser of stolen goods may be held liable for conversion. The law is unwilling to grant the defendant leniency for fear of undermining the plaintiff's underlying rights.

Exceptionally, however, liability is imposed even though the defendant was not at "fault," at least in any of the usual ways. In this chapter, we examine two concepts: *strict liability* and *vicarious liability*.

(a) STRICT LIABILITY

Strict liability is triggered simply by the breach of an obligation. The court does not demand proof that the breach was intentional, careless, or unreasonable. It is sufficient that the defendant acted in a prohibited manner. The classic examples address injuries inflicted by dangerous animals and losses falling under the rule in *Rylands v. Fletcher* (1868), L.R. 3 H.L. 330. The basic explanation is the same in each instance: by choosing to engage in a particularly dangerous activity, the defendant assumes responsibility for (almost) all damage that may occur. Consequently, if the defendant owns a dog with a history of aggression, the law bluntly says "Do not keep a dangerous animal that causes harm." If the dog subsequently bites the plaintiff, liability will be imposed even if, in the circumstances, the defendant neither encouraged the animal to attack nor carelessly failed to control its actions. Likewise, if the defendant chooses to store a large quantity of fireworks in a warehouse, the law imposes a strict obligation that says "Do not allow this danger to escape your property and injure another person." If the fireworks explode and destroy a neighbouring house, the plaintiff probably will be entitled to relief even if the defendant took every precaution possible.

Because this concept of strict liability sometimes is difficult to understand, it may be useful to draw comparisons with two other areas of private law: *contract* and *unjust enrichment*.

- *Strict Liability in Contract*: The law of contract generally shares tort law's notion of strict liability. Leaving aside exceptional circumstances (*e.g.* frustration), each party is strictly liable to perform its contractual obligations. The law bluntly says "Perform the agreement." In the event of breach, it is irrelevant that the defendant made every reasonable effort to fulfill the promise.
- *Strict Liability in Unjust Enrichment*: Although unjust enrichment also involves "strict liability," it defines that term much differently than do tort and contract. If the plaintiff mistakenly pays $5,000 to the defendant, the law *prima facie* will demand restitution (*i.e.* the defendant must reverse the transfer by repaying the money). Moreover, that liability is *strict*, in the narrowest sense of the word. Once again, there is no question of intentional or careless wrongdoing. Beyond that, however, there is no question of any wrongdoing at all. Breach of an obligation simply never enters into the analysis. Consequently, liability may be imposed even if the defendant was entirely unaware of the transfer (*e.g.* because the plaintiff mistakenly deposited $5,000 into the defendant's bank account while the defendant was on vacation). An unjustified transfer, regardless of culpability or fault, is sufficient to trigger the law of unjust enrichment.

(b) VICARIOUS LIABILITY

Strict liability in tort law occurs when the defendant breaches an obligation, albeit non-intentionally and non-negligently. The concept of *vicarious liability* goes one step further. It allows liability to be imposed on one person as a result of the tortious conduct of another. The most common example occurs in the employment context. If an employee commits a tort, the employer may be held responsible for the damage even though it did nothing wrong and even though it did not itself breach any obligation.

Within a generally fault-based regime of tort law, the concepts of strict liability and vicarious liability are anomalous and hence controversial. As explained in the last section of this chapter, the Supreme Court of Canada has recently provided policy justifications for vicarious liability. Strict liability, in contrast, remains highly contentious. Elsewhere in the Commonwealth, courts have begun to re-interpret areas of strict liability along more orthodox (*i.e.* fault-based) lines. As yet, there is no similar development in Canada.

NOTES AND QUESTIONS

1. Explain the difference between (a) the intention required for liability under the intentional torts, (b) the nature of fault under the strict liability torts, and (c) the nature of strict liability under the action in unjust enrichment.

2. Why is the law of unjust enrichment able to impose liability in the absence of a breach, whereas tort invariably requires proof that the defendant failed to fulfil an obligation? In answering this question, consider the nature of the remedies that are available in each instance. Does restitution (as awarded in unjust enrichment) ever hurt the defendant or help the plaintiff, relative to the *status quo ante*? Do compensation and disgorgement (as awarded in tort) ever hurt the defendant or help the plaintiff, relative to the *status quo ante*? See McInnes, "The Measure of Restitution" (2002) 52 U.T.L.J. 163.

2. Strict Liability for Escape of Dangerous Substances: *Rylands v. Fletcher*

(a) INTRODUCTION

The prime example of strict liability falls under the rubric of *Rylands v. Fletcher*. The defendants built a reservoir on their property in order to provide a regular supply of water to their mill. Unfortunately, the defendants did not realize that their reservoir was constructed over an abandoned mineshaft that was connected to the plaintiff's property. Water from the reservoir broke through the hidden shaft and flooded the plaintiff's adjoining mine. The House of Lords' decision has generated a large, complex body of law concerning liability for non-natural uses of land. The terms "non-natural use" and "escape" have resisted definition, and many of the defences remain somewhat unsettled. The decision and the judicial interpretations of its main elements are considered in this section.

RYLANDS v. FLETCHER
(1868), L.R. 3 H.L. 330

THE LORD CHANCELLOR (Lord Cairns): – My Lords, in this case the plaintiff . . . is the occupier of a mine and works under a close of land. The defendants are the owners of a mill in his neighbourhood; and they proposed to make a reservoir for the purpose of keeping and storing water to be used about their mill upon another close of land, which, for the purposes of this case, may be taken as being adjoining to the close of the plaintiff, although in point of fact some intervening land lay between the two. Underneath the close of land of the defendants on which they proposed to construct their reservoir there were certain old and disused mining passages and works. There were five vertical shafts, and some horizontal shafts communicating with them. The vertical shafts had been filled up with soil and rubbish; and, it does not appear that any person was aware of the existence either of the vertical shafts or of the horizontal works communicating with them. In the course of the working by the plaintiff of his mine, he had gradually worked through the seams of coal underneath the close, and had come into contact with the old and disused works underneath the close of the defendants. In that state of things the reservoir of the defendants was constructed. It was constructed by them through the agency and inspection of an engineer and contractor. Personally the defendants appear to have taken no part in the works, nor to have been aware of any want of security connected with them. As regards the engineer and the contractor, we must take it from the case that they did not exercise, as far as they were concerned, that reasonable care and caution which they might have exercised, taking notice, as they appear to have taken notice, of the vertical shafts filled up in the manner which I have mentioned. However, my Lords, when the reservoir was constructed and filled, or partly filled, with water, the weight of the water, bearing upon the imperfectly filled-up and disused vertical shafts, broke through those shafts. The water passed down them and into the horizontal workings and from the horizontal workings under the close of the defendants, it passed on into the workings under the close of the plaintiff and flooded his mine, causing considerable damage, for which this action was brought. The Court of Exchequer, when the special case stating the facts to which I have referred was argued before them, were of opinion that the plaintiff had established no cause of action. The Court of

Exchequer Chamber, before whom an appeal from their judgment was argued, were of a contrary opinion, and unanimously arrived at the conclusion that there was a cause of action, and that the plaintiff was entitled to damages. My Lords, the principles on which this case must be determined appear to me to be extremely simple. The defendants, treating them as owners or occupiers of the close on which the reservoir was constructed, might lawfully have used that close for any purpose for which it might, in the ordinary course of the enjoyment of land, be used; and if in what I may term the natural user of that land there had been any accumulation of water, either on the surface or underground, and if by the operation of the laws of nature that accumulation of water had passed off into the close occupied by the plaintiff, the plaintiff could not have complained that that result had taken place. If he had desired to guard himself against it, it would have lain on him to have done so by leaving or by interposing some barrier between his close and the close of the defendants in order to have prevented that operation of the laws of nature. . . . On the other hand, if the defendants, not stopping at the natural use of their close, had desired to use it for any purpose which I may term a non-natural use, for the purpose of introducing into the close that which, in its natural condition, was not in or upon it – for the purpose of introducing water, either above or below ground, in quantities and in a manner not the result of any work or operation on or under the land; and if in consequence of their doing so, or in consequence of any imperfection in the mode of their doing so, the water came to escape and to pass off into the close of the plaintiff, then it appears to me that that which the defendants were doing they were doing at their own peril; and if in the course of their doing it the evil arose to which I have referred – the evil, namely, of the escape of the water, and its passing away to the close of the plaintiff and injuring the plaintiff – then for the consequence of that, in my opinion, the defendants would be liable. . . . My Lords, these simple principles, if they are well founded, as it appears to me they are, really dispose of this case. The same result is arrived at on the principles referred to by Blackburn, J. in his judgment in the Court of Exchequer Chamber, where he states the opinion of that court as to the law in these words:

> We think that the true rule of law is that the person who, for his own purposes, brings on his land and collects and keeps there anything likely to do mischief, if it escapes must keep it in at his peril, and if he does not do so is *prima facie* answerable for all the damage which is the natural consequence of its escape. He can excuse himself by showing that the escape was owing to the plaintiff's default, or, perhaps, that the escape was the consequence of *vis major* or of the act of God; but, as nothing of this sort exists here, it is unnecessary to inquire what excuse would be sufficient. The general rule as above stated seems on principle just. The person whose grass or corn is eaten down by the escaping cattle of his neighbour, or whose mine is flooded by the water from his neighbour's reservoir, or whose cellar is invaded by the filth of his neighbour's privy, or whose habitation is made unhealthy by the fumes and noisome vapours of his neighbour's alkali works, is damnified without any fault of his own; and it seems but reasonable and just that the neighbour who has brought something on his own property (which was not naturally there), harmless to others so long as it is confined to his own property, but which he knows will be mischievous if it gets on his neighbour's, should be obliged to make good the damage which ensues if he does not succeed in confining it to his own property. But for his act in bringing it there no mischief could have accrued, and it seems but just that he should at his peril keep it there so that no mischief may accrue, or answer for the natural and anticipated consequence. And upon authority this,

we think, is established to be the law, whether the things so brought be beasts, or water, or filth, or stenches.

My Lords, in that opinion, I must say, I entirely concur. Therefore I have to move your Lordships that the judgment of the Court of Exchequer Chamber be affirmed, and that the present appeal be dismissed with costs.

LORD CRANWORTH. – My Lords, I concur with my noble and learned friend in thinking that the rule of law was correctly stated by Mr. Justice Blackburn in delivering the opinion of the Exchequer Chamber. If a person brings or accumulates on his land anything which, if it should escape, may cause damage to his neighbour, he does so at his peril. If it does escape and cause damage, he is responsible, however careful he may have been, and whatever precautions he may have taken to prevent the damage. In considering whether a defendant is liable to a plaintiff for damage which the plaintiff may have sustained, the question in general is, not whether the defendant has acted with due care and caution, but whether his acts have occasioned the damage. . . . And the doctrine is founded on good sense. For when one person in managing his own affairs causes, however innocently, damage to another, it is obviously only just that he should be the party to suffer. He is bound *sic uti suo ut non loedat alienum*.

NOTES AND QUESTIONS

1. What are the elements of an action under the rule in *Rylands v. Fletcher*?

2. In the court below (1866), L.R. 1 Exch. 265, Blackburn J. stated (at 282):

> There does not appear to be any difference in principle, between the extent of the duty cast on him who brings cattle on his land to keep them in, and the extent of the duty imposed on him who brings on his land water, filth, or stenches, or any other thing which will, if it escape, naturally do damage.

Should these two instances of strict liability (*i.e. Rylands v. Fletcher* and animals) be governed by the same principle? See *Read v. J. Lyons & Co.*, [1947] A.C. 156 at 166-67 (H.L.).

3. Other authorities, including Lord Macmillan's *obiter dicta* in *Read v. J. Lyons & Co.*, *supra* at 173, indicate that *Rylands* applies to personal injuries as well as property damage. See *Shiffman v. Order of St. John*, [1936] 1 All E.R. 557 (K.B.); *Schubert v. Sterling Trusts Corp.*, [1943] 4 D.L.R. 584 (Ont. H.C.); *Aldridge v. Van Patter*, [1952] 4 D.L.R. 93 (Ont. H.C.); *Perry v. Kendricks Transport Ltd.*, [1956] 1 All E.R. 154 (C.A.); and *Gertsen v. Municipality of Metropolitan Toronto* (1973), 41 D.L.R. (3d) 646 (Ont. H.C.). In *Transco plc v. Stockport Metropolitan Borough Council*, [2004] 2 A.C. 1 (H.L.), the House of Lords held that *Rylands v. Fletcher* protects only against property damage. That decision, however, was based on the fact that (as explained below) English law now narrowly views *Rylands* as a particular species of nuisance.

4. The rule in *Rylands* has been the topic of considerable academic attention. See for example Fridman, "The Rise and Fall of *Rylands v. Fletcher*" (1956) 34 Can. Bar Rev. 810; Fleming, "Comment: The Fall of a Crippled Giant" (1995) 3 Tort L. Rev. 56; Husak, "Varieties of Strict Liability" (1995) 8 C.J.L.J. 189; Pardy, "Fault and Cause:

Rethinking the Role of Negligent Conduct" (1995) 3 Tort L. Rev. 143; Stanton, "The Legacy of *Rylands v. Fletcher*" in Mullany & Linden, eds., *Torts Tomorrow: A Tribute to John Fleming* (1998) at 84-101; Shugerman, "The Floodgates of Strict Liability: Bursting Reservoirs and the Adoption of *Fletcher v.Rylands* in the Guilded Age" (2000) 110 Yale L.J. 333; and Abraham, "*Rylands v. Fletcher*: Tort Law's Conscience" in Rabin & Sugarman, eds., *Torts Stories* (2003) at 207.

5. The rule in *Rylands* is popular among proponents of enterprise liability. Although enterprise liability can be supported on loss distribution principles, it is most closely associated with market deterrence. The essential feature of enterprise liability was summarized in Lang, "The Activity-Risk Theory of Tort: Risk, Insurance and Insolvency" (1961) 39 Can. Bar Rev. 530 at 530: "The basic proposition and starting point is that activity should bear the risks of harm that it produces. Unless the act is sufficiently worthwhile to pay for the increase in risks that accompany it, the act should not be done at all." See generally Calabresi, *The Cost of Accidents* (1970); and Cane, *Atiyah's Accidents, Compensation and the Law*, 6th ed. (2006).

6. One of the most interesting criticisms of enterprise liability is found in Coase, "The Problem of Social Cost" (1960) 3 J.L. & Econ. 1. He suggests that it is difficult to determine which party should be assigned the cost of a particular activity. For example in *Rylands*, is the damage a cost which ought to be attributed to constructing the reservoir or to maintaining the mine? Presumably, the defendant's conduct would have been harmless if the plaintiffs had not been engaged in an equally "non-natural" use of their land. Since no trespass was committed, should it matter that the water escaped from the defendant's land to the plaintiffs'? Why should the plaintiffs' interest be preferred to that of the defendant, particularly when both are commercial enterprises? See also Morris, "Hazardous Enterprises and Risk-Bearing Capacity" (1951) 61 Yale L.J. 1172; Calabresi, *supra*; Fletcher, "Fairness and Utility in Tort Theory" (1972) 85 Harv. L. Rev. 537; Coleman, "The Morality of Strict Tort Liability" (1976) 18 William & Mary L. Rev. 259; and Schwartz, "The Vitality of Negligence and the Ethics of Strict Liability" (1981) 15 Georgia L. Rev. 963.

(b) ESCAPE

READ v. J. LYONS & CO.

[1947] A.C. 156 (H.L.)

VISCOUNT SIMON L.C.: My Lords, in fulfilment of an agreement dated Jan. 26, 1942, and made between the Ministry of Supply and the respondents, the latter undertook the operation, management and control of the Elstow Ordnance Factory as agents for the Ministry. The respondents carried on in the factory the business of filling shell cases with high explosives. The appellant was an employee of the Ministry, with the duty of inspecting this filling of shell cases, and her work required her (although she would have preferred and had applied for other employment) to be present in the shell filling shop. On Aug. 31, 1942, while the appellant was lawfully in the shell filling shop in discharge of her duty, an explosion occurred which killed a man and injured the appellant and others. No negligence was averred or proved against the respondents. The plea of *volenti non fit injuria*, for whatever it might be worth, has been expressly withdrawn before this

House by the Attorney-General on behalf of the respondents, and thus the simple question for decision is whether in these circumstances the respondents are liable, without any proof or inference that they were negligent, to the appellant in damages, which have been assessed at £575 2*s*. 8*d*, for her injuries.

. . .

Now, the strict liability recognized by this House to exist in *Rylands v. Fletcher* is conditioned by two elements which I may call the condition of "escape" from the land of something likely to do mischief if it escapes, and the condition of "non-natural use" of the land. This second condition has in some later cases, which did not reach this House, been otherwise expressed, *e.g.*, as "exceptional" user, when such user is not regarded as "natural" and at the same time is likely to produce mischief if there is an "escape". . . . The American Restatement of the Law of Torts, III, s. 519, speaks of "ultra-hazardous activity," but attaches qualifications which would appear in the present instance to exonerate the respondents. It is not necessary to analyse the second condition on the present occasion, for in the case now before us the first essential condition of "escape" does not seem to me to be present at all. "Escape," for the purpose of applying the proposition in *Rylands v. Fletcher* means escape from a place which the defendant has occupation of, or control over to a place which is outside his occupation or control. Blackburn J., several times refers to the defendant's duty as being the duty of "keeping a thing in" at the defendant's peril and by "keeping in" he means, not preventing an explosive substance from exploding, but preventing a thing which may inflict mischief from escaping from the area which the defendant occupies or controls. In two well-known cases the same principle of strict liability for escape was applied to defendants who held a franchise to lay pipes under a highway and to conduct water (or gas) under pressure through them: *Charing Cross Electric Co. v. Hydraulic Power Co.* [[1914] 3 K.B. 772]; *Northwestern Utilities, Ltd. v. London Guarantee, etc., Co.* [[1936] A.C. 108].

In *Howard v. Furness Houlder Argentine Lines, Ltd.* [[1936] 2 All E.R. 781] Lewis, J., had before him a case of injury caused by an escape of steam on board a ship where the plaintiff was working. The judge was, I think, right in refusing to apply the doctrine of *Rylands v. Fletcher* on the ground that the injuries were caused on the premises of the defendants. Apart altogether from the judge's doubt (which I share) whether the owners of the steamship by generating steam therein are making a non-natural use of their steamship, the other condition on which the proposition in *Rylands v. Fletcher* depends was not present, any more than it is in the case with which we have now to deal. Here there is no escape of the relevant kind at all and the appellant's action fails on that ground.

In these circumstances it becomes unnecessary to consider other objections that have been raised, such as the question of whether the doctrine of *Rylands v. Fletcher* applies where the claim is for damages for personal injury as distinguished from damages to property. It may be noted, in passing, that Blackburn, J., himself when referring to the doctrine of *Rylands v. Fletcher* in the later case of *Castle v. Stockton Waterworks* [(1875), L.R. 10 Q.B. 453] leaves this undealt with. He treats damages under the *Rylands v. Fletcher* principle as covering damages to property, such as workmen's clothes or tools, but says nothing about liability for personal injuries.

. . .

LORD MACMILLAN: . . . The doctrine of *Rylands v. Fletcher*, as I understand it, derives from a conception of the mutual duties of adjoining or neighbouring landowners and its congeners are trespass and nuisance. If its foundation is to be found in the injunction *sic utere tuo ut alienum non laedas*, then it is manifest that it has nothing to do with personal injuries. The duty is to refrain from injuring not *alium* but *alienum*. The two prerequisites of the doctrine are that there must be the escape of something from one man's close to another man's close and that that which escapes must have been brought on the land from which it escapes in consequence of some non-natural use of that land whatever precisely that may mean. Neither of these features exists in the present case. I have already pointed out that nothing escaped from the defendants' premises, and, were it necessary to decide the point, I should hesitate to hold that in these days and in an industrial community it was a non-natural use of land to build a factory on it and conduct there the manufacture of explosives. I could conceive it being said that to carry on the manufacture of explosives in a crowded urban area was evidence of negligence, but there is no such case here and I offer no opinion on the point.

It is noteworthy in *Rylands v. Fletcher* that all the counts in the declaration alleged negligence and that on the same page of the report on which his famous *dictum* is recorded (L.R. 1 Exch. 265, at p. 279), Blackburn J., states that:

> the plaintiff . . . must bear the loss, unless he can establish that it was the consequence of some default for which the defendants are responsible.

His decision for the plaintiff would thus logically seem to imply that he found some default on the part of the defendants in bringing on their land and failing to confine there an exceptional quantity of water. Notwithstanding the width of some of the pronouncements, particularly on the part of Lord Cranworth, I think that the doctrine of *Rylands v. Fletcher*, when studied in its setting, is truly a case on the mutual obligations of the owners or occupiers of neighbouring closes and is entirely inapplicable to the present case, which is quite outside its ambit.

. . .

LORD SIMONDS: . . . My Lords, in this branch of the law it is inevitable that reference should be made to what Blackburn, J., said in *Fletcher v. Rylands* and what Lord Cairns said in *Rylands v. Fletcher*. In doing so I think it is of great importance to remember that the subject-matter of that action was the rights of adjoining landowners and, though the doctrine of strict liability there enforced was illustrated by reference to the responsibility of the man who keeps beasts, yet the defendant was held liable only because he allowed, or did not prevent, the escape from his land onto the land of the plaintiff of something which he had brought onto his own land and which he knew or should have known was liable to do mischief if it escaped from it. I agree with the late Mackinnon, L.J., that this and nothing else is the basis of the celebrated judgment of Blackburn J., and I think it no less the basis of Lord Cairns' opinion. For it is significant that he emphasises that, if the accumulation of water (the very thing which by its escape in that case caused the actionable damage) had arisen by the natural user of the defendant's land, the adjoining owner could not have complained. The decision itself does not justify the broad proposition which the appellant seeks to establish, and I would venture to say that the word "escape" which is used so often in the judgment of Blackburn, J., meant to him escape from the defendant's premises and nothing else. It has been urged that escape means escape from control and that it is irrelevant where damage takes place if there has been such an escape, but, though it is arguable that that ought to be the law, I see no logical necessity for it and much less any judicial authority. For as I have said, somewhere the line must be drawn unless full rein be given to the doctrine that a man acts always at his peril, that "coarse and impolitic idea" as O.W. Holmes somewhere calls it. I speak with all deference of modern American text books and judicial decisions, but I think little guidance can be obtained from the way in which this part of the common law has developed on the other side of the ocean, and I would reject the idea that, if a man carries on a so-called ultra-hazardous activity on his premises, the line must be drawn so as to bring him within the limit of strict liability for its consequences to all men everywhere. On the contrary, I would say that his obligation to those lawfully on his premises is to be ultra-cautious in carrying on his ultra-hazardous activity, but that it will still be the task of the injured person to show that the defendant owed to him a duty of care and did not fulfil it. It may well be that in the discharge of that task he will sometimes be able to call in aid the maxim *res ipsa loquitur*.

My Lords, I have stated a general proposition and indicated that there are exceptions to it. It is clear, for instance, that, if a man brings and keeps a wild beast on his land or a beast known to him to be ferocious of a species generally *mansuetae naturae*, he may be liable for any damage occurring within or without his premises without proof of negligence. Such an exception will serve to illustrate the proposition that the law of torts has grown up historically in separate compartments, and that beasts have travelled in a compartment of their own. So, also, it may be that in regard to certain chattels a similar liability may arise though I accept and would quote with respect to what Lord Macmillan said in *Donoghue v. Stevenson* [[1932] A.C. 562 at 611]:

> I rather regard this type of case as a special instance of negligence where the law exacts a degree of diligence so stringent as to amount practically to a guarantee of safety.

There may be other exceptions. Professor Winfield, to whose "Textbook of the Law of Tort," 3rd edn., 1946, I would acknowledge my indebtedness, is inclined to include certain "dangerous structures" within the rule of strict liability. This may be so. It is sufficient for my purpose to say that, unless a plaintiff can point to a specific rule of law in relation to a specific subject-matter he cannot, in my opinion, bring himself within the exceptions to the general rule that I have stated. I have already expressed my view that there is no rule which imposes on him who carries on the business of making explosives, though the activity may be "ultra-hazardous" and an explosive "a dangerous thing," a strict liability to those who are lawfully on his premises.

. . .

[Lords Porter and Uthwatt delivered separate concurring speeches.]

NOTES AND QUESTIONS

1. What must the plaintiff establish to meet the "escape requirement" that was articulated in *Read*? What are the rationale and purpose for this requirement? Are losses inherently worse if they are suffered off the defendant's land? Are other torts available with respect to losses that occur on the defendant's land?

2. In *Deyo v. Kingston Speedway Ltd.*, [1954] 2 D.L.R. 419 (Ont. C.A.), aff'd [1955] 1 D.L.R. 718 (S.C.C.), two spectators at a stock car race were injured by a racing car that went out of control. A claim based on *Rylands* was dismissed because there had

been no escape. In *Aldridge v. Van Patter*, [1952] 4 D.L.R. 93 (Ont. H.C.), a stock car went out of control, crashed through a fence and injured the plaintiff, who was in an adjoining park. One of the bases upon which liability was imposed was the rule in *Rylands*. Can you justify the results in these two cases?

3. Because the escape requirement may defeat otherwise meritorious claims, it occasionally is ignored or loosely interpreted. See Linden & Feldthusen, *Canadian Tort Law*, 8th ed. (2006) at 538.

4. Compare and contrast the rule in *Rylands* with the rules governing occupiers' liability discussed in Chapter 23 and private nuisance discussed in Chapter 24. What are the advantages and disadvantages of each regime? Under what circumstances will the two sets of rules reach different conclusions?

5. An easement exists when a landowner is entitled to exercise some right with respect to a neighbouring property (as when a homeowner is entitled to drive over a neighbour's land in order to reach a highway). For the purposes of *Rylands*, is there an "escape" if a dangerous thing initially located on the defendant's land causes damage to another part of the defendant's land that is subject to an easement in the plaintiff's favour? Is it sufficient that the plaintiff's property interest was damaged, even though the dangerous thing remained on land owned by the defendant? See *Transco plc v. Stockport Metropolitan Borough Council*, [2004] 2 A.C. 1 (H.L.).

6. In *Dokuchia v. Domansch*, [1945] 1 D.L.R. 757 (Ont. C.A.), the plaintiff was injured while pouring the defendant's gasoline into the defendant's truck, which was on a highway. *Rylands* was applied, notwithstanding that there was no connection with either party's land, let alone an escape. Do you agree with this application of *Rylands*? Can you justify a rule that makes the owner of dangerous substances strictly liable for any injuries they cause?

(c) NON-NATURAL USE

GERTSEN v. MUNICIPALITY OF METROPOLITAN TORONTO
(1973), 41 D.L.R. (3d) 646 (Ont. H.C.)

[Two municipalities, Toronto and York, reached an agreement whereby Toronto dumped putrescible organic waste into a landfill site in York. Methane gas seeped from the site, some of which accumulated in the plaintiff's garage and exploded when he started his car. The plaintiff sued both municipalities in nuisance, negligence, and strict liability. The following excerpt is limited to the court's discussion of strict liability.]

LERNER J.: . . . Blackburn, J., in [*Rylands v. Fletcher*], stated the rule which has been sometimes distinguished and sometimes restricted in its application:

We think that the true rule of law is, that the person who for his own purposes brings on his lands and collects and keeps there anything likely to do mischief if it escapes, must keep it in at his peril, and, if he does not do so, is prima facie answerable for all the damage which is the natural consequences of its escape.

This rule, if applicable on the facts of the case, makes liability absolute. The defendants by joint agreement brought putrescible organic matter on the lands of York as a means of disposing of same. This organic matter generated methane gas, admittedly a dangerous substance in itself. The gas escaped onto the plaintiffs' land and caused them damage. *Prima facie* the defendants should be liable without proof of negligence. . . . However, there are sometimes other considerations brought to bear which, if applicable, somewhat restrict the rule.

York argued that the work was under the control of Metro which would relieve it from liability. It has, however, been held that a defendant (York) cannot avail itself of the absence of negligence on its part and even of those over whom it has control. The owner (York) is charged with keeping a dangerous substance at its peril. . . .

Another submission of York is that waste disposal was a natural user of these lands. If the owner uses his land in the exercise of his ordinary rights, he incurs no liability under the rule if he injures his neighbour. . . .

In *Rickards v. Lothian*, [1913] A.C. 263, the Privy Council withdrew a wide range of activities from the ambit of strict liability under this rule on the basis that it applied only to damage due to non-natural use of land. As an incident thereof, since the non-natural user thereof is an essential element of liability, the burden of proving it rests on the plaintiff. . . .

When the use of the element or thing which the law regards as the potential source of mischief is an accepted incident of some ordinary purpose to which land is reasonably applied by the occupier, the *prima facie* rule of absolute responsibility for the consequences of its escape must give way. In applying this qualification, the Courts have looked not only to the thing or activity in isolation, but also to the place and manner in which it is maintained and its relation to its surroundings. Time, place and circumstance, not excluding purpose, are most material. The distinction between natural and non-natural user is both relative and capable of adjustment to the changing patterns of social existence: Fleming, *Law of Torts*, 4th ed. (1971), p. 283.

> The distinction between natural and non-natural user has served the function principally of lending the rule in *Rylands v. Fletcher* a desirable degree of flexibility by enabling the courts to infuse notions of social and economic needs prevailing at a given time and place . . . Yet caution should be observed lest the qualification be pushed too far. There is no merit, for example, in occasional suggestions to exempt all activities redounding to the "general benefit of the community", such as nationalized industries or even the manufacture of munitions in time of war. Not only is there no warrant in principle for prejudicing private rights by the facile pleas of overriding public welfare, at least in the absence of statutory authorization, but many are the decisions which have attached strict liability to enterprises engaged in community services such as public utilities and the like.

I must now decide whether this garbage-fill project was natural or non-natural user of the land. I am emboldened by the statement of Lord Porter in *Read v. J. Lyons & Co., Ltd.*, [[1947] A.C. 156 (H.L.)] at p. 176, where he states:

> Possibly a further requisite is that to bring the thing to the position in which it is found is to make a non-natural use of that place . . . Manifestly these requirements must give rise to difficulty in applying the rule in individual cases and necessitate at least a decision as to what can be dangerous and what is a non-natural use . . . For the present I need only say that each seems to be a question of fact subject to a ruling of the judge as to whether the particular object can be dangerous or the particular use can be non-natural, and in deciding this question I think that all the circumstances of the time and place and

> practice of mankind must be taken into consideration so that what might be regarded as dangerous or non-natural may vary according to those circumstances.

In the same case Viscount Simon stated at pp. 169-70:

> I think it not improper to put on record, with all due regard to the admission and dicta in that case, that if the question had hereafter to be decided whether the making of munitions in a factory at the Government's request in time of war for the purpose of helping to defeat the enemy is a "non-natural" use of land, adopted by the occupier "for his own purposes", it would *not seem to me* that the House would be bound by this authority to say that it was.

(The italics are mine.) That statement seems to have been provoked by the opinion of Lord Buckmaster in *Rainham Chemical Works, Ltd. (in Liquidation) et al. v. Belvedere Fish Guano Co., Ltd.*, [1921] 2 A.C. 465 at p. 471. Injuries had been sustained by the inspector in the factory of the defendants who were making munitions when an explosion occurred. Lord Buckmaster stated that the making of munitions was certainly not "the common and ordinary use of the land."

I take judicial notice, supported by the exhibits and all testimony, that this was a relatively small ravine surrounded by heavily populated urban areas. It was originally subdivided apparently for occupation by the citizenry but because of its difficult contours and a stream in the lower areas, it appears to me that it was not practicable for such use. This does not, however, in my view, alter the case and the fact that Metro was seeking garbage and waste disposal areas does not change the situation either. I find that the primary purpose for filling this ravine in this manner was a selfish and self-serving opportunity for Metro who held out a "carrot" to York that if this were permitted York would end up with a level area instead of an "eyesore" and also gain attractive facilities, at no expense. This, in my view, having regard to its location together with the known temporary and permanent problems caused by such a garbage-fill project, cannot be said to be supported by the "overriding public welfare" theory. The initial benefits were to Metro which was responsible for disposing of garbage, etc. and not to the general benefit of the community directly affected by this use, *i.e.*, the owners and occupiers of the surrounding land. They were the community that I must consider. Applying the propositions of time, place and circumstances and not excluding purpose, I find that this was a non-natural user of the land and, therefore, that exception to the rule of strict liability also fails.

. . .

[Both defendants were held liable under the rule in *Rylands*, as well as in nuisance and negligence.]

NOTES AND QUESTIONS

1. In *Rylands*, Lord Cairns suggested that non-natural land use involved the introduction of "that which in its natural condition was not in or upon it." Why was mining considered any less natural a use than milling? In *Rickards v. Lothian*, [1913] A.C. 263 at 280 (P.C.), the court said: "There must be some special use bringing with it increased danger to others . . . not merely the ordinary use of the land or such a use as is proper for the general benefit of the community." This latter interpretation of non-natural use was

adopted in both *Read* and *Gertsen*. How has the definition of non-natural use changed, and what is the significance of this change? Which interpretation is preferable?

2. For a criticism of the restrictive definition of non-natural use see Linden & Feldthusen, *Canadian Tort Law*, 8th ed. (2006) at 532. See also Newark, "Non-Natural User and *Rylands v. Fletcher*" (1961) 24 Mod. L. Rev. 557; and Williams, "Non-Natural Use of Land" [1973] C.L.J. 310.

3. The escaping object or substance must be likely to cause harm: it must be a "dangerous thing." This may include both (a) objects that are dangerous in themselves and (b) objects that are likely to escape and thereby pose risks to others. It is difficult to determine which objects and substances would be considered "dangerous things" without resort to the case law. The answer sometimes is surprising. *Rylands* has been applied to water, gas, electricity, sparks from a steam locomotive, strips of metal foil, caravan dwellers, and a car with a full gas tank in a garage.

4. For Canadian cases interpreting the related concepts of non-natural use and dangerous things see *Heintzman & Co. v. Hashman Const. Ltd.* (1973), 32 D.L.R. (3d) 622 (Alta. S.C.); *Schenck v. R.*; *Rokeby v. R.* (1981), 34 O.R. (2d) 595 (H.C.); *Quondam v. Francis Belliveau Excavations Ltd.* (1983), 46 N.B.R. (2d) 352 (C.A.); *Palma v. Stora Kopparbergs Berslags Aktiebolag* (1983), 26 C.C.L.T. 22 (N.S.T.D.); *Beaudry v. Tollman*, [1983] 6 W.W.R. 660 (Alta. Q.B.); *Chu v. Dawson* (1984), 31 C.C.L.T. 146 (B.C.C.A.); *John Campbell Law Corp. v. Strata Plan 1350* (2001), 8 C.C.L.T. (3d) 226 (B.C.S.C.); and *Tock v. St. John's Metropolitan Area Board* (1989), 64 D.L.R. (4th) 620 (S.C.C.).

5. The early common law held an occupier strictly liable if a fire in his or her control escaped and caused damage to another's property. This common law rule has been supplanted by legislation in all the Canadian provinces that eliminates strict liability for accidental fires. However, it has been held that these statutes do not affect the rule in *Rylands*. Therefore, the escape of a "non-natural fire," such as that used in an industrial setting, may give rise to strict liability. For examples of fires that constitute a non-natural use see *A.G. Can. v. Diamond Waterproofing Ltd; Pillar Const. v. Defence Const. (1951) Ltd.* (1974), 48 D.L.R. (3d) 353 (Ont. C.A.) (storing highly flammable material near a heater); and *Hudson v. Riverdale Colony of Hutterian Brethren* (1980), 114 D.L.R. (3d) 352 (Man. C.A.) (grass fire started to contain larger fire). For examples of fires that constitute a natural use see *O'Neill v. Esquire Hotels Ltd.* (1972), 30 D.L.R. (3d) 589 (N.B.C.A.) (propane gas used for cooking); *Lickoch v. Madu* (1973), 34 D.L.R. (3d) 569 (Alta. C.A.) (farmer burning trash); *Dudeck v. Brown* (1980), 33 O.R. (2d) 460 (H.C.) (homeowner using wood-burning stove); and *Dahler v. Bruvold*, [1981] 5 W.W.R. 706 (B.C.S.C.) (logger starting fire to clear land pursuant to a provincial permit). But see *Smith v. Widdicombe* (1987), 39 C.C.L.T. 98 (Man. Q.B.), where the court held that a fire used to burn stubble prior to cultivation was a natural use. See also Ogus, "Vagaries in Liability for the Escape of Fire" [1969] C.L.J. 104

(d) DEFENCES TO THE RULE IN *RYLANDS v. FLETCHER*

As we have seen, the courts have narrowly interpreted and applied *Rylands*. They have further limited its impact by recognizing six defences: consent, common benefit, default of the plaintiff, act of God, act of a stranger, and statutory authority. This situation led J. Fleming to state that "[t]he aggregate effect of these exceptions makes it doubtful whether there is much left of the rationale of strict liability as originally contemplated in 1866": *The Law of Torts*, 9th ed. (1998) at 385.

(i) *Consent*

The defendant who establishes that the plaintiff implicitly or explicitly consented to the presence of the danger enjoys a complete defence to a claim under *Rylands*. The courts may imply consent from the nature of the legal relationship between the parties or from the physical circumstances. For example, a tenant in a lower floor is taken to implicitly consent to the presence of water pipes in the upper floors and cannot invoke *Rylands* if water seeps into his premises causing damage. The tenant's remedy, if any, would lie in negligence. See generally *Peters v. Prince of Wales Theatre (Birmingham) Ltd.*, [1943] 1 K.B. (C.A.); *Holinaty v. Hawkins* (1965), 52 D.L.R. (2d) 289 (Ont. C.A.); *Federic v. Perpetual Investments Ltd.* (1968), 2 D.L.R. (3d) 50 (Ont. H.C.); *Elfassy v. Sylben Invts. Ltd.* (1978), 21 O.R. (2d) 609 (H.C.); and *Pattison v. Prince Edward Region Conservation Authority* (1984), 30 C.C.L.T. 305 (Ont. H.C.).

(ii) *Common Benefit*

If the source of the danger is maintained for the common benefit of both the plaintiff and the defendant, liability will not be imposed under *Rylands*. In the classic case of *Carstairs v. Taylor* (1871), L.R. 6 Exch. 217, rain water was collected in a special box on the roof and flowed through the drains. When a rat made a hole in the box, water flowed into the plaintiff's ground floor premises, damaging his property. The plaintiff's action under *Rylands* was dismissed because the water was collected for the mutual benefit of both the defendant and the plaintiff. Since the defendant had not been careless, the plaintiff's claim also failed in negligence. The common benefit defence sometimes is treated as a form of implied consent. See generally *Danku v. Town of Fort Frances* (1976), 73 D.L.R. (3d) 377 (Ont. Dist. Ct.); and *Gilson v. Kerrier District Council*, [1976] 3 All E.R. 343 (C.A.).

(iii) *Default of the Plaintiff*

A person who voluntarily and unreasonably encounters a known danger cannot recover under *Rylands*. Recovery also will be denied if the plaintiff's wanton, wilful, or reckless misconduct materially increased the probability of injury. Nor will the defendant be held liable for damages which are caused by the abnormal sensitivity of the plaintiff's property. See *Dunn v. Birmingham Canal Co.* (1872), L.R. 8 Q.B. 42 (Ex. Ch.); *Ponting v. Noakes*, [1894] 2 Q.B. 281; and *Hoare v. McAlpine*, [1923] 1 Ch. 167.

(iv) *Act of God*

An act of God is a force of nature that arises without human intervention. To provide a defence, the natural force must be so unexpected that it could not have been reasonably foreseen, and thus its effects could not have been prevented. See *Nichols v. Marsland* (1875), L.R. 10 Exch. 255, aff'd (1876), 2 Ex. D. 1 (C.A.); *Greenock Corp. v. Caledonian*

Railway Co., [1917] A.C. 556 (H.L.); *Smith v. Ont. & Minnesota Power Co.* (1918), 45 D.L.R. 266 (Ont. C.A.); and *Goldman v. Hargrave*, [1967] 1 A.C. 645 (P.C.).

(v) *Act of a Stranger*

The owner of a dangerous thing generally is strictly liable for foreseeable harm caused by third parties. However, liability will not be imposed under *Rylands* if the defendant proves that the escape of the dangerous thing was caused by a stranger's deliberate and unforeseeable act. The onus is on the defendant to show that the escape could not have been prevented through reasonable care. Unfortunately, it is not always clear whether an intermeddler will be considered a stranger (whose deliberate actions may exempt the defendant from responsibility) or someone for whom the defendant may be accountable. That latter category includes the defendant's servants, independent contractors, invitees, licensees, and possibly even family members acting under the defendant's control. Notice that the defence of an act of a stranger introduces into this area concepts commonly associated with negligence. See *Rickards v. Lothian*, [1913] A.C. 263 (P.C.); *Northwestern Utilities Ltd. v. London Guarantee & Accident Co.*, [1936] A.C. 108 (P.C.); and *Hale v. Jennings Brothers*, [1938] 1 All E.R. 579 (C.A.). For a discussion of people who are considered to be strangers see *Schubert v. Sterling Trusts Corp.*, [1943] 4 D.L.R. 584 (Ont. H.C.); *Holinaty v. Hawkins* (1965), 52 D.L.R. (2d) 289 (Ont. C.A.); *Saccardo v. Hamilton* (1970), 18 D.L.R. (3d) 271 (Ont. H.C.); *Smith v. Scott*, [1973] Ch. 314; and *Holderness v. Goslin*, [1975] 2 N.Z.L.R. 46 (S.C.).

(vi) *Statutory Authority*

Many of the activities that potentially involve the escape of dangerous substances (such as water, electricity, and sewage) are now managed by public utilities operating under statutory authority. Liability under *Rylands* may be denied if the defendant acted pursuant to statutory authority.

Legislation seldom expressly addresses the issue of tort liability, and the scope of this defence often is a matter of statutory interpretation. If the statutory language is *mandatory* (*i.e.* it imposes an obligation on the defendant to supply the service), then, in the absence of negligence, the defendant will not be held liable for acts done pursuant to that duty. However, if the statutory language is *permissive*, the courts generally will not interpret it as authorizing the defendant to violate the rule in *Rylands*. See *Benning v. Wong* (1969), 43 A.L.J.R. 467 (H.C.A.); *Himmelman v. Nova Const. Co.* (1969), 5 D.L.R. (3d) 56 (N.S.S.C.); *Gertsen v. Municipality of Metropolitan Toronto* (1973), 41 D.L.R. (3d) 646 (Ont. H.C.); *Schenck v. R.*; *Rokeby v. R.* (1981), 34 O.R. (2d) 595 (H.C.); and *Lyon v. Village of Shelburne* (1981), 130 D.L.R. (3d) 307 (Ont. Co. Ct.).

(e) A COMMENT ON *RYLANDS v. FLETCHER*

Like all other common law cases, the decision in *Rylands v. Fletcher* was the product of particular legal and historical circumstances. Three factors appear to have been especially important to the outcome. First, as an English landowner who innocently had suffered serious property damage, Rylands was an ideal plaintiff in the Victorian era. Second, Rylands was a deserving plaintiff with no obvious legal remedy. When it became clear that Rylands could not establish a case in negligence, sympathetic Law Lords felt compelled to identify some alternative theory of liability. Third, historical research reveals that the *Rylands* case had been preceded by a number of notorious burst-reservoir disasters. The judges who formulated the strict liability rule appear to have been motivated, in part, by the desire to deter future calamities of this kind. See Simpson, "Bursting Reservoirs and Victorian Tort Law" in *Leading Cases in the Common Law* (1995) at 194.

Elsewhere in the Commonwealth, however, judges have grown uncomfortable with the doctrine of strict liability underlying *Rylands v. Fletcher*. At least two aspects of that doctrine are problematic. The first is the imprecision of the action's constituent elements. Phrases such as "dangerous substance" and "non-natural use" resist consistent interpretation and application. Second, many judges question the fairness of strict liability and note the anomaly of allowing *Rylands* to operate within a tort regime that generally is premised upon negligent and intentional fault. In recent years, several leading Commonwealth jurists have concluded that *Rylands* is a doctrinal anachronism, a legal principle that has outlived whatever rationale or usefulness that might once have justified its existence. In the 1990s this view hardened and affected the appellate judges of England and Australia.

Recent developments in England begin with *Cambridge Water Co. v. Eastern Counties Leather plc*, [1994] 2 A.C. 264 (H.L.). The defendant was a leather manufacturer and the plaintiff was its distant neighbour. Over a 20-year period, 1,000 gallons of chemical solvent seeped from the defendant's property and into the plaintiff's well. When the contamination was discovered and traced, the plaintiff sued in negligence, nuisance, and on the principles established in *Rylands v. Fletcher*. The first two claims failed for lack of reasonable foreseeability. With regard to strict liability, the Law Lords unanimously decided that "knowledge, or at least foreseeability of the risk" is a requirement for even so-called "strict" liability. Since the plaintiff could not prove that the seepage of solvents into his distant well had been foreseeable, the defendant was not liable under the rule in *Rylands v. Fletcher*.

Some commentators interpreted the House of Lords' focus on reasonable foreseeability as proof that *Rylands* had been subsumed within the law of negligence. See Fleming, "The Fall of a Crippled Giant" (1995) 3 Tort L. Rev. 56. Significantly, however, both the English Court of Appeal and House of Lords in *Cambridge Water* deliberately refrained from overruling *Rylands*.

In *Transco plc v. Stockport Metropolitan Borough Council*, [2004] 2 A.C. 1 (H.L.), the House of Lords once again was invited to abolish the independent doctrine of *Rylands v. Fletcher*. And the court once again declined. Aside from the fact that substantial developments are best left to Parliament, a principle of strict liability was thought to remain important, albeit in relatively few cases. However, the House of Lords did take the opportunity to restate the doctrine. In England, *Rylands* now exists as a species of the tort of private nuisance. As a result, strict liability no longer is available with respect to personal injuries, as opposed to property damage. The court also attempted to refine *Rylands* by restating the conditions of liability. The traditionally troublesome requirements of dangerousness and non-natural use of land now are combined into a single concept that is governed by "ordinary contemporary standards." Unfortunately, the various judges each expressed that focus in different terms: "extraordinary and unusual" (Lord Bingham), "special" (Lord Walker), "non-natural user" (Lord Hoffmann), and "natural" and "ordinary" (Lord Scott). Other aspects of *Transco* were mentioned in earlier notes in this section. For discussion of recent developments in English law, see Nolan, "The Distinctiveness of *Rylands v. Fletcher*" (2005) 121 L.Q.R. 421; Bagshaw, "*Rylands* Confined" (2004) 120 L.Q.R. 388; and Amirthalingam, "*Rylands* Lives" [2004] C.L.J. 273. See also *Hamilton v. Papakura District Council*, [2000] 1 N.Z.L.R. 265 (C.A.).

In *Burnie Port Authority v. General Jones Pty. Ltd.* (1994), 179 C.L.R. 520 (H.C.A.), the High Court of Australia was bolder. The case involved a fire that had spread from part of a building owned by the defendant to part of the same building that the plaintiff rented for cold storage. Prior to the fire, the defendant had brought a large quantity of a highly flammable substance onto its property. The defendant did this with the knowledge that welding would take place in close proximity. After the ensuing fire, the plaintiff sued in both strict liability and negligence.

Writing for five of seven judges, Mason C.J. criticized the notorious "obscurity" and "quite unacceptable uncertainty" of strict liability principles. The Chief Justice further noted that in the hundred years since *Rylands*, tort law had experienced a crucial development: the "emergence of a coherent law of negligence to dominate the territory of tortious liability for unintentional injury." Mason C.J. therefore concluded that the rule in *Rylands* had been "absorbed by the principles of ordinary negligence." The defendant in *Burnie Port Authority* was found liable in negligence for failing to take reasonable care in storing a highly flammable substance, but it was not held strictly liable. In short, *Burnie Port Authority* appears to have expunged strict liability from the common law of Australia.

Canada's highest appellate court has not similarly reviewed the rule in *Rylands v. Fletcher*. For this reason, the myriad of cases on "dangerous substances" and "natural use," as well as the common law defences to allegations of strict liability, remain relevant to Canadian lawyers.

NOTES AND QUESTIONS

1. In *Transco*, the House of Lords characterized *Rylands* as a species of nuisance. Do both torts truly operate on the basis of the same rationale? What is the purpose of each tort? Must either or both parties occupy land for the purposes of nuisance? Has the same answer traditionally been given with respect to *Rylands*?

2. In *Transco*, the House of Lords held that since *Rylands* is a species of private nuisance, it cannot redress personal injury. Is the tort of private nuisance confined to property damage in Canadian law?

3. Many of the traditional difficulties associated with *Rylands* stem from the requirements of unusual danger and non-natural use of land. Has the House of Lords overcome those difficulties in *Transco*?

4. Given the developments elsewhere in the Commonwealth, how should Canadian law treat *Rylands*? Should the doctrine be abolished? Subsumed within the tort of private nuisance? Subsumed within negligence? Does *Rylands* serve any useful purpose that cannot better be served by other means?

3. Strict Liability for Animals

In formulating the rule in *Rylands v. Fletcher*, several members of the House of Lords referred to cases of strict liability involving damage caused by animals. For the purposes of discussion, it is best to subdivide this topic according to whether the instrument of harm was a dangerous animal or "cattle."

(a) DANGEROUS ANIMALS

COWLES v. BALAC
(2005), 29 C.C.L.T. (3d) 284 (Ont. S.C.J.)

[David Balac and Jennifer Cowles were dating in 1996. He worked as an accordion player and studied at Sheridan college; she worked as an exotic dancer. On a warm spring day, they visited African Lion Safari (ALS). ALS offers a unique wildlife experience. In a typical zoo, the animals are enclosed and the customers roam freely from one exhibit to the next. At ALS, the roles are reversed. The animals roam freely within their reserves and it is the customers who are enclosed (in their own vehicles) as they drive through the park.

Tragically, while the attraction of ALS is close contact with wild animals, the couple's encounter was *too* close. Shortly after they had entered the tiger reserve, their car was attacked by the tigers. Although the facts were disputed and unclear, the judge found that the initial attack startled Balac, who accidentally hit a button that rolled down Cowles' window. A Siberian tiger named Paca then lunged through the window and mauled the couple. The injuries were severe. Because of permanent scarring to her scalp and hip, Cowles was unable to continue work as a "featured dancer." David suffered physical injuries that prevented him from playing the accordion and psychological injuries that further limited his employment prospects.]

MACFARLAND J.: . . .

Liability . . .

This case raises the question whether the keeper of a wild vicious animal will be strictly liable for damage caused by that animal regardless of fault and in effect whether the law of strict liability in such circumstances remains a part of law of Ontario today. For the reasons that follow I have concluded that it does.

The learned authors of the tort texts distinguish between the two classes of dangerous animals. The first category is of animals *ferae naturae* such as bears and lions – and quite obviously tigers would be included in this first category and the second category is of animals *mansuetae naturae* like cows, dogs and horses. . . .

In his text, Fridman, G.H.L. *The Law of Torts in Canada* 2nd edition Carswell), Fridman notes at page 250-1:

> Under the *scienter* doctrine it is very relevant that harm has resulted from the keeping of an animal. The common law developed special rules to deal with the situation where damage was caused by animals, even before the emergence of the modern law of negligence, and quite distinct from the action for cattle-trespass, or under the much later doctrine of *Rylands v. Fletcher*. The *scienter* doctrine was, and remains a form of strict

liability, that is to say, liability without proof of negligence. In this respect it is akin to both cattle-trespass and the *Rylands v. Fletcher* doctrine. . . .

and at page 254-255:

The Scienter Doctrine

. . . Where harm is caused by the behaviour of an animal, whether on the property of the defendant or elsewhere, this kind of liability depends upon the type of animal concerned. The law distinguishes between the wild animals, i.e., animals *ferae naturae*, and tame or domestic animals, i.e., animals *mansuetae naturae* or *domitae naturae*. For damage resulting from the act of a wild animal, the defendant is strictly liable, without proof of negligence or other wrongful conduct, and without the necessity of proving that the defendant was aware of the dangerous character of the particular animal that caused the harm, or of the class of animals to which it belonged. If the animal is mansuetae naturae, that is, one which ordinarily did not cause the kind of harm that is involved, the common law requires that the particular animal concerned have the dangerous or mischievous propensity to commit the harm or damage that it inflicted, and that the defendant knew of such propensity or characteristic of the individual animal. To keep such an animal with knowledge of its potential for causing harm is not in itself negligence, or indeed wrongful in any other way (any more than to keep a wild animal is *per se* unlawful or negligent). Indeed, despite some judicial discussion that appears to introduce elements of negligence into liability for animals, at common law there is no need to prove negligence in the way in which the animal in question was controlled or kept in order to establish liability, as long as the requisite elements of dangerous propensity or character and knowledge are present. Nor will negligence in controlling the animal, so that it is able to escape from the property of the defendant and cause harm, entail liability under the *scienter* doctrine in the absence of knowledge of the dangerous propensity, or if the animal is not normally dangerous. There might be liability based on negligence if other ingredients of such liability, such as a duty of care, exist, as frequently occurs where dogs or cattle escape onto the highway, or get out of control while on the highway, with consequent damage to other road users or adjoining landowners. Such liability, if it arises, is not strict as is the situation where the *scienter* doctrine is applicable: it will depend upon the resolution of the issues of duty, remoteness and causation that are an integral part of the law of negligence.

The underlying rationale for the strict liability of the *scienter* doctrine is that anyone who maintains an animal that is known to be dangerous to humans or other animals or in any other way does so at his peril. He has created a dangerous, or potentially dangerous situation involving risk to others. In the case of the wild animals, such knowledge is irrebutably presumed by the law. Domestic animals are not normally harmful. Therefore, knowledge of the vicious nature of the particular animal must be established. In the days when pleadings in the common law courts were written in Latin, the allegation of the plaintiff was that the defendant knowingly kept (*scienter retinuit*) a dangerous animal which caused harm to the plaintiff. Hence arose the appellation of this kind of liability.

Sometimes it has been suggested that liability is absolute, where the animal is wild or a domestic animal known to be dangerous. This cannot be accurate, because it is clear that there are limits upon the liability of the defendant, for example, contributory negligence on the part of the plaintiff, voluntary assumption of risk or consent, the act of a stranger, or an act of God. Hence, liability although strict in the sense of without proof of negligence, is not absolute, which could mean that it would be imposed whatsoever the circumstances, as long as the animal caused the harm.

and p. 262:

> The question of who is the owner or keeper, or the person whose duty it is to exercise control, is a question of fact. The real test of responsibility is not ownership. There may be many circumstances under which a person who is not the owner and indeed one who has not the actual possession of the animal may be under a duty to exercise control and will be responsible if it injures somebody.
>
> What appears to be the crucial factor in liability is the issue of control. Hence, it has been suggested that liability is founded upon the failure of a defendant, who was under a duty to confine or control the offending animal, to maintain a sufficient degree of control to prevent the injury that occurred. Language of this nature carries overtones of negligence, i.e., the failure to exercise reasonable care. However, there is no doubt that, where the *scienter* doctrine applies, the duty is strict. Negligence in controlling the animal does not need to be proved. But reference to control suggests that it is escape from control that is vital to liability. Thus, if an animal is caged, chained or leashed, but nevertheless manages to inflict injury on a plaintiff, it has been held in some cases that the *scienter* doctrine is inapplicable, although some other form of action, such as negligence, might be invoked. In such instances, it is said that for *scienter* to apply, the animal must have escaped from control. In *Maynes v. Galicz*, the plaintiff, aged seven, put her fingers inside a wolf cage constructed of heavy duty two-inch square mesh. The cage was located at the defendant's zoo. The wolf grabbed the child's fingers and pulled her hand into the cage, in the course of which the hand was split. The *scienter* doctrine was held to be inapplicable because the wolf had not escaped from the cage (and the person in charge of the wolf had sufficiently restrained the animal so that injury would not ordinarily happen). A similar view was taken in *Lewis v. Oeming*. There, the tiger which caused the plaintiff's injury was properly housed in a safe enclosure and never did escape from the custody and control of the owner. Moreover, the tiger was segregated into a part of the enclosure off from the main area where the cap, which the plaintiff sought inside the tiger's cage, was lying. For these reasons, Miller J. held that the concept of strict liability, i.e. *scienter*, did not apply.

and p. 263-4:

> (vi) *Defences*
>
> (A) *Contributory negligence* If the circumstances justify such a conclusion, a court may find that the injured plaintiff has brought about his injury, in part at least, by his own neglect for his safety. Indeed, the plaintiff may be totally responsible, as in *Dowler v. Bravender*, where the owner of a horse which kicked the plaintiff did not discharge the onus of proving that he lacked knowledge of the horse's dangerous propensity, yet the defendant was not liable because the plaintiff brought the injury on herself by shouting and frightening the horse. Whether a plaintiff is guilty of contributory negligence is a question of fact. Once such conduct is established, its effect in law depends upon the application of common law or statutory principles relevant to the apportionment of liability in consequence of contributory negligence.
>
> (B) *Consent* Where the *scienter* doctrine is invoked, as in other situations, a defendant must plead that the plaintiff consented to the risk of being injured, or voluntarily assumed that risk: *volenti non fit injuria*. Whether a plaintiff has done so is a question of fact that depends on the circumstances. Such a plea was successful in *Young v. Green*, where the plaintiff, an odd-job man working with a traveling show or midway, volunteered to move a sign warning the public not to go near a lion cage. The sign was on top of the cage, from which position the plaintiff had previously retrieved it. On this occasion, while the plaintiff was trying to get hold of the sign, the lion put its paw through the

> bars and drew the plaintiff's arm into the cage, causing him injury. That plaintiff was denied an action on the ground that he was *volens*. He had consented to run the risk involved in his actions. . . .

Here the defendant ALS suggests that claims such as the one at bar should, in modern times, be resolved "within the modern and flexible parameters of negligence law". . .

The ALS is a unique game farm experience in Canada and the United States. It is the only such facility to display tigers in an open environment. Tigers roam freely and patrons to the ALS drive in their vehicles among the animals. As it was described in the evidence - the patrons are caged and the animals roam freely - in contrast to the traditional zoo situation. . . .

It remains to consider whether any defence is, on the facts of this case available to the defendant, ALS.

The defendant, ALS relies on three defences, contributory negligence, consent and/ or voluntary assumption of risk and act of stranger.

Contributory Negligence

The defence in this respect relies on the passage in Fridman referenced above at p. 255 of the text more fully discussed by the author at page 263 also set out above.

It seems to me contradictory to hold a defendant strictly liable – i.e. whether negligent or not – and then to consider a plaintiff's "contributory" negligence. If one reads Fridman carefully I don't think he is really speaking of contributory "negligence" per se. He refers to the British Columbia decision of *Dowler v. Bravender* (1968), 67 D.L.R. (2d) 734 (B.C.S.C.). In that decision the court did not find the defendant liable under the scienter doctrine because it was not persuaded that she knew her horse was vicious or mischievous "in the sense that it would kick out purposely at human beings as alleged by the plaintiffs here". He concluded that the female plaintiff had "brought the accident upon herself" by doing something that upset the horse with the result that the accident did not flow from any failure to control the animal but from a quite different cause – i.e. the actions of the plaintiff.

In any event, I have found that the injuries to and the damages suffered by both plaintiffs resulted from the unprovoked attack on their vehicle by the tiger PACA. That forceful assault on the vehicle caused Mr. Balac's body to inadvertently come into contact with the window switch resulting in the lowering of the windows on the vehicle which admitted the tiger into the vehicle. There was no conduct, in my view on the part of either David or Jennifer which would constitute contributory negligence on their part even if such defence were available. Their windows were up when they entered the Carnivore Section and were not deliberately put down for any purpose while in that Section before the attack, by either of them.

. . .

Consent/Voluntary Assumption of Risk

There is in my view on the factual findings made no basis for such a defence. Had the plaintiffs rolled their windows down or one of them, there might have been some basis for such a defence. On the facts as I have found them there is not.

It is clear on the evidence that the plaintiffs were aware that tigers are dangerous animals and it would be dangerous to put one's car window down in close proximity to a tiger. That knowledge – absent a finding that the plaintiffs put the window down – does not absolve the defendant ALS of liability. Unlike the situation in *Lewis v. Oeming*, [1983] A.J. No. 734 (Alta. Q.B.) where the plaintiff did something he had no business to do – i.e. enter the tiger's locked cage at night to retrieve his girlfriend's ball cap – these plaintiffs I have found, did nothing they had no business doing. On the contrary, they were, as I have found, merely driving through the compound, in their own vehicle with the windows up stopping occasionally to take photos – just as the owners of ALS contemplated they should do.

In *Crocker v. Sundance*, [[1988] 1 S.C.R. 1186], the Supreme Court of Canada made it clear that the volenti defence will only apply where the plaintiff assumed both the physical risk and the legal risk of his/her activity. The court stated that this defence would rarely be applicable. . . .

By analogy to this case there were but two signs – both just outside the main gate leading to the game reserves – one on each side of the road that are relevant to this argument. They read "All visitors enter the park at their own risk. No responsibility for damage to vehicle or person however caused is accepted". . . . Neither Jennifer nor David recalled seeing the signs and no one from ALS drew their attention to them.

On the brochure probably handed to them when they paid the admit fee it is stated: "All persons entering the reserves do so entirely at their own risk" and "No responsibility is accepted for damage to vehicles or trailers, their car bras, tires, lights or canvas covers, vinyl roofs or other accessories . . .". Neither read the brochure and no one from ALS pointed out the stated limitation to them. Although the employees at the booth were instructed to warn patrons of the possibility of damage to their vehicle, the only evidence on this point came from Jennifer and David who said they received no such warning. ALS called no evidence to contradict them. I accept their evidence on this point and note that employees in any event were only ever instructed to warn about damage to vehicles – nothing was said in relation to any injury to person.

There is simply no evidence – which it was the defence's burden to call – to support the argument that either David or Jennifer assumed any legal risk of their visit into the game reserves that day.

In my view the volenti defence is inapplicable. . . .

[The trial judge awarded $1,701,032 to David Balac and $813,169 to Jennifer Cowles. The Court of Appeal for Ontario upheld that decision: *Cowles v. Balac* (2006), 83 O.R. (3d) 660 (C.A.).]

NOTES AND QUESTIONS

1. As explained in *Cowles*, the common law distinguishes between animals that, by nature of their species, are ordinarily ferocious (*ferae naturae*), and animals that, as a species or by virtue of long domestication, are not usually dangerous (*mansuetae naturae*). A keeper is held strictly liable for injuries caused by *ferae naturae*, but is held strictly liable only for injuries caused by *mansuetae naturae* with *scienter*.

What is the *scienter* requirement? How does it differ from proof of negligence? Is it accurate to state that actions requiring proof of *scienter* involve strict liability?

2. English courts have held that a keeper is strictly liable for any injury caused by a *ferae naturae*, even if the injury is unrelated to the animal's ferocity. However, a keeper

is held strictly liable only for injuries attributable to the dangerous propensity of a *mansuetae naturae*. See *Behrens v. Bertram Mills Circus*, [1957] 1 All E.R. 583 (Q.B.); and *Glanville v. Sutton*, [1928] 1 K.B. 571.

3. Traditionally, a keeper was held strictly liable in these actions even if the animal was on the keeper's land and was restrained when it caused the injury. See Fleming, *The Law of Torts*, 9th ed. (1998) at 400-402; and *McNeill v. Frankenfield* (1963), 44 D.L.R. (2d) 132 (B.C.C.A.). However, as noted in *Cowles*, some courts have held that strict liability applies only if the keeper loses control or custody of the animal. See *Maynes v. Galicz*, [1976] 1 W.W.R. 557 (B.C.S.C.); *Lewis v. Oeming* (1983), 24 C.C.L.T. 81 (Alta. Q.B.); and Irvine, "Annotation" (1983), 24 C.C.L.T. 82.

4. Voluntary assumption of risk is the only generally recognized defence to actions involving dangerous animals. It is not clear whether the defendant can raise the plaintiff's contributory negligence. *Cowles* suggests not. See also *Higgins v. William Inglis & Sons Pty. Ltd.*, [1978] 1 N.S.W.L.R. 649 (C.A.). It is also doubtful whether "acts of God" or "acts of a stranger" are applicable defences. See Fleming, *The Law of Torts*, 9th ed. (1998) at 405-406. See also *McNeill v. Frankenfield, supra*; *Lewis v. Oeming, supra*; and *Witman v. Johnson* (1990), 5 C.C.L.T. (2d) 102 (Man. Q.B.).

5. A person injured by a wild animal enjoys the option of suing in both strict liability and negligence. In what circumstances would the plaintiff have a remedy in strict liability but not negligence? Are there circumstances in which the reverse is true? See *Fleming v. Atkinson*, [1959] S.C.R. 513; *Morris v. Baily* (1970), 13 D.L.R. (3d) 150 (Ont. C.A.); *Maynes v. Galicz, supra*; and *Moffett v. Downing*; *Downing v. Moffett* (1981), 16 C.C.L.T. 313 (Ont. C.A.).

6. Compensatory relief is the usual remedy. In exceptional cases, however, the plaintiff may also receive aggravated or punitive damages. See *Meloche v. Bezaire*, 2005 CarswellOnt 938 (S.C.J.) (WLeC) (confusing aggravated and punitive damages).

7. Many provinces have enacted legislation governing liability for dangerous animals. Some of the statutes simply embody the common law rules, but other legislation imposes significantly different principles. For example Ontario, Manitoba, and Newfoundland and Labrador impose liability on dog owners for the personal injuries caused by their pets without proof of *scienter*. See the *Dog Owner's Liability Act*, R.S.O. 1990, c. D.16, s. 2. While the Ontario legislation is based on strict liability, it also provides that damages shall be adjusted in proportion to the defendant's degree of fault. See *Strom (Litigation Guardian of) v. White* (1994), 21 O.R. (3d) 205 (Gen. Div.); the *Animal Husbandry Act*, R.S.M. 1987, c. A90, s. 26; and the *Dog Act*, S.N. 1990, c. D-26, s. 8. See *Whitehorse (City) v. Domingue* (1988), 3 Yukon R. 273 (Terr. Ct.)

As a result of several well-publicized incidents, Ontario amended its legislation in 2005 to introduce several new provisions affecting "pit bulls" (as defined by the statute). The new laws place severe restrictions upon the ownership and control of such animals.

8. Many actions resulting from animal attacks are brought under the common or statutory law of occupiers' liability, as discussed in Chapter 23. What are the advantages and disadvantages of this approach? See *Taller (Guardian ad litem of) v. Goldenshtein*, [1994] 3 W.W.R. 557 (B.C.C.A.). However, where loss or injury is caused by a dog

attack on the owner's property, s. 3 of the Ontario *Dog Owner's Liability Act*, *supra*, states that liability must be resolved under that statute rather than under the *Occupiers' Liability Act*, R.S.O. 1990, c. O.2.

9. Liability for animals is partially governed by statute in England. If the *Animals Act 1971* does not apply, then liability falls to the general action in negligence. If the statute does apply, then liability is strict. The statute applies to dangerous animals. Dangerous animals fall into two categories. The first category includes animals that are not commonly domesticated in the British Isles and are likely to cause severe harm. The second category includes other animals that are known to be dangerous in accordance with a three-part test.: (1) "a kind of animal, unless restrained, was likely to cause or which, if caused by the animal, was likely to be severe," (2) " the likelihood of the damage or of its being severe was due to characteristics of the animal which are not normally found in animals of the same species or are not normally so found except at particular times or in particular circumstances," and (3) "those characteristics were known to that keeper or were at any time known to a person who at that time had charge of the animal."

While that entire test is opaque, the second element is most contentious. Over the years, it generated two interpretations. The broad view applied strict liability if the relevant risk either was not normal for the species *or* was normal for the species, but only in unusual circumstances. The narrow view applied strict liability only if the relevant risk was abnormal for the species under either normal or abnormal circumstances. The essential difference between the two interpretations pertained to damage caused by animals acting normally in abnormal circumstances (*e.g.* domesticated dogs normally do not bite, but female dogs frequently snap when protecting their young).

The debate was resolved in *Mirvahedy v. Henley*, [2003] 2 A.C. 491 (H.L.). The defendant exercised reasonable control over its horses. Nevertheless, during a thunderstorm, the animals panicked, broke free from their paddock, and ran onto the road. The claimant was injured when his car collided with one of the horses. Although horses seldom panic and stampede under normal conditions, they frequently do so when spooked. The court therefore was required to select from between the broad and narrow interpretations of the statutory provision. By a three-to-two majority, it preferred the broader approach, largely on the belief that it better reflected Parliament's intention. The defendant consequently was strictly liable for the claimant's losses. For discussion, see Howarth, "The House of Lords and the Animals Act: Closing the Stable Door" [2003] C.L.J. 548; and Amirthalingam, "Animal Liability – Equine, Canine and Asinine" (2003) 119 L.Q.R. 563.

(b) CATTLE TRESPASS

ACKER v. KERR

(1973), 42 D.L.R. (3d) 514 (Ont. Co. Ct.)

THOMPSON CO. CT. J.: – This action is brought by the plaintiff as the owner of lot No. 11, Concession 4 in the Township of Proton, in the County of Grey, against the defendant as the owner of adjoining lot No. 12, Concession 4 in the said Township of Proton for damages which the plaintiff alleges were sustained by him as a result of the failure of the defendant to properly confine cattle owned by him and placed by him on his property so that such animals were permitted to stray onto the property of the defendant.

The plaintiff alleges that the straying in question took place in the years 1969, 1970 and 1971 and that as a result of the same, he sustained damages in the sum of $2,650.

Evidence was tendered by both parties which satisfies me that indeed the cattle of the defendant did get onto the property of the plaintiff during the years just mentioned doing some damage to crops of the plaintiff, the extent of which will be more fully referred to later on in my reasons for judgment.

The matter of the liability, if any, of the defendant for the damages in fact sustained by the plaintiff is rather complex and has many ramifications as will be seen.

Counsel for the plaintiff takes the position that once cattle are allowed to stray and damage is done, a trespass has been committed and the injured party is entitled to such damages as he may have sustained regardless of anything done or omitted to be done by such injured party which may have been a contributing factor to the damages so sustained. On the other hand, counsel for the defendant takes the position that the plaintiff was the author of his own misfortune as in essence he failed to keep up and repair a portion of the line fence which existed between the two farms and the cattle were thereby permitted to stray onto his property. Counsel for the plaintiff further contends that whether or not the plaintiff was obliged to maintain the fence and whether or not the fence was in a state of disrepair has nothing whatever to do with the end result and that unless the plaintiff was guilty of some positive act which enabled the defendant's cattle to get onto the plaintiff's land, he could not be held responsible either in whole or in part for the damage resulting from the cattle straying.

. . .

[The judge considered the *Line Fences Act*, R.S.O. 1970, c. 248, s. 2(1), and concluded that it imposed no affirmative duty on the plaintiff to maintain the fence.]

Counsel for the plaintiff cited innumerable authorities for the proposition that the defendant in circumstances as they exist here is liable to the plaintiff for damages for trespass.

I take it from these cases to be the law that the owner of animals *domitae naturae* is bound to keep them under control and is liable if they escape for such damage as it is ordinarily in their nature to commit. The liability is an absolute liability independent of negligence unless the escape or trespass was involuntary or caused by an Act of God or was due to the act or default of the plaintiff or of a third party for whom the defendant is not in law responsible. No case has been referred to me by counsel for the defendant which in any way detracts from this statement of the law.

[The judge then analyzed the *Pounds Act*, R.S.O. 1970, c. 353, s. 2, which, in his view, set out in statute form the requirements of the common law.]

In the cases to which I have made reference there is none which contains exactly the factual situation with which we are confronted here, but none the less I am of the opinion that the principle which I have enunciated is applicable, and on finding as I do, that the escape or trespass was not involuntary or caused by an Act of God or was due to the act or default of the plaintiff or of a third person for whom the defendant is not responsible, liability on the defendant does arise for such escape and subsequent trespass and damages.

As I have indicated, it would be almost impossible to tell just at which part of the fence in question the animals escaped but on the other hand as I have also indicated, it is not necessary for the purposes of my decision to make a finding in that regard because, in my view, it makes no difference whether it was in that portion of the fence which it might be argued was the responsibility of the plaintiff to maintain and repair or that portion of the fence which it might be argued was the responsibility of the defendant to maintain and repair or both. It was the defendant's cattle that escaped and it was the responsibility of the defendant when he put the cattle in the field to see that the fences were kept in such a state of repair as to contain the cattle within such field whether by himself seeing to the necessary work in that connection or by some agreement with the plaintiff which would exonerate the defendant from that responsibility, which agreement I find to be lacking.

NOTES AND QUESTIONS

1. Based on *Acker*, what are the principles governing cattle trespass and its defences? Why was the condition of the plaintiff's fences not considered relevant in determining if there was a defence? In *Singleton v. Williamson* (1861), 158 E.R. 533 (C.A.), the plaintiff's breach of an affirmative obligation to maintain his fence provided the defendant with a defence to cattle trespass. Can you reconcile *Acker* and *Singleton*?

2. The English common law cases provided that an owner of a straying animal was not liable for damages it caused on the highway. See *Searle v. Wallbank*, [1947] A.C. 341 (H.L.). In *Fleming v. Atkinson*, [1959] S.C.R. 513, three judges clearly rejected this principle and held that liability in such cases was governed by negligence. The other two judges for the majority did not find it necessary to reject *Searle*, but they did limit its application to narrow circumstances. The two dissenting judges followed *Searle*. Since *Fleming*, the great majority of Canadian courts have held that liability for straying animals on highways is governed by negligence. See for example *Crosby v. Curry* (1969), 7 D.L.R. (3d) 188 (N.S.S.C.); *MacKinnon v. Ellis* (1978), 20 Nfld. & P.E.I.R. 297 (P.E.I.S.C.); *Windrem v. Hamill* (1978), 95 D.L.R. (3d) 381 (Sask. C.A.); *Rozon v. Patenaude* (1982), 35 O.R. (2d) 619 (Co. Ct.); and *Ruckheim v. Robinson*, [1995] 4 W.W.R. 284 (B.C.C.A.).

3. At common law, if an animal was lawfully on a highway and then escaped onto the plaintiff's land, the case was governed by negligence. See *Goodwyn v. Cheveley* (1859), 157 E.R. 989 (Exch.). However, if the animal escaped from the defendant's land to the highway and then entered the plaintiff's land, strict liability applied. Should the place from where an animal strays affect the owner's liability? See Williams, *Liability for Animals* (1939) at 369-76.

4. Although cattle trespass cases usually involve only property damage, the action can be invoked to recover for personal injuries: see *Wormald v. Cole*, [1954] 1 Q.B. 614 (C.A.).

5. The term "cattle trespass" is misleading. The governing rules apply not only to cattle, but also to other straying animals (*e.g.* goats, pigs, horses, chickens). The same rules do not, however, apply with respect to cats and dogs. What is the rationale for that exception? Most provinces have enacted legislation making the owner of a dog liable

for injuries to livestock. In some provinces, the protection extends to any kind of property damage. See the *Dog Act*, R.S.N. 1990, c. D-26.

6. Most provinces have now enacted legislation to deal with straying animals. In *Acker*, it was held that the *Pounds Act*, R.S.O. 1970, c. 353 (now R.S.O. 1990, c. P.17) did not alter the common law action for cattle trespass. This is not the case in all provinces. See the *Livestock Act*, S.B.C. 1996, c. 270.

7. What was the rationale for imposing strict liability in cattle trespass? Can this principle still be justified? Would you favour the adoption of negligence principles for all cases of straying animals?

8. If a cow damaged the plaintiff's property after straying from the defendant's land, could the plaintiff successfully invoke the rule in *Rylands v. Fletcher*?

9. For a detailed discussion of liability for animals see North, *The Modern Law of Animals* (1972); and Sandys-Winsch, *Animal Law* (1984).

4. Products Liability: Negligence or Strict Liability?

In the Canadian common law jurisdictions, the roots of contemporary products liability lie in *Donoghue v. Stevenson*, [1932] A.C. 562 (H.L.). As a general proposition, a consumer injured by a product must sue the manufacturer in negligence. The plaintiff therefore must prove that the manufacturer breached the requisite standard of care in the design, production or distribution of the product, and that the defendant's carelessness caused or contributed to actual harm. The situation is different if the injured party acquired the item under contract. Contractual obligations are strict. Moreover, by virtue of consumer protection legislation (particularly the provincial statutes on the sale of goods), most consumer contracts impose obligations upon vendors to, *inter alia*, provide goods that are "fit for their intended purpose" and of "merchantable quality." If a contractual obligation is breached, and the purchaser consequently suffers injury, the vendor is strictly liable. Notice, however, that the legislation applies only as between contractual parties. That is why May Donoghue was forced to sue in negligence. She received her bottle of ginger beer as a gift from a friend.

In contrast, products liability in Quebec and the United States is based on principles of strict liability. A plaintiff need prove only that the product was defective and that the defect caused his or her injury. Considerable effort has been devoted to comparing the relative merits of negligence and strict liability. Manufacturers undoubtedly are held liable more often under principles of strict liability. Advocates of strict liability defend that result. They argue that manufacturers are profit-driven to create risks, that consumers rarely are in a position to evaluate the risks associated with products, and that manufacturers are in the best position to minimize defects and insure against the losses.

Strict liability also has its critics, particularly in the United States. In the 1960s, juries in the United States began making very large general and punitive damage awards in product liability cases, both to generously compensate injured plaintiffs and to punish and deter irresponsible manufacturers. Critics argue that the real beneficiaries were plaintiffs' lawyers, who orchestrated thousands of products liability claims and reaped enormous contingency fees for their efforts. It is often contended that strict liability is a major hindrance to the efficiency and competitiveness of American industry.

In the 1990s, American manufacturers and their insurers lobbied intensively for what they dubbed "tort reform." Essentially, this movement sought legislation to narrow the common law principles of strict liability, limit the discretion of juries, minimize or cap punitive damage awards, and otherwise protect industry from product liability claims. Although some industries were quite successful in restricting their exposure, the tort reform movement has enjoyed only limited success. Needless to say, consumer associations and trial lawyers have vigorously opposed the tort reform efforts.

NOTES AND QUESTIONS

1. There has been very little public debate on products liability in Canada. What aspects of Canadian tort law and the legal profession might explain this lack of controversy? What other important differences between Canada and the United States have helped shape their respective products liability laws?

2. Until recently, the Canadian alcohol and tobacco industries have been largely immune to major products liability litigation. Given the deaths, injuries and illnesses attributable to these products, what political and economic factors explain the relative invulnerability of these industries to products liability claims?

3. In recent years, the most widely publicized products liability claims in Canada have related to breast implants and various aspects of the "tainted-blood scandal." What explains the relative success of this litigation in contrast to the lack of progress in claims against tobacco and alcohol manufacturers?

4. An allegation of strict liability for injuries caused by defective products may be struck out as disclosing no cause of action. See *Andersen v. St. Jude Medical Inc.*, 2002 CarswellOnt 150 (S.C.J.) (WLeC).

5. In some cases, the victim of a defective product will enjoy a right of recovery under statute. See for example *Morse v. Cott Beverages West Ltd.* (2001), [2002] 4 W.W.R. 281 (Sask. Q.B.), applying the *Consumer Products Warranties Act*, R.S.S. 1978, c. C-30, s. 2(h)(i). However, consumers must accept some responsibility for their own safety: see *Tudor Inn Reception Hall (1992) Ltd. v. Merzat Industries Ltd.*, 2006 CarswellOnt 5496 (S.C.J.) (WLeC).

6. For a review of the various issues, see Boivin, "Strict Liability Revisited" (1996) 33 Osgoode Hall L.J. 487; "Symposium on Products Liability: Comparative Approaches and Transnational Litigation" in (1999) 34 Tex. Int. L.J.; Waddams, "New Directions in Products Liability" in Mullany and Linden, eds., *Torts Tomorrow: A Tribute to John Fleming* (1998) at 119-29; and Waddams, *Products Liability*, 4th ed. (2002), ch. 11.

5. Vicarious Liability

Under the doctrine of strict liability, the defendant may be held liable without acting intentionally, carelessly, or unreasonably. It is enough that the relevant obligation was breached. The doctrine of vicarious liability goes even further. Liability may be imposed even though the defendant did not breach any obligation at all.

As the following sections indicate, vicarious liability may arise under three headings: (1) *statutory vicarious liability*, (2) *agency*, and (3) *employment* or *master-servant* relationship. Because of a common misperception, however, it is important to identify one other situation that does *not* attract the doctrine. Parents are not vicariously liable for their children's torts. That is true even under "parental responsibility legislation." As explained in Chapter 3, those statutes merely impose a presumption, in some circumstances, that a parent negligently failed to control or supervise the child, and therefore is *personally* liable.

(a) STATUTORY VICARIOUS LIABILITY

A vehicle may be owned by one person, but driven by another, at the time of an accident. Under the common law principles examined below, the vehicle's owner could be held vicariously liable only if the driver was its employee or agent. As a result of legislation, however, the scope of vicarious liability is cast more widely. Unfortunately, the statutes vary somewhat from jurisdiction to jurisdiction. One common approach is exemplified by s. 192 of Ontario's *Highway Traffic Act*, R.S.O. 1990, c. H.8:

> 192. (1) The driver of a motor vehicle or street car is liable for loss or damage sustained by any person by reason of negligence in the operation of the motor vehicle or street car on a highway.
> (2) The owner of a motor vehicle or street car is liable for loss or damage sustained by any person by reason of negligence in the operation of the motor vehicle or street car on a highway, unless the motor vehicle or street car was without the owner's consent in the possession of some person other than the owner or the owner's chauffeur.
> (3) A lessee of a motor vehicle or street car is liable for loss or damage sustained by any person by reason of negligence in the operation of the motor vehicle or street car on a highway, unless the motor vehicle or street car was without the lessee's consent in the possession of some person other than the lessee or the lessee's chauffeur.
> (4) Where a motor vehicle is leased, the consent of the lessee to the operation or possession of the motor vehicle by some person other than the lessee shall, for the purposes of subsection (2), be deemed to be the consent of the owner of the motor vehicle.

Another model appears in Alberta's *Highway Traffic Act*, R.S.A. 2000, c. H.8:

> 181. In an action for the recovery of loss or damage sustained by a person by reason of a motor vehicle on a highway,
>
> > (a) a person driving the motor vehicle and living with and as a member of the family of the owner of it, and
> > (b) person who is driving the motor vehicle and who is in possession of it with the consent, express or implied, of the owner of it,
>
> is deemed to be the agent or servant of the owner of the motor vehicle and to be employed as such, and is deemed to be driving the motor vehicle in the course of that person's employment, but nothing in this section relieves any person deemed to be the agent or servant of the owner and to be driving the motor vehicle in the course of that person's employment from the liability for the damages.

Whatever form the special rule takes, its rationale is clear. In modern society, vehicles are frequently instruments of harm. Liability insurance is prevalent, but normally it is purchased in connection with the ownership, rather than the operation, of a vehicle. Consequently, if traffic accident victims are to be compensated, they require access to the owner's insurance.

NOTES AND QUESTIONS

1. Explain the difference between the approaches adopted in Ontario and Alberta. Which is more straightforward? Which is more likely to impose liability upon an owner?

2. Because the purpose of such legislation is to protect the public, vicarious liability will not be defeated merely because the owner purported to provide permission to use a vehicle, but only on the condition that the borrower refrain from drinking and driving: *Mugford v. Weber* (2004), 348 A.R. 332 (C.A.).

3. For examples of the difficulties created by the statutory provisions see *MacDonald v. Mitchell* (1969), 10 D.L.R. (3d) 240 (N.B.C.A.); *Deakins v. Aarsen* (1970), 17 D.L.R. (3d) 494 (S.C.C.); *Hayduk v. Pidoborozny* (1971), 19 D.L.R. (3d) 160 (Alta. C.A.); *Daigle v. Theo Couturier Ltd.* (1973), 43 D.L.R. (3d) 151 (N.B.C.A.); *Honan v. Gerhold* (1974), 50 D.L.R. (3d) 582 (S.C.C.); *Schroth v. Innes* (1976), 71 D.L.R. (3d) 647 (B.C.C.A.); *Mader v. MacPhee* (1978), 84 D.L.R. (3d) 761 (N.S.C.A.); *Lajeunesse v. Janssens* (1983), 3 D.L.R. (4th) 163 (Ont. H.C.); *Barreiro v. Arana*, [2003] 4 W.W.R. 391 (B.C.C.A.); and *Pugsley v. Rahbar* (2002), 41 C.C.L.I. (3d) 62 (Ont. S.C.J.). See also *Pawlak v. Doucette*, [1985] 2 W.W.R. 588 (B.C.S.C.), where the test of vicarious liability in motor vehicle cases was applied to the owner of a boat.

4. For a general discussion of the legislation, see Fridman, *The Law of Torts in Canada*, 2d ed. (2002) at 286-89.

(b) PRINCIPAL-AGENT RELATIONSHIP

In an agency relationship, the principal authorizes the agent to act on its behalf. Quite commonly, for example, a company will empower a person to enter contracts for its benefit. As illustrated in the case extracted below, the principal may be held liable for the agent's torts. It is important to bear in mind, however, that an agent may also be an employee. If so, the doctrine of vicarious liability may also arise as a result of that employment relationship. The principles are much the same in either event and, indeed, there may no longer be much need to distinguish between the two situations. See Fridman, *The Law of Torts in Canada*, 2d ed. (2002) at 292.

T.G. BRIGHT & CO. v. KERR
[1939] 1 D.L.R. 193 (S.C.C.)

[The court considered whether the defendant, a wine dealer, was vicariously liable for the negligence of its motorcycle deliveryman. Although the deliveryman was held to be the defendant's agent, the majority concluded that he was not the defendant's servant or employee because the defendant had no control over the precise manner in which the task was performed. The following excerpt from Duff C.J.C.'s dissenting judgment is limited to the issue of vicarious liability.]

DUFF C.J.C. (dissenting).: . . . It would appear to be necessary to make some reference to the ground upon which the responsibility of a principal for the acts of his agent rests.

Respondant superior is a rule which does not rest upon any notion of imputed guilt or fault. The fallacy that it does was responsible for the difficulty that great lawyers of the last century felt (Bramwell, B., for example) in admitting the liability of a corporation for the fraud of its agents. In *Hern v. Nichols*, 1 Salk. 289, 91 E.R. 256, the point in issue was the responsibility of a merchant for the deceit of his factor beyond the sea. Holt, C.J., states the broad ground of responsibility thus: –

> . . . for seeing somebody must be a loser by this deceit, it is more reason that he that employs and puts a trust and confidence in the deceiver should be a loser, than a stranger . . .

In *Hall v. Smith*, 2 Bing. 156, at p. 160, 130 E.R. 265, Best, C.J., says: –

> The maxim of *respondeat superior* is bottomed on this principle, that he who expects to derive advantage from an act which is done by another for him, must answer for any injury which a third person may sustain from it.

The principal having the power of choice has selected the agent to perform in his place a class or classes of acts, and, to adapt the language of Collins, M.R., in *Hamlyn v. Houston & Co.*, [1903] 1 K.B. 81, at pp. 85-6, it is not unjust that he who has selected him and will have the benefit of his services if efficiently performed should bear the risk of his negligence in "matters incidental to the doing of the acts the performance of which has been delegated to him."

The rule has been precisely explained in the House of Lords. . . . In *Percy v. Glasgow Corp.*, [1922] 2 A.C. 299, at pp. 306-7, Viscount Haldane said: –

As was laid down by Story in a passage adopted in an earlier case by Blackburn J. and approved in this House in *Lloyd v. Grace, Smith & Co.* [[1912] A.C. 716 at 737] "the principal is liable to third persons in a civil suit 'for the frauds, deceits, concealments, misrepresentations, torts, negligences, and other malfeasances or misfeasances, and omissions of duty of his agent *in the course of his employment*, although the principal did not authorise, or justify, or participate in, or indeed know of such misconduct, or even if he forbade the acts, or disapproved of them. The limitation is that 'the tort or negligence occurs in the course of the agency. For the principal is not liable for the torts or negligences of his agent in any matters beyond the scope of the agency, unless he has expressly authorised them to be done, or he has subsequently adopted them for his own use and benefit.' "

NOTES AND QUESTIONS

1. According to Duff C.J.C., does the principal's liability arise from its own culpability?

2. A partnership is based on a principle of mutual agency. As a result, if one partner commits a tort, every other partner may be held vicariously liable. See *Blyh v. Fladgate*, [1891] 1 Ch. 377; *McDonic v. Hetherington* (1997), 142 D.L.R. (4th) 648 (Ont. C.A.); and *Partnership Act*, R.S.O. 1990, c. P-5, s. 11

In some situations, however, the traditional rules may now be displaced for the purposes of a *limited liability partnership* (LLP). As the name suggests, such partnerships are unusual insofar as the liability of the individual partners is limited. Sections 11-13 of Alberta's *Partnership Act*, R.S.A. 2000, c. P-3 illustrate the distinction between traditional partnerships and limited liability partnerships:

> *Liability of partner*
>
> 11(1) This section is to be applied subject to section 12.
>
> (2) Each partner in a firm is liable jointly with the other partners for debts and obligations of the firm incurred while that partner is a partner. . ..
>
> *LLP limited liability*
>
> 12(1) Subject to subsections (2) and (4), a partner in an Alberta LLP is not individually liable, directly or indirectly by means of indemnification, contribution, assessment or otherwise, for debts, obligations or liabilities of the partnership or another partner that arise from the negligence, wrongful acts or omissions, malpractice or misconduct of
>
> (a) another partner, or
>
> (b) an employee, agent or representative of the partnership
>
> that occur in the ordinary course of carrying on practice in an eligible profession within the meaning of section 81 while the partnership is an Alberta LLP.
>
> (2) Subsection (1) does not operate to protect a partner from liability
>
> (a) where the partner knew of the negligence, wrongful act or omission, malpractice or misconduct at the time it was committed and failed to take reasonable steps to prevent its commission, or
>
> (b) where
>
> (i) the negligence, wrongful act or omission, malpractice or misconduct was committed by an employee, agent or representative of the partnership for whom the partner was directly responsible in a supervisory role, and
>
> (ii) the partner failed to provide such adequate and competent supervision as would normally be expected of a partner in those circumstances.
>
> (3) A partner in an Alberta LLP is not a proper party to a proceeding by or against the partnership that claims relief in respect of negligence, wrongful acts or omissions, malpractice or misconduct referred to in subsection (1).
>
> (4) The protection from liability given to a partner under subsection (1) shall not be construed as offering any protection from claims against that partner's interest in the partnership property.
>
> *Liability of firm for wrongs*
>
> 13 When, by a wrongful act or omission of a partner acting in the ordinary course of the business of the firm or with the authority of the partner's co-partners, loss or injury is caused to a person not being a partner in the firm, or a penalty is incurred, the firm is liable for it to the same extent as the partner so acting or omitting to act.

Similar provisions were enacted across the country (with the exception of Newfoundland) around the turn of the last century. Can you suggest any explanation for the sudden proliferation of such statutes? Who benefits from the existence of LLPs? Do LLPs adversely affect anyone?

3. A group of people who wish to establish a business generally are free to select from among several models, including partnership and incorporation. For present pur-

poses, there is a significant difference between those two options. Partners normally are vicariously liable for each other's acts. In contrast, the shareholders in a corporation are at risk only to the extent that the company's assets are available to the company's creditors. If those assets are insufficient to satisfy a tort judgment, the claimant is not entitled to extract the shortfall from the shareholders. Likewise, while the courts occasionally "pierce the corporate veil," corporate directors generally are not responsible for a company's debts.

4. For a general discussion of vicarious liability in the agency context, see Fridman, *The Law of Agency*, 7th ed. (1996), ch. 13.

(c) MASTER-SERVANT RELATIONSHIP

Vicarious liability most often arises in a master-servant relationship. That is not to say, however, that the doctrine is uncontroversial or well understood in the employment context. On the contrary, in the past decade, appellate courts throughout the Commonwealth have struggled to identify the doctrine's underlying rationale and to establish clear criteria for determining when an employer will be vicariously liable for an employee's torts.

The Supreme Court of Canada has contributed eight decisions to this area since 1999. The following extract is taken from the leading case of *Bazley v. Curry*, [1999] 2 S.C.R. 534. The court's other decisions are examined in the notes that follow, along with recent decisions from England and Australia.

Before turning to the cases, however, it will be useful to note several aspects of vicarious liability. While the following propositions are presented in the context of employment relationships, the first, second, and fourth ideas govern vicarious liability in other circumstances as well.

- *Alternative Liability*: Vicarious liability does not relieve a tortfeasor of responsibility. Take a simple example. The plaintiff brought a car to a garage for repairs. The vehicle's paint was scratched after an employee of the garage negligently dropped a tool on it. A court may hold the employer *vicariously* liable and the employee *personally* liable. The doctrine of vicarious liability provides the plaintiff with an alternative source of relief; it does not relieve the employee of responsibility.

- *Right of Indemnification*: If the employer satisfies judgment under the doctrine of vicarious liability, it generally has the right to recover the same amount from the employee. See *Lister v. Romford Ice & Cold Storage Co.* (1956), [1957] A.C. 555 (H.L.). As between the two defendants, the primary burden falls on the actual tortfeasor. Typically, however, employers do not exercise that right to indemnification. An employment contract or collective agreement may prevent it from doing so. In any event, the employer may conclude that enforcement of its right would be counterproductive if it would damage employee morale, or useless if the wrongdoing employee is impecunious.

- *Third Party Protection*: The next point involves a slight digression from tort law. If the plaintiff's repair contract with the defendant garage included an exclusion clause that eliminated or reduced the defendant's exposure to liability, the protection of that clause may extend to the defendant's employees as well. As a general rule, of course, the benefit of an agreement is limited to parties that enjoy privity of contract. As a matter of practical justice and commercial reality, however, the Supreme Court of Canada has created an exception in favour of employees. See *London Drugs Ltd. v. Kuehne & Nagel International Ltd.*, [1992] 3 S.C.R. 299; and *Fraser River Pile & Dredge Ltd. v. Can-Dive Services Ltd.*, [1999] 3 S.C.R. 108.

- *Vicarious and Personal Liability*: The final point returns more narrowly to the issue of tort liability. An employer may be held *vicariously* liable for its employee's tort. It is important to remember, however, that an employer also may be held *personally* liable for its own tort. For instance, assume that the employee who committed the primary tort in our example was, because of an intellectual disability, completely ill-suited to working in a garage. The employer itself might have acted negligently in hiring such a person. If so, the plaintiff could sue the employee personally and the employer both vicariously and personally.

BAZLEY v. CURRY

(1999), 174 D.L.R. (4th) 45 (S.C.C.)

[The plaintiff had been sexually assaulted as a young child in a residential care facility for emotionally troubled youths. The Children's Foundation, the non-profit organization that operated the facility, had undertaken a thorough background check of Curry, the perpetrator, prior to hiring him. As soon as Curry's criminal conduct was discovered, the facility fired him.]

MCLACHLIN J.: – . . .

A. May Employers Be Held Vicariously Liable for Their Employees' Sexual Assaults on Clients or Persons Within Their Care?

Both parties agree that the answer to this question is governed by the "Salmond" test, which posits that employers are vicariously liable for (1) employee acts authorized by the employer; or (2) unauthorized acts so connected with authorized acts that they may be regarded as modes (albeit improper modes) of doing an authorized act. Both parties also agree that we are here concerned with the second branch of the test. They diverge, however, on what the second branch of the test means. The Foundation says that its employee's sexual assaults of B. were not "modes" of doing an authorized act. B., on the other hand, submits that the assaults were a mode of performing authorized tasks, and that courts have often found employers vicariously liable for intentional wrongs of employees comparable to sexual assault.

The problem is that it is often difficult to distinguish between an unauthorized "mode" of performing an authorized act that attracts liability, and an entirely independent "act" that does not. Unfortunately, the test provides no criterion on which to make this distinction. In many cases, like the present one, it is possible to characterize the tortious act either as a mode of doing an authorized act (as the respondent would have us do), or as an independent act altogether (as the appellants would suggest). In such cases, how is the judge to decide between the two alternatives?

One answer is to look at decided cases on similar facts. As Salmond and Heuston, [*The Law of Torts*, 19th ed. (1987)], put it, "the principle is easy to state but difficult to apply. All that can be done is to provide illustrations on either side of the line" (p. 438).

The problem is that only very close cases may be useful. Fleming observes that "[n]o statistical measurement is possible [of when such torts are properly said to be within the "scope of employment"], and precedents are helpful only when they present a suggestive uniformity on parallel facts" (J.G. Fleming, *The Law of Torts* (9th ed. 1998), at p. 421).

Where decided cases do not help, Salmond and Heuston, *supra*, at p. 522, suggest the impasse may be resolved by the devices of a *prima facie* case and shifting evidentiary burden. If the plaintiff establishes that the employee's act was done on the employer's premises, during working hours, and that it bears a close connection with the work that the employee was authorized to do, then the responsibility shifts to the employer to show that the act is one for which it was not responsible. But this is not so much a test as a default position, and it remains unclear exactly what the employer would need to show to escape responsibility.

Increasingly, courts confronted by issues of vicarious liability where no clear precedent exists are *turning to policy for guidance*, examining the purposes that vicarious liability serves and asking whether imposition of liability in the new case before them would serve those purposes. . . .

This review suggests that the second branch of the Salmond test may usefully be approached in two steps. First, a court should determine whether there are precedents which unambiguously determine on which side of the line between vicarious liability and no liability the case falls. If prior cases do not clearly suggest a solution, the next step is to determine whether vicarious liability should be imposed in light of the broader policy rationales behind strict liability. This Court has an additional duty: to provide guidance for lower tribunals. Accordingly, I will try to proceed from these first two steps to articulate a rule consistent with both the existing cases and the policy reasons for vicarious liability.

1. Previous Cases

This is one of those difficult cases where there is little helpful precedent to guide the Court in determining whether the employee's tortious act should be viewed as an unauthorized mode of an authorized act, or as an altogether independent act. Apart from one recent case in the United Kingdom, the issue before us appears not to have been previously considered in depth by higher tribunals. Nevertheless, it may be useful to review the situations where courts have held employers vicariously liable for the unauthorized torts of employees. At very least, they may suggest recurring concepts and policy considerations that shed light on how the issue should be resolved.

The relevant cases may usefully be grouped into three general categories: (1) cases based on the rationale of "furtherance of the employer's aims"; (2) cases based on the employer's creation of a situation of friction; and (3) the dishonest employee cases. If we can find a common thread among these three categories of cases, it may suggest how the test should be interpreted.

The cases confirming vicarious liability on the basis that the employee was acting in furtherance of the employer's aims rely on the agency rationale implicit in the Salmond test. . . . Because the employee was acting in furtherance of the employer's aims, he or she is said to have "ostensible" or "implied" authority to do the unauthorized act. This rationale works well enough for torts of negligent accident. It does not suffice for intentional torts, however. It is difficult to maintain the fiction that an employee who commits an assault or theft was authorized to do so, even "ostensibly". . . . I would put the line of cases addressing the distinction between a "frolic" and a "detour" in this group.

The cases based on the employer's creation of a situation of friction rest on the idea that if the employer's aims or enterprise incidentally create a situation of friction that may give rise to employees committing tortious acts, an employee's intentional misconduct can be viewed as falling within the scope of the employment and the employer is vicariously liable for ensuing harm. This rationale was used to extend vicarious liability to intentional torts like a provoked bartender's assault on an obnoxious customer. While it does not rest on ostensible or implied authority, it builds on the logic of risk and accident inherent in the cases imposing vicarious liability on the basis that the employee was acting to further the employer's aims. Intentional torts arising from situations of friction are like accidents in that they stem from a risk attendant on carrying out the employer's aims. Like accidents, they occur in circumstances where such incidents can be expected to arise because of the nature of the business and hence their ramifications appropriately form part of the cost of doing business. . . .

Neither furtherance of the employer's aims nor creation of situations of friction, however, suffice to justify vicarious liability for employee theft or fraud, according to cases like *Lloyd v. Grace, Smith & Co.*, [1912] A.C. 716 (H.L.), and *The Queen v. Levy Brothers Co.*, [1961] S.C.R. 189. The language of authority, whether actual or ostensible, is inappropriate for intentional, fraudulent conduct like the theft of a client's property. A bank employee stealing a client's money cannot be said to be furthering the bank's aims. Nor does the logic of a situation of friction apply, unless one believes that any money-handling operation generates an inexorable temptation to steal. Nevertheless, courts considering this type of case have increasingly held employers vicariously liable, even when the employee's conduct is antithetical to the employer's business. . . .

At the heart of the dishonest employee decisions is consideration of fairness and policy. . . . As P.S. Atiyah, *Vicarious Liability in the Law of Torts* (1967), at p. 263, puts it, "certain types of wilful acts, and in particular frauds and thefts, are only too common, and the fact that liability is generally imposed for torts of this kind shows that the courts are not unmindful of considerations of policy." The same logic dictates that where the employee's wrongdoing was a random act wholly unconnected to the nature of the enterprise and the employee's responsibilities, the employer is not vicariously liable. Thus an employer has been held not liable for a vengeful assault by its store clerk: *Warren v. Henlys, Ltd.*, [1948] 2 All E.R. 935 (K.B.D.).

Looking at these three general classes of cases in which employers have been held vicariously liable for employees' unauthorized torts, one sees a progression from accidents, to accident-like intentional torts, to torts that bear no relationship to either agency-like conduct or accident. In search of a unifying principle, one asks what the three classes of cases have in common. At first glance, it may seem little. Yet with the benefit of hindsight it is possible to posit one common feature: in each case it can be said that the employer's enterprise had created the risk that produced the tortious act. The language of "furtherance of the employer's aims" and the employer's creation of "a situation of friction" may be seen as limited formulations of the concept of enterprise risk that underlies the dishonest employee cases. The common theme resides in the idea that where the employee's conduct is closely tied to a risk that the employer's enterprise has placed in the community, the employer may justly be held vicariously liable for the employee's wrong. . . .

2. Policy Considerations

Vicarious liability has always been concerned with policy. . . . The view of early English law that a master was responsible for all the wrongs of his servants (as well as his wife's and his children's) represented a policy choice, however inarticulate, as to who should bear the loss of wrongdoing and how best to deter it. The narrowing of vicarious responsibility with the expansion of commerce and trade and the rise of industrialism also represented a policy choice. Indeed, it represented a compromise between two policies – the social interest in furnishing an innocent tort victim with recourse against a financially responsible defendant, and a concern not to foist undue burdens on business enterprises. . . . The expansion of vicarious liability in the 20th century from authorization-based liability to broader classes of ascription is doubtless driven by yet other policy concerns. "[V]icarious liability cannot parade as a deduction from legalistic premises, but should be frankly recognized as having its basis in a combination of policy considerations" (Fleming, at p. 410).

A focus on policy is not to diminish the importance of legal principle. It is vital that the courts attempt to articulate general legal principles to lend certainty to the law and guide future applications. However, in areas of jurisprudence where changes have been occurring in response to policy considerations, the best route to enduring principle may well lie through policy. The law of vicarious liability is just such a domain.

Recognizing the policy-driven perspective of the law of vicarious liability, La Forest J. in [*London Drugs Ltd. v. Kuehne & Nagel International Ltd.* (1992), 97 D.L.R. (4th) 261 (S.C.C.)] opined that vicarious liability was traditionally considered to rest on one of two logical bases: (1) that the employee's acts are regarded in law as being authorized by the employer and hence as being the employer's acts (the "master's tort theory" or "direct liability theory"); or (2) that the employer was the employee's superior in charge or command of the employee (the "servant's tort theory"). . . . La Forest J., quoting Fridman [*The Law of Torts in Canada* (1990), vol. 2 at 315], went on to note, however, that "neither of the logical bases for vicarious liability succeeds completely in explaining the operation of the doctrine . . . express[ing] 'not so much the true rationale of vicarious liability but an attempt by the law to give some formal, technical explanation of why the law imposes vicarious liability'.".. . Faced with the absence in the existing law of a coherent principle to explain vicarious liability, La Forest J. found its basis in policy. . .: "[T]he vicarious liability regime is best seen as a response to a number of policy concerns. In its traditional domain, these are primarily linked to compensation, deterrence and loss internalization."

Fleming has identified similar policies lying at the heart of vicarious liability. In his view, two fundamental concerns underlie the imposition of vicarious liability: (1) provision of a just and practical remedy for the harm; and (2) deterrence of future harm. While different formulations of the policy interests at stake may be made (for example, loss internalization is a hybrid of the two), I believe that these two ideas usefully embrace the main policy considerations that have been advanced.

First and foremost is the concern to provide a just and practical remedy to people who suffer as a consequence of wrongs perpetrated by an employee. Fleming expresses this succinctly (at p. 410): "a person who employs others to advance his own economic interest should in fairness be placed under a corresponding liability for losses incurred in the course of the enterprise". The idea that the person who introduces a risk incurs a duty to those who may be injured lies at the heart of tort law. As Cardozo C.J. stated in

Palsgraf v. Long Island R. Co., 162 N.E. 99 (N.Y. 1928), "[t]he risk reasonably to be perceived defines the duty to be obeyed, and risk imports relation; it is risk to another or to others within the range of apprehension." This principle of fairness applies to the employment enterprise and hence to the issue of vicarious liability. While charitable enterprises may not employ people to advance their economic interests, other factors, discussed below, make it fair that they should bear the burden of providing a just and practical remedy for wrongs perpetrated by their employees. This policy interest embraces a number of subsidiary goals. The first is the goal of effective compensation. "One of the most important social goals served by vicarious liability is victim compensation. Vicarious liability improves the chances that the victim can recover the judgment from a solvent defendant." (B. Feldthusen, "Vicarious Liability For Sexual Torts", in *Torts Tomorrow* (1998), 221, at p. 224). Or to quote Fleming, the master is "a more promising source of recompense than his servant who is apt to be a man of straw" (p. 410). . . .

Reviewing the jurisprudence, and considering the policy issues involved, I conclude that in determining whether an employer is vicariously liable for an employee's unauthorized, intentional wrong in cases where precedent is inconclusive, courts should be guided by the following principles:

(1) They should openly confront the question of whether liability should lie against the employer, rather than obscuring the decision beneath semantic discussions of "scope of employment" and "mode of conduct".

(2) The fundamental question is whether the wrongful act is sufficiently related to conduct authorized by the employer to justify the imposition of vicarious liability. Vicarious liability is generally appropriate where there is a significant connection between the creation or enhancement of a risk and the wrong that accrues therefrom, even if unrelated to the employer's desires. Where this is so, vicarious liability will serve the policy considerations of provision of an adequate and just remedy and deterrence. Incidental connections to the employment enterprise, like time and place (without more), will not suffice. Once engaged in a particular business, it is fair that an employer be made to pay the generally foreseeable costs of that business. In contrast, to impose liability for costs unrelated to the risk would effectively make the employer an involuntary insurer.

(3) In determining the sufficiency of the connection between the employer's creation or enhancement of the risk and the wrong complained of, subsidiary factors may be considered. These may vary with the nature of the case. When related to intentional torts, the relevant factors may include, but are not limited to, the following:

(a) the opportunity that the enterprise afforded the employee to abuse his or her power;

(b) the extent to which the wrongful act may have furthered the employer's aims (and hence be more likely to have been committed by the employee);

(c) the extent to which the wrongful act was related to friction, confrontation or intimacy inherent in the employer's enterprise;

(d) the extent of power conferred on the employee in relation to the victim;

(e) the vulnerability of potential victims to wrongful exercise of the employee's power.

Applying these general considerations to sexual abuse by employees, there must be a strong connection between what the employer was asking the employee to do (the risk created by the employer's enterprise) and the wrongful act. It must be possible to say that the employer significantly increased the risk of the harm by putting the employee in his or her position and requiring him to perform the assigned tasks. The policy considerations that justify imposition of vicarious liability for an employee's sexual misconduct are unlikely to be satisfied by incidental considerations of time and place. For example, an incidental or random attack by an employee that merely happens to take place on the employer's premises during working hours will scarcely justify holding the employer liable. Such an attack is unlikely to be related to the business the employer is conducting or what the employee was asked to do and, hence, to any risk that was created. Nor is the imposition of liability likely to have a significant deterrent effect; short of closing the premises or discharging all employees, little can be done to avoid the random wrong. Nor is foreseeability of harm used in negligence law the test. What is required is a material increase in the risk as a consequence of the employer's enterprise and the duties he entrusted to the employee, mindful of the policies behind vicarious liability. . . .

In summary, the test for vicarious liability for an employee's sexual abuse of a client should focus on whether the employer's enterprise and empowerment of the employee materially increased the risk of the sexual assault and hence the harm. The test must not be applied mechanically, but with a sensitive view to the policy considerations that justify the imposition of vicarious liability – fair and efficient compensation for wrong and deterrence. This requires trial judges to investigate the employee's specific duties and determine whether they gave rise to special opportunities for wrongdoing. Because of the peculiar exercises of power and trust that pervade cases such as child abuse, special attention should be paid to the existence of a power or dependency relationship, which on its own often creates a considerable risk of wrongdoing. . . .

C. Application to the Case at Bar

Applying these considerations to the facts in the case at bar, the Foundation is vicariously liable for the sexual misconduct of Curry. The opportunity for intimate private control and the parental relationship and power required by the terms of employment created the special environment that nurtured and brought to fruition Curry's sexual abuse. The employer's enterprise created and fostered the risk that led to the ultimate harm. The abuse was not a mere accident of time and place, but the product of the special relationship of intimacy and respect the employer fostered, as well as the special opportunities for exploitation of that relationship it furnished. Indeed, it is difficult to imagine a job with a greater risk for child sexual abuse. This is not to suggest that future cases must rise to the same level to impose vicarious liability. Fairness and the need for deterrence in this critical area of human conduct – the care of vulnerable children – suggest that as between the Foundation that created and managed the risk and the innocent victim, the Foundation should bear the loss.

NOTES AND QUESTIONS

1. In what circumstances will an employer be held vicariously liable for the torts of an employee?

2. What policy considerations support the imposition of vicarious liability?

3. What is the "Salmond" test of vicarious liability? Is McLachlin J.'s test of vicarious liability any more certain or predictable than Salmond's? How do those two tests differ with respect to unauthorized acts by employees?

4. What impact will *Bazley* have on the availability and cost of liability insurance for non-profit organizations that provide free services to children? What impact will it have on the screening procedures for both employees and volunteers of such organizations? Exactly what steps should employers take in their screening processes? Would such measures be subject to possible human rights and problems under the *Canadian Charter of Rights and Freedoms*, Part I of the *Constitution Act, 1982*, being Schedule B to the *Canada Act 1982* (U.K.), 1982, c. 11?

5. Are the tests outlined in *Bazley* limited to cases of childhood sexual abuse or would they apply to any vulnerable population? Would similar principles apply to high school and university students, and nursing and retirement homes? What are the implications of *Bazley* for other types of employers, such as military or the police, that have a clear hierarchical structure?

6. The basic issues that were addressed in *Bazley* subsequently came before the House of Lords in *Lister v. Hesley Hall Ltd.*, [2002] 1 A.C. 215 (H.L.). The claimant, who lived in a residential home for boys with behavioural difficulties, was sexually abused by the facility's warden. The House of Lords adopted the essence of McLachlin J.'s test, but phrased the governing rules in more general terms. It similarly refrained from elaborating on the "sufficiently close connection" test in *Dubai Aluminium Co. Ltd. v. Salaam*, [2003] 2 A.C. 366 (H.L.). See Hopkins, "What is the Course of Employment?" [2001] C.L.J. 458; Glofcheski, "A Frolic in the Law of Tort: Expanding the Scope of Employers' Vicarious Liability" (2004) 12 Tort L. Rev. 18; Gilliker, "Rough Justice in an Unjust World" (2002) 65 Mod. L. Rev. 269; Elvin "The Notion of Vicarious Liability for Sexual Abuse in English law" (2002) 13 King's College L.J. 97; McIvor, "The Use and Abuse of the Doctrine of Vicarious Liability" (2006) 35 Common Law World Rev. 268; McIvor, *Third Party Liability in Tort* (2006); and McBride, "Vicarious Liability in England and Australia" [2003] C.L.J. 255.

Unsurprisingly, the Privy Council followed the same approach in *Bernard v. Attorney General of Jamaica*, [2004] I.R.L.R. 398 (P.C.). A man presenting himself to be a police officer demanded use of a public telephone that the claimant was holding, saying: "I am going to make a long distance call. . . boy leggo this, police." When the claimant refused, the officer pulled out his revolver and shot point blank. In finding the officer's employer vicariously liable, the Privy Council focussed on three facts: (1) the tortfeasor presented himself as a police officer, (2) the tortfeasor subsequently arrested the victim in the hospital, on the grounds of interfering with the administration of justice, and (3) the police department's policy of allowing officers to possess firearms while off-duty.

In contrast, the High Court of Australia rejected the *Bazley* approach and reaffirmed the Salmond test: *New South Wales v. Lepore* (2003), 212 C.L.R. 511 (H.C.A.). The court expressed a number of concerns regarding the new Canadian approach: (1) it was too vague to provide certainty and consistency in practice, (2) it potentially cast the net of vicarious liability too widely, and (3) employers' liability could be more sensitively addressed under a generalized action in negligence. See Wangmann, "Liability for Institutional Child Sexual Assault: Where Does *Lepore* Leave Australia?" (2004) 28 Melb. U. L. Rev. 169; White & Orr, "Precarious Liability: The High Court in *Lepore, Samin* and *Rich* on School Responsibility for Assaults by Teachers" (2003) 11 Torts L.J. 101; and Luntz, "Round-up of Cases in the High Court of Australia in 2003" (2004) 12 Torts L.J. 1.

7. A master's vicarious liability for a servant's tort may arise in countless contexts. Particular circumstances may raise unusual or unique considerations. For instance, doctors at one time were considered to be employees of the patient, and not the hospital. In recent years, however, there has been a trend to extend the scope of a hospital's vicarious liability for doctors and other staff. See *Jaman Estate v. Hussain*, [2002] 11 W.W.R. 241 (Man. C.A.); Magnet, "Liability of a Hospital for the Negligent Acts of Professionals" (1977) 3 C.C.L.T. 135; Picard, *Legal Liability of Doctors and Hospitals in Canada*, 2d ed. (1984) at 313-28; and Fridman, *The Law of Torts in Canada*, 2d ed. (2002) at 282-84.

If a player injures an opponent in a way that is not only contrary to the rules of the game, but also tortious, should the offending player's team be vicarious liable? See James & McArdle, "Player Violence or Violent Players? Vicarious Liability for Sports Participants" (2004) 12 Tort L. Rev. 131.

A nightclub employs a doorman to vet guests and remove unruly customers. After becoming involved in an incident with a patron, the doorman leaves the premises, fetches a knife from his apartment, and returns to stab the patron. Is the nightclub vicarious liable for the doorman's actions? Is vicarious liability precluded by the fact that the tort was unauthorized and personally motivated behaviour? See *Mattis v. Pollock*, [2003] 1 W.L.R. 2158 (C.A.); and *Vasey v. Wosk's Ltd.*, [1988] B.C.J. No. 2089 (S.C.) (QL).

8. Even if a tort is committed by an employee, the employer will not be vicariously liable if, on the facts, the doctrine would not serve the underlying goals of compensation and deterrence. In *Schultz v. Miki* (2006), 264 D.L.R. (4th) 201 (B.C.C.A.), a landlord hired his cousin to make repairs in an apartment. While in the apartment, the cousin sexually assaulted the tenant. The court did not hold the landlord vicariously liable for the tort. Southin J.A. explained that "[t]he policy considerations of fair compensation and deterrence are eliminated in the circumstances of this case. If the appellant's arguments were to succeed, we would be dangerously close to imposing absolute liability on employers for the intentional torts of their employees." On vicarious liability for criminal conduct, see also *Royal Bank of Canada v. Intercon Security Ltd.*, 2005 CarswellOnt 5922 (S.C.J.) (WLeC); and *Weingerl v. Seo* (2005), 256 D.L.R. (4th) 1 (Ont. C.A.).

9. At common law, the Crown was not vicariously liable for the torts of its agents and servants. That immunity has been abrogated by statute. See for example *Crown Liability and Proceedings Act*, R.S.C. 1985, c. C-50, s. 3(a); and *Proceedings Against the Crown Act*, R.S.A. 2000, c. P-25. Nevertheless, the courts will not lightly visit vicarious liability upon a Minister or Premier. See for example *Tottrup v. Lund* (2000), 186 D.L.R. (4th) 226 (Alta. C.A.); *Decock v. Alberta* (2000), 186 D.L.R. (4th) 265 (Alta. C.A.); *P.(N.I.) v. B.(R.)* (2000), 193 D.L.R (4th) 752 (B.C.S.C.); and *Williams v. Attorney General of Canada* (2005), 257 D.L.R. (4th) 704 (Ont. S.C.J.). See also Fridman, *The Law of Torts in Canada*, 2d ed. (2002) at 284-85.

10. Vicarious liability covers compensatory damages, but not punitive relief, where the master is not guilty of "high-handed, malicious, arbitrary or highly reprehensible misconduct that departs to a marked degree from ordinary standards of decent behaviour": *Blackwater v. Plint*, [2005] 3 S.C.R. 3 at 35. A master nevertheless may be vicariously liable for aggravated damages: *T.W.N.A. v. Clarke* (2003), 235 D.L.R. (4th) 13 (B.C.C.A.); and *Weingerl v. Seo, supra.*

11. Although the doctrine of vicarious liability arose under the common law, it extends, as a matter of logic and principle, to equitable wrongs and statutory wrongs as well: *Majrowski v. Guy's and St Thomas's NHS Trust*, [2006] 3 W.L.R. 125 (H.L.).

12. *Bazley* did not resolve all of the issues arising from vicarious liability of servants. The Supreme Court of Canada consequently has delivered judgment in several other cases since *Bazley*. The first of those judgments was rendered contemporaneously with *Bazley*. In *Jacobi v. Griffiths*, [1999] 2 S.C.R. 576, a four-to-three majority of the court ruled that the Boys and Girls Club of Vernon was not vicariously liable for the sexual assaults committed by the Club's program director. The majority emphasized that the assaults did not take place at the Club, that the Club offered only recreational activities and occasional outings and not residential services, and that the director was responsible for developing and supervising the recreational programs. In the words of the majority, the director was not placed in a special relationship of trust for the children's "care, protection and nurturing." McLachlin J. wrote a strong dissent.

13. In light of *Griffiths*, how would you respond to the questions raised in notes 4 and 5? For comments on *Bazley* and *Griffiths*, see Cane, "Vicarious liability for sexual abuse" (2000) 116 L.Q.R. 21; Hall, "Responsibility Without Fault" (2000) 79 Can. Bar Rev. 474; Black & Wildeman, "Parsing the Supreme Court's New Pronouncements on Vicarious Liability for Sexual Battery" (1999) 46 C.C.L.T. 126; and Rafferty, "Developments in Contract and Tort Law: The 1998-1999 Term" (1999) 11 S.C.L.R. (2d) 183. See also *H.L. v. Canada* (2002), [2003] 5 W.W.R. 421 (Sask. C.A.), varied on other grounds, [2005] 1 S.C.R. 401.

14. In 2003, the Supreme Court of Canada rendered three more decisions dealing with vicarious liability: *B.(K.L.) v. British Columbia*, [2003] 2 S.C.R. 403; *B.(M.) v. British Columbia*, [2003] 2 S.C.R. 477; and *G.(E.D.) v. Hammer*, [2003] 2 S.C.R. 459. The general effect was to somewhat reduce the scope of the doctrine. The facts of *B.(K.L.)* and *B.(M.)* were substantially the same. The plaintiffs were sexually, physically and psychologically abused while living in foster homes. Because they had been placed in those homes under the authority of the *Protection of Children Act*, R.S.B.C. 1960, c. 303, they claimed that the provincial government was vicariously liable for the torts. The court held that vicarious liability would be appropriate only if the claimants satisfied two conditions. First, the relationship between the parties had to be sufficiently close or proximate to warrant the doctrine's application. A crucial factor in that respect is the level of control that the master exercised over the servant. Second, the wrongful conduct had to be "sufficiently connected" to the servant's assigned tasks so that the impugned conduct may be regarded as a "materialization of the risks created by the enterprise." The court concluded those conditions were not met on the facts of *B.(K.L.)*and *B.(M.)*. Independence is the essence of the foster home program. The government does not, and

practically speaking could not, exercise substantial control over the day-to-day lives of the foster children. Moreover, the court feared that the imposition of vicarious liability might deter the government from placing children in foster homes, rather than less effective institutional settings. Looking ahead to the final sections of this chapter, the court also held that the government had not been subject to a *non-delegable duty of care* to the claimants. In *B.(K.L.)*, however, the court did find that the government had been subject to a standard duty of care in negligence insofar as it was required to exercise care in placing children in foster homes and in supervising their stay. The court also found that the government had breached the standard of care. The defendant nevertheless escaped liability because of the lapse of time under the *Limitations Act*, R.S.B.C. 1996, c. 266, ss. 3(2) and 7(1)(a)(i).

G.(E.D.) v. Hammer, the third case in the trilogy, arose in a different context. The plaintiff was sexually assaulted by a janitor at her school. The perpetrator was liable. The plaintiff, however, also alleged that the school board was liable for breach of a non-delegable duty, liable for breach of a fiduciary duty, and vicariously liable for the janitor's torts. The first claim is discussed below. The second claim was dismissed on the ground that, while the school board owed a fiduciary duty to the claimant, the wrongs in question were not of a fiduciary nature. Finally, the claim for vicarious liability was denied at trial and was pursued not on appeal to the Supreme Court of Canada.

15. The Supreme Court of Canada continued its development of vicarious liability the next year in *John Doe v. Bennett*, [2004] 1 S.C.R. 436. The parish priest in a remote village in Newfoundland committed a series of sexual assaults on several young boys. Although some of the victims complained to the priest's supervising bishops, and to an Archbishop of a neighbouring diocese, nothing was done to stop the attacks. The victims sued many years later. The priest was held personally liable. The local diocese (a corporate body, under the authority of local bishops) was directly liable on the basis of the bishops' failure to act. The final question concerned the diocese's vicarious liability for the priest's actions. Because the issue was not settled by precedent, McLachlin C.J.C. examined whether vicarious liability would promote the policy concerns underlying enterprise liability. She found, following *Bazley* and *B.(K.L.)*, that (1) the diocese closely controlled the priest, and (2) the priest's wrongs were closely connected to his assigned tasks. In ultimately siding with the claimants, McLachlin C.J.C. also emphasized the special circumstances of the case. Given the geographical and social context, the priest held enormous authority within the community. The boys (and their parents) regarded the priest as absolute authority and lacked any other role models. By encouraging the community to defer to the priest's wishes, the diocese effectively created a situation ripe for abuse.

16. The most recent two cases, decided in 2005, involved the abuse of aboriginal students in residential schools. In *B.(E.) v. Order of the Oblates of Mary Immaculate in the Province of British Columbia*, [2005] 3 S.C.R. 45, the claimant was subject to a series of sexual assaults by a lay employee who served the school as a baker, boat driver, and odd-job labourer. The claimant sought damages, on the basis of vicarious liability, against the Catholic Order that operated the school. The claim was dismissed. Binnie J. (writing for the majority) stressed the need for something more than "mere opportunity" to commit a wrongful act. While vicarious liability does not require proof that the tortfeasor was given parent-like authority over the victim, it does presume a "strong

connection" between the assigned tasks and the wrongful conduct. On the facts, however, the tortfeasor was neither required, nor permitted, to become involved intimately in the plaintiff's life.

The second case, *Blackwater v. Plint*, [2005] 3 S.C.R. 3, concerned a series of sexual assaults committed by a dormitory supervisor. The assaults occurred within a residential school that was operated by the federal government and the United Church of Canada. Although the plaintiff pursued several claims (including one, discussed below, against the government for breach of a non-delegable duty), the most interesting for present purposes is the allegation that both the government and the church were vicariously liable. The argument alleged that the tortfeasor was employed by both defendants. While the Church was Plint's immediate employer (because, for instance, it nominated the school's principal and hired the staff), the government also was an employer (because, for instance, it hired the principal, selected the students, and funded the program). McLachlin C.J.C. accepted the allegation on two grounds: (1) dual responsibility would further the policy goals underlying the doctrine of vicarious liability, and (2) various members of a partnership may be held vicariously liable for the tort of an employee.

The Chief Justice's reasons were surprisingly thin. They refer to no cases and they do not explore the conceptual difficulties raised by the prospect of dual vicarious liability. Most surprisingly of all, McLachlin C.J.C. failed to mention the fact that there has been a strong presumption, for nearly two centuries, that vicarious liability may be imposed on only one employer: *Laugher v. Pointer* (1826), 108 E.R. 204 (K.B.); and *Mersey Docks and Harbour Board v. Coggins & Griffiths (Liverpool) Ltd.*, [1947] A.C. 1 (H.L.). Nor did she mention the Canadian cases that either accepted or rejected the orthodox view. See for example *McKee v. Dumas* (1977), 12 O.R. (2d) 670 (C.A.); *Hardisty v. 851791 N.W.T. Ltd.* (2004), 26 C.C.L.T. (3d) 305 (N.W.T.S.C.), aff'd (2005), [2006] 4 W.W.R. 199 (C.A.); and *Gemco Equipment Ltd. v. Westen* (1965), 54 W.W.R. 513 (B.C. Co. Ct.). The Supreme Court of Canada's decision therefore compares very poorly with the masterful treatment that the issue received at the hands of May L.J. in *Viasystems (Tyneside) Ltd. v. Thermal Transfer (Northern) Ltd.*, [2006] Q.B. 510 (C.A.). While the English Court of Appeal ultimately arrived at the same conclusion, it did so only after thoroughly canvassing the issues and precedents. On the question of "borrowed employees," see Fridman, *The Law of Torts in Canada*, 2d ed. (2002) at 289-92; and Fleming, *The Law of Torts*, 9th ed. (1998) at 418.

(d) INDEPENDENT CONTRACTORS

There are several options open to a person who wants to retain the services of a worker. We already have seen two possibilities: agency and employment. The doctrine of vicarious liability applies to both. Significantly, however, an employer will not be held vicariously liable for torts committed by an "independent contractor." The classification of a worker is therefore critically important. Unfortunately, it often is very difficult as well.

671122 ONTARIO LTD. v. SAGAZ INDUSTRIES CANADA INC.

(2001), 204 D.L.R. (4th) 542 (S.C.C.)

[The plaintiff manufactured synthetic sheepskin car seat covers. It sold its product to Canadian Tire for over thirty years. At the time of the events in question, sales to Canadian Tire accounted for more than half of the plaintiff's annual business.

The defendant also manufactured car seat covers. It hired a marketing company called AIM in an effort to obtain Canadian Tire's business. AIM achieved that goal by bribing the head of Canadian Tire's automotive division.

The loss of Canadian Tire's business devastated the plaintiff. It sued several parties. One of its claims was against the defendant. For present purposes, the key issue was whether the defendant was vicariously liable for the torts (*i.e.* conspiracy and unlawful interference with economic relations) committed by AIM. The resolution of that issue depended upon the classification of AIM as either an employee or an independent contractor.]

MAJOR J.: –

A. Vicarious Liability

(1) Policy Rationale Underlying Vicarious Liability

Vicarious liability is not a distinct tort. It is a theory that holds one person responsible for the misconduct of another because of the relationship between them. Although the categories of relationships in law that attract vicarious liability are neither exhaustively defined nor closed, the most common one to give rise to vicarious liability is the relationship between master and servant, now more commonly called employer and employee.

In general, tort law attempts to hold persons accountable for their wrongful acts and omissions and the direct harm that flows from those wrongs. Vicarious liability, by contrast, is considered to be a species of strict liability because it requires no proof of personal wrongdoing on the part of the person who is subject to it. As such, it is still relatively uncommon in Canadian tort law. What policy considerations govern its discriminate application?

. . .

First, vicarious liability provides a just and practical remedy to people who suffer harm as a consequence of wrongs perpetrated by an employee. Many commentators are suspicious of vicarious liability in principle because it appears to hold parties responsible for harm simply because they have "deep pockets" or an ability to bear the loss even though they are not personally at fault. The "deep pockets" justification on its own does not accord with an inherent sense of what is fair (see also R. Flannigan, "Enterprise Control: The Servant-Independent Contractor Distinction" (1987), 37 U.T.L.J. 25, at p. 29). Besides an ability to bear the loss, it must also seem just to place liability for the wrong on the employer. McLachlin J. addresses this concern in *Bazley*. . .:

> Vicarious liability is arguably fair in this sense. The employer puts in the community an enterprise which carries with it certain risks. When those risks materialize and cause injury to a member of the public despite the employer's reasonable efforts, it is fair that the person or organization that creates the enterprise and hence the risk should bear the loss. This accords with the notion that it is right and just that the person who creates a risk bear the loss when the risk ripens into harm.

Similarly, Fleming stated that "a person who employs others to advance his own economic interest should in fairness be placed under a corresponding liability for losses incurred in the course of the enterprise" [*The Law of Torts*, 9th ed. (1998) 410]. McLachlin J. states that while the fairness of this proposition is capable of standing alone, "it is buttressed by the fact that the employer is often in the best position to spread the losses through mechanisms like insurance and higher prices, thus minimizing the dislocative effect of the tort within society". . . . Finally on this point, it is noteworthy that vicarious liability does not diminish the personal liability of the direct tortfeasor. . . .

The second policy consideration underlying vicarious liability is deterrence of future harm as employers are often in a position to reduce accidents and intentional wrongs by efficient organization and supervision. This policy ground is related to the first policy ground of fair compensation, as "[t]he introduction of the enterprise into the community with its attendant risk, in turn, implies the possibility of managing the risk to minimize the costs of the harm that may flow from it" (*Bazley, supra*).

(2) Employee Versus Independent Contractor

The most common relationship that attracts vicarious liability is that between employer and employee, formerly master and servant. This is distinguished from the relationship of an employer and independent contractor which, subject to certain limited exceptions. . ., typically does not give rise to a claim for vicarious liability. If a worker is determined to be an employee as opposed to an independent contractor such that vicarious liability can attach to the employer, this is not the end of the analysis. The tortious conduct has to be committed by the employee in the course of employment. For the reasons that follow, this second stage of the analysis is not relevant and need not be analysed in the present appeal.

What is the difference between an employee and an independent contractor and why should vicarious liability more likely be imposed in the former case than in the latter? This question has been the subject of much debate. The answer lies with the element of control that the employer has over the direct tortfeasor (the worker). If the employer does not control the activities of the worker, the policy justifications underlying vicarious liability will not be satisfied. See Flannigan, *supra*, at pp. 31-32:

> This basis for vicarious liability discloses a precise limitation on the scope of the doctrine. If the employer does not control the activities of the worker it is clear that vicarious liability should not be imposed, for then insulated risk-taking [by the employer] does not occur. Only the worker, authorized to complete a task, could have affected the probability of loss, for he alone had control in any respect. Thus, because there is no mischief where employer control is absent, no remedy is required.

Explained another way, the main policy concerns justifying vicarious liability are to provide a just and practical remedy for the plaintiff's harm and to encourage the deterrence of future harm. . . . Vicarious liability is fair in principle because the hazards of the business should be borne by the business itself; thus, it does not make sense to anchor liability on an employer for acts of an independent contractor, someone who was in business on his or her own account. In addition, the employer does not have the same control over an independent contractor as over an employee to reduce accidents and intentional wrongs by efficient organization and supervision. Each of these policy justifications is relevant to the ability of the employer to control the activities of the employee, justifications which are generally deficient or missing in the case of an independent contractor. [T]he policy justifications for imposing vicarious liability are relevant where the employer is able to control the activities of the employee but may be deficient in the case of an independent contractor over whom the employer has little control. However, control is not the only factor to consider in determining if a worker is an employee or an independent contractor. For the reasons discussed below, reliance on control alone can be misleading, and there are other relevant factors which should be considered in making this determination.

Various tests have emerged in the case law to help determine if a worker is an employee or an independent contractor. The distinction between an employee and an independent contractor applies not only in vicarious liability, but also to the application of various forms of employment legislation, the availability of an action for wrongful dismissal, the assessment of business and income taxes, the priority taken upon an employer's insolvency and the application of contractual rights. . . . Accordingly, much of the case law on point while not written in the context of vicarious liability is still helpful.

The Federal Court of Appeal thoroughly reviewed the relevant case law in *Wiebe Door Services Ltd. v. M.N.R.*, [1986] 3 F.C. 553. As MacGuigan J.A. noted, the original criterion of the employment relationship was the control test set out by Baron Bramwell in *Regina v. Walker* (1858), 27 L.J.M.C. 207, and adopted by this Court in *Hôpital Notre-Dame de l'Espérance v. Laurent*, [1978] 1 S.C.R. 605. It is expressed as follows: "the essential criterion of employer-employee relations is the right to give orders and instructions to the employee regarding the manner in which to carry out his work" (*Hôpital Notre-Dame de l'Espérance, supra*, at p. 613).

This criterion has been criticized as wearing "an air of deceptive simplicity" [Atiyah, *Vicarious Liability in the Law of Torts*, (1967) 41]. The main problems are set out by MacGuigan J.A. in *Wiebe Door*. . .:

> A principal inadequacy [with the control test] is its apparent dependence on the exact terms in which the task in question is contracted for: where the contract contains detailed specifications and conditions, which would be the normal expectation in a contract with an independent contractor, the control may even be greater than where it is to be exercised by direction on the job, as would be the normal expectation in a contract with a servant, but a literal application of the test might find the actual control to be less. In addition, the test has broken down completely in relation to highly skilled and professional workers, who possess skills far beyond the ability of their employers to direct.

An early attempt to deal with the problems of the control test was the development of a fourfold test known as the "entrepreneur test." It was set out by W. O. Douglas (later Justice) in "Vicarious Liability and Administration of Risk I" (1928-1929), 38 Yale L.J. 584, and applied by Lord Wright in *Montreal v. Montreal Locomotive Works Ltd.*, [1947] 1 D.L.R. 161 (P.C.), at p. 169:

> In earlier cases a single test, such as the presence or absence of control, was often relied on to determine whether the case was one of master and servant, mostly in order to decide issues of tortious liability on the part of the master or superior. In the more complex conditions of modern industry, more complicated tests have often to be applied. It has been suggested that a fourfold test would in some cases be more appropriate, a complex involving (1) control; (2) ownership of the tools; (3) chance of profit; (4) risk of loss. Control in itself is not always conclusive.

As MacGuigan J.A. notes, a similar general test, known as the "organization test" or "integration test" was used by Denning L.J. (as he then was) in *Stevenson Jordan and Harrison, Ltd. v. Macdonald*, [1952] 1 The Times L.R. 101 (C.A.), at p. 111:

> One feature which seems to run through the instances is that, under a contract of service, a man is employed as part of the business, and his work is done as an integral part of the business; whereas, under a contract for services, his work, although done for the business, is not integrated into it but is only accessory to it.

This decision imported the language "contract of service" (employee) and "contract for services" (independent contractor) into the analysis. The organization test was approved by this Court in [*Co-operators Insurance Association v. Kearney*, [1965] S.C.R. 106] . . . where Spence J. observed that courts had moved away from the control test under the pressure of novel situations, replacing it instead with a type of organization test in which the important question was whether the alleged servant was part of his employer's organization. . . .

However, as MacGuigan J.A. noted in *Wiebe Door*, the organization test has had "less vogue in other common-law jurisdictions". . ., including England and Australia. For one, it can be a difficult test to apply. If the question is whether the activity or worker is integral to the employer's business, this question can usually be answered affirmatively. For example, the person responsible for cleaning the premises is technically integral to sustaining the business, but such services may be properly contracted out to people in business on their own. . . . As MacGuigan J.A. further noted in *Wiebe Door*, if the main test is to demonstrate that, without the work of the alleged employees the employer would be out of business, a factual relationship of mutual dependency would always meet the organization test of an employee even though this criterion may not accurately reflect the parties' intrinsic relationship. . . .

Despite these criticisms, MacGuigan J.A. acknowledges . . . that the organization test can be of assistance:

> Of course, the organization test of Lord Denning and others produces entirely acceptable results when properly applied, that is, when the question of organization or integration is approached from the persona of the "employee" and not from that of the "employer," because it is always too easy from the superior perspective of the larger enterprise to assume that every contributing cause is so arranged purely for the convenience of the larger entity. We must keep in mind that it was with respect to the business of the employee that Lord Wright [in Montreal] addressed the question "Whose business is it?"

According to MacGuigan J.A., the best synthesis found in the authorities is that of Cooke J. in *Market Investigations, Ltd. v. Minister of Social Security*, [1968] 3 All E.R. 732 (Q.B.D.), at pp. 737-38. . .:

> The observations of LORD WRIGHT, of DENNING, L.J., and of the judges of the Supreme Court in the U.S.A. suggest that the fundamental test to be applied is this: "Is the person who has engaged himself to perform these services performing them as a person in business on his own account?". If the answer to that question is "yes", then the contract is a contract for services. If the answer is "no" then the contract is a contract of service. No exhaustive list has been compiled and perhaps no exhaustive list can be compiled of considerations which are relevant in determining that question, nor can strict rules be laid down as to the relative weight which the various considerations should carry in particular cases. The most that can be said is that control will no doubt always have to be considered, although it can no longer be regarded as the sole determining factor; and that factors, which may be of importance, are such matters as whether the man performing the services provides his own equipment, whether he hires his own helpers, what degree of financial risk he takes, what degree of responsibility for investment and management he has, and whether and how far he has an opportunity of profiting from sound management in the performance of his task.

Finally, there is a test that has emerged that relates to the enterprise itself. Flannigan, *supra*, sets out the "enterprise test" . . . which provides that the employer should be vicariously liable because (1) he controls the activities of the worker; (2) he is in a position to reduce the risk of loss; (3) he benefits from the activities of the worker; (4) the true cost of a product or service ought to be borne by the enterprise offering it. According to Flannigan, each justification deals with regulating the risk-taking of the employer and, as such, control is always the critical element because the ability to control the enterprise is what enables the employer to take risks. . . .

In my opinion, there is no one conclusive test which can be universally applied to determine whether a person is an employee or an independent contractor. Lord Denning stated in *Stevenson Jordan* . . . that it may be impossible to give a precise definition of the distinction . . . and, similarly, Fleming observed that "no single test seems to yield an invariably clear and acceptable answer to the many variables of ever changing employment relations" (p. 416). Further, I agree with MacGuigan J.A. in *Wiebe Door* . . . that what must always occur is a search for the total relationship of the parties:

> [I]t is exceedingly doubtful whether the search for a formula in the nature of a single test for identifying a contract of service any longer serves a useful purpose. . . . The most that can profitably be done is to examine all the possible factors which have been referred to in these cases as bearing on the nature of the relationship between the parties concerned. Clearly not all of these factors will be relevant in all cases, or have the same weight in all cases. Equally clearly no magic formula can be propounded for determining which factors should, in any given case, be treated as the determining ones.

Although there is no universal test to determine whether a person is an employee or an independent contractor, I agree with MacGuigan J.A. that a persuasive approach to the issue is that taken by Cooke J. in *Market Investigations*. . . . The central question is whether the person who has been engaged to perform the services is performing them as a person in business on his own account. In making this determination, the level of control the employer has over the worker's activities will always be a factor. However, other factors to consider include whether the worker provides his or her own equipment, whether the worker hires his or her own helpers, the degree of financial risk taken by the worker, the degree of responsibility for investment and management held by the worker, and the worker's opportunity for profit in the performance of his or her tasks.

On the facts, Major J. concluded that AIM was "in business on its own account" – *i.e.* it was an independent contractor, rather than an employee, of the defendant. The defendant consequently was not vicariously liable for AIM's torts. In reaching that decision, Major J. was particularly influenced by a number of factors: (i) AIM had separate offices, (ii) AIM paid all of its own costs, (iii) AIM was free to take on other business, (iv) AIM decided when, where and how to perform the job, and was otherwise generally in control of the project, and (v) AIM was in a position to either suffer a loss or earn a profit, depending upon its performance of the job.

NOTES AND QUESTIONS

1. In terms of a worker's relationship with an employer, what is the difference between an employee and an independent contractor? Why does that difference affect the availability of vicarious liability?

2. Do the governing principles sufficiently take into account the plaintiff's interests? How can a potential plaintiff determine whether a particular task is to be performed

by an employee, rather than an independent contractor? Are there circumstances in which a potential plaintiff's business decision may be affected by such knowledge?

3. What is the "control test?" What is the "organization test?" What are the deficiencies of each of those tests?

4. The categories concerning vicarious liability are not mutually exclusive. Accordingly, it sometimes is necessary to consider more than one possibility. For instance, a life insurance company may be held vicariously liable for theft by its sales agent, despite the fact that the agent was not an employee: *Thiessen v. Mutual Life Assurance Co. of Canada* (2002), 219 D.L.R. (4th) 98 (B.C.C.A.).

(e) NON-DELEGABLE DUTIES

It often is difficult to distinguish between employees and independent contractors. Nevertheless, as *Sagaz* demonstrates, once that threshold issue has been resolved, the general conclusion is straightforward: vicarious liability may attach to the torts of an employee but not to those of an independent contractor. That is not to say, however, that liability is never imposed on a person who retained a contractor's services. McLachlin J. enumerated the exceptions in *Lewis (Guardian ad litem of) v. British Columbia* (1997), 153 D.L.R. (4th) 594 at 614 (S.C.C.):

> The general rule at common law is that a person who employs an independent contractor will not be liable for loss flowing from the contractor's negligence. This rule for a long time admitted only three exceptions: (1) where the employer was negligent in hiring the contractor; (2) where the employer was negligent in supervising the contractor; and (3) where the employer hired the independent contractor to do something unlawful. A fourth exception crystallized in *Pickard v. Smith* (1861), 10 C.B. (N.S.) 470, 142 E.R. 535. Lord Blackburn stated the rule as: "a person causing something to be done, the doing of which casts on him a duty, cannot escape from the responsibility attaching on him of seeing that duty performed by delegating it to a contractor" (*Dalton v. Angus* (1881), 6 App. Cas. 740 (H.L.) at p. 829). This exception is referred to as the "non-delegable duty" rule.

Perhaps the most important exception to the employer's general immunity is the last one: *non-delegable duty*. A person subject to such an obligation can delegate *performance* but not *responsibility*. In other words, despite being entitled to retain an independent contractor to execute the relevant task, the obligee bears the risk of liability if anything goes tortiously wrong. In *Lewis*, for instance, a public authority was statutorily required to maintain a highway in a certain condition. The public authority was free to assign the actual work to an independent contractor. Nevertheless, when the plaintiff was killed as a result of the independent contractor's negligence, the public authority bore responsibility along with the actual tortfeasor.

The primary difficulty with the concept of a non-delegable duty concerns its scope of application. Historically, the courts merely recognized various instances in which a person could not escape responsibility by delegating a task to an independent contractor. The list included cases involving the rule in *Rylands v. Fletcher*, ultra-hazardous activities, the duty to refrain from creating a nuisance, the duty to provide lateral support for adjacent land, and the duty of a bailee for reward to safeguard goods in his or her possession.

In *Lewis*, the Supreme Court of Canada began the task of extracting a general principal from those discrete circumstances. Cory J. said that:

> . . .a party upon whom the law has imposed a strict statutory duty to do a positive act cannot escape liability simply by delegating the work to an independent contractor. Rather a defendant subject to such a duty will always remain personally liable for the acts or omissions of the contractor to whom it assigned the work.

McLachlin J. continued the analysis in a concurring judgment:

> In essence, a non-delegable duty is a duty not only to take care, but to ensure that care is taken. It is not strict liability, since it requires someone (the independent contractor) to have been negligent. But if it applies, it is no answer for the employer to say, "I was not negligent in hiring or supervising the independent contractor." The employer is liable for the contractor's negligence. The employer already has a personal duty at common law or by statute to take reasonable care. The non-delegable duty doctrine adds another obligation – the duty to ensure that the independent contractor also takes reasonable care.
>
> While the nature of the exception is clear, when it applies is not. Some courts have held that it applies only in certain categories of cases, such as harm done by inherently dangerous objects or activities, harm done in the course of the exercise of statutory powers and duties, or in the United States, harm caused by failure to maintain highways and other public places in a reasonably safe condition. . . . The problem with the category approach is that the existing categories have evolved for reasons that may not be acceptable under modern theories of tort liability. . . . Thus Glanville Williams writes that "the courts have extended, seemingly without any reference to considerations of policy, the liability for independent contractors" ("Liability for Independent Contractors," [1956] Cambridge L.J. 180, at p. 180).
>
> Rather than confirm or add to a hodgepodge of categories, we should seek the underlying principles that justify the imposition of a non-delegable duty on a person who hires an independent contractor to have work done. This is the approach that Cory J. takes. Whether a non-delegable duty arises "will depend upon the nature and the extent of the duty owed by the defendant to the plaintiff". "In some circumstances, the duty to take reasonable care may well be discharged by hiring and, if required, supervising a competent contractor to perform the particular work". There is no categorical rule that common law duties arising from the exercise of a statutory power are never non-delegable. Rather, "[w]hether or not there will be liability for the negligence of the acts of the independent contractor will depend to a large extent upon the statutory provisions involved and the circumstances presented by each case". Cory J. goes on to conclude that in this particular case, the wording of the statute, combined with policy considerations, imposes on the Crown, not only a duty to be careful in hiring or supervising independent contractors, but an additional non-delegable duty to ensure that the work of its contractors is done without negligence.
>
> I agree with this analysis. I am not so sure as my colleague that s. 48 of the Ministry of Transportation and Highways Act, R.S.B.C. 1979, c. 280, which provides that the Ministry "shall direct the construction, maintenance and repair" of all highways, demonstrates clearly that the Ministry must "personally direct" and supervise these works in all their aspects. It seems to me that those words are also consistent with a basic direction that works be undertaken. Yet I am satisfied in this case that the circumstances, taken together with the statutory provisions, suffice to establish a non-delegable duty of care on the Ministry with respect to highway maintenance. To determine whether a non-delegable duty should be imposed, the Court should examine the relationship between the parties and ask whether that relationship possesses elements that make it appropriate

to hold the defendant liable for the negligence of its independent contractor. In the case at bar, the fact that road maintenance is entirely within the power of the Ministry is an important element to consider. So is the correlative fact that this renders the public, who often have no choice but to use the highway, totally vulnerable as to how, and by whom, road maintenance is performed. Finally, the fact that safety and lives are at issue is of critical importance. Cory J. correctly stresses these factors in concluding that the Ministry cannot discharge its duty in this case merely by proving that it exercised reasonable care in hiring and supervising the contractor. The Ministry must go further and ensure that the contractor's work was carried out without negligence.

NOTES AND QUESTIONS

1. Is the rule governing non-delegable duties an instance of vicarious liability? Fleming, *The Law of Torts*, 9th ed. (1998) at 437 draws a distinction:

> [A] non-delegable duty includes responsibility not only for the delegate's failure to perform the duty (for example to carry out a repair), but also negligence in the course of performing it (for example injuring a bystander). But it does not extend to "casual" or "collateral" acts of negligence. This limitation provides the most important distinction between a principal's liability for the acts of an independent contractor and the genuinely vicarious liability of a "master" because the latter is accountable for any wrongdoing of his servant, however incidental to the main job, so long as it falls within the course of employment. Suppose a contractor is instructed to carry out a dangerous work on the highway and negligently knocks down a pedestrian while bringing up machinery for the job; his employer would not be liable, because the negligence is collateral to the work itself. In the same circumstances, though, a master would clearly have to pay.

2. The Supreme Court of Canada's reasons in *Lewis* were applied in the companion case of *Mochinski v. Trendline Industries Ltd.* (1997), 154 D.L.R. (4th) 212 (S.C.C.). For other discussions of non-delegable duties, see *Kitchener (City of) v. Robe & Clothing Co.*, [1925] S.C.R. 106; *St. John (City) v. Donald*, [1926] S.C.R. 371; *Darling v. Attorney-General*, [1950] 2 All E.R. 793 (H.L.); *Hole v. Sittingbourne & Sheerness Railway Co.* (1861), 158 E.R. 201 (Ch.); *Kondis v. State Transport Authority* (1984), 154 C.L.R. 672 (H.C.A.); *Burnie Port Authority v. General Jones Pty. Ltd.* (1994) 179 C.L.R. 520 (H.C.A.); and *New South Wales v. Lepore* (2003), 77 A.L.J.R. 558 (H.C.A.).

3. Many commentators initially interpreted *Lewis* as indicating that the Supreme Court of Canada intended to adopt a broad conception of non-delegable duty and thereby substantially increase the incidence of liability. Subsequent decisions, however, have taken a more restricted view of the doctrine. See Rafferty, "Developments in Contract and Tort Law: The 2003-2004 Term" (2004) 26 S.C.L.R. (2d) 147.

The opportunity for reconsideration arose in connection with many of the cases previously discussed under the rubric of vicarious liability: *B.(K.L.) v. British Columbia*, [2003] 2 S.C.R. 403; *G.(E.D.) v. Hammer*, [2003] 2 S.C.R. 459; and *Blackwater v. Plint*, [2005] 3 S.C.R. 3. In each instance, the plaintiff, who had been sexually assaulted while living in a foster home or a residential school, claimed that the government had breached a non-delegable duty to protect the children. On that theory, the government was entitled to delegate the actual operation of the facilities to other parties, but it remained responsible for any harm that occurred. The court consistently rejected that theory. For instance, in *Blackwater* (at 290) McLachlin C.J.C. examined the *Indian Act*, S.C. 1951, c. 29, and found "that none of 'the general duties gives school boards full responsibility for students' welfare while on school premises, in the way that the statutes in Lewis gave the Ministry full responsibility for overseeing maintenance projects and for ensuring that workers exercised reasonable care.'" Likewise, in *B.(K.L.)* (at 426-27) she found that the *Protection of Children Act*, R.S.B.C. 1960, c. 303:

> offers no basis for imposing on the Superintendent a non-delegable duty to ensure that no harm comes to children through the abuse or negligence of foster parents. Foster parents provide day-to-day care for the children. But the Act does not suggest that the Superintendent is responsible for directing this day-to-day care and for ensuring that no harm comes to the children in the course of this care. . . . Although the Act makes the Superintendent solely responsible for the well-being of a child before placement, it does not suggest that this is work for which the Superintendent retains responsibility after placement. Indeed, if the Superintendent were responsible for all of the wrongs that might befall children in foster care, there would be no need to set out his particular duties with respect to placement and supervision.

4. For a recent discussion of the topic see Stevens, "Non-Delegable Duties and Vicarious Liability" and Murphy, "Juridical Foundations of Common Law Non-Delegable Duties" in Neyers, Chamberlain & Pitel, eds., *Emerging Issues in Tort Law* (2007), chs. 13 and 14.

26

BUSINESS TORTS

1. Introduction
2. Deceit (Fraud)
3. Passing Off
4. Intimidation
5. Conspiracy
6. Interference with Contractual Relations
7. Intentional Interference With Economic Relations by Unlawful Means

1. Introduction

Tort law plays a significant role in the business world. We already have seen several illustrations. The issues of negligent misrepresentation (Chapter 13) and pure economic loss (Chapter 14) frequently arise in commercial contexts. In some circumstances, business people should be particularly attentive to the rules governing occupiers' liability (Chapter 23) and nuisance (Chapter 24). A store that detains a suspected shoplifter should be concerned about false imprisonment, and a tavern that employs a bouncer should be concerned about battery (Chapter 3). And, of course, the doctrine of vicarious liability (Chapter 25) was designed to extend the scope of liability from an employee to a employer.

In this chapter, we turn our attention to so-called "business torts." Obviously, there is no discrete tort of that name and, as an organizing concept, the phrase is somewhat open-ended. We use the rubric to focus on six torts: (1) deceit (fraud), (2) passing off, (3) intimidation, (4) conspiracy, (5) interference with contractual relations, and (6) the innominate action for intentional interference with economic interests by unlawful means. Several related torts, such as injurious falsehood and misappropriation of personality, will be introduced by the accompanying notes.

Before beginning, however, it is important to set the scene by briefly considering tort law's default position. The Canadian economy is based on capitalism, which is in turn based on vigorous, even ruthless, competition. Success in the business world often depends upon an ability to strike a good bargain for oneself – and, by extension, a bad bargain for the other side; upon an ability to hire the most skilful workers – and, by extension, an ability to lure those people away from competitors; and so on. Indeed, the best way to deal with a rival sometimes is to simply get rid of it. Within fairly broad parameters, our legal system condones that strategy.

The common law initially was more protectionist. *Keeble v. Hickeringill* (1707), 103 E.R. 1127 stood for the proposition that "he that hinders another in his trade or livelihood is liable to an action for so hindering him." During the 19th century, however, *laissez-faire* philosophies took hold and the courts began to espouse a much different line. *Allen v. Flood* (1897), [1898] A.C. 1 (H.L.) is the seminal decision. A ship, the *Sam Waller*, was under repair. Woodwork was being done by the plaintiffs, who belonged to a small union. Ironwork was being done by members of a much larger union, which was represented by the defendant. The two unions were not on good terms. The defendant told the company overseeing the repairs that unless the plaintiffs were dismissed, the ironworkers would not perform. The threat was effective and the plaintiffs were replaced with other woodworkers. The House of Lords held that this conduct did not constitute intimidation, conspiracy, or interference with contractual relations, the last of which was precluded by the fact that the plaintiffs had been hired on a day-to-day basis. The court also held that the defendant's malicious motive, in itself, did not render his conduct tortious. As long as he did not achieve his goal by otherwise unlawful means, the defendant was free to deliberately drive the plaintiffs out of business. In the dog-eat-dog world of commerce, the law favours the survival of the fittest.

The remainder of this chapter should be read against the backdrop of *Allen v. Flood.* Although modern Canadian courts and legislatures are more willing to regulate the marketplace, they also remain attentive to the need for healthy competition. Not surprisingly, it is often difficult to strike an appropriate balance.

2. Deceit (Fraud)

Deceit (or fraud) is a very serious matter, especially in a commercial context. While success in the business world depends largely on facts and choices, deceit consists of misinformation that skews the decision-making process. The courts consequently are keen to sanction and deter it. At the same time, however, they appreciate the debilitating stigma that may attach to a finding of deceit. To say that a person has committed fraud is, in the common law, to call that person a liar. And few people are willing to deal with a business person who has a reputation for dishonesty. (In equity, in contrast, the term "fraud" may refer to actual deceit, but it also may refer, in a very broad and misleading way, to any failure to act as required.) The following case illustrates the tension created by the need to both (1) protect the plaintiff from fraud, and (2) protect the defendant from unfair stigma.

DERRY v. PEEK
(1889), 14 A.C. 337 (H.L.)

[A company intended to operate a tramway line. The defendants, who were the directors of that company, issued a prospectus stating that they had "the right to use steam or mechanical power instead of horses." If that statement was true, the venture would have much greater prospects for profitability. In fact, while the defendants honestly believed that government approval of steam or mechanical power was a mere formality, the Board of Trade held a very real discretion. The Board eventually exercised that discretion against the defendants. The plaintiff, who had purchased company shares on the strength of the prospectus, sued the defendants for deceit in an effort to recover his lost investment.]

LORD HERSCHELL: . . .

"This action is one which is commonly called an action of deceit, a mere common law action." This is the description of it given by Cotton L.J. in delivering judgment. I think it important that it should be borne in mind that such an action differs essentially from one brought to obtain rescission of a contract on the ground of misrepresentation of a material fact. The principles which govern the two actions differ widely. Where rescission is claimed it is only necessary to prove that there was misrepresentation; then, however honestly it may have been made, however free from blame the person who made it, the contract, having been obtained by misrepresentation, cannot stand. In an action of deceit, on the contrary, it is not enough to establish misrepresentation alone; it is conceded on all hands that something more must be proved to cast liability upon the defendant, though it has been a matter of controversy what additional elements are requisite. I lay stress upon this because observations made by learned judges in actions for rescission have been cited and much relied upon at the bar by counsel for the respondent. Care must obviously be observed in applying the language used in relation to such actions to an action of deceit. Even if the scope of the language used extends beyond the particular action which was being dealt with, it must be remembered that the learned judges were not engaged in determining what is necessary to support an action of deceit, or in discriminating with nicety the elements which enter into it.

There is another class of actions which I must refer to also for the purpose of putting it aside. I mean those cases where a person within whose special province it lay to know a particular fact, has given an erroneous answer to an inquiry made with regard to it by a person desirous of ascertaining the fact for the purpose of determining his course accordingly, and has been held bound to make good the assurance he has given. *Burrowes v. Lock* [10 Ves. 470] may be cited as an example, where a trustee had been asked by an intended lender, upon the security of a trust fund, whether notice of any prior incumbrance upon the fund had been given to him. In cases like this it has been said that the circumstance that the answer was honestly made in the belief that it was true affords no defence to the action. Lord Selborne pointed out in *Brownlie v. Campbell* [5 App. Cas. 935] that these cases were in an altogether different category from actions to recover damages for false representation, such as we are now dealing with.

One other observation I have to make before proceeding to consider the law which has been laid down by the learned judges in the Court of Appeal in the case before your Lordships.

> An action of deceit is a common law action, and must be decided on the same principles, whether it be brought in the Chancery Division or any of the Common Law Divisions, there being, in my opinion, no such thing as an equitable action for deceit.

This was the language of Cotton L.J. in *Arkwright v. Newbould* [17 Ch. D. 320]. It was adopted by Lord Blackburn in *Smith v. Chadwick* [9 App. Cas. 193], and is not, I think, open to dispute.

In the Court below Cotton L.J. said:

> What in my opinion is a correct statement of the law is this, that where a man makes a statement to be acted upon by others which is false, and which is known by him to be false, or is made by him recklessly, or without care whether it is true or false, that is, without any reasonable ground for believing it to be true, he is liable in an action of deceit at the suit of anyone to whom it was addressed or anyone of the class to whom it was addressed and who was materially induced by the misstatement to do an act to his prejudice.

About much that is here stated there cannot, I think, be two opinions. But when the learned Lord Justice speaks of a statement made recklessly or without care whether it is true or false, *that is* without any reasonable ground for believing it to be true, I find myself, with all respect, unable to agree that these are convertible expressions. To make a statement careless whether it be true or false, and therefore without any real belief in its truth, appears to me to be an essentially different thing from making, through want of care, a false statement, which is nevertheless honestly believed to be true. And it is surely conceivable that a man may believe that what he states is the fact, though he has been so wanting in care that the Court may think that there were no sufficient grounds to warrant his belief. I shall have to consider hereafter whether the want of reasonable ground for believing the statement made is sufficient to support an action of deceit. I am only concerned for the moment to point out that it does not follow that it is so, because there is authority for saying that a statement made recklessly, without caring whether it be true or false, affords sufficient foundation for such an action.

. . .

Having now drawn attention, I believe, to all the cases having a material bearing upon the question under consideration, I proceed to state briefly the conclusions to which I have been led. I think the authorities establish the following propositions: First, in order to sustain an action of deceit, there must be proof of fraud, and nothing short of that will suffice. Secondly, fraud is proved when it is shewn that a false representation has been made (1) knowingly, or (2) without belief in its truth, or (3) recklessly, careless whether it be true or false. Although I have treated the second and third as distinct cases, I think the third is but an instance of the second, for one who makes a statement under such circumstances can have no real belief in the truth of what he states. To prevent a false statement being fraudulent, there must, I think, always be an honest belief in its truth. And this probably covers the whole ground, for one who knowingly alleges that which is false, has obviously no such honest belief. Thirdly, if fraud be proved, the motive of the person guilty of it is immaterial. It matters not that there was no intention to cheat or injure the person to whom the statement was made.

. . .

In my opinion making a false statement through want of care falls far short of, and is a very different thing from, fraud, and the same may be said of a false representation honestly believed though on insufficient grounds. Indeed Cotton L.J. himself indicated, in the words I have already quoted, that he should not call it fraud. But the whole current of authorities, with which I have so long detained your Lordships, shews to my mind conclusively that fraud is essential to found an action of deceit, and that it cannot be maintained where the acts proved cannot properly be so termed.

. . .

[Lord Herschell concluded that the plaintiff had failed to establish deceit. Lords Watson, Halsbury, Bramwell, and Fitzgerald delivered separate concurring judgments.]

NOTES AND QUESTIONS

1. Flowing from *Derry v. Peek*, the tort of deceit often is said to contain four elements: (1) the defendant must have made a *false statement*, (2) the defendant must have *known* that the statement was false, (3) the defendant must have made the statement with the *intention of misleading* the plaintiff, and (4) the plaintiff must have suffered a

loss as a result of *reasonably relying* on the statement. The next four notes address those elements. See also Perell, "The Fraud Elements of Deceit and Fraudulent Misrepresentation" (1996) 18 Adv. Q. 23; Hoyano, "Lies, Recklessness and Deception: Disentangling Dishonesty in Civil Fraud" (1996) 75 Can. Bar. Rev. 474; and Fridman, *The Law of Torts*, 2d ed. (2002) at 745-55.

2. The idea of a *false statement* usually is straightforward. In most successful cases, the defendant says or writes something that is positively untrue. That statement is a lie. Occasionally, however, the analysis is more complicated.

First, although the defendant's statement is usually spoken or written, liability may also be imposed on the basis of misleading actions: see *Abel v. McDonald* (1964), 45 D.L.R. (2d) 198 (Ont. C.A.).

Second, although the actionable statement usually consists of a simple lie, liability exceptionally may be imposed in other situations. The defendant may be held responsible for a *half-truth*. For instance, while selling a business, the defendant may present revenue figures so as to suggest that they refer to net profits, rather than gross profits. Liability also may be imposed for a *failure to update information*. For instance, the defendant might refrain from correcting a statement that, while true when stated, has to the defendant's knowledge become untrue.

Third, although mere silence otherwise is not actionable, there are situations in which the law places an obligation on a person to speak up. This is true, for instance, if a person selling a house knows of a hidden defect that renders the premises dangerous or unfit for habitation. It is also true if a fiduciary relationship exists between the parties. See Fleming, *The Law of Torts*, 9th ed. (1998) at 695-97 for a list of exceptions to the general rule. See also *Sorensen v. Kaye Holdings Ltd.*, [1979] 6 W.W.R. 193 (B.C.C.A.); *C.R.F. Holdings Ltd. v. Fundy Chemical Int. Ltd.* (1981), 19 C.C.L.T. 263 (B.C.C.A.); *Francis v. Dingman* (1983), 43 O.R. (2d) 641 (C.A.); *Canson Enterprises Ltd. v. Boughton & Co.* (1991), 85 D.L.R. (4th) 129 (S.C.C.); and *Freeman v. Perlman* (1999), 169 D.L.R. (4th) 133 (B.C.C.A.).

An issue may arise as to whether a false statement was that of the defendant. In *Derry v. Peek*, for instance, the plaintiff was misled by statements made by a company's directors. In such circumstances, who is the proper defendant: the directors or the company? The question is interesting because company law is based on the fundamental principle that the corporation is a separate entity, even though it acts through human agents (such as its directors). Nevertheless, the House of Lords recently affirmed that, notwithstanding the general rule of corporations, "No one can escape liability for his fraud by saying 'I wish to make it clear that I am committing this fraud on behalf of someone else and I am not to be personally liable'": *Standard Chartered Bank v. Pakistan National Shipping Corp. (Nos. 2 and 4)*, [2003] 1 A.C. 959 at 968 (H.L.). *Cf. Sealand of the Pacific v. Robert C. McHaffie Ltd.* (1974), 51 D.L.R. (3d) 702 (B.C.C.A.) (liability imposed on company, but not human agent, under claim for *negligent* misstatement).

Personal liability was imposed in *1318777 Ontario Ltd. v. 1004847 Ontario Inc.*, 2006 CarswellOnt 2922 (S.C.J.) (WLeC). The plaintiff purchased goods and leased property from a company called "100." Before doing so, it received an affidavit from Karp, the controlling and directing mind of 100, swearing to the fact that that company had no unsecured creditors and only one secured creditor. In fact, Karp had no reason to believe that that information was correct. Some time later, the situation deteriorated and the plaintiff received a judgment against 100 for $30,540. Unfortunately, because of 100's other debt, it was unable to pay the plaintiff. The plaintiff then successfully sued Karp on the basis of his fraudulent affidavit.

3. The plaintiff must prove that the defendant *knew* that the relevant statement was false when it was made. Actual dishonesty normally is required. As explained in *Derry v. Peek*, however, liability may be imposed if the defendant was reckless to the truth or falsity of a statement, and therefore had no belief in its accuracy.

4. The defendant must have *intended to deceive* the plaintiff, or have been substantially certain that the statement would deceive the plaintiff.

5. The plaintiff must have suffered a loss as a result of *reasonably relying* upon the defendant's statement. The idea of a loss simply demonstrates that deceit is not actionable *per se*. Significantly, however, once the plaintiff has established that the false statement was made with an intention to deceive, the defendant bears the burden of proving that the plaintiff did not actually rely upon it: *Sidhu Estate v. Bains* (1996), 25 B.C.L.R. (3d) 41 (C.A.); but *cf. Smith v. Chadwick* (1884), 9 App. Cas. 187 (H.L.).

One of the more difficult aspects of the tort of deceit is the requirement of *reasonable reliance*. Reasonable people refrain from relying on certain types of statements. Because they know that sales people tend to exaggerate, reasonable people do not place stock in empty *puffery*. Because they know that the future is uncertain and unknowable, reasonable people not rely on *predictions*. And because they know that values and perceptions vary, reasonable people are not swayed by personal *opinions*.

For the most part, then, the reasonable person relies only on statements of *past* or *present facts*. Significantly, however, such a statement may be *implied* by a puff, a prediction, or an opinion. Suppose, for instance, that a sales person assures a buyer that a particular vehicle will pass a government roadworthiness test. On its face, the statement is a prediction of the government's future conduct. Underlying it, however, may be an implicit statement regarding the car's *present* mechanical condition.

A reasonable person does not rely upon a statement for which the speaker has *disavowed responsibility*. In *Antorisa Investments Ltd. v. 172965 Canada Ltd.* (2006), 20 B.L.R. (4th) 211 (Ont. S.C.J.), the defendant sold a gas station "as is" to the plaintiff. The sale contract excluded liability for the condition of the property and for pre-contractual statements. Several years after the sale, the plaintiff discovered that the property was contaminated. He then sued the defendant for deceit. Liability was denied on several grounds, including the fact that the claimant, a sophisticated businessman, had not relied on the defendant's purportedly fraudulent statements.

6. Although most deceit actions involve pure economic loss, the action also provides redress for physical harm. In *Graham v. Saville*, [1945] 2 D.L.R. 489 (Ont. C.A.), a married man induced an unmarried woman to believe that he was single and that they had undergone a valid marriage ceremony. That was not true. The woman subsequently gave birth to a child and sued in battery and deceit. The court found for the plaintiff in deceit and awarded her $4,000, which included compensation for the "physical injury, pain, and suffering in consequence of her pregnancy and the birth of a child." See also *Beaulne v. Ricketts* (1979), 96 D.L.R. (3d) 550 (Alta. S.C.).

Likewise, while most deceit actions arise in commercial contexts, the same rules extend to social and family settings. In *Raju v. Kumar* (2006), 265 D.L.R. (4th) 632 (B.C.S.C.), the defendant duped the plaintiff into marrying him. His real goals were (1) to have her pay for his immigration to Canada from Fiji, and (2) to use his marriage status as a basis for legally remaining in this country. In addition to damages for the expenses that the plaintiff incurred in connection with the immigration process and the wedding, the court awarded $10,000 in general damages to reflect the plaintiff's humiliation and lost marriage prospects. Do you agree that the tort of deceit is an appropriate method for resolving such disputes?

The High Court of Australia addressed a different set of familial issues in *Magill v. Magill*, [2006] HCA 51. The defendant had three children while she was married to the plaintiff. The parties divorced and the plaintiff paid child support for several years. He then discovered that two of the children had been fathered by another man. The plaintiff sought damages for various expenses (*e.g.* psychiatric counselling) that he incurred upon learning the shocking truth. The action was based on the allegation that, in having the plaintiff sign the two birth certificates, the defendant falsely misrepresented that he was the father and she thereby committed the tort of deceit. The court unanimously dismissed the action. First, it found that, while the plaintiff had acted on the assumption that he was the children's father, he had not relied upon the birth certificates specifically. Second, and much more significantly, a majority of the court held that the tort of deceit was inappropriate on the facts. The individual judges, however, differed on their reasons for that conclusion. Gummow, Kirby and Crennan JJ. said that "conduct which constitutes a breach of promise of sexual fidelity and any consequential false representation about paternity, occurring within a continuing sexual relationship, which is personal, private and intimate, cannot be justly or appropriately assessed by reference to bargaining transactions, with which the tort of deceit is typically associated." In sharp contrast, Heydon J. held that while the claim failed on the facts, there was no reason to exclude the tort from family matters. Gleeson C.J. and Hayne J. fell somewhere between those two extremes. What arguments can be offered for and against the application of the tort of deceit in intimate settings? See also *S.(F.) v. H.(C.)* (1994), 120 D.L.R. (4th) 432 (Ont. Gen. Div.), aff'd (1994), 133 D.L.R. (4th) 767 (Ont. C.A.) (no duty to disclose; silence not a representation; action was against public policy); *Fleming v. Fleming* (2001), 19 R.F.L. (5th) 274 (Ont. S.C.J.) (no duty to disclose); and *D.(D.R.) v. G.(S.E.)* (2001), 14 R.F.L. (5th) 279 (Ont. S.C.J.) (no duty to disclose; man liable to support child to whom he acted as parent).

7. Damages in tort law normally are calculated to provide compensation for the plaintiff's losses. Exceptionally, however, the plaintiff may elect instead to receive disgorgement of the benefits that the defendant received as a result of the tort. See *Amertek Inc. v. Canadian Commercial Inc.* (2003), 229 D.L.R. (4th) 419 (Ont. S.C.J.), rev'd on other grounds (2005), 76 O.R. (3d) 241 (C.A.); *Evans v. MacMicking* (1909), 2 Alta L.R. 5 (S.C.); *Lang v. Giraudo*, 40 N.E.2d 707 (Mass. S.C. 1942); and *Janigan v. Taylor*, 344 F.2d 781 (1st Cir. C.A. 1965). English courts, however, have questioned the availability of purely gain-based relief: *Halifax Building Society v. Thomas*, [1996] Ch. 217 (C.A.); *Smith New Court Ltd. v. Scrimgeour Vickers*, [1997] A.C. 254 (H.L.); but *cf. Kettlewell v. Refuge Assurance Co.*, [1908] 1 K.B. 545 (C.A.). Suggest a situation in which it would be preferable to receive disgorgement rather than compensation.

8. Property (including money) that is acquired by theft or fraud may be impressed with a constructive trust while it remains in the possession of the guilty party or anyone who received the property from the guilty party. An exception exists only once the property is acquired by a *bona fide* purchaser for value. Even in that situation, however, the constructive trust may shift onto the traceable proceeds of the original property, as long as those proceeds are not held by a *bona fide* purchaser. For a discussion of the causes of action and remedies that may arise in such situations, see *iTrade Finance Holdings Inc. v. Webworx Inc.*, 2006 CarswellOnt 5939 (S.C.J.) (WLeC).

9. In addition to compensation, a successful plaintiff in a case of fraud may also receive punitive damages. As the Supreme Court of Canada stressed in *Performance Industries Ltd. v. Sylvan Lake Golf & Tennis Club Ltd.*, [2002] 1 S.C.R. 678 at 711, fraud invariably entails "a type of misconduct that to some extent 'offends the court's sense of decency' and which 'represents a marked departure from ordinary standards of decent behaviour,' yet not all fraud cases lead to an award of punitive damages." Consistent with the governing rules, punitive damages are "rational," and hence available, "'if, but only if' compensatory damages do not adequately achieve the objectives of retribution, deterrence and denunciation."

10. For general discussion of damages in deceit, see *West Coast Finance Ltd. v. Gunderson, Stokes, Walton & Co.* (1974), 44 D.L.R. (3d) 232 (B.C.S.C.), rev'd (1975), 56 D.L.R. (3d) 460 (B.C.C.A.); *Siametis v. Trojan Horse (Burlington) Inc.* (1979), 25 O.R. (2d) 120 (H.C.); *C.R.F. Holdings Ltd. v. Fundy Chemical Int. Ltd.* (1981), 33 B.C.L.R. 291 (C.A.); *Bitton v. Jakovljevic* (1990), 75 O.R. (2d) 143 (H.C.); and Fridman, *The Law of Torts in Canada*, 2d ed. (2002) at 755-58. For a discussion of the circumstances in which the plaintiff is entitled to both rescission of a contract and damages in deceit, see *Burrows v. Burke* (1982), 36 O.R. (2d) 737 (H.C.); and *Archer v. Brown*, [1984] 2 All E.R. 267 (Q.B.).

11. Deceit appears to have emerged centuries ago as an independent tort, later becoming associated with contractual warranties. See generally Waddams, *Products Liability*, 4th ed. (2001) at 1-11. This connection was severed by *Pasley v. Freeman* (1789), 100 E.R. 450 (K.B.), which held that the tort remedy in deceit lay against only a party who intentionally induced another to act to his or her detriment upon a knowingly false statement.

Deceit remained the major cause of action for recovery of pure economic losses caused by misrepresentations until *Hedley Byrne & Co. v. Heller & Partners Ltd.*, [1964] A.C. 465 (H.L.) created a broad right of recovery within the law of negligence. Furthermore, recent developments in contract law have made it easier to establish that a misrepresentation is part of a contract. See Swan, *Canadian Contract Law* (2006) at 550-61; and Waddams, *The Law of Contracts*, 5th ed. (2005), ch. 13.

12. For a discussion of the elements of deceit and how it differs from mere "sharp" or "hardball" business practices, see *Harland v. Fancsati* (1993), 13 O.R. (3d) 103 (Gen. Div), aff'd (1994), 21 O.R. (3d) 798 (Div. Ct.).

13. As suggested by the high threshold for liability, the issue of fraud is taken very seriously. Another indicia of the legal system's attitude is seen in the fact that an allegation

of fraud must be specifically pleaded and proven and that a failure to sustain such an allegation may result in having to pay costs to the other side. Likewise, a discharge from bankruptcy does not release the bankrupt from "any debt or liability for obtaining property by . . . fraudulent misrepresentation": *Bankruptcy Act*, R.S.C. 1985, c. B-3, s. 178(1).

14. The tort of deceit is not vulnerable to the defence of contributory negligence: *Standard Chartered Bank v. Pakistan National Shipping Corp. (Nos. 2 and 4)*, [2003] 1 A.C. 959 (H.L.). It therefore is irrelevant that, for instance, the plaintiff carelessly failed to verify the information received from the defendant. What is the explanation for denying the defence in such circumstances?

3. Passing Off

Reputations, good and bad, play a crucial role in the business world. Consumers favour goods or services that are known (or thought) to be of a high quality, reliable, fashionable, or otherwise desirable. At the same time, they avoid inferior products, at least unless there is a reduction in price. Likewise, personal images can both enhance and diminish sales. Professional athletes may not know a great deal about soft drinks, but their mere association with a company may attract customers.

Reputations are hard won and easily lost. They often are also easily manipulated. An unscrupulous business may take advantage of that fact. It may usurp a competitor's goodwill or exploit a celebrity's image without permission. It may sully a competitor's name or denigrate its products. Tort law responds to each of those wrongs. The extract that appears below is concerned with the tort of *passing off*. The notes that follow introduce the torts of *misappropriation of personality*, *defamation*, and *injurious falsehood*.

CIBA-GEIGY CANADA LTD. v. APOTEX INC.

(1992), 95 D.L.R. (4th) 385 (S.C.C.)

[Ciba-Geigy, a pharmaceutical company, sold a drug called "metroprolol" under licence. In 1984, Apotex legally began to manufacture and sell the same drug, but in tablets of different size, shape, and colour. In 1986, Apotex changed its marketing strategy and started to market the metroprolol drug in tablets that were virtually identical to the plaintiff's. Ciba-Geigy brought a passing off action against Apotex and another corporate defendant. The lower courts rejected the claim on the basis that the plaintiff had not shown that physicians or pharmacists would be confused by the defendants' actions. The plaintiff appealed to the Supreme Court of Canada.]

GONTHIER J.: . . .

A. *Passing-off action*

(1) *General principles developed by the courts*

The concept of passing-off was developed in 1842 in *Perry v. Truefitt* (1842), 6 Beav. 66, 49 E.R. 749, which seems to have been the first case in which the expression "passing-off" appeared: "A man is not to sell his own goods under the pretence that they are the goods of another man". In *Singer Manufacturing Co. v. Loog* (1880), 18 Ch. D.

395 (C.A.) at pp. 412-13; affirmed 8 App. Cas. 15 (H.L.), James L.J. described passing-off and its origins:

> . . . no man is entitled to represent his goods as being the goods of another man; and no man is permitted to use any mark, sign or symbol, device or other means, whereby, without making a direct false misrepresentation himself to a purchaser who purchases from him, he enables such purchaser to tell a lie or to make a false representation to somebody else who is the ultimate customer . . . he must not, as I said, make directly, or through the medium of another person, a false representation that his goods are the goods of another person.

The House of Lords has set out the requirements for a passing-off action on many occasions. In *Erven Warnink B.V. v. J. Townend & Sons (Hull) Ltd.*, [1980] R.P.C. 31, Lord Diplock identified five conditions. . .: there must be (1) misrepresentation (2) by a trader in the course of trade (3) to prospective customers of his or ultimate customers of goods or services supplied by him, (4) which is calculated to injure the business or goodwill of another trader, and (5) which causes actual damage to the business or goodwill of the trader bringing the action.

More recently, in *Reckitt & Colman Products Ltd. v. Borden Inc.*, [1990] 1 All E.R. 873 (H.L.), Lord Oliver reaffirmed, at p. 880:

> The law of passing off can be summarised in one short general proposition, no man may pass off his goods as those of another. More specifically, it may be expressed in terms of the elements which the plaintiff in such an action has to prove in order to succeed. These are three in number. First, he must establish *a goodwill or reputation attached to the goods or services which he supplies* in the mind of the purchasing public *by association with the identifying "get-up"* (whether it consists simply of a brand name or a trade description, or the individual features of labelling or packaging) under which his particular goods or services are offered to the public, such that the get-up is recognised by the public as distinctive specifically of the plaintiff's goods or services. Second, he must demonstrate *a misrepresentation* by the defendant to the public (whether or not intentional) leading or likely to lead the public to believe that goods or services offered by him are the goods or services of the plaintiff . . . Third, he must demonstrate that he suffers or, in a quia timet action, that he is likely to suffer *damage* by reason of the erroneous belief engendered by the defendant's misrepresentation that the source of the defendant's goods or services is the same as the source of those offered by the plaintiff. (Emphasis added.)

The three necessary components of a passing-off action are thus: the existence of goodwill, deception of the public due to a misrepresentation and actual or potential damage to the plaintiff. . . .

In *Consumers Distributing Co. v. Seiko Time Canada Ltd.* (1984), 10 D.L.R. (4th) 161 at p. 175, this court noted that the requirements of a passing-off action have evolved somewhat in the last 100 years:

> . . . attention should be drawn to the fact that the passing off rule is founded upon the tort of deceit, and while the original requirement of an intent to deceive died out in the mid-1800s there remains the requirement, at the very least, that confusion in the minds of the public be a likely consequence by reason of the sale, or proffering for sale, by the defendant of a product not that of the plaintiff's making, under the guise or implication that it was the plaintiff's product or the equivalent.

A manufacturer must therefore avoid creating confusion in the public mind, whether deliberately or not, by a get-up identical to that of a product which has acquired a secondary meaning by reason of its get-up.

. . .

(2) *Purposes of the passing-off action and target clientele*

In considering those upstream and downstream of the product, two separate aspects must be distinguished. I refer in this regard to the persons who manufacture or market the products, on the one hand ("the manufacturers"), and on the other to those for whom the products are intended, the persons who buy, use or consume them ("the customers").

It is clear that however one looks at the passing-off action, its purpose is to protect all persons affected by the product.

(a) *Protection of manufacturers*

This corresponds to the third point mentioned by Lord Oliver. The right to be protected against the "pirating" of a brand, trade name or the appearance of a product is linked to a kind of "ownership" which the manufacturer has acquired in that name, brand and appearance by using them.

In *Pinard v. Coderre* [1954] 3 D.L.R. 463 at p. 468, Marchand J.A. of the Quebec Court of Appeal noted (translation): "It would seem that the first occupant of this name or these words acquired a right to use them exclusive of all other persons, comparable in many ways to *a true right of ownership*" (emphasis added).

Accordingly, to begin with, from what might be called the individual or manufacturer's standpoint, the passing-off action is intended to protect a form of ownership.

There is also the concept of ownership, protected by the passing-off action in relation to goodwill, a term which must be understood in a very broad sense, taking in not only people who are customers but also the reputation and drawing power of a given business in its market. In *Consumers Distributing Co. v. Seiko Time Canada Ltd., supra*, Estey J., at p. 13 C.P.R., p. 173 D.L.R., cites *Salmond on the Law of Torts*, by R.F.V. Heuston, 17th ed. (London: Sweet & Maxwell, 1977), at pp. 403-4:

> "The courts have wavered between two conceptions of a passing-off action – as a remedy for the invasion of a quasi-proprietary right in a trade name or trade mark, and as a remedy, analogous to the action on the case for deceit, for invasion of the personal right not to be injured by fraudulent competition. The true basis of the action is that *the passing off injures the right of property in the plaintiff*, that right of property being his right to the goodwill of his business.
>
> . . .
>
> "Indeed, it seems that the essence of the tort lies in the misrepresentation that the goods in question are those of another . . .". (Emphasis added.)

It will then be necessary to look at the relationship between the various merchants or manufacturers, and it is at that point that questions of competition have to be considered. As Chenevard says (*Traité de la concurrence déloyale en matière industrielle et commerciale*, vol. 1 (Paris: L.G.D.J., 1914), at pp. 6-7) (translation) "[c]ompetition is the soul of commerce; it requires unceasing effort and as such is the chief factor in economic progress". Drysdale and Silverleaf, *Passing Off: Law and Practice* (London: Butterworths, 1986), are substantially of the same opinion, at p. 1:

> In countries with a free market system the proper functioning of the economy depends upon competition between rival trading enterprises. It is the mechanism of competition which controls the price, quality and availability of goods and services to the public.

. . .

The purpose of the passing-off action is thus also to prevent unfair competition. One does not have to be a fanatical moralist to understand how appropriating another person's work, as that is certainly what is involved, is a breach of good faith.

Finally, another more apparent, more palpable aspect, a consequence of the preceding one, must also be mentioned. The "pirated" manufacturer is very likely to experience a reduction in sales volume and therefore in his turnover because of the breaking up of his market. When such a situation occurs in the ordinary course of business between rival manufacturers, that is what one might call one of the rules of the game, but when the rivalry involves the use of dishonest practices, the law must intervene.

(b) *Protection of customers*

In the Anglo-Saxon legal systems (translation), "the person chiefly concerned is the competitor affected by the unfair act": Louis Mermillod, *Essai sur la notion de concurrence déloyale en France et aux États-Unis* (Paris: Pichon & Durand-Auzias, 1954), at p. 176. He is frequently in fact the first party affected by the practice or aware of it.

However, "[i]t should never be overlooked that . . . unfair competition cases are affected with a public interest. A dealer's good will is protected, not merely for his profit, but in order that the purchasing public may not be enticed into buying A.'s product when it wants B.'s product": *General Baking Co. v. Gorman*, 3 F. 2d 891 (1st Cir., 1925). Accordingly (translation), "the power of the court in such cases is exercised, not only to do individual justice, but to safeguard the interests of the public": *Scandinavia Belting Co. v. Asbestos & Rubber Works of America, Inc.*, 257 F. 937 (2d Cir., 1919) at p. 941. The ordinary customer, the consumer, is at the heart of the matter here. According to the civilian lawyer Chenevard, *op. cit.*, at p. 20, in a case of unfair competition it is (translation) "the buyer who is the first to be injured".

The customer expects to receive a given product when he asks for it and should not be deceived. It often happens that products are interchangeable and that a substitution will have little effect. However, the customer may count on having a specific product. There are many reasons for such a choice: habit, satisfaction, another person's recommendation, the desire for change, and so on. I have no hesitation in using the classic saying, taken from popular imagery: "the customer is always right". Merchants must respect his wishes, choices and preferences as far as possible. Where this is simply not possible, no substitution must be made *without his knowledge*. That is the minimum degree of respect which manufacturers and merchants, who we should remember depend on their customers, should show.

There is no shortage of fraudulent or simply misleading practices: one may think, for example, of products having a similar get-up, the use of similar labelling, use of the same trade name, counterfeiting, imitation of packaging. These are all possible ways of attempting, deliberately or otherwise, to mislead the public. The courts and authors have unanimously concluded that the facts must be weighed in relation to an "ordinary" public, "average" customers: ". . . you must deal with the ordinary man and woman who would take ordinary care in purchasing what goods they require, and, if desiring a particular brand, would take ordinary precautions to see that they get it" (Neville J. in *Henry Thorne & Co. v. Sandow* (1912), 29 R.P.C. 440 (Ch. D.) at p. 453.)

The average customer will not be the same for different products, however, and will not have the same attitude at the time of purchase. Moreover, the attention and care taken by the same person may vary depending on the product he is buying: someone will probably not exercise the same care in selecting goods from a supermarket shelf and in choosing a luxury item. In the first case, the misrepresentation is likely to "catch" more readily.

. . .

[Gonthier J. allowed the appeals and held that the plaintiff was required to show only that the defendants' actions were likely to confuse physicians, pharmacists or patients and customers]

NOTES AND QUESTIONS

1. In *Ciba-Geigy*, Gonthier J. said that the cause of action requires proof of "actual or *potential* damage to the plaintiff." Notice that the plaintiff is not required to prove that it actually suffered any loss as a result of the defendant's deception. Suggest an explanation for that rule. In doing so, consider the evidentiary difficulties that the plaintiff would face if required to prove actual loss.

If the defendant intended to deceive the public, the court readily will assume that deception took place. Otherwise, the plaintiff bears the onus of proving that the defendant's practices were likely to mislead: Fleming, *The Law of Torts*, 9th ed. (1998) at 783. In that regard, the courts recognize that consumers do not always carefully inspect products before using them. As Lord Macnaghten said, "Thirsty folk want beer, not explanations": *Montgomery v. Thompson*, [1891] A.C. 217 at 225 (H.L.). The question, therefore, is whether or not the reasonable customer might have been misled.

2. The Supreme Court of Canada revisited the tort of passing off in *Kirkbi AG v. Ritvik Holdings Inc.*, [2005] 3 S.C.R. 302. The patent protecting the plaintiff's Lego building blocks expired. The defendant company therefore began manufacturing Mega Bloks, with essentially the same design as Lego products (*i.e.* each piece was topped by raised studs that allowed pieces to be joined together). The plaintiff sued (1) under statute for trademark infringement, and (2) at common law for the tort of passing off. Both claims failed.

Trademark laws exist to protect distinctive guises or appearances, not to create monopolies over utilitarian features. The court held that the raised studs traditionally used for Lego blocks fell into the latter category and therefore were not protected. The plaintiff previously had enjoyed such protection under the *Patent Act*, R.S.C. 1985, c. P-4, but that protection had expired. Patent legislation strikes a balance between competing interests. In exchange for disclosing the relevant secret, an inventor is entitled to exclude competitors for 20 years. After that time, however, everyone is free to use the new process.

The court affirmed that the tort of passing off consists of three elements: (1) goodwill attached to a distinctive product belonging to the plaintiff, (2) deception of the public, either deliberately or carelessly, by the defendant, and (3) actual or potential damage to the claimant. On the facts of *Kirkbi*, the tort claim, like the trademark claim, was defeated by the doctrine of *functionality*. LeBel J. explained:

> The alleged distinctiveness of the product consisted precisely of the process and techniques which were now common to the trade. Again, Kirkbi could not overcome another form of the functionality problem. Granting such a claim in these circumstances would amount to recreating a monopoly contrary to basic policies of the laws and legal principles which inform the various forms of intellectual property in our legal system. The appellant is no longer entitled to protection against competition in respect of its product. It must now face the rigours of a free market and its process of creative destruction.

Do you agree with the court's decision? Have you ever played with Lego blocks and Mega Bloks? Are both products essentially interchangeable or is one noticeably better than the other? If one is superior, should the law protect consumers against the risk of confusion?

3. As in *Kirkbi AG v. Ritvik Holdings Inc.*, a plaintiff may claim both violation of trademark and passing off on the same facts. Those two concepts may also combine in another way. Registration of a trademark under the federal *Trademark Act*, R.S.C. 1985, c. T-13, entitles the owner to exclusive use throughout Canada. A registered trademark accordingly is a complete defence to an allegation of the common law tort of passing off: see *Molson Canada v. Oland Breweries Ltd.* (2002), 214 D.L.R. (4th) 473 (Ont. C.A.).

4. The tort of passing off frequently is litigated. Many of the cases arise in the context of the sports and entertainment industries. See for example *Paramount Pictures Corp. v. Howley* (1991), 5 O.R. (3d) 573 (Gen. Div.); *National Hockey League v. Pepsi Cola Ltd.* (1992), 70 B.C.L.R. (2d) 27 (S.C.), aff'd (1995), 2 B.C.L.R. (3d) 3 (C.A.); *Walt Disney Productions v. Triple Five Corp.* (1994), 149 A.R. 112 (C.A.); and *Walt Disney Productions v. Fantasyland Hotel Inc.* (1996), 184 A.R. 110 (C.A.).

For other examples, see *Molson Canada v. Oland Breweries Ltd., supra*; *Eli Lilly & Co. v. Novopharm Ltd.* (2000), 195 D.L.R. (4th) 547 (Fed. C.A.); and *Campomar v. Nike* (2000), 169 A.L.R. 677 (H.C.A.).

5. In a typical passing off case, the defendant misrepresents its goods as having been produced by the plaintiff. However, the tort extends to other situations as well. For instance, a business cannot usurp goodwill by falsely suggesting that its product was produced in a geographical region known for particularly high quality. Champagne comes from a particular region of France, not from Spain, just as Advocaat comes from the Netherlands, not England. See *Bollinger v. Costa Brava Wine Co.*, [1960] Ch. 262 (Ch. Div.); and *E.W.B. Venootschap. v. J. Townend & Sons (Hull) Ltd.*, [1979] A.C. 731 (H.L.).

6. The courts generally have been reluctant to extend the economic torts beyond the commercial law contexts in which they were first recognized: see *Polsinelli v. Marzilli* (1987), 42 C.C.L.T. 46 (Ont. H.C.).

7. See generally MacInnis, "Commercial Morality and Passing Off: A Model for a Modern Tort" (1998) 30 C.B.L.J. 415.

8. Damages in tort law usually are calculated to compensate for the plaintiff's losses. Having established the tort of passing off, however, the plaintiff enjoys the option of demanding either compensation or disgorgement of the defendant's wrongful gain (if there is one): *Draper v. Trist* (1939), 56 R.P.C. 429 (C.A.); and *Procea Products Ltd. v. Evans & Sons Ltd.* (1951) 68 R.P.C. 210 (Ch. D.). In *My Kinda Town Ltd. v. Soll*, [1982] F.S.R. 147, rev'd as to liability [1983] R.P.C. 407 (C.A.), the defendant passed off its restaurant ("Chicago Pizza Company") as the plaintiff's ("The Chicago Pizza Pie Factory"). Slade J. ordered the defendant to give up *all* of its wrongful profits and not merely those that otherwise would have been earned by the plaintiff.

9. The tort of passing off is concerned with goods and services. The tort of *misappropriation of personality* is available if the defendant made unauthorized use of the plaintiff's image. Consequently, a company will be held liable if it attempts to increase sales through the use of a famous athlete's photograph: *Athans v. Canadian Adventure Camps* (1977), 80 D.L.R. (3d) 583, (Ont. H.C.). See also *Krouse v. Chrysler Canada Ltd.* (1973), 1 O.R. (2d) 225 (C.A.); and *Horton v. Tim Donut Ltd.* (1997), 45 B.L.R. (2d) 7 (Ont. Gen. Div.). Protection also is provided by privacy statutes in British Columbia, Manitoba, Newfoundland, Nova Scotia and Saskatchewan.

10. The torts of misappropriation of personality and passing off generally involve situations in which the defendant seeks to take advantage of the plaintiff's reputation and goodwill. The torts of defamation and injurious falsehood are available if, to the contrary, the defendant acts in a way that could be harmful to the plaintiff's reputation.

Defamation occurs when the defendant makes a false statement to a third party that could lead a reasonable person to have a lower opinion of the plaintiff. Defamation is discussed in Chapter 27.

Whereas defamation protects a person's reputation, *injurious falsehood* protects a person's business or commercial interests. The plaintiff must prove four elements: (1) the defendant made a disparaging statement to a third party regarding the plaintiff's land, goods, services or business, (2) the statement was false, (3) the defendant acted out of "malice," and (4) the plaintiff suffered a loss as a result. See Fridman, *The Law of Torts in Canada*, 2d ed. (2002) at 814-29; Fleming, *The Law of Torts*, 9th ed. (1998) at 778-82; and Osborne, *The Law of Torts*, 2d ed. (2003) at 286-87.

4. Intimidation

The tort of intimidation may occur if: (1) the defendant threatened to commit an unlawful act, such as a crime, a tort or, in some circumstances, a breach of contract, (2) the defendant's threat was effective insofar as it induced someone to act in particular way, and (3) the plaintiff consequently suffered a loss. Significantly, the court need not be satisfied that the defendant actually implemented the threat. Of course, if the unlawful act is carried out, it will support legal proceedings on its own.

Intimidation has two forms: two-party intimidation and three-party intimidation. As illustrated by the extract that appears below, the general principles are the same in either form, but some of the specific rules do vary.

The leading case of *Rookes v. Barnard*, [1964] A.C. 1129 (H.L.) involved three-party intimidation. The plaintiff was a member of the defendant union. He also was an employee of B.O.A.C., an airline. The plaintiff became involved in a dispute with the union and resigned his membership. The union then threatened to withdraw all of its services from B.O.A.C. unless the airline terminated the plaintiff's employment. That threat was unlawful insofar as it was made pursuant to a conspiracy between various members of the union. B.O.A.C. succumbed to the pressure and fired the plaintiff. Notice the vulnerability of the plaintiff's position. Because the defendant's threatened breach of contract was directed toward the third party, there was no way for the plaintiff to directly combat it. Furthermore, while B.O.A.C. terminated the plaintiff's contract without cause, it had also given him payment in lieu of notice. It therefore could not be held further liable for breach of contract. Fortunately, the plaintiff was not entirely vulnerable. He was entitled to succeed against the defendant under the tort of intimidation.

CENTRAL CAN. POTASH v. GOVT. OF SASK.

(1979), 88 D.L.R. (3d) 609 (S.C.C.)

MARTLAND J.: . . . Pursuant to the *Mineral Resources Act*, a scheme for the control of production of potash in Saskatchewan had been put into effect. The appellant, as a potash producer, was prohibited from producing potash in excess of the amounts prescribed by the licences issued to it. It was required after receiving a licence to submit a production schedule, showing monthly production during the 12-month term of the licence not exceeding the total production authorized.

The appellant, being understandably unhappy with the quota allotted to it, endeavoured to persuade the Minister to increase its allocation, but without success. It sought to compel such an increase by *mandamus*, again without success. It failed to submit a proper production schedule within 30 days of the receipt of its licence for the 1972-73 year. It continued its production upon a scale beyond that which was contemplated by its licence.

This was the situation in which the Deputy Minister wrote the letter of September 20, 1972, calling on the appellant to reduce its production or to face the possibility of a cancellation of its mineral lease. That lease, as has been noted, included a requirement that the appellant, as lessee, would observe, perform and abide by all obligations imposed upon holders of mineral leases by the Act or Regulations thereunder in effect from time to time.

In the present case, the threat by the Deputy Minister was the possible exercise by the Minister of powers which he had reasonable grounds for believing the Minister possessed. In *Rookes* the threat was to pursue a course of action which the defendants knew would be a breach of the collective agreement between the union and B.O.A.C.

In the present case, the Deputy Minister sought to induce the appellant to limit the amount of its production to conform with the prorationing scheme which had been established. In the *Rookes* case, the object of the threat was to compel B.O.A.C. to discharge the plaintiff, an action which, except for the pressure, it did not wish to take and which it was under no legal obligation to take.

In the *Rookes* case, the threat was not made to the plaintiff. It was made to a third party, B.O.A.C., with a view to compel it to take a course of action detrimental to the plaintiff. In the present case, the threat was made directly to the appellant and no third party was involved.

I will deal with this distinction now, and will revert to the other distinctions later. It is significant because the plaintiff, in the *Rookes* case, was not in a position to claim a breach of contract by his employer when he was dismissed. The only recourse he could seek was against the defendants who had threatened a breach of the collective agreement between the union and the employer as a means to compel the employer to discharge Rookes. Here the appellant is a party to the contract which it says was threatened to be breached, *i.e.*, the lease, and would have been entitled to pursue its contractual remedies had that contract been illegally breached.

On this point, I am in agreement with the view expressed by the author of *Winfield and Jolowicz on Tort*, 10th ed., p. 458, as follows:

> It is submitted, therefore, that the two-party situation is properly distinguishable from the three-party situation and that it does not necessarily follow from *Rookes v. Barnard* that whenever A threatens B with an unlawful act, including a breach of his contract with B, he thereby commits the tort of intimidation. In fact the balance of advantage seems to lie in holding that where A threatens B with a breach of his contract with B, B should be restricted to his contractual remedies. The law should not encourage B to yield to the threat but should seek to persuade him to resist it. If he suffers damage in consequence he will be adequately compensated by his remedy in damages for breach of contract, as his damage can scarcely be other than financial. Where, however, what is threatened is tort, and especially if the threat is of violence, it is both unrealistic to insist that proceedings for a *quia timet* injunction afford him adequate protection against the consequences of resistance and unreasonable to insist that if violence is actually inflicted upon him he is adequately compensated by an award of damages thereafter. The view is preferred, therefore, that although A commits the tort of intimidation against B where he threatens B with violence or perhaps with any other tort, no independent tort is committed when all that is threatened is a breach of contract.

In my opinion the tort of intimidation is not committed if a party to a contract asserts what he reasonably considers to be his contractual right and that other party, rather than electing to contest that right, follows a course of conduct on the assumption that the assertion of right can be maintained.

I am also of the view that if the course of conduct which the person making the threat seeks to induce is that which the person threatened is obligated to follow, the tort of intimidation does not arise. If, in the *Rookes* case, the collective agreement between the union and B.O.A.C. had contained a closed shop provision so as to require B.O.A.C. to discharge the plaintiff upon his ceasing to be a member of the union, the plaintiff could not have succeeded in his suit because of the threat of a strike, even though the agreement provided that there should be no strikes.

In the present case the *Potash Conservation Regulations, 1969* made under the *Mineral Resources Act* prohibited the appellant from exceeding a specified production of potash. By conforming to the requirements of the Regulations, the appellant would not suffer damage and, therefore, the claim for intimidation is not well founded.

What, then, is the position if, subsequently, it is found that the Regulations were *ultra vires*? Does that finding then mean that there has been intimidation?

In my opinion it does not. The conduct of the Deputy Minister in relation to the tort of intimidation must be considered in relation to the circumstances existing at the time the alleged threat was made. The Deputy Minister was then seeking to induce conformity with the prorationing plan which had been created by legislation which it was his duty to enforce. At the time the threat was made, the legislation stood unchallenged.

. . .

In my opinion it would be unfortunate, in a federal state such as Canada, if it were to be held that a government official, charged with the enforcement of legislation, could be held to be guilty of intimidation because of his enforcement of the statute whenever a statute whose provisions he is under a duty to enforce is subsequently held to be *ultra vires*.

This brings me to the latter portion of the definition of intimidation from Clerk & Lindsell which I have adopted. "The tort is one of intention and the plaintiff, whether it be B or C, must be a person whom A intended to injure." The authority for this statement is found by the authors in the judgments of Lord Devlin and Lord Evershed in the *Rookes* case, and I am in agreement with it. There is no evidence that the Deputy Minister intended to injure the appellant. The correspondence, and particularly the letter of September 20, 1972, make it clear that his purpose was to induce compliance with an existing legislative scheme.

. . .

I would dismiss the appellant's claims for damages.

NOTES AND QUESTIONS

1. For an interesting forerunner to *Rookes*, see *Int. Brotherhood of Teamsters v. Therien*, [1960] S.C.R. 265, in which the same principles were applied without specific reference to the tort of intimidation. See also *J.T. Stratford & Son v. Lindley*, [1965] A.C. 307 (H.L.); *Mintuck v. Valley River Band No. 63A* (1977), 75 D.L.R. (3d) 589 (Man. C.A.); and *Selig v. Mansfield* (1982), 53 N.S.R. (2d) 246 (C.A.). For a general discussion of the tort of intimidation, see Fridman, *The Law of Torts in Canada*, 2d ed. (2002) at 777-89; Osborne, *The Law of Torts*, 2d ed. (2003) at 296-98; Wedderburn, "Intimidation and the Right to Strike" (1964) 27 Mod. L. Rev. 257; and Burns, "Tort Injury to Economic Interests: Some Facets of Legal Response" (1980) 58 Can. Bar Rev. 103 at 126-40.

2. *Allen v. Flood*, [1898] A.C. 1 (H.L.) was discussed in the introduction to this chapter. Why was the plaintiff in that case unable to succeed in intimidation?

3. In terms of the governing rules, what is the difference between two-party intimidation and three-party intimidation? Is there a difference if the defendant threatens to commit a crime or a tort? What if the defendant threatens to breach a contract?

4. Do you agree with Martland J. that the defendant did not intend to injure the plaintiff? Was the injury a necessary consequence? Should the defendant's motive be

relevant in intimidation? Is there something special about this case that justifies the concern with motive?

5. The issues of intent, motive, and justification are further complicated by Martland J.'s statement in *Central Can. Potash* that:

> In my opinion the tort of intimidation is not committed if a party to a contract asserts what he reasonably considers to be his contractual right and that other party, rather than electing to contest that right, follows a course of conduct on the assumption that the assertion of the right can be maintained.

According to Martland J., does the defendant's mistaken belief that the threat is lawful preclude liability in intimidation? In the alternative, must both the defendant and the plaintiff mistakenly believe that the threat is lawful? See *Roehl v. Houlahan* (1990), 74 D.L.R. (4th) 562 (Ont. C.A.); and *Roth v. Roth* (1991), 4 O.R. (3d) 740 (Gen. Div.).

In *J.C. Kerkhoff & Sons Contracting Ltd. v. XL Ironworks Co.* (1983), 26 C.C.L.T. 1 (B.C.S.C.), this principle was applied in a situation involving three-party intimidation. Even though the threat was unlawful, the defendant was absolved of liability because it reasonably believed that the threat was lawful. Should this principle apply in three-party intimidation cases, given the different relationships that exist in the two types of intimidation actions?

6. The operative threat may be implicit or explicit, and there is no legal distinction between a threat and a warning. It is essential that the threat or warning be unlawful, but this issue is controversial. Clearly, a threat to commit a crime or a tort is considered unlawful. However, in J. Fleming's words, "beyond that, the approach has been casuistic, without any evident rationale related to policy ends, and suffering from some inexplicable inconsistencies": *The Law of Torts*, 9th ed. (1998) at 767. In *Rookes v. Barnard*, [1964] A.C. 1129, the House of Lords established that, at least in regard to three-party intimidation, a threatened breach of contract is an unlawful threat. This principle has been criticized. Can you suggest why? Should this principle apply to two-party intimidation cases?

7. Damages in tort law are usually calculated to provide compensation for losses sustained by the plaintiff. However, a plaintiff who proves the action in intimidation may alternatively recover any gains that the defendant enjoyed as a result of the tort. See *Rookes v. Barnard*, [1964] A.C. 1129 at 1232 (H.L.); and *Universe Tankship Inc. of Monrovia v. I.T.W.F.*, [1983] 1 A.C. 366 (H.L.) (transfer between the parties reversed on the basis of the independent action in unjust enrichment). Suggest a situation in which it would be preferable to receive disgorgement rather than compensation.

5. Conspiracy

Conspiracy is a strange tort. As we saw in the introduction to this chapter, *Allen v. Flood* stands for the general proposition that, so long as otherwise lawful means are used, it is not tortious to deliberately destroy someone's business. And yet, if two or more people act together for the same purpose, they may be held liable under the tort of conspiracy.

That "magic of combination" remains a mystery. It sometimes is said that there is an inherent moral difference between being victimized by several conspirators, rather than by a single competitor. On that view, the common law condones aggressive competition, but its sense of fair play is offended when several people "gang up" on someone. Particularly in modern times, however, that explanation leaves something to be desired. As a matter of both moral intuition and sheer brute force, a large multinational corporation often poses much more of a threat than two local enterprises that temporarily have banded together.

Tort law recognizes two species of conspiracy, as indicated in *Canada Cement LaFarge Ltd. v. B.C. Lightweight Aggregate Ltd.* (1983), 145 D.L.R. (3d) 385 (S.C.C.):

- *Conspiracy to Injure*: If the conspirators agreed to execute an otherwise *lawful act*, then they may be held liable only if their *predominant purpose* was to hurt the claimant. That burden often is difficult to discharge. *Daishowa Inc. v. Friends of the Lubicon* (1998), 158 D.L.R. (4th) 699 (Ont. Gen. Div.) is illustrative. The defendants organized a consumer boycott of the plaintiff's paper products in order to draw attention to Aboriginal land claim issues. The plaintiff lost a great deal of money because many of its usual customers purchased elsewhere. The action in conspiracy nevertheless failed because the defendants' primary purpose was not to hurt the plaintiff, but rather to raise public awareness of a political agenda.

- *Conspiracy to Commit an Unlawful Act*: In contrast, if the conspirators agreed to execute an otherwise *unlawful act* (*e.g.* a tort, a crime or a breach of contract, or a violation of licensing, competition or labour legislation), they may be held liable as long as (1) their scheme was directed toward the plaintiff, and (2) they *should have known* that they might thereby hurt the plaintiff. Of course, liability also may be imposed if the defendants' predominant purpose was to hurt the plaintiff, or if they actually knew that their scheme would do so.

POSLUNS v. TORONTO STOCK EXCHANGE

(1964), 46 D.L.R. (2d) 210 (Ont. H.C.)

[Employees of firms in the Toronto Stock Exchange ("TSE") required approval from the TSE before participating in various trading activities. The TSE formed the opinion that Posluns had engaged in such activities without approval. It then informed Posluns' employer, Daly Co., that he no longer was entitled to act in any capacity for any firm in the TSE. Daly Co. promptly fired Posluns. Posluns subsequently sued the TSE for both conspiracy and interference with contractual relations. The first claim is considered in this excerpt. The second claim is addressed later in this chapter.]

GALE J.: . . . While his counsel did not exhibit much confidence in the plaintiff's alleged cause of action for damages for conspiracy, it was not abandoned and I must therefore give attention to it.

It was pleaded that the defendant George Gardiner along with the other members of the Board who participated in the events of February 28th and March 2nd and the Exchange itself, all combined together to unlawfully injure the plaintiff by sending out the notice, ex. 33, which probably had the result, not only of bringing about his dismissal as an employee and his removal as a director and shareholder, but also of precluding him from obtaining immediate employment with any other member or member corporation of the Exchange, and of damaging his reputation to some extent. Both compensatory and punitive damages were asked for on this branch of the case, and it will be observed, as stated above, that the complaint was not confined to interference with the plaintiff's contract of employment only.

It need hardly be said that a conspiracy consists of an agreement of two or more to do an unlawful act or to do a lawful act by unlawful means. Thus, the tort of conspiracy is committed if a person is damaged by a combination which is formed for the purpose of harming him in his trade, business or other interests, whether or not a breach of contract is the result, or if that damage is caused by an unlawful act on the part of those acting in concert.

. . .

In my opinion, the claim based upon a supposed conspiracy fails for several reasons. To begin with, there was not any agreement to injure the plaintiff or any agreement to do something the doing of which would harm him. All the governors did was to vote in the same way, but, because they had agreed upon nothing before voting, and were not at any time actuated by malice or any other improper motive, they did not merely, by so voting, enter into an agreement, express or implied, to do something which had not yet been done, the requisite of any conspiracy. As Mr. Arnup said, the directors of a corporation do not make an "agreement" in the conspiracy sense by voting the same way. They individually make the same decision. In the popular sense they are "in agreement", but in the sense in which the law of conspiracy uses "agree" they were not. Each simply expressed an individual opinion and the majority opinion prevailed. A contrary view would bring extraordinary consequences. One of its implications would be that each time the majority of a Board of Directors voted to have the corporation pursue a course of action which ultimately turned out to be illegal, those who were in favour of having the corporation act as it did would be conspirators by reason solely of having so voted.

The proposition that the mere taking of a decision by directors or others at a meeting cannot constitute an agreement to conspire unless some of them have entered into a compact in advance of the meeting to induce others to cause the organization on whose behalf they are acting to do something which is wrong, is supported by authority. In *De Jetley Marks v. Greenwood (Lord) et al.*, [1936] 1 All E.R. 863, Porter, J., as he then was, observed at p. 872:

> . . . I think it is true that directors in a board meeting could not induce or conspire to induce that meeting to break a contract – at any rate, not without malice.

That language does not substantiate Mr. Williston's suggestion that there is a difference between a vote to have a company break one of its own contracts and a vote to wrongfully procure the breach of a contract between others. I should add that Porter, J., was careful to qualify the quoted statement by pointing out that some or all of the directors could conspire before the meeting to cause the Board to wrongfully break a contract.

. . .

[Gale J. dismissed the claim in conspiracy.]

NOTES AND QUESTIONS

1. As previously noted, a distinction generally is drawn between two situations: (1) conspirators who agreed to commit an otherwise *lawful* act, who may be held liable only

if their *predominant purpose* was to hurt the plaintiff, and (2) conspirators who agreed to commit an otherwise *unlawful* act, who may be held liable even if they *primarily* were acting out of self-interest, as long as their act was *directed toward* the claimant and they at last *should have known* that the plaintiff could be injured.

English courts, however, have debated whether there should be liability where the defendants did not *primarily* intend to hurt the claimant. This issue received considerable attention during the 1980s and 1990s in a series of cases initiated by the Lonrho corporation. In *Lonrho Ltd. v. Shell Petroleum Co. (No. 2)*, [1982] A.C. 173, Lord Diplock suggested that while the second species of conspiracy ought not to exist, it was too well-entrenched to be discarded judicially. He nevertheless did insist that it should be narrowly confined. In *Lonrho Ltd. v. Fayed*, [1992] 1 A.C. 448 (H.L.), however, Lord Bridge held that liability should be possible as long as conspirators used *unlawful* means with *an intention* to injure the claimant, even if their *primary* aim was to advance their own interests.

2. Why did the conspiracy action fail in *Posluns*? Was Gale J. suggesting that corporate directors could only be liable in conspiracy if they agreed to a course of conduct in advance of a board meeting?

3. As in *Posluns*, the same events often trigger claims in both conspiracy and interference with contractual relations. For a discussion of the difference between those two torts, see Cameron J.A.'s analysis in *Garry v. Sherritt Gordon Mines Ltd.* (1987), 59 Sask. R. 104 (C.A.).

4. Conspiracy differs from the other intentional economic torts in that the defendant's purpose or motive is an element of the cause of action. The defendant's motive also is relevant in establishing the *defence of justification*. Unfortunately, the nature and scope of that defence are somewhat unclear. At the risk of oversimplification, however, a distinction can be drawn. If the defendants banded together in order to advance their own legitimate interests, their conduct is less likely to be labelled tortious. In contrast, if they joined together out of malice, ill-will or spite, they are more likely to be held liable.

In *Mogul S.S. Co. v. McGregor, Gow & Co.*, [1892] A.C. 25 (H.L.), the defendants conspired together in an effort to cut prices and thereby drive the claimant out of business. Because they acted out of self-interest, their scheme was acceptable to the court. Likewise, the court in *Crofter Hand Woven Harris Tweed Co. v. Vietch*, [1942] 1 All E.R. 142 at 148 (H.L.), stated that the tort is not committed if the defendants acted in the genuine belief that their scheme served their "*bona fide* and legitimate interests." Does the defence of justification require the courts to make policy decisions in areas in which they lack expertise? See *Hersees Ltd. v. Goldstein* (1963), 38 D.L.R. (2d) 449 (Ont. C.A.); and Heydon, "The Defence of Justification in Cases of Intentionally Caused Economic Loss" (1970) 20 U.T.L.J. 139.

5. Although the second species of conspiracy does not require proof that the defendants' primary purpose was to hurt the plaintiff, a claim will fail if the court is unable to find at least constructive knowledge that the scheme would hurt the plaintiff: *Golden Capital Securities Ltd. v. Holmes* (2005), 33 B.C.L.R. (4th) 1 (C.A.).

6. The second species of conspiracy requires proof that the defendants joined together to commit an *unlawful* act: *Pro-Sys Consultants Ltd. v. Microsoft Corp.* (2006), 57 B.C.L.R. (4th) 323 (S.C.).

Interestingly, however, the wrongfulness of that act need not arise in tort law. The act may be unlawful for some *other* reason. That fact creates an oddity: an unlawful, though non-tortious, act may become tortious merely because it is committed by two people acting in concert. This anomaly may seem innocuous if the act is unlawful because it is a crime. Significantly, however, the tort of conspiracy also extends much farther. In *Canadian Training and Development Group v. Air Canada* (1986), 57 O.R. (2d) 659 (Div. Ct.), the defendant was a member of an air traffic controllers' union. In an attempt to pressure his employer, he falsely called in sick and thereby breached the collective agreement and the provisions of the *Public Service Staff Relations Act*, R.S.C. 1970, c. P-35. The court accordingly held that the defendant had conspired with other air traffic controllers in an *unlawful* act. It further held that the defendant *prima facie* was liable for the losses suffered by the plaintiffs, who were passengers on flights that had been affected by the industrial action. The claim nevertheless ultimately failed on the ground of an immunity provided by the *Rights of Labour Act*, R.S.O. 1980, c. 456. Should otherwise non-tortious acts be rendered tortious by the "magic of combination?"

7. The tort of conspiracy is not confined to the business world: it may also arise in social or family settings. In *Helmy v. Helmy* (2000), 36 E.T.R. (2d) 100 (Ont. S.C.J.), a husband won $2,500,000 in a lottery. He did not tell his wife, from whom he separated a short time later. With the help of several family members, he continued to hide the winnings from his estranged wife while she was seeking a division of the matrimonial assets. The wife did not discover the truth until after those proceedings were closed. She then commenced several claims, including one in conspiracy against her husband and the relatives who had participated in his scheme. The court held that the wife was entitled to (1) a half-interest in the lottery winnings and their traceable proceeds, (2) compensatory damages under the tort of conspiracy against her husband and his complicit relatives, to the extent that she was otherwise unable to actually recover her share of the lottery winnings, and (3) punitive damages of $50,000 against her husband and his complicit relatives.

8. For additional judicial discussion of conspiracy, see *Apotex Inc. v. Hoffman-LaRoche Ltd.* (2000), 195 D.L.R. (4th) 244 (Ont. C.A.); *Newswest Corp. v. Glendar Holdings Ltd.*, [2001] 9 W.W.R. 312 (Sask. Q.B.); *Claiborne Industries Ltd. v. Nat. Bank of Can.* (1989), 69 O.R. (2d) 65 (C.A.); *Normart Management Ltd. v. West Hill Redevelopment Co.* (1998), 41 C.C.L.T. (2d) 282 (Ont. C.A.); and *Daishowa Inc. v. Friends of the Lubicon* (1998), 158 D.L.R. (4th) 699 (Ont. Gen. Div.). See also *Surrey (District) v. Marall Homes Ltd.* (1988), 48 C.C.L.T. 70 (B.C.S.C.), where the tort of conspiracy was described as an "anachronism" that ought to be restricted to the labour and commercial disputes from which it originated. See also Carthy & Miller, "Civil Conspiracy" in *L.S.U.C. Special Lectures: New Developments in the Law of Torts* (1973) at 495; Burns, "Civil Conspiracy: An Unwieldy Vessel Rides a Judicial Tempest" (1982) 16 U.B.C.L. Rev. 229.

9. The tort of conspiracy must be distinguished from the crime of conspiracy. Section 465 of the *Criminal Code*, R.S.C. 1985, c. C-46, states:

465. (1) Except where otherwise expressly provided by law, the following provisions apply in respect of conspiracy:

(a) every one who conspires with any one to commit murder or to cause another person to be murdered, whether in Canada or not, is guilty of an indictable offence and liable to a maximum term of imprisonment for life;
(b) every one who conspires with any one to prosecute a person for an alleged offence, knowing that he did not commit that offence, is guilty of an indictable offence and liable

(i) to imprisonment for a term not exceeding ten years, if the alleged offence is one for which, on conviction, that person would be liable to be sentenced to imprisonment for life or for a term not exceeding fourteen years, or
(ii) to imprisonment for a term not exceeding five years, if the alleged offence is one for which, on conviction, that person would be liable to imprisonment for less than fourteen years;

(c) every one who conspires with any one to commit an indictable offence not provided for in paragraph (a) or (b) is guilty of an indictable offence and liable to the same punishment as that to which an accused who is guilty of that offence would, on conviction, be liable; and
(d) every one who conspires with any one to commit an offence punishable on summary conviction is guilty of an offence punishable on summary conviction

10. Conspiracy also is an offence under section 45 of the *Competition Act*, R.S.C. 1985, c. C-34. The main provisions state:

45. (1) Every one who conspires, combines, agrees or arranges with another person

(a) to limit unduly the facilities for transporting, producing, manufacturing, supplying, storing or dealing in any product,
(b) to prevent, limit or lessen, unduly, the manufacture or production of a product or to enhance unreasonably the price thereof,
(c) to prevent or lessen, unduly, competition in the production, manufacture, purchase, barter, sale, storage, rental, transportation or supply of a product, or in the price of insurance on persons or property, or
(d) to otherwise restrain or injure competition unduly,

is guilty of an indictable offence and liable to imprisonment for a term not exceeding five years or to a fine not exceeding ten million dollars or to both.

Although private actions occasionally are available under the *Competition Act*, they are narrowly confined and relatively infrequent.

6. Interference with Contractual Relations

Contracts are the lifeblood of commerce. They are used to secure supplies of raw materials and labour, and to sell finished products and services. A breach of contract consequently can be very disruptive to a business. Contractual remedies are available, but often they are inadequate. Specific enforcement is limited to exceptional circumstances and, whatever the position in theory, monetary damages frequently are a poor substitute for actual performance. As a result, there is a strong temptation for an unscrupulous business person, searching for a competitive advantage, to target the agreements that a rival has created with third parties (*e.g.* suppliers, employees, and customers).

To effectively deal with such situations, our legal system offers two avenues of relief: (1) an action for *breach of contract* against the part that actually failed to perform as promised, and (2) an action for *accessory liability* against the party that induced or assisted that breach of contract. The concept of accessory liability is well known in criminal law. Most lawyers, for instance, recognize the possibility of being held responsible for aiding or abetting a criminal act. See for example *Criminal Code*, R.S.C. 1985, c. C-46, s. 21(1). Although less familiar, a similar principle occasionally applies in private law. Equity has developed a general principle of accessory liability that applies if, for instance, a stranger knowingly assists in a trustee's breach of trust: *Air Canada v. M & L Travel Ltd.* (1993), 108 D.L.R. (4th) 592 (S.C.C.). Law, in contrast, traditionally has been more reluctant to impose liability on accessories. See generally Sales, "The Tort of Conspiracy and Civil Secondary Liability" [1990] C.L.J. 491. It nevertheless does offer a tort of *interference with contractual relations* (often known as *inducing breach of contract*).

The tort of interference with contractual relations consists of four elements:

- *Defendant's Knowledge*: The defendant must have known about the contract between the plaintiff and the third party, though not necessarily about all of its details.

- *Defendant's Intention*: The defendant must have intended the third party to break its agreement with the plaintiff, though the defendant need not have been motivated by a malicious desire to hurt the plaintiff.

- *Causation of Breach*: The defendant in fact must have caused the third party to break its contract with the plaintiff. However, the courts draw an important distinction between merely providing information regarding the possible benefits of breach and actually encouraging a breach of contract.

- *Plaintiff's Loss*: The plaintiff must have suffered a loss as a result of the third party's breach, though mere lack of contractual performance normally is sufficient.

As discussed in the case extract and notes that appear below, the tort comes in two varieties. Although the general principles are the same in either event, there is a slight difference regarding the nature of the interfering act.

- *Direct Interference*: In a case of *direct* interference, liability may be imposed even if the defendant's conduct was otherwise lawful. This would be true if, for instance, the defendant secured the services of a third party by promising a higher salary than that person was receiving from the plaintiff.

- *Indirect Interference*: In a case of *indirect* interference, liability will be imposed only if the defendant's behaviour was unlawful in itself. This would be true if, for instance, the defendant prevented a third party from fulfilling a contract with the plaintiff by stealing the tools that that person required for the job.

The leading case in this area is *Lumley v. Gye* (1853), 118 E.R. 749 (Q.B.). An opera singer named Johanna Wagner agreed to sing for one season with the plaintiff's company, Her Majesty's Theatre. The defendant subsequently induced Ms Wagner to break that contract by offering to pay her a higher fee to sing with his company, the Royal Italian Opera. The plaintiff suffered a financial loss as a result of losing the diva's services. He therefore sued the defendant for inducing breach of contract. The claim ultimately failed only because the defendant believed, at the time that he hired Ms Wagner, that she legally had discharged her contract with the plaintiff. However, in another case arising from of the same set of facts, the court awarded an injunction to prevent Ms Wagner from singing for the defendant's company: *Lumley v. Wagner* (1852), 42 E.R. 687 (Ch. Div.). For a fascinating discussion of the cut-throat world of opera, see Waddams, "Johanna Wagner and the Rival Opera Houses" (2001) 117 L.Q.R. 431. The following extract contains an important Canadian application of the same principles.

POSLUNS v. TORONTO STOCK EXCHANGE
(1964), 46 D.L.R. (2d) 210 (H.C.)

[Employees of firms in the Toronto Stock Exchange ("TSE") required approval from the TSE before participating in various trading activities. The TSE formed the opinion that Posluns had engaged in such activities without approval. It then informed Posluns' employer, Daly Co., that he no longer was entitled to act in any capacity for any firm in the TSE. Daly Co. promptly fired Posluns. Posluns subsequently sued the TSE for both conspiracy and interference with contractual relations. The first claim was considered above. The second claim is addressed in this extract.]

GALE J.: . . .

(a) *General Principles*

I propose first to examine the plaintiff's claim against the Exchange for damages for having procured a breach of his contract with the Daly company.

While a contract cannot impose the burden of an obligation on one who is not a party to it, a duty is undoubtedly cast upon any person, although extraneous to the obligation, to refrain from interfering with its due performance unless he has a duty or a right in law to so act. Thus, if a person without lawful justification knowingly and intentionally procures the breach by a party to a contract which is valid and enforceable and thereby causes damage to another party to the contract, the person who has induced the breach commits an actionable wrong. That wrong does not rest upon the fact that the intervenor has acted in order to harm his victim, for a bad motive does not *per se* convert an otherwise lawful act into an unlawful one, but rather because there has been an unlawful invasion of legal relations existing between others.

. . .

To sustain the cause of action now being discussed, and in the circumstances which prevailed, it must be shown that:

1. A valid and enforceable employment contract subsisted between the plaintiff and the Daly company; and
2. The defendant Exchange was or can be assumed to have been aware of the existence of that contract; and
3. A breach of that contract was procured by the Exchange; and
4. Such breach was effected by wrongful interference on the part of the Exchange; and
5. The plaintiff suffered damage as a result thereof. If all of those elements have been proved the plaintiff is entitled to relief.

[Subject to a complication regarding the third point, which need not concern us, Gale J. accepted that the first three points were established and continued.]

(d) *Was there unlawful interference on the part of the Exchange?*

I now pass to the next link in the plaintiff's chain of action. Does he show that the interference, if any, on the part of the Exchange with his contractual rights was such as to sustain his claim, for the law stipulates that to be tortious the interference which is the source of damage to another must be "unlawful" before it will be actionable. It is unnecessary to consider the various kinds of particular interference which have been held to be wrongful; it will suffice to say that to procure a breach of contract by direct intervention is "unlawful", and will give rise to a cause of action to the person who is thereby injured unless it is justifiable. For that proposition I rely, amongst others, upon *D.C. Thomson & Co. Ltd. v. Deakin*, [1952] Ch. 646, where, at pp. 677 and 681 respectively, Lord Evershed, M.R., stated:

> At any rate, it is clear that, when there is such a direct intervention by the intervener [causing a party to break his contract], the intervention itself is thereby considered wrongful.

And:

> Dealing first with individual contractors, it seems to me that the intervener, assuming in all cases that he knows of the contract and acts with the aim and object of procuring its breach to the damage of B, one of the contracting parties, will be liable not only (1) if he directly intervenes by persuading A to break it, but also (2) if he intervenes by the commission of some act wrongful in itself so as to prevent A from in fact performing his contract . . .

In the same case Jenkins, L.J., had this to say at p. 694:

> Direct persuasion or procurement or inducement applied by the third party to the contract breaker, with knowledge of the contract and the intention of bringing about its breach, is clearly to be regarded as a wrongful act in itself, and where this is shown a case of actionable interference in its primary form is made out: *Lumley v. Gye*, 2 El. & Bl. 216.

I pause here to point out that when considering this tort, care must be taken always to distinguish between a cause of action based upon the procurement of a breach of a contract and one for interference with other civil rights. The House of Lords in England has restricted the scope of the principle which I have just outlined to interference with actual contracts; see *Allen v. Flood*, [1898] A.C. 1 and *Sorrell v. Smith*, [1925] A.C. 700.

. . .

Here, there was direct and deliberate interference by the Exchange with the contractual relations between the plaintiff and the Daly company. On the authorities, that interference, unless justifiable, must be deemed to be unlawful action on the part of the Exchange if a breach of those contractual relations was the result. True, it did not act for the purpose of causing damage to Mr. Posluns or with malice or spite, but that is immaterial, for if the Exchange intended to bring an end to the employment contract and such was clearly its purpose, that intention is sufficient and does not have to be accompanied by a wish to do harm.

. . .

In short, therefore, it would seem that the plaintiff is entitled to reparation from the

Exchange if the latter by direct, intentional and unjustified intervention through the Daly company, effected a breach of contract of which it was or ought to have been aware.

. . .

(e) *Was the Exchange justified in procuring a breach of contract?*

The limits of the doctrine of justification as it applies to the tort under discussion have never been defined with any degree of precision. Perhaps the only safe guide in the matter is to follow, and try to enlist, the words of Romer, L.J., at p. 574 in the report of the judgments in the Court of Appeal in *Glamorgan Coal Co. Ltd. v. South Wales Miners' Federation*, [1903] 2 K.B. 545, where this appears:

> I will only add that, in analyzing or considering the circumstances, I think that regard might be had to the nature of the contract; the position of the parties to the contract; the grounds for the breach; the means employed to procure the breach; the relation of the person procuring the breach to the person who breaks the contract; and I think also to the object of the person in procuring the breach.

If the act of interference is in itself a lawful one, both as to purpose and means, then no vindication is required unless it was committed in the course of a conspiracy to injure the victim. If, on the other hand, unlawful intervention has been the source of the harm, justification must be shown if the claim is to be avoided. The defence rarely succeeds. Self-interest, alone or with others, or the fulfilment of an undertaking to protect others in the same interest, will not of themselves amount to justification. . .; nor where there is an honest belief that there is a duty to act. . .; nor where a person is induced to break a contract because the other party to it has breached his contract with the intervenor. . .

On the other hand, in several instances the Courts have sanctioned interference, particularly where it has been promoted by impersonal or disinterested motives. For example, in some of the early cases it was intimated that a defendant might be excused from the consequences of his otherwise illegal act if he was under the influence of some great moral or religious force, reference being made to a father who might induce his impressionable daughter to break a contract for the promise of marriage with a scoundrel. And I suppose if a doctor were to cause a patient to end a contract of service for health reasons, he would likewise be protected. Even in those examples, however, the distinction between inducement and mere advice is significant and should be heeded.

In two instances interference which otherwise would have been illegal was held to be privileged on the ground that it was effected in the public interest. I have in mind *Stott v. Gamble*, [1916] 2 K.B. 504, where a licensing body banned an objectionable film which the plaintiff had arranged to exhibit at another theatre, and *Brimelow v. Casson*, [1924] 1 Ch. 302, where a protective committee was held to be justified in procuring breaches of employment contracts under which chorus girls were so grossly underpaid as to compel them to resort to immorality. In the first case, however, reliance was placed upon a condition attached to the licence, and the second is today of doubtful authority. . . . In any event, those cases do not cover the situation before me. The Exchange was not here primarily engaged in upholding the public interest. That certainly was one of the purposes in the minds of the governors but not the predominant one. They were disciplining the Daly firm, Mr. Posluns and, later, Mr. Robb. I am inclined to the view, therefore, that the action of the Exchange, if otherwise illegal, cannot be excused on the theory that it was acting in the public welfare.

Lastly, a person may be justified in encroaching upon another's civil rights because of some statutory or contractual privilege, in which case he can be said to be acting in accordance with a right conferred by contract or a duty imposed upon him by competent authority as distinct from the mere protection of his own interest. Really, this has been already touched upon, for if that person is under such a cloak, he is not deemed to be acting unlawfully. In *Read v. Friendly Society of Operative Stonemasons of England, Ireland & Wales*, [1902] 2 K.B. 88 and 732, for example, Darling, J., stated at p. 95 that a person would be justified in causing the breach of a contract which was incapable of being carried out without infringing his rights under another contract. That appears to be an illustration of a contractual privilege and, in a sense, the *Stott* case exemplifies recourse to a statutory one. Here, the Exchange could not say that it was acting under an explicit statutory licence, but, by reason of its relations with the plaintiff, it enjoyed a very considerable measure of control over him, for he submitted himself to its jurisdiction when he applied to become, and was approved as, a customers' man . . . I think it is only reasonable to conclude that he thereby impliedly agreed that so long as he continued under the aegis of the Exchange, he would submit to any control *properly* exerted by it. . . . A correlative obligation was, however, cast upon the Exchange to act within its own rules and within the realm of natural justice when exerting that control, and unless it did both when dealing with Mr. Posluns, any implied contractual right to interfere was lost.

[Gale J. concluded that the TSE had fulfilled its correlative obligations, and dismissed the claim for inducing breach of contract.]

NOTES AND QUESTIONS

1. Based on *Posluns*, define the tort of intentional interference with contractual relations. To what extent does the law protect rights that are held under a contract? To what extent does the law protect other sorts of rights? Consider, for example, the manner in which tort law protects rights to real property (trespass to land), personal property (conversion, detinue and trespass), reputation (defamation), and bodily integrity (battery). Do contractual rights receive relatively more or relatively less protection? What is the explanation for your answer to that question?

2. In light of the fact that the plaintiff cannot recover twice for the same loss, why is it necessary to allow an action in tort against the accessory as well as the action in contract against the party that actually failed to perform the agreement? Are compensatory damages calculated in the same way in both tort and contract? Are other forms of relief (*e.g.* punitive damages) governed by the same rules in tort and contract? Is the rule against double recovery triggered if judgment against one defendant cannot actually be satisfied (*e.g.* because of insolvency)?

3. Do you agree with Gale J. in *Posluns* that the defendant's motive should not affect the question of liability? Would the result have been the same if Posluns had proven that the TSE normally overlooked transgressions such as his and that it had taken action against him out of spite? See also *Gerrard v. Manitoba* (1993), 81 Man. R. (2d) 295 (C.A.).

Liability initially was said to require proof that the defendant acted *maliciously*: *Lumley v. Gye* (1853), 118 E.R. 749 (Q.B.). It soon was accepted, however, that the real standard is *intention*: *Allen v. Flood*, [1898] A.C. 1 (H.L.); and *Quinn v. Leathem*, [1901]

A.C. 495 (H.L.). An issue sometimes arises as to whether the tort may be committed *negligently*. Canadian courts occasionally have answered in the affirmative. See for example *Nicholls v. Richmond (Township)* (1983), 43 B.C.L.R. 162 (C.A.); and *Yellow Submarine Deli Inc. v. A.G.F. Hospitality Associates Inc.* (1998), 118 Man. R. (2d) 270 (C.A.). The better view, however, is that the tort ought to remain based on intention. As evidenced by the late development of *Hedley Byrne & Co. Ltd. v. Heller & Partners Ltd.*, [1964] A.C. 465 (H.L.), courts generally have been reluctant to impose liability for negligently caused economic loss. It arguably would be undesirable to weaken the restrictions that currently exist under the intentional torts. See *Ed Miller Sales & Rentals Ltd. v. Caterpillar Tractor Co.*, [1994] 5 W.W.R. 473 at 541 (Alta. Q.B.); and Danforth, "Tortious Interference with Contract: A Reassertion of Society's Interest in Commercial Stability and Contractual Integrity" (1981) 81 Colum. L. Rev. 1491.

Because interference with contractual relations is an intentional tort, the plaintiff must identify the particular defendant who purportedly possessed the relevant intention: *Lysko v. Braley* (2006), 79 O.R. (3d) 721 (C.A.). The plaintiff also must show that the defendant was aware of the relevant contract: *Super-Save Enterprises Ltd. v. 249513 B.C. Ltd. (c.o.b. Mike's Auto Towing)* (2004), 43 B.L.R. (3d) 23 (B.C.C.A.).

4. The fact that interference with contractual relations presumes the existence of a valid contract generally is non-problematic. Difficulties nevertheless occasionally arise. In *Unident v. DeLong* (1981), 50 N.S.R. (2d) 1 (T.D.), the plaintiff was awarded damages even though the contract was unenforceable because it violated the *Sale of Goods Act*, R.S.N.S. 1967, c. 274, s. 6(1). The judge emphasized that the contract was valid in substance and only unenforceable due to a technical defect. In *Royal Bank v. Wilton*, (1995), 165 A.R. 261 (C.A.), liability was imposed for interference with a sale contract that was subject to a true condition precedent, even though the condition was never satisfied. Should liability be imposed if the defendant persuaded a third party to dismiss the plaintiff from a *volunteer* position? See *Potter v. Rowe*, [1990] B.C.J. No. 2912 (S.C.) (QL).

5. In an action for *indirect* interference with contractual relations, the plaintiff must prove that the defendant used independently unlawful means to procure the breach. A criminal offence, independently tortious conduct, or a breach of the defendant's own contractual obligations can satisfy this "unlawful means" requirement. In *Verchere v. Greenpeace Canada Ltd.* (2004), 29 B.C.L.R. (4th) 75 (C.A.), for instance, the defendants were liable for chaining themselves to loggers' equipment in order to prevent them from felling timber. A violation of the rules of natural justice, or a breach of a regulatory statute, may suffice as well. No firm rule has emerged, and the issue has been determined on a case-by-case basis. See *Body v. Murdoch*, [1954] 4 D.L.R. 326 (Ont. C.A.), for an illustration of the difficulty that arises in attempting to balance the conflicting interests involved in this type of case.

6. There has been a trend towards expanding the tort of interference with contractual relations. Several English decisions extended liability to cases in which the defendant's conduct merely *interfered* with the plaintiff's contractual relations, but did not result in a *breach* of contract. See *Stratford (J.T.) & Son Ltd. v. Lindley*, [1965] A.C. 269 (H.L.); *Emerald Const. Co. v. Lowthian*, [1966] 1 All E.R. 1013 (C.A.); and *Torquay Hotel Co. v. Cousins*, [1969] 2 Ch. 106 (C.A.). Some Canadian courts have been similarly inclined:

Potechin v. Yashin (2000), 186 D.L.R. (4th) 757 (Ont. S.C.J.); *College of Dental Surgeons (Saskatchewan) v. Thorvaldson* (1991), 93 Sask. R. 22 (C.A.); and *Garry v. Sherritt Gordon Mines Ltd.* (1987), 59 Sask. R. 104 (C.A.). That development nevertheless has drawn comment and criticism: see Burns, "Tort Injury to Economic Interests: Some Facets of Legal Response" (1980) 58 Can. Bar Rev. 103 at 114-25; Richardson, "Interference with Contractual Relations: Is *Torquay Hotel* the Law in Canada?" (1983) 41 U.T. Fac. L. Rev. 1; and Carty, "Unlawful Interference with Trade" (1983) 3 J. Legal Stud. 193.

7. The tort of interference with contractual relations potentially places certain types of people in a precarious position. Lawyers occasionally are asked for advice as to whether a contract ought to be performed. If the lawyer responds in a way that is interpreted as an inducement to breach, liability might be imposed. Likewise, a corporate director might form the opinion that it would not be in the company's best interest to perform a contract. In recognition of those potential dilemmas, courts generally refrain from imposing liability for advice or decisions taken in good faith. See *Spectra Architectural Group Ltd. v. Eldred Sollows Consulting Ltd.* (1991), 7 C.C.L.T. (2d) 169 (Alta. Master); and Welling, "Individual Liability for Corporate Acts: The Defence of Hobson's Choice" (2000) 12 S.C.L.R. (2d) 55.

In such circumstances, a defendant also may be protected by a proposition put forcefully by the House of Lords in *OBG Ltd. v. Allan; Douglas v. Hello!; Mainstream Properties Ltd. v. Young*, [2007] UKHL 21. That proposition arose in connection with the third named case. Two directors of a company approached the defendant seeking funds for a new business venture. The defendant asked whether that venture would place the directors into a conflict of interest by requiring them to breach their contracts of employment. They untruthfully told him that their employer already had declined the opportunity to pursue the venture and that there consequently was no problem. After the defendant financed the new venture, however, he was sued by the employer. The House of Lords held that he was not liable. Even if his belief in the directors' assertions had been "muddle-headed and illogical," it also was honest. An honest belief in the legality of a venture is sufficient to preclude liability.

8. Liability may be defeated by the defence of *justification*. Not surprisingly, however, the courts are reluctant to accept an argument that the defendant was justified in inducing a third party to break a contract with the plaintiff. Consequently, the defence seldom succeeds. Although they have not devised any clear tests, the courts generally consider several factors, including the nature of the breached contract, the nature of the breach, the relationship between the various parties, the defendant's motivation, and the means by which the breach was procured: *Glamorgan Coal Co. v. South Wales Miner's Federation*, [1903] 2 K.B. 545 at 573-74 (C.A.), aff'd [1905] A.C. 239 (H.L.). The cases fall into two groups, depending upon the nature of the purported justification.

Self-interest can provide a justification only if the defendant's own *rights* were in jeopardy (as when a purchaser persuades a vendor to honour a contract of sale, despite the fact that the vendor will thereby breach a contract with the plaintiff, to whom the vendor mistakenly agreed to sell the same property). See *Franklin Supply Co. v. Midco Supply Co.* (1995), 33 Alta. L.R. (3d) 362 (Q.B.); and *Rogers Cable TV Ltd. v. 373041 Ontario Ltd.* (1996), 69 C.P.R. (3d) 85 (Ont. Gen. Div.). Self-interest will not provide a defence, however, if the defendant simply acted in pursuit of some general *interest* (as when a person steals away an employee from a competitor and claims that the deed was done in the name of "freedom of contract").

Public interest and morality may provide a justification for otherwise tortious conduct. Liability therefore may be denied if the defendant's purpose in persuading a third party to breach a contract with the plaintiff was to draw attention to environmental destruction or exploitation of migrant workers, for example. So too if a government agency intervenes to prevent performance of a contract that would violate a statute or regulation: *Atcheson v. College of Physicians and Surgeons (Alta.)* (1994), 148 A.R. 395 (Q.B.). More intimately, it previously was suggested that a father would be justified in persuading his daughter to break off her engagement to a cad: *Crofter Hand Woven Harris Tweed Co. v. Veitch*, [1942] A.C. 435 (H.L.). In such circumstances, however, the court may deny the defence if the same objectives could have been pursued or secured through lawful means. See generally *Brimelow v. Casson*, [1924] 1 Ch. 302; and *Verchere v. Greenpeace Canada Ltd., supra.*

9. In *Posluns*, Gale J. said that unlawful interference is one of the elements of the tort, but then noted that "direct interference" in the contract is *per se* unlawful. Consequently, many cases for direct interference with contractual relations will depend on the issue of justification. Why did Gale J. conclude that the defendant was justified in *Posluns*? For a discussion of the relationship between intent and justification, see *Babcock v. Carr; Babcock v. Archibald* (1981), 34 O.R. (2d) 65 (H.C.); *Thermo King Corp. v. Proincial. Bank of Can.* (1981), 34 O.R. (2d) 369 (C.A.); and *Bank of N.S. v. Gaudreau* (1984), 48 O.R. (2d) 478 (H.C.).

10. For an interesting contrast between the alleged tortious interference of governmental and private sector actors, see *Cheticamp Fisheries Co-operative Ltd. v. Canada* (1994), 134 N.S.R. (2d) 13 (T.D.), rev'd (1995), 139 N.S.R. (2d) 224 (C.A.); and *A. & B. Sound Ltd. v. Future Shop Ltd.* (1995), 25 C.C.L.T. (2d) 1 (B.C.S.C.).

11. Claims for interference with contractual relations are common. For important examples, see *Powder Mountain Resorts Ltd. v. British Columbia* (2001), 94 B.C.L.R. (3d) 14 (C.A.); *565486 Ontario Inc. v. Tristone Properties Inc.* (2001), 54 O.R. (3d) 689 (S.C.J.); *Berry v. Pulley* (2000), 2 C.C.L.T. (3d) 103 (Ont. C.A.); *Rummery v. Matthews*, [2001] 11 W.W.R. 473 (Man. C.A.); *369413 Alberta Ltd. v. Pocklington* (2000), 194 D.L.R. (4th) 109 (Alta. C.A.); *No. 1 Collision Repair & Painting (1982) Ltd. v. I.C.B.C.* (2000), 1 C.C.L.T. (3d) 1 (B.C.C.A.); *Harry Winton Investments Ltd. v. CIBC Development Corp.* (2001), 199 D.L.R. (4th) 709 (Ont. C.A.); *Swift Current (City) v. Saskatchewan Power Corp.* (2007), 31 M.P.L.R. (4th) 161 (Sask. C.A.); and *Kay Aviation b.v. v. Rofe* (2001), 202 D.L.R. (4th) 683 (P.E.I.C.A.).

12. Damages in tort law are usually calculated to provide compensation for the losses sustained by the plaintiff. See for example *Colborne Capital Corp. v. 542775 Alberta Ltd.*, [1999] 8 W.W.R. 222 (Alta. C.A.). There also is authority suggesting that the plaintiff may elect to receive disgorgement of the benefits (if any) that the defendant wrongfully received: *Federal Sugar Refining Co. v. United States Sugar Equalization Bd.*, 268 F. 575 (S.D. N.Y. 1920). Suggest a situation in which it would be preferable to do so. Depending upon the circumstances, the plaintiff also may be entitled to punitive

damages and injunctive relief. Suggest situations in which each of those remedies would be appropriate.

13. As the preceding notes suggest, important issues remain unresolved with respect to the tort of interference with contractual relations. Some authors go further, suggesting that the entire area must be re-considered and re-analyzed. See Simester & Chan, "Inducing Breach of Contract: One Tort or Two?" [2004] C.L.J. 132 (arguing for recognition of two distinct torts: one dealing with cases in which the defendant persuades the third party to breach its contract with the plaintiff, and the other dealing with cases in which the defendant prevents the third party from performing its agreement with the plaintiff).

14. Quite often, the same facts will support various claims by the same plaintiff. See for example *Daishowa Inc. v. Friends of the Lubicon* (1998), 39 O.R. (3d) 620 (Gen. Div.) which involved allegations of interference with contractual relations, interference with economic relations, intimidation, conspiracy, and defamation. As a general rule, the plaintiff is, of course, entitled to plead in the alternative: *Enviro-Tex Products Ltd. v. Fibrex Insulations Inc.* (2006), 80 O.R. (3d) 641 (C.A.). See also *Roman Corp. v. Hudson's Bay Oil & Gas Co.*, [1973] S.C.R. 820; and *Lysko v. Braley* (2006), 79 O.R. (3d) 721 (C.A.).

7. Intentional Interference with Economic Relations by Unlawful Means

We opened this chapter with a brief examination of *Allen v. Flood*, in which the House of Lords formulated the general proposition that the defendant's intentional, though otherwise *lawful*, interference with the plaintiff's business interests is not tortious. Consistent with that rule, we have seen that liability may be imposed, at least in some circumstances, if the defendant's interference with the plaintiff's business interests was both intentional and *unlawful*. Consequently, a tort may be committed if the defendant threatens an unlawful act in order to *intimidate* the plaintiff or a third party, *conspires* with another person to perform an unlawful act that injures the claimant, or *indirectly induces a breach of contract* by unlawful means. There are, admittedly, exceptions to this pattern of analysis. Actionable *conspiracy* may involve otherwise lawful actions, and a *direct interference with contractual relations* may occur by otherwise *lawful* means.

The question for present purposes is whether intimidation, unlawful conspiracy, and indirect interference with contractual relations are discrete instances of a larger principle. Before 1932, negligence was actionable only in specific categories of cases. The genius of *Donoghue v. Stevenson*, [1932] A.C. 562 (H.L.), was to extract a unifying principle from those categories and to use that principle as the basis for a generalized cause of action. Should the same process occur in the context of business torts? While there is no suggestion that the discrete actions for intimidation, conspiracy, and interference with contractual relations should be abolished, there is growing support for an as yet unnamed (hence "innominate," as it sometimes is called) tort of *intentional interference with economic relations by unlawful means*. Should that tort encompass all of the others? Could it do so?

The innominate tort has yet to receive the Supreme Court of Canada's imprimatur. It nevertheless is appearing with increasing frequency in the lower courts. And while its contents have yet to be settled, it often is said to require proof of four elements: (1) *interference* with business interests, (2) by *unlawful* means, (3) with an *intent to injure*, (4) resulting in *loss or injury*. See for example *Barretts & Baird (Wholesale) Ltd. v. Institution of Professional Civil Servants*, [1987] 1 R.L.R. 3.

There is much to be said for the emerging tort. As a matter of both legal and commercial morality, the existing actions sometimes seem unnecessarily constrained and there is a danger that worthy claims may fall through the cracks. At the same time, however, there is some need for caution. The discrete torts have been crafted over many years, by many minds, in many situations. Experience has eliminated most of the defects and deficiencies. In contrast, it is impossible to foresee all of the potential problems with a generalized cause of action. Moreover, at least in the interim, the innominate tort raises several questions. Which "economic interests" are protected? Which acts will be considered "unlawful?" To what extent must the defendant "intend" to harm the plaintiff (*e.g.* must the plaintiff's injury be the defendant's primary purpose)? What defences will apply to negate a *prima facie* claim? And so on.

REACH MD INC. v. PHARMACEUTICAL MANUFACTURERS ASSN. OF CANADA

(2003), 227 D.L.R. (4th) 458 (Ont. C.A.)

[The plaintiff ("Reach") sold "Herman M.D." calendars to health care professionals. As the name suggests, the calendars featured the cartoon character "Herman" in a variety of medical settings. The enterprise initially was an enormous success, largely because the calendars also contained advertisements purchased by drug companies. The situation changed, however, when the calendars caught the attention of the defendant ("PMAC"). PMAC was an organization of companies involved in the drug industry. On March 28, 1990, it told its members that advertisements in the Herman M.D. calendars violated its Code of Conduct. In fact, that was not true. While PMAC could have prohibited its members from purchasing advertising space in the plaintiff's calendar, its Code of Conduct did not actually do so. The impact on the Reach's business was devastating. Annual sales immediately plummeted from $850,000 to $200,000, and the business was dead within a short time.

Reach sued under all of the headings included in this chapter, as well as breach of fiduciary duty and breach of confidence. All of the claims failed at trial. Most significantly for present purposes, while PMAC was found to have committed the tort of interference with economic relations, Reach was denied damages. The judge reasoned that while PMAC's Code of Conduct did not actually prohibit the advertisements when the defendant communicated with its members on March 28, 1990, a valid prohibition was in place five months later, on August 20, 1990. The plaintiff appealed.]

LASKIN J.A.: [The appellate court began by holding that the trial judge had erred in finding that PMAC's action on August 20, 1990 validly prohibited its members from advertising in Reach's calendars.]

Reach cannot succeed on its main ground of appeal merely by showing that the Committee's . . . ruling was unauthorized. Instead, it must show that this ruling amounted to the tort of intentional interference with economic relations. To establish this tort, Reach must prove three elements:

(i) PMAC intended to injure Reach;

(ii) PMAC interfered with Reach's business by illegal or unlawful means; and

(iii) as a result of the interference Reach suffered economic loss.

. . .

To satisfy the first element, Reach need not prove that PMAC's predominant purpose was to injure it. This first element of the tort will be met as long as PMAC's unlawful act was in some measure directed against Reach. That is so even if–as PMAC claims–its predominant purpose was to advance its own interest and those of its members. In short, "The defendant's manoeuvre must have been targeted against the plaintiff, although its predominant purpose might well have been to advance his own interests thereby rather than to injure the plaintiff". See John G. Fleming, *The Law of Torts*, 9th ed., (1998) at p. 769. . . .

Even though PMAC may have acted to protect its members, its ruling was in some measure directed against Reach. Indeed the trial judge found at para. 23, "PMAC was clearly aware of the current and potential effects of its efforts on third parties such as the plaintiff". . . . The Committee must also have recognized these effects when it ruled in August 1990. On all the evidence, I see no other reasonable inference. See *Lonhro plc. v. Fayed*, [1989] 2 All E.R. 65 (C.A.), and *Daishowa Inc. v. Friends of the Lubicon* (1996), 27 O.R. (3d) 215 (Div. Ct.).

The second element of the tort–that PMAC interfered with Reach's business by illegal or unlawful means–on the facts of this case is the most contentious element. Unquestionably, the Committee's August 1990 ruling interfered with Reach's business, but did this ruling satisfy the "illegal or unlawful means" branch of the tort?

The case law reflects two different views of "illegal or unlawful means", one narrow, the other broad. The narrow view confines illegal or unlawful means to an act prohibited by law or by statute. . . .Though unauthorized, the Committee's August 1990 ruling was not prohibited either by law or by statute.

The broader view, however, extends illegal or unlawful means to an act the defendant "is not at liberty to commit"–in other words, an act without legal justification. Lord Denning espoused this broader view in *Torquay Hotel Co. Ltd. v. Cousins*, [1969] 1 All E.R. 522 at 530 (C.A.):

> I must say a word about unlawful means, because that brings in another principle. I have always understood that if one person deliberately interferes with the trade or business of another, and does so by unlawful means, that is, by an act which he is not at liberty to commit, then he is acting unlawfully, even though he does not procure or induce any actual breach of contract. If the means are unlawful, that is enough.

The trial judge adopted the principle in *Torquay Hotel* in finding that [the] March 28 letter was "an improper and unwarranted act" that satisfied the second element of the tort. Several Canadian appellate courts have taken the same view. For example, the Nova Scotia Court of Appeal applied this principle in finding a franchisor liable for unlawful interference with economic interests because of its unauthorized instruction to a franchisee's bank not to honour certain cheques. See *Volkswagen Canada Ltd. v. Spicer* (1978), 91 D.L.R. (3d) 42 (N.S.S.C. App. Div.). . . .

I think that the trial judge was right to take a broader view of illegal or unlawful means. It is, however, unnecessary to decide the outer limits of the principle in *Torquay Hotel*. Unlawful means at least include what occurred here: the Committee made a ruling that it was not authorized to make. Its ruling was beyond its powers. I see no policy reasons for taking a narrower view of unlawful means. Indeed, to do so would preclude redress against organizations like PMAC and others for any number of unauthorized acts that on a common sense view would be considered unlawful, but nonetheless, were not prohibited by law or by statute.

Taking this broader view of unlawful means, I conclude that the Committee's August 1990 ruling was an act PMAC "was not at liberty to commit". Reach has, thus, met the second element of the tort of intentional interference with economic relations. It has shown that PMAC interfered with its business by unlawful means.

Reach has also satisfied the third element of the tort. As a result of PMAC's interference, Reach obviously suffered economic loss. The Committee's . . . ruling caused Reach's advertising sales to plummet. Within a couple of years, Herman M.D. could no longer survive. I therefore conclude that because of the Committee's August 1990 ruling, PMAC is liable to Reach for the tort of intentional interference with economic relations.

[Having found PMAC liable to Reach under the tort of interference with economic relations, Laskin J.A. turned to the issue of damages. He held that if PMAC had known that it had not validly prohibited the advertisements on August 20, 1990, it would have immediately taken steps to rectify the situation. A prohibition therefore would have come into force within a year. Damages therefore were limited to the losses that Reach suffered in the twelve months following the commission of the tort.]

NOTES AND QUESTIONS

1. As illustrated by *Reach MD*, it is common for lawyers to plead some, if not all, of the business torts together. Is there any justification for retaining so many separate torts? Would it be possible and preferable to consolidate all of those actions into a single species of claim?

2. Describe a situation in which liability would be imposed under (1) the innominate tort, but not the torts of conspiracy or interference with contractual relations, (2) the tort of conspiracy, but not the innominate tort or the tort of interference with contractual relations, and (3) the tort of interference with contractual relations, but not the tort of conspiracy or the innominate tort.

3. How did the plaintiff in *Reach MD* satisfy the requirement of *unlawfulness*? Was the court's treatment of the concept consistent with the concept of unlawfulness in other business torts? What purpose is served by the requirement? Did Laskin J.A. sufficiently explain that purpose? Is it possible or prudent to define a concept without first establishing its precise nature and purpose?

Which types of misconduct will satisfy the requirement of unlawfulness? Will every breach of a legal obligation suffice? Should only breaches of legal obligations suffice? Leaving aside the role that it played under the tort of unlawful interference with economic interests, was the defendant's conduct otherwise actionable? If not, why should the defendant be liable for the plaintiff's loss?

Aside from *Reach MD*, several cases have taken a broad view of the requirement of unlawfulness. See for example *U.F.C.W., Local 1252 v. Cashin* (2002), 216 Nfld. & P.E.I.R. 41 (Nfld. C.A.); *Tran v. Financial Debt Recovery Ltd.* (2000), 193 D.L.R. (4th) 168 (Ont. S.C.J.), set aside on other grounds (2001), 40 C.C.L.T. (3d) 106 (Ont. Div. Ct.); and *A & B Sound Ltd. v. Future Shop Ltd.* (1995), 25 C.C.L.T. (2d) 1 (B.C.S.C.). Many of the leading authorities are reviewed by Lambert J.A. in *No. 1 Collision Repair*

& Painting (1982) Ltd. v. Insurance Corp. of British Columbia (2000), 80 B.C.L.R. (3d) 62 (C.A.).

The House of Lords has taken a far more restricted approach to the issue: *OBG Ltd. v. Allan; Douglas v. Hello!; Mainstream Properties Ltd. v. Young*, [2007] UKHL 21. Lord Nicholls, in dissent, said that "unlawful means" should include both civil wrongs and crimes. The majority, led by Lord Hoffmann, took an even narrower view and insisted on proof that the defendant had interfered with the claimant's business interests by committing a civilly actionable wrong against a third party (or would have done so, but for the fact that the third party did not suffer a loss). Would the facts of *Reach MD* satisfy either test articulated in the House of Lords? Which approach is best?

4. Despite a generally liberal approach, liability will be denied, notwithstanding purported damage to the claimant, if the defendant's actions were entirely innocent. In *Culhane v. ATP Aero Training Products Ltd.* (2004), 238 D.L.R. (4th) 112 (F.C.), aff'd (2005), 252 D.L.R. (4th) 340 (F.C.A.), both parties sold flight training manuals and examinations. The defendant began to offer the examinations free of charge over the Internet. The plaintiff claimed that the defendant's conduct constituted "predatory pricing" aimed at driving him out of business. The court rejected that allegation. It found that while the plaintiff undoubtedly had suffered a loss of profits, many causal factors were at play. It further found that while the defendant no longer received profits directly from the sale of its examinations, it had not been motivated by a desire to eliminate the plaintiff. Rather, the defendant's strategy was to attract customers to its website, where they might be persuaded to purchase other products, and where they would leave contact information that could be sold to marketers. Finally, the court found that since the defendant's conduct did not violate the terms of the *Competition Act*, R.S.C. 1985, c. C-34, it was not unlawful.

In *1175777 Ontario Ltd. v. Magna International Ltd.* (2001), 200 D.L.R. (4th) 521 (Ont. C.A.), it was held that the tort is not committed if a corporate director orders a subsidiary to refrain from signing an agreement and thereby creating a contract with the claimant. Nor is the tort committed if a municipality, in good faith and *intra vires*, created a mandatory recycling program that devastated the business of a private firm. It is irrelevant that the city foresaw the damage: *People Recycling Inc. v. Vancouver (City)* (2002), 13 C.C.L.T. (3d) 312 (B.C.S.C.). See also *Conversions by Vantasy Ltd. v. General Motors of Canada Ltd.* (2006), 205 Man. R. (2d) 131 (C.A.).

5. The tort of unlawful interference with economic relations may be used if the defendant "backballs" the plaintiff, so as to prevent the claimant from securing employment: see *Drouillard v. Cogeco Cable Inc.* (2005), 42 C.C.E.L. (3d) 222 (Ont. S.C.J.), aff'd 2007 CarswellOnt 2624 (C.A.) (WLeC).

6. How did Laskin J.A. define the requirement of *intention*? Was the court's treatment of the concept consistent with the concept of intention in other business torts?

7. Which defences are available in this context? Should justification defeat liability, as it does in the context of interference with contractual relations? See *Gerrard v. Manitoba* (1992), 81 Man. R. (2d) 295 (C.A.); and *Worthman v. Assessmed Inc.* (2006), 80 O.R. (3d) 249 (Div. Ct.).

8. In the United States, many of the issues governed by our nominate intentional economic torts are governed by a single *prima facie* tort doctrine. That doctrine holds the defendant liable for any deliberate and unjustified interference with the plaintiff's economic interests. See *Tuttle v. Buck*, 119 N.W. 946 (Minn. S.C. 1909); Forkosch, "An Analysis of the '*Prima Facie* Tort' Cause of Action" (1975) 42 Cornell L. Rev. 465; and Shapiro, "The *Prima Facie* Tort Doctrine: Acknowledging the Need for Judicial Scrutiny of Malice" (1983) 63 Boston U.L. Rev. 1101.

The same doctrine might have developed in England. In *Keeble v. Hickeringill* (1706), 103 E.R. 1127 at 1128 (Q.B.), the court stated: "[H]e who hinders another in his trade or livelihood is liable to an action for so injuring him." However, that *prima facie* tort approach was rejected by the House of Lords in *Allen v. Flood*, [1898] A.C. 1 (H.L.), which held that in the absence of a conspiracy, the intentional interference with economic interests by lawful means is not actionable.

The High Court of Australia previously recognized a principle that was very similar to the *prima facie* tort doctrine: *Beaudesert Shire Council v. Smith* (1966), 120 C.L.R. 145 (H.C.A.). The court had stated that "independently of trespass, negligence or nuisance but by an action upon the case, a person who suffers harm or loss as the inevitable consequence of the unlawful, intentional and positive acts of another is entitled to damages from that other." However, the court subsequently ruled that such a principle was unsound and should not be followed: *Northern Territory v. Mengel* (1995), 185 C.L.R. 307 (H.C.A.). See Mullany, "Beaudesert Buried" (1995) 111 L.Q.R. 583; Orr, "Abrogating the Beaudesert Aberration: the High Court on Governmental Liability in *Northern Territory v. Mengel*" (1996) 15 U. Tasm. L. Rev. 136; and Cane, "The Inexorable Advance of Negligence" (1995) 3 Torts L.J. 205.

In theory and in practice, what is the difference between the *prima facie* tort doctrine and the nominate economic torts? Is the tort that was applied in *Reach MD* the same as the *prima facie* tort doctrine found in American law and previously in Australian law?

9. The House of Lords thoroughly reviewed the "business torts" in *OBG Ltd. v. Allan*; *Douglas v. Hello!*; *Mainstream Properties Ltd. v. Young*, [2007] UKHL 21. It recognized four heads of liability: (1) procuring or inducing breach of contract, (2) unlawful interference with a trade or business, (3) intimidation of a third party causing the claimant loss, and (4) conspiracy. In doing so, it reiterated the general rule that bad faith, though an important element of some of the individual torts, is itself insufficient to trigger responsibility.

Much of the judgment is devoted to rejecting the "unified theory," previously popular in England, that blurred the line between inducing breach of contract and unlawful interference with business interests. Lord Hoffmann, with whom the other members of the panel agreed, drew a clear and sharp distinction. True, both torts presume the involvement of a third party. The differences between the two torts nevertheless are more substantial.

> (1) Inducing breach of contract obviously requires the existence of an agreement between the claimant and the third party, whom the defendant persuaded to breach. Unlawful interference does not so require.
>
> (2) Inducing breach of contract is a form of *accessory liability*. The claimant's primary action lies against the third party for breach of contract and the defendant's responsibility arises in conjunction with that breach. Unlawful interference, in

contrast, is a form of *primary liability*. It does not presume that the third party committed a wrong against the claimant.

(3) The defendant's actions in inducing a breach of contract need not themselves be wrongful. In contrast, as the name indicates, a claim of unlawful interference requires proof that the defendant committed the tort by acting in an otherwise unlawful manner.

(4) Inducing breach of contract is actionable as long as the defendant intended the third party to break its contract with the claimant, even if the defendant did not intend to hurt the claimant. Unlawful interference, in contrast, occurs only if the defendant intended to harm the claimant.

(5) Perhaps the easiest way to distinguish between the two torts is to consider the possibility of other actions arising from the same facts. If the claimant could sue the third party, then the defendant's liability likely consists of inducing breach of contract. If, however, the third party could successfully sue the defendant, then the claimant's action against the defendant probably consists of unlawful interference. Of course, in the right circumstances, both branches of that test may be met, thereby allowing the claimant a choice of torts against the defendant.

10. For other examples of the innominate action, see *Gersham v. Manitoba Vegetable Producers' Marketing Board* (1975), 65 D.L.R. (3d) 181 (Man. Q.B.), aff'd (1976), 69 D.L.R. (3d) 114 (Man. C.A.); *Int. Brotherhood of Teamsters, Local 213 v. Therien*, [1960] S.C.R. 265; *Volkswagen Can. Ltd. v. Spicer* (1978), 28 N.S.R. (2d) 496 (C.A.); *Ed Miller Sales & Rentals Ltd. v. Caterpillar Tractor Co.* (1994), 151 A.R. 1 (Q.B.), rev'd (1996), 187 A.R. 81 (C.A.); *Mintuck v. Valley River Band No. 63A* (1977), 75 D.L.R. (3d) 589 (Man. C.A.); *White Hatter Limousine Service Ltd. v. Calgary (City)* (1993), 144 A.R. 379 (Q.B.); *Paragon Properties (Finance) Ltd. v. Del Swan Trucking Inc.* (1998), 68 Alta. L.R. (3d) 165 (Q.B.); *Mead Johnson Canada v. Ross Pediatrics* (1996), 31 O.R. (3d) 237 (Gen. Div.); and *Canada Safeway Ltd. v. Man. Food & Commercial Workers Local 832* (1983), 22 Man. R. (2d) 12 (C.A.). For a critique of *Canada Safeway*, see Vincent, "Everything You Want in a Tort – and a Little Bit More" (1983) 25 C.C.L.T. 10.

REVIEW PROBLEM

Import Company purchased 50 mink coats and contracted to supply them to its best customer, Bridget Furs. The wholesale price of the furs was so low that Bridget advertised them at 25% below the regular price in a brochure that it mailed to 250 preferred customers. It offered to sell the coats to the first 50 customers who presented preferred customer cards on January 20.

Retail Union represented the employees of Bridget and was engaged in a lawful strike at the time. The strike was proving ineffective because customers were ignoring the picket lines around the store. Consequently, Retail Union set up "secondary picket" lines around suppliers of Bridget, including Import. Secondary picketing is not referred to in any relevant legislation. The employees of Import, members of another union, refused to cross the picket line, thereby preventing the delivery of the mink coats to Bridget.

Steven, an independent trucker, telephoned Import and volunteered to deliver the coats for a fee. Import's management doubted that Steven would be able to do so, but indicated that it would agree if he could enter its premises. Import's guess proved correct as Steven was turned back at the gates by an angry mob of picketers.

Import's management then met with Retail Union, which agreed to remove the picket line if Import returned the furs to the American supplier. Import agreed on January 19. As a result, Bridget was forced to turn away 100 preferred customers, who had lined up at the store on January 20 for the sale.

Discuss the possible economic torts arising from this incident.

27

DEFAMATION

1. Introduction
2. Elements of a Defamation Action
3. Defences
4. Remedies

1. Introduction

The torts discussed in the preceding chapters involve the protection of one's person, property and financial interests. The tort of defamation is unique in protecting one's reputation from unjustified attacks. While chattels can be replaced, and many physical injuries will heal, damage to one's reputation can often be irremediable. Thus, the damages awarded for defamation are aimed not only at compensating the plaintiff for damage to his or her personal or professional reputation, but also at vindicating the plaintiff's reputation and deterring future defamatory publications.

Nevertheless, the protection of reputation has to be balanced against another fundamental legal principle: the freedom of expression, enshrined in s. 2(b) of the *Canadian Charter of Rights and Freedoms*, Part I of the *Constitution Act, 1982*, being Schedule B to the *Canada Act 1982* (U.K.), 1982, c. 11. While the *Charter* does not apply directly to the common law tort of defamation, the Supreme Court of Canada affirmed in *Hill v. Church of Scientology*, [1995] 2 S.C.R. 1130, that the law of defamation should develop in light of *Charter* values. Further, as explained by LeBel J. in *Gilles E. Néron Communication Marketing Inc. v. Chambre des notaires du Québec*, [2004] 3 S.C.R. 95, freedom of expression predates the *Charter* and lies at the heart of our democratic institutions.

The tort of defamation recognizes the competing values of reputation and freedom of expression. This is reflected in the fact that, while it is relatively easy for a plaintiff to prove a *prima facie* case of defamation, there are also numerous defences available. Indeed, most of the law on the tort of defamation involves the applicability of the various defences. The defences signal that, in some situations, the value of free and uninhibited speech outweighs the need to protect a person's reputation. At the same time, however, a defendant who speaks falsely and maliciously will often lose the benefit of the defences. As you proceed through this chapter, ask yourself whether the current law strikes the appropriate balance between protecting reputation and freedom of expression.

Many of the principles underlying the law of defamation stem from older English case law. For example, the common law historically distinguished between slander (spoken defamation) and libel (written defamation, films, pictures, or other concrete forms of expression). Because slander is transitory, it was considered to be less damaging than libel and was actionable only in certain situations or on proof of special damages. The types of slander that were historically actionable *per se* were imputations of the commission of a crime, a loathsome disease, a lack of chastity (women only), and unfitness to practice one's trade or profession. On the other hand, damage is presumed in cases of libel. However, several Canadian jurisdictions have removed the distinction between libel and slander, replacing them with the broader notion of "defamation."

All Canadian jurisdictions have introduced some legislation regarding defamation. The legislation varies from province to province, but often contains provisions specific to the media and guidelines on the applicability of certain defences. Nevertheless, the common law principles are still predominant, and are the main focus of this chapter.

The tort of defamation is somewhat unusual in that it continues to involve the use of civil juries. Some jurisdictions provide an absolute right to a jury trial for defamation claims. The reasons for this are twofold. First, particularly in cases where the defendant has spoken out against a public official, it is believed that a jury provides protection from indirect censorship by the state. Second, as will be seen throughout this chapter, many of the issues in a defamation claim refer to community standards. For instance, "how would a reasonable person understand the defendant's remarks?" or "would this damage the plaintiff's reputation in the eyes of a reasonable person?" It can be argued that using a jury is the best way to apply such community standards.

Finally, the advent of the internet and electronic communications has had, and will continue to have, a significant effect on the law of defamation. The internet provides the opportunity to publish defamatory statements instantly to a worldwide audience, and the author of the statements is often permitted to use a pseudonym. It also raises questions with respect to jurisdiction (*e.g.*, where is an electronic communication "published?"); and with respect to those responsible for the publication (*e.g.*, should an internet service provider or the host of a chat room be liable for defamatory statements published there?). If the defamatory statements are "published" in a foreign jurisdiction, a plaintiff might have difficulty, as a practical matter, obtaining compensation or having the defamatory remarks removed from the website. All of these issues will need to be addressed as the law of defamation enters the information age.

NOTES AND QUESTIONS

1. For general texts on the law of defamation, see Brown, *The Law of Defamation in Canada*, 2d ed. (1994); McConchie & Potts, *Canadian Libel and Slander Actions* (2004); Milmo & Rogers, *Gatley on Libel and Slander*, 9th ed. (1998); and Price & Duodu, *Defamation Law, Procedure & Practice*, 3d ed. (2004). For an historical review of the competing values in this area of the law, see Jones, *Insult to Injury: Libel, Slander, and Invasions of Privacy* (2003).

2. The United States Supreme Court has attempted to balance free speech against the protection of reputation in a different way. In *New York Times Co. v. Sullivan*, 376 U.S. 254 (Ala. 1964), the court decided that the existing common law of defamation violated freedom of speech and unduly prevented the press from speaking out against public officials. The court ruled that, where the plaintiff is a public figure, he or she must establish that the defendant knew the statements were false or was reckless as to whether they were false at the time they were made. This has come to be known as the "actual malice" rule.

In *Hill v. Church of Scientology*, [1995] 2 S.C.R. 1130, the Supreme Court of Canada considered and rejected the approach in *Sullivan*, finding that the existing law of defamation struck the appropriate balance between competing values. Thus, in Canada, once the plaintiff proves that the defendant's statements were defamatory, they are presumed to be false and the burden is on the defendant to prove otherwise.

Do you prefer the approach in *Sullivan* or in *Hill*? At least one author has criticized the Supreme Court of Canada for not adopting *New York Times v. Sullivan*. See Boivin, "Accommodating Freedom of Expression and Reputation in the Common Law of Defamation" (1997) 22 Queen's L.J. 229. See also Tingley, "Reputation, Freedom of Expression and the Tort of Defamation in the United States and Canada: A Deceptive Polarity" (1999) 37 Alta. L. Rev. 620.

For criticism of the actual malice rule, see Lewis, "*New York Times v. Sullivan* Reconsidered: Time to Return to 'The Central Meaning of the First Amendment'" (1983) 83 Col. L. Rev. 603; Epstein, "Was *New York Times v. Sullivan* Wrong?" (1986) 53 U. Chi. L. Rev. 782; and Leval, "The No-Money, No-Fault Libel Suit: Keeping *Sullivan* in its Proper Place" (1988) 101 Harv. L. Rev. 1287. It has been argued that the decision in *Sullivan* actually increased the number of defamation actions, and has also made them longer and more expensive to litigate.

3. For articles discussing the actual or desired impact of the *Charter* on defamation actions, see Ross, "The Common Law of Defamation Fails to Enter the Age of the *Charter*" (1996) 35 Alta. L. Rev. 117; and Boivin, *supra*. The authors suggest that the current common law of defamation does not adequately protect freedom of expression, citing the Supreme Court of Canada's rejection of *Sullivan* as an example. They also suggest that the value of a good reputation is outdated and ought not to be protected as fiercely in modern society. Do you agree?

4. For examples of provincial legislation regarding defamation, see *Libel and Slander Act*, R.S.B.C. 1996, c. 263; *Libel and Slander Act*, R.S.O. 1990, c. L.12; *Defamation Act*, R.S.N.S. 1989, c. 122; and *Defamation Act*, R.S.A. 2000, c. D-7.

5. For an examination of the jurisdictional issues implicated in actions for defamation via the internet, see Martin, "*Tolofson* and Flames in Cyberspace: The Changing Landscape of Multistate Defamation" (1997) 31 U.B.C.L. Rev. 127.

2. Elements of a Defamation Action

In order to succeed in a defamation action, the plaintiff must prove on the balance of probabilities that the impugned statements (i) were defamatory, (ii) made reference to the plaintiff, and (iii) were published or disseminated.

(a) DEFAMATORY MATERIAL

It is relatively easy for a plaintiff to establish that statements are defamatory, and few cases are dismissed at this stage. A plaintiff may allege that the statements were defamatory in the plain and ordinary sense (sometimes referred to as their "literal" meaning). However, even if the plain and ordinary meaning of the words seems innocent, the plaintiff may establish defamatory meaning in two other ways. First, if there are facts or circumstances extraneous to the publication that are known to those receiving the publication and would give the publication a defamatory meaning, the plaintiff may succeed on the basis of "legal innuendo" or "true innuendo." For example, a photo caption describing a man and his "girlfriend" seems innocent enough on its face. Nevertheless, if extraneous materials prove that the man was married, there is an innuendo that the man is having an illicit affair, and the publication could be considered defamatory. See the similar circumstances in *Duval v. O'Beirne* (1912), 20 O.W.R. 884 (H.C.); and *Cairns v. John Fairfax & Sons Ltd.*, [1983] 2 N.S.W.L.R. 708 (C.A.). Legal innuendo may also arise if the statements make use of slang or technical language that would be known to the particular audience. The plaintiff has the burden of proving the extraneous facts or circumstances necessary to support the plea of innuendo.

Second, if the plaintiff can establish that an ordinary person would infer something defamatory from apparently innocent remarks, even without special knowledge of the plaintiff or the circumstances, then the plaintiff may succeed on the basis of "false innuendo" or "popular innuendo." This is not an independent pleading: a plaintiff arguing false innuendo is essentially arguing that a reasonable person would understand the "plain and ordinary" meaning of the statements to be something more than their literal meaning. In other words, the plain and ordinary meaning of a statement includes those things that a reasonable person would infer from them. The plaintiff raised false innuendo in the case below.

SIM v. STRETCH

[1936] 2 All E.R. 1237 (H.L.)

[A housemaid, Edith, worked for the defendant and then for the plaintiff. She later returned to her employment with the defendant, who sent the following telegram to the plaintiff: "Edith has resumed her service with us to-day. Please send her possessions and the money you borrowed, also her wages to Old Barton.—Sim." Old Barton was the defendant's home.]

LORD ATKIN: – . . .Before dealing with the appeal it is necessary to explain the reference in the telegram to "money borrowed." It appears that at the end of March, "a week just before Easter," which that year fell on Apr. 1, Mrs. Sim had been away for a week. She had left money with Edith to pay the books, but had arranged on Edith's suggestion that anything over Edith should pay out of her own money. Apparently Edith paid two small items amounting to 14s., which sum was outstanding on Apr. 12, and was in fact paid on Apr. 15.

The statement of claim, after alleging publication of the words of the telegram to the officials of the post office whose duty it was to transmit and deal with the telegram, alleged in para 7:

> By the said words the defendant meant and was understood to mean that the plaintiff was in pecuniary difficulties, that by reason thereof he had been compelled to borrow and had in fact borrowed money from the said housemaid, that he had failed to pay the said housemaid her wages and that he was a person to whom no one ought to give any credit.

At the close of the plaintiff's case counsel for the defendant submitted that the words were incapable either of the meaning alleged in the innuendo or of any defamatory meaning. The learned judge rejected the submission, and counsel for the plaintiff urged the innuendo before the jury as he has done both in the Court of Appeal and in your Lordships' House. My Lords, it appears to me that the alleged innuendo is fantastic and that the words used are in their ordinary meaning incapable of being understood by reasonable persons as conveying an imputation upon the plaintiff's financial credit. It was, in my opinion, the duty of the judge so to hold, and to withdraw the count alleging the innuendo from the jury. . ..

. . .

The question, then, is whether the words in their ordinary signification are capable of being defamatory. Judges and textbook writers alike have found difficulty in defining with precision the word "defamatory." The conventional phrase exposing the plaintiff to hatred, ridicule and contempt is probably too narrow. The question is complicated by having to consider the person or class of persons whose reaction to the publication is the test of the wrongful character of the words used. I do not intend to ask your Lordships to lay down a formal definition, but after collating the opinions of many authorities I propose in the present case the test: would the words tend to lower the plaintiff in the estimation of right-thinking members of society generally? Assuming such to be the test of whether words are defamatory or not there is no dispute as to the relative functions of judge and jury, of law and fact. It is well settled that the judge must decide whether the words are capable of a defamatory meaning. That is a question of law: is there evidence of a tort? If they are capable, then the jury is to decide whether they are in fact defamatory. Now, in the present case it is material to notice that there is no evidence that the words were published to anyone who had any knowledge at all of any of the facts that I have narrated above. There is no direct evidence that they were published to anyone who had ever heard of the plaintiff. The post office officials at Maidenhead would not be presumed to know him, and we are left without any information as to the officials at Cookham Dean. The plaintiff and his wife dealt at the shop at which was the sub-post office, but there is no evidence that the shopkeeper was the telegraph clerk; the probability is that he was not. It might, however, be inferred that the publication of the telegram at Cookham Dean was to someone who knew the plaintiff. What would he or she learn by reading the telegram? That Edith Saville had been in the plaintiff's employment; that she had that day entered the defendant's employment; and that the former employer was requested to send on to the new place of employment the servant's possessions together with the money due to her for money borrowed and for wages. How could perusal of that communication tend to lower the plaintiff in the estimation of the right-thinking peruser who knows nothing of the circumstances but what he or she derives from the telegram itself. The defamatory imputation is said to be in the words "the money you borrowed," coupled with the request for the return of it sent in a telegram. It was said by the learned judge at the trial and accepted by the two members of the Court of Appeal who affirmed the judgment that the words were capable of conveying to anybody that the plaintiff had acted in a mean way borrowing money from his own maid and not paying her as he was required to and required to by telegram and also withholding her wages. With the greatest respect, that is imputing to the words a suggestion of meanness both in borrowing and in not repaying which I find it impossible to extract from their ordinary meaning. The sting is said to be in the borrowing. It happens that the phrase is substantially true. I myself have no doubt that if we were merely regarding legal technicalities the transaction which I have described as to the 14s. which was still unpaid could be covered by an indebitatus count for money lent as well as for money paid. In substance and in fact a justification of money borrowed would have been made out. But I am at a loss to understand why a person's character should be lowered in anyone's estimation if he or she has borrowed from a domestic servant. I should have thought it such a usual domestic occurrence for small sums to be advanced in such circumstances as the present, and with the assent of everyone concerned to be left outstanding for some days that the mere fact of borrowing from a servant bears not the slightest tinge of "meanness." Of course there may be special circumstances, and so large an amount may be borrowed or left so long unpaid that the facts when known would reflect on the character of the master. But to make an imputation which is based upon the existence of facts unknown and not to be inferred from the words attacked is surely exactly to come under the ban of Lord Esher [then Brett L.J.] cited in *Nevill v. Fine Art & General Insurance Co*, [[1897] A.C. 68 (C.A.)] at p 73:

> It seems to me unreasonable that, when there are a number of good interpretations, the only bad one should be seized upon to give a defamatory sense to the document.

It is not a case where there is only the choice between two reasonable meanings, one harmless and one defamatory. It is a case where there is only one reasonable meaning which is harmless, and where the defamatory meaning can only be given by inventing a state of facts which are not disclosed, and are in fact non-existent. . ..

[Lord Atkin discussed several cases cited by counsel which he found to be unhelpful.]

I only cite *Clay v. Roberts* [(1863), 8 L.T. 397] because of its reference to social conditions 70 years ago. It was held that it could not be defamatory to say of a physician that he met homopathists in consultation.

Would it be libellous, asked Pollock, C.B., at p. 398, to write of a lady of fashion that she had been seen on the top of an omnibus; or of a nobleman, that he was in the habit of burning tallow-candles? There is a distinction between imputing what is merely a breach of conventional etiquette, and what is illegal, mischievous, or sinful.

I think that no importance can be attached to the words being published by a telegram. The defendant who had acted quite unjustifiably repaired his wrong to some extent by giving immediate notice as to what had happened to the maid. It was quite natural and proper that he should ask for the maid's possessions to be sent to a named address and natural that he should in the same communication ask that the money, which in fact was due to her, should be sent to the same place. The truth of this case is that the whole matter is a trumpery affair and that the alleged libel would probably never have been heard of but for the wounded feelings caused by the improper enticement. That juries should be free to award damages for injuries to reputation is one of the safeguards of liberty. But the protection is undermined when exhibitions of bad manners or discourtesy are placed on the same level as attacks on character; and are treated as actionable wrongs. In the present case I find myself in complete agreement with the judgment of Slesser LJ. Being of opinion with him that the words complained of are incapable of a defamatory meaning, I am of opinion that the appeal should be allowed. The order of the Court of Appeal should be set aside and the verdict and judgment at the trial on the issue of libel should be set aside and judgment entered for the defendant. . .. I move your Lordships accordingly.

[Lord Macmillan and Lord Russell of Killowen agreed.]

NOTES AND QUESTIONS

1. How does Lord Atkin identify "defamatory" statements? Is the test objective or subjective?

2. The courts have gone to considerable lengths to define an "ordinary" or "right thinking" person. For instance, in *Lewis v. Daily Telegraph*, [1964] A.C. 234 at 259-60 (H.L.), Lord Reid remarked,

> Ordinary men and women have different temperaments and outlooks. Some are unusually suspicious and some are unusually naive. One must try to envisage people between these two extremes and see what is the most damaging meaning that they would put on the words in question. . .
>
> What the ordinary man, not avid for scandal, would read into the words complained of must be a matter of impression.

Similarly, in *Saunders v. Randolph Hotel Co. Ltd.*, [1945] O.R. 600 at 604 (C.A.), Laidlaw J.A. warned against assuming the position of someone "of prejudice, bias or evil mind" or someone "of low mentality and intellect." See also *Macdonald v. Mail Printing Co.* (1900), 32 O.R. 163 (H.C.J.), rev'd on other grounds (1901), 2 O.L.R. 278 (C.A.); *W. v. A.* (1908), 13 B.C.R. 333 (C.A.); *I.W. Holdsworth Ltd. v. Assoc. Newspapers Ltd.* (1937), 53 T.L.R. 1029 (C.A.); *Botiuk v. Toronto Free Press Publications Ltd.*, [1995] 3 S.C.R. 3; *Color Your World Corp. v. Canadian Broadcasting Corporation* (1998), 38 O.R. (3d) 97 (C.A.); *Hodgson v. Canadian Newspapers Co.* (1998), 39 O.R. (3d) 235 (Gen. Div.), varied with respect to damages (2000), 49 O.R. (3d) 161 (C.A.); and *Mantini v. Smyth Lyons LLP (No. 2)* (2003), 64 O.R. (3d) 516 (C.A.).

3. Is there a difference between an ordinary person and a right thinking person? Should a plaintiff be allowed to succeed in a defamation action if the statements would lower his or her reputation in only part of the community? For example in *Mawe v. Pigott* (1869), I.R. 4 C.L. 54, an Irish priest claimed that he had been defamed by accusations that he was an informer against Irish criminals. He argued that a certain class of Irishmen would therefore think ill of him. The court found that "right thinking" men would likely think better of the priest as a result of the accusations, so they could not be defamatory just because they might cause a smaller class of persons to think less of him.

The test of "right thinking" persons has been criticized as impractical in modern pluralistic society: Deakin, Johnston & Markesinis, *Markesinis and Deakin's Tort Law*, 5th ed. (2003) at 645-48. For example, it has historically been considered defamatory to call someone a homosexual, and some people might still consider it to be so. However, given changing attitudes and recent equality jurisprudence, it may be difficult to maintain that "right thinking" members of society continue to find this defamatory.

Courts will consider community standards when deciding whether a statement would be understood as defamatory. For example the label of "papist" has been considered defamatory at different times during the history of England (see for example *Walden v. Mitchell* (1692), 86 E.R. 431 (K.B.)) and the label of "freemason" was considered actionable by a candidate running for office in a Catholic community of Québec (*Lareau v. La Compagnie d'Imprimerie de la Minerve* (1883), 27 L.C. Jur. 336 (S.C.)).

4. In determining whether something is defamatory, one must examine both the context of the words and the mode of publication. The courts will generally view the publication as a whole, rather than focus on isolated passages, because that is how the ordinary reader would understand it. This includes headlines, pictures and illustrations. See *Slim v. Daily Telegraph Ltd.*, [1968] 2 Q.B. 157 (C.A.).

If the allegedly defamatory remarks are made during a radio or television broadcast, the court should consider gestures, facial expressions, and tone of voice. Esson J. wrote in *Vogel v. Canadian Broadcasting Corporation*, [1982] 3 W.W.R. 97 (B.C.S.C.):

> [T]elevision programs. . . by reason of their transitory nature, tend to leave the audience with an impression rather than a firm understanding of what was said. Images, facial expressions, tones of voice, symbols and the dramatic effect which can be achieved by juxtaposition of segments may be more important than the meaning derived from careful reading of the words of the script.

See also *Lougheed v. Canadian Broadcasting Corporation*, [1979] 3 W.W.R. 334 (Alta. C.A.); *Color Your World, supra*; and *Pressler v. Lethbridge* (2000), 86 B.C.L.R. (3d) 257 (C.A.).

5. If the court concludes that ordinary people would find a statement to be defamatory, it is not a defence to argue that the defendant did not intend the statement to be defamatory (*E. Hulton & Co. v. Jones*, [1910] A.C. 21 (H.L.)) or that the defendant had a commendable motive (*Dennis v. Southam Co.* (1954), 13 W.W.R. (N.S.) 494 (Man. C.A.)).

6. The types of allegations that have been considered defamatory are legion, and are limited only by the human imagination. The allegations in the following cases have been found to be defamatory: *Mychajluk v. Kolisnyk*, [1923] 4 D.L.R. 724 (Man. K.B.) (corruption); *Lawrence v. Finch* (1930), 66 O.L.R. 451 (C.A.) (dishonesty); *Patching v. Howarth* (1930), 43 B.C.R. 108 (C.A.) (sexual immorality); *Houseman v. Coulson*, [1948] 2 D.L.R. 62 (Sask. K.B.) (having a venereal disease); *Warren v. Green* (1958), 25 W.W.R. 563 (Alta. S.C.) (doctor referred to as a "quack"); *Theaker v. Richardson*, [1962] 1 W.L.R. 151 (C.A.) (prostitution); *Wheeler v. Somerfield*, [1966] 2 Q.B. 94 (C.A.) (glibness); *Bonham v. Pure Water Association* (1970), 74 W.W.R. 617 (B.C.S.C.) (hypocrisy); *Murphy v. LaMarsh*, [1971] 2 W.W.R. 196 (B.C.C.A.) (being detested by others); *Loan v. MacLean* (1975), 58 D.L.R. (3d) 228 (B.C.S.C.) (stupidity); *Cherneskey v. Armadale Publishers Ltd.*, [1979] 1 S.C.R. 1067 (racism); *Bennett v. Stupich* (1981), 30 B.C.L.R. 57 (S.C.) (habitual drunkenness of politician); *Moores v. Salter* (1982), 37 Nfld. & P.E.I.R. 128 (Nfld. Dist. Ct.) (profanity); *Planned Parenthood Newfoundland/Labrador v. Fedorik* (1982), 135 D.L.R. (3d) 714 (Nfld. S.C.) (causing a rise in illegitimacy and abortion rates); *Berkoff v. Burchill*, [1996] 4 All E.R. 1008 (C.A.) (ugliness); *Seraphim v. Sterling Newspapers Ltd.*, 2001 CarswellBC 2107 (S.C.) (WLeC) (criminal conviction); and *Newman v. Halstead*, 2006 CarswellBC 52 (S.C.) (WLeC) (suggesting that teachers were bullies and associated with pedophiles).

For a more complete catalogue, see Brown, *The Law of Defamation in Canada*, 2d ed. (1994), ch. 4. However, Brown warns that precedents on what constitutes defamation do not carry as much weight as precedents in other area of tort law, due to changes in social conditions and the meaning of language, as well as the context and circumstances of any given case.

(b) REFERENCE TO THE PLAINTIFF

The plaintiff in a defamation action has the burden of showing, on a balance of probabilities, that the defamatory statement made reference to the plaintiff. This requirement has historically been known as "colloquium." The case is simple if the defamatory statement refers to the plaintiff by name. However, the requirement can also be satisfied in the absence of express reference, as explained in the case below.

KNUPPFER v. LONDON EXPRESS NEWSPAPER, LTD.
[1944] A.C. 116 (H.L.)

[The defendants published an article regarding a group known as "Young Russia." The article claimed that the members of this group were pro-Hitler and expected that one of them would be selected as a "puppet fuehrer" by Hitler to head up a fascist Russian state. The plaintiff was the leader of the British branch of Young Russia, but was not named in the article. At trial, he called four witnesses who were asked, "To whom did your mind go when you read that article?" Each one indicated the plaintiff. The plaintiff was awarded £3,500 at trial, but this was reversed by the Court of Appeal. The plaintiff appealed to the House of Lords.]

VISCOUNT SIMON L.C.: – My Lords, it is an essential element of the cause of action for defamation that the words complained of should be published "of the plaintiff." If the words are not so published, the plaintiff is not defamed and cannot have any right to ask that the defendant should be held responsible to him in respect of them.

In the words complained of in this case there is no specific mention of the appellant from beginning to end, and the only countries in which it is stated that this group of emigrés is established are France and the United States. Evidence was given at the trial that the appellant had joined the Young Russia Party in 1928, that in 1935 he became assistant representative of the Young Russia movement in Great Britain, and that in 1938 he was appointed representative of the movement in Great Britain and head of the British branch of the movement. The headquarters of the movement were in Paris until June, 1940, when they were removed to America.

These facts, standing alone, however, do not justify the conclusion that the words complained of are capable of being read as a defamation of the appellant. The words make allegations of a defamatory character about a body of persons - some thousands in number - who belong to a society whose members are to be found in many countries.

. . .

There are two questions involved in the attempt to identify the appellant as the person defamed. The first question is a question of law - can the article, having regard to its language, be regarded as capable of referring to the appellant? The second question is a question of fact - Does the article, in fact, lead reasonable people, who know the appellant, to the conclusion that it does refer to him? Unless the first question can be answered in favour of the appellant, the second question does not arise, and where the trial judge went wrong was in treating evidence to support the identification in fact as governing the matter, when the first question is necessarily, as a matter of law, to be answered in the negative. I move that this appeal be dismissed.

NOTES AND QUESTIONS

1. What error in the trial judge's reasoning did Viscount Simon L.C. identify?

2. The test in *Knuppfer* has been affirmed in Canada. See for example *Arnott v. College of Physicians and Surgeons (Sask.)*, [1954] S.C.R. 538; *Booth v. B.C.T.V. Broadcasting Systems* (1982), 139 D.L.R. (3d) 88 (B.C.C.A.); and *Butler v. Southam Inc.* (2001), 197 N.S.R. (2d) 97 (C.A.).

3. There are many ways that a plaintiff can be identified without being specifically named. See for example *Barnes v. Carter* (1910), 16 O.W.R. 911 (H.C.J.) (obituary indicating that plaintiff's mother was an unmarried woman, leading to the inference that the plaintiff was conceived out of wedlock); *Byrne v. Deane*, [1937] 1 K.B. 818 (C.A.) (play-on-words involving the plaintiff's name); *Jozwiak v. Sadek*, [1954] 1 W.L.R. 275 (Q.B.) (allegedly fictional character closely resembled the plaintiff); *Scelfo v. Rutgers University*, 282 A.2d 445 (N.J. 1971) (photograph of plaintiff accompanying article); *E.W. Scripps Co. v. Cholmondelay*, 569 S.W.2d 700 (Ky. App. 1978) (news article identified one party to a fight but not the plaintiff); and *Hayward v. Thompson*, [1981] 3 W.L.R. 470 (C.A.) (reference to political donations for which plaintiff had gained notoriety).

4. *Knuppfer* also addresses the more specific issue of when a plaintiff can be considered "identifiable" through membership in a group that has been defamed. The general rule is that the individual members of a large group cannot succeed in an action for defamation unless there is something in the statement that identifies a particular member: *Abraham v. The Advocate Co.*, [1946] 2 W.W.R. 181 (P.C.); and *Elliott v. Canadian Broadcasting Corporation* (1993), 16 O.R. (3d) 677 (Gen. Div.), aff'd on other grounds (1995), 25 O.R. (3d) 302 (C.A.). But see *A.U.P.E. v. Edmonton Sun* (1986), 75 A.R. 253 (Q.B.), where the court found that a group of nearly 200 officers employed at a Correction Centre were defamed by an editorial that described officers at the centre as "goons" and a "gang of bumbling yo-yos." The writer had not taken care to restrict his comments to the individuals involved in a recent incident with a photographer, and a reasonable person who knew one of the plaintiffs or identified the plaintiffs through their distinctive uniforms would be of the opinion that the comments referred to the plaintiffs.

Where the group in question is small and the statement refers to the entire group, *Knupffer* indicates that each member may have an action for defamation.

Some jurisdictions have enacted legislation allowing members of religious or racial groups that have been defamed by racist comments to sue for an injunction to end such remarks. See for example *Defamation Act*, C.C.S.M. c. D20, s. 19(1).

5. If a plaintiff satisfies the colloquium requirement, it is not a defence to argue that the defendant did not intend to identify the plaintiff. Nor can the defendant argue that he or she did not know the plaintiff existed. The test is not what the defendant meant, but how the defendant's statement would be understood by a reasonable person to whom it was published: *Clarke v. Stewart* (1916), 10 Alta. L.R. 393 (C.A.). In making this determination, the court will consider the surrounding circumstances (*e.g.*, who the speaker was, the knowledge the speaker would be presumed to have, and the likely audience). See *Booth, supra.*

However, it is not sufficient if only the *plaintiff* believed that the statements made reference to him or her. The plaintiff must show that the reasonable person to whom the statements were published would understand them to be referring to the plaintiff. See *Willows v. Williams* (1950), 2 W.W.R. (N.S.) 657 (Alta. S.C.); and *Risk v. Zeller's Ltd.* (1977), 27 N.S.R. (2d) 532 (S.C. (T.D.)). Furthermore, it is likely not sufficient for the plaintiff to call his or her relations or close friends to testify as to how they understood the statement: *Halprin v. The Sun Publishing Company Ltd.*, [1978] 4 W.W.R. 685 (B.C.S.C.); and *Dale's Trad'N Post v. Rhodes* (1987), 19 B.C.L.R. (2d) 73 (S.C.).

(c) PUBLICATION

Since the essence of this tort is injury to reputation, defamatory remarks are not actionable unless they are communicated to someone other than the plaintiff. This element of the tort is known as "publication," and will be satisfied as long as the statement is communicated, in any way, to a third party who understands the statement. Accordingly, there is no liability if the defendant made a remark to an empty room, or to a person who did not hear it or understand the language, or to the plaintiff alone.

As a general rule, every repetition of a defamatory statement is considered a new publication that is independently actionable: *Lambert v. Thomson*, [1937] O.R. 341 (C.A.), rev'd on other grounds [1938] S.C.R. 253. Thus, someone who repeats a statement that originated with someone else may be held liable in defamation, even if he or she believed the statement to be true, specifically named the source of the statement, or did not adopt the defamatory remark. As Grimmer J. noted in *Trafton v. Deschene* (1917), 44 N.B.R. 552 at 559 (S.C. (A.D.)), "Tale bearers are as bad as tale makers."

Further, any party who had a part in communicating the defamatory statements may be subject to liability. Thus, a defendant may be liable not only for originating the statement, but also for repeating it, printing it, or allowing it to be posted on premises over which the defendant has control. Similarly, an employer may be liable for defamatory remarks made by an employee acting within the scope of employment. Nevertheless, the person who originated the defamatory remarks will not be liable for their repetition by others unless (i) he or she has given express or implied authority for the remarks to be republished, (ii) he or she made the remarks to someone who had a moral, legal or social duty to republish those remarks, or (iii) the republication is a natural and probable consequence of the original publication.

NOTES AND QUESTIONS

1. Publication can occur orally, in writing, by posters, signs or cartoons, by gestures, or any other form of communication. In some, but not all, American states, publication has even been found to occur when a will is probated. Thus, the estate may be liable if the testator made defamatory remarks when explaining why certain distributions were made: see for example *Harris v. Nashville Trust Co.*, 128 Tenn. 573 (1914); and *Brown v. Mack*, 56 N.Y.S.2d 910 (1945).

2. Publication does not occur when a person makes a defamatory remark about the plaintiff to his or her own spouse. See *Wennhak v. Morgan* (1888), 20 Q.B.D. 635; and *Huth v. Huth*, [1915] 3 K.B. 32 (C.A.). What do you think is the reason for the special treatment of conversation between spouses? Is it justifiable? Should it apply to other relationships?

3. A defendant may not be liable if a defamatory remark is overheard entirely by accident: *McNichol v. Grandy*, [1931] S.C.R. 696. Similarly, if the statement is read by someone for whom it was not intended, and the defendant had no reason to believe that it would be read by such a person, the defendant may avoid liability. For instance, in *Huth*, *supra*, the defendant wrote a letter to his wife which was opened and read, out of curiosity, by the wife's servant. This was found not to be "publication" to the servant, since the husband had no reason to believe that the letter would be opened by the servant.

However, if a writer knows that the addressee's mail is normally opened and screened by someone else, then the writer may be considered to have "published" the statement to that person: see *Delacroix v. Thevenot* (1817), 171 E.R. 573 (K.B.). See also *O'Malley v. O'Callaghan* (1992), 128 A.R. 28 (Q.B.).

4. Where defamatory material is contained in a newspaper, magazine or book, the plaintiff may sue anyone who takes part in its publication, including the author, editor, proprietor and printer: see *Popovich v. Lobay (No. 2)* (1937), 45 Man. R. 327 (C.A.). These parties should be sued as joint tortfeasors in a single cause of action: *Thomson v. Lambert*, [1938] S.C.R. 253. It is no defence to claim that the defendant was not aware of the defamatory remarks. However, those playing a subordinate role in the distribution of such material (*e.g.* vendors, newspaper carriers, or librarians) are not liable unless they know or ought to suspect that the material is defamatory. See *Vizetelly v. Mudie's Select Library Ltd.*, [1900] 2 Q.B. 170 (C.A.).

In *Menear v. Miguna* (1996), 30 O.R. (3d) 602 (Gen. Div.), rev'd (1997), 33 O.R. (3d) 223 (C.A.), on a motion for summary judgment the judge had concluded that a printing company played a subordinate role in the publication of defamatory material and could succeed on a defence of "innocent dissemination." The judge relied on evidence that modern technology does not require a printer to read or edit the material that is being printed. The Court of Appeal reversed the granting of summary judgment on the grounds that the argument ought to be examined more fully at trial. Do you think that printers should be considered subordinate players, or should they be liable as joint tortfeasors even if they are unaware of defamatory content?

5. *Botiuk v. Toronto Free Press Publications Ltd.*, [1995] 3 S.C.R. 3, examined the issue of joint liability for defamation. The plaintiff, a lawyer, had performed substantial legal services on behalf of the Ukranian-Canadian Committee (UCC) during a public inquiry. He did not expect to be paid for his services because the UCC did not have sufficient funds for this purpose. However, the UCC received an award of costs and the plaintiff then submitted a bill for his services. The first defendant, Maksymec, submitted a report to the UCC complaining about the plaintiff's fees, and the report was later reprinted in a Ukranian-Canadian newspaper. Maksymec alleged that, in accordance with his agreement to provide services pro bono, the plaintiff should not receive any payment. Maksymec then wrote and published a declaration signed by the second defendants, a group of Ukranian lawyers who had provided very minimal services at the inquiry and suggested that there was an understanding that the work was to be performed pro bono. Maksymec later wrote another article on the subject that was reproduced in a Ukranian-Canadian publication, making reference to the declaration signed by the second defendants.

The plaintiff claimed in defamation for the damage done to his personal and professional reputation by all three publications, and was successful at trial and on appeal. Before the Supreme Court of Canada, the second defendants argued that they should not be held liable for the full defamatory effect of all three publications, since they had only participated in one of them. However, a majority of the Supreme Court of Canada affirmed that the second defendants were liable as joint tortfeasors for the consequences of all three publications. In doing so, the court relied on the notion of conspiracy, suggesting that the second defendants acted with Maksymec for a common intention and purpose, and knew that he would make extensive use of their declaration.

Is there any way that the second defendants could have avoided such liability? Is *Botiuk* consistent with the principle that each publication is a separate incidence of defamation? In a concurring opinion, Major J. doubted whether a common intention existed on the facts, and suggested that similar cases might be treated as separate instances of defamation in the future.

6. *Carter v. B.C. Federation of Foster Parents Assn.* (2005), 257 D.L.R. (4th) 133 (B.C.C.A.) examined the liability of those who host internet chat rooms for defamatory statements that are posted by subscribers. The defendant had a website with a chat room. One subscriber posted statements in the chat room that defamed the plaintiff. The plaintiff complained to the defendant, a representative of which undertook to remove the defamatory remarks. Two years later, however, the remarks remained on the website. The defendant's argument of "innocent dissemination" was rejected by the British Columbia Court of Appeal because the defamatory statements were brought to the defendant's attention and the defendant was clearly negligent.

Can you think of situations where a defence of innocent dissemination might be successful by the host of an internet chat room? How closely should such sites be monitored? How soon after a defamatory comment is posted should the host be expected to remove it?

What is the role of internet service providers in circulating defamatory statements? See Gosnell, "Hate Speech on the Internet: A Question of Context" (1998) 23 Queen's L.J. 369; and Savage, "Between a Rock and a Hard Place: Defamation and Internet Service Providers" (2002) 2 Asper Rev. of Int'l Bus. and Trade Law 107.

3. Defences

As with other torts, the defendant has the burden of proving any defence on a balance of probabilities. Since it is relatively easy for plaintiffs to make out a *prima facie* case of defamation, most of the litigation about this tort is focused on the various defences that can be raised. The first defence, justification, applies if the defendant can prove that the allegedly defamatory statements were true. The next three defences – absolute privilege, qualified privilege, and fair comment – do not rely on the truth of the statements but on the types of circumstances in which the statements were published. In these circumstances, the importance of free and open communication takes precedence over the damage to reputation that the plaintiff may suffer. The final defence, consent, rests on the principle that a person who has agreed to the publication of certain information cannot thereafter complain that it is defamatory.

In addition to these defences, of course, the defendant may argue that the impugned statements were not defamatory, did not refer to the plaintiff, or were not published.

(a) JUSTIFICATION

Once the plaintiff has proven that the statements made by the defendant were defamatory, the court will presume that those statements were false. Thus, it falls to the defendant to prove that the statements, though defamatory, were true. This defence is known as "justification." Justification is a complete defence to defamation: if the defendant proves that the statements were true, then the plaintiff's claim will be dismissed. A variety of reasons are typically offered for this result. In *McPherson v. Daniels* (1829), 109 E.R. 448 at 451 (K.B.), Littledale J. defended justification on the grounds that "the law will not permit a man to recover damages in respect of an injury to a character which he either does not, or ought not to possess." It has also been said that "What is true cannot be defamatory": *Courchene v. Marlborough Hotel Co.* (1971), 20 D.L.R. (3d) 109 (Man. Q.B.), aff'd [1972] 1 W.W.R. 149 (C.A.). Finally, as a matter of policy, the common law refuses to restrict free speech to the point that the truth is actionable. Thus, even though the plaintiff may be embarrassed by the revelation of certain facts about his or her life, and even though the revelation of those facts is of no benefit to the public interest, the plaintiff's claim will be defeated if those facts turn out to be true. A defendant can even succeed on a defence of justification if the statements were made maliciously.

A defendant pleading justification must show that "the whole of the defamatory matter is substantially true": *Meier v. Klotz* (1928), 22 Sask. L.R. 385 at 388 (C.A.). It is not sufficient for the defendant to show that he or she believed the statements to be true or relied on information provided by a third party. Nevertheless, the defendant need not prove the literal truth nor the truth of every single fact in the allegation. Generally speaking, the defendant needs to prove the truth of the statements that comprise the "sting" of the defamation. As discussed below in *Williams v. Reason* (1983), [1988] 1 All E.R. 262 (C.A.), a defamatory statement that is general in character may be justified by proving the truth of specific instances that support the general imputation. However, a single instance will not suffice. For example, in *Wakley v. Cooke* (1849), 154 E.R. 1316 (Exch.), the statement that the plaintiff was a "libellous journalist" was not justified by proving that the plaintiff had published one libellous story.

There is a disincentive to bringing a plea of justification: the defence is considered a re-publication of the impugned statements and, if the defence fails, the defendant will be liable for a separate instance of defamation. This may serve to aggravate damages, as discussed later in this chapter. Indeed, Idington J. warned in *Price v. Chicoutimi Pulp Co.* (1915), 51 S.C.R. 179 at 193-94, "A defence of justification involving the truth in substance and in fact of an alleged libel is often a perilous sort of proceeding."

WILLIAMS v. REASON

(1983), [1988] 1 All E.R. 262 (C.A.)

[The plaintiff was an amateur rugby player. The defendant was a sports correspondent for a national newspaper. The defendant wrote two articles accusing the plaintiff of "shamateurism" (*i.e.*, playing amateur rugby while accepting money from outside sources). The articles specifically referred to money that the plaintiff had received for writing a book about his rugby career. The plaintiff was successful at trial, but on appeal the defendant requested a new trial and sought to introduce new evidence that the plaintiff had received "boot money" from Adidas. The excerpts below discuss whether such evidence would be relevant to the defendant's plea of justification.]

STEPHENSON L.J.: – . . . In support of his submission that the evidence is admissible and leave to amend should be granted, counsel for the defendants cites, and I think is content to adopt, Duncan and Neill *Defamation* (1978) p 58, para 11.12 as an accurate statement of a difficult and developing branch of the law; cf *Gatley on Libel and Slander* (8th edn, 1981) pp 151-152, para 354. The former paragraph reads:

> 'In some cases the defendant may wish to contend that the words bear a less defamatory meaning than that alleged by the plaintiff and that in the less defamatory sense they are true. On the other hand, a defendant, with a view perhaps to introducing evidence of

"similar facts", may wish to contend that the words, which ex facie relate to a specific incident, would be understood in a wider sense, for example, as conveying a general charge of dishonesty. The law on this matter appears to be at a stage of development. If the plaintiff himself pleads an inferential meaning to the effect that the words meant, for example, that he was a dishonest man or unfit to be a director, the defendant will then be free to introduce evidence of other incidents which are relevant to prove the truth of the inferential meaning. But where the plaintiff, exercising perhaps a wise discretion, does not allege that the words impute, for example, general dishonesty, the position is less clear. It is submitted, however, that the scope of the defence of justification should not depend upon the way in which the plaintiff pleads his case but on the meaning which the words are found to bear. It is submitted therefore that the defendant is entitled to put before the jury evidence of any facts which are relevant to justify the words in any meaning which they are capable of bearing.'

. . .

None of the authorities comes very near the present case, and I have not found it easy to decide whether the evidence of boot money is relevant to the words which Mr Reason wrote of the plaintiff, understood in any meaning which they are reasonably capable of bearing. But I conclude that counsel for the defendants is right in contending that the sting of the libel here is 'shamateurism', the charge, still tied to his book but nevertheless carrying with it a charge of hypocrisy and deviousness, that the plaintiff was a professional while claiming to be an amateur, that the evidence which alleges that he regularly took boot money, if accepted, would prove that he had by reason of [the regulations governing amateur rugby] no amateur status to infringe or lose at the time he wrote the book because he had already lost it by taking boot money and that a jury which heard evidence that he had accepted boot money might have been influenced into finding that he had, on any interpretation of the regulations, infringed them by writing a book for money which he never intended to give to charity until the publication of the first of Mr Reason's articles in the Daily Telegraph.

A jury might think that to take comparatively small sums of boot money was much less serious than to get thousands of pounds for writing a book, even for one who put a high value on amateur status in Rugby Union football. They might consider the distinction between 'gentlemen' and 'players' long since dead and buried, not only on the cricket field, and, to give a new meaning to the words which Shakespeare's Jacques spoke in a theatrical context (*As You Like It* II. vii. 140), in every field of sport nowadays 'all the men and women merely players'. But a jury might take a more serious view of boot money and consider that by undermining the plaintiff's claim to amateur status its acceptance would provide justification for the more general allegation of 'shamateurism' which the defendants' articles might reasonably be understood to make. Accordingly, I cannot say that evidence of taking boot money would be irrelevant to the sting of the libel, and therefore inadmissible if this court allows the defendants' amendment.

The first trial was conducted on the basis that the sting of the libel was shamateurism and hypocrisy. . .. The trial developed, as counsel for the plaintiff described it, into 'a slanging match' between the plaintiff and the defendant Mr Reason, the only two witnesses called. In a comprehensive cross-examination, counsel for the defendants had taken the plaintiff through a number of documents which seemed on their face to require explanation if they were to be consistent with the plaintiff's evidence that he never intended to make anything out of his book but always intended to give what he or his agents received for it to a charity. Before the plaintiff left the witness-box counsel for the defendants was rightly compelled by the judge to admit that he was challenging the plaintiff's honesty and the truth of his evidence that he decided to donate the proceeds of the book to charity at the very outset. The defendants were calling him a liar and that was made doubly sure by Mr Reason in his cross-examination. Mr Reason not merely disagreed with the opinion of the Welsh Rugby Union that the plaintiff had not lost his amateur status when he contracted to write the book but went further. The judge asked him:

> 'Q. Worse than that, Mr Reason, you think he is a shamateur because he is professing to be an amateur when in reality he is a professional? A. He was for a period of time, yes.
> Q. And a shamateur is a hypocrite? A. That is right.'

The jury can have been left in no doubt how serious was the charge Mr Reason was making against the plaintiff's character in court. Though it was not for Mr Reason to say what his articles meant but for the judge to rule what they were capable of meaning and for the jury to say what they meant, they were in my judgment capable of meaning what the judge suggested to the jury they meant: that the plaintiff was a shamateur; that his evidence that he always genuinely intended to give the proceeds of his book to charity was a lie, his conduct in relation to the book devious, his claim to amateur status sheer hypocrisy. Since that was a meaning which the articles, or at any rate the second article, could reasonably bear, evidence that he had earlier lost his amateur status by being paid like a professional such remuneration as boot money seems to me admissible to justify the allegation of shamateurism, on the authority of those cases to which I have referred.

[O'Connor and Purchas LL.J. rendered concurring judgments. The appeal was allowed and a new trial ordered.]

NOTES AND QUESTIONS

1. How does Stephenson L.J. define the scope of the justification defence? What is the relevance of the plaintiff's pleadings? What meaning of the defamatory statements is the defendant required (or permitted) to justify? See also *Hare & Grolier Society v. Better Business Bureau*, (1946), [1947] 1 D.L.R. 280 (B.C.C.A.); *Polly Peck (Holdings) plc v. Trelford*, [1986] 2 All E.R. 84 (C.A.); and *Pizza Pizza Ltd. v. Toronto Star Newspapers Ltd.* (1998), 42 O.R. (3d) 36 (Div. Ct.), aff'd (2000), 49 O.R. (3d) 254 (C.A.).

2. A defendant cannot justify a defamatory allegation by proving that the plaintiff engaged in other reprehensible behaviour. See *London Computer Operators Training Ltd. v. British Broadcasting Corporation*, [1973] 1 W.L.R. 424 (C.A.).

3. A defendant cannot succeed by showing that the defamatory statements were literally true if they were expressed in a way to create an overall false impression. See *Dunlap v. Philadelphia Newspapers Inc.*, 301 Pa. Super. 475 (1982); and *Bank of British Columbia v. Canadian Broadcasting Corporation* (1995), 126 D.L.R. (4th) 644 (B.C.C.A.).

4. A discrepancy in material facts will normally defeat a claim of justification: *Green v. Minnes* (1892), 22 O.R. 177 (Q.B.). The difficulty lies in determining whether something is a material fact or an insignificant detail. Generally, the court should consider

whether the discrepancy would change the overall impression in the minds of the reader or listener: *Thomson v. Herman* (1931), 39 O.W.N. 375 (H.C.).

5. Where the defendant has stated that the plaintiff is guilty of a criminal offence, proof that the plaintiff was convicted of the offence is sufficient: see *York v. Okanagan Broadcasters Ltd.*, [1976] 6 W.W.R. 40 (B.C.S.C.). Historically, however, the defendant had to meet the criminal burden of proof, *i.e.*, beyond a reasonable doubt: *Meier v. Klotz* (1928), 22 Sask. L.R. 385 (C.A.).

In England, this issue is resolved by the *Civil Evidence Act, 1968* (U.K.), c. 64, s. 13, which states that proof of the plaintiff's conviction for a criminal offence is conclusive evidence that the plaintiff committed the offence.

6. Where the plaintiff claims for multiple defamatory statements, a defendant can bring a defence of partial justification at common law to justify one or more of the defamatory imputations. The defendant will remain liable for any statements that have not been justified. However, the court may consider the partial justification in assessing damages for the unjustified statements. For example in *Makow v. Winnipeg Sun* (2003), 172 Man. R. (2d) 213 (Q.B.), aff'd (2004), 184 Man. R. (2d) 97 (C.A.), the defendants justified only 3 of 12 statements made about the plaintiff. The trial judge considered this in assessing damages for lost reputation, stating that "the plaintiff should not be viewed as a university lecturer of unimpeachable character, but one whose reputation has been partially blemished" (at para. 146). Thus, the award reflected that the plaintiff's reputation was not impeccable at the time the libel was published.

Ontario's *Libel and Slander Act*, R.S.O. 1990, c. L.12, s. 22, provides as follows with respect to the defence of partial justification: "In an action for libel or slander for words containing two or more distinct charges against the plaintiff, a defence of justification shall not fail by reason only that the truth of every charge is not proved if the words not proved to be true do not materially injure the plaintiff's reputation having regard to the truth of the remaining charges."

7. Should a defendant succeed on a plea of justification even if the defendant acted maliciously and there was no public interest at stake? Should those who wish to air others' dirty laundry in public be protected from liability? See Wright, "Note" (1939) 17 Can. Bar Rev. 276; Thayer, "The Changing Libel Scene" [1943] Wisc. L. Rev. 331; and Harnett & Thornton, "The Truth Hurts: A Critique of a Defense to Defamation" (1949) 35 Va. L. Rev. 425.

Should justification be limited to situations involving matters of public interest? Are there other avenues of redress for a plaintiff whose indiscretions have been made a matter of public knowledge by a malicious defendant? Is this an area where the emerging tort of invasion of privacy might have a role?

(b) ABSOLUTE PRIVILEGE

As its name suggests, absolute privilege provides complete immunity in tort for statements falling within the privilege. There are three categories of communication attracting absolute privilege: statements by executive officers relating to affairs of the state, statements made during Parliamentary proceedings, and statements made in the course of judicial or quasi-judicial proceedings. In all of these situations, immunity from defamation claims is thought necessary to maintain the independence of those involved and to promote honest and candid speech in the public interest.

(i) *Executive Officers*

DOWSON v. THE QUEEN
(1981), 124 D.L.R. (3d) 260 (F.C.A.)

[A member of the Ontario Legislative Assembly requested, during a session of the Assembly, that the Attorney-General seek information about an alleged RCMP investigation into certain members of the New Democratic Party. The Attorney-General agreed to the request and wrote a letter to the Solicitor-General to ask for the information. The Solicitor-General then asked Sexsmith, the Deputy Director General, Operations, of the RCMP, to provide the requested information. Sexsmith, in turn, asked Chief Superintendent Vaughan to make the inquiries and prepare a report. Vaughan submitted the report to the Solicitor-General. Sexsmith then met with the Acting Assistant Deputy Attorney-General of Ontario, McLeod, to discuss the findings. It was during this meeting that the defamatory statements about the plaintiff were made. In particular, the statements suggested that some members of the NDP might support change "by violent and undemocratic means." The excerpt below addresses whether Sexsmith and Vaughan were entitled to assert absolute privilege with respect to the statements.]

The judgment of the Court was delivered by

LE DAIN J: — . . .. The respondent's defence of absolute privilege is based on two categories of privileged occasion recognized by the authorities: communications between officers of state in relation to state affairs, and proceedings in Parliament or the Legislature. The learned trial Judge held that there was absolute privilege in the present case on the basis of both of these categories of privileged occasion.

The law with respect to the first category of privileged occasion is stated in 28 Hals., 4th ed., p. 54, para. 107, as follows: "An official communication relating to state affairs, including commercial matters, made by one officer of state to another in the course of his official duty is absolutely privileged." The authority cited for that proposition is *Chatterton v. Secretary of State for India in Council*, [1895] 2 Q.B. 189 (C.A.). That was a case of an action for libel that was dismissed as vexatious on the ground that the statement complained of was protected by absolute privilege. The statement was made by the Secretary of State for India to the Parliamentary Under-Secretary for India to enable the latter to answer a question in the House of Commons concerning the treatment of the plaintiff as an officer in the Indian Army by the Indian military authorities and Government. Lord Esher M.R. said at pp. 190-1:

> The substance of the case is that it is an action brought against him in respect of a communication in writing made by him as Secretary of State, and, therefore, a high official of the state, to an Under-Secretary of State in the course of the performance of his official duty. The master, the judge at chambers, and the Divisional Court have all come to the conclusion that the action is one which cannot by any possibility be maintained; that it is not competent to a civil Court to entertain a suit in respect of the action of an official of state in making such a communication to another official in the course of his official duty, or to inquire whether or not he acted maliciously in making it. I think that conclusion was correct.

And after referring to the authorities, he concluded at pp. 191-2:

> In my opinion, the statement of which the plaintiff complains, being a communication relating to a state matter made by one state official to another, was absolutely privileged.

I conclude from what was said in the *Chatterton* case that there are three conditions for this category of absolute privilege: (a) the statement must have been made by one officer of state to another officer of state; (b) it must relate to state matters; and (c) it must be made by an officer of state in the course of his official duty.

The issue with respect to the first condition is whether the statement that was made by Chief Superintendent Vaughan to Acting Assistant Deputy Attorney-General McLeod at the meeting that was also attended by Assistant Commissioner Sexsmith can be said to have been made by one officer of state to another officer of state within the meaning of the principle affirmed in the *Chatterton* case.

In some judicial expressions of this category or occasion of absolute privilege the expression used has been "high officer of state". . .. In *Chatterton*, Lord Esher M.R., after referring to the Secretary of State for India as a "high official of state", used the unqualified expressions "official of state", "officer of state" and "state official" in referring to this occasion of absolute privilege. On the other hand, the passage from *Fraser on the Law of Libel and Slander*, 6th ed., which was adopted by the Court as correctly stating the law, gave as an example of this case of absolute privilege "every communication relating to state matters made by one minister to another, or to the Crown", and the statement in the *Chatterton* case was made by a Minister of the Crown. The case is not clear authority as to the other officers of state who should, on grounds of public policy, enjoy the protection of absolute privilege.

[Le Dain J. surveyed other Commonwealth authorities on the types of officials permitted to claim absolute privilege, ending with a quotation from Denning M.R. that reviewed the state of the law]:

> The authorities do show that a report by a very senior military or naval officer to his superior is absolutely privileged; but nothing else is settled. It is doubtful whether reports by the middle or lower ranks of the army and navy are absolutely privileged. The middle ranks of the police do not appear to be absolutely privileged. It has been held by the High Court of Australia that a report made by an inspector of police to his superior officer is not absolutely privileged; see *Gibbons v. Duffell* [(1932), 47 C.L.R. 520 (H.C.A.)]. It is a nice question whether the secret service should be treated like the police force or like the army or navy. Apart from these difficulties about our own English forces in this country, it is very difficult to say how far this absolute privilege applies to the visiting forces of a friendly foreign power. In *Szalatnay-Stacho v. Fink* [[1946] 2 All E.R. 231] a letter written in England by a senior Czecho-Slovakian officer to his government was held not to be the subject of absolute privilege.

The appellant relied particularly on this passage in his contention that it was arguable whether a statement by a chief superintendent of the R.C.M.P. should be subject to absolute privilege. I would certainly agree, if the statement made by Chief Superintendent Vaughan is to be regarded as his own statement, made on his own behalf and on his own initiative. But it is clear in my opinion that it cannot be so regarded in the light of the facts which must be taken as established. It was a statement that was made for and on behalf of the Solicitor-General of Canada and pursuant to his instructions. The request for information was addressed by the Attorney-General of Ontario to the Solicitor-General. The Solicitor-General replied by letter on November 30, 1977, setting out the substance of his reply to the Attorney-General's question in two sentences and indicating that he had instructed Assistant Commissioner Sexsmith to provide any further information that the Attorney-General might require at a meeting to be arranged at his convenience. The statement made by Vaughan under Sexsmith's direction at the meeting with McLeod was thus simply an elaboration of the Solicitor-General's reply to the Attorney-General. Vaughan should therefore be likened to a person who makes a statement as the agent of another, and as such should be regarded as having the benefit of the absolute privilege that would clearly apply, on the authority of the Chatterton case, to a statement in relation to a state matter made by the Solicitor-General in the course of his official duty. This principle – that an agent who makes a statement takes the benefit of the privilege that would attach to the statement if made by the person on whose behalf it is made – has been recognized in cases of qualified privilege. . .and I can see no reason why it should not apply to the occasion of absolute privilege created by the statement of a Minister of the Crown in relation to a matter of state, particularly, in view of the necessary delegation that is involved in the exercise of that office: cf. Powell, *The Law of Agency*, 2nd ed. (1961), pp. 279-80.

By the same reasoning the statement must be taken to have been made to Mr. McLeod as an officer acting for and on behalf of the Attorney-General of Ontario and thus to have been made to the Attorney-General, who, like the Solicitor-General of Canada, is clearly an officer of state within the principle in *Chatterton*.

As for the other two conditions for this occasion of absolute privilege, there can be no doubt, in my view, that the statement complained of related to state affairs and that it was made in the course of official duty. It was concerned with surveillance by the R.C.M.P. for security purposes, and it was made in response to a question in the Legislature of Ontario and a formal request for information addressed by the Attorney-General of Ontario to the Solicitor-General of Canada. Because of his responsibility for the R.C.M.P. the Solicitor-General and those acting under his instructions were in the exercise of their official duty in making the statement.

It was the appellant's contention that whether or not the officers of the R.C.M.P. who engaged in the preparation and communication of the report were in the exercise of their official duty was a question of fact that should be allowed to go to trial. It was his contention that the pleadings alleged in effect that the R.C.M.P. had seized an occasion of absolute privilege to pursue an object other than a response to the request for information by the provincial Attorney-General. He argued that on its face the statement complained of did not address the questions raised by the request, but evaded them in the pursuit of some other purpose. It is necessary not to confuse the question whether the statement was made in the exercise of official duty with the question of the intention or motive with which it might have been made – that is, the question of malice, which is irrelevant in a case of absolute privilege. Whether the statement was an adequate answer to the request for information from the Attorney-General or whether it was intended to serve some other purpose at the same time is, in my opinion, beside the point. It purported to be an answer to that request and it was acted on as such.

For these reasons I am of the opinion that the statement made by Chief Superintendent Vaughan to Mr. McLeod was clearly made on an occasion of absolute privilege, and that accordingly the action cannot possibly succeed in so far as it is based on the statement having been made on this occasion. The learned trial Judge was therefore right in striking out the statement of claim and dismissing the action for so much as he did, and accordingly the appeal should be dismissed.

(ii) *Parliamentary Privilege*

Parliamentary privilege provides immunity for defamatory statements made during parliamentary proceedings. Such statements are protected as a matter of policy: legislators should be encouraged to speak freely for the public interest and ought not to be inhibited by fear of actions for defamation. The privilege extends to parliamentary proceedings, including testimony before committees, parliamentary reports and papers. However, it does not protect a member who makes or repeats defamatory statements outside of the assembly.

(iii) *Judicial Proceedings*

There is absolute privilege for statements made in the course of judicial or quasi-judicial proceedings: *Stark v. Auerbach*, [1979] 3 W.W.R. 563 (B.C.S.C.). The rationale for this privilege is that participants in such proceedings should be encouraged to speak honestly and candidly. The privilege also seeks to avoid a multiplicity of proceedings, as when a litigant who is unsuccessful in one proceeding goes on to bring a defamation action against witnesses who testified during that proceeding: *Cinapri v. Guettler* (1997), 33 B.L.R. (2d) 289 (Ont. Gen. Div.). The privilege extends to anyone involved in a judicial or quasi-judicial proceeding, including the judge, jury, counsel, parties and witnesses. It includes not only the trial proper, but also any proceedings leading up to the trial (*e.g.* pleadings, preliminary motions, discovery, written submissions) or following it (motions for a new trial, the assessment of costs, and the satisfaction of judgments). Moreover, the privilege applies even if the statements were made maliciously and without justification: *Royal Aquarium and Summer & Winter Garden Society Ltd. v. Parkinson*, [1892] 1 Q.B. 431 (C.A.).

HUNG v. GARDINER

(2003), 227 D.L.R. (4th) 282 (B.C.C.A.)

The judgment of the court was delivered by
LEVINE J.A.: —

Introduction

At issue in this appeal is whether a person who provides information to a professional disciplinary body about the conduct of one of its members is liable in an action brought by that member. The clear answer is that the communication of the information is subject to absolute privilege, which provides a defence to all claims.

The appellant, Christine Hung, is a member of the Law Society of British Columbia and the Certified General Accountants Association of British Columbia (the "CGA Association"). Actions taken by her while she was employed by a firm of chartered accountants resulted in an investigation and reprimand of her supervisor by the Professional Conduct Enquiry Committee (the "PCEC") of the respondent, the Institute of Chartered Accountants of British Columbia (the "ICABC"). The members of the PCEC. . . decided that the Law Society and the CGA Association should be informed of the appellant's conduct. The respondent, Brian Gardiner, the Director of Ethics for the

ICABC, forwarded to those professional bodies the report of the investigator, the respondent, Wayne McIlroy. Both professional bodies declined to investigate further or to take any disciplinary action against the appellant.

The appellant brought an action for damages for defamation, malicious prosecution, negligence, breach of confidentiality under the *Freedom of Information and Protection of Privacy Act*, R.S.B.C. 1996, c. 165, breach of the *Accountants (Chartered) Act*, R.S.B.C. 1996, c. 3, and bylaws, misfeasance in public office, breach of the *Privacy Act*, R.S.B.C. 1996, c. 373, invasion of privacy and conspiracy.

Mr. Justice Joyce, after a summary trial under Rule 18A of the Supreme Court Rules, dismissed all of the appellant's claims, finding that they were barred by the absolute privilege that surrounded the act of providing the report to the professional bodies. . ..

. . .

Absolute Privilege

The trial judge began his discussion of the application of the defence of absolute privilege by quoting the decision of Smith J. in *Sussman v. Eales* (1985), 33 C.C.L.T. 156 (Ont. H.C.J.) at 157, appeal allowed in part (1986), 25 C.P.C. (2d) 7 (Ont. C.A.).

. . .

Smith J. explained the rationale for the immunity [regarding complaints to professional bodies] (at pp. 159-60):

> The principle is the same. It is a question of balancing two interests. The public interest should outweigh that of the individual for at least two reasons. Firstly the immunity will only be conferred upon a citizen complaining in a confidential way to a body created by statute. A communication of that kind can hardly be said to be a publication of the kind that is apt to harm one's reputation in the community to a degree sufficient to attract an award of compensation.
>
> Secondly, the right to engage in professional activities must be the subject of rules governing them. These rules cannot be enforced without a corresponding right in the members of the public to complain uninhibited and without fear of being found wrong and as a result being subject to actions in defamation. Surely it is a small price for a professional person to pay.

The Court of Appeal agreed that the doctrine of immunity applied to statements made to a disciplinary body [p. 8]:

> In our view, the doctrine of immunity by reason of absolute privilege with respect to statements made in the course of proceedings before a statutory body, exercising disciplinary powers over a member with respect to unprofessional conduct, applies to statements made in a letter of complaint addressed to the Registrar of the Royal College of Dental Surgeons. It is a document incidental to the initiation of quasi-judicial proceedings, and it matters not that the Complaints Committee has investigatory powers which may or may not lead to a direction that the matter be referred to the Discipline Committee. A complainant in the respondent Eales' position should not be deterred by the fear of proceedings and "the vexation of defending actions". (*Lincoln v. Daniels*, [1962] 1 Q.B. 237, [1961] 3 All E.R. 740 at 748 (C.A.).)

In *Sussman*, the issue was whether the body to which the complaint was sent was quasi-judicial or whether it was merely administrative in nature.

That is not an issue on this appeal. The trial judge found, and the appellant does not dispute that both the Law Society and the CGA Association are quasi-judicial bodies, empowered by statute, and each having a duty, to investigate complaints and hold disciplinary proceedings. The trial judge concluded that the act of sending the report to the Law Society and the CGA Association was the necessary first step in quasi-judicial proceedings, and was sufficiently proximate to potential disciplinary proceedings to be protected by absolute privilege.

The appellant claims that the trial judge erred in finding that the respondents enjoyed absolute privilege where neither the Law Society nor the CGA Association commenced disciplinary proceedings against her. She argues that absolute privilege extends to a complaint submitted to a quasi-judicial body only if proceedings ensue.

[Levine J.A. reviewed similar arguments in other cases.]

In support of her argument that neither the Law Society nor the CGA Association exercised any quasi-judicial functions when they decided not to proceed with disciplinary action, the appellant relies on *Lincoln v. Daniels*, [1962] 1 Q.B. 237 (C.A.); *Rajkhowa v. Watson* (1998), 167 N.S.R. (2d) 108 (S.C.); and *O'Connor v. Waldron*, [1935] A.C. 76, [1935] 1 D.L.R. 260 (P.C.), reversing [1932] S.C.R. 183, [1932] 1 D.L.R. 166.

[The discussion of *Lincoln v. Daniels* is omitted.]

In *Rajkhowa*, the defendant investigated and audited claims submitted by doctors under the Medical Services Insurance Plan. He gave information to the police concerning the plaintiff's billing practices, so that they could conduct a criminal investigation. No charges were laid and the investigation came to an end.

Hood J., citing from *Sussman*, set out the test to determine whether the information was protected by absolute privilege (at para. 36):

> The proper question to be asked in this case is that set out by Smith, J. in Sussman: "whether the body to which the complaint . . . was sent is quasi-judicial or whether it is merely administrative in nature."

Citing from *Boyachyk v. Dukes* (1982), 136 D.L.R. (3d) 28 (Alta. Q.B.), he applied the test as follows (at para. 46):

> If the question is asked: Do the police exercise quasi-judicial or administrative functions? to ask the question is to answer it. The police investigate, they do not adjudicate. Or to paraphrase Adams, J. in *Boyachyk*: they do not have the duty and authority to determine guilt or innocence nor the disciplinary powers to enforce sanctions. The police are therefore in a position similar to that of the Bar Council in the *Lincoln* case: they do not exercise judicial or quasi-judicial functions.

It is noteworthy that in *Boyachyk*, the court found that a complaint to the chief of police concerning the conduct of a police officer was subject to absolute privilege, because:

> Unlike the commissioner in the *O'Connor* case and the bar council in the *Lincoln* case, the chief of police in the present case had not only the authority but the duty to determine the guilt or innocence of the plaintiff and the disciplinary powers to enforce sanctions.

The appellant also relies on *O'Connor*, arguing that it settled the law on absolute privilege in Canada. The *O'Connor* case concerned words uttered by a commissioner appointed under the *Combines Investigation Act*, R.S.C. 1927, c. 26, alleging misconduct by the plaintiff, who was a barrister, during proceedings under the Act. In his defence, the commissioner claimed he uttered the words on an occasion of absolute privilege. In determining the issue, Lord Atkin, writing for the Privy Council, stated (at p. 81):

> The question therefore in every case is whether the tribunal in question has similar attributes to a court of justice or acts in a manner similar to that in which courts act?

He applied the test to the facts of the case as follows:

> Has then a commissioner appointed under the Combines Investigation Act attributes similar to those of a court of justice; or does he act in a manner similar to that in which such courts act? In their Lordships' opinion the answer must be in the negative.

He explained (at p. 82):

> It is only necessary to remember that the commissioner by the Act is empowered to enter premises and examine the books, papers and records of suspected persons to see how far his functions differ from those of a judge. His conclusion is expressed in a report; it determines no rights, nor the guilt or innocence of any one. It does not even initiate any proceedings, which have to be left to the ordinary criminal procedure.

In the result, the Privy Council reversed the decision of the Supreme Court of Canada and adopted the dissenting reasons of Hodgins J.A., of the Appellate Division of the Supreme Court of Ontario ([1931] O.R. 608, [1931] 4 D.L.R. 147). In reaching the conclusion that absolute privilege did not apply, Hodgins J.A. (at pp. 614-5) cited the following passage from *Odgers on Libel and Slander*, 6th ed. (1929), at p. 195:

> "An absolute privilege also attaches to all proceedings of, and to all evidence given before, any tribunal which by law, though not expressly a Court, exercises judicial functions—that is to say has power to determine the legal rights and to effect (*sic*) the status of the parties who appear before it."

On close reading, the authorities cited by the appellant are consistent with those relied on by the trial judge. He applied the proper test to determine whether the report was sent on an occasion of absolute privilege. The test is whether the Law Society and the CGA Association, exercising their disciplinary powers, have attributes similar to a court of justice or act in a manner similar to that in which such courts act. There is no real question that they do.

The Law Society and the CGA Association are quasi-judicial bodies and are not merely administrative in nature. They have the power to determine the legal rights and to affect the status of their members. Thus, a complaint made to them in a confidential way concerning a member's conduct is absolutely privileged.

There are important public policy reasons for this finding. Absolute privilege allows a member of the public to raise a concern about the conduct of a professional person, without fear of reprisal. In this way, the immunity afforded by absolute privilege protects both professionals and the public.

The purpose of the immunity would be undermined if absolute privilege only applied where the complaint leads to proceedings, as contended by the appellant. Nor is the defence of absolute privilege affected by the fact that the Law Society and the CGA Association declined to pursue the matter further.

Thus, the trial judge was correct in finding that the respondents sent the report to the Law Society and the CGA Association on an occasion of absolute privilege.

The trial judge was also correct in concluding that the absolute privilege applies to all causes of action arising from that act. That is clear from the reasons for judgment of Sellers L.J., concurred in by Willmer and Diplock L.JJ., in *Marrinan v. Vibart*, [1962] 3 All E.R. 380 (C.A.) where, after citing the Court's decision in *Lincoln*, he said (at p. 383):

> Whatever form of action is sought to be derived from what was said or done in the course of judicial proceedings must suffer the same fate of being barred by the rule which protects witnesses in their evidence before the court and in the preparation of the evidence which is to be so given. . ..

Sellers L.J. quoted further from *Royal Aquarium* [*and Summer and Winter Garden Society v. Parkinson*, [1892] 1 Q.B. 431 (C.A.)], as follows:

> "But it does not matter whether the action is framed as an action for defamation or as an action analogous to an action for malicious prosecution or for deceit or, as in this instance, for combining or conspiring together for the purpose of injuring another: the rule of law is that no action lies against witnesses in respect of evidence prepared (*Watson v. M'Ewan, Watson v. Jones* [[1905] A.C. 480], given, adduced or procured by them in the course of legal proceedings. The law protects witnesses and others, not for their benefit, but for a higher interest, namely, the advancement of public justice."

. . .

The appellant's action against the respondents cannot be maintained. All of the respondents are entitled to claim absolute privilege and are immune from liability for their actions in sending information to the Law Society and the CGA Association concerning the appellant's professional conduct.

NOTES AND QUESTIONS

1. Based on the authorities cited in *Hung v. Gardiner*, how is a quasi-judicial body identified for the purposes of absolute privilege? The following bodies have been found to be quasi-judicial: a board of review under the *Workers Compensation Act* (*Stark v. Auerbach* (1979), 11 B.C.L.R. 355 (S.C.)); the registrar of the Royal College of Dental Surgeons initiating a complaint against a dentist (*Sussman v. Eales* (1985), 33 C.C.L.T. 156 (Ont. H.C.), rev'd on other grounds (1986), 25 C.P.C. (2d) 7 (Ont. C.A.); the Ontario New Home Warranty Plan when receiving complaints against builders (*Gala Homes Inc. v. Flisar* (2000), 48 O.R. (3d) 470 (S.C.J.), aff'd on other grounds 2000 CarswellOnt 3584 (C.A.) (WLeC)); arbitration proceedings under residential tenancy legislation (*Zanetti v. Bonniehon Enterprises Ltd.*, 2002 CarswellBC 1945 (S.C.) (WLeC), aff'd 2003 CarswellBC 1278 (C.A.); and a hospital board cancelling a doctor's hospital privileges under a statutory regime (*Cimolai v. Hall* (2004), 25 B.C.L.R. (4th) 117 (S.C.)). See also *Trapp v. Mackie*, [1979] 1 W.L.R. 377 (H.L.), where Lord Diplock summarized the criteria identifying a quasi-judicial body.

2. Although statements made by witnesses in court are generally protected by absolute privilege, it is doubtful whether this protects statements that are completely

irrelevant to the proceedings. Thus, a witness cannot use the courtroom as an opportunity to utter gratuitous defamatory statements: see *Duke v. Puts* (2004), 241 Sask. R. 187 (C.A.).

3. According to *Dowson*, what officials qualify for executive privilege? Is there good reason to restrict such privilege to "high officials?" See *Gibbons v. Duffell* (1932), 47 C.L.R. 520 (H.C.A.); *Merricks v. Nott-Bower* (1964), [1965] 1 Q.B. 57 (C.A.); and Williams, "Absolute Privilege for Licensing Justices" (1909) 25 L.Q.R. 188.

4. For the law on parliamentary privilege, see generally Veeder, "Absolute Immunity in Defamation: Legislative and Executive Proceedings" (1910) 10 Col. L.R. 131.

(c) QUALIFIED PRIVILEGE

Qualified privilege protects defamatory materials that are communicated on certain occasions. It applies even if the statements are untrue. Unlike absolute privilege, however, it does not apply if the plaintiff can establish that the statements were made maliciously. Moreover, there are no clear rules as to the occasions attracting qualified privilege. Generally speaking, it applies in situations where the speaker has an interest or duty (legal, social or moral) to make the statement, and the recipient has a reciprocal interest to receive the statement: see *Toogood v. Spryring* (1834), 149 E.R. 1044 (Exch.). Qualified privilege also applies to statements made in protection of one's own interests. The types of occasions attracting qualified privilege can be roughly (and non-exhaustively) categorized as follows.

First, qualified privilege applies to statements made by the defendant in protection of his or her own interests. Thus, a person who is being subjected to an attack on his or her character is permitted to utter statements to defend him or herself. Such statements will be protected by qualified privilege unless they are excessive or irrelevant to the original attack. The occasion cannot be used as an opportunity to launch gratuitous insults. At the same time, the courts will not be overly critical of statements uttered in self-defence. Lord Atkinson wrote in *Adam v. Ward*, [1917] A.C. 309 at 334 (H.L.) that the defendant will be protected "even though his language should be violent or excessively strong, if, having regard to all the circumstances of the case, he might have honestly and on reasonable grounds believed that what he wrote or said was true and necessary for the purpose of his vindication, though in fact it was not so." See also *Davies & Davies Ltd. v. Kott*, [1979] 2 S.C.R. 686.

Second, qualified privilege applies in situations where the defendant publishes the relevant statements in order to protect the interests of another person. The defendant must show that he or she had a legal, social or moral duty to communicate the information. It typically applies in situations where, for example, credit or character references are provided with respect to the plaintiff. It is less clear what situations will qualify as creating a "moral duty" to communicate information. A leading English case, *Watson v. Longsdon*, [1930] 1 K.B. 130 (C.A.), decided that qualified privilege did not apply when a friend of the plaintiff's wife informed the wife of the plaintiff's alleged infidelity.

Third, communications made in the furtherance of a common interest may be protected by qualified privilege, as long as there is a reciprocity of interests. For instance, in *McLoughlin v. Kutasy*, [1979] 2 S.C.R. 311, the defendant was a physician who was hired to examine prospective employees for a hazardous construction project and make reports about the candidates to the Ontario Ministry of Labour, Construction Safety Branch. The plaintiff was denied employment as a result of the doctor's report, which suggested the plaintiff had a psychopathic personality and "would be dangerous" to the safety of the project. The defendant successfully argued that the statements were protected by qualified privilege, since he had a duty to make the report to the government and the government had a duty to receive it.

Finally, qualified privilege will attach to statements that are made in the protection of the public interest. This category covers a broad spectrum of occasions, including some political speech, as well as communications among public officials over matters of public interest, health or safety. It also applies to speech in municipal politics: *Prud'homme v. Prud'homme*, [2002] 4 S.C.R. 663; and *Wells v. Sears*, 2007 CarswellNfld 102 (C.A.) (WLeC). Again, it is generally necessary that the speaker have a duty to publish the information and the recipient have a reciprocal interest to receive it. For this reason, defamatory statements made by the media are not generally covered under the rubric of public interest: there is no *duty* for the media to report matters of public interest. See *Globe & Mail Ltd. v. Boland*, [1960] S.C.R. 203; and *Banks v. Globe & Mail Ltd.*, [1961] S.C.R. 474.

The qualified privilege with respect to public interest was extended in *Campbell v. Jones* (2002), 209 N.S.R. (2d) 81 (C.A.). During an investigation into a theft at a school, the plaintiff police officer conducted a strip search of three female students, in view of each other and an open window facing a hallway. The plaintiff conceded that she had violated the students' *Charter* rights to be free from arbitrary detention and unreasonable search. The lawyers representing the students then held a press conference in which they suggested that the searches would not have occurred if the students had not been black and poor. A majority of the Nova Scotia Court of Appeal held that the statements at the press conference were protected by qualified privilege. The majority reasoned at para. 58 that "lawyers, by virtue of their role as officers of the court with a specific duty to improve the administration of justice and uphold the law, have a special relationship with and responsibility to the public to speak out when those involved in enforcing our laws violate the fundamental rights of citizens." Thus, the public interest in receiving the information about the officer's conduct was more important than the plaintiff's right not to be defamed to "the world at large." For commentary see Duckworth, "The Impact of 'Charter Values' and Campbell v. Jones: Is It Now Easier to Establish Qualified Privilege Against Defamation?" (2006) 29 Dal. L.J. 277.

A separate form of qualified privilege is that of "fair and accurate reporting." This applies to reports of proceedings that are open to the public, such as judicial proceedings, legislative proceedings, public meetings and public documents. This privilege is available at common law as long as the reporting is fair and accurate, and not blasphemous, indecent, seditious or malicious. Fair and accurate reporting is also covered by legislation in some jurisdictions. For example, ss. 3-4 of the Ontario *Libel and Slander Act*, R.S.O. 1990, c. L.12, define the qualified privilege afforded to the media for fair and accurate reporting.

The common law privilege for fair and accurate reporting of a judicial proceeding was discussed in *Hill v. Church of Scientology*, [1995] 2 S.C.R. 1130. In particular, the court had to determine whether the privilege applied to a report about court documents that had not yet been filed.

HILL v. CHURCH OF SCIENTOLOGY
[1995] 2 S.C.R. 1130

[The plaintiff, Casey Hill, was a Crown attorney working in Toronto. The first defendant, the Church of Scientology, intended to initiate contempt of court proceedings against the plaintiff, alleging that he had misled a judge and opened sealed documents pertaining to the defendant. Before filing the notice of motion, the defendants organized a press conference on the steps of Osgoode Hall. The second defendant, Morris Manning, represented the Church of Scientology and appeared at the press conference wearing his barrister's gown. Manning read out the notice of motion at the press conference, including the accusations against the plaintiff and the desired sanction of fine or imprisonment. Copies of the notice of motion were also distributed to the reporters in attendance. The plaintiff was exonerated at the contempt proceedings and then brought a defamation claim against the defendants. The following excerpt deals with the defendants' argument that their statements were covered by qualified privilege, *i.e.*, that they constituted a report on court proceedings.]

Cory J.: – . . .Qualified privilege attaches to the occasion upon which the communication is made, and not to the communication itself. As Lord Atkinson explained in *Adam v. Ward*, [1917] A.C. 309 (H.L.), at p. 334:

> . . . a privileged occasion is . . . an occasion where the person who makes a communication has an interest or a duty, legal, social, or moral, to make it to the person to whom it is made, and the person to whom it is so made has a corresponding interest or duty to receive it. This reciprocity is essential.

This passage was quoted with approval in *McLoughlin v. Kutasy*, [1979] 2 S.C.R. 311, at p. 321.

The legal effect of the defence of qualified privilege is to rebut the inference, which normally arises from the publication of defamatory words, that they were spoken with malice. Where the occasion is shown to be privileged, the *bona fides* of the defendant is presumed and the defendant is free to publish, with impunity, remarks which may be defamatory and untrue about the plaintiff. However, the privilege is not absolute and can be defeated if the dominant motive for publishing the statement is actual or express malice. See *Horrocks v. Lowe*, [1975] A.C. 135 (H.L.), at p. 149.

Malice is commonly understood, in the popular sense, as spite or ill-will. However, it also includes, as Dickson J. (as he then was) pointed out in dissent in *Cherneskey* [*v. Armadale Publishers*, [1979] 1 S.C.R. 1067] at p. 1099, "any indirect motive or ulterior purpose" that conflicts with the sense of duty or the mutual interest which the occasion created. See, also, *Taylor v. Despard*, [1956] O.R. 963 (C.A.). Malice may also be established by showing that the defendant spoke dishonestly, or in knowing or reckless disregard for the truth. See *McLoughlin, supra*, at pp. 323-24, and *Netupsky v. Craig*, [1973] S.C.R. 55, at pp. 61-62.

Qualified privilege may also be defeated when the limits of the duty or interest have been exceeded. . .. As Loreburn E. stated at pp. 320-21 in *Adam v. Ward, supra*:

> . . . the fact that an occasion is privileged does not necessarily protect all that is said or written on that occasion. Anything that is not relevant and pertinent to the discharge of the duty or the exercise of the right or the safeguarding of the interest which creates the privilege will not be protected.

In other words, the information communicated must be reasonably appropriate in the context of the circumstances existing on the occasion when that information was given. For example, in *Douglas v. Tucker*, [1952] 1 S.C.R. 275, the defendant, during an election campaign, stated that the plaintiff, who was the officer of an investment company, had charged a farmer and his wife an exorbitant rate of interest causing them to lose their property. The plaintiff maintained that the allegation was without foundation. In response, the defendant asserted that the plaintiff was facing a charge of fraud which had been adjourned until after the election. This Court held that the defendant had an interest in responding to the plaintiff's denial, thereby giving rise to an occasion of qualified privilege. However, it ruled that the occasion was exceeded because the defendant's comments went beyond what was "germane and reasonably appropriate" (p. 286).

In *Sun Life Assurance Co. of Canada v. Dalrymple*, [1965] S.C.R. 302, the district manager of the defendant insurance company threatened to resign and take the district agents with him. This Court held that it fell within the scope of the privilege for the company to make certain defamatory comments about the plaintiff in order to dissuade its agents from leaving.

The principal question to be answered in this appeal is whether the recitation of the contents of the notice of motion by Morris Manning took place on an occasion of qualified privilege. If so, it remains to be determined whether or not that privilege was exceeded and thereby defeated.

The traditional common law rule with respect to reports on documents relating to judicial proceedings is set out in *Gatley on Libel and Slander* (8th ed. 1981), at p. 252, in these words:

> The rule of law is that, where there are judicial proceedings before a properly constituted judicial tribunal exercising its jurisdiction in open court, then the publication without malice of a fair and accurate report of what takes place before that tribunal is privileged.

. . .

The rationale behind this rule is that the public has a right to be informed about all aspects of proceedings to which it has the right of access. This is why a news report referring to the contents of any document filed as an exhibit, or admitted as evidence during the course of the proceedings, is privileged. However, the common law immunity was not extended to a report on pleadings or other documents which had not been filed with the court or referred to in open court. Duff C.J. explained the reasoning for this in *Gazette Printing Co. v. Shallow* (1909), 41 S.C.R. 339, at p. 360:

> The publicity of proceedings involving the conduct of a judicial authority serves the important purposes of impressing those concerned in the administration of justice with a sense of public responsibility, and of affording every member of the community an opportunity of observing for himself the mode in which the business of the public tribunals is carried on; but no such object would appear to be generally served by applying the privilege to the publication of preliminary statements of claims and defence relating only to private transactions; formulated by the parties themselves; in respect of which no judicial action has been taken, and upon which judicial action may never be invoked. It is only when such preliminary statements or the claims or defences embodied in them form the basis or the subject of some hearing before, or some action by, a court or a judicial officer, that their contents can become the object of any real public concern as touching the public administration of justice.

In *Edmonton Journal* [*v. Alberta (Attorney General)*, [1989] 2 S.C.R. 1326] at pp. 1338-40, I noted that the public scrutiny of our courts by the press was fundamentally important in our democratic society and that s. 2(*b*) protected not only speakers, but listeners as well. This right to report on court proceedings extended to pleadings and court documents filed before trial, since access to these documents served the same societal needs as reporting on trials. Even in private actions, such as those for wrongful dismissal or for personal damages, the public may well have an interest in knowing the kinds of submissions which can be put forward.

Both societal standards and the legislation have changed with regard to access to court documents. When the qualified privilege rule was set out in *Shallow*, *supra*, court documents were not open to the public. Today, the right of access is guaranteed by legislative provision, in this case s. 137(1) of the *Courts of Justice Act*, R.S.O. 1990, c. C.43. As well, s. 2(*b*) of the *Charter* may in some circumstances provide a basis for gaining access to some court documents. However, just as s. 137(1) provides for limitations on the right of access to court documents, so too is the s. 2(*b*) guarantee subject to reasonable limits that can be demonstrably justified in a free and democratic society. This Court's reasons in *Canadian Newspapers Co. v. Canada (Attorney General)*, [1988] 2 S.C.R. 122, provide an illustration of the kind of restriction that has been upheld in relation to information flowing from court proceedings. In that case, the constitutionality of s. 442(3) of the *Criminal Code* was upheld. It imposed a publication ban on the identity of a complainant in sexual assault cases (or any information that might disclose her identity) upon the request of that complainant. There is no need to elaborate further on the scope of access, however, since it does not arise on the facts of this case. It is sufficient to observe that, in appropriate circumstances, s. 2(*b*) may provide the means to gain access to court documents. It follows that the concept of qualified privilege should be modified accordingly.

The public interest in documents filed with the court is too important to be defeated by the kind of technicality which arose in this case. The record demonstrates that, prior to holding the press conference, Morris Manning had every intention of initiating the contempt action in accordance with the prevailing rules, and had given instructions to this effect. In fact, the proper documents were served and filed the very next morning. The fact that, by some misadventure, the strict procedural requirement of filing the documents had not been fulfilled at the time of the press conference should not defeat the qualified privilege which attached to this occasion.

This said, it is my conclusion that Morris Manning's conduct far exceeded the legitimate purposes of the occasion. The circumstances of this case called for great restraint in the communication of information concerning the proceedings launched against Casey Hill. As an experienced lawyer, Manning ought to have taken steps to confirm the allegations that were being made. This is particularly true since he should have been aware of the Scientology investigation pertaining to access to the sealed documents. In those circumstances he was duty bound to wait until the investigation was completed before launching such a serious attack on Hill's professional integrity. Manning failed to take either of these reasonable steps. As a result of this failure, the permissible scope of his comments was limited and the qualified privilege which attached to his remarks was defeated.

The press conference was held on the steps of Osgoode Hall in the presence of representatives from several media organizations. This constituted the widest possible dissemination of grievous allegations of professional misconduct that were yet to be tested in a court of law. His comments were made in language that portrayed Hill in the worst possible light. This was neither necessary nor appropriate in the existing circumstances. While it is not necessary to characterize Manning's conduct as amounting to actual malice, it was certainly high-handed and careless. It exceeded any legitimate purpose the press conference may have served. His conduct, therefore, defeated the qualified privilege that attached to the occasion.

[La Forest, Gonthier, McLachlin, Iacobucci and Major JJ. concurred with Cory J.]

L'HEUREUX-DUBÉ J.: – I have had the advantage of reading the reasons of my colleague Justice Cory and, except on one point, generally agree with them as well as with his disposition of this appeal.

. . .

. . .the one issue on which I part company with my colleague concerns the scope of the defence of qualified privilege. Traditionally, this Court has held that the defence of qualified privilege is available with respect to reports of judicial proceedings, but not with respect to reports of pleadings in purely private litigation upon which no judicial action has yet been taken: *Gazette Printing Co. v. Shallow* (1909), 41 S.C.R. 339. The appellants, however, argue that *Shallow* is no longer good law as it had been overtaken by this Court's more recent decision in *Edmonton Journal v. Alberta (Attorney General)*, [1989] 2 S.C.R. 1326. My colleague appears to accept this argument. Accordingly, he broadens the scope of the defence of qualified privilege, making it available with respect to reports of pleadings upon which no judicial action has yet been taken. I disagree. In my view, *Shallow* and *Edmonton Journal* are entirely consistent. In this respect, I adopt the following statement from the judgment of the Court of Appeal in the case at hand ((1994), 18 O.R. (3d) 385, at p. 427):

> We were urged to extrapolate from *Edmonton Journal* the proposition that the common law of defamation should respect such constitutional forms of expression as the reporting of information pertaining to intended court proceedings by conferring qualified privilege on the occasion of the publication of such reports. With respect, we do not agree. *Edmonton Journal* struck down, in the name of freedom of expression, statutory provisions which sought to inhibit the publication of the details of pending matrimonial and other civil actions. But it by no means follows that the publication of such details should be accorded the mantle of qualified privilege if they are defamatory.
>
> *Edmonton Journal* and *Gazette Printing* stand together without conflict: there is a right to publish details of judicial proceedings before they are heard in open court, but such publication does not enjoy the protection of qualified privilege if it is defamatory. As Duff J. noted in the extract from p. 364 of *Gazette Printing* set out above, no such privilege is necessary if the statements published are true, and no such privilege is desirable if they are not true.

Subject to the above, I would dispose of this appeal as does my colleague Cory J.

[The appeal was dismissed. The portions of the judgment pertaining to damages are reproduced later in this chapter.]

NOTES AND QUESTIONS

1. What does Cory J. mean when he says that qualified privilege "attaches to the occasion upon which the communication is made, and not to the communication itself?"

2. What is the *ratio decidendi* of the majority's decision on the issue of qualified privilege?

3. How does L'Heureux-Dubé J. reconcile *Edmonton Journal* and *Gazette Printing*? If statements are defamatory, how can they be considered "fair and accurate reporting?"

4. In England, the media have a broader qualified privilege when reporting on matters of public interest. They may be protected from liability for publishing defamatory, untrue statements as long as they engage in "responsible reporting." See *Reynolds v. Times Newspapers Ltd.*, [2001] 2 A.C. 127 (H.L.); and *Jameel v. Wall Street Journal Europe Sprl*, [2006] UKHL 44.

(d) FAIR COMMENT

The defence of fair comment reflects the importance of free speech in Canada. As its name suggests, it provides a defence to those who comment fairly on matters of public interest. In order to establish the defence, the defendant must show that the material in question was (a) a comment, as opposed to an accusation or allegation of fact, (b) made honestly and in good faith, (c) based on facts that are true, and (d) pertaining to a matter of public interest. The defence will fail if it is shown that the comments were made maliciously. However, there is generally no need for the defendant to show that the comments were "fair," so the name of this defence is slightly misleading. As Diplock J. (as he then was) famously remarked to the jury in *Silkin v. Beaverbrook Newspapers Ltd.*, [1958] 1 W.L.R. 743 (Q.B.) at 747:

> People are entitled to hold and to express freely on matters of public interest strong views, views which some of you, or indeed all of you, may think are exaggerated, obstinate or prejudiced, provided – and this is the important thing – that they are views which they honestly hold. The basis of our public life is that the crank, the enthusiast, may say what he honestly thinks just as much as the reasonable man or woman who sits on a jury, and it would be a sad day for freedom of speech in this country if a jury were to apply the test of whether it agrees with the comment instead of applying the true test: was this an opinion, however exaggerated, obstinate or prejudiced, which was honestly held by the writer?

The decision in *Cherneskey v. Armadale Publishers Ltd.*, [1979] 1 S.C.R. 1067, excerpted below, focuses largely on the requirement of honest belief. It also addresses more generally the importance of public debate and the obligations of the media in reproducing opinions of third parties.

CHERNESKEY v. ARMADALE PUBLISHERS LTD.
[1979] 1 S.C.R. 1067

The Chief Justice and Pigeon and Pratte JJ. concurred with the judgment delivered by

RITCHIE J.: — This is an appeal brought pursuant to leave granted by the Court of Appeal of Saskatchewan from a judgment of that Court setting aside a judgment rendered at trial by Mr. Justice MacPherson sitting with a jury and ordering a new trial of this libel action which was brought by the appellant, a practising lawyer and alderman of the Saskatoon City Council, as a result of a letter published in the correspondence column of The Star-Phoenix a newspaper published in Saskatoon, of which the respondent, Armadale Publishers Limited (hereinafter referred to as "Armadale") is the owner and publisher and the respondent Sterling King is the editor.

The facts giving rise to this litigation are accurately and fully stated in the dissenting judgment of Mr. Justice Brownridge in the Court of Appeal which is now conveniently reported at 79 D.L.R. (3d) 180 (hereinafter referred to as the "Report"), at pp. 183 *et seq.*, but in order to fully understand the questions to which this appeal gives rise it will be necessary for me to summarize them briefly.

The alleged libel of which the appellant complains is contained in a letter written to The Star-Phoenix by two law students concerning a petition which was presented to the Saskatoon City Council and which was apparently drafted with the assistance of the appellant. The petition presented on behalf of fifty-four citizens was directed against the establishment of an Alcoholic Rehabilitation Centre in what was alleged to be a residential section of Saskatoon and the report of its presentation to Council as published in The Star-Phoenix referred in particular to Indians and Metis whose use of the centre was alleged to be detrimental to the area. In this regard Mr. Yaworski, who presented the petition, was reported as saying that the establishment of the centre was going to turn the area into "an Indian and Metis ghetto".

. . .

Having read this article, the two law students proceeded to write a letter to The Star-Phoenix which was published in a column headed "Editor's Letter Box" at the foot of which the following statement was printed:

> Letter writers are requested to provide addresses and phone numbers to allow checking for authenticity and accuracy. Letters must be signed – no pseudonyms will be published. *All are subject to editing for* length, *general interest*, grammar, style *and good taste*. Letters under 250 words are preferred. (Emphasis added.)

In his charge to the jury, the learned trial judge touched on this phase of the matter saying:

> The Star-Phoenix, as the evidence indicates has a right to decline to publish. They chose to publish and they, as they indicated, have a right to insist upon their right to edit. That's their privilege naturally.

The letter complained of was itself headed "Racist Attitude" and it is reproduced in full at pp. 183 and 184 of the D.L.R. Report, but the real sting of the language complained of is contained in the last three paragraphs which read:

> As a law student and an articling law student, we are appalled by the stance adopted by Alderman Cherneskey, himself a lawyer. We appreciate his sympathy with the concerns of certain members of the white community; however, we thoroughly disagree with his contention the centre should cease its operation until such time as the application of the relevant zoning bylaw has been clarified. We feel this situation is not unlike that of a man charged with a criminal offence. Such a man is deemed innocent until proven guilty. That Alderman Cherneskey should imply the onus is upon those operating the centre to establish their right to remain in the neighbourhood until further clarification, is abhorrent to all concepts of the law. At the very least, it flies flagrantly in the face of the

> principles of natural justice. It is unbecoming a member of the legal profession to adopt such an approach.
> Although we do not reside in the particular neighbourhood in question, we would have no objection whatsoever to such a centre operating in our neighbourhood. We entirely support the project initiated by Clarence Trotchie and hope the racist resistance exhibited will be replaced by the support and encouragement which the project deserves.

In the course of his reasons for judgment in the Court of Appeal, Mr. Justice Brownridge points out that:

> Prior to the trial the defendants sought leave to join as third parties the two authors of the offending letter but this application was refused on appeal:. . . *At the trial it was agreed by counsel that both letter writers were out of the jurisdiction and neither was called as a witness.* (Emphasis added.)

By his statement of claim the appellant claimed damages for defamation of his personal character in relation to his profession and in his office as an alderman. . ..

[Ritchie J. examined the definition of "defamatory."]

Accordingly, as I agree with the trial judge that the words used are capable of being construed as tending to lower the plaintiff in the estimation of right-thinking members of society generally, a *prima facie* cause of action arises and in my view a plea of fair comment by way of defence does not of itself have the effect of saddling the plaintiff with the burden of proving that the comment was unfair. This plea constitutes a vital part of the case for the defendants and in my view the burden of proving each ingredient of the defence so pleaded should rest upon the party asserting it. One of these ingredients is that the person writing the material complained of must be shown to have had an honest belief in the opinions expressed and it will be seen that, in my view, the same considerations apply to each publisher of that material.

. . .

In cases where the essential ingredients of either the plea of "qualified privilege" or that of "fair comment" have been established by the defence, then if it can be proved that the statements complained of were made or written maliciously, the plea must fail; but in my view no burden lies upon the complainant to prove malice unless and until either plea has been shown to be supported by the evidence.

. . .

Honesty of belief has been characterized by Lord Denning M.R., in *Slim et al. v. Daily Telegraph Ltd. et al.* [[1968] 1 All E.R. 497.], at p. 503, as "the cardinal test" of the defence of fair comment, and in the context of the present case this must mean honesty of belief in the opinions expressed in the letter complained of.

. . .

Perhaps the most singular feature of the present case is that the state of mind of the defendants is established by their own evidence to the effect that they did not honestly hold the opinions expressed in the letter. This is illustrated by the following excerpt from the evidence of the defendants in relation to the comments complained of Mr. R. Struthers, who was the executive vice-president of the defendant, Armadale, stated in the course of cross-examination as follows:

Q. But of course there is no question but what you do not believe Morris Cherneskey to be a racist?
A. No, I do not.
Q. You do not believe Morris Cherneskey to be a person with a racist attitude?
A. I do not believe him to be so.
Q. And in any capacity, as a lawyer, you don't believe him to be a lawyer with a racist attitude?
A. No.
Q. Or an alderman with a racist attitude?
A. No.

The same witness had given the same answers when speaking as the officer examined for discovery on behalf of the defendant, Armadale.

The second defendant, Sterling King, who was the editor of The Star-Phoenix, stated that he had no opinion as to the approach of Cherneskey in relation to the white community in the area in question but it was his honest opinion that Cherneskey had a reputation for honesty and integrity as a lawyer and an alderman.

. . .

[Ritchie J. reviewed the authorities in which the defence of fair comment was raised with respect to defamatory statements written by third parties but published by the defendants. Ritchie J. then referred to the Saskatchewan Court of Appeal's decision in the present case.]

Mr. Justice Bayda, however, expressed the following opinion:

> Where, however, the defendant is a publisher of the impugned words and in particular is a newspaper which publishes in its letters-to-the-editor column a letter capable of being defamatory, what is the acceptable standard? It is indisputable that if such a newspaper honestly holds the opinions expressed in the impugned writing, and was not actuated by malice, then as in the case of the writer, condition (c) [honesty] would be satisfied (*Slim v. Daily Telegraph, Ltd., supra*; *Lyon and Lyon v. Daily Telegraph, Ltd.*, [[1943] 2 All E.R. 316]). But is a different (I hesitate to say "lower") standard acceptable? Suppose the newspaper cannot be said to hold the opinions expressed in the impugned writing but honestly believes that they represent the real opinions of the writer (in other words, an honest belief that they were publishing a letter in which the writer was making a fair comment upon a matter of public interest) and, in addition, is not actuated by malice in publishing the letter, is that an acceptable state of mind for a plea of fair comment to succeed? I have concluded that it is.

This conclusion which lies at the very heart of this case, is based on an *obiter dictum* of Lord Denning in the case of *Slim v. Daily Telegraph, supra*, where, as in the *Lyon* case, it was found that the newspaper honestly held the views expressed and Lord Denning observed at p. 503:

> . . . the right of fair comment is one of the essential elements which go to make up our freedom of speech. We must ever maintain this right intact. It must not be whittled down by legal refinements. When a citizen is troubled by things going wrong, he should be free to "write to the newspaper": and the newspaper should be free to publish his letter. It is often the only way to get things put right. The matter must, of course, be one of public interest. The writer must get his facts right: and he must honestly state his real opinion. But that being done, both he and the newspaper should be clear of any liability. They should not be deterred by fear of libel actions.

In the penultimate paragraph of the same judgment, Lord Denning stated:

> On the face of these letters, I think that the comments made by Mr. Herbert and the Daily Telegraph were fair comments on a matter of public interest. *They* honestly said what *they* thought. (Emphasis added.)

It must be apparent, as it seems to me, that the sentence last above quoted refers to the honesty of both the writer and the newspaper so that this case in my opinion affords no authority for the proposition that comments published in a newspaper need not be honest expressions of the newspaper's opinion in order to support a defence of fair comment so long as the newspaper can show its belief that the comments were an honest expression of the real opinion of the writer.

If the publication of the libel had been confined to the letter and the writers had been sued, or alternately, if it had originated with the newspaper and its publisher, it would in either case have been necessary to show honest belief in order to sustain the defence of fair comment. The same considerations would thus in my opinion apply to the newspaper and the writers.

In my opinion each publisher in relying on the defence of fair comment is in exactly the same position as the original writer. . ..

It appears to me to follow from this that where, as here, there is no evidence as to the honest belief of the writers of the letter, and the newspaper and its publisher have disavowed any such belief on their part, the defence of fair comment cannot be sustained.

In this regard the language employed by Lord Shaw in *Arnold v. The King-Emperor* [(1914), 83 L.J.P.C. 299.], at p. 300, is appropriate. He there said:

> Their Lordships regret to find that there appears on the one side of this case the time-worn fallacy that some kind of privilege attaches to the profession of the Press as distinguished from the members of the public. The freedom of the journalist is an ordinary part of the freedom of the subject, and to whatever lengths the subject in general may go, so also may the journalist, but, apart from statute law, his privilege is no other and no higher. The responsibilities which attach to his power in the dissemination of printed matter may, and in the case of a conscientious journalist do, make him more careful; but the range of his assertions, his criticisms, or his comments is as wide as, and no wider than, that of any other subject. No privilege attaches to his position.

These views were adopted in this Court in *Globe and Mail v. Boland* [[1960] S.C.R. 203], at p. 208.

These authorities satisfy me that the newspaper and its editor cannot sustain a defence of fair comment when it has been proved that the words used in the letter are not an honest expression of their opinion and there is no evidence as to the honest belief of the writers. In view of this finding, I do not consider it necessary to deal with the other submissions made on behalf of the appellant.

. . .

This does not mean that freedom of the press to publish its views is in any way affected, nor does it mean that a newspaper cannot publish letters expressing views with which it may strongly disagree. Moreover, nothing that is here said should be construed as meaning that a newspaper is in any way restricted in publishing two diametrically opposite views of the opinion and conduct of a public figure. On the contrary, I adopt as descriptive of the conclusion which I have reached, the language used by Brownridge

J.A., in the following excerpt from his reasons for judgment in the Court of Appeal where he said at p. 192 of the Report:

> What it does mean is that a newspaper cannot publish a libellous letter and then disclaim any responsibility by saying that it was published as fair comment on a matter of public interest but it does not represent the honest opinion of the newspaper.

For all these reasons I would allow this appeal and restore the judgment at trial. The appellant is entitled to his costs throughout.

The judgment of Spence, Dickson and Estey JJ. was delivered by

DICKSON J. (dissenting): — This case involves a letter written to the editor of the Saskatoon Star-Phoenix by two law students. They were concerned with an issue of public interest and importance which had evoked substantial controversy in the City of Saskatoon, namely, whether an Indian and Metis rehabilitation centre for alcoholics would be permitted in a predominantly white neighbourhood. The letter was published in The Star-Phoenix. The appellant, Morris T. Cherneskey, who is an alderman and a practising lawyer in Saskatoon, alleges that the tenor of the letter was such as to charge him with being "racist" and with conduct unbecoming a barrister and solicitor. He brought an action for libel against Armadale Publishers Limited, owner and publisher of The Star-Phoenix, and Sterling King, editor of the paper. The writers of the letter were not sued, nor did they appear as witnesses, as both were out of the province at the time of trial.

. . .

The law of defamation must strike a fair balance between the protection of reputation and the protection of free speech, for it asserts that a statement is not actionable, in spite of the fact that it is defamatory, if it constitutes the truth, or is privileged, or is fair comment on a matter of public interest, expressed without malice by the publisher. These defences are of crucial importance in the law of defamation because of the low level of the threshold which a statement must pass in order to be defamatory. The virtually universally accepted test is that expressed by Lord Atkin "after collating the opinions of many authorities" in *Sim v. Stretch* [(1936), 52 T.L.R. 669.], at p. 671. He stated that the test of whether a statement is defamatory is: "Would the words tend to lower the plaintiff in the estimation of right-thinking members of society generally?" In the earlier case of *O'Brien v. Clement* [(1846), 15 M. and W. 435.] at p. 436 Baron Parke said that, subject to any available defences, "[e]verything printed or written, which reflects on the character of another" is a libel. It is apparent that the scope of defamatory statements is very wide indeed. In particular, a great deal of what is printed in the Letters to the Editor columns of newspapers unquestionably has the effect of lowering the subject's reputation in the estimation of right-thinking people generally. In all cases, nevertheless, the statement is not actionable if it is the truth, or fair comment, or protected by privilege. This is the reason why most defamation actions centre on the defences of justification, fair comment, or privilege. It is these defences which give substance to the principle of freedom of speech.

The important issue raised in this appeal is whether the defence of fair comment is denied a newspaper publishing material alleged to be defamatory unless it can be shown that the paper honestly believed the views expressed in the impugned material. It does not require any great perception to envisage the effect of such a rule upon the position of a newspaper in the publication of letters to the editor. An editor receiving a letter containing matter which might be defamatory would have a defence of fair comment if he shared the views expressed, but defenceless if he did not hold those views. As the columns devoted to letters to the editor are intended to stiumlate uninhibited debate on every public issue, the editor's task would be an unenviable one if he were limited to publishing only those letters with which he agreed. He would be engaged in a sort of censorship, antithetical to a free press. One can readily draw a distinction between editorial comment or articles, which may be taken to represent the paper's point of view, and letters to the editor in which the personal opinion of the paper is, or should be, irrelevant. No one believes that a newspaper shares the views of every hostile reader who takes it to task in a letter to the editor for error of omission or commission, or that it yields assent to the views of every person who feels impelled to make his feelings known in a letter to the editor. Newspapers do not adopt as their own the opinions voiced in such letters, nor should they be expected to.

III

The issue is broader than that. A free and general discussion of public matters is fundamental to a democratic society. The right of persons to make public their thoughts on the conduct of public officials, in terms usually critical and often caustic, goes back to earliest times in Greece and Rome. The Roman historian, Tacitus, spoke of the happiness of the times when one could think as he wished and could speak as he thought (1 Tacitus, *History*, para. 1). Citizens, as decision-makers, cannot be expected to exercise wise and informed judgment unless they are exposed to the widest variety of ideas, from diverse and antagonistic sources. Full disclosure exposes, and protects against, false doctrine.

It is not only the right but the duty of the press, in pursuit of its legitimate objectives, to act as a sounding board for the free flow of new and different ideas. It is one of the few means of getting the heterodox and controversial before the public. Many of the unorthodox points of view get newspaper space through letters to the editor. It is one of the few ways in which the public gains access to the press. By these means, various points of view, old and new grievances and proposed remedies get aired. The public interest is incidentally served by providing a safety valve for people.

Newspapers will not be able to provide a forum for dissemination of ideas if they are limited to publishing opinions with which they agree. If editors are faced with the choice of publishing only those letters which espouse their own particular ideology, or being without defence if sued for defamation, democratic dialogue will be stifled. Healthy debate will likely be replaced by monotonous repetition of majoritarian ideas and conformity to accepted taste. In one-newspaper towns, of which there are many, competing ideas will no longer gain access. Readers will be exposed to a single political, economic and social point of view. In a public controversy, the tendency will be to suppress those letters with which the editor is not in agreement. This runs directly counter to the increasing tendency of North American newspapers generally to become less devoted to the publishers' opinions and to print, without fear or favour, the widest possible range of opinions on matters of public interest. The integrity of a newspaper rests not on the publication of letters with which it is in agreement, but rather on the publication of letters expressing ideas to which it is violently opposed.

I do not wish to overstate the case. It is my view, however, that anything which serves to repress competing ideas is inimical to the public interest. I agree that the publisher of a newspaper has no special immunity from the application of general laws, and that in the matter of comment he is in no better position than any other citizen. But he should not be in any worse position. That, I fear, will be the situation if one fails to distinguish between the writer of a letter to the editor, and the editor, or if one compresses into one statement the several steps in the requisite process of analysis of the defence of fair comment.

Here, the newspaper, as such, had no opinion on the matter published. Although the executive vice-president of Armadale and the editor happened to know the appellant, and did not share the opinion expressed by the writers of the letter in question, the newspaper, in fact, operated merely as a conduit for the opinion.

. . .

[Martland J. delivered a separate concurring opinion on behalf of himself, Laskin C.J.C. and Beetz J. The appeal was allowed and the trial award of $25,000 plus costs was restored.]

NOTES AND QUESTIONS

1. Is the majority decision in *Cherneskey* realistic? How would it affect the ability of newspapers to act as a forum for public debate? Are the fears of the dissenting judges well-founded? Does the majority adequately address them?

2. The decision in *Cherneskey* was severely criticized and has been addressed by legislation in most provinces. See for example *Defamation Act*, R.S.A. 2000, c.D-6, s. 9(1); *Defamation Act*, R.S.O. 1990, c. L.12, s. 24; and *Defamation Act*, C.C.S.M. c. D-20, s. 9(1). Although the provisions are slightly different, they essentially provide that the defence of fair comment will not fail simply because the defendant did not share the defamatory opinion expressed by another person. In most jurisdictions, however, the defence will fail if the defendant knew that the *original* opinion was dishonestly expressed.

British Columbia, Nova Scotia and Saskatchewan have not overturned the effects of *Cherneskey* by legislation. Do you think that, since the advent of the *Charter*, the decision in *Cherneskey* will be able to stand in those provinces?

3. According to *Cherneskey*, what does each party have to prove in a defamation action involving the defence of fair comment? Was the defendant's case hampered by the fact that the writers of the impugned letter were out of the jurisdiction and unable to testify?

4. It is important to distinguish between comment and allegations of fact. The defence of fair comment protects freedom of discussion; it does not provide licence to make unsubstantiated accusations against those in the public eye. Thus, to suggest that a politician has taken bribes is an allegation of fact that is not protected by the defence of fair comment. However, fair comment may apply if a politician has been found guilty of taking bribes, and the defendant has commented that such conduct is disgraceful or dishonourable. These latter comments are subjective statements of opinion and, as long as they are honestly expressed, can be defended as fair comment.

Nevertheless, it is often difficult to distinguish between comments and statements of fact. The burden is on the defendant to show that the impugned statements were comments, and the test is whether they would "be recognizable to the ordinary reasonable man as a comment upon true facts, and not as a bare statement of fact": *Vander Zalm v. Times Publishers* (1980), 18 B.C.L.R. 210 at 213 (C.A.). Generally, facts are statements that are susceptible to proof: their truth or falsity can be determined. For instance, witnesses can testify whether a politician has, in fact, taken bribes. Conversely, comments are subjective opinions that cannot be proved or disproved.

It must be clear to the reader or listener that the impugned statements were comments rather than facts. If the facts and commentary are so intermingled as to be indistinguishable, the defence of fair comment will not apply. See *Jones v. Bennett*, [1969] S.C.R. 277; and *Mitchell v. Times Printing and Publishing Company Limited (No. 2)*, [1944] 1 W.W.R. 400 (B.C.S.C.).

If the defendant fails to establish that the impugned statements were comments, they will be treated as facts and will only be protected if the defendant can satisfy the defence of justification (*i.e.*, if the defendant can prove the truth of those facts) or some other privilege. See *Murphy v. LaMarsh* (1970), 73 W.W.R. 114 (B.C.S.C.), aff'd (1970), [1971] 2 W.W.R. 196 (B.C.C.A.).

5. A defendant raising the defence of fair comment must prove that the facts underlying its opinion are true. The defence is not available if the underlying facts are unproven or misstated: *Holt v. Sun Publishing Co. Ltd.* (1979), 100 D.L.R. (3d) 447 (B.C.C.A.); *Hodgson v. Canadian Newspapers Co.* (1998), 39 O.R. (3d) 235 (Gen. Div.), aff'd (2000), 49 O.R. (3d) 161 (C.A.); and *Rogacki v. Belz* (2004), 243 D.L.R. (4th) 585 (Ont. C.A.). Nor is it available if the facts are fabricated or twisted: *Price v. Chicoutimi Pulp Co.* (1915), 51 S.C.R. 179; *Leenen v. Canadian Broadcasting Corporation* (2000), 48 O.R. (3d) 656 (S.C.J.), aff'd (2001), 54 O.R. (3d) 612 (C.A.); and *Myers v. Canadian Broadcasting Corporation* (1999), 47 C.C.L.T. (2d) 272 (Ont. S.C.J.), aff'd (2001), 54 O.R. (3d) 626 (C.A.).

If facts are sufficiently notorious to have become public knowledge, they do not need to be provided as long as they are clearly identifiable. For instance, political cartoons do not necessarily need to set out the facts upon which they are based. See *Ross v. New Brunswick Teachers' Association* (2001), 238 N.B.R. (2d) 112 (C.A.). However, mere rumour is not sufficient to be "fact" for the purposes of fair comment: *Pressler v. Lethbridge* (2000), 86 B.C.L.R. (3d) 257 (C.A.).

Although the defendant must show that the facts underlying the comment are true, there is no need to show that the comment itself is true. There is no need to show that the defendant made a correct inference on the facts. Indeed, evidence regarding the falsity of the comment is inadmissible. See *Leech v. Leader Publishing Co.* (1926), 20 Sask. L.R. 337 (C.A.); and *Boys v. Star Printing and Publishing Co.* (1927), 60 O.L.R. 592 (C.A.).

6. The decision in *Simpson v. Mair* (2006), 55 B.C.L.R. (4th) 30 (C.A.) illustrates that the defendant must have a factual basis for his or her commentary. The defendant made editorial comments about the plaintiff on his radio broadcast. The plaintiff was a public opponent of teaching homosexual lifestyles in public schools. The defendant described the plaintiff as an intolerant bigot, compared her to Hitler and the Ku Klux

Klan, among others, and suggested that she would condone violence against homosexuals. The Court of Appeal rejected the defence of fair comment because, although the defendant honestly believed that the plaintiff was an intolerant bigot, there was no evidentiary basis for the claim that the plaintiff would condone anti-homosexual violence.

7. The defence of fair comment is only available for subjects that are matters of public interest. The public interest may be satisfied by the importance of the person about whom the comments are made, or by the event or occasion giving rise to the comment. A person may be the legitimate target of fair comment if he or she is a public figure or official (*e.g. Boland v. Globe and Mail Ltd.*, [1961] O.R. 712 (C.A.)); or has sought out the public spotlight (*e.g. Pound v. Scott*, [1973] 4 W.W.R. 403 (B.C.S.C.)). However, the defence of fair comment is not available for defamatory statements about the private life of a public official (*Vander Zalm, supra*). Is the private conduct of a public official ever a matter of public importance? See *Coleman v. MacLennan*, 78 Kan. 711 (1908).

The types of events and occasions capable of giving rise to fair comment are numerous. They include, not surprisingly, governmental affairs and the administration of justice, political elections, and public health. They also include criticism of literary or artistic exploits, sporting events and coaching decisions, and restaurant cuisine.

8. The defence of fair comment will fail if the plaintiff can prove on a balance of probabilities that the comments were made maliciously. Thus, even if a defendant honestly believes a statement, the defence is not available if it can be shown that the statement was published for an improper reason or motive. See *Christie v. Westcom Radio Group Ltd.* (1990), 75 D.L.R. (4th) 546 (B.C.C.A.). Media defendants may be tainted by malice if their primary motives are to enhance their own reputations through sensational programming rather than to serve the public interest: *Vogel v. Canadian Broadcasting Corporation*, [1982] 3 W.W.R. 97 (B.C.S.C.). Moreover, media defendants who do not provide an opportunity for the subject of a story to respond to the allegations made therein may be tainted by malice: *Munro v. Toronto Sun Publishing Corp.* (1982), 39 O.R. (2d) 100 (H.C.J.).

In *WeGo Kayaking Ltd. v. Sewid*, 2007 CarswellBC 71 (S.C.) (WLeC), the plaintiffs and defendant were commercial rivals competing for eco-tourism business in the Broughton Archipelago and Johnstone Strait of Vancouver Island. The defendant posted defamatory material on his website regarding the plaintiffs' businesses. Among other things, he alleged that guests on tours operated by the plaintiffs would have to stay in soggy, wet, dirty tents, that their tours had environmental concerns, and that they took advantage of "token Indians." The defence of fair comment was defeated, in part, due to the malicious nature of the publication. In particular, the defendant had the improper motive of trying to injure the plaintiffs' businesses and gain economic advantage.

9. Special rules apply if the defendant has imputed "corrupt or dishonourable motives" to the plaintiff. Such comments will only be protected if the imputations were warranted on the facts, *i.e.*, that the conclusion is one that a fair-minded person might make in the circumstances. See *Masters v. Fox* (1978), 85 D.L.R. (3d) 64 (B.C.S.C.). The rules apparently originated in *Campbell v. Spottiswoode* (1863), 122 E.R. 288 (Q.B.), where Cockburn C.J. feared that lesser treatment might discourage persons of honour and integrity from enlisting in public affairs. These rules have been criticized, but have

so far been upheld in the Canadian courts. See *Vogel, supra*; *Hodgson v. Canadian Newspapers Co.* (1998), 39 O.R. (3d) 235 (Gen. Div.), aff'd without comment on point (2000), 49 O.R. (3d) 161 (C.A.); and *Leenen, supra.*

(e) CONSENT

The defence of consent is based on the maxim *volenti non fit injuria.* It applies when statements have been put into circulation by the plaintiff him or herself, or by someone acting on the plaintiff's behalf. It also applies to statements that have been invited or elicited from the defendant at the plaintiff's instigation in situations where it is reasonable to conclude that the plaintiff consents to their publication. For instance, if the plaintiff asks the defendant a question in which a defamatory remark is invited or anticipated, the defendant will have a good defence of consent.

The plaintiff's consent can be express or implied, but is typically construed narrowly and applies only to statements that the plaintiff could reasonably have anticipated. Further, as with the defence of consent more generally, a defendant who exceeds the scope of the plaintiff's consent will not be permitted to rely on the defence.

JONES v. BROOKS

(1974), 45 D.L.R. (3d) 413 (Sask. Q.B.)

[The plaintiff, a lawyer, provided services to a municipality with respect to a development project. He was removed from the project when it was learned that he had a financial conflict of interest. The plaintiff's legal practice soon began to suffer, and the plaintiff suspected that the defendants, Mayor Brooks and Councillor Bracken, were circulating defamatory remarks about him. He hired Flaman and Poley, who were private detectives, to elicit and secretly record defamatory statements from the defendants.]

MACPHERSON J: – [The judge reviewed the background facts and continued.] Each detective had a cover story. He was investigating the plaintiff on behalf of national corporations who proposed to invest in West Bay, that the inquiry was confidential and the source would not be reported to anyone. In his interview with Flaman, Brooks said of the plaintiff that he was unethical, that he had no character, that he was a shyster, that he had no scruples. To Poley, Brooks referred to the plaintiff as a crooked son-of-a-bitch and as a real shyster. Flaman and Brooks drove to West Bay and picked up Bracken on the way. Bracken said, according to Flaman, that Jones had used his influence as town solicitor to get land for his companies. This is the only allegation of slander against Bracken. It is denied by Bracken and not mentioned by any other witness. Kondra said to Poley that he thought the plaintiff was about the most corrupt lawyer there is, that he had the legal know-how to shaft anyone and that he was a manipulator.

I have no difficulty in finding as a fact that the defendants Brooks and Kondra did say the words identified to their voices on the tapes by the two detectives and appearing in the transcripts of the tapes filed. Neither defendant when testifying made any effort to deny them. But I comment, too, that much of what was said of a defamatory nature by Brooks and Kondra to the detectives was provoked and cajoled and indeed invited by the words and manner of the detectives, particularly Poley.

. . .

[MacPherson J. reviewed the Canadian authorities and found them unhelpful.]

Whereas our law seems to have atrophied, there has been considerable judicial debate in the United States. There the leading case is *Teichner v. Bellan*, (1959) 181 N.Y.S.2d 842, a decision of the appellate division of the Supreme Court of the State of New York. Justice Halpern for the Court of five said at p. 845:

> There are decisions in some States that a communication of defamatory matter to an agent of the person defamed in response to an inquiry does not constitute a publication to a third person . . .
>
> But the better view seems to us to be that taken in another line of cases, holding that the communication to the plaintiff's agent is a publication, even though the plaintiff's action may ultimately be defeated for other reasons. The agent is, in fact, a different entity from the principal; the communication to the agent is, in fact, a publication to a third person . . .
>
> Consent is a bar to a recovery for defamation under the general principle of *volenti non fit injuria* or, as it is sometimes put, the plaintiff's consent to the publication of the defamation confers an absolute immunity or an absolute privilege upon the defendant . . . However, a plaintiff who had authorized an agent to make an inquiry on his behalf is not to be charged with consent to a defamatory statement made in reply to the inquiry, unless he had reason to anticipate that the response might be a defamatory one . . . Only in such a case can it be said that he had impliedly agreed to assume the risk of a defamatory communication to his agent . . .

I have omitted only the learned Judge's authorities.

I think that this passage represents a fair statement of the law to be applied to the present case insofar as it concerns the defences of no publication and *volenti*. . .

It follows. . . that what was said by the defendants to the detectives constituted publication notwithstanding that they were agents for the plaintiff.

. . .

The detectives were experienced investigators and they were paid by the plaintiff. Each had a tape recorder and a cover story and was told by the plaintiff what to ask. Flaman was told to talk to Brooks. Poley was told to talk to all three defendants and the former defendant Miller. The whole purpose of each detective was to get the defendants to make slanderous remarks about the plaintiff and to record them on tape as evidence for this action which the plaintiff then had in contemplation.

Unquestionably the plaintiff knew when he dispatched the detectives that he had been defamed. The plaintiff testified that he instructed Flaman to learn the nature of the statements Brooks was making about him. Flaman said that the plaintiff felt he was being slandered and he was to find out what was being said. Poley said that his purpose was "to check out the slanders". When the plaintiff instructed Poley the plaintiff knew what Brooks had said to Flaman. He knew also the Mittelstadt evidence which I shall discuss presently. The plaintiff knew the nature of his difficulties with the town council.

The plaintiff therefore had good reason when he sent the detectives to anticipate that the response by the defendants to the inquiries might be defamatory.

This is the very essence of *volenti non fit injuria* - the knowing consent of the plaintiff to the defendant's wrong which the plaintiff expected. . .

. . .

In my view, the defendants have successfully met the burden and with respect to the evidence of the detectives concerning all three defendants the defence of *volenti* succeeds.

When *volenti* applies the issues of privilege and malice become redundant. Because he had assumed the risk of being slandered the plaintiff cannot now be heard to say that a defendant exceeded his privilege or was malicious. The defendants have, as Justice Halpern said above, an absolute privilege.

NOTES AND QUESTIONS

1. As indicated above, the defence of consent will fail if the defendant has exceeded the scope of the plaintiff's consent. For example, in *Syms v. Warren* (1976), 71 D.L.R. (3d) 558 (Man. Q.B.), the plaintiff had agreed to participate in a radio show to explain defamatory comments that had been made about him. The court found that he had given implied consent for the republication of those statements in order that he might clarify them. However, after the plaintiff went off the air, a caller to the show repeated the rumours circulating about him. The court held that the plaintiff's consent was thereby exceeded and the radio station was held liable. The court stressed that the defence of consent must be construed narrowly, or else "consent to the merest publication would open the door to wide dissemination that might be very damaging and never intended to be authorized by the person giving the initial consent" (at 563).

2. The defence of consent has been criticized in situations, like *Jones*, where the plaintiff elicits defamatory remarks in an effort to provide evidence of remarks that the defendant has already made. In England, the law appears to favour the plaintiff who thereby seeks to "trap" or "challenge" the defendant into repeating defamatory remarks. See Milmo & Rogers, eds., *Gatley on Libel and Slander*, 9th ed. (1998) at §18.19.

4. Remedies

(a) INJUNCTION

A plaintiff claiming in defamation may seek an injunction prior to trial to enjoin further publication of the allegedly defamatory statements. However, the courts are quite reluctant to grant such injunctions. A plaintiff will not be granted an injunction unless (i) the statements are clearly defamatory, and (ii) either the defendant does not plead justification or it is impossible for the defence of justification to succeed: *Canada Metal Co. Ltd. v. Canadian Broadcasting Corporation* (1975), 55 D.L.R. (3d) 42 (Ont. Div. Ct.). Further, as with interlocutory injunctions more generally, an injunction will not be granted if the continued publication of the defamatory material could be adequately compensated by damages at trial.

If there is any doubt over whether the statements are defamatory or whether a successful defence could be raised, then the court will not award an injunction prior to trial. It is feared that awarding injunctions too readily would have a chilling effect on democratic dialogue and freedom of the press. Thus, they are limited to situations where the impugned statements are clearly defamatory and false.

Of course, this issue will only arise in situations where the defendant threatens to continue publishing the allegedly defamatory statements. For instance, if the defendant refuses to remove the impugned material from a website, refuses to take down an allegedly defamatory poster, or continues to broadcast an allegedly defamatory advertisement, the plaintiff may wish to seek an injunction.

Recall that each publication of defamatory material is a new instance of defamation for which the defendant may be held liable. Thus, even if no injunction is sought, it may be advisable for a defendant to refrain from republishing allegedly defamatory statements to prevent an increase in damages if the defendant is ultimately found liable.

(b) DAMAGES

HILL v. CHURCH OF SCIENTOLOGY
[1995] 2 S.C.R. 1130

[The facts in *Hill* were explained in the earlier section on qualified privilege. At trial, the jury awarded $300,000 in general damages against Morris Manning and the Church of Scientology jointly. The jury also awarded $500,000 in aggravated damages and $800,000 in punitive damages against the Church of Scientology alone. These awards were upheld by the Court of Appeal for Ontario. The Supreme Court of Canada's decision on damages is below.]

Cory J.: —

(1) *The Standard of Appellate Review*

The appellants do not contend that the trial judge made any substantive error in his careful directions to the jury. Thus, there is no question of misdirection of the jury or of its acting upon an improper basis or of any jury consideration given to wrongfully admitted or excluded evidence. The sole issue is whether the quantum of the jury's award can stand.

Jurors are drawn from the community and speak for their community. When properly instructed, they are uniquely qualified to assess the damages suffered by the plaintiff, who is also a member of their community. This is why, as Robins J.A. noted in *Walker v. CFTO Ltd.* (1987), 59 O.R. (2d) 104 (C.A.), at p. 110, it is often said that the assessment of damages is "peculiarly the province of the jury". Therefore, an appellate court is not entitled to substitute its own judgment as to the proper award for that of the jury merely because it would have arrived at a different figure.

The basis upon which an appellate court can act was very clearly enunciated by Robins J.A. in *Walker, supra*. He stated at p. 110 that the court should consider:

> . . . whether the verdict is so inordinately large as obviously to exceed the maximum limit of a reasonable range within which the jury may properly operate or, put another way, whether the verdict is so exorbitant or so grossly out of proportion to the libel as to shock the court's conscience and sense of justice.

The history of this action emphasizes the reasonableness of the jury's verdict. It was the [Church of Scientology] who had always insisted upon the jury assessing damages for the libel. . ..

. . .

If guidelines are to be provided to juries, then clearly this is a matter for legislation. In its absence, the standard which must be applied remains that the jury's assessment should not be varied unless it shocks the conscience of the court. With this in mind, let us first consider the jury's assessment of damages.

(2) *General Damages*

It has long been held that general damages in defamation cases are presumed from the very publication of the false statement and are awarded at large. See *Ley v. Hamilton* (1935), 153 L.T. 384 (H.L.), at p. 386. They are, as stated, peculiarly within the province of the jury. These are sound principles that should be followed.

The consequences which flow from the publication of an injurious false statement are invidious. The television report of the news conference on the steps of Osgoode Hall must have had a lasting and significant effect on all who saw it. They witnessed a prominent lawyer accusing another lawyer of criminal contempt in a setting synonymous with legal affairs and the courts of the province. It will be extremely difficult to correct the impression left with viewers that Casey Hill must have been guilty of unethical and illegal conduct.

The written words emanating from the news conference must have had an equally devastating impact. All who read the news reports would be left with a lasting impression that Casey Hill has been guilty of misconduct. It would be hard to imagine a more difficult situation for the defamed person to overcome. Every time that person goes to the convenience store, or shopping centre, he will imagine that the people around him still retain the erroneous impression that the false statement is correct. A defamatory statement can seep into the crevasses of the subconscious and lurk there ever ready to spring forth and spread its cancerous evil. The unfortunate impression left by a libel may last a lifetime. Seldom does the defamed person have the opportunity of replying and correcting the record in a manner that will truly remedy the situation. It is members of the community in which the defamed person lives who will be best able to assess the damages. The jury as representative of that community should be free to make an assessment of damages which will provide the plaintiff with a sum of money that clearly demonstrates to the community the vindication of the plaintiff's reputation.

(a) *Should a Cap be Imposed on Damages in Defamation Cases?*

The appellants contend that there should be a cap placed on general damages in defamation cases just as was done in the personal injury context. In the so-called "trilogy" of *Andrews v. Grand & Toy Alberta Ltd.*, [1978] 2 S.C.R. 229, *Arnold v. Teno*, [1978] 2 S.C.R. 287, and *Thornton v. Board of School Trustees of School District No. 57 (Prince George)*, [1978] 2 S.C.R. 267, it was held that a plaintiff claiming non-pecuniary damages for personal injuries should not recover more than $100,000.

In my view, there should not be a cap placed on damages for defamation. First, the injury suffered by a plaintiff as a result of injurious false statements is entirely different from the non-pecuniary damages suffered by a plaintiff in a personal injury case. In the latter case, the plaintiff is compensated for every aspect of the injury suffered: past loss of income and estimated future loss of income, past medical care and estimated cost of future medical care, as well as non-pecuniary damages. Second, at the time the cap was placed on non-pecuniary damages, their assessment had become a very real problem for the courts and for society as a whole. The damages awarded were varying tremendously not only between the provinces but also between different districts of a province. Perhaps as a result of motor vehicle accidents, the problem arose in the courts every day of every week. The size and disparity of assessments was affecting insurance rates and, thus, the cost of operating motor vehicles and, indeed, businesses of all kinds throughout the land. In those circumstances, for that *one* aspect of recovery, it was appropriate to set a cap.

A very different situation is presented with respect to libel actions. In these cases, special damages for pecuniary loss are rarely claimed and often exceedingly difficult to prove. Rather, the whole basis for recovery for loss of reputation usually lies in the general damages award. Further, a review of the damage awards over the past nine years reveals no pressing social concern similar to that which confronted the courts at the time the trilogy was decided. From 1987 to 1991, there were only 27 reported libel judgments in Canada, with an average award of $30,000. Subsequent to the decision in this case, from 1992 to 1995, there have been 24 reported libel judgments, with an average award of less than $20,000. This later figure does not include the award in *Jill Fishing Ltd. v. Koranda Management Inc.*, [1993] B.C.J. No. 1861 (S.C.), which involved the assessment of damages for a number of different causes of action. Therefore, there is no indication that a cap is required in libel cases.

There is a great difference in the nature of the tort of defamation and that of negligence. Defamation is the *intentional* publication of an injurious false statement. While it is true that an actual intention to defame is not necessary to impose liability on a defendant, the intention to do so is nevertheless inferred from the publication of the defamatory statement. This gives rise to the presumption of malice which may be displaced by the existence of a qualified privilege. Personal injury, on the other hand, results from negligence which does not usually arise from any desire to injure the plaintiff. Thus, if it were known in advance what amount the defamer would be required to pay in damages (as in the personal injury context), a defendant might look upon that sum as the maximum cost of a licence to defame. A cap would operate in a manner that would change the whole character and function of the law of defamation. It would amount to a radical change in policy and direction for the courts.

[Cory J. reviewed the issue of placing a cap on awards for defamation in other Commonwealth jurisdictions.]

In any event, I would observe that, if the trilogy were to be applied, the value of the cap in 1991 would be approximately $250,000. It follows that even if the appellants' contention on this issue was accepted, the general damages of $300,000 assessed by the jury would come very close to the range said to be reasonable by the appellants.

(b) *Joint Liability for General Damages*

Manning complains that the judge erred in refusing to accept his request that the verdict in general damages be rendered separately. He argues that his liability should be limited to the statement he made at the press conference and should not extend to the subsequent circulation of the notice of motion. The trial judge's error, he argues, contributed to the very high award by the jury. This position cannot be accepted.

It must be remembered that at trial: a) it was the position of Manning's counsel that Manning and Scientology should be jointly and severally liable for general damages in respect of each of the defamatory statements published by them; b) Scientology admitted that it published each of the defamatory statements at issue in the action; c) Manning admitted that he published each of the defamatory statements with the exception of the notice of motion; and d) the jury specifically found that Manning published the notice of motion.

Thus, both Manning and Scientology published the notice of motion. It is a well-established principle that all persons who are involved in the commission of a joint tort are jointly and severally liable for the damages caused by that tort. If one person writes a libel, another repeats it, and a third approves what is written, they all have made the defamatory libel. Both the person who originally utters the defamatory statement, and the individual who expresses agreement with it, are liable for the injury. It would thus be inappropriate and wrong in law to have a jury attempt to apportion liability either for general or for special damages between the joint tortfeasors Manning and Scientology. See *Lawson v. Burns*, [1976] 6 W.W.R. 362 (B.C.S.C.), at pp. 368-69; *Gatley on Libel and Slander* (8th ed.). . . at p. 600. However, this comment does not apply to aggravated damages, which are assessed on the basis of the particular malice of each joint tortfeasor.

(c) *Application of Principles to the Facts Established in this Case*

It cannot be forgotten that at the time the libellous statement was made, Casey Hill was a young lawyer in the Crown Law office working in the litigation field. For all lawyers their reputation is of paramount importance. Clients depend on the integrity of lawyers, as do colleagues. Judges rely upon commitments and undertakings given to them by counsel. Our whole system of administration of justice depends upon counsel's reputation for integrity. Anything that leads to the tarnishing of a professional reputation can be disastrous for a lawyer. It matters not that subsequent to the publication of the libel, Casey Hill received promotions, was elected a bencher and eventually appointed a trial judge in the General Division of the Court of Ontario. As a lawyer, Hill would have no way of knowing what members of the public, colleagues, other lawyers and judges may have been affected by the dramatic presentation of the allegation that he had been instrumental in breaching an order of the court and that he was guilty of criminal contempt.

This nagging doubt and sense of hurt must have affected him in every telephone call he made and received in the course of his daily work, in every letter that he sent and received and in every appearance that he made before the courts of the province of Ontario. He would never know who, as a result of the libellous statement, had some lingering suspicion that he was guilty of misconduct which was criminal in nature. He would never know who might have believed that he was a person without integrity who would act criminally in the performance of his duties as a Crown counsel. He could never be certain who would accept the allegation that he was guilty of a criminal breach of trust which was the essential thrust of the libel.

The publication of the libellous statement was very carefully orchestrated. Members of the press and the television media attended at Osgoode Hall in Toronto to meet two prominent lawyers, Morris Manning and Clayton Ruby. Osgoode Hall is the seat of the Court of Appeal and the permanent residence of the Law Society. The building is used as the background in a great many news reports dealing with important cases emanating from the Court of Appeal. In the minds of the public, it is associated with the law, with the courts and with the justice system. Manning went far beyond a simple explanation of the nature of the notice of motion. He took these very public steps without investigating in any way whether the allegations made were true.

At the time this press conference was called, Scientology members had been working with the sealed documents for some time and they had not yet discovered any of the sealed documents to have been opened. Yet, Scientology persisted in the publication of this libel against Hill, who was listed in their files as an "enemy".

Hill movingly described the effect the reading of the press reports of the press conference had upon him and of viewing the television broadcast. He put it in this way:

> I was sick. I was shocked. I understood from reading it that it related to access to the documents. The type of thing that Mr. Ruby and I had been dealing with over many months, and I was just incredulous.
>
> . . .
>
> I was horrified when I saw it. I had had a long history of dealing with counsel for the Church of Scientology. Small problems, medium-sized problems and very serious problems had been raised between us.
> Every effort was made to answer those issues as they came up. When I saw the newscast, I realized that there was really nothing I could do to stop the information from getting out. I thought it was false. I thought it was a very dramatic representation. A well-known lawyer as Mr. Manning was—and he was gowned.
>
> . . .
>
> And he was standing before the High Court. The indication that I had been involved in opening sealed documents and giving permission was totally false. For me, in seeing it, it was equivalent to saying I was a cheat and that I had obstructed the course of justice. It was an attack on my professional reputation and I had no way of stopping it.
>
> . . .
>
> I also have no way of knowing whether there are people in the community who would be in a position to place some reliance on the fact that regardless of the outcome of the criminal case, Manning, a prominent lawyer, and the Church of Scientology of Toronto, had still expressed a view on September 17th.

The factors which should be taken into account in assessing general damages are clearly and concisely set out in *Gatley on Libel and Slander* (8th ed.). . . at pp. 592-93, in these words:

> Section 1. Assessment of Damages
> **1451. Province of the jury.** In an action of libel "the assessment of damages does not depend on any legal rule." The amount of damages is "peculiarly the province of the jury," who in assessing them will naturally be governed by all the circumstances of the particular case. They are entitled to take into their consideration the conduct of the plaintiff, his position and standing, the nature of the libel, the mode and extent of publication, the absence or refusal of any retraction or apology, and "the whole conduct of the defendant from the time when the libel was published down to the very moment of their verdict. They may take into consideration the conduct of the defendant before action, after action, and in court at the trial of the action," and also, it is submitted, the conduct of his counsel, who cannot shelter his client by taking responsibility for the conduct of the case. They should allow "for the sad truth that no apology, retraction or withdrawal can ever be guaranteed completely to undo the harm it has done or the hurt it has caused." They should also take into account the evidence led in aggravation or mitigation of the damages.

There will of necessity be some overlapping of the factors to be considered when aggravated damages are assessed. This can be seen from a further reference to the Gatley text at pp. 593-94 where this appears:

> **1452. Aggravated damages.** The conduct of the defendant, his conduct of the case, and his state of mind are thus all matters which the plaintiff may rely on as aggravating the damages. "Moreover, it is very well established that in cases where the damages are at large the jury (or the judge if the award is left to him) can take into account the motives and conduct of the defendant where they aggravate the injury done to the plaintiff. There may be malevolence or spite or the manner of committing the wrong may be such as to injure the plaintiff's proper feelings of dignity and pride. These are matters which the jury can take into account in assessing the appropriate compensation." "In awarding 'aggravated damages' the natural indignation of the court at the injury inflicted on the plaintiff is a perfectly legitimate motive in making a generous, rather than a more moderate award to provide an adequate *solatium*. . . that is because the injury to the plaintiff is actually greater, and, as the result of the conduct exciting the indignation, demands a more generous solatium."

In considering and applying the factors pertaining to general damages in this case it will be remembered that the reports in the press were widely circulated and the television broadcast had a wide coverage. The setting and the persons involved gave the coverage an aura of credibility and significance that must have influenced all who saw and read the accounts. The insidious harm of the orchestrated libel was indeed spread widely throughout the community.

The misconduct of the appellants continued after the first publication. Prior to the commencement of the hearing of the contempt motion before Cromarty J., Scientology was aware that the allegations it was making against Casey Hill were false. Yet, it persisted with the contempt hearings as did Morris Manning. At the conclusion of the contempt hearing, both appellants were aware of the falsity of the allegations. Nonetheless, when the libel action was instituted, the defence of justification was put forward by both of them. The statement of defence alleging justification or truth of the allegation was open for all the public to see. Despite their knowledge of its falsity, the appellants continued to publish the libel. Although Manning withdrew the plea of justification, this was only done in the week prior to the commencement of the trial itself. For its part, Scientology did not withdraw its plea of justification until the hearing of the appeal. Finally, the manner in which Hill was cross-examined by the appellants, coupled with the manner in which they presented their position to the jury, in light of their knowledge of the falsity of their allegations, are further aggravating factors to be taken into account.

When all these facts are taken into account there is no question that the award of $300,000 by way of general damages was justified in this case.

(d) *Comparison with Other Libel Cases*

At the outset, I should state that I agree completely with the Court of Appeal that each libel case is unique and that this particular case is in a "class by itself". The assessment of damages in a libel case flows from a particular confluence of the following elements: the nature and circumstances of the publication of the libel, the nature and position of the victim of the libel, the possible effects of the libel statement upon the life of the plaintiff, and the actions and motivations of the defendants. It follows that there is little to be gained from a detailed comparison of libel awards.

(3) *Aggravated Damages*

(a) *General Principles*

Aggravated damages may be awarded in circumstances where the defendants' conduct has been particularly high-handed or oppressive, thereby increasing the plaintiff's humiliation and anxiety arising from the libellous statement. The nature of these damages was aptly described by Robins J.A. in *Walker v. CFTO Ltd., supra*, in these words at p. 111:

> Where the defendant is guilty of insulting, high-handed, spiteful, malicious or oppressive conduct which increases the mental distress – the humiliation, indignation, anxiety, grief, fear and the like – suffered by the plaintiff as a result of being defamed, the plaintiff may be entitled to what has come to be known as "aggravated damages".

These damages take into account the additional harm caused to the plaintiff's feelings by the defendant's outrageous and malicious conduct. Like general or special damages, they are compensatory in nature. Their assessment requires consideration by the jury of the entire conduct of the defendant prior to the publication of the libel and continuing through to the conclusion of the trial. They represent the expression of natural indignation of right-thinking people arising from the malicious conduct of the defendant.

If aggravated damages are to be awarded, there must be a finding that the defendant was motivated by actual malice, which increased the injury to the plaintiff, either by spreading further afield the damage to the reputation of the plaintiff, or by increasing the mental distress and humiliation of the plaintiff. [Examples omitted.] The malice may be established by intrinsic evidence derived from the libellous statement itself and the circumstances of its publication, or by extrinsic evidence pertaining to the surrounding circumstances which demonstrate that the defendant was motivated by an unjustifiable intention to injure the plaintiff. . ..

There are a number of factors that a jury may properly take into account in assessing aggravated damages. For example, was there a withdrawal of the libellous statement made by the defendants and an apology tendered? If there was, this may go far to establishing that there was no malicious conduct on the part of the defendant warranting an award of aggravated damages. The jury may also consider whether there was a repetition of the libel, conduct that was calculated to deter the plaintiff from proceeding with the libel action, a prolonged and hostile cross-examination of the plaintiff or a plea of justification which the defendant knew was bound to fail. The general manner in which the defendant presented its case is also relevant. Further, it is appropriate for a jury to consider the conduct of the defendant at the time of the publication of the libel. For example, was it clearly aimed at obtaining the widest possible publicity in circumstances that were the most adverse possible to the plaintiff?

(b) *The Application to the Facts of this Case*

In this case, there was ample evidence upon which the jury could properly base their finding of aggravated damages. The existence of the file on Casey Hill under the designation "Enemy Canada" was evidence of the malicious intention of Scientology to "neutralize" him. The press conference was organized in such a manner as to ensure the widest possible dissemination of the libel. Scientology continued with the contempt proceedings although it knew its allegations were false. In its motion to remove Hill from the search warrant proceedings, it implied that he was not trustworthy and might act in those proceedings in a manner that would benefit him in his libel action. It pleaded justification or truth of its statement when it knew it to be false. It subjected Hill to a demeaning cross-examination and, in its address to the jury, depicted Hill as a manipulative actor.

It is, as well, appropriate for an appellate court to consider the post-trial actions of the defendant. It will be recalled that Scientology, immediately after the verdict of the jury, repeated the libel, thus forcing the plaintiff to seek and obtain an injunction restraining Scientology from repeating the libel. It did not withdraw its plea of justification until the hearing of the appeal. All this indicates that the award of aggravated damages was strongly supported by the subsequent actions of Scientology.

In summary, every aspect of this case demonstrates the very real and persistent malice of Scientology. Their actions preceding the publication of the libel, the circumstances of its publication and their subsequent actions in relation to both the search warrant proceedings and this action amply confirm and emphasize the insidious malice of Scientology. Much was made of their apology tendered at the time of the hearing in the Court of Appeal. There is a hollow ring to that submission when it is remembered that it was not until the fifth day of oral argument before the Court of Appeal that the apology was tendered. Scientology can gain little comfort from such a late and meaningless apology.

These damages were awarded solely against Scientology and are based upon the misconduct of that appellant. There is no question of Manning being in any way responsible for these damages. Indeed, there cannot be joint and several responsibility for either aggravated or punitive damages since they arise from the misconduct of the particular defendant against whom they are awarded. . .. Scientology's behaviour throughout can only be characterized as recklessly high-handed, supremely arrogant and contumacious. There seems to have been a continuing conscious effort on Scientology's part to intensify and perpetuate its attack on Casey Hill without any regard for the truth of its allegations.

(4) *Punitive Damages*

(a) *General Principles*

Punitive damages may be awarded in situations where the defendant's misconduct is so malicious, oppressive and high-handed that it offends the court's sense of decency. Punitive damages bear no relation to what the plaintiff should receive by way of compensation. Their aim is not to compensate the plaintiff, but rather to punish the defendant. It is the means by which the jury or judge expresses its outrage at the egregious conduct of the defendant. They are in the nature of a fine which is meant to act as a deterrent to the defendant and to others from acting in this manner. It is important to emphasize that punitive damages should only be awarded in those circumstances where the combined award of general and aggravated damages would be insufficient to achieve the goal of punishment and deterrence.

Unlike compensatory damages, punitive damages are not at large. Consequently, courts have a much greater scope and discretion on appeal. The appellate review should be based upon the court's estimation as to whether the punitive damages serve a rational purpose. In other words, was the misconduct of the defendant so outrageous that punitive damages were rationally required to act as deterrence?

This was the test formulated by Robins J.A. in *Walker v. CFTO Ltd., supra*. In that case, he found that the general damages award of $908,000 was obviously sufficient to satisfy whatever need there was for punishment and deterrence. He found that, in those circumstances, the $50,000 punitive damage award served no rational purpose. The Court of Appeal, in the case at bar, applied the same reasoning and upheld the award of punitive damages.

Punitive damages can and do serve a useful purpose. But for them, it would be all too easy for the large, wealthy and powerful to persist in libelling vulnerable victims. Awards of general and aggravated damages alone might simply be regarded as a licence fee for continuing a character assassination. The protection of a person's reputation arising from the publication of false and injurious statements must be effective. The most effective means of protection will be supplied by the knowledge that fines in the form of punitive damages may be awarded in cases where the defendant's conduct is truly outrageous.

(b) *The Application to the Facts of this Case*

There can be no doubt that the conduct of Scientology in the publication of the injurious false statement pertaining to its "enemy" was malicious. Its publication was carefully planned and carried out in a manner which ensured its widest possible dissemination in the most damaging manner imaginable. The allegation made against Hill was devastating. It was said that he had been guilty of breach of trust, breach of a court order and that his conduct and behaviour was criminal. Scientology's actions from the time of publication, throughout the trial, and after the trial decision was rendered constituted a continuing attempt at character assassination by means of a statement which it knew to be false. It was such outrageous conduct that it cried out for the imposition of punitive damages.

There might have been some concern that, in light of the award of general and aggravated damages totalling $800,000, there might not be a rational basis for punitive damages. However any lingering doubt on that score is resolved when Scientology's persistent misconduct subsequent to the trial is considered. On the very next day following the verdict, Scientology republished the libel in a press release delivered to the media. It then brought a motion to adduce fresh evidence which it stated would have a bearing "on the credibility and reputation of the plaintiff S. Casey Hill" which, if presented at trial, "would probably have changed the result". Its actions were such that Hill was forced to bring an application for an injunction enjoining Scientology from republishing the libel. In his reasons for granting the injunction, Carruthers J. stated that he was forced to take that action because "no amount awarded on account of punitive damages would have prevented or will prevent the Church of Scientology from publishing defamatory statements about the plaintiff". Even the injunction did not deter Scientology which moved to set it aside. Further, in its notice of appeal of the libel judgment, Scientology alleged that the trial judge had erred in ruling the decision of Cromarty J. in the contempt proceedings was *res judicata* of the issues raised in the libel trial.

During the appeal, it was conceded and the evidence and events confirmed that in all likelihood, no amount of general or aggravated damages would have deterred Scientology. Clearly then, this was an appropriate case for an award of punitive damages. Scientology did not withdraw its plea of justification until the first day of the oral argument in the Court of Appeal. Nor was any apology tendered by Scientology until the fifth day of oral argument before the Court of Appeal.

The award of punitive damages, therefore, served a rational purpose in this case. Further, the circumstances presented in this exceptional case demonstrate that there was such insidious, pernicious and persistent malice that the award for punitive damages cannot be said to be excessive. Scientology has alleged that the size of the award of punitive damages had a chilling effect on its right to freedom of expression. However as stated earlier, in spite of the slow and methodical progress of this case to trial and appeal, and despite the motion brought six years before the trial which drew attention to the need for evidence, Scientology adduced no evidence as to the chilling effect of the award. In its absence, this argument should not be considered. It may be that different factors will have to be taken into consideration where evidence is adduced and where a member of the media is a party to the action. However, those are considerations for another case on another day.

[The court upheld the damages awarded by the jury and dismissed the appeal with costs.]

NOTES AND QUESTIONS

1. Why is it important for the jury to assess damages for defamation? What does Cory J. mean when he says that damages in a defamation case are "at large?" See *Farrell v. Canadian Broadcasting Corporation* (1987), 66 Nfld. & P.E.I.R. 145 (Nfld. C.A.).

2. Why did Cory J. decide that a cap on defamation awards was not warranted, as compared to personal injury awards? Are his reasons convincing?

3. According to *Hill*, what factors are to be considered when assessing aggravated damages in defamation? How are these different from the factors considered when assessing punitive damages?

4. What mitigating factors might serve to lower an award in a defamation case? Most provincial legislation permits the defendant to argue mitigation if the defendant has provided a written apology or, in the case of broadcast libel, broadcast a full apology at the earliest opportunity. See for example *Libel and Slander Act*, R.S.O. 1990, c. L.12, ss. 9 and 20; *Libel and Slander Act*, R.S.B.C. 1996, c. 263, s. 10; and *Defamation Act*, R.S.N.S. 1989, c. 122, s. 5. See the recent case of *Second Cup Ltd. v. Eftoda* (2006), 41 C.C.L.T. (3d) 111 (Ont. S.C.J.), where damages were increased because the defendant refused to apologize.

5. Why was the defendants' plea of justification relevant to the award of damages?

REVIEW QUESTION

Heidi is the host of a local radio call-in show. Since there have recently been several complaints against the local police for excessive use of force, Heidi decided to produce a show on that topic. As background research, Heidi read a few local news stories and editorial columns. She learned that one officer, John Fraser, was implicated in several of the complaints. However, the investigation into the complaints was ongoing, and there had not yet been any criminal charges or disciplinary action taken.

On the day of the show, Heidi began her broadcast by describing the complaints according to the information she had read in the local papers. She then quoted directly from an editorial in the Daily Dirt, which read, "It seems like the police in this area have let power go to their heads. It is time for heads to roll." Heidi continued by adding her own comments, saying, "John Fraser is at the centre of these complaints. He is willing to beat up anyone who gets in his way. It is an outrage when officers of the law turn into criminals."

Heidi then turned to the call-in portion of the show. Her assistant, whose job it is to screen callers, informed her that one of the complainants was on the line. Heidi was thrilled and told her assistant to put the caller on. The caller, who refused to be identified for fear of further police brutality, described in detail her complaint of excessive force against John Fraser. She ended her call by saying "I've heard that he cheated on his wife, too. I don't know if that's true, but I wouldn't put it past him." Heidi did not comment on this last accusation, and immediately took a commercial break.

Some officers at the police station were listening to Heidi's show and heard the accusations against Fraser and the rest of the force. A senior officer decided he wanted to call into the show to set the record straight. However, Heidi's assistant refused to put him on the air. When he protested, she told him he could write the manager of the radio station to complain.

The local police and John Fraser have come to you for advice on their potential claims in defamation.

28

TORT LAW: THEORIES, CRITICISMS AND ALTERNATIVES

1. Introduction
2. Theoretical Criticism of Tort Law
3. The No-Fault Alternatives

1. Introduction

We have now completed our examination of the rules of tort law. Before concluding, however, it is appropriate to take stock of the area as a whole. Why do we have tort law? Does it do what it purports to be doing? Does it do what it should be doing? Are there any preferable alternatives?

There is a great deal of academic literature devoted to tort law's theoretical bases and its role in modern society. It is not possible, in this final chapter, to consider that literature in any great depth. Our aim, instead, is to provide an overview and, hopefully, to spur further thought. The discussion is divided into two parts. The first reviews some of the more important theories of tort law and highlights the debates they have generated. The second examines the concept of "no-fault" recovery. As we shall see, tort law provides only one means by which losses can be redressed. Many commentators believe that tort law has outlived its usefulness.

2. Theoretical Criticism of Tort Law

(a) INTRODUCTION

Theoretical criticism of tort law falls into two general categories: analytical and normative. Analytical criticism is concerned with the basic concepts of tort law. In particular, analytical critics identify and evaluate both the supposed functions of tort law and foundational tort concepts, such as intent, consent, duty of care and fault. The work of analytical critics can be either empirical (*i.e.* observational investigations of the actual operation of tort systems) or more philosophical (*i.e.* rigorous investigations of the internal logic of concepts).

The second category of tort criticism involves the use of normative theory. Normative critics engage in the moral evaluation of tort concepts and systems. These critics are interested in the degree to which tort principles and outcomes conform to concepts of "justice." While some normative theorists analyze the morality of particular tort decisions or doctrines in terms of their consequences, others are more interested in the inherent moral qualities and defects of the law.

The first two parts of this section concern the analytical theory of two purported functions of tort law: deterrence and compensation. The third part investigates some recent normative criticisms of tort law.

NOTES

1. See generally Deakin, "The Evolution of Tort" (1999) 19 O.J.L.S. 537; Cane, *The Anatomy of Tort Law* (1997); Owen, ed., *Philosophical Foundations of Tort Law* (1995); Goldberg, "Twentieth-Century Tort Theory" (2003) 91 Geo. L.J. 513; and Madden, ed., *Exploring Tort Law* (2005).

2. Before reading this chapter, it may be helpful to review section 6 of Chapter 1.

(b) DETERRENCE

Many authors suggest that one of the primary goals of tort law is, or should be, the deterrence of intentional and negligent wrongdoing. In this section, we will examine some of the limits on the effectiveness of tort law as a deterrent and the recent contributions that economists have made to deterrence theories.

The object of deterrence is to prevent undesirable conduct. Tort liability has the potential to deter both particular defendants (specific deterrence) and other members of the public (general deterrence). The level of deterrence is often defined as the product of the swiftness, certainty and severity of an action's consequences. Moreover, effective deterrence requires a precise definition of the objectionable conduct, and a sanction that discourages such conduct without inhibiting desirable conduct.

There are several inherent limitations on the deterrent impact of tort law. Much of the conduct giving rise to tort liability involves spontaneous, careless behaviour, which is not particularly amenable to deterrence. For example, drivers do not contemplate liability when making the complex, split-second decisions that are part of driving. The available empirical evidence suggests that individuals who are risk-takers are greatly over-represented in car and other types of accidents and that they are not easily deterred. If dangerous drivers are not deterred by the risk of death or injury to themselves and others, the risk of criminal prosecution and licensing sanctions, or the risk of higher insurance costs, it is questionable whether the risk of a tort claim will deter them in any significant way.

Tort law probably has its greatest impact on planned decision-making in business. For example, profit-maximizing industrial managers would presumably weigh potential liability costs against the costs of safety precautions, and take cost-justified measures of accident avoidance. In Chapter 15, we saw that R. Posner explains the standard of reasonable care in this manner. However, if this theory is to create efficient levels of accident prevention, it must assume that defendants will actually incur liability for losses caused by their unreasonable conduct. In reality, many legitimate tort claims are not pursued, and damage awards rarely reflect all of the personal and social losses that are suffered. In this sense, tort law may encourage careless conduct.

The deterrent impact of tort law is also affected by an individual's perception of the likelihood of both litigation and a finding of liability. The typically long delay between the tortious conduct and the imposition of liability lessens the law's deterrent effect. In addition, the contingencies of litigation and deficiencies in evidence mean that some tortfeasors may not be found liable in court, and others will settle for amounts far less than the damages they cause. Finally, the fact that almost all drivers, businesses and industries carry some form of liability insurance further reduces tort law's deterrent impact: even if found liable, the actors responsible for tortious harms may not bear the financial consequences of their actions. As J. Fleming famously remarked in "The Role of Negligence in Modern Tort Law" (1967) 53 Va. L. Rev. 815 at 823: "the deterrent function of the law of torts was severely, perhaps fatally, undermined by the advent of liability insurance."

In recent years, legal economists have entered the debate over deterrence theory. They suggest that tort law can operate as an efficient deterrent in two ways. First, tort rules may address the problem of "externalities" by allocating accident costs to the activities that generate them. Second, tort rules can lower the cost of accidents by allocating these costs to the party who is able to avoid them at the lowest possible cost.

The basic premise of economic analysis is that society chooses how much of a good, service or activity its members want through the price system. Other things being equal, demand will fall as prices rise. Provided prices accurately reflect the cost of the activity in question, the price system will produce an efficient allocation of resources. Given the existing distribution of wealth, society is obtaining the optimum mixture of the goods and services that it wants, based on its members' willingness to pay.

Since perfect market conditions rarely exist, our economy does not automatically produce an efficient allocation of resources. One major problem is that prices will not accurately reflect costs if a portion of those costs have been externalized. Economists have recognized that legal rules can be important in preventing the externalization of such costs. For example, if motorists are required to have liability insurance, they must take this cost into account in deciding whether to drive. The law internalizes the cost of accidents and ensures that it is reflected in the price of driving.

If the law were changed so that liability insurance was paid for out of general tax revenue, the cost of accidents would be externalized from the activity of driving in two ways. First, some of the costs of accidents would be paid by taxpayers who do not drive. More importantly, drivers would not have to consider the cost of accidents in deciding whether to drive; they would have to pay the tax regardless. Consequently, some people who would not have driven because of the insurance costs would now choose to drive, thereby increasing the number of cars on the roads and the number of accidents. By externalizing part of the insurance costs of driving, the law would have produced an inefficiently high number of automobile accidents.

Once costs have been internalized, tort law may play a role in determining who should bear them. For example, should the costs of defective brakes be borne by automobile owners or manufacturers? If tort law held owners liable, they would incur the personal and third-party accident costs. In response, they might attempt to reduce their liability by arranging for inspections, repairs or modifications. If manufacturers were held liable, they would either pay damage awards or minimize these costs by designing a safer braking system. An economist would argue that tort law should impose liability on the party who is able to minimize these accidents at the lowest cost and that the law should provide that party with an incentive to adopt the lowest cost solution. Thus, if manufacturers are the cheapest cost-avoiders, liability should be imposed on them. Such a rule would encourage manufacturers to install safe braking systems, rather than risk incurring liability costs.

In summary, according to economic theory, tort law can serve as a deterrent in two ways. First, it can internalize costs, which allows the price system to determine the level of accidents for which society is willing to pay. Second, tort law can reduce total accident costs by allocating liability to the cheapest cost-avoider.

NOTES AND QUESTIONS

1. For a helpful discussion of specific and general deterrence in tort law, see Brown, "Deterrence and Accident Compensation Schemes" (1978-79) 17 U.W.O.L. Rev. 111; and Williams, "Second Best: The Soft Underbelly of Deterrence Theory in Tort" (1993) 106 Harv. L. Rev. 932.

2. There are many rules of tort law that are not predicated on deterrence. For example, does the defence of private necessity serve to deter the relevant conduct? Can the rules of tort law governing duress be explained in terms of deterrence?

3. For a comprehensive critique of the deterrent aspects of tort law, see Sugarman, "Doing Away with Tort Law" (1985) 73 Cal. L. Rev. 555.

4. Several studies suggest that tort liability has little deterrent impact on driving. See for example Brown, "Deterrence in Tort and No-Fault: The New Zealand Experience" (1985) 73 Cal. L. Rev. 976; and Osborne, *Report of Inquiry Into Motor Vehicle Accident Compensation in Ontario* (1988). But see Dewee, Duff & Trebilcock, *Exploring the Domain of Accident Law* (1995) at 21-22, who conclude that "several features of the current automobile liability system comport relatively well with the ideal deterrence model."

5. Deterrence is also undermined by the doctrine of vicarious liability, which makes employers liable for the torts committed by employees in the course of their work. As a practical matter, few employers go on to seek contribution from their employees for the amounts they have had to pay to injured plaintiffs. This means that many employees who make loss-creating decisions will not bear the financial consequences of their actions, and will not feel the deterrent impact of the law. See Sykes, "The Economics of Vicarious Liability" (1984) 93 Yale L.J. 1231.

6. R. Posner has argued that tort damages are awarded to induce plaintiffs to initiate legal proceedings, thereby maintaining a private system of deterrence: "A Theory of Negligence" (1972) 1 J. Legal Stud. 29. See also Holmes, *The Common Law* (1881) at 95-96; White, "Risk-Utility Analysis and the Learned Hand Formula: A Hand that Helps or a Hand that Hides?" (1990) 32 Ariz. L. Rev. 77; and Englard, "Law and Economics in American Tort Cases: A Critical Assessment of the Theory's Impact on Courts" (1991) 41 U.T.L.J. 359.

7. For an explanation of the role of tort law in internalizing the costs of accidents, see Calabresi, *The Cost of Accidents* (1970). Calabresi's thesis is reassessed by Attanasio in "The Calabresian Approach to Products Liability" in Owen, ed., *Philosophical Foundations of Tort Law* (1995) 299.

8. In contrast to Calabresi's thesis, the 1967 *Report of the Royal Commission of Inquiry on Compensation for Personal Injury in New Zealand* expressly rejected economic efficiency as an appropriate social goal (at 177-88). The Commission favoured a general pooling of all risks on the theory that activities are interdependent. Calabresi's analysis suggests that the Commission's approach distorts efficient consumption choices,

creating more dangerous activities and fewer safe ones than would be the case if costs were assigned properly.

9. The main thrust of the law and economics approach to tort law is that compensatory damages represent the cost of accidents and, if a tortfeasor prefers to pay damages rather than take precautions to prevent the harm, it is efficient to allow the harm. Even assuming the tort system worked perfectly to achieve such efficiency, is this a sound or desirable premise? Are some accidents "worth having?" See Schwartz, "The Myth of the Ford Pinto Case" (1991) 43 Rutgers L. Rev. 1013.

10. What role should punitive damages play in deterring actors from choosing to sacrifice human safety in the name of economic efficiency? See Calabresi, "The Complexity of Torts — The Case of Punitive Damages" in Madden, ed., *Exploring Tort Law* (2005) 333.

11. Under perfect market conditions, society would always find the lowest cost solution, regardless of how the law allocated responsibility. For example, assume that the law did not hold a manufacturer liable for injuries caused by defective brakes. If the lowest cost solution was to have manufacturers design and install an improved braking system, owners and accident victims would be better off to pay manufacturers to develop such a system than to incur the accident costs themselves. However, the transaction costs of getting these people together, allocating a fair share to each driver and enforcing this system are far too great to make it practical. Thus, in the real world, the proper choice of the liability rule is essential to ensure the lowest cost solution. See Coase, "The Problem of Social Cost" (1960) 3 J.L. & Econ. 1.

12. Some have argued that the threat of tort liability actually over-deters and discourages socially desirable behaviour. For instance, the risk of malpractice claims and rising insurance costs may discourage doctors from entering certain specialist fields that have high rates of lawsuits (*e.g.* obstetrics). See Domin, "Where Have All the Baby-Doctors Gone? Women's Access to Healthcare in Jeopardy: Obstetrics and the Medical Malpractice Insurance Crisis" (2004) 53 Cath. U.L. Rev. 499. Other doctors may engage in defensive medicine, ordering unnecessary tests and making compendious records to protect them in the event of litigation, leading to an inefficient level of medical costs. But see Hyman & Silver, "The Poor State of Health Care Quality in the U.S.: Is Malpractice Liability Part of the Problem or Part of the Solution?" (2005) 90 Cornell L. Rev. 893.

(c) COMPENSATION

Accident compensation is widely regarded as one of the most important functions of tort law, particularly in negligence. As noted in Chapter 1, compensation serves important social goals and acts as the major motivating factor for individual plaintiffs. However, the present tort system is increasingly difficult to justify as a rational compensation scheme. For example, in *The Damages Lottery* (1997), P.S. Atiyah provides a scathing criticism of the tort system as a coherent and predictable means of compensating accident victims. He contends that the current tort regimes fail miserably at their principal task: providing speedy and adequate reparations to the injured. The complexity of the law, its clumsy procedures, and its arcane doctrines of fault, causation, proof and damages generally conspire against the plaintiff. While a handful of tort victims receive generous, even over-generous, compensation from the tortfeasor's insurer, most victims get nothing at all. To make matters worse, corporate retailers and purchasers of insurance pass on the costs of this system to consumers. Atiyah advocates replacing the tort system with a comprehensive accident insurance system that will end tort litigation while guaranteeing a measure of compensation to all accident victims.

Many potential defendants carry liability insurance, and many potential plaintiffs are eligible for some public and private first party insurance benefits. Most of these collateral compensation systems were created independently of tort law. The overlap among and *ad hoc* development of collateral sources have created a very complicated system of accident compensation, only tangentially related to tort law. Critics argue that tort law has become largely irrelevant in accident compensation. They favour a comprehensive and rationalized approach to accident compensation, free from the historical fetters of tort law.

There is overwhelming evidence that tort law performs poorly in terms of accident compensation. For example, The Ontario Law Reform Commission stated in its *Report on Motor Vehicle Accident Compensation* (1973) at 48 that:

> All the studies demonstrate that the tort system pays only about one-third of the total pecuniary losses (called "economic losses" in the studies) and further that the money paid out is distributed very unevenly among the victims. Less than half the people who suffer losses receive compensation through the tort regime. More important, perhaps, is the consistent finding in all studies that the more serious the accident, and therefore, generally speaking, the greater the loss, the lower the recovery percentage. Even with non-tort sources added, a large fraction of pecuniary losses remain uncompensated and the pattern of maldistribution does not improve.

Furthermore, the administrative costs of the tort law system are remarkably high relative to the amount of compensation actually paid. It has been estimated that the administrative expenses of the tort system amount to approximately 85% of the sums paid out, *i.e.*, for every dollar paid in compensation, 85 cents are spent on administrative costs. P. Cane explains the reasons for these costs in *Atiyah's Accidents, Compensation and the Law*, 6th ed. (1999) at 338:

> First, it is necessary (in theory, at least) to ascertain in every case who, if anyone, was at fault and whether that fault caused the plaintiff's injuries. These are very difficult questions to answer in many cases, and the process of investigation may be time-consuming (and time is money); it requires expertise (which costs money); and it may require the interviewing of witnesses, the taking of statements, the commissioning of technical or medical experts to analyse the evidence, and so on. . .. Secondly, the compensation payable in a tort case depends on the medical condition and other circumstances of the particular plaintiff; there are no rigid tariffs or formulae for assessing tort compensation: every case is different. Thirdly, because of the adversarial nature of the tort process, both parties will employ advisers to make the same inquiries about the causes and consequences of the accident. This duplication itself accounts for a considerable portion of the total cost.

It quickly becomes clear why the tort system is so expensive to operate. This can be contrasted to the social welfare system, where administrative costs run at only 12% of the sums paid out. Thus, tort law not only fails to adequately compensate a large proportion of accident victims, but does so on a very uneconomical basis.

It is perhaps unfair to criticize tort law as an accident compensation scheme. Indeed, there is no historical evidence to indicate that tort law was ever intended to operate solely as an accident compensation plan. The tort law system is a means of empowering private individuals to seek redress for the civil wrongs they have suffered, and compensation is only one component of the overall scheme. Even staunch supporters of the current tort system would admit that it is hardly comprehensive in the compensation it offers, and that no society should rely solely on tort law to compensate injured parties. It is not, therefore, surprising that most countries have found it necessary to supplement tort law with alternative accident compensation programs.

NOTES AND QUESTIONS

1. Is the goal of compensation compatible with the other goals of tort law like deterrence and punishment? P.S. Atiyah has observed that the more we limit liability to morally blameworthy conduct, the less likely we are to achieve adequate compensation for accident victims. On the other hand, if the compensation objective is treated as paramount, defendants may be held liable in the absence of subjective fault. See Atiyah, *Accidents, Compensation and the Law* (1970) at 456.

2. Judicial disagreements on breach of the standard of care often reflect the incompatibility of the goals of deterrence and compensation. To hold a defendant who has taken cost-justified precautions liable in negligence secures compensation for the victim at the expense of discouraging efficient conduct. To encourage "efficient" safety measures may leave many accident victims uncompensated. For example, contrast the views of Spence J. and de Grandpré J. on the issue of the mother's negligence in *Arnold v. Teno*, [1978] 2 S.C.R. 287. See also Laskin C.J.C. and de Grandpré J. on the liability issue in *Wade v. C.N.R.*, [1978] 1 S.C.R. 1064. This case involved a young child who, as the result of a dare, jumped aboard a moving train. Can you think of other examples? Is it realistic to expect tort law to achieve all of the goals that have been set for it?

3. Several scholars have criticized compensation under the tort system as being arbitrary, in that it depends on the "good fortune" of someone else being at fault for an accident. Leading examples are Ison, *The Forensic Lottery* (1967); and Atiyah, *supra*. Injured persons who are equally in need of compensation, but cannot prove that the accident was caused by the fault of another, receive nothing from the tort system.

4. In the *Report of the Royal Commission on Compensation for Personal Injury in New Zealand* (1967) at 39-41, the Commissioner identified the following as objectives of a compensation scheme: community responsibility, comprehensive entitlement, complete rehabilitation, real compensation, and administrative efficiency. Are these the proper goals of a compensation scheme? Does the present tort system adequately serve these goals?

5. The New Zealand Royal Commission Report was very critical of tort law's performance in providing accident compensation. Other critical studies include Ison,

supra; Elliott & Street, *Road Accidents* (1968); O'Connell, *The Injury Industry and the Remedy of No-Fault Insurance* (1971); Ontario Ministry of Financial Institutions, *Ontario Task Force on Insurance, Final Report* (1986); McLaren, "The Theoretical and Policy Challenges in Canadian Compensation Law" (1985) 23 Osgoode Hall L.J. 609; Sugarman, "Doing Away With Tort Law" (1985) 73 Cal. L. Rev. 555; Dewees & Trebilcock, "The Efficacy of the Tort System and Its Alternatives: A Review of Empirical Evidence" (1992) 30 Osgoode Hall L.J. 57; and Abel, "A Critique of Torts" (1994) 2 Tort L. Rev. 99.

6. One of the chief obstacles in the way of an improved understanding of tort systems is the lack of systematic empirical data. See generally Saks, "Do We Really Know Anything about the Behavior of the Tort Litigation System — and Why Not?" (1992) 140 U. Pa. L. Rev. 1147.

7. For an examination of the public and private insurance regimes that constitute the hidden reality of the tort system in the field of automobile compensation, see Osborne, *Report of Inquiry Into Motor Vehicle Accident Compensation in Ontario* (1988). The Report was critical of the role of tort law in accident compensation and recommended substantial changes to damage quantification rules and greatly expanded add-on, no-fault benefits. See also Priest, "The Current Insurance Crisis and Modern Tort Law" (1987) 96 Yale L.J. 1521.

8. Even if the tort law system provides inadequate compensation at high administrative costs, does it serve other useful purposes? Is there value in having one's "day in court" and seeing a wrongdoer held liable? This notion of responsibility was cited in the report of the British *Royal Commission on Civil Liability and Compensation for Personal Injury* (1978) as one reason to maintain the tort law system in preference over a no-fault compensation scheme. See also Fleming, "The Pearson Report: Its 'Strategy'" (1979) 42 Mod. L. Rev. 249. The goal of vindication may be particularly important to plaintiffs suing large corporations or government entities. See Koenig & Rustad, *In Defense of Tort Law* (2001).

(d) THEORIES OF TORT LAW BASED ON CONCEPTS OF JUSTICE

To this point, we have discussed several goal-based theories of tort law, namely those which focus on deterrence, efficiency and accident compensation. In this subsection, we examine those theories that evaluate the principles of tort according to notions of "justice." The various concepts of justice underlying these theories are purportedly derived independently of desirable social consequences. It is important to distinguish these "pure theories" of justice from those that assert that a principle of tort law is "just" because it promotes a desirable goal, such as accident compensation. The most provocative articles concerning the concepts of justice in tort law have been written in the past 35 years, largely in response to the literature claiming that tort law is based on principles of economic efficiency.

Corrective and Distributive Justice: The concepts of corrective and distributive justice are typically traced back to Aristotle's account of justice in Book V of his *Nicomachean Ethics*:

> [p]articular justice on the other hand, and that which is just in the sense corresponding to it, is divided into two kinds. One kind is exercised in the distribution of honour, wealth, and the other divisible assets of the community, which may be allotted among its members in equal or unequal shares. The other kind is that which supplies a corrective principle in private transactions.

Distributive justice seeks to effect the just distribution of a particular benefit or burden based on some measure of merit or desert, and theories of distributive justice are accordingly concerned with the appropriateness of the distribution of wealth and entitlements in society. There are many different views, most based on concepts of natural rights or equality. It is generally conceded that tort law plays a relatively minor role in achieving distributive justice. However, some tort rules and decisions have explicit distributional aims, such as those involving the "deep pocket" approach to loss allocation, or rules that apportion liability among defendants based on their market share.

Most tort rules have distributional consequences, although these are often subtle and perhaps unintended. For example, it can be demonstrated that, in theory, strict liability and negligence promote precisely the same level of deterrence. But by adopting principles of negligence rather than strict liability, society imposes the costs of "unavoidable" injuries on accident victims and not on those who cause accidents. Moreover, compensatory damage awards usually protect the pre-existing distribution of wealth. For instance, the damages awarded for loss of income to an unemployed labourer will be significantly lower than those awarded to an established accountant. However, the liability insurance premiums paid by the labourer guard against his or her potential liability to higher income earners.

Over the last few decades, tort theory has been largely dominated by the concept of corrective justice, which seems to persuasively explain the operation of modern tort law. The basic premise of corrective justice is that when one party has committed and another has suffered a wrong, the law should rectify or "correct" the wrong and return the parties to their initial positions. In tort law, this corrective principle is manifested in the objective of *restitutio in integrum*, according to which the remedy ordered by the court seeks to restore the plaintiff to the position he or she would have enjoyed, had the defendant not committed the tort.

Many scholars have propounded theories of corrective justice, and they cannot all be surveyed here. The flavour of the debate can be captured by noting the positions of two leading corrective justice theorists: J. Coleman and E. Weinrib. In his influential book, *Risks and Wrongs* (1992), Coleman argues that tort law is concerned with the rectification of wrongful losses. The plaintiff has suffered a loss through no fault of his or her own. If the plaintiff wishes to shift that loss to the defendant, the plaintiff must prove that the defendant (i) committed a wrong and (ii) caused the plaintiff's loss. It is the fact that the plaintiff's wrongful loss came through the agency of the defendant that permits corrective justice to shift the loss to the defendant.

Weinrib, however, argues that corrective justice is aimed at rectifying not wrongful losses, but the wrongs themselves. It is not sufficient that the defendant has committed a wrong and caused loss to the plaintiff; rather, the factors that made the defendant's conduct wrongful toward the plaintiff must be the same factors that caused the plaintiff's loss. In his book, *The Idea of Private Law* (1995), Weinrib illustrates his theory by reference to Justice Cardozo's famous opinion in *Palsgraf v. Long Island Railroad*, 248 N.Y. 339 (1928), excerpted in Chapter 10. In that case, the railroad employee committed a wrong by carelessly pushing a running passenger onto the train, causing him to drop his package of explosives. The plaintiff, who was standing further down the platform, suffered a loss when the explosion caused a set of scales to fall on her. However, Cardozo J. dismissed the plaintiff's claim because the plaintiff did not fall within the scope of the risk created by the defendant's careless conduct, *i.e.*, he had not been negligent *toward her*. Although the defendant had committed a wrong, it was not a wrong with respect to the plaintiff.

Thus, Weinrib's account of corrective justice stresses the notion of correlative rights and duties. He explains in "Corrective Justice in a Nutshell" (2002) 52 U.T.L.J. 349 at 352-53:

> The injustice that liability rectifies consists in the defendant's having something or having done something that is incompatible with a right of the plaintiff. Right and duty are correlated when the plaintiff's right is the basis of the defendant's duty and, conversely, when the scope of that duty includes avoiding the kind of right-infringement that the plaintiff suffered. Under those circumstances the reasons that justify the protection of the plaintiff's right are the same as the reasons that justify the existence of the defendant's duty.
>
> . . ..Then correlativity obtains because the parties are the doer and sufferer of the same injustice, and the reason for the plaintiff's entitlement to win the lawsuit would be the same as the reason for the defendant's liability to lose it.

Weinrib's account thus explains the structure of modern tort law: the defendant's wrongful infringement of the plaintiff's right explains why the defendant (and no one else) has an obligation to compensate the plaintiff. And the plaintiff's suffering of a correlative loss explains why the plaintiff (and no one else) can demand that the defendant pay compensation. Corrective justice links the doer and sufferer of the harm in a single normative unit.

Corrective justice is oblivious to the "justice" of the initial distribution of wealth between the parties. As Aristotle wrote, "it makes no difference whether a good man has defrauded a bad man or a bad one a good one. . . the law looks only at the nature of the damage, treating the parties as equal, and merely asking whether one has done and the other suffered injustice, whether one inflicted and the other has sustained damage." For instance, assume that the plaintiff is incredibly wealthy, not because of his or her own merit, but only through a privileged birth. The defendant, by contrast, is hopelessly poor due to a disadvantaged birth. If the defendant carelessly injures the plaintiff, and the plaintiff has to spend money on medical treatment, the situation is arguably better from the perspective of distributive justice: the plaintiff now has less undeserved wealth than before. But this is irrelevant to the notion of corrective justice, which requires the defendant to compensate the plaintiff for the loss irrespective of the apparent inequality of their initial positions.

Corrective justice provides a formalist or procedural account of tort law, but not necessarily a substantive one. Theories of corrective justice seek to explain how tort law works, and seldom ask whether this is fair or whether the tort system, itself, is justifiable. Further, while corrective justice theories generally invoke some concept of wrongdoing, they typically avoid defining what a "wrong" is. Thus, while it can provide a stimulating intellectual debate and help to make the operation of tort law more intelligible, corrective justice theory does not necessarily explain why tort law is an important aspect of the modern legal system or overall compensation scheme.

Retributive Justice: A tort system based on retributive justice would impose liability on blameworthy actors to penalize, punish or nullify their moral fault. A "pure" theory of retribution is solely concerned with ensuring that wrongful acts are appropriately punished. In contrast, retribution could be imposed not because it is just, but rather as a means of appeasing the plaintiff and society by having the wrongdoer's conduct judged and condemned.

There are two criticisms of retributive theories of modern tort law. First, some authors argue that society should not provide an institutionalized vehicle for retribution. Even if retribution is an appropriate social concern, many feel it should be a matter for the criminal law. These concerns are reflected in the debates over punitive damages, the area of tort law in which concepts of retributive justice most obviously arise.

Second, most tort actions, and in particular negligence cases, rarely involve morally reprehensible conduct that would warrant retribution. Thus, it has been argued that modern tort law cannot be explained or justified on the basis of retributive justice. However, retribution is a powerful notion both on an individual and societal level. The belief that tort law serves a retributive purpose may explain much of the support for the continued existence of the present tort system.

NOTES AND QUESTIONS

1. The most influential modern work on distributive justice is Rawls, *A Theory of Justice* (1971). From his famous starting point of the "veil of ignorance," Rawls derives, *inter alia*, his "Difference Principle," which posits that inequalities can only be justified to the extent that they benefit the least advantaged members of society. Rawls is often contrasted with Nozick's *Anarchy, State and Utopia* (1974), a libertarian work which argues that the role of the state should be limited to protection against force, theft or fraud.

2. Libertarian theories of tort law rest on notions of ownership and the belief that individuals have complete dominion over themselves and the activities they undertake. If those activities cause losses to others, then those losses are as much the "property" of the actors as any benefits of the activity would be. Thus, libertarian theories of tort law tend to focus on causation and favour strict liability for the consequences of one's activities. See Coleman & Ripstein, "Mischief and Misfortune" (1995) 41 McGill L.J. 91.

3. Cases on "gendered earnings" provide an example of how tort law can serve the interests of distributive justice. For an overview and criticism, see McInnes, "The Gendered Earnings Proposal in Tort Law" (1988) 77 Can. Bar Rev. 152. Can you think of other ways that tort law can foster distributive justice? Is this a legitimate goal for tort law? See Keren-Paz, "An Inquiry into the Merits of Distribution Through Tort Law: Rejecting the Claim of Randomness" (2003) 16 C.J.L.J. 91.

4. Distributive justice theories can also be applied to tort doctrine itself. That is, rather than examining the distribution of benefits and burdens within society generally, they can be used to examine the distribution of the benefits and burdens of risky, but valuable activities. See Keating, "Distributive and Corrective Justice in the Tort Law of Accidents" (2000) 74 S. Cal. L. Rev. 193.

5. The correlativity aspect of corrective justice theory stresses that tort law is aimed at putting matters right between two parties. Even though wrongful acts could be addressed through criminal or regulatory law, and wrongful losses could be compensated through alternative compensation schemes, only tort law combines the retribution for wrongs and compensation for losses in a unitary whole. Do you think that an element of "justice" would be sacrificed if litigation between the parties were not permitted?

6. Historically, studies indicate that accident victims are far more concerned with fair and efficient compensation than with fault-based compensation and the notions of retributive and corrective justice. See for example Linden, *Osgoode Hall Study on Compensation for Victims of Automobile Accidents* (1965); and Harris, *Compensation and Support for Illness and Injury* (1984).

7. As indicated, corrective justice is a popular topic for tort theorists and the literature is vast. In addition to the works listed above, see Fletcher, "Fairness and Utility in Tort Theory" (1972) 85 Harv. L. Rev. 537; Perry, "The Moral Foundations of Tort Law" (1992) 77 Iowa L. Rev. 449; Keating, "Reasonableness and Rationality in Negligence Theory" (1996) 48 Stan. L. Rev. 311; Perry, "The Distributive Turn: Mischief, Misfortune and Tort Law" in Bix, ed., *Analyzing Law: New Essays in Legal Theory* (1998) 141; Zipursky, "Rights, Wrongs, and Recourse in the Law of Torts" (1998) 51 Vand. L. Rev. 1; Ripstein, *Equality, Responsibility, and the Law* (1999); Coleman, *The Practice of Principle: In Defence of a Pragmatist Approach to Legal Theory* (2001); Zipursky, "Civil Recourse, Not Corrective Justice" (2003) 91 Geo. L.J. 695; and Walt, "Eliminating Corrective Justice" (2006) 92 Va. L. Rev. 1311.

8. Recent tort reforms in the United States have sought to reduce or cap punitive damage awards to halt what is perceived as a litigation crisis. See generally Daniels & Martin, "The Strange Success of Tort Reform" (2004) 53 Emory L.J. 1225; Carlson, "Tort Reform: Redefining the Role of the Court and the Jury" (2005) 47 S. Tex. L. Rev. 245; and Galligan, "U.S. Supreme Court Tort Reform: Limiting State Power to Articulate and Develop Tort Law — Defamation, Preemption, and Punitive Damages" (2006) 74 U. Cin. L. Rev. 1189. But see Hemphill, "Smoke Screens and Mirrors; Don't be Fooled Get the Economic Facts Behind Tort Reform and Punitive Damages Limitations" (1997) 23 T. Marshall L. Rev. 143; and Boulton, "The Farmer's Retort to Tort Reform: Why Legislation to Limit or Eliminate Punitive Damages Hurts the Agricultural Sector" (2004) 9 Drake J. Agric. L. 415.

9. Some authors have argued for an increased role for punitive damages in tort law. For example, I. Englard argues that, given the deplorable state of public enforcement, the self-initiated private action for punitive damages has an important role to play in achieving society's penal goals: "The System Builders: A Critical Appraisal of Modern American Tort Theory" (1980) 9 J. Legal Stud. 27. See also Galanter & Luban, "Poetic Justice: Punitive Damages and Legal Pluralism" (1993) 42 Am. U.L. Rev. 1393.

(e) FEMINIST PERSPECTIVES

Tort law has not received as much attention from feminist legal scholars as areas where women's concerns are more obvious (*e.g.* family law, human rights, employment law). Nevertheless, feminist torts scholarship has increased in recent years and addresses a wide range of issues. A useful summary can be found in Bender, "An Overview of Feminist Torts Scholarship" (1993) 78 Cornell L. Rev. 575.

First, some feminist scholars examine existing issues in tort law that are of particular concern to women. For example, claims for wrongful conception and birth have a disproportionate effect on women, and the issue of liability for injuries suffered *in utero* has particular implications for the autonomy of pregnant women. Further, the litigation surrounding pharmaceutical products like DES and Dalkon Shield necessarily raises issues about women's reproductive health.

Second, feminist scholars have begun to create what they describe as a "woman-centred" perspective on the law of torts. The major premise of this work is that the body of judge-made law and critical commentary on torts has assumed a false posture of inclusiveness and neutrality. It is asserted that the common law of torts has, at best, ignored the unique concerns of women and, at worst, contributed to their position of social inequality.

Feminist criticism of tort law has both analytical and normative aims. One strand addresses the "gendered" nature of specific legal concepts and standards. For example, it is argued that tort law concepts like "injury" and "harm" are determined on a patriarchal basis: there is greater concern for losses traditionally claimed by men (property damage, economic loss) than for those traditionally claimed by women (sexual abuse, harassment, emotional distress). Indeed, claims for domestic abuse were historically barred by the doctrine of spousal immunity and, even where this bar was removed, were sometimes seen as non-tortious or distasteful to litigate.

Another important task is the critical evaluation of tort concepts such as the "reasonable man" standard of prudent action. In "A Lawyer's Primer on Feminist Theory and Tort" (1988) 38 J. Legal Educ. 3, L. Bender argues that "reasonableness" is a concept which has disguised and suppressed the seemingly divergent standards by which men and women evaluate conduct. The recent re-naming of the reasonable man as the reasonable person, Bender further asserts, should not be taken to indicate that the courts have come to accept a less male-centred view of the negligent blameworthiness (or not) of particular actions.

In a similar line of discourse, some feminist scholars have advocated a "reasonable woman" standard for certain types of claims, especially workplace sexual harassment: the level of workplace sexual innuendo acceptable to a reasonable man might not be acceptable to a reasonable woman. Other scholars suggest that, if the reasonable person test drew more heavily on feminine values like care, compassion and responsibility, the current cost-benefits calculus could be replaced by a more humane standard of care.

At the same time, feminist tort scholars are also interested in the larger social and moral implications of the tort system for women. Common points of concern include the undervaluation of women's work, as reflected in damage awards for lost earning capacity, and the minimization of the psychological harms suffered by women in cases of sexual battery, workplace harassment, or the loss of a loved one. Finally, on a more pragmatic basis, some scholars have lamented the difficulties encountered by female plaintiffs in persuading the largely male-dominated judiciary of the harms they have suffered.

NOTES AND QUESTIONS

1. Feminist legal historians have described the role of gender ideology in historical tort doctrines, particularly in the reluctance to award damages for so-called "nervous

shock." See Chamallas & Kerber, "Women, Mothers, and the Law of Fright: A History" (1990) 88 Mich. L. Rev. 814; and Welke, *Recasting American Liberty* (2001).

2. For an illustration of the difficulties faced by women making sex-based complaints in the tort system, see *Waters v. Metropolitan Police Commissioner*, [2000] 1 W.L.R. 1607 (H.L.). The plaintiff, a female police officer, alleged that she had been raped by a fellow officer while off duty. She filed a complaint with senior officers, but the ensuing investigation did not lead to charges. On account of her complaint, the plaintiff's coworkers subjected her to continued bullying, aggression, offensive or pornographic literature, and job-related sabotage. The plaintiff claimed, *inter alia*, in negligence against the Police Commissioner for breaching his duty, as employer, to not cause foreseeable injury to her. After a lengthy court battle in which her claims were struck out as "doomed to fail" by an Industrial Tribunal, the High Court and the Court of Appeal, the House of Lords finally allowed the plaintiff's claim to proceed. See the analysis of *Waters* in Conaghan, "Law, Harm and Redress: a Feminist Perspective" (2002) 22 L.S. 319.

3. Some feminist scholars have argued that a woman-centred tort law would be more likely to adopt a duty to rescue, due to a preference for values like interconnectedness, responsibility and safety over the "masculine" values of autonomy, profit and efficiency. Do you agree? See Bender, "A Lawyer's Primer on Feminist Theory and Tort" (1988) 38 J. Legal Educ. 3 at 33-36. But see Posner, "Conservative Feminism" [1989] U. Chicago Legal F. 191 at 213-14; and McClain, "'Atomistic Man' Revisited: Liberalism, Connection, and Feminist Jurisprudence" (1992) 65 S. Cal. L. Rev. 1171.

4. On the application of the "reasonable woman" standard in sexual harassment litigation, see Conaghan, "Tort Law and the Feminist Critique of Reason" in Bottomley, ed., *Feminist Perspectives on the Foundational Subjects of Law* (1996) 47.

5. Is there such a thing as a universal standard of reasonable behaviour, whether male or female? Is it preferable to recognize diversity in outlook and experience, and to adapt the standard of care depending on the particular context?

6. What aspects of the damages calculation are potentially unfair to women? See Cassels, "Damages for Lost Earning Capacity: Women and Children Last!" (1992) 71 Can. Bar. Rev. 445. This issue is discussed further in Chapter 18.

3. The No-Fault Alternatives

(a) INTRODUCTION

No-fault accident compensation plans are designed to compensate victims of accidents. These schemes are usually a form of first-party insurance under which victims are compensated by their own insurers for their own losses. In contrast, liability insurance covers insured individuals for liability they incur to others. The term "no-fault" indicates only that the victim need not prove fault of another to obtain compensation, and that the victim's compensation does not depend generally on his or her own conduct having been blameless. Moreover, no-fault compensation has no impact on the significance of the parties' fault for other purposes. For example, a reckless or impaired driver may still be subject to criminal prosecution.

It is misleading to describe no-fault insurance as an alternative to tort law. Tort law purports to achieve other goals than accident compensation. No-fault is premised on isolating compensation from other goals, such as deterrence or punishment. Typically, the compensatory goals of tort law are different from those under no-fault schemes. The purpose of no-fault is to make compensation more widely and swiftly available to all victims of accidents.

In theory, tort law could co-exist unmodified with no-fault plans, much as it co-exists with other forms of first-party insurance. In practice, the broader coverage of no-fault tends to be funded in part from restrictions on traditional tort rights. This is usually done by restricting the right to sue to the victims of relatively serious injuries and by curtailing the right to recover for non-pecuniary loss.

There is no such thing as a typical no-fault insurance plan. The activities covered by the schemes vary from jurisdiction to jurisdiction. The degree to which they replace the victim's right to maintain a common law tort action also differs. Some are administered by government agencies and others by private insurers. The schemes may be funded by general tax revenue or by levies on the participants in the plan. These categories are not mutually exclusive.

Comprehensive no-fault plans, which provide compensation for all accident losses, are relatively rare. Activity-specific compensation plans are far more common, such as those that deal exclusively with employment or automobile accidents.

A "pure" no-fault plan abolishes all tort actions for personal injuries within the scope of the plan. Victims of accidents are paid compensation entirely from the plan. This is the basis upon which most workers' compensation systems operate. It is also an essential feature of Quebec's government-run compensation program for personal injuries caused by automobile accidents.

Many no-fault plans are what J. O'Connell and R. Henderson describe in *Tort Law, No-Fault and Beyond* (1975) as either "add-on" or "modified" plans. The add-on plans provide some no-fault coverage without eroding the right to sue in negligence. Injured persons are entitled to compensation up to the no-fault policy limit for pecuniary loss, regardless of their own fault or ability to sue another party. The injured persons may also sue in tort, subject to provisions to prevent double recovery. In some American states, no-fault automobile insurers have a right to reimbursement if the injured person collects from the defendant. In most Canadian provinces, the no-fault fund is the primary source, in that amounts received through the no-fault scheme are deducted from the tortfeasor's liability.

"Modified" plans are similar, but they impose some limitations upon the victim's right to maintain a tort action. In some instances, the right to sue for pecuniary damages is retained, while the right to sue for non-pecuniary damages is severely restricted. For example, the right to sue for pain and suffering might be limited to individuals who have suffered at least $1,000 in medical expenses. The point at which this threshold is placed has been a source of concern. It is argued that such fixed criteria provide an incentive to increase medical bills. Thresholds limiting the right to sue to certain types of injuries or to injuries that necessitate missing work for a specified number of days are also common. Other modified plans abolish not only the right to sue for pain and suffering, but also the right to sue for pecuniary losses that are provided for by the no-fault coverage.

These various plans can be administered either by a government agency or by private insurance companies. Whether public or private, the schemes can be compulsory or voluntary. There are a number of possible funding mechanisms for no-fault plans, and each funding alternative would have different deterrent and loss allocation effects. Although a no-fault scheme can incorporate whatever compensatory principles are desired, most set modest compensatory goals. Proponents of comprehensive no-fault schemes prefer rapid and adequate compensation for all accident victims, rather than "full" compensation for the more limited class of successful plaintiffs.

(b) NO-FAULT ACCIDENT COMPENSATION IN NEW ZEALAND

In 1974, New Zealand abolished all statutory and common law damage claims arising out of accidental death and personal injury. In their place, the government created a comprehensive no-fault accident compensation scheme. The scheme, administered by a Crown Corporation, was designed to provide compensation for all injuries except those that were deliberately self-inflicted. The legislation is lengthy and complicated and the following is a brief summary.

The scheme was comprehensive, governing all accidental injuries, regardless of how or where the accident occurred. Although the injured party simply applied to the Crown Corporation, for internal purposes the payment was drawn from one of three separate funds. The Earner's Fund covered both employees and self-employed persons, and was financed by levies against employers and the self-employed. The Motor Vehicle Fund covered all victims of automobile accidents, and was financed by levies on owners and drivers of motor vehicles. The Supplementary Fund, which was financed by general taxation, covered all other cases, such as non-earners injured otherwise than by motor vehicles. The Corporation was empowered to vary the levies against employers or drivers according to the individual's safety record, but this power was seldom used. Claims were assessed by agents of the Corporation. There were numerous provisions for appeal, first within the Corporation, then to an independent agency, and ultimately to the courts in some cases.

Since its inception in 1974, both the boundaries and the costs of New Zealand's Accident Compensation Scheme have grown steadily. As a consequence, there have been at least 13 major reviews of the plan. In 1992, the New Zealand government substantially amended the original legislation. The main aim of the reform was to create a more tightly controlled and cost efficient system that respected the objectives of the 1974 plan. This was to be achieved by a combination of measures, including narrower definitions of compensable injury and the elimination of lump sum compensation for non-economic loss. In 2001, the government introduced the Injury Prevention, Rehabilitation and Compensation Act, which again redefined personal injury and, in an effort to curb claims arising from alleged medical malpractice, provided a limited definition of the "medical misadventure" for which victims could claim through the fund. The 1992 and 2001 reforms appear to have increased certainty in the scope and cost of the scheme. However, the internal consistency and adequacy of accident compensation, especially for very seriously injured claimants, continues to be debated.

NOTES AND QUESTIONS

1. For an assessment of the New Zealand Accident Compensation Scheme, see Keith, "Compensation in New Zealand 1974-1991," in Wall, ed., *Proceedings of the Medical Defence Union Conference* (1991); and Palmer, "New Zealand's Accident

Compensation Scheme: Twenty Years On" (1994) 44 U.T.L.J. 223. For an earlier assessment of the New Zealand system, see Harris, "Accident Compensation in New Zealand: A Comprehensive Insurance System" (1974) 37 Mod. L. Rev. 86; Palmer, *Compensation for Incapacity* (1979); Klar, "New Zealand's Accident Compensation Scheme: A Tort Lawyer's Perspective" (1983) 33 U.T.L.J. 80; and Brown, "Deterrence in Tort and No-Fault: The New Zealand Experience" (1985) 73 Cal. L. Rev. 976. For a description of an alternative to the New Zealand model, see Atiyah, *The Damages Lottery* (1997) at 188-93.

2. Several notable exceptions to New Zealand's plan are exemplary (punitive) damages, damages for stress and mental injury, and secondary trauma (*i.e.* shock suffered by witnesses to an accident). Due to the limited definitions of "personal injury" and "accident," other potential exclusions include: nervous shock arising from a "near miss" (not actual impact); certain negligently caused diseases (*e.g.* infecting one's partner with HIV); heart attacks and strokes caused by negligent or intentional conduct outside the spheres of employment or medical misadventure; and unwanted pregnancy and birth. Further, the common law of tort survives for the protection of other interests (*e.g.* defamation, wrongful imprisonment, damage to property and economic interests). Thus, it is misleading to suggest that the New Zealand accident compensation scheme has "eliminated" tort actions in that country. See Todd, ed., *The Law of Torts in New Zealand*, 4th ed. (2005).

3. J. O'Connell states in "Elective No-Fault Liability Insurance for All Kinds of Accidents: A Proposal" [1973] Ins. L.J. 495 at 497-98: "Much more than half – 56 cents – of every auto insurance premium dollar is chewed up in administrative and legal costs. This is in contrast to administrative and legal expenses of 3 cents for Social Security, 7 cents for Blue Cross, and 17 cents for Health and Accident plans." The administrative cost of the New Zealand plan is 10% of the total amount paid into it. Can you explain or justify the marked differences in the costs of operating these plans? What are the implications of these data? Unfortunately, these data have not been comprehensively updated since the no-fault debate reached its peak in the 1970s. Nevertheless, some recent American data suggest that the administrative costs of the tort system have not changed significantly. See Council of Economic Advisers, *Who Pays for Tort Liability Claims? An Economic Analysis of the U.S. Tort Liability System* (2002).

4. What was the rationale for the three separate compensation funds in the New Zealand plan? How does this compare to a wholly tax-funded system? Why did the legislature provide for differential levies against certain industries, employers and drivers?

5. What are the advantages and disadvantages of having a fixed schedule and statutory maximums for lost earnings and non-pecuniary damage awards? Which groups benefit the most from the principles that govern the common law assessment of damages?

6. Liability insurance is compulsory for Canadian automobile owners and is commonly carried by all persons likely to be exposed to negligence liability. Compared to the New Zealand plan, how efficient is liability insurance at spreading losses and ensuring that funds will be available? Would you favour making liability insurance compulsory

for activities other than driving? What effect might such compulsory liability insurance and/or comprehensive no-fault accident compensation plan have on the notion of the personal responsibility of individuals? See Solender, "New Zealand's No-Fault Accident Compensation Scheme Has Some Unintended Consequences: A Caution to U.S. Reformers" (1993) 27 Int'l Law. 91.

7. The most common activity-specific schemes are the Workers' Compensation and no-fault automobile insurance plans, which are discussed below. Another activity-specific no-fault scheme was recommended for Canadian victims of medical malpractice in Prichard (Chair), *Liability and Compensation in Health Care* (1990). The report stated that over $200 million were paid out each year on direct insurance costs, but that only 250 victims, fewer than 10% of the total number of malpractice victims, received any compensation from the tort system. The report nevertheless called for retention of the tort system for the purpose of deterrence. See also Weiler, "The Case for No-Fault Medical Liability" (1993) 52 Md. L. Rev. 908; Brown, "Eight Questions About No-Fault Compensation for Blood-Product Harm" (2000) 18 Windsor Y.B. Access Just. 217; Tappan, "Medical-Malpractice Reform: Is Enterprise Liability or No-Fault a Better Reform" (2005) 46 B.C.L. Rev. 1095; and Hitzhusen, "Crisis and Reform: Is New Zealand's No-Fault Compensation System a Reasonable Alternative to the Medical Malpractice Crisis in the United States?" (2005) 22 Ariz. J. Int'l & Comp. L. 649.

8. It has also been proposed to treat domestic and sexual abuse through a no-fault system. See Brown & Randall, "Compensating the Harms of Sexual and Domestic Violence: Tort Law, Insurance and the Role of the State" (2004) 30 Queen's L.J. 311. See also Brown, "School Board Liability, the Insurance Crisis and Accident Compensation" (2003) 12 E.L.J. 273.

(c) WORKERS' COMPENSATION

Although no-fault insurance received a great deal of attention toward the end of the last century, the idea is by no means new. Most jurisdictions had no-fault compensation schemes for work-related injuries by the early 20th century. Germany was the first country to establish a comprehensive workers' compensation system, including medical treatment and sick benefits. England established a more modest plan in 1897, and all but six American states had workers' compensation systems by 1920.

British Columbia established a compensation scheme based on the English model in 1902, and most of the other provinces followed suit shortly thereafter. In 1914, Ontario introduced the first Canadian workers' compensation scheme administered by an independent government agency. Similar agencies have since been created in every Canadian jurisdiction.

Workers' compensation boards are public bodies created by statute. Employers and employees governed by the scheme are required to participate. As the title suggests, workers' compensation is an activity-specific scheme which provides compensation for personal injuries that occur in the course of employment. Minor injuries are excluded from most schemes by a requirement that the employee must be disabled beyond the day of the accident to make a claim. In part, the Canadian schemes are "pure" no-fault, because the legislation prohibits employees from suing their employers in tort for personal injuries suffered at work. However, employees have the option of claiming from the fund or bringing a tort action against persons other than their employers. Nevertheless, the vast majority of work-related accident claims are dealt with by workers' compensation boards and not courts.

The damages payable under workers' compensation schemes differ significantly from those awarded in negligence. For example, there is no recovery for pain and suffering or loss of amenities. The statutes classify the worker's injury as "temporary total disability," "temporary partial disability," "permanent total disability," or "permanent partial disability." Statutory guidelines are provided for assessing compensation in each category. For example, workers with a temporary total disability are entitled to 75% of their average weekly earnings, subject to statutory minimums and maximums.

The legislation provides compensation for other special medical expenses, such as the cost of medical attendants and equipment. The board has discretion to authorize expenditures that it deems necessary for a worker's expedient re-entry into the work force. The schemes also provide for benefits in the case of fatal accidents.

NOTES AND QUESTIONS

1. R.C.B. Risk suggests several reasons why workers' compensation plans were initially introduced. First, he indicates that litigation was generally regarded as a nuisance. Second, the notion that every accident involved individual responsibility on the part of either the actor or victim was falling into disfavour. Finally, there was increased social concern with the plight of accident victims. He goes on to provide an interesting analysis of why employment injuries were singled out for special treatment. See Risk, "This Nuisance of Litigation: The Origins of Workers' Compensation in Ontario" in Flaherty, ed., *Essays in the History of Canadian Law*, vol. 2 (1983) 418. For a historical analysis of workers' compensation in the United States, see Witt, *The Accidental Republic* (2004).

2. Given the positive experience with workers' compensation, why have the provinces not introduced more comprehensive no-fault insurance programs?

3. Although workers' compensation claims are considered by an administrative tribunal and not a court, both the board and the claimant may have legal representation. It has been suggested that lawyers have thwarted the drafters' intentions by injecting tort principles into the proceedings. See Glasbeek & Hasson, "Fault — The Great Hoax" in Klar, ed., *Studies in Canadian Tort Law* (1977) 395 at 418. See also Ison, "The Infusion of Private Law in Public Administration" (1976) 17 C. de D. 799.

4. Workers may be denied recovery if their injuries are attributable solely to their own serious and wilful misconduct. What is the purpose of this rule? Is it consistent with the overall objectives of the legislation? How does it compare to the provisions of New Zealand's plan?

5. A contentious issue over the last two decades was whether workers' compensation schemes should provide compensation for mental stress arising out of employment. See for example Troost, "Workers' Compensation and Gradual Stress in the Workplace" (1985) 133 U. Pa. L. Rev. 847; Cook, "Workers' Compensation and Stress Claims: Remedial and Restrictive Application" (1987) 62 Notre Dame L. Rev. 879; Noble, "Workers' Compensation Stress Claims: Is it Really a Brave New World?" (1994) 10

J.L. & Soc. Pol'y 71; and Nisbet, "Workers' Compensation and Teacher Stress" (1999) 28 J.L. & Educ. 531. Are there good reasons to include or exclude such claims from the workers' compensation system?

6. Depending on the industry involved, employers may be required to either contribute to the general workers' compensation fund or provide equal or greater benefits to their workers through private insurance. See for example *Workplace Safety and Insurance Act*, S.O. 1997, c. 16 and its associated regulations: O. Reg. 175/98, Schedules 1 and 2.

7. See generally Egner, "Personal Injury Awards and Workmen's Compensation" (1980) 18 U.W.O.L. Rev. 269; and Derstine & Nathu, "Workers' Compensation in Ontario: A Decade of Reform" (1990) 48 U.T. Fac. L. Rev. 22.

(d) NO-FAULT AUTOMOBILE INSURANCE IN CANADA

Apart from workers' compensation, no-fault insurance has had its greatest impact in Canada in the field of automobile accidents. The majority of academic writing about no-fault insurance has focused on automobile accidents, reflecting the importance of the automobile in our society, the staggering number of deaths and injuries which occur on the nation's highways, and the potentially huge number of legal proceedings that automobile crashes could engender.

Saskatchewan introduced the first no-fault automobile accident insurance plan in the English-speaking world in 1946. Similar plans have since been adopted in many other jurisdictions. No-fault automobile accident benefits are now available in every Canadian province, but the plans vary considerably. Coverage for no-fault accident benefits is compulsory in most jurisdictions. The maximum amounts and the duration of the payments differ considerably from province to province. These no-fault benefits are provided by private insurers in most provinces. Only Quebec and Manitoba provide something resembling a "pure" no-fault plan. Most of the other provinces have add-on plans that give rise to problems of overlapping compensation. Generally, the no-fault benefits are intended to be the primary source of compensation; plaintiffs can only seek damages in tort if their losses exceed the no-fault benefits.

In 1990, Ontario adopted a modified threshold scheme, administered by private insurers. The legislation was designed to preserve common law tort actions for the comparatively small group of persons who were killed, seriously disfigured or permanently and significantly disabled in car accidents. During the 1990s, successive governments submitted the original no-fault scheme to significant reforms. This tinkering generated extensive litigation regarding the original and reformulated thresholds of private tort actions. Despite these skirmishes over the boundaries of the no-fault scheme, Ontario continues to have a relatively comprehensive no-fault compensation system for automobile accidents.

Saskatchewan's automobile insurance plan is unique: it provides residents with the option of being subject to either the no-fault scheme or the tort law system. By default, everyone is subject to the no-fault plan, which provides comprehensive benefits in the case of a collision, but severely limits claims for pain and suffering. Those wishing to choose the tort system must file a written declaration indicating this desire. Although those subject to tort coverage still receive a basic package of benefits, they are required to sue if they wish to recover additional expenses or pain and suffering. Whatever coverage is in effect at the time of the accident will govern the parties' rights. However, it is the plaintiff's coverage that is potentially the most crucial. For example, even if the at-fault driver has chosen no-fault coverage (and will thus have his or her own injuries covered by the no-fault plan), the at-fault driver can still be sued in tort if the plaintiff has elected for the tort law system.

NOTES AND QUESTIONS

1. Typical no-fault auto schemes, even fairly extensive ones such as those in Quebec, Manitoba and Ontario, do not deal with property damage on a no-fault basis. Does this make sense?

2. For reviews of the no-fault automobile legislation in Ontario, see Brown, "No-Fault Automobile Insurance in Ontario: A Long and Complicated Story" (1998) 66 Assurances 399; and Feldthusen, "Have the Politics of Rate Regulation Produced a Better No-Fault Regime for Ontario" (1998) 39 C. de D. 473. For a national overview, see Solomon *et al.*, "Automobile Insurance, Impaired Driving and Victim Compensation Across Canada" (2005) 12 M.V.R. (5th) 22.

3. In 1978, Quebec abolished entirely the right of traffic accident victims to sue for bodily injury damages. Victims are entitled to recover no-fault compensation from the Regie de l'assurance automobile du Quebec, a public carrier. The plan is funded by fees paid by registered owners and drivers of motor vehicles. Benefits are indexed to the consumer price index. Employed workers may recover wage replacement to a maximum gross income of approximately $55,000. There are provisions to address lost earning potential and special provisions for homemakers, the unemployed and students. Limited lump-sum awards for non-pecuniary loss are paid. The Regie operates extensive rehabilitation programs. In 1989, the legislation was amended to allow reduced income replacement for victims detained under a judicial process for an indictable offence committed while driving a motor vehicle. See *Automobile Insurance Act*, R.S.Q. 1989, c. A-25, s. 38.30.

4. Reports on Quebec's no-fault system indicate that it provides benefits in a timely and cost-efficient manner. For instance, a 2001 report from SAAQ, the body that administers the no-fault system in Quebec, indicated that the first income compensation cheques are issued to accident victims on average 22 days after the receipt of a claim. Moreover, 88 cents out of every dollar are paid toward compensation: SAAQ, *Quebec's Automoile Insurance Plan* (2001).

5. Manitoba's no-fault plan came into force in 1994. The plan is administered by the government-owned Manitoba Public Insurance Corporation. It provides compensation for any bodily injury (including death) caused by an automobile, irrespective of fault. Apart from some limited exceptions regarding non-residents, the right to sue for bodily injury caused by automobiles has been abolished in the province. For a review of the legislation, see Schnoor, "No-Fault Automobile Insurance in Manitoba: An Overview" (1998) C. de D. 27. See also *McMillan v. Rurual Municipality of Thompson* (1997), 115 Man. R. (2d) 2 (C.A.), where the plaintiffs unsuccessfully alleged that a

crash caused by a gap in the road was not "caused by" an automobile and could be the subject of a tort claim against the municipality. A decision in the plaintiff's favour would have seriously undermined the efficiency of the no-fault system, effectively requiring a judicial determination of the proximate cause of every accident.

6. For an academic proposal to allow motorists to select either no-fault or tort coverage, see O'Connell & Joost, "Giving Motorists a Choice Between Fault and No-Fault Insurance" (1986) 72 Va. L. Rev. 61. Should motorists be required to elect their coverage prior to the accident (as in Saskatchewan) or should they be allowed to choose the most beneficial system after the accident? See Brown, "A Choice of Choice: Adding Postaccident Choice to the Menu of Non-fault Models" (1989) 26 San Diego L. Rev. 1095.

7. When assessing the income replacement provisions of the no-fault plans, keep in mind that they are usually based on gross income and that the no-fault benefits themselves are tax free.

8. Based on the earlier discussion of the different types of no-fault schemes, categorize the no-fault automobile plan in your province.

9. Automobile liability insurance has been common, if not compulsory, throughout Canada for some time. Thus, even before the introduction of no-fault plans, there was more comprehensive accident compensation in this area than in most others.

10. Given that most employment accidents and an increasing number of automobile accidents are now dealt with by no-fault insurance, what is the rationale for treating other accident victims differently? What is the rationale for treating accident victims differently from victims of serious illness and disease?

11. Although Ontario's no-fault auto scheme will reduce litigation, legal counsel may still be needed given the three concurrently operating auto injury compensation systems and the disparities in bargaining power between the insurers and injured claimants. See generally Lackman & Firestone, "Ontario Lawyers Still Needed to Negotiate Complex Benefits Web in No-Fault Auto Insurance Scheme" *The Lawyers Weekly* (31 March 1995) 9. See also Sachs, "Dispute Resolution in a Statutory Accident Benefits Compensation Scheme: The Ontario Model" (1994) 16 Adv. Q. 218.

12. A continuing debate regarding no-fault automobile insurance is whether it reduces incentives to drive safely. See for example Kochanowski & Young, "Deterrent Aspects of No-Fault Automobile Insurance: Some Empirical Findings" (1985) 52 J. Risk and Ins. 269; Brown, "Deterrence and No-Fault: The New Zealand Experience" (1985) 73 Cal. L. Rev. 976; Schwartz, "Auto No-Fault and First-Party Insurance: Advantages and Problems" (2000) 73 S. Cal. L. Rev. 611; Cummins, Phillips & Weiss, "The Incentive Effects of No-Fault Automobile Insurance" (2001) 44 J.L. & Econ. 427; and Loughran, *The Effect of No-Fault Auto Insurance on Driver Behavior and Auto Accidents in the United States* (2001).

REVIEW PROBLEM

Iris earns $1,000 a week (gross) as a graphic artist. She is extremely talented and much sought after in the industry. She is also independently wealthy and notoriously indifferent to her work. This is her first job in two years. Otherwise, she sketches at home, but does not sell her work. She has told co-workers she plans to quit within the year. Her absentee rate is unusually high and she has been cautioned about this by her employer. She was struck by an automobile while crossing the street. It is agreed she will be unable to work for 52 weeks and will be completely recovered thereafter. Under an employee benefit plan, she is entitled to $400 a week in disability benefits to replace lost wages.

Compare how Iris would fare in receiving compensation for loss of income under the no-fault scheme in Ontario and Quebec to how she would fare under the scheme in effect in your province. How do these outcomes compare to how she would fare under the lost earning capacity head under a pure tort system? Make the same assessments of how you would fare if you suffered the same injuries as Iris.